Global Political Economy

Global Political Economy

SEVENTH EDITION

Edited by

Erin Hannah and John Ravenhill

OXFORD
UNIVERSITY PRESS

OXFORD

UNIVERSITY PRESS

Great Clarendon Street, Oxford, OX2 6DP,
United Kingdom

Oxford University Press is a department of the University of Oxford.
It furthers the University's objective of excellence in research, scholarship,
and education by publishing worldwide. Oxford is a registered trade mark of
Oxford University Press in the UK and in certain other countries

Fourth Edition 2014
Fifth Edition 2017
Sixth Edition 2020

Published in the United States of America by Oxford University Press
198 Madison Avenue, New York, NY 10016, United States of America

British Library Cataloguing in Publication Data

Data available

Library of Congress Control Number: 2023947351

ISBN 978–0–19–284755–3

Printed in the UK by
Bell & Bain Ltd., Glasgow

MIX
Paper | Supporting
responsible forestry
FSC® C007785

Preface and Acknowledgements

This book was established by John Ravenhill almost twenty years ago as one of the leading text-books in the field of Global Political Economy (GPE). It is widely regarded as authoritative, balanced, and comprehensive, offering empirically rigorous and theoretically rich chapters written by leading scholars in the field. This new edition seeks to expand on these existing strengths by bringing to light aspects of GPE that tend to be excluded from textbooks. Enhanced coverage of colonialism, race, gender, and the Global South, for example, are central to the seventh edition. It also offers a wider range of theoretical approaches, integrating critical GPE approaches, non-Western viewpoints, and greater diversity of contributors. Thank you to John Ravenhill for encouraging me to take on this challenge and for trusting me with his legacy.

Thank you also to the contributors for so thoroughly and brilliantly fulfilling my vision for the seventh edition. I want to acknowledge the very challenging circumstances under which we all worked over the past several years. The COVID-19 pandemic and its aftermath compounded the everyday double burdens that many contributors shoulder behind the scenes. I am grateful to each contributor for their unwavering commitment to the project, despite enduring various disruptions.

Maria Bajo Gutiérrez, Katie Staal and Sarah Iles at Oxford University Press were constant and enthusiastic champions of the seventh edition. Their experience, guidance, and editorial support throughout the process were essential to bringing the new edition to life. I believe this book is as much a labour of love for them as it is for me.

A book of this magnitude was only made possible by the invaluable contributions of my editorial assistance team: Tyler Girard, Lucy Hinton, and Madison Paisley.

Tyler Girard served as Editorial Assistant in which he had the major responsibilities of shepherding chapters, preparing the manuscript to OUP's requirements, and preparing and updating the tables and figures. Notably, the vision for the seventh edition was born, in part, through a GPE course that Tyler and I cocreated and instructed, and shaped through our mutual exchange of ideas and collaboration over many years. I am immensely grateful for his exceptional insights, attention to the finest details, and unwavering support for this project from the beginning.

As Online Editorial Assistant Lucy Hinton brought highly innovative ideas to the creation of new online pedagogical resources for instructors and students. By taking a unique equity approach to pedagogy that makes learning accessible and inclusive and which challenges traditional power dynamics, Lucy brilliantly aligned the online resources with the spirit of the new edition.

Madison Paisley, a MA student in Global Governance at the Balsillie School of International Affairs, provided assistance in updating the glossary, meticulously formatting the references, assisting with the manuscript formatting, and copyediting. Most importantly, she read the new edition from cover to cover, providing constructive feedback on every chapter from a student's perspective.

This book is dedicated to our students who inspire and challenge us.

ERIN HANNAH

New to this Edition

- Thirteen new contributors
- Four thoroughly revised chapters
- Twelve new chapters with enhanced coverage of colonialism, race, gender, the everyday, the Global South, non-Western viewpoints, public opinion, populism, technology, migration, and climate change
- New material on global production, globalization, inequality, and poverty
- New pedagogical features including Case Studies, GPE of the Everyday Boxes, Key Theory Boxes, Key Concept Boxes

A Note on the Cover

The cover art showcases wicker baskets in a market in Axum in the Tigray region of Ethiopia which serve as a visual tapestry for the themes of the seventh edition. By highlighting informal economy, markets in the Global South, feminized labour, and the intricacies of social reproduction and precarity, the cover centres some of the peripheries of GPE. The Tigrayan women and children who likely crafted these baskets have faced immense challenges, including sexual violence and displacement, especially since the start of the 2020 war in the region. The baskets serve as a poignant reminder of the interconnections between the global economy and the world's most vulnerable and marginalized people.

The cover art also has deep personal significance as it connects to my journey to Tigray with students as part of an experiential learning course in February 2020. We learned from the Tigrayan people how these baskets are interwoven into the economy, politics, traditional dances, and daily life. The selection of this cover art serves as a tribute to the many beautiful people we met along our journey and an expression of gratitude for their profound generosity.

Economics for Non-economists

Students in Global Political Economy courses are often concerned about their lack of background in economics. While we provide concise explanations in this book for all of the key concepts that we use (and the book contains a comprehensive Glossary), students often want to go beyond this basic information to improve their knowledge of economics. The following books are useful introductions, written with the non-specialist in mind:

John Black, Nigar Hashimzade, and Gareth Myles, *Oxford Dictionary of Economics*, 5th edition (Oxford University Press, 2017).

James Gerber, *International Economics*, 8th edition (Pearson, 2021).

Donald Rutherford, *Economics: The Key Concepts* (Routledge, 2007).

Donald Rutherford, *Routledge Dictionary of Economics*, 3rd edition (Routledge, 2012).

For those who are comfortable with basic economic concepts, the following provide very good introductory overviews of major theoretical approaches to international economics:

Peter B. Kenen, *The International Economy*, 4th edition (Cambridge University Press, 2000).

Paul Krugman, Maurice Obstfeld, and Marc Melitz, *International Economics: Theory and Practice*, 12th edition (Pearson, 2023).

Brief Outline

Detailed Contents

About the Contributors

Vinod K. Aggarwal is Distinguished Professor and Alann P. Bedford Professor in Asian Studies in the Travers Department of Political Science; Affiliated Professor in the Haas School of Business; Director of the Berkeley APEC Study Center at the University of California, Berkeley; and Fellow in the Public Law and Policy Program, Berkeley Law. He is Editor-in-Chief of the journal *Business and Politics*, and has two forthcoming coedited books: *Great Power Competition and Middle Power Strategies* and the *Oxford Handbook on Geoeconomics and Economic Statecraft*.

Ali Bhagat is Assistant Professor of Racial Equity and Public Policy in the School of Public Policy at Simon Fraser University. His book, *Governing the Displaced: Race and Ambivalence in Global Capitalism*, is forthcoming with Cornell University Press (2024). He has published in journals relevant to international political economy, global development, and geography such as *Review of International Political Economy*, *New Political Economy*, and *Antipode*.

Chris Clarke is Reader in Political Economy at the University of Warwick. He has published on a range of topics associated with International Political Economy and finance. His first book is entitled *Ethics and Economic Governance: Using Adam Smith to Understand the Global Financial Crisis*, and he is currently writing a monograph on the political economy of FinTech.

Cédric Dupont is Professor of Political Science and co-Chair of the Thinking Ahead on Societal Change (TASC) platform at the Graduate Institute of International and Development Studies, Geneva. He has published widely on governance and negotiation processes at the global and regional levels. He is the coauthor of a forthcoming book: *Investment Arbitration as a Complex System*.

Kate Ervine is Associate Professor in the Department of Global Development Studies at Saint Mary's University and a Faculty Associate with SMU's School of the Environment. Her publications include *Carbon* (Polity Press), *Beyond Free Trade: Alternative Approaches to Trade, Politics and Power* (coedited with Gavin Fridell; Palgrave Macmillan), and the short documentary film *The Carbon Cage* (with Duy Linh Tu; Scientific American).

Tyler Girard is Assistant Professor in the Department of Political Science at Purdue University. His work broadly explores the political economy of digital technologies and the promotion of global norms and agendas. His research is published in such journals as the *American Political Science Review* and the *Review of International Political Economy*, among others.

Ellie Gore is Lecturer in Global Political Economy in the Department of Politics at the University of Manchester. Their expertise are in feminist and queer international political economy, with a particular focus on sexuality, labour relations, and the political economy of development. Their publications include *Between HIV Prevention and LGBTI Rights: The Political Economy of Queer Activism in Ghana* (forthcoming with University of Michigan Press, 2024) and journal articles in *New Political Economy*, *International Feminist Journal of Politics*, and *The Journal of Development Studies*.

Alexandra Guisinger is Associate Professor of the Department of Political Science and a faculty fellow of the Public Policy Lab at Temple University. Her publications include *American Opinion on*

Trade: Preference without Politics (Oxford University Press, 2017). She is currently a principal investigator of *The Foreign Policy in a Diverse Society* project which seeks to expand our understanding about how gender, race, and ethnicity shape public opinion on economic foreign policy.

Erin Hannah is Professor of Politics and International Relations and Associate Dean of Research at King's University College at the University of Western Ontario, Canada. She has published widely in the areas of global political economy, gender and trade, sustainable development, global governance, global civil society, the role of expert knowledge in global trade, and innovative pedagogy. She is author of *NGOs and Global Trade: Non-State Voices in EU Trade Policymaking* (Routledge), and coeditor of *Expert Knowledge in Global Trade* (Routledge) (with James Scott and Silke Trommer).

Adam Harmes is Associate Professor in the Department of Political Science at the University of Western Ontario. His most recent book is *The Politics of Fiscal Federalism: Neoliberalism vs Social Democracy in Multilevel Governance* (McGill-Queen's University Press, 2019).

Eric Helleiner is Professor and University Research Chair in the Department of Political Science and Balsillie School of International Affairs at the University of Waterloo. His most recent books are *The Contested World Economy: The Deep and Global Roots of International Political Economy* (Cambridge: Cambridge University Press, 2023) and *The Neomercantilists: A Global Intellectual History* (Ithaca: Cornell University Press, 2021).

Lucy Hinton is Assistant Professor in Politics and International Relations at King's University College, Canada, and a Balsillie School of International Affairs (BSIA) Fellow. Her work examines the intersections of food systems and political economy, with a focus on the interactions of the English-speaking Caribbean in global food governance. Most recently, she has published about corporate power in policymaking in the Caribbean Community (CARICOM) (2022) and on how sustainable diets fit in global governance (2022).

Erin Lockwood is Assistant Professor in the Department of Political Science at the University of California, Irvine. Her research explores how private financial authority is exercised and the politicization of global inequality, including the intersection between both domains. Her work is published in the *Review of International Political Economy*, *New Political Economy*, and *Theory and Society*.

Louis W. Pauly is the J. Stefan Dupré Distinguished Professor of Political Economy at the University of Toronto. He is a former editor of the journal *International Organization*, and his publications include *Opening Financial Markets* and *Who Elected the Bankers?* (both from Cornell University Press), *The Myth of the Global Corporation* (Princeton University Press), and *Complex Sovereignty* (University of Toronto Press).

John Ravenhill is Professor in the Department of Political Science at the University of Waterloo, Canada. His publications include *The Political Economy of Automotive Industrialization in East Asia* (Oxford University Press) [with Richard F. Doner and Gregory W. Noble], *The Oxford Handbook of the International Relations of East Asia* (Oxford University Press) [coedited with Saadia Pekkanen and Rosemary Foot], *Crisis as Catalyst: Asia's Dynamic Political Economy* (Cornell University Press), and *APEC and the Construction of Pacific Rim Regionalism* (Cambridge University Press).

Adrienne Roberts is Senior Lecturer in International Politics at the University of Manchester. She has published widely in the area of feminist international political economy, with a particular focus on the gendered relations of finance, debt, development, and trade. Her recent books include *Feminist Global Political Economies of the Everyday* (with Juanita Elias), *Handbook of the International Political Economy of Gender* (with Juanita Elias), and *Gendered States of Punishment and Welfare*.

James Scott is Reader in International Political Economy in the Department of Political Economy at King's College London. He works on global governance, with a primary focus on trade, and mainly with regard to the relationship between trade governance and development. James has published widely across the fields of trade, global governance, International Political Economy, and development. He coedited the books *Trade, Poverty, Development: Getting beyond the WTO's Doha Deadlock* (2013) and *Expert Knowledge in Global Trade* (2015).

J. P. Singh is Distinguished University Professor at George Mason University, USA, and Richard von Weizsäcker Fellow with the Robert Bosch Academy, Berlin. He works at the intersection of technology, culture, and political economy in global contexts, examining transformative impacts from the provision of telephone services in poor countries to the use of artificial intelligence in global value chains in cutting-edge industries. J. P. has consulted or advised international organizations such as the British Council, UNESCO, the World Bank, and the World Trade Organization, and has conducted field research in thirty-six countries.

Silke Trommer is Senior Lecturer in Politics in the School of Social Sciences at the University of Manchester, UK, and Director of the Manchester Jean Monnet Centre of Excellence. Her publications include *Transformations in Trade Politics: Participatory Trade Politics in West Africa* (Routledge, 2014), and *Expert Knowledge in Global Trade* (with Erin Hannah and James Scott; Routledge, 2015).

Matthew Watson is Professor of Political Economy in the Department of Politics and International Studies, University of Warwick, and from 2013 to 2019 was a UK Economic and Social Research Council Professorial Fellow. His publications include *The Market*, *Uneconomic Economics and the Crisis of the Model World*, *The Political Economy of International Capital Mobility*, and *Foundations of International Political Economy*.

PART I

Theoretical Approaches to Global Political Economy

1

The Study of Global Political Economy

John Ravenhill and Erin Hannah

Chapter contents

Reader's guide

The multilateral economic order is facing several major challenges, including the persistent impact of COVID-19 on global output and growth, the shift towards decoupling and fragmentation in economic relations with China, the Russian invasion of Ukraine, the disruption of global value chains, and the rise of conservative populism, which, together, challenge the principles of liberal internationalism. These challenges provide a clear illustration of the relationship between trade, finance, international institutions, and the difficulties governments face in coping with the problems generated by complex interdependence.

Before 1945, the spectacular increase in economic integration that had occurred over the previous century was not accompanied by institutionalized governmental collaboration on economic matters. International trade patterns also changed very little over several centuries before 1945. The end of the Second World War marked a significant disjuncture: global economic institutions were created, the transnational corporation emerged as a major actor in international economic relations, and patterns of international trade began to change markedly from the traditional North–South exchange of manufactured goods.

Global political economy (GPE) has developed as a rich field of study that aims to make sense of the complex interactions between states, markets, and, often, societies by addressing the prevailing question: 'who benefits?'. The field of GPE is defined by its theoretical plurality, and scholars are increasingly attuned to the need to centre the conceptual and empirical margins of the field by paying attention to issues such as colonialism, gender, race, and the intersections of GPE with everyday life.

1.1 Prologue: The multilateral economic order under threat

The onset of the COVID-19 pandemic in 2020 was the single largest shock to the global economy since the Second World War. For the first time in half a century, global output declined (Figure 1.1). Although the global economy experienced a bounce-back the following year, the impact of the pandemic is likely to be enduring. It set a new (lower) trajectory for economic growth—the International Monetary Fund (IMF) (2023: 3) predicted that post-COVID global growth would settle around 3 per cent, substantially below the average of 3.8 per cent for 2000–2019, which in turn was lower than in the two preceding decades. Moreover, performance in the early years of recovery was markedly uneven across countries; whereas the US economy grew at 5.7 per cent in 2021, the average figure for sub-Saharan Africa was only 3.2 per cent (UNTAD 2022a: 2). The COVID-19 pandemic was projected to cause growth rates in developing economies to be 4 per cent lower than they otherwise would have been (IMF 2022a: 10, figure 1.15).

The impact of the pandemic also interacted with domestic and geo-strategic developments—most notably, the rise of conservative populism, the continued growth in the economic and military strength of China, and the Russian invasion of Ukraine. Together, these combined to challenge the principles of liberal internationalism (see Key Concept Box 1.1) that underlie the global economic system constructed since 1945.

The election of Donald Trump to the US Presidency in 2016 and the pro-Brexit referendum in the UK in the same year, part of a more general resurgence of populism (see Key Concept Box 1.2), challenged the trend towards closer integration that had been dominant in the global economy over the previous half century.

Although often considered together as examples of popular backlash against globalization, the two developments differed in some fundamental ways in their implications for the global economy. Both did threaten the institutional order that had evolved since the end of the Second World War. In the case of the UK, Brexit marked a fundamental setback for regionalism—one of the dominant trends in closer economic integration over the last fifty years (see Trommer, Chapter 5). Trump's foreign economic policies with their emphasis on unilateralism and protectionism (albeit not unprecedented in the US, given the unilateral imposition of protectionist measures by Presidents Bush senior and junior and Reagan) were the most important challenge to the rules-based economic order for a

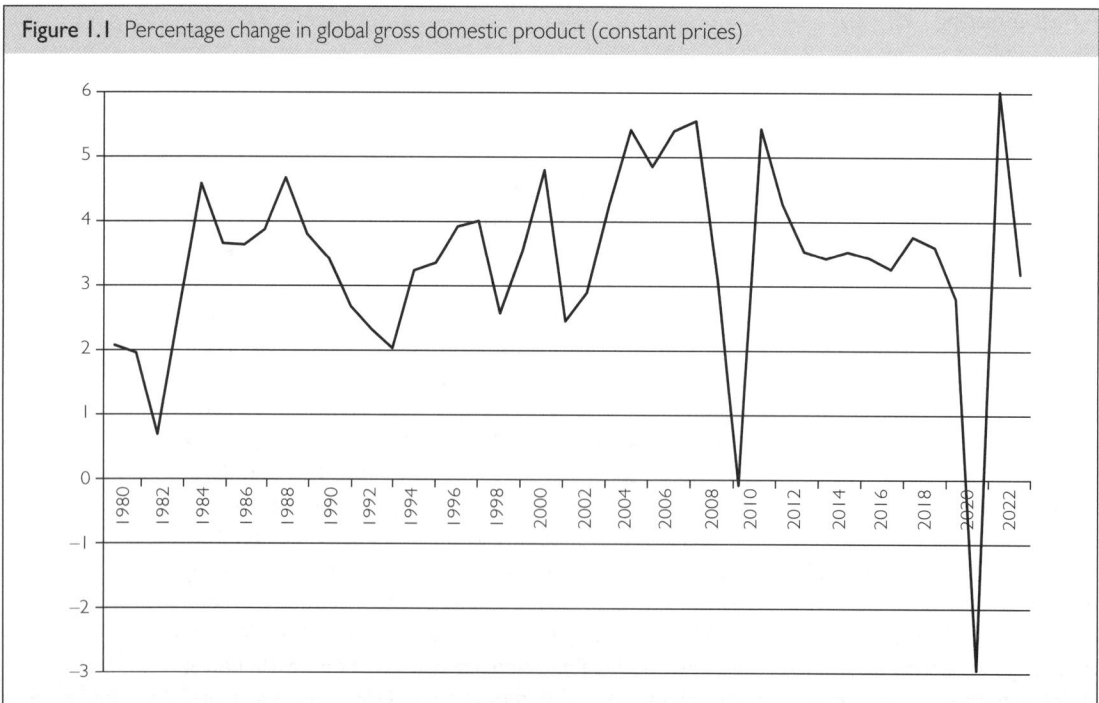

Figure 1.1 Percentage change in global gross domestic product (constant prices)

KEY CONCEPT BOX 1.1 LIBERAL INTERNATIONALISM

As with other labels for theoretical approaches to global political economy (see Watson, Chapter 2), authors differ on exactly what constitutes liberal internationalism. Most would agree, however, that it has both political and economic dimensions, drawn from a long tradition of liberal thought. The economic dimension reflects the classic liberal preference for free markets (Cobden, Mill, etc.)—in this instance manifested in a push to remove constraints on the international movement of goods, services, and capital to foster economic interdependence. The political dimension contains two key elements. The first is governance of the global economy through multilateral (preferably global) economic institutions—as seen in the Bretton Woods 'twins' (the World Bank and the International Monetary Fund—see Helleiner, Chapter 8) and the World Trade Organization (see Trommer, Chapter 5). The second is the promotion of democratization worldwide, a manifestation of the Kantian belief that a world of democratic states will provide the foundations for the growth of economic interdependence and the elimination of inter-state conflict (for further discussion, see Hoffmann 1995; Ikenberry 2011; Ikenberry 2018).

KEY CONCEPT BOX 1.2 WHAT IS POPULISM?

Populism is a political programme or movement that champions the ordinary person, usually by contrasting them with political elites and the 'establishment'. Populism is often hostile to representative politics, preferring a direct relationship between people and their leaders. In the US in the late nineteenth century, the term was applied to a movement that united farmers and workers against the gold standard and the Eastern financial establishment, culminating in the People's Party in 1892. The movement demanded direct democracy through popular initiatives and referenda. In the twentieth and twenty-first centuries, populism became associated with personalized rule by leaders who claimed to embody the will of the people. As Rodrik (2017) notes, contemporary populism is associated with 'an anti-establishment orientation, a claim to speak for the people against elites, opposition to liberal economics and globalization, and often (but not always) a penchant for authoritarian governance'. For further discussion, see Harmes, Chapter 11.

half century. But whereas US policies leaned towards a system of managed trade between Washington and its major partners (especially China and the EU), Brexit, at least in the eyes of the leadership of Britain's ruling Conservative Party, offered the opportunity to usher in a new era of liberalized trade—somewhat ironic given the concerns of many who had voted in favour of the UK leaving the EU. As Colin Hay (2019: 15) points out, the vote for Brexit, given the lack of detail on what Britain's withdrawal from the EU would entail, was not for a particular Brexit, but 'for as many different Brexits as it was possible to imagine wishing to vote for'. Post-Brexit, the UK government has found it more difficult to negotiate new trade agreements than it had assumed, signing only three new trade agreements by the end of 2022, two of which (with Australia and New Zealand) had not entered into force at that date. Negotiations with two of the world's larger economies (India and the United States) had stalled (Webb 2022).

The rise of populism and nationalist economic policies across the globe—from Viktor Orbán in Hungary to Donald Trump to Jair Bolsonaro in Brazil—was a response to multiple factors, predominantly but not exclusively economic in origin. Slowing rates of economic growth after the Global Financial Crisis (GFC) of 2008–2009 (or 'Great Recession' in the IMF's terminology) provided a context. These slow rates of growth contributed to and were compounded by a growth in income inequality, which occurred in a large number of economies, developed and developing alike, from the 1980s onwards (see Figure 1.2; Lockwood, Chapter 13). Across the world, the share of the top 10 per cent of income earners in national income grew steadily while in most countries the shares of the middle 40 per cent and bottom 50 per cent of the population declined. These changes coincided with a marked liberalization of international trade. Critics of globalization saw a direct link between these two phenomena. Recent evidence from economists indicates that they were correct—but that the relationship was complicated by other factors, notably technological change and government policies, particularly on taxation.

Figure 1.2 Gini coefficients for selected industrialized economies

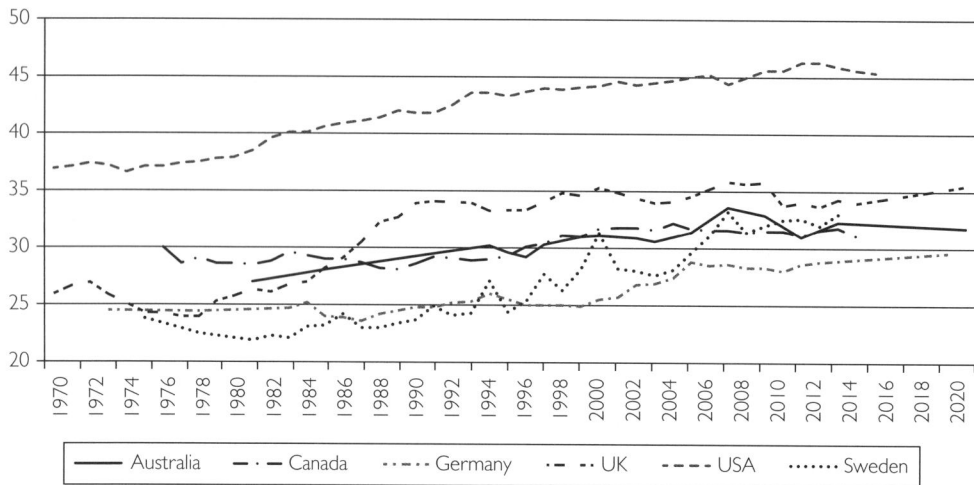

Source: Derived from data from the 'Chartbook of Economic Inequality', http://chartbookofeconomicinequality.com/wp-content/uploads/DataForDownload/AllData_ChartbookOfEconomicInequality.xlsx. Consulted 15 March 2023, updated with data from the Organization for Economic Cooperation and Development (OECD), 'Income Inequality'.

Conventional economic wisdom since David Ricardo has portrayed trade as a win-win situation. Those theories that did acknowledge that international trade would generate losers as well as winners nonetheless asserted that trade would improve national welfare in the aggregate—so that winners would be able to compensate losers. It was assumed that governments would pursue adjustment policies that facilitated such transfers: moreover, they would provide effective retraining schemes that equipped workers to compete in an increasingly globalized economy (see Guisinger, Chapter 6).

In the 1990s, when concerns were first raised about the impact of imports from low-income economies on employment in the industrialized world, the consensus among most economists was that technological change was a greater contributor to job loss than were imports from lower-income economies (Wood 2018). Moreover, it seemed that industrialized economies were adjusting successfully to increased competition generated by imports from lower-wage economies. Unemployment rates remained relatively low.

Since the turn of the century, the economic position of less skilled workers in industrialized economies has deteriorated markedly (IMF 2017). Employment in manufacturing, traditionally the source of (often relatively well-paying) jobs for workers with low levels of education, has declined sharply. In the years since the 2008–2009 Global Financial Crisis, casual employment, frequently with few or no associated benefits, has become the norm in many industries—bringing into being a precariat, a term coined by French sociologists in the 1980s to describe a new army of unprotected, temporary workers.

Technological change continues to be a significant source of loss of employment in manufacturing industries in industrialized economies. It is clear, however, that another factor has been at work: new competition from China's emergence as the world's assembly plant (see Scott, Chapter 12). China's role was facilitated by a new transnationalization of production, driven by the growth of global value chains (see Key Concept Box 1.3).

Economic reforms that began in China in the early 1980s released huge numbers of un- or under-employed labourers from agricultural production. More than 250 million workers moved from farms to cities, providing China with a huge advantage in labour-intensive manufacturing. Very substantial inflows of **foreign direct investment** in the 1990s and domestic policies of privatization laid the foundations for a rapid growth in China's share in global manufacturing exports,

KEY CONCEPT BOX 1.3 GLOBAL VALUE CHAINS

The global value chain (GVC), sometimes called 'global production network' or 'global supply chain', refers to 'the full range of activities that firms and workers perform to bring a product from its conception to end use and beyond' (Gereffi and Fernandez-Stark 2016: 7). It embraces every stage from research and development of a product to its manufacturing to marketing and after-sales service. GVCs are distinguished from the **multinational corporation (MNC)**, defined as an enterprise that owns and operates assets in more than one country, in that they typically involve more than one company. These companies may themselves be multinationals (for instance, a key supplier in Apple's supply chain is its principal rival in the cellphone market, Samsung, from which it sources the displays for the iPhone). Or they may be firms that operate only in a single country. The distinguishing feature of the GVC is that, unlike the MNC, the relations between firms do not necessarily involve investment; they may be entirely 'arm's-length', based on market transactions.

GVCs developed when companies decided that it was more profitable and/or politically expedient to outsource some activities rather than conduct them in-house. Their growth was facilitated by the very substantial reductions in the costs of moving information, goods, and people across national boundaries brought about by the technological revolution that we associate with **economic globalization**. Although by definition they operate transnationally, very few 'global' value chains are truly global in character. More typically, they operate predominantly within major geographical regions—Richard Baldwin (2012: 20) refers to 'Factory Asia', 'Factory Europe', and 'Factory North America'. Few African economies participate in such value chains except as suppliers of raw materials that are usually refined elsewhere.

In the years after the Global Financial Crisis of 2008–2009, the key multilateral economic institutions—the WTO, IMF, the World Bank—became enthusiastic advocates of participation in GVCs as a means for less developed economies to grow more rapidly, increase domestic employment opportunities, and upgrade their technology. There is little evidence to suggest, however, that merely making oneself attractive to lead firms in GVCs in itself will produce the desired results (Ravenhill 2014). Studies have shown that there were relatively few instances where domestic firms were successful in upgrading their capabilities within GVCs (Pipkin and Fuentes 2017; Doner, Noble, and Ravenhill 2021). It always needs to be remembered that the very reason why lead firms choose to outsource some activities is because these are the least profitable parts of their operations. And sub-contracting, particularly within textile and clothing value chains, has sometimes produced the labour exploitation that Gore discusses in Chapter 7.

---

which rose from 2.3 per cent in 1991 to 18.8 per cent in 2013 (Autor, Dorn, and Hanson 2016). China's entry into the WTO in 2001 provided it with new security of access to the markets of industrialized economies. By 2009, China had overhauled Germany as the world's single largest exporting economy, and it overtook the US as the world's largest manufacturer the following year (see Scott, Chapter 12, for further discussion).

Conventional expectations in economic theory regarding the consequences of rising exports from China would be that the increased incomes generated would lead to new demand for more technologically advanced products from other countries. Labour displaced from low-skilled manufacturing in these countries would be retrained and ultimately find higher-skilled employment in other sectors. A win-win situation would prevail. The reality has been different. China, to be sure, has rapidly expanded its imports of some high-technology goods such as passenger jet aircraft, machinery, and vehicles—in the process becoming the largest market for many economies.

But trade with China for major industrialized economies remains substantially imbalanced: only Ireland among the twenty-seven members of the EU ran a trade surplus with China in 2022. The region's overall trade deficit with China that year totalled €395 billion (Eurostat 2023). In the same year, the US experienced a record US$383 billion trade deficit with China (US Census Bureau 2023).

What explains China's persistent trade surpluses and the failure of adjustment mechanisms to trade imbalances to work in the manner that economic theory predicts? A large component of the explanation is China's persistently high rates of savings (in 2021, close to 45 per cent of GDP, nearly twice the global average (World Bank 2023)).[1] This rate of savings inevitably reduces demand for imports. Although China's per capita GDP is similar to that of Brazil, household

---

[1] 'Gross Savings (% of GDP)', https://data.worldbank.org/indicator/NY.GNS.ICTR.ZS?order=wbapi_data_value_2011%20wbapi_data_value%20wbapi_data_value-first&sort=desc, consulted 13 March 2023.

consumption is half that of the Latin American country. The high savings ratio in part reflects societal preferences: in a country where there is no significant social security, families have a strong incentive to save to counter uninsurable risks. Such tendencies are reinforced by extraordinarily high property prices in large cities and by the costs of education and health care. And overall household savings have been boosted by the growing inequality of income, higher-income households tending to save a larger proportion of their incomes. Household savings account for around one half of China's total savings: the balance is derived from corporate savings and government savings (budgetary surpluses), both of whose rates are substantially above the global average.

China's persistent trade surpluses have been one reason why industrialized economies have not adapted successfully to its rise to economic powerhouse status. Another has been that labour markets have been far less flexible than anticipated, which has led to the 'China shock' (see Scott, Chapter 12). In the United States, regions that suffered the largest 'China shock' experienced larger reductions in average weekly wages (Autor, Dorn, and Hanson 2016). Exposure to imports from China consequently has had political as well as economic repercussions. Studies of voting in the United States have found that geographical areas most

subject to imports, particularly from China, disproportionately supported less moderate politicians—and in the 2016 presidential election shifted towards Republican candidates (Autor et al. 2017). In Europe, exposure to Chinese imports was associated with an increase in support for nationalist and isolationist parties, an increase in support for right-wing parties, and a general shift to the right in the electorate (Colantone and Stanig 2018a). Support for Brexit was systematically stronger in regions hit harder by economic globalization, particularly imports from China (Colantone and Stanig 2018b).

The growth of China's economic and military prowess has prompted a fundamental reconsideration of international economic policies in Brussels and Washington (as well as the capitals of most other smaller Western economies). The European Commission (2019: 2) noted, for instance, 'a growing appreciation in Europe that the balance of challenges and opportunities presented by China has shifted', and the need for Europe to adopt a 'more realistic, assertive, and multi-faceted approach'. Increasingly, industrialized economies have adopted techno-nationalist approaches (see Key Concept Box 1.4).

The view from many Western capitals was that China had long followed this strategy through policies such as investment subsidies, lack of enforcement of intellectual property rights, industrial policies

---

KEY CONCEPT BOX 1.4 TECHNO-NATIONALISM

The term 'techno-nationalism' was coined by the American economist Robert Reich (1987) to refer to US moves to protect technological breakthroughs by domestic companies from being captured by foreign competitors (in the context of an attempt by the Japanese company Fujitsu to acquire the US chipmaker Fairchild). Richard Samuels (1993), in his study of Japanese economic development, elaborated the concept to refer to the belief that technology is a fundamental element in national security: the role of the state, consequently, must be to help develop, indigenize, and diffuse core technologies to promote both economic development and military prowess. Luo (2022) discusses how the concept has evolved and its use in contemporary discourse.

Figure 1.3 Techno-nationalism, a strategy whereby certain countries prioritize technological innovation and self-sufficiency as part of their national economic and security strategies, is on the rise.

Source: Shutterstock.

including the ambitious 'Made in China 2025' plan, and various non-tariff barriers that discriminated against foreign companies (European Commission 2023). It had simply refused to respect the rules of the multilateral trade system. Western countries took increasingly aggressive retaliatory action, the most blatant being the Trump administration's 'trade war' which was initiated in March 2018, following a study of China's trade practices by the Office of the United States Trade Representative (USTR), whose primary focus was technology transfer rather than trade imbalances (Kwan 2020). Washington imposed new tariffs on China's exports, took measures to restrict investment by Chinese companies in key technology sectors, and filed a case at the WTO against China's alleged discriminatory licensing practices.

The Trump administration's actions demonstrated clear links between conservative populism, a retreat from multilateralism and the principles of a liberal international economic order, the priority given to national security issues, and the promotion of domestic manufacturing. The concerns that gave rise to these policies were exacerbated by two developments at the start of this decade: the Coronavirus outbreak and the Russian invasion of Ukraine. Both served as reminders of the fragility of global value chains, and they reinforced techno-nationalist sentiments in the United States and the EU alike.

Contrary to expectations among some commentators that the removal of the populist Trump administration would lead to a return to policies more supportive of liberal internationalism, the Biden administration doubled down on sanctions against China, broadening the bans on the export of US technology and on the operations of some Chinese companies in the United States. Moreover, it simply rejected the decision of the WTO Dispute Settlement Body that the duties imposed by the Trump administration in 2018 on imports of steel and aluminium were inconsistent with US obligations. In its submission to the WTO, the Biden administration asserted: 'At issue in this dispute is the sovereign right of a state to take action to protect its essential security in the manner it considers necessary ... WTO Members did not relinquish this inherent right in joining the WTO' (United States Trade Representative 2021). And it continued to refuse to allow new appointments to the WTO's Appellate Body (a policy that began under Obama and was maintained by Trump), which rendered it inoperative. One of the justifications was that the actions of the

Appellate Body had 'favored non-market economies at the expense of market economies [and] rendered trade laws ineffective' (United States Trade Representative 2020: 2) (see Trommer, Chapter 5, and Scott, Chapter 12).

The onset of the COVID-19 pandemic led to an unseemly scramble among governments of industrialized economies to secure supplies of vaccines for their own populations. Together with the substantial disruptions to global trade that lockdowns caused, this competition reinforced techno-nationalist tendencies and led to calls for the 're-shoring' of manufacturing capabilities. They were further boosted by the Russian invasion of Ukraine, which called into question the wisdom of relying on suppliers located in countries that were potential military adversaries: value chains were to be redirected towards 'friend-sourcing'. Techno-nationalist approaches were most obvious in massive increases in state subsidies for domestic companies. The US Inflation Reduction Act of 2022 included US$369 billion of subsidies and tax credits for clean energy technologies. The CHIPS and Science Act, signed into law by President Biden in the same year, provided an additional US$280 billion to encourage the construction of microprocessor manufacturing facilities in the US. To prevent loss of investment, the European Union decided in March 2023 to permit its member states to match incentives offered outside Europe (Espinoza and Fleming 2023).

Even before the COVID-19 pandemic and the Russian invasion of Ukraine, countries had imposed an increasing number of restrictions on international trade, particularly in high-tech sectors linked to national security or strategic competition (Global Trade Alert 2021). During the pandemic, these restrictive actions spilled over into the financial sector, again frequently linked to national security considerations (IMF 2022a: 51, figure 3.4). The increased scepticism towards multilateralism and the trend towards unilateral restrictions on cross-border economic transactions led the IMF to suggest that 'the global economy may be on the brink of a reversal of the steady increase in integration that characterized the second half of the 20th century' (Aiyar et al. 2023: 5). It warned that 'geo-economic fragmentation', manifested in the elimination of trade in high-tech manufacturing and energy across rival blocs, could lead to losses equivalent to 1.2 per cent of global GDP (Aiyar et al. 2023: 14, Box 1).

The pandemic and the economic consequences of Russia's invasion of Ukraine disproportionately

Figure 1.4 Regions in sub-Saharan Africa have been most affected by the Russian-Ukrainian conflict due to an increase in food price inflation, especially in Zimbabwe, Burkina Faso, Ghana, Nigeria, and Zambia.

Source: Shutterstock.

affected developing economies. In 2020, for the first time in the twenty-first century, the number of people living in poverty increased. The pandemic increased the numbers in extreme poverty by 77 million (UNCTAD 2022a: 1). The pandemic had its greatest impact on the most vulnerable in labour markets, especially migrants and women. Higher interest rates, introduced by central banks in industrialized economies as they sought to contain the pandemic-induced inflation, increased the already significant burden of debt-servicing for developing economies. Because they already had sizeable debt problems, most developing economies lacked the policy space to pump resources into their economies in the same manner as the industrialized economies. The stimulus, measured as a percentage of GDP, that low-income economies were able to provide is estimated to have been less than a quarter of that provided by the advanced economies (UNCTAD 2022a: 59, figure 5.1).

The conflict between Russia and Ukraine directly impacted the poorest in developing economies because of the disruptions to exports of foodstuffs and fertil-izers. The prices of food staples in Africa rose by 24 per cent between 2020 and 2022 (Okou, Spray, and Unsal 2022). According to the World Food Programme (2023), more than 345 million people were expected to be food insecure in 2023, more than double the pre-COVID number in 2020. One third of these are in Africa. The cost of fertilizer doubled. The Ukraine conflict also led to soaring costs for imports of energy: by August 2022, the global price of the energy index was seven times the pandemic-induced level of mid-2020, and more than three times the level at the end of 2019.[2]

The multilateral economic order has come under unprecedented assault since 2015. For the first time, it has not just been a matter of the United States occasionally ignoring the rules when it suited its interests. Rather, both the Trump and the Biden administrations have explicitly repudiated core elements of multilateral economic cooperation. In their policies towards China, both the United States and the European Union have

[2] Federal Reserve Bank of St. Louis, https://fred.stlouisfed.org/series/PNRGINDEXM.

moved from engagement to decoupling, increasing the risks of global fragmentation into rival economic and security blocs. 'Re-shoring' and 'friend-sourcing' threaten to undermine the economic integration fostered by global value chains (although it should be noted here that companies are not always compliant instruments of government policies and have their own interests to pursue in creating cost-effective supply chains). The following section briefly sketches how the world economy evolved to reach its present state.

KEY POINTS

- The COVID-19 pandemic had a significant impact on the global economy, leading to major disruptions in global value chains, a decline in global output, and setting a lower trajectory for economic growth. Developing economies were particularly affected, with projected growth rates being 4 per cent lower than they would have been without the pandemic.

- Economic factors, including slowing rates of economic growth, income inequality, and the liberalization of international trade, contributed to the rise of populism and nationalist economic policies worldwide. Workers in industrialized economies, especially those with lower levels of education, faced deteriorating economic conditions and job losses due to factors such as technological change and competition from China.

- China's emergence as a global manufacturing powerhouse, facilitated by its entry into the WTO and the growth of global value chains, created imbalanced trade relationships with major industrialized economies. China's persistent trade surpluses, high savings rates, and inflexible labour markets in other countries have hindered successful adaptation to its economic rise and have had political repercussions.

- The rise of conservative populism, exemplified by events such as the election of Donald Trump as US President and the Brexit referendum, challenged the principles of liberal internationalism that had shaped the global economic order since the Second World War.

1.2 The world economy pre-1914

The 'modern world economy', most historians agree, came into existence in the late fifteenth and sixteenth centuries. It was in large part a response to a deepening economic crisis within feudal systems as agricultural productivity declined (Wallerstein 1974). This was a period in which despotic monarchs in Western Europe, seeking to consolidate their power against both internal and external foes, pushed to extend the boundaries of markets. In this era of **mercantilism**, political power was equated with wealth, and wealth with power (Viner 1948). Wealth, in the form of bullion generated by trade surpluses or seized from enemies, enabled monarchs to build the administrative apparatus of their states and to finance the construction of military forces. The new concentration of military power could be projected, both internally and externally, to extract further resources. The consolidation of the state went hand in hand with the extension of markets. Gradually, most parts of the world were enmeshed in a Eurocentric economy as suppliers of raw materials and 'luxury' goods. Britain adopted domestic reforms largely pioneered by the Netherlands (which had the world's highest per capita income in the seventeenth and eighteenth centuries) to supplant the Dutch in many world markets: armed conflict and the use of the **Navigation Acts** (1651–1849), which restricted the use of foreign vessels in British trade, enabled it to monopolize trade with its ever-expanding empire.

The era of mercantilism did not, however, bring a notable increase in overall global wealth. Before 1820, per capita incomes in most parts of the world were not significantly different from those of the previous eight *centuries* (they increased by less than an average of one tenth of 1 per cent each year between 1700 and 1820). And, despite the striking extension of the global market during the seventeenth and eighteenth centuries, the vast majority of commerce continued to be conducted within individual localities until the advent of the Industrial Revolution. The introduction of steam power in the first half of the nineteenth century revolutionized transportation, both internally and internationally. And in the second half of the nineteenth century, further technological advances—the introduction of refrigerated ships, the laying of submarine telegraph cables—contributed to a 'shrinking' of the world and to a deepening of the international division of labour. The value of world exports grew tenfold (from a relatively small base) between 1820 and 1870: from 1870 to 1913, world exports grew at an annual average rate of 3.4 per cent, substantially above the 2.1 annual increase in world GDP (Maddison 2001: 262, table B-19, and 362, table F-4).

Trade was becoming increasingly important to world welfare, yet the pattern of international commerce in 1913—indeed, even in 1945—was not dramatically different from that of the eighteenth century. The industrialized countries of the world—essentially a Western European core to which had been added the US and Japan by the turn of the twentieth century—exported principally manufactured goods, while the rest of the world supplied agricultural products and raw materials to feed the industrialized countries' workforces and to fuel their manufacturing plants. As a relative latecomer to industrialization, and as an economy with significant **comparative advantage** in agricultural production, the US was an exception to this generalization: cotton remained the single most important export for the US in 1913, contributing nearly twice the value of exports of machinery and iron and steel combined. It was not until 1930 that machinery exports exceeded those of cotton, although by 1910 the US had become a net exporter of manufactured goods (data from Mitchell 1993: 504, table E3; and Irwin 2003).

With the exception of the US, trade among the industrialized countries in manufactured goods remained relatively unimportant. In 1913, for example, agricultural products and other primary products constituted two thirds of the total imports of the UK. To be sure, some changes had occurred in the composition of imports. Although the 'luxury' imports of the previous centuries—sugar, tea, coffee, and tobacco—had become staples in the diet of the new urban working and middle classes, their aggregate importance in European imports had shrunk relative to other commodities, notably wheat and flour, butter and vegetable oils, and meat (Offer 1989: 82, table 6.1).

For the early European industrializers, trade with their colonies, dominions, or with the other lands of recent European settlement, such as Argentina, was more important than trade with other industrialized countries (Key Theory Box 1.5 discusses the political economy of colonialism). For the UK, a larger share of imports was contributed by Argentina, Australia, Canada, and India together than by the US, despite the latter's importance in British imports of cotton for its burgeoning textiles industry. These four countries also took five times the American share of British exports in 1913 (Mitchell 1992: 644, table E2). Similarly, Algeria was a larger market for French exports in 1913 than was the US.

Tariffs continued to constitute a significant barrier to international trade even in what is often termed the 'golden age' of liberalism before 1914. Most industrialized countries (the significant exceptions being the UK and the Netherlands) had actually raised the level of their tariffs in the last three decades of the nineteenth century to protect their domestic producers against the increasing import competition that had been facilitated by lower transport costs. In 1913, the average tariff level in Germany and Japan was 12 per cent, in France 16 per cent, and in the US 32.5 per cent (Maddison 1989: 47, table 4.4). The post-1870 increase in tariffs offset some of the gains from lower transportation costs. Lindert and Williamson (2001) estimate that nearly three quarters of the closer integration of markets that occurred in the century before the outbreak of the First World War is attributable to these lower transport costs.

Governments continued to erect barriers to the movement of goods in the second part of the nineteenth century, but capital and people moved relatively freely across the globe, their mobility facilitated by developments in transportation and communication. From 1820 to 1913, 26 million people migrated from Europe to the US, Canada, Australia, New Zealand, Argentina, and Brazil. Five million Indians followed the British flag in migrating to Burma, Malaya, Sri Lanka, and Africa, while an even larger number of Chinese are estimated to have migrated to other countries on the Western Pacific rim (Maddison 2001: 98). The opening up of the lands of 'new settlement' required massive capital investments—in railways in particular (and stands in marked contrast to the paucity of investment in most other colonies). By 1913, the UK, France, and Germany had investments abroad totalling over US$33 billion: after the 1870s, Britain invested more than half its savings abroad, and the income from its foreign investments in 1913 was equivalent to almost 10 per cent of all the goods and services produced domestically (Maddison 2001: 100).

The spectacular growth in international economic integration was not accompanied by any significant institutionalization of intergovernmental collaboration. Even though the Anglo-French Cobden–Chevalier Treaty of 1860 had introduced the principle of **most-favoured nation (MFN)** status into international trade agreements (see Trommer, Chapter 5, Key Concept Box 5.1), governments conducted trade negotiations on a bilateral basis rather than under the auspices of an international institution.

The international financial system was similarly characterized by a lack of institutionalization. The rapid growth of economic integration was facilitated by the international adoption of the **gold standard** (see Key Concept Box 1.6). The origins of the nineteenth-century gold standard lay in action by the Bank

KEY THEORY BOX 1.5 THE POLITICAL ECONOMY OF COLONIALISM

Over the past 250 years, debate has raged over the role that economic factors played in driving imperialism, the impact of empire on the economies of industrialized countries, and that of colonialism on the Global South. As Watson demonstrates in Chapter 2, classical liberals, although generally in agreement that the maintenance of empire and of a preferential trading system that favoured the colonies were a misallocation of scarce resources, were divided on whether empire was beneficial to the colonies given their often racist views regarding Indigenous populations. Writers in the socialist (Hobson) and Marxist (Lenin, Rosa Luxemburg, Hilferding) traditions believed that structural features of contemporary capitalism (under-consumption, excessive capital accumulation) drove imperialism (Etherington 1984; Brewer 1990). Others believed that strategic rivalry was more important than economic issues (Waltz 1979).

The calculus of benefits for imperial countries and colonies is complex, interweaving various strands of arguments: that companies in the imperial centre benefitted because of their capacity to pay workers even less than at home; that 'merchants' and thus the City of London were the principal beneficiaries of imperial commerce; that imperialism extracted 'surplus' from the periphery to the benefit of the metropolitan economies; and that the destruction of traditional handicraft industries in the colonies was positive because it paved the way for industrialization, which in turn would be facilitated by the infrastructure built by the colonizers.

Estimating the economic impact of imperialism on the colonies is particularly challenging given the number of factors besides colonial rule itself that might affect outcomes (differences in pre-colonial structures and factor endowments, the number of colonial settlers, who the colonizing power was, etc.). It is evident, for instance, that the impact of colonialism was very different in Australia or Canada than it was in sub-Saharan Africa. Dilley (2008) provides a useful introduction to the complexities involved. And, assumptions have to be made about the counter-factual situation, that is, what would have occurred in the absence of colonialism. A number of econometric studies have reached the conclusion, however, that it is difficult 'to argue that there is any country today in sub-Saharan Africa that is more developed because it was colonised by the Europeans. Quite the contrary' (Heldring and Robinson 2018). They argue that the poor post-independence economic performance of most African countries is directly linked to the impact of colonialism through mechanisms such as the immiseration (including falls in real wages) of Africans that resulted from land alienation, a lack of investment in human and physical capital (with investments in infrastructure only to facilitate exports and to extend colonial rule), the suppression of prices through agricultural marketing boards, the use of forced labour to build infrastructure, etc.

It is not just colonialism itself that has to be considered, but the impact of the slave trade. As Nunn (2008: 140) reminds us, whereas official colonial rule in most parts of Africa lasted for around seventy-five years, from the Congress of Berlin in 1884–1885 to around 1960, Africa simultaneously experienced four forms of slave trade (trans-Atlantic; trans-Saharan; Red Sea; and Indian Ocean) for nearly 500 years, from 1400 to 1900. He finds a strong association between the number of slaves taken from African countries and poor economic performance (measured as real GDP). A crucial mechanism is the impact that the slave trade had on state formation by weakening political institutions. Nunn argues that engagement with the slave trade frequently fractured ties between villages because of conflicts over supplying slaves, and consequently discouraged the formation of larger communities and ethnic identities. The slave trade thus was directly linked to subsequent political instability, which was compounded by the lack of political development during colonial rule. Post-independence rulers inherited weak and unstable states, a major factor underlying African countries' poor economic performance (Herbst 2014).

---

of England in 1821 to make all its notes convertible into gold (although Britain had operated a *de facto* gold standard from as early as 1717). The US, though formally on a bimetallic (gold and silver) standard, switched to a *de facto* gold standard in 1834 and turned this into a *de jure* arrangement in 1900. Germany and other industrializing economies followed suit in the 1870s. Because every country fixed the value of its national currency in terms of gold, each currency had a fixed exchange rate against every other in the system (assume, for example, that the US sets the value of its currency as US$100 per ounce of gold, while the UK sets its value at £50 per ounce of gold: the exchange rate between the two currencies would be £1 = US$2).

The great contribution of the gold standard to facilitating international commerce was that economic agents generally did not have to worry about foreign exchange risks: the possibility that the value of the currency of a foreign country would change vis-à-vis their domestic currency and thus, for example, reduce the value of their foreign investments. British investors in American railways could be confident that the dollars they had bought with their sterling investments would buy the same amount of sterling at the

KEY CONCEPT BOX 1.6 THE GOLD STANDARD

A gold standard requires a country to fix the price of its domestic currency in terms of a specific amount of gold. National money (which may or may not consist of gold coins, because other metallic coins and banknotes were also used in some countries) and bank deposits would be freely convertible into gold at the specified price.

Under the gold standard, because the level of each country's economic activity is determined by its money supply, which in turn rests on its gold holdings, a disequilibrium in its balance of trade in principle would be self-correcting. Let us assume, for example, that Britain is running a trade deficit with the US because inflation in Britain has made its exports relatively unattractive to US consumers. Because British exports do not cover the full costs of imports from the US, British authorities would have to transfer gold to the US Treasury. This transfer would reduce the domestic money supply, and hence the level of economic activity in Britain, by reducing the demand for goods and labour, thereby having a deflationary effect on the domestic economy, and depressing its demand for imports. In the US, the opposite would occur: an inflow of gold would boost the money supply, thereby generating additional economic activity in the US and increasing inflationary pressures there. Higher levels of economic activity would also increase the country's demand for imports. Changes in the money supplies in the two countries brought about by the transfer of gold, therefore, would bring their demand for goods back into balance and lead to a restoration of the ratio of the two countries' prices to that reflected in the exchange rate between their currencies.

In principle, the gold standard should act to restore equilibrium automatically in international payments. Central banks, however, were also expected to facilitate adjustment by raising their interest rates when countries were suffering a payments deficit (thereby further dampening domestic economic activities and making domestic investments more attractive to foreigners) and, conversely, to lower interest rates when their economies were experiencing a payments surplus. For most of the period from 1870 to 1914, the Bank of England played by the rules of the game reasonably consistently. Other central banks—including those of France and Belgium—did not. They frequently intervened to attempt to shield the domestic economy from the effects of gold flows (to 'sterilize' their effects) by buying or selling securities (thereby reducing or increasing the volume of gold circulating in the domestic economy).

The gold standard was vulnerable to 'exogenous' shocks (those coming from outside the financial system itself), which were often transmitted quickly from one country to another. The discovery of gold in California in 1848, for example, led to an increase in the US money supply, domestic inflation, and an outflow of gold to its trade partners, which in turn raised their domestic price levels. Countries on the periphery were particularly vulnerable to shocks: interest-rate increases in the industrialized countries, for example, often drew capital from the periphery, leaving the peripheral countries with the major burden of adjustment. For further discussion, see Eichengreen (1985) and Officer (2001).

date their investment matured, and that the US Treasury would convert the dollars back into gold at this time. Meanwhile, they received interest on the sums invested. Confidence in the gold standard did not rest on any international institution, but rather on the commitment of individual governments to maintain the opportunity for individuals to convert their domestic currencies into gold at a fixed exchange rate. Ultimately, the implementation of the gold standard rested on the assumption that governments had both the capacity and the will to impose economic pain on their domestic populations when deflation was needed in order to bring their economy back into equilibrium when experiencing trade deficits. These domestic costs became less acceptable with the rise of working-class political representation, and with the growth of expectations that a fundamental responsibility of governments was to ensure domestic full employment.

KEY POINTS

- The modern world economy came into existence in the fifteenth and sixteenth centuries.

- Despite the significant changes that occurred in the three centuries before the outbreak of the First World War, the fundamental composition and direction of international trade remained unchanged.

- Neither in the field of trade nor finance was any significant international institution constructed in the years before 1914.

- Advances in technology were the main driving force behind the integration of markets, and they facilitated the enormous growth in investment and migration in the nineteenth century.

- The great merit of the gold standard was that it provided certainty for international transactions because it largely removed the risk of foreign exchange losses.

1.3 The world economy in the interwar period

The outbreak of the First World War was a devastating blow to cosmopolitan liberalism: it destroyed the credibility of the liberal argument that economic interdependence in itself would be sufficient to foster an era of peaceful coexistence among states. The war brought to an end an era of unprecedented economic interdependence among the leading industrial countries. For many industrialized economies, indicators of economic openness and interdependence did not regain their pre-First World War levels until the 1970s.

The war devastated the economies of Europe: subsequent political instability compounded economic disruptions. Economic reconstruction was further complicated by demands that Germany make reparations for its aggression, and that Britain and other European countries repay their wartime borrowings from the US. The economic chaos of the interwar years was a sorry reflection of the inability of governments to agree on measures to restore economic stability, and of their resort to beggar-thy-neighbour policies in their efforts to alleviate domestic economic distress. Although the collapse of international trade in the 1930s is the feature of the interwar economy that figures most prominently in stories of this era, the most fundamental problem of the period was the inability of states to construct a viable international financial system.

The international gold standard broke down with the outbreak of war in August 1914 when a speculative attack on sterling caused the Bank of England to impose exchange controls—a refusal to convert sterling into gold and a *de facto* ban on gold exports. Other countries followed suit. Leading countries agreed to reinstate a modified version of the international gold standard in 1925. They failed to act consistently, however, in re-establishing the link between national currencies and gold. The UK restored the convertibility of sterling at the pre-war gold price, despite the domestic inflation that had occurred in the intervening decade. The consequence was that sterling was generally reckoned to be over-valued by at least 10 per cent, making British exports uncompetitive. It proved very difficult for the British government to establish an equilibrium in its **balance of payments** without imposing severe deflation domestically. Other countries—notably

France, Belgium, and Italy—restored convertibility of their currencies at a much lower price of gold than had prevailed before 1914.

The resulting misalignment of currencies was compounded by higher trade barriers than had existed before 1914, the absence of a country/central bank with the resources and the will to provide leadership to the system, and by a failure of central banks to play by the 'rules of the game' of the gold standard. Their inclination to intervene to 'sterilize' the domestic impact of international gold flows was symptomatic of a more fundamental underlying problem: in an era when the working class had been fully enfranchised, when trade unions had become important players in political systems, especially in Western Europe, and when governments were expected to take responsibility for maintaining full employment and promoting domestic economic welfare, the subordination of the domestic economy to the dictates of global markets in the form of the international gold standard was no longer politically acceptable. Polanyi (1944) is the classic statement of this argument; on the misguided attempts by Britain to restore the convertibility of sterling at pre-1914 levels, see Keynes (1925).

The abandonment of the international gold standard followed another speculative attack on sterling in the middle of 1931. The Bank of England lost much of its reserves in July and August of that year, and Britain left the gold standard in September, a move that precipitated a sharp depreciation of the pound (testimony to its over-valuation in the brief period in which the gold standard was restored). Other countries again quickly followed in breaking the link between their currencies and gold. By then, the world economy was in depression, following the shocks to it transmitted from the US after the Wall Street collapse of October 1929. The gold standard almost certainly exacerbated the effects of the depression, because government efforts to maintain the link between their currencies and gold constrained the use of expansionary (inflationary) policies to combat unemployment and low levels of domestic demand (Eichengreen 1992).

The world economy was already in depression before the US Congress, in response to concerns about the intensification of import competition for domestic farmers, passed the infamous Smoot–Hawley Tariff of 1930. This raised US tariffs to historically high levels (an average *ad valorem* tariff of 41 per cent, although tariff rates were already very high as a result of the Tariff Act of 1922, the Fordney–McCumber Tariff). Retaliation from US trading partners quickly followed, with European countries giving preferential tariff treatment to their colonies. The value of world trade declined by two thirds between 1929 and 1934, and became increasingly concentrated in closed imperial blocks.

As in the pre-1914 period, international institutions played no significant role in the governance of international economic matters. The League of Nations had established an Economic and Financial Organization with subcommittees on the various areas of international economic relations. It enjoyed success in the early 1920s in coordinating a financial reconstruction package of £26 million for Austria. It also held various conferences aimed at facilitating trade by promoting common standards on customs procedures, compilation of economic statistics, and so on. But the economic and political disarray of the interwar period simply overwhelmed the League's limited resources and legitimacy: the move to restore international economic collaboration awaited effective action by the world's leading economy, the US. This began with the passage by Congress in 1934 of the Reciprocal Trade Agreements Act (RTAA), which gave the president the authority to negotiate foreign trade agreements (without Congressional approval). The RTAA and the subsequent signing before 1939 of trade agreements with twenty of America's trading partners laid the foundations for the multilateral system that emerged after the Second World War (the reasons why US trade policy changed so dramatically between 1930 and 1934 have been a focus of significant work in GPE; see Irwin and Kroszner 1997; Hiscox 1999).

KEY POINTS

- Misalignment of exchange rates contributed to the problems of economic adjustment in the 1920s.

- The world economy was already in recession before tariffs were raised in the early 1930s—but higher tariffs exacerbated the decline in international trade.

- States did not negotiate any significant institutionalization of international economic relations in the interwar period.

1.4 The world economy post-1945

The world economy that emerged after the Second World War was qualitatively different from anything experienced before. John Ruggie, a leading theorist of political economy, identified two fundamental principles that distinguish the post-war economy from its predecessors: the adoption of what Ruggie (1982), following Polanyi (1944), termed **embedded liberalism**, and a commitment to **multilateralism** (Ruggie 1992). Embedded liberalism refers to the compromise that governments made after 1945 between safeguarding their domestic economic objectives, especially a commitment to maintaining full employment, on the one hand, and an opening up of the domestic economy to allow for the restoration of international trade and investment on the other. The 'embedding' of the commitment to economic openness—the liberal element—within domestic economic and political objectives was attained through writing into the rules of the game an acknowledgement that governments could give priority to the pursuit of domestic economic objectives. Provisions in the rules of international trade and finance allowed governments to opt out, on a temporary basis, from their international commitments should these threaten fundamental domestic economic goals. The adoption of the principle of embedded liberalism was a recognition by governments that international economic collaboration rested on their capacity to maintain domestic political consensus—and that international economic collaboration was, fundamentally, a political bargain. This recognition explains, for example, why the agricultural sector was for many years excluded from trade liberalization: governments judged the domestic political costs of negotiating freer trade in agricultural products to be so high as to jeopardize otherwise politically feasible trade liberalization in other sectors.

The institutionalization of international economic cooperation was another fundamental change in international economic relations in the post-war period. Neither in the period of relative stability of the pre-First World War gold standard era nor in the chaos of the 1930s did leading economies create significant international economic institutions. A commitment to multilateralism is one of the defining characteristics of the post-1945 order. For Ruggie (1992: 571), multilateralism is not merely a matter of numbers—it involves collaboration among three or more states,

---

KEY CONCEPT BOX 1.7 BRETTON WOODS

In 1944, the Western allies brought together their principal economic advisers for a conference at the Mount Washington Hotel in the village of Bretton Woods, New Hampshire, to chart the future of the international economy in the post-war period. Forty-four governments, including a number of developing economies, participated in the negotiations at what was officially known as the United Nations Monetary and Financial Conference (Helleiner 2014a) and agreed on the principles that would govern international finance in the post-war years. Additionally, they agreed to establish two major international institutions to assist in the management of these arrangements: the International Monetary Fund, and the World Bank (formally

known as the International Bank for Reconstruction and Development). For details of the discussions at the conference, see van Dormael (1978) and Helleiner (2014a).

These institutions and the rules for managing international finance that were agreed became known collectively as the Bretton Woods regimes. In 1947, a United Nations Conference on Trade and Employment in Havana, Cuba, drew up a charter[3] for an International Trade Organization (ITO), to complement the Bretton Woods financial institutions. The ITO never came into existence, however—see Trommer, Chapter 5.

---

not necessarily among all members of the system—but it also has a *qualitative* element in that the coordination of relations is on 'the basis of "generalized" principles of conduct, that is, principles which specify appropriate conduct for a class of actions, without regard to the particularistic interests of the parties or the strategic exigencies that may exist in any specific occurrence'. A classic example is the most-favoured-nation principle, with its requirement that products from all trading partners must be treated in the same manner regardless of the characteristics of the countries involved. This principle for the conduct of trade contrasts, for example, with the largely bilateral trade agreements of the interwar years, where governments, rather than applying a generalized principle to their trade relations, discriminated in their treatment of individual trading partners.

The commitment to multilateralism that developed in the late 1930s and during the Second World War bore immediate fruit in the founding of the **Bretton Woods** multilateral financial institutions: the International Monetary Fund and the World Bank (see Key Concept Box 1.7). Note, however, that these global or universal institutions, membership of which is open to all states in the international system, are just one form of multilateralism. For the whole of the period since 1945, but especially since the mid-1990s, regional institutions have also played an important role in international economic (as well as security) affairs (see Trommer, Chapter 5). States have increasingly enmeshed themselves in a dense web of multilateral institutions.

The unprecedented rates of economic growth achieved in the years after 1945 attest to the success of the pursuit of multilateral economic collaboration in

this period. Global GDP grew at close to 5 per cent in the period 1950–1973. The recessions that followed the oil price rises of 1973–1974 and 1979–1980, and the debt crises that afflicted Latin America and Africa, contributed to a slowing of growth in the quarter-century after 1973. World GDP nonetheless grew after 1945 at an average of 3 per cent per annum, a faster rate than in any other historic era (Maddison 2001: 262, tables 8–19). Moreover, world trade grew more rapidly than world production: world exports expanded by close to 8 per cent per annum in the years 1950–1973, and by 5 per cent annually in the subsequent twenty-five-year period (Maddison 2001: 362, table F-4). The internationalized sector consequently grew in importance in most economies, with important implications for the balance of domestic political interests on trade policy issues (see Guisinger, Chapter 6).

Aggregate rates of economic growth disguised substantial variations across different regions of the world economy. The gap between rich and poor widened substantially. In 1500, little difference existed in per capita incomes across various regions of the world. Incomes per head in the US did not exceed those of China until the second quarter of the eighteenth century. By the third quarter of the nineteenth century, however, a marked gap had developed between incomes per capita in the US and Western Europe on the one hand, and those of the rest of the world (Figure 1.5). Per capita incomes in Africa and in most parts of Asia stagnated (and in China actually regressed for a century). Despite the economic turmoil and

---

[3] For more details on the agreement, refer to www.wto.org/english/docs_e/legal_e/havana_e.pdf.

Figure 1.5 Per capita income 1000–1998 (US$)

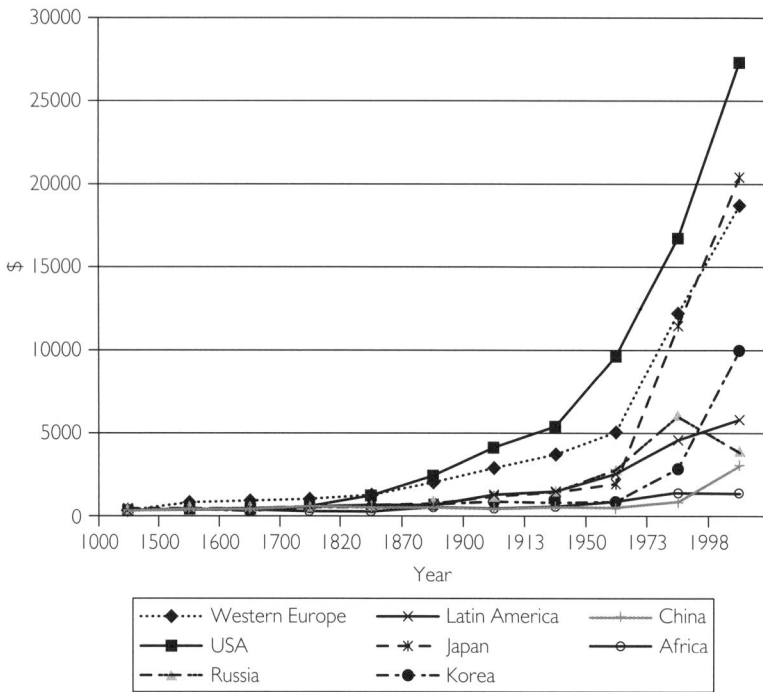

Legend:
····◆···· Western Europe ——✕—— Latin America ——+—— China
——■—— USA – –✱– – Japan ——⊙—— Africa
– –▲– – Russia – –●– – Korea

slower rates of growth of the interwar years, the absolute gap between the industrialized economies and the rest of the world continued to widen.

Contrary to the expectations of mainstream economics, a striking feature of the global economy over the last half-century has been the widening income gap between industrialized economies (which although encompassing only 14 per cent of the world's population contribute 42 per cent of global GDP and 62 per cent of world exports) and those in other parts of the world (see Lockwood, Chapter 13). Even allowing for the likelihood of substantial differences in performance between countries in the same grouping, Figure 1.5 provides a clear illustration of this trend.[4]

Whereas in 1980 per capita incomes in advanced economies were roughly double those in Latin

---

[4] The graph uses the terminology of the International Monetary Fund, from which these data are drawn. The Fund's group of **'advanced'** economies (forty in total) consists of Andorra; Australia; Austria; Belgium; Canada; Cyprus; Czech Republic; Denmark; Estonia; Finland; France; Germany; Greece; Hong Kong; Iceland; Ireland; Israel; Italy; Japan; Korea, Republic of; Latvia; Lithuania; Luxembourg; Macao; Malta; The Netherlands; New Zealand; Norway; Portugal; Puerto Rico; San Marino; Singapore; Slovak Republic; Slovenia; Spain; Sweden; Switzerland; Taiwan; UK; and the USA.

Sub-Saharan Africa comprises forty-five countries: Angola; Benin; Botswana; Burkina Faso; Burundi; Cabo Verde; Cameroon; Central African Republic; Chad; Comoros; Democratic Republic of the Congo; Côte d'Ivoire; Equatorial Guinea; Eritrea; Eswatini; Ethiopia; Gabon; The

Gambia; Ghana; Guinea; Guinea-Bissau; Kenya; Lesotho; Liberia; Madagascar; Malawi; Mali; Mauritius; Mozambique; Namibia; Niger; Nigeria; Rwanda; São Tomé and Príncipe; Senegal; Seychelles; Sierra Leone; South Africa; South Sudan; Tanzania; Togo; Uganda; Zambia; and Zimbabwe.

Latin America and the Caribbean consists of thirty-three countries: Antigua and Barbuda; Argentina; Aruba; the Bahamas; Barbados; Belize; Bolivia; Brazil; Chile; Colombia; Costa Rica; Dominica; Dominican Republic; Ecuador; El Salvador; Grenada; Guatemala; Guyana; Haiti; Honduras; Jamaica; Mexico; Nicaragua; Panama; Paraguay; Peru; St Kitts and Nevis; St Lucia; St Vincent and the Grenadines; Suriname; Trinidad and Tobago; Uruguay; and Venezuela.

The **ASEAN-5** are: Indonesia; Malaysia; the Philippines; Thailand; and Vietnam.

America, by 2022 they were more than four times the figure. For sub-Saharan Africa, the ratio had increased from around ten to more than twenty. Even though GDP in many developing economies grew more rapidly than in advanced economies (Table 1.1), the slower growth rates in the latter nonetheless generated larger *absolute* increases in GDP (in that they started from a much higher base—a 6 per cent growth rate on a $10,000 base, for instance, generates $600, whereas a 3 per cent growth on $30,000 generates $900). And in sub-Saharan Africa in particular, relatively high rates of population growth ensured that growth in *per capita* incomes remained low. In the more than forty years covered by this graph, per capita incomes in sub-Saharan Africa grew by little more than 20 per cent, a mere half per cent a year on average. The last twenty years of the twentieth century were 'lost decades' for economies in Latin America and sub-Saharan Africa, with stagnant or declining per capita incomes, as they struggled with significant external debt problems (for further discussion see Pauly, Chapter 9). By the end of the twentieth century, average per capita income in Africa was no more than Western Europe had experienced in 1820 (Maddison 2001).

In the whole period since the Second World War, only a small number of economies have 'graduated' to high income status (Wade 2016: 469). These have been a handful of oil-exporting economies with small populations, a few economies on the periphery of major industrialized areas (for example, Mexico, Ireland, Slovenia), and the East Asian **newly industrializing countries** (NICs) (Hong Kong, Republic of Korea, Singapore, and Taiwan, all four of which are now included in the IMF's category of 'advanced' economies). The performance of the East Asian NICs raises the question of why they have been exceptional. This is too large a topic to explore here in detail—explanations in the scholarly literature range from their geo-political location and significance (Korea and Taiwan benefitted from substantial US assistance in the 1950s and 1960s), their colonial experiences (both Korea and Taiwan were briefly colonies of Japan), the sound macroeconomic policies they followed, and their incorporation within GVCs. Many commentators believe that the strength of state institutions was a fundamental reason for their success (see, for instance, Amsden 1989; Wade 1990; Wade 2018). Such reasoning reinforces the importance of the argument about how the colonial experience weakened political institutions in Africa.

The structure of the post-war global economy arguably constrained the opportunities of many developing economies in significant ways (see Bhagat, Chapter 14). The emphasis in the colonial period was on the export of commodities valued by the metropolitan countries: at independence, many former colonies were essentially mono-crop economies. The structure of international tariffs until the 1980s typically made it easier for raw materials than processed products to enter the markets of industrialized economies, discouraging efforts at upgrading and adding value locally. And in the financial system, developing economies received few of the assets (**Special Drawing Rights**—see Helleiner, Chapter 8, and Pauly, Chapter 9) created internationally. They were unwisely encouraged by the international financial institutions, developed countries, and private banks to take on debt in the 1970s and 1980s, leading to unsustainable debt burdens that have constrained their growth over the last forty years.

The contemporary global economy is characterized by more frequent financial crises than during the era of fixed exchange rates under the Bretton Woods system (until August 1971—see Helleiner, Chapter 8, and Pauly, Chapter 9). The Global Financial Crisis of 2008–2009 caused a drop in world output by over 2 per cent, the first such fall since the 1930s, and world trade declined by close to 40 per cent. A similar decline occurred in inflows of **foreign direct investment** (**FDI**). That problems that began in the home lending market in the US could plunge the world into its

Table 1.1 Average annual GDP growth 1995–2007 and 2011–2019 (%)		
	1995–2007	2011–2019
World	4.1	3.6
Advanced economies	2.9	1.3
Eurozone	2.4	1.3
Emerging market and developing*	5.5	4.9
Latin America	3.1	1.7
Sub-Saharan Africa	4.9	3.8

* Average for 155 countries including China and India

Source: Calculated from IMF, World Economic Outlook Database, March 2023.

Figure 1.6 Per capita income, purchasing power parity, constant prices 2017 international dollar

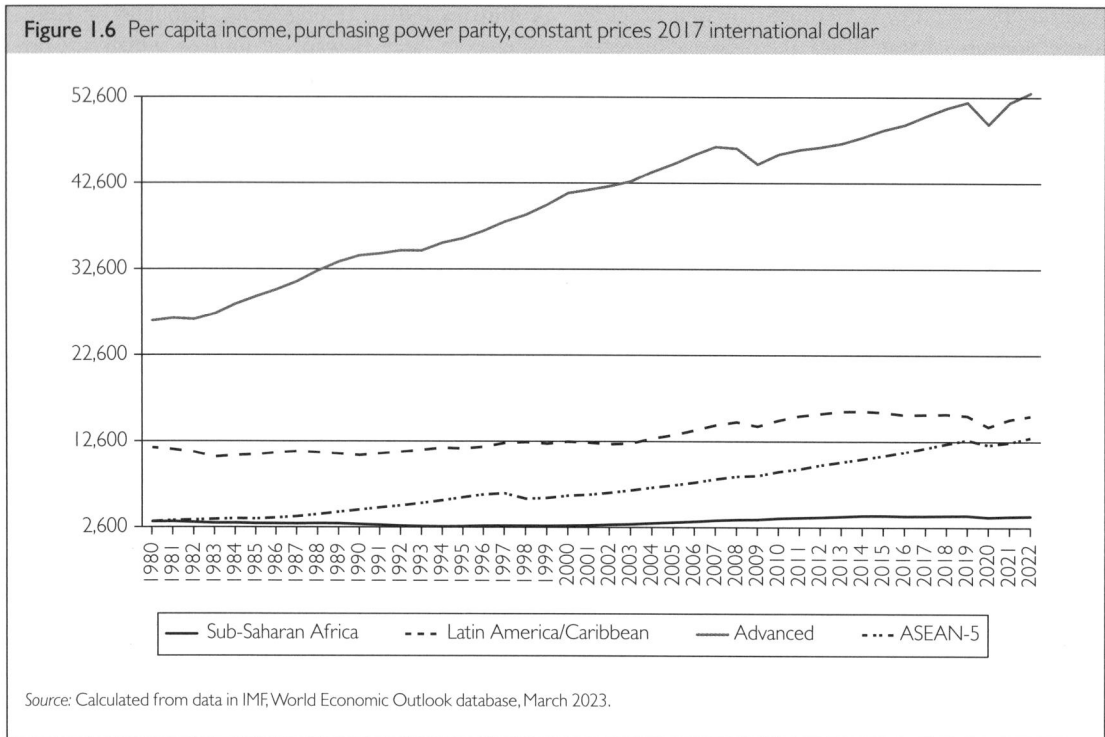

Legend: Sub-Saharan Africa — Latin America/Caribbean — Advanced — ASEAN-5

Source: Calculated from data in IMF, World Economic Outlook database, March 2023.

worst recession since the 1930s is powerful testimony to the integration of the contemporary global economy. Difficulties originating in the US financial sector were quickly transmitted to financial institutions in other advanced economies and then to the 'real' economy when banks curtailed their lending (and, in many instances, had to be bailed out by their governments). Firms (and households) lacked the finance not only to invest for the future, but even to conduct their daily operations. Finance for international trade dried up. The world economy quickly went into reverse. Although national governments and international organizations implemented measures that were intended to reduce the likelihood of similar crises occurring in the future, neither financial sector professionals nor academic commentators were confident that some of the core weaknesses in the system had been addressed. Although there are commonalities across crises, the triggers frequently differ. As one review published by the IMF concluded, 'it should be possible to prevent crises. Yet that seems to have been an impossible task' (Claessens and Kose 2013: 35).

Another defining characteristic of the post-1945 international economy has been the growth in the number of **transnational corporations (TNCs)** (also

referred to in some chapters of this volume as **multinational enterprises**). An increase in the number of significant private economic enterprises with international operations had accompanied the emergence of the modern world economy in the fifteenth century. These, however, were primarily *trading* companies, such as the East India Company, specializing in moving goods between national markets. And when foreign investment took off in earnest, in the half-century before the First World War, the vast majority of it was **portfolio investment**—that is, investment in bonds and other financial instruments that did not give investors management control over the borrowing company. Companies that engaged in FDI—that is, the ownership and management of assets in more than one country for the purposes of production of goods or services (the definition of a TNC)—were relative rarities before 1945 (with some notable exceptions, such as the major oil companies and IBM). In the post-Second World War years, FDI accelerated rapidly, and has grown more quickly than either production or international trade.

The TNC has become the key actor in the globalizing economy. By 2009, it was estimated that there were 82,000 TNCs in operation, controlling more than 810,000 subsidiaries worldwide (UNCTAD 2009: 18). Foreign direct investment increased substantially between 1990 and 2021: whereas the value at current prices of global FDI inflows in the 1990s was US$205 billion, by 2021 the figure had reached US$1,582 billion. In the latter year, the global stock of FDI amounted to about US$45 trillion, equivalent to fully one half of the world's GDP in that year (UNCTAD 2022b: table 1.16). Moreover, sales by the subsidiaries of TNCs were nearly 50 per cent more than the total value of world trade: an estimated US$33 trillion. The significant financial transfers associated with TNC activities should also be noted: in 2021, TNCs benefitted from royalties and licence fee receipts in excess of US$471 billion (UNCTAD 2022b: table 1.16).

Whereas in the period before 1960 the vast majority of FDI and TNCs came from the US, in subsequent years the American presence has been supplemented by corporations with their headquarters in Europe, Japan, Korea, and, increasingly, in less developed countries such as Brazil, China, and India (for further discussion, see Dicken 2015). **Sovereign wealth funds** have also become major sources of foreign investment.

The activities of TNCs, in turn, have fundamentally transformed the nature of international trade. Both the composition and direction of trade have changed dramatically since 1945. Whereas in the interwar years the composition of trade differed little from that of the previous centuries—that is, it was based on the exchange of raw materials and agricultural products for manufactured goods—since the post-war reconstruction of Europe and Japan the principal component of trade has been the international exchange of manufactured goods. At first, this trade (and most FDI) was primarily among the industrialized countries. In many instances, it involved **intra-industry trade**, that is, the international exchange of products from the same industry. For example, intra-industry trade occurs when Sweden exports Volvo cars to Germany and imports BMW vehicles from Germany. As this example suggests, product differentiation by brand name often provides the basis for intra-industry trade and bears little resemblance to the comparative advantage-based explanation for trade that underlies conventional economic theory. Over the last four decades, the growth in intra-industry trade has occurred not so much in the exchange of finished products but of components that are often moved across several national boundaries before assembly and then exported to their final markets—a process

that economists have termed the 'fragmentation' of production.

Since the 1980s in particular, less developed countries have also been integrated into the GVCs led by TNCs (see Key Concept Box 1.3). Many developing countries have changed the structure of their tariffs to give preference to the processing and assembling of components, which they subsequently export. The imported content of processed manufactured exports ranged from more than 50 per cent in China to 66 per cent in Mexico to 63 per cent in relatively developed Korea (Koopman et al. 2010). The WTO estimates that at the turn of the century such processing activities accounted for more than 80 per cent of the exports of the Dominican Republic, close to 60 per cent of the exports of China, and nearly 50 per cent of the exports of Mexico (WTO 2001). This participation in GVCs is the most significant factor in a dramatic change in the commodity composition of the exports of less developed countries. Contrary to some popular impressions, by the end of the 1990s manufactured exports constituted 70 per cent of the total exports from the developing world. The share of manufactures in their exports had increased threefold since the end of the 1970s (UNCTAD 2001: xviii).

Reference to these less developed economies provides a timely reminder of another dramatic change in international economic relations since 1945—a huge augmentation in the number of independent states in the system. As noted in Key Concept Box 1.7, only forty-four countries were represented at the Bretton Woods conference, which was dominated by the industrialized countries of Europe and North America, but also included a few of the long-independent countries of Central and South America. Within two decades, almost all of the colonies of the European countries had gained their independence. This development had profound implications for the international system. One was simply the consequence of an increase in both the number of states and in the diversity of the international community: the number of states in the system more than doubled. Collaboration in international economic relations and the management of various dimensions of this collaboration became increasingly complex, illustrated very clearly in the trade sphere by the difficulties in negotiating the Uruguay and Doha Rounds of WTO talks (see Trommer, Chapter 5, for details of these discussions, and Aggarwal and Dupont, Chapter 3, for a discussion of the problems that larger numbers pose for collaboration).

The growth in the number of less developed countries also brought institutional changes, most notably in the foundation of the United Nations Conference on Trade and Development (UNCTAD) in 1964. And the new arithmetic in the international system generally, and particularly within the United Nations system, contributed to a change in international norms with the adoption, first, of decolonization (Jackson 1993), and then of development as core norms of the modern system (most recently seen in the Sustainable Development Goals). As Singh discusses in Chapter 15, countries from the Global South have been active agents in promoting new international agendas.

Another defining characteristic of the contemporary system contributed to the enshrining of the development norm—the vast expansion in the number of non-governmental organizations (NGOs), many of which focused on the alleviation of poverty (Bhagat, Chapter 14). NGOs have also been prominent in global environmental affairs (see Ervine, Chapter 16) and, increasingly, in international trade (Trommer, Chapter 5). Relations between industrialized and less developed countries, and issues relating to global poverty and inequality, emerged as an important dimension of the study of GPE, the evolution of which is discussed in Section 1.5 of this chapter.

KEY POINTS

The post-war international economy was qualitatively different from anything that preceded it, in several dimensions:

- states made a commitment to multilateralism, reflected in the construction of institutions at the global and regional levels;

- the world economy grew at unprecedented rates after 1945—the internationalized component of economies became more significant as trade and foreign investment grew more rapidly than production;

- TNCs and FDI emerged as key agents in the process of internationalization;

- the composition and direction of international trade changed dramatically, with intra-industry trade among industrialized economies constituting the majority of aggregate world trade; and

- the number of countries in the international system rose substantially.

1.5 The study of global political economy

1.5.1 The origin stories of GPE

Global political economy has multiple origin stories. Most commonly, GPE textbooks position the development of GPE as a significant subfield of International Relations (IR) that emerged in the 1970s in response to real-world changes and to trends in theorizing within and outside the field of study (see Key Concept Box 1.10).

In the early 1970s, the global economy entered a period of turbulence following an unprecedented period of stable economic growth. The 'long boom' from the early post-war years through to 1970 benefitted developed and less developed economies alike. Because of the comparative stability of this period, it was commonplace to regard international economic relations as a relatively uncontentious issue area that technocrats could be left to manage. All this changed in the late 1960s, however, when the US economy encountered increasing problems because its commitment to a **fixed exchange rate** constrained its policy options at a time when domestic inflation was being fuelled by high levels of government expenditure—domestically, on social programmes, and internationally on the pursuit of the Vietnam War. In August 1971, a new era of instability in the global economy was ushered in when the Nixon administration unilaterally devalued the dollar, the so-called Nixon Shock (for further discussion, see Helleiner, Chapter 8). In doing so, it set in motion events that were to end the system of fixed exchange rates, one of the pillars of the Bretton Woods financial regime.

The new instability in international finance reinforced perceptions that the global economy was about to enter an era of significant upheaval. Commodity prices had risen substantially in the early 1970s; Western concerns about the future availability and pricing of raw materials were compounded by the success of the Organization of the Petroleum Exporting Countries (OPEC) during the Arab–Israeli war of 1973 in substantially increasing the price of crude oil. Less developed countries believed that they could use their new-found 'commodity power' to engineer a dramatic restructuring of international economic regimes, a demand they made through calls at the United Nations for a **New International Economic Order (NIEO)** (see Bhagat, Chapter 14, and Singh, Chapter 15). Industrialized economies were already having difficulty in coping with a surge in imports of manufactured goods from Japan and the East Asian NICs, causing them to revert to various discriminatory measures to protect their domestic industries, in disregard of their obligations under the international trade regime (for a discussion of these obligations see Trommer, Chapter 5). In trade and finance regimes alike, new pressures were causing governments to seek to rewrite the rules governing international economic interactions.

Although the early 1970s were characterized by the greatest instability in international economic relations since the depression of the 1930s, inter-state relations in the security realm, which had been the principal focus of the study of post-war international relations, appeared to be on the verge of entering a new era of collaboration. The US was winding down its involvement in Indochina; Henry Kissinger was negotiating détente with the Soviet Union; and President Nixon's visit to China in 1972 appeared to presage a new epoch in which China would be integrated peacefully into the international system. For many scholars of international relations, the traditional agenda of the discipline was incomplete, and the preoccupation of the dominant, realist approach with security issues and military power seemed increasingly irrelevant to the new international environment (Keohane and Nye 1972; Morse 1976).

The new turbulence in international economic relations prompted political scientists to take an interest in a subject matter that had previously been left largely to economists. It was not, as some commentators suggested, that international economic relations had suddenly become 'politicized'. Politics and asymmetries in power had always underlain the structure of global economic relations, seen, for example, in the content of the various financial regimes negotiated at Bretton Woods. Rather, what was novel was that the turbulence of the early 1970s suggested that the fundamental rules of the game were suddenly open for renegotiation, and that a return to post-war stability was both desirable and achievable.

Political scientists' new interest in international economic relations also coincided with the abandonment by the economics profession of what had previously been taught and researched as institutional economics. As the discipline of economics aspired to more 'scientific' approaches through the application of statistical and mathematical models, it also increasingly abandoned the study of international economic institutions. Political scientists discovered a vacuum that they quickly filled.

This also coincided with the rise in prominence of **rational choice theory** and its offshoots in GPE's parent field, International Relations, in the 1970s. Rational choice theory is based on the assumption that actors engage in utility-maximizing behaviour. This means that actors' self-interests or preferences are known, fixed, and prioritized. Actors make decisions given the available options and certain constraints, such as limited resources and availability of information. Actors assign subjective values to outcomes and assess the probability of each outcome occurring. They weigh these factors to calculate the expected utility of different choices and select the option with the highest expected utility. Critics argue that this type of theorizing naturalizes a particular type of economic agency akin to *homo economicus*, who is only suited to life inside free markets. Some even argue that the rise in prominence of rational choice theory reflects and reinforces free market **hegemony** that GPE scholars might otherwise wish to critique (Cox 1981; Watson 2020). Nevertheless, rational choice theory was inscribed onto the three main approaches to GPE that rose to prominence in the field after 1970—liberalism, realism (sometimes referred to as neo-mercantilism), and Marxism—and it is the basis of many methodological and theoretical divides in GPE today.

While some scholars have acknowledged that the field has deeper roots (Strange 1984; Cohen 2008), these real world and theoretical advancements in the 1970s ushered in the formal 'discipline' of GPE from the 1970s onwards and built in a normative bias in favour of a return to the type of 'stability' experienced during the post-war period and a theoretical bias in favour of three approaches—liberalism, realism, and Marxism—each of which is grounded in assumptions about rationality. Indeed, for Watson (2020), 'writing GPE's history as if there is nothing of relevance before 1970 has the potential to inadvertently bind it to the very modern predilection for viewing the world through the interlocking prisms of pro-market ideology and rational choice theory.'

Reading this origin story, students would be forgiven for thinking that GPE is a strictly modern field of study that was born on the eve of the 1971 Nixon Shock. This dominant story notwithstanding, GPE has a very deep, historical, and global intellectual lineage that is often obscured in textbook accounts of the field. In perhaps the most significant intervention to date, Eric Helleiner (2023) has uncovered an altogether different origin story that challenges the very notion that GPE has a single received canon or that it can be traced intellectually to the European Enlightenment. In an effort to source the global intellectual roots of GPE in the pre-1945 era, Helleiner brings into view thinkers from all over the world who were concerned with many topics of contemporary relevance including environmental degradation, gender inequality, racial discrimination, religious worldviews, civilizational values, national self-sufficiency, and varieties of economic regionalism. For example, Helleiner (2023: 164) shines a spotlight on early feminists who worked to varying degrees in liberal, socialist, neo-mercantilist, and Pan-African ideological traditions but who all shared 'the broad normative goal of challenging patriarchal practices and structures in order to end women's subordination within the world economy'. In addition to the 'three orthodoxies', Helleiner (2023: 4) shows us that the pre-1945 theoretical landscape included many approaches, including 'autarkism, environmentalism, feminism, Pan-Africanism, Pan-Islamism, Pan-Asianism, and some distinctive visions of economic regionalism'. Examining the historical debates and trajectories of different approaches highlights the cross-germination of ideas over time as well as important internal divisions within the different approaches which continue to influence GPE thinking today.

Many early thinkers are invoked in contemporary debates about GPE, but little scholarly attention has been devoted to understanding their influence. Quoting John Maynard Keynes, Helleiner (2023: 2) describes the ideas from the pre-1945 period as 'voices in the air': 'madmen in authority, who hear voices in the air, are distilling their frenzy from some academic scribbler of a few years back'. In Chapter 2 of this volume, Matthew Watson helps fill these silences by 'decolonizing' the historical roots of GPE (Shilliam 2021), or destabilizing foundational knowledge, by showing: (1) who said that a subject field's foundations could only be framed in one particular way; (2) what motivations they had for declaring the search for foundations over; (3) how subsequent generations of scholars allowed their own thinking to be organized around such a restricted vision; and (4) who was erased as a consequence from the stories that a subject field's practitioners tell themselves about disciplinary origins. Watson's contribution to decolonizing GPE is to reassess eighteenth- and nineteenth-century political economy on the basis of what it said about race, empire, and colonialism and what it means for the contemporary study of GPE.

1.5.2 What is GPE and how can we study it?

GPE is a field of inquiry that has as its subject matter the dynamic relationship between power, economics, and politics (see Key Concept Box 1.8). It is not

---

KEY CONCEPT BOX 1.8 WHAT'S IN A NAME? INTERNATIONAL VS GLOBAL POLITICAL ECONOMY

When international relations scholars began to examine economic issues in depth, the new subfield inherited the rather misleading adjective 'international' as the leading word in its title. Commentators have often pointed out that 'international' relations is a misnomer for its subject matter in that it confuses 'nation' with 'state', and it fails to acknowledge the significance of private actors in global politics. It also fails to account for domestic- or local-global interactions or the politics of the global economy as a whole. But labels, like institutions, are often 'sticky'—once adopted, it is difficult to displace them, even if a better alternative is available. The abbreviation, IPE, has become synonymous with the field of study. Nevertheless, we prefer 'global political economy' in this book because it reflects more accurately the contemporary subject matter of this field, although many scholars still follow conventional usage in employing the abbreviation IPE and in referring to 'international' political economy.

While the study of GPE achieved a new prominence in the 1970s, a variety of work in what would now be recognized as the field of GPE was published much earlier than this. Prominent examples include Albert Hirschman's (1945) study of asymmetries in Germany's economic relations with its East European neighbours, and Karl Polanyi's (1944) *The Great Transformation*, which examined the evolution of relations between markets and the state. Much of the work in the field of development economics that blossomed in the post-war period included a significant focus on political and international components. And the Marxist tradition of political economy remained vibrant, particularly in Europe. For discussion of pre-1945 work in the field of GPE, see Helleiner (2023).

To confuse matters, the study of economics was known in the eighteenth and nineteenth centuries as political economy (see, for example, John Stuart Mill's (1970) *Principles of Political Economy* (first published in 1848)). The titles of some leading journals in the field of economics—for example, the *Journal of Political Economy*, first published in 1892—continue to reflect this older usage.

KEY THEORY BOX 1.9 OPEN ECONOMY POLITICS

The 'open economy politics' (OEP) approach has become increasingly popular among political scientists especially in the US and in some universities in the UK and continental Europe. OEP adopts the assumptions and methods of neo-classical economic theory. The focus is on individuals, firms, and sectors—the premise being that they act rationally in pursuing their economic interests in a context in which alternative policies will have distributional consequences. As with the study of economics, the goal has been to search for law-like regularities (for a sympathetic exploration see Lake 2009; Cohen (2017) and Oatley (2017) offer interpretations that are more critical).

Critics of OEP deny that GPE can be reduced to the study of individual pursuit of self-interest. For them, efforts to mimic economic theory render the OEP approach vulnerable to the same criticisms that Susan Strange made of economics in her 1970 article 'International Economics and International Relations: A Case of Mutual Neglect' (Strange 1970), which many see as the foundational piece for GPE outside the US. In particular, economics typically has little interest in institutions, in structures through which power is exercised, and in the role of ideas (beyond economic self-interest) in shaping behaviour. Critics of OEP generally reject methodological individualism (the idea that social phenomena can be explained by the aggregation of individual actions), or the possibility that the study of GPE can be 'scientific' in the sense of discovering universal laws, and notions that individuals are rational maximizers in their behaviour. For critics of OEP, an understanding of GPE requires a far more eclectic approach that embraces theoretical and methodological pluralism.

---

a specific approach or set of approaches to studying this subject matter. Rather GPE is defined by its theoretical and methodological **pluralism**. Indeed, the full range of theoretical and methodological approaches from international and comparative politics has been applied to the study of GPE.

Alongside the origin story which places GPE's birthday in 1970, GPE textbooks commonly present three main theoretical positions through which introductions to GPE are then typically taught—realism, liberalism, and Marxism. This follows Robert Gilpin's publication of the best-selling GPE textbook *The Political Economy of International Relations* (1987), which identified what he called 'three ideologies' of GPE: nationalism, liberalism, and Marxism (Gilpin 1987: 25; see also Gilpin 1975: 21).[5] Of these three labels, only liberalism has been used universally in other categorizations. Other writers have substituted 'statism', 'mercantilism', 'realism', or 'economic nationalism' for nationalism. In a similar vein, the approaches that Gilpin subsumed under the label Marxism have variously been identified as 'radical', 'critical', 'structuralist', 'dependency', 'under-development', and 'world systems'. In itself, the use of a variety of labels points to one of the problems with the 'trichotomous' categorization of approaches to the study of GPE: the (sometimes misleading) lumping together of substantially different perspectives within a single category which is presented as a coherent 'ideology'.

[5] In Gilpin's original terminology these were liberalism, nationalism, and Marxism. He changed some of his labels in the updated version of his book: Gilpin 2001.

Although Gilpin is widely recognized as having set the parameters within which the field continues to be located today (Cohen 2008), the trichotomous categorization does not capture the wealth of methodological and theoretical approaches used in the contemporary study of GPE or provide an accurate signpost to the breadth of fascinating questions that currently preoccupy researchers in the field. Indeed, the continued use of this categorization serves to silence and marginalize important contributions to the field. For these reasons, we do not use the trichotomous categorization in this book.

We adopt a more open-ended distinction—'conventional' and 'critical'—to help organize our engagement with different approaches to GPE (see Hannah and Hinton, Chapter 4, for additional discussion). Rather than representing self-contained and coherent world views—like the different positions in Gilpin's formulation—we understand conventional and critical approaches to represent big, theoretically plural tents which can be distinguished based on whether they encompass approaches to studying GPE that problem-solve within dominant orders (conventional) or problematize dominant orders themselves (critical) (for a discussion of problem-solving and critical theory, see Ervine, Chapter 16). Within the critical tent we can locate critical constructivist, Marxist, Gramscian, critical feminist, postcolonial, decolonial, and post-structural scholarship. Within the conventional tent we can locate the multitude of GPE approaches that ascribe to realism or liberalism, including open economy politics (see Key Theory Box 1.9).

All GPE scholars address the question posed by Susan Strange (1996), 'ciu bono', or 'who benefits?' Indeed, questions of distribution are central to GPE: who gets what, when, and how? Nevertheless, how scholars approach answering this question (and others) depends very much on what they see and do not see when they look out into the world. This is related to *ontology*.

Ontology is the study of the nature of reality, of what 'exists'. It is concerned with the identification of core objects of study, their characteristics, and their relationships to other objects. Importantly, scholars cannot 'see' everything at once. In order to reduce complexity, they must make choices about what is important to study and not to study. This is akin to wearing different coloured blinders to make sense of the world. While this might seem very abstract, when applied to GPE, ontology asks: what are the basic building blocks of the social and economic world and how do they interact with one another? Answering these questions involves a series of and/or constitute normative choices about the things that should be elevated and the things that should be neglected in the study of GPE (see Hannah and Hinton, Chapter 4, for further discussion).

For many scholars who adopt conventional approaches to GPE, the basic building blocks of GPE are states and markets and the central focus is on the interplay between public and private power in the distribution or allocation of scarce resources both globally and locally. The main actors in GPE include states, international organizations, and private actors such as multinational corporations and non-governmental organizations operating across a range of policy domains such as trade, finance, and development which are treated as if they are rational and utility maximizing. In this vein, the study of GPE is often top-down, conducted from the vantage point of the so-called governors of the GPE, whether it be international organizations such as the IMF or states such as the United States or China. Economic and social spheres are treated as analytically distinct; what happens within societies, communities, or households is generally treated as separate from or peripheral to the workings of the global economy.

For scholars working within conventional approaches to GPE, power tends to be seen as the capacity of one actor to change the behaviour of another (Dahl 1963). Power may be exercised through coercion and domination, but power is also exercised through the capacity of actors to set agendas (Bachrach and Baratz 1970; Lukes 1974) and to structure the rules in various areas of international economic relations so as to privilege some actors and disadvantage others (Strange 1988).

Besides focusing on questions of distribution and of power, scholars working within conventional approaches to GPE have also been preoccupied with one of the central issues in the study of international relations: which conditions are more favourable for the evolution of cooperation among states in an environment where no central enforcement agency is present? For many observers, this problem of 'cooperation under anarchy' is even more pertinent in the economic than in the security realm. This is because greater potential exists in the economic sphere, particularly under conditions of interdependence, for cooperation on a win-win basis, but states have a considerable temptation to 'cheat' by attempting to exploit concessions made by others while not fully responding in kind (see Aggarwal and Dupont, Chapter 3).

Much of the early GPE work in the 1970s and early 1980s, particularly in North America, married two of these central concerns—the distribution of power within the global economy, and the potential for states to engage in collaboration. Conducted at a time when many perceived US economic power to be waning, this work focused on the link between hegemony and an open global economy (see Key Concept Box 1.10).

In contrast to conventional approaches, scholars who use critical approaches apply different ontologies to the study of GPE (see, for example, Shields et al. 2011). As Hannah and Hinton discuss in Chapter 4, many critical scholars are interested in the social and cultural dimensions of GPE which are considered key to understanding the prevailing question in GPE, 'who benefits?', and uncovering various forms of domination, exploitation, and inequality that arise from global economic arrangements. Public and private spheres of life are seen as deeply intertwined. Rather than draw distinctions or boundaries between economy and society, many critical scholars are attuned to the highly complex interactions between states, markets, and *societies* at different sites and scales, including communities and households. The study of GPE is often bottom-up from a critical perspective, conducted from the vantage point of people and perspectives conventionally on the margins of GPE (see, for example, Clarke and Roberts, Chapter 10). Critical scholars see the centrality of social relations to the global economy *and* the centrality of hierarchical power relations to society. Economic activities in GPE are seen as embedded within broader social contexts and influenced by social interactions and power relations. Power is understood as embedded in dominant ideas, norms, institutions, and discourses. In Chapter 4, Erin Hannah and Lucy Hinton show that by examining the interplay of ideas, social hierarchies, and practices of resistance in everyday life—within the complex interactions of states, markets, and societies—we can begin to make sense of how structural inequalities and power relations along class, gendered, and racialized lines are central to GPE. Similarly, in Chapter 7 Ellie Gore shows us how severe labour exploitation in the global economy is part of a broader set of interactions between market forces, state and supra-state institutions and practices, and social relations, including class relations and hierarchies of race, gender, and citizenship. While critical scholars may

see many of the same actors as conventional scholars in GPE—the US, the International Monetary Fund, Amazon, and so on—the building blocks of GPE are understood very differently, and this has implications for the way GPE is studied.

Likewise, we find substantial variation in epistemology and methodology within and across conventional and critical approaches to GPE (see Key Concept Box 1.11). Many scholars find this rich mix of theories and methodologies a cause for celebration rather than concern. This is certainly the view of the contributors to this volume, which reflects much of the current lively debate in the study of GPE.

As discussed earlier in this section, all GPE scholars have to make a series of difficult normative choices about what is important to study or not to study, and this has inevitably resulted in major empirical and conceptual blind-spots across the field of GPE (Best et al. 2021;

KEY CONCEPT BOX 1.10 POWER AND COLLABORATION

The theory of hegemonic stability suggests that international economic collaboration in pursuit of an open (or liberal) economic order is most likely to occur when the global economy is dominated by a single power. The reasoning is that the dominant country, the hegemon, will have both the desire and the capacity to support an open economic system—the dominant economy is likely to benefit most from free trade; moreover, its relatively large size will give it leverage over other states in the system. Theorists pointed to the experience of the mid-nineteenth century when Britain was the hegemonic power, and to the period of US dominance from 1945 to 1971, as demonstrating the relationship between hegemony and an open world economy. In contrast, the interwar period, when no single country enjoyed equivalent pre-eminence, was characterized by a breakdown in international economic collaboration. The decline in the relative position of the US economy in the 1960s, following the rebuilding of the Western European and Japanese economies, appeared to coincide with renewed closure (a rise in protectionism in response to imports from Japan and the

East Asian NIEs) and the general turbulence in global economic regimes noted above.

Subsequently, however, the hegemonic stability argument was undermined both by trends in the real world and by new theoretical work. In the 1990s, countries extended their collaboration on international economic matters, especially in trade, despite a relatively more even dispersion of economic power in the global system. The recent trend towards populism, however, particularly in the US where one dimension has been support for a pulling back from America's international commitments, has revived interest in the relationship between the distribution of power in the global system and systemic stability.

For statements of the hegemonic stability argument, see Kindleberger (1973) and Krasner (1976); for alternative theoretical perspectives, see Keohane (1984; 1997), Snidal (1985b), and Pahre (1999). For further discussion, see Aggarwal and Dupont, Chapter 3.

KEY CONCEPT BOX 1.11 ONTOLOGY, EPISTEMOLOGY, AND METHODOLOGY

Ontology is the study of being and of what 'exists'. It is concerned with the identification of the core objects of study, their characteristics, and their relationships to other objects. Epistemology is the study of knowledge and justified belief. It is

concerned with questions about the necessary and sufficient conditions of knowledge, the sources of knowledge, and how knowledge is created. Methodology refers to a procedure or set of procedures used to study a subject matter.

Cammack 2021; LeBaron et al. 2021; Hall 2023). For example, topics such as colonialism, race, and gender have typically fallen outside the purview of most textbook analyses of GPE. Although much scholarship has been dedicated to these topics, they are often served up as side dishes or excluded from GPE textbooks altogether. Likewise, non-Western perspectives have been marginalized in both the study and teaching of GPE. This volume considers these to be central axes of inequality in GPE that need to be addressed. The contributors to this volume centre the margins of GPE by being attuned to the legacies of colonialism and considering topics such as North-South dynamics, race, and gender from a range of theoretical viewpoints from across the conventional and critical landscape.

Contributors to this volume also fill blind-spots by considering the intersections of GPE with everyday life (see Hobson and Seabrooke 2007). This is intended to shift students' gaze from the 'global governors' to the 'globally governed' to better understand how everyday people experience the global political economy and how contestations and resistance play out on a daily basis. It also brings to light the ways that everyday practices such as going to work, buying coffee, driving a car, are central to how the global economy operates. Inspired by Brassett et al. (2023), contributors have selected an object or practice that people are likely to use in everyday life (such as beer, cheap clothes, and coffee) and consider how it intersects with major themes in each chapter. In so doing, contributors conduct bottom-up analyses and centre everyday social relations while considering themes such as human rights, sustainability, gender equality, and health.

The first part of the volume engages theoretical approaches to the study of global political economy. In Chapter 2, Matthew Watson contributes to the decolonization of GPE by reassessing the intellectual 'prehistory' of global political economy on the basis of what it said about race, empire, and colonialism and considering what it means for the contemporary study of GPE. In Chapter 3, Vinod Aggarwal and Cédric Dupont consider the conditions that are the most conducive to the emergence of collaborative behaviour among states on economic issues. In Chapter 4, Erin Hannah and Lucy Hinton highlight the interplay of ideas, social hierarchies, and the everyday in order to shed light on some of the most important but often neglected aspects of GPE: gender, race, and everyday life.

The second part of the volume focuses on the global political economy of trade and production. In Chapter 5, Silke Trommer examines the evolution of historical and contemporary global trade relations. Paying particular attention to class, race, and gender, Alexandra Guisinger examines the role of identity in shaping domestic-level attitudes towards trade in Chapter 6. In Chapter 7, Ellie Gore shifts the focus to global production and the centrality of severe labour exploitation in the supply chains of key commodities—from garments to electronics, fishing to agriculture.

The third part of the volume focuses on the global political economy of global money and finance. In Chapter 8, Eric Helleiner takes stock of the development of the international monetary and financial regime since 1944. Louis Pauly assesses the politics of global financial stability and the prospects for collaborative financial governance in Chapter 9. Chris Clarke and Adrienne Roberts offer a bottom-up analysis of global finance in Chapter 10 by adopting 'the everyday' as a lens to explore the worlds of finance, debt, and money.

The resurgence of the state in the face of 'deglobalization' trends and shifting power dynamics is examined in part four of the volume. In Chapter 11, Adam Harmes discusses how political ideologies can help to explain the contemporary politics of globalization, anti-globalization, and global governance, including new forms of populism and economic nationalism. In Chapter 12, James Scott assesses how China and other new powers are impacting GPE and the institutions that govern it.

The penultimate part of this volume focuses on the global political economy of development and inequality. In Chapter 13, Erin Lockwood examines global economic inequality, the role of historical forces in structuring today's wealth distribution, and the impact of contemporary economic institutions of trade, finance, and development in this equation. In Chapter 14, Ali Bhagat problematizes globalized development, its link to crisis-prone tendencies of globalization and to everyday practices in global political economy. In Chapter 15, J. P. Singh considers the important role of 'institutionalized' culture in shaping relations between the Global North and Global South in the global political economy.

Finally, the volume turns its attention to two of the most important and pressing issues in the global political economy today: environmental crises and the digital transformation of the global economy. As we stand on the precipice of catastrophe, Kate Ervine shows in Chapter 16 that the environment is central to the functioning of the global economy and that uneven development and global inequality—two areas that require urgent attention—are deeply connected to ecological decline. Tyler Girard concludes the volume

in Chapter 17 by showing how digital technology—indeed, digital globalization—is fundamentally reconfiguring power relations, and disrupting global labour markets, the structure of international trade, and the very nature of global finance.

1.6 QUESTIONS

1. What were the principal economic factors contributing to the rise of populism?

2. How have COVID-19, the economic and military growth of China, the Russian invasion of Ukraine, and the rise of conservative populism challenged the principles of liberal internationalism?

3. In what ways do we still see and experience the legacies of colonialism in the contemporary global economy?

4. How did the gold standard operate automatically to bring the payments positions of countries into equilibrium?

5. What were the principal reasons for the breakdown of international economic relations in the interwar period?

6. What are the defining characteristics of the post-1945 world economy?

7. What factors led to the emergence of GPE as a significant field of study?

8. What is GPE?

9. What are some key differences between conventional and critical approaches to GPE?

10. From a critical perspective, power is understood as embedded in dominant ideas, norms, institutions, and discourses. It is seen as a central aspect of social relations and hierarchical power relations in society. How do these power relations along class, gendered, and racialized lines shape and influence the global political economy?

1.7 FURTHER READING

Blyth, M. (ed.) (2009), *Routledge Handbook of International Political Economy (IPE): IPE as a Global Conversation* (London: Routledge). This book highlights the diverse and plural nature of GPE scholarship across different regions and theoretical perspectives. It maps different approaches worldwide, encouraging readers to engage with the intellectual diversity in the field rather than seeking a single definitive approach.

Brassett, J., Elias, J., Rethel, L., and Richardson, B. (2023), *I-PEEL: The International Political Economy of Everyday Life* (Oxford: Oxford University Press). This is an innovative textbook that explores the field of GPE through topics like social media, debt, food, and clothing, using everyday experiences to illustrate and challenge key concepts in understanding the world around us.

Cohen, B. J. (2008), *International Political Economy: An Intellectual History* (Princeton, NJ: Princeton University Press). This book provides a detailed examination of the development of contemporary international political economy in various parts of the world.

Cohen, B. J. (2022), *Rethinking International Political Economy* (Northampton, MA: Edward Elgar Publishing). This book examines the problems facing the field of GPE and offers solutions to revive its vitality. Cohen explores the purpose of GPE, its diverse research traditions, and the need for collaboration and policy engagement to rejuvenate the field.

Cox, R. W. (1987), *Production, Power, and World Order: Social Forces in the Making of History* (New York: Columbia University Press). This seminal book examines power in the global political economy by identifying the connections between production, the state, and world order.

Gilpin, R. (1987), *The Political Economy of International Relations* (Princeton, NJ: Princeton University Press). Widely regarded as the seminal introductory textbook which laid the foundation for the 'three orthodoxies' in GPE.

Helleiner, E. (2023), *The Contested World Economy: The Deep and Global Roots of International Political Economy* (Cambridge: Cambridge University Press). This book offers a ground-breaking exploration of the intellectual roots of international political economy, revealing a diverse and global tradition of thought that predates the post-1945 era, shedding new light on current debates and emphasizing the importance of a global understanding of their origins.

Strange, S. (1988), *States and Markets* (London: Pinter). Written by one of the foundational thinkers in GPE, this book provides an idiosyncratic framework of power dynamics, encompassing security, production, finance, and knowledge, to illuminate the intricate relationship between politics and economics in the global arena.

Tooze, R., and Murphy, C. (1996), 'The Epistemology of Poverty and the Poverty of Epistemology in IPE: Mystery, Blindness and Invisibility', *Millennium: Journal of International Studies*, 25/3: 681–707. This article discusses the limits of orthodox approaches in understanding and addressing global poverty in the field of GPE, highlighting the need for more inclusive approaches that consider prevailing power dynamics, historical contexts, cultural factors, and the perspectives of the poor themselves.

Wallerstein, I. (1974), *The Modern World-System* (New York: Academic Press). The first volume of a highly influential multipart work examining the emergence and evolution of the modern world across centuries.

CONTRIBUTOR NOTES

John Ravenhill is Professor in the Department of Political Science at the University of Waterloo, Canada. His publications include *The Political Economy of Automotive Industrialization in East Asia* (Oxford University Press) [with Richard F. Doner and Gregory W. Noble], *The Oxford Handbook of the International Relations of East Asia* (Oxford University Press) [coedited with Saadia Pekkanen and Rosemary Foot], *Crisis as Catalyst: Asia's Dynamic Political Economy* (Cornell University Press), and *APEC and the Construction of Pacific Rim Regionalism* (Cambridge University Press).

Erin Hannah is Professor of Politics and International Relations and Associate Dean of Research at King's University College at the University of Western Ontario, Canada. She has published widely in the areas of global political economy, gender and trade, sustainable development, global governance, global civil society, the role of expert knowledge in global trade, and innovative pedagogy. She is author of *NGOs and Global Trade: Non-State Voices in EU Trade Policymaking* (Routledge), and coeditor of *Expert Knowledge in Global Trade* (Routledge) [with James Scott and Silke Trommer].

2

Race, Empire, Colonialism, and the Pre-history of Global Political Economy

Matthew Watson

Chapter contents

Reader's guide

Global political economy (GPE) scholars have often claimed an interest in thinking historically, contextualizing how the world economy is managed today through reference to the dilemmas faced by older generations of policymakers. Yet their historically oriented analyses often seem to be divorced from some of the biggest issues on which they might be asked to adjudicate. Taking race, empire, and colonialism as my subject matter, I show how restrictive the GPE approach to history has often been. As a rule, it emphasizes policy over people, elite contexts over the everyday, the most recent past over the **longue durée**, and what classic texts would have said about today's conditions of existence over what their authors actually said about their own time. From this perspective, empire and colonialism often disappear from view as relics of a dim and distant past, of no obvious consequence to standard GPE historical fare such as Bretton Woods, the Cold War, the move to a floating exchange rate regime, and the institutionalization of new forms of economic globalization. Race, meanwhile, is understood through its modern manifestations, not through links between past and present. This chapter reveals how narrowly GPE typically draws the parameters of intellectual history, as well as how much it simplifies the multidimensional arguments of the early modern political economists. They may have often written in a way that looks to the contemporary reader to be hesitant, superficial, overly qualified, downright awkward, or even plain wrong, but they did address at length many of the issues that GPE scholars have recently 'discovered' should have been central to their own research all along.

2.1 Introduction

Every subject field is in some sense beholden to its own origin story. Whoever enjoys most success in popularizing their version of how the field emerged and to what questions it was initially oriented will also be likely to shape its present sense of self and its future development. Global political economy (GPE) is curious in this regard, because it seems to operate on the basis of two origin stories. One is its own history, which begins when the first scholars began openly identifying with the new field they had brought into existence. This was during the systemic breakdown of international economic stability during the 1970s. The other might be seen more precisely as its pre-history. The first people to announce that they were engaged in the practice of GPE were quite clearly not the first to be studying political economy more broadly. The PE in GPE had a head start of many centuries, and it focused much of its energy on earlier incarnations of globalization, a topic that the G in GPE likes to claim as its own unique subject matter.

GPE scholars usually connect the history and the pre-history of their subject field by assuming that they have a shared substantive focus on the political conditions under which economic stability can be secured for the inter-state system. However, this involves imposing a distinctly modern template onto older intellectual concerns. GPE's origin story promotes as its fundamental rationale the search for management techniques that allow the world economy to avoid the frequent onset of crises. It then tends to reduce the centuries-old tradition of political economy scholarship to how it approached the same question. How might the economy be organized domestically to ensure that each generation enjoys a higher standard of living than its predecessors? How might the inter-state system be organized internationally to ensure that each state has the chance to develop economically to the benefit of its own population?

The earliest GPE scholars came to the subject field from International Relations (IR), at a time when IR was engaged in its so-called **Third Great Debate**, the inter-paradigm debate between liberals, realists, and radicals (see Key Concept Box 2.1). Each sought authority for their own theoretical position in the present through appeal to foundational texts in political economy's past. IR liberals found a convenient historical starting point for their new venture into GPE scholarship in Smithian economic liberalism, IR realists in the mercantilist reflections of Listian nationalism, and IR radicals in Marxian structuralism. IR liberals in general believed that the world economy could once again be regulated for the good of all through allowing market price signals to be restored to centre stage. IR realists wanted systemic governance to better reflect enhanced capacity for states to choose their own course beyond what markets would allow if left to their own devices. IR radicals said that GPE was asking the wrong questions and that the system would lurch from one crisis to another and remain essentially ungovernable for as long as it was specifically a capitalist system.

This is likely to be a familiar sketch for anyone whose knowledge of the history of economic thought is restricted to what introductory GPE textbooks have told them that they need to know about it. The textbooks' approach to intellectual history is almost always to treat each of these inherently diverse political economy traditions as if they provided a straightforward answer to the question of what is next for the world economy following the breakdown of the **Bretton Woods** system in the early 1970s. Two centuries of liberal thought were condensed into the view that markets know best. A century and a half of modern mercantilist thought was consolidated into the counterview that states should always legislate for political overrides to purely market-based decisions, and a century of Marxist thought was reduced to regretting that the world was not yet ready to dispense with the capitalist mode of production once and for all.

KEY CONCEPT BOX 2.1 THE GPE CANON

Imagine a Matryoshka doll. Each time you remove one of the dolls you discover that there are more inside. Something similar appears true of GPE. The debate about the GPE canon has evolved through a series of stages to the point where the most compelling image is of a canon within a canon within a canon. When one layer of canonical thinking is peeled away, another is revealed. Perhaps the most important feature of GPE's Matryoshka doll effect is that it appears to be constructed out of other subject fields' claims to foundational knowledge, not its own.

When the discussion first turned to the GPE canon in the 1990s, it was really about how it had imported an overly narrow choice of theoretical frameworks from IR. GPE scholars appeared to have restricted themselves to operating within the confines of the neorealist/neoliberal turn in IR's inter-paradigm debate of the 1970s and 1980s. Quickly though, the discussion was refocused on what this outward appearance masked, with a second emphasis on what IR had itself imported from political science. The neorealist and neoliberal frameworks merely mimicked the political science obsession with rational choice theory since the 1960s. The idea here is that all social theory can

be explained as the result of individuals seeking to do the best for themselves in every situation. This, of course, in turn merely mirrors earlier restrictions on how economists had elected to view the world. In 1932, Lionel Robbins introduced his famous definition of economics as 'the science which studies human behaviour as a relationship between ends and scarce means which have alternative uses' (Robbins 1984: 16). Increasingly since then, the Robbins definition has erected a rather oppressive cordon around what might be considered 'proper' economics.

It has been a more recent development to think of GPE's foundations through the perspective of the history of economic thought, and much more recent still to insist that this perspective is suitably decolonized. This latter approach offers opportunities to escape the Matryoshka doll effect through which GPE was presented as a reflection of prior decisions made in IR, themselves a reflection of prior decisions made in political science, themselves a reflection of prior decisions made in economics. Yet maybe it merely reinforces the impression that GPE lacks a standalone **intellectual history** of its own and is always in some sense borrowing that history from somewhere else.

The pre-history of GPE is easy to teach when whole traditions are presented in such simplistic terms, and perhaps this is why the textbooks have been reluctant to take a markedly different approach to the relationship between GPE and the history of economic thought. This chapter might therefore be seen as a consciously anti-textbook offering. It will focus on what the textbooks do not. Indeed, it will focus on what the textbooks cannot. They present the history of economic thought as being an entirely separate endeavour to GPE, but two results ensue from successful attempts at unpacking the history of economic thought rather more fully.

First, it allows us to see how the search for politically acceptable understandings of prevailing economic arrangements endures across a considerable expanse of time, even as the underlying economic structure changes so profoundly, and even as new political struggles emerge to challenge what previous generations treated as acceptable. Second, it allows us to see ourselves more fully in GPE debates. If both the history and the pre-history of those debates is locked in place and directed only at the question of how to impose efficient international regulation, then it is difficult for any of us to truly see ourselves within the resulting

analysis. We may be affected by the regulatory outputs of the global system, but how many of us truly exist in close proximity to the process through which such outputs arise? However, if we widen the lens of the intellectual history that is to be allowed into GPE, we are much more likely to spot the imprints of the lives we lead in the writing of much older scholars.

Of course, extensions of the frame of reference immediately invite the question of how far is enough to have adequately expanded the discussion. Much of the early modern political economy scholarship reflected on issues of a genuinely global nature, and GPE would be much enriched by deeper appreciation of this fact. At the same time, it did so in a knowingly parochial manner. This was the European gaze looking outwards to where other people lived and how they conducted their lives. It was definitely not a conversation of equals between Europe and its others. GPE scholars today must take care not to replicate the asymmetries that are evident in such one-way knowledge flows. They are thus presented with the delicate balancing act of engaging more comprehensively with the history of economic thought but without reproducing the hierarchies of 'self' and 'other' that permeate older texts in political economy.

KEY CONCEPT BOX 2.2 EMPIRE AND IMPERIALISM

The adjective 'imperial' simply means 'related to empire'. However, the nouns 'imperialism' and 'empire' have subtly different meanings and should not be used interchangeably as if they were direct synonyms. 'Empire' refers to a political unit that comprises territory extending beyond the state with which that particular empire is most closely associated. For instance, the British Empire was governed as a single unit from the seat of the British Parliament in London, but also included many other countries as well. 'Imperialism' refers to the political strategy of extending the boundaries of the territory over which the centralized political authority exerts control. We can therefore think of the rise and fall of the British Empire in relation to periods of time in which initially more and subsequently fewer countries were under London's explicit command. The former process occurred almost always through military conquest, the latter through political independence.

The following pages should be read as one such attempt to walk this tightrope. It has taken GPE a long time to recognize how many lives are diminished by the continuing presence around the world of **imperialism**, and there is still little sense of how the subject field's economic concepts continue to carry within them content that reflects their origins in the age of empire (see Key Concepts Box 2.2). Much remains unknown about the way in which issues of race, empire, and colonialism are subsumed within the very vocabulary we use to talk about the economy. Learning more about what the early modern political economists wrote on such matters helps us to further understand GPE's conceptual inheritance and its continued conceptual limits.

In other words, studies in intellectual history are of more than merely historical relevance. Older texts are always going to be of their own time, written in a language that reflects the specific debates in which their authors were involved. But if we allow ourselves to look beneath the surface of those debates to the broader philosophical issues that inform them, we find that their pursuits were not so very different to ours. We might have developed new ways to express our objectives, but in philosophical terms modern-day GPE often merely re-asks questions that have been doing the rounds in political economy scholarship for hundreds of years. We would do well to remember that we are not the first people to worry about how we might learn to live well together when the world's entire population has only one global economic system through which to satisfy its social provisioning needs. The same is true when attention turns to how to organize access to meaningful and dignified existence in a globally equitable manner. The responses

modern-day GPE scholars deliver must reflect the specificities of our own world, but if we wish them to meet the test of being suitably decolonized, there are worse places to start than by applying the same standard to the answers our predecessors gave to the same questions. Decolonizing their thoughts helps to decolonize our own, and it therefore brings greater clarity to how we understand our world.

2.2 Globalizing the history of economic thought

The phrase 'political economy' has been in use since the publication in 1615 of *Traicté de l'Œconomie Politique* by Antoine de Montchrestien (1575–1621). When consulting the GPE textbooks, though, it is as if nothing of this nature existed before Adam Smith (1723–1790) published *The Wealth of Nations* in 1776. Such a view certainly reinforces his reputation as the 'father of economics', but it is misleading. *The Wealth of Nations* was almost certainly the first economic principles book to go global, at least in the sense of generating adherents in many countries, but the pattern of reception around the world was marked by concerns to understand how closely Smith's work reflected forms of economic theory that were already commonplace in their own societies (see Chen 2017; Sakamoto 2017). Moreover, even though the text is not structured in the same way we would expect today—there is no stand-alone chapter dedicated to reviewing the literature and no straightforward attempt to direct the reader to what he thought his main contribution to the literature was—Smith was at pains to show that he was entering pre-existing conversations.

Two distinct strategies therefore present themselves when seeking a greater understanding of how Smith's ideas relate to those whose own work has been put into dialogue with his. The first is to place Smithian economic liberalism in the global context of who else had previously written similar things. Instead of treating *The Wealth of Nations* as the ultimate grand departure and hailing the European Enlightenment as the factor that revolutionized the whole of economic thought, the task is to study potential sources of pre-emption and to ask about the specific national, cultural, and societal conditions under which such prior intellectual discoveries took place. Should the origin story of the pre-history of GPE be traced back to the mid-eighteenth-century Qing dynasty official Chen Hongmou (1696–1771), who operated in the longstanding Confucian tradition to suggest that markets might be internally self-organizing around a century before anyone in the West began to interpret Smith's **invisible hand** metaphor as saying the same thing? Or what about the fourteenth-century North African Muslim scholar Ibn Khaldun (1332–1406), who produced what today look like rudimentary theories of value, demand and supply, and the division of labour 400 years before Smith turned his mind to the same subjects?

The second strategy is to think of *The Wealth of Nations* as part of an evolving conversation between Smith, his most immediate predecessors, and those of later generations who expressed loyalty to his vision. Three predecessors are never far from the surface of his text: the Genevan Jean-Jacques Rousseau (1712–1778), the Scotsman James Steuart (1712–1780), and the Englishman Thomas Mun (1571–1641). Smith's self-declared 'system of natural liberty' consistently engaged economic critique to define his position against Rousseau's anti-Enlightenment ethics and the varying shades of **mercantilism** found in the work of Steuart and Mun. What do we learn about the pre-history of GPE when stepping outside the textbook claims about Smith's decisive break with the past to view *The Wealth of Nations* instead as an intervention into an existing debate about Europe's insertion into the global economy of the time? What more do we learn about it when also considering how the meaning of *The Wealth of Nations* was reconstituted by his followers in multiple countries to make it speak to

debates about empire and colonialism that long post-dated his death?

These two strategies for widening the historical lens in turn suggest two distinct ways in which GPE might be considered ripe for **decolonization**. The former challenges the very idea of a received canon in the history of economic thought, and it certainly dispels the implicit assumption that modern lineages of political economy must all have their origins in the European Enlightenment. Eric Helleiner's (2023) important new book, *The Contested World Economy*, performs this function much more convincingly than I could ever attempt within the confines of a single chapter. It reimagines the very basis of how the pre-history of GPE might be visualized in thoroughly comprehensive fashion, drawing into the narrative thinkers from all around the world.

I will instead follow the latter route towards a potential decolonization of GPE (see Key Theory Box 2.3). I start from the presumption that nobody ever sets out to be a canonical author, mainly because to ascend to such status involves ad hoc attempts by later generations to repackage your message in a series of simplified soundbites when you are no longer around to defend the integrity of your text as a whole. Much valuable work therefore remains to be done to connect GPE to what its textbooks do not say about the books they place on a canonical pedestal. Helleiner begins his account of the global origins of GPE with European liberalism, before reconstructing the rich tapestry of what lies beyond it. I also start with European liberalism, but my aim is to show how much more there is within it than is commonly recognized. GPE textbooks tend to present it as a hermetically sealed tradition founded on a small number of big abstract claims, hence the regularity with which Smith's invisible hand concept is introduced as a supposed commitment to the principle of self-regulating markets. I also turn next to Smith, but it is an explicitly non-canonical Smith who catches my interest. Introductory GPE textbooks are highly unlikely to say as much, because to do so would undermine their message that Smithian liberalism bequeaths to contemporary scholars the political idea that markets always know best. However, the text of *The Wealth of Nations* reveals his deep concerns for the way in which the global markets of his time were being forged through a political project of empire.

KEY THEORY BOX 2.3 DECOLONIZING GLOBAL POLITICAL ECONOMY

According to Robbie Shilliam (2021), successful decolonization consists of three core manoeuvres: it is simultaneously an attempt to recontextualize, reconceptualize, and reimagine received forms of knowledge. Decolonizing strategies attempt to destabilize foundational knowledge by showing: (1) who said that a subject field's foundations could only be framed in one particular way; (2) what motivations they had for declaring the search for foundations over; (3) how subsequent generations of scholars allowed their own thinking to be organized around such a restricted vision; and (4) who got erased as a consequence from the stories that a subject field's practitioners tell themselves about disciplinary origins.

Simply by allowing these questions to be debated, it becomes immediately obvious how narrow and how self-serving most disciplinary self-knowledge is. It is typically constructed around the question 'why do people like me think like I do about the economy?', rather than 'how many traditions of political economy scholarship have flourished somewhere in the world at some point in time?', let alone 'why do I not know more about these alternative traditions than I do?' The last of these questions invites everyone to reflect back on what they were

taught as the basic economic knowledge that feeds into GPE and to wonder whether they should have been taught more widely. There is no national, regional, or even hemispherical monopoly on legitimate ways of thinking about the economy. Every society throughout history has reflected on the same issues of how first to secure subsistence and then how to lift people out of poverty.

Recognizing the multidimensionality of such debates both geographically and historically is the first step to overcoming the blinkers that canonical thinking introduces. It recontextualizes foundational knowledge about the economy by making us think in terms of competing points of origin, leading to divergent trajectories and multiple traditions of thought. The history of GPE can then be reconceptualized in a genuinely global manner, introducing into the conversation a more diverse body of thinkers and the cultural practices that their writings embody. The ultimate goal is to challenge the various ways in which orthodox economic theory reflects the historical experiences of white, Western populations and their Judeo-Christian cultural practices, reimagining GPE in a more suitably inclusive manner.

KEY POINTS

- The history of economic thought has incalculably more dimensions than those revealed by GPE textbook accounts of liberalism versus realism versus Marxism.

- GPE scholars appear to have been more eager to self-credentialize their work by finding supposed precursors in classic texts than to allow the authors of those texts to speak in their own words.

- One strategy for decolonizing the pre-history of GPE is to put European Enlightenment scholars into conversation with economic thinkers from different times and different places.

- Another strategy for decolonization is to reassess eighteenth- and nineteenth-century political economy on the basis of what it said about race, empire, and colonialism.

2.3 Adam Smith and the contested politics of British imperialism

It is the standard misfortune of authors who are elevated to the canon that their work ceases to be known for what it actually says in the text, in preference for

what their followers believe they 'really meant to say' (see Key Theory Box 2.4). This is perhaps never more the case in the history of economic thought than with Smith. His mythical status as the subject field's founding father has turned him into such an important authority figure that others have subsequently sought credibility for their own views through a self-serving reading of his original work. The editors of posthumous editions of *The Wealth of Nations*—amongst them William Playfair in 1818, John Ramsay McCulloch in 1838, Thorold Rogers in 1869, Joseph Shield Nicholson in 1895, and Edwin Cannan in 1904—allowed themselves to comment on Smith's work as if he was a contemporary who should have been as aware as they were of how the world was going to change. From the 1830s onwards, the fashion became to insert comment boxes alongside the text to indicate what, in the editor's opinion, Smith should have written at that point but did not. 'What Smith really meant to say' was thus transformed into 'what he would have said back then had he been me today'.

Nicholson's own changing opinions on empire are instructive in this regard, because they also forced a change in his interpretation of what Smith had written. When he first assumed the editorship of *The Wealth*

KEY THEORY BOX 2.4 CLASSIC THEORETICAL TEXTS IN POLITICAL ECONOMY

Nobody is ever going to be able to read everything of potential interest. Is it an acceptable time-saving device, then, simply to take other people's word on the underlying meaning of a classic text?

The answer probably depends on what that person's intention is. If they have made an in-depth study of the relationship between text and context and can be trusted not to impose their favoured understanding of their own world onto the author's earlier work, they are likely to act as a reliable guide. This will still deprive the person who accepts somebody else's account as given of the rewards of discovering for themselves the secrets contained in the text. There can be a feeling of wonder when finding yourself transported back in time to learn what the world looked like to economic theorists in their own day and to see their hopes and fears for the future come to life in front of you. Nevertheless, at times needs must, and it will be necessary to defer to authoritative interpretations as a short-cut to identifying essential characteristics of classic texts.

However, it is a different matter if the guide proves to be less reliable because their intention is to launder the reputation of a long-dead predecessor for their own ends. Many have succumbed to the temptation of using a self-imagined link back to a text that is widely believed to speak on behalf of the profession as a whole to enhance the perceived standing of their own claims. Classic texts are often put at the service of modern arguments with which they bear no real connection. Canonical knowledge frequently forms in this way, reducing a text to a single quote or a single concept that serves much more purpose today than it did at the time it was originally committed to the page. All references to context are immediately removed in the pretence that the original content reveals a universal truth. It can be with a different sense of wonder that reading a classic text enables such claims to be challenged. The moment it becomes apparent that the content of a particular book is not as the canon presents it typically lasts long in the memory. It also often leads to disbelief at how the canon survives.

of Nations in 1895, there were already many British supporters of **imperial federation** who were claiming that Smith licensed their views. Not so, retorted a defiant Nicholson at that time. He had yet to be won over to protectionist schemes of **imperial preference** and, reading *The Wealth of Nations* through that perspective, he could see nothing within it to doubt his own view. It still read to him as advocating imperial dissolution in favour of a **Cobdenite** version of global free trade.

Within a decade, however, Nicholson had warmed first to the theoretical system of protection outlined in the *National System of Political Economy* by Friedrich List (1789–1846)—he was simultaneously editor of up-to-date English-language editions of both Smith and List—and then to the practical system of **Tariff Reform** to which it pointed. In 1909, he published *A Project of Empire: A Critical Study of the Economics of Imperialism, with special reference to the ideas of Adam Smith*. In it, he repositioned Smith not as a forerunner of the contemporary Cobdenite resistance to the protectionism inherent in imperial preference, but as the intellectual inspiration for Tariff Reform itself. Smith had certainly argued that, as a last resort, if imperial dissolution proved politically impossible then an imperial parliament should be constructed to provide the colonial population with both the right to a voice and the responsibility to contribute to British

treasury funds. In the later Nicholson's hands, though, this was turned into open advocacy of imperial federation (Palen 2014: 193). 'What Smith really meant' was therefore always rendered consistent with Nicholson's position, even though it experienced a complete about-turn between 1895 and 1909. Such can be the fate of a canonical work when the maintenance of its core meaning passes into the possession of those with a vested interest in it being remembered in a particular way. For forty years from the 1870s, British politics was consumed with the question of what to do about its empire. The canonical Smith came to be cited approvingly on both sides of a polarized debate.

2.3.1 **Empire in *The Wealth of Nations***

The text of *The Wealth of Nations* would seem to provide the most assured means of adjudicating between the factions, but it does so only within limits. It provides insights into Smith's considered thoughts about the *economics* of Britain's late eighteenth-century imperial position, but no more than that. The transcripts of the lectures Smith (1982) delivered at the University of Glasgow in the 1760s are a better indicator of his overall view of empire than any of his published work. His lecture course was divided into four parts, covering the four realms of morals, the economy, the law, and the policymaking process. His position on empire is woven throughout these sections. The lectures make clear his objections to Britain's contemporary imperial ventures: to the immorality of settling lands already populated by an Indigenous population; to the horrors of the plantation economy that allowed British colonists to turn a profit; to the inefficiency of granting commercial monopolies to those who dominated the colonial trade; to the system of laws that preserved such waste at the expense of the population's subsistence needs; and to the policies enacted by those who personally stood to gain from the maintenance of the status quo.

However, something less than all these criticisms made it into Smith's published work. The ethical objections did appear (albeit often at one stage removed) in *The Theory of Moral Sentiments* (1759) and the economic objections (this time directly) in *The Wealth of Nations* (1776). But his big book on jurisprudence was never completed, which meant that his criticisms of the legal system that permitted empire were unknown to the Victorian public who were being told that he was stationed simultaneously on both sides of the debate. Meanwhile, some of his lectures on government policy were incorporated into later editions of *The Wealth of Nations*, but others were dropped entirely.

The chapter 'On Colonies' is the longest in *The Wealth of Nations* at around 35,000 words. It was also one of the last to be drafted, helping to delay publication by anything up to three years. Smith set off for London in 1773, sending advance notice to his publisher that he had the completed manuscript already in his possession. He spent the intervening time until the eventual publication date of 1776 using his circle of London friends to further familiarize himself with Britain's eastward colonial trade (Muthu 2008: 199). He had already informed his students about the losses that were entailed in allowing the **East India Company** to be free of competitors for that trade ('they must be detrimentall to the opulence of the nation'). He had also told them how consumers back home incurred the costs of those losses in the higher prices that were necessary to ensure that monopolistic companies paid dividends to their shareholders ('the people engaged in them make the price what they please') (Smith 1982: LJ(A) vi.87, LJ(B) 232). Yet it was only when he was physically on the spot in London that he witnessed first hand the personal networks that the East India Company had established in parliament to secure its monopoly position against more exacting regulation (see Case Study Box 2.5). Some of

this critique made its way into *The Wealth of Nations*, but usually only incidentally as a by-product of the economic argument against corporate waste and inefficient consumer pricing structures. More of the overtly political critique of the East India Company's capture of the policymaking process might have been expected had the intended books on the law and on the policymaking process ever been written, but they were not.

In Smith's day, Britain's westward imperial trade was also established on a corporate monopoly, but to reflect the different nature of the monopoly this time he presented a different economic critique. The trade with Britain's American colonies, he said, was imposing an unnatural course of development. Smith understood development in stadial terms, whereby a society passed through numerous economic stages: from an agricultural society serving only subsistence needs, to an agricultural society permitting localized trade, to an increasingly industrial society where the boundaries of the immediate market for both agricultural and industrial goods were expanding within the confines of the nation, and only then to international trade (Smith 1776/1981: III.i.3). However, the Navigation Acts required Britain's American colonists to sell their produce bound for European markets only to British merchants. Many port towns on Britain's west coast consequently grew very rich by exploiting to the full their lack of competitors for importing and then re-exporting the agricultural produce coming from the Americas (Smith 1776/1981: IV.ii.24, IV.vii.c.24, 30, cf. IV.vii.c.25). They circumvented many of what Smith thought were the natural stages of development, moving in double-quick time from being, at most, the centres of localized agricultural trade to the stage after international trade. Their economic structures were reorganized to facilitate the so-called **carrying trade**, profiting from local merchants inserting themselves as intermediaries to transport someone else's products to third-party markets (Smith 1776/1981: IV.ii.6).

2.3.2 Smith's personal connections to empire

No town prospered more in this way than the one in which Smith lived and worked between 1751 and 1764. Glasgow had become a bustling global **entrepôt** on the back of its domination of the American tobacco trade, and Smith counted many of the city's tobacco lords amongst his closest acquaintances (Perelman

2000: 173). His biographers point to the significance of these interactions for the evolution of his economic thinking, the constant conversation about contemporary business practices allowing him to clarify where he stood on matters of economic principles. Yet if his thoughts did cohere through companionable chats with his friends, the outcome of that process was still that he took a position against the activities through which great wealth was being delivered to their home town. At no stage, though, did he make this case explicitly. Glasgow merits hardly any mention in *The Wealth of Nations*, and its tobacco lords are completely absent (Watson 2022: 976). Whether in deference to the Enlightenment standard of politeness, or maybe just out of fear of embarrassing his friends, Smith's critique of the exclusive privileges of Britain's westward colonial trade took place at a highly abstract level. The directors of the East India Company were called out openly for their offences against his economic system of natural liberty, but the merchants operating westwards of Britain were spared the same

fate. Their specific activities remained hidden within a more general critique of the maldevelopment enacted by the carrying trade.

The same is true of Smith's critique of the plantation system through which Britain's American colonies flourished throughout his lifetime. The plantation owners' profits were indelibly linked to the transatlantic slave trade, and they re-emerged as secondary profits for the Glaswegian merchants of Smith's acquaintance. Whilst he attacked the institution of slavery in general, the specific actions of those who made their money from it were left unremarked upon. Once again in *The Wealth of Nations* there is little beyond the complaint that the plantation economy could have been organized more efficiently, even though he was surrounded by evidence from Glasgow of the riches it was creating for some. '[T]he work done by slaves', he lamented, 'is in the end the dearest of any' (Smith 1776/1981: III.ii.9). However, in a parallel lament from *The Theory of Moral Sentiments*, he did wonder whether the American colonists might

---

CASE STUDY BOX 2.5 BRITISH LIBERAL ECONOMIC THOUGHT AND THE EAST INDIA COMPANY

It can come as a surprise to learn how close many of the leading lights of early modern British liberal economic thought were to the East India Company. After all, the world they imagined bringing into being was usually the very antithesis of the one it had created for itself. Yet it was the East India Company that established the first academic post with 'political economy' in the title. This was at its own finishing school, Haileybury College in Hertfordshire, with its initial occupant in 1805 being Thomas Robert Malthus (1766–1834).

James Mill (1773–1836), one of the influential circle of friends and correspondents including Malthus, David Ricardo (1772–1823), and Jeremy Bentham (1748–1832), joined the service of the Company in 1819, on the back of his rampantly pro-empire *History of British India*. The book has recently been described as 'the single most important source of British Indophobia and hostility to Orientalism' (Trautmann 1997: 117). Mill's son, John Stuart (1806–1873), followed the same career path. A child prodigy in intellectual terms, he nevertheless did as his father demanded and found employment as a lowly Company clerk at the age of 17, working there alongside writing his philosophical and economic treatises until the government disbanded the Company in 1858. He failed to ever distance himself from his father's view that Indian people were generically incapable of self-government—Malthus voiced similar objections to local independence movements—thus justifying the Company's

appropriation of sovereign executive functions throughout society. Those who believed that Britons ought to be treated significantly more liberally by their own government denied that Indians were similarly deserving.

However, not everyone amongst the early economists acted as paid Company advocates. Adam Smith eagerly accepted a position on an independent commission appointed in 1772 to investigate alleged malpractices of the East India Company (Barber 1975: 88). His lectures at the University of Glasgow were already widely known for their attacks on what he later called the 'strange absurdity' of the Company's activities (Smith 1776/1981: IV.vii.c.103). He looked forward to playing his part in presenting to parliament how these abuses of natural justice translated into numerous harms perpetrated on the general masses both locally and back at home. Perhaps because of the known pre-existing opinions of the commissioners, the government eventually baulked at letting them do their job, transferring responsibility for oversight of the Company's activities to a parliamentary committee including some members who were in its pay. Smith was therefore deprived of what was meant to be a three-year on-the-ground fact-finding mission. He was left to bemoan in *The Wealth of Nations* that corporate entities who seized sovereign executive functions in the manner of the East India Company were 'nuisances in every respect' (Smith 1776/1981: IV.vii.c.108).

Figure 2.1 The victims of enslavement made many attempts to resist their captivity and subvert their owners' financial interests. Here, onlookers watch as the plantation house of the Roehampton Estate in north-west Jamaica is set on fire, eighteen months before the Slavery Abolition Act was passed by the British Parliament in 1833. The plantation's absentee owner was granted compensation under that act of around £1,000,000 in today's money, which could now be worth hundreds of millions of pounds given successful investments.

The Destruction of Roehampton Estate in the parish of St James's in January 1832, the property of J. Baillie Esq. 1833, lithograph by Adolphe Duperly.

Source: Alamy.

unlearn the habits of the 'sordid master' by observing the self-command of those they oppressed (Smith 1759/1982: V.2.9) (see Figure 2.1).

The rather different nature of these arguments drew different objections from those who defended the slave owners' interest. In Smith's day, this was most people with public platforms. His economic critique was gently mocked in the House of Commons, with William Pulteney, at one time Smith's student but now an anti-abolitionist MP, suggesting it was founded only on 'a supposition, a mere theory' (Hansard 1805: vol. 3, col. 658). But his broader concerns about the colonial character touched a more personal nerve, being denounced by Arthur Lee (1764: 10), an Edinburgh law student from Virginia, for articulating 'as bitter an invective as ever fell from the tongue of man'.

The strength of the dismissal of Smith's views by his enraged contemporaries seems to be out of proportion to the views themselves. Emma Rothschild (2011: 213–214) points to the problem he encountered in having a moral theory based on immediate visual experience but then needing to comment on the treatment of people many thousands of miles away. Did Smith 'know anyone who was a slave?' she asks, 'did he know anyone who knew anyone who knew a slave?' The implication seems to be that the imaginative leap

required to close this perceptual gap in moral terms meant that an economic critique was all that was left to him. However, Smith clearly knew many people who made their fortunes from the existence of the plantation system (Rothschild 2010: 31). He was also cited on behalf of the claimant in Joseph Knight v John Wedderburn, the legal case that finally ended the practice of slavery in Scotland. The Court of Sessions, with Smith's mentor Lord Kames as one of the justices, granted Knight his legal freedom. Yet acting as the counsel for the slave owner was Robert Cullen, son of his friend William Cullen, and formerly his favourite student. Smith's social circles were populated by those who moved freely around the Atlantic world, revelling in its glamour, but also hardly ignorant of its terrors. Marvin Brown (2010: 22) concludes: 'Once the gap between what Smith said and what he knew is acknowledged, one wonders how he kept these two stories isolated from each other'.

Such silences are clearly very important. Yet the absence of a bolder dismissal of empire and its connections to the transatlantic slave trade is not the same as support for it. This still leaves it necessary to explain how late-Victorian opinion-formers managed to put their words into Smith's mouth one hundred years after his death to transform him into an advocate of empire. Nicholson seems to have taken what Smith perceived to be the least-worst option once all other political alternatives had been exhausted and presented it as his outright preference. Certainly there are passages in *The Wealth of Nations* that begin to sketch what an imperial federation would look like both economically and politically. This was to be activated as a fall-back position if his reasoning on the economic advantages of imperial dissolution proved unacceptable to the ruling elites. But the wholesale removal of empire as the predominant form of contemporary **economic globalization** remained his primary objective.

KEY POINTS

- *The Wealth of Nations* provides only one of many liberal viewpoints on the future of the British Empire in the late eighteenth century.

- Smith's critique looks very narrow to modern eyes, telling us why an economic liberal but not a political liberal might object to the institution of empire.

- Smith's earliest critics in print all objected to his anti-slavery position.

- *The Wealth of Nations* was re-read as a pro-empire text by many late nineteenth-century British scholars.

2.4 Nineteenth-century British imperial liberalism

The story of how Smith's views got turned on their head in pursuit of a late-Victorian imperial liberalism is, predictably, a complicated one. Yet even being prepared to acknowledge the scope of these complexities is confirmation in itself of the limitations of the usual GPE textbook treatment of the history of economic thought. This typically begins by identifying one all-important forerunner of contemporary schools of GPE and then drawing a straight line to connect past with present (see Watson 2020). The struggle over Smith's intellectual legacy, of the critic of empire increasingly being presented as an advocate of imperial federation, is surely evidence that any such line is necessarily fuzzy in character and subjected to frequent political reinterpretation. The GPE textbooks present the subject field's historical roots in terms of the search for a single essence that transcends the

economic relations of both time and place. But it is also necessary to think about who these theories were created for and how they might have been expected to land. Smith wrote at a time of elite support but general public agnosticism regarding empire. Importantly, though, the late Victorians pitched their pro-imperial federation version of Smith to a public that was overwhelmingly sympathetic to Britain continuing to enjoy some sort of imperial role (MacKenzie 1984: 7).

The Wealth of Nations was written against the backdrop of a significant gap in the popular consciousness where patriotic images were subsequently to be, because everyday economic experiences in the 1770s remained largely untouched by anything beyond highly localized subsistence activities. It required a century of cultural evolution before Britain became what Frank Trentmann (2008: 8) has described as a 'Free Trade nation'. Even then, this was only rarely an unqualified endorsement of the pure Cobdenite vision of a world without economic borders, what Smith (1776/1981: IV.ii.43) himself called the 'Utopia' to be found within his economic writings. The late-Victorian debate about free trade in Britain has often been misinterpreted in GPE due to a failure to pay sufficient attention to the imperial context underpinning that debate. It was conducted within the limits enforced by general public support for the image of a globally ascendant Britannia. Where Smith's economic critique only had to persuade the policymakers of his day (Brown 1994: 43), his late-Victorian successors had to persuade both policymakers and the public. This led to what, to the modern eye, can often appear to be tortuous tensions between the political and economic dimensions of nineteenth-century liberal scholarship on empire.

2.4.1 The Mills: Economic critics but political supporters of empire

James Mill today usually enters the liberal canon at one stage removed, as the friend and correspondent of Jeremy Bentham and David Ricardo or as the father and teacher of John Stuart Mill. In his day, though, he was an important thinker in his own right, moving so effortlessly between various spheres of influence that he was something of a bellwether for contemporary liberal opinion. Economically, he positioned himself squarely in the tradition of Smith, Bentham, and Ricardo. From this perspective, the maintenance of empire in general and of imperial preference trading structures more specifically constituted an unconscionable drain on resources. The economy's full potential, he said, could never be realized whilst such distortions were allowed to persist. Yet politically he continued to accept such losses in championing British despotism as the right form of government for India, whose people he believed were fundamentally incapable of attending to their own needs. Empire came at an economic cost, then, but this was a price worth paying for political reasons. Mill remained throughout his later life a utilitarian imperialist who could not reconcile his liberal economic theory with the harm enacted by empire's misallocation of available resources, but overruled this concern by assuming that a greater good was satisfied if Britain continued its colonial administration of India. To truly decolonize GPE involves the difficult task of accounting for the ambiguities inherent in all those conceptions of empire, like Mill's, that resist characterization in such easy binary terms as being either strictly for or strictly against.

Writing about John Stuart Mill's equally Janus-faced approach to imperial realities half a century later, Jonathan Riley (1998: 294) draws a distinction between '**Ricardian science**' and 'liberal utilitarian art' that applies just as well to James's. Father and son were both sufficiently ardent devotees of Ricardo's (1817) *Principles of Political Economy and Taxation* to know that they could find no justification in abstract economic laws for the British establishment's urge to imperial expansion. James had written an article for the *Encyclopaedia Britannica* in 1823 entitled 'Colony'. He used it to assess the various alleged benefits of colonization purely in economic terms, concluding that each one of them was a mirage produced by a faulty imagination (Majeed 1992: 158). For him, the refusal to accept the combined Smithian-Benthamite-Ricardian dismissal of the economic case for empire amounted to a clear cognitive failure to grasp what he believed to be the settled principles of political economy (Mill 1823: 17). Yet the art of governing, he argued, lay not in simply transposing scientific principles onto lived reality as some sort of template, but in devising a set of rules for taking you to where you ultimately wanted to be. The science would therefore often have to give way to the art.

This allowed both Mills to protect their reputations within two different communities of concern. They were able to burnish their liberal credentials when speaking with the leading intellectuals of the day by continuing to criticize the prevailing British system of government for its illiberal nature and to speak up for the downtrodden at home. Simultaneously, they maintained their popular credentials by arguing for a solution to India's governing problem that was wantonly more illiberal still and would do nothing to assist the distantly downtrodden. They consistently argued that Britain had a duty to impose its rule on backward, uncivilized, underdeveloped India. It was the Indian people who made the country so irredeemably ungovernable, as is evident from how frequently James's writings are littered with observations about the 'rude mind', the 'uncultivated mind', the 'barbarous mind'. John Stuart was less direct, but also identified similar psychological failings that legitimated stripping their bearers of all political rights. James argued that British despotic rule in India was a moral duty to an inferior people undertaken in the knowledge that its own interests lay elsewhere, with John Stuart later presenting it as a selfless act undertaken to advance the economic interests of the world as a whole. Both accused the colonized, in Uday Singh Mehta's (1990: 443) evocative phrase, of a 'civilizational infantilism' that justified removing from them the right to self-determination (see also Sen 2004: 140).

James had been very critical of the East India Company in his 1817 *History of British India*, but by 1819 he was in the Company's employ. He was given the role of assistant examiner of correspondence, helping to sustain political support for the Company's activities by replying to letters questioning the legitimacy of its rule. It governed through a combination of martial law and secret deals with local leaders, and it was subjected to persistent challenge by those back in Britain who continued to operate in the Smithian tradition of treating its seizure of sovereign executive functions as a gratuitous infringement of natural justice. The older Mill's job was to popularize the defence of British despotism so that the East India Company's antagonistic correspondents might be thwarted in their efforts to turn their often very obvious revulsion at its abuses into widespread popular concern. He was writing letters to individual correspondents but constructing arguments to try to sway public opinion. Interestingly, he was also involved in simultaneous attempts to popularize the principles of political economy and to show a public becoming increasingly attuned to life lived within an imperial **metropole** how the British empire could be defended as a matter of practical economics, if not necessarily by economic theory. Others were doing the same, the most successful being two women whose presence in these debates has left no imprint on the GPE textbooks (cf. Watson 2020).

2.4.2 Marcet, Martineau, and economic fictions of empire

Jane Marcet (1769–1858) and Harriet Martineau (1802–1876) attempted to open up the black box of Ricardian science to bring basic economic principles to life as something of explicit relevance to everyday experiences. They inserted guides into their prose to allow readers to overcome initial uncertainties on abstract economic matters and develop increasingly sophisticated understandings. Marcet had a single guide throughout her 1816 *Conversations on Political Economy*, the worldly wise governess Mrs B (we never do discover her full name). Martineau, by contrast, inserted a variety of guides into the twenty-five monthly instalments of her *Illustrations of Political Economy*, each one published as a standalone novella between 1832 and 1834 (see Everyday GPE Box 2.6). It was a significant departure for the time that both

---

EVERYDAY GPE BOX 2.6 POLITICAL ECONOMY AND THE RISE OF THE NOVEL

Due to the development of the novel in the late seventeenth and early eighteenth centuries, European populations were becoming increasingly familiar with calling to mind the image of Black people. From the perspective of the European gaze, however, they were always racialized as 'other'. They were presented defiantly as unlike fellow Europeans, in terms of looks, dispositions, instincts, and conduct. The economic roles they were designated were equally defiantly not ones that Europeans of the time would consider filling themselves. This restricted the development of empathetic relations between Black characters and the books' overwhelmingly white readership.

Two examples from early English language novels show how this empathetic gap was sustained.

In the 1688 novel *Oroonoko*, by Aphra Behn (1640–1689), white readers are invited to commiserate with the eponymous hero for the fate that befalls him after he is tricked into slavery. Yet the pity being solicited is not for every person languishing in that condition, but for the fact that here it has happened to a royal prince. Readers are not invited through their engagement with the text to arrive at judgements about the dehumanizing effects of the economic institution of slavery as a whole, only that Oroonoko's princely status should have sheltered him from such a loss.

In the 1719 novel *Robinson Crusoe*, by Daniel Defoe (1660–1731), this time the eponymous hero is white rather than Black. The first-person narrative constantly justifies Crusoe's attempts to make money from the transatlantic slave trade, to shoot on sight every time he feels fear at the presence of those he racializes as 'other', and to claim property rights in the island he settles following his shipwreck. At no stage does the text require any other emotional or moral response than to confirm that Crusoe is perfectly within his rights to also treat Friday as his property once he has saved him from what he assumes is a cannibal attack.

Economic theory has typically developed entirely in isolation from how economic relations have been captured in the novels of the age. This is a somewhat puzzling omission, seeing as economists have used characters from fiction to illustrate core theoretical propositions when no living person could be found for that task. It is next-to-impossible, for instance, to open an economics textbook and not encounter exercises showing Crusoe to have organized his desert island according to the insights of economic theory. By contrast, everyday GPE scholarship has been much less reticent in attempting to bridge this gap to literary presentations. As part of an ongoing effort to bring popular culture more broadly into discussions of economic life, it has asked how 'the economy' of economic theory relates to 'the economy' as presented in novels. The relationship proves to be complex but close.

Decolonial literary techniques have certainly helped everyday GPE scholars in such a task. In particular, the process of 'writing back' to acknowledged classics has produced valuable new insights into English language novels of the seventeenth and eighteenth centuries. By proceeding in this way, contemporary authors have provided agency to those characters who are rendered inert in the original telling of the story, where the plot lines invariably revolve around the aspirations of the books' white protagonists. Such techniques have now inspired the publication of historical novels regarding the experience of people of colour within the global economy of empire. One excellent example is James Robertson's 2003 novel, *Joseph Knight*. In 1777, the previously enslaved Knight was declared free under Scottish law by the Court of Sessions in Edinburgh, a judgment that thereafter made slave ownership illegal in Scotland. Almost without exception, the historical literature focuses on the construction of the legal arguments as the case was referred all the way to the highest court in the land. Robertson, though, builds on the technique of writing back to reimagine for a modern readership the thoughts of Knight and the nobleman who had previously claimed property in him, and he puts those thoughts into vicarious conversation. The objective is to rehumanize Knight in the face of the historical literature having previously reduced him to an abstract legal datum.

relied extensively on female figures to 'correct' the initial misgivings of a political economy beginner so that standard liberal arguments would eventually win out in their mind.

Mrs B's role throughout Marcet's (1816) *Conversations* is to provide answers to the ever-inquisitive Caroline, who wants to know as she stands on the threshold of adulthood how a young woman of good social standing is to conduct herself in a world that seems to be increasingly in thrall to brute economic logics. Mrs B is at her persuasive best in comforting Caroline that her background will still allow her to marry well but that the society she is destined for will benefit from following Ricardian principles on how best to create investible surpluses (Klaver 2003: 54–55). She is told to expect to enact the **bourgeois** manners of her upbringing in deference to the men who will ultimately loom large in her life, but that she must understand practical lessons of capital formation if she is to support their views in the way she must (Hollis 2002: 386). Caroline's role will be restricted to the home, and she is not to be encouraged to think beyond the terms of her future husband's economic opinions. However, her new-found familiarity with economic theory will allow her to understand how he has come to form those opinions and why she should defer to them as he pursues greater wealth for their family.

Martineau, by contrast, wrote from well outside contemporary gender norms. In confronting social anxiety at the time about the onset of the **industrialization** that was powering empire, in 'The Hill and the Valley' she used a female character (Mrs Wallace) to overturn the view of a male character (Mr Armstrong) that this was a regrettable, retrograde step (Martineau 1832–1834, number 2: 51–79). Marcet's Caroline was a role model for young women who wished to reaffirm the social status quo, but Martineau's Mrs Wallace showed what was possible if women were genuinely to free their minds from their inherited social subordination. Mr Armstrong is castigated for failing to see the future even when it stands before him as an ironworks pumping fire, smoke, steam, and filth into the air, at the same time as it pumps greater gusto into the global circulation of British capital (Freedgood 1999: 219). As with Marcet's guide, Martineau's talk about a future that is already in important ways part of the present, as society sought to adapt to the morals and the mores of industrialization and consequently became more tolerant of empire.

2.4.3 Marcet, Martineau, and the moulding of public opinion

Marcet's audience became wider over time, as she began to consider how her mix of liberal economics and conservative social thought might be presented to the labouring classes. She published *John Hopkins's Notions of Political Economy* in 1833, at the mid-point of the appearance of Martineau's *Illustrations*. The title character persists in wondering whether there might be more to his life than back-breaking toil for a pittance of a wage, only to eventually be convinced that deference to market-bound laws of price and wage determination is his best course of action. This point is underlined most obviously in an allegory entitled 'Rich and Poor'. 'Here I am half-starving', John sighs at the start of the tale, 'while my landlord rides about in a fine carriage; his children are pampered with the most dainty fare, and even his servants are bedizened with gaudy liveries'. He summons a fairy to remove the worst manifestations of ostentatious wealth, believing that 'rich men, by their extravagance, deprive us poor men of bread' (Marcet 1833: 1). The fairy does as asked but prevents John from issuing his thanks for a week, until he has seen the full effects of his most earnest wish. In the meantime, the economy grinds to a halt because the rich have no incentive to keep earning money if there are no luxuries on which to spend it, and first his brother and then John himself lose their jobs and are deprived of the means of providing for their families. Suitably chastised at having forgotten that a harmony of interests exists between rich and poor, he requests that the fairy undoes her work, confirming that he should have been grateful for his lot all along.

Martineau, by contrast, seemed to genuinely believe the position that Marcet initially ascribed to Hopkins, complaining that a wealthy elite was 'pampered above-stairs while others are starving below' (Martineau 1832–1834: v). The liberal economic inheritance she sought to popularize was therefore very different to Marcet's. Marcet took a harmony-of-interests reading of Smith's system of natural liberty to insist on a greater deference to existing social structures than he ever did, whereas Martineau took a rent-seeking reading of Ricardo to urge her working-class readers to understand the extent to which political decisions that protected landowners' privileges kept them poor. Salvation from a political system that was so clearly skewed against them was captured in the *Illustrations* by proletarian characters exhibiting bourgeois habits of mind. In this way, according to Sangeeta Ray (2000: 54), Martineau assisted 'the consolidation of the hegemony of the middle class to which she belonged'.

The working classes could engage in economic self-improvement, we are told, simply by acting as though they had the same opportunities as the middle classes: aping their aspirations, taking on their affectations, voicing their expectations of what they should get out of life. Martineau believed that colonial territories offered the possibility of spatial overflows into which the surplus population of Britain could be poured (Çelikkol 2011: 67). They were places where the working classes could make themselves anew, where their mimicking of middle-class manners would raise their social standing to previously unimagined heights. If only those who were trapped in subsistence conditions in Britain could will themselves into a life at the colonial frontier, then they would have the equality that was denied them at home. The *Illustrations* can therefore often come across as a character book, of how best the working classes might take responsibility for their own conditions of existence.

Marcet's *Conversations*, by contrast, more closely resembles a conduct book. The British Empire is not mentioned once in nearly 400 pages, but the tortured way in which the elites of the time presented their Janus-faced views on empire is a persistent background presence to the text. Over the many editions of the *Conversations*, Mrs B continued to extol her opening position that laissez-faire is best for everyone (Düppe 2011: 124). Caroline's often naïve reconciliation with the inequalities of a hierarchically ordered society serves to naturalize the practice of capital formation within a laissez-faire economy. The distinctive feel of Marcet's writing is always that it is grounded in the realities of the day, and the realities of the practice of capital formation in Victorian Britain cannot be understood other than in relation to the economic conditions of empire. If readers today must work hard to make the relevant connections, her audience would presumably have regarded them as second nature. They would have known that Mrs B's paean to an unqualified laissez-faire always had to confront the counter-reality that the profits currently being recycled around the British economy were in considerable part the outcome of the country's colonial fixation.

The allegorical tale 'The Three Giants' in the later *John Hopkins* removes all of this pretence (Marcet 1833: 27–64). A pedlar trades for a night's lodging with the Hopkins household a classic nineteenth-century **Robinsonade**, a story of emigrants shipwrecked on an uninhabited island having set off from England in search of a better life. There, they meet Aquafluens, Ventosus, and Vaporifer—water power, wind power, and steam power respectively—whose voluntary labour is harnessed to turn the new settlement into a microcosm of the contemporary British economy. The story acts as a clear advertisement for the promise of empire, delivered to an audience that by the 1830s was increasingly receptive to the message. It was then reprinted in the *Story-Book* of 1858, whose title page says that it is aimed at 'little children', indicating how early in life future British citizens would be exposed to the hortatory appeal to empire (Marcet 1858: 93–137). The teenagers in the tale display their good manners in deferentially accepting the economic morals bound into the very fabric of that appeal, and they join their parents in finding wonder that a colony can begin with nothing but very soon be trading on an equal footing with the mother country.

> **KEY POINTS**
>
> - Empire was the important contextual factor underpinning all economic writings in Britain in the nineteenth century, whether they were principles books, character books, or conduct books.
>
> - The Mills were at the forefront of the nineteenth-century trend of saying that there was no justification for empire in economic theory but that it should be pursued as a political strategy nonetheless.
>
> - Marcet and Martineau used a storytelling form populated by fictional characters to try to reach sections of society that might otherwise have remained ignorant of basic political economy principles.
>
> - The various ways in which empire entered economic writings reflected the fact that public opinion now seemed to have swung decisively behind it.

2.5 Racial dynamics in the pre-history of GPE

The pre-history of GPE contains nothing that looks like the modern conception of race. The economics of empire typically bypassed the issue altogether, as it was reduced to a straightforward but dispassionate comparison of costs and benefits. The politics of empire, meanwhile, revolved primarily around whether Britain had a responsibility both to itself and to others to persist with its colonizing mission wherever local people were ill-suited to self-government. It is not as if the question of race was altogether absent in this latter regard, because the hierarchy of national character posited by British imperial liberals mapped very closely onto assumptions about racial hierarchies. It is just that explicit discussions of race in GPE's pre-history were usually masked by and concealed within a whole series of prejudices based on national, religious, and political stereotypes.

As popular support for empire deepened, the nineteenth-century British public increasingly operated within a consent structure that responded to such prejudices. They had to be taught how to identify difference in others in a way that reflected the new geopolitical strategies on which the country's leaders had embarked. Previously it had been necessary only to nurture popular distrust of fellow Europeans to meet the objectives of British statecraft. As late as the 1840s, John Stuart Mill (1843) was still working within the broad outlines of his father's assessment of national character to suggest that it was only really Germany that had a population whose sober industriousness might allow it to match Britain's economic achievements. Irish, French, and southern European peoples were all much more excitable and therefore much more likely to lack the self-control necessary for the improvement of the country as a whole. By the mid-nineteenth century, though, the need to create a popular support structure for the project of empire meant that the distrust that had been nurtured of Catholic Europe had to now also encompass new countries and new sources of difference. Eighteenth-century British liberals had tended to view such differences as interesting intellectual puzzles in the context of assuming that all people were generically the same. By contrast, nineteenth-century British liberals politicized the feeling of unfamiliarity to license white rule over anyone who did not look the same as the audiences they were addressing at home.

2.5.1 The path from Enlightenment liberalism to imperial liberalism

The relationship between Enlightenment liberalism and imperial liberalism is nothing if not complex. Even with its widespread distrust of the economics of empire, Enlightenment liberalism was by no means

blameless in the construction of a superiority complex that today we would understand as being clearly racialized. In perhaps the most important example, David Hume (1711–1776), doyen of British Enlightenment thinking, argued in his essay 'On National Characters' that there were different 'species of men' and that 'I am apt to suspect the Negroes to be naturally inferior to the Whites' (Hume 1748: 213). Hume very rarely enters the consciousness of GPE scholars as anything more than Smith's friend, confidante, and intellectual inspiration. But Smith took a very different position in *The Theory of Moral Sentiments*. He believed that the content of the sympathy one person might express for another through an imaginative act of fellow-feeling would be likely to differ depending on cultural upbringing. Yet the all-important moral capacity to imagine what it might be like to have experienced what had just happened to someone else was a common human faculty that transcended cultural context. If there was a shared capability to engage one another sympathetically, there must also be a shared capability to accept that others hold a right to be treated sympathetically, and therefore Hume's idea of separate 'species of men' according to the colour of their skin was entirely groundless.

Sixty years later, James Mill appeared to revive important aspects of Hume's racial theory, absent some of the explicit racial markers. He presented himself as the spiritual heir to the Scottish conjectural historians—Hume and Smith, but also Adam Ferguson (1723–1816) and John Millar (1735–1801)—in asserting a philosophical account of the past that must be true if society was to evolve to its current state. However, the lineage is dubious (Pitts 2005: 129). Mill certainly used much of the same language of progress as his Scottish predecessors, and he also invoked their idea that society had passed through many distinct stages prior to the present. Yet he also repeatedly doubled down on the claim that the early adoption of commercial society proved the greater reason and thereby the moral superiority of Europeans. The Scottish conjectural historians believed, by contrast, that this was merely the fortunate happenstance of other, entirely incidental social changes. Hume aside, the furthest they typically went was to treat the customs and practices of their own society as a better fit for the type of society it had become, but never better in any objective sense. Smith, Ferguson, and Millar offered a complex multidimensional grid onto which the evolution of each individual society might be mapped and then studied in depth. Its current state of progress was to be understood via the interaction of many factors: the scope that the individual was granted to act upon their own moral judgement; the support that the legal system provided for free and fair economic exchange; the robustness of the legal protection of civil liberties; and the general relationship between government and society. Mill, by contrast, erased all the subtlety made possible by this way of thinking, in preference for an all-encompassing one-dimensional distinction. There were societies that had achieved the state of civilization, but everyone else remained in a state of rudeness. The reason why some countries had left the earlier state behind, he argued, was due to the superior mental capabilities of their members. Some were simply more suited to reasoned judgement and for creating social institutions out of that judgement.

Mill did not appeal to Hume's separate 'species of men', but he hardly needed to. The Scottish conjectural historians saw their task as explanation rather than appraisal, much less a self-serving appraisal in which Britons would learn to be grateful for living in a country with so few equals. Their refusal to condemn other countries for being different was transformed by Mill into a desire wherever possible to avow British superiority. He began his *History of British India* by writing that his predecessors' probing accounts of contemporary states of development across multiple dimensions of explanation could be replaced with his simple 'scale of excellence, or defect' (Mill 1817: 133). The specific differences exhibited by countries outside the European core were washed away in the assertion of their shared developmental backwardness. Mill (1809: 413) had previously expressed his irritation at how easily the European mind was deceived by distance into assuming that India and China had the potential to match Europe's economic pre-eminence and probably already would have done had European settlers not frustrated their more recent development. In his review of Chretien-Louis-Joseph de Guignes's *Voyages à Peking, Manille et l'Île de France*, he insisted instead that there were inherent similarities between those who lived in complex agricultural societies in India and China, the largely nomadic Indigenous people across North and South America and the South Sea Islands, and the 'savages of New Holland' (Mill 1809: 426). Perhaps the only thing they actually had in common was that they could be very easily racialized as 'other' relative to Mill himself, a fact he presented as indisputable evidence of their inherent backwardness (see Figures 2.2a and 2.2b).

2.5.2 **John Stuart Mill's science of ethology**

The younger Mill was without doubt the most important nineteenth-century liberal philosopher in the English-speaking world. However, his permissive approach to personal freedom extended no further than the boundaries of the most immediate political community. People in other countries who were subjected to British rule had no such recourse as the British themselves to object to government infringements of their right to freedom based on the principles of natural justice. Mill was a consistent critic of colonial administrators who overstepped the mark in their mistreatment of local populations, '[k]nowing what the English are, when they are left alone with what they think an inferior race' (Mill 1963a: 1136). Yet this was never turned into a question of whether colonial administration in general contravened his most basic understanding of moral laws. He recoiled at particular actions taking place within the institutional framework of empire, but not at the institutional framework itself (Curthoys and Mitchell 2018: 245).

Mill's reasoning followed from his science of ethology (from the Greek *ēthos*, originally meaning disposition). In his 1859 essay 'A Few Words on Non-Intervention', he declared it 'a grave error' to 'suppose that the same international customs, and the same rules of international morality, can obtain between one civilized nation and another, and between civilized nations and barbarians'. Those peoples still in thrall to the customary traits of barbarism, he said, 'have no rights as a nation, except a right to such treatment as may, at the earliest possible period, fit them for becoming one' (Mill 1859: 772). Britain's role would therefore seem to be less that of the imperial power and more the model society whose imprint would help deliver to other people the freedoms that Britons were already entitled to claim as their own. The later language of the '**white man's burden**' is not used, but its image is nonetheless never far away (Justman 1991: 123–125).

Mill's sketch of his new science of ethology is a curious mix. True to his time, he revealed a concern for elucidating abstract laws—here a combination of psychological and sociological laws—but only as a smokescreen for validating Britain's expanded geopolitical role (Ball 2010: 35). In providing a clear distinction between who deserved to experience liberal institutions of personal freedom and who did not, he

Figures 2.2a and 2.2b The European imagination and the Indigenous 'other'

The diversity of Indigenous people was often wilfully overlooked by European writers of the eighteenth and nineteenth centuries. The attempt by de Guignes to depict everyone not of European ancestry as equally inferior and inherently the same was by no means an isolated display of ignorance. The pictures show people today from regions with their own distinctive histories and cultures but stereotyped by de Guignes. They are from lands that became European settler colonies in North America and Australia. 2.2a. Zuni dancer from New Mexico, USA; 2.2b. Aboriginal warrior from North Queensland, Australia.

(a)

(b)

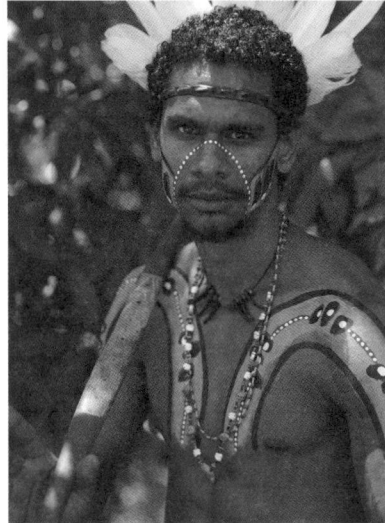

Source: Alamy.

was thus able to shift the terrain of the ethical justification of empire in a way that ultimately eluded his father. James seems to have thought that asserting British superiority was enough in itself, but John Stuart focused his argument on the nature of subject peoples (Skorupski 2021: 436). For James, Britain deserved to enjoy its imperial role because of its exceptional moral status. For John Stuart, it was the colonized who got what they deserved because their deficiencies of moral character meant they required guidance from those who knew better.

The younger Mill's attempts to psychologize politically relevant differences of the rude, primitive, or savage mind avoids the need to explicitly racialize arguments for empire, but it does nothing to remove the underlying racial connotations (Mantena 2010: 35). The most potent example in this regard concerns his divergent treatment of India and Ireland, both of course part of nineteenth-century Britain's sphere of imperial influence. India's backwardness

was attributed to Asiatic habits of mind that infected its entire culture, whereas Ireland's was the result of systematic misgovernment. The Indian people therefore laboured under an adverse ethological inheritance of 'the Hindoo character', which deprived them of the right to be free of British rule, but the adversity faced by the Irish people followed directly from solutions— 'the old bad means'—the British had adopted to manage their affairs (Mill 1868: 22, 24). 'The English nation', he wrote (Mill 1963b: 903), 'owes a tremendous debt to the Irish people for centuries of misgovernment'. In forty-three articles for the *Morning Chronicle* written at the height of the Irish potato famine in 1846–1847, he made the case for a new system of peasant proprietorship of marginal lands to restore moral dignity to their means of existence (Maurer 2012: 65). No parallel scheme was considered necessary for the Indian peasantry, because no such account of their autonomy as moral beings was forthcoming. Mill was often at pains to emphasize the ethological proximity between Irish peasants and Britain's Saxon race, even if the former often lacked the latter's 'dogged tenacity for work' (Mill 1963b: 916). This translated into a moral proximity through which he insisted that the Irish famine could not be reduced to a matter of national character, a point conspicuously absent in his treatment of Indian famines (Bigelow 2003: 69). The differential treatment of European and non-European populations is glaring, but it somehow seems to pass Mill by.

2.5.3 Marcet, Martineau, and dual narratives of character formation

Marcet's Robinsonade in *John Hopkins* has an important feature that distinguishes it from Daniel Defoe's original story. Defoe placed Crusoe on his desert island with no feasible means of escape. If he is to

secure safe passage home, he must come into contact with other people, and given that he was originally shipwrecked on a slave-running voyage those other people are almost certainly going to include the native populations of surrounding islands (see Key Theory Box 2.7).

Marcet, though, ensured that nobody else ever enters the lives of her colonists. Their story is of a struggle against nature alone, in which they are given prodigious help by the three giants Aquafluens, Ventosus, and Vaporifer. Defoe's Crusoe, by contrast, proves to himself that he can subdue nature only as a prelude to the ultimate test he has to pass if he is to achieve redemption. He must also be able to bend to his will everyone else he encounters on the island. The well-known interactions between Crusoe and Friday show his colonization strategy to have the most overt

---

KEY THEORY BOX 2.7 THE MILLS, MARCET, AND MARTINEAU ON SLAVERY

The variety of views that the four held on slavery is merely a further indication of the lack of unity in nineteenth-century British liberalism. Even on this most fundamental of questions there was a marked absence of agreement. It was not of the same nature as the discord over empire, where there were many in favour even though their economic theories told them to be against. A strong abolitionist core ran throughout liberal opinion at this time, but there were marked differences in how the argument was put and what practical implications were read into it.

As Seymour Drescher (2002: 55) has noted, none of the early modern British liberals used their own economic theories to enter the debate about free versus slave labour when the political argument was moving decisively in favour of abolition: not Ricardo, Malthus, or Bentham, and certainly not the older of the Mills. In his famous 'Essay on Government' of 1820, James entirely dismissed the ability of economic theory to speak to the issue of slavery. Noting that it was a 'matter of evil', he nonetheless wrote that it was a 'mode of procuring labour we need not consider' when attention was focused on the utilitarian question of how the government should organize everyday economic life for the greatest happiness of the greatest number (Mill 1820: 5).

Marcet was only marginally more forthcoming. In the *Conversations* published four years previously, she allowed Caroline to broach with Mrs B the topic of abolition. Caroline takes up the issue by reflecting on 'the poor Africans in the West Indies', and when Mrs B tells her that the economic limits of the use of enslaved labourers will be revealed in due course,

Caroline returns to the idea that abolition is above all a moral question by commenting: 'I wish the West-Indian planters could be induced to adopt this opinion'. Like the older Mill, Marcet was writing between the British Parliament outlawing involvement in the slave trade in 1807 and outlawing the ownership of slaves in the countries' colonies in 1833. In Mrs B's rebuke to Caroline to not run ahead of the argument, we presumably see Marcet's own opinion on the benefits of proceeding incrementally from one to the other: 'important changes ought not to be introduced without extreme caution' (Marcet 1819: 110–111).

Martineau and the younger Mill, by contrast, were writing after the dual abolition had taken place in their own country, focusing particularly on the prevailing situation in the United States. Both saw abolition as primarily a moral crusade and, if there were also economic arguments in its favour, then these were strictly secondary. Martineau travelled extensively throughout the US, beginning very soon after she had delivered the last of her *Illustrations* to the publisher, and she wrote ethnographic accounts of what she saw. She spared herself from witnessing few of the human horrors of slavery, attending auctions where enslaved people were sold as property and observing the plantation economy to see how they were put to work. She concluded that the mere existence of a structure of slavery demoralized the white families who benefitted economically from it as well as the Black families who were subjected to it (Logan 2007: 255).

Not long after the start of the **American Civil War** (1861–1865), John Stuart Mill asked his fellow Britons to put

EVERYDAY GPE BOX 2.7 THE MILLS, MARCET, AND MARTINEAU ON SLAVERY (continued)

aside their recent quarrels with the Union government to acknowledge where moral right existed in the conflict, even if their own government was unwilling to be moved from its official stance of strict neutrality. The only position, he argued, 'which becomes a people who are as sincere enemies of slavery as the English really are' is to hope for a Union victory that will end the practice for good (Mill 1862: 6). This was entirely consistent with his earlier writings, in which he

lamented how enslaved people his earlier writings, in which he lamented how enslaved people were 'worked to death, literally to death' merely to satisfy their owners' 'love of gold … I have yet to learn that anything more detestable than this has been done by human beings towards human beings in any part of the earth'. 'If "the gods" will this', he stressed, 'it is the first duty of human beings to resist such gods' (Mill 1850: 26–25) (see Figure 2.3).

Figure 2.3 In 1788, the Society for Effecting the Abolition of the Slave Trade commissioned an engraving of the conditions in which people from Africa were trafficked to plantations in British colonies as part of the infamous Middle Passage. The engraving of the Brookes toured the country as part of the abolitionists' campaign. Its content and its message were evoked in a 2018 protest artwork temporarily installed at the foot of the statue to the Bristol slave trader Edward Colston.

Source: Bristol Post.

racial dimension imaginable, but Marcet managed to eliminate this dimension by ensuring that her colonizers never meet anyone they do not already know. Both are allegories of empire, but only Defoe forced his reader to confront the imperial reality of racial subordination.

Martineau's 1845 economic parable 'Dawn Island' reinstates the racial dimension. It was written for the **Anti-Corn Law League** but contains a very different message to its leading light, Richard Cobden's anti-imperialism (Edmond 1997: 135). 'Dawn Island' is

simultaneously a free-trade fantasy and an imperial fantasy, encircling in one story the tensions inherent in nineteenth-century British liberalism. It acts as another Robinsonade, but it stands out from others of its genre in the nineteenth century by depicting the colonial encounter from the perspective of the Indigenous islanders. The British trading vessel that lands on the island comes in search of commercial opportunities and not societal suppression. Indeed, societal suppression is unnecessary, because the savage code by which the islanders live is undermining their long-term survival (Logan 2016: 103). Miava, a particularly perceptive member of the community, alerts the British sailors to the death spiral created by local customs, and welcomes the enlightened attitudes the newcomers bring along with their commitment to trade (Martineau 1845: 30). The 'dawn' of the title is the arrival of commercial society to overwrite what Patrick Brantlinger (1996: 186) has called the self-servingly imagined 'autogenocide' of savage society. Martineau's (1838/2020) earlier *How to Observe: Morals and Manners* had laid down a series of simple liberal rules to avoid describing other cultures through Western stereotypes. However, 'Dawn Island' appears to fall some way short of this standard. It indulges the imperialist defence of the wilful displacement of native populations by claiming that their primitive state was in any case propelling them towards collective suicide, a fate that only the 'higher disclosure' of European civilization could circumvent (Martineau 1845: 62).

There are dual narratives of character formation in operation in these Robinsonades. Marcet's can only possibly be focused on the Britons who have set sail in search of a new life, because nobody but them appears in her story. Her readers are being encouraged to accept the new economic structures in which their lives are to be conducted and to think expansively about the terrain over which those structures now spread. The geographical boundaries of the nation state are not to be treated as the outer limits of economic possibility, because there is an abundance of virgin land still to be settled. However, Britons might well have to act upon their own character to ensure that they are made of the right stuff to prosper economically in far-off lands, because there is no obvious endorsement of the Mills' insistence that this character is given to them at birth. Meanwhile, Martineau's Robinsonade focuses on the good that can be done for humanity as a whole when the imperial spirit takes hold. The British, she says, can engage in a civilizing mission by exporting their character at the same time as trading their goods. There are role model effects they can enact to the benefit of those whose prevailing customs have hampered their economic development, and free trade is the means through which they can place their character on a pedestal for emulation. The availability of genuinely uninhabited land was no longer a prerequisite for asserting the British way of life if existing inhabitants could be persuaded to look beyond their own embedded customs towards a future commercial society.

KEY POINTS

- Racialized rationales for empire entered much of nineteenth-century imperial liberalism, but often under cover of debates about character.

- The British seemed at this time in little doubt about the superiority of their character, using this as justification for their 'civilizing' mission.

- Enlightenment liberalism treated empire as an impediment to free trade, but imperial liberalism presented Britain's free trade traditions as a reason to push the project of empire.

- Popular culture became an increasingly important site for the reproduction of Britain's imperial mindset.

2.6 Conclusion

The GPE textbooks tell us that liberalism is all about free markets and free trade. These are presented as universal features of all liberal thought, an unchanging core on which all liberals always and everywhere agree. This chapter has shown just how partial, narrow, and indeed misleading the textbook view is. I have barely begun to scratch the surface of the multiple ways in which eighteenth- and nineteenth-century British liberals challenged one another's positions on the question of empire and what this meant for their preferred state of economic affairs. It would be perfectly possible to select an altogether different cast list but still come to the same general conclusion. The route to today's GPE liberalism passes through a patchwork quilt of claim and counterclaim regarding the compatibility of liberal economic theory and the political institutions of empire. Liberal economic theory might today still tend towards discussions of free markets and free trade, but for so long these were discussions set specifically within the context of empire. The imprint of that context continues to be evident within the models, the concepts, and the very language that has been handed down in the liberal GPE tradition, even when its history remains resolutely undisturbed by scholars today.

It is not just the case that it is possible to get a more rounded view of where GPE has come from by engaging that history. Without embracing suitably decolonized understandings of the main points of contestation in the history of economic theory, it might not be possible to genuinely grasp where GPE has come from at all. The textbooks typically present a clear, crisp, and precise account of the essence of different theoretical positions, but it is always necessary to wonder what they leave out of the story. Who would know solely from what the textbooks say that so many points of contestation existed between the Enlightenment liberalism of the eighteenth century and the imperial liberalism of the nineteenth century on what a world constructed on liberal economic principles would look like? Who would be able to tell that the relationship between liberal economics and liberal politics would become so murky that, one hundred years after his death, Adam Smith would be cited approvingly in Britain on both sides of the debate about empire?

This is not to claim, of course, that the insights from the preceding pages complete the task of decolonizing the historical roots of GPE. At most, I have shown what might be done to decolonize one aspect of one way of operationalizing that desire. I have focused solely on restoring questions of race, empire, and colonialism to an understanding of texts that GPE scholars frequently treat as being part of the economics canon. I have left completely untouched the Eurocentric construction of that canon, and I have not asked how economic thought was evolving at the same time outside Europe. Even then, I have focused only on the precursors of GPE liberalism and have not mentioned any other theoretical perspective. This chapter is merely the start of something much bigger. Now that the general case for decolonization is beginning to be accepted, the realization is sinking in amongst GPE scholars about how much remains to be done.

2.7 QUESTIONS

1. Why should we take the time to read classic texts in political economy if the economic structures they depict are different to those we are faced with today?

2. Is it possible to avoid replicating the Eurocentric biases of early modern political economy when studying canonical texts?

3. How might the depth of reflection contained in the work of the modern political economy pioneers be reconciled with how simplistically it is characterized in GPE textbooks?

4. To what extent does the typical textbook treatment of liberalism versus realism versus Marxism obscure the significance of societal cleavages such as race, gender, class, sexuality, and religion?

5. What did eighteenth- and nineteenth-century British liberals say about the stability of the inter-state economic system, the primary question on which GPE has traditionally focused?

6. Is it necessary to adopt a consciously everyday perspective to understand how empire entered the popular consciousness in nineteenth-century Britain?

7. Why did some scholars think support for the system of slavery was compatible with the principles of political economy, but most did not?

8. Where might we turn in attempts to find a genuinely global discussion of empire rather than one that narrates colonial experiences from the perspective of the imperial metropole?

2.8 FURTHER READING

Classic texts

Nothing beats the rewards that come from going back to a classic text and discovering what is in it for yourself. But it is obviously impossible to read everything. Some short-cuts might therefore be necessary.

History of economic ideas

There are several very good introductions to the history of economic thought that are comprehensive in their coverage but do not get too bogged down in theoretical detail. They are written with a student audience uppermost in mind, but they exhibit a familiar Eurocentric feel in their choice of authors:

Backhouse, R. (2002), *The Penguin History of Economics* (London: Penguin). Written with the beginner student in mind, requiring some knowledge of basic economic concepts but otherwise an accessible introduction to the history of economic thought.

Barber, W. (2001), *A History of Economic Thought* (London: Penguin). Assumes no prior training in economics, and therefore provides GPE students with what they need to know without sending them scurrying off to find a dictionary of economic terms.

Heilbroner, R. (2000), *The Worldly Philosophers: The Lives, Times, and Ideas of the Great Economic Thinkers* (London: Penguin). An instant classic in its first edition and now into its ninth, it presents the history of economic thought in detailed but concise and plain language.

Alternative history of economic ideas

There are now some important alternative texts that attempt to widen the discussion to include many other authors, standpoints, arguments, and ways of thinking:

Helleiner, E. (2023), *The Contested World Economy: The Deep and Global Roots of International Political Economy* (Cambridge, MA: University of Cambridge Press). An encyclopaedic demonstration that what is usually presented as 'the' history of economic thought silences alternative traditions of scholarship about global economic relations from all around the world.

Hobson, J. M. (2012), *The Eurocentric Conception of World Politics: Western International Theory, 1760–2010* (Cambridge: Cambridge University Press). Takes as its starting point the fact that GPE questions of international engagement, interaction, cooperation, and order have not historically been the sole province of Western thinkers.

Madden, K., and Dimand, R. W. (eds.) (2018), *The Routledge Handbook of the History of Women's Economic Thought* (London: Routledge). Introduces students to many women who are conventionally overlooked in mainstream histories of economics, particularly those whose work has deepened feminist approaches to the subject.

CONTRIBUTOR NOTE

Matthew Watson is Professor of Political Economy in the Department of Politics and International Studies, University of Warwick, and from 2013 to 2019 was a UK Economic and Social Research Council Professorial Fellow. His publications include *The Market*, *Uneconomic Economics and the Crisis of the Model World*, *The Political Economy of International Capital Mobility*, and *Foundations of International Political Economy*.

3

Cooperation and Conflict in the Global Political Economy

Vinod K. Aggarwal and Cédric Dupont

Chapter contents

Reader's guide

How can one understand the problems of collaboration and coordination in the global political economy (GPE)? In situations of global interdependence, individual action by states often does not yield the desired result. Many argue that the solution to the problem of interdependence is to create international institutions. Yet this approach itself raises the issue of how states might go about creating such institutions in the first place. This chapter examines the conditions under which states might wish to take joint action and provides an introduction to game theory as an approach to understanding interdependent decision-making. It then discusses the conditions under which international institutions are likely to be developed and how they may facilitate international cooperation. Finally, the chapter examines dimensions of institutional variation, with a discussion of factors that shape the design of international institutions.

3.1 Introduction

It is now commonplace to hear about the phenomenon of globalization. Much of the current analytical debate on globalization has its roots in the international political economy literature on interdependence of the early 1970s (Cooper 1972; Keohane and Nye 1977). At that time, political scientists began to identify the characteristics of the changing global economy, including the increased flows of goods and money across national boundaries, as well as the rise of non-state actors, as a challenge to traditional conceptions of international politics.

Although increasing interdependence among states was a relatively new phenomenon when considered against the baseline of the 1950s, high levels of interdependence had existed in earlier historical periods, including the period prior to the First World War (Bordo, Eichengreen, and Irwin 1999). This interdependence, however, was not matched by high levels of institutionalization, in stark contrast to the post-Second World War Bretton Woods organizations of the International Monetary Fund (IMF), the World Bank, and the General Agreement on Tariffs and Trade (GATT), and now its successor, the World Trade Organization (WTO) (see Figure 3.1). The problems that institutions such as the IMF faced with the breakdown of the Bretton Woods gold-dollar-based standard in 1971 (Reinhart and Trebesch 2016), the movement towards trade protectionism that appeared to undermine the GATT, and instability in the oil market with the 1973–1974 oil crisis also drove the debate on interdependence in the early 1970s.

A key issue in considering the implications of interdependence revolves around the question of how to achieve collaboration and coordination among states. In particular, scholars have focused on how states respond to perceived problems in the global economy that they cannot deal with solely on their own. An important starting point is to distinguish interdependence from interconnectedness based on the costs of interaction. According to Keohane and Nye (1977: 9),

Figure 3.1 This is a general view of a plenary session of the United Nations Monetary Conference in Bretton Woods, NH, on 4 July 1944. Delegates from forty-four countries are seated at the long tables. Sen. Charles W. Tobey, R-NH, is speaker in centre background. (AP Photo/Abe Fox).

Source: Alamy.

'[w]here interactions do not have significant costly effects, there is simply interconnectedness'. With costly effects (or high benefits), however, we can consider countries as mutually dependent on each other, or interdependent. In attempting to cope with interdependence, then, countries will be faced with making decisions that will affect their direct wellbeing, and thus the sharing of costs and benefits can be potentially controversial.

This chapter considers the problem of collaboration by first characterizing situations that might require states to work with each other to achieve a desired outcome. It then turns to a focus on basic game theory as an analytical tool to tackle the nature of collaboration and coordination efforts. Finally, we consider how institutions might play a role in enhancing the prospects for cooperative behaviour.

3.2 Globalization and the need for international cooperation

According to international economics textbooks, worldwide economic openness has clear benefits. Integrated world markets help to ensure an optimal allocation of factors of production and therefore help to maximize both aggregate world welfare and individual national welfare. By contrast, sealing off national borders fosters economic inefficiency and has negative consequences for poverty alleviation and development prospects. Yet, in practice, the benefits of globalization cannot always be realized by states pursuing independent policies: cooperative action is required.

The process of global integration forces significant adjustments in production patterns across states. In particular, the changing distribution of costs and benefits from trade liberalization can result in strong political opposition, mainly against, but sometimes for further liberalization (see Guisinger, Chapter 6, for discussion). Adjustment has been all the more difficult in that it leads to unpredictable outcomes and instability in the prices of traded goods. This has proven particularly problematic for many developing countries because they strongly rely on a few primary commodities for the bulk of their exports (UNCTAD 2021). Not only have the prices of most non-fuel commodities declined over the long term, but they have also been increasingly volatile (UNDP 2011; UNCTAD 2012; UNGA 2013; World Bank 2018).

From this perspective, the price surges from 2003 to mid-2008, in 2009–2011, and since 2016 for non-agricultural commodities may not be indicative of a long-term reversal. The abrupt drop of prices in the second half of 2008 is an acute reminder of the long-term boom and bust pattern in commodity **terms of trade** (Spatafora and Tytell 2009; IMF 2012a). Ultra-specialization by some countries in specific commodities has therefore brought severe adjustment costs on the one hand and, on the other hand, failed to provide stable and increasing revenues and significantly hurt their growth prospects (Cavalcanti, Mohaddes, and Raissi 2012). This is an increasing source of concern, as the number of countries whose value of commodity exports exceeds 60 per cent of the value of total merchandise exports has been rising since 2010 (UNCTAD 2019). Price volatility, and often associated supply shortages, has also been a high concern for importing countries, as seen during the global food crisis in 2007–2008, or more recently as a result of the war in Ukraine (FAO 2022). Developing countries that rely on the export of manufactures have also faced significant adjustment challenges. For example, many Latin American countries have increasingly faced a loss of market share in the United States (US) and Europe with the rapid rise of the Chinese export juggernaut. The COVID-19 crisis has highlighted that adjustment challenges may come from import shortages when global trade routes get choked or global supply chains are no longer synchronized (Dadush 2022).

Liberal analysts often argue that countries will be able to manage the process of adjusting to a rapidly shifting division of labour. From their perspective, the prospect of growth in a large number of newly competitive sectors, combined with state capacity to provide social and fiscal transfers, should serve as means to address the challenges of world competition. Yet developing countries, particularly the poorest among them, often have a pre-industrial economic structure. As a consequence, economic openness has brought about a radical transformation of their socio-economic structures, particularly in rural areas, leading to massive migration flows to urban areas. The state structures of developing states are often simply unable to cope with such a rapid and radical transformation. This has led to chaos and, in many instances, to famine and violence, as well as to further political instability and insecurity. For their part, rich countries have often faced strong domestic lobbies in agriculture, textiles, steel, and other older sectors of the economy, creating pressure for trade distorting restrictions of various kinds including subsidies, tariffs, quotas, **voluntary export restraints**, and the like (see Aggarwal, Keohane, and Yoffie 1987). Although such demand, in line with the Ricardo-Viner competitive trade logic (see Guisinger, Chapter 6, Key Theory Box 6.2), seems to be in decline due to the increasing multinationalization of the production chain, the rise of trade in intermediary products, and product differentiation, governments are increasingly facing opposition from pro-environmental groups, human-rights activists, or consumer-protection groups.

Given these political constraints, countries may either be unwilling or unable to sustain processes of economic liberalization by themselves. We need to distinguish between two situations. Facing political difficulties, some countries may no longer view international economic cooperation as highly beneficial and will adopt more nationalistic approaches, relying on selective domestic economic closure or selective domestic support measures while trying to preserve market access abroad. For most countries, however, such a choice would be politically too costly given previous international commitments, but also because they have become too economically, financially, and technologically dependent on the rest of the world. Reneging on economic liberalization mostly comes from the difficulty of resisting domestic demands for some protection, from the hope of levelling or tilting the international playing field in their favour, and more recently from the need to manage the 'green transition'. The temptation by some countries to slow or halt liberalization may induce others to reconsider their commitments, leading to an action–reaction cycle that slows global integration and decreases economic welfare. This cycle has been readily evident in the imposition of tariffs by the Trump Administration in the US and retaliation against these measures by China. It has also been at work in the decisions by the US and the EU to subsidize so-called game changer technologies, in particular in the digital sector and renewable energy, as we discuss below.

International cooperative action may therefore be required to avoid the unfortunate effects of this **temptation to free ride**. This temptation varies according to the socio-political organization of countries, their degree of economic flexibility, their competitiveness, and the extent of their integration into global value chains. On the socio-political dimension, the political insulation of governments from lobbying by those who are affected by adjustment costs can ease the process of economic liberalization, as was the case in the first wave of globalization in the second half of the nineteenth century when few countries had democratic systems of government. But with the spread of democracy, such political insulation has drastically diminished, forcing governments to at best 'talk' protectionist or, worse, adopt protectionist policies during economic recessions. Another way to make liberalization politically palatable has been the development in some countries of corporatist deals between the government, unions, and business to share the costs of adjustment. The temptation to free ride also depends on the economy of countries and on their flexibility, particularly regarding labour markets, as well as labour skill levels. More generally, countries with deregulated markets and few and lean state-owned companies should be less tempted to free ride on the globalization process because adjustment would be less costly. Lastly, the globalization of the supply chain has increased the number of firms that would suffer from any reversal in economic liberalization, making countries with high integration into global supply chains less likely to be tempted to renege on existing commitments.

International cooperation may also be required to remedy what we call the 'inhibiting fear' that countries may feel when facing a decision to either engage in economic liberalization or to continue it. Although countries may be convinced that liberalization will yield benefits, they may be hesitant to risk the instability that might come from the ebbs and flows of the international market. This fear is particularly problematic in the domain of financial liberalization. In contrast to trade integration, financial integration has produced sudden and violent shocks to national economies (see Pauly, Chapter 9). The massive increase in capital flows in the last thirty years has been accompanied by extreme volatility, particularly for developing countries that have been experiencing sharp fluctuations in the flow of short-term capital (Calvo and Talvi 2005; Edwards 2005; Reinhart and Rogoff 2009; Caceres et al. 2017). This volatility is particularly strong for countries that are highly dependent on commodity prices (Pagliari and Hannan 2017). For example, the series of crises that hit East Asia in the period 1997–1998 led to drastic economic contractions. South Korea's growth rate dropped seven percentage points below its pre-crisis, five-year-average growth rate,

Indonesia's performance was similar, and Thailand's was even worse (Eichengreen and Bordo 2002). Recent work on the Asian financial crises and the Argentinean crisis in 2001, both at the aggregate and case-specific levels, has shown that governments are highly vulnerable to such profound economic contractions. On average, the chances of losing office in the six months immediately following a currency crash seem to be twice as likely as at other times (Frankel 2005). Long believed to be limited to the developing world, this financial and political reality has nowhere been more vivid than in the Eurozone since 2010, with the tense dynamics around the situation of Greece foremost but also around other countries, including larger economies such as Spain and Italy. Economic globalization has created profound and far-reaching policy challenges to states that, in turn, have an impact on key pillars of their economic and political organization.

International cooperative action in the financial realm may reassure countries through promises of assistance either by individual states or international institutions before or during difficult times. This may facilitate states' adjustment efforts in responding to shocks and prevent them from taking the wrong action at the wrong time, which could lead to massive negative contagion effects. As with trade, the need for international support varies across countries depending on the socio-political and economic characteristics that we have discussed. The inadequate response of rich states and financial institutions to the problems faced by countries affected by the financial crises of the late 1990s led many countries to rapidly build up their holdings of foreign reserves to counter speculative attacks on their currency and to avoid an IMF **structural adjustment programme** (SAP). But this individual response has come at a significant price. Most central banks hold foreign exchange reserves in the form of low-yielding, short-term US Treasury bonds and other securities. The accumulation of reserves by developing countries created an important opportunity cost (the difference between what governments might have earned by investing these assets elsewhere versus keeping them in low-yielding securities). In most cases, for instance, investing the same amount in the domestic economy would have yielded a significantly higher return. According to a recent study, the income loss due to this difference in yields amounts to close to 1 per cent of GDP (Rodrik 2006). Leaving aside the question of whether this insurance against the vagaries of financial integration comes at an acceptable price, such a solution is only available to a small number of countries, and therefore is not a viable alternative to international action to provide **liquidity** to countries facing financial crises.

KEY THEORY BOX 3.1 GOODS AND THE PROBLEMS OF COOPERATION

In examining the problem of collaboration, we can use the concept of 'type of goods' to examine more rigorously the problem of incentives to free ride, fear that one's counterparts will fail to follow good policies, and the distributive conflicts that might ensue over where to meet. In a capitalist economy, private firms produce goods such as wheat, clothing, and computers, and services such as financial products, insurance, and the like. Such goods are generally referred to as **private goods**, based on two characteristics: the goods are generally excludable and are not joint in consumption. The concept of *excludable* means that goods can be withheld from those who do not pay for them; *not joint in consumption* means that when a consumer utilizes the good, it is exhausted and cannot be used by others without additional production.

In addition to private goods, other goods may be desired, such as national defence or parks. These goods are characterized by the difficulty in creating exclusion and the jointness of their consumption, and they are known as **public goods**. Because anyone can have access to these goods once they are produced, consumers will misrepresent their demand for such goods as they can obtain them and 'free ride'. In such cases, the private sector will not produce public goods, and governments will coerce citizens to pay for such goods through mechanisms such as taxation.

If a good is characterized by lack of exclusion and lack of jointness, then such a good is referred to as a **common pool of resources**. Examples of such goods include fish in the oceans, or even, as a limiting case, a public park. Thus, if the ocean is overfished, fish will cease to reproduce and die out. Similarly, while parks are often seen as public goods, too many users of a park create crowding, which impairs the enjoyment of the good for others. Private actors will be particularly reluctant to produce such goods, and even governments will be concerned about the problem of too many users.

Finally, **inclusive club goods** refers to goods that may be excludable and yet be joint in consumption. These include goods

KEY THEORY BOX 3.1 GOODS AND THE PROBLEMS OF COOPERATION (continued)

such as software, music, and literature, which the private sector has a great incentive to produce. Once a unit of the good is produced, it can be distributed at either little or no cost (in more formal terms, the marginal cost of extension is near zero). Indeed, firms may quickly develop a monopoly in the production of such goods if they are the first movers who make the good, and thus face regulation. For example, if a firm decides to launch a satellite to beam television programmes to consumers, the initial cost to pay for a rocket to put the satellite in orbit will be high. Once the satellite is in operation, however, the programmes can be disseminated to large numbers of consumers. Private firms will generally attempt to regulate consumption by encoding the transmission to prevent free riding. Alternatively, governments may simply regulate the industry and consumer

behaviour to prevent consumption without paying (for example, penalties for copyright infringement). Figure 3.2 summarizes the four types of goods.

Figure 3.2 Summary of the four types of goods

		Jointness in Consumption?	
		YES	NO
Exclusion Possible?	NO	Public	Common Pool Resources
	YES	Inclusive Club Goods	Private

CASE STUDY BOX 3.2 COOPERATION AND GLOBAL WARMING

How do the problems of creating various types of goods play out in the international arena, and what obstacles do states face in achieving cooperation? Consider the case of cooperation with respect to global warming. It is now well documented that emissions of greenhouse gases, in particular CO_2, due to human activity (in particular the burning of fossil fuels) have reached levels that lead to an important warming of average temperatures on earth with a potentially dramatic impact on populations in the medium to long term. Yet, because reducing the emissions of greenhouse gases is a costly process that may require deep restructuring of energy production and use, the negotiations over how much or how quickly to limit those gases has been an internationally contentious issue. The public good nature of the problem can be seen in the incentives to free ride by various countries who wish to benefit from the reduction in emissions of greenhouse gases but do not want to bear the costs of reducing their emissions. There is a severe distributive conflict ('where to meet') as actors debate the appropriate levels of reduction for developed and developing countries. The latter fear derailing economic development to fight a phenomenon largely associated with

the economic development since the mid-1800s of current developed economies. After more than three decades of difficult discussions on how to combine binding mechanisms and flexibility provisions, the agreement reached in December 2015 at the 21st Session of the Conference of the Parties (COP 21) in Paris brought hope of change and progress towards the objective of curbing warming. According to the agreement, all parties have to 'undertake ambitious efforts' (Article 3) in the view of reaching the objective to hold 'the increase in the global average temperature to well below 2 °C above pre-industrial levels' (Article 2). Although the pace and intensity of efforts will take into account differences in levels of economic development, the Paris agreement extends the obligation of taking concrete action to all countries. This came about at the price of significant financial assistance given by developed countries to developing ones, which could open new discussions on the distribution of costs and benefits, and also at the price of delaying for three additional years until COP 24 held at Katowice in December 2018 the tricky issue of finding a common standard on how governments measure and monitor their individual efforts.

Finally, when countries address the issues of 'temptation to free ride' and 'inhibiting fear', they may encounter a third problem—how to negotiate the distribution of gains and losses from a possible agreement (see Case Study Box 3.2). This 'where to meet' problem can be seen in cases of international cooperation such as a decision on how much to contribute to common support funds, how and to what extent

to intervene in currency markets, and in the trade-off between quotas, tariffs, and subsidies in trade negotiations (see Key Theory Box 3.1). For example, as part of the bargaining over the creation of a **common pool of resources** to support financial stability, there is likely to be considerable debate about the criteria for which country should contribute how much. This burden-sharing decision has often been a problem historically.

Intervention in currency markets is also controversial. Although some national intervention to maintain stable currencies may be warranted in that it helps governments to obtain various national economic objectives such as controlling the rate of inflation, the US has often accused Japan and China (and other East Asian states) of manipulating their exchange rate to gain a competitive advantage in trade.

Burden-sharing problems may also be part of the problem of trade liberalization. A good example has been the ongoing conflict with respect to the reduction of agricultural support schemes used by developed countries (and often by developing countries as well) to protect their farmers. Addressing the free riding temptation has been hampered by the difficulty of finding an agreement at a lower level of support.

3.3 International cooperation: A strategic interdependence approach

Our discussion so far has highlighted the potentially important role of international cooperation in enhancing the prospects for global economic integration. Yet, as the 'where to meet problem' shows, such cooperation may itself entail varying costs and benefits for participating states, and its successful negotiation is therefore not a foregone conclusion. To further explore the challenges of international cooperation, we can utilize a game-theoretic approach to examine interdependent decision-making. A country's choice depends both on its cost–benefit evaluation of the various outcomes and on its expectations regarding the choices of other actors. Game theory provides useful tools to analyse actors' behaviour in such a context. Key features of actors' interactions are captured through 'games' that describe the choices available to actors (players in the game), their evaluations of potential outcomes, as well as the information they have when they make their choices.

To keep this chapter's discussion of game theory as parsimonious as possible, we focus on simple games with two persons and two strategies per person (see Key Theory Box 3.3). We further assume that actors have extensive knowledge of the other actor's preferences but that they cannot observe their actual choices. Obviously, in real-life situations actors may have less information about preferences and/or may be able to observe the other's behaviour. Our modelling choices may appear to oversimplify real-life examples but, as

---

KEY POINTS

- International cooperation can help to address three typical problems associated with the process of global integration: a temptation to free ride, an inhibiting fear, and a need to find meeting points in situations where collaboration will produce differing costs and benefits to governments.

- A country's need for international cooperation depends on its socio-political structure as well as on the structure and flexibility of its economy.

- Different types of problems associated with the process of global integration call for different solutions to address these three typical problems, ranging from the provision of binding rules to facilitating mechanisms.

KEY THEORY BOX 3.3 GAME THEORY AND ITS CRITICS

Game theory has become a standard tool for analysing situations of interdependence in social sciences. Aside from its predictive aim, game theory has a strong appeal for anyone engaged in explanation, investigation, or prescription. It often makes ostensibly puzzling processes intelligible, without attributing causality to factors such as the incompetence, irresponsibility, or lack of concern of decision-makers.

Whatever its value, however, the use of game theory poses severe methodological problems that have prompted intense debates in the literature. Critics have traditionally emphasized (1) the overstretching of the concept of rationality and (2) the gap between abstract theoretical concepts and real phenomena. Regarding the notion of rationality, most applications of game theory assume that players, interacting under conditions of imperfect information, possess a very high computational ability. To make their decisions, players must evaluate a host of possible worlds on the basis of the knowledge commonly shared with others or privately known. This kind of situation often implies that players engage in comparative reasoning about a large set of possible worlds. Leeway in their interpretation often leads to a myriad of possible equilibria, which significantly decreases the predictive power of game theory. To avoid this indeterminacy, most game theorists have refined the concept of 'rationality' to allow the selection of one or very few equilibria among the vast initial array. For example, one might assume that people always choose to buy the cheapest product available (even though we

several authors have already shown, simple models can clearly reveal the decisions that governments face in attempting to deal with fundamental aspects of interdependence (Cooper 1975; Snidal 1985b; Martin 1992; Aggarwal and Dupont 1999; Drezner 2007).

Each of the three typical problems discussed in the previous section can be depicted with a specific game. We address them in turn and then focus on situations that represent mixed situations.

3.3.1 'Free riding temptation': The Prisoners' Dilemma

As we have seen, global economic integration remains fragile due to countries' political difficulties in implementing potentially costly economic changes—albeit ones that are economically positive. They may be tempted to free ride on others' policy changes to take advantage of the gains from their trading partners opening their markets, which may in turn affect others' policy choices, and possibly bring an end to global economic liberalization. This situation is aptly captured with the game called the Prisoners' Dilemma (see Key Concept Box 3.4)

Figure 3.4 illustrates the Prisoner's Dilemma for the case of two players, Alpha and Beta, each with two strategies, S1 and S2. The numbers in the various cells indicate the preferences of players on an ordinal ranking scale, with 4 being the most preferred situation and 1 the least preferred. In Figure 3.4, and the following ones, the first number in each box refers to Player Alpha's preference, while the second number refers to

Player Beta's preference (thus '4,1' is Alpha's most preferred outcome and Beta's least preferred outcome).

As Figure 3.4 shows, strategy S2 brings each player the highest utility whatever strategy the other is planning to use—it is a so-called dominant strategy. The choice of S2 by the two players leads to what is called the **Nash Equilibrium** outcome, which is in the lower-right cell of the matrix. A Nash Equilibrium is an outcome in which none of the players can improve their situation by changing their individual strategy. But if both players switch to Strategy 1 in the matrix in Figure 3.4, each of them gets a better outcome (upper-left cell). Yet ironically, this collectively optimal situation, also known as a **Pareto-optimal outcome**, defined as outcomes from which no actor could become better off without worsening the pay-offs to another actor, is unstable because each actor can improve their own welfare by individually switching strategy to the cells in the upper-right or lower-left corners of the matrix.

Within global political economy, the Prisoners' Dilemma has been widely used to illustrate the problem of reciprocal trade liberalization (Grossman and Helpman 1995; Hoekman and Kosteki 1995; Maggi 1999). The difficulties in monitoring partners' trade policies, and the potential political benefits to governments from open export markets and closed domestic markets, often push states to back out of their commitments to reciprocate trade liberalization measures. As Conybeare (1984) shows, this argument particularly applies to countries with large domestic markets, as these countries are less dependent on the success of

KEY CONCEPT BOX 3.4 THE PRISONER'S DILEMMA

The Prisoners' Dilemma (PD) models a situation in which the actors face a structure of interaction that prevents them from reaching a cooperative solution even though such a solution would be optimal for both of them (see Figure 3.3). It is best illustrated with the example of two persons who are involved in a robbery and are caught near the scene of the crime. The district attorney (DA, or prosecutor) does not have sufficient evidence to convict either of the suspects of robbery unless at least one of them reveals additional information to them, but there is evidence to convict both of them of a lesser crime (for instance, reckless driving or carrying a firearm). The DA wants more information to convict both suspects for a long period.

The two prisoners are placed in separate interrogation rooms. The DA tells each prisoner that if he confesses and reveals the truth, he will get a much lighter sentence. Confessing to the DA could bring the minimal sentence if the other one does not confess but could also lead to a lengthier sentence if the other also confesses. Remaining silent, on the other hand, may lead to either a moderate sanction if the other prisoner remains silent, or the maximum penalty if the other one speaks to the attorney. Facing this situation, and unable to communicate, the rational strategy for both prisoners is to choose to confess, as this choice is individually always a safer strategy than remaining silent, thus leading to a collectively suboptimal outcome.

Figure 3.3 Visual representation of the Prisoners' Dilemma

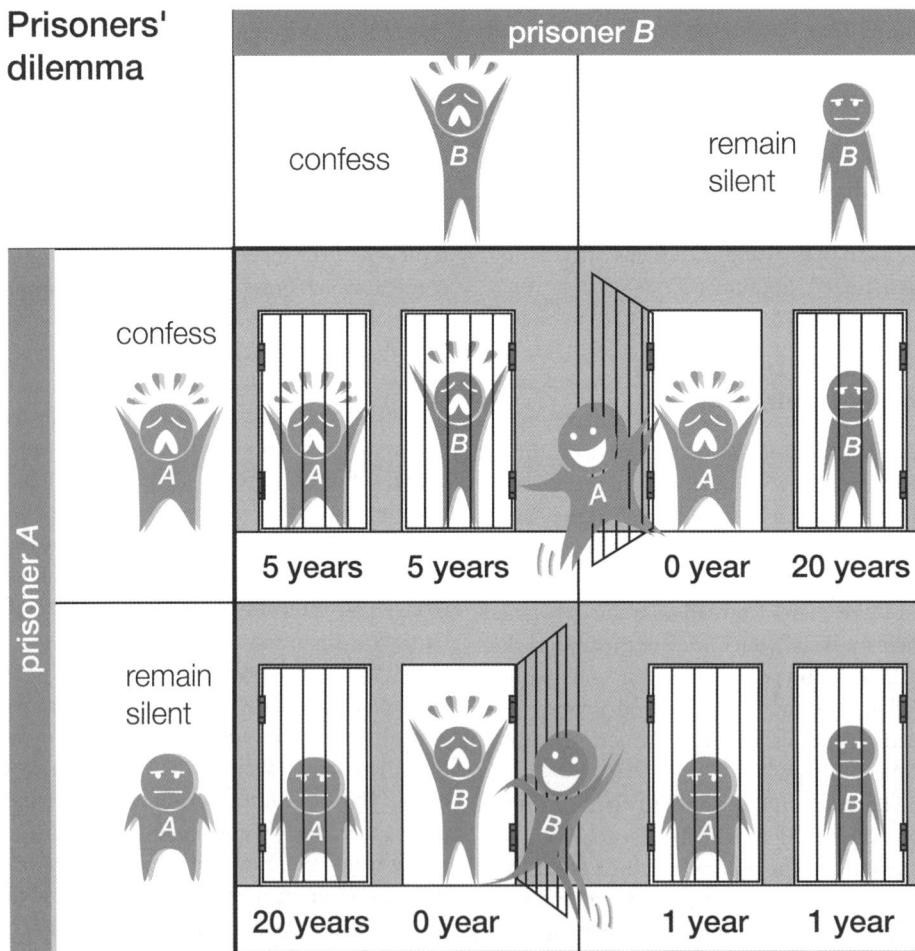

Figure 3.4 Prisoner's Dilemma Game (ordinal form)

		Player Beta	
		S1	S2
Player Alpha	S1	3, 3	1, 4
	S2	4, 1	**2, 2**

trade liberalization (this makes the utilities of the lower-right cell in Figure 3.4 relatively acceptable) and such countries can also positively affect world prices through their tariff policy (imposing a tariff on imports lowers the price that other countries will receive for their exports). A recent example of how the PD game can illustrate the problem of '**beggar thy neighbour policies**' concerns the trend towards a semiconductor subsidy war. In the context of increasing tension between the US and China, and a chip shortage in 2021, the US, EU, China, South Korea, and other countries started to devote large sums of money to bolster their own chip production. With each country attempting to capture a larger share of the global chip market, we could well see overproduction of chips. Cooperation to avoid a costly outcome (mutual defection in PD) could involve sharing research and development costs, coordinating supply chains, and establishing international standards. These policies of advanced states contrast with the case of smaller countries. Here, the Prisoners' Dilemma is not an adequate depiction of their trade situations. Rather, smaller countries tend to have preferences that reflect the game of Chicken, a situation that we discuss later. Furthermore, for countries with firms integrated into multinational supply chains, reciprocal trade liberalization may be superior to asymmetric liberalization, a situation that better reflects the game of assurance that we discuss next.

3.3.2 'Inhibiting fear': Assurance games

The second typical problem that a country seeking to enter international cooperation faces comes from the uncertainty of benefits and costs linked to integration in the world economy. Global economic integration brings its full benefits when most countries are part of it and adopt appropriate policies. When some countries make mistakes, or if liberalization policies lose momentum, international markets may react abruptly. If states become paralysed by this likelihood,

the whole world may revert to a much lower level of integration. This situation is best modelled through another category of game—assurance games.

One specific example of an assurance game is 'Stag Hunt', depicted in Figure 3.5. The name of the game comes from the story of two hunters chasing a stag. They go out before dawn and take positions on different sides of an area where they think a stag is hiding. They have a mutual understanding to shoot only at the stag (Strategy S1 in the game depicted in Figure 3.5). Shooting at any other wild animal, say a hare (Strategy S2), would lead them to miss shooting the stag because the stag would be frightened by the noise and stay put in its hiding place. As time goes by and as dawn arrives, however, both hunters start thinking that going back home with a hare might be better than continuing to wait for the stag to come out of hiding. If each of them thinks that the other one will eventually yield to the temptation to shoot at a hare, they will both end up killing a hare—a better outcome than not catching anything but clearly much less attractive than sharing a stag.

In Stag Hunt, players share a single most preferred outcome—that is, a Pareto-optimal Nash Equilibrium—but they do not have dominant strategies. As a result, there is a second, Pareto-deficient, equilibrium outcome. In such a game, reaching the Pareto-optimal equilibrium is not a foregone conclusion. Doubts about the willingness of one's counterpart to choose strategy S1 (shoot the stag) might push a player to choose strategy S2 (shoot a hare), which guarantees for that individual the highest minimal gain. Yet, such an outcome is rather unlikely because of the attraction of the upper-left cell. In contrast to the Prisoners' Dilemma game, it is not the temptation to reap additional gains that may prevent actors from being in the upper-left cell of the game, but their anticipation of a possible mistake or unintentional move by the other one.

Financial globalization has features of a stag hunt game. With increasing capital flows among countries, global capital markets become deeper and provide

Figure 3.5 Assurance game (Stag Hunt) (ordinal form)

		Player Beta	
		S1	S2
Player Alpha	S1	**4, 4**	1, 3
	S2	3, 1	**2, 2**

greater opportunities for individual countries. Yet, policy mistakes by some countries, or sharply different health conditions as revealed by the COVID-19 crisis, or changing priorities, may quickly destabilize markets. Fear of the potential negative impact of such a destabilization may lead countries to implement measures to slow down or restrict capital movements. Such a move may lead to changes in other actors' expectations and quickly drive the world, or at least a region of the world, to a much lower level of integration. This new situation could have the advantage of being less risky for countries but is unlikely to bring as many opportunities for investment and therefore reduces growth prospects.

3.3.3 'Where to meet': Coordination games

Whereas market liberalization is essential for global economic integration and increased prosperity, sustainable global integration requires some market supervision. This supervision in turn requires cooperative action by countries. The difficulty, however, is that there are often many ways to supervise markets, and countries may differ on their preferred coordination point because potential solutions vary in their costs and benefits. This strategic context corresponds to a game of coordination. In the specific game depicted in Everyday GPE Box 3.5, actors have to choose *among* pareto-optimal outcomes.

In global political economy, efforts by developed countries to choose mutually compatible macroeconomic policies typically reflect games of coordination (Putnam and Bayne 1987). For instance, when there is high volatility in financial and exchange rate markets, coordinated responses by leading countries would often be best, but each country would like to choose the policy mix that fits its own domestic constraints. Coordination was a key challenge in efforts to address the 2008–2009 Global Financial Crisis and the ensuing 2009–2012 global recession. Whereas major central banks were able to coordinate their actions to contain the stress in financial markets to a reasonable extent, governments have had more difficulty in implementing concerted fiscal responses. Some countries, such as the US, engaged in large fiscal stimulus, while others were more reluctant to use **fiscal policy** out of concern for the health of their public finances. This asymmetry fuelled a concern for free riding where a country would benefit from the efforts of its neighbours, as their stimulus plans boost its exports without affecting its fiscal stance. As a result, countries resorting to large stimulus tended to adopt 'nationalist' or protectionist policies to channel government funding to national firms. To offset this suboptimal

---

EVERYDAY GPE BOX 3.5 'BATTLE OF THE SEXES'

'Battle of the Sexes' comes from the story of a husband and wife who have to decide where to spend their evening after work. They can either go to the opera or watch a football match. Neither spouse derives much pleasure by being without the other one, but they differ on the best choice. The husband would prefer to watch football (strategy S1 in Figure 3.6) whereas the wife would prefer the opera (strategy S2 in Figure 3.6). In the story, both are getting off work and have to rush to either the stadium or the opera. They cannot communicate with each other (say, the batteries of their cell phones are dead!) and have to meet at one of the locations. If each of them follows their preferred solution, they end up at different locations, which both regard as a bad outcome. Perversely, if both of them want to please the other one by choosing the location that they know their partner prefers, they also end up being separated. Thus, they have to somehow implicitly coordinate, with one making a concession and the other getting their first choice. Figure 3.6 provides a generalization of that story.

In the 'Battle of the Sexes', none of the players has a dominant strategy. Player Alpha prefers to play Strategy 1 when Player Beta chooses Strategy 1 and prefers Strategy 2 when Player Alpha chooses Strategy 2. With Player Beta having the same preferences as Alpha, the game has two equilibrium outcomes— the upper-left and lower-right cells in Figure 3.5. These two outcomes are clearly Pareto-superior to the two other possible outcomes, but actors will disagree on which one to choose. Player Alpha prefers the upper-left cell whereas Player Beta prefers to end up in the lower-right cell. Both players want to avoid being separated but each player prefers a different outcome.

Figure 3.6 Coordination game (Battle of the Sexes)

		Player Beta	
		S1	S2
Player Alpha	S1	4, 3	1,1
	S2	1, 1	3, 4

dynamic, major economies have repeatedly committed to concerted plans of action and pledged to refrain from protectionist measures, as for instance under the G20 motto of 'recover together, recover stronger' (G20 2022).

3.3.4 **Mixed situations: Chicken, Called Bluff, and Suasion**

We now turn to games that capture situations in which more than one typical problem of cooperation may be present or in which the actors may view the structure of the problem differently. We begin with the game of Chicken, which combines the features of the temptation to free ride as well as distributive tensions between the actors. This game, depicted in Figure 3.7, builds on the story of two cars, travelling in opposite directions, speeding down the middle of the road towards one another. Inside each car sits a driver who wants to impress her respective passenger that she is a tough person (that is, demonstrate resolve). The best way to do so is to continue driving straight down the middle of the road (strategy S2 in the game depicted in Figure 3.7)—even when the car coming in the opposite direction comes dangerously close. Yet, if at least one driver does not swerve, the outcome will be disastrous and both cars will crash, killing everyone. To avoid this unfortunate outcome, at least one driver will have to yield and swerve (strategy S1 in Figure 3.7), but both would like the other one to be the 'chicken' who swerves.

The distributive tension between two equilibrium outcomes is a typical feature of the **coordination games** discussed earlier. But in contrast to those games, the game of Chicken has a third outcome that is collectively optimal—the compromise solution in the upper-left cell. As in the Prisoners' Dilemma, however, this outcome is not stable, and actors have a strong temptation to revert to one of the two equilibriums represented in boldface in Figure 3.7. As such, the Chicken game helps to capture more complex situations faced by countries attempting to engage in international cooperation (Stein 1982).

In the context of the global political economy, chicken games are useful depictions of the complex structure of burden sharing that occurs within a group of powerful players. For instance, when there is monetary and financial stability in the global economy, the US and the EU may tend to resist making public commitments to international cooperation unless there is a clear sign that the other party will act similarly. Getting out of a trade negotiation stalemate or dispute such as the US–China tariff war can also be a Chicken-like situation in which each actor is unwilling to agree on any asymmetric solutions.

To this point, we have only considered cases where actors have symmetrical preferences. We now examine two interesting *asymmetric* games, the first of which has one player whose preferences are those of the Prisoners' Dilemma game, and a second player with a structure of preferences of the Chicken game. The resulting asymmetric game, known as the game of 'Called Bluff', is depicted in Figure 3.8.

Player Alpha has Prisoners' Dilemma preferences with a dominant strategy to play S2, whereas Player Beta has Chicken preferences with a preferred choice of S2 if Alpha chooses S1 and a choice of S1 if Alpha chooses S2. Yet in this game, owing to the asymmetry in payoffs, Beta knows that Alpha has a dominant strategy of S2, and Beta therefore should choose S1, leading to the equilibrium outcome in the lower-left cell in Figure 3.8. Here, Player Alpha gets their most preferred outcome, whereas Player Beta gets their second-worse outcome. This scenario can be used to analyse situations where stronger countries or actors can take advantage of the other's weakness and shift the burden of cost of cooperative action onto the weaker party. This outcome is caused by the difference in actors' sensitivity (vulnerability) to the need for cooperation itself. The player with the less dependence on the need for cooperation (Beta in Figure 3.8) is able to free ride on the other player (Alpha in Figure 3.8). Given the lack of capacity of the weaker actor to sustain cooperation alone, this often leads to a breakdown of international action.

Figure 3.7 Chicken game (ordinal form)

		Player Beta	
		S1	S2
Player Alpha	S1	3, 3	**2, 4**
	S2	**4, 2**	1, 1

Figure 3.8 Called Bluff (ordinal form)

		Player Beta	
		S1	S2
Player Alpha	S1	3, 3	1, 4
	S2	**4, 2**	2, 1

A good illustration of this situation is the **monetary policy** of Germany and Japan in the 1960s, in the context of the Bretton Woods fixed exchange rate system. The stronger player, the US, asked these countries to revalue their currencies to help boost the competitiveness of US exports and relieve the pressure on the dollar. These countries refused to undertake significant revaluations, which thus had increasingly costly implications for the US economy, and, ultimately under the Nixon administration, the US simply forced the burden of adjustment on the weaker countries by breaking the link between the dollar and gold and imposing a 10 per cent across-the-board tariff. This action led to the end of the Bretton Woods system (see Helleiner, Chapter 8).

A second case of asymmetry is a game with one player having preferences oriented towards cooperation and the other one having Chicken preferences. In the game of 'Suasion', Player Beta has preferences similar to a player in the Chicken game, but Player Alpha has preferences that are typical of another game, the game of Harmony. The basic feature of harmony games (see Figure 3.9) is that both players not only dislike acting separately (as in the case of coordination games), but they also do not differ on the best outcome. They both therefore have a dominant strategy to do the same thing. Cooperation is, so to speak, naturally guaranteed (as, for instance, in nineteenth-century liberal assumptions about international economic relations, which argued that everyone would generally be made better off with free trade and open markets more generally).

Combining a player with Chicken preferences and a player with Harmony preferences yields the game depicted in Figure 3.10, known as the game of 'Suasion' (Martin 1992).

The predicted outcome of the Suasion game shares some similarity with that of the game of Called Bluff illustrated in Figure 3.8. Both games feature a situation in which one player gets its most preferred outcome. However, the difference between these two games is that in Suasion, the 'stronger' player (Alpha in Figure 3.9) gets his second-best outcome, which results from the

Figure 3.10 Suasion (ordinal form)

		Player Beta	
		S1	S2
Player	S1	4, 3	**3, 4**
Alpha	S2	2, 2	1, 1

choice of his dominant strategy (S1 in Figure 3.9). Put into the context of international cooperation, this clearly reflects a situation in which an actor perceives the benefits of international action to be much more than its associated costs. Because this actor (Alpha) absolutely wants to carry through action at the international level and is assumed to have the capability to do so, other actors (Beta) are in a situation whereby they will let him (Alpha) undertake the bulk of the effort, and will enjoy the benefits at low or no costs to themselves.

One can view this situation as one of the tyranny of the weak, which is in sharp contrast to the game of Called Bluff. Note, however, that the stronger player is not forced into an asymmetric outcome by the behaviour of the weak, but by his own preferences. From this perspective, the Suasion game features an opportunistic attitude by the weak rather than a deliberately tyrannical outlook. This attitude calls for action by the stronger player if it undermines his own action. For example, tax havens in small countries were 'tolerated' by bigger countries as long as the latter could use capital movement restrictions to secure financial stability. When capital restrictions were dismantled, there were significant increases in the efforts to circumvent the free-riding behaviour of tax havens. Such free riding became politically intolerable with the advent of the Global Financial Crisis, which required global coordination efforts. The G20 countries put significant pressure on 'renegade' countries with the preparation of a blacklist by the Organization for Economic Cooperation and Development (OECD). The 2021 OECD tax, with 137 members and accounting for over 90 per cent of global GDP, is an example of a solution to the taxation free riding problem. The first pillar of this accord addresses multinational corporations (MNCs) that might sell in a particular country but that don't have a physical presence. The agreement provides a redistribution mechanism among countries to address this concern. The second pillar of this agreement is a 15 per cent minimum tax, which sets a floor in this tax haven competition. Still, controversy continues on the ratification of this accord.

Figure 3.9 Harmony (ordinal form)

		Player Beta	
		S1	S2
Player	S1	**4, 4**	3, 2
Alpha	S2	2, 3	1, 1

3.4 International cooperation: A variety of solutions

The discussion of cooperation problems in the global political economy highlights the varied nature of the challenges facing actors. We now turn to the question of how to address these challenges. In particular, we focus on the role that international institutions can play in addressing cooperation problems. Our analysis begins with situations where the problems can be addressed without institutions, and then turns to cases where institutions can help the process of cooperation.

3.4.1 International action without international institutions

In many of the games that we have examined, individual actions by both players lead, or may lead, to an outcome that we can characterize as collectively optimal because there is no welfare loss. Yet, this notion of optimality tends to be short-sighted because the asymmetric outcomes of the Called Bluff, Suasion, Chicken, and even coordination games are optimal only in terms of a narrow view of *collective welfare*. Such a conception of welfare does not obviate the problems of the distribution of gains that may either make the road to an agreement difficult or plague the likelihood of collaboration. As we discuss later, institutions may play useful roles in addressing these problems, but collaboration may also occur through individual actions.

Individual, decentralized action can also be optimal in the thorny case of the Prisoners' Dilemma. Yet for this to happen, we must relax the baseline assumption that players play the game only once and allow them to have repeated interactions through time (Axelrod and Keohane 1986; Taylor 1987; Sandler 1992; Cornes and Sandler 1996). When players expect to meet again in the future, they may be more willing to cooperate. Yet even under such conditions of iteration, however, cooperation is not a foregone conclusion. For example, if the expected net value of cooperation is too low (for example, actors may overly discount the importance of future iterations owing to a dire economic or political situation at home for governments), the temptation to free ride cannot be overcome. The Prisoners' Dilemma game demonstrates that if defection by one actor would generate high costs for the other actor, or if actors cannot gather information easily, actors may not reach a Pareto-optimal outcome.

Applied to the case of trade liberalization, repeated interaction is not sufficient to ensure cooperative behaviour for governments that are under heavy domestic pressure, as the temptation to reap immediate political gains through defection may simply be too great. Domestic pressure may be particularly high in democratic countries where economic groups or citizens have easy access to the political sphere, in countries with a political system that tends to favour coalition governments, or in countries without strongly embedded social consultation mechanisms. Conversely, the cost of defection may be too high when actors invest heavily in cooperative efforts and highly value the outcome produced by cooperation. In such cases, they are significantly more reluctant to jeopardize cooperation, even if others free ride.

A world without international institutions is also not universally effective in securing the exchange of goods. As long as trading partners have access to other markets for their products, an institution-free world can work in the context of global trade, because countries can simply turn to another market if a breach in the trading relationship occurs. Yet if there is only one partner that is interested in the goods produced, or if it would be more costly to trade with other partners, such an option does not exist. If a country cannot threaten to sell its goods elsewhere, another country may take advantage of it. Another important qualification for successful institution-free contexts is if one (or both) of the parties has made relation-specific investments, for instance in supply chains.

In such a case, these investments will discourage, or even disable, defection and may encourage cooperative behaviour. Private infrastructure substitutes for public governance, sometimes at high cost (Gjesvik 2022; LeBaron and Lister 2022).

What other factors might impede cooperation when actors cannot rely on international institutions? Monitoring will be much more difficult if states only have limited information-gathering capability. If an actor has so little information that, for example, it is unsure whether the other actor 'defected' on the last round, then the prospect of repeated interactions does not increase the chances of cooperation. Similarly, an expanding number of states, with an expanding range of trade products that use increasingly sophisticated policies to intervene in markets, makes monitoring trade policies increasingly difficult. It is therefore more difficult to detect non-compliance without the help of a third party.

3.4.2 **The role of institutions**

As our discussion earlier suggests, actors may need help to sustain collectively optimal outcomes. One way that individuals might be able to coordinate their choices to achieve desired goals is through the creation or use of international institutions or regimes (see Key Concept Box 3.6).

We structure our discussion in the following sections around three major functions of institutions (see Table 3.1).

First, institutions can act as channels for the third-party enforcement of agreements. To successfully overcome players' temptation to free ride, international institutions should be strong, meaning that member countries should have specific and binding obligations. In particular, agreements that credibly restrain actors' temptation to free ride in trade and monetary policy, for instance, need to rely on some sort of enforcement mechanism delegated to an international institution. At its strongest expression, in the EU or in the WTO, such a mechanism relies on an organization—the EU has two such entities, the Commission and the Court of Justice—with supranational power to monitor, evaluate, and sanction (if needed) the behaviour of its members.

The chances of a cooperative agreement can also be enhanced through a different kind of centralization— one that ensures a prompt and undistorted dissemination of information. This type of facility helps identify the requirements of multilateral action and protects against possible defections. Enforcement can also be achieved through either positive incentives, as when the IMF provides funds to countries that are following its policy recommendations, or through punitive action, as when the WTO rules against a particular state policy.

Second, international institutions can help craft responses to situations characterized by distributive tensions among states. They can help states choose one among several collective outcomes and eliminate some sharply asymmetric outcomes. Institutions may also be useful for gathering information about the preferences of actors, and through appropriate use of agenda setting, may help find focal point solutions for both cost sharing and benefit splitting. Institutions with a firmly and widely established meta-regime tend to perform these tasks extremely well. In contrast, institutions lacking a strong meta-regime may have difficulty generating possible solutions that are

---

KEY CONCEPT BOX 3.6 INTERNATIONAL REGIMES

International regimes have been defined broadly as 'sets of principles, norms, rules and decision-making procedures upon which actors' expectations converge' (Krasner 1983). To refine this definition, we can distinguish between the principles and norms, or 'meta-regime', and the regime itself, defined as the rules and procedures, to allow us to distinguish between two very different types of constraints on the behaviour of states (Aggarwal 1985). In this case, we can use the term institution to refer to the combination of a meta-regime and a regime— rather than Krasner's definition. Note that an institution is not the same thing as an international organization: one can find areas of international collaboration where there are well-defined principles, norms, rules, and procedures for actors' behaviour in the absence of a formal international organization. A prominent example was the gold standard in the second half of the nineteenth century that provided international monetary stability through unilateral pegs to gold. With the increase in the number of states after 1945, most regimes now include one or several formal organizations as they help reduce transaction costs and serve as pools of resources and expertise. The IMF is now a central player in the international monetary regime.

Table 3.1 Problems, games, and institutional roles

	From problems to institutional solutions		
	'Free riding temptation'	'Inhibiting fear'	'Where to meet'
Strategic game	Prisoners' Dilemma	Stag Hunt (assurance games)	'Battle of the Sexes'
Illustrations	Trade liberalization	Financial integration	Managing adjustments
	Debt rescheduling	Trade liberalization and specialization	Multilateral negotiations
Role(s) of institutions	Channel to enforce contracts monitoring/surveillance sanctioning mechanisms policy transfer	Enhancers of cooperation pools of resources suppliers of knowledge and capacity	Providers of solutions to distributive conflicts negotiation fora agenda setting linkages
Examples of institutional solutions	*Monitoring/Surveillance*: Articles IV and VIII of IMF; Trade Policy Review mechanism WTO *'Sanction'*: Conditionality IMF; DSB's authorization of sanctions WTO *Policy transfer*: Common Trade policy and Economic and Monetary Union in the EU	*Pools of resources*: quota system in IMF *Suppliers of knowledge and capacity*: WTO (technical cooperation), World Bank, IMF, UNCTAD	*Negotiation fora*: WTO General Council; Executive Boards IMF and World Bank; UNCTAD *Agenda setting*: IMF and World Bank staff

attractive to all members. This has often been considered as the source of difficulties for the GATT, and its successor the WTO. Deep disagreements among GATT members led to the creation of another forum, the United Nations Conference on Trade and Development (UNCTAD), in the 1960s, and to serious hurdles in the negotiations of the extension of the scope of GATT/WTO, as revealed during the Doha Round of negotiations (see Trommer, Chapter 5). The members of UNCTAD had shared principles and norms that they felt were not importantly addressed in GATT/WTO (see Singh, Chapter 15, for discussion).

Third, international institutions can do a lot to allay actors' fear or reluctance to engage in cooperative behaviour. Rather than enforcing a particular outcome, institutions should enable actors to reach it (by pooling resources, for example). To help the integration of developing countries into the global financial system, the IMF provides cheap credit opportunities through the contributions subscribed by all members. The World Bank finances the development of basic infrastructure in developing countries to help them reduce poverty. At the European regional level,

the European Monetary System (EMS) has relied on a decentralized system of very short lending facilities among members to help them defend the parity grid that served as an anchor to the set of national currencies.

To address enforcement and distribution problems, institutions can establish rights for members that either define mechanisms of exclusion or determine compensation schemes. In relation to our previous discussion of games and cooperation, careful institutional design can sometimes 'privatize' the benefits of cooperation, reducing the temptation to free ride. The reduction of trade barriers almost always applies to countries that belong to particular clubs, be they regional or global. Assigning rights and obligations can also produce decentralized cooperation when institutions also provide information about the preferences of actors and reduce the costs of their discussions to their minimum. When actors are more certain about who owns and is responsible for what (a result of the assignment of rights and obligations), cooperation may result.

Under these conditions, as Coase (1960) suggests, actors do not need any centralized power to remedy the problem of **negative externalities** (situations where an individual's action negatively affects the wellbeing of another individual in ways that need not be paid for according to the existing definition of **property rights**) (Conybeare 1980; Keohane 1984) but should find a mutually satisfactory solution through financial compensation. The crucial aspect, in the Coasian framework, is establishing liabilities for externalities. The history of international monetary agreements provides several examples of the difficulties associated with determining satisfactory schemes assigning responsibilities to the involved parties. For instance, the collapse of the fixed exchange rate systems was largely due to the inability of IMF members to redistribute the burden of adjustment from the US to Germany and Japan.

Our brief discussion of the roles of institutions reveals the value associated with information gathering and dissemination. Long-term enforcement requires identifying prospects for defection, finding a focal point based on the constellation of positions, and informing actors of the overall global context. Therefore, a major activity of international institutions is to collect information about actors' behaviour, preferences, and the state of the international environment.

KEY POINTS

- Institutions are key instruments for resolving enforcement, distribution, and assurance problems.
- Institutions help assign rights and obligations to benefactors of cooperation as well as defining those benefactors.
- Institutions help make the international scene an information-rich environment.

3.5 The formation and evolution of institutions

We have seen that institutions can help cooperation in several ways. But how might institutions be formed in the first place? And what factors may impact the design of institutions? We begin with a broad discussion from the literature on international relations and then turn to more specific issues. In examining institutions, four different approaches in international relations have been brought to bear on this problem: neo-realism, neo-realist institutionalism, neo-liberal institutionalism, and cognitivism. (Aggarwal 1998).

Neo-realists assume that in an anarchic international system, states must rely primarily on their own resources to ensure their security. For neo-realist scholars, international institutions have no significant role in international relations because power considerations are predominant in an anarchic world (Waltz 1979; Mearsheimer 1990). In this view, as we discussed earlier, collaboration will only be sustainable if states highly value future interactions, have symmetric resources, and are highly interdependent.

Still within a power-based tradition, though, some scholars have examined changes in and the effects of international institutions. In this literature, labelled neo-realist institutionalism, the central concern is on how regimes affect the distribution of costs and benefits of state interaction. For analysts in this school (Krasner 1983; Aggarwal 1985; Krasner 1991; Knight 1992), institutions have distributional consequences (in other words, the benefits of cooperation may be unequal) and can be used as devices to seek and maintain asymmetric gains. They can more broadly help control other actors' behaviour, both at home and abroad (Aggarwal 1985). For example, within the domestic context, state elites can argue that their hands are tied and thus attempt to circumvent pressure for particular actions from domestic actors. Examples of this include the Mexican government signing onto the North American Free Trade Agreement (NAFTA) (tying the hands of the Mexican government to a more open market posture in the face of domestic protectionist groups) or the American use of the Multi-Fibre Arrangement (MFA) to prevent textile and apparel interests from pressing for excessive trade protection.

A central theme in this literature has been the role of hegemonic powers in fostering the development of institutions through both positive and negative incentives (Kindleberger 1973; Gilpin 1975; Krasner 1976). Benevolent hegemons, for example, may provide public goods (a special type of good, for example national defence, that cannot practically be withheld from an individual without withholding them from all—the 'non-excludability criterion'—and for which the marginal cost of an additional person consuming them, once they have been produced, is zero; the 'non-rival consumption' criterion) because their large size makes it worthwhile for them to take action on their own to overcome collective action problems. But while suggesting that regimes may form when powerful states desire them, this approach does not tell us much about the nature of regimes. Moreover, scholars in this school over-emphasize tensions arising from the differences in the distribution of benefits between actors and downplay the possibility that actors may not necessarily and as acutely think in comparative terms but focus on the positive impact of institutions on their situations. Finally, this approach has little to say about actors' desire to pursue multilateral versus bilateral solutions to accomplish their ends.

Building on these criticisms of the neo-realist approach, neo-liberal institutionalists have examined the specific incentives for states to create institutions—as opposed to simply engaging in ad hoc bargaining. This body of work, taking off from seminal research by Oliver Williamson, examines the role of institutions in lowering the costs involved in choosing, organizing, negotiating, and entering into an agreement (what he calls **transaction costs**), and has garnered a considerable following in the field of international relations (Keohane 1984). As we have seen, institutions provide many useful functions in helping actors to coordinate their actions or achieve collaboration. This theoretical approach assumes that collaborative action is primarily demand-driven—that is, actors will create institutions because they are useful—but does not really specify a mechanism for how they would go about actually creating them.

An important theme of this work has been how existing institutions may constrain future institutional developments (Keohane and Nye 1977; Keohane 1984). One aspect of this constraint is the possibility that existing institutions with a broad mandate will affect the negotiation of more specific institutions, leading to the 'nesting' of regimes within one another (Aggarwal 1985). Thus, while the notions of transaction costs and **sunk costs** (the investments that actors have made in specific institutions) are central elements in this thinking, the role of regimes in providing states with information and reducing organizational costs can be distinguished from the role of existing institutions in constraining future actions.

A fourth approach to examining institutional innovation and change places emphasis on the role of expert consensus and the interplay of experts and politicians (Haas 1980; 1992). New knowledge and cognitive understandings may lead decision-makers to calculate their interests differently. For example, work by Ernst Haas focused on the efforts of politicians to use linkages across various issues (sometimes from quite distinct areas) to create new issue packages in international negotiations. The objective is to provide benefits to all, in an effort to facilitate the formation of international regimes (Haas 1980).

3.5.1 The characteristics of international institutions

The four general approaches just discussed are a useful starting point for the understanding of how institutions are created and of the key drivers of their subsequent evolution, but they clearly are of limited help in understanding specific variations in the forms of institutions. Based on the existing literature and on our own work, we characterize institutions in terms of their membership, the stringency of their rules (the degree to which they constrain state behaviour), their scope, their membership, the extent of delegation of power from member states to institutional bodies, and the centralization of tasks within the institution (see Case Study Box 3.7).

The Bretton Woods Institutions, the WTO, and UNCTAD have quasi-universal *membership*. By contrast, the Group of Seven (G7) most industrialized countries only welcomed one new member in the last thirty years (Russia formally joined the Group in 1997, transforming it into the G8). Moreover, it is interesting to underline that the G7/8 remains autonomous from the larger G20, with the latter becoming the most visible global economic steering forum. Similarly, most regional integration arrangements have remained selected clubs with limited membership. Membership also varies in terms of the type of actors who can participate. While most institutions remain state-centric, some have started to include private actors. For instance, the Financial Stability Forum (FSF) was created in 1999 and upgraded to the Financial Stability Board by the G20 in 2009 (Helleiner 2014b) to promote international financial stability groups' representatives from national ministries, international financial institutions, and sector-specific groups (insurance, accounting standards, securities commissions). Controversy continues at the WTO over whether non-state

---

CASE STUDY BOX 3.7 IMF AND WTO: SELECTED ORGANIZATIONAL CHARACTERISTICS

Set up in order to promote international monetary cooperation, the IMF exerts a surveillance function over member states' financial and economic policies and provides financial and technical assistance to member states. Day-to-day business is conducted by the Executive Board, a restrictive body with twenty-four executive directors representing directly or indirectly all members. The IMF's six largest shareholders—the US, Japan, China, Germany, France, and the United Kingdom (UK)—along with Russia, and Saudi Arabia, have their own seats whereas the other sixteen executive directors are elected by groups of countries. The Executive Board gets its powers from the Board of Governors, the highest authority of the IMF in which each member has a seat. To assist it in the conduct of IMF affairs, the Executive Board in turn selects a managing director who is the chief of the Fund's operating staff of 2,800 employees, with half of them being economists.

Within the Executive Board, the normal *de jure* decision-making mode is simple majority, but important issues are decided by qualified majority, either 70 per cent (suspension of one member's rights in case of non-respect of obligations) or by 85 per cent (for example, modification of quotas, change in the seats of the Executive Board, provisions for general exchange arrangements). Qualified majority voting increases the power of the biggest contributors, in particular the US, which has a veto power over issues requiring 85 per cent majority decisions. *De facto*, however, voting rarely occurs in the Executive Board. Instead, executive directors use consensus to adopt decisions.

The institutional structure of the WTO differs significantly from the IMF model. It reflects very clearly what the organization considers to be its primary role, that is, a forum for the negotiation of liberalization agreements. In the WTO, the principal institutional structures are a ministerial conference meeting every two years, the General Council, and three councils in the area of goods, services, and intellectual property. All members have a seat in these councils. The default

decision-making mode is consensus, but decisions may also be made at unanimity (suspension of most-favoured nation (MFN) treatment), at 75 per cent majority (interpretation of an existing multilateral agreement, or a waiver of an obligation for a particular country), or with two-thirds majority (for admission of new members, for instance).

The WTO General Council also serves as the Trade Policy Review Body that adopts reviews of member states' trade policies. Reviews are conducted on the basis of a policy statement by the member under review and a report prepared by economists in the WTO Secretariat. That Secretariat, headed by a director-general, has around 640 staff and its main function is one of administrative and technical support to WTO councils, committees, and working groups.

Delegation of authority in the WTO is therefore restricted to the mechanism for solving trade disputes between members. Delegation is conferred first to small groups of experts (three or five) which are established when members fail to settle disputes in a conciliatory way. Panel members are independent individuals under instruction from no government. Their role is to make an objective assessment of the dispute and issue a report with findings and recommendations (establishing the legality of member states' policies in the case under dispute). This report has then to be adopted by the General Council serving as the Dispute Settlement Body. The latter, however, can only reject the panel report by consensus.

The second body with delegated authority from the member state is the Appellate Body, which reviews appeals made by member states on panel reports. The seven members of the Appellate Body serve for four-year terms and are legal experts with international standing. The appeal can uphold, modify, or reverse the panel's legal findings and conclusions. As for the case of panel reports, the Dispute Settlement Body must endorse the appeal report. Rejection is only possible by consensus.

---

actors should be permitted to participate in deliberations. (For other efforts paying particular attention to membership issues, see Sandler 1992; Koremenos, Lipson, and Snidal 2001; and Aggarwal and Dupont 2002).

The second dimension, *stringency of rules*, covers both the precision and the obligation of rules in the literature on legalization of world politics (see Aggarwal 1985 on regime strength, and Abbott and Snidal 2000 on legalization). From this perspective, authors have often contrasted the so-called European and Asian models of regional economic integration. The first one is built upon a wide set of specific and binding

rules (called the *acquis communautaire* in the jargon of European integration), whereas the second is built upon declarations, intentions, and voluntary commitments (Ravenhill 1995; 2001). The lack of any precise and concise definition of a balance of payments problem in the IMF severely affected the constraining power of this institution in preventing its members from running imbalances.

Third, we consider the *scope* of agreements defined as issue coverage (Aggarwal 1985; Koremenos, Lipson, and Snidal 2001). The evolution of the GATT from its origins in 1947 to the creation of the WTO in 1995 reveals an important increase in the scope of the agreements. Whereas GATT initially focused on the liberalization of trade in goods, the WTO covers services, agriculture, and trade related aspects of intellectual property rights and investment. Similarly, the G7/8 agenda has drastically expanded from a focus on macroeconomic management at its creation in the mid-1970s to a broad range of international security and economic issues, including terrorism, energy, environment, and arms control, in the 1990s and early 2000s. At the other end of the range, one finds sector-specific institutions such as the International Organization of Securities Commissions (IOSCO), the International Associations of Insurance Supervisors (IAIS), and the International Accounting Standards Board (IASB), as well as product-specific organizations such as the International Coffee Organization (ICO), the International Cocoa Organization (ICCO), the International Copper Study Group (ICSG), and the International Sugar Organization (ISO).

The fourth dimension is the extent of *institutional delegation*, the authority ceded by members to an institution, a dimension central to several existing studies (Abbott and Snidal 2000; McCall Smith 2000; Dupont and Hefeker 2001; Hawkins et al. 2006). International agreements may or may not include the creation of institutional organs, and these organs may or may not be given some autonomy from members for making new rules or monitoring and enforcing existing ones.

The extent of delegation may vary significantly across organs of the same institution. For instance, while the dispute settlement process in the WTO features an independent Appellate Body, the governing body of the organization—the General Council—relies upon consensus decision-making, and the members have kept the size and the prerogatives of the Secretariat down to a minimum. At the regional level, the extent of delegation strongly distinguishes the EU from the small secretariats found in other regional institutions. Whereas the EU includes organs with supranational power, governments remain in full control of negotiation and implementation processes in most other regional agreements, including the NAFTA, the Association of Southeast Asian Nations (ASEAN), and the Asia-Pacific Economic Cooperation (APEC) grouping.

A fifth dimension is *institutional centralization* (Koremenos, Lipson, and Snidal 2001). Is there a concentration of tasks performed by a single institutional entity? Centralization may refer to such tasks as the

diffusion of information, monitoring of members' behaviour, or the imposition of sanctions, as well as the adoption of new rules or modification of existing ones. Strong administrative bodies are natural candidates for the centralization of many tasks, as exemplified by the case of the European Commission in the EU, or the administration of the IMF or the World Bank. Yet, in the latter two, key decisions and tasks go through the Executive Board with a limited membership of twenty-four countries or groups of countries represented by executive directors elected by member states (see Helleiner, Chapter 8).

It is often difficult to understand these five dimensions as being separate, but they are conceptually distinct. As an example, although it is hard to imagine an agreement with lax rules and high delegation, strict rules do not necessarily imply high delegation (good instances are the numerous bilateral treaties on investment and, to a lesser extent, bilateral free trade treaties). Similarly, centralization and delegation may reinforce each other but none of them requires the other one. Conferences or councils of heads of governments and states centralize most of the activities of several regional economic organizations (including monitoring and dispute settlement). Yet, decision-making remains either consensual (where no state publicly dissents from the agreement) or based on unanimity.

3.5.2 Explaining institutional design

How can one account for institutional variation on these five dimensions? Consistent with a functionalist approach to the study of international institutions, we should expect the five dimensions to be affected by the type of problems that institutions should address (Stein 1982; Snidal 1985b; Aggarwal and Dupont 1999; Koremenos, Lipson, and Snidal 2001; Ostrom 2003). In Table 3.1, we linked our three typical problems with specific roles for international institutions. Keeping these in mind, the 'temptation to free ride' problem is the one that clearly calls for strong rules, with delegation and centralization to international bodies. Cooperation is difficult and thus requires relatively strong institutions. In such cases, membership tends to be restricted to well-'socialized' governments. An inclusive membership makes monitoring more difficult and costly, and thus creates many opportunities for members to free ride.

As for scope, on the one hand enforcement of the agreements is more likely to occur when institutions have a broad scope and are able to link different issues (Aggarwal 1998). Linkages across issues help in deterring defection on a single issue when actors have broad interests (McGinnis 1986; Lohmann 1997). For example, members of the WTO cannot subscribe to the agreement on goods (GATT) without also accepting the agreement on services (GATS) as well as the agreements on intellectual property rights (TRIPS) and investment (TRIMs), and the dispute settlement mechanism. On the other hand, adding issues to an institution's agenda requires strong capacity to monitor behaviour, which may often not be present. In the context of the Doha Round of talks within the WTO, now collapsed, there was increasing concern about the negative impact of the willingness to support an all or nothing approach—to make the WTO a **single undertaking** as a means to achieve a negotiation breakthrough (Elsig and Dupont 2012).

The 'inhibiting fear' and 'where to meet' problems call for quite different institutional features. For these cases, there is a positive link with centralization for the pooling of resources, knowledge, and information provision, or the reduction of costs of negotiations. Addressing the 'inhibiting fear' may require some clear and binding rules on access to resources and knowledge. Yet in these cases, restricting the size of membership may not be a strong prerequisite for success. Solving distribution problems may require a softening of rules to allow some room for different interpretations of the agreements. Delegation of power is not essential in both situations, except for a potential benefit of agenda-setting power to find mutually acceptable solutions.

As for scope, there is no clear link between 'inhibiting fear' and issue coverage. But a diverse set of issues can provide greater ground for compromise when players have different preferences and when they do not assign equal value to all of the issues. For instance, trade liberalization and monetary cooperation in the European Community (EC) has often been facilitated by the development of social or regional policies or packages to 'compensate' countries that might not immediately be major beneficiaries of the other policies. But, as the case of agriculture in the GATT/WTO shows, having different issues on the agenda is not helpful when countries categorically exclude certain issues from consideration in making trade-offs. Finally, with respect to membership, selected, restrictive groupings tend to reinforce the fear of being left out and thus should be avoided in addressing the 'inhibiting fear' problem. As for problems of distribution, more members may on the one hand help in the quest for new solutions. Yet, new members may also add as many new conflicts as complementarities among players.

As we have seen, then, different types of problems call for appropriate institutional design. Although focusing on general tendencies in institutional design in view of the problems they need to address provides a useful first step, we are still faced with some anomalies. For instance, given that trade liberalization is widely portrayed as embodying a 'temptation to free ride', how can one explain that some institutions (for instance the European Free Trade Association) that focus on trade liberalization have remained informal and thus lack organs with delegated power? Why is it that some institutions do not have clear rules and preconditions for membership (for instance the GATT/WTO, or the EU until the early 1990s)? And lastly, why do some countries prefer very loose rules in designing institutions (such as ASEAN and APEC)?

To increase our ability to understand such choices, we can consider three other key influences. First, an important issue is what we call *potential participants* in the institution. In particular, the number of these actors and their relative power—two factors considered by Koremenos, Lipson, and Snidal (2001)—as well as their overall financial and 'social' capital (Ostrom 2000) influence the design of institutions. Relatively little concern about membership rules in GATT 1947 can be accounted for by the fact that the international system was much smaller and more homogeneous than the one that emerged in the 1960s as a result of decolonization. Similarly, the need to define strict criteria for entering the EU only became salient when the iron curtain fell and former communist countries with still very different political systems expressed an interest in joining the EU. Turning to the financial and social capital among potential actors, the disparities in size of financial reserves held by East Asian economies surely explains the very decentralized form of the regional financing arrangement known as the Chiang Mai Initiative (an East Asian mechanism that is intended to provide emergency finance to member economies facing a run on their currencies). In turn, the fact that there has been little formalization of relationships between central banks in the developed, democratic world builds upon a joint understanding and on a high level of expertise on how to address problems.

Second, the *information and knowledge available to actors* affects institutional design. Institutions comprised of actors with rich and reliable information usually require less centralization or less delegation (Coase 1960; Williamson 1975; Koremenos, Lipson, and Snidal 2001), as illustrated by the loose structure of the European Free Trade Association from its creation in 1960 to its upgrading in 1993. The founding members of that association—the UK, Denmark, Norway, Sweden, Austria, Switzerland, and Portugal—did not have the mutual distrust that characterized French–German relationships in the EC, and information from partner countries was thus considered by all members to be rich and reliable. Existing knowledge about the issue area(s) covered by the agreement may affect the stringency of rules, the delegation of power, issue scope, and membership. Poor knowledge about the issues at stake tends to make actors wary of making hard commitments (rules and delegation)—a tendency particularly present in the discussions in the domain of the environment (see Ervine, Chapter 16). Better knowledge may affect issue scope and the contours of membership, as clearly illustrated by the key influence of the work of the Intergovernmental Panel on Climate Change (IPCC)—the intergovernmental body that reviews and assesses the scientific information on climate change—on the evolution of commitments in the domain of climate change. In trade, whereas the politics of trade liberalization may call for careful selection of members for inclusion in the WTO, the widespread belief in the veracity of international trade theory (which argues that global membership yields the greatest efficiency in the allocation of resources) helps to account for the pressure to increasingly universalize membership in this institution.

Third, and finally, we can focus on the *outside institutional setting*. When actors create new institutions, they generally do not do so in a vacuum. Thus, when new institutions are developed, they often must be reconciled with existing ones. One approach to achieving such reconciliation is by nesting broader and narrower institutions in hierarchical fashion. Another means of achieving harmony among institutions is through an institutional division of labour, or 'horizontal' linkages (Aggarwal 1998). The challenge of institutional reconciliation is not, however, unique to the creation of new ones. In lieu of creating new institutions, policymakers might also modify existing institutions for new

purposes. For instance, faced by seemingly intractable balance of payments problems in Africa in the 1990s, the IMF developed new **SAPs** that overlapped substantially with those of the World Bank. When modifying institutions, members therefore must also focus on issues of institutional compatibility. Moreover, bargaining over institutional modification is likely to be strongly influenced by existing institutions.

A few examples will illustrate these ideas. One can think about the problem of reconciling institutions from both an issue area and a regional perspective (Oye 1992; Gamble and Payne 1996; Lawrence 1996). Nested institutions in an issue area are nicely illustrated by the relationship between the international regime for textile and apparel trade (the Long-Term Arrangement on Cotton Textiles and its successor arrangement, the **Multifiber Arrangement** (**MFA**), that was phased out completely in 2005) and the broader regime in which it was nested, the GATT. When the Executive Branch in the US faced pressure from domestic protectionist interests simultaneously with international pressures to keep its market open, the American administration promoted the formation of a sector-specific international regime under GATT auspices. This nesting effort ensured a high degree of conformity with both the GATT's principles and norms as well as with its rules and procedures (Aggarwal 1985; 1994). Although the textile regime deviated from some of the GATT's norms in permitting discriminatory treatment of developing countries' exports, it did follow the MFN norm, which called for developed countries to treat all developing countries alike.

The APEC grouping, created in 1989, illustrates the concept of regional nesting. APEC's founding members were extremely worried about undermining the GATT, and sought to reconcile these two institutions by focusing on the notion of 'open regionalism'—that is, the creation of APEC would not bar others from benefitting from any ensuing liberalization in the region. APEC members saw this non-discriminatory liberalization as a better alternative to using Article 24 of the GATT, which permits the formation of discriminatory **free trade areas** and **customs unions**, to justify this accord. Rather than forming an institution that could conflict with the promotion of GATT initiatives, therefore, APEC founding members attempted to construct an institution that would complement the GATT. Furthermore, APEC members wanted to avoid undermining existing sub-regional organizations, in particular ASEAN. This clearly restricted the level of obligation and delegation that could have been transferred to the newly created pan-regional organization (Dupont 1998).

An alternative mode of reconciling institutions would be to simply create 'horizontal' institutions to deal with separate but related activities, as exemplified by the division of labour between the GATT and the Bretton Woods monetary system (IMF and World Bank). In creating institutions for the post-Second World War era, policymakers were concerned about a return to the 1930s era of competitive devaluations, marked by an inward turn among states and the use of protectionist measures. These 'beggar-thy-neighbour' policies were found across economic issue areas, and individual action by each state worked to the detriment of all. As a consequence, the founders of the Bretton Woods monetary system also turned their focus to creating institutions that would help to encourage trade liberalization. By promoting fixed exchange rates through the IMF and liberalization of trade through the GATT, policymakers hoped that this horizontal institutional division of labour between complementary institutions would lead to freer trade.

Finally, on a regional basis, one can see the development of the European Economic Coal and Steel Community and the Western European Union (WEU) as horizontal organizations. The first was oriented towards strengthening European cooperation in economic matters (with, of course, important security implications), while the WEU sought to develop a coordinated European defence effort.

3.6 Conclusion

This chapter has sought to provide a systematic analysis of the problem of collaboration in global political economy through the lenses of types of problems, games, and institutions. We have seen that states may need to collaborate or to coordinate their actions to keep economic globalization on track because they may face problems of free riding, an inhibiting fear that their efforts will lead to instability for their economy, and the need to find coordination points that have varying costs and benefits to the participants.

The problem of free riding or the difficulty of finding a coordination equilibrium is a common one in a number of issues, including trade, monetary cooperation, the environment, human rights, and the like. Despite some limitations, game theory provides useful

insight into the diverse set of problems that states may face in collaborating or in coordinating their actions. One of the most commonly used games, the Prisoners' Dilemma, has been utilized to show that in many issue areas, actors have a strong incentive to defect despite the potential joint gains that they may receive. Yet as we have shown, many problems in global political economy are not Prisoners' Dilemma games, but instead may be better characterized as Chicken, Assurance, Suasion, or even Harmony games. By carefully examining the types of problems that actors face in a particular issue area and the structure of pay-offs, game theory provides insight into the constraints on joint action.

It is worth keeping in mind that the preferences that go into creating games are often assumed by many analysts—particularly those in the neo-realist institutionalist and neo-liberal institutionalist camps. Where do preferences come from and are such preferences amenable to change? It is on this dimension that arguments focusing on the role of experts, changing knowledge, and possible shifts in preferences through learning may provide significant insight that can help us to create more logically compelling games.

Once we can establish the basic game structure that actors face, we can better examine what role institutions might play in ensuring more favourable outcomes. In some cases, contrary to the perspective often taken by neo-institutionalists, institutions may not really be necessary for ensuring cooperative state action. Hence, we examined the types of situations in which self-help might lead to a positive outcome versus those in which institutions might play a genuinely useful role in overcoming collective action problems.

The role of institutions in fostering collaboration itself raises two puzzles. First, how might states collaborate in the first place to create institutions? This in itself raises an analytical problem that various theories have attempted to address. As we have seen, hegemons may have strong incentives to create institutions to constrain the behaviour of other actors and possibly their own domestic lobbies. Other approaches such as neo-liberal institutionalism focus on the strong incentives that major states may have in creating institutions and suggest that small numbers of actors may be able to overcome the usual collective action problems that may lead to free riding behaviour.

A second puzzle concerns the design of institutions. We focused on five dimensions to characterize institutions: membership, the stringency of their rules, their scope, the extent of delegation of power from member states to institutional bodies, and the centralization of tasks within the institution. The types of problems which actors face can partially account for specific institutional characteristics. Yet other factors also influence the design of institutions. These include the potential participants in the specific issue area, the knowledge and information available to actors, and the pre-existing institutional context. In particular, with respect to the last factor, an important issue has been about reconciling new and old institutions in increasingly dense institutional contexts, such as in trade governance with the proliferation of bilateral and regional arrangements or in international and development finance with the creation of regional monetary mechanisms and new development banks.

? 3.7 QUESTIONS

1. Why does globalization increase the pressure for international collaboration?

2. What is the most frequent problem of collaboration in global political economy?

3. What is the thorniest situation of collaboration in global political economy?

4. How can game theory help us understand problems of collaboration?

5. Can enforcement really be carried out in international political economy?

6. How can institutions help overcome obstacles to collaboration?

7. What is the link between the types of problems that countries face in the global economy and their choice of an institution?

8. What are some key characteristics that can be used to describe international institutions?

9. What theories or variables help to account for the choice of specific international institutional characteristics?

≋ 3.8 FURTHER READING

Aggarwal, V. K. (ed.) (1998), *Institutional Designs for a Complex World: Bargaining, Linkages and Nesting* (Ithaca, NY: Cornell University Press). A collective volume that focuses on the relationships between institutions and the stability of dense institutional settings.

Aggarwal, V. K., and Dupont, C. (1999), 'Goods, Games and Institutions', *International Political Science Review*, 20/4: 393–409. The original and technical presentation of our theory that links goods, games, and institutions.

Cooper, R. N. (ed.) (1989), *Can Nations Agree?* (Washington, D.C.: Brookings Institution). An insightful collection of work on coordination attempts of economic policies among nations outside of institutional settings.

Hasenclever, A., Mayer, P., and Rittberger, V. (eds.) (1997), *Theories of International Regimes* (Cambridge: Cambridge University Press). A collective volume on developments in theories of international regimes with application to all domains of international politics.

Kaul, I., Grunberg, I., and Stern, M. A. (eds.) (1999), *Global Public Goods* (Oxford: Oxford University Press). A collective volume with a range of examples of global public goods in economics, politics, and environment with interesting lessons for the future provision of such goods.

Keohane, R. O. (1984), *After Hegemony: Cooperation and Discord in the World Political Economy* (Princeton, NJ: Princeton University Press). The classic work on the links between regime change and change in power distribution.

Kormenos, B., Lipson, C., and Snidal, D. (2001), 'The Rational Design of International Institutions', *International Organization*, 55/4: 761–799. Introductory article to the latest collective work on institutional design, using insights from game theory and considering various facets of institutions.

Krasner, S. D. (ed.) (1983), *International Regimes* (Ithaca, NY: Cornell University Press). The seminal collective volume on international regimes that includes the classic definition of regimes as well as a range of examples in various domains of international politics.

Olson, M. (1965), *The Logic of Collective Action: Public Goods and the Theory of Groups* (Cambridge, MA: Harvard University Press). Classic work on collective action and the conditions under which groups of actors may produce public goods.

Sandler, T. (1992), *Collective Action: Theory and Applications* (Ann Arbor, MI: University of Michigan Press). A comprehensive treatment of the problem of collective action using both basic and advanced formal analytical tools.

Snidal, D. (1985), 'Coordination versus Prisoners' Dilemma: Implications for International Cooperation', *American Political Science Review*, 79: 923–942. The seminal article on the contrast between Prisoners' Dilemma and coordination games applied to international relations.

Taylor, M. (1987), *The Possibility of Cooperation* (Cambridge: Cambridge University Press). An advanced treatment of the problem of cooperation using repeated games.

Yarbrough, B. V., and Yarbrough, R. M. (1992), *Cooperation and Governance in International Trade* (Princeton, NJ: Princeton University Press). An elegant analysis of the problem of governance in trade approached through the lens of transaction costs.

CONTRIBUTOR NOTES

Vinod K. Aggarwal is Distinguished Professor and Alann P. Bedford Professor in Asian Studies in the Travers Department of Political Science; Affiliated Professor in the Haas School of Business; Director of the Berkeley APEC Study Center at the University of California, Berkeley; and Fellow in the Public Law and Policy Program, Berkeley Law. He is Editor-in-Chief of the journal *Business and Politics*, and has two forthcoming coedited books: *Great Power Competition and Middle Power Strategies* and the *Oxford Handbook on Geoeconomics and Economic Statecraft*.

Cédric Dupont is Professor of Political Science and co-Chair of the Thinking Ahead on Societal Change (TASC) platform at the Graduate Institute of International and Development Studies, Geneva. He has published widely on governance and negotiation processes at the global and regional levels. He is the coauthor of a forthcoming book: *Investment Arbitration as a Complex System*.

4

Ideas, Social Hierarchies, and the Everyday

Erin Hannah and Lucy Hinton

Chapter contents

Reader's guide

This chapter begins with the premise that unequal relations of power along classed, racialized, and gendered lines are central to the functioning of the global political economy (GPE) which is defined as the highly complex interaction between states, markets, and societies. These relations of power have nevertheless been hidden from view in much of GPE scholarship. This chapter centres some of the empirical and conceptual margins of GPE and highlights the interplay of ideas, social hierarchies, and the everyday in order to shed light on some of the most important but often neglected aspects of GPE: gender, race, and everyday life. The role of ideas in establishing and legitimizing different patterns of authority and power is explored in Section 4.1. Next, we discuss how social hierarchies—which are underpinned by dominant ideas, discourses, material conditions, and power dynamics—are cemented into the GPE in ways that produce different life chances for different categories of people along class, gendered, and racialized lines. Finally, we turn our gaze to the 'globally governed' to better understand how everyday people experience the GPE and exercise agency, power, and resistance on a daily basis. In so doing, we show how some GPE scholars explore the intersection of the global economy with everyday life at the level of households, local communities, informal economies, and more.

4.1 Introduction

What constitutes the global political economy (GPE)? In whose interest is the GPE constructed, and by whom? What is the role of public and private power in the distribution of scarce resources both globally and locally? How can different types of inequalities in the GPE best be redressed? These are some of the perennial questions that underpin the field of global political economy (GPE).[1] By tackling them, scholars aim to make sense of the highly complex interactions between states, markets, and societies at different sites and scales. Scholars approach these questions in very different ways, making a series of normative choices about what we see and do not see when we look out into the world. Silences, marginalizations, and exclusions are the inevitable consequences of making such choices. The purpose of this chapter is to shine a light on some of the most important but often neglected aspects of the GPE: **gender**, race, and everyday life.

As discussed in the introduction to this volume and in Section 4.3.1, by attending to the **intersectional** dimensions of inequality and including *societies* in the complex interactions we seek to unpack, we make a normative commitment to elevate parts of the GPE that have previously received insufficient attention in much of GPE scholarship. Indeed, attending to the blind-spots in the study of GPE has become impossible to ignore.[2] We show that by examining the interplay of ideas, social hierarchies, and **the everyday**—within the complex interactions of states, markets, and societies—we can begin to make sense of how **structural inequalities** and power relations along class, gendered, and racialized lines are central to the GPE.

Critical approaches to GPE are particularly well suited to shining a light on these neglected aspects, although they have not always done so (Waylen 2006; Elias 2011). We situate critical approaches to GPE

under a very broad tent and draw insight from critical constructivist, Marxist, Gramscian, feminist, post-colonial, decolonial, and post-structural scholarship in this chapter. Whilst our treatment is plural and inclusive of a range of theoretical, conceptual, and methodological approaches, there is coherence with the critical GPE scholarship from which we draw. 'Critical' means to problematize the current world order of capitalism, its power relations, and the dominant ideas and institutions that established and comprise it. Critical approaches aim to uncover and challenge forms of domination, exploitation, and inequality that arise from global economic arrangements. Critical approaches seek to understand how the existing world order came about and how it produces and sustains the major problems we seek to address. In this respect, this body of scholarship centres structural inequalities and 'the human faces behind economic transformations' (Elias 2010: 608). Fundamentally, the GPE is understood as a site of struggle and contestation where people's life chances are at stake. Finally, the scholars from whom we draw insight seek to locate resistance and the prospects for transforming or challenging the current world order in ways that can solve those very problems. Many critical GPE scholars, though certainly not all, also advance a normative agenda in favour of a more inclusive and equitable GPE, which prioritizes ecological sustainability, and the needs of poor, marginalized, and vulnerable people the world over.

We do not offer a comprehensive survey of critical GPE scholarship in this chapter (see Shields et al. 2011; Murphy and Tooze 1991), nor is the purpose to show that conventional GPE scholarship has it wrong and critical GPE scholarship has it right (see Key Theory Box 4.1). Themes such as gender, race, and the everyday have historically been neglected by large parts of both bodies of scholarship, and efforts to redress this situation are taking place across the field. Here we bring attention to some of the ways that certain conceptual and analytical tools have been deployed by critical GPE scholars in order to make sense of the intersectional dimensions of inequality in the GPE and the related implications for different communities of people.

The chapter unfolds in three parts. Section 4.2 introduces the crucial role of ideas in the GPE and illustrates several key ways that ideas have been operationalized in critical scholarship: ideas as knowledge,

---

[1] In this chapter, we differentiate between *the* GPE (the dynamic and empirical interplay between states, markets, and societies) and GPE (the analysis or study of the former).
[2] See, for example, two special issues that were published in 2021 in the *Review of International Political Economy* and *New Political Economy* that called for scholars to be more attuned to the empirical and conceptual blind-spots in GPE, and a recentring of previously marginalized perspectives in the discipline. See also critical engagements with these special issues by Cammack (2021) and Hall (2023).

KEY THEORY BOX 4.1 CONVENTIONAL VS CRITICAL, ELEVATED VS NEGLECTED

In the introduction to this chapter, we noted that GPE scholars are always making decisions about what they study and what they do not study. We call these 'normative choices'. In other words, GPE scholars are always deciding what they think *should* be studied, elevating those issues and neglecting others. However, as we make the case in this chapter, ideas, social hierarchies, and everyday life are important, and the field of GPE is no different. What GPE scholars choose to study is also subject to the ideas that dominate in the discipline and the social hierarchies that have often determined whose voices are considered authoritative.

Most GPE textbooks rely on a 'three-way split' to explain the dominant approaches to studying the GPE (Watson 2014). These are usually *realism*, *liberalism*, and *Marxism*. In some cases, the third core theoretical position is considered as a more general 'critical theories' bucket. We similarly use the framing of 'critical' as a big tent, aiming to encompass approaches to studying the GPE that problematize dominant orders. We can take from this, then, that realism and liberalism are more often considered 'dominant' (or what we tend to call 'conventional') approaches to studying the GPE. In this textbook, we do not eschew conventional approaches, and indeed many chapters exemplify excellent and important contributions to our

understanding of GPE (see, for example, Aggarwal and Dupont, Chapter 3, and Gulsinger, Chapter 6). Rather, in this chapter, we invert the usual centralization of dominant or conventional approaches (with critical approaches served up as a side dish), and aim instead to hone in on some of these more 'neglected' theoretical approaches and topic areas.

Finally, recent approaches to an intellectual history of GPE have highlighted several trends that are helpful for students to be aware of. Cohen (2008) argues that GPE as a field of study could largely be thought of along the lines of a British school (more akin to critical approaches and grand theories), an American school (more based in quantitative, economics analyses; similar to what is also known as Open Economy Politics), and everyone else. Blyth (2009) showcases the geographical and theoretical diversity of GPE by engaging different versions found in North America, the UK, Asia, and Australia. Helleiner (2023) argues that the lineage of GPE is much older, more global, and much more diverse than traditionally considered in the Anglophone world. These are major oversimplifications of these intellectual histories, but they help us point to why a plurality of views in GPE is important, and especially when we consider neglected areas.

---

ideas as meaning, and ideas as culture. Three illustrative vignettes—trade orthodoxy, gender equality, and corporate Islam—show the power of ideas in establishing and legitimizing existing patterns of authority and power in the GPE, as well as ways of thinking and doing in GPE, the field of study.

Section 4.3 discusses how social hierarchies and shared ideas about who and what is valued are cemented into the GPE to produce different life chances for different categories of people. Here we operationalize key concepts such as **feminism**, **decolonization**, and **racial capitalism** in order to spotlight certain intersectional identities that have historically been marginalized in GPE scholarship but are key to understanding global structural inequalities.

Finally, Section 4.4 considers the prospects for resisting the dominant power dynamics and structural inequalities in the GPE by examining bottom-up practices of resistance in everyday life. We provide three illustrative examples of everyday resistance by looking to feminist activism and solidarity economies, everyday activism and ethical consumerism, and Indigenous activism and food sovereignty movements.

4.2 Ideas

4.2.1 Understanding the role of ideas in the global political economy

Power in the GPE is not solely derived from material capabilities, such as military strength or economic resources. Power is also exercised through the control of knowledge, the shaping of ideas, and the construction of **discourses**. Things that we might consider strictly material—gross domestic product (GDP), balance of trade, debt levels, financial flows, foreign direct investment, ownership of the means of production, access to technology, the distribution of natural resources such as oil and minerals—are all shaped by prevailing ideas and power dynamics. As we discuss in Section 4.3, humans share ideas about who and what is valued. Importantly, ideas are historically and geographically contingent rather than universal and, as we discuss in more detail in Section 4.3, they are mediated by dominant power relations. While ideas are initially socially constructed, they are made into material reality in social systems when they are embedded in institutions and discourses. Ideas also give material factors meaning and power. Indicators like GDP are not objective or neutral measures. Rather, they are the product of social interactions and human agreement that are themselves underlined by certain power dynamics that serve particular political agendas (DeRock 2021; Mügge 2016).

The study of ideas in GPE has a long lineage (see Ravenhill and Hannah, Chapter 1), and they are pivotal to a wide range of different approaches in GPE. Drawing on the work of the German sociologist Max Weber, scholars have examined the role that ideas play in defining the range of policy options that governments consider, and in providing a focal point for agreement in international negotiations (Hall 1989; Goldstein and Keohane 1993; Garrett and Lange 1996). Also derived from Weberian analysis are constructivist approaches, which emphasize the significance of ideas in constituting actors' perceptions of their interests and identities, rather than taking these for granted (for example, Abdelal et al. 2010). In this vein, Ruggie (1982) very famously attuned us to the conceptual and empirical importance of 'social purpose' in understanding economic systems. Social purpose has been defined as collectively held, normative ideas about what constitutes a 'desirable or good economic system, derived from combinations of economic analysis and ethical reasoning' (Baker 2018: 293). Ideas have been the central focus of scholarship which builds on the arguments of the former Italian communist party leader Antonio Gramsci, on how ideas help ruling classes to legitimate their domination (Cox 1987; Gill 1990). As we discuss in Section 4.3, feminist, postcolonial, and decolonial scholars show us that ideas about what, or who, has value can generate powerful hierarchies in the GPE. These ideas can act as governing or signifying codes to systematically privilege (or marginalize) various identities, types of labour, livelihoods, and more.

Many foundational interventions on the role of ideas offered by constructivist scholars in GPE made the case that ideas matter by showing how they shape policy agendas, help states to reach agreement in various international negotiations, and legitimize current economic, political, and **social structures** (for example, Blyth 1997; 2002; Finnemore and Sikkink 1998; Abdelal et al. 2010; Béland and Cox 2016). Today, this point is largely uncontested by conventional and critical scholars alike, and there exists a vast literature that seeks to understand the power and dynamics of ideas in the GPE.

In this section, we explore how certain critical GPE scholars treat ideas and study how particular, intersubjective, taken-for-granted ways of thinking and talking cement ideational and material inequalities in the GPE (Strange 1998; Wilkinson 2009; Siles-Brügge 2013). We draw specific insight from critical constructivist and feminist scholarship to distil three overlapping ways that ideas have been operationalized to shine new light on neglected areas of study: ideas as knowledge, ideas as meaning, and ideas as culture. In so doing, we provide illustrative vignettes of the power of ideas in the GPE—demonstrating how to use the tools of critical GPE to understand the world around us.

4.2.2 Ideas as knowledge

For many critical GPE scholars, dominant ideas and ways of thinking and doing help to establish and legitimize existing structures of authority and power in the GPE. A helpful starting point in understanding the power of ideas is the concept of episteme (Foucault 1970; Adler and Bernstein 2005; see Key Theory Box 4.2).

KEY THEORY BOX 4.2 EPISTEMES

Epistemes are composed of background knowledge, ideological and normative beliefs, and shared intersubjective causal and evaluative assumptions about how the world works. They are invisible lenses that allow people to interpret, categorize, simplify, and make sense of the world. For Adler and Bernstein, '[e]pisteme thus refers to the "bubble" within which people happen to live, the way people construe their reality, their basic understandings of the causes of things, their normative beliefs, and their identity, the understanding of self in terms of others' (Adler and Bernstein 2005). Epistemes are not reducible to material interests because they are embedded in institutions and in common discourses through which people communicate, which are part of social structures. They are powerful because they demarcate the boundaries within which people reason and make choices, define the range of problems that can be addressed, and determine which policy options are conceivable, who has a voice, and which agendas are prioritized (Hannah 2016; Trommer 2015). Notably, epistemes—different ways of thinking and doing—are numerous and permeable; the predominant episteme is just one among several possible sets of lenses through which to view the world.

4.2.2.1 Spotlight: Understanding the trade orthodoxy through epistemes

We can use the concept of epistemes to understand the trade orthodoxy in the GPE—in other words, a distinct set of ideas that dominate in trade policy circles (Hannah et al. 2015; Hannah 2016).[3] Central to the trade orthodoxy is the belief that open markets and free trade are engines of economic growth and thus desirable ends in themselves (Eagleton-Pearce 2016). Social goals such as environmental sustainability or gender equality are treated as secondary to economic growth. Markets are seen as inherently rational in that they distribute the gains from trade efficiently and ultimately 'lift all boats', suggesting that everyone will collectively benefit from open markets and free trade even if there are individual losers in the short term.

Relatedly, the trade orthodoxy tends to separate trade policy from its societal and environmental impacts. Trade is understood to involve, primarily, the movement of goods and services through global markets. States and corporate actors are considered the most important stakeholders. Seen through this strictly economistic lens, the impact of trade on communities and people in their multiple roles as producers, workers, consumers (including consumers of public services), carers, eaters, and more—as well as the broader environment in which global trade takes place— tend to be treated as second-order issues, or ignored altogether.

The trade orthodoxy is also marked by a trend towards legalization. The idea is to 'lock-in' trade policy through the creation of enforceable rights and obligations in binding legal mechanisms such as the World Trade Organization (WTO), Dispute Settlement Understanding (DSU), or Investor-State Dispute Settlement Mechanisms (ISDS). This serves to entrench rights for investors and corporations, deter deviation from free market principles, and insulate market transactions from public scrutiny and social and environmental regulation. In other words, enshrining trade rules in law is thought to bind the hands of future governments from protectionist or regulatory temptations (see, for example, Gill 2002; Gill and Cutler 2014).

Finally, the trade orthodoxy serves to empower 'insider' trade experts. Trade is a highly technical and complex issue area. Technical language, metaphors, myths, and common sense narratives serve as blueprints for policymaking and work to establish trade experts' monopoly over trade knowledge and empower experts as gatekeepers over trade policymaking (Strange 2013; Siles-Brügge 2014; Trommer 2015). This means that trade experts possess an authoritative claim on knowledge relative to other actors who might be critical of the trade agenda, such as NGOs (Hannah et al. 2015).

The more technical an issue is, the more experts can shape policy to the exclusion of other actors. Actors who do not know how to speak technical trade language may be excluded from trade policymaking altogether, even if they have valuable and important contributions to make (Hinton 2022). By contrast, according to Trommer, using the technical trade language to gain a seat at the table could have the effect of 'discursively reproducing its underlying perspectives and normative commitments, irrespective of the speaker's own worldviews and understandings of reality' (Trommer 2015; see also Del Felice 2014; Trommer 2014). In other words, by 'talking the talk' actors may cement the ideas, norms, consensual scientific knowledge, and ideological beliefs that constitute the orthodoxy. Trade experts can also strengthen orthodox views on trade by coopting, marginalizing, and silencing critical, 'in-expert' voices (Trommer 2015; Hannah 2016).

In sum, the trade orthodoxy privileges economic growth over social goals such as gender equality, thereby marginalizing their significance in trade policy discussions. It ignores losers from trade, empowers trade experts who apply trade-specific epistemes and marginalizes critics, minimizes the capacity of domestic governments to engage in social and environmental regulation, and generally prevents trade experts from considering the intersection of trade with everyday life. This is not to say that trade policy is uncontested. But rather that the trade orthodoxy serves to cement dominant ways of thinking about trade that make it difficult for critics/detractors to gain traction in policymaking circles.

4.2.3 Ideas as meaning

In the GPE, ideas help to assign meaning to the material world. Ideas tell us—consciously or unconsciously—what to elevate and what to neglect, what to value and what to devalue. Ideas also help individuals and institutions to define goals, to drive policy agendas

---

[3] This discussion draws heavily from Hannah, Roberts, and Trommer 2022.

forwards, and to set the boundaries of what makes 'legitimate' policymaking and acceptable practices. Yet, in these actions, ideas can sometimes *mean* different things to different actors. This raises questions like, where does meaning come from? Under what circumstances is meaning contested? How are contestations resolved? Big global policy ideas, like 'development', 'economic empowerment', and 'gender equality', are central to the GPE. Do these big global policy ideas mean the same thing to everyone? Who decides the demarcations of meaning, and is it always clear cut?

Contestations over big global policy ideas are a central preoccupation for many critical GPE scholars, particularly critical constructivist and feminist GPE scholars. Here, scholars consider the role of different actors in operating as 'ideational entrepreneurs', which can include anyone involved in contesting and fixing meanings and thereby setting the boundaries of legitimate policymaking: knowledge-based experts, intergovernmental organizations, NGOs or transnational advocacy networks, think tanks, corporate actors, international commissions, and so on.

Much GPE scholarship has been dedicated to the role of civil society organizations. While civil society organizations are wildly diverse in their goals and ideological orientations, their inclusion is considered key to making macroeconomic policymaking more equitable and sustainable. Civil society organizations are thought to give voice to marginalized groups, and channel the concerns of the grassroots upwards to policymakers through various tactics ranging from protest and media campaigns, to lobbying for policy change, to the provision of analysis and expertise. Indeed, they are widely understood to constitute an autonomous group of 'outsider-insiders' that play an essential role in:

[p]roviding a forum for debate; generating ideas and policies; legitimating ideas and policies; advocating for ideas and policies; implementing or testing ideas and policies in the field; generating resources to pursue ideas and policies; monitoring progress in the march of ideas and the implementation of policies; and occasionally burying ideas and policies (Weiss et al. 2009: 123, 128–129).

Given these multiple roles, civil society organizations are central players in contesting the meaning of big global policy ideas in the GPE.

Increasingly, attention is also paid to 'resistant insiders', experts that work inside international organizations that are involved in governing the GPE. Perhaps surprisingly, prevailing ideas, structures, and ways of thinking are often contested and even transformed by the everyday acts of knowledge production and dissemination by insider experts. The South Center is an example of an intergovernmental organization that is very much part of the global trade landscape, but which helps countries from the Global South push back against the trade orthodoxy discussed above. Trade experts working for the South Center strategically provide expertise, research, technical assistance, and advice to Global South trade delegations so that they can better defend or advance their trade interests. The meaning of food security and protectionism have both been the subject of the South Center's advocacy on behalf of the Global South (Hannah, Ryan, and Scott 2017).

In the example that follows, we draw attention to contestations over the meaning of gender equality and the role played by civil society organizations and resistant insiders in pushing back against the business case for gender equality.

4.2.3.1 Spotlight: Understanding meaning through the 'business case' for gender equality

Gender equality is enshrined as a global policy idea in several key international conventions including the United Nations (UN) Beijing Platform for Action, Goal 5 of the Sustainable Development Goals (SDGs), and the Convention on the Elimination of all Forms of Discrimination Against Women (CEDAW). More recently, gender equality has shown up as a global policy idea in places where we have not seen it before, such as in the field of global trade, and it has become the centrepiece of many public and private (corporate and NGO-led) women's empowerment initiatives worldwide (Roberts 2015). Although this may seem like a positive move, there is a great deal of contestation around the meaning of gender equality.

In Section 4.3, we draw from feminist approaches to GPE to undertake a detailed discussion of gender which is presented as an analytical category— something that helps us make sense of the world. In this view, gender equality means problematizing gender and all of the unequal power relations that underlie it. For example, it means acknowledging and supporting social reproduction, and addressing the intersectional dimensions of inequality, the denigration of feminized and unpaid labour, the pervasiveness of double burdens, that is, situations where people work for wages and are responsible for the majority of unpaid domestic work, and more. In other words, for feminists gender equality is something that is fundamentally transformative and which challenges **neoliberal capitalism**, which entails economic liberalization, privatization, deregulation, and the deepening of corporate power (Peterson 2006). Many women's organizations advance a feminist understanding of gender equality. The Gender and Trade Coalition, for example, was established to bring together feminist and progressive activists to advance gender equality in the global economy in a way that does not instrumentalize gender equality as a means of furthering neoliberal capitalism (Gender and Trade Coalition n.d.).

Many, however, consider gender an empirical category, often synonymous with women and in relation to men, and gender equality simply means adding more women (Peterson 2006). Governments, intergovernmental organizations, and private actors alike are increasingly attuned to helping women achieve parity, not only in political representation, but also in economic power, market share, and decision-making. The 'business case' for gender equality claims that investing in women and girls so that they can participate more fully in the market economy as producers and consumers of goods and services is good for business and good for economic growth. We can look to the UN Women/UN Global Compact's Women's Empowerment Principles (WEPs), subtitled 'Equality Means Business', the World Bank's 'Smart Economics' paradigm, Nike's 'Girl Effect', and the International Trade Center's 'She Trades Initiative' as a few illustrative examples (see Roberts and Soederberg 2012; Prügl and True 2014).

From a feminist GPE perspective, integrating women into existing economic structures (or 'adding women and stirring') reinforces neoliberal capitalism. Rather than achieving gender equality, the 'business case' is, according to Prügl (2017), 'feminism with a neoliberal face'—it cements gender-based and other inequalities that underpin and are reproduced by its continued expansion (Fraser 2009; Roberts 2015). Notably, feminist gender experts are working as resistant insiders in organizations such as the World Bank and UN Women to move the needle on gender equality in more transformative directions, but with limited success (Ferguson 2015).

4.2.4 Ideas as culture

In the same way that we can explore the role of ideas in the GPE by examining knowledge and meaning, we can also explore ideas by looking at culture.

As Appadurai succinctly puts it: 'culture mediates between economy and politics' (in Singh 2020: ix). While states and markets are often portrayed as devoid of culture, and interests and preferences are often calculated as existing outside of history and culture, the humans and institutions that make up states and markets are socialized through core sets of values (Singh 2021; Singh, Chapter 15). Best and Patterson (2009) argue that much of the mainstream understanding of the GPE builds on a rhetorical foundation of *separation* of market and social phenomena, as in Polanyi's (1944) disembedding markets.

Hirschman (1978) expanded on this idea by showing that the logic of the market was both morally and socially disruptive, since religious constraints (like charging interest)—a form of culture—needed to be overcome. The results of such a rhetorical separation led to the idea of a theoretical, acultural market, rather than understanding the market as not detached from culture, but simply reconstituting the content of that culture (Best and Patterson 2009).

In recent years, critical constructivist approaches have examined culture more often, aiming to undo this separation and especially to give light to the ways that interests and ideas are culturally informed. Culture can be thought of as toolkits for making sense of the world, made up of values that are malleable and dynamic. In the study of GPE, values might be considered 'weights, importance, or rank given to some things or issues, and manifested through rituals, symbols, social interactions and stratifications, and (in economic conduct) prices' (Singh 2021: 324; see also Singh, Chapter 15). Scholars can fail to grasp some of the intangible factors that shape outcomes in the GPE (Best and Patterson 2009) if they do not consider culture in their examination of states, markets, and societies. For Murphy and Rojas de Ferro (1995: 63):

[when conventional GPE] sees the rise of capitalism as a story of changes in the production and circulation of things it overlooks the linkage between capitalism and its accompanying messages about who is 'wealthy' and who is 'poor', who is 'advanced' and who is 'behind', who is 'rational' and who is 'irrational', who is 'peaceful' and who is 'violent'. Perhaps even more significantly, [conventional GPE] overlooks *whose* representations of the world have ended up answering those questions for most of us, and whose have not.

Importantly, we can use culture to explore some of the problems, issues, or phenomena that we encounter in the GPE. Indeed, using a cultural approach to analyse the GPE can help draw attention to the *pre-conditions* that determine different groups' economic needs and grievances, which Sau (2021) argues is especially important given the recent surge in far-right ideas and state policy. Sau (2021) extends cultural political economy approaches so that we can explain policies that are not traditional 'economic' policies, further expanding the reach of pluralist political economy scholarship.

4.2.4.1 Spotlight: Understanding corporate Islam and economic moralities through cultural values

For example, we can use the concept of cultural values to understand the recent expansion of the Islamic economy and corporate Islam. The Islamic revival of the 1970s and 1980s spurred on attempts to build an Islamic economy, an economic system built around Islamic values like social justice, equity, and prosperity for all, but also on respect for property rights. The burgeoning Islamic economy needed to straddle the ideological economic systems of the time—capitalism and communism (Hefner 2006; Siddiq 2006). And while slow to develop comprehensively, the post 9/11 world saw greater enmeshment between emerging Islamic economies, other broader and conventional forms of global economic governance, and the actors operating in the Organisation for Islamic Cooperation (OIC) framework that was developed earlier (Rethel 2019).

The Islamic economy, Rethel argues (2019), can be defined both narrowly and more broadly, but both definitions encompass cultural conceptions of the intersections of politics and economics. Narrowly, Rethel defines the Islamic economy as the 'economic activity which is conducted in compliance with Islamic law'—therefore differentiating between *halal* (permissible) and *haram* (prohibited) (2019: 352). More broadly though, the Islamic economy can refer to the sectors of the global economy that produce goods and services directed towards Muslim consumers, like family tourism (especially pilgrimage), modest fashion, or specific news media (Rethel 2019). Yet the central nodes of importance in the Islamic economy are not necessarily the centres of political or intellectual authority in the Islamic world (Bano and Sakurai 2015), and global Islamic economic governance forums are focusing more on capitalist values of entrepreneurship and business networking (Rethel 2019), raising questions as to the scale of values in defining this alternative economy.

Rethel (2019) also suggests some other ways we might understand the Islamic economy. In the first,

the Islamic or *halal* economy is simply viewed through the lens of consumer segmentation, as in the tradition of moral markets (Jones 2010; Tobin 2016). In other words, the cultural values that distinguish some consumers are used strategically by actors in markets. Whereas previously consumption habits were seen as 'antithetical to Muslim ethical traditions' (Hefner 2005: 21), Islamic values are now 'realised precisely through consumption' (Rethel 2019). Moreover, these values can now be standardized and certified in a regime complex (Fischer 2016), as required when states like Australia and Brazil are some of the world's biggest exporters of *halal* meat (Thompson Reuters 2015). Finally, Rethel (2019: 355) raises the question of a normative space: 'can we speak of global capitalism/Muslim style?'

Ideas are often invisible until they are made visible, and a cultural lens can help us to see some of what shapes the GPE. And while there have been more efforts towards this approach in recent years, Singh (2020; Chapter 15 this volume) reminds us that further theorization into the internal dynamics of culture is required, especially in relation to race.

KEY POINTS

- *Ideas* have long been examined by scholars to understand their impact on the GPE. Since actors are influenced by their social context—shared rules, meanings, and ideas—ideas are historically and geographically contingent rather than universal, and are always mediated by power relations.

- Thinking about *epistemes* can be a helpful way to analyse dominant sets of ideas (knowledge) that keep people in 'bubbles' of understanding. Trade experts are an example of 'insiders' who share epistemes—invisible lenses about what is acceptable—that often end up marginalizing the views of 'outsiders'.

- Ideational entrepreneurs including civil society organizations and other actors can help shape *meaning* in the GPE. Our understanding of ideas like 'development' or 'gender equality' have changed substantially over time, and these meanings show us that ideas are continuously constructed and reconstructed.

- *Culture* is a toolkit of values that can shape both the ways that people interact with the world and the economy. *Culture*, like other ideas in the GPE, is historically contingent and dynamic. It is shaped and reshaped over time, subject to social forces in its interactions with economic issues.

4.3 Social hierarchies

4.3.1 **Understanding the role of social hierarchies and structural inequalities in the GPE**

All GPE scholars address the question so succinctly posed by Susan Strange (1996) 'ciu bono', or 'who benefits?' They are concerned with who gets what, when, and how. As noted by Ravenhill and Hannah (Chapter 1), how we approach answering this question depends very much on what we see (and do not see) when we look at the GPE. Conventional approaches generally 'see' states and markets. They are concerned with top-down governance and the interplay between public and private power in the distribution or allocation of scarce resources both globally and locally. Economic and social spheres tend to be treated as analytically distinct, with the latter falling outside the scope of much GPE scholarship. In other words, in conventional approaches to the study of GPE, what happens within societies, communities, or households is treated as separate from or peripheral to the workings of the global economy. By contrast, many critical GPE scholars reject the distinction between economy and society and take as their starting point the centrality of gendered, racialized, and other social hierarchies at different sites and scales to the workings of the global economy which assign some people higher status or value than others. These scholars bring the identities and inequalities people experience in society into the analysis of states and markets.

Feminist, postcolonial, and decolonial scholars in particular take issue with the conventional 'states and markets' approach to studying the GPE. By adopting an intersectional approach, they put marginalized and/or vulnerable people including women, racialized people, LGBTQ2S+, Indigenous people, and those living with disabilities squarely into view and show how social identities can overlap and create compounding experiences of prejudice and discrimination. They ultimately aim to uncover and redress structural inequalities that result from social hierarchies. Inequalities are structural when they are baked into the ideas and institutions that comprise a given world order (such as capitalism) and they are material when they produce different life chances for different categories of people. Historically, class was understood by many to be the main source of structural inequalities. In this chapter, we place a spotlight on other intersectional identities such as gender and race that have traditionally received less attention in GPE scholarship but which are at least as, if not more, important in understanding global inequalities. Indeed, there are a multitude of gendered and racialized inequalities that are baked into the global political economy which are discussed throughout the various chapters in this book, including access to resources (Bhagat, Chapter 14) and technology (Girard, Chapter 17), divisions of labour (Gore, Chapter 7), wealth and income (Lockwood, Chapter 13), climate change (Ervine, Chapter 16), and debt (Clarke and Roberts, Chapter 10).

4.3.2 **How gender matters in GPE**

As discussed in Key Theory Box 4.3, feminist approaches to GPE are multidisciplinary, intellectually eclectic, and methodologically plural. There is no single 'feminist' approach, just as there is no single 'critical' approach to GPE. That said, all feminist approaches invite us to consider the ways in which the global economy is gendered. When we say that something is gendered, we mean that it privileges or is biased in favour of one gender over others.

Gender is a set of socially constructed ideas and assumptions 'describing what men and women ought to be' as opposed to sex, which is biologically determined (Tickner and Sjøberg 2011: 196). Gender provides a signifying or governing code that tells people what it means to be a man or a woman in the world, which behaviours are appropriate and inappropriate (Peterson 2006). They are shaped by culture and vary across time and space (see Shepherd 2022). Gender not only informs people's everyday practices, but also their political practices, including those who are engaged in governing the GPE (Griffin 2009).

Gender is also a discourse, a way of thinking and talking that is underlined by power. It privileges or empowers the 'masculine' over the 'feminine' in different sites and scales such as in the home or in the workplace. Certain types of men and 'masculinities' are privileged or valorized while certain types of women and 'feminine' practices tend to be devalued, stigmatized, or even ignored in GPE (Peterson 2006: 502; Elias and Roberts 2018: 4). Unpaid care work and informal textile work that takes place inside households, for example, are unaccounted for in conventional economic analyses even though they are part of what keeps the capitalist global economy turning. Meanwhile, as discussed by Gore in Chapter 7 of this volume, the feminization of global assembly lines often relegates women

KEY THEORY BOX 4.3 FEMINIST APPROACHES TO GPE

While feminist approaches to GPE are characterized by theoretical and methodological **pluralism** and feminist scholars cover a vast array of issues areas (see Elias and Roberts 2018 for a comprehensive overview), there is coherence to feminist GPE research 'whose central premise is that political economic structures and discourses constitute, reproduce, and/or change gender norms, relations, and inequalities in a multilayered manner' (Altan-Olcay 2022; see also Bedford and Rai 2010). Further, we can distil five key feminist insights to help guide our efforts to uncover the role of gender in the GPE.[4]

First, feminist scholars ask us to be attuned to the operation of structural gender inequalities in the global economy. This means that we should consider the ways in which gender norms and power relations shape people's participation in the economy and society at different sites and scales, including at home and in workplaces. It also means taking seriously gender-based divisions of unpaid labour for which women are overwhelmingly responsible the world over. The double and triple burdens of women performing multiple and overlapping roles such as entrepreneur, worker, and carer should be taken seriously.

Second, and relatedly, we should adopt a holistic and intersectional approach to understanding the global economy. When we think about economics, we tend only to think about people in their roles as economic actors—traders, workers, entrepreneurs, and so on. A more holistic approach helps us see people in their multiple roles as business owners as well as workers, consumers, users of public services, paid and unpaid carers, citizens, and more. Given that these roles are shaped not only by gender norms and power relations, but also by relations of class, caste, race, ethnicity, nationality, citizenship status, sexuality, age, ability, etc., there is a need to adopt an explicitly intersectional approach to understanding gender in the GPE.

Third, feminist scholars ask us to challenge the false distinction between society and economy and to see private and public spheres of life as deeply intertwined (Prügl 2020). This means being attuned to the human, social, and environmental conditions in which global economic activity takes place. One way to approach this is through the concept of social reproduction, which refers to all those activities (paid and unpaid, formal and informal) involved in reproducing, both biologically and socially, people and communities (Bakker 2003; Luxton 2018; see also Gore, Chapter 7, Key Theory Box 7.6). Social reproduction includes the biological reproduction of the species—motherhood—and the conditions under which this work is performed. It includes the reproduction of the labour force which includes subsistence, education, and training. Care work, the provisioning of caring needs for children, the elderly, those with disabilities, is also part of social reproduction. Social reproductive activities include domestic labour that takes place inside households, as well as paid and unpaid/volunteer work in schools, hospitals, and communities. Activities aimed at environmental sustainability and care for the planet on which human life depends are also considered an integral dimension of social reproduction (Hannah, Roberts, and Trommer 2021). Importantly, responsibility for social reproductive labour is shouldered disproportionately by women, migrants, and racialized minorities in every corner of the world.

Feminist scholars have shown us how to be attuned to social reproduction by turning to 'the everyday' aspects of life which are central to social reproduction by '[l]ooking to the practices and routines of daily life in order to raise important questions about the gendered power relations that underpin foreign direct investment, development, globalization, the transformation of the state, the nature of work, and/or financial crisis' (Elias and Roberts 2018: 790).

Finally, feminist scholars are focused on efforts to resist or challenge structural gender inequality in the global economy. For example, feminists are interested in initiatives that aim to address gender inequalities in and through trade.

to low-wage, low-skill, export-oriented work which is characterized by exploitative working conditions (see also Bair 2010; Gunawardana 2018).

Ultimately, gender is a structural relation of inequality, and it is baked into the GPE in ways that produce different life chances for different people.

4.3.2.1 Spotlight: Gender and global trade

Let us turn our attention to an example of how we can apply these insights. Until recently, conventional wisdom among trade policymakers was that trade is gender neutral, in the sense that it targets neither women nor men (Roberts, Trommer, and Hannah 2019). Open markets and free trade were seen as engines of economic growth and thus desirable ends in themselves, as opposed to other social goals such as gender equality, human rights, environmental protections, and so on (Hannah, Roberts, and Trommer 2022). In other words, trade was considered a technical matter and goals like gender equality and human rights were seen as totally separate from trade policy, and certainly not the business of trade institutions such as the World Trade Organization (WTO).

[4] Drawn from Hannah, Roberts, and Trommer 2023.

This began to change in 2017 when policymakers started to talk about the importance of gender mainstreaming in trade policy. This shift in thinking gained traction with the signing, in December 2017, of the WTO Joint Declaration on Trade and Women's Economic Empowerment (WTO Declaration) by 118 members and observers. Since then, more than one hundred gender and trade initiatives have been developed globally (Hannah, Roberts, and Trommer 2018).

Despite the relative 'newness' of this agenda, global trade is and always has been gendered (Hannah, Roberts, and Trommer 2018; 2021; 2022; Roberts, Trommer, and Hannah 2019). Trade policy affects almost every area of public policy, and it impacts people in their multiple roles as business owners as well as workers, consumers, users of public services, paid and unpaid carers, citizens, and more. As discussed above, these different roles are shaped by gender norms and power relations in society, as well as other intersecting identities. For example, gender norms in a country can impact women's access to education, employment, and earnings relative to men. The impacts of trade policy are gendered as a result of the different position of women and men in these roles, and policymakers are increasingly attuned to the differential impacts of trade in four key areas: paid work, consumption, public services, and care work (see Case Study Box 4.4).

CASE STUDY BOX 4.4 THE GENDERED IMPACTS OF TRADE

Paid Work: Trade liberalization often results in an increase in jobs, particularly in those countries that specialize in production for export, and this may give women increased income and purchasing power. However, women are responsible for the majority of unpaid care work for children and the elderly the world over. This means that they are over-represented in precarious and temporary forms of work. Countries that specialize in goods for export may also have wide gender wage gaps as the payment of low wages or poor working conditions in feminized sectors of the economy are the ways that countries are able to compete in a global economy (Roberts, Trommer, and Hannah 2019).

The 'feminization' of labour that occurred in Mexico following the signing of the North American Free Trade Agreement (NAFTA) in 1994 is one example of the complex ways in which trade liberalization can impact the conditions of paid work for women and other vulnerable communities. The impacts are often complex and context specific. An often-rehearsed argument is that greater employment opportunities for women, even if initially poorly paid and precarious, will in time reduce gender pay inequalities when wages begin to rise in response to declining unemployment. However, the evidence for this is rather weak. To take one example, Domínguez-Villalobos and Brown-Grossman (2010) find that after twenty years of Mexican export production (primarily by women), '[t]here is consistent evidence of the negative impact of export orientation on men's and women's wages and the gender wage ratio, signifying that women lose in both absolute and relative terms'.

That said, there may be important positive effects on women's position in society that come through their greater incorporation into paid employment. For instance, in Turkey, even though women are integrated into textile and clothing production on the basis of long hours, low pay, and low security, it nonetheless opens some limited opportunities for positive change, such as enabling greater personal choice of whom they marry (Dedeoglu 2010: 22–23). Many of these complicated dynamics are explored by Gore in Chapter 7 of this volume.

Consumption: Generally speaking, trade liberalization is thought to benefit consumers by lowering prices of goods and services, but the picture in practice is not always so clear. For example, sometimes trade liberalization leads to increases in the cost of food imports, which disproportionately affect the poorest households and women, who tend to have less access to and control over income while also being the primary persons responsible for food purchase and preparation (Roberts, Trommer, and Hannah 2019). Moreover, when there are dramatic price fluctuations in international markets for food staples like rice, as occurred in 2007–2008 and 2022, those costs of provisioning households tend to be borne most heavily by women.

Public services: Women, along with Indigenous and other racialized groups, are over-represented among those who use public services. This is often due to their disproportionate responsibility for care work. Women also tend to make up the majority of workers in public service sectors like health, education, and social work. If public services are privatized and opened to global competition through trade liberalization, these groups will be most heavily impacted. Sometimes trade liberalization leads to improved access to public services, including those that are essential for women's reproductive health. At other times the capacity of governments to invest in public services is undermined through marketization or privatization, and this makes it more difficult for women and other vulnerable groups to access public services (Roberts, Trommer, and Hannah 2019).

> ### CASE STUDY BOX 4.4 THE GENDERED IMPACTS OF TRADE (continued)
>
> *Care work*: When new trading arrangements succeed in drawing women into formal, paid work, there is a need for additional resources—either from the state or from families—to make up for the potential reduction of care work that was previously performed by women. Unless governments dedicate additional resources to support the provisioning of public services in the health and care sectors, there may be a decline in levels of care overall, with poor households experiencing the greatest losses (Roberts, Hannah, and Trommer 2019).
>
> It is important to emphasize that trade does not cause gender inequalities. Trade can improve the lives of women and other vulnerable groups by redressing existing gender inequalities, or it can make them more precarious by exacerbating already existing gender inequalities. Nevertheless, by placing gender at the centre of analysis, we can see the centrality of gendered and other social hierarchies to the deeper workings of the global political economy and look for ways to challenge or even dismantle them.

4.3.3 How race matters in GPE

While gender has (slowly and incrementally) been embraced in the study of GPE, there has, perhaps, been an even more lethargic adoption when it comes to race as an analytical lens. That is not to say that scholars have ignored racial elements in the global economy, but that race has frequently been marginalized in conventional approaches. While race began as a social construct, human action made race material over time (Tilley and Shilliam 2018). In aiming to understand how race is central to the operation of the GPE, it can be useful to start with theories of dependency and world systems (de Oliveira and Kvangraven 2023; Lockwood, Chapter 13, Key Theory Box 13.3). From the 1950s, some economists, sociologists, and historians, especially from Latin America and Africa, argued that colonial efforts had created 'cores' and 'peripheries' in the global economy, and that these relationships were continuing through the independence era (see Key Theory Box 4.6 on decolonization) (Prebisch 1950; Nkrumah 1966; Frank 1969; Rodney 1972; Galeano 1973; Wallerstein 1974; Cardoso and Faletto 1979). These scholars argued that Europe's development could be tied directly to the extractive activities (for example, human/slavery and natural resources such as timber, palm oil, aluminium, cotton, cocoa) conducted in colonies, and that the contemporary global economy is built on these structural qualities (see Lockwood, Chapter 13, Section 13.2.1 for a discussion of the colonial origins of global inequality).

Despite the intellectual history of inequality in the global economy based on the structural legacies of colonialism, race is missing from some of the most critical perspectives on neoliberal capitalism. In an important special issue in *New Political Economy*, Tilley and Shilliam (2018) argue that such significant critical scholars as Wendy Brown, William Davies, and David Harvey all fail to adequately address race in their critiques of neoliberalism. Perhaps an unintentional effect of Hall's (1979) entrenchment of a divide between race as ideology and class as materiality, scholars have been slow to fully grasp the totality of the race-as-construct turned reality. Instead, and especially given the recent rise in racist rhetoric propelled by leaders of countries around the world, GPE scholars must 'attend to the ways that race functions in structural and agential ways, integrally reproducing raced markets and social conditions' (Tilley and Shilliam 2018: 534).

4.3.3.1 Spotlight: Raced markets

In exploring the way that race has moved from fiction/ideas to materiality over time, 'reproduced in relation to the manifold raced markets of the global political economy', Tilley and Shilliam (2018: 534) introduce *raced markets* as a way to understand the GPE. Putting race at the centre of the analysis shows that race has the same materiality as class to constitute social hierarchies (Gilmore 2007; Chakravatty and da Silva 2012). Race has, of course, been crucial to the European visioning of proper political and economic subjects, enabling the justification for colonial domination by shifting some people into a class of non-human (and foregoing any need for ethical norms of treatment) (Tilley and Shilliam 2018). The entire edifice of *homo economicus* can be traced to a wealthy

Western approximation (Wynters 2003), emphasizing the ethno-classed foundations of modern economics. Further exemplified through Watson's (2018) exploration of the Robinson Crusoe story (discussed in Watson, Chapter 2) in many modern political economy textbooks, understanding our ideas about race (or its erasure) is also vital to understanding the construction of the global economy. As Tilley and Shilliam summarize (2018: 538), '[w]hen the historical evidence is surveyed, it becomes clear that race has been integral to centuries of colonization in the service of dispossession, extraction and enslavement, and continues to play a role in the ordering of accumulation and impoverishment in the present'.

Raced markets are, therefore, an analytical tool to explore the racial ordering that is, and always has been, required for global markets to work. Colonial relations both established and continue to reproduce the global political economy (Bhambra 2021). It makes visible the possibility to consider neoliberalism as a raced market, and to therefore see the co-constitutive relationship among race, racism, and neoliberalism (Tilley and Shilliam 2018). Rajaram (2018) provides an illustrative example of the raced market dynamic by examining the struggles that some groups in society have in valorizing their body power in capitalism.

Rajaram (2018) shows that while capitalism is premised on the idea that a labourer freely enters into labour contracts with the owners of capital (their employer)—that is, they formally valorize their body power—migrants and refugees are often unable to valorize their body power. These are 'surplus populations' in capitalism. In the colonial era, Rajaram argues, 'native' 'work' was dismissed in favour of civilized 'labour', and the failure to relinquish the cultural traits would constrain an individual from becoming a reliably good labourer (Alatas 1977). These same cultural traits would be used long past the colonial era to judge an individual's capacity to engage in labour, structuring different groups' possibilities in the labour market. Importantly though, Rajaram (2018: 628) argues that these surplus populations are not excluded from capitalism. Indeed, '[s]urplus populations work the dark underbelly of capitalism, its backstage operations where cheap and irregular labour is used up in the search for hyperprofit'. As explored in more detail by Gore in Chapter 7 of this volume, today migrants and refugees, from undocumented Mexican workers in the United States, to precarious Bangladeshis in Malaysia, to migrants and Roma in Hungary, all work to support this underbelly of capitalism, showcasing not that neoliberalism is colour-blind, but that it relies on raced markets to prop it up.

Critical GPE scholars often use race as a central analytical lens to show that global inequality is not colour-blind—in fact it is anchored to colour. In particular, they tie histories of extraction to the perpetuation of race-based inequalities in the GPE, understanding race alongside other social hierarchies and, often, actively seeking to dismantle them (see Key Concept Box 4.5).

KEY CONCEPT BOX 4.5 RACIAL CAPITALISM

Capitalism is more than an economic system. The system of 'free' exchange between labour and owners of capital is built on histories and social relations, and these histories and social relations structure the resulting exchanges. Rather than arguing that capitalist modes of production can create a racialized structure or an ideology of racism, scholars show that capitalism is constituted by the histories and superstructure of racism (Hall 1996; Dirlik 2002). Importantly, racial capitalism is 'not a way of understanding capitalism as a racist conspiracy or racism as a capitalist conspiracy' (Bhattacharya 2018: ix). Bhattacharya warns us not to read racial capitalism as an allegation of intentionality.

Initially described by Cedric Robinson (1983/2000) in his seminal work *Black Marxism: The Making of the Black Radical Tradition*, Robinson worked to shine light on areas Marx had failed to adequately acknowledge. Robinson argued that the appearance and codification of racism during the feudal period had enduring effects on the way the global economy has been structured. Importantly, Robinson shows that the emergence of the racial order under European feudalism was not simply restricted to ordering European and non-European relations, but actually a consequence of internal European labour ordering. This foundation, he argued, led to the organization and expansion of racial directions in capitalist society, developed in parallel with a corresponding social ideology. It could be expected, then, Robinson writes, that 'racialism would inevitably permeate the social structures emergent from capitalism'. While scholars, such as W. E. B. Du Bois (see Figure 4.1) of the United States, and Eric Williams and C. L. R. James of Trinidad, had all previously tied capitalism to the foundations of slavery.

Figure 4.1 William Edward Burghardt Du Bois, more commonly known as W. E. B. Du Bois, was born in Massachusetts in 1868. Du Bois was the first African American to receive a PhD from Harvard University in 1895. In 1903, Du Bois published *The Souls of Black Folks*, based on many of his own experiences, and would go on to cofound the National Association for the Advancement of Colored People (better known as the NAACP) and be a major actor in the civil rights movement. W. E. B. Du Bois was a major intellectual force in a tumultuous time in the United States.

Source: Shutterstock.

Traditionally, decolonization has been referred to in political science as the period where former colonial rulers left colonized territories, whether actively pushed out or through a phased agreement (*literally*, de-colonization). In this way, decolonization is the pursuit of political sovereignty, or the temporal period where former colonies gained independence and the right to self-determination, and the term was popularized during the 1960s–1980s. However, long before the period traditionally thought of as 'decolonization', there were outliers both in terms of geographies where sovereign autonomy was achieved and postcolonial thinkers who brought the related philosophies to life.

The Haitian slave revolt of 1789 initiated the first Black republic in 1804. Yet recent reporting shows that the reparations imposed by France for the loss of the colony left most of Haiti's revenues unavailable for any sovereign development initiatives, keeping Haiti in a constant and unequal relationship with its former ruler (Porter et al. 2022). Haiti's experience shows that the removal of a colonial sovereign is not the same as true, national self-determination.

Long before the temporal period of 'decolonization', thinkers like Haiti's Toussaint L'Ouverture engaged with ideas that problematized colonial occupation and motivated resistance. Mahatma Gandhi helped to spur on resistance to British rule

KEY THEORY BOX 4.6 DECOLONIZATION (continued)

characterized by *ahimsa* (non-violence), and though India achieved independence in 1947, he was assassinated in 1948 (Gandhi 2019). Gandhi, like W. E. B. Du Bois of America, Marcus Garvey of Jamaica, Aimé Césaire and Frantz Fanon of Martinique, and Walter Rodney of Guyana, helped the world begin to think of decolonization not simply as a political process, but as a revolution in material and ideological terms for the oppressed people of the world—or those who Fanon called *The Wretched of the Earth*. The work of these thinkers helped to invigorate a new political class of Third World[5] leaders who would demand greater concessions from the First and Second Worlds in the second half of the twentieth century, such as Sukarno of Indonesia, Jawaharwal Nehru of India, and Kwame Nkrumah of Ghana.

The work of scholars like Du Bois, Césaire, Fanon, Rodney, and many others is experiencing a resurgence today as

contemporary scholars try to make sense of global inequality (Acharya 2014). Decolonization can take on different meanings in different parts of the world, such as the former plantation economies in the Caribbean (N. Roberts 2015; Kamugisha 2019), or through scholars' and activists' work in settler-colonial contexts like Turtle Island (what we often call North America) (Tuck and Yang 2012; Martens et al. 2020; Manuel and Derrickson 2021). In these contemporary contexts, there is some controversy as to whether decolonization must be specific about giving land back (Tuck and Yang 2012), or whether decolonization can happen in other spheres, such as public health and diets (Eni et al. 2021) or the decolonization of the mind (Thiong'o 1986). No matter the context though, decolonization can be understood as the removal of an occupying power and the right to self-determination.

KEY POINTS

- Humans share ideas about who and what is valued and these ideas—though initially social constructs—are made into material reality in social systems (social hierarchies). Structural inequalities result when shared ideas about gender, race, and other identity characteristics are baked into the GPE and produce different life chances for different categories of people.

- Feminist scholars have shown how the GPE is constituted through unequal *gender* relations, emphasizing the ways that unpaid care work, double burdens, and the feminization of global work (amongst other issues) all contribute to the foundation on which the GPE is built.

- From dependency theories onwards, scholars of GPE have grappled with the relationship of race with markets. While conventional GPE has often disassociated the two, critical scholars have shown that race is not ignored by or secondary to the global economy, but rather that the global economy relies on unequal relations of race to operate in its current form.

- At the same time, scholars have long tried to push race into the forefront of scholarship, showing that without meaningful decolonization, true equality will not be possible within the GPE.

4.4 The everyday (resistance)

4.4.1 Thinking about everyday resistance in the GPE

As discussed in Section 4.1, critical GPE problematizes the current world order of capitalism, its power relations, and the dominant ideas and institutions that comprise it. Scholars ask questions like 'how did we get here?', 'how did these power relations come to be?', 'how does the current world order produce and sustain particular problems?' Critical GPE also opens the door for considering solutions that resist and challenge the dominant order. Scholars seek out, analyse, and, where possible, assist social processes that can bring about emancipation from dominant power relations / hierarchies (Cox 1996). Although often overlooked, an important place we can look for transformative alternatives to the current world order is in everyday practices of resistance.

It has been observed that 'where there is resistance, there is power' (Abu-Lughod 1990: 42). Resistance simply means 'to push against', but from a critical GPE perspective resistance has a normative agenda in favour of a 'better world', one that is more equitable

---

[5] In this chapter we have mostly used 'Global South'. However, during the independence era the term 'Third World' was much more common, and so it is used here to refer to the newly independent nations of the time. There are some

signs of the 'Third World' terminology resurging (Temin 2022), as scholars apply critical lenses to the GPE and more globalizing approaches to International Relations (Acharya 2014) take hold.

and inclusive. It is a counter-hegemonic movement that prioritizes ecological sustainability and centres the needs of the marginalized, of the vulnerable, of the poor. But who exercises it? How does it lead to transformative change? In answering these questions, we push back against two tendencies in GPE scholarship. The first is a tendency to focus on the conditions for resistance and/or the structural constraints on resistance. Some scholars think of full-scale and violent revolution when they think of popular resistance to global capitalism. From this vantage point, resistance is fundamentally constrained by structural and material factors and can only succeed if it is led by working classes who operate outside of dominant power structures. Other constraint-focused research includes some scholars' focus on the structural power of discursive and social contexts that ultimately limit agency and cement ideas about appropriate subjects for dialogue and debate, thereby limiting the potential for resistance. Tucker (2014), Strange (2013), and Hannah (2016), for example, seek to demonstrate how the assimilation and reproduction of the trade orthodoxy discussed in Section 4.2.1 blunt the teeth of resistance movements in global trade governance. Notwithstanding these important insights, here we highlight important critical GPE scholarship that locates some hopeful prospects for resistance in the agency of people and communities engaged in practices of everyday life.

Second, the study of GPE has conventionally taken a top-down view and been centred on broad structural trends, macro-level power dynamics, and key actors such as states and institutions of global economic governance, the 'global governors of GPE', so to speak. Likewise, there has been a tendency to focus on global civil society actors—NGOs and social movements—as the sole agents of resistance and sources of political and economic transformations away from neoliberal orthodoxy, such as the Occupy Movement. Often conceived as acting upon the institutions of global economic governance and/or in opposition to a neoliberal agenda, Gramscian-inspired scholars, in particular, see a **dialectical** relationship between the globalization of power and globalized forms of resistance (Cox 1999; Gill 2000). As Lafferty (2000: 19) writes, 'the politics of civil society, articulated primarily through new social movements, have superseded the politics of class', meaning that resistance and counter-hegemony are addressed almost exclusively through the work of transnational NGOs and popular resistance movements.

There is no question that global civil society actors play important roles in the GPE, even as international mega-protests such as the so-called Battle of Seattle or the Occupy Movement are on the wane (Tarrow 2005), radical social movements in major centres of power and decision-making such as Davos and Geneva have been quieted, displaced, or coopted (Paterson 2009), and NGOs have become more professionalized, or 'NGO-ized' (Roy 2014). Indeed, there is an expansive literature that showcases the crucial role of global civil society actors in the GPE and beyond (Davies 2019). Nevertheless, by taking a bottom-up approach, it is our objective to bring into view acts of resistance that tend to fall outside the purview of GPE scholarship and take place at the level of individuals and local communities.

Here we shine a light on acts of resistance that come from the 'everyday', by which we mean the 'mundane practices and minutiae of everyday life' (Elias and Roberts 2016: 788; see also Hobson and Seabrooke 2007; Brasset et al. 2023). Practices of everyday life such as going to work, buying groceries, borrowing and saving money, or caring for children, the sick, and the elderly are all integral to the global economy. In the sections that follow, we place a spotlight on three efforts to reshape, resist, and redress structural inequalities through everyday acts of resistance: banker ladies, ethical consumerism, and food sovereignty.

4.4.2 Feminist resistance: Solidarity economies and Banker Ladies

As outlined in Section 4.3.2, feminist approaches to GPE show us 'how the mundane matters' (Enloe 2013). By offering a bottom-up analysis of everyday life and placing a spotlight on social reproduction, feminist approaches to GPE elucidate the ways in which gendered and racialized hierarchies at different sites and scales such as inside the home, local community, workplace, and more are central to global capitalism. Feminist approaches to GPE (critical to decolonial) also locate resistance—gendered political struggles for emancipation and equality—at the level of the everyday. For Elias and Roberts (2016: 795), the feminization of everyday resistance means that the everyday 'is a site within which battles are fought over women's appropriate role in economic life, who cleans and cares for the children, how working lives are experienced and whose leisure time counts for most.

It is also a site within which economic reforms touch down and reshape the lives of the most vulnerable and a site within which neoliberal reform projects are resisted and challenged'

One example of feminist activism and everyday resistance is the emergence of so-called Banker Ladies, informal, women-led savings collectives for diaspora communities which are based on the principles of mutual aid and self-help. Located in the solidarity economy or 'Black social economy', Banker Ladies offer a distinct alternative to racialized capitalism, a point we return to in Section 4.3.3.

Social and solidarity economies (SSEs) are widely recognized as a 'third sector' in a capitalist economy. They have a long and global history, and they exist to fill needs that are not met by the state or the private sector. According to the International Labour Organization (ILO), '[t]he SSE encompasses enterprises, organizations and other entities that are engaged in economic, social, and environmental activities to serve the collective and/or general interest, which are based on the principles of voluntary cooperation and mutual aid, democratic and/or participatory governance, autonomy and independence, and the primacy of people and social purpose over capital in the distribution and use of surpluses and/or profits as well as assets' (ILO 2022a: para. II.5) Further, SSEs are seen to contribute to the goals of 'decent work, inclusive and sustainable economies, social justice, sustainable development, and improving standards of living for all' (ILO 2022a: para. III.6.a). Given this expansive definition, SSEs may include cooperatives, associations, mutual societies, foundations, social enterprises, and entrepreneurial non-profit organizations that operate in both formal and informal economies. The UN estimates that the social economy accounts for approximately 7 per cent of the world's GDP (UN 2017a).

Many consider SSEs to be essential bridges between governments and the private sector, often cooperating, interacting, and working towards common goals including tackling socio-economic inequalities (for example, Quarter et al. 2017; World Economic Forum 2022). Others focus on the inherently adversarial relationship between governments, the private sector, and SSEs by emphasizing that many SSEs emerged in response to the exclusion of racialized minorities from formal economies and the under-provision of human and social needs for marginalized people in both the Global South and Global North. From this view, SSEs are sites of resistance against racial and gendered inequities and economic exclusion.

Hossein and Pearson (2023), for example, ask us to distinguish between social economies—which support the existing order and thereby maintain the marginalization of certain groups—and solidarity economies or 'Black social economies'—which involve struggle against the existing order and centre the lived experiences of women, Black and Indigenous people, and other vulnerable groups in informal arenas (see also Hossein 2019).

We can look around the world and across history to find numerous examples of economically excluded people struggling and working from the bottom up through local communities to transform the prevailing economic order (Amin 2009; Hossein and Christabell 2022). A few illustrative examples include Black Lives Matter in the United States, the Zapatistas in Mexico, the Indigenous Neechi Co-Op in Winnipeg, Canada, the Quilombos in Brazil, and the Banker Ladies in Toronto, Canada, to which we now turn.

The Banker Ladies of Toronto, Canada, are small groups of women who have established Rotating Savings and Credit Associations (ROSCAs). They are informal, women-led, community-based initiatives established by and for Black African diaspora women who are excluded from or discriminated against in the mainstream banking system in Canada. ROSCAs are based on imported community lending practices found in the Global South, for example, 'susu' in Ghana, 'hagbad' in Somalia, 'partner' in Jamaica, 'sol' in Haiti, and 'njangi' in Cameroon. The ROSCAs are democratic and laterally organized, with one woman organizing the collection and distribution of funds. Each participant pays a fixed amount to a common fund each month. The entire fund is paid to one member per month on a rotating basis and no interest is charged. While the premise is quite simple, women who participate in ROSCAs describe the experience as transformational and empowering. Diaspora women have access to a pool of funds that would otherwise be unavailable to them. The pooled funds are used to pay for children to attend university, down payments on houses, personal spending money, small business start-up costs, and so on. Not only does the ROSCA represent an 'intentional community' (Nembhard 2014) in which Black women form their own economic livelihoods and financial independence, it fosters a sense of community based on inclusion, trust, and mutual empowerment, which are missing from conventional economies.[6] This example of women-led cooperative banking is but one of a multitude of ROSCAs initiatives that exist globally and which reflect W. E. B. Du Bois's powerful vision set forth in *The Souls of Black Folk* (1903) of communal and collective forms of African business that have been deployed to resist racial capitalism (see Hossein, Austin, and Edmonds 2023).

4.4.3 Consumer resistance: Ethical consumerism at the grocery store

Earlier we noted that resistance means 'to push against', and that in critical GPE resistance has a normative agenda in favour of a 'better world'. One way that people often engage in a normative vision of the world—in other words, a world they want society to move towards—is through food. Food has both major cultural significance, since many of our traditions and habits centre around food, and it is also a major component of the global political economy. Many scholars have sought to understand the ways that food both shapes and is shaped by political and economic forces (Friedmann and McMichael 1989; McMichael 2013; Margulis 2017; Clapp 2020). Because people care a lot about the food they eat, and because most people purchase most (if not all) of the food they eat, food is one way that individuals can use their purchases to communicate their normative wishes for society, enacting what is more broadly known as *ethical consumption*. This strategy is referred to as 'voting with your fork', and it encourages consumers to use the power of their dollars to change the direction of everything from poor labour practices (Fridell 2014; Guthman 2019) to better sustainability practices (Jaffee et al. 2004).

Voting with your fork requires two major actions from individual consumers. First, consumers need to have committed to a normative vision of the food system, and second they need to take action to move that vision forwards (Maniates 2002; 2014). For example, consumers might be concerned about pollution from pesticides and buy organic foods as a result. Or they might be concerned about methane emissions from livestock production, or simply the ethics of eating animals, and buy only vegan food as a result.

As a result of these trends, different food companies and corporate-NGO partnerships have formed to help

consumers quickly identify foods that relate to their preferred normative vision (Morrison 2021). These initiatives often use different labels or symbols to indicate to consumers that a particular product fits their vision of the world. For example, Fair Trade-certified tea and coffee carries the Fair Trade symbol, which is highly recognizable to consumers (G. Fridell et al. 2021). These labels and symbols are examples of *heuristics*; they act as shortcuts for human understanding (Cohen and Babey 2012). So, if you are concerned with equitable labour practices, a Fair Trade label might help you to 'vote with your fork'. In other words, heuristics help individual consumers enact their normative agendas for society through ethical consumerism. In this way, voting with your fork is an act of resistance, and that resistance is made easier for consumers to engage with through food company and NGO heuristics.

However, the definition of resistance examined above has a second half. It argues that resistance is counter-hegemonic, and it centres the needs of the marginalized, the vulnerable, and the poor. Ethical consumption, as a narrative of transformative action, relies on individuals making lifestyle changes through their purchase habits. This raises the question as to whether everyday practices of ethical buying really are acts of resistance. Do the purchase efforts of individuals in a market-based system lead to meaningful transformative change?

The logic of ethical consumption as a theory of change is more complicated than 'vote with your fork' would have us imagine at first glance. 'Vote with your fork' or 'vote with your money' suggests that purchases impose change. In reality, this logic relies on several invisible steps in between. A consumer must first make a decision to purchase a product with a particular vision in mind, as described above. But for the purchase to make an impact, one of two parallel actions must also take place, both of which rely on the producer or manufacturer of the product in question. The first way is that the company who produces the product must have designed that product in a way that it is coherent with the consumer's vision, and that vision has been adequately communicated to the consumer (for example, through a label or certification—*a heuristic*). In this case, the consumer must take a leap of faith that the company is communicating with integrity; in other words, that the heuristic is communicating the truth, and that the company is not engaging in *greenwashing* (Delmas and Burbano 2011; Czarnezki et al. 2014). Essentially, the consumer is buying the product

---

[6] ROSCA members share their experiences as Banker Ladies in this documentary: https://www.youtube.com/watch?v=fXMYRtLTYP0.

based on the assumption that the producer is actually engaging in the change they have communicated, making an *upstream* change in a value chain, such as growing organically or ensuring fair trade labour. The second way this can happen is that the consumer makes a decision to communicate their desires about upstream changes to the market in general. In other words, the consumer might *boycott* or *buycott* certain products in an attempt to communicate their demands to producers, who will then (theoretically) meet market demand. This approach to ethical buying is also known as *political consumerism* (see Figure 4.2).

In both of these cases, a consumer's purchases do not represent actual change. They simply aim to encourage upstream changes. The result is that ethical consumption's theory of change is not as straightforward as we might first assume. At their heart, ethical consumption and political consumerism both rest well within the conventional market-based system. Alternatively, other efforts to influence food systems change might take place through state intervention or regulation (for example, states can impose taxes on sugar-sweetened beverages, or limit the amount of sodium per 100 grams), or through more radical efforts on the part of citizens to reorientate the food

Figure 4.2 Individuals practising ethical consumerism have different normative goals, including those who want companies to reduce packaging waste. Consumers enact these normative visions by buying products with minimal or no packaging, especially plastic packaging. The 'Zero Waste' movement is a good example of a guiding normative vision for ethical consumerism.

Source: Alamy.

system away from the conventional market logic. We now turn to an example of just such an effort (see GPE of the Everyday Box 4.7).

GPE OF THE EVERYDAY BOX 4.7 FAIR TRADE

Fairtrade labels, as heuristics, help consumers make decisions about which products they want to put their money behind. But what exactly is fair trade? How does Fairtrade support this mission? And why is it necessary in the first place (see Figure 4.3)?

The starting point of the fair trade movement is that trade, as it exists today, is inherently *unfair*. As Akram-Lodhi (2021) argues, a trade system developed first through mercantilist policies and then through the colonial era continues to reproduce the same patterns of exploitation. Recalling the discussion in Section 4.3.3 on dependency theories, raced markets, and racial capitalism, the unequal foundation of trade will be unsurprising to readers. Fair trade movements are normative. In other words, proponents of fair trade offer it up as a solution to existing systems.

Fairtrade (Fairtrade.ca 2023) seeks to 'change [sic] the way trade works through better prices, decent working conditions, and a fairer deal for farmers and workers' with the goal of enabling them to 'have more control over their lives and decide to invest in their future'. Fairtrade aims to accomplish this mission by using a Fairtrade Minimum Price, essentially a safety net guarantee for farmers should the world price drop below that price. Fairtrade has expanded sales substantially since it was established, and most studies show it has modestly raised incomes for those

Figure 4.3 Fairtrade coffee has spread widely through coffee chains and suppliers answering the customers' expectations of consuming socially responsible and sustainable products. Fair trade of coffee started in response to the struggles of Mexican coffee farmers in the late 1980s; it aims to guarantee fair and stable prices for the coffee, covering sustainable production costs.

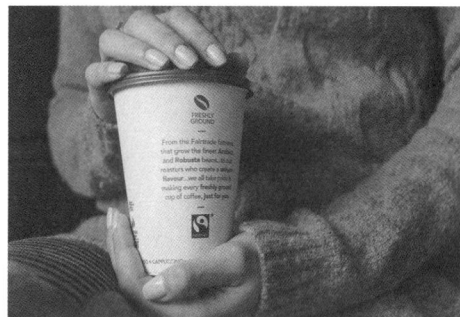

Source: Alamy.

GPE OF THE EVERYDAY BOX 4.7 FAIR TRADE (continued)

involved (M. Fridell et al. 2021). Fair trade movements also often aim to improve sustainability and social issues (G. Fridell et al. 2021). Yet critics of fair trade movements suggest that the power of northern consumers to substantially impact trade through their purchases is overblown (M. Fridell et al. 2021; Williams 2021). Indeed, some argue that '[t]he fair trade fantasy is often more powerful than fair trade itself' (G. Fridell 2014: 1180).

Fridell argues that while Fairtrade has had a positive impact on the thousands of families who have participated, they are still generally relatively poor. For example, many coffee farmers cannot find enough market space to sell all their beans, since only 2 per cent of global coffee sales are fair trade (Fairtrade.ca 2023), and the result is that farmers have to sell at conventional prices. And while the Minimum Price is helpful, the extra income is often put towards the extra labour and inputs required to meet the fair trade standards, making the impact less meaningful

(Jaffee et al. 2004; Bacon 2008; Fridell 2014; Jaffee 2014). Fair trade has been criticized for developing onerous standards that are developed largely in the North, with little representation from farmers (Frundt 2009). And perhaps most pertinent to our discussion on forms of resistance, fair trade has been criticized for perpetuating the dependence of commodity growers in the South on the benevolent whims of consumers in the North (Dawson 2004).

In his (2014) comparison of the explosion in Vietnamese coffee production around the same time that fair trade coffee expanded considerably, Fridell demonstrates that both projects have advantages and disadvantages, impacts, and successes. Ultimately, Fridell argues, scholars and media have paid much more attention to fair trade because it more closely aligns with underlying North American values of what 'free trade' *should* be, rather than the reality of what both systems are.

4.4.4 Indigenous resistance: Food sovereignty movements

In 1996, at the UN World Food Summit, a little-known (at the time) peasant organization called La Via Campesina challenged dominant approaches to food in the international multilateral system (see Figure 4.4). Until that point, states mostly organized around the idea of *food security* which had been introduced in 1974 and was embedded in and evolved alongside conventional economic paradigms in the global economy

Figure 4.4 Nearly a thousand protestors marched in downtown Cancun, Mexico, during La Via Campesina's Global Day of Action for Climate Justice in December 2010 during the 16th Conference of the Parties. The march's main slogan was 'Peasants cool the planet', summarizing the proposal to solve climate change by combating the destruction of the environment, and concerns for farmers, landless peasants, and Indigenous people.

Source: Alamy.

(UN 1974, cited in FAO 2003; Patel 2009). The idea of food security came about in a particular moment in time, when the Third World was gaining momentum through its calls for a New International Economic Order and a UN Conference on Trade and Development (Agarwala 1983). The era propelled major state commitments in making food available to all people, everywhere. Yet by 1996, Patel (2009) argues, the dominant neoliberal paradigm meant that food security was increasingly seen by world leaders as something to be achieved through market-based initiatives.

La Via Campesina's intervention in 1996 therefore marked a major shift in thinking about food systems. '[F]ood sovereignty is a call for peoples' rights to shape and craft food policy . . . ' (Patel 2009: 663). In contrast to the ways that ethical consumption and political consumerism are embedded in markets, food sovereignty calls for a complete reorientation as to who makes decisions about food. Rather than consumers relying on a lengthy chain of communication with producers through heuristics and purchases, food sovereignty calls for the rights of producers and eaters to be made central to conversations about food. More importantly, it consistently places the rights of the landless, Indigenous people, and other marginalized folks at the forefront of its demands (Grey and Patel 2015).

What, exactly, is food sovereignty then, and how do those who call for it enact everyday resistance? Patel (2009) argues that while food sovereignty is intentionally and explicitly a 'big tent', it is possible to drill down to important core tenets. If, as outlined above, food sovereignty is the call for peoples' rights to shape and craft food policy, there are two prior commitments that are made. The first is a commitment to a deliberative and direct democracy, where people are deeply engaged in the ability to shape decisions around food. The second must come even earlier. To enable people to engage in this way, underlying power dynamics that prevent and shape engagement must also be tackled. It is for this reason that food sovereignty is not just about food. The Nyéléni Declaration calls for a living wage, cultural rights, and an end to the dumping of goods below the cost of production, an end to colonialism and imperialism (Via Campesina 2007). A commitment to women's rights and resistance to the patriarchal relations that structure society must also be enacted to ensure an egalitarian approach to engaging with food decisions.

In what is today called Canada, there are strong food sovereignty movements taking place amongst wider Indigenous peoples' movements. Robin (Martens) (2019) argues that the food sovereignty efforts in Western Canada must be seen within broader efforts to expand Indigenous sovereignty more generally, writing that:

The ability to self-determine both food and political systems works toward achieving harmony and balance in community and ultimately supports well-being. Self-determination must exist within and beyond food to include the ability of Indigenous peoples to self-determine their own futures.

Robin's (2019) exploration reveals four common elements of Indigenous food sovereignty: history, connection to the land, relationships, and cultural identity. The projects and programmes undertaken in the name of Indigenous food sovereignty prioritize learning from history (including how plants were grown and the way lands have been lost); connecting to land (both in terms of land-based practices such as hunting and harvesting, but also nourishing the body and soul through returning to the land); 'embrac[ing] an awareness of the intimate connection between people and all of creation' (Robin 2019: 92); and showed that participating in cultural food practices helped to contribute to a sense of being Indigenous and building community. The efforts in Robin's study range from school, market, or community gardens, to food boxes and food conferences. By examining the everyday efforts of Indigenous peoples to (re)build Indigenous food sovereignty, Robin demonstrates the multiple ways that Indigenous peoples are resisting both the dominant and conventional food system, and also the multiple and overlapping ways that Indigenous land and culture have been colonized.

Indigenous food sovereignty is then a fundamentally different form of resistance when compared to ethical consumption or political consumerism. One takes place within the realm of the dominant market system, whereas the other pushes back against it. Instead of aiming to shift the food system through an incremental chain of indicating supply and demand, those working towards food sovereignty, and especially Indigenous food sovereignties, show that a more radical approach to dismissing conventional patterns of power is possible.

KEY POINTS

- Many GPE scholars problematize the current world order of capitalism, its power relations, and the dominant ideas and institutions that comprise it, which opens the door for considering solutions that resist and challenge the dominant order. Where possible, scholars analyse and assist social processes (*resistance*) that can bring about emancipation from dominant power relations and social hierarchies.

- *Solidarity economies* or *Black social economies* are one way that those outside dominant power structures can exercise power and resistance. Rotating Savings and Credit Associations (ROSCAs) are an example of women-led savings collectives for diaspora communities which are based on the principles of mutual aid and self-help, and which offer a distinct alternative to racialized capitalism.

- When trying to influence the conventional food system, many consumers use *ethical consumerism* as a form of (questionable) resistance. This action relies on a long chain of supply and demand to impact production practices, and in the end stays within the dominant market-based food system.

- In contrast, the *food sovereignty* movement resists the capitalist food system by reasserting autonomy over food production and consumption patterns. In some examples of Indigenous food sovereignty, efforts are especially made towards re-engaging with historical practices and putting relationships at the heart of actions. Food sovereignty is ultimately about undoing patterns of social domination to ensure everyone has equal capacity to engage in food systems.

4.5 Conclusion

This chapter introduced readers to the way that some scholars have aimed to make sense of the highly complex interactions between states, markets, and societies at different sites and scales. By exploring trade orthodoxy, gender equality, and the Islamic economy, we showed how ideas can help explain how different patterns of authority and power are established and legitimized in the GPE. We examined different social hierarchies in the GPE and the ways in which they can help to explain both individual life chances within the GPE and also existing global structural inequalities. At the same time, by examining social hierarchies we can also learn about theoretical perspectives that have historically been marginalized in GPE scholarship.

Finally, in part three we showcased one of these marginalized approaches in the study of GPE by discussing everyday, bottom-up practices of resistance. Banker Ladies in Toronto show how solidarity economies are alternative approaches to partaking in the conventional capitalist system, whereas ethical consumerism in regular grocery shopping relies on the interplay of supply and demand and the market itself

to enact forms of resistance. In contrast, the food sovereignty movement aims to reassert autonomy over decisions about food production and consumption, and in so doing also aims to reset power at the dinner table. Food sovereignty movements therefore embrace more than just food issues, but prioritize resetting power relations to ensure that everyone can engage in self-determination around food.

This chapter has placed a spotlight on one small part of the broad tent of critical GPE approaches that aim to draw attention to and problematize the current world order of capitalism, its power relations, and the dominant ideas and institutions that comprise it. While we could not and do not attempt to comprehensively survey the important interventions of all critical GPE scholars, this chapter should set the stage for readers' own explorations into the GPE, including both the 'dark underbelly of capitalism' (Rajaram 2018: 629) and by inviting students to find and explore more of the 'blind-spots' in the study of GPE. It also prepares readers to engage with the critical interventions in Chapters 2, 7, 10, 14, 15, and 16 of this volume that aim to centre the empirical and conceptual margins of GPE.

? 4.6 QUESTIONS

1. This chapter aimed to bring light to some of the 'blind-spots' in the study of GPE. Hall (2023) suggests one way to incorporate different perspectives in the discipline is to ask non-academics or scholars from outside of GPE to review GPE textbooks and identify what might be missing. Think about what you have seen so far in this chapter, and briefly review the other chapters through the Table of Contents. What 'blind-spots' do *you* recognize in GPE? Why might better coverage of these issues help to strengthen GPE?

2. Understanding the GPE through a lens of culture can help explain specific forms of economic development, such as Corporate Islam. Have you noticed economic development looks different in different places? How might culture help explain some of these differences?

3. How and why does the trade orthodoxy prioritize economic growth over social and environmental concerns, and what are the implications of this prioritization in trade policy discussions?

4. Several sections in this chapter deal with the legacies of imperialism and colonialism, such as through the ideas of raced markets or racial capitalism. Bhattacharya (2018: ix) warns us not to think of 'capitalism as a racist conspiracy' and yet also invites us to think about reparations—not simply as a matter of reconciliation, but as a question of economic justice (see Bhattacharyya 2018: Ch. 3). Do you think economic justice is possible within the current global order?

5. What is decolonization and why is it important to the study of GPE?

6. Is the business case for gender equality a progressive movement towards gender equality, or is it 'neoliberalism with a feminist face', a neoliberal strategy that perpetuates existing inequalities under the guise of economic empowerment?

7. Social hierarchies are defined as systems of social organization in which individuals or groups are ranked or valued differently, often according to intersecting factors such as race, class, and gender. How do social hierarchies contribute to structural inequalities in the GPE?

8. The 'everyday' refers to mundane practices, routines, and activities such as going to work, buying groceries, and borrowing money. Have you ever engaged in an everyday practice of resistance in order to push back against oppression, inequality, or injustice?

9. Have you engaged with ethical consumerism? Having read this chapter, do you feel that ethical consumerism is an effective way to achieve your normative vision for the world?

10. Food sovereignty is a movement that is transnational—that is, it connects people across borders. What other movements of everyday resistance can you think of that connect people across borders?

4.7 FURTHER READING

Bhambra, G. K. (2021), 'Colonial Global Economy: Towards a Theoretical Reorientation of Political Economy', *Review of International Political Economy*, 28/2: 307–322. This book shows that standard explanations for the emergence of the global political economy overlook the importance of colonial relations that shaped and continue to shape it. It calls for a reorientation of historical analysis and a transformative framework that includes the appropriate consideration of colonial relations.

Bhattacharyya, G. (2018), *Rethinking Racial Capitalism: Questions of Reproduction and Survival* (Landham, MD: Rowman & Littlefield). This book calls for the centring of racial capitalism in analyses of global political economy. Only by showing the interconnections between capitalism and histories of racist appropriation can we fully understand how historical legacies of racial oppression continue to shape contemporary economic and social structures.

Clapp, J. (2020), *Food* (Cambridge, UK: Polity). This book explores global food systems from a GPE perspective, showcasing the way the world food economy works. It explores aspects of the food system of interest to GPE students, including growing corporate control and expanding financialization of food. The book also covers justice and sustainability challenges in a world food economy.

Elias, J. and Roberts, A. (eds.) (2018), *Feminist Global Political Economies of the Everyday* (London and New York: Routledge). This book examines the gendered dynamics of global transformations at the level of everyday practices, emphasizing the importance of feminist perspectives in understanding how the global political economy operates at the local level.

Hannah, E., Roberts, A., and Trommer, S. (2022), 'Gender in Global Trade: Transforming or Reproducing Trade Orthodoxy?', *Review of International Political Economy*, 29/4: 1368–1393. Drawing on critical trade and feminist International Political Economy (IPE) literature, this article examines the growing inclusion of gender considerations in trade policymaking, assessing whether these initiatives reproduce the existing trade orthodoxy or have the potential to bring about transformative changes.

Prügl, E. (2021), 'Untenable Dichotomies: De-Gendering Political Economy', *Review of International Political Economy*, 28/2: 295–306. This article explores how feminist global political economy challenges foundational dichotomies in conventional GPE, specifically questioning the opposition between production and reproduction as well as the public-private divide, and highlights the need for alternative perspectives that consider the interconnections between logics of accumulation and public purpose, self-interest and care, and private household governance and the state.

Rodney, W. (2018/1972), *How Europe Underdeveloped Africa* (Verso Books). This book explores the historical connection between slavery, colonialism, and the underdevelopment of Africa within the context of international capitalism. Rodney challenges the notion that Africa's economic struggles are due to geographic limitations, emphasizing instead the ongoing effects of imperial exploitation, providing valuable insights into the historical and contemporary dynamics of global inequality.

Sheilds, S. et al. (2011), *Critical International Political Economy: Dialogue, Debate and Dissensus* (London: Palgrave Macmillan). This book addresses the need to reconsider the concept of 'critical' within IPE, examining whether the theoretical foundations of critical IPE have reached their potential. The contributors engage in a diverse range of approaches to reassess the purpose of critical approaches, explore the selective preference for certain social theorists, and emphasize the importance of engaging in substantial critical social inquiry within IPE.

Shilliam, R. (2021), *Decolonizing Politics* (Polity Press). This book explores the colonial origins and assumptions that have shaped the field of political science, offering students a framework to decolonize its main themes and issues by incorporating diverse intellectual resources from the (post)colonial world, ultimately challenging mainstream approaches and highlighting the potential for deeper political understanding from marginal positions.

CONTRIBUTOR NOTES

Erin Hannah is Professor of Politics and International Relations and Associate Dean of Research at King's University College, Canada. She has published widely in the areas of global political economy, gender and trade, sustainable development, global governance, global civil society, the role of expert knowledge in global trade, and innovative pedagogy. She is author of *NGOs and Global Trade: Non-State Voices in EU Trade Policymaking*, and coeditor of *Expert Knowledge in Global Trade* (with James Scott and Silke Trommer).

Lucy Hinton is an Assistant Professor in Politics and International Relations at King's University College, Canada, and a Balsillie School of International Affairs (BSIA) Fellow. Her work examines the intersections of food systems and political economy, with a focus on the interactions of the English-speaking Caribbean in global food governance. Most recently, she has published about corporate power in policymaking in the Caribbean Community (CARICOM) (2022) and on how sustainable diets fit in global governance (2022).

PART II
Global Trade and Production

5

Global Trade

Silke Trommer

Chapter contents

Reader's guide

Across history, all successful human civilizations have engaged in one form of cross-cultural trade or another. Following decades of contested but successful trade multilateralism under the General Agreement on Tariffs and Trade (GATT) established in 1947 and the World Trade Organization (WTO) established in 1995, hybrid governance structures characterize the global trade system of the twenty-first century. In this system, multilateral, regional, and bilateral institutions provide overlapping and separate rules and regulations for the conduct of global trade. Meanwhile, global trade is widely perceived as a key arena within which we need to address key challenges, from climate change and big data to economic and social inequalities within and between countries. This chapter reviews the history, politics, and recent trends and challenges of the global trade system.

5.1 Introduction

All human societies trade. Long-distance circulation of valuable materials can be traced back in human history into the Neolithic era. The first cross-cultural trading network is usually dated to the Sumer economy of Mesopotamia in the fourth millennium BC. By the fifteenth century AD, trade routes encompassed most of the globe (Kristiansen et al. 2018). All long-distance trading arrangements rely on the availability of materials to trade; a medium of exchange; technologies of transport and communication; political and legal structures to facilitate exchange; and social structures in which the production, circulation, and consumptions of traded items are embedded. These foundational elements determine the particular shape of different trading orders across time and space.

In today's globalized economy, we hold an extensive understanding of tradable materials, including not only primary commodities and consumer items, but also services and data, which prior to recent technological innovations had been inconceivable as objects of trade. Traders, investors, and consumers rely on the global financial system in order to provide a medium of exchange via convertible currencies, as well as a source of trade finance and, increasingly, consumer finance via credit and loan arrangements. The internet, the container and maritime and air cargo, as well as the energy sources on which these run, have revolutionized the speed and ease with which we trade (see Figure 5.1). These revolutions have led to previously unimaginable volumes of trade flows in the post-Second World War era, with the value of global trade reaching US$28.5 trillion in 2021—that is almost 347 times its value in the 1950s (WTO 2022a).

Governments provide many of the political and legal structures that are central to the stability and predictability that trade requires. They do this through domestic laws and policies, and through international cooperation in global trade governance institutions from the World Trade Organization (WTO) to a global network for preferential trade agreements (PTA). Traders also develop private rules and regulatory standards that are recognized and used by governments worldwide. One such example is the International Chambers of Commerce's 'Incoterms', which define liabilities and procedures in the arrangement of shipments. Capitalism in its many varieties provides the near universal social order in and through which global trade operates. Indeed, trade is often regarded as one of the central drivers of economic globalization. Accordingly, trade is also a central battlefield for the key questions of our time, from global hegemony, to inequality, to the natural limits to economic expansion.

This chapter deals with the political contestations in and around the contemporary global trade order. While it will be impossible to explore all dimensions of this complex and contested order, the chapter conveys an advanced-level understanding of how and why global trade is contested along economic, political, legal, environmental, and social dimensions. Readers are encouraged to delve into other chapters of this book, as well as the suggested readings, to further grasp the nature, causes, and consequences of these contestations.

To begin our journey of understanding how and why global trade is politically contested, the next section takes a quick glimpse at historical antecedents, to trace the political, economic, and ideational foundations of today's global trade order.

Figure 5.1   Rescue vessels work at the site of the stuck container ship Ever Given on the Suez Canal, Egypt, 28 March 2021. The massive container ship Ever Given, carrying approximately US$1 billion in cargo, was successfully refloated after being stranded in the Suez Canal for almost a week. This illustrates the scale and importance of container shipping to global trade. (Suez Canal Authority/Handout via Xinhua).

Source: Alamy.

5.2 Historical antecedents

From the sixteenth to the eighteenth century, global trade was based on **mercantilism** and centred around China, India, and Southeast Asia, with spices, silk, tea, porcelain, and silver constituting the main traded commodities. As a result of the Mexican War of Independence in 1815 and the gradual European colonization of Asia and Southeast Asia, Europeans became the chief actors in the global trade order across the nineteenth century, at the same time as **liberalism** began emerging within Europe.

The period 1860–1945 set the scene for the global trade order that was to be established following the Second World War. This time period saw the first modern trade treaties being signed and ambitious plans for international trade governance institutions being drafted. It also witnessed dramatic shifts in how global trade was organized across the globe and how trade affected different regions. In much of global political economy (GPE), we do not normally tell the restructuring of world trade that occurred in 1860–1945 as one global trade story. Instead, we tend to focus on the lessons of free trade and international trade cooperation that the period seems to have held for industrialized countries of the Global North. This partial storytelling erases the experiences of the Global South from the history of the contemporary trade system, where trade in 1860–1945 was heavily associated with unequal exchange, colonialism, as well as uneven and combined development.

In this section, we trace both trade histories of 1860–1945, once as the age of liberalism, and once as the age of empire. Bifurcating the historical backdrop to the post-Second World War trade order in this way will help us better understand the intractable nature of some of the key contemporary challenges of global trade that we explore throughout the chapter.

5.2.1 **The age of liberalism**

Adam Smith presented his **absolute advantage** theory in *The Wealth of Nations* in 1776, whereby global welfare rises if every country produces the product that they are best at making (see Watson, Chapter 2). Advocates of free trade in Britain and western Europe subsequently demanded that governments abandon age-old measures such as tariffs, duties, and other levies on trade, arguing that these economic policy tools diminish the wealth of nations, rather than augmenting it. In 1817, David Ricardo introduced the notion of **comparative advantage** in his *Principles of Political Economy and Taxation*. Ricardo argued that even for countries that are not best at producing anything, the free trade logic still holds. This is because we need to

ask how much of the production of one product we give up in order to produce another. If we compare opportunity costs of production, a country that does not hold an absolute advantage in any product can still be comparatively better at producing the product than any other country. Specialization and exchange still increase global welfare in this scenario.

In 1848, following a campaign for free trade led by Manchester-based manufacturer and politician Richard Cobden (as discussed by Watson in Chapter 2 of this volume), Britain unilaterally repealed the Corn Laws, which had restricted imports of wheat and other grains. Over the next two decades, Britain put free trade into practice. In 1860, the Cobden–Chevalier treaty liberalized trade bilaterally between Britain and France. It contained a **most-favoured-nation** (**MFN**) clause, whereby the tariff concessions granted by France and England to each other were extended to other countries with whom they concluded bilateral trade agreements. This led to the emergence of a regional network of interlocking bilateral trade agreements across Europe (Rosecrance 1986), which was a precursor to the multilateral trade system established a century later (Brown 2003).

The most prominent opponents of free trade were Alexander Hamilton (*Report on the Subject of Manufactures*, 1791) and Friedrich List (*National System of Political Economy*, 1841), both of whom advocated interventionist trade policies and tariffs for **infant industry promotion** (Gilpin 1987). Their ideas influenced tariff and trade policy in the United States (US) and Germany during this time.

As a result of technological improvements in the mid-1850s, the comparative advantage in grain growing shifted to the Americas, with grain prices falling sharply in European markets. At the same time, a slump occurred in industrial production, in the form of low prices and low return on capital for manufactured products. The global economic recession of the 1870s that ensued ushered in an era of **protectionism**. By the 1870s, Austria–Hungary, Italy, Germany, France, and the US all deployed protectionist trade policies. By the end of the century, the UK was the only major nation practising free trade (Kindleberger 1951).

The US emerged from the First World War (1914–1918) as the largest trading nation in the world. The trade policy debates and initiatives that shook the US in the context of the 1929 Great Depression set the overall tone for the global trade order in the early twentieth century.

The Smoot–Hawley Act of 1930 raised US duties to historic levels and increased the scope of tariff coverage. The Smoot–Hawley tariff provoked widespread retaliation by other countries, contributing to tariff increases around the world and openly discriminatory trade relations, based on prohibitions, quantitative restrictions, and exchange controls (Irwin 2011). In 1932, Great Britain abandoned its century-old commitment to liberal trade when it established the Imperial Preference system through a combination of tariff increases and tariff preferences for the British Empire. By the mid-1930s, world trade fell by about two thirds.

In the US presidential election of 1932, Democratic candidate Franklin D. Roosevelt attacked Smoot–Hawley as contributing to the Depression. Two years after Roosevelt's election, in 1934, Congress enacted a new tariff legislation under the title Reciprocal Trade Agreements Act (RTAA). The RTAA empowered the president to lower (or raise) tariffs up to 50 per cent from Smoot–Hawley levels in the course of trade negotiations with other countries. From the standpoint of American politics, the RTAA transferred tariff-setting policy to the presidency and away from Congress and substantially increased the control the executive exercised over trade policy. From the standpoint of international politics, the RTAA advanced the notion that setting tariff rates should no longer be exclusively a unilateral policy, but, rather, was a bilateral matter to be settled through negotiations among states.

By 1939, the US had concluded twenty-one reciprocal trade agreements, which made reductions in approximately 1,000 duties. All agreements were made on a most-favoured-nation (MFN) basis, which slowed the negotiation because it engaged more parties, but also for the same reason extended the impact of the agreements. The RTAA provided a corpus of experience in trade liberalization that became integrated after the Second World War, which was demonstrated by the fact that most of the GATT articles drawn up in 1947 were taken from various agreements reached under the RTAA system. It was concurrent with a sea change in US and world public opinion, which generally speaking had begun to favour free trade over protectionism. It also underlined the leadership of the US in the international trading system in the twentieth century.

This leadership was on full display at the 1944 **Bretton Woods** Conference, where the global economic order for the post-Second World War era was being forged (see also Helleiner Chapter 8, for discussion).

The Bretton Woods Conference established the **International Bank for Reconstruction and Development (World Bank)** and the **International Monetary Fund (IMF)**. In the arena of trade, under US leadership, delegates decided trade should be managed multilaterally via the **International Trade Organization (ITO)**. Although the ITO never came into existence, one of its draft chapters, the General Agreement on Tariffs and Trade (GATT), became the seed of the multilateral trade system of the twentieth century, to which we return below when we discuss the birth of GATT and its eventual transformation into the World Trade Organization.

5.2.2 **The age of empire**

While witnessing the dawn of economic liberalism and international cooperation, the period 1860–1945 was also an age of empire. In the nineteenth century, global trade flows began increasing due to technological innovations, while the epicentres of global trade shifted from China, India, and Southeast Asia to Europe and its growing empires. The 1860s also saw the gradual ending of the most devastating episode in global trade history, namely the **transatlantic slave trade**, also known as the triangular trade.

The transatlantic slave trade operated between Europe, Africa, and the Americas from the sixteenth century until the 1860s. It consisted of one-directional trade patterns among the three regions and was chiefly organized initially by Portuguese and Spanish traders and then by British traders. Slaves captured in or purchased from African kingdoms were sold in the Americas, including the Caribbean. Cash crops grown in the Americas, such as sugar, cotton, and tobacco, as well as rum and iron, were sold in Europe. Goods manufactured in Europe, such as cloth, weapons, and ammunition and ironware, were sold, or bartered for slaves, on the West African coast. It is estimated that up to 15.4 million people fell victim to the transatlantic slave trade (Inikori 1981).

In 1807, the UK Parliament's Slave Trade Act and the US Act Prohibiting Importation of Slaves outlawed international slave trading in the two nations that had been at its centre. However, the US Act did not affect the domestic slave trade, nor did it prohibit slavery, which remained legal in the US until the end of the American Civil War in 1865. A vibrant illegal slave trade thus continued throughout the nineteenth century. In 1870, Portugal ended the last remaining slave trade route worldwide with Brazil, which was the last country to outlaw slavery in 1888.

Much like its establishment in the sixteenth century, the abolition of the transatlantic slave trade in the 1860s upset regional economies and trading systems that had organized around the slave trade for many centuries. In West Africa, from where most slave ships departed and an estimated half of victims originated, both the massive expansion of slave trading during the eighteenth century and its abolition in the early nineteenth century created economic strain, political tension, and social hardship. It upset many of the trade routes and provisioning systems that had worked to support slave trading, which interacted with existing political tensions among regional groups and kingdoms. In this context, which coincided with the global economic recession of the 1870s, European traders found it increasingly impossible to generate profits in their overseas trading posts across the African and Asian continents. Over the second half of the nineteenth century, fierce competition between European and local traders in these regions led European traders to lobby their governments for full political control over these regions, which was one important factor in the expansion of European empires (Zeleza 1997).

By the turn of the century, most of Africa, Southeast Asia, and Oceania were under imperial control. Most imperial countries operated regimes of **colonial trade** with their colonies and dependent territories, using a mix of military and political suppression and economic measures such as imperial preferences in the form of low-duty or duty-free trade, quantitative restrictions (quotas) on imports from third countries, and currency restrictions. Colonial trade produced a system of unequal exchange which tended to support the economic development of the core regions and tended to undermine the economic development of the peripheral regions. Colonies specialized in the production of raw materials and agricultural products, while importing manufacturing and industrial products from the metropolitan country, under unfavourable terms of trade. These trade imbalances, whereby Global South countries are heavily reliant on exports of primary products, while high-value activities are mainly carried out in the Global North, persist until the present day, although the rise of emerging economies is shaking up these patterns for some countries (see Scott, Chapter 12).

At the Bretton Woods Conference of 1944, officials and analysts from under-developed regions, including Brazil, China, India, Mexico, and another twenty-eight delegations from Latin American, African, Asian, and East European countries, openly promoted state-led development policies, such as **import-substitution industrialization**, which calls for protective tariffs so consumers purchase domestic-made products over imports. Theorists such as Argentina's Raúl Prebisch or China's Sun Yat-sen represented a nascent intellectual tradition at Bretton Woods that believed in the power of domestic industrialization, supported by international institutions, in order to help with improving their terms of trade and catching up with the living standards of Global North countries (Helleiner 2014a; Singh, Chapter 15).

By the end of the Second World War, the decolonization movement was in full bloom and all territories had gained independence by the 1970s. However, as we shall see throughout the chapter, the manner and effect of their integration into the global trading system remains a perennial source of political conflict in global trade politics until the present day.

KEY POINTS

- Organized efforts to establish freer and non-discriminatory trade in Europe began in the middle of the nineteenth century and continued with the US RTAA of 1934.

- Throughout the period, industrialized countries continued to pursue protectionist trade policies in the context of the world wars and economic depressions.

- Countries in the Global South experienced colonialism and relationships of unequal exchange and began suggesting means to redress this at the 1944 Bretton Woods Conference.

5.3 The GATT years

The General Agreement on Tariffs and Trade started out as a chapter of a failed agreement that was never ratified but was provisionally applied by its original signatories who were keen to participate in a non-discriminatory system to manage trade among nations. Despite, or maybe because of its informal and diplomatic beginnings, the GATT turned out to be highly successful, overseeing the successive fall in tariff levels in the second half of the twentieth century; a steady increase in membership numbers, although some of them were newly decolonized countries that had effectively already been part of the GATT system under the various empires; and the eventual creation of the WTO in 1995. This section recounts the history of the GATT, paying particular attention to the features that remain relevant in global trade politics today.

5.3.1 The birth of GATT

The US was in a position of global economic leadership in the immediate post-war period. By 1950, the US accounted for nearly 17 per cent of world trade, which was about one and a half times the share of the UK, the next leading nation (Krasner 1976). By 1960, US trade was 20 per cent of world trade, which was roughly equal to the combined total of the three leading European economies: the UK, France, and West Germany. The US also went from an initial foreign investment stock of US$7 billion in 1946 to over US$100 billion in 1973, representing 51 per cent of total world foreign investment in that year (UN 1978). Security concerns of the Cold War with the Soviet Union encouraged other Western nations to follow US leadership in designing post-war global economic institutions, although the intellectual contributions of the British economist and Bretton Woods delegate John Maynard Keynes are generally recognized. Delegations from Global South countries did not represent a unified group at Bretton Woods, but a number of ideas by Prebisch, Sun, and others also proved influential (Helleiner 2014a).

In the realm of trade, countries concluded and signed an agreement to establish the ITO in 1948, which was to complete the triad of international economic organizations imagined at Bretton Woods in 1944. When the US Congress failed to ratify the agreement, countries relied on the GATT, established in 1947 as part of ITO negotiations, to provide structure for the rapidly expanding trade system. The GATT itself was a contract embodying trade rules for industrial and manufactured products, built around contested principles of trade liberalization, multilateralism, and a legal approach to trade relations.

Following the Second World War, policymakers in the US believed that trade liberalization would drive full employment and economic growth. Trade liberalization was also consistent with the US national interest, since the US was favourably positioned to benefit from freer trade. Because of the uncertain circumstances facing European economies after the war, policymakers in European nations believed that full employment and economic growth were a precondition of trade liberalization, which chimed with some of the Southern countries' efforts around import substitution.

A second American value was that of multilateralism, intended to guarantee non-discrimination between all countries in the trade regime. The Americans blamed European discriminatory trading blocs, most notably Great Britain's 1932 Imperial Preferential Trade system, for the collapse of international trade in the interwar years. The Europeans instead promoted economic regionalism, which later came to fruition in the gradual formation of the European Union (EU). Some members of the Imperial Preferential Trade system were also keen to preserve their preferential trade relations with Great Britain and its empire.

A third American value was a legal approach to trade relations, built on a code of international trade law coupled with a mechanism for settling trade disputes. The Europeans sought instead to preserve governments' administrative discretion. They preferred a global trading system built on practice rather than legal commitments (Gardner 1969).

In the end, the trade regime was based on what Ruggie (1982) has characterized as **embedded liberalism**. It established a middle ground between various forms of unfettered economic liberalism and Keynesian domestic interventionism and provided some room for the Global South's desire for import substitution industrialization. As such, the global trade regime has always been based on a negotiated consensus, which in the real world is often only achieved through compromises that are unpalatable to the purists.

The twenty-three original signatories of the GATT 1947 were Australia, Belgium, Brazil, Burma, Canada, Ceylon, Chile, China, Cuba, Czechoslovakia, France, India, Lebanon, Luxembourg, Netherlands, New Zealand, Norway, Pakistan, South Africa, Southern Rhodesia, Syria, the UK, and the US. In addition to liberalization, the most important principles of the GATT are non-discrimination, reciprocity, development, and safeguards (Finlayson and Zacher 1981).

Non-discrimination is principally embodied in Articles I and III of the GATT, as well as a number of other articles. Article I ensures that a country cannot discriminate externally between countries and Article III ensures it cannot discriminate internally within countries. Article I is known as the most-favoured-nation principle (see Key Concept Box 5.1). It requires that any advantage—such as a lowered tariff—granted by one

KEY CONCEPT BOX 5.1 MOST-FAVOURED-NATION PRINCIPLE (MFN)

The MFN principle required GATT Contracting Parties to extend to all signatories the most favourable trade conditions it granted any other country (that is, the 'most-favoured-nation'). The effect of the MFN principle was to eliminate discrimination between trade partners, as countries were obliged to have one MFN tariff that applied to all countries, and were prohibited from applying different tariffs on the same product coming from different countries. The overall purpose of MFN and non-discrimination was to create a unified trading system, and to prevent a fragmented and discriminatory system of regional preferences. The proliferation of preferential free trade agreements (FTAs) (also known as regional trade agreements) in the twenty-first century has heavily compromised the norm of non-discrimination in the global trade regime.

contracting party to any other country is immediately accorded to all contracting parties. MFN attacked the practice of discriminatory tariff preferences commonly employed before the Second World War.

A second dimension of non-discrimination is the National Treatment rule (Article III), which obliges nations to treat imported products no less favourably than domestic products with respect to taxes and all laws and regulations affecting the product's placement on the domestic market. Article III removed a whole range of policy tools (such as internal taxes or distribution requirements) that governments traditionally used to benefit domestic producers.

Another important principle of the GATT is **reciprocity**. The GATT provided a forum and a legal regime within which countries were encouraged to lower tariffs on a reciprocal basis. Negotiations were normally undertaken on a bilateral basis between the principal supplier and the principal buyer of a good. For example, in the 1950s the US, as the major buyer of wool (to clothe its troops fighting the Korean War), negotiated tariff reductions with Australia, the principal supplier of wool. It would be assumed that Australia would reciprocate by offering concessions to the US. The resulting lowered tariffs would be accorded to all GATT members.

Reciprocity encourages export interests to support liberalization (because they will benefit from concessions granted by other countries) in the face of domestic interest groups that will lose as a result of trade liberalization (see Guisinger, Chapter 6). In the GATT's early history, the principle worked reasonably well, as the steady drop in industrial tariffs illustrates (see Figure 5.2). Free riding, whereby a country

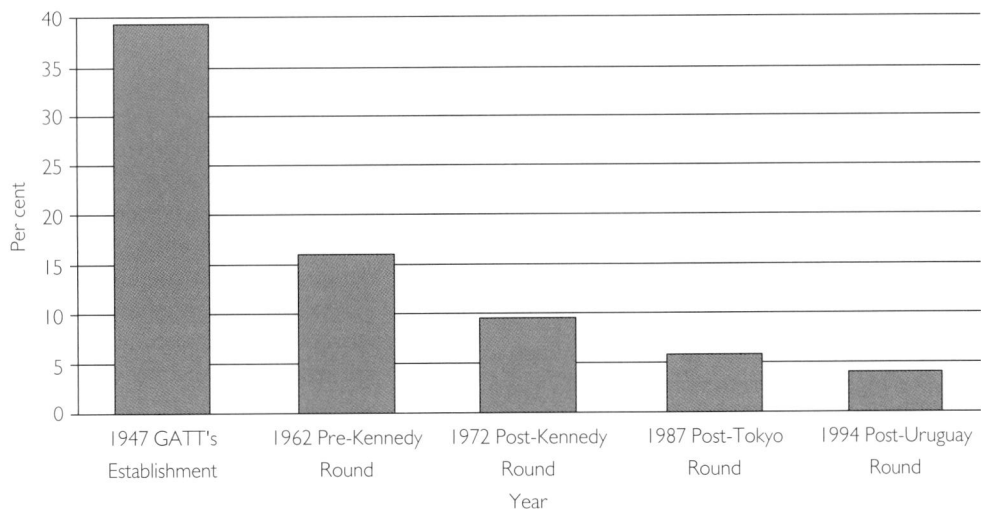

Figure 5.2 Average industrial tariffs in developed countries since 1947

Source: WTO and Department of Trade and Industry.

draws unreciprocated benefits from a lowering of tariffs by other countries, was regarded as a lesser problem, in part because free trade theory predicts that even unreciprocated liberalization is economically beneficial.

Reciprocity ran into difficulties when developing countries found a unified voice in the GATT following the decolonization process. The developing countries' comparative advantages lay mainly in areas that were not covered under the GATT, namely agriculture and textiles. In various negotiations beginning in the mid-1950s, attempts were made to mitigate the obligations of GATT membership for developing countries through the concept of **special and differential treatment (SDT)**. This involved exemptions from the principle of reciprocity, preferential access for developing country exports to rich country markets (that is, exemption from MFN), and development assistance to help developing countries compete in export markets (Hoekman and Kostecki 2009).

Exceptions to non-discrimination had always been part and parcel of GATT, as significant tariff reductions could only be achieved if exceptions could be included in the trade regime. The main exceptions concern regionalism, general exceptions, and **safeguards**. Article XXIV of the GATT allows the formation of regional trade agreements and **customs unions**, subject to specific conditions. Under the 'General Exceptions' of Article XX, governments reserve the right to take measures that serve a restricted list of public policy goals, such as the protection of public morals, the protection of human, animal, or plant life or health, or the conservation of exhaustible natural resources. Article XII allows governments to reimpose trade restrictions in the face of balance-of-payments difficulties, while Article XIX permits governments to raise tariffs for a period of time when a particular industry is confronting significant economic problems.

The rules of the GATT provided a basis for governance in a narrow, but fundamentally important, sector of international relations. The GATT was only ever intended to be a temporary agreement until the ITO Charter came into force. The fact that the GATT came to look and function like an international organization is the result of a largely unplanned and incremental accretion of political and legal powers, to which we turn in the next section.

5.3.2 **The GATT to 1994**

The GATT sponsored multilateral negotiations, known as 'rounds', in 1949 (Annecy), 1951 (Torquay), 1956 (Geneva), 1960–1961 (Dillon Round), 1963–1967 (Kennedy Round), 1973–1979 (Tokyo Round), and 1986–1993 (Uruguay Round). The first four negotiations did not make significant progress in liberalizing trade. On the one hand, the European post-war recovery did not occur as quickly as expected. Most newly independent developing countries pursued import-substitution industrialization. In practice, the US offered most of the tariff concessions.

The Kennedy Round of 1963–1967 was the first significant GATT round (Preeg 1970). It was the first GATT negotiation in which the European Community (EC)[1] participated as a single unit, engaging European nations and the US on an apparent basis of equality and reciprocity. It also signalled the willingness of governments to tackle long-standing problems in the trade system.

The Kennedy Round led to significant tariff cuts on industrial goods in developed countries. It produced an anti-dumping code that helped to standardize national policies geared to prevent unfair competition in international trade, and an international grain agreement that provided price ranges for wheat and multilateral sharing of international food aid. It also broadly agreed the principle of non-reciprocity for developing countries, codified as Part IV of the GATT. The inclusion of agriculture was significant, as agriculture trade was highly distorted by interventionist policies designed to detach domestic prices from international markets. However, disagreement between the US and the EC stymied progress on bringing agriculture into the discipline of GATT rules.

Prompted by chaos in the international monetary system and the increasing use of non-tariff barriers (NTBs) against exports surges from Japan and the **newly industrializing economies (NIEs)**, the Tokyo Round of the 1970s was also comprehensive and far-reaching (Winham 1986). It produced six legal codes that dealt with NTBs (plus a sectoral code for trade in aircraft); tariff reductions; and the 'Enabling Clause',

[1] In 2009, the Treaty of Lisbon legally replaced the European Community (EC) and the three-pillar system—EC, Common Foreign and Security Policy, and Justice and Home Affairs—with a single, legally consolidated organization, the European Union (EU).

explicitly allowing favourable treatment of developing countries. The six codes covered customs valuation procedures, import licensing, technical standards for products, subsidies, and countervailing duty measures, government procurement, and anti-dumping duty procedures. The code negotiations improved the openness, certainty, and non-arbitrariness of the rules governing international trade.

Although tariffs were not the major focus of the Tokyo Round, the average reductions of about 35 per cent of industrial nations' tariffs covered more than US$100 billion of imports, and were phased in over an eight-year period (Cline 1983). Once again, agriculture proved to be an intractable issue, with the US and the EC agreeing to remove the two major issues in agriculture trade—market access and the use of subsidies—from the negotiating table halfway through the round.

A major outcome of these negotiations was the '**Enabling Clause**', which allowed GATT signatories to accord differential and more favourable treatment to developing countries, without according the same treatment to other countries. Notwithstanding the Enabling Clause, developing countries were disappointed with the results of the Tokyo Round, as it failed to tackle non-tariff measures used by developed countries to restrict imports in industry sectors where developing countries were competitive, including food products, textiles, clothing, and footwear, iron and steel, shipbuilding, and consumer electronics (UNCTAD 1982). However, the active involvement of a large number of developing countries in the Tokyo Round negotiation was unprecedented in the GATT, and set the scene for the Uruguay Round a decade later.

In contrast with past GATT negotiations, the Tokyo Round was a rule-making exercise of major proportions. It produced legal rules that reached further into the nation state and impacted on domestic regulatory systems more deeply than was the case with most international agreements.

KEY POINTS

- Trading nations established the GATT under US leadership in 1947, and attempted in 1948 to create an ITO, which failed to receive ratification by the US Congress.
- The objectives of the GATT were to promote economic growth and prosperity through the expansion of international trade. This was to be achieved through the gradual reduction of tariffs and the elimination of discrimination in industrial and manufactured products, alongside safeguards and other exceptional measures that provided members with a range of policy tools to continue intervening in global trade.
- GATT negotiations were conducted on a multilateral and reciprocal basis.
- The Kennedy Round (1963–1967) was the GATT's first significant tariff-cutting round, whereas during the Tokyo Round (1973–1979) countries focused on reducing non-tariff measures that afforded protection in international trade and codified the principle of non-reciprocity for developing country members, demonstrating the importance of multilateral negotiation to the management of the international trade system.

5.4 The Uruguay Round

In the 1980s, there was deep division among countries about the desirability of new multilateral trade negotiations. The US advocated a new round, partly to counter growing protectionist pressures at home, and to expand the GATT regime to include new issues of concern to US business and industry, such as services, investment, and intellectual property (IP). The US also wanted to deal with high levels of agricultural protectionism, especially in the EC and Japan. A group of agriculture exporters including Australia, Canada, New Zealand, and a group of developing countries in South America and Southeast Asia supported the US position. Some of these developing countries had moved from import-substitution industrialization towards export-oriented development under the structural adjustment programmes and loan conditionalities of the **International Monetary Fund (IMF)** and the **World Bank**. Market-based reforms designed to deregulate national economies often led developing countries to move from opposition to support for multilateral agreements.

Many other countries opposed a new round, including the EC and Japan, who wanted to maintain their agricultural trade barriers, and ten developing countries led by India and Brazil, the 'G10', who argued that they were not sufficiently developed to negotiate the new issues. The 1982 GATT ministerial meeting, which was convened to launch a new round, failed, and brought the GATT close to breakdown (Croome 1995). In response, the US began to negotiate bilateral and regional trade agreements with key trade and security partners, including Israel and Canada (Ostry 1997). These talks provided an early indication that the US commitment to multilateralism could not be taken for granted.

Opposition to a new round was overcome through the efforts of an informal working group of nine developed and twenty developing countries. The so-called Café au Lait group was led by Colombia and Switzerland, giving the group its name. It developed the negotiating mandate that became the basis for the Uruguay Round. Henceforth, coalitional diplomacy was a central feature of multilateral negotiations.

The Uruguay Round was launched after a week-long special ministerial session at Punta del Este in September 1986 (Winham 1998). Negotiations on services, investment, and intellectual property were separated from those on traditional GATT issues, which was expected to lessen the prospects that developed countries could force trade-offs between new and traditional trade topics. The agenda of the Uruguay Round (Key Concept Box 5.2) comprised fifteen negotiating groups arranged initially in four principal categories: market access (including the critical areas of agriculture and textiles); reform of GATT rules; measures to strengthen the GATT as an institution; and the new issues: services, investment, and intellectual property.

5.4.1 New issues: Services, investment, and intellectual property

For the GATT, the incorporation of services was not a straightforward matter (Arup 2000). Services are not goods, which had always been the focus of GATT rules, but processes in which skills and knowledge are exchanged in order to meet consumer needs. They can include processes as widely differentiated as engineering consulting, financial **intermediation**, tourism, transport, and legal advice. Services were traditionally considered to be domestic activities. But by the 1980s, as a combined result of communication, transportation, and technology revolutions and changes in the global financial system, services had come to account for well over half of the **gross domestic product (GDP)** of developed countries.

Governments generally seek to provide consistent regulation over markets, and this might require discrimination against trade partners that apply different standards for trade in services. It may also require

the protection of an entire service sector from international competitors. However, in the 1980s many governments began to undertake regulatory reform through the breaking up of monopolies, privatization, and liberalization (for example, public utilities, postal services, telecommunications, and national airlines). Combined with pressure from other economic sectors who wanted access to cheaper services, as well as changing consumer preferences, and facilitated by rapid advances in information communications technology, services increasingly became seen as contestable and tradeable—hence the willingness of governments to contemplate multilateral rules and disciplines in services trade.

Translating GATT principles such as non-discrimination and national treatment to the services sector proved to be a major conceptual challenge for the Uruguay Round negotiators, and private sector lobbying (particularly in the US financial services sector) played a significant role in advancing this work. The result of the negotiations was the creation of the General Agreement on Trade in Services (GATS), which established a code of conduct for all measures affecting trade in services. GATS Article I defines trade in services by specifying four modes of supply. They are: cross-border supply (where a service crosses a border, for example call centres and online education); consumption abroad (where a service consumer crosses a border, for example, tourism, education, healthcare); commercial presence (where a service provider establishes a subsidiary in order to provide a service abroad, for example, foreign subsidiaries of hotels, universities, or insurance companies); and presence of natural persons (where a service provider temporarily crosses a border to provide a service, for example, architects, engineers, management consultants). The GATS requires MFN treatment with some time-bound exceptions (Article II) and exemptions for regional trade agreements (Article V). National treatment (Article XVII) is required for any sectors that are listed in a member's schedule of commitments. The GATS explicitly recognizes the right of governments to regulate services in order to meet national policy objectives, but requires that these regulations be applied in 'a reasonable, objective, and impartial manner' (Article VI).

Annexed to the GATS is each member's schedule of commitments, which lists each service sector for which a member has granted market access and national treatment to foreign service suppliers. There is wide variation in these schedules. Developed countries included a greater number of services sectors in their schedules than developing countries, and the poorest developing countries scheduled very few commitments at all. Rarely did these commitments extend new market access; in most cases they were simply a legal commitment to 'bind' existing regulatory regimes. Trade liberalization was left to future negotiations.

Alongside changing attitudes towards regulation in services, by the 1980s governments were abandoning capital controls and saw the liberalization of investment regimes as a valuable tool in stimulating international economic exchanges (see Helleiner, Chapter 8, and Pauly, Chapter 9, for discussion). Investment has always attracted considerable domestic regulation because of risks to sovereignty associated with high levels of foreign investment in sensitive industries. In the Uruguay Round, the negotiation of a multilateral investment agreement eventually proved to be impossible, and the agreement that was concluded on **Trade-Related Investment Measures (TRIMs)** dealt with only a small proportion of the issues raised in the negotiation.

Trade-Related Aspects of Intellectual Property Rights (TRIPs) was the third of the new issues. Intellectual property rights (IPRs) grant state protection to producers of new ideas. The 1886 Berne and 1896 Paris Conventions had provided for international cooperation on these rights, but protection had not been mandatory in the international economy up until this point (Maskus 2000). Producers of high-tech products sought to internationalize the intellectual property protections they enjoyed in their home country, and producers' associations such as the Pharmaceuticals Manufacturers Association demanded constraints on generic industries.

Developed countries asserted in the Uruguay Round that inadequate protection of intellectual property rights was a serious non-tariff barrier to trades. In contrast, developing countries, led by India and Brazil, viewed intellectual property protection itself as a non-tariff barrier to trade, as it can stymie competition, and were concerned over the monopolies granted in developed countries for products such as pharmaceuticals, which they considered crucial to the public interest. The developing countries acquiesced on this issue because they felt their losses were compensated by gains elsewhere in the overall accord (for example in agriculture, textiles, and clothing), and an agreement was concluded that set international standards for certain protections dealing with copyrights and patents (Winham 1998). However, the controversy over the TRIPs Agreement continued as a mainstay of WTO politics, and resurged during the COVID-19 pandemic, to which we return at the end of the chapter.

5.4.1.1 Agriculture

At the outset of the negotiation, a coalition of fourteen agricultural exporters from among the developed and developing countries formed under Australian leadership to promote the liberalization of global agricultural markets. Known as the 'Cairns Group', these countries played an important role in the early stages of the negotiation in ensuring that agriculture was not abandoned as in previous rounds (Capling 2001). However, by January 1992 it became clear that the Uruguay Round was blocked over agricultural negotiation between the major players. The US–EU differences stemmed mainly from the fact that, since the 1960s, Europe had established a protectionist policy under the Common Agricultural Policy, while the US was moving towards a comparative advantage in agricultural exports. For eighteen months, the main activity of the multilateral negotiation was a series of bilateral encounters between US and EU officials, with the Cairns Group keeping pressure on the parties to reach agreement. This blockage halted progress in other areas and even between other countries. The US and the EU eventually reached a resolution of their differences in the 'Blair House' accords on agriculture, but agriculture continued to be the major stumbling block to a general agreement until very late in the negotiation. The Agreement on Agriculture for the first time in history bound agricultural tariffs and restricted the use of domestic and export subsidies. While it did not achieve additional trade liberalization, the agreement created a basis for future negotiations.

5.4.1.2 Rules

The Uruguay Round Agreements were concluded on 15 December 1993. The Uruguay Round substantially altered the legal nature, modus operandi, and scope of the trade regime (see Table 5.1). First, the agreements created the WTO, which is a formally constituted international organization and not—as the GATT was—a contract regarding trade rules between countries. Internally, the WTO maintained consensus as one chief negotiating principle, which was a traditional GATT principle for decision-making. It means that a decision is adopted when no member actively disagrees. Consensus effectively gives each WTO member the right to veto a decision. The Uruguay Round results added the Single Undertaking as a new WTO principle. As a negotiating procedure, Single Undertaking meant that all issues were treated as a single package so that 'nothing was agreed until everything was agreed'. In effect, this required a balance of concessions from developed countries (for example, in agriculture, textiles and clothing, and SDT) and developing countries (for example, in services, intellectual property) in order to make a deal acceptable to all members. The principles of consensus and the Single Undertaking combined to increase the power of small and middle-sized countries in the Uruguay Round, which was demonstrated dramatically at the 1988 ministerial meeting in Montreal when five Latin American countries prevented consensus on an interim package agreement because the US and the EC did not meet their concerns over agriculture. The Single Undertaking also requires all parties to accept

Table 5.1 Results of GATT negotiations: 1960–1994

Negotiation	No. of countries	Results
Dillon Round 1960–1961	26	• Average tariff cut of 10% on US$4.9 billion of trade
Kennedy Round 1963–1967	62	• Average tariff cut of 35% on US$40 billion of trade • Anti-dumping code • Part IV of the GATT for developing countries
Tokyo Round 1973–1979	102	• Average tariff cut of 35% on more than US$100 billion of trade • Six codes dealing with non-tariff measures, plus aircraft code • Revision of GATT articles for developing countries
Uruguay Round 1986–1994	128	• Average tariff cut of 39% on US$3.7 trillion of trade • Twelve agreements (including agriculture, textiles, subsidies, safeguards) • New issues: GATS and trade related • Aspects of intellectual property rights (TRIPs) • DSU • Creation of WTO, new legal footing for the multilateral trade regime

and implement all elements of a negotiated agreement. Any GATT members that wanted to join the WTO in 1995 had to accept all agreements negotiated in the round. This was a departure from GATT practice where countries could adopt rules on an opt in/opt out basis. Internally, these institutional changes provided for clearer rules on trade, and reduced the fragmentation and inconsistency that had existed between various GATT-sponsored agreements. Externally, the WTO reinforced the role of trade in international economic relations, and it permitted trade concerns to be represented more fully in relations with the World Bank and the IMF.

Second, the various agreements reached at the Uruguay Round greatly expanded the rules of the international trading system. New issues were brought under multilateral rules for the first time, while old issues such as agriculture and textiles were finally brought under multilateral rules (Paarlberg 1997).

Third, the Uruguay Round Agreements advanced the rules-based nature of trade relations between countries, and thereby increased the economic security of smaller and middle-sized countries in their relations with larger powers. In particular, the agreements consolidated and strengthened the dispute settlement system that had evolved under the GATT. The agreements created an obligation for countries to adjudicate an issue if a trading partner seeks this recourse. Conversely, countries are obligated not to use unilateral trade sanctions as an alternative to WTO dispute settlement. Both provisions increase the prospects that countries, regardless of their size and power, would be equal before the law in trade disputes.

KEY POINTS

- The Uruguay Round (1986–1994) comprised a lengthy negotiating agenda, including new issues such as trade in services and TRIPs.

- The most difficult issue in the Uruguay Round was trade in agriculture, particularly between the major parties, the EU and the US, and a group of export competitive as well as developing country members.

- The Uruguay Round expanded the scope of international trade rules, and created the WTO and a more effective dispute settlement system. Its purpose was to establish a rules-based international trade system.

5.5 The age of WTO multilateralism

5.5.1 Organization and functions

The WTO is headquartered in Geneva and headed by a ministerial conference convening in principle every two years (see Table 5.2). It has near universal membership (164 countries at the time of writing, with 24 more in the queue for accession).

The ministerial conference brings together trade ministers of all member countries and is the WTO's top decision-making organ. The General Council acts on behalf of the ministerial conference between these meetings. Members typically have permanent representations in Geneva, and ambassadors come together regularly in order to carry out the functions of the WTO. The General Council may also convene as the Dispute Settlement Body (DSB), which adopts reports on international trade disputes, and as the Trade Policy Review Body, an organ that regularly examines individual members' domestic trade policy measures. A range of subsidiary councils, committees, and working groups supports the principal political organs of the WTO. They are aided in their work by the WTO's Director-General, with the support of a small Secretariat of 620 staff in 2023 (WTO 2023).

Table 5.2 WTO ministerial conferences

Year	City
1996	Singapore
1998	Geneva
1999	Seattle
2001	Doha
2003	Cancún
2005	Hong Kong
2009	Geneva
2011	Geneva
2013	Bali
2015	Nairobi
2017	Buenos Aires
2020	Kazakhstan

Source: WTO (www.wto.org/english/thewto_e/minist_e/mc12_e/mc12_e.htm).

Although decision-making by consensus puts all members on equal footing in procedural terms, a country's influence in WTO politics is determined not only by market size, but also by the quality of its representation in Geneva. There are significant variations in the size of members' permanent representations. While big trading nations such as the US, the EU, and China have separate, well-staffed WTO missions in addition to their UN missions and diplomatic representations to Switzerland, the least developed countries' (LDCs) missions had 4.1 staff members on average in 2008, with many of them representing their country in all international organizations in Geneva as well as taking on consular functions (DiCaprio and Trommer 2010).

The WTO is a 'member-driven' organization, meaning that the members and not the Secretariat are mainly responsible for setting the agenda and carrying out the functions of the organization (Blackhurst 1998). Dialogue and exchange on international trade issues occurs through regular exchanges among country officials in Geneva as well as the publication of members' Trade Policy Reviews. The main purpose of a review is information dissemination and transparency, but the reviews also help to evaluate whether members are in full compliance with their WTO obligations.

The WTO agreements and domestic law pertaining to international trade flows constitute the hard core of rules. Rules can be renegotiated in WTO negotiations. The Single Undertaking in principle excludes the possibility that new rules will apply in certain areas before the entire set of rules being negotiated has been agreed. As explored later in this chapter, this principle has gradually eroded during the Doha Round. Particularly over the last three WTO ministerial conferences, critical mass voting and plurilateral agreements among subsets of members have been used.

Where there is disagreement on the application of trade rules, the Dispute Settlement Body has been created to find a legal resolution to such issues. Dispute settlement was once hailed as the jewel in the crown of international economic cooperation, because its procedural rules turned WTO law into the only body of public international law that retained instruments allowing the enforcement of legal obligations. Although the WTO dispute settlement system is in crisis at the time of writing, it is important to comprehend the legal and political impact of WTO dispute settlement, which is explored in the next section.

5.5.2 **Dispute settlement**

During the GATT years, if two parties could not put their differences on trade rules aside in diplomatic consultations, a GATT panel of international trade experts adjudicated the dispute. Then and now, only members can bring disputes, although non-state actors including businesses lobby their governments to file complaints in Geneva. To date, the majority of disputes have been settled in the consultation stage, indicating that dialogue and negotiation remain crucial tools in multilateral trade governance. Only if consultations have failed may the complaining member request the establishment of a panel. Panels are made up of three or five international trade experts on a case-by-case basis.

Non-compliance with GATT reports among members became a problem from 1980 onwards (Hudec et al. 1993). To resolve this problem, the WTO's DSU introduced a number of changes to dispute settlement, notably the reverse consensus rule and an appeals process. Negative or reverse consensus stipulates that a report is adopted unless members decide by consensus not to adopt it. It has made the adoption of WTO dispute settlement reports quasi-automatic (Palmeter and Mavroidis 1999). In the WTO, members may also submit appeals on legal questions, which are heard before three of the seven members of the Appellate Body. The Appellate Body is a standing body of international legal experts appointed by the DSB that brings consistency, coherence, and stability into the interpretation of WTO law. In case of noncompliance with a DSB report, the complaining member may request authorization to suspend concessions under the WTO agreements.

In order to make this so-called retaliation effective, members are not confined to issuing measures in the economic sector in which the violations occurred. In the famous *EC–Hormones* case taken by the US against the EU, for example, the report required the EU to lift its import ban on hormone-treated beef products because, in the eyes of the Appellate Body, it had not conducted a scientific risk assessment of the health risks associated with the products before implementing the ban. When the EU did not comply, the US was allowed to introduce a 100 per cent *ad valorem* duty on a variety of agricultural products (Sien 2007).

As this example indicates, WTO dispute settlement is political. On the one hand, the DSU prohibits judicial law-making at the WTO, as concessions and new trade rules can only be made by members in negotiations. As the body of WTO law is often incomplete, this presents a difficult exercise for WTO judges. As we will see below, the debate over judicial law-making is one of the reasons for the current crisis in WTO dispute settlement which has led to an empty-chair crisis at the Appellate Body.

On the other hand, WTO dispute settlement is a highly technical exercise requiring extensive and specialized legal expertise and experience, which is not always readily available in poor countries. To address this imbalance, a range of international lawyers do *pro bono* work for developing countries and LDCs, and the Advisory Centre on WTO Law was created as an independent organization in Geneva in 2001. The size of a member, however, also matters at the implementation stage of a ruling. For example, for the EU even the African heavyweight Nigeria only accounts for 1.2 per cent of EU merchandise trade (DG Trade 2015). In a context of severe economic asymmetry, sanctions risk hurting the country issuing them as much or more than the sanctioned country. In this context, the possibility for members to compensate across WTO agreements can enable small, trade-dependent nations to retaliate against a trade giant. This was markedly demonstrated in the *US–Gambling* case that pitched the US against the tiny island state of Antigua and Barbuda. In this case, the Appellate Body sided with Antigua and Barbuda in arguing that certain US laws restricting online gambling violated US market access commitments under the GATS. When the US failed to comply with the DSB report, the DSB thus authorized Antigua and Barbuda to retaliate under TRIPs instead.

On balance, the Dispute Settlement Mechanism (DSM) has been highly effective in assuring compliance with WTO law. This has been one important factor in the WTO's relationship with civil society and trade critics. To this we turn in the next section.

5.5.3 **The WTO and civil society**

The unprecedented extension of international trade rules into domestic legal and regulatory systems under the WTO attracted criticism from a broad range of civil society groups. In addition to their concerns about the impact of WTO agreements on domestic policy regimes, these groups were critical of the lack of transparency in trade policymaking, the privileged access that governments afforded to business interests in trade policy matters, and their inability to participate directly in WTO negotiations (Capling and Low 2010).

A number of early WTO dispute settlement cases, such as *US–Gasoline* and *US–Shrimp Turtle*, signalled to environmental groups that decisions taken in Geneva could impact on the regulatory victories they had registered at home. In both cases, WTO members successfully challenged domestic measures taken in the interest of environmental protection, namely certain aspects of the US Clean Air Act (in *US–Gasoline*) and a prohibition on shrimp fished with nets that did not feature turtle excluder devices (in *US–Shrimp Turtle*). The DSB confirmed that members have the right, under GATT Article XX, to assure air quality or protect certain species. However, it found that the US could have implemented the environmental measures in a less trade restrictive manner, a condition foreseen in Article XX. Both domestic regulations thus needed to be amended. One bone of contention in the trade and environment debate today is the question of where the right balance between enabling trade flows and enabling environmental protection and preservation lies, and which governmental or international body is best placed to make the decision.

The lowest point to date in the relationship between the WTO and civil society was reached during the 1999 Ministerial Conference held in Seattle. Negotiations collapsed over agricultural subsidies, competition, investment, and the dismay of many developing countries about long-standing institutional practices that effectively excluded them from the negotiating room. Meanwhile, in the streets of Seattle at least 40,000 protesters assembled and periodically clashed with armed police in what became known as the Battle of Seattle. Similarly outspoken, if less violent, protests that critiqued the WTO as being anti-democratic and biased in favour of the interests of rich nations and corporations were registered during every ministerial conference held in the first decade of the twenty-first century.

Since the events of Seattle, efforts have been made to increase the WTO's transparency and engagement with civil society. NGOs can become accredited to attend plenary sessions at WTO ministerial conferences and can cooperate with the Secretariat to arrange issue-specific symposia. The WTO Secretariat has established a dedicated NGO unit in its External Relations Division which maintains contact with the NGO community and channels information flows between the WTO and civil society. Since 2001, the WTO opens its doors annually during its Public Forum event, where representatives from civil society, academia, business, the media, governments, parliamentarians, and intergovernmental organizations present their views on the multilateral trade regime. The Appellate Body held in *US–Shrimp Turtle* that it is permissible for the DSB to use unsolicited NGO submissions as *amicus curiae* briefs.

Commentators on the evolving relationship between the WTO and civil society are divided along two broad lines. Some hold that the natural constituency of a trade organization is economic interests, including business, workers, and consumer representatives, and they see more far-reaching societal engagement with a critical eye. Others argue that as the trade agenda expands to cover behind-the-border measures that protect the environment and society more broadly, excluding these interests from trade governance makes the WTO illegitimate. The question of the appropriate level and form of civil society input also remains unresolved. Under the current ad hoc modes of engagement, some worry that the type of civil society representation that effectively reaches trade policy circles reproduces existing biases in favour of well-resourced political actors from wealthy countries (Chimni 2006), and crowds out alternative voices from the debate (Hannah 2014). More recently, trade critics have turned their attention to regional trade agreements, which often include controversial subjects that are not negotiated at the WTO. Indeed, during the course of its most recent round of multilateral negotiations, the Doha Round, the WTO has ceased to be the principal forum for global trade governance. We explore the beginnings of the Doha Round in the next section.

5.5.4 The beginnings of the Doha Round

With the adoption of the Doha Ministerial Declaration on 14 November 2001, members launched the WTO's first round of multilateral trade negotiations. The road to Doha contained the seeds of many political problems that led key members to abandon the round *de facto* in 2015. The EU wanted a new round to include four new issues in the negotiating agenda, namely competition policy, investment, trade facilitation, and government procurement—the so-called Singapore Issues. The US proposed reductions in trade barriers in industrial goods and raised the controversial issues of linking labour and the environment into the trade regime. Developing countries argued that before any new negotiation could begin, further efforts should be made to redress the inequities resulting from the Uruguay Round results, notably in the areas of agriculture, textiles, and TRIPs.

Following the collapse of the Seattle meeting, the EU and the US stepped back from their most contentious demands on investment and competition policy, and labour rights and the environment, respectively. By September 2001, it was clear that the major issues were those dear to developing countries, mainly relating to agriculture. When the 9/11 attacks struck in New York and Washington, a sense that the international community needed to stand as one gave political momentum to the Doha Ministerial Conference in November 2001. Ministers set out an ambitious work programme covering, *inter alia*, agriculture, implementation issues, intellectual property, services, Singapore Issues, and trade and environment. The agenda became known as the Doha Development Agenda (DDA), and a promise was made that the new round would be 'a round for free' for the developing countries. It was unclear what this would mean in practice, but many understood it to signal that no new concessions would be expected from developing country members in return for concessions given to them. The DDA was scheduled to conclude on 1 January 2005.

At the first Ministerial Conference of the Doha Round in Cancún, Mexico, in 2003, it became clear that the old negotiating paradigm of the GATT, whereby a deal was struck once the US, the EU, Canada, and Japan were in agreement, was defunct under the WTO. Spearheaded by Brazil, China, India, and South Africa, a group of developing countries formed a new coalition, known as the G20. The G20 demanded increased access to developed country markets for their agricultural products, an end to agricultural export subsidies, and the elimination of domestic support measures that act as export subsidies.

Over the next four years, a profound malaise enveloped the Doha Round. Priority areas were narrowed down to agricultural subsidies and tariffs, non-agricultural market access (mainly, industrial tariffs), and, to a lesser degree, trade in services, and all Singapore Issues except trade facilitation were dropped. With the EU and the US unwilling to make substantial offers in agriculture, developing countries were

not willing to offer concessions in services or manufactured goods.

In July 2008, ministers from around thirty key
members met in Geneva in a 'mini-Ministerial' to
resolve the deadlock. While progress was made on
agricultural subsidies and industrial tariffs, the negotiations collapsed over the Special Safeguard Mechanism (SSM) in agriculture, an issue that had attracted
little attention until that point. In 2005 the G33 coalition of developing country members had proposed
a SSM methodology that would allow developing
countries under certain conditions to increase duties
on farm imports in excess of pre-Doha tariff ceilings.
In a dramatic meeting of Australia, Brazil, China,
the EU, Japan, India, and the US on 29 July 2008, US
demands for predictable market access for farm products clashed with the concerns of import-sensitive
China and India.

While economic historians will debate at what
exact point the Doha Round collapsed for generations to come, many observers argue that after the
2008 mini-Ministerial, things were looking bleak for
the WTO's negotiation function. By then, new trade
rules were increasingly being developed within the
realm of regional and preferential agreements. These
developments set the scene for an emerging hybrid
governance model for trade, to which we turn in the
next section.

KEY POINTS

- The WTO is an international economic institution that
  combines elements of procedural equality and factual
  political asymmetry among members. Its main functions
  are making international trade rules, providing a forum for
  dialogue on trade issues for countries, and adjudicating
  international trade disputes among its members. The
  negotiation and adjudication functions are now in crisis.

- The WTO Dispute Settlement Mechanism has been highly
  effective in assuring compliance with WTO obligations.
  Because economic power and legal expertise matter, not
  all countries have equal access to dispute settlement.

- Disagreement over market access for agricultural goods,
  manufactures, and services has been at the heart of
  deadlock in the Doha Round negotiations. As a result
  of the rise of large and fast-growing economies, the US
  and the EU no longer exercise unrivalled dominance
  in multilateral trade negotiations. The emphasis on
  development issues exposed profound differences in

members' understandings of the trade and development
nexus.

- The expansion of the trade agenda and the introduction
  of binding dispute settlement procedures drew the
  attention of broader societal interests to the global
  trade regime. Following the 1999 Battle of Seattle, WTO
  initiatives to promote transparency and accessibility have
  improved the relationship between civil society and the
  WTO.

5.6 The age of hybrid trade governance

In 2011, ministers formally declared that the Doha
Round was at an impasse. Despite a number of subsequent WTO negotiating successes, most notably the
Trade Facilitation Agreement concluded at the 2013
Bali Ministerial Conference, the multilateral trading
system of the twentieth century was now giving way
to a twenty-first-century hybrid model of trade governance. Under hybrid trade governance, the WTO provides for a baseline of multilateral trade rules, while
many new trade rules are developed in a large network of overlapping regional and preferential trade
agreements. The WTO reserves the right to review
members' preferential agreements. Many preferential
agreements actively incorporate WTO rules in certain areas, most commonly on safeguards, and some
refer back to WTO dispute settlement. Major players
strategically pursue their trade political interests in
this integrated, if highly complex network. They may
develop new rules in preferential agreements that they
may later hope to multilateralize at the WTO, or set
up trade agreements with large numbers of members
in specific regions, so-called mega-regionals, that are
so vast that they may provide the seeds of an alternative multilateral system. Smaller countries are more
in a position of rule-takers in this hybrid governance
model than they were during the age of WTO multilateralism, not least because their veto and collective
bargaining powers are jeopardized. While preferential
agreements usually contain dispute settlement provisions including sanctioning mechanisms, they lack
a third party, such as the GATT/WTO Secretariat,
that could drive the procedural aspects of a dispute
forwards, should countries fail to come to agreement
in consultations. On the whole, these features render the twenty-first-century hybrid trade governance

model less rules-based than WTO multilateralism, and more based on power (Trommer 2017; Wilkinson 2017). This section will first discuss the rise and politics of regional and preferential trade agreements. It will then consider the evolution of WTO negotiations in the twenty-first century, as well as the WTO Appellate Body Crisis and ongoing debates about WTO reform.

5.6.1 The rise of regional and preferential trade agreements

The number of regional trade agreements (RTAs) has grown rapidly since the WTO came into existence in 1995 (see Figure 5.3). Roughly one half of world trade is now conducted within these preferential arrangements, the most significant exception to the WTO's principle of non-discrimination. By the end of April 2019, of the WTO's 164 members only one, Mauritania, was not a party to one or more RTAs (for a complete listing of RTAs by country, see WTO 2019). In the twenty years since the foundation of the WTO, members notified the organization of more than 400 new RTAs, more than twice the number notified to the GATT in the period 1948–1994. By 2019, more than 467 regional agreements were in force (WTO 2019).

Three sets of rules in the WTO permit the creation of RTAs:

- Article XXIV of the GATT lays down conditions for the establishment and operation of free trade agreements and customs unions covering trade in goods.
- The Enabling Clause permits regional agreements among developing countries on trade in goods.
- Article V of the GATS establishes conditions that permit liberalization of trade in services among regional partners.

Parties to regional arrangements are obliged to notify the WTO of the details of their agreements; the Committee on RTAs has responsibility for ensuring that the agreements comply with the WTO's provisions (for agreements only involving developing economies, the responsibility lies with the Committee on Trade and Development). Table 5.3 shows the various strategies that governments use to liberalize trade.

For most of the post-Second World War period, regional economic integration had been associated with an arrangement between geographically contiguous states. The EU is the best known of such agreements, but consider also the East African Cooperation (Kenya, Tanzania, and Uganda) and the

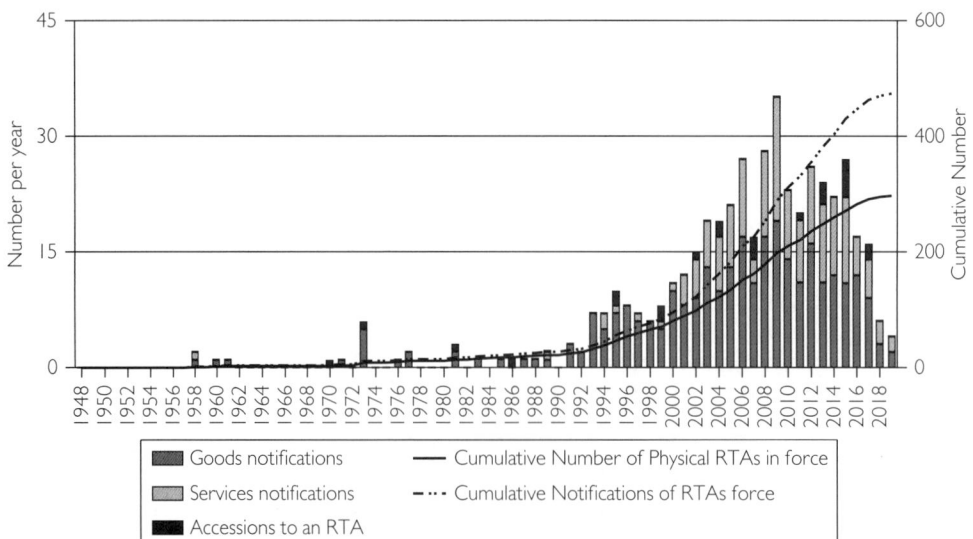

Figure 5.3 Regional trade agreements notified to the GATT/WTO, 1948–2018

Source: http://rtais.wto.org/UI/charts.aspx#.

Table 5.3 Example of the geographical scope of trade liberalization strategies

Unilateral	Bilateral		Minilateral			Multilateral
	Geographically concentrated	Geographically dispersed	Geographically concentrated	Geographically dispersed		
	Bilateral within region	Bilateral transregional	Regionalism	Transregionalism	Interregionalism	
Trade liberalization in Britain in the nineteenth century, in Latin America, SE Asia, Sub-Saharan Africa, Australia, and NZ in the 1980s and 1990s	Cobden–Chevalier Treaty Australia–New Zealand Closer Economic Relations Trade Agreement (ANZCERTA)	Singapore–US	EU USMCA SADC	Trans-Pacific Partnership RCEP	EU–MERCOSUR ANZCERTA–AFTA	GATT/WTO

Andean Community of Nations (Bolivia, Colombia, Ecuador, and Peru). Today, however, a large number of trade agreements are signed that involve only two parties (for example, China–Hong Kong). Sometimes these bilateral agreements link parties that are not geographically contiguous (for example, Korea and Chile). Because all non-global agreements are subject to the scrutiny of the WTO's Committee on RTAs, the WTO applies to them the label 'regional'. Many commentators prefer the term preferential trade agreement because many of the recent agreements are not 'regional' in the conventional sense and do not free all trade between the parties.

RTAs take various forms that range in scope of cooperation, from free trade areas to **economic unions** (see Key Theory Box 5.3).

But it is not just the terminology that is problematic. Economists assert that an economy's welfare can be maximized if governments lower trade barriers on a non-discriminatory basis (either through unilateral action or through multilateral negotiations at the WTO). Preferential Trade Agreements (PTAs) can reduce global welfare by distorting the allocation of resources, and may even lead to welfare losses (see Case Study Box 5.4). Moreover, from the political scientist's perspective, it is usually more efficient to negotiate a single agreement with a large number of states than to undertake a series of negotiations with individual states or with small groupings (because it both economizes on the public resources and increases the opportunities for trade-offs).

Why, then, has regionalism become increasingly attractive to governments in the last two decades? The combination of reasons why governments enter regional economic agreements includes political/strategic as well as economic factors.

Regionalism frequently involves the use of economic means to pursue political ends: the improvement of interstate relations and/or the enhancement of security within a region. In international relationships that have a history of conflict or where no tradition of partnership exists, cooperation on economic matters can be a core element in a process of confidence-building (for example, the creation of the EU or ASEAN). The negotiation of an RTA has also been used by large powers, most notably the US, to reward its security partners (Aggarwal and Govella 2013). Offers by industrialized countries in recent years to extend regional economic cooperation to less developed neighbours have frequently been encouraged by concerns about 'non-traditional' security threats emanating from such partners. These threats include environmental damage, illegal migration, organized crime, drug smuggling, and terrorism. Regional cooperation may help address these issues directly, for example, through USMCA provisions on the environment.

RTAs may also be easier to negotiate and 'sell' at home. The international relations literature is inconclusive on the relationship between the number of participants and the successful negotiation and

KEY THEORY BOX 5.3 REGIONAL ECONOMIC ARRANGEMENTS

A *free trade area* exists when countries remove barriers to the free movement of goods and services between them. Governments are free to choose how they treat goods and services imported from non-regional-partner states. Membership in one free trade area therefore does not prevent a country from joining other free trade areas. Because free trade areas impose relatively few constraints on national decision-making, they are the easiest of the regional arrangements to negotiate. More than 90 per cent of regional partnerships take the form of free trade areas. Examples include USMCA (and its predecessor, NAFTA), the Japan–Singapore Economic Partnership Agreement, and the Baltic Free Trade Area.

A *customs union* goes beyond the removal of trade barriers within the region to adopt a common set of policies towards imports from countries outside the region. This includes a common level of tariffs on all extra-regional imports. Such agreements inevitably cost governments autonomy in their foreign economic policies (joint institutions are usually required to negotiate and administer the common external trade policies). They also have distributive effects, depending on the level at which the common external tariff is set for various items. Consequently, customs unions are usually more difficult to negotiate than free trade areas. Of the 472 regional agreements notified to the WTO by May 2019, only eighteen were customs unions. This includes the Andean Community, Caribbean Community and Common Market (CARICOM), Common Market of the South (MERCOSUR, comprising Argentina, Brazil, Paraguay, and Uruguay), and the Southern African Customs Union.

A *common market* includes a customs union and also allows for free movement of labour and capital within the regional partnership. Such free flows of factors of production inevitably require governments to collaborate in additional policy areas to ensure comparable treatment in all countries within the regional grouping. Historically, few governments have been willing to accept the loss of policymaking autonomy. The best-known example today is the EU.

CASE STUDY BOX 5.4 THE COSTS AND BENEFITS OF PREFERENTIAL TRADE AGREEMENTS—TRADE DIVERSION AND TRADE CREATION

Jacob Viner (1950) first presented a systematic assessment of the economic effects of regional economic integration. He argued that increased trade between parties to a regional arrangement can occur through two mechanisms. **Trade creation** occurs when imports from a regional partner displace goods that have been produced domestically at higher cost. **Trade diversion** occurs when imports from a regional partner displace imports originating outside the regional arrangement, because the extra-regional imports are no longer price-competitive when regional tariffs are removed. Let's consider a hypothetical example (see Table 5.4). Let's say Indonesia was the lowest-cost source of cotton T-shirts for the US, manufacturing and delivering a T-shirt to the US at US$5, while a Mexican T-shirt was US$5.40. Before USMCA, both countries faced the same 10 per cent *ad valorem* tariff duty, and the US preferred importing from Indonesia. After the implementation of USMCA, only Indonesian imports face the duty, raising their price to US$5.50. Mexican T-shirts would now seem more cost-competitive and US imports would divert to Mexico.

Several consequences follow from this trade *diversion*. The consumer in the US *may* gain because the cost to the importer of purchasing a T-shirt falls from US$5.50 to US$5.40. The US government, however, loses the tariff revenue (50 cents for each imported T-shirt), the new imports from Mexico not being subject to a tariff. For the US economy as a whole, therefore, the potential gain to consumers is significantly exceeded by the loss of tariff revenue (which is a form of taxation income for the government). The Indonesian economy will also suffer a welfare loss because of the decline in export revenue.

If trade diversion outweighs trade creation, the net welfare effect can be negative.

Table 5.4 The potential for trade diversion after the removal of tariffs on intraregional trade (US$)

	Cost of production	Tariff cost pre-NAFTA	Cost to importer pre-NAFTA	Tariff post-NAFTA	Cost to importer post-NAFTA
Indonesia	5.00	0.50 (10%)	5.50	0.50 (10%)	5.50
Mexico	5.40	0.54 (10%)	5.94	Zero	5.40

implementation of agreements. There are plenty of instances where regional negotiations have failed to produce agreements or have taken a very long time to complete (for example, the FTA between Japan and Korea took twenty years to negotiate, and the Transatlantic Trade and Investment Partnership (TTIP) between the US and the EU failed). Of greater importance, however, are the perceptions that governments hold, and there is little doubt that many *believe* that regional agreements are easier to negotiate, given the WTO stalemate we discussed above. In addition, the political advantage of an RTA to governments is that they may be able to respond to protectionist pressures by excluding 'politically sensitive' non-competitive domestic sectors from the trade liberalization measures negotiated regionally, whereas such exclusion would be more difficult multilaterally. Meanwhile, they will push for liberalization in those sectors where there are competitive domestic exporters.

As for economic factors, governments may believe that domestic producers will be successful in competition with regional partners and will benefit from the larger (protected) market that a regional scheme creates, but that they would not survive a competition with producers located outside the region. Rather than liberalizing with all the world, RTAs provide a larger 'home' market for domestic industries, possibly enabling them to benefit from economies of scale (see Key Concept Box 5.5).

Such reasoning is often—but not only—implied in the formation of RTAs in the developing world. Raul Prebisch (1963; 1970) had argued that regional integration was essential to provide a sufficiently large market to enable the efficient local production of goods that had previously been imported. Related to this is the idea that regionalism can increase the attractiveness of an economy to potential investors. Companies that previously supplied the separate national markets through exports from outside the region may now find that the unified regional market is of sufficient size to make local production (and hence foreign investment into the region) attractive.

Regionalism may also be more attractive than a multilateral treaty because it enables agreement on issues that would not be possible in the WTO where membership is more diverse. It may include, for instance, agreements on the environment, on the treatment of foreign direct investment (FDI), on domestic competition (anti-trust) policies, on intellectual property rights, on regulatory standards, and on labour standards—sometimes referred to as twenty-first-century trade issues (Baldwin 2011). Regional agreements, especially bilateral free trade areas, may also enable more powerful states to bring their weight to bear more effectively on weaker parties, for whom the price of gaining security of access to a larger market may be to accept undertakings on issues that they veto at the WTO (on this issue of unequal bargaining power in regional agreements, see Helleiner 1994; Perroni and Whalley 1994; Shadlen 2005).

Overall, it is not possible to point to one particular dynamic that by itself can explain the rise of regionalism. Instead, RTAs are determined by complex institutional and political environments which are region-specific (Duina 2007).

5.6.2 The rush to preferential trade agreements

The rush to regionalism that began in the mid-1990s is the second major wave of RTAs since the Second World War: the first occurred in the early 1960s,

---

KEY CONCEPT BOX 5.5 ECONOMIES OF SCALE

In modern manufacturing, which frequently depends on the use of expensive machinery and large investments in research and development, large-scale production often enables firms to produce at a lower average cost per unit. These *economies of scale* can result not just from a more efficient use of machinery and of labour, but also because specialist managers and workers can be employed, savings can be made in borrowing on financial markets (which generally charge higher interest rates to smaller borrowers), raw materials can be purchased more cheaply when bought in bulk, and advertising costs are spread across a higher volume of output.

A related concept is *economies of scope*. These occur when firms can spread various costs (including, for example, research and development, accounting, marketing) across various products, which may—although not necessarily—be related (for example, production of calculators and of liquid crystal display (LCD) screens for laptop computers).

largely in response to the 1957 establishment of the European Economic Community (EEC). Two factors were to change the global context to make it far more favourable to regionalism in the 1990s. First, the end of the Cold War and the disintegration of the Soviet Union opened the way for East European countries to enter into economic agreements with the EU (and, eventually, EU membership). It also required new arrangements to be established amongst former Soviet bloc members. In Asia, the end of the Cold War broke down the barriers that had previously prevented regional economic integration. In 1991, China joined the APEC grouping, which included its former Cold War foes Japan, the US, and South Korea. In 2001, China began to negotiate a free trade agreement with ASEAN (see Figure 5.4).

The second contextual factor was the growth in global interdependence, and the ascendancy of neoliberal ideas in Western governments and international financial institutions (IFIs). The growing integration of markets placed increasing pressure on governments to pursue market-friendly policies. Potential foreign investors quickly voted with their feet when faced by governments that attempted to impose conditions on them. From the early 1980s onwards, the balance of bargaining power between investors and governments shifted dramatically so that investors were increasingly able to demand concessions from host governments on issues such as taxation, rather than accepting restrictions on their activities.

Similarly, financial markets were quick to punish governments that were perceived to be inward-looking or interventionist.

In this new context, the regional arrangements that developed were often designed to enhance states' participation in the global economy, to signal their openness to foreign investment, and to seek access to the markets of industrialized countries. Unlike the arrangements from the 1960s and 1970s, the new regionalism frequently involved partnerships between industrialized and less developed economies, that is, they were often North–South rather than South–South in orientation. In the last decade, an increase in the number of agreements between industrialized and emerging economies has reflected a desire to facilitate the operation of production networks. Again, the focus has been less on traditional barriers to trade and more on facilitating the movement of components around a region. Richard Baldwin has characterized these '21st Century Trade Agreements' as being driven by a new reciprocity: 'the basic bargain is "foreign factories for domestic reforms"—not "exchange of market access"' (2011: 1).

Very significantly, by the 1990s the US had also shifted from its long-standing 'multilateralism-only' approach to trade liberalization. The US attitude towards regional economic agreements changed in the early 1980s, as it despaired of the slow multilateral progress and bristled at the European Community's Common Agricultural Policy (CAP). The new approach to trade

Figure 5.4 Geographical distribution of RTAs

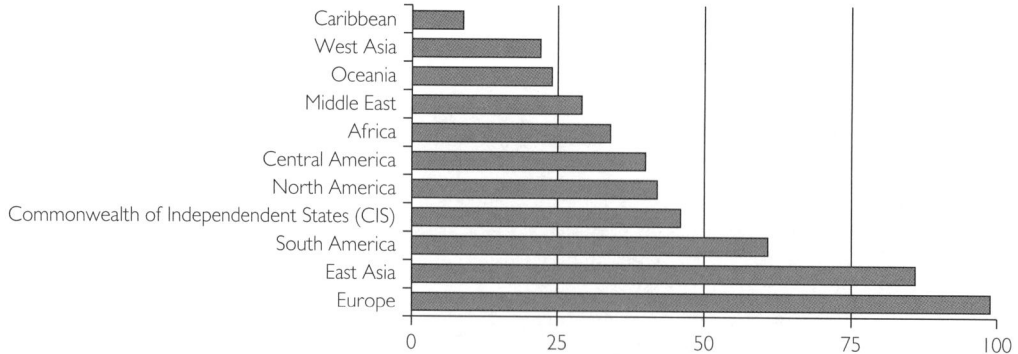

Note: The country composition of regions may be found in the WTO's RTA database User Guide (http://rtais.wto.org/userguide/User%20Guide_Eng.pdf). RTAs involving countries/territories in two (or more) regions are counted more than once.

Source: WTO Secretariat (http://rtais.wto.org/UI/charts.aspx#), accessed 2 May 2019.

policy in the early 1990s was succinctly stated by Lawrence Summers, who became under-secretary of the Treasury for International Affairs in the first Clinton administration: that there should be a 'presumption in favor of all the lateral reductions in trade barriers, whether they be multi, uni, tri, plurilateral' (quoted in Frankel 1997: 5). In other words, the new policy was one of 'anything goes' in trade policy so long as it contributed to trade liberalization.

Some of the new free trade areas also came into being because industrialized countries wished to make their trade arrangements with developing countries compatible with WTO regulations. Here, the EU has again been the most important actor. The EU had previously constructed a network of preferential trade arrangements with the countries of the southern Mediterranean, and with the African, Caribbean, and Pacific (ACP) grouping, which comprises over seventy countries. These arrangements had largely grown out of imperial preference systems of former European colonies. They offered duty-free access to the European market for most ACP exports without obliging the ACP countries to provide preferential treatment to European exports. The arrangements had been challenged under the GATT and then again by the WTO under the famous *EC–Bananas* cases. Ultimately, a WTO Dispute Settlement panel found that the European provisions on bananas contravened several WTO articles. The Europeans eventually committed themselves to introducing arrangements that were compatible with their WTO obligations and chose the tool of FTAs to do so (Ravenhill 2004).

Finally, the rush to regionalism was aided by difficulties in the GATT/WTO negotiating function. When the Uruguay Round of GATT negotiations stalled, governments turned to regional agreements both as a substitute for a global agreement and as a means of increasing pressure on other countries to persuade them to make concessions in global talks. A decade later, the failure of the WTO's ministerial meeting in Seattle in December 1999 convinced many governments (including some that had previously been hostile towards RTAs, for example, Japan, see METI 2000) that negotiation of a new global agreement would not bring early results and that they should therefore look to RTAs to advance their trade agendas. The deadlock in the Doha Round—and a more general frustration on the part of the US and the EU about the prospects for advancing 'deeper' integration agendas in global institutions—were

significant precipitants of the Trans-Pacific Partnership and TTIP negotiations.

Today, PTAs cover many policy areas in which new trade rules are needed but cannot be negotiated at the WTO. These PTA rules may be WTO-+, meaning that they exist in areas that are also covered by the WTO, but where PTA rules go further. They may also be WTO-X, meaning that they exist in areas where there are no WTO rules in place. Table 5.5 shows the

Table 5.5 Policy areas covered in PTAs

WTO-+	WTO-X
• Tariffs industrial goods	• Anti-corruption
• Tariffs agricultural goods	• Competition policy
• Customs administration	• Environmental laws
• Export taxes	• Investment measures
• SPS measures	• Labour market regulation
• State trading enterprises	• Movement of capital
• TBT measures	• Consumer protection
• Countervailing measures	• Data protection
• Anti-dumping	• Approximation of legislation
• State aid	• Audiovisual
• Public procurement	• Civil protection
• TRIMS measures	• Innovation policies
• GATS	• Cultural cooperation
• TRIPS	• Economic policy dialogue
• Agriculture	• Education and training
	• Energy
	• Financial assistance
	• Health
	• Human Rights
	• Illegal immigration
	• Illicit drugs
	• Industrial cooperation
	• Information society
	• Mining
	• Money laundering
	• Nuclear safety
	• Political dialogue
	• Public administration
	• Regional cooperation
	• Research and technology
	• Small- and medium-sized enterprises (SMEs)
	• Social matters
	• Statistics
	• Taxation
	• Terrorism
	• Visa and asylum

Source: Hofmann et al. (2017).

WTO-+ and WTO-X policy areas covered in PTAs today.

In the minds of today's policy community, the WTO is the central pillar of the global trading system that provides a fundamental set of trade rules under which all members can trade. Yet, when it comes to making trade rules for the twenty-first century, all eyes are currently set on preferential trade agreements as the preferred tool. Meanwhile, negotiations in the WTO also continue, along with debates on the Appellate Body crisis and WTO reform. To this we turn in the next section.

5.6.3 **The WTO in the twenty-first century**

Following the 2011 ministerial declaration that the Doha Round was at an impasse, various initiatives led to a negotiating outcome that few had thought possible, namely the adoption of the Bali Package at the 2013 Ministerial Conference in Bali. The Bali Package included a new Trade Facilitation Agreement (TFA), a decision on LDCs, and a decision on agriculture. In order to reduce the cost of trading, the TFA obliges members to speed up their customs procedures and underlines the need for technical assistance for the poorest countries. The TFA entered into force on 22 February 2017 when two thirds of the membership had ratified it. The Bali Ministerial also witnessed the disintegration of the G33 developing country group, with India remaining in an isolated position demanding that the SSM issue needed to be permanently resolved before closing the Bali Package. The year 2014 saw a dramatic stand-off between the US and India over the Bali 'peace clause', which stated that no country would be barred from food security programmes even if it breached the support limits specified in the WTO Agreement on Agriculture. While India's issue was resolved in this instance, the episode demonstrated that members' trust of the multilateral process was eroding.

At the next three Ministerial Conferences, 2015 in Nairobi, 2017 in Buenos Aires, and 2022 in Geneva, members managed to reach a number of decisions on long-standing and new issues. At Nairobi, the WTO reached decisions on the elimination of export subsidies in agriculture, SSM, public stockholding for food security purposes, cotton, and LDCs. A group of members also reached a plurilateral deal on information technology. The devil for the DDA however

lies in the detail of the Nairobi Ministerial Declaration. The text notes that 'many members reaffirm the Doha mandate', while others have 'different views on how to address negotiations'. This effectively means that there is no longer a consensus among members on the Doha Mandate. At Buenos Aires, plurilateral initiatives were taken to engage in negotiations on e-commerce, investment for development, and micro, small, and medium-sized enterprises (MSMEs). One hundred and nineteen WTO members and observers also adopted the Declaration on Trade and Women's Economic Empowerment. The Declaration is significant because it brings gender mainstreaming, which has long been a prerogative of global financial and development institutions, within the realm of multilateral trade governance for the first time (Hannah, Roberts, and Trommer 2018). The next Ministerial Conference was delayed by the COVID-19 pandemic but eventually took place in Geneva in June 2022. It reached a historical agreement on fisheries subsidies, as well as agreements on food security, a World Food Programme exemption, pandemic response, an IP waiver, e-commerce moratorium, and WTO reform. While some see these negotiating outcomes as displaying the continued relevance of the WTO, others argue that many of these agreements fall short of their own ambitions and fail to resolve the various trade problems that they aim to address (Narlikar 2022).

Some of the problems that plague multilateral negotiations include the high level of sensitivity of issues on the table. WTO institutional features have also been blamed. The consensus principle—which effectively gives any member a veto—can be cumbersome, and it can promote a lowest common denominator approach to decision-making. The obligation of Single Undertaking has made some countries resistant to the inclusion of new issues in the WTO agenda. Since the Nairobi meeting, there has been a return to plurilateral negotiations among subsets of WTO members, which had already been deployed during the Tokyo Round. For developed countries, this reintroduces a more flexible and supple approach to deal-making where smaller groups can advance their common interests within the WTO. However, many developing countries fear that this undermines their ability for collective bargaining and lessens the possibilities for trade-offs within the WTO. This could make it harder for them to secure wins in key areas of interest.

Since the launch of the Doha Round, the global economy has also changed. In 2013 China replaced the US as the world's largest trading nation, and the ongoing trade frictions between China and the US over aluminium, steel, and intellectual property and, increasingly, digital trade have led some commentators to question whether the WTO is equipped to deal with a confrontation of this magnitude. Ultimately, it is clear that the days when the US and the EU could shape the contours of a deal and when developing countries were not expected to make 'concessions' in negotiations are long gone. Smaller developing countries and LDCs have continuously built negotiating capacity and use coalition-building as an effective negotiating strategy. There is also no new coalition of major players in sight, with the US, the EU, China, and India all at loggerheads over international trade.

Finally, the Doha Round has also exposed the difficult relationship between trade and development policy. In the Doha Declaration, the objectives specified by all signatories clearly identified the main concern to be the betterment of developing and least developed countries. This was expressed in statements of belief that trade could play a major role in economic development and the alleviation of poverty and in statements of action, such as the intent to place the needs of the developing countries at the heart of the Doha Work Programme. This shift has politicized negotiations, because it has brought controversies over the appropriate trade and development policy mix into the WTO's negotiating arena.

Over recent years, disagreement has arisen in trade policy circles on whether the WTO is in crisis. The WTO's rule-making function appears dysfunctional from the perspective of most members. The WTO DSM remains popular and cannot easily be replaced by preferential trade deals. Nonetheless, it is also currently in crisis, with the US refusing to appoint members to the Appellate Body until the system has been reformed. The stance is often attributed to the hostility that the Trump Administration held for multilateralism and the WTO in particular. However, the blocking of new Appellate Body members was begun by the Obama administration and continued under President Biden (Narlikar 2022). On this issue, the US is at the helm of a group of members who believe that the Appellate Body has overstepped its mandate by adding rights and obligations that members had not agreed on in negotiations in order to adjudicate cases. The term of the last member of the Appellate Body expired on 30 November 2020, and there are currently no appeals heard in this organ. At the same time, consultations and panel hearings continue under the WTO's DSU, and members are still bringing cases. Led by the EU, an interim appeal arrangement under the DSU's arbitration clause has also been set up, allowing for appeals to take place under this temporary format.

These developments notwithstanding, it is clear that the multilateral system is in need of reform. Various WTO members and observers have been making reform proposals for some time (Hoekman 2011; Hoekman and Mavroidis 2021). Proposals range from changes to decision-making practices and clarifying developing country status, to rules dealing with the rise of China, as well as agriculture, digital trade, and climate change. At the same time, many, often poorer members still wait for their long-standing issues with the multilateral trade regime to be fully addressed. Any reforms that undermine their (limited) bargaining powers, and most notably changes to consensus decision-making, are unlikely to find their approval. At the time of writing, the political conflicts that have led to the WTO stalemate appear set to also plague any reform process.

For the time being, it is safe to say that we live in an era in which global trade is governed across a hybrid system relying both on the WTO and the network of regional and preferential trade agreements. This takes away the non-discriminatory character of the GATT/ WTO regime of the second half of the twentieth century. Negotiating on every issue separately with all trading nations is time- and resource-intensive for bureaucracies, and the resulting network of overlapping agreements can be difficult for business and civil society organizations to navigate. These pragmatic problems with the twenty-first-century hybrid trade regime may explain why many refuse to give up on WTO reform, despite the difficult politics that underlie it. In the final section, we discuss present challenges that the global trade system must address from within the hybrid model of trade governance.

KEY POINTS

- Governments often enter RTAs for political reasons. These include: enhancing security; improving their international bargaining positions; signalling to potential investors the seriousness of their commitment to reforms; satisfying domestic constituencies' demands for 'reciprocity'; and because they perceive that regional agreements are easier to negotiate than those within the WTO.

- Today, trade is governed in a hybrid format whereas certain matters are addressed at the WTO, while other topics are negotiated in the network of preferential and regional trade agreements.

- The hybrid model of trade governance allows for new rules to be developed even in the face of WTO deadlock. At the same time, it is by definition discriminatory and creates a complex and at times unintelligible rule book for global trade.

- While continually negotiating new PTAs, WTO members are also engaged in talks about WTO reform. These talks need to address the underlying political conflicts that have led to WTO stalemate in the twenty-first century in order to allow the organization to move forwards.

5.7 Global trade challenges

The challenges of WTO reform, of the role and position of emerging economies in the global political economy (see Scott, Chapter 12), and of persistent global inequalities (see Lockwood, Chapter 13) are all central for global trade moving forwards. In this final section, we focus on three trade topics that are important bones of contention within the trade regime and where we can also see a number of these wider challenges playing out. These are the linkages between trade and climate, the question of e-commerce and digital trade, and the debate about access to medicines.

5.7.1 **Trade and climate change**

Global trade and climate change are intimately linked. Trade can exacerbate climate change, climate change can alter trade patterns, and trade can be a tool in the global response to climate change. At the same time, the global governance regimes for climate and for trade have evolved separately from each other, and there is much potential for clashes between the two regimes, which needs addressing (Low et al. 2012). First, there remain significant trade barriers in environmental goods and services that plurilateral negotiations at the WTO have failed to remove. Second, trade barriers tend to be lower in carbon-intensive industries than in green industries (Shapiro 2021). Climate policies that increase the costs of energy

and carbon-intensive production can affect economic competitiveness, prompting governments to protect vulnerable sectors. Third, states may use the non-discrimination rules of the trade regime to challenge climate measures. Finally, there is an underlying difference in the goals and rationales of both regimes, whereby governments have set up the climate regime to constrain markets, whereas they have set up the trade regime to constrain their ability to shape markets. Both regimes have also been plagued by similar and linked political controversies about differential historical responsibilities for the current situation, and about appropriate forms of redress (Charnovitz 2003).

Nonetheless, the WTO recognizes climate change as an 'existential threat' in its 2022 World Trade Report titled *Climate Change and International Trade* (WTO 2022b). Efforts to address climate change at the WTO are aided by the fact that the Marrakesh Agreement establishing the WTO sets out sustainable development and environmental protection as goals of the multilateral trade system. Accordingly, WTO members are increasingly adopting climate-related trade measures, which can be reviewed in the WTO Environmental Database. These measures include technical regulations or specifications, grants and direct payments, conformity assessment procedures and tax concessions, among others, and fall mainly under WTO rules on subsidies and on technical barriers to trade (WTO 2022c). Explicit provisions on climate change can also be found in an increasing number of preferential agreements (WTO 2022d). Members are also beginning to discuss trade measures more within the spirit of trade as a means for achieving global public goods, rather than focusing on trade distortions. This is evidenced by the Trade and Environmental Sustainability Structured Discussions, the Informal Dialogue on Plastics Pollution and Environmentally Sustainable Plastics Trade, and the Fossil Fuel Subsidy Reform initiative (WTO 2022b).

At the same time, critics lament that environmental and climate rules in trade agreements are often unenforceable and that governments do too little to assess the true environmental impact of trade agreements. While they welcome climate-related trade measures, they point out that existing trade rules work to entrench carbon-intensive production and farming methods, slow down technology transfer, and give special rights to companies that allow them to enact measures geared at decarbonizing the economy (for a discussion of decarbonization see Ervine,

Chapter 16). They argue for a complete overhaul of the global trade system in order to put it on a sustainable footing (Klein 2015).

5.7.2 Digital trade

The digital transformation has brought about a new form of trading that the founders of the GATT regime could not have imagined, namely e-commerce and digital trade. While there is no authoritative definition of digital trade, there is growing consensus that it includes digitally enabled transactions of goods and services that can either be digitally or physically delivered and that involve consumers, firms, and governments (OECD 2023). At its core, digital trade involves the movement of data, for instance when an order is placed and processed online, or global value chains are managed and organized. Data transfer is also implicated in certain aspects of trade facilitation, 3D printing, the Internet of Things, and crowdfunding, all of which are relevant for digital trade. As such, digital trade brings about complex legal and regulatory issues linked to the arenas of data flows and data protection, logistics, IP protection, consumer and worker protection, and customs and excise (OECD 2023; Girard, Chapter 17).

Within the global trade regime, the WTO's second Ministerial Conference adopted a Declaration on Global Electronic Commerce in 1998, which launched a work programme on e-commerce and declared a moratorium stipulating that governments will not charge customs duties on electronic transmissions. In 2019 a plurilateral Joint Initiative on E-Commerce was begun, which by now involves eighty-seven members and covers over 90 per cent of world trade. Every Ministerial Conference since 1998 has confirmed the e-commerce moratorium. This practice has been critiqued by WTO members such as India and South Africa as well as UNCTAD as leading to revenue losses, particularly in developing countries where governments depend more on tariffs for revenue than in the developed world, and as being the 'equivalent to developing countries giving the digitally advanced countries duty-free access to markets' (WTO 2020c). A coalition of digitally advanced countries including Australia, Canada, Chile, China, South Korea, Norway, and Switzerland argue that the benefits of duty-free e-commerce outweigh the foregone government revenues (IISD 2020).

Meanwhile the regulatory issues raised by e-commerce and digital trade are starting to be addressed under a variety of domestic regimes of data economy, notably in the US, Europe, and China, which are slowly spilling into the FTAs of these players (Janow and Mavroidis 2019). The various regimes define digital trade and market access in digital trade, and devise regulatory models for data flow management and data protection. These issues are politically sensitive, as digital trade rules have a bearing on whether and how data flows across borders, how citizens' personal data is protected, and on the governance of the Internet and of new technologies such as artificial intelligence and algorithmic decision-making (Jones and Kira 2020).

5.7.3 Access to medicines

The implications of the WTO TRIPS Agreement on access to medicines has been a highly politicized issue in trade politics on numerous occasions.

When the HIV/AIDS epidemic ravaged Sub-Saharan Africa in the 1980s/1990s, a controversy arose around flexibilities on patenting rules in the WTO TRIPs Agreement. Members such as the EU and the US were initially keen to actively defend the protection of intellectual property rights. NGOs such as Médecins sans Frontières, Treatment Action Campaign, and Oxfam ran campaigns across the world to support the developing countries' position that provisions in TRIPs enabling the use of generic drugs to combat national health epidemics should not be undermined. By building and maintaining a successful coalition around TRIPs flexibilities, developing countries attained the adoption of the Doha Declaration on the TRIPs Agreement and Public Health at the 2001 Ministerial Conference in Doha (Abbott 2002). The declaration created a presumption that WTO members would be able to exercise their rights to procure generic medicines, and, more importantly, that other members (particularly the US) would be unlikely to take dispute settlement actions against members that exercised those rights.

The episode showed that business and civil society organizations often use similar strategies and tools to get trade policymakers on their side (Sell and Prakash 2004). In the lead-up to the TRIPs Agreement, the business community successfully managed to sell policymakers the idea that patent protection, free trade, and investment would be cornerstones of development across the global economy. In the lead-up to the Doha Declaration, transnational NGOs managed to frame the HIV/AIDS crisis as a problem of excessive intellectual property protection that made HIV/AIDS medication unaffordable. In each case, agenda-setting, coalition-building, and normative framing were key components of a successful trade campaign.

The pendulum on the TRIPS/access to medicines debate swung again when the COVID-19 pandemic spread across the globe in 2020 (see, for example, Furlong et al. 2022; Everyday GPE Box 5.6). COVID-19 killed millions of people and led to the biggest drop in global trade on record (WTO 2020a). In October 2020, India and South Africa proposed a WTO waiver to suspend patents and other TRIPS provisions in relation to the prevention, containment, and treatment of COVID-19 for the duration of the pandemic (WTO 2020b). The proposal carved out policy space for governments to scale up manufacturing capacities of medicines, vaccines, diagnostics, and other medical products essential to fight COVID-19. The EU, the UK, and Norway, among others, believed that existing IPRs enable the effective development and supply of medical products. They pointed to the 2001 Doha Declaration that reconfirmed TRIPS flexibilities. The US backed the TRIPS waiver in May 2021, with the important caveat that it supported a patent waiver only, when the original proposal targeted all products necessary to fight the pandemic. After intense negotiations, the WTO adopted the Ministerial Decision on the TRIPS Agreement at the 2022 Ministerial Conference in Geneva, which allows developing country members to authorize 'the use of the subject matter of a patent required for the production and supply of COVID-19 vaccines without the consent of the right holder to the extent necessary to address the COVID-19 pandemic' (WTO 2022e). While many members welcomed the decision, a group of developing country members, civil society coalitions, and critical observers argued that the waiver was not enough to help developing countries comprehensively address the COVID-19 and future pandemics. They argue that the COVID-19 waiver sets a bad precedent for pandemic preparedness, because it does not tackle systemic issues in unequal access to health technologies (Furlong et al. 2022).

EVERYDAY GPE BOX 5.6 TRADE, HEALTH, AND SOCIAL REPRODUCTION

The COVID-19 pandemic exposed the ambivalent links between trade and health. Trade helps produce welfare, knowledge, and technology, which can support health, but also acts as a vector for disease transmission and social and economic inequalities, which give rise to poor health (Woodward et al. 2002). COVID-19 destabilized global trade flows, which provoked crises in 'supplies of drugs and medical equipment, nutrition and food security, and government income necessary to pay for health services' (Barlow et al. 2021: 102).

Social reproduction is a useful analytical concept to consider the links between trade and health from a feminist standpoint. Social reproductive work includes care work for children, the sick, and the elderly, food provisioning, and other domestic and household chores necessary for daily life. Social reproduction aims to achieve or maintain health (Elson 2012) but can be carried out under conditions that undermine health (Doyal 1995). Social reproductive work is generally unpaid or underpaid, and, where it takes place in domestic spheres, it is not seen as forming part of 'the economy' (Bakker 2007), despite being essential for the productive economy to exist and function. Trade policymakers generally regulate trade based on the gendered view that

transnational flows of goods, services, money, and knowledge primarily affect the productive economy (Trommer 2022).

Trade agreements typically make liberalization commitments in goods and services trade and directly regulate trade-related areas, such as product and safety standards, IP, or investment, based on the idea that increased economic competition within the productive economy maximizes the welfare of society. Seen through a growth-focused, productive economy lens, the health effects of trade policy and the gendered impacts of trade appear as second-order issues in trade policymaking. Trade agreements typically include general exceptions and dedicate clauses or chapters to broader societal issues, such as health, gender, labour, the environment, etc., in order to balance the effects of standard commercial commitments on ostensibly wider areas of public policy. However, the orthodox view of trade as centred within the productive economy alone does not stand up to feminist scrutiny. Standard commercial commitments in trade agreements directly affect the global distribution of medical products, nutrition and food safety, health services, and a clean environment (Barlow et al. 2021), all of which

EVERYDAY GPE BOX 5.6 TRADE, HEALTH, AND SOCIAL REPRODUCTION (continued)

impact on human health and social reproductive labour. Trade agreements therefore directly affect health and social reproduction, although in complex and differential ways.

Trade agreements in their current form support good health and social reproductive conditions for some populations, but undermine these conditions for other populations (Trommer 2022). This is a feminist issue because women continue to be the primary providers of social reproductive work across the productive economy and domestically. Feminist trade research

furthermore suggests that women and other vulnerable groups tend to lack the economic, social, and political resources to absorb trade shocks (Van Staveren et al. 2007), and therefore tend to be disproportionately represented among those populations whose health and social reproductive conditions are undermined by trade agreements. The feminist view that social reproductive work is the essential work of society implies that the links between trade, health, and social reproduction are central trade issues, and not second-order, trade-related issues.

KEY POINTS

- WTO reform, the role and position of emerging economies in global trade, and persistent global inequalities present key challenges for global trade governance going forwards.

- Key controversies in the topics of trade and climate, digital trade, and access to medicines highlight how difficult these challenges are to tackle.

- At the same time these controversies underscore why a global and inclusive trade regime is needed, as no member of the trade policy community can resolve the various challenges on their own.

5.8 Conclusion

The focus of the global trade regime that was gradually established following the Second World War has been to create international agreements that allow the transnational exchange of goods and services with a reduced interference by national governments. Such agreements are an important form of regulation, or system management, in the international economy. The GATT, and now the WTO, are central features of the international trade system. Through negotiations in these institutions, countries established a rules-based regime for regulating international trade. The negotiation process is critically important to the success of the WTO, but it is a fickle and sometimes fragile process. When it is successful, the rules of the

regime are advanced, and all countries can be said to benefit from the greater stability and predictability that comes from a regime based on rules rather than on the play of power politics. But the negotiation process is not always successful, and the absence of consensus also stops the WTO from dealing with problems that many members think need to be addressed. When an impasse occurs in the WTO, there is always the fear that the organization will be eclipsed, and that countries will use other means, including unilateral actions, to resolve the problems they face in the international trade system. We can point to GATT/WTO history and see that multilateral trade cooperation has known many moments of crisis.

As it looks to the future, the greatest challenge facing the WTO will be to incorporate countries at varying levels of development fully into one multilateral organization and particularly to do this as countries graduate from 'developing' to more fully 'developed' status. The various recent crises in the negotiating and adjudicating functions may ultimately serve as a political wake-up call for all members to use their diplomatic skill and political power to realize their multilateral aspirations. As attractive as unilateral and plurilateral approaches appear in the here and now, they ultimately fragment the trading landscape, which comes at economic and political costs to all countries.

Since the 1950s, the GATT and the WTO have endured despite many challenges, but the task of implementing a global and inclusive trade regime continues to be the most imposing test of all.

? 5.9 QUESTIONS

1.   What is the significance of historical antecedents for global trade today? Give examples.

2.   What does non-discrimination mean in international trade and how is it put into effect by the rules of the GATT?

3.   What was the role of the developing countries in the Uruguay Round negotiation? Why was it historically significant?

4.   What were the challenges encountered in negotiating rules for trade in services in the Uruguay Round negotiation?

5.   How does the WTO differ from the GATT?

6.   What is the WTO DSU? Why is it necessary? What are some of the difficulties with its operations?

7.   What were the challenges for the WTO in conducting the Doha Round?

8.   For what reasons might governments prefer trade liberalization at the regional rather than global level?

9.   Is a hybrid global governance model for trade desirable? Why or why not?

10.   What are the major challenges facing the global trading regime and how could they best be addressed?

≋ 5.10 FURTHER READING

Bhagwati, J. (2008), *Termites in the Trading System: How Preferential Agreements Undermine Free Trade* (Oxford: Oxford University Press). Jagdish Bhagwati shines a critical light on preferential trade agreements (PTAs) to reveal how the over-saturation of PTAs endangers the world trading system by undermining principles of non-discrimination and has slowed the liberalization of trade.

Chang, H. J. (2002), *Kicking Away the Ladder: Development Strategy in Historical Perspective* (London: Anthem Press). Through this historiographical account of economic development, Ha-Joon Chang shows the tariff-dependence of early United States and Britain in the process of industrialization, and questions free trade arguments for development based on this history.

Deese, D. (2016), *Handbook of the International Political Economy of Trade* (Cheltenham: Edward Elgar). This handbook provides an overview of the politics of trade in the current era. Contributors from the fields of political economy, politics, economics, law, and policy studies examine trade policy and governance on its own terms in relation to key governance issues of our time.

Gallagher, K. P. (2004), *Free Trade and the Environment: Mexico, NAFTA and Beyond* (Stanford: Stanford University Press). Through this book, Kevin P. Gallagher examines two opposing views about free trade and the environment using the case of Mexico. The book concludes with suggestions for free trade policies that couple environmental benefits with economic integration.

Goldstein, J. (1993), *Ideas, Interests and American Trade Policy* (Ithaca: Cornell University Press). In a first-of-its-kind analysis of America's political past, Judith Goldstein seeks to expose and understand the contradictions in American policy and trade decisions.

Hoekman, B. M. and Kostecki, M. (2009), *The Political Economy of the World Trading System: The WTO and Beyond* (Oxford: Oxford University Press). A comprehensive textbook on the economics, politics, and institutional workings of the WTO.

Hopewell, K. (2021), *Clash of Powers: US–China Rivalry in Global Trade Governance* (Cambridge: Cambridge University Press). Kristen Hopewell provides critical insight into the question of how global trade has fared in the face of increasing tension between the United States and China.

Irwin, D. (1996), *Against the Tide: An Intellectual History of Free Trade* (Princeton, NJ: Princeton University Press). Tracing the origins of trade doctrine from pre-mercantilist times to Adam Smith and the classical economists, Irwin shows how Smith's ideas overtook those of protectionists and have endured the test of time.

Kay, T., and Evans, R. L. (2018), *Trade Battles: Activism and the Politicization of International Trade Policy* (Oxford: Oxford University Press). The book shows the impact of activism on the politicization of trade. Kay and Evans demonstrate how activism shapes trade policy and reveal the linkages between institutional opportunities and democratic practices.

Mansfield, E. D., and Milner, H. V. (2012), *Votes, Vetoes, and the Political Economy of International Trade Agreements* (Princeton: Princeton University Press). Through the critical study of PTAs, the authors integrate systemic and institutional influences on PTAs into a succinct and comprehensive framework for analysis.

Narlikar, A. (2003), *International Trade and Developing Countries: Bargaining Together in the GATT and WTO* (London, New York: Routledge). An analysis of coalition-building behaviour of developing countries in the multilateral trading system from the GATT to the Uruguay Round.

Sell, S. K. (2003), *Private Power, Public Law: The Globalization of Intellectual Property Rights* (Cambridge: Cambridge University Press). By examining the political landscape leading up to the TRIPS agreement, the first seven years of its institution, and the backlash it has faced in the wake of political and social crises, the book shows the power of private interests in international politics.

Singh, J. P. (2017b), *Sweet Talk: Paternalism and Collective Action in North-South Trade Relations* (Stanford: Stanford University Press). J. P. Singh exposes the 'emptyness' of Western trade benevolence through in-depth critical analysis of post-colonial paternalism and structural racism.

Van Staveren I., Elson, D., Grown C., and Cagatay, N. (2007), *The Feminist Economics of Trade* (London, New York: Routledge). This book explores the intersection of trade and gender through a feminist economics analysis of how gender inequality affects trade policy and vice versa.

Wilkinson, R. (2014), *What's Wrong with the WTO and How to Fix It* (London: John Wiley & Sons). A diagnosis of the ills of the WTO and a reform proposal that promises development for all.

CONTRIBUTOR NOTE

Silke Trommer is Senior Lecturer in Politics in the School of Social Sciences at the University of Manchester, UK, and Director of the Manchester Jean Monnet Centre of Excellence. Her publications include *Transformations in Trade Politics: Participatory Trade Politics in West Africa* (Routledge, 2014), and *Expert Knowledge in Global Trade* (with Erin Hannah and James Scott; Routledge, 2015).

6

Identity and Attitudes Towards Trade

Alexandra Guisinger

Reader's guide

International trade shapes everyday lives and life chances the world over. It helps determine what people eat, the clothes they wear, where they work, and how much they get paid for that work. At a more abstract level, trade flows can serve to strengthen global alliances or break them. Regulating who has the right to access markets has catalysed both international cooperation and conflict for centuries. While trade policy is often considered the purview of domestic and international elites, throughout modern history and across the globe, the public's preferences for increased or decreased market access have both shaped elite behaviour and at times stymied it.

Understanding how individuals develop preferences about trade policy is challenging but can help explain when and how the public matters. Economic explanations based on individuals' employment and consumption patterns have served as the basis for much of the scholarship on the public's attitude towards trade. Yet, such models fall short in predicting individuals' stated preferences and voting patterns. Notably, when directly asked, some individuals offer opinions incorporating different economic concerns or non-economic concerns such as national security. Many others express high levels of uncertainty.

The rest of the chapter considers alternative explanations for individuals' preferences for trade policy. In many societies, gender, race, and ethnicity shape individuals' economic outcomes. Trade—and especially change in trade flows—can serve to strengthen some forms of gender, race, and ethnic discrimination and shake up others. Trade policy distributes economic costs and benefits within societies and across countries. Individuals' beliefs about which people and which countries deserve the benefits or should bear the costs are themselves influenced by racial, ethnic, and gender concerns. Furthermore, the public's uncertainty about trade provides opportunities for political elites to shape public opinion on trade. The chapter concludes that political and media messaging serve to highlight and replicate gender, ethnic, and race-based biases in trade.

6.1 Introduction

Across the globe, we can observe contradictory trends. In opinion polls such as the 2018 Pew Research Global Attitudes Survey (Figure 6.1), acceptance and support for globalization as a concept appears high across advanced and emerging economies. At the same time and in many of the same countries, public backlash against trade in practice has slowed, stopped, or reversed specific trade liberalization policies.

The 2018 survey of the British public found that 89 per cent of respondents believed that trade was good for their country and only 8 per cent thought it was bad. In fact, compared globally, British respondents espoused some of the highest levels of support for trade among the advanced economies. Yet, only two years previously, via the Brexit referendum, the British public voted in favour of the United Kingdom's withdrawal from the European Union, the European Union Customs Union, and the European single market.

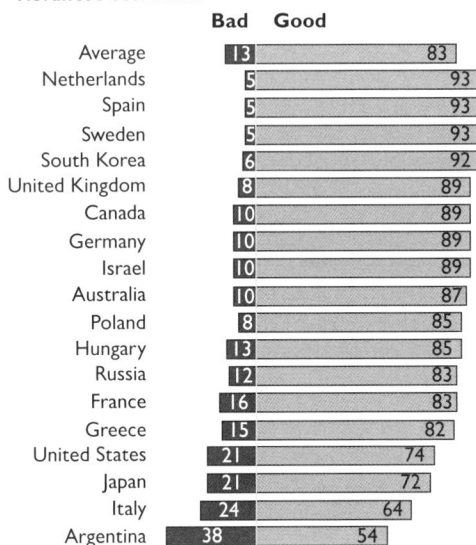

Figure 6.1 Cross-national public opinion on the national benefsts of trade

Growing trade and business ties with other countries is a _____ thing for our country.

Advanced economies	Bad	Good		Emerging economies	Bad	Good
Average	13	83		Average	14	81
Netherlands	5	93		Kenya	10	90
Spain	5	93		Indonesia	10	86
Sweden	5	93		Philippines	12	86
South Korea	6	92		Nigeria	15	83
United Kingdom	8	89		Tunisia	15	83
Canada	10	89		South Africa	17	81
Germany	10	89		Mexico	19	79
Israel	10	89		Brazil	23	72
Australia	10	87		India	9	71
Poland	8	85				
Hungary	13	85				
Russia	12	83				
France	16	83				
Greece	15	82				
United States	21	74				
Japan	21	72				
Italy	24	64				
Argentina	38	54				

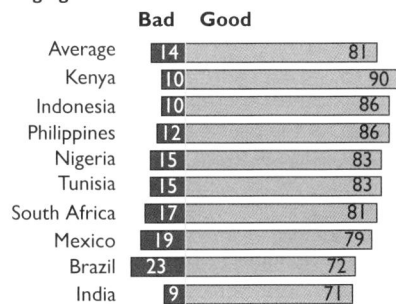

Source: Pew Global Attitudes Survey, 2018. https://doi.org/10.25940/ROPER-31115445.

Across the Atlantic, after decades of bi-partisan domestic support, the United States' global leadership on trade liberalization increasingly faces domestic pushback. Since the start of the twenty-first century, Americans' concerns about trade related job losses have hamstrung American trade diplomacy, supported tariffs targeting China, and led to US politicians on both the left and the right disavowing high profile, US-led multilateral agreements such as the Trans-Pacific Partnership (TPP). The 2018 Pew survey found that over 21 per cent of respondents believed that trade was bad for America and only 74 per cent thought that trade was good for the country, some of the lowest support among advanced economies. Hidden behind the averages is another cultural shift: individuals' beliefs about trade appear increasingly dependent on their partisan affiliation, a stark break from polls taken prior to Donald Trump's entrance into politics. In 2018, 46 per cent of Republicans stated that trade was a 'bad' thing for the US, compared to only 19 per cent of Democrats.

To the South, the belief among the Mexican public that trade is good has generally trended upwards since the implementation of the North American Free Trade Agreement (NAFTA) in 1994. In fact, the 2018 Pew research survey found higher support for trade among the Mexican public than among the American public, with 79 per cent of those surveyed saying that trade was good for the country and 19 per cent saying that trade was bad. But as in the US case, national averages hide a societal divide. In 1994, on the day that NAFTA came into effect, the Zapatista Army of National Liberation (EZLN), a militant political group representing Indigenous groups, publicly declared war against the Mexican government in an effort to counter the rise of neoliberalism and protest NAFTA-related agricultural reforms and changes to the constitution which undermined Indigenous land claims. Two decades later, the EZLN continues to control much of Chiapas—the southernmost state of Mexico—and continues to espouse its opposition to economic globalization.

These three snapshots of trade policy and trade opinion highlight a variety of puzzles in the literature: Why does the public both believe trade is good and vote against policies that support trade? How can individual preferences shift so radically in a short period of time? How does community and identity shape preferences for national-level policies?

Understanding trade attitudes requires identifying the types of costs and benefits individuals perceive

trade brings to themselves, their communities, and their nations, as well as where individuals receive information about the costs and benefits. While trade policy shapes the world around us—the goods we consume, the jobs available, and our country's strategic alliances—individuals often have limited information concerning the role of trade in their countries and communities. The setting of trade policy—whether through unilateral domestic legislation or through international negotiations—occurs away from their everyday experiences. For individuals to develop clear preferences for trade policy, they must directly (and correctly) perceive the effect of trade on themselves and their community or indirectly integrate explanations provided by motivated information purveyors such as unions, firms and industry groups, the media, and local and national politicians.

This chapter starts with traditional egocentric (or pocketbook) models of individual attitudes towards trade: models which predict preferences based on individuals' role in the economy. Later sections discuss models which focus on individuals' incorporation of community, national, and international considerations. The chapter concludes with the still open puzzle of the global gender gap in trade attitudes. At each level, a recurring question arises. How do individuals incorporate information about trade into their decision-making and how does identity shape individuals' access and response to information?

The chapter relies heavily on research from the United States and other economically advanced and democratic countries both for examples and quantitatively rich analysis. As outlined by Silke Trommer in Chapter 5, since the Second World War such countries have driven global trade liberalization in ways that have highlighted the conflicts between elite and public preferences in democracies and thus drawn the attention of scholars. These countries also have robust individual-level data collection programmes funded by governments and non-government entities that make possible extensive cross-time, individual-level research which would otherwise be too costly for many scholars. However, the tide is shifting both in terms of politically important actors and access to individual-based measures of public opinion. After the United States withdrew from the Trans-Pacific Partnership (TPP), Japan took the lead in organizing its next iteration. Emerging countries have been vocal globalizers at the World Trade Organization (WTO) and other forums. Mechanically, the spread of phones and tablets and the global proliferation of low-cost survey firms provides the opportunity to retest and expand theories using a broader and more diverse set of countries and individuals within those countries.

6.2 Egocentric models of individual attitudes towards trade

The starting point for most economic models of individual preference formation is how trade influences their individual economic circumstances via income and consumption or, in other words, how much individuals earn and how much they can purchase with their earnings. Due to the narrow focus on individual economic outcomes, these models tend to be classified as pocketbook or egocentric models, even when the calculation for the individual may incorporate broad costs or benefits to their community or nation.

6.2.1 Consumption models

Generally speaking, it is thought that individuals benefit economically from free trade through lower prices and a greater variety of goods.[1] Thus, if consumption concerns were primary, the public would favour increasing trade. Yet public support varies substantially over time and across countries. One explanation might lie in the disconnect between the expectation of economic models and public perceptions. In a 2018 Pew Research Center survey fielded in twenty-seven advanced and emerging economies, in only two countries (Israel and Sweden) did the majority of respondents perceive trade as decreasing prices (Stokes 2018). In the other twenty-five, the public believed that trade increased or made no difference to prices. Of surveyed respondents, 70 per cent in the set of advanced economies and 80 per cent in the set of emerging economies held beliefs counter to economic assumptions about the benefit of trade for domestic consumers. Everyday

---

[1] The preferences of consumers can be more nuanced. In some countries, the poor—and especially those outside of the wage economy—may purchase few to no imported goods, making the impact of trade on their household consumption negligible. In contrast, individuals in countries which export agricultural and raw materials widely used domestically might recognize that trade in the form of exports drives up prices for staples such as rice, wheat, and palm oil.

GPE Box 6.1 discusses why consumers may find it difficult to incorporate the cost of tariffs into their economic and political decision-making.

6.2.2 Class vs industry models of preference formation

The effect of trade on individuals' earnings is more complicated to model than that of consumption as it depends on assumptions about trade flows and on assumptions about how tied individuals are to their current profession and industry. When individuals are characterized by their role in production, scholars can identify more distinct groups of trade-policy-affected individuals, especially those in society who see their future earnings threatened by free trade agreements and increased trade in goods and services.

To predict the impact of trade on individual wages, models must first consider global trade flows. Despite advancements in trade flow models, the starting point for many trade preference models remains the Heckscher-Ohlin model (Heckscher 1919/1949; Key Theory Box 6.2). The H-O model predicts that countries liberalizing trade will export goods whose production intensively uses a country's abundant resources and will import goods whose production intensively uses a country's scarce resources. Countries characterized by an abundance of labour relative to capital, such as Bangladesh or Columbia, will tend to export goods whose production requires a lot of labour (for example, textiles or labour-intensive agricultural goods) and import goods whose production requires a lot of capital (for example, computers and machinery.)

One outcome of H-O trade is that domestic prices for scarce resources will fall while prices for abundant resources will rise, the so-called factor-price equalization theorem (Samuelson 1949). Owners of abundant resources would thus expect to see a benefit from trade liberalization, and owners of scarce resources, a loss (Stolper and Samuelson 1941). However, specifically who wins and who loses from changing trade policy depends greatly on how broadly these resources for production are defined.

Early work in this area (such as Rogowski 1987) recognized three classes of resources—land, labour, and capital—and predicted cleavages in public opinion based on individuals' ownership of one type of resource or another. In countries in which labour is relatively scarce compared to land and capital—such as the United States in the twentieth and twenty-first

EVERYDAY GPE BOX 6.1　BEER, FABRIC, AND THE INVISIBILITY OF TARIFFS

In comparison to other taxes, tariffs are relatively invisible to the standard consumer. Consider payroll taxes, income taxes, or sales taxes—common sources of government revenue in many countries. My paystub from Temple University in Philadelphia, USA, details eight different taxes deducted from my gross earnings, including healthcare tax, federal tax, state tax, township tax, and a tax for working but not living in Philadelphia. Each year, I file both a US federal and Pennsylvania state income tax return in which I detail every source of income from my wages to investments, look up my tax bracket, and calculate individual taxes on each. At the grocery store, the receipt shows not just the itemized purchase but the additional state sales tax on the last line—both as a proportion to total sales and the absolute number. Some gas stations publicize the current gas tax on top of their pumps. I know these taxes in detail, but how much do I pay each year due to taxes on trade?

Most countries post detailed, itemized lists of their tariff schedules. Interested consumers could go to the WTO website or a national website and download the information specific to an imported pair of shoes or a cotton T-shirt. However, unless they were personally importing the goods from abroad, they would not necessarily pay the specific tariff costs. Domestic firms sourcing goods from abroad pay different tariff rates depending on the country and can choose how much of the tariff to pass through to the final consumer. Pass-through is the proportion of increased costs that firms choose to offset by increasing or lowering prices. Just as firms face a choice to lower profits or raise prices when facing increased gas, food, or labour prices, firms must choose how much of the tariff cost to pass

through to customers when tariff rates suddenly change due to a change in supplier origin or a change in the tariff rate itself.

Generally invisible to the public, the tariff pass-through choice hit the US news cycle in 2018 when President Donald Trump instigated a series of tariffs directed against China on goods ranging from fabric to steel and semiconductor chips to washing machines. US household names like JOANN Fabrics—the largest fabric and craft retailer in the US—and MillerCoors brewing company spoke directly to consumers about the extra costs they would incur. The CEO of JOANN Fabrics emailed their customers to note that the proposed 25 per cent tariffs would jeopardize 'your ability to continue creating at an affordable cost'. In newspapers and on air, Pete Coors laid out the math of why tariffs would increase the cost of a 'cold can of beer on a hot summer day'. Other domestic retailers kept more silent, but their pass-through choices still hit the news for a different reason. The Trump Administration's China tariffs first increased to 20 per cent and then 50 per cent for washing machines. Domestic retailers not only passed through most of the tariff costs to consumers by raising prices for washing machines, but they also raised prices on the frequently paired product of clothes dryers. US consumers spent an additional US$1.5 billion a year on washers and dryers as a result of the tariffs, according to economists at the Federal Reserve. Typically such costs would go unnoticed, but the sudden imposition and public response by some corporations and researchers raised the issue of consumer costs of tariffs to the forefront of the news cycle and into consumer email boxes—albeit briefly.

KEY THEORY BOX 6.2　HECKSCHER-OHLIN

The Heckscher-Ohlin (H-O) model of international trade and its extensions is a widely used economic model developed to discuss the implications of lowered trade barriers on the flows of exports and imports between countries. A more technical version of David Ricardo's original theory of **comparative advantage**, the Heckscher-Ohlin starts from the assumption that countries vary in their **factor endowments**—or, in other words, the three resources needed to produce goods and services: land, labour, and capital.

Some countries have relatively abundant land and labour but a scarcity of capital. Other countries may have high reserves of capital but relatively scarce access to land and labour. Since scarce inputs will be more expensive, goods using domestically abundant resources will be cheaper to produce than goods using domestically

scarce resources. The production cost benefits of using abundant resources drive the implications for trade. Countries have a comparative advantage in goods that intensively use abundant resources and thus should specialize in the production of those goods for sale domestically and abroad while, in turn, importing goods that intensively use domestically scarce resources.

Heckscher-Ohlin predicts strong trade flows between capital-abundant (developed) countries and capital-scarce (developing) countries. For example, think about the international flows of agricultural products. The US (a capital- and land-abundant, labour-scarce country) produces capital-intensive agricultural goods such as wheat, corn, and soybeans while importing labour-intensive agricultural goods like soft fruits and organic produce from Mexico and other more labour-abundant countries.

KEY THEORY BOX 6.2 HECKSCHER-OHLIN (continued)

The model underpins the related Stolper-Samuelson theorem, which provides expectations about the effect of trade flows on labour and capital. Stolper-Samuelson states that if the price of a good increases—for any reason—then the returns to factors it uses intensively will also rise. Thus, if, following the H-O expectations, labour-abundant countries export goods that intensively use labour (such as textiles) for higher prices on the international market, then labour should see a relative rise in wages. Conversely, in capital-abundant countries the export of capital-intensive goods brings higher returns to capital to the detriment of labour, who will see the real value of their wages fall. Whether labour in labour-abundant countries has, in fact, benefitted from trade openness remains a contentious debate (for example, Feenstra and Hanson 1996; Dorn, Fuest, and Potrafke 2022).

Heckscher-Ohlin-based models have received criticism for their restrictive assumptions and poor predictive power. The bulk of modern international trade occurs between similarly endowed industrial countries. In the face of empirical divergence from Heckscher-Ohlin expectations, rising inequality, and increased anti-globalization sentiment, GPE scholars have revisited more specialized models to account for trade in primary commodities (Harvey et al. 2010), the influence of returns to scale and network effects (the New Trade Theory, for example, Krugman and Helpman 1985), and trade in intermediaries (the updated New New Trade Theory, Melitz and Redding 2015). Yet, Heckscher-Ohlin remains the standard reference for considering the domestic economic implications of trade and subsequent political cleavages over trade policy.

centuries—trade would be expected to lower labour's wages while raising the profits of capital and landowners. More sophisticated models distinguish between different levels of labour—generally skilled and unskilled workers as defined by educational attainment (see, for example, Leamer 1984)—but the prediction structure remains similar: individuals of similar socio-economic status should share similar preferences for trade.

Class-based models create easily identifiable societal cleavages both in the US and elsewhere but rest on the assumption that resources (labour, capital, and land) flow with a low cost between different industries. When resources are less mobile—that is, tied to particular industries—then individuals' preferences may be less influenced by their identity as capital, land, or labour and more influenced by their industry

identity. In sectoral models, scholars assume that the owners of the **factors of production** (see Key Concept Box 6.3) (land, labour, and capital) participating in the economic activity of a specific industry share the impact of trade and thus share preferences for trade policies. If trade creates increased competition for the auto industry, then all individuals bound to the industry—from stockholders and the CEO to engineers and custodians—should share preferences on trade policy which affects the growth and profitability of the auto industry and, more narrowly, the specific firms to which they are linked financially. For models assuming limited **mobility** (that is, owners of a factor of production would pay a high cost to exit from one industry and enter into another), understanding individual preferences requires knowing both individuals' industry affiliations but also whether those industries

KEY CONCEPT BOX 6.3 FACTORS OF PRODUCTION

The primary factors of production are traditionally defined as land (natural resources), labour (workers), and capital (money) necessary for the production of goods and services. Some recent works simplify the factors to focus on two types of labour—skilled and unskilled—as measured by education.

The endowment of these factors of production—the relative abundance within a country of land, labour, and capital—helps determine which goods a country can make most efficiently. Abundant resources are relatively cheaper than scarce resources. Thus, countries have a **comparative advantage** when

producing goods that intensively use their abundant resources and a **comparative disadvantage** in producing goods that intensively use their scarce resources.

With free trade, countries should export goods that intensively use their abundant resources. Stolper-Samuelson (see Key Theory Box 6.2) predicts that trade will thus increase the returns for owners of abundant resources and decrease returns for owners of scarce resources. These relative gains and losses should then produce political coalitions based on the ownership of the resources (Rogowski 1987).

are export-oriented import-competing, or neither (so-called non-tradables such as education, healthcare, and public services).

In sectoral models, low mobility theoretically binds workers (skilled or unskilled) and capital together, cutting across class lines. Yet, low mobility alone is not necessarily enough to ensure shared preferences for trade policy within an industry. Dean (2015) noted that unions in the steel and textile industries of the late nineteenth century supported higher tariffs as long as both labour and capital benefitted from higher tariffs, but when structures that ensured profit sharing via formal negotiations ceased, then the unions publicly spoke against the tariffs their employers supported. Additionally, not all factors of production need to be equally tied to an industry. Some scholars, such as Alt and Gilligan (1994), envision capital tied to industries but labour mobile. Rather than make assumptions about mobility, Hiscox (2001; 2002) uses wage and profit differentials to calculate the mobility of factors across time in different countries in order to predict whether trade preferences will be organized by class or by sector.

6.2.3 **Empirical testing of economic models**

As a whole, these production-based models of individual preferences offer clearly defined, testable predictions linking individual skill level and employment to trade preference in the United States and elsewhere. Furthermore, the groups defined by production-based theories fit neatly into existing political interest groups, be they defined broadly by classes or specifically by industry: labour parties, unions, and industry coalitions. That said, numerous surveys conducted to test these models of individuals' preferences have shown that respondents' economic welfare narrowly defined can explain only a small portion of the variation in preferences for trade protection (see, for the debate, Fordham Kleinberg 2012).

Not only do individuals' responses in surveys often differ from theoretical expectations, but also many individuals' responses to questions about trade policy take the form of a non-answer: they 'don't know', 'can't choose', or 'neither agree nor disagree', depending on the options available. In 2013, the International Social Survey Programme (ISSP Research Group 2015) asked representative samples of the public across thirty-three developed and emerging economies whether they agreed or disagreed with the statement

that their country 'should limit the import of foreign products in order to protect its national economy'. On average, a quarter of the public in each country answered either 'Neither agree nor disagree' or 'Can't choose'. The public in some countries expressed little uncertainty. In Croatia, only 11 per cent offered a non-answer, while 80 per cent agreed. In contrast, in Japan, 47 per cent expressed uncertainty.

Kleinberg and Fordham (2018) note that individuals express greater uncertainty about foreign policy in general but especially foreign economic policy. In the US, uncertainty about trade policy preferences appears to be on the rise. Since 1986, the American National Election Studies (1986–2012; 2010) has regularly asked a representative sample of Americans whether they would support or oppose 'new limits on foreign imports'. The question wording is a little tricky, framing the question in terms of a policy change from current levels and requiring individuals' ability to decode what is meant by limits on foreign imports. However, with minor changes, the question has remained the same across four decades. During that time, Americans have expressed greater and greater uncertainty. In 1986 when the question was first asked, less than one third of respondents failed to provide a definitive 'support' or 'oppose' answer. In 2016, the proportion providing a non-response answer was 48 per cent.

One potential explanation for a large number of 'don't know' responses and the gap between theoretically based predictions of individuals' responses and actual survey responses may be due to individuals being simply unaware of trade's economic impact on their personal circumstances. In surveys fielded in the United States in 2006 and 2010, Guisinger (2017) found that although individuals expressed clear beliefs about how trade affected employment in the United States, relatively few—less than 30 per cent—could identify how trade affected their own employment. Most individual preference models expect individuals to understand trade's effect on their own economic outcomes.

To better understand how much misperception or a lack of perception about one's own economic circumstances matters when forming preferences for trade, Rho and Tomz (2017) designed a research project to measure the effect of educating participants in the expectations of current economic theory. First, they asked a sample of approximately 1,500 Americans to predict the distributional consequence of limiting imports intensively using non-college-educated labour and the consequence of limiting imports intensively using college-educated labour on the economic outcomes for domestic college-educated and non-college-educated workers. In the US case, the Stolper-Samuelson model (Key Theory Box 6.4) predicts that limits on imports of low-skilled labour-intensive goods (for example, textiles, labour-intensive agricultural goods, furniture, etc.) help non-college degree holders at the expense of college-degree holders and vice versa in the case of limits on imports using college-educated labour (for example, chemicals, pharmaceuticals, software, etc.). Less than a third of respondents' answers matched the expectations provided by economic theory. As a follow-up, Rho

and Tomz then implemented a survey experiment in which they trained a randomly selected group in the class-based expectations of the Stolper-Samuelson model and then compared their preferences for trade protection to the preferences of the control group. The effect of information was mixed. On average, college-degree holders informed of Stolper-Samuelson expectations of the winners and losers of trade limits on specific types of goods decreased their support for trade protection on goods using non-college-educated labour and increased their support for trade protection on goods using college-educated labour. In other words, information narrowed (although notably did not close) the gap between individuals' responses and

---

KEY THEORY BOX 6.4 RICARDO-VINER VS STOLPER-SAMUELSON MODELS OF ECONOMIC INTERESTS

When considering the distributional effect of trade, the political economy literature generally uses one of two assumptions to characterize individuals' interests: the sectoral-based Ricardo-Viner model or the class-based Stolper-Samuelson model. Both start by assuming individuals' ownership of a single factor of production: traditionally, land, labour, or capital. These factors of production do not themselves cross borders, although the goods they produce can. Furthermore, owners of these factors of production cannot switch their type (that is, use the wages of their labour to become capital). The primary difference between these models is the assumption about their mobility, or the ability to move from one sector to another in response to changing market conditions.

In the Stolper-Samuelson model, factors of production are fully mobile domestically. As trade liberalizes, the abundant factor can move to the sector which is able to export and thus can benefit from higher returns. In contrast, the importation of goods that intensively use a country's scarce resources generates competition for the owners of that resource, whether or not the owner is directly involved in import-competing production. As such, Stolper-Samuelson predicts winners and losers to be organized by class, with trade-affected labour sharing their interests with all labour, trade-affected capital owners sharing their interests with all capital owners, and trade-affected landowners sharing their interests with all landowners.

Many recent articles update the Stolper-Samuelson model to identify two types of labour: skilled and unskilled labour (generally measured by education level). A developed (capital-abundant) country should, according to Heckscher-Ohlin expectations, export goods that intensively use skilled labour and import goods that intensively use unskilled labour. The result is that trade economically helps skilled labour and economically

hurts unskilled labour, leading to an expectation that political coalitions will divide these two groups and their preferences for trade.

In the Ricardo-Viner model, the factors are not fully mobile domestically. As a result, the economic outcomes of owners of the factors of production are primarily determined by the outcomes of the industries to which they are linked, regardless of whether they own a scarce or abundant resource. For example, returning to a simplified two-factor model in which there exist two types of labour—skilled and unskilled—we can observe the distributional consequences of increased trade. As before, a developed (capital-wealthy) country should, according to Heckscher-Ohlin expectations, export goods that intensively use skilled labour and import goods that intensively use unskilled labour. However, because labour cannot easily move between different sectors, in the Ricardo-Viner model both the skilled and unskilled labour associated with the export industry 'win' while both the skilled and unskilled labour associated with the import-competing industry 'lose'. The economic outcome creates cross-class cleavages as both types of workers will wish to increase or decrease trade protection according to the benefits of their sector rather than their class.

The two models offer predictions based on either end of the spectrum of mobility from non-mobile to full mobility. The ability of factors of production to move between sectors is historically and institutionally contextual. Some scholars, such as Hiscox (2001; 2002), have explored how changes in mobility result in shifting political coalitions. Others have offered empirical tests to better understand which best predicts preferences and political behaviour in a specific context (see, for example, Magee, Brock, and Young 1989; Scheve and Slaughter 2001).

economic expectations of their responses. However, non-college degree holders informed of the distributional consequences of trade limits on specific types of goods decreased their support for limits on imports intensively using non-college-educated labour. In other words, information increased the gap between their material self-interest and their responses. Rho and Tomz's findings suggest that information provision matters but not always in predictable ways, that individuals may mix both self-interest and altruism, and that much of individuals' preference formation process still remains to be explained.

The economic models remain popular for a reason. They are parsimonious yet help explain many general observations of trade policy discussion among the public. Yet their simplicity can obscure other economic considerations and the way in which political structures and discourse shape individuals' beliefs and behaviour. The remaining components of the chapter assume individuals incorporate additional concerns about the influence of trade on themselves, their communities, and the country. Doing so requires attention to how individuals incorporate their own and others' identities into their calculations, how identity issues—gender, race, and ethnicity—interact to reshape preferences, and how political discourse can aid, exacerbate, or suppress such identity-based divisions.

KEY POINTS

- Traditional economic models of trade preferences focus on an individual's role in production or consumption patterns.

- Production-focused models tend to group individuals either by their economic class (land, labour, or capital) or by their industry affiliation. If trade liberalization hurts the group, individuals within the group should support protection, whereas if trade liberalization helps the group, individuals within the identified group should support liberalization.

- Consumption-focused models tend to classify individuals in terms of the types of goods they purchase (domestic or imported). Those for whom trade decreases the price of goods they buy should support increased trade liberalization.

- Empirical tests of the production- and consumption-based models find that such groupings imperfectly predict individuals' responses in surveys.

- A potential explanation for the inconsistent link between individuals' economic characteristics and their trade preferences is that individuals may lack the necessary information to calculate the economic cost or benefits of trade for their own outcomes.

- One attempt to provide individuals with the necessary information to make decisions according to the economic models results in mixed outcomes in terms of closing the gap between economic predictions and individual responses.

6.3 Incorporating individuals' community and national considerations

When asking the public's beliefs and opinions about trade, national opinion surveys tend to ask about general rather than individual effects of trade: Is trade good for your country? Does trade increase or decrease wages in your country? Does trade with other countries lead to job creation or job losses in your country? Does trade with other countries lead to an increase or a decrease in products sold in your country? Should the government impose trade restrictions to protect American . . . or British . . . or Mexican jobs?

To highlight the contrast between pocketbook- or egocentric-based policy evaluations and nationally based policy evaluations, Kinder and Kiewiet (1981) coined the term 'sociotropic politics'. In sociotropic political decision-making, individuals look beyond their own outcomes to consider how policies would impact the broader community. Kinder and Kiewiet assumed that citizens moved by sociotropic information—such as whether trade is good for the country—would vote for politicians (and thus policies) that 'furthered the nation's economic well-being' despite their own economic concerns. Kinder and Kiewiet recognized that the information costs for sociotropic politics are substantially higher than for pocketbook voting but voiced the opinion that citizens need only develop 'rough evaluations' of national economic conditions, leaving open the question of how these evaluations come to be and how wholistically individuals incorporate other citizens into their considerations.

The insight that voters incorporate national- and community-level considerations about the benefits to others into their evaluations of government policies is firmly ingrained in the comparative public policy literature but is relatively new to the study of trade preferences, despite clear theoretical expectations that self-interest, community interest, and national interest might differ. Economic theory predicts that while the nation as a whole should benefit from freer trade in the long run, certain groups of individuals—particularly those with skill sets or in industries that are at a comparative disadvantage—pay the short-term costs.

Structures within society can further concentrate gains and losses among societally defined groups. While trade liberalization—particularly in developing countries—has created new opportunities for some groups previously denied access to markets due to their gender or ethnicity (Beviglia Zampetti and Tran-Nguyen 2004), trade liberalization can also reaffirm existing divides (Hannah et al. 2022). In particular, those who are more economically vulnerable may struggle with both trade liberalization and de-liberalization as both bring costs, volatility, and added uncertainty (Roberts et al. 2019; Brutger and Guisinger 2022). Increased volatility from trade can create additional burdens for women already balancing work inside and outside the home, yet such concerns only recently began to appear in trade policy discussion, and with mixed results (Hannah et al. 2023). Indigenous groups have also faced additional burdens from trade and trade liberalization. Historically trade agreements have overlooked and undermined their interests (Borrows and Schwartz 2020). For example, in preparation for the North American Trade Agreement, the Mexican government removed a constitutional provision protecting communal lands from privatization. Other trade agreements failed to protect communities' cultural property and left traditional economic structures vulnerable to foreign imports. The new iteration of NAFTA—the United States–Mexico–Canada (USMCA) agreement signed in 2018—provides specific protections for Indigenous rights, their environmental concerns, and preferential treatment of Indigenous benefits (albeit less than initially proposed). Similarly, the 2021 Indigenous Peoples Economic and Trade Cooperation Arrangement (IPETCA), endorsed by Australia, Canada, New Zealand, and Taiwan, highlights advancements in recognition and inclusion while also calling attention to the specific costs incurred by Indigenous groups in the face of globalization. Both the examples of women and Indigenous groups serve as reminders that the losers of increased globalization are not uniformly distributed across a nation, nor are individual perceptions of national benefits as uniform (or as positive) as might be expected.

Early work in this field that considered sociotropic influences, such as Mansfield and Mutz (2009), examined the broad dichotomy between perceived benefits to oneself and perceived benefits to the nation. Incorporating beliefs about national benefits helps to close the gulf between individuals' perceptions of their own self-interest and their preferences for policy. In the run-up to the 2016 US presidential election, in which trade policy played a prominent role, a much smaller proportion of individuals (less than 25 per cent) thought trade hurt their own employment than thought trade hurt national employment (more than 60 per cent), and their support for trade protection reflected both considerations (Guisinger 2017). In developed and developing countries in which individuals have a more positive outlook on trade's effect on the nation, individuals express less support for trade protection.

Yet beliefs about national-level benefits are only one definition of sociotropism. Sociotropism also incorporates friends and family, neighbours and neighbourhoods, communities and regions. Scholars (for example, Niemi, Bremer, and Heel 1999) have found that individuals can and do assess distinct economic outcomes for the nation, sub-national communities, and themselves. However, these perceptions can rely heavily on word-of-mouth rather than direct experience and thus are malleable to the influence of motivated information providers. Furthermore, for individuals to incorporate sociotropic considerations into their preferences requires that they also determine who matters to them. This section on sociotropic concerns thus focuses on these two factors: how individuals form their perceptions about others' benefits from trade and the extent to which individuals privilege some beneficiaries over others.

6.3.1 Media

Economists have often noted the inconsistency that while their economic models suggest that trade is beneficial for a country as a whole, the public tends to hold more cautious views of trade. One standard assumption is that the risk of losses—not just at an individual level but at a national level—concerns the public. Thus, the potential for job losses from a trade agreement weighs more heavily than the potential for job gains. A related explanation relies on the concept of negative news bias: that the media's selection of coverage-worthy stories appears to privilege bad news over good news. Whether the bias arises from bad news making better press, the media's focus on holding actors accountable, or simply that journalists like the mass public—are more responsive to negative events, media coverage of economic issues is highly correlated with negative news about those issues.

News on international trade appears to follow the same pattern as economic news more generally: the frequency of trade-related stories increases with negative news, the coverage of trade focuses on negative news, and news stories are more likely to incorporate negative consumer and producer narratives than positive (Guisinger 2017). For example, when the US trade deficit shot up at the start of the 1980s, so did the frequency of trade-related articles in the *New York Times*, whereas decreases in the trade deficit received less attention. As individual events, job losses, especially factory closures, receive more press than job gains and factory openings. Furthermore, Brutger and Strezhnev (2022) find that Canadian and American newspapers are more likely to run articles about their countries' respective losses in trade courts than their countries' wins.

Scholars of social media see similar trends. Analysing Twitter discourse on the Transatlantic Trade and Investment Partnership (TTIP), Ciofu and Stefanuta (2016) calculated negative hashtag use outstripped positive hashtag use 99–1, or in other words, positive statements concerning the TTIP constituted approximately 1 per cent of all Twitter coverage. Finally, in terms of content, news stories concerning trade liberalization or 'globalization' tend to focus on the threats rather than on the benefits. The highlighted threats extend past economic job losses and labour concerns. Analysis of US national newscasts reveals that the most common framing of trade links trade to safety concerns about food, health, the environment, and security. Representative titles included 'China–US Trade Relations: Import Safety Worries'; 'Food Supply Safety, Poisoning Prevention Measures'; and 'Children's Toy Imports from China Safety Worries'. Representative top stories covered a House of Representatives' hearing into FDA import inspections flaws, the monitoring of lead paint in Chinese products, the FDA's ban of generic pharmaceuticals from a plant in India, and traces of Brazilian pesticides found in orange juice imports. Even trusted neighbours and trading partners appear suspect in trade news. In 2003, a year in which the US's top trading partner was Canada, the only two stand-alone stories about Canadian trade on the most watched of American evening news programme (the ABC Evening News) were the possible danger from imported Canadian pharmaceuticals and the US government's ban on Canadian beef imports because of fears over mad cow disease.

Only recently, as developed countries have reversed their position on trade liberalization, has the **negative news bias** swung around in trade's favour. Both prior to and in the aftermath of the United Kingdom's 2016 referendum on staying part of the European Union and consequently part of its common market, attention turned to individuals and industries that would suffer from a less free exchange of trade (see Harmes, Chapter 11). In contrast to prior years in which the news was about trade liberalization and its risks, here the news was about a return to trade restrictions and their risks, especially in terms of higher consumer prices, a narrative whose salience increased in the early 2020s as the country faced rising inflation. At the same time, in the United States Donald Trump was threatening and subsequently imposing a series of new tariffs. Each roll-out of new tariffs against lumber, steel, and washing machines received media attention focused on the consumer costs of these tariffs—a shift from the previous period of media concern about the employment costs of trade protection. Although Trump's proposal of a broad-ranging Border Adjustment Tax (the so-called BAT Tax) via an executive order imposing a 15 to 35 per cent tax on imported goods never came to fruition, the threat stirred a response from US retailers and many domestic manufacturers who relied on imports. The National Retail Federation (NRF) created a public-facing fake infomercial entitled the 'B.A.T. Tax is a BAD tax' (Figure 6.2) which not only

Figure 6.2 The National Retail Federation's response to Trump's proposed Border Adjustment Tax (the BAT Tax)

INCOME-CHILLING
TAX-BRINGING
JOB-KILLING

B.A.T. TAX

Source: National Retail Federation

informed Americans of the range of goods taxed, 'it will tax your car, your food, your gas, your medicine, your clothes', but also promised them 'the new job-killing formula' as a special bonus. The ad turned on its head the traditional way political ads discuss trade in the United States.

Although the developed world and the United States in particular have pushed internationally for the expansion of trade liberalization since the end of the Second World War (see Trommer, Chapter 5), domestic political discourse has centred on protecting those made vulnerable from trade expansion. As discussed in Everyday GPE Box 6.5, since the start of the twenty-first century in the United States, only a handful of

political campaign ads for presidential, Senate, or House of Representative races have described trade in a positive light. The vast majority of trade-related campaign ads depict the negative consequences of trade—closed factories, lost jobs, and blighted communities. Even politicians who sign trade-liberalizing bills run trade-protecting campaign advertisements. In 2012, Public Citizen—a progressive think tank—highlighted half a dozen Republican incumbents running ads against trade liberalization despite what Public Citizen characterized as a '100 percent track record of support for every single NAFTA-style trade deal arising under their tenure' and called out another eighteen Democrats and Republicans who supported the Korea

EVERYDAY GPE BOX 6.5 POLITICAL CAMPAIGN ADS

Trade policy is generally decided by national legislatures or executives—not referendums—and thus discussion of trade policy tends to coincide with national elections. In the United States, the currently standard thirty-second television campaign ad provides very little time for nuance. Incumbents and challengers have a limited time to signal their merits and distinguish themselves from competitors. While candidates hone the content of their ads strategically to focus on framing key issues for the constituency most likely to support their candidacy, the campaign ads play in front of a general, relatively uninformed audience. Analysis of campaign ads can highlight both the types of individuals for whom trade policy is politically salient and also how elite discourse can influence beliefs about trade more broadly.

Compared to other issues, trade-related campaign ads are relatively scarce in twentieth-century US campaign cycles. Even in the 2016 US election, when trade rose to prominence, only 3 per cent of the 2,753 campaign ads run in major media markets discussed trade, and trade-related campaign ads ran for less than 2.5 per cent of the total airtime and only 2.8 per cent of the time for presidential ads.[2] Furthermore, the distribution is uneven, with the majority of US major media markets (fourteen of twenty-three) showing no trade-related political ads. Even though trade affects many US industries, trade-related ads tend to be highly concentrated in manufacturing districts. Where they are run, trade-related ads can be hard to avoid. Almost a quarter of all campaign ads shown on air during the Wisconsin Senate race and 12 per cent during the Ohio Senate race included references to trade.

The content of trade-related campaign ads is almost never positive. Take a look at some US trade-related campaign ads on YouTube or from the online Political TV Ad Archive. In US trade-related campaign ads, trade destroys American jobs or ships them overseas. In recent years, despite substantial US trade with Canada and Mexico, trade-related campaign ads focus on Chinese–US trade relations. Images of sweatshops, red-washed backgrounds, and claims of 'stealing' generate an ominous backdrop for claims that the US government must do more to protect Americans against trade.

The campaign ads also provide context for who would be protected and from whom. The beneficiaries in the campaign ads are predominantly hard-hatted, white, and male blue-collar workers. Women workers appear infrequently and at much lower proportions than their employment in trade-protected industries merits. Asian Americans almost never appear, and Asian-appearing faces are almost universally shown as an external threat.

Anti-China rhetoric, white faces, and a focus on traditional manufacturing sell trade protection in today's United States. This limited presentation of the effect of policies serves to highlight one segment of trade-affected society while effectively erasing others, such as the consumers who pay the cost of tariffs, workers whose jobs depend on trade exports, or women and non-white men who work in the trade-affected industry but due to their exclusion from campaign ads may view such policies (and politicians) as doing little to benefit them. With a broader information environment, the specific presentation of trade policy in campaign ads would matter less; but in a society in which voters learn about policies in the period preceding the election, the specific frames of trade-campaign ads strongly shape general perceptions.

[2] The raw data is available from the Political TV Ad Archive and is on file with the author.

free trade agreement yet still ran ads against offshoring (Public Citizen 2012). More commonly, politicians choosing to liberalize trade policy minimize discussion of trade policy. The combined result is a stream of negative political information on trade with little public pushback from trade-liberalizing policymakers.

6.3.2 **Privileged industries**

The second characteristic of developed country discourse is the focus on a core set of industries. In Britain, during the debate over Brexit, trade discussions focused on industries such as fishing, more traditional manufacturing, and steel. Across Europe, textiles, apparel, steel, and agriculture are considered sensitive industries capable of mobilizing public opinion in ways that technology, chemical, and, until COVID-19, pharmaceutical industries do not. Within developed countries, the protection of agriculture resonates strongly, even as negotiators push developing countries to liberalize on their behalf. Why do some industries and workers galvanize the public or segments of the public when others do not?

One explanation lies in geographic concentration. Concentrated industries support a strong informational infrastructure. Trade policy has the potential to pit industries against each other and create confusion about whether trade policy is good or bad for a region or a country. A geographically concentrated set of related firms provides a less complex calculation of pros and cons. Thus, the more unified the economic base of a community, the easier it is for community-focused organizations and political leaders to develop specific and uncontroversial recommendations and the clearer their message about preferences for trade protection. Concentrated industries can also interact with local media, where such media still remain. Local media, particularly print media, provide a different economic picture than the national media (Goidel et al. 2010), which is particularly important in considering trade policy. To the extent that economic characteristics differ at the local and national levels, the effects of trade also differ. Local media, where they remain, can propel narrow and deep trade narratives. In turn, the concentration of industry influences individuals' preferences as well as behaviour. Marc Busch and Eric Reinhardt (2000) show that high industrial concentration is linked with stronger preferences among regional workers, high contributions to political campaigns, and higher voter turnout.

The concentration of industry, especially during developed countries' manufacturing boom, now has, in general, served to heighten attention to competition from imports. Many developed countries have specific regions with high concentrations of import-affected industries: the northern manufacturing cities of the United Kingdom; East Germany; the Rust Belt in the US; Nord–Pas-de-Calais and Lorraine. The economic decline of these regions has received substantial media and political attention. In the UK both the rise of the far right and support for Brexit appear correlated to geographic centres of industrial decline (Power 2018). In the US, some scholars have found evidence of a positive correlation between the concentration of job losses from China's entry into the WTO—the so-called China shock—and increasingly negative perceptions of trade (see Scott, Chapter 12, for further discussion). The extent to which these changes arise in individuals' own perceptions of regional economic consideration versus political messaging and other partisan and cultural factors remains under dispute. As shown in Figure 6.3, in the United States the distribution of trade-related campaign ads shows disproportionate attention to so-called rust-belt regions. Individuals in export-oriented states such as Texas and California may not see a single trade-related campaign ad throughout an election cycle, while in Pennsylvania, Michigan, and Ohio, residents may struggle to avoid them. Such communications can propel a small group of individuals' economic concerns into larger regional and even national concerns. Political campaign ads targeting affected individuals can influence the larger community via saturation. As the large community's preferences coalesce, in specific circumstances these can become national discussions. Pennsylvania, Michigan, and Ohio are 'swing' states whose outcome can determine the US presidency and the partisan majority within the trade-setting Senate. In contrast, the trade policy concerns of the diverse industries of California—the most populous US state, the largest state contributor to the US gross domestic product, and the second largest state in terms of exports—receive almost no national campaign attention.

Not all salient industries benefit from geographical concentration, and concentration alone cannot explain why certain industries gain broader national support, especially when trade protection can raise national consumer prices. The widespread public support across developed countries for the protection of agriculture offers a particular puzzle. Trade-related subsidies, import restrictions, and import tariffs raise food prices

Figure 6.3 Concentration of pro-protection trade-related ads in the 2008 election (as a percentage of total ads in each market)

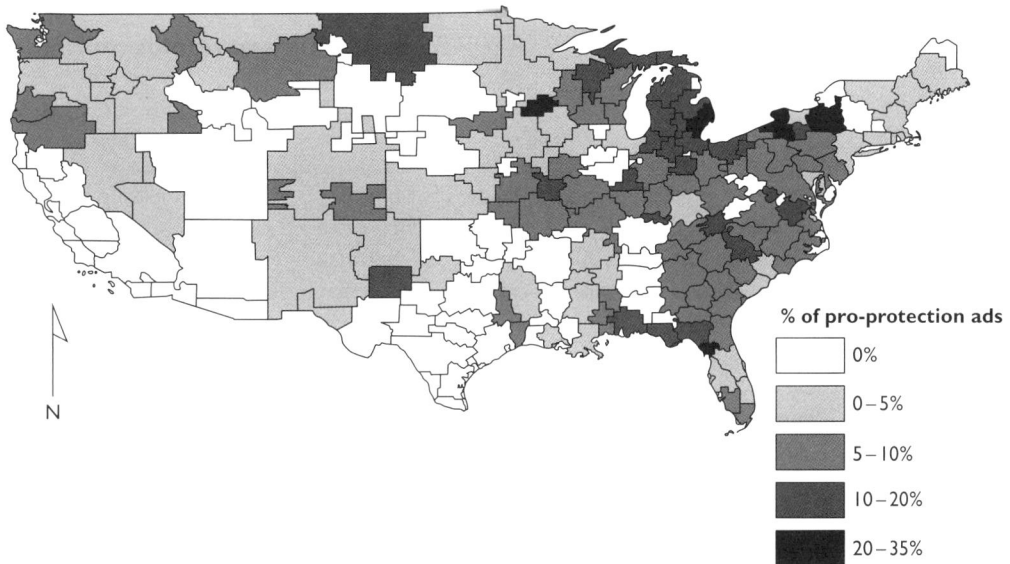

% of pro-protection ads

- 0%
- 0–5%
- 5–10%
- 10–20%
- 20–35%

N

Source: https://elections.wisc.edu/wisconsin-advertising-project/.

across developed countries. And while the concentrated political power of agriculture versus the diffuse political interests of consumers might explain the sector's political success in achieving protection, it does not explain the support for these protectionist policies among the public. In a compilation of surveys, Naoi and Kume (2011) found that across Organization for Economic Cooperation and Development (OECD) countries in the late 2000s, in the midst of a global recession, and despite the consumer costs, public support for the protection of the agricultural industry was equivalent to or exceeded opposition: 43 to 44 per cent in the US (March 2009); 50 to 36 per cent in Europe (fall of 2007), and 55 to 38 per cent in Japan (February 2009).

It is important to understand why Megumi and Kume designed a survey experiment in which they primed participants to think in terms of consumers or producers. They found surprisingly that while the consumer primes insignificantly influenced individuals' responses, producer primes consisting of photos of Japanese farmers increased concern about food imports. Further analysis suggested that respondents related to producer images via projection: individuals with the greatest concerns about their own job security responded most strongly to pictures of Japanese farmers whose livings would

be endangered by greater trade liberalization. In other words, the consumers with the most to gain from cheaper food imports most strongly aligned with farmers.

Projection could also partially explain the powerful influence of trade-related political campaign ads which focus on firms and industries that provide relatively few jobs. In the United States, manufacturing and steel industries repeatedly star in trade-related political campaign ads. Yet, manufacturing employs an increasingly smaller number of Americans (less than 10 per cent) and steel even fewer (just 0.04 per cent). The demographic shift means not only that fewer individuals are directly concerned with trade protection, but also that fewer communities have a reason to be directly concerned with increasing or decreasing trade protection. By 2006, in the majority of all US counties, manufacturing accounted for less than 10 per cent of employment. In half of these counties, manufacturing accounted for less than 5 per cent of employment. In such counties with relatively few involved in import-competing manufacturing, the community benefits of trade protection may not be readily apparent. And yet, manufacturing-heavy trade-related ads effectively shift the opinion of viewers who do not themselves depend on manufacturing jobs and in regions without a concentration of manufacturing jobs.

To demonstrate the power of narratives about specific industries, Guisinger (2017) designed an experiment to measure the response to a protectionist campaign ad narrowly focused on the protection of US steel workers from import competition. In 2014, from a sample of 500 adults from across the United States, Guisinger randomly selected 250 to watch 'A Couple of Miles', a trade-related television advertisement for Sal Pace, an unsuccessful Democratic challenger in Colorado's 3rd congressional district in 2012. In the ad, a steelworker narrates how Pace changed regulations to prevent non-American steel from being used in Colorado building projects as the ad provides visual images of the narrator himself, a bridge built with Chinese steel, and multiple shots of American steelworkers such as that shown in Figure 6.4. All participants (those who had watched 'A Couple of Miles' and those in the control group who watched an unrelated ad campaign) then answered questions both about their support for trade protection and their perceptions of the beneficiaries of trade protection. Those who watched 'A Couple of Miles' were 14.1 percentage points more likely to support limits on trade and 5.2 percentage points less likely to oppose new limits on trade protection than those who did not—nearly a 20-percentage-point difference in favour of trade protection. When asked who they thought benefitted from trade protection, those who had watched 'A Couple of Miles' were more likely to respond that trade protection helped blue-collar workers, but this doesn't alone explain the swing since this is not a characteristic that most respondents shared with the steel workers. One characteristic that many respondents did share with those in the Sal Pace ad, and those in the US trade-related ads

Figure 6.4 Steelworkers shown in 'A Couple of Miles', a trade-related television advertisement for Sal Pace

Source: Library of Congress

more generally, was their race. In the absence of shared employment or socio-economic status, how much difference does shared identity make?

6.3.3 Deserving and non-deserving beneficiaries

Which individuals deserve government support? In considering the answer to how societies determine the distribution of benefits, comparative political science offers a rich set of theories linking community characteristics to preferences regarding collective and public goods that have yet to be incorporated into discussions of trade policy. Trade policy is redistributive in that it creates economic winners and losers, and although individuals typically support some level of redistribution in response to inequality, redistributive policies propel debates about who deserves redistribution. Societies may differ in their identity groupings, but across different contexts scholars have found that individuals distinguish between in- and out-groups when considering who is deserving of redistribution.

Lü, Scheve, and Slaughter (2012) consider the role of self-centred inequity aversion: the assumption that individuals use their own economic standing to determine whether others deserve altruism or not. In terms of who deserves trade protection, the authors assume that individuals will support policies that provide benefits to lower-earning, less-skilled workers. Class distinctions matter, but unlike Stolper-Samuelson- or Ricard-Viner-based models in which expectations of trade support vary conditionally upon the characteristics of the country, expectations are similar across developed and developing countries. Individuals should support policies geared towards those whose economic fortunes are well below theirs but not policies geared towards those whose economic fortunes are well above theirs. The focus is on relative equity rather than solely self-interest. Using a paired experiment in the United States and China, the authors found evidence that respondents incorporated other workers' economic outcomes into their policy preferences, but only for those in sectors in which workers' incomes are substantially lower than the respondents'. While the theory can provide some insight into sectoral differences in trade protection when pay differentials are known, it raises other questions about identifying the deserving beneficiaries. In the United States case, many of the jobs shown as worthy of protecting pay well over minimum wages and yet receive general support from poor and wealthy alike. Individuals may be misinformed about the beneficiaries' economic expectations. For example, information campaigns concerning agriculture seldom discuss corporate farms and almost universally show small family farmers. Individuals may also simply be uninformed. Without clear pay differentials allowing for inequality aversion calculations, individuals in the United States and elsewhere may seek cues about other considerations when forming their preferences.

For countries with more diverse publics, perceptions of who benefits from trade protection can highlight identity-based concerns about the relative protection of in-groups versus out-groups. Public policy scholars have already noted that racial divisions decrease support for redistribution (see, for example, Austen-Smith and Wallerstein 2006). Not only is trade protection a form of redistribution, but also the combination of race- and ethnicity-based employment sorting as well as choice in framing the beneficiaries of trade protection can highlight the cross-group distributional consequences.

Gaikwad and Suryanarayan (2019) focus particularly on support for trade liberalization in developing countries characterized by 'ranked ethnic systems': societies where ethnicity and economic class overlap (Horowitz 2000). In such countries, members of low-ranked groups face employment discrimination regardless of their skill level. Under the status quo, individuals from low-ranked groups have few opportunities for advancement and may even choose to under-invest in their skills development because of lower rates of return than for individuals from high-ranked groups. In such conditions, trade liberalization in a developing country offers individuals in low-ranked groups both the potential for occupational mobility in a changing and less discriminatory economy and the potential for low-skilled workers who are a developing country's comparative advantage in the world market.

To test their theory, Gaikwad and Suryanarayan analyse individual support for trade protection and liberalization in three ranked and one non-ranked ethnic societies: India, the Philippines, South Africa, and Nigeria. As expected by a Heckscher-Ohlin (class-based) model, low-skilled individuals were more supportive of trade liberalization. But specifically in the ranked ethnic societies of India, South Africa, and the Philippines, both high- and low-skilled individuals expressed greater support for trade liberalization.

In contrast, in Nigeria, a country in which ethnic groups are differentiated but not clearly ranked in society, identification with an ethnic group did not correlate with support for trade liberalization.

As a further test of their theory, in 2017 Gaikwad and Suryanarayan fielded a survey experiment on a large, nationally representative sample of voting-age citizens in India. Before asking about individuals' support for trade liberalization, the researchers provided information about which types of individuals were likely to benefit or lose from trade liberalization. The experiment randomly varied whether the information provided focused on ethnic identities, skill level, both, or neither. By comparing the average responses of participants, Gaikwad and Suryanarayan could observe a difference between individuals in high- and low-ranked ethnic groups. Individuals in low-ranked ethnic groups—regardless of their skill level—increased their support for trade liberalization when they learned that trade would help coethnics. In contrast, the knowledge that coethnics would benefit did not increase support among individuals in high-ranked ethnic groups.

In developed countries, trade liberalization creates a different set of winners and losers. One of the most visible effects of trade liberalization in developed countries has been the loss of jobs in manufacturing and related sectors and diminished incomes for those without a college degree. The job losses receive disproportionate media and political attention, as would be expected by psychological theories of risk aversion. Political campaign ads frame these trade-affected workers as particularly deserving of government support, in contrast to much of the rhetoric surrounding welfare recipients whose need is often framed as their own responsibility. As a general rule, Americans—especially white Americans—support trade protection at much higher levels than other types of redistribution, such as welfare.

Yet, the gap between support for redistribution via trade protection and via welfare may only be partially explained by the different presentations of responsibility. In the US, the manufacturing jobs threatened by trade have traditionally been disproportionately held by white men. Furthermore, political campaign ads disproportionately feature white men (Guisinger 2017), a stark contrast to the disproportionate representation of African-American women in discussions of welfare (Kellstedt 2000; 2003). To understand how much of the difference arises from racialized concerns, Guisinger

(2017) fielded an experiment that varied the race of the worker benefitting from trade protection (see details in Case Study 6.6). Guisinger found that white people are more likely to support trade protection when the beneficiaries appear as other (in-group) white people rather than (out-group) African Americans. Thus, a portion of domestic support for trade protection relies on expectations of benefits accruing to the in-group.

CASE STUDY 6.6 WHO DESERVES GOVERNMENT SUPPORT? RACE AND REDISTRIBUTION

Like many tax policies, trade protection is redistributive: some citizens pay more so that others receive a direct or indirect subsidy. Whether the government places a tariff on imports or restricts their entry, trade protection causes domestic consumers to pay more than they would otherwise for protected goods and their immediate substitutes. Domestic producers of protected goods directly benefit, as do related industries, related workers, and potentially their local communities. As such, trade policies in general—and trade protection in particular—can economically privilege some segments of society at a cost to others. In other words, trade protection generates economic redistribution.

In the US, as in many countries, societal cleavages—be they linguistic, religious, ethnic, or racial—appear to influence support for redistributive policies. For example, Martin Gilens (1999) and Paul Kellstedt (2000; 2003) found that the disproportionate political and media depiction of welfare beneficiaries as minorities diminished white American support for welfare.

In the case of trade protection, the current depiction of beneficiaries in the US is the reverse. In an analysis of 531 trade-related congressional, gubernatorial, and presidential campaign advertisements running in the country's largest media markets between 2000 and 2012, Guisinger (2017) found that pro-protection campaign ads overwhelmingly depict the face of trade as white, working-class, and male. On average, one minority worker for every nine white workers was depicted as a beneficiary of trade policy. Sixty per cent of the time, there were no minority faces. While many depictions of the American populace skew white and male, this portrayal is unusual for a redistributive policy.

To find out whether the depiction of white beneficiaries mattered, Guisinger conducted a survey experiment on a sample of 850 US respondents and randomly assigned each participant to read one of three subtly different versions of a brief newspaper-style article, entitled 'Data Shows Struggling Manufacturers, Costly Imports and Gloomier Consumers'.

One group read a short version of the news story that provided no individual depiction of affected workers. The story was illustrated with a picture of a factory floor captioned 'Jobs in the U.S. manufacturing sector have declined as imports have doubled'. The two other groups read a longer version

that began with the same text but also included a brief description of a recently laid-off worker and his difficulties making ends meet:

[Name] worked for Delphi auto parts until being laid off last month. His union job once earned him $50,000 a year, enough to support his family comfortably and send his oldest daughter to college. 'At my age I don't know if I will be able to find a different job and I don't have the savings some do. I just don't know what I am going to do now,' said [Name].

In the 'Black' beneficiary version, the laid-off worker was named 'Cedric Washington', and the accompanying picture showed two unnamed, middle-aged Black men at an employment fair. In the 'White' beneficiary version, the laid-off worker was named 'Randy Snyder', and the accompanying picture was of two unnamed, middle-aged white men at an employment fair. After reading their respective versions, all respondents answered whether they supported, opposed, or had no opinion concerning a policy of increased trade protection.

Changing the depiction of the beneficiary of trade protection diminished whites' support of trade protection. White participants who read the 'Black' beneficiary version of the news story demonstrated higher opposition to increased trade protection than those who read the 'White' beneficiary version of the news story (36 per cent to 29 per cent). Similarly, support for increased trade protection was lower (41 per cent to 45 per cent). The combined effect totals an 11-percentage-point swing in support—although nothing else changed in the article, and the respondents were randomly assigned the article version.

By itself, the finding that the framing of trade in terms of white, male, and blue-collar workers increased support might not be surprising, but in contrast with other redistributive policies such as welfare—which are predominantly illustrated with non-white and female faces—the presentation and different response is stark. White Americans are more comfortable offering redistribution to the beneficiaries shown in trade-related ads than they are with spending on welfare.

Source: Guisinger (2017).

6.4 Trade and attitudes towards foreign countries

Although economists since Adam Smith have viewed trade as a cooperative endeavour benefitting both importer and exporter, the public appears to strongly weigh not just the distributional consequences but also the identity of the trading partner. As Herrmann, Tetlock, and Diascro (2001) noted, the mass public makes judgements like 'intuitive Realists and intuitive Rawlsians'; in other words, the public would prefer that trade benefits their own country over others, that it benefits allies over enemies and the disadvantaged over the advantaged. These traits leave public opinion on trade agreements vulnerable to framing by political entrepreneurs.

6.4.1 **Perceived fairness**

Public concern with the fairness of trade has served as a hook for both protectionists and liberalizers. During the post-Second World War development of multilateral trade agreements, supporters of the General Agreement on Tariffs and Trade (GATT) and the WTO framed the benefits of institutional arrangements as creating the rules, adjudication processes, and punishment mechanisms necessary to diminish unfair trading practices between countries (see Trommer, Chapter 5). As Davidson, Matusz, and Nelson (2006) note, in the short term this focus on fairness via institutionalization served to insulate trade liberalization from public debate by enshrouding trade regulation in technical terminology. However, in the longer term, losers from trade liberalization have reclaimed the rhetoric of fair trade to rail against trade agreements.

What do various publics see as fair? The question arises both in prospective expectations of trade agreements and retrospective evaluations. Brutger and Rathbun (2021) argue and find support for a definition of fairness based on equality rather than equity. In their survey of Americans, they found that participants believed trade agreements that structure concessions and benefits equally across all member countries are fairer than ones that provide participants with gains relative to their contributions. Since countries can substantially differ in their initial economic conditions, this preference for equality generates a hurdle for trade agreements across dissimilar economies on both sides. For example, as discussed in Chapter 5, developing countries have long criticized the WTO for prioritizing developed countries' access to developing markets and stalling on developing countries' access to developed countries' agricultural markets. For their part, developed countries point to provisions both in the GATT and the WTO for more favourable treatment of developing countries.

One complicating factor for domestic publics evaluating the fairness of trade or any international agreement is the asymmetry of information once an agreement is in place. Looking at investment disputes, Brutger and Strezhnev (2022) found that not only is the media more likely to cover negative news concerning international institutions' impact on domestic companies, but also that reading such news has a strong negative effect on support for international institutions. In the case of China, Tanya Schweinberger (2022) notes a disproportionate use of fairness terms in both the media and political discussion surrounding US–China trade. She finds that this language successfully influences preferences both in China and in the US and thus offers a tool for political elites seeking to shape public preferences.

Furthermore, the power of perceived fairness and the relative lack of information available to the average citizen creates the opportunity for predispositions to matters. Brutger and Li (2019) find that publics are more likely to trust the outcomes of trade agreements when members are similar ('like-minded') rather than dissimilar, suggesting the identity of trading partners and their non-economic characteristics influences public opinion. As they note, the identity of trading partners is a commonplace and salient component of news and political media surrounding trade agreements.

6.4.2 The identity of the trading partners

What aspects of a country do individuals consider when forming their opinion about trade? In many developed countries, trade has become synonymous with imports from China. Guisinger (2017) found that even before China became the United States' top trading partner the majority of respondents already believed it to be so, and that their perceptions mattered in their support for trade protection. Those who received a correction that it was, in fact, Canada that was (at the time) the primary trading partner were substantially less supportive of trade protection and more likely to oppose increasing trade protection. Despite their breadth of trading partners, political discussions of trade in the US and, to a lesser extent, Europe continue to focus on China, mixing the economic concerns of trading with a rapidly developing country with cultural, political regime, and security concerns (see Scott, Chapter 12).

The role of cultural similarities in public support for trade can be difficult to distinguish from the natural tendency to trade more with neighbouring countries than distant countries. Spilker, Bernauer, and Umaña (2016) made use of a distinct type of trade agreement—preferential trading agreements, or PTAs—in order to test the theory that cultural similarities would influence support for trade from specific countries. They fielded a survey experiment in Costa Rica, Nicaragua, and Vietnam in which they varied multiple characteristics of a proposed PTA partner. As well as the economic characteristics of the size of the country and distance, they randomly selected potentially important characteristics such as types of public holidays, religion, type of political regime, and security alliances. They found that respondents in all three countries strongly preferred partner countries with a similar culture and religion as well as democracies.

Cultural identity does not appear to be equally important across the public. Looking specifically at consumer choices, Sabet (2013) found that the name of the firm affected by a trade tariff only mattered to the most prejudiced respondents. In a similar vein, Mutz and Kim (2017) found that individuals with higher levels of in-group favouritism were, in general, less supportive of trade liberalization. More specifically, in the United States Mutz, Mansfield, and Kim (2021) found that both observationally and in survey experiment, white respondents in America preferred trade when they believed the trade would be with more culturally and racially similar countries, but that these racialized preferences did not influence non-white respondents.

Additionally, cultural similarities do not guarantee positive perceptions across the public as a whole. In his analysis of European support for the TTIP, Nils Steiner (2018) found a strong correlation between individuals' negative perceptions of the United States and, specifically, its role in world politics and country-level support for the TTIP agreements.

Early work in public opinion on trade preference found support for the idea that, unlike elites, the public preferred trade agreements with allies rather than enemies (Herrmann, Tetlock, and Diascro 2001). However, the primary source of empirical evidence came from the US. More recently, Carnegie and Gaikwad (2020) have fielded new surveys in both the US and India to better understand how strongly geopolitics shapes public opinion on trade. They find that whether a country is an ally or an adversary is central to the respondents' support for trade with a country unless trade with an adversary is explicitly framed as a strategic decision to foster peace and only if trade with an adversary will not improve the adversary's military capability.

The question of who constitutes an ally and who constitutes an adversary is influenced by a large number of factors, including race and ethnicity. Búzás argues that since the Second World War, the liberal international order has been structured along racial lines. The entrance of China into the WTO highlighted existing fractures in the trade agreement but also brought to the forefront the conflict between choices to integrate or isolate China in light of its growing economy and increased geopolitical influence (for further discussion see Scott, Chapter 12).

6.5 The gender gap in trade preferences

The 2017 Pew Survey (Figure 6.5) showed a definite pattern in trade preferences: a gender gap. As shown in Figure 6.5, in many developed and developing countries, women—on average—express greater support for trade protection than men. Although not the case for every country-year, scholars have noted the consistency of the finding in analyses of US surveys (see, for example, Scheve and Slaughter 2001; Guisinger 2009;

Mansfield and Mutz 2009), Latin America surveys (see Beaulieu, Yatawara, and Wang 2005), and international surveys (see, for example, O'Rourke and Sinnott 2001; Mayda and Rodrik 2005). Given the reliance on economic models to predict preferences, researchers first considered how gender might influence consumption and employment patterns and through them attitudes towards tariffs.

Tariffs both directly and indirectly affect consumer prices. Recognizing a gendered division of economic activities in which women undertake a higher proportion of consumption, some scholars have linked increases in women's political participation to increases in trade liberalization (Hall, Kao, and Nelson 1998). However, this assumed causal relationship appears to run counter to empirical findings that women are on average more supportive of protectionist policies. Recent literature does, however, find support that women face a so-called pink tax in tariff rates for women's goods and that the gap is lower in countries with higher proportions of women representatives at the national level (Betz, Fortunato, and O'Brien 2020). Most countries utilize a version of the Harmonized Commodity Description and Coding Systems (HS) when setting trade tariff schedules. The HS system differentiates clothing

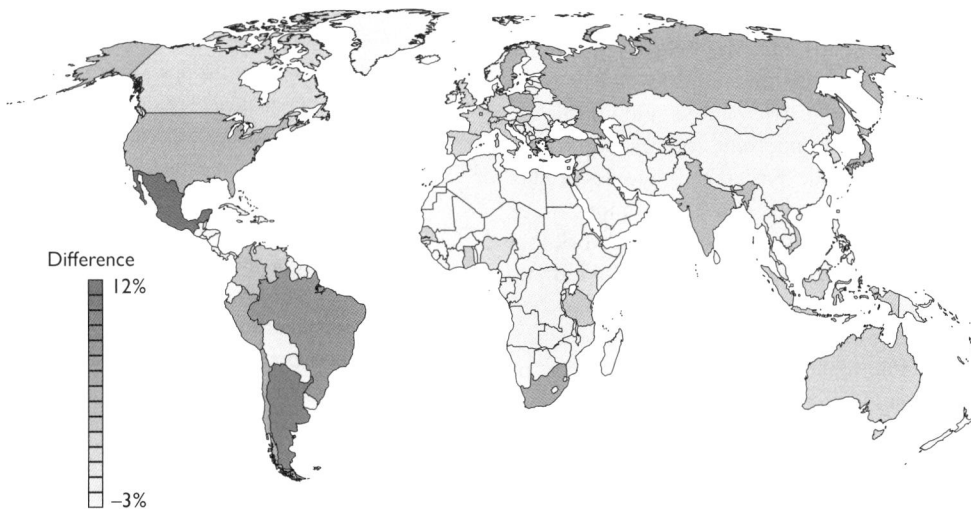

Figure 6.5 Difference between men's and women's belief that trade is good for the country (PEW 2017)

Difference
12%

−3%

Source: Pew Research Center. Question 5a from International Social Survey Programme ISSP 2013—'National Identity III'—ZA No. 5950, http://dx.doi.org/10.4232/1.12312.

by gender, allowing for a direct comparison of pairs of goods (for example, cotton pants) differentiated only by whether they are marketed towards men or women. When Betts et al. analysed approximately 200,000 such paired tariff rates on men's and women's apparel products in 167 countries between 1995 and 2015, they found nearly 40 per cent of the pairs differed in the applied tariffs. Overall, women's apparel carried a higher tariff. The opacity of the HS coding system and tariff schedules would, in general, prevent the average consumer from relating the price of their purchases to these differentials. But legislators and their staff are in a position to identify and respond to such discrepancies, especially as the WTO and the World Bank have moved to highlight the gendered effects of trade. Betts et al. find that as the proportion of women legislators increases, the differential 'pink tax' generated by applied tariff rates diminishes. Their findings suggest a specific role of women legislators in equalizing, if not lowering, the consumer cost of tariffs on specific goods, but again this does not explain the average women's greater support for protection across imported goods as a whole.

Tariffs also both directly and indirectly affect domestic wages and, as discussed in Section 6.2.2, do so systematically but unequally across occupational skill levels and sectors. Many developed and developing countries exhibit gender-based educational, occupational, and sector segregation in which men and women disproportionately sort into high- and low-skilled work and into different industries. If women in developed countries select—by choice or by necessity—occupations requiring fewer years of education or industries more vulnerable to trade, then Stolper-Samuelson- and Ricardo-Viner-based models of trade preferences would predict that they would be more concerned about wage losses from trade. Yet, the same empirical work that showed the gender gap already controlled for individuals' skill level and sector of employment. Furthermore, in developing countries these same selection processes should make women more supportive of trade than men. Developing countries export goods utilizing less educated labour, and export industries such as textiles have provided women new outlets for their labour, allowing many to enter the wage economy and generate an independent income. Considerations of selection processes do not close the gap and, at times, serve to exacerbate the gender gap in preferences.

6.5.1 | Gender and differences in attitudes

A rich literature has considered both essential and socially constructed differences across genders as a source for women's greater support for protectionism. One strand of this literature considers other observed differences in attitudes as a source for the gender gap in attitudes towards trade. For example, scholars have attempted to explain the gender gap in trade via empirically identified gender differences in views towards competition, willingness to move, greater altruism and concern for disadvantaged groups, and the relative importance placed on societal welfare. Identifying the relationship is a first step that can create further scholarship teasing out potential underlying causes and developing research designs to test causality.

Take, for example, findings that men and women differ in risk-orientation and that risk-averse individuals are more likely to support trade protection (for example, Eckel and Grossman 2008; Ehrlich and Maestas 2010). While some scholars assume innate differences, others consider how constructed differences might shape women's willingness to accept increased risk. Globally, childcare is unequally divided between fathers and mothers, and, additionally, the proportion of women-headed households is increasing (Craig and Mullan 2011). At the same time, workforce structures continue to disadvantage working women—single or married, with or without children. The COVID-19 economic crisis starting in 2019 highlighted the dual pressures of caregiver responsibilities and labour force inequities. Globally, women's unemployment dropped by 4.2 per cent compared to men's 3 per cent, according to the International Labour Organization (ILO 2021). Well before COVID-19, in many countries, women experienced higher chances of getting fired and lower chances of getting hired than men. Given the costs of job loss and the difficulties of regaining a job with conditions amenable to household burdens, women may value stability more than men because of societal structures in place, not just innate differences. These preferences can then transfer to other welfare-affecting policies, such as trade. Trade offers the opportunity for economic growth but at the cost of increased economic volatility and increased potential for job losses. If trade protection lessens the potential for lay-offs, then, according to risk-orientation models, women should prefer protection, regardless of their socio-economic status and regardless of whether they live in a developed or developing country.

6.5.2 **Gender and political knowledge**

A second strand focuses on empirically identified differences in knowledge and survey-taking behaviour. Across a wide variety of Western developed countries (Ferrín, Fraile, and García-Albacete 2019) and some developing countries, scholars have identified a political knowledge gap that appears to lessen women's political participation and policy preference formation. In addition, GPE scholars have also identified trade-specific knowledge gaps; or, in other words, the general trend of women being more likely to respond 'don't know' or provide incorrect answers to questions about trade policy in surveys (Hiscox and Burgoon 2004; Kleinberg and Fordham 2018). Whether the difference arises from differences in education and coursework, differences in workplace opportunities to discuss trade, or differences in interest in domestic and international news remains under debate.

Regardless of the source of the gap, the knowledge gap hypothesis predicts that women—and, for that matter, men—with specific knowledge should be observed to differ from other women and be more similar to men with specific knowledge. Furthermore, if differences in knowledge are the source of the gender gap, then correcting erroneous information about trade and trading partners should reduce the gender gap in trade preferences. To test this hypothesis, in 2010, as part of a national omnibus election survey in the United States, Guisinger (2017) compared the gender gap in trade preferences of two groups: the control group with its average distribution of those with information and those without information about trade and a treatment group which had been presented with trade information. The first experiment provided the treatment group with general information in the form of positive but factual information about the rank of the United States as the largest trading country and the link between exports and jobs in both the service and manufacturing sectors. The second experiment provided specific information by reinforcing, correcting, or supplying the name of the United States' main trading partner at the time (Canada). The analysis of the control group showed the expected gender gap in knowledge: women were more likely than men to answer 'don't know' and to provide the wrong top trading partner. In both cases, providing the treatment group with trade-related information resulted in a greater change in men's responses than women's and exacerbated rather than closed the gender gap in preferences.

6.5.3 **Gender and structural discrimination**

More recently, scholars and organizations such as the World Bank have begun to consider structural and institutional explanations for the gender gap. The size of the gender gap in trade attitudes is not consistent across countries and is sometimes reversed. The variation across countries poses an interesting puzzle that forces scholars to move past generalizations about essential and socially constructed differences between men and women.

Economic models of trade preferences assume similar economic outcomes for individuals based on class, skill level, or industry affiliation. Yet, empirical evidence highlights that men and women in the same jobs and in the same industries do not always receive the same treatment. As a result of discrimination in hiring, retention, and wages, women may face higher levels of economic vulnerability than men. At the same time, in societies with greater gender discrimination, women are more likely than men to be exposed to the downside risks associated with trade liberalization and other economic shocks (Kushi and McManus 2018; Roberts et al. 2019). Recent work (Guisinger and Kleinberg, 2023) suggests that women's attitudes towards trade are shaped by these inequalities, but conditionally according to domestic structures in place. Using two different indices of gender inequalities (The World Bank's Women, Business and the Law Index 2020, and the World Economic Forum's Global Gender Gap Index 2020) as a measure of societal structures of discrimination, they find that women's not men's beliefs about the benefits of trade are correlated with the level of discrimination: in countries with lower levels of discrimination, women are more likely to express a belief that trade is 'good' for the country. Additionally, cross-national differences in women's beliefs about the benefit of trade, not men's, drive the size of the gender gap in trade attitudes. More research needs to be done to consider how gender discrimination shapes the gender gap in developing countries.

Despite increased attention in current scholarship, the gender gap in trade attitudes offers a variety of open research questions. Theories and empirical studies exploring the role of economic selection, the influence of essential and socially constructed gender differences, and the impact of norms and institutions have generated new avenues for research as much as they have provided answers to the initial question.

One potentially fruitful direction might consider when gender and trade preferences interact politically. In the US, the 2016 US election saw increased discussion about the loss of male, white, and blue-collar jobs in the rust belt, but by-and-large left women out of the picture. Women are less likely to appear as workers in US trade-related campaign ads than minorities, and US women-oriented political organizations prioritize other issues. Understanding when and where trade preferences organize around gender and how that will shape political outcomes is the next frontier for the research on the gender gap.

KEY POINTS

- Empirical evidence across developed and developing countries finds that women are, on average, more protectionist than men, although the size of the gap varies substantially across countries.

- Economic explanations based on consumption patterns and employment sorting explain some but not all of the gender gap.

- An alternative set of explanations seeks to explain women's greater protectionism as consistent with the gender gap in risk-aversion and competitiveness.

- Some scholars have focused on a knowledge gap between men and women both in general foreign policy knowledge but also specific to trade-related policies.

- Recent work argues that gender differences in trade preference arise from structural discrimination within countries. As such, this argument could explain both the gender gap and also why the gender gap varies so much across otherwise similar developed countries.

6.6 Conclusion

For the most part, trade policy is set by domestic political elites and international negotiators, far away from the control of countries' citizens. Yet, across time and around the globe, domestic public opinion has served to push the direction of trade policy directly through referendums or voting and indirectly through politicians proactively responding to public preferences. How those preferences arise is complicated.

Empirical work has demonstrated that economic models of individual preferences for trade are only a starting point to understanding public responses to increased trade. Individuals seek to incorporate their concerns about others into their consideration but also the position of their country within the international system. In doing so, the public faces a lack of information and thus relies on political and media elite presentations. Furthermore, the public itself is multifaceted. Their perceptions of the costs and benefits from trade depend as much on their individual characteristics (especially their race, ethnicity, and gender) as their attitudes towards others domestically and internationally.

Too much of current scholarship relies on research based on the United States and other advanced economies. As different countries seek to influence global trade patterns, new research is needed to better understand public sentiment in non-Western powers and emerging economies, especially as internal society structures appear to strongly influence opinion formation and the power of public opinion in shaping national policies.

? 6.7 QUESTIONS

1. Thinking about your local community (your county, district, or state), what are the primary industries in the region? Are they easily identifiable? If so, are they import-competing, export-oriented or non-tradeable? If not, why not? Do you see a link between the industry in your local community and its national-level representative's position on trade?

2. Under what conditions do you think that people will perceive themselves in terms of class interest versus in terms of their industry affiliation? Which do you think is more important in organizing trade opinions in your country?

3. What do your friends and family think about trade policy? Do they focus on national concerns or more local concerns? Are these concerns economic, security, or other?

4. Where do you learn about trade? The media? Politicians? Your workplace? How might those sources of information influence your opinions?

5. Who appears as the beneficiary of trade policy in campaign and other political discussions in your country? Why do you think they are considered deserving of government intervention?

6. How do race, ethnicity, and gender influence employment in your country? Does your country's trade-related industry disproportionately include those from an identifiable sub-group?

7. Identify the top three countries from which your country imports and the top three countries to which your country exports. Do they receive similar levels of attention? What are the similarities or differences in the news and in political discourse?

8. The gender gap in political knowledge and in trade preferences varies across nations and across time. What factors do you think might influence the gender gap? Would you expect these to be static or in the process of changing?

6.8 FURTHER READING

Baker, A. (2005), 'Who Wants to Globalize? Consumer Tastes and Labor Markets in a Theory of Trade Policy Beliefs', *American Journal of Political Science*, 49/4: 924–938, 10.1111/j.1540-5907.2005.00164.x. Baker incorporates the role of consumer preferences into a standard labour-based model to explain individual- and country-level support for liberalization across forty-one developed and developing countries. In doing so, he shows how a taste for cheap imports can override concerns about the environmental, employment, and sovereignty costs of globalization.

Borrows, J., and Schwartz, R. (eds.) (2020), *Indigenous Peoples and International Trade: Building Equitable and Inclusive International Trade and Investment Agreements* (Cambridge, MA: Cambridge University Press). Borrows and Schwartz provide a unique compilation of scholarship on the subject of Indigenous peoples, international trade, and international law. Recently updated to include the US–Mexico–Canada Trade Agreement (USMCA), the book's chapters offer both critiques of past practices of exclusion and analysis of still evolving strategies for inclusion of Indigenous peoples' interests.

Brutger, R., and Rathbun, B. (2021), 'Fair share? Equality and Equity in American Attitudes Toward Trade', *International Organization*, 75/3: 880–900. Across the world, politicians decry or tout the 'fairness' of trade agreements. This article considers different definitions of fairness and finds that—at least among current day Americans—public assessment of fairness is crucial but egoistically biased to national interests.

Guisinger, A. (2017), *American Opinion on Trade: Preferences without Politics* (Oxford, UK: Oxford University Press). For much of the late twentieth and early twenty-first centuries, US trade policy diverged from Americans' preferences. In this book, Guisinger seeks to explain how the gap lasted so long and in doing so identifies previously overlooked sources of protectionist sentiment such as gender and race-based employment concerns and race-based ideas about which groups deserve redistribution.

Hannah, E., Roberts, A., and Trommer, S. (2022), 'Gender in Global Trade: Transforming or Reproducing Trade Orthodoxy?', *Review of International Political Economy*, 29/4: 1368–1393. Through text analysis of four trade and gender initiatives, Hannah et al. adopt a feminist approach to GPE and assess the extent to which the current trade agenda reaffirms rather than transforms how trade impacts women around the globe.

Hiscox, M. J. (2001), 'Class versus Industry Cleavages: Inter-Industry Factor Mobility and the Politics of Trade', *International Organization* 55/1: 1–46. In this article, Hiscox offers a unifying theory to explain why sometimes trade divides society by class (as predicted by the Stolper-Samuelson theory) and other times by industry (as predicted by the Ricardo-Viner theory). Drawing on six country case studies across a two-century timeframe, he shows how changing conditions of factor mobility explain how both theories can appear valid at different times and in different places.

Kleinberg, K. B., and Fordham, B. O. (2018), 'Don't Know much about Foreign Policy: Assessing the Impact of "Don't Know" and "No Opinion" Responses on Inferences about Foreign Policy Attitudes', *Foreign Policy Analysis*, 14/3: 429–448. Kleinberg and Fordham highlight how the methods used by political science may obscure differences in foreign policy attitudes across sub-groups of the population.

Mutz, D. C., and Kim, E. (2017), 'How Ingroup Favoritism Affects Trade Preferences', *International Organization*, 71/4: 827–850. Mutz and Kim offer an exploration of how identity shapes preferences for the structure of trade agreements, especially among those with a strong sense of in-group favouritism.

Naoi, M., and Kume, I. (2011), 'Explaining Mass Support for Agricultural Protectionism: Evidence from a Survey Experiment During the Global Recession', *International Organization*, 65/4: 771–795. Naoi and Kume explore the public's acceptance of agricultural protection by selecting a time in which consumer preferences should be strongest—when a global recession is creating hardship for Japanese households.

Rho, S., and Tomz, M. (2017), 'Why Don't Trade Preferences Reflect Economic Self-Interest?', *International Organization*, 71/S1: S85–S108. Rho and Tomz challenge the assumption that individuals base trade attitudes on their individual economic circumstances via a survey experiment that provides a randomly selected set of participants with the necessary economic knowledge to make decisions as some economists assume that they will.

CONTRIBUTOR NOTE

Alexandra Guisinger is an Associate Professor of the Department of Political Science and a faculty fellow of the Public Policy Lab at Temple University. Her publications include *American Opinion on Trade: Preference without Politics* (Oxford University Press, 2017). She is currently a principal investigator of the *Foreign Policy in a Diverse Society* project which seeks to expand our understanding about how gender, race, and ethnicity shape public opinion on economic foreign policy.

7

Global Production and Unfree Labour

Ellie Gore

Reader's guide

The presence of extremely exploitative labour conditions in the supply chains of key commodities—from garments to electronics, fishing to agriculture—is now widely recognized. Yet there is relatively little agreement over what causes severe labour exploitation, commonly referred to as 'forced' or 'unfree labour', in global production and how to address it. Is unfree labour an aberration within an otherwise free market, the result of a few unscrupulous employers and recruiters? Or is exploitation a routine and systematic aspect of work for the millions of people employed in commodity supply chains around the globe? This chapter explores these debates by examining the patterns, prevalence, and drivers of severe labour exploitation in global production. The first part of the chapter looks at key frameworks and concepts, focusing on the divide between proponents of the 'modern slavery' paradigm and their critics, who prefer the conceptual framing of 'unfree labour'. The second part of the chapter examines the structural drivers of labour exploitation in global supply chains, which include: outsourcing and the globalization of production; state policies and practices; and commercial dynamics rooted in the vast political and economic power of multinational corporations (MNCs). The third part of the chapter considers what makes workers vulnerable to labour exploitation, including its most extreme forms, with a focus on poverty, migration, and the intersections of gender, race, class, ethnicity, caste, and citizenship. The final section evaluates the effectiveness of current public and private initiatives to address unfree and forced labour in global production.

7.1 Introduction

The growth and intensification of severe labour exploitation—commonly referred to as 'forced labour'—is now recognized as one of the most pressing global issues of our time. In mainstream media, the plight of workers in global supply chains has increasingly hit the headlines. This includes accounts of extreme exploitation and violence in the Thai fishing industry (Dow 2019), debt and deception in electronics factories in Malaysia (Ramchandani 2018), labour abuses on palm oil plantations in Southeast Asia (Gould 2016), and the systematic underpayment of tea-pickers in India (Bannerji and Hussain 2018), to name just a few widely reported cases. In the UK, attention has also turned to labour conditions within domestic supply chains; in June 2020, for example, a report into garment production in Leicester—the UK's largest manufacturing hub—sparked widespread media interest (Lewis 2020). The report found that many of Leicester's garment factories had defied instructions to close during the first national coronavirus lockdown, putting workers at increased risk of illness and mortality from COVID-19. As well as pervasive health and safety violations, workers reported excessive overtime, a lack of formal employment contracts, and illegally low wages (as little as £2–3 an hour, well below the UK's National Minimum Wage).

Media, activist, and consumer concern over the ethical risks of globalized production has proliferated over the last three decades. In the 1990s, activists began to highlight the human and environmental costs of corporate profit-making practices, particularly targeting 'superbrands' like Nike, Coca-Cola, Microsoft, Disney, and McDonalds. This anti-corporate backlash was, in part, a reaction to changes in the structure of global production, namely increased **outsourcing**. Broadly speaking, this process entailed the relocation of labour-intensive manufacturing from the Global North to countries with lower-cost labour supplies and weaker labour laws, typically in the Global South. Since the 1990s, the links between the offshoring and outsourcing of production and labour exploitation have been widely documented. While reliable statistics on the prevalence of forced labour in the global economy remain lacking, there is now a broad body of evidence highlighting extremely exploitative labour conditions across a range of sectors and industries: fishing; agriculture and food processing; manufacturing; construction; and natural resource extraction (ILO 2013). This evidence illuminates the foundational role of severe labour exploitation in producing key commodities—clothing, shoes, mobile phones, fish, meat, tea, chocolate, sugar, palm oil—and in the production of services, such as care, domestic, and sex work.

In the contemporary juncture, a diverse range of actors has converged around the issue of forced labour in global production. These actors include unions, NGOs, campaign and advocacy groups, and international bodies and agencies, such as the United Nation's International Labour Organization (ILO). Against this backdrop, governments and policymakers have sought to demonstrate a commitment to eradicating forced labour in their supply chains. These initiatives have been typically located within broader efforts to tackle 'modern slavery', of which forced labour is considered a key subset. Some jurisdictions have brought in specific legislation aimed at tackling modern slavery, such as the UK's 2015 Modern Slavery Act and the California Transparency in Supply Chains Act (2012) in the US. At a global level, commitments to tackling labour exploitation have been enshrined in the Sustainable Development Goals (SDGs), including SDG 8 on Decent Work, which includes targets on the eradication of modern slavery and the protection of labour rights. Global corporations and brands have also adopted a raft of private governance measures intended to improve labour and environmental standards in their supply chains, such as transparency initiatives, benchmarking and auditing, codes of conduct, ethical certification schemes, and other **corporate social responsibility (CSR)** activities.

While there may be consensus in government, policy, and civil society spheres over the importance of addressing severe labour exploitation in the global economy, there has been considerably less agreement over its causes and solutions. This relative dissensus extends to the academic literature, which is characterized by multiple and at times competing approaches and frameworks. Put otherwise, as interest in the impacts of globalized production on labour standards and practices has grown, so too has the diversity of the academic literature. One key divide is between proponents of the modern slavery paradigm (sometimes called 'new' or 'neo-slavery') and their critics, who often prefer the conceptual framing of 'unfree labour'.

This diverse scholarship is informed by a range of key questions: Why does labour unfreedom persist in the contemporary global economy? How can we measure the incidence of extreme exploitation and abuse? How does labour unfreedom relate to poverty and inequality and who is most vulnerable? What role have shifts in the organization of global production played in increasing and intensifying labour unfreedom? And what kinds of governance and regulatory measures are required to improve labour standards in supply chains? The latter three questions have been of particular interest to scholars of global political economy (GPE), who have sought to study severe labour exploitation as part of a broader set of interactions between market forces, state and supra-state institutions and practices, and social relations, including class relations and hierarchies of race, gender, and citizenship.

How we understand the nature of a problem informs how we formulate policy and legislative interventions to address it. Contrasting accounts of severe labour exploitation therefore lead to disagreements over practical solutions, particularly in relation to the perceived effectiveness of anti-slavery and trafficking approaches. This paradigm, which brings together anti-human trafficking initiatives with efforts to eradicate modern slavery, has become increasingly embedded in policy and governance frameworks in the Global North over the last two decades. It has also provided a powerful and emotive rallying point for NGOs and other advocacy groups. Like the concept of modern slavery, however, anti-slavery and trafficking approaches are highly contested. We will consider some of the reasons for this in the final section of this chapter.

Section 7.2 of the chapter provides an overview of key frameworks and definitions, focusing on modern slavery, forced labour, and unfree labour. Section 7.3 examines the structural drivers of unfree labour, particularly as they relate to the globalization of production, the rise of MNCs, state policies and practices, and other shifts in the global economy under neoliberalism. Section 7.4 explores the factors shaping workers' vulnerability to unfree labour in global production, with a particular focus on the role of poverty, migration, and intersections of gender, race, caste, ethnicity, nationality, and citizenship status. Finally, Section 7.5 examines the limitations of existing public and private initiatives to prevent labour exploitation in supply chains. The chapter makes three interrelated arguments: (1) we cannot understand the most extreme forms of labour unfreedom in isolation from broader dynamics of exploitation, insecurity, and precarity in the global economy; (2) there are structural and institutional drivers of unfree labour in supply chains that are rooted in (and reproduce) the vast political and economic power of MNCs; and (3) certain *types* of worker—informal, contract, and casualized workers and workers at the base of global supply chains—and certain *groups* of workers—poor and working-class people, women, migrants, people of colour, Indigenous people, and people from low-status castes—are systematically exploited in global supply chains and are disproportionately vulnerable to the most extreme forms of abuse.

7.2 Key frameworks

This section reviews some of the key frameworks and concepts used to study severe labour exploitation in the global economy. We will begin with one of the most influential paradigms among policy, governance, and advocacy actors: modern slavery.

7.2.1 Modern slavery

Modern slavery is an umbrella term used to encompass a range of exploitative practices and relations, including slavery, forced labour, and human trafficking (see Key Theory Box 7.1). It became popular in development studies in the late 1990s and has since gained widespread traction; the concept has notably been adopted by the UK government in the 2015 Modern Slavery Act. Modern slavery is not defined in international law, however, and there is no single, agreed-upon account of modern slavery. Rather, definitions vary across political and disciplinary contexts and may include diverse phenomena: compulsory labour; debt bondage; contract slavery; forced sexual exploitation. Advocates of this framework argue that the fluidity of the concept is one of its strengths; it allows for a dynamic and context-specific understanding of slavery. It also unifies an ostensibly disparate range of exploitative practices and relations by emphasizing their historical antecedent (that is, slavery) and by identifying three common elements: control, coercion, and exploitation (Mende 2019).

While early work in the modern slavery paradigm drew primarily on qualitative research (including personal accounts from researchers), more recently scholars have sought to measure the prevalence of modern slavery in the global economy (Datta and Bales 2013).

KEY THEORY BOX 7.1 MODERN OR 'NEW SLAVERY'

In the academic literature, Kevin Bales' (2012) book *Disposable People: New Slavery in the Global Economy* made an important contribution to the 'modern' or, what he terms, 'new slavery' paradigm. In this work, Bales documents an 'epidemic' of new slavery in the Global South, using a multi-country case study of Thailand, Mauritania, Brazil, Pakistan, and India. According to Bales, contemporary slavery can take many forms, but it is linked to past forms of slavery by its key characteristics. These are: 'the state of control exercised over the slave based on violence or its threat, a lack of any payment beyond subsistence, and the theft of the labor or other qualities of the slave for economic gain' (Bales 2005: 9). In essence, Bales (2005: 9) conceptualizes slavery as 'the violent control of one person by another'. Bales' account expands conventional definitions of slavery, which are premised on the ownership of one person by another, to include other types of control, such as: 'debt bondage', where a person pledges their service against the loan of money and where the length and nature of this service is generally undetermined (see also Key Concept Box 7.2); and 'contract slavery', where a worker is given a written or verbal contract but discovers this misrepresents the actual conditions of their employment, which are akin to slavery. Extreme forms of labour exploitation—for example, workers trapped by indebtedness in stone quarries in India—are therefore understood as one modality of 'new slavery' (that is, debt bondage). Other modalities of 'new slavery' range from young children undertaking hazardous work on fishing boats in Ghana (that is, child labour) to women trafficked from Eastern Europe into sex work in Turkey (that is, human trafficking—see also Key Concept Box 7.3).

This research has informed the development of a Global Slavery Index (GSI) and the Global Estimates of Modern Slavery, which were produced through a collaboration between the Walk Free Foundation, an NGO cofounded by the academic Kevin Bales, and the ILO. According to the most recent global estimates (ILO 2022a), there are 27.6 million people in situations of forced labour globally, with 63 per cent in the private economy in sectors other than commercial sexual exploitation, 23 per cent in forced commercial sexual exploitation, and 14 per cent in state-imposed forced labour. This is a significant increase from the 2016 figures (ILO 2017), which indicated that there were 24.9 million people in conditions of forced labour, and represents 'a rise in the prevalence of forced labour from 3.4 to 3.5 per thousand people in the world' (ILO 2022a: 2).

The modern/new slavery framework has no doubt been influential, particularly as it has informed growing international advocacy and policy activities. This combination of research and activism has helped to push the issue of modern slavery—and its subsets, forced labour and human trafficking—up the global policy agenda. However, the empirics and methodology used to develop both the GSI and the ILO/Walk Free estimates have come under close scrutiny, with scholars (Gallagher 2017; Mügge 2017) raising concerns about the limitations of the underlying data and how it was extrapolated to arrive at the global estimates. The modern slavery paradigm has also been challenged at a theoretical level for creating a binary between 'slavery' and 'non-slavery' (O'Connell Davidson 2013) and

for what Janie Chuang (2014) calls 'exploitation creep', whereby all forced labour is interpreted as trafficking and all trafficking as slavery. Conflating terms such as 'modern slavery', 'human trafficking', and 'forced labour'—and locating them within a broader binary of slavery vs non-slavery—creates conceptual and analytical fuzziness. This fuzziness is unhelpful for identifying different types of exploitation, varying degrees of severity in exploitation, and the key drivers of exploitation across different spatial and temporal contexts.

Elsewhere, scholars have critiqued the modern slavery paradigm for its lack of systemic analysis, that is, for disconnecting the most severe forms of labour exploitation from their political-economic, social, and legal contexts (Barrientos, Kothari, and Phillips 2013). Modern slavery is thus presented as an essentially transhistorical phenomenon that is enacted through micro-level relations of violence and control; as LeBaron argues, it is viewed as 'a series of *individualized* instances of domination rather than as a social relationship of insecurity and exploitation' (LeBaron 2015: 2, italics mine). With its focus on extreme forms of exploitation, this framing obscures less overt and more everyday forms of labour unfreedom and the reality that—for large swathes of workers around the world—labour conditions are routinely exploitative and highly precarious. This is especially the case for workers located at the base of global supply chains and in informal and unprotected forms of work. Bunting and Quirk (2018: 9) refer to this as modern slavery's 'politics of exceptionality, wherein slavery is promoted as a unique and exceptional evil that stands apart from other "lesser" challenges'.

Looking beyond academia, the industry of NGOs working on modern slavery and the wider 'abolitionist' movement have also attracted criticism, notably for othering victims and perpetuating 'white saviour' narratives that deny agency to individuals (and specifically people of colour) experiencing the most extreme forms of exploitation (Kempadoo 2015). Again, this movement tends to frame extreme forms of labour exploitation in moral and exceptional terms, rather than locating these relations *within* the structures, norms, and practices of capitalist states and markets. As Bernstein summarizes (2007: 144): 'For modern-day abolitionists, the dichotomy between slavery and freedom poses a way of addressing the ravages of neoliberalism that effectively locates all social harm outside of the institutions of corporate capitalism and the state apparatus. In this way, the masculinist institutions of big business, the state, and the police are reconfigured as allies and saviors, rather than enemies, of unskilled migrant workers'.

Bernstein's (2007) point about the modern slavery paradigm obscuring the key role of the state in shaping dynamics of labour unfreedom is an important one: not only do states *respond* to 'modern slavery' as a policy issue—for example, through the introduction of legislation like the UK's Modern Slavery Act—but state policy and practices can also *facilitate* the conditions in which extreme exploitation flourishes (Lebaron and Phillips 2019). This can occur through the deregulation of labour markets, the establishment of restrictive immigration systems, and policies that enhance the power of business (Strauss and Fudge 2014). As we will see, the assumptions underpinning the modern slavery framework stand in contrast to the case made in the GPE literature, which holds that: the most severe forms of labour unfreedom *cannot* be understood as categorically discrete or external to other exploitative labour relations under capitalism; and that governments and corporations play a key role in (re)producing the structural conditions and power relations through which extreme labour exploitation occurs.

KEY CONCEPT BOX 7.2 DEBT BONDAGE

Debt bondage, also sometimes referred to as 'bonded labour', is a key mechanism of exploitation included within the ILO definition of 'forced labour'. According to the ILO (2019a), 'debt bondage exists when labourers (sometimes with their families) are forced to work for an employer in order to pay off their own debts or those they have inherited'. Although the worker may receive pay or other compensation, the debt prevents them from exiting the job (and the worker may be returned forcibly if they try to leave). Debt bondage can take many forms, ranging from older semi-feudal forms of servitude to the ways in which contemporary migrant workers are forced to accrue large debts in order to cover recruitment fees and travel costs (ILO 2019a).

KEY CONCEPT BOX 7.3 HUMAN TRAFFICKING

The internationally recognized definition of human trafficking comes from the UN Trafficking in Persons Protocol. According to the Protocol, human trafficking entails 'the recruitment, transportation, transfer, harbouring or receipt of persons, by means of the threat or use of force or other forms of coercion … for the purpose of exploitation' (UNODC 2000: 42). Trafficking is commonly understood to take various forms, including: trafficking for forced labour; trafficking for forced criminal activities, such as begging; trafficking for sexual exploitation; trafficking for forced marriage; and trafficking for organ harvesting. In academic and policy discourse, considerable attention has been paid to sex trafficking, with relatively less interest in labour trafficking. In line with critiques of the modern slavery paradigm, some critical scholars (Kempadoo 2005) have questioned the tendency of anti-trafficking approaches to assume that all sex work is sex trafficking (and relatedly that all trafficking is sex trafficking).

7.2.2 **Forced labour**

In policy and legal discourse, forced labour is often referred to as a subset of modern slavery. Unlike modern slavery, however, forced labour does have an established definition in international law. Article 2(1) of the ILO Forced Labour Convention, 1930 (No. 29) defines forced labour as: 'all work or service which is exacted from any person under the menace of any penalty and for which the said person has not offered himself [or herself] voluntarily'. According to the ILO, forced labour can take various forms, including slavery or slave-like practices, debt bondage, and human trafficking.

At a conceptual level, the ILO definition of forced labour can be broken down into three key components: work, which includes all forms of work, including in the informal economy; the **menace** or threat of penalty, which may take various forms, such as 'penal sanctions' and 'direct or indirect coercion, such as physical violence, psychological threats or the non-payment of a wage'; and **involuntariness**, which refers to a worker's 'free and informed consent' to take a job and their freedom to exit it at any time (ILO 2022b).

In order to operationalize the legal definition of forced labour, the ILO (2012) have developed a set of indicators. These indicators are intended to distinguish forced labour from less severe forms of exploitative or 'sub-standard' work. The indicators include:

- Abuse of vulnerability
- Deception
- Restriction of movement
- Isolation
- Physical and sexual violence
- Intimidation and threats
- Retention of identity documents
- Withholding of wages
- Debt bondage
- Abusive working and living conditions
- Excessive overtime

According to this rubric, the presence of a single indicator does not necessarily indicate the presence of forced labour; rather it is the combination of multiple indicators that suggests forced labour is present.

The ILO's definition of forced labour and the indicators devised to accompany it provide a clear and consistent framework for identifying the most severe forms of labour exploitation. The ILO definition avoids 'exploitation creep' (Chuang 2014) by emphasizing degrees of severity and by cautioning against the over-determination of modern slavery as a concept, that is, its use as an all-encompassing term. According to Beate Andrees from the ILO's Special Action Programme to Combat Forced Labour, it is important to use precise concepts and avoid slippages between terms, since 'not all children who are exposed to hazardous work are "slaves", and not all workers who don't receive a fair wage are "forced"' (Andrees 2014).

However, the ILO definition of forced labour is not without limitation. One key issue is the exclusion of economic coercion, that is, compulsion on the grounds of destitution or starvation, from its understanding of 'direct and indirect coercion'. In the ILO account, coercion can only operate through individualized acts and relations, for example, by employers or governments compelling a person to work, as an *extra-economic* force (LeBaron et al. 2018). However, evidence suggests that economic coercion is a key factor determining workers' entry into and ability to exit highly exploitative working conditions; this coercive force is located at a structural level, not only an individual one (LeBaron and Gore 2020). In other words, a worker's decision to accept an employer's dangerous or degrading job offer or a moneylender's predatory loan terms is influenced by the economic and social conditions of their existence, notably poverty, hunger, and other forms of vulnerability; it is not exclusively determined by the power exerted by one person upon another. A worker may therefore enter into and stay in highly exploitative and coercive forms of work due to a lack of viable economic alternatives. Like the concept of 'modern slavery', a definition of forced labour that excludes economic coercion is inconsistent with a GPE analysis that emphasizes how relations of exploitation are structurally embedded and (re)produced within the global economy, as part of capitalist labour relations. In terms of coercion, this type of analysis also shifts the focus away from the micro and individual level, that is, from the control of one person over another, towards 'the forms of compulsion that are … exerted by a worker's social and economic circumstances' (Barrientos, Kothari, and Phillips 2013: 1039). Judy Fudge (2019: 109) summarizes this helpfully as a focus on 'structural causes' rather than 'individual pathologies'. Finally, it is important to note that unfreedom is not only constituted at the point of entry into or exit from work, as per the ILO definition, but may be produced through the conditions of work itself; for example, by the use of debt as a mechanism to keep a worker in their job (Barrientos, Kothari, and Phillips 2013).

7.2.3 Unfree Labour

In light of these shortcomings, some critical scholars have returned to longstanding political economy debates about 'free' and 'unfree labour' (McGrath and Strauss 2015). The origins of these categories can be traced to liberal and neo-classical economics, as well as some strands of Marxist theory, which have tended to view free labour as a quintessential feature of capitalism. Unfree labour—which includes slavery and other forms of indentured and coerced labour—is seen as incompatible with the capitalist mode of production; it is a 'pre-capitalist' or 'non-capitalist' type of labour (see Key Theory Box 7.4).

The academic debates on unfree labour are wide-ranging and theoretically dense. For our purposes, it is sufficient to note that the argument that unfree labour is incompatible with capitalism has long been challenged by scholars within the Black radical tradition, who have highlighted how coercive, violent, and highly exploitative forms of work persisted after the formal abolition of chattel slavery, particularly for racialized groups such as African Americans and Asian migrants working as 'indentured labourers' in the Caribbean, that is, workers who were contractually bound to an employer for a fixed period of work, typically in exchange for transportation to the colonies (Robinson 1983; Singh 2022; see also Kempadoo

2017). Other scholars of political economy have challenged existing accounts of unfree labour for failing to capture the 'many "un-decent" forms and aspects of labour relations' under neoliberalism (Lerche 2011: 4). By adopting a binary understanding of freedom and unfreedom, liberal, neo-classical, and some Marxist scholarship is seen to reproduce the propensity to 'ringfence' extreme labour exploitation characteristic of the modern slavery paradigm (Barrientos, Kothari, and Phillips 2013).

Far from disappearing under capitalism, unfree labour has persisted across space and time in multiple forms; in this sense, capitalism is able to operate through a remarkably diverse range of labour relations and regimes, some of which are more unfree than others (Fudge 2019). However, contemporary forms of labour unfreedom are distinct from historic ones in that they often include elements of both freedom and unfreedom (Phillips 2011). They may also be time-specific, that is, unfreedom may occur within a certain period of time as part of a contract (as opposed to it being a permanent state or relation) (Bastia and McGrath 2011). These characteristics mean that it is extremely difficult to separate 'severe' forms of exploitation from more 'everyday' ones, since workers may move between more and less exploitative conditions over time, across different jobs, and even within the same job. Research into cocoa supply chains (LeBaron and Gore 2020, discussed in detail in Case Study Box 7.5), shows how below-subsistence wages and a lack of savings create fertile terrain for more severe forms of exploitation amongst cocoa workers in Ghana. In the context of generally inadequate incomes and poor working conditions, a worker may be forced to take out a loan at an exorbitant interest rate, for example,

---

KEY THEORY BOX 7.4 FREE AND UNFREE LABOUR

In the liberal and neo-classical accounts, free labour is characterized by a *voluntary* exchange between capital and labour. Since the market is made up of self-determining, 'utility-maximizing' agents, it is understood as an arena of freedom. These assumptions mean that 'unfreedom' in labour relations must occur in an anomalous, involuntary, and *extra-economic* fashion. Marxists differ from liberals and neo-classical economists in that they conceptualize workers' 'freedom' in a dual sense; a worker is 'free' firstly because they have been dispossessed from the means of production, and secondly because they are 'free' to sell their labour power to capital in return for a wage. Rather than viewing the labour market as an arena of freedom and consent, Marxists understand it as a locus of economic coercion (see McGrath 2017; Fudge 2019 for an overview). Despite the differences between these approaches, one point of commonality is the assumption that unfree labour would become obsolete as capitalism progressed through different stages of economic development.

CASE STUDY BOX 7.5 GENDER, MIGRATION, AND UNFREE LABOUR IN COCOA SUPPLY CHAINS

Research into cocoa supply chains (see Figure 7.1) underscores why it is impossible to understand labour exploitation without analysing gender and migration (LeBaron and Gore 2020). Drawing on data collected in Ghana in 2017–2018, namely a survey of 500 cocoa workers and sixty in-depth interviews with workers, LeBaron and Gore's (2020) study reveals that labour exploitation is endemic in cocoa production. Specifically, employers seek to offset costs by imposing a complex system of fines, fees, and deductions on cocoa workers. This system works to systematically underpay workers and engender situations of indebtedness. While all workers in cocoa farming have very low wages—an average of just over 5 GHS or US$1.04 per day—there are important gendered differences in workers' experiences of exploitation. Firstly, women cocoa workers earn less than men. For example, women carrying out caretaking work on cocoa farms earn on average 4.41 GHS per day, or US$0.92. This compares to an average of 6.45 GHS per day, or US$1.35, for male workers performing the same role. Various factors explain women's lower incomes, namely that women workers tend to be concentrated in the least well-paid activities in cocoa farming, such as weeding; wages are often paid to male family members, such as husbands, who do not share the wages equally; and employers discriminate against women because of their gender, namely by paying them less for the same work.

The study also found that migrant women workers are especially vulnerable to being exploited in cocoa production, typically through a combination of underpayment and non-payment of wages and indebtedness. Migrant women workers further reported that they felt unable to challenge these exploitative and unfair practices, since their position as women

and as migrants made them effectively powerless in the eyes of the employer. This shows how structural inequalities and forms of discrimination arising from gender and migration status make it harder for workers to challenge or exit exploitative labour conditions.

Finally, intra-household inequalities in the allocation of resources and the division of labour adversely impact on women's work in the cocoa sector. Since women often work as 'family labour', that is, alongside male family members who are directly hired by the farm owner, they depend on these family members to give them their share of the wages or crop. As a result, women cocoa workers do not always receive an equitable portion of the earnings. Moreover, women's other household responsibilities, which include more subsistence-based activities such as fetching water, weeding, and looking after other crops on the cocoa farm, as well as childcare, cooking, and cleaning, mean that they have less time to dedicate to paid productive work in cocoa. These social reproductive activities act as a powerful constraint on women's earning power and increase their vulnerability to exploitation and abuse.

In sum, the findings from this study indicate that business models in cocoa production are configured to rely on the exploitation of poor and informalized workers, especially women and migrants, at the bottom of the supply chain. These workers lack formal work contracts, earn well below the poverty line, and are at risk of more extreme forms of exploitation, which include involuntary labour and debt bondage. Women workers are disproportionately vulnerable to abuse, which is related to gender norms and the organization of social reproduction.

Figure 7.1 Simplified cocoa-chocolate value chain

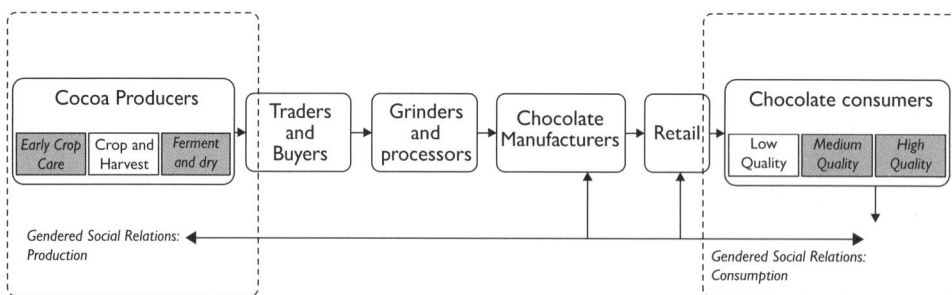

Source: Barrientos (2014).

to pay for a child's medical care, leaving them trapped in debt. It is this combination of long-term factors—poverty wages and an inability to save—with short-term ones—the unexpected expense of a child's illness—that gives rise to more extreme forms of exploitation in cocoa supply chains.

Against this background, some scholars have argued that it is more fruitful to understand labour unfreedom as part of a spectrum or **continuum of unfreedom**, which ranges from decent work to the most extreme forms of exploitation and abuse (Lerche 2011; LeBaron 2015; Strauss and McGrath 2017). Conceptualizing labour unfreedom as a spectrum has important analytical and methodological implications; rather than studying 'forced labour' or 'modern slavery' as a unique or isolated phenomenon, the most extreme forms of unfreedom must be studied in relation to other patterns and dynamics of labour exploitation. This framework allows for recognition of the diversity of types of labour unfreedom in the global capitalist economy and the extent to which 'freedom' and 'unfreedom' are interconnecting dynamics in the lives of many workers. This critical GPE account of unfree labour is therefore the preferred conceptual framing for this chapter.

KEY POINTS

- There are a number of different (and competing) frameworks for understanding severe labour exploitation in the global economy, which include: modern slavery; forced labour; and unfree labour.

- Modern slavery is an umbrella term used to encompass a range of exploitative practices, such as slavery, forced labour, and human trafficking. The modern slavery paradigm has gained widespread traction among policymakers, but has also attracted considerable critique. One key concern is that it frames extreme forms of exploitation as 'exceptional', that is, rather than the outcome of relations and dynamics that are internal to the global capitalist economy.

- Forced labour is often referred to as a subset of modern slavery. Unlike modern slavery, forced labour has a clear definition in international law and can be identified using the ILO's indicators of forced labour. However, the ILO definition has been critiqued for its exclusion of economic coercion, that is, compulsion on the grounds of destitution or starvation.

- Debates on 'free' and 'unfree' labour have a long lineage in political economy. Recently, some critical scholars have sought to challenge binary understandings of free versus unfree by conceptualizing labour unfreedom along a continuum. This means studying unfree labour not as an exception, but in relation to less overt and more routine forms of labour exploitation within the global economy.

7.3 Understanding the structural drivers of unfree labour

Sweeping changes in the organization of global production have occurred since the late 1960s, as part of a wider set of transformations associated with neoliberal globalization. Understanding these structural shifts is essential to identifying how and why unfree labour has persisted and proliferated across many sectors of the global economy, including in key commodity supply chains.

7.3.1 The changing nature of global supply chains

Let us start with the reconfiguration of global supply chains linked to processes of outsourcing noted in the introduction. A **global supply chain**—also called a 'global value chain' or 'global production network'—refers to the sequence of processes and activities that facilitate the movement of goods through the economy from production to distribution. With the dismantling of trade barriers and advances in technology and transportation, **multinational corporations** (MNCs) have been incentivized to offshore and outsource major elements of production. From the 1970s onwards, labour- and other cost-intensive activities within manufacturing were relocated to countries with large pools of lower-cost labour and weaker labour laws, the majority of which were in the Global South. Scholars of political economy conceptualized this shift as introducing a 'new international division of labour' (Fröbel, Heinrichs, and Kreye 1978). As these processes accelerated through the 1980s, supply chains became characterized by an increasing fragmentation of tasks and activities, with the production and distribution of commodities occurring through vast chains or networks of supplier firms, often stretching across multiple countries and continents. In the contemporary context, not all 'lead firms' (that is, the companies at the top of the supply chain) are located in the Global North; regional and domestic supply chains have also emerged led by firms in Asia, Africa, and Latin America (Barrientos 2022).

As a result of these shifts, employment in commodity supply chains has expanded rapidly; according to the ILO, 453 million people were employed in global supply chains in 2013, a massive increase from 296 million in 1995 (ILO 2015). Alongside the geographic reorganization of supply chains, the development of these new labour markets has been facilitated by the entry of 'rising power' economies or 'new powers'— China, India, Brazil—into the global economy (see Scott, Chapter 12). In Information and Communications Technology (ICT) manufacturing, for example, there has been a significant concentration of jobs towards China and other parts of Asia (Delautre 2017). Thus, while the total number of people working in ICT globally has increased significantly since 2000, there are stark regional variations; huge growth in ICT jobs in China, Vietnam, and Taiwan has occurred alongside major decreases in jobs in the US, Japan, and other Global North countries. Figures suggest that, as of 2017, nearly two thirds of all jobs in ICT manufacturing were located in China, compared to only one third of jobs in 2003 (Delautre 2017: 2; see also Girard, Chapter 17). In textile and clothing manufacturing, India, China, Vietnam, Bangladesh, and Pakistan have similarly seen major spikes in employment; there were over 1 million people employed in textiles and clothing manufacturing in Vietnam in 2010, a 52 per cent increase since 2004. Again, in Europe, the same period saw significant job losses within this sector, with an estimated 50 per cent of jobs lost in clothing and textiles between 2004 and 2014 (ILO 2014: 10). These changes reflect the broader reorientation of Global North countries away from manufacturing towards more service-based economies.

One key effect of this restructuring has been the distancing of companies at the top of the supply chain from the workers who provide their labour (see Figure 7.2). While firms at the top of the chain exert considerable power over dynamics within it, they are formally disconnected from the labour that is used to produce the goods. In the garment sector, for example, production is characterized by 'deep' supply chains, with multiple and complex layers of outsourcing and subcontracting. Since global buyers are located outside the jurisdictions in which the labour is contracted, they are not subject to national labour laws. Furthermore, in key garment-producing countries

Figure 7.2 Gloves production line in a factory

Source: iStock

like India, the workforce typically has very low levels of unionization (Dutta 2021). These dynamics create issues around governance, transparency, and accountability, sometimes referred to as the 'governance gap' (Crane et al. 2019). This 'gap' denotes the challenges of regulating labour standards and practices across large, complex, and transnational supply chains and the extent to which this enables labour exploitation.

Another way that increased outsourcing in global supply chains is linked to unfree labour is through the expansion of labour contracting. With goods increasingly sourced through multitiered global, regional, and domestic networks, labour intermediaries (also called labour contractors) have taken on a more significant role in supply chains, essentially acting as a third party between employers and workers. While some intermediaries take the form of recruitment agencies that help find temporary workers, other intermediaries operate informally or semi-informally (Barrientos 2013). Evidence from South African and UK horticulture supply chains indicates that labour contracting is an important vector of exploitation, with contract workers experiencing a range of labour abuses, such as excessive recruitment fees, high burdens of debt, extremely low wages and the underpayment of wages, and long working hours (Barrientos 2013). This is especially the case in the lower tiers of the chain and where the labour intermediaries are largely informal. While not all labour contracting results in unfreedom, it compounds the geographic and regulatory distance between producers and buyers and opens up new potential channels of exploitation. Again, this highlights how the drivers of unfree labour are built into the structure and political economy of contemporary supply chains; labour contracting is directly linked to outsourcing and attempts by companies at the top of the supply chain to maximize flexibility and minimize costs and risks, namely by pushing them down the chain (Barrientos 2013).

MNCs have been able to amass huge power and profits over the past forty years, fortified by light-touch regulatory approaches from states in areas such as corporate tax, trade, and competition policy, and by policies to promote greater labour market flexibility (Phillips 2017). In this way, the 'governance gap' has been actively facilitated by the rolling back of the state in key areas of labour governance, such as labour inspections, and by the rolling out of pro-business regulatory frameworks, policies, and laws (Crane et al. 2019). As highlighted in Section 7.2.1, state policies and practices are therefore not only important in tackling unfree labour, but can play a key role in engendering or facilitating the conditions in which unfree labour proliferates. This can occur across three primary areas: the regulation of labour mobility (for example, through restrictive immigration and citizenship laws); the regulation of labour markets (for example, through policies to promote greater labour market 'flexibility' and to restrict the power of trade unions); and the regulation of businesses (for example, by downscaling state-led labour regulation in favour of private governance measures) (LeBaron and Phillips 2019). While specific policies and practices vary according to country context, across many parts of the globe neoliberal state regulatory regimes have contributed to a rebalancing of power away from workers towards corporations. In essence, this means that states are key agents shaping dynamics of unfree labour in the global economy.

7.3.2 **MNCs and the distribution of power in the supply chain**

Widening economic inequality is often seen as one of the defining characteristics of the neoliberal era (see Lockwood, Chapter 13). This is reflected in an unprecedented concentration of wealth upwards over the last forty years (Piketty 2014). Anti-capitalist activists have pushed back against the accumulation of vast wealth by a tiny minority of the world's population—a sentiment memorably encapsulated in the 2011 Occupy Wall Street slogan, 'we are the 99%'. Yet figures from 2021 reveal the continuing extent of global inequality; the richest 10 per cent of the global population makes 52 per cent of global income, whereas the poorest half of the population makes just 8.5 per cent (Christiensen 2021). Global inequalities in wealth (that is, what people own) are even starker than global inequalities in income (that is, what people earn); the poorest half of the global population possesses just 2 per cent of total wealth, while the richest 10 per cent owns 76 per cent. While inequality *between* countries has decreased since the 1980s, largely as a result of rapid economic growth in China and India, inequality *within* countries has intensified (Christiensen 2021). This suggests that the 'benefits' of economic development have been unevenly distributed, with a relatively small number of businesspeople, shareholders, and other members of the global corporate elite disproportionately profiting.

There was a total of 2,153 billionaires in the world in 2019, who together owned more wealth than 4.6 billion people, that is, 60 per cent of the world's population (Oxfam 2020). According to the 2022 Forbes list, the wealthiest person globally is Elon Musk, the founder and CEO of SpaceX, who has an estimated net worth of US$219 billion. Second on the Forbes list is Jeff Bezos, the founder and former CEO of Amazon, who has an estimated net worth of US$171 billion. In July 2021, Bezos sparked controversy by saying 'thank you' to his employees for helping to fund his Blue Origin rocket launch, as part of the so-called billionaire space race between Bezos, Musk, and Richard Branson (the British businessman who founded the Virgin Group). Bezos' expression of gratitude was criticized by unions and NGOs, who pointed out the sharp contrast between the profits accrued by Bezos and the degrading and dangerous working conditions experienced by Amazon workers. The president of the Retail, Wholesale and Department Store Union in the US, Stuart Applebaum, for example, stated that 'He [Bezos] could have done a lot more for humanity if instead he paid his workers fairly and spent the money that was necessary to protect their health and safety and their lives' (NYCCLC 2021). In Europe and the US, Amazon workers have reported poor and unsafe working conditions, which include high injury rates, a lack of paid sick leave, gruelling and unrealistic fulfilment targets, and insufficient bathroom breaks (Alimahomed-Wilson and Reese 2021).

The accumulation of vast profits by billionaire businessmen has accompanied the growth and concentration of corporate power. As discussed in Girard, Chapter 17, Big Tech companies such as Alphabet, the parent company of Google, have become synonymous with the excesses of corporate power, as a small number of 'mega-corporations' have taken near-monopoly control over whole industries and sectors. In food production, for example, ten companies control almost every major brand of food and drink in the world: Nestlé, PepsiCo, Coca-Cola, Unilever, Danone, General Mills, Kellogg's, Mars, Associated British Foods, and Mondelez. At the same time, new types of mega-corporations have emerged. Amazon, for example, operates as an online retailer and marketplace, a delivery and logistics infrastructure, an online streaming platform and subscription services provider, and a producer of digital devices and gadgets, among many other functions. For these types of companies, growing corporate power has translated into record profits;

in 2021, Alphabet recorded a profit of US$21 billion (France24 2021), nearly three times its pre-pandemic figure, while Nestlé, the world's largest food and drink corporation, saw its profits surge by 38 per cent in 2021 to 16.9 billion Swiss Francs (£13.5 billion) (Cristea 2022). In the same year, Amazon's net income reached US$33.4 billion, up from US$21.3 billion the previous year.

Shifting patterns of corporate ownership, power, and profit have fundamentally reconfigured the structural position of big business within the global economy. Put simply, less competition means that an increasingly small number of MNCs are wielding an increasingly large amount of market power, in key areas such as price-setting, sourcing practices, and the distribution of value in the supply chain. This shift is sometimes referred to as a transformation away from producer-driven supply chains towards buyer-driven ones. From a GPE perspective, the growth and concentration of corporate power over the past three decades is key to understanding how the 'business demand' for unfree labour arises in supply chains, as part of the drive to reduce costs and risks and increase revenue for businesses (LeBaron et al. 2018). This relationship also demonstrates how shifts in outsourcing, governance, and profit-making processes within supply chains relate to bigger-picture trends in neoliberal globalization, notably trade liberalization and deregulation.

On the 'supply-side', widening inequality is also part of the broader material conditions that help to produce a pool of labour highly vulnerable to exploitation (see also Section 7.4). In this sense, inequality can be understood as both a driver and an outcome of unfree labour in the global economy. Viewed through this lens, record corporate profits and record levels of inequality are interrelated rather than parallel phenomena. This means that inequality is not an inevitable or even accidental outcome of neoliberal economic transformation: it is hardwired into the political economic system on which the global economy is built, including the global supply chain regime. We will explore how insecurity and exploitation are structurally embedded and (re)produced through supply chains in more detail in the following section.

7.3.3 MNCs and the distribution of value in the supply chain

The question of how and by whom value is generated and captured in the supply chain has attracted interest within the literature on global supply chains and unfree labour, with a specific focus on the low value accorded to labour (Phillips 2017; LeBaron et al. 2018). Dedrick et al. (2011) usefully break down the distribution of value within Apple supply chains. They document that Apple captured a staggering 58 per cent of value—that is, the share of gross profit—on their iPhone 4 and 30 per cent of value on their iPad. In addition to the overwhelming concentration of value in the hands of Apple, the breakdown shows that only 2 per cent of gross profits go to the Chinese workers at the base of the supply chain, that is, the workers in the assembly plants (Dedrick et al. 2011). These patterns underscore how the devaluation of productive labour at the bottom of the supply chain is linked to the generation and capture of value, in the form of profits, higher up the chain; they are essentially two sides of the same coin. Garment supply chains are similarly notable for the disproportionately low value attributed to productive labour, despite the labour-intensive character of production. Faced with high levels of competition, big retail brands use their structural power to keep prices low. In so doing, suppliers' margins further downstream in the supply chain are increasingly squeezed. As a result, labour costs and practices have been targeted as a key area for savings by firms (Phillips 2017).

7.3.4 **MNCs and sourcing practices**

Not only does Apple's large value share squeeze the wages of the assembly plant workers, but the company's emphasis on fast turnaround times negatively impacts on labour practices. Research on labour conditions at Foxconn, Apple's chief supplier in China (and a major manufacturer of electronic goods globally), finds that the 'compressed delivery time of new products has repeatedly taken precedence over protecting workers' health, safety and rights, at times with tragic consequences' (Pun et al. 2016: 9). Foxconn employs over 1 million people in China alone, with approximately 85 per cent of the workforce made up of internal migrants (Pun et al. 2016: 172). Workers' productivity is constantly surveilled within Foxconn factories and any perceived lapses in productivity, such as a failure to meet a target, are harshly punished. This can involve dismissal, forms of public humiliation, and verbal abuse. Workers also experience routine overtime and extremely long working hours in order to meet production timelines, up to sixty to seventy hours per week (Pun et al. 2016: 173). As this

evidence demonstrates, demands for flexible, fast, and low-cost production from lead firms like Apple exert downward pressures on wages and labour standards among supplier firms. This encourages the lowering of labour standards and the use of exploitative labour practices, for example, the imposition of excessive overtime (that is, the intensification of work), wage depression (that is, the underpayment of workers), or other more extreme forms of labour control, such as the use of threats and punishments (that is, coercion).

Labour practices at Foxconn factories must be contextualized within a broader political economic context in which China's sizeable temporary migrant population—estimated to comprise 244 million people in 2017 (Shen 2020: 31)—frequently lack basic labour rights and protections, as well as access to welfare, health, and other social services. This is linked to the strict laws and policies that govern internal mobility in China, including the *hukou* system of household registration (Swider 2015). The experiences of Foxconn workers in China thus illuminate how states—and specifically the state regulation of labour mobility—can serve to facilitate migrant workers' vulnerability to exploitation. It also shows how the impact of state regulatory regimes varies across geographic contexts; in Europe and North America, for example, it is state regulation of mobility in terms of restrictive immigration and citizenship laws that underpins (international and particularly Global South) migrant workers' vulnerability to exploitation; in China and other contexts such as India and Brazil, it is the state's governance of *internal* mobility that is especially significant (Lebaron and Phillips 2019).

KEY POINTS

- MNCs' extensive market power has wide-ranging implications for labour practices and standards in global supply chains.

- Companies at the top of lucrative supply chains have sought to maximize flexibility and offset costs and risks by pushing them further down the chain.

- MNCs also exert control and influence over key areas like price-setting, value capture, and sourcing practices. These dynamics put pressure on turnaround times and squeeze the financial margins of suppliers. This, in turn, increases the demand for cheap and flexible labour and encourages non-regular forms of work—contract, temporary/casualized, and informal—some of which are highly exploitative.

- Key structural and institutional factors in supply chains that shape unfree labour include: increased outsourcing and subcontracting, including labour contracting; the rolling back of the state in labour governance; a shift towards rapid, low-cost production and demands for greater flexibility from capital; the uneven distribution of value within the chain; and the extensive political and economic power wielded by MNCs.

7.4 Understanding workers' vulnerability to unfree labour

Changes in the structure, balance of power, and political economy of global supply chains are key to understanding how and why unfree labour occurs. In addition to this, it is useful to consider what factors make workers vulnerable to highly exploitative and coercive forms of work, that is, which workers are most at risk in global supply chains and why? This discussion is especially important since recent critical scholarship on unfree labour has sought to move beyond a focus on workers as abject and passive 'victims' to emphasize both structure and agency in shaping workers' entry into exploitative working conditions (Brace and O'Connell Davidson 2018). This section therefore considers what LeBaron et al. (2018) conceptualize as 'supply-side' factors, that is, the factors that help to create a pool of workers vulnerable to labour exploitation in the global economy. These factors include: poverty, global migration regimes, and social hierarchies arising from gender, race, class, caste, ethnicity, sexuality, nationality, and citizenship.

7.4.1 **Poverty**

One thing that scholars within both the modern slavery and unfree labour camps broadly agree on is the role of poverty in shaping workers' vulnerability to labour exploitation. For millions of people around the world, making enough money to cover their basic needs—food, water, clothing, shelter—is an everyday struggle. Figures from 2022 indicate that 8.5 per cent of the global population—approximately 682 million people—are living in extreme poverty, which is calculated as living on less than US$2.15 a day. Twenty-three per cent of the global population (1.8 billion people) are living on less than US$3.65 a day—an increase of 46 million people since 2019—and over two fifths of the

global population (4.2 billion people) are living on less than US$6.85 per day (Development Initiatives 2023: 8). A worker's ability to turn down or exit exploitative and coercive forms of work is severely constrained if they lack viable economic alternatives. With so many people living in poverty around the world, there is evidently a huge pool of labour that is potentially vulnerable to predation.

As discussed in Bhagat, Chapter 14, within mainstream development policy and academic discourse globalized production is understood to bring benefits to countries in the Global South, in terms of promoting economic growth and reducing poverty and unemployment. Export-oriented production in sectors such as garments, footwear, and electronics in particular are seen as 'good for development' by actors like the World Bank because they generate 'low-skill' jobs and boost workforce participation. This is especially the case for women workers in geographic regions such as South Asia, whose workforce participation has historically been low. According to the World Bank, export-oriented apparel production is therefore a key means to 'unleash South Asia's export and job potential' (Lopez-Acevado and Robinson 2016: 3). In the same vein, scholars and policymakers have sought to establish the extent to which 'economic upgrading', that is, the repositioning of southern firms and economies within global supply chains, can lead to the 'social upgrading' of workers, that is, improvements in workers' employment and living conditions (Barrientos, Gereffi, and Rossi 2011; Delautre 2017).

However, expanding employment opportunities in global supply chains have not translated into decent work for millions of workers around the globe. At best, gains for workers have been partial and differentiated, with stark variations across and within different sectors and geographic contexts. At worst, employment in global supply chains has led to increased precarity, informality, and insecurity. This is particularly the case for certain types of workers, such as low-skill and irregular workers located on the bottom rungs of global labour markets. Arianna Rossi's (2013) study of the garment supply chain in Morocco sheds light onto some of these complex dynamics. The study reveals how social upgrading in garment production—in terms of improved labour conditions and protections—has occurred primarily among *regular* workers, that is, workers on permanent contracts, who are employed in senior and/or high-skill jobs. 'Upgrading' for those workers, however, has occurred alongside 'downgrading' for other workers, namely through the expansion of an *irregular* workforce, that is, workers on casualized contracts in low-skill jobs, who are concentrated in the final segments of the garment supply chain. These workers are not only excluded from the benefits of upgrading experienced by regular workers, but encounter low wages, poor working conditions, exploitative practices, and discrimination.

While much of the focus within development discourse has been on getting people into work, the 'working poor' refers to people who are in work but whose wages are inadequate to provide a decent standard of living. According to ILO estimates from 2019, 13 per cent of the global employed population are moderately poor and 8 per cent are in extreme poverty. This works out as a global working poverty rate of 8 per cent (ILO 2019c: 2). The number of working poor is, in part, linked to expansion of the '**informal economy**', which is defined as 'all economic activities by workers and economic units that are—in law or in practice—not covered or insufficiently covered by formal arrangements' (ILO 2015). The informal economy is typically characterized by high levels of worker poverty and vulnerability and what the ILO terms 'decent work deficits'. In 2018, there were over 2 billion people working in the informal economy globally, which amounts to over 60 per cent of the global employed population (ILO 2018). Not all informal work is necessarily 'bad for workers', and there is huge diversity in the types and character of economic activities that take place within the informal sector around the world. However, informal work is associated with increased precarity and vulnerability to exploitation, primarily because workers lack formal labour rights and protections (Phillips 2011).

The figures and trends discussed above challenge the assumption that employment alone is sufficient to reduce poverty. They also underscore why wages and working conditions matter, both for understanding how the most extreme forms of exploitation that constitute unfree labour arise, and for identifying more generally who benefits from processes of economic globalization. Indeed, rather than viewing globalized production as inherently 'good for development', critical GPE scholars have highlighted its negative impacts on labour, particularly poor and working-class people, women, and migrants. According to Nicola Phillips (2013), the global productive economy and its labour markets operate through (and are shaped by) the social relations of poverty, which act as a form of '**adverse incorporation**'. It is the interconnection of these labour and social relations that generates workers' vulnerability and gives rise to unfree labour. In other words, the participation of poor workers in global supply chains forms part of a cycle of exploitative work that (re)produces chronic poverty and vulnerability. This challenges the liberal expectation that it is workers' exclusion from labour markets that drives poverty. Since these dynamics are systemic in character, the 'adverse incorporation' of poor and vulnerable workers is central to profit-making processes in the global economy (Phillips 2013: 172).

The key role of exploitative and degrading labour relations in generating value within global supply chains is similarly highlighted by Selwyn (2019). Selwyn uses evidence from garment supply chains in Cambodia and electronics supply chains in China to show how jobs in globalized, export-oriented production engender chronic poverty among their workers. Central to this dynamic is a systematic failure to pay workers a 'living wage', that is, a wage that is sufficient to cover rent, food, healthcare, clothing, childcare, and transportation and which would allow workers to save for unexpected costs. Research from Workers' Rights Consortium (2013: 2) found that workers' wages in leading apparel-exporting countries to the US, such as China, Cambodia, and Vietnam, on average covered just over a third—36.8 per cent—of a living wage. In Bangladesh, workers' wages were providing just 14 per cent of a living wage. There is also a gendered dimension to these patterns of exploitation, since garment production relies on a largely female workforce. Again, Selwyn (2019) conceptualizes these dynamics as *internal* to the structures and political economy of global supply chains (or global value chains), which he renames 'global poverty chains'. This reformulation directly links the generation of value in supply chains to the exploitation of workers. Although Phillips and Selwyn differ in terms of their theoretical and conceptual emphases, they share the analysis that rather than helping to lift workers out of poverty, global supply chains rely on and reproduce the exploitation and impoverishment of poor and working-class labour, especially (but not limited to) women and other workers in the Global South. Furthermore, these more 'minor' or routine forms of labour exploitation—for example, poverty wages and a lack of labour rights and protections—provide the conditions in which more extreme forms of labour unfreedom flourish.

7.4.2 Migration and intersections of gender, race, and citizenship

While poverty is no doubt crucial to understanding why some people may be vulnerable to unfree labour, there are other factors that drive workers' vulnerability to exploitation. As we have seen, at the bottom rungs of global supply chains labour is often carried out by informal, casualized, and/or contract workers (that is, non-regular workers). These *types* of workers lack key labour rights and protections, which in turn leaves them open to exploitation. Yet evidence also suggests that certain *groups* of workers—women, people of colour, Indigenous people, people from low-status castes, and migrants (and the intersections between these social identities)—are at disproportionate risk of exploitation and abuse. As discussed in Chapter 4, this vulnerability is rooted in hierarchies and patterns of exploitation dating back to slavery and colonialism, which are reconfigured and reproduced through the practices, norms, and relations of the contemporary global economy. Put simply, this means that some (racialized and gendered) workers in the global economy are deemed less valuable and more 'disposable' than others (Mezzadri 2016) (see also Key Theory Box 7.6).

In both the Global North and Global South, migrant workers are especially likely to experience precarious and exploitative working conditions, including the most extreme forms of unfreedom. Migrant workers' insecurity is intimately linked to restrictive border and immigration regimes, which limit workers' access to labour rights and protections, as well as their ability to engage in collective bargaining and association (Crane et al. 2019). Broadly speaking, workers who are excluded from citizenship and who are worried about their immigration status are less able to contest exploitative practices. Structural inequalities also mean that certain gendered and racialized groups find it more difficult to challenge or refuse poor and unsafe working conditions (Evans 2017). In this way, restrictive border and immigration regimes in the Global North create fertile terrain for exploitation among undocumented workers, asylum seekers, and other types of migrant workers, especially women, people of colour, and those migrating from the Global South.

Elsewhere, scholars have highlighted how South–South and internal migration shapes vulnerability to labour exploitation (McGrath 2013; Piper, Rosewarne, and Withers 2017; Deshingkar et al. 2019). Temporary intra-regional migrant workers in Asia, for example, are rendered precarious by a lack of formal legal rights and protections, which facilitates various forms of labour exploitation, including the substitution of contracts, the non-payment and underpayment of wages, and exploitative recruitment systems (Piper, Rosewarne, and Withers 2017). Temporary intra-regional migrants experience 'protracted precarity' not only as a result of their migration status, but because of their position within the global division of labour, that is, on the lowest rungs of the global labour market where they carry out predominantly informal, casualized,

---

KEY THEORY BOX 7.6 SOCIAL REPRODUCTION AND UNFREE LABOUR

Since the 1970s, feminist political economists have argued that production and reproduction are not separate but integrated 'spheres'; in order to understand the functioning and structure of the global economy, we must recognize the labour (paid and unpaid, formal and informal) that goes into (re)producing life, as well as goods and services (see also Hannah and Hinton, Chapter 4). Social reproductive labour includes child- and elder-care, looking after the sick, cleaning, and domestic work, such as doing the laundry and cooking. This labour is key to the daily and intergenerational reproduction of the working class, but has been historically undervalued. Social reproductive labour is also gendered, racialized, and geographically differentiated. Put simply, this means that women, migrants, and people of colour carry a disproportionate burden of responsibility for 'life-making activities' in the contemporary global economy (Bhattacharya

2017). In light of this, it is insufficient to focus exclusively on unfree labour relations in global production. Rather, we must pay attention to the labour involved in social reproduction and to the types of exploitation and oppression this entails. As we saw in the discussion of cocoa supply chains, the organization of social reproduction fundamentally shapes women workers' experiences of productive work, including unfree labour.

The global care economy is another example that blurs the boundary between production and reproduction, since it is a key site of reproductive labour, but also operates as an industry in which care is commodified and sold on the market (Prügl 2021). Thus, as Elizabeth Prügl notes (2020: 300) 'the production of life is increasingly integrated in circuits of commodity production'. We can recognize this integration through the concept of 'global (re)production'.

and otherwise unprotected types of work. Again, these forms and patterns of exploitation are not local or regional anomalies, but are rooted in the political economy of neoliberal globalization. Elsewhere, in the context of India, research has also documented the links between internal migration, discrimination on the basis of ethnicity and caste, and labour exploitation. Rameez Abbas' (2016) study, for example, found that North Indian labour migrants in Mumbai and Kolkata tend to be concentrated in low-paid informal jobs, particularly in the manufacturing and service sectors. In addition to low pay and insecure working conditions, this group of workers faces barriers to accessing citizenship rights, which are compounded by discrimination on the basis of ethnicity (Abbas 2016: 159).

Global agricultural supply chains are another case in point of how race, class, and migration intersect to (re)produce workers' exploitation. As Ben Rogaly

(2021) points out, the history of food production under capitalism is bound up with the history of slavery. From chattel slavery, enforced migration, and indentureship on plantations, to the super-exploitation that underpins contemporary agricultural supply chains, people across Africa, Asia, Latin America, and the Caribbean have been systematically exploited in agriculture (Manjapra 2018). In today's global economy, agricultural workers, many of whom are migrants, remain some of the most exploited in the world. Examples include West African migrant workers experiencing highly exploitative working conditions in tomato farming in Italy (Melossi 2021), workers trapped in debt bondage in sugarcane cutting and cattle farming in Brazil (Phillips 2013), and Mexican migrants facing precarity and disposability as temporary agricultural labourers in Canada (Castell Roldán and Alvarez Anaya 2022), to name just a few. As this discussion has shown (see also Everyday GPE Box 7.7),

---

EVERYDAY GPE BOX 7.7 HIGH-STREET CLOTHES

From the Nike sweatshop exposés of the 1990s to the Rana Plaza building collapse in Bangladesh in 2013 (see Figure 7.3), which killed 1,138 garment workers, the garment sector has long been dogged by scandal and tragedy. As a result, consumers are increasingly conscious of the provenance of high-street clothes and the potential environmental and labour issues involved in their production. As we discussed in Section 7.4.1, the garment sector's reliance on low wages has been roundly criticized by labour scholars and activists, with chronic poverty providing the context in which more extreme forms of labour exploitation can flourish. Sourcing practices and rapid, low-cost production systems also create structural and commercial dynamics that stimulate and reinforce labour exploitation. While the pace of global production has increased across many sectors and industries, the 'fast fashion' industry is an example of these dynamics par excellence. 'Fast fashion' refers to a business model whereby retailers seek to continuously refresh product lines for consumers, as frequently as once a week. With retailers like Primark offering new T-shirts for as little as £2, who is profiting and who is losing out from the 'fast fashion' trend?

The Leicester manufacturing scandal discussed in the Introduction to this chapter—in which manufacturers defied orders to close during the UK's national coronavirus lockdown—illustrates how these dynamics work in practice. Boohoo Group, an online fashion retailer, is the largest of the big brand companies linked to the Leicester factories. Boohoo hit record profits in 2020, with revenue of £600.7 million, up

39 per cent in the UK and 51 per cent internationally (Boohoo Groups PLC 2020: 2). According to evidence compiled by the campaign group Labour Behind the Label (LBH) (Lewis 2020), Boohoo sourced around 60–70 per cent of its production from Leicester at the beginning of 2020, a proportion that increased to 80 per cent by June 2020. During the same period, the company is estimated to have ordered up to 400,000 units per week from suppliers in Leicester (Lewis 2020). This demand helped to fuel unsafe labour practices and non-regular and highly exploitative forms of work: forced overtime; work intensification; the underpayment of wages; and a lack of adequate health and safety measures. While reports of labour abuses in the garment industry in Leicester are not new, these dynamics were intensified in the context of the coronavirus pandemic, with some workers being forced to work even when they were sick. Again, the speed, flexibility, and prices demanded by firms at the top of the garments supply chain acted as key structural drivers of exploitation; according to LBH (Lewis 2020): 'Industry sources state that it is impossible to produce the units/garments requested by Boohoo for the product price *and* pay workers the national minimum wage'. As a result of the controversy, Boohoo promised to launch a multi-million-pound audit of labour standards within their supply chains. However, subsequent reports indicate that no legal actions were taken against employers in Leicester. Moreover, the only prosecution arising from the investigation was the deportation of an undocumented migrant worker.

Approximately one third of workers in Leicester's garment factories are migrants, largely from Pakistan, India, Bangladesh, Somalia, and Eastern Europe, and the majority are people of colour (Lewis 2020: 5). These demographic patterns reflect, to an extent, the makeup of the garment workforce globally, in which migrant workers, especially women in the Global South, are significantly overrepresented. In key exporting countries such as Bangladesh, Sri Lanka, Myanmar, and Cambodia, women comprise upwards of 80 per cent of the garment workforce (Evans 2017). Migrant women are systematically exploited as a cheap and 'disposable' source of labour in the garment sector (Mezzadri 2016). These dynamics are not just about gender—although that is a key factor—but about how gender and class relations are co-constituted through the garment sector's exploitative and patriarchal labour regimes.

While garment workers globally have relatively low levels of unionization, some trade unionists within the sector have sought to organize against abusive and dangerous working conditions. Thivya Rakini is the president of the Tamil Nadu Textile and Common Labour Union, a major hub of garment production in India, with a largely female workforce. Rakini is highly sceptical of the efforts made by the global fashion industry to prevent the exploitation of workers like herself and the women she represents. In an interview with the *Guardian* newspaper (2022), Rakini stated: 'The truth is that sexual harassment, rape, even murder has become part and parcel of the lives of women working in garment factories in my district. International brands who buy from Tamil Nadu know very well that women in their supply chains are exploited to the core, they know the impact that their production targets and their poverty wages have on the workers' lives. Their auditors know their inspections are meaningless. Their whole system is a lie'. Rakini's comments sum up the realities of the structural and political economic factors shaping unfree labour: the unequal distribution of value; predatory sourcing and purchasing practices; the devaluing of feminized and racialized labour; and the impact of poverty wages. She also highlights the flaws within existing private governance initiatives to tackle unfree labour, notably in terms of audit initiatives, which we will discuss further in Section 7.5.

Figure 7.3 Dhaka, Bangladesh. 24 April 2021. A general view of the site during the eighth anniversary of the Rana Plaza building disaster in Savar. One of the world's most devastating factory disasters, Rana Plaza, an eight-story building, collapsed due to structural failure and has led to international safety monitoring in Bangladesh. Campaigners are warning of 'grim consequences' if such oversight is abandoned.

Source: Alamy.

workers' vulnerability to unfree labour is often rooted in the intersection of *multiple* axes of oppression and relations of exploitation: gender, race, class, sexuality, geography, and migration status. These dynamics are contextualized by uneven patterns of global development arising from the history and legacies of slavery and colonialism (see Bhagat, Chapter 14).

KEY POINTS

- Labour exploitation in global production occurs systematically, with certain types and groups of workers, in certain industries, and in certain sections of the supply chain at greater risk of unfree labour. This includes: informal, casualized, and contract workers employed at the base of global supply chains; people living in poverty; women; people of colour; migrants; Indigenous people; and people from low-status castes.

- Some of these axes of oppression and exploitation can be traced back to slavery and colonialism. But they are also reproduced through the relations and structures of the contemporary global economy.

- Export-oriented production is seen as 'good for development' in the Global South by actors like the World Bank because it reduces poverty and increases workforce participation, including by providing low-skill jobs for women.

- Rather than providing a route out of poverty and unemployment, however, critical GPE scholars have argued that global supply chains are configured to rely on and reproduce the exploitation and impoverishment of workers at the bottom of the chain.

7.5 Addressing unfree labour in supply chains

Initiatives to combat unfree and 'forced labour' in global supply chains have multiplied since the 2000s. With trade liberalization, deregulation, and the rolling back of the state, there has been a particular emphasis on enhancing private responsibility for labour governance, namely by corporations. Corporate governance initiatives have taken on renewed urgency as consumer concerns over the ethics of global production have grown. MNCs have therefore invested heavily in activities aimed at improving their environmental and social credentials. Much of this investment has been channelled into **corporate social responsibility**

(**CSR**) activities, which include voluntary codes of conduct, audit programmes, and ethical certification schemes. These activities are based on an essentially voluntary set of commitments, principles, and activities. While on the surface this may seem laudable, scholars have outlined a number of weaknesses in company codes of conduct as a means to raise labour standards. Key weaknesses include: vague definitions; unclear responsibilities and parameters; failures in enforcement and monitoring; a lack of independent verification; and the exclusion of major sourcing companies from the codes (Soederberg 2007). Evidence also suggests that voluntary compliance programmes aimed at improving 'worker voice' have been largely ineffective in promoting greater freedom of association for workers (Anner 2017). This is because they are voluntary and lack strong enforcement mechanisms, particularly in countries where employers or the state control trade unions, as is the case with much garment production.

Alongside voluntary compliance programmes and codes of conduct, audits have become a central mechanism of corporate supply chain governance in the contemporary era. Audits require companies to monitor and report on their own supply chains, effectively as a form of self-regulation. Again, however, evidence suggests that audits are largely ineffective in identifying and addressing labour abuses in supply chains (LeBaron, Lister, and Dauvergne 2017). One significant limitation is that they often exclude key sections of the supply in which exploitation is more likely to take place. Auditing and benchmarking are also a key component in ethical certification schemes, an increasingly popular form of multi-stakeholder initiative since the 2000s. According to the logic of these initiatives, companies address governance gaps in their supply chains by adhering to a set of international standards, engaging in benchmarking and monitoring activities, and participating in collective governance systems. Many of these initiatives have been rolled out in partnership with civil society organizations, who then certify the products as 'sustainable', 'ethical', or 'fair trade'. Well-known examples include Rainforest Alliance and Fairtrade International. Again, however, evidence shows that ethical certification schemes are failing to fulfil their environmental and social objectives (LeBaron et al. 2022). In terms of labour, this is because the schemes fail to tackle the key structural, institutional, and commercial dynamics in supply chains that drive labour exploitation, such as the vast market power of MNCs, sourcing practices, and the low value accorded to labour. Moreover, some critical GPE scholars have argued that not only are these schemes inadequate to address the key drivers of labour exploitation—such as poverty wages—they are reinforcing them, by giving corporations a veneer of accountability and respectability, and by coopting and neutralizing more radical calls for change (Soederberg 2007). As LeBaron et al. (2022: 101) put it, 'MNCs strategically use CSR to fend off criticism of their business models and supply chain dynamics while refusing to redistribute value down the supply chain in the form of higher wages for workers'.

7.5.1 Public initiatives: Modern slavery and trafficking

Alongside the expansion of corporate supply chain governance, governments around the world have brought in legislative and policy measures intended to address modern slavery in supply chains, as part of wider 'anti-trafficking and slavery' activities. The UK's Modern Slavery Act (MSA) is one prominent example, which was passed into law in 2015. The MSA contains the Transparency in Supply Chains (TISC) clause, which requires businesses grossing over £36 million to publish an annual statement on the steps they have taken to eradicate modern slavery in their supply chains. This clause is intended to help close the 'governance gap' in supply chains. However, in practice, the TISC clause is a relatively weak measure, since it continues to place the onus on companies (and effectively consumers) to self-regulate the industry, rather than the state. Indeed, the MSA has attracted criticism more broadly for its weak enforcement mechanisms, which are seen to lack requisite regulatory power (Fudge 2018).

In addition to these issues, the interpretation of modern slavery in legislation like the MSA has been critiqued for largely limiting its focus to migrant labour (Fudge 2018). This focus is linked to a political agenda of restricting immigration and controlling borders. The UK model is therefore best understood as a criminal justice and border control approach to tackling slavery. Indeed, across the Global North, anti-slavery and trafficking policy efforts have tended to prioritize criminal justice interventions. These interventions seek to target 'bad apple' employers or labour recruiters and provide protection to victims. They have been operationalized through actors such as the police and immigration and border forces. However, critics of this approach highlight the role of anti-slavery and

trafficking policy in bolstering restrictive immigration and border regimes, which, as we discussed in Section 7.3.4, negatively impact on migrant workers, particularly from the Global South. As Judy Fudge puts it: 'the modern slavery paradigm tends to reinforce the view that labour exploitation and unfreedom are the result of morally culpable individuals who should be publicly vilified, rather than systemic and institutional features of state policies and practices' (2018: 415). This means that, in practice, criminal justice interventions work to extend the power of some of the key purveyors of discrimination and insecurity towards undocumented migrant workers, namely the police and border forces. They also obscure the central role of the state in manufacturing the types of transnational migrant precarity that leave workers vulnerable to unfree labour (LeBaron and Phillips 2019). In this way, dominant policy approaches to anti-slavery and trafficking in the Global North not only fail to support workers who experience the most extreme forms of exploitation, but form part of a wider set of legal, policy, and institutional practices that create the conditions in which labour exploitation can flourish. From a critical GPE perspective, alternative solutions must be found that address the underlying political economic drivers of exploitation and insecurity, notably strengthening labour rights and protections, curbing corporate power through increased state governance and regulation, dismantling restrictive immigration regimes, and increasing the value accorded to labour, including by paying workers a living wage.

Calls for greater state regulation may seem optimistic in light of the dominance of private corporate governance regimes and the broader institutional entrenchment of neoliberalism. However, some governments and policymakers have at least begun to acknowledge the risks of excessive corporate power. The power of the Big Tech companies in particular has become a source of concern, even though their growth has been facilitated by pro-business regulatory frameworks and policies. In the US, for example, an investigation by the House Judiciary Committee into the four Big Tech giants Google, Amazon, Facebook, and Apple recommended curbing their monopoly power. Lawmakers from the Democratic Party have since introduced five bills aimed at reducing the monopoly power of Big Tech companies (Godwin 2021). Similarly, the United Nations Conference on Trade and Development (UNCTAD) Report *Beyond Austerity* highlights the risks associated with the concentration of corporate power within global supply chains, calling it 'a new form of global rentier capital-ism to the detriment of balanced and inclusive growth for the many' (2017: 119).

7.6 Conclusion

The problem of unfree labour goes to the core of debates around development, poverty, and economic growth. Is export-oriented growth 'good for workers'? Can 'economic upgrading' lead to 'social upgrading'? And who benefits from processes of economic glo-balization, including the expansion of global supply chains? In order to explore these issues, this chapter began by looking at liberal and critical GPE accounts of severe labour exploitation, as well as influential pol-icy and legal instruments, such as the ILO's definition of forced labour. Using a critical approach, the chap-ter highlighted how labour exploitation is structurally embedded and (re)produced within the global econ-omy, with particular types and groups of workers, in particular sectors, and in particular sections of the supply chain at greater risk of exploitation and abuse. This includes: contract, casualized, and informal

workers; workers at the base of global supply chains; poor and working-class people; migrants (including internal and South–South migrants); women; people of colour; Indigenous people; and people from low-status castes. Sectors that are known to profit from unfree labour include garments, electronics, agricul-ture and food processing, mining, fishing, construc-tion, domestic work, care services, and sex work. Thus, rather than viewing labour unfreedom as an excep-tional form of labour relation, that is, one that occurs in isolated, individualized, and otherwise anomalous circumstances, it constitutes a routine aspect of work for millions of people employed in global (re)produc-tion. The pervasive character of unfree labour chal-lenges conventional accounts of 'modern slavery', in which slavery and unfreedom are seen as essentially individualized relations and practices that are external to the global capitalist economy. The theoretical roots of this interpretation can be traced to the liberal idea that labour unfreedom is an aberration within an oth-erwise free market and can be rectified by a combina-tion of market-based and policy solutions (LeBaron 2015; Fudge 2019).

Using a critical GPE lens, the chapter went on to explore the role of institutional and structural driv-ers of labour unfreedom, namely: the organization of globalized (re)production and the changing nature of supply chains; deregulation and the rolling back of the state; the extensive political and economic power of MNCs and their impact on supply chain dynamics; vast disparities in wealth and income associated with neo-liberal economic transformation; and global migration regimes and hierarchies of gender, race, and citizen-ship. Finally, the chapter considered 'anti-trafficking and slavery' approaches as adopted by policymakers and governments in the Global North and the turn towards corporate supply chain governance as a means to identify and remediate labour and environmental issues in supply chains, as exemplified in CSR. While these efforts may seem like an important step forward, the chapter argued that they have largely failed to address the *political economy* of unfree labour in global supply chains. In terms of practical implications, this perspective translates into a concern for pro-worker, pro-migrant solutions: increased labour rights and pro-tections; strengthening workers' collective bargaining power and freedom of association; dismantling restric-tive immigration regimes; greater state involvement in labour governance; initiatives to regulate and curb corporate power and profits; and the redistribution of power and value across supply chains.

7.7 QUESTIONS

1. Why have scholars critiqued the modern slavery framework in theory and in practice?

2. What are the pros and cons of understanding severe labour exploitation using the concept of 'forced labour'?

3. What does it mean to think of labour unfreedom as a 'continuum'?

4. Who is most vulnerable to unfree labour in global production and why?

5. How does migration and citizenship relate to unfree labour?

6. What are the limitations of private corporate governance efforts, such as corporate social responsibility, to improve labour standards in supply chains?

7. Why should we be concerned about the political and economic power of MNCs?

8. How should we address unfree labour in global supply chains?

7.8 FURTHER READING

Bales, K. (2012), *Disposable People: New Slavery in the Global Economy, Updated with a New Preface*, 3rd ed. (Oakland, CA: University of California Press). An influential account of 'new slavery'.

Barrientos, S., Kothari, U., and Phillips, N. (2013), 'Dynamics of Unfree Labour in the Contemporary Global Economy', *Journal of Development Studies* 49/8: 1037–1041. A short article that helpfully situates the study of unfree labour in the context of broader debates about labour conditions and the globalization of production.

Brace, L., and O'Connell-Davidson, J. (eds.) (2018), *Revisiting Slavery and Antislavery: Towards a Critical Analysis* (London: Palgrave Macmillan). Interdisciplinary collection that develops a critique of modern slavery discourse.

ILO (International Labour Organization) (2012), *ILO Indicators of Forced Labour* (Geneva: ILO). The ILO's explanation of their indicators of forced labour.

ILO (International Labour Organization) (2022), *Global Estimates of Modern Slavery: Forced Labour and Forced Marriage* (Geneva: ILO, Walk Free, and IOM). The global and regional estimates of modern slavery produced by the International Labour Organization (ILO), Walk Free, and the International Organization for Migration (IOM).

LeBaron, G. (2015), 'Unfree Labour Beyond Binaries', *International Feminist Journal of Politics* 17/1: 1–19. A detailed discussion of how shifts in power, production, and social reproduction under neoliberalism have given rise to unfree labour.

Lerche, J. (2011), 'The Unfree Labour Category and Unfree Labour Estimates: A Continuum within Low-End Labour Relations', *Manchester Papers in Political Economy No. 10* (Manchester: University of Manchester), 1–45. A critical account of unfree labour that proposes the 'continuum of unfreedoms'.

McGrath, S. (2017), 'Unfree Labor', in *International Encyclopedia of Geography* (London: John Wiley). A concise overview of the debates surrounding unfree labour, forced labour, new slavery, and trafficking.

Phillips, N. (2013), 'Unfree Labour and Adverse Incorporation in the Global Economy: Comparative Perspectives on Brazil and India', *Economy and Society* 42/2: 171–196. A detailed critical examination of the links between unfree labour, poverty, and vulnerability in the global economy.

CONTRIBUTOR NOTE

Ellie Gore is a Lecturer in Global Political Economy in the Department of Politics at the University of Manchester. Their expertise are in feminist and queer international political economy, with a particular focus on sexuality, labour relations, and the political economy of development. Their publications include *Between HIV Prevention and LGBTI Rights: The Political Economy of Queer Activism in Ghana* (forthcoming with University of Michigan Press, 2024) and journal articles in *New Political Economy, International Feminist Journal of Politics*, and *The Journal of Development Studies*.

PART III

Money and Finance

8

The Evolution of the International Monetary and Financial System

Eric Helleiner

Chapter contents

Reader's guide

The international monetary and financial system plays a central role in the global political economy (GPE). The contemporary system is still shaped by many legacies of the Bretton Woods monetary and financial order established in 1944 and the political priorities of its architects. That order has also undergone several pivotal transformations. An important gradual change has been dramatic globalization of financial markets since the 1960s. A more sudden one was the abandonment of the Bretton Woods gold exchange standard in 1971. The dollar standard that replaced it faces a number of challenges in the contemporary era. Also significant has been the breakdown of the adjustable peg exchange rate regime in the early 1970s, as well as regionalization and decentralization trends.

8.1 Introduction

It is often said that money makes the world go round. Indeed, international flows of money today dwarf the cross-border trade of goods in their size. If money is so influential, it is fitting that it should have a prominent place in the study of GPE.

Scholars working on the political economy of international monetary and financial issues share the belief that the study of money and finance must embrace a wider lens than that adopted by most economists. Economists are trained to view money and finance primarily as economic phenomena. They highlight how money serves as a medium of exchange, a unit of account, and a store of value, while financial activity allocates credit within the economy. But monetary and financial systems are also designed to serve many political purposes (not to mention social and cultural ones), including the pursuit of power, ideologies, and interests. Their functioning also has many political consequences (as well as, once again, social and cultural ones). Understanding these interrelationships between politics and systems of money and finance is a goal of GPE scholars (e.g. Strange 1998; Kirshner 2003).

These interrelationships are particularly evident at the international level, where no single political authority exists. What money should be used to facilitate international economic transactions, and how should it be managed? What should the nature of the relationship between national currencies be? How should credit be created and allocated at the international level? The answers to these questions have profoundly important implications for politics, not just within countries, but also between them. Not surprisingly, they are also the subject of domestic and international political struggles, often of an intense kind.

This chapter provides an overview of the evolution of the international monetary and financial system since the creation of the Bretton Woods order in 1944. The first section examines the core features of that order as well as its initial implementation. The following three sections analyse some important transformations of the Bretton Woods order relating to the globalization of financial markets and the nature of the international monetary standard, as well as the content of exchange rate regimes and trends of regionalization and decentralization. In Chapter 9, Louis W. Pauly addresses another feature of the contemporary international financial order: its vulnerability to crises. In Chapter 10, Chris Clarke and Adrienne Roberts offer a bottom-up perspective by adopting 'the everyday' as a lens to examine the politics of finance, debt, and money.

8.2 The Bretton Woods order

The contemporary international monetary and financial system is shaped by many legacies of a 1944 conference that took place in Bretton Woods, New Hampshire (Conway 2014). The meeting was attended by forty-four governments from around the world that were on the side of the Allies during the Second World War. Its goal was to design a new international monetary and financial order for the post-war world in the event that the Allies won the war (which was not entirely clear at the time of the conference). At the end of the meeting, the delegates endorsed a very innovative design.

8.2.1 The Bretton Woods Institutions

To begin with, they established two new public multilateral financial institutions that remain influential today: the International Monetary Fund (IMF) and the International Bank for Reconstruction and Development (now World Bank). No institutions of this kind had ever been created before. At the time, the only existing international financial institution was the Bank for International Settlements (BIS), which had been created in 1930 to foster cooperation among a small number of central banks, many of which were private institutions at the time. By contrast, the IMF and World Bank were designed to be intergovernmental institutions with membership open to all countries that were willing to accept their goals. They also had much more ambitious mandates than the BIS.

Their core mandate was a liberal economic one of cultivating a more open world economy than had existed during the 1930s. In that previous decade, international trade and investment had collapsed in the context of financial instability, currency fluctuations, and rising national controls on cross-border trade and payments. In the view of the Bretton Woods architects, those developments had contributed not just to the Great Depression, but also to the war itself. They hoped that the IMF and World Bank could help to revive and protect a more open global economic order in order to avoid repeating those traumatic economic and political experiences.

The Bretton Woods Institutions were designed to play this role partly through their lending activities. The IMF was empowered to offer short-term loans to governments whose countries were experiencing temporary external payments deficits. With the loans, governments could finance the deficits instead of resorting to the kinds of policies used in the 1930s to cope with payments imbalances, such as controls on trade and payments or currency devaluations. The World Bank was designed to mobilize long-term capital for reconstruction and development after the war (both with its own loans and by guaranteeing private loans). In the words of its charter, its support for these long-term loans was designed to 'promote the long-range balanced growth of international trade and the maintenance of equilibrium in balances of payments' (Article I(iii)).

An open world economy would also be fostered by new international legal obligations on all member governments of a kind that had never existed before in international monetary and financial relations. Two such obligations embodied in the IMF's charter were particularly important. First, to foster international trade, the IMF's rules required members to keep their currencies freely convertible into other currencies for trade (or, more precisely, '**current account**') payments. Second, to reduce currency volatility that disrupted international trade and investments, member governments had to maintain a fixed value of their national currency vis-à-vis that of the US dollar, which itself was convertible into gold at a fixed rate of US$35 per ounce.

8.2.2 **A different kind of gold standard**

By requiring the pegging of all national currencies to gold via the US dollar, the IMF rules created an international 'gold exchange' standard. With its tie to gold, the Bretton Woods system bore some likeness to the **international gold standard** that had supported the open world economy of the late nineteenth and early twentieth centuries. That international monetary regime had earned a reputation as a market-oriented international monetary system in which governments played little role (see Key Concept Box 8.1). The Bretton Woods system, however, endorsed a more activist economic role for public authorities.

A number of features of the Bretton Woods agreements highlight this endorsement of public economic activism. One was the international lending roles of the IMF and World Bank themselves. Another was the fact that IMF member governments were given the right to control all cross-border capital movements (in contrast to their obligation to maintain 'current account' convertibility). While the Bretton Woods

---

KEY CONCEPT BOX 8.1 THE PRE-1930S INTERNATIONAL GOLD STANDARD

In the last third of the nineteenth century, an international gold standard emerged in an ad hoc fashion across the world, as many governments unilaterally fixed the value of their national currencies to gold. The result was a fixed exchange rate regime with an almost global reach. The system broke down during the First World War, but it was resurrected briefly in the 1920s, only to collapse again in the early 1930s. In theory, the international gold standard was a self-regulating international monetary order that relied on market dynamics to resolve international payments imbalances. For example, if a country experienced a trade deficit, the export of gold would depress domestic wages and prices in such a way that the country's international competitive position—and thus its trade position—improved. That simple process was complicated, however, by the fact that domestic monetary systems were increasingly made up of bank notes and deposits rather than gold coins (see Figure 8.1). In that context, a national monetary authority which issued notes and regulated the banking system was expected to simulate the automatic adjustment process by following 'rules of the game'. In the event of a trade deficit, it would tighten monetary conditions by curtailing the issue of notes and raising interest rates. The latter was designed not just to induce deflationary pressures (by increasing the cost of borrowing), but also to attract short-term capital flows to help finance the payments

imbalance while the underlying macroeconomic adjustment process was taking place. In practice, however, governments did not always follow these 'rules of the game', and the financing of, and adjustment to, payments imbalances did not always take place in the automatic manner that the theory of the gold standard anticipated (e.g. De Cecco 1974; Eichengreen 1985; Bryan 2010).

Figure 8.1 American US Canadian Australian Dollar, Euro, Japanese Yen, and Chinese Yuan banknotes

Source: iStock.

architects welcomed productive international investment flows, this right to use '**capital controls**' was designed to enable governments to stop speculative and disequilibrating private financial flows that could disrupt their policy autonomy and stable exchange rates (Helleiner 1994).

Underlying the desire to protect policy autonomy was an endorsement of public economic activism at the domestic level. Delegates from the two leading powers at the Bretton Woods conference—the US and Britain—were interested in building welfare states and pursuing new activist macroeconomic policies to promote full employment. Many governments from less industrialized countries (which made up well over half of the delegations) backed state-led industrialization and development policies that were designed to boost local standards of living. Another important conference attendee, the Soviet Union, was committed to a centrally planned economy. Capital controls would help to protect each of these forms of domestic economic activism from being undermined by cross-border financial movements that sought, for example, to evade high taxes, low interest rates, or various kinds of domestic financial regulations (Helleiner 1994; 2014a).

A further innovation of Bretton Woods was a provision in the IMF's rules that allowed national governments to adjust the pegged value of their national currencies whenever their country experienced a 'fundamental disequilibrium', such as a large and sustained trade deficit. Under the pre-1930s international gold standard, trade deficits were expected to be resolved through market dynamics that did not involve this kind of exchange rate adjustment (see Key Concept Box 8.1). This IMF rule enabled more government agency and activism in resolving a payments imbalance of this kind. For example, a government could choose to devalue its national currency vis-à-vis the US dollar as a way of discouraging imports (which would suddenly be more expensive for citizens) and encouraging exports (which would suddenly be cheaper for foreigners). Unilateral devaluations of this kind had taken place in the 1930s, but the IMF was designed to place these types of national decisions within a more cooperative international framework that looked out for the interests of the world economy as a whole (Best 2005).

Finally, and more generally, the IMF was given a broad mandate to promote active intergovernmental monetary cooperation and encourage governments to, in the words of its charter, 'shorten the duration and lessen the degree of disequilibrium in the international balances of payments of members' (Article 1(vi)). To discourage international economic imbalances, the IMF's lending capacity gave it some potential influence over deficit countries. Another provision in its charter—the scarce currency clause—provided a means for official pressure to come to bear on surplus countries. Although never applied in the post-war years, the clause enabled the Fund to declare the currency of such a country 'scarce', in which case other member governments were permitted to impose temporary restrictions on trade with that country (Patalano 2019).

8.2.3 Embedded liberalism and its limits

John Ruggie (1982) famously described the innovative vision of the Bretton Woods architects as an 'embedded liberal' one. On the liberal side, this vision was centred around two new public multilateral financial institutions whose activities and rules were meant to promote an open world economy. At the same time, the commitment to a new kind of institutionalized liberal multilateralism was 'embedded' in social priorities by being combined with an endorsement of various kinds of activist economic roles for public authorities (Helleiner 2019).

It is important to recognize that the multilateralism of Bretton Woods had important hierarchical and exclusionary elements. The hierarchy stemmed from the fact that the voting rules in the IMF and World Bank were set up in a manner that gave the major financial powers—and the US in particular—a dominant voice in these institutions (see Key Concept Box 8.2 for the IMF). The exclusionary side arose from the fact that most colonized parts of the world were not represented at the conference or in the new institutions being established; the only two exceptions were the Philippines (which had been promised independence by the US after the war) and India (which had already been represented at international conferences before the war). When Indian delegates called for the IMF to address enormous sterling debts that the British had accumulated to their Indian colony during the war, the conference's rejection of this idea also highlighted how intra-empire monetary relations would be insulated from the multilateralism of Bretton Woods (Helleiner 2014a).

It is also important to recognize the limits of the social 'embeddedness' of the Bretton Woods vision. Ruggie borrowed the concept of 'embeddedness'

KEY CONCEPT BOX 8.2 QUOTAS AND DECISION-MAKING IN THE IMF

On joining the IMF, all member governments pay a 'quota' to the institution, a contribution whose size reflects attributes such as their relative size within the world economy. The amount of money they can borrow from the Fund is determined by their quota size. Quotas also play a very significant role in determining voting shares within the Fund. All countries are allocated some 'basic votes', but most of their voting share is determined by their quota size. Quotas are reviewed at least every five years, and the relative share of various countries has changed over time in response to these reviews. The US share of total votes, for example, has fallen from over 30 per cent of the total in 1944 to 16.50 per cent today. The next three largest holders of votes currently are Japan (6.14 per cent), China (6.08 per cent), and Germany (5.31 per cent). Major decisions in the Fund—including changes to quotas—must be approved by an 85 per cent majority of the total votes. The IMF is governed by its Board of Governors, which meets annually. Day-to-day decision-making, however, is delegated to the Executive Board, which meets several times a week. The Board has twenty-four members, with some executive directors representing single countries (the US, Japan, China, Germany, France, Britain, and Saudi Arabia), while others head up groups of countries or 'constituencies' (such as India, which represents both itself and several other countries in its region).

from the scholar Karl Polanyi (1944: 59) who argued, in the same year as the Bretton Woods conference, for a socialist economic order that was more 'embedded in social relations' than a market economy. Polanyi's ambitious conception of embeddedness was not shared by the lead American and British architects of Bretton Woods. They also did not share Polanyi's view that a socially embedded economy needed to address environmental issues such as soil erosion, dust bowls, deforestation, river pollution, and 'defiled' landscapes. These issues received very little attention at the 1944 conference. Two months before the Bretton Woods meeting began, the International Labour Organization also urged that the social goals of promoting gender equality and ending racial discrimination be addressed in post-war international financial planning. But these issues, too, were ignored in the formal deliberations at Bretton Woods (Helleiner 2022).

8.2.4 Implementing Bretton Woods

Soon after the conclusion of the 1944 conference, it became clear that some of the ambitions of the Bretton Woods delegates would not easily be realized. They had hoped to build an international monetary and financial order of worldwide scope. In 1946, however, the Soviet Union refused to join the system that it had helped to negotiate, and Soviet allies also withdrew once the Cold War began. After the 1949 Chinese revolution, the People's Republic of China was also outside the system, as China was represented in the IMF and World Bank by the government in Taiwan.

Even for the countries that remained members of the Bretton Woods system, the IMF and World Bank played only very limited roles for the first decade and a half after the Second World War. Many governments also did not make their currencies convertible in this period, including most West European countries which did not restore current account convertibility until 1958 (the Bretton Woods agreements had allowed for a 'transition' period during which countries could keep currencies inconvertible). Further, imperial powers who were members of the Bretton Woods Institutions imposed monetary and financial policies on their colonies that were far from the 'embedded liberal' ideals of Bretton Woods, including through 'currency boards' that managed money in a manner similar to the pre-1930s gold standard (Helleiner 2019).

At the same time, however, some of the principles outlined at Bretton Woods were endorsed by many governments outside the Soviet orbit and colonial contexts, such as support for capital controls, the gold exchange standard, and the maintenance of an **adjustable peg** exchange rate regime. Moreover, although the Bretton Woods Institutions were side-lined, other bodies—particularly the US government, but also regional institutions such as the European Payments Union—acted in the ways that the Bretton Woods architects had hoped the IMF and World Bank would; that is, they provided public international lending for temporary balance of payments support, as well as for reconstruction and development (Helleiner 1994; 2019).

The period between 1958 and 1971 is often described as the heyday of the Bretton Woods order, as its key provisions came into place in this era. The membership of the IMF and World Bank also expanded dramatically as many newly independent countries in Africa and Asia joined the institutions. In addition, both institutions became more active lenders, although they still had a less central role in the system than the Bretton Woods architects had hoped for (and the IMF began to impose stringent conditions on their loans to less industrialized countries in ways that had not been discussed at Bretton Woods).

What has become of the Bretton Woods order since then? In some respects, it seems to be still alive. The IMF and World Bank still exist (although their roles have changed in ways described at various places in this chapter). Indeed, their membership has widened to include almost all countries in the world (including the People's Republic of China and Russia, which joined the institutions in 1980 and 1992, respectively), just as the Bretton Woods architects had hoped. Most countries' currencies are also still convertible for current account transactions. Another key sign of continuity is the fact that the US dollar remains the key international currency. At the same time, however, the Bretton Woods order has also been transformed in important ways.

KEY POINTS

- The 1944 Bretton Woods conference created two new kinds of public international institutions—the IMF and World Bank—to foster a more open world economy.

- It also endorsed public economic activism via their lending roles as well as the IMF's endorsement of capital controls, adjustable currency pegs, and active intergovernmental monetary cooperation.

- 'Embedded liberalism' describes the Bretton Woods vision of creating a new kind of institutionalized liberal multilateralism that was compatible with public economic activism.

- Some of the features of the Bretton Woods order were in place between 1945 and 1958, but this order reached its heyday between 1958 and 1971.

8.3 The globalization of financial markets

The globalization of private financial markets has been one of the most important of these transformations. Recall that the Bretton Woods architects endorsed an international financial order in which governments could control cross-border private financial flows, and public international institutions played a new role in international lending. Although the Bretton Woods architects had certainly hoped to revive productive private international investment flows, few at the time expected the world in which we now live, where enormous sums of private capital flow around the world quite freely on a 24-hour basis.

8.3.1 Explaining financial globalization

How did we get from there to here? The growth of global telecommunications networks has enabled money to be moved around the world much more easily and cheaply than in the past. The dramatic expansion of international trade and multinational corporate activity in recent decades has also generated growing demand for private international financial services. Other market trends have encouraged financial globalization, such as growing competitive pressures within leading financial systems, and the creation of new financial products such as derivatives (see Pauly, Chapter 9).

Governments have also fostered the trend by supporting the emergence of a more liberal environment for cross-border financial flows (Helleiner 1994; Abdelal 2007). A first step was taken by the British government when it encouraged the growth of a 'euro-market' in London during the 1960s, where international financial activity in foreign currencies could be conducted on a largely unregulated basis. After the early 1970s, many governments began to fully dismantle capital controls they had employed at various times during the postwar years, led by the US (1974) and UK (1979). By the 1990s, an almost fully liberal pattern of financial relations had emerged among Organization for Economic Cooperation and Development (OECD) countries, giving market actors a degree of freedom in cross-border financial activity unparalleled since the 1920s. Many lower income countries also began to abolish capital controls, including many small jurisdictions—such as the Cayman Islands—that offered their territories as locations for 'offshore' international financial activity via loose regulatory environments (Palan et al. 2009; Ogle 2017).

What explains states' growing support for financial globalization? The increasing influence of more free market or 'neoliberal' ideology among financial policymakers in this period played a part in some countries. Neoliberals argued that 'free money'—like their view of free trade—would enhance individual liberty and market efficiency. While 'embedded liberals' sought to protect the policy autonomy of governments, many neoliberals also applauded how global financial markets could discipline governments that pursued inflationary or fiscally unsustainable policies. Some policymakers have also seen the liberalization of capital controls as a kind of competitive strategy to attract mobile financial business and capital to their national territory. Further, as their country's firms became increasingly transnational and had access to foreign financial markets, policymakers worried that national capital controls were becoming increasingly difficult to enforce in an effective manner that was not costly to the national economy (Goodman and Pauly 1993).

Alongside governments' unilateral decisions to abolish capital controls, there have been efforts to codify the commitment to financial liberalization in international rules (Abdelal 2007). Some of these efforts have been successful, such as a 1988 European Union directive to liberalize capital controls among its members, and a 1989 amendment to an OECD code which committed OECD countries to liberalizing all financial flows. Less successful was an effort that began in the mid-1990s to remove IMF members' right to control capital movements that had been granted at Bretton Woods. That initiative was abandoned at the height of the 1997–1998 East Asian financial crisis, which highlighted the costs of unrestricted capital mobility to many policymakers in the region and elsewhere (see Pauly, Chapter 9).

The experience of the global financial crisis of 2008 further undercut support for financial liberalization. In the wake of the crisis, many observers noted that countries which had maintained capital controls—such as China and India—were more insulated from the severe financial turmoil in US and European markets. When US and European authorities dramatically lowered interest rates during and after the crisis, countries such as Brazil and South Korea also employed various capital account restrictions to prevent large-scale financial inflows from driving up their exchange rates and/or generating domestic financial bubbles. These experiences prompted the IMF in 2012 to declare that 'in certain circumstances, capital flow management measures can be useful' (IMF 2012b: 2). In 2022, it widened the circumstances in which their use was endorsed. These declarations represented

a shift in the IMF's position from that of the 1990s, but they were still far from the strong endorsement of capital controls at Bretton Woods (Gallagher 2015; Grabel 2015). More generally, no major advanced industrialized country has reimposed capital controls, and global financial markets remain an enduring, central feature of the GPE.

8.3.2 Implications for national policy autonomy

What have been the implications of the post-war globalization of finance? One set of implications is addressed in Pauly, Chapter 9: the vulnerability of global financial markets to financial crises. A second set of implications relates to the concerns of the Bretton Woods architects. As noted earlier in this chapter, they worried that a liberal international financial order would undermine their efforts to create a stable exchange rate system and to protect national policy autonomy. We will see later in this chapter how financial globalization did complicate the task of maintaining fixed exchange rates. But what about its implications for the autonomy of national governments to pursue their preferred economic policies?

This question has generated much debate in the field of GPE. Some have argued that financial globalization has severely undermined national policy autonomy by giving investors a powerful 'exit' option to exercise against governments that stray too far from global investors' preferences. Proponents of this view argue that this discipline is felt particularly strongly by governments that pursue policies disliked by wealthy asset-holders, such as large budget deficits, high taxation, expansionary macroeconomic policies that risk inflation, or, more generally, policies that reflect left-of-centre political values (Gill and Law 1989; Kurzer 1993; Cerny 1994; Sinclair 1994). Less industrialized countries are seen to be especially vulnerable to the discipline of global financial markets because their financial systems are often very small relative to the enormous size of global financial flows and because investors are often more skittish about the security of their assets in these contexts. If asset-holders (domestic or foreign) lose confidence, these countries can experience an enormously damaging flight of private capital. Their vulnerability to the structural power of global financial markets is seen to reinforce their wider and longstanding position of 'international financial subordination' and financial 'dependency' (Musthaq 2021; Alami et al. 2022).

When **flight capital** helps to trigger external debt crises, countries have often turned to the IMF and World Bank for financial support. During the 1980s and 1990s, that support came with increasingly tough conditions, such as demands for austerity and neoliberal structural reforms (see Pauly, Chapter 9). When imposing conditionality of this kind, these institutions were acting in a different role from that envisioned by the Bretton Woods architects. The IMF and World Bank faced much criticism for this shift and have adjusted their policies in some contexts and responded in other ways, including by demonstrating new interest in issues such as gender equality and environmental protection. Their responses have triggered much scholarly debate about the degree and direction of change in their behaviour (e.g. Grabel 2017; Prügl 2017; Coburn 2019; Ramos et al. 2022).

Not all GPE scholars are convinced that financial globalization has severely undermined the policy autonomy of national governments. They point to open macroeconomic theory, which explains that governments face trade-offs among an 'impossible trinity' of exchange rate stability, national monetary policy autonomy, and capital mobility. Governments can achieve two of these goals, but not all three simultaneously (see Key Theory Box 8.3). As they liberalized cross-border capital movements, governments could still maintain monetary policy autonomy if they were willing to allow their national currency's exchange rate to fluctuate in value (Andrews 1994).

Governments could, for example, continue to pursue autonomous expansionary monetary policies as long as they were willing to accept a depreciation of the national currency.

Some authors suggest that the disciplining effect of global finance on governments with high levels of government spending, high taxation, or a more general left-of-centre political orientation has also been exaggerated. Mosley (2003) found that international financial market actors were concerned primarily with national inflation rates and aggregate levels of fiscal deficits rather than governments' overall level of spending, taxation, or political orientation (although this result was less true when they considered investments in less industrialized countries). More recent scholarship has also shown how global financial markets have not constrained governments in places as diverse as Bolivia, Hungary, and South Korea from pursuing increasingly activist national financial policies after the 2008 financial crisis (Johnson and Barnes 2015; Thurbon 2016; Naqvi 2021). Scholars have noted further that the policy autonomy of the US, in particular, has been *boosted* by the globalization of finance as private investors around the world have been attracted to its uniquely deep and liquid financial markets in ways that have helped fund US current account and fiscal deficits (e.g. Strange 1986; Helleiner 1994; Schwartz 2009). Some governments in lower income countries have also found their policy autonomy boosted by inflows of remittances which are sometimes

---

KEY THEORY BOX 8.3 THE 'IMPOSSIBLE TRINITY' OF OPEN MACROECONOMICS

Economists have pointed out that national governments face an inevitable trade-off between the three policy goals of exchange rate stability, national monetary policy autonomy, and capital mobility. Only two of these goals can be realized at the same time. If, for example, a national government wants to preserve free capital mobility and a fixed exchange rate, it must abandon an independent monetary policy. An independent expansionary monetary policy in an environment of capital mobility will trigger capital outflows—and downward pressure on the national currency—as domestic interest rates fall. In this context, it will be possible to maintain the fixed exchange rate only by pushing interest rates back up and thereby abandoning the initial monetary policy goal. If, however, the government chooses to maintain the expansionary policy, it will need either to introduce capital controls (as a way of stopping the capital outflows) or to embrace currency depreciation (the latter may also reinforce

domestic expansionary pressures by boosting exports and discouraging imports), thereby sacrificing one of the other goals within the 'impossible trinity'.

Historically, during the era of the pre-1930s international gold standard, governments embraced fixed exchange rates and capital mobility, while abandoning national monetary policy autonomy. During the early post-1945 years, national policy autonomy and fixed (although adjustable) exchange rates were prioritized, while capital mobility was deemed to be less important. Since the early 1970s, the leading powers have sacrificed a global regime of fixed exchange rates in order to prioritize capital mobility and preserve a degree of monetary policy autonomy. Many governments within this system, however, have embraced fixed rates at the regional or bilateral level by using capital controls or by abandoning national policy autonomy.

counter-cyclical; that is, they increase when the recipient country is undergoing difficult economic times (see, for example, Kapur and McHale 2003).

The growing significance of '**sovereign wealth funds**' (SWFs) in global financial markets also complicates debates about the impact of global financial markets on governments' policy autonomy by blurring the analytical distinction between 'global markets' and 'states'. The governments that control the largest such funds (especially Abu Dhabi, China, Kuwait, Norway, and Singapore) have become significant global investors and their policy priorities now play a role in shaping the behaviour of global financial markets. For example, Norway's SWF is mandated to invest in ways that uphold various international social and environmental conventions that Norwegian politicians have prioritized. The overseas investments of SWFs may also be used to gain economic or political leverage abroad, or to bolster the power of the state that owns them in other ways (Shemirani 2016; Braunstein 2019).

One further issue in GPE debates about the erosion of national policy autonomy concerns the control of illicit financial activity. Many GPE scholars have highlighted how financial globalization has encouraged a dramatic growth of illicit financial activity, such as money laundering, terrorist finance, and tax evasion. International capital mobility has enabled citizens to evade national rules, particularly with new access to offshore financial centres that offer secrecy and lax regulation (Palan et al. 2009). But states have also developed creative cooperative mechanisms to boost their ability to combat illicit finance. Through the Financial Action Task Force (created in 1989), many states have joined together to share information, cooperate legally, and tighten domestic regulations on money laundering and (after 2001) terrorist finance. The FATF member countries have also collectively pressured offshore financial centres to do the same (Morse 2021). Since 2014, over one hundred countries—including leading tax havens—have also begun sharing information to combat tax evasion in ways that have encouraged some governments to raise taxes on capital for the first time in decades (Hakelberg 2020; Hakelberg and Rixen 2021).

8.3.3 Environmental and social implications

Scholars have also been interested in some other implications of financial globalization that attracted less attention at Bretton Woods, such as its environmental

implications. Some analysts have argued that speculative and volatile international financial flows reward instant economic results and short-term thinking in ways that greatly complicate the kind of long-term planning that is required for the promotion of environmental values. For example, as far back as 1996, Schmidheiny and Zorraquin (1996: 10) argued that 'the globalization of investment flows is speeding the destruction of natural forests' as investors push firms to harvest forests for short-term windfall profits. But others have noted that one powerful actor in global finance—the global insurance sector—has a longer-term perspective that may encourage it to lobby for action on climate change in order to reduce the risk of future claims in this area (Haufler 1997; Paterson 2001). At the same time, insurance companies have also been capitalizing on climate change by 'financializing' the adaptation to its risks with new products, such as catastrophe bonds and micro-insurance for low-income peasants (Keucheyan 2018; Aitken 2022).

In recent years, powerful private financial actors have been developing investment products and private standards that promote 'sustainable finance' or 'green finance', including through greater disclosure of environmental risks. These initiatives have also received some official support, including from the World Bank (e.g. Hiss 2013; Mörth 2014; Pattberg 2017). Since 2017, leading central banks and financial supervisors have also been exploring how to strengthen 'greening the financial system' through initiatives such as 'achieving robust and internationally consistent climate and environment-related disclosure' and 'integrating climate-related risks into financial stability monitoring and micro-supervision' (NGFS 2019: 4–6). While some GPE scholars see promise in these kinds of initiatives, others are more sceptical, questioning their effectiveness and seeing them simply as an elite effort to promote a new neoliberal 'Wall Street Consensus' in global environmental policymaking (quote from Dafermos et al. 2021; see also Harmes 2011; Langley and Morris 2020).

Another important implication of financial globalization is its distributive impact on different social groups. Many scholars highlight how financial globalization has contributed to rising intra-country inequality by enabling the rich and corporations to escape high taxation and regulations by moving their wealth and business abroad, including to offshore locations (Palan et al. 2009). Neo-Marxist scholars have argued more generally that it has bolstered the power of an emerging, internationally mobile capitalist class, while eroding that of labour. The emerging transnational capital class has gained 'structural power' through its new ability to exit—or simply to threaten to exit—domestic political settings (Gill and Law 1989).

Frieden (1991) has also highlighted new political divisions that have emerged within the business sector. While **transnational corporations** (TNCs) and owners of financial assets and services have gained from financial globalization, businesses that are more nationally based often have not. In a world of heightened capital mobility, he argues, these two groups are, in fact, increasingly at loggerheads over policy choices within the 'impossible trinity'. The former generally prefer exchange rate stability because of their involvement in international trade and finance, even if this involves a cost of abandoning monetary policy autonomy. Those in the non-tradable sector are inclined to defend monetary policy autonomy, even if this involves accepting a floating exchange rate.

Some scholars have also analysed how financial globalization intersects with racial discrimination and gender inequality. Charles Dannreuther and Oliver Kessler (2017: 358) argue that modern risk management in global financial markets acts as a global structure of power that 'operates through three qualities of de-socialisation, de-humanisation, and de-territorialising' in order to 'stabilize risk as a quantitative rationality'. Its origins, they argue, are in Europe's past, including the racism of the slave trade whose growth was associated with the emergence of modern European financial markets. Feminist scholars have also highlighted gendered implications of financial globalization. For example, to the extent that global financial integration has been associated with the retrenchment of the welfare state, the costs have often been borne more by women than men (Singh and Zammit 2000; van Staveren 2002). They have also highlighted the gendered nature of the global financial markets themselves, which are constructed and legitimated by gendered narratives and discourses, and made up overwhelmingly of male traders operating within a culture that is hyper-masculinized (McDowell 1997; De Goede 2000; Prügl 2012; Griffin 2019).

8.3.4 The global power of new private authorities and practices

Finally, GPE scholars have been interested in how the globalization of finance has empowered private authorities and practices in the global markets to have worldwide influence. At the Bretton Woods conference, the US Treasury Secretary Henry Morgenthau told the delegates that the new public institutions they were creating would 'limit the control which certain bankers have in the past exercised over international finance' (quoted in Helleiner 2014a: 121). As global financial markets assumed a more central place in the world economy, private bankers have regained some of the influence they had in the pre-Bretton Woods era. Other private actors that are major authorities in the markets have also become powerful.

Some examples include the dominant bond rating agencies: Moody's, Standard and Poor's, and Fitch. Their authority stems not from control of money itself, but from the ratings that they assign to private and public bonds that are sold and traded in global markets. Those ratings are closely followed by investors worldwide, shaping their decisions and thus influencing the price of borrowing for firms and governments around the globe. Although governments have sometimes tried to challenge the authority of these agencies, their efforts have not been very effective to date (Helleiner and Wang 2018; Sinclair 2021; Mennillo 2022).

Another set of important private authorities are the Big Four accountancy firms: Deloitte, Ernst and Young, KPMG, and PricewaterhouseCoopers. Their power stems partly from the fact that financial actors depend on them to make decisions about how assets are valued, a process that is not always simple or politically neutral. For example, if the Big Four decided to take climate risks very seriously, Thistlethwaite and Paterson (2016) highlight how the valuation of many assets would be affected in ways that could steer capital around the world away from 'dirty' activities towards 'cleaner' ones. The broader expertise and global reach of the Big Four has also led transnational corporations to increasingly hire them as consultants to reduce corporate taxes through the use of offshore structures and other complicated accounting mechanisms. In this context, they have become what Ajdacic et al. (2021) call a global 'wealth defense industry' that not only undermines governments' ability to raise tax revenue, but also distorts competition.

Two other kinds of private authorities have emerged from the rapid post-2008 growth of passive investment products that follow equity markets. The first are the dominant sellers of these products:

BlackRock, Vanguard, and State Street. Because these firms now manage enormous sums of money (over $10 trillion in BlackRock's case, as of early 2022), the statements by their leaders—such as Larry Fink of BlackRock—now carry huge weight in global financial markets (Wigglesworth and Agnew 2022). Second, the providers of the indices themselves have also assumed a new authoritative role because their decisions to include or exclude certain countries or firms from an index steer large volumes of capital in one direction or another in very consequential ways. Recognizing this, governments have begun to adjust their behaviour in ways that might enhance the chances of being included in specific indices, and some have even tried to lobby the index providers directly (Petry et al. 2021).

GPE scholars have also pointed to the global influence of some specific private *practices* in the markets. For example, Brooks (2019) analyses the growing investor acceptance of 'collective action clauses' in sovereign debt contracts that constrain the ability of hold-out private creditors to block debt restructuring initiatives. As Brooks notes, this changed market practice has the potential to have huge consequences for people living in highly indebted countries by preventing wealthy 'vulture funds' from suing low-income governments for full repayment of their debts. Lockwood (2015) also highlights the enormous importance of the private practice of managing risks via 'value-at-risk' models since the 1990s (which quantify potential financial losses in a given time period). As she notes, the widespread use of these models has transformed them into a form of governance over the world.

KEY POINTS

- The globalization of financial markets has been driven not just by technological and market pressures, but also by the decisions of states to liberalize capital controls that had been popular in the early post-war years.

- A hotly contested subject among GPE scholars concerns the degree to which global financial markets have eroded the policy autonomy of national governments.

- Financial globalization has also had important environmental and social consequences.

- It has also given private authorities and practices in the global markets worldwide influence.

8.4 The demise of gold and the future of the dollar

While the globalization of financial markets took place in a gradual fashion, the Bretton Woods' gold exchange standard broke down more suddenly when then-US president Richard Nixon suspended the convertibility of the US dollar into gold in August 1971. Since other currencies had been tied to gold only via the US dollar, this 'Nixon shock' signalled the end of gold's role as a standard for other currencies as well.

8.4.1 Before and after the Nixon shock

The collapse of the gold exchange standard had in fact been predicted as far back as 1960, when Triffin (1960) had highlighted its inherent instability. In a system where the dollar was the central reserve currency, he argued that international liquidity could be expanded only when the US provided the world with more dollars by running larger external deficits. But the more it did so, the more it risked undermining confidence in the dollar's convertibility into gold.

One potential solution to the **Triffin Dilemma** was to create a new international currency whose supply would not be tied to the balance of payments condition of any one country. The chief British negotiator at Bretton Woods, John Maynard Keynes, had, in fact, proposed such a currency—which he called 'bancor'—in his initial plans for the post-war international monetary and financial order. In 1969, the IMF membership did create **Special Drawing Rights** (SDRs) to be used by national monetary authorities as a reserve asset for settling inter-country payments imbalances (and subject to certain conditions). But they were initially issued by the IMF only in small amounts to supplement the US dollar's international role.

As US external deficits grew during the 1960s, driven partly by the costs of the Vietnam War, dollar holdings abroad increased. If all holders of dollars suddenly decided to convert the US currency into gold, US officials recognized that they would not be able to meet the demand. A crisis of confidence in the dollar's convertibility into gold was initially postponed when some key foreign allies—notably Germany and Japan—agreed not to convert their reserves into gold (sometimes as part of an explicit trade-off for US security protection, Zimmermann 2002). But other countries that were more critical of US foreign policy in this period—France in particular—refused to adopt this practice, seeing it as a reinforcement of American hegemony and the 'exorbitant privilege' that they believed the US gained from issuing the world's leading currency (Kirshner 1995: 192–203). When speculative pressures against the dollar reached a peak in 1971, Nixon chose simply to 'close the gold window' in order to free the US from the constraint on its policies that gold convertibility had previously imposed (Gowa 1983).

When US policymakers ended the dollar's convertibility into gold, some predicted that the US currency's role as the dominant world currency would be quickly challenged, since the dollar was no longer 'as good as gold'. In fact, however, the dollar's central global role has endured up to the present day. It has continued to be the currency of choice for settling international economic transactions and for denominating international trade and investments across much of the world. Among countries that peg their currencies, the dollar is also the most popular anchor currency. In addition, the greenback has remained the most common currency in which most governments hold their foreign exchange reserves.

The US dollar's enduring central global position is partly a product of inertia and the enormous size and significance of the US economy in the world. There are many '**network externalities**' that reinforce the continued use of existing currencies, particularly when the issuing country is such a major player in the global economy; the more a currency is used, the greater the incentive for others to use it for convenience reasons. The dollar's global role is also supported by the fact that US financial markets have remained the most liquid in the world because of their depth, breadth, resilience, and openness to foreigners. These attributes have made the holding and use of US dollars very attractive to private actors and foreign governments. Some scholars suggest that the broader military power of the US also helps to bolster confidence in its currency. Further, GPE literature has shown that foreign governments have continued to support the dollar's global role in various ways because of their economic and political ties with the US (Chey 2012; Helleiner 2014b; Norloff et al. 2020).

8.4.2 Emerging challenges to the dollar's dominant position

Will the dollar's global dominance continue? At the moment, the euro is the second most widely used currency internationally, but its international use is held back by a number of factors, including the fragmented nature of European financial markets and the absence of a common fiscal authority in Europe. Both of those factors have meant that no equivalent exists in the eurozone to the uniquely liquid and deep US Treasury bill market. If these kinds of factors were addressed in ways that strengthened the eurozone, the euro could become a more significant international currency in the coming years.

As China's significance in the world economy has grown, analysts have increasingly speculated about whether its currency, the renminbi (RMB), might begin to challenge the dollar's international dominance. This speculation has been encouraged by the sudden interest shown by the Chinese government in internationalizing the RMB after the 2008 global financial crisis (Subacchi 2017; Cohen 2018). The crisis highlighted to the Chinese leadership the vulnerabilities associated with their country's dependence on the dollar, including those stemming from the fact that the vast bulk of its foreign assets are held in dollar-denominated assets. Most powerful creditor countries in the past have lent abroad in their own currency in order to avoid exposure to the kinds of exchange rate risks which China now faces. While this vulnerability has left Chinese officials with strong incentives in the short term to defend the dollar (in order to protect the value of China's existing assets), it has also encouraged them to explore ways of reducing their dependence on the dollar over the medium term. Promoting the RMB's international use will also reduce exchange rate risks and transaction costs for Chinese firms involved in international commerce, as well as diminish China's vulnerability to US sanctions (discussed in the next section) and boost China's international influence more generally.

Since the 2008 crisis, Chinese officials have engaged in a flurry of initiatives to promote the internationalization of the RMB. These have ranged from the removal of many of the controls that were previously imposed on its international use, to the signing of bilateral currency swap agreements with many foreign monetary authorities that can help to encourage the growth of RMB use abroad (McDowell 2019). But the attractiveness of China's currency to foreigners has been undermined by its enduring use of capital controls as well as the absence of well-developed, liquid, and open RMB financial markets that are backed by a stable legal infrastructure and property rights. While some groups within China favour the kinds of reforms that are necessary for RMB internationalization, those reforms threaten to undermine the regulated financial system that has been core to the Chinese export-oriented, state-led development model. They thus have powerful opponents in the Chinese political economy (Li 2018). As Eichengreen (2011: 7) puts it, if the euro is challenged by being a 'currency without a state', the RMB faces the opposite situation of being a 'currency with too much state'.

In addition to promoting RMB internationalization, Chinese officials have supported the strengthening of the SDR's role in the international monetary system. In March 2009, Chinese central bank governor Zhou Xiaochuan released a prominent paper that, citing Keynes and Triffin, argued for the SDR to assume a larger role in the international monetary system. At that time, US officials agreed to back the first new SDR allocation since the early 1980s as a way of bolstering the IMF's resources to help buffer countries from balance of payments shocks (Helleiner 2014b: 68–78). In 2015, US officials also supported the inclusion of the RMB for the first time in the basket of currencies that make up the SDR's value, another reform that Zhou had called for. The US and other IMF members then backed a further—larger—SDR allocation in 2021 in response to the global pandemic. Despite these recent allocations, the SDR's role still remains a relatively minor one in the international monetary system.

Could emerging private digital currencies threaten the dollar's international role? Created in 2009 by an anonymous person or group, bitcoin does not pose much of a threat. Although its supporters believe this stateless form of money could soon replace national currencies, its attractiveness as a currency has been undermined by its unstable value and high transaction costs as a means of payment (see Clarke and Roberts, Chapter 10; Girard, Chapter 17). A more serious potential threat was posed by Facebook's 2019 proposal to create a global currency called the Libra (and subsequently renamed Diem) (Vasudevan 2020). In contrast to bitcoin, Libra was to be a 'stablecoin' whose value was fixed to a basket of leading national currencies and backed up by a reserve of assets such as US Treasury bills. Given Facebook's enormous global customer base, policymakers across the world feared that it would quickly be used alongside national currencies in many countries, thus undermining their country's monetary sovereignty (see Figure 8.2). In addition to challenging states' monetary sovereignty, Libra would have consolidated Facebook's broader

Figure 8.2 Golden ripple, bitcoin, and Ethereum coins lying on the homepage of Facebook launching its digital wallet Calibra and cryptocurrency Libra

Source: iStock.

global power. Not only could the currency become a new source of profits for Facebook, but the company would have gained access to payments data of millions of people and locked more users into its broader platforms. Libra would also have provided a new channel for illicit financial flows. At a broader level, it risked becoming a new source of potential global financial instability if, for example, its reserves were not stable or if it was subject to panic selling (Vasudevan 2020).

The concerns about Libra prompted Western regulatory officials to impose many regulatory hurdles in front of its initiative, hurdles that eventually led Facebook to abandon the proposal by early 2022. But Facebook's proposal had a lasting legacy in prompting policymakers to begin much more serious work on creating their own '**central bank digital currencies**' (CBDCs) to meet changing consumer preferences in the digital age and to fend off future competition from other private stablecoins (see Key Concept Box 8.4). Among the major powers, China is furthest along in developing a CBDC that it hopes may also promote the RMB's international role. Indeed, some GPE scholars anticipate new 'digital currency wars', as the US begins exploring the idea of issuing its own CBDC (Aggarwal and Marple 2020). But it is also evident that the US dollar's global position is less threatened by private stablecoins because they are likely to be heavily linked to the US dollar. Indeed, Facebook's CEO, Mark Zuckerberg, even suggested that Libra had the potential to *boost* the dollar's international position because it would 'be backed mostly by dollars and …

KEY CONCEPT BOX 8.4 WHAT ARE CENTRAL BANK DIGITAL CURRENCIES?

The most general definition of a central bank digital currency is 'a digital payment instrument denominated in the national unit of account, which is a direct liability of the central bank' (BIS 2022: 93). That definition includes deposits that commercial banks have long held in electronic form at their country's central bank as reserves or settlement balances. Some of the contemporary debates about CBDCs focus on reforming those existing 'wholesale' CBDCs to offer new kinds of transactions via distributed ledger technology (or blockchain) to a wider group of financial intermediaries or to facilitate wholesale cross-border payments. But much of the debate is focused instead on the idea of creating new kinds of 'retail' CBDCs that would be widely available to the general public for everyday payments.

These new CBDCs would enable the general public to hold and transact central bank money (or 'public money') in digital form rather than in the form of cash. Under one model, they could do this directly via digital tokens issued by the central banks or accounts that people held at the central bank. But the more popular model is a two-tiered one in which licensed private firms (such as banks and payment service providers) would handle the customer-facing activities, competing to provide CBDC services such as token-based products or accounts in which people could hold their CBDCs and transact with them. Under this two-tiered system, customers would not experience a great difference from existing digital ways of storing value and making payments, but the money involved would now be a direct claim on the central bank rather than being a liability of a private firm.

---

will extend America's financial leadership around the world, as well as our democratic values and oversight' (quoted in Huang and Mayer 2022: 330).

In addition to these potential external challenges to the dollar's dominant global role, could US behaviour itself play a role in encouraging a downsizing of the greenback's international position? It is certainly true that domestic US economic mismanagement could undermine confidence in the currency. Some foreigners may also become more wary of dollar dependence as US policymakers increasingly leverage access to dollar clearing and payments systems as a tool of their foreign policy. US threats to cut off that access have played an important role in encouraging foreign governments (including those hosting offshore financial centres) to cooperate with US regulatory initiatives combating illicit financial flows (Hakelberg 2020; Morse 2021). Actual bans on access have also become a key tool in US sanctions against foreigners, including Russians during the Ukraine conflict that began in 2021. In the latter case, the US also

took the dramatic step—in cooperation with its allies—of freezing over half of the Russian central bank's foreign exchange reserves. The more that the US officials have 'weaponized' the dollar's global role in these ways, the more some foreign governments—including Russia and China—have been trying to reduce their exposure to the currency and to create alternative clearing and payments systems to minimize their vulnerability (Wigglesworth, Ivanova, and Smith 2022; McDowell 2023).

An erosion of the US dollar's global role would have important consequences for the US. As foreign dependence on dollar-clearing and payments networks diminished, the US would lose an important foreign policy tool. It would also lose seigniorage revenue (see Key Concept Box 8.5), as well as the international prestige that comes from issuing a dominant world currency. In its current position as the sole producer of the world's key currency, the US also plays a decisive role during international financial crises because of its unique ability to make advances of dollars to foreign governments or private institutions in distress

---

KEY CONCEPT BOX 8.5 WHAT IS 'SEIGNIORAGE'?

Seigniorage is the difference between the nominal value of money and its cost of production. This difference is a kind of 'profit' for the issuer of money. In the pre-modern era, this source of revenue was often very important for ruling authorities. National monetary authorities earn seigniorage not just from the

use of the money they issue to citizens within their borders, but also from its international use. When foreigners hold US dollar bills, they provide the equivalent of an interest-free loan to the US. According to some estimates, the value of this perk for the US is approximately US$15–20 billion per year (Cohen 2015: 21).

(see Pauly, Chapter 9). To the extent that the dollar's global role generates higher foreign demand for the services of US financial firms (e.g. trade finance, foreign exchange business, the buying and selling of securities), those companies also earn some '**denomination rents**'. In addition, the dollar's global role has bolstered the US capacity to finance current account deficits, as well as to subsequently deflect the costs of adjustments onto foreigners by depreciating its currency. During international political and economic crises, investors also often flock to dollar investments in ways that boost the US' macroeconomic room to manoeuvre. More generally, dependence on the US dollar may encourage foreigners to identify their interests more closely with those of the US (Kirshner 1995; Cohen 2018; Norloff et al. 2020).

The erosion of the dollar's central global position would also have consequences for the world as a whole. Drawing on the historical experience of Britain's decline (see Case Study Box 8.6), the hegemonic stability theory—developed by GPE scholars in the 1970s—suggests that the erosion of US monetary hegemony is likely to generate a more unstable global monetary system. But some scholars challenge the theory and suggest the exact opposite, arguing that hegemonic powers are inevitably tempted to exploit their dominant position over time to serve their own interests rather than the interests of the stability of the system (Calleo 1987: Ch. 8). Another critique of the hegemonic stability theory as it applies to the US has been that there is an 'inherent instability in the global dollar-based system' linked to 'periods of expansionary and contractionary policy in the United States' in which low US interest rates trigger a 'surge of financialized capital into world markets' followed by dramatic and destabilizing pull-backs when US rates tighten (Gallagher and Kozul-Wright 2022: 51–52). Still others have gone further to suggest that the hegemonic nature of the international monetary system contributes to deeper ecological instabilities (Svartzman and Althouse 2020). Even if we accept these cases for a less hegemonic order, it is important to recognize that the transition away from a dollar-centred one is likely to contain risks for the world economy and usher in broader geopolitical shifts (Kirshner 2014).

CASE STUDY BOX 8.6 BRITAIN'S DECLINE AND THE HEGEMONIC STABILITY THEORY

The hegemonic stability theory was initially developed in the 1970s, drawing heavily on Charles Kindleberger's (1973: 105) argument that 'for the world economy to be stabilized, there has to be a stabilizer—one stabilizer'. That argument drew lessons from the history of Britain's world economic leadership and decline. According to the theory, the pre-1914 international financial and monetary regime remained stable as long as British hegemonic leadership sustained it. Before the First World War, the UK's currency, sterling, was seen to be 'as good as gold', and it was used around the globe as an international currency. Britain was also the largest creditor to the world, and London's financial markets held a pre-eminent place in global finance. The UK's capital exports helped to finance global payments imbalances, and they were usefully counter-cyclical; that is, foreign lending expanded when the UK entered a recession, thus compensating foreign countries for the decline in sales to the UK. During international financial crises, the Bank of England is also said to have played a leadership role in stabilizing markets through lender-of-last-resort operations (see Pauly, Chapter 9).

After the First World War, however, the UK lost its ability to perform its leadership role in stabilizing the global monetary and financial order, as the US replaced it as the lead creditor to the world economy. New York also began to rival London's position as the key international financial centre, and the US dollar emerged as an important international currency. In these new circumstances, the US might have taken on the kind of leadership role that the UK had played before the war. But it proved unwilling to do so because of isolationist sentiments and domestic political conflicts between internationally oriented and more domestically focused economic interests. Hegemonic stability theorists criticize several aspects of US behaviour during the 1920s and early 1930s. Its capital exports during the 1920s were pro-cyclical; they expanded rapidly when the US economy was booming, but then came to a sudden stop in the late 1920s, just as the growth of the US economy was slowing down. The collapse of US lending generated balance of payments crises for many foreign countries that had relied on US loans to cover their external payments deficits. The US then exacerbated these countries' difficulties by raising tariffs against imports with the passage of the 1930 Smoot–Hawley Act. As confidence in international financial markets collapsed in the early 1930s, the US also refused to take on the role of international **lender-of-last-resort**, or even to cancel the war debts that were compounding the crisis. In these ways, Kindleberger (1973) argued that the absence of a hegemonic leader contributed to the collapse of the world economy during the Great Depression.

8.5 Exchange rate regimes, regionalization, and decentralization

Alongside the gold exchange standard, another feature of the Bretton Woods monetary order that broke down in the early 1970s was the adjustable peg system. This development took place in 1973, when leading powers allowed their currencies to float in value vis-à-vis one another. In 1978, a new international exchange rate regime was formalized when an amendment to the IMF's Articles of Agreement came into force, which legalized floating exchange rates by declaring that each country could now choose its own exchange rate regime. At the same time, countries also committed to 'avoid manipulating exchange rates or the international monetary system in order to prevent effective balance of payments adjustment or to gain an unfair competitive advantage over other members'. To police this commitment, the IMF was given a new mandate to 'exercise firm surveillance over the exchange rate policies of members' (Article IV, sections 1 and 3) (Pauly 1997).

8.5.1 **Floating exchange rates and their critics**

The end of the adjustable peg system was partly triggered by the growing size of speculative international financial flows, which complicated governments' efforts to defend their **currency pegs**. Also important was the fact that some influential policymakers began to argue that floating exchange rates could play

a very useful role in facilitating smooth adjustments to external imbalances (Odell 1982). The idea of using exchange rate changes for this purpose had, of course, been endorsed at Bretton Woods; governments could adjust their currency's peg when the country was in '**fundamental disequilibrium**'. But, in practice, governments had been reluctant to make these changes because exchange rate adjustments often generated political controversy, both at home and abroad. Adjustments usually came only when large-scale speculative financial movements left governments with no option. A floating exchange rate system, it was hoped, would allow external imbalances to be addressed more smoothly and continuously.

Since their introduction in the early 1970s, floating exchange rates have undoubtedly played a useful role in facilitating adjustments to international economic imbalances. But as foreign exchange trading has grown dramatically, critics have argued that exchange rates have also sometimes been subject to considerable short-term volatility and longer-term misalignments. In these circumstances, floating exchange rates have sometimes been a source of—rather than the means of adjusting to—external economic imbalances. To curb the adverse effects of speculative foreign exchange trading, some have suggested that a currency transaction tax be levied against all cross-currency transactions. But this proposal has encountered strong political opposition from the financial industry and others (Kalaitzake 2017).

When speculative financial flows have exacerbated external economic imbalances, there have been brief episodes when leading economic powers attempted to collectively manage exchange rates. The most famous of these took place between 1985 and 1987 when the G5 (the US, the UK, the Federal Republic of Germany, France, and Japan) worked together to encourage a depreciation of the US dollar after speculative financial flows had pushed up its value dramatically in the early 1980s, worsening the US trade deficit at the time (and generating widespread protectionist sentiments within the US by 1984–1985) (Funabashi 1988). This enthusiasm for a more managed exchange rate system between the world's major currencies proved to be short-lived. The leading economic powers at the time were not prepared to accept the kinds of serious constraints on their macroeconomic policy autonomy that were required to make such a system effective.

Another criticism of the new post-1978 international exchange rate regime is that it has enabled governments to deliberately undervalue their national currencies for **competitive advantage** in ways that have exacerbated global economic imbalances. For example, after the turn of the millennium, many analysts accused China of purchasing foreign exchange (usually dollars) in order to keep the value of its currency low for this 'mercantilist' purpose (for discussions, see Steinberg 2015; Pauly, Chapter 9). Indeed, its foreign exchange reserves grew in a particularly dramatic fashion, reaching a peak of close to US$4 trillion by 2014 (of which a majority were estimated to be held in US dollar-denominated assets). Watching this development, many US policymakers argued that the IMF had not been sufficiently critical of China in its 'surveillance' role. If the IMF would not act, they pressed for unilateral US action, such as trade restrictions (Blustein 2016).

Against this backdrop, the G20 leaders' forum became another international setting in which issues relating to exchange rates and macroeconomic coordination could be discussed. The forum was created at the height of the global financial crisis in November 2008 and included leaders from all the world's major economies (the G20 had already met regularly at the level of finance ministers and central bankers since 1999). At their third summit in September 2009, the G20 leaders committed to a new 'consultative mutual assessment process' to evaluate whether national economic policies remained consistent with shared goals outlined by the G20 as a whole (Rommerskirchen and Snaith 2017). The IMF (along with the World Bank) was assigned a role of supporting this process through analyses that built on its existing surveillance activities. Some hoped that the new G20 mutual assessment process would reinvigorate the kind of multilateral exchange rate management and macroeconomic coordination that characterized the 1985–1987 period. But it did not, and the fundamental political challenge identified at Bretton Woods of reconciling countries' desire for national policy autonomy with their commitment to an open multilateral world economy remains (Knaack and Katada 2013).

8.5.2 Europe's monetary union

Although international efforts to coordinate the relationship between the values of the world's major currencies have been limited since the early 1970s, some governments have created stable monetary relations in smaller regional contexts. The most ambitious regional initiative of this kind has taken place in Europe, culminating with the creation of its common currency, the euro, in 1999. The initiative built upon efforts since the 1970s to stabilize intra-European exchange rates in order to prevent currency volatility and misalignments from disrupting their efforts to build a closer economic community.

The euro's creation was also backed for various political reasons (McNamara 1998). For example, some policymakers outside Germany hoped a common regional currency and central bank would dilute German financial power in Europe. At the same time, others saw it as a way to import the German central bank's successful anti-inflationary monetary policy and lower domestic interest rates. Indeed, like the German Bundesbank, the new European central bank was given a strict mandate to pursue price stability as its primary goal. More generally, the euro has been seen as a tool for deepening European political integration as well as challenging the US dollar's international role.

The eurozone's subsequent experiences have highlighted the difficulties of creating a currency union, particularly in a context which is not what economists call an 'optimum currency area' (see Key Theory Box 8.7). Within large national currency zones such as the US or Canada, economic imbalances between regions of the country are addressed by mechanisms such as labour migration and large fiscal transfers from the national government. In the eurozone, however, migration has not usually been extensive and large-scale fiscal transfers do not yet take place. In that context, eurozone countries with persistent payments deficits have been forced to adopt painful and unpopular austerity programmes that push down wages and prices, as under the gold standard (see Key Concept Box 8.1) (Matthijs and McNamara 2015; Johnson 2016). Not surprisingly, those measures have encouraged anti-euro sentiment.

If the euro is to flourish, its member countries must also improve other aspects of the eurozone's governance, such as fiscal cooperation (including not just larger fiscal transfers, but also the issuing of common eurozone debt). Some recent initiatives point in these directions, but advocates of the euro call for more pooling of sovereignty while others resist those calls. The outcomes of these political battles will shape not just the future of Europe, but also the evolution of the international monetary system as a whole, because a more politically consolidated eurozone would accelerate the move towards a more multipolar currency order.

KEY THEORY BOX 8.7 MONETARY UNIONS AND THE THEORY OF OPTIMUM CURRENCY AREAS

The theory of optimum currency areas was first developed by the Nobel Prize winning economist Robert Mundell (1961), to evaluate the pros and cons of forming a monetary union among a selected group of countries. While assuming the union will produce microeconomic benefits in the form of lower transaction costs for cross-border commerce, the theory focuses its analytical attention on the potential macroeconomic costs associated with abandoning the exchange rate as a tool of macroeconomic adjustment. If these costs are low, the region is said to approximate more closely an 'optimum currency area' that should be encouraged to create a monetary union.

To evaluate how significant these costs are in each regional context, the theory examines a number of criteria. If selected countries experience similar external shocks, for example, the theory notes that they are more likely to be good candidates for monetary union, since they will each have less of a need for an independent exchange rate. Even if they experience asymmetric shocks, the macroeconomic costs of abandoning national exchange rates may still be low if wages and prices are very flexible within each country, if labour is highly mobile between countries, or if there are mechanisms for transferring fiscal payments among the countries. Each of these conditions would enable adjustments to be made to external shocks in the absence of an exchange rate.

8.5.3 Regionalization and decentralization elsewhere?

The euro's creation in 1999 triggered some policy and scholarly debate about the prospects of closer monetary cooperation in other regions. Some monetary unions already exist, such as the CFA (Communauté Financière Africaine) franc zone involving many former French colonies in West and Central Africa. Its members chose at the moment of their political independence to maintain a colonial monetary union created by France, and its evolution has continued to be shaped by the power and political interests of France in the post-colonial context (Stasavage 2003). Another common currency—the Eastern Caribbean dollar, which is shared by eight countries—has been one of the first to issue a CBDC in 2021–2022 (Campbell-Verduyn et al. 2022).

At the time of the euro's creation, there was a brief debate about constructing a monetary union either in North America or the Americas as a whole, based on the US dollar. Two countries that were already extensively *de facto* dollarized—Ecuador and El Salvador—introduced the US dollar as their national currency, in 2000 and 2001, respectively, but the idea of formal **dollarization** attracted little serious political support elsewhere in the region. Most governments were very wary of abandoning the exchange rate tool of adjustment in the absence of any alternative adjustment mechanisms such as free labour movement to and from the US, or arrangements for inter-country fiscal transfers. In addition, US policymakers made it clear that the US Federal Reserve would not offer dollarized countries any role in its decision-making,

extend lender-of-last-resort support to their banks, or share seigniorage revenue with them. While European countries have shared sovereignty in creating the euro, countries in the Americas had only the unattractive option of becoming a monetary dependency (Helleiner 2006).

Although formal dollarization is not very attractive, some governments in the region (and elsewhere) have maintained a fixed exchange rate vis-à-vis the US dollar. This policy eliminates exchange rate volatility and can help establish monetary stability domestically in a context where the credibility of local monetary authorities may be questioned (Subacchi 2020). But countries with this policy are subject to US monetary policy decisions and they give up the exchange rate tool of adjustment, forcing external deficits to be resolved through other mechanisms such as deflationary policies designed to put downward pressure on wage and price flexibility. Those policies can be very economically painful, as was demonstrated very vividly by Argentina's deflation of the late 1990s that was pursued to maintain its peg to the US dollar. That deflation contributed to Argentina's spectacular financial crisis of 2001 (see Pauly, Chapter 9). It also prompted many local community groups across the country to issue their own 'community currencies' to address the shortage of money in the country (see Everyday GPE Box 8.8). Indeed, at one point, these alternative currencies—which were denominated in their own units of account—were being used by as many as 2 million people in the country (Gomez 2015).

In the East Asian region, there has been little talk of monetary union, but other forms of monetary and financial cooperation grew after the 1997–1998 East

---

EVERYDAY GPE BOX 8.8 CREATE YOUR OWN CURRENCY?

Why do GPE scholars usually focus only on currencies issued by large institutions such as states (national currencies), the IMF (SDRs), and big corporations (Facebook's Libra)? Everyday people working in local communities can, and do, issue currencies too. Since the 1980s, many 'community currencies' have been created in this way around the world for use only within a local context. Some community currencies are denominated in the national currency, while others have a unique unit of account, including even ones based on hours of labour. Many of these currencies are issued in physical form (and often emblazoned with local imagery). But others exist in digital form, with debts and credits among the participants being recorded in a centralized database. Some advocates of digital community currencies have even proposed using a new decentralized blockchain technology that can be geo-fenced via IP addresses (Alcantara and Dick 2017).

Advocates of community currencies highlight how they can encourage people to consume locally made goods and services as opposed to those coming from farther away. In that context, they may encourage a more ecologically sustainable economy as well as greater value to be placed on informal, household, or subsistence activities that are often unpaid. When local currencies are denominated in units such as labour hours, they may also promote equity goals, by reorientating traditional concepts of valuation to reward work that is poorly compensated by the mainstream economy. Further, community currencies can foster economic activity that was inhibited by

monetary scarcity in ways that reduce local unemployment and poverty. The community organizations that issue the money can also choose to allocate some of the funds to specific community causes. More generally, community currencies are seen as tools for fostering a sense of local community and self-determination. In all these ways, this form of money is seen as one that can reflect community values and preferences rather than those of distant authorities (Helleiner 2000; Rasillo 2021).

Community currencies have their critics (see, for example, Larue 2022). It is also important to note that users of community currencies rarely transact most of their economic life with this form of money. Indeed, advocates often emphasize that they are attempting not to de-link from the mainstream economy entirely, but simply to boost the relative significance of this alternative economic realm within people's everyday lives. Some have even sought to build international links to other groups with similar ideals. For example, supporters of community currencies created 'Faircoin' in 2014 to allow for trade between like-minded communities around the world. This currency uses blockchain with transactions being validated at dozens of approved nodes around the world (Rasillo 2021). In this way, local community currencies can coexist not just with established national currencies, but also with this transnational currency in a world of multilevel currency pluralism similar to that which existed before the emergence of modern nation-states and their territorially homogenous national currencies (Helleiner 2003).

Asian financial crisis. That crisis exposed the vulnerability of the region to outside market and political pressures, encouraging policymakers from China, Japan, South Korea, and the Association of Southeast Asian Nations (ASEAN) countries to explore ways to boost their collective monetary and financial independence. The first major cooperative venture of this 'ASEAN + 3' grouping was the Chiang Mai Initiative, created in 2000 to provide short-term financial assistance to member countries suffering from balance of payments crises. This initial bilateral swap network was soon transformed under the Chiang Mai Initiative Multilateralization (CMIM) into a US$120 billion multilateral fund that opened in 2010 (and whose size was doubled to US$240 billion in 2012), accompanied in 2011 by a new region-wide economic surveillance mechanism (Helleiner 2014b; Grabel 2017).

This initiative points towards a decentralization of the balance of payments lending role that the IMF was

assigned at Bretton Woods. But the trend should not be overstated: the CMIM has been explicitly designed to work with the IMF through its rule that the majority of the funds can be accessed only if a country has an IMF programme in place. Other multilateral funds with partial links to the IMF have also been created elsewhere, such as the US$100 billion Contingent Reserve Arrangement created by the BRICS (Brazil, Russia, India, China, and South Africa) in 2014 (Grabel 2017).

It is in the field of multilateral development lending where the decentralization trend is more pronounced. As far back as the 1960s, the World Bank had already begun sharing its policy space with new regional multilateral development banks (MDBs) created in Latin America, Africa, and Asia. New MDBs have continued to be created since then, including the BRICS' New Development Bank and the Chinese-led Asian Infrastructure Investment Bank in 2014–2015. This trend is both responding to and reinforcing the broader decentralization of power in the global economy. It also reflects the increasingly ambitious financial statecraft of emerging powers, as well as their discontent with lack of reform of the Western-dominated Bretton Woods Institutions (Grabel 2017; Roberts, Armijo, and Katada 2018; Bazbauers and Engel 2021).

Some see these decentralization trends as a worrying development, because of their potential to undermine the global cooperative framework of Bretton Woods. In an era when the US is less willing to perform leadership roles (and China is not yet able or willing to fill a leadership vacuum), that framework is seen as more important than ever, particularly to avoid the kind of instability experienced during the interwar years (Subacchi 2020). Others, however, argue that the growing incoherence of global financial governance may be 'productive' in the sense of enhancing resilience and national policy space, as well as encouraging useful experimentation and incremental innovation (Grabel 2017).

> • The emergence of new regional and other multilateral lending institutions is generating a more decentralized international financial order with uncertain consequences.

8.6 Conclusion

The contemporary international monetary and financial system is still shaped by many legacies of the 1944 Bretton Woods conference, including the still-prominent role of the IMF and World Bank, ongoing commitments to current account convertibility, and the dollar's enduring global pre-eminence. But the system has also undergone many important transformations since the creation of the Bretton Woods order and its implementation during the early post-war years. This chapter has focused on the globalization of financial markets, the collapse of the gold exchange standard, new challenges to the dollar's global role, the breakdown of the adjustable peg exchange rate regime, and regionalization and decentralization trends.

Each of these transformations in the nature of the international monetary and financial system has had important implications for the key question of who gets what, when, and how in the GPE. Monetary and financial systems—at both the domestic and international levels—do not just serve economic functions. They also have important political consequences. Not surprisingly, this makes them the subject of heated political debate and hard-fought political struggles. For this reason, the study of money and finance cannot be left only to economists, who have traditionally dominated scholarship in this area. It also needs the attention of students of GPE who have an interest in their wider political dimensions.

KEY POINTS

- After the 1973 breakdown of the adjustable peg exchange rate regime, IMF rules were amended in 1978 to allow countries to choose their own exchange rate regime, subject to IMF surveillance and to the provision that exchange rates cannot be manipulated to gain unfair competitive advantage.

- Concerns about exchange rate misalignments and manipulation have prompted occasional intergovernmental efforts to manage the relationship between the values of the world's major currencies.

- Other alternatives to floating exchanges include regional monetary unions, currency pegs, and formal dollarization.

? 8.7 QUESTIONS

1. Is a hegemonic leader necessary for a stable international monetary and financial system? Is the US able and willing to be a leader of the system?

2. To what extent has financial globalization undermined the policy autonomy of national governments? What are the most important environmental and social consequences of financial globalization?

3. What are the most powerful private authorities in global financial markets? What can be done about their new power?

4. Can financial globalization be reversed?

5. For how much longer will the US dollar remain the world's key currency? What is most likely to challenge its global role?

6. Should a big technology company such as Facebook be allowed to create a global currency? What would be the costs and benefits?

7. Should the leading powers try to stabilize the relationship between the values of the major currencies? Should the IMF be empowered to play a more active role in preventing exchange rate manipulation?

8. Has the creation of the euro been a positive move for Europeans? Should other regions emulate the European example, and are they likely to do so?

9. Should the move to a more decentralized international monetary and financial system be welcomed or feared? Can it be reversed?

10. Should a new Bretton Woods meeting be called? What could and should it try to achieve?

8.8 FURTHER READING

Bello, W. (2019), *Paper Dragons: China and the Next Crash* (London: Zed Books). An analysis of the fragility of the global financial system in the context of China's growing financial influence.

Cohen, B. (2018), *Currency Statecraft: Monetary Rivalry and Geopolitical Ambition* (Chicago, IL: University of Chicago Press). An analysis of the relationship between power and money by one of the pioneers of the study of the GPE of money and finance.

Grabel, I. (2017), *When Things Don't Fall Apart: Global Financial Governance and Developmental Finance in an Age of Productive Incoherence* (Boston, MA: MIT Press). An award-winning analysis and defence of the move to a more decentralized global financial order.

Kindleberger, C. (1973), *The World in Depression* (Berkeley: University of California Berkeley Press). A classic analysis of the Great Depression that helped to popularize the hegemonic stability theory.

Morse, J. (2021), *The Bankers' Blacklist: Unofficial Market Enforcement and the Global Fight Against Illicit Financing* (Ithaca: Cornell University Press). An examination of the growth of illicit finance and states' efforts to control it.

Ocampo, J. A. (2017), *Resetting the International Monetary (Non)System* (Oxford: Oxford University Press). A comprehensive overview of the contemporary international monetary system with a programme of reform.

Prasad, E. (2021), *The Future of Money: How the Digital Revolution is Transforming Currencies and Finance* (Cambridge, MA: Harvard University Press). An examination of the emergence and consequences of digital currencies, both private and public.

Roberts, C., Armijo, L., and Katada, S. (2018), *The BRICS and Collective Financial Statecraft* (Oxford: Oxford University Press). An analysis of the increasingly important role of the BRICS countries in international monetary and financial politics.

Strange, S. (1998), *Mad Money: When Markets Outgrow Government* (Ann Arbor, MI: University of Michigan Press). A classic critique of the international monetary and financial system from one of the pioneers of the study of the GPE of money and finance.

Subacchi, P. (2020), *The Cost of Free Money: How Unfettered Capital Threatens Our Economic Future* (New Haven: Yale University Press). A critique of financial globalization and defence of the need for a strengthened multilateral monetary and financial order.

CONTRIBUTOR NOTE

Eric Helleiner is Professor and University Research Chair in the Department of Political Science and Balsillie School of International Affairs at the University of Waterloo. His most recent books are *The Contested World Economy: The Deep and Global Roots of International Political Economy* (Cambridge: Cambridge University Press, 2023) and *The Neomercantilists: A Global Intellectual History* (Ithaca: Cornell University Press, 2021).

9

The Politics of Global Financial Stability

Louis W. Pauly

Chapter contents

Reader's guide

After the early 1970s, capital flowed ever more freely across the borders of advanced as well as emerging economies. Many countries acquiesced in a broadening movement away from capital controls as they came to depend on ever greater inflows of external financing. National capital markets became more deeply linked and more volatile. The ultimate stability of those markets now rests on a rough consensus, especially among leading states, on policy collaboration in the face of crises. In the late twentieth century, most cross-border financial crises began in emerging-market economies. In 2008, however, the system came close to collapse when policy mistakes in the United States—the central node in now dense financial networks—combined with large national payment imbalances and a global economic downturn to spawn a worldwide emergency. Europeans faced down a related regional crisis a few years later. The resilience of border-spanning financial markets was tested again during the past decade by new digital technologies, as well as by whip-saw economic pressures coincident with the COVID-19 pandemic, Russia's invasion of Ukraine, and geopolitical concerns focused on China. Although private authorities now play important roles in trying to ensure productive and fair competition across borders, global capital markets in the end remain governed by legally sovereign public authorities whose effective power is constrained not only by their deepening dependence upon one another, but also by new technologies enhancing the mobility of wealthy citizens, entrepreneurial firms, and illicit organizations. Progress has been made in the collaborative assessment of systemic financial risks, even if serious questions remain on the policies needed to prevent future crises. As the periodically unsteady experiment in financial openness continues, domestic and international struggles over the distribution of its benefits and costs deepen.

9.1 Introduction: Opening capital markets

Promoting **interdependence** among the economies of the world was a key strategic objective of the United States and its main allies after 1945. Although it was true that the intensifying economic linkages characteristic of industrial capitalism did little to prevent the catastrophic and vast shedding of blood on a global scale in the decades after 1914, no better idea for rebuilding world order was on offer. During the 1970s, the political logic of expanding trade and productive investment extended to markets for financial services.

The broadening movement towards financial openness hearkened back to the situation at the leading edge of the world economy before the First World War. Just as then, globalizing finance was soon marked by cross-border crises that spilled into everyday life (DeLong 2022). In Chapter 8, Eric Helleiner provides essential historical background for understanding the monetary dynamics behind the globalization of finance, which accelerated after the end of the Cold War and the opening of China. In Chapter 10, Chris Clarke and Adrienne Roberts explore the deep implications within societies around the world by showing how broader structural trends in the global economy affect the day-to-day experiences of individuals and households. This chapter focuses on the state-level politics involved in effectively and legitimately managing what is in effect an increasingly complex policy experiment signalled by openness and financialization at the global scale. In the end, it poses the question of whether collaborative financial governance can ever reliably be delivered in the absence of systemic political transformation.

9.1.1 **Policy changes**

Economists still argue about the precise effects of financial liberalization on the efficient and fair functioning of 'real' economies, where tangible goods and services are produced, exchanged, and consumed. In the decades following 1945, to be sure, leading states were wary of repeating the worst experiences of the nineteenth century, when speculative excesses, financial crises, and economic depressions commonly coincided. As their economies recovered from war and entered a period of rapid expansion, however, those same states proved unwilling to permanently bear the costs of the functional or geographic regulations imposed during the Great Depression. As well, **capital controls** imposed during the wartime years that followed gradually fell away. International direct investments by corporations again began to grow, while markets for short- as well as long-term financing reconnected and deepened. Participation of more domestic and also foreign participants was encouraged, while innovation, especially in telecommunications' technologies, was actively promoted. Productive capital movements within and across political boundaries once again became difficult to differentiate from unproductive speculation. Constructing risks in uncertain environments and shifting them across increasingly diverse portfolios, after all, was the essence of finance capitalism. Although few serious voices with any claim to political authority ever favoured completely open and deregulated capital markets, over time even fewer could justify closure and restriction in the face of rapid economic expansion.

Competing banks, following their clients, found it more urgent to diversify their balance sheets internationally, while competing governments faced ever fewer incentives to stop them. Firms, banks, and eventually non-bank financial intermediaries sought competitive advantages by engaging in arbitrage, playing one government's policies off against those of another. The states licensing and hosting them, in turn, tried more energetically to attract inflows of foreign capital and to build employment-rich financial centres within their borders. Barriers between commercial banking and investment banking gradually eroded as a range of old and new intermediaries devised novel financial instruments and innovative ways to use leverage to bolster rates of return (Copelovitch and Singer 2020).

Private credit rating agencies then became more significant arbiters in the allocation of credit globally (Sinclair 2021).

Over the past half century, financial restrictions have simply become more difficult to sustain or justify, except on a temporary basis. In the name of national security, controls are occasionally reimposed—for example, in the midst of the 2008 global financial catastrophe discussed below and, more recently, in emerging-market economies threatened by sudden speculative outflows. In the absence of world war, however, the possibility of systemic movement back towards financial closure has become remote. Even in the context of national security, the political leverage provided by financial openness is increasingly relied upon as dominant states seek non-military means to exert pressure on adversaries (Jentleson 2022). Despite the probability that target states will eventually find ways to counter such 'weaponization', threats of exclusion from vital financial networks have become increasingly attractive as bargaining tools (Farrell and Newman 2019b).

9.1.2 Policy implications

Over time, financial intermediaries, their corporate clients, and wealthy individuals built the idea of progressive openness into their strategic expectations. Their influence, policy-framing, and everyday operating decisions pushed ever less reluctant governments along the path towards deeper financial integration.

As collective movement along that path accelerated, however, globalizing capital markets, like their historic analogues, periodically exhibited the behaviour of a manic depressive. Years of ecstatic euphoria were routinely followed by moments of black despair, marked by threatened paralysis (or 'illiquidity') in more intimately linked payment systems—the basic plumbing upon which modern economies rest. Firms and individuals that appeared one day to be financially strong threatened to become insolvent the next. Although some volatility is expected in any dynamic financial system, the fragility of the social and psychological underpinnings of open capital markets has revealed itself time and again throughout contemporary history (Minsky 1986). Periods of apparent stability and creative growth repeatedly end in systemic crisis.

When capital mainly stayed within national boundaries, national authorities developed the competence to oversee them and the last-resort lending and investing policies to stabilize them when necessary. Although often controversial, finance ministries and central banks knew what to do. It takes a fair amount of wishful thinking, however, to imagine that such knowledge and experience is readily transportable to the system level in a world of still sovereign states. Figure 9.1 suggests the expanding scale of both the economic opportunities and the political challenges the experiment in capital market openness has posed for governments since the early 1980s.

Figure 9.1 Global cross-border capital inflows of portfolio and foreign direct investment (US$ trillion)

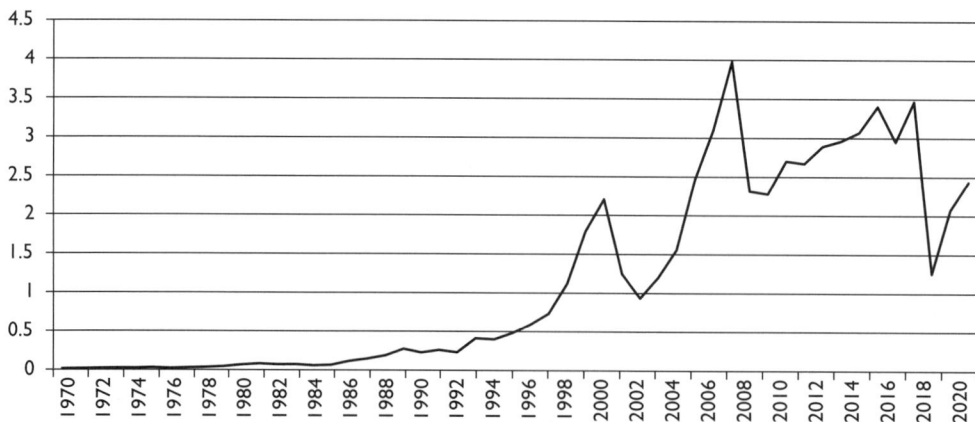

Source: World Bank Development Indicators 2022 https://databank.worldbank.org/source/world-development-indicators.

Practical governing capacities in this context are as fragile or as strong as the relationships among those who will be blamed if globalizing capital markets collapse. Put differently, if countries continue to depend upon external sources of private capital, if the markets through which that capital now flows occasionally become unstable, and if one does not share the ahistorical, indeed quite utopian, libertarian faith that states as currently constituted will ever again let deeply troubled markets self-correct, then one conclusion follows. As the global experiment in capital market openness continues, some kind of reliable collective authority needs to be in place during systemic emergencies to restore confidence. Some such authority also eventually needs to be in place to protect the unscrupulous few from taking financial advantage of the naïve many. And once general market failure is ruled out, authoritative systemic arrangements need to be in place to limit the '**moral hazards**' posed when intermediaries are tempted to take excessive risks because they expect to be bailed out if they get into trouble.

The idea that financial regulation and supervision is necessary in modern societies to engineer politically tolerable trade-offs among the objectives of market efficiency, safety, justice, and resilience has a long pedigree. The related notion that capital markets are inherently dangerous and prone to instability also rests on plenty of historical evidence (Minsky 1986). John Maynard Keynes gave such ideas a prominent place at Bretton Woods. Research reinforcing them has deepened ever since then (Wade 1990; Abdelal 2007; Skidelsky 2009; Rodrik 2011). Despite those ideas, we are once again caught up in a seemingly inexorable attempt to extend the stability programme to the global level. In a still inherently uncertain world, the experiment in political economy often seems to depend on disaster myopia, the human proclivity to quickly forget past catastrophes (Reinhart and Rogoff 2009; Abdelal 2022). The challenge of reviving memories and learning from them is now necessarily as global in scope as capital markets themselves.

9.2 Local politics, global markets

In principle, capital markets exist mainly to support economic development and growth. The prices of most financial assets and liabilities continuously fluctuate. But rapid and severe fluctuations in the value of financial claims can significantly disrupt economic expansion, societal development, and even basic trade in goods and services. In the democratic systems currently lying at the heart of the global economy, price fluctuations in capital markets are conventionally viewed as constructive. They steer resources to promising sectors and away from failing ones. Well-functioning markets are seen as essential tools of policy; their price-signalling instruments are useful for advancing short- and long-term economic, social, and political objectives. Cross-border capital flows can in principle do the same globally. High and rising imbalances in the current accounts of individual countries can signal the need for adjustment, and capital inflows can allow such adjustment to occur gradually (Figure 9.2). Inward and outward flows can certainly expand social inequalities and disrupt traditional social structures. They can also provide governments both political buffers and scapegoats for difficult decisions.

Excessively volatile flows can readily become socially and politically destructive. Examples abound of otherwise reasonable economic policies disrupted and reversed by damaging capital flight precipitated by unrelated sources of regional or systemic turbulence. Calls for capital controls (or in recent jargon, 'capital-flow management measures') typically ensue (Grabel 2017). Such controls can sometimes provide governments with breathing space, even if they soon become difficult to maintain (Ghosh, Ostry, and Qureshi 2018). Restrictions on inflows, say, on foreign purchases of local real estate, are not uncommon around the world. Limits on outflows, for example, from heavily indebted countries during unanticipated crises, may be justifiable. Nevertheless, maintaining the effectiveness of controls, forestalling corruption, and reversing course in a timely fashion have often proven problematic, even in advanced economies (Goodman and Pauly 1993).

Some volatility in well-functioning capital markets is quite normal and expected as buyers and sellers of financial claims seek new opportunities, recalibrate risk tolerances, or respond to unexpected shocks as well as to routine changes in tax and other policies. A high degree of volatility, however, may be the consequence of excessive leverage and unproductive speculation. Unstable and inflexible capital markets often reflect deeper sources of dysfunction. In modern history, they have been associated with disasters of the first order.

Figure 9.2 Current account balances ($US billions)

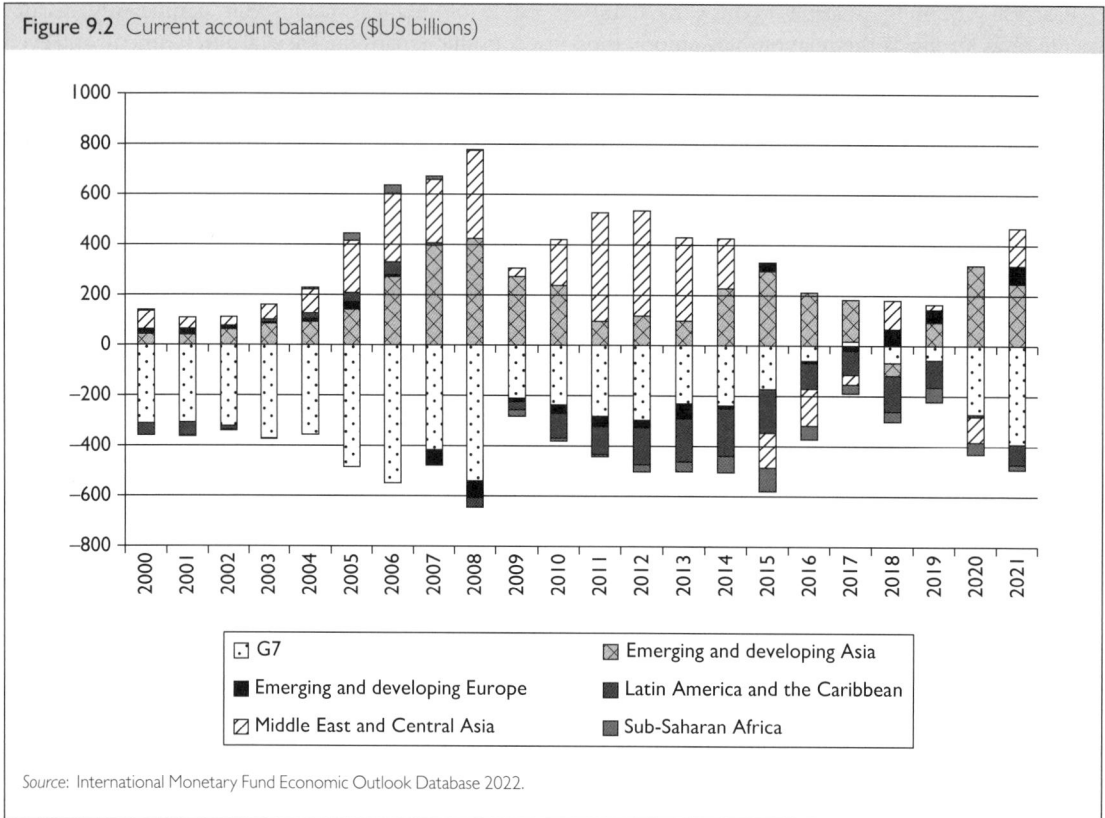

Legend:
- ☐ G7
- ■ Emerging and developing Europe
- ▨ Middle East and Central Asia
- ▨ Emerging and developing Asia
- ■ Latin America and the Caribbean
- ▨ Sub-Saharan Africa

Source: International Monetary Fund Economic Outlook Database 2022.

From the 1870s until today, the world economy has grown rapidly and consistently, except during periods marked by serious financial crisis. Significant downturns occurred after the financial panic of 1907, during the First World War, between 1929 and 1931, and during the period of demobilization immediately after the Second World War (IMF 2009: 129). Not coincidentally, the economic policies of leading states after 1945 shared an abiding aversion to repeating those experiences. The US in particular, while rarely putting international commitments ahead of its domestic priorities, tied a broad set of its policies to the promise of a widening global circle of shared prosperity (Ikenberry 2001; 2020; Rauchway 2015). That promise eventually entailed acquiescence in capital market openness at home and abroad (Pauly 1988; Helleiner 1994; Germain 1997). The political costs of returning to a regime of fixed exchange rates or strong capital controls were consistently judged as too high (See Helleiner, Chapter 8). That the benefits of capital mobility would actually be widely shared, though, was never guaranteed. What gradually became obvious was that

the financial effects of bursting asset bubbles, financial accidents, and other afflictions within the United States would be more easily transmitted globally (Ba 2021).

The die was cast when the Cold War began and vast amounts of capital were required rapidly to rebuild broken European and Asian economies and then to promote economic development in the rest of the world. American public funds, most prominently those allocated in Europe through the Marshall Plan, kick-started the process (Steil 2018). They were soon quite intentionally dwarfed by private capital flows in the form of payments for imports, foreign bank lending, private remittances, and foreign direct investment. Facilitating those flows were telecommunications networks continuously being reshaped by both policy and technological innovations and accommodating governmental policies on both ends of the pipeline.

Regulatory and tax arbitrage—firms and individuals moving across political borders in search of least costly operating environments—arguably enhanced competitive efficiency. They also expanded 'offshore' opportunities for avoidance and evasion at a global scale (Friman and Andreas 1999; Palan 2006). Critics quite reasonably feared a policy of 'race to the bottom', the increasing concentration of financial income and wealth, and the facilitation of corruption by autocratic regimes and criminal networks. The empirical evidence is scattered, often opaque, and diversely interpreted (Drezner 2001; Applebaum 2021). The less debatable view was that much more intense political collaboration would be required either to move back feasibly and safely towards capital market closure or to move forwards decisively towards a system that was both more efficient, more transparent, and more just.

KEY POINTS

- The opening of capital markets and the liberalization of cross-border capital movements during the past half century reflected policy shifts across the advanced industrial and developing world.

- International capital in its various forms facilitated trade, investment, and development. But the markets through which capital flowed more freely were subject to bouts of instability and debates over distributive fairness.

9.3 Uncertainty, risk, and financial crises

Financial crises commence with sharp breaks in the prices of key financial instruments. The expectations of market participants suddenly change, and the *uncertainty* always underlying the human condition becomes vivid. 'Shocks' course through markets, and participants seek to adjust their financial holdings rapidly. Unable to accommodate demands, markets freeze up and soon the physical commerce depending on them stops. Since the dawn of modern capitalism, financial crises have varied in their type, severity, and ultimate impact.

Capitalist economies as well as their precursors rest on foundations of debt (Graeber 2011). Borrowing and lending fuel economic growth even as they reshape social structures (see Clarke and Roberts, Chapter 10). In principle, the aggregate financial claims created by the interaction of consumers, producers, savers, and investors in an economy are supportable as long as expected future revenues exceed the expected future costs of debt servicing and repayment. The same logic

applies internationally when once-separated economies become more integrated. At base, this involves the integration of markets for the information that is embedded in the prices of financial claims.

Market expectations are always shifting and subject to doubt. When enough borrowers and lenders share enough information to form common expectations of the future, it becomes feasible to speak of probabilities, or *risks* capable of being managed (Knight 1921; Arnoldi 2009). This is precisely what banks do when they accept deposits from savers in the short run, pool them, and make longer-term loans to borrowers who agree to pay interest and ultimately repay principal. In more advanced economies, various non-banking financial institutions and asset managers facilitate 'portfolio' investing, or the buying and selling of securities, like stocks, bonds, futures, options, and more exotic derivative instruments that derive their value from anticipated movements in the prices of underlying assets or market indicators. Insurance and reinsurance firms do something similar when they accept premiums, invest the proceeds in diversified investment portfolios, and plan for probable future claims.

Even when financial intermediation occurs smoothly, say through efficient and prudent banks, the prices of specific instruments (assets from the point of view of creditors, liabilities from the point of view of borrowers) can change abruptly. Misjudgements occur, risks are incorrectly estimated, or market conditions suddenly shift. In the wake of unexpected shocks, creditors become *uncertain* about the payment capacity of debtors and the adequacy of available or contingent reserves. When national markets are open, information 'asymmetries' during crises complicate assessments of the probability of default (Nelson and Katzenstein 2014). When a radical sense of systemic uncertainty sets in, 'manias, panics, and crashes' can spread around the world like highly contagious viruses (Kindleberger 1978; Flandreau and Zumer 2004; Frieden 2006; Katzenstein 2022).

No matter how they are themselves constituted, states have lately proven willing to intervene in their national capital markets in the face of extreme confidence-sapping shocks, especially when currency crises and banking crises coincide (Bordo and Eichengreen 2002). By opening monetary and fiscal spigots, they seek to administer a powerful counter-shock to bring market participants psychologically out of the realm of radical uncertainty and back into the realm of risk, where productive trade and investment can resume.

9.4 Financial policy coordination

In 1974, the failure of the German Bankhaus I. D. Herstatt to honour its foreign exchange contracts led to the collapse of the Franklin National Bank of New York (Spero 1980). Long memories recalled the failure of the Credit-Anstalt Bank in Austria in 1931 and the contagion it spread through world markets (Schubert 1992; Marcus 2018). This time, the American central bank intervened decisively to contain the damage. Similarly, in 1984 the Federal Deposit Insurance Corporation intervened when the Continental Illinois Bank threatened to fail. To mitigate the moral hazards then threatening to make increasingly interconnected markets more, not less, fragile, the United States and other governments started collaborating more deeply on bank regulation and supervision.

Following their multinational corporate clients, those same banks accelerated the global diversification of their investment and trading activities, especially in Central and South America. Capital infusions from abroad seemed for a time to promise faster real economic growth. In such an environment, few asked how the benefits and costs of financial openness should be distributed when debt servicing and repayment problems arose?

9.4.1 **Distributive politics in a more open world**

Before the 1970s, some developing countries had in fact sought to limit the future role of private international capital in their national economies. They demanded a **New International Economic Order** (**NIEO**), engineered through some kind of political redistribution of real and financial resources. By the 1980s, though,

most had abandoned a quest that never attracted serious support from leading capitalist states (Boughton 2001; Martinez-Diaz 2009). Economic liberalization across much of the developing world then reflected changing domestic interests, the waning of the Cold War, and ideological shifts in policymaking circles (Chwieroth 2010). Although few immediately assigned priority to financial openness over exchange rate stability, painful experiences in attempting to maintain unrealistic exchange-rate pegs were often repeated. With the rise of East Asian economies and especially the opening of China in ensuing decades, foreign capital inflows would soon be permitted by country after country to expand dramatically, even if formal capital flow management measures were sometimes only gradually and tentatively loosened (Figure 9.3).

In line with the experience of advanced industrial countries before the collapse of the Bretton Woods system, when financial markets across the developing world opened up, exchange rates and therefore debts denominated in foreign currencies became much more difficult to manage. More complicated as well became the task of foreign lenders and investors in calculating the probability of default or payment problems. After the 1980s, bouts of uncertainty led repeatedly across many emerging-market economies to sudden stops in capital inflows.

The global experiment upon which many states had effectively embarked by the 1980s rested on the hidden assumption that sharp reversals in cross-border capital movements would encourage disciplined domestic policies conducive to systemic stability. In practice, the stronger the country, the weaker such disciplinary effects turned out to be. Fundamental issues of effective governance, economic fairness, and distributive justice became ever clearer as the experiment in capital market openness continued (Best 2005; Sen 2009). Deeper financial integration seemed to imply the need for more intrusive political instruments designed to negotiate and implement a widening array of policy trade-offs.

9.4.2 **Sovereignty and financial interconnectedness**

When capital markets are booming, it is difficult to plan for downturns. But when confidence-withering financial contagion spills over national boundaries, who is ultimately responsible for bailing out intermediaries suddenly confronting the prospect of collapse?

Figure 9.3 Capital inflows to developing countries ($US billions)

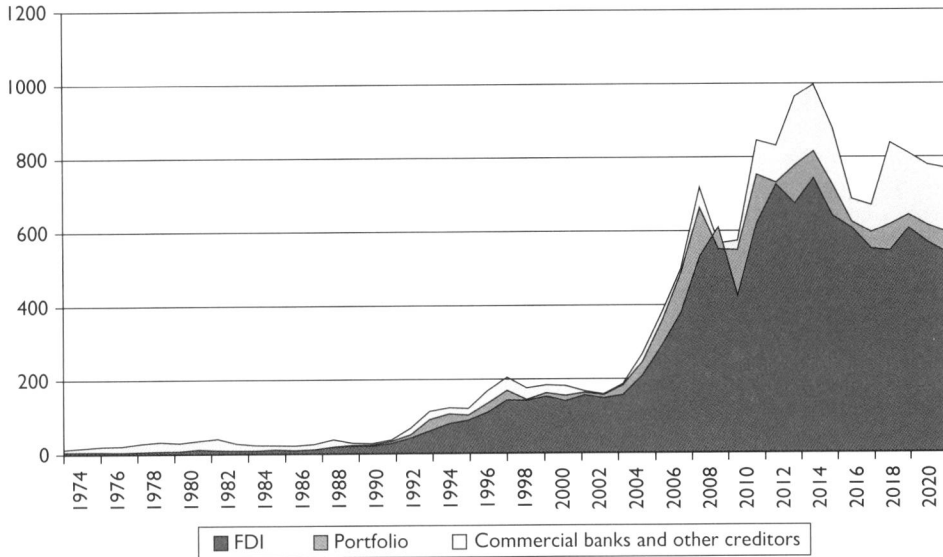

Source: World Bank Development Indicators 2022.

During actual financial crises in the decades following the breakdown of the Bretton Woods exchange rate system, the answer gradually emerged (Kapstein 1994). Last-resort lending and investing facilities remained under the exclusive purview of individual states themselves, and the home states of globally active financial intermediaries therefore bore primary regulatory and supervisory responsibilities. Treaty-based intergovernmental organizations like the **International Monetary Fund (IMF)** could sometimes assist financially

and play the role of scapegoats, but those states and their central banks would have to lead in resolving any systemic crisis. At points of emergency, a modicum of trust between home and host states was both crucial and tenuous. Every cross-border financial crisis in recent years has therefore refocused attention on the underlying political fragility of the experiment in capital market openness. The crisis of the late 1990s emanating from East Asia illustrates the point well (see Case Study Box 9.1).

CASE STUDY BOX 9.1 THE FINANCIAL PANIC OF THE LATE 1990s

In the mid-1990s, interest rates fell and stock markets boomed in North America and Western Europe. Banks and portfolio investors, including rapidly expanding mutual funds and hedge funds that pooled and leveraged the capital of institutional and wealthy investors, increasingly looked abroad for higher returns. With those higher returns came higher risks. They manifested themselves in localized currency crises, as in Mexico in 1994, but they seemed manageable in an expanding array of opening markets. Japanese banks in particular, confronting stagnant demand in a slumping

home market, considered it an ideal time to expand aggressively across the East Asian region. Both public sector and private sector borrowers in many emerging-market economies discovered new and ready sources of funds, and they borrowed heavily.

In Thailand, much of this new debt was denominated in the local currency, which the Thai government valued at a pegged, not floating rate. By buying local debt, investors and creditors, in essence, bet that the Thai baht would hold its value. Early in

KEY CONCEPT BOX 9.1 THE FINANCIAL PANIC OF THE LATE 1990S (continued)

1997, however, Japanese banks, which then held about half of the country's foreign debt, began to lose confidence. They sought to reduce their exposures in Thailand as well as in a number of neighbouring countries. Their pullback prompted a regional **liquidity** crunch. Soon, generalized fears of a devaluation of the baht became self-fulfilling, and other Asian nations needed to defend the competitive advantages of their exporting industries by allowing their own currencies to depreciate.

Capital suddenly flew out of South Korea, Indonesia, and Malaysia. Just as a bank hit by a run of depositors is forced hurriedly to raise cash by calling in loans, investment funds had to meet demands for withdrawals by liquidating their assets. As their Thai assets declined in redeemable value, they withdrew what they could as quickly as possible from their Asian portfolios. Liquidity dried up across the region, and very quickly the solvency of local banks recently considered sound came into question.

The government of Malaysia tried to stem the panic by imposing capital controls to forbid the repatriation of what its prime minister labelled the immoral gains of speculators. Others took the more conventional route of calling in the IMF to provide emergency funding. Such support came, but often with conditions attached that seemed to the recipients excessively intrusive. Political backlash came quickly. Whereas borrowing countries saw themselves struggling against a short-term problem, the IMF insisted on more fundamental kinds of reform designed to make East Asian markets, including capital markets, more open and more transparent. Talk of neo-imperialism by Western powers became commonplace as national incomes fell across the region, imports declined, and a cut-throat competition to maintain exports ensued.

In the midst of the East Asian debacle, Russia's post-1991 experiment with rapid economic liberalization crashed into a wall of unsustainable foreign debt. It certainly seems in

retrospect that many foreign investors had unwisely discounted the possibility that Russia's new class of tycoons would take careful measures to spirit their own capital out of the country. By the summer of 1998, even a massive IMF loan could not bolster confidence in the value of the rouble. It also failed to attract back private Russian capital invested in safe Western investments. Not coincidentally, American and European investors pulled out what they could. When the Russian government defaulted in August and simultaneously devalued the rouble, seismic shocks immediately hit the core of the world's financial system. Loans extended to hedge funds were called in by banks, and stock markets plummeted around the world. Fearing that other emerging-market economies would follow Russia, panicked financiers around the world pulled vast amounts of capital out of Mexico, Brazil, Argentina, and elsewhere.

In September 1998, Long-Term Capital Management (LTCM), a prominent and highly leveraged American hedge fund with little direct exposure in emerging markets, found its leveraged investment strategies wrecked as the crisis spread unexpectedly from Asia to Russia (Lowenstein 2001). While the consensus view among American financial market regulators would ordinarily have been to let such an entity bear the cost of its mistakes, even if that meant failure and liquidation, panic had by now gripped Wall Street itself. The Federal Reserve therefore encouraged a consortium of LTCM's creditors to take over the firm's dwindling assets, gradually unwind its bad bets, and replace its management. No one doubted then that the full faith and credit of the US government would be available if required. Calm returned, and soon many emerging-market economies reverted to liberalizing policies in an effort to stimulate the resumption of capital inflows (Boughton 2012). China's opening and expansion vastly increased pools of available capital for cross-border investment, and both formal and informal channels widened in the decade before the COVID-19 pandemic opened a new era of regional uncertainty.

KEY POINTS

- Following the end of the Bretton Woods exchange rate system, shocks mainly emanating from emerging-market economies only briefly interrupted the global if still incomplete experiment in capital market openness.

- Regional financial crises proved difficult but not impossible to manage. International financial institutions like the IMF

were often useful, but serious crises required intervention by leading states.

- Sovereignty remains an important legal doctrine in a globalizing economy, but in practical policy terms the need to manage border-spanning financial risks collaboratively became ever more obvious.

9.5 Recognizing systemic risk

No modern capital market exists for long without a base of common standards understood by all participants. At the most fundamental level, financial information must be expressed in an understandable form so that risks may be recognized and measured. The intermediaries between the buyers of financial claims and the sellers must be deemed trustworthy. In legal markets, common property, accounting, auditing, licensing, and dispute-settlement rules form the bedrock. In all but the most limited local markets, or in all but the most libertarian utopias, such rules are not spontaneously generated. Some recognized authority has to provide the collective goods of rule adjudication, reform, and, ultimately, enforcement. Cryptocurrency and even illicit markets, if they are to persist, require some source capable of instilling confidence in the finality of payments and settlements. In most cases, that is what governments do, either directly or through central banks. The failure of the FTX cryptocurrency exchange in 2022 vividly demonstrated what happens when confidence in settlement finality suddenly disappears. Firms with any connections to the failing entity begin to falter. Systemic risk crystallizes until the disaster burns itself out or until some outside force steps in. As we have seen in the modern era, that force has come from government, and its intervention has mainly been limited to its responsibility for maintaining a stable payments system at the core of the economy it oversees. In the case of cryptocurrency trading and what has generally come to be known as FinTech innovation (see Girard, Chapter 17), the pattern set by debt crises in the 1980s and 1990s remains evident. As long as the exposure of major clearing banks to probable future speculative losses is low, monetary and fiscal authorities are slow to engage in the cause of crisis pre-emption. Even as private payment systems arise, some based on cryptocurrencies and possibly decentralized blockchains, central banks prepare to offer digital versions of their own currencies in order to maintain their own capacities to restore market stability in the midst of future disasters. (See Helleiner, Chapter 8, and Clarke and Roberts, Chapter 10, for related discussions.)

9.5.1 Defending public and private interests

Not surprisingly, given the picture painted above, financial crises spilling over political borders expose jurisdictional gaps. Even the most severe crises yet confronted, however, have not been followed by the establishment of an unquestioned global standard-setter or supranational agency capable of final dispute settlement or rule enforcement. The frontiers of markets integrating across legal boundaries, moreover, are intentionally only weakly patrolled by intergovernmental agencies and voluntary industry associations. At most, they have been expected to promote and monitor normative understandings that leave room for interpretation (Bryant 2003). In the US, the United Kingdom (UK), and elsewhere, governments have sometimes been willing to let market participants attempt to clarify such understandings among themselves, for example, on best operating and risk-reduction practices.

Contemplating the ever present possibility that systemically significant financial intermediaries they do regulate could fail, however, governments retain the ultimate capabilities either to dip into national treasuries or to turn to their central banks for the funding required to withstand market turmoil. Over time, other kinds of financial intermediaries found ways to provide services analogous to those provided by banks. Following the Herstatt experience, and after the emergence and expansion of financial intermediaries more lightly regulated than commercial banks, the logic of international collaboration on standard setting and rule enforcement began to spread. Most firms in globalizing insurance, securities, and asset-management businesses were still reliably supervised in their home markets, which helped explain the home bias of risk-averse investors. The governmental agencies licensing and overseeing them nevertheless tried to support the expansion of those firms overseas while deliberately trying to limit their own responsibilities for regulating 'offshore' activities. So when non-bank financial institutions (like hedge and private equity funds, wealth managers, and others now conventionally labelled 'shadow banks') began expanding globally, their home governments attempted to reduce their own potential liabilities by participating in international standard-setting exercises, which often specified the responsibilities of host countries to step up when problems arose within their jurisdictions. As in the banking sector, though, establishing common norms, defining enforcement roles, and limiting official liabilities became much more difficult as functional and geographic barriers were permitted to erode. Whether by intentional design or not, dividing lines between public and private interests often became very difficult to draw (Pauly 2009; McKeen-Edwards and Porter 2013; O'Connell and Elliott 2023).

9.5.2 **Prudential risk assessment**

During the 1980s, with the temptations of regulatory arbitrage and the threat of 'races to the bottom' in the background, promoting multilateral collaboration on cross-border financial regulation emerged as an important rationale for regular meetings of a central bankers' club hosted by the **Bank for International Settlements (BIS)**. Originally established to manage reparations payments after the First World War, the BIS survived attempts to close it down after 1945. Thirty years later, after having developed a profitable business managing central-bank reserves, it proved a convenient venue for meetings of monetary and financial officials and a vital source of staff support. The Basel Committee on Banking Supervision (BCBS) was the first of a new set of clubs to benefit.

The focus of the BCBS is at the micro level. Its policy recommendations typically target large banks active across national borders. In 1999, having just come through the Asian crisis, G20 governments complemented BCBS initiatives by establishing the Financial Stability Forum (FSF) to draw attention to the macroeconomic implications of integrating financial markets and to try to come to grips with the widely perceived expansion of systemic risk. Designing 'macroprudential policies' to reduce vulnerabilities exposed by intensifying cross-border linkages came to the forefront of discussion when the FSF became the Financial Stability Board (FSB) ten years later (Key Theory Box 9.2). Other bodies were also established or upgraded to promote regulatory and supervisory collaboration across increasingly complex markets (Moschella 2017; Key Concept Box 9.3). Together, the often overlapping risk-assessment and standard-setting activities of the BCBS and many of these other groups came to be called the 'Basel Process'.

Banking crises initially led the BCBS to propose a concordat to clarify the respective responsibilities of the home and host country supervisors of cross-border banks, and then to promote minimum standards for capital reserves expected to be available to absorb losses and reduce the likelihood that national monetary and fiscal resources would be called upon during periods of instability (Basel I). It also commenced work with other national and regional bodies to bolster the effectiveness of prudential supervision within and beyond the banking sector narrowly defined. In 2006, the most extensive and detailed effort to ensure capital adequacy came in an accord commonly dubbed Basel II. Under its terms, international lenders were encouraged to bring sophisticated and self-disciplined risk-management techniques into calculations of capital adequacy. The politics of policymaking through technocratic clubs here reached a limit, not least because underlying risk cultures across major states and regions remained distinctive, but also because 'self-discipline' in a competitive environment often proved to be an oxymoron.

The fact that the implementation of Basel II left much discretion for national supervisors was only one source of future trouble. The accord enhanced the **competitive advantages** of large money-centre banks. Astute observers pointed out that its impact might also be 'pro-cyclical'. That is, banks around the world would be encouraged to excessively restrict lending during recessions and to imprudently expand lending during booms. They proved to be correct. The Basel Process could promote common risk-assessment standards, but the enforcement of actual operating rules potentially capable of preventing future systemic crises would continue to depend upon local agencies mainly responsive to diverse and sometimes conflicting domestic policy priorities (Singer 2007). The proliferation of global supervisory initiatives and the gradual diffusion of geopolitical power, moreover, continued to underline the risk of fragmentation at readily imaginable moments when systemic emergency management was required.

9.5.3 **Policy failures**

The main symptom of mounting systemic problems in the decades immediately following the end of the Bretton Woods system took the form of enduring imbalances in the current accounts of leading countries. By the turn of the twenty-first century, it was clear that the US was routinely importing too much, saving too little, and depending for its financing needs on vast inflows of capital from China, Japan, Germany, and even many middle-income and developing countries. Instead of encouraging macroeconomic adjustments, expanding capital markets permitted payments imbalances to grow.

These imbalances, combined with other factors set out below, are commonly blamed for what happened next. Real estate-related bank failures were not unusual in American history, but after 2007 staggering numbers occurred, and their effects were now global.

KEY THEORY BOX 9.2 MACROPRUDENTIAL POLICY

Just like closer interaction across human communities increases the risk that microbial diseases will spread, intensifying banking and investment linkages across national borders provide expanding vectors for financial contagion. In the aftermath of financial crises in the 1970s, national financial regulators and supervisors began paying more attention to the theory and practice of managing systemic financial risk, the probability that financial shocks elsewhere in the world will disrupt domestic macroeconomies.

In many countries, microprudential regulation focused on individual financial intermediaries had long been routinized. The need was clear to prevent banks understood to have access to last-resort loans from central banks from taking on excessive risks. Also rendered undeniable, often by bitter experience, was the necessity to protect consumers from fraudulent financial practices. Minimum capital ratios and rules related to the treatment of anticipated loan losses, among many other indicators, provided measurable standards that supervisors could enforce. Experience also increasingly indicated, however, that differential national policies at this level were ineffective in preventing the spread of financial contagion globally. Systemic risks were broadly perceived to be growing. The effects of many market and regulatory failures, not only related to large intermediaries but also to deeply interconnected ones, could not reliably be contained within national borders. Information suggestive of excessive speculation was harder to detect within globe-spanning financial networks. Similarly, cycles of euphoria or despair, justified or not, proved harder to contain or counteract through adjustments in discrete national policies. As capital markets opened and integrated during the past fifty years, the need for coordinated macroprudential policies became ever more obvious.

The demand for such policies has provided a focal point for the Basel Process ever since its inception (Goodhart 2011).

A universal toolkit has not been agreed, but understandings on the design and implementation of regulatory and supervisory standards are emerging. In general, the aim is to moderate financial booms and busts and prevent concentrations of excessive financial risks and losses. Common loan-loss provisions for like-sized banks, dynamically adjustable capital requirements, aggregate limits on the uncovered debt like intermediaries are permitted to carry, required amounts of liquid assets intermediaries in the same business and same networks are expected to maintain—experiments with these and other rules targeting macroeconomic stability are underway. At the same time, regulators and supervisors are insisting on more rigorous and expansive balance-sheet stress testing, the imagining of future scenarios and the analysis of their effects on the abilities of particular intermediaries to meet their obligations and of key national systems of intermediation to remain stable. They are also requiring better specific and general modelling of the effects of interconnectedness across national networks.

Although their efforts ostensibly try to clarify plausible risks, the most sophisticated practitioners of macroprudential policy know that they are really aiming to manage deepening uncertainty (Kay and King 2020). When financial markets become unstable, the initial reaction of nationally constituted governments is to try to put up walls, ring-fence local markets, and assure citizens that their particular interests will be protected. In the United States, Europe, and elsewhere, organizations charged with overseeing financial stability now take a wider view of their responsibilities. The steady evolution of macroprudential policy indicates a broadening acceptance of the view that both the benefits and the costs of more open capital markets must be borne collaboratively (Edge and Liang 2019).

KEY CONCEPT BOX 9.3 INSTITUTIONS FOR FINANCIAL POLICY COLLABORATION

Bank for International Settlements (BIS): Established in 1930 to oversee Germany's war reparation payments. With its headquarters in Basel, Switzerland, its continuing role in facilitating a multilateral payments system in Europe made it an obvious venue during the 1960s for intensifying dialogue among central bankers, now including the US and other non-European countries, on a broad range of financial regulatory and supervisory issues. Today, the BIS provides a meeting place and secretariat for several collaborative committees, including the BCBS, the Committee on the Global Financial System, the Committee on Payments and Market Infrastructures (CPMI),

the Markets Committee, the Central Bank Governance Forum, and the Irving Fisher Committee on Central Bank Statistics.

Basel Committee on Banking Supervision (BCBS): Originally a Standing Committee of the Central Bank Governors of the G10, its 1975 mandate was to promote collaborative approaches on issues of common concern. (Actually numbering eleven, the informal G10 includes the central banks of the leading advanced industrial states. The IMF turns to them through the General Arrangements to Borrow when it needs to augment its resources.) BCBS participants also now include

KEY CONCEPT BOX 9.3 INSTITUTIONS FOR FINANCIAL POLICY COLLABORATION (continued)

Argentina, Australia, Brazil, China, the European Union (EU), Hong Kong SAR, India, Indonesia, Korea, Luxembourg, Mexico, Russia, Saudi Arabia, Singapore, South Africa, Spain, and Turkey. The Committee cooperates with other regional groups as it develops international standards on capital adequacy for banks and core principles for the effective supervision of cross-border banking. The Committee also works with related central bank committees convening at the BIS as well as with the International Organization of Securities Commissions (IOSCO), the International Association of Deposit Insurers (IADI), and the International Association of Insurance Supervisors (IAIS) (see below) on issues related to the operations of transnational financial institutions (Goodhart 2011).

Financial Action Task Force (FATF): Initiated at the 1989 summit meeting of the G7 to combat money laundering. With a secretariat based in the Organization for Economic Cooperation and Development (OECD), but not technically part of that organization, it coordinates national efforts and also aims to disrupt the financing of terrorism in a world of more open capital markets (Kahler et al. 2018).

Financial Stability Board (FSB): Following the international financial crises of the late 1990s, the G7 finance ministers and central bank governors brought together national financial regulators from a wide range of countries hosting important international financial centres, together with international organizations involved in financial policy matters. The FSF began meeting in April 1999 and maintained a small secretariat at the BIS. In April 2009, the G20 expanded its membership to include Spain and the European Commission and transformed it into a more ambitious effort with the mandate of fostering 'macroprudential' policy collaboration among central banks and financial supervisors, that is, on ensuring that the oversight of financial institutions included not only analysis of the effects of institutional failure on the system as a whole, but also rigorous assessment of the effects of systemic shocks on the institutions themselves. The FSB, with an expanded secretariat comprised mainly of officials seconded from central banks, was to be a vehicle for consultation across various standard-setting groups and organizations. It was to link its country-level work to the Financial Sector Assessment Programs of the World Bank and the IMF and to the IMF's surveillance operations. Especially after the crisis of 2008, particular emphasis was placed on complex issues related to the regulation of capital adequacy and liquidity management in cross-border and systemically significant financial institutions.

Group of 7/Group of 20 (G7/G20): Dating back to informal meetings of European finance ministers after the collapse of the Bretton Woods exchange rate arrangements, regular annual

meetings of financial officials and heads of government now occur under these rubrics. The G7 includes the US, France, the UK, Germany, Japan, Canada, and Italy. The G20, which includes China, India, Brazil, South Africa, Indonesia, and other emerging-market economies, came to prominence after the emerging-market debt crises of the late 1990s. Meetings aim to develop key relationships in advance of a widening variety of crises. Neither the G7 nor the G20 have permanent secretariats, but the most comprehensive archive of communiques, other group documents, and independent accountability reports is located in the library system of the University of Toronto.

International Accounting Standards Board (IASB) and *International Federation of Accountants*: Private sector bodies organized by industry associations to encourage international standardization of accounting principles and auditing practices.

International Association of Deposit Insurers (IADI): Established in 2002 to enhance the effectiveness of national deposit insurance systems. Its secretariat is in Basel, where it receives technical assistance from the BIS.

International Association of Insurance Supervisors (IAIS): Established in 1992 to encourage cooperation among regulators and supervisors of insurance companies. Since 1998, its secretariat has been supported by the BIS.

International Bank for Reconstruction and Development (World Bank): Designed at Bretton Woods, its advice to developing members has encouraged financial sector adjustment and reform.

International Monetary Fund (IMF): Designed at the Bretton Woods Conference, July 1944. From the 1970s onwards, it became increasingly involved in conditional financing programmes to assist members facing payments crises caused by financial shocks and in the incrementally elaborated mission of bilateral, multilateral, and financial surveillance for individual members and for the system as a whole.

International Organization of Securities Commissions (IOSCO): With a secretariat now based in Madrid, Spain, since 1983, IOSCO has facilitated the sharing of information and best practices among market regulators.

Organization for Economic Cooperation and Development (OECD): Evolved out of efforts after the Second World War to facilitate the use of Marshall Plan resources. Often now considered a think tank for industrial countries contemplating various forms of economic policy coordination.

Regional development banks and financial arrangements: With local mandates akin to that of the World Bank, regional organizations and informal arrangements sometimes including currency swap facilities (in Africa, Latin America, East Asia, Eastern Europe, and

---

KEY CONCEPT BOX 9.3 INSTITUTIONS FOR FINANCIAL POLICY COLLABORATION (continued)

Central Europe) are now involved in providing technical advice and financial backstops as markets open and deepen. In 2015, China established new longer-term financing facilities for the East and Central Asian regions in the intergovernmental Asian Infrastructure and Investment Bank (AIIB) and its own Belt and Road Initiative (BRI).

United Nations (UN): Various UN commissions, agencies, and departments, such as the Department of Economic and Social Affairs in the New York-based secretariat, have mandates to promote understanding among member states on issues of

equity and efficiency in the global economy. In this context, they advocate for adequate and reliable financing to achieve internationally agreed Millennium and Sustainable Development Goals for poverty and inequality reduction, economic development, and environmental protection.

World Trade Organization (WTO): Having grown out of the General Agreement on Tariffs and Trade (GATT), under which national trade policies were liberalized on a multilateral basis after 1948, the WTO now oversees trade in various services, including a widening range of financial services.

In their wake, the capacity of existing multilateral arrangements to pre-empt contagion across the markets to which banks and other intermediaries were by then directly or indirectly connected proved inadequate. The most severe systemic financial emergency since the Great Depression ensued.

KEY POINTS

- Since the collapse of the Bretton Woods exchange rate regime, governments have attempted to cooperate more intensively to prevent financial crises.

- Fundamental macroeconomic policy choices condition the flow of capital across national borders, but capital flight can sometimes occur unexpectedly.

- Before the Global Financial Crisis of 2008, private as well as official efforts to render integrating capital markets more resilient occurred mainly in fragmented regulatory and supervisory arenas.

9.6 Managing emergencies and preventing future crises

As outlined in Case Study Box 9.4, governments around the world intervened heavily and directly in global markets beginning in the fall of 2008. The US in particular lent and invested monetary and fiscal resources lavishly. The beneficiaries included most of its own large financial institutions and many foreign-headquartered institutions operating within and across its borders. The equivalent of a systemic run had started in securities firms,

and it very quickly threatened to bring down the clearing banks upon which they and everyone else ultimately depended. Central bank funding and eventually fiscal resources managed by the US Treasury flowed to an array of domestic and foreign financial intermediaries.

In circumstances where illiquidity and insolvency were not easy to differentiate, between 2007 and 2010 190 firms benefitted from the provision of US$1.2 trillion in low-cost emergency loans from the Federal Reserve (2019). These included the subsidiaries and branches of many European, Japanese, and Canadian banks, which also benefitted from reinforcing actions by central banks in their home markets. Expanded currency swap arrangements among central banks at the core of a now deeply integrated global payments system worked in the same direction.

Swap lines are hardly new. Typically at fixed exchange rates for limited terms at modest interest rates, currency swaps help central banks meet liquidity requirements in their local markets. The originating central bank bears no credit risk reflective of direct exposure to ultimate beneficiaries and no foreign exchange risk. It does, however, take on the risk that the counterparty central bank may default when the time comes to reverse the swap. The recipient central bank, in turn, can offer foreign-currency loans to local financial institutions (including the subsidiaries or branches of foreign institutions) under its purview, and by doing so it assumes *credit risk*. During the crisis of 2008, US dollar liquidity in American and foreign markets quickly became scarce. Similarly, demand for other reserve currencies, especially the euro and to a lesser extent the Swiss franc and the Japanese yen, spiked.

CASE STUDY BOX 9.4 TIMELINE OF THE GLOBAL FINANCIAL CRISIS OF 2008 AND ITS AFTERMATH

June 2007: In the midst of rising turbulence in US housing markets, two highly leveraged hedge funds owned by the investment bank Bear Stearns report large losses and are forced to begin selling assets at distressed prices. The trouble spreads to major Wall Street firms, which had lent the funds money. Similar problems surface in the UK, and it would later emerge that many European and Asian institutions owned vast amounts of subprime mortgage-backed securities.

August 2007: Early in the month, US stock markets fall sharply. 'Credit crunch' spreads around the world as subprime mortgage-backed securities are disclosed in portfolios of banks from BNP Paribas to the Bank of China. To provide market liquidity, the Federal Reserve cuts interbank interest rates and injects nearly US$100 billion into the US banking system. The European Central Bank (ECB) and the central banks of Japan, England, Canada, and Australia make coordinated moves in their own markets.

16 August 2007: Stricken by losses in investments related to US subprime mortgages, the German regional bank, Sachsen LB, is taken over by Landesbank Baden-Wuerttemberg. The same day, Countrywide Financial Corporation, the biggest US mortgage lender, narrowly avoids bankruptcy by taking out an emergency loan of US$11 billion from a group of banks. (Bank of America will acquire it for US$4 billion a few months later.) Shortly thereafter, the UK bank Northern Rock requests Bank of England assistance in the face of a run by depositors. (It would be nationalized in early February 2008.) One month later, staggering losses are announced by international giants like the Union Bank of Switzerland and Merrill Lynch.

12 December 2007: As an economic recession begins, the Federal Reserve's Open Market Committee negotiates currency swap lines with the ECB and the Swiss National Bank for up to US$20 billion and US$4 billion, respectively.

28 January 2008: Four days after the first nationwide decline in housing prices since the 1930s is reported, the Economic Stimulus Act of 2008 is proposed in the US Congress. The next day, the House of Representatives passes a US$146 billion aid package to speed up tax rebates for most taxpayers. The Senate increases the package, and the legislation is sent to the president on 7 February.

16 March 2008: JPMorgan Chase & Co acquires what is left of Bear Stearns, in a deal engineered and backstopped by the Federal Reserve. The G7 finance ministers launch a review of the global financial regulatory system.

16 June 2008: The New York investment bank Lehman Brothers reports a catastrophic loss. Within the firm, capital begins to flow from overseas offices back to New York. Three days later, ex-Bear Stearns managers are arrested by the FBI for allegedly misrepresenting the fiscal health of their funds heavily invested in subprime mortgages.

31 August 2008: German Commerzbank AG takes over Dresdner Kleinwort investment bank. Seven days later, US Treasury Secretary Henry Paulson announces a public 'conservatorship' for cash-starved Fannie Mae and Freddie Mac, which provide mortgage guarantees.

15 September 2008: Lehman Brothers files a Chapter 11 bankruptcy petition after the failure of official attempts to arrange for the 158-year-old firm to be taken over by another private firm. The next day, under pressure from government officials, the Bank of America acquires Merrill Lynch.

16 September 2008: In coordinated operations, central banks around the world pump billions of dollars into money markets. Panic increases, and the US government announces an unprecedented blanket guarantee for money market funds once thought to be low-risk investments. The same day, the Federal Reserve lends insurance giant American International Group (AIG), an arm of which had become a key insurer of rapidly depreciating mortgage-backed securities, US$85 billion in exchange for nearly 80 per cent of its stock. The price of gold soars by over 8 per cent, equity markets continue a broad global retreat, and governments around the world begin moving to ban the speculative short selling of financial stocks.

21 September 2008: Goldman Sachs and Morgan Stanley, the two remaining giants in US investment banking markets, change their legal charters to become bank holding companies, thus gaining access to the emergency liquidity facilities of the Federal Reserve. Three days later, in the largest bank failure in US history, Washington Mutual collapses and with government support is sold to JPMorgan Chase.

29 September 2008: The US Congress rejects a US$700 billion plan to bail out the US financial system. As various banks are nationalized or merged into stronger institutions around the world, the Federal Reserve continues supporting markets with massive liquidity operations, while the Securities and Exchange Commission and the Financial Accounting Standards Board announce moves to relax 'mark-to-market' accounting rules that have the effect of exaggerating the effects of panic-induced credit losses. The next day, spreads on short-term lending between top-tier banks, normally quite low, spike to 7 per cent, the highest levels ever recorded.

1 October 2008: Following a dramatic plea from the US Treasury Secretary, the US Congress reverses course. Two days later, President Bush signs the US$700 billion Emergency Economic Stabilization Act into law. Three days later, EU leaders travel to Paris for an emergency summit. G7 finance ministers also meet. During the next week, stock markets around the world record their worst week since the early 1930s. Iceland's banking system collapses, while major British banks suffer large losses and are partly nationalized. Germany, France, and other EU countries take steps to stabilize failing local banks. Fearing a global economic collapse, many central banks around the world simultaneously slash interest rates and lift limits on bilateral swap lines.

10 November 2008: China announces a US$586 billion stimulus package, the largest in the country's history. Two weeks later, the World Bank launches a new Debt Management Facility to help developing countries. Meanwhile, the IMF negotiates large standby arrangements with vulnerable countries around the world. As global investors seek the relative safety of US government debt, the yield on three-month Treasury bills soon falls below zero for the first time ever, and the Federal Reserve begins planning for highly unusual new measures (quantitative easing) to bolster market liquidity.

9 January 2009: The German government takes a 25 per cent stake in Commerzbank through a €10 billion capital injection in an effort to help Commerzbank acquire Dresdner Bank. Ireland bails out Anglo-Irish Bank. A few days later, Standard & Poor's cuts the credit rating of debt issued by Greece, while Portugal, Spain, and Ireland are put on watch lists.

20 January 2009: Barack Obama is sworn in as the forty-fourth president of the US. The IMF projects world economic growth to fall to just 0.5 per cent this year, its lowest rate since just after the Second World War. Three weeks later, the US Treasury announces a Financial Stability Plan involving purchases of convertible preferred stock in eligible banks, the creation of a Public-Private Investment Fund to acquire troubled assets from financial institutions, expansion to US$1 trillion of the Federal Reserve's Term Asset-Backed Securities Loan Facility, and new initiatives to stem residential mortgage foreclosures. One week later, after the Obama administration fails to convince the Congress to approve a larger amount, a new US$787 billion fiscal stimulus plan, the American Recovery and Reinvestment Act, is signed into law.

1 March 2009: The Federal Reserve and the US Treasury provide US$30 billion in capital to AIG and completely take over two divisions of the company after it announces a US$61.7 billion loss, the largest in US corporate history. One month later, G20 leaders meet in London, where they agree to convert the FSF, born after the Asian crisis, to the better-resourced FSB.

9 December 2009: The US Congress begins work that culminates in the sweeping Dodd-Frank Wall Street Reform and Consumer Protection Act on 21 July 2010. Among other things, it establishes the Financial Stability Oversight Council (FSOC) to monitor markets and coordinate financial regulatory policies across the complicated US federal system.

7 June 2010: Euro area member states establish the European Financial Stability Facility temporarily to provide financing to members in distress. Two years later, it would be succeeded by the permanent **European Stability Mechanism** to manage debt rescheduling and restructuring operations. The ESM issues bonds guaranteed by the most creditworthy members of the euro area, sells them to sovereign wealth funds, reserve managers (not least in China), and other global investors, and

extends the proceeds, with structural adjustment conditions attached, to members in distress. In cases like that of Greece in 2010 and 2011, IMF financing programmes ran alongside those of the ESM and the European Central Bank. More expansively, in addition to its normal provision of liquidity, the ECB was later charged with providing a Single Supervisory Mechanism for systemically significant intermediaries in a planned European Banking Union, and the ESM was expected to provide a backstop for a Single Resolution Fund aimed at helping troubled intermediaries in the future.

January 2011: The Financial Crisis Inquiry Commission (FCIC) established by the US Congress explored the reasons for the sudden collapse of a classic 'bubble' in US housing markets. It blamed loose monetary policies, lax regulation and supervision, excessive leverage, opaque financial innovation, and dramatic failures of corporate governance and risk management at many systemically important financial institutions. Its final report concluded, 'There was a systemic breakdown in accountability and ethics' (FCIC 2011). For an illustration of public reactions to the Financial Crisis, see Figure 9.4.

Figure 9.4 Protester at Liberty Square, the symbolic home of Occupy Wall Street. This movement started on 17 September 2011 when hundreds of protesters gathered at Zuccotti Park, occupying it for fifty-eight days. This movement pursued tighter banking regulations from the US government, asked for financial accountability of those considered responsible for the 2008 crisis, and stood against corruption and misrepresentation. Their main slogan was 'We are the 99%'. The occupation ended on 15 November; the protesters were removed by the police ordered by the New York City mayor at that time, Michael Bloomberg, due to public health concerns.

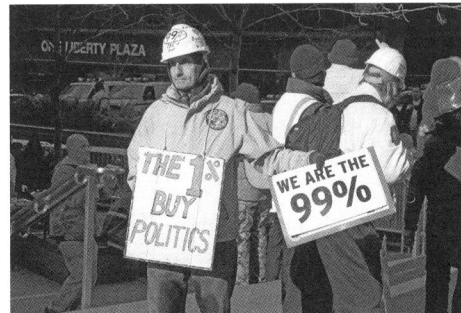

Source: Alamy.

In response, mutually self-interested, informally coordinated, and structurally tiered actions by the US Federal Reserve and other key currency central banks activated and significantly deepened swap networks centred on the dollar, the euro, the Japanese yen, and the Swiss franc (Broz 2015; Murau, Pape, and Pforr 2022). Additionally, regional swap arrangements put in place during and after previous crises in Asia and Latin America were revived. From 2007 onwards, nearly half of all potential foreign-currency demand from local financial institutions around the world was for US dollars, including demand originating from US bank subsidiaries and branches whose parent banks had pulled liquidity home when US markets were dramatically contracting. Swap facilities from the Federal Reserve, in essence, played a crucial global role, directly by keeping US dollar markets liquid and indirectly by reassuring market participants that routine funding risks would remain low. In all, fourteen swap lines were set up by the Federal Reserve after 2007. Drawings, mainly by European, Japanese, and Korean central banks, peaked at US$554 billion in the fourth quarter of 2008 (Allen and Moessner 2010). Others benefitted indirectly from the market-calming influence of their very existence.

The biggest jump in swap line usage occurred after the Lehman Brothers' default. It was accompanied by an unprecedented Federal Reserve decision to expand without limit the lines available to the central banks of Europe, the UK, Japan, and Switzerland. These lines expired early in 2010, but new swap facilities for Canada, Europe, the UK, Japan, and Switzerland were established in the spring as the rough waves generated in the United States came crashing down on the weaker economies within the Eurozone. In October 2013, the Federal Reserve, the ECB, and the central banks of Canada, the UK, Japan, and Switzerland agreed to make those new swap arrangements permanent.

Again, central banks were not alone in their emergency management activities during this period. Between September 2008 and June 2009, advanced-economy governments around the world announced some thirty-four systemic or institution-specific programmes involving bank recapitalization, debt guarantees, asset purchases, and increases in deposit-insurance limits. The politics of emergency management at the national level essentially permitted assertive and informally coordinated fiscal action at the core of the system. Although these ad hoc policy responses appeared quite consistent with earlier technocratic work aimed at crisis prevention, they clearly marked the reassertion of finance ministries and legislatures in the actual face of systemic emergency.

The most visible recent efforts to make the post-crisis system more resilient were coordinated by the FSB as it resumed its project to increase private capital buffers and ensure sound liquidity management in the banking sector, but now also in other sectors like insurance and asset management. By late 2015, leading central banks and supervisors had agreed in principle to impose 'Basel III' rules on large, systemically significant banks. As a macroprudential measure, their 'total loss-absorbing capacity', including capital and subordinated debt, was expected to rise to 18 per cent of their risk-weighted assets. Systemic crisis prevention remained the ultimate objective, but the new capital standard and an evolving liquidity standard for those same institutions were once again to be implemented at a time of rising cross-national competition and fading memories of crises past. As analysts soon pointed out, moreover, it remained curious that macroprudential goals were still being pursued mainly by upgrading microprudential rules at the level of individual institutions (Kranke and Yarrow 2018). Logically, an open and integrating system requires systemic regulation if crisis prevention policies are truly to be effective.

All that seemed politically feasible as the Basel III rules began being implemented, however, there was a gradual movement back towards Basel-I-style requirements for cross-border banks, with less discretion allowed for internal risk-management models. Discussions on refining them continued among supervisors, and pressure for deferred deadlines soon mounted. In principle, the new regime was now more expansive and extensive, as it included not only explicit and generally higher requirements for bank capital, but extra capital buffers during periods of high credit growth, new standards for leverage and liquidity, and routine stress testing. In practice, concerns about the international competitiveness of still nationally regulated intermediaries began coming back to the fore. Lists of 'systemically significant' intermediaries subject to the new rules were soon pared down, and some deadlines were postponed. Even in countries that had agreed internally to tougher rules than those enshrined in Basel III, what some bankers were already calling Basel IV, political winds soon started moving in the opposite direction. Moves to keep the City of London attractive after the UK reconfigured its relationship with its

European partners, as well as mounting deregulatory pressures in the US, once again stimulated regulatory competition.

The question remained whether the collaborative energy reflected in the Basel Process, together with national policy changes designed to curtail future bail-outs of banks and, increasingly, bank-like competitors, would prove more successful than analogous efforts had been in the past. Would they send adequate signals to global markets to constrain moral hazards and induce better risk management practices? Would they help forestall future 'doom loops', the situation where the downgraded bonds of troubled sovereigns threaten to destabilize their own bond-holding banks?

In yet another financial crisis occurring in the early months of the COVID-19 pandemic, the US Federal Reserve pumped nearly US$200 billion into faltering money markets to keep them liquid. It also reactivated swap lines with central banks around the world to help them meet panic-driven demand for dollars. Fiscal authorities also moved jointly to stabilize the system. Governments and central banks succeeded in keeping capital markets open and fluid, but the specific allocation of the economic and social costs involved, the expansion of inequalities, and the long-term implications of post-crisis policies became matters of intense debate (Drezner 2014; Geithner 2014; Helleiner 2014b; Bernanke 2015; Mody 2018; ESM 2019; Tooze 2019; Petrou 2021). The policy responses to the most damaging financial crises of the post-1945 period may have avoided even worse outcomes. Perceptions of deepening inequities and basic human tragedies associated with financial stabilization operations, however, had readily observable political consequences around the world. As discussed in more detail in Harmes, Chapter 11, widespread populist reactions were plausibly associated with opposition to the costs of quelling market turmoil and to the apparently unequal distribution of the benefits of financial openness (Everyday GPE Box 9.5; Drache and Froese 2022).

In the aftermath of these crises, and despite the constructive if often passive roles it played in resolving them, it was hardly surprising to see China try to reduce its dependence on US and European financial policies. At the same time, Russian aggression and the rising assertiveness of autocratic regimes in China and elsewhere suggested that deeper changes were underway in the geopolitical settlements emerging from the Second World War and the subsequent Cold War. In such a context, continuing to rely on ad hoc emergency financial management based on assumptions of a stable political hierarchy seemed increasingly risky.

KEY POINTS

- The resolution of global financial crises since 2008 depended on assertive action by the US Federal Reserve and Treasury, but also on supportive and complementary policy responses by leading governments around the world.

- After systemic and regional crises subsided, central banking and sectoral supervisory networks became ever more prominent in efforts to prevent future financial emergencies. Because of legislative and fiscal restraints in the United States and elsewhere, as well as ongoing shifts in the geopolitical underpinnings of global finance, systemic crisis management may be more difficult in the future.

EVERYDAY GPE BOX 9.5 FAMILIES AND FINANCIAL CRISES

Financial crises can seem abstract. Although they can have broad effects, like spawning economic recessions, many people in many places are able to carry on with their everyday lives with little disruption. But others can suffer greatly. Financial crises therefore open a window into the social and political structures underpinning societies and unevenly distributing what economists call the burdens of adjustment. In Chapter 10, Clarke and Roberts dig deeply into that theme. It is worth taking a moment here to consider an idea that is just beginning to be explored systematically: the effects of financial crises on individuals, as well as in aggregate across diversely structured societies, are mediated by families.

Research by economic geographers and sociologists has isolated several important features of family structure that can buffer or exacerbate the impact of financial crises (Harker and Martin 2012; Hally 2016). Because of its suddenness and severity, the Global Financial Crisis of 2008 provided ideal circumstances for ethnographic studies. They highlighted the enduring importance of gendered and interpersonal relationships within families, of multigenerational representation in immediate family units, of

---

EVERYDAY GPE BOX 9.5 FAMILIES AND FINANCIAL CRISES (continued)

shared experiences and memories, and of diverse applications of norms of reciprocity.

Findings suggested that daily spending and budgeting were typically gendered activities, with maximum stress from crisis moments borne by the parent in charge of daily nutrition and shopping. In families whose members range from infants to grandparents, moreover, the understanding of individuals as rational calculators or risk takers seems completely unrealistic; the sacrifices required by strained budgets tend to be concentrated. In day-to-day interactions, any abstract notion of fairness breaks down at the family level. Close observers also found that the roles of debt and credit, tools that are commonly thought of as potentially useful in making adjustment burdens easier to bear over time, needed to be viewed in light of distinct family histories, especially in multigenerational families. Likewise, perceptions of the security of investments tended to depend on whether grandparents were around. Different expectations regarding responsibilities for elder care, again typically gendered, and the passing on of legacies from one generation to

the next also shaped the way crisis-driven stressors were experienced.

There is no doubt that the financial crisis of 2008 had severe aggregate effects on poor families. Given the correlation between poverty and race in the United States, it was hardly surprising for researchers to find that racialized families bore a disproportionate share of the pain caused, for example, by the crisis-induced collapse of housing markets (McArthur and Edelman 2017). The differential consequences for families were particularly pronounced in societies with high numbers of single-parent families and limited social welfare programmes, where wealth gradually built up by homeownership effectively provides a major source of insurance for any hard times ahead (Schwartz 2009).

In debates over more effective and fairer policies to prevent or manage future financial crises, the everyday lens highlights important and differential roles played by family structure. To bolster societal resilience in the face of economic shocks, the case for means-tested universal basic income programmes is solid (Haagh 2019). But families will still experience those shocks in different ways.

9.7 Financial stability and debt restructuring

Despite the scope and drama of systemic financial emergencies in the advanced industrial world, crises in emerging-market and developing countries remain much more frequent. They are often occasioned by high sovereign debt loads and sudden increases in carrying costs. Local monetary and fiscal constraints leave few options for halting runs by creditors and for redistributing adjustment burdens. A relatively poor country facing a currency or banking crisis in an open and integrating system is in a position somewhat analogous to that of a domestic firm unable to meet its obligations, with an important exception. Where the firm may have access to undoubted and binding bankruptcy arrangements, a country does not.

When debts are perceived to have become unsustainable, creditors can try to demand repayment even as the resources available to settle accounts rapidly lose value. Crisis conditions can be generated by government overspending, by excessive imports, by the building up of private-sector debt that cannot be financed domestically, or by exogenous shocks. Any of these situations might motivate the government

to increase the rate of production of its monetary printing press. Inflation would normally be the consequence, and if the fundamental problem is one of temporary illiquidity this might just provide the political space for necessary internal adjustments to occur. If much of a country's debt is owed to foreigners and is denominated in foreign currency, however, loose monetary policies may quickly deepen the problem (see Figure 9.5). Inflation in the local currency by definition pushes up the value of foreign currency liabilities. Expecting further declines in the purchasing power of the local currency, domestic as well as foreign investors may well rush to take hard-currency assets out of

Figure 9.5 Inflation and its cascading effects

Source: Alamy.

the country and resist calls to jump back in. A deteriorating real exchange rate would then make debt repayment more difficult and imports more expensive. The debtor government can try to impose capital controls, default on its debt, or allow private firms under its purview to walk away from their obligations to foreign creditors. Each option is costly, and countries caught in debt traps have no easy way out. The experience of Argentina over many decades provides a vivid case in point (Case Study Box 9.6).

Missing at the system level is a formal sovereign debt restructuring mechanism. Two successive deputy managing directors of the IMF, in fact, made proposals along this line, one for the IMF to be legally empowered to play the role of lender-of-last-resort and the next for the IMF to play the role of ultimate bankruptcy court (Fischer 2000; Goodhart and Illing 2002; Krueger 2002). Even in the aftermath of the Asian and Argentine crises, however, neither proved politically acceptable. What did prove feasible were ideas on the middle ground, including provisions of 'soft law' that would provide incentives for cooperation among bondholders in future debt restructurings (Brummer 2012). Still absent is a legal system capable of ordering

---

CASE STUDY BOX 9.6 DEVELOPMENT, DEBT, AND POLITICS IN ARGENTINA

Blessed with abundant natural resources, diversified industries, and a well-educated labour force, Argentina might have become a regional beacon of prosperity and stability. After decades of internal political conflict between populist and anti-populist factions and inconsistent economic policies, however, it was caught in a seemingly intractable debt trap. In April 1991, a populist government embarked upon a bold policy experiment to reverse the economy's course, pay down its debts, and induce productive capital inflows. Its Convertibility Plan rigidly pegged the value of the peso to the US dollar and thereby constrained the ability of the central bank to engage in inflationary monetary policies. Simultaneously, the government announced a wide range of structural reforms to make the economy more flexible, competitive, and open. Initially, the plan achieved dramatic results. Inflation fell, capital flowed in, and the economy grew by an average of 6 per cent through 1997. Late in 1998, however, a surprisingly severe recession began, and its effects were compounded by the unusual turbulence in global financial markets. Some observers later argued that the government did not react quickly enough with policy adjustments to give itself flexibility and to reassure investors. Others pointed to large loans from the IMF inadequately conditioned on such adjustments, and to a currency devaluation by Brazil that undercut Argentina's export competitiveness. In any event, bank runs, the suspension of IMF loans, and severe political and social unrest ensued. In December 2001, the country began defaulting on its international debts; the next month it abandoned its currency peg, and as the peso's value plummeted, the value of its debt, now largely denominated in US dollars, exploded. In 2002, the economy contracted by 20 per cent and unemployment exceeded 20 per cent of the workforce (Allen 2003: 131; see also Blustein 2005).

In 2002, depressed asset prices had tempted some investors to move back in and rekindle export-oriented production. Growth in commodity markets also accelerated. The government then in place, widely viewed as having a left-leaning populist orientation, then took several measures further to stimulate economic recovery and growth, including repaying IMF loans, partly by borrowing from Venezuela at very high interest rates, and nationalizing state pension funds. By 2005, general economic growth had been restored and much of the country's foreign debt had been restructured, but within a few years the economy began to look overheated. Early in 2010, the government engaged in an intense political struggle with its own central bank over the use of foreign currency reserves, the retention of foreign exchange controls, and dealings with certain private foreign hedge funds who refused to cooperate in debt restructuring. The struggle with those creditors would only conclude under a new government a few years later with significant and controversial pay-outs after final court rulings abroad.

Stability proved short lived. A new chapter in a seemingly perennial saga of inconsistent economic policies opened in the summer of 2019, when Argentina's financial markets crashed once again. The COVID-19 pandemic and then the explosion in energy costs caused by Russia's invasion of Ukraine soon complicated the search for compromise between dominant political factions. Durable economic prosperity for the average citizen appeared to remain out of reach. Painful as ever, sovereign debt deferral agreements were reached with private creditors later in 2020, and new refinancing arrangements with the IMF were negotiated in January 2022. Within the year, however, inflation accelerated, fresh reserves were depleted, the peso spiralled downward, and new and only partially effective controls on capital outflows were tightened. Argentina was forced to pay 80 per cent per annum on its short-term bonds and nearly 50 per cent on ten-year bonds. (Compare that to Ukraine at war, which in mid-2022 was paying less than 40 per cent on ten-year bonds.) The election of a populist right-wing government at the end of 2023 seemed no coincidence.

the replacement of government officials and the mandatory adjustment of the national balance sheet. This remains no accident. In the conceptual extreme, the sovereignty of a state implies the absolute right both to resort to war and to default on debts. As a political realist might nevertheless argue, the ability in practice to exercise such a right is in the final analysis dependent on the raw power a state possesses to absorb any negative consequences and the willingness of other states to defer. In the midst of the 2008 crisis, the case of Iceland vividly demonstrated this logic as the country defaulted on its debts, imposed draconian capital controls on itself, and embarked on a contentious but successful negotiation with its creditors.

In the decade following 2008, emerging-market economies came back to the fore in global discussions on crisis prevention (Best 2014; Gallagher 2015). The BCBS and FSB, for example, moved towards comprehensive supervision of individual intermediaries, whether they had big footprints outside advanced industrial countries or not, through multilateral 'colleges' involving both home- and host-country supervisors. Following internal adjustments in voting power and staff representation that partially acknowledged the rise of China and other emerging-market members, the IMF also linked itself more completely to G20

discussions on what its Executive Board now called the Global Financial Safety Net. Still a work in progress, collaborative resources were in place to supplement the foreign exchange reserves countries maintained as buffers to reduce the domestic impact of exogenous financial shocks (Figure 9.6). They included central bank swap facilities, regional financing arrangements, and an expanding array of IMF programmes often committed in tandem with funding from other multilateral and national development agencies (Henning 2020; Moschella 2024).

Note the essential mutualization of systemic risks implied by these arrangements. On their own, foreign exchange reserves may be viewed as self-insurance against external shocks. Reserve accumulation above a prudent level required for routine and predictable international payments, however, represents the purchase of very expensive insurance and, since reserves are generated by trade surpluses, invites retaliation. Indeed, as discussed in Helleiner, Chapter 8, forestalling retaliatory actions, building trust, and reducing the need for such 'insurance' provided key rationales for multilateralizing reserve management after 1945. At Bretton Woods the architects of the post-war monetary system took the first steps to design an instrument that would limit the extent to which sovereign

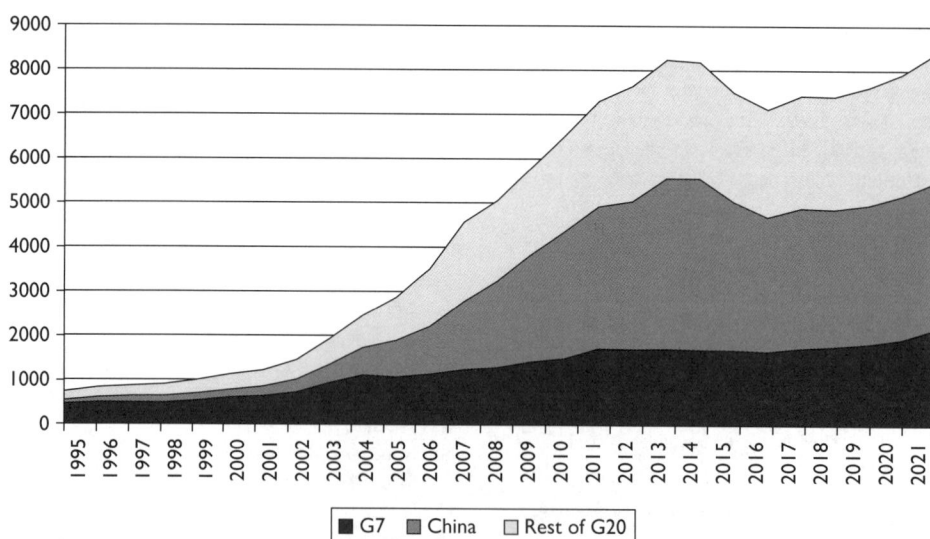

Figure 9.6 G20 foreign exchange reserves ($US billions)

Legend: G7 ■ China ▨ Rest of G20 □

Source: IMF, International Financial Statistics 2022.

states would find themselves pushed by the fear of financial chaos to restrict imports or renege on their debts. Time and again in succeeding decades after their grand plan had to be revised, the main creditor states acting collaboratively were similarly inspired by the spectre of cascading crises to bail out troubled debtors.

Ad hoc sovereign debt restructurings for developing countries have in fact been commonplace since the 1980s. International banks as well as official agencies providing export credits organized themselves into negotiating groups (the London Club and Paris Club, respectively) to manage such arrangements. Ad hoc debt rescheduling and restructuring proved challenging but manageable. With the rapid growth in cross-border purchases of bonds, stocks, and other kinds of securities in recent decades, however, the number and interests of potential participants have increased dramatically and made constructive debt restructuring much more difficult. Over time, novel initiatives, like embedding collective-action clauses in new bonds in anticipation of potential defaults, were designed to encourage constructive last-resort negotiations if the need arose.

When it was called upon, the immediate objective of the IMF at such moments was to help break the psychology of fear and mistrust among creditors and debtors. That the IMF was not dissolved after 1973, when the exchange rate system it was meant to defend broke down, reflected much more than bureaucratic inertia. Its financing facilities, which had grown over time in both size and flexibility, proved to be extremely convenient to its major member states. Arguably still not adequate to the scale of predictable problems today, they at least provide a workable mechanism for creditor states to share the burden of providing emergency financial assistance to debtors and indirectly to attempt to enforce necessary policy adjustments. Although the willing acceptance of IMF programmes is typically critical to their success, through the **conditionality** tied to the use of its financing facilities, the IMF could sometimes exert pressure on borrowers in a manner that would be politically difficult for individual creditor states to exert directly. Recently, the IMF began loosening its traditional stance against extending new financing to members in arrears on previous IMF packages. It demonstrated a willingness to extend financing in situations where troubled members were at least engaged in good-faith negotiations with all creditors. At times, this enabled difficult

restructuring operations to occur (Hagan 2020). In addition, the IMF's *surveillance* activities after the mid-1970s still offered the promise of rendering all members accountable for the external consequences of their economic policy choices (Pauly 1997). In practice, as now transmitted mainly through skittish capital markets, such consequences were more often felt by the weak than by the strong or the well connected (Lipscy and Lee 2019).

For its part, China complicated the process of prudently managing national debts in many emerging-market and developing countries when it provided non-transparent financing through the BRI and related programmes. In fact, the extent and opacity of its domestic and international financial exposures raise questions about its own stability and reliability as a constructive participant in future debt restructuring negotiations (Shih 2017; also see Scott, Chapter 12). Its broader interests may change over time, but those questions help explain the continuing expansion of foreign exchange reserves across East Asia and the caution of many countries in deepening regional financial arrangements.

KEY POINTS

- High sovereign debt loads, the legacy of past policies, and basic structural constraints suggest the need for a formal debt restructuring mechanism for troubled economies.

- Creditors nevertheless continue to rely on voluntary club arrangements to help stave off systemic turmoil when significant defaults are threatened.

- Foreign exchange reserves can provide policy space for prudent and gradual economic adjustments, but excessively high reserves signal lost opportunities and risk, setting off cycles of trade and investment restriction.

9.8 Conclusion: Building global governing capacity?

Three crucial facts stand out. First, as the global, if still partial and incomplete, experiment in capital market openness continues, border-spanning financial crises recur. Second, when market activity crosses legal and political borders, and last-resort back-up facilities become unclear or contested, the probability of systemic emergencies increases. The extent of interconnectedness becomes more difficult to estimate and the information embedded in prices becomes less readily accessible to all market participants. In the deep structure of contemporary capital markets, the information asymmetries highlighted by economists and the power asymmetries analysed by political scientists thus overlap (Kirshner 2014; Pauly and Jentleson 2014). Third, in the contemporary period, leadership and policy improvisation by key creditor states, sometimes assisted by multilateral institutions, have managed to restore confidence at moments of systemic emergency. After those moments have passed, however, the crisis-borne idea of more formally constituting supervisory and debt restructuring authority at the system level has proved fleeting. At most, the Basel Process and continuing plurilateral and sectoral policy coordination aim to constrain systemic risks, discipline systemically significant intermediaries, and bolster an informal global safety net.

After systemic emergencies subside, the interests of investors, intermediaries, and governments soon lean once again in the direction of freer markets, albeit with all market participants aware that political authorities are now willing to play last-resort lending and investing roles on an ad hoc basis. Moral hazard problems have thus become endemic, requiring prudential oversight. Even inside a European Union formally committed to establishing a single market for banking and other financial services, however, robust prudential policies remain difficult formally to coordinate, and reliable arrangements for fiscal burden sharing during crises remain elusive (Henning 2017; Rommerskirchen 2019). The prospect of future joint gains from serious policy coordination among the world's leading creditor states turns out to be a weak motivator for anything more than incremental reform (Fioretos 2016; Hagan 2016). On the other hand, the credible and shared prospect of massive national and systemic losses when financial shocks become systemic has thus far proven successful in concentrating minds and encouraging a minimally adequate degree of collaborative management during crises.

The relationships between financial intermediaries and the states licensing them remain profound, and the social structures underpinning those states remain quite diverse. There is no guarantee therefore that collaboration will always emerge when required. The actual capacity to manage global financial risks is in fact today evolving differentially across the spectrum of risk assessment, crisis prevention, and emergency management. Shaping arrangements and future expectations in each of these three policy arenas are different kinds of politics.

The politics of risk assessment mainly involves social learning, common knowledge, and technical coordination by experts, leavened by competitive market dynamics. In this regard, proponents of the Basel Process can claim some success. The politics of emergency management, however, relies thus far on assertive and short-term governance in a hierarchical order now challenged by political fragmentation and the gradual diffusion of systemic power (Carré and Le Maux 2020; Pape 2022). Finally, the politics of crisis prevention is complicated by popular expectations of national policy autonomy and by persistent cross-national differences on the meaning and requirements of social justice. This makes the basic principles of insurance systems—risk pooling, portfolio diversification, burden sharing, and joint regulation to reduce moral hazards—very difficult to translate into practice in the governance of global capital markets. The experiment in global financial openness thus inclines both towards more complex interdependence *and* more contentious political conflict (Zürn 2018; Quaglia 2022).

The challenge of sustaining global financial stability cannot be wished away. There is no a priori reason, however, to rule out the probability of political transformation in anticipation of future systemic emergencies. The social inequalities exacerbated by crisis-driven financial policies in the recent past are not written in stone. Higher degrees of institutionalized solidarity, after all, have emerged in and across discrete human communities in the past (Grande and Pauly 2005). Until an adequate degree of monetary and fiscal authority moves decisively to the levels implied by the scale and scope of integrating capital markets, however, the political capacity to govern them will rest on uneasy foundations. Organizational innovations like the Basel Process, the FSB, reforms in IMF surveillance procedures, central-bank swap facilities, and subtle reinsurance arrangements may for a time help us to cope with rising systemic financial risks. More robust standards promoted by private authorities may instil greater managerial discipline in cross-border intermediaries and force a broadening range of investors to participate in more efficient and fairer debt restructuring operations. Some uncertainties surrounding complex new techniques for transferring risks may be reduced by new public and private initiatives. Fiscal authorities may collaboratively begin to undercut the attractiveness of tax havens. A more vivid sense of shared fate across deeply interconnected polities might eventually move official and ultimate practices of prudential oversight to the appropriate governing level (Subacchi 2020). In the meantime, although clear and binding *ex ante* burden-sharing agreements across still diverse societies may remain rare, the repeated if ad hoc sharing of fiscal and monetary burdens during actual systemic emergencies is giving rise to reasonable expectations of more coordinated official interventions in the future.

Despite deepening geopolitical uncertainty, the continuing global experiment in financial openness rests on such hopes. History suggests the existence of no apolitical power capable of justifying them. It suggests instead no alternative to remembering the past together, jointly imagining a better future, and struggling collectively to constitute more effective and just governing institutions at the levels required.

? 9.9 QUESTIONS

1. Why did an unsteady but persistent movement towards more open capital markets occur in the aftermath of the collapse of the Bretton Woods pegged exchange rate system?

2. What special risks are associated with open capital markets, and how have regulatory authorities tried to improve their assessments of them?

3. Can regulatory and tax arbitrage by business firms and banks be restrained in the absence of a world government?

4. What are the implications of China's rise for the effective management of future systemic financial emergencies?

5. What practical measures hold promise for preventing future global financial crises?

6. What should be done to discourage the expansion of unsustainable external debts by sovereign states and to reduce the risks associated with financial innovation?

7. Why has the construction of smoothly functioning sovereign debt restructuring instruments been so difficult?

8. Does a Global Financial Safety Net exist? If so, what are its consequences for financial intermediaries as well as for states?

9. How should issues of distributive justice raised by capital market openness be evaluated?

≋ 9.10 FURTHER READING

DeLong, J. B. (2022), *Slouching Towards Utopia: An Economic History of the Twentieth Century* (New York: Basic Books). An engaging introduction to the world economy within which repeated experiments in financial globalization emerged.

Eichengreen, B. (2003), *Capital Flows and Crises* (Cambridge, MA: MIT Press). A readily accessible account of the causes and consequences of international financial crises.

Henning, C. R. (2017), *Tangled Governance: International Regime Complexity, the Troika, and the Euro Crisis* (Oxford: Oxford University Press). A thorough study of the institutions that struggled to contain the euro crises between 2010 and 2015.

Katzenstein, P. J., and Kirshner, J. (2022), *The Downfall of the American Order?* (Ithaca, NY: Cornell University Press). A probing examination of systemic stability in the aftermath of the Global Financial Crisis.

Kindleberger, C. P. (1978), *Manias, Panics, and Crashes: A History of Financial Crises* (New York: Basic Books). A path-breaking orientation to the fragile financial underpinnings of modern capitalism.

King, M. (2016), *The End of Alchemy, Money, Banking, and the Future of the Global Economy* (New York: W.W. Norton). At once a memoir of the Global Financial Crisis by a former governor of the Bank of England and an accessible primer on the fundamental role of financial markets in helping people cope with uncertainty.

Martinez-Diaz, L. (2009), *Globalizing in Hard Times: The Politics of Banking-Sector Opening in the Emerging World* (Ithaca, NY: Cornell University Press). A compelling political analysis of financial liberalization in emerging-market countries.

Minsky, H. (1986), *Stabilizing an Unstable Economy* (New Haven, CT: Yale University Press). The original and prescient analysis of the inherent fragility of financial markets.

Obstfeld, M., and Taylor, A. (2004), *Global Capital Markets: Integration, Crisis, and Growth* (Cambridge: Cambridge University Press). A useful history of market development and deepening since the late nineteenth century.

Pauly, L. (1997), *Who Elected the Bankers? Surveillance and Control in the World Economy* (Ithaca, NY: Cornell University Press). An examination of the development of the IMF and its systemic oversight role in the wake of twentieth-century monetary and financial crises.

Sen, A. (2009), *The Idea of Justice* (Cambridge, MA: Belknap/Harvard University Press). Behind the technical discussions of globally minded financial experts lie significant issues of legitimacy and justice, and this book provides a foundation for grappling with them.

Tooze, A. (2019), *Crashed: How a Decade of Financial Crises Changed the World* (New York: Penguin). A brisk assessment of the causes and consequences of the systemic and regional crises that began in 2007.

CONTRIBUTOR NOTE

Louis W. Pauly is the J. Stefan Dupré Distinguished Professor of Political Economy at the University of Toronto. He is a former editor of the journal *International Organization*, and his publications include *Opening Financial Markets* and *Who Elected the Bankers?* (both from Cornell University Press), *The Myth of the Global Corporation* (Princeton University Press), and *Complex Sovereignty* (University of Toronto Press). He thanks William O'Connell for research assistance and wise advice in the preparation and revisions of this chapter.

10

Global Finance and the Everyday

Chris Clarke and Adrienne Roberts

Chapter contents

Reader's guide

This chapter uses 'the everyday' as a lens to explore the worlds of finance, debt, and money. It complements the previous two chapters by offering a 'bottom up' perspective on broader structural trends in the world economy, showing both how these affect the day-to-day experiences of individuals and households and how everyday financial practices are constitutive of the world economy. The chapter uses debt and money as entry points for this discussion. It begins by discussing how and why households have come to rely on debt in everyday life, and shows how this has unequal consequences. It then surveys the use of money by ordinary people and the everyday political economy of monetary governance.

10.1 Introduction

When scholars of Global Political Economy (GPE) study finance, they typically focus on broad structural trends and the actions of a group of actors including states, institutions of global economic governance, and large financial institutions. However, for some time now GPE scholarship has argued that it is equally important to understand how financial trends, actors, policies, and practices are experienced and constituted at the level of 'the everyday' (Martin 2002; Langley 2008). On the one hand, structural trends and institutional actors affect the everyday lives of individuals and households. On the other hand, the practices and routines of everyday life are central to how the world economy operates. That is, the world economy would not function if people did not go to work, spend, borrow, share, invest, and so on, making these practices constitutive of that world economy. Feminist GPE scholars would add to this list the work of caring, for instance for the young, the sick, the elderly, the disabled, and the next generation of workers—an activity that is usually considered to be 'non-economic' but which is actually a foundational part of the world economy (Elias and Roberts 2018). Contestations and resistance to economic practices also play out at the level of the everyday.

Studying global finance through the lens of 'the everyday' offers an opportunity to explore dynamics that often remain overlooked in more institutional accounts of high finance. For example, it allows us to think about how and why people engage in mundane practices such as borrowing money from family or friends, or altering spending habits to try to keep up with rising food bills. It enables us to centre sites of finance that are not usually privileged. In this chapter the household is one such site. The everyday focus further offers openings to consider events and practices that take place outside the usual corridors of power, including in Global South countries and contexts that might otherwise be overlooked in predominantly Eurocentric scholarship. Finally, thinking in intersectional terms about the everyday allows us to consider how finance is deeply entwined in broader relations of class, gender, race, sexuality, and more. By **intersectional**, we mean a way of seeing the world that acknowledges that people's experiences are not shaped by just one system of exploitation or oppression, such as sexism or racism, but by many axes of inequality that work together and influence each other (Hill Collins and Bilge 2016).

This chapter uses debt and money as entry points for this discussion. It begins by discussing a political economy of debt from the perspective of the household. It asks how and why households have come to rely so centrally on debt as part of everyday life (Section 10.2) and shows how this has unequal consequences (Section 10.3). To better engage an everyday political

economy of money, the second half of the chapter explores two aspects of the everyday life of money in recent decades. These are the uses of money by ordinary citizens (Section 10.4) and the everyday political economy of monetary governance (Section 10.5). These themes are chosen not to cover the totality of the everyday experience of debt and money, but to highlight key issues and trends in the everyday political economy of finance.

10.2 Indebted life

Traditionally, when GPE scholars have analysed how debt operates in the world economy, they have tended to focus on **sovereign debt** (also called government debt or public debt), which is debt owed by states. A considerable number of countries owe more in debt (which might include loans made to present or past governments, debt securities such as government bonds, and government employee pension obligations) than they produce each year as measured by gross domestic product (GDP) (Institute of International Finance n.d.). From an everyday perspective, sovereign debt levels are significant for numerous reasons. One reason is that governments with high debt burdens may feel a need and/or be compelled to reduce their debt. They generally do this either by cutting spending on public services and infrastructures or by raising taxes, both of which have impacts on everyday life. We know, for example, that when the international financial institutions (IFIs) bailed out a number of countries in Latin America, Africa, and elsewhere in the wake of debt crises in the 1980s, the conditions attached to loans forced governments to prioritize debt repayment above all else. This fuelled poverty among the masses. In Latin America, the poverty rate rose from 40.5 per cent in 1980 to 48.3 per cent in 1990. In both Latin America and Sub-Saharan Africa, poverty rates did not return to the levels of 1980–1981 until 2005 (United Nations 2017b: 60).

It is equally important to look beyond sovereign debt to consider how household debt is an integral aspect of the world economy. The next section offers a brief overview of household debt and considers some of the factors that have led to its proliferation. It then turns to a discussion of debt as a relation of power and reflects on some of the ways that states actively create the conditions for household indebtedness.

10.2.1 **The drivers of household debt**

In most countries, household debt has grown substantially over the past several decades. Though there is geographical unevenness, in most advanced industrialized countries household debt levels are extremely high (see Figure 10.1). After dropping slightly in the wake of the Global Financial Crisis of 2007–2008, they have been increasing year on year since then.

In many countries in the Global South, consumer spending and household debt are not as prolific, though they are also seeing a precipitous increase. For example, China's households used to be considered among the world's best savers. But household debt more than tripled between 2007 and 2020 in China, much of this being related to a rise in mortgage debt (Apostolou et al. 2022).

The reasons for the growth of household debt are not straightforward, nor are they the same across the world. When examining the advanced industrialized countries, GPE scholars often attribute the proliferation of household debt to a credit boom in the late 1990s. During this period, banks and other lenders were able to lend at much lower interest rates than

during other periods in history, and new financial techniques such as securitization, explained in Key Concept Box 10.1, allowed them to shift some of the risk of lending onto investors in financial markets. Banks and financial firms were also searching for new asset streams, looking to create new forms of revenue by introducing novel financial products and/or finding new consumers.

The deepening of household debt in many countries has been shaped by broader trends in the world economy since the 1970s, including wage stagnation, the growth of precarious forms of labour, and the reduction of certain forms of social provisioning and welfare support. This has led to a situation in which households increasingly rely on private debt to pay for consumption and necessities such as food, fuel, and rent. It is also used to pay for things that governments in richer countries could, and sometimes have, provided in previous historical periods, such as health care services and access to a university education. Some have been able to use debt to acquire assets in ways that increase their wealth, while others, including the young, households headed by single parents (who are

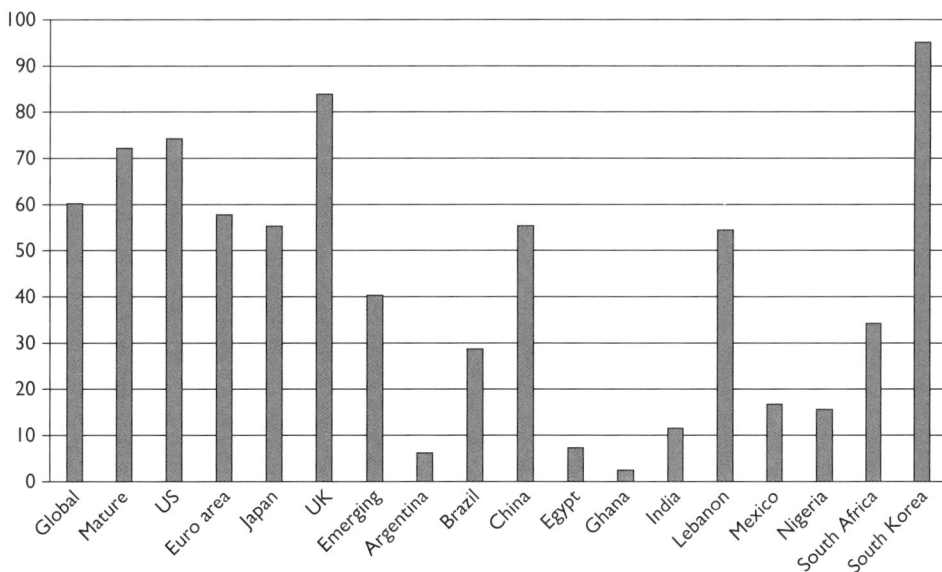

Figure 10.1 Household debt as a % of GDP

Source: Institute of International Finance.

KEY CONCEPT BOX 10.1 SECURITIZATION

Securitization is a process that involves combining (that is, 'pooling') different types of assets (for example, mortgages) into a new type of investment (that is, 'security'), which is then sold to investors. What is the purpose of this process? On the one hand, the original lender (the 'originator') can relinquish responsibility for the loans. This reduces the liabilities on the originator's balance sheet and allows them to make new loans. On the other hand, investors can make money from the purchase of these new securities through the interest generated by the combined underlying assets. Additionally, these securities can be divided into different pieces (that is, 'tranches'), each of which has a different level of risk associated with it, and therefore generates different rates of return (with less risky securities generating a lower return). Though securitization was initially used to finance self-liquidating assets such as mortgages (that is, via mortgage-backed securities), it is also now applied to corporate and sovereign loans, consumer credit, microcredit, student loans, and other lending agreements.

Securitization can increase market liquidity (that is, how easily assets can be bought and sold) while also reducing systemic risks (by diffusing exposure to credit risks). At the same time, securitization creates—and even hides—a variety of important risks. This form of 'financial innovation' was a key factor driving the subprime mortgage crisis that swept through the US in 2007. Securitization encouraged lenders to engage in lax screening and monitoring procedures, and to extend loans to high-risk borrowers, including those with little or no collateral. There was also a lack of transparency around how these securities were constructed and the 'real' risks across the different tranches, making it difficult for investors to make informed decisions and for regulators to identify the formation of systemic risks.

mostly women), and those on low or no incomes, have not been able to access these same privileges. We will return to this discussion in Section 10.3.2 below.

It is clear that over the past several decades, debt has become increasingly central to the ability of individuals, households, and communities to reproduce themselves on a daily and generational basis—a process that feminist GPE scholars call **social reproduction** (Bakker and Gill 2003; Roberts 2013). In rich countries, this signals a shift away from a reliance on governments and/or employers to support social reproduction, that is, through the provision of publicly funded services by the former and adequate wages and benefits by the latter, towards a new reliance on financial markets. It has also become central to how some national economies function, for instance as debt keeps people and families alive and working, it generates demand that would not otherwise exist, and contributes to economic growth via the increase in house prices (for more, see Key Concept Box 10.3).

10.2.2 Everyday debt and power in the world economy

Many GPE scholars understand debt to be constituted by power relations and shaped by the broader dynamics of the world economy. From this perspective, the growing indebtedness of households should be understood as part of a broader process of 'financialization'

(see Key Concept Box 10.2), which signals the growing power of financial actors, financial markets, and financial ways of thinking in the global economy.

GPE scholars have stressed that debt is not a normal, natural, or apolitical market transaction, and is constituted by the uneven distribution of power. This unevenness can be seen, for instance, in the *privatization* and *individualization of risk* faced by growing numbers of people around the world who are dependent on debt to pay for the necessities of everyday life. The counterpart to this is the offloading of risk by banks and lenders through processes of securitization (see Key Concept Box 10.1 above) and its socialization via government bail-outs in times of financial crises. At the same time, for many GPE scholars debt is not simply a question of rational time/money management, but is a social relation premised on a claim to future income which means that it is connected to the exploitation of workers who have to dedicate more and more of their wages to paying interest and fees (Bryan et al. 2009; Soederberg 2014a).

Though often overlooked, debt relations also depend on the unpaid labour, including the emotional labour, of those who do the work of managing debt payments, balancing household accounts, and dealing with debt collectors (Deville 2015; Montgomerie and Tepe-Belfrage 2016). People may change their everyday practices so that they are able to service their debts, that is, by making more food from scratch to

KEY CONCEPT BOX 10.2 FINANCIALIZATION

While uses of the term differ, two commonly cited definitions of financialization include the following:

> . . . financialization means the increasing role of financial motives, financial markets, financial actors and financial institutions in the operation of the domestic and international economies (Epstein 2005: 3).

> . . . financialization is a pattern of accumulation in which profits accrue primarily through financial channels rather than through trade and commodity production (Krippner 2005: 174).

These are both broad definitions that are focused on what Mader et al. (2020: 6–7) call the *macro level* of analysis. Others have focused on the *meso level*, which involves considering how corporations have themselves undergone important transformations as a result of financialization. Stockhammer (2004: 720), for instance, views financialization as involving the 'increased activity of non-financial businesses on financial markets . . . measured by the corresponding income streams', while Froud et al. (2000) focus on how firms have come to prioritize 'shareholder value'—or the value delivered to the shareholders in the form of dividends or capital gains—above other corporate aims or objectives.

Still others have focused on the operation of financialization at the *micro level*. They point to how the growing prevalence and power of finance is manifest in the everyday, shaping how individuals behave and how they think about themselves and the world around them. Randy Martin (2002: 43) writes about the 'financialization of daily life', which 'insinuates an orientation toward accounting and risk management into all domains of life'. As will be further discussed below, being in debt leads people to behave in certain ways that they might not otherwise, so it is a crucial part of the everyday politics of the market subject.

What unites different theories of financialization is a recognition that finance is a set of relations and practices that increasingly influence and may even dominate other realms of economy and society. They also generally understand this as being a harmful development in how the world economy is organized, fuelling financial instability (up to and including financial crises), as well as poverty, insecurity, and inequalities along the lines of class, gender, race, nationality, and more (Mader et al. 2020: 5).

---

stretch household budgets or caring for the sick and elderly at home rather than paying for care. This is highly gendered work, predominantly performed by women, especially those who are most marginalized. This sort of gendered reproductive labour has also been found to increase in the wake of economic and financial crises as states cut back on social spending to comply with the requirements of the IMF and/or other lending bodies such as the European Central Bank (Elson 2013; Pauly, Chapter 9).

Some emphasize the important roles states play in upholding the social relations of debt that shape everyday life. For Susanne Soederberg (2014a), capitalist states act as **debtfare states**, which use a combination of both *indirect* and *direct* power to make debt seem normal and natural, and to create an institutional and disciplinary structure that supports debt-driven forms of accumulation. In terms of *indirect power*, politicians in various countries have long promised that households will be better off if they buy houses, invest in the stock market, put their savings for old age into private pensions plans, and more. This discussion of the benefits to be gained from 'democratizing' access to credit and/or finance rests on the idea that removing barriers to access, particularly for poor people or those with no credit history, will lead to greater prosperity.

Debt relations are also projected as legitimate, and even desirable, through wider growth and development discourses, such as the World Bank's promotion of the need to 'bank the unbanked', and its focus on **financial inclusion** which, it explains, 'is a key enabler to reducing poverty and boosting prosperity' (World Bank 2008). The United Nations (2006: 4) also shares this view, explaining that access to financial services 'economically and socially empower[s] individuals, in particular poor people, allowing them to better integrate into the economy of their countries, actively contribute to their development and protect themselves against economic shocks'. These sorts of claims are rooted in a belief that poverty is the outcome of market exclusion, and that prosperity can be achieved by better connecting individuals to formal financial institutions.

More *direct* forms of power are also used by states (and global governance institutions) to support debt-driven forms of accumulation. This includes state policies that govern things like lending standards and

> **KEY CONCEPT BOX 10.3 PRIVATIZED KEYNESIANISM AND ASSET-BASED WELFARE**
>
> **Privatized Keynesianism** is a concept used to denote a shift in how demand is stimulated in economies. Whereas Keynesian policies usually entail the government taking on additional debt that is spent to stimulate the economy in times of need, this newer model relies on households taking on debt to stimulate it. They do so by using debt to pay for consumption (for instance, by buying goods with credit cards), but also crucially by using mortgages to purchase houses, which further fuels economic growth driven by house price inflation.
>
> The term **asset-based welfare** is a related term that has been used to describe the ways in which certain countries, primarily the Anglo (or English-speaking) countries, but also
>
> some European and East Asian countries, have promoted the individual accumulation of assets (such as houses, stocks, bonds, financial securities, pension plans, and more) to sustain economic and social development (Gamble and Prabhakar 2005). For proponents, the accumulation of assets encourages people to act responsibly and works to alleviate poverty without having to depend on state social provisioning. For critics, asset-based welfare shifts responsibilities from states onto citizens, perpetuates inequalities (since not everyone is in a position to save and invest in asset ownership), and fuels unsustainable levels of household indebtedness (Montgomerie and Büdenbender 2015). We return to this point in Section 10.3.2.

interest rates. States also play a role in regulating—or failing to regulate—predatory lenders, which are lenders that charge exorbitant interest rates and fees, and usually target vulnerable consumers who may have difficulties accessing less costly forms of credit. This includes women (especially single women with children), many racial and ethnic minorities, LGBTQ+ groups, low-income earners, informal workers, and the elderly. These lenders often operate at the fringes of the global financial system, extracting value from vulnerable populations (Aitken 2015), and may include payday lenders, car title pawn operators, small loan and mortgage companies, rent-to-own schemes, check cashing outlets, and microfinance lenders, among others.

More broadly, GPE scholars have argued that over the past several decades, states have been restructured in ways that have involved the transfer of a whole host of financial responsibilities and risks onto individuals and households, which privatizes and/or individualizes risk. Colin Crouch (2009) coined the term 'privatized Keynesianism', explained in Key Concept Box 10.3, to refer to the fact that in a number of (mostly rich) countries, the decline in social spending and the retrenchment of the welfare state has been accompanied by an increase in indebtedness amongst the poor and those with middle incomes. Though this may not have been a planned outcome of reforms to welfare states, indebtedness 'is as much about government household provisioning and labour market practice as about the transformations in financial markets' (Montgomerie 2013: 872). Welfare states increasingly

expect households to commit their earnings (which have been stagnating) to building assets via home ownership, private pensions plans, etc., to support them in old age.

> **KEY POINTS**
>
> - Household debt has grown substantially over the past several decades due to changes in the world economy that have made it more profitable for lenders to extend credit and more necessary for individuals and households to rely on debt for everyday life.
>
> - The growing indebtedness of households is part of broader processes of financialization, which signal the growing power of financial actors, financial markets, and financial ways of thinking at multiple scales in the world economy.
>
> - Debt relations are inherently political. They are relations of power that are supported by the direct and indirect power of states and international institutions.

10.3 Debt and inequality

It should be apparent from the discussion above that there are different forms of debt, and that not all debt works the same way. It is also true that different groups of people have different relationships with debt. For example, while some people are able to access credit at low interest rates, others are not. This not only impacts how much debt costs, but also how long people are likely to stay in debt, how much of their income it takes up, and even how much mental and physical energy goes towards repaying that debt. This section looks at different types of debt and considers which types of debt are most problematic for which groups of people. It uses the COVID-19 pandemic as an entry point into thinking about how crises fuel indebtedness amongst particular sectors of the global population and ends with a discussion of how debt affects the very way that we think about ourselves and our relationships with others.

10.3.1 The many faces of debt

One way to characterize different types of debt is to consider whether it is 'secured' or 'unsecured'. Secured debt is backed by some sort of asset as collateral, such as a car or a house. If you default on the repayment of the loan, the creditor is able to take the collateral rather than using other forms of debt collection or legal action. This type of debt is usually thought to be less risky than unsecured debt because the lender can regain losses by seizing property. It also tends to come with lower interest rates, especially if the borrower has a good credit rating. Unsecured debt is not backed by collateral, and may include things such as credit cards, student loans, and medical loans, and so on. It is often considered to be more risky than secured debt, and may come with higher interest rates, though these can vary considerably depending on what type of credit is being extended, to whom, and by whom.

Finance and debt might also be classified as being either formal or informal. 'Formal finance' is that which comes from banks and other lenders that are recognized and (usually) regulated by governments. 'Informal finance' comes from lenders that operate outside of these recognized structures, such as private moneylenders, **FinTech** lenders, family, or friends. When governments and institutions such as the World Bank talk about the need to extend financial inclusion to the poor, this is partly based on their desire to move people from the informal into the formal sphere of finance. However, these distinctions are not always clear cut. For example, research done in the Indian state of Andhra Pradesh has revealed that (formal) microfinance institutions have relied on (informal) intermediaries such as village moneylenders to find borrowers as well as to enforce repayment of loans, which has involved highly coercive tactics including abduction and extortion (Arunachalam 2011; Taylor 2012). Research done in Uttar Pradesh, also in India,

suggests that even when moneylenders are registered with the state and are therefore technically regulated, they straddle the formal/informal divide. For instance, they may engage in transactions that fall outside of regulations by charging higher interest rates or taking a cut of the principal, and may have less access to legal redress in the case of default (Schwecke 2022: 280–282).

GPE scholars have also drawn attention to the shifting geographies of debt, as the line between what constitutes legal/formal and extra-legal/informal finance changes over time. This sometimes happens because of challenges to the legitimacy of some forms of lending that come to be seen as unethical or predatory (De Goede 2005; Aitken 2015). Payday lending is a good example of a type of lending that has become increasingly *de*-legitimized in recent years. The distinction between formal and informal credit may also shift as a result of advocacy by certain financial interests that wish to become regulated in order to legitimize their businesses, such as new FinTech lending firms (Rogers and Clarke 2016; Girard, Chapter 17, Section 17.5.1).

10.3.2 Debt and leverage

When looking across the landscape of debt relations, it is clear that not all debt is equal. Interest rates can vary immensely across the different types of debt, as can payment terms and conditions. Think of the difference between a mortgage that can be paid off over a period of thirty years versus a payday loan that must be repaid within one to two weeks or risk additional charges.

At the same time, some people are more negatively impacted by debt than others. This is both because different types of debt are used by different groups for different purposes, and because some groups of people are able to access loans on more advantageous terms than others. As Johnna Montgomerie writes:

Debt is not a problem for everyone. Some segments of the population (the top 5 per cent) have done very well from their highly leveraged investments. For this group, debt is a source of wealth . . . If the young wish to get a university education or buy their first home, very high debt levels are a necessity. For them, debt is the means to achieve a middle-class lifestyle. For others, debt is how they pay the bills from month to month; it is for consumption. For others still, for example elderly people, singletons, single parents, or low- and middle-income households, debt is a safety net (2019: 30).

Indeed, in contrast to the growing burden of debt faced by middle-to-lower income groups, the wealthiest members of society have used debt as a lever to accumulate vast wealth as they borrow for investment purposes (Adkins et al. 2020; Samman and Sgambati 2022). The rich tend to have a higher leverage ratio, meaning that they can borrow more money proportional to their income than others. For instance, in the UK most mortgage calculators assume that borrowers can borrow up to four and a half times their annual salary, but this jumps to as much as seven times annual salary for those on higher incomes (Jones 2021). Meanwhile, rather than borrowing from banks, the very wealthiest, that is, those in the top 1 per cent globally, borrow through hedge funds, private equity funds, and other investment vehicles, as well as non-financial corporations. This type of borrowing does not appear in the usual accounts of household debt, which masks the vast inequality that exists between those who are able to achieve remarkably high returns as the result of leveraging asset portfolios and the rest of the population (Samman and Sgambati 2022).

An everyday political economy of leverage draws attention to the difference between the negative connotations of the word debt as compared to the language of leverage, which is imbued with 'magical qualities of multiplication' (Allon 2015: 688). Within this uneven geography of debt/leverage, certain people and groups are also more vulnerable to the depreciation or the loss of assets. This came to light most obviously during the 'subprime mortgage crisis' that emerged in the US in 2007. Subprime lending is a trend that emerged in the US and elsewhere in the 1990s when lenders began selling mortgages to higher-risk households. These households usually had limited access to other sources of credit, which made the mortgages appealing (Dymski 2009: 164). In the US, lenders targeted particular 'redlined' areas, which are neighbourhoods—usually with large Black and Latino populations—where lenders had previously refused to make credit available. Subprime lending grew exponentially throughout the 1990s, growing 900 per cent between 1993–1999, with African Americans more than twice as likely and Latinos up to 220 per cent more likely than white applicants to receive these loans (2009: 164).

Throughout the 2000s, more and more people signed up for subprime mortgages, not least because while the value of houses increased steadily, there was limited access to social housing which was being privatized, commercialized, and de-legitimized through discourses extolling the benefits of the 'Ownership Society' (Roberts 2013). Even though wages and incomes remained stagnant while house prices appreciated, growing numbers of people wanted to get onto 'the property ladder'. Banks and financial firms were keen to lend to them, especially given that they could then sell the loans on to financial markets. By 2006, almost 20 per cent of mortgage loans were subprime, of which almost 80 per cent were securitized (Dymski 2009: 172). Researchers have also estimated that during the peak of lending more than half of subprime loans were given to people with credit scores high enough to merit conventional mortgages (Brooks and Simon 2007).

When housing prices started to collapse, it led to mortgage delinquencies and foreclosures, as well as a devaluation of housing-related securities, ultimately triggering the Global Financial Crisis. This had severe implications for everyday life as the net worth of US households fell by about 20 per cent—or US$13 trillion overall—and the losses were disproportionately felt by those communities targeted by subprime lenders. This meant that rather than leading to the accumulation of assets and long-term security as many believed it would, buying homes on these terms actually led to a 'dis-accumulation' of wealth and the deepening of gender- and race-based inequalities (Montgomerie and Young 2011) (see Figure 10.2).

Figure 10.2 Due to soaring house prices, many properties have been left abandoned, including this house in Detroit, Michigan, US.

Source: Shutterstock.

10.3.3 **Debt and COVID-19**

While debt is sometimes used as leverage in the ways noted above, for many poor and working-class households it is a crucial safety net of last resort that allows them to be able to buy life's necessities, especially in times of crisis. This was the case for many individuals and households during the COVID-19 crisis that emerged in 2020, which has heightened inequalities along the intersecting lines of class, race, gender, disability, and more.

In many countries, the COVID-19 pandemic emerged in a context of already high levels of household debt. As governments imposed lockdowns, some households, especially those that already had relatively high incomes, were able to increase their savings and pay down their existing debts as they cut back on spending. Research from the Organization for Economic Cooperation and Development (OECD) (OECD 2020) shows that there was an increase in aggregate savings for the household sector overall. But this obscures the very different situation felt by different households. For those on low incomes, with precarious jobs, with childcare responsibilities, and with already high levels of unsecured debt, the COVID-19 crisis only worsened their financial position. Looking beyond the OECD countries, research published by the IMF suggests that given the unprecedented levels of debt pre-crisis, the COVID-19 crisis is likely to trigger extensive debt distress, particularly amongst small- to medium-sized enterprises (SMEs) and households (Liu et al. 2020)—a situation that has been further exacerbated by the rise in interest rates globally since 2021, which will be outlined below.

While the lasting impacts of the COVID-19 crisis and its aftermath are not yet fully clear, in countries such as the UK early evidence suggested that it had an important impact on household debt. In 2019 there were 3.2 million people in severe problem debt and 9.8 million people showing signs of financial distress (Step-Change 2020: 1). While the government put in place a number of measures to try to protect businesses and households in the wake of the national lockdown, not everyone was protected against income losses. Those who were younger, female, responsible for children, and/or in insecure forms of work were most likely to be negatively affected. The Bank of England found that households with unsecured debt were more likely to have experienced a drop in income, as they were more likely to be in lower paid and less secure jobs compared to those with secured debt (that is, homeowners) (Franklin et al. 2021). When faced with the loss of income, better-off households were able to use their savings and/or cut back on spending. Others, however, fell into arrears on debt or bills and/or took on additional debt.

Researchers found that less than ten months into the crisis, nearly 9 million people in the UK had to borrow more money than usual because of the pandemic (Francis-Devine 2021: 13). Between March 2020 and January 2021, an estimated 10.6 million people borrowed to make ends meet. Of these, 48 per cent borrowed on a credit card, 35 per cent used a bank overdraft facility, 32 per cent borrowed from family or friends, and 26 per cent used high-cost credit. These are disproportionately low-income households, with 54 per cent of those in the lowest fifth income bracket borrowing to cover everyday costs such as food and housing (2021: 14). People from a minority ethnic group, single parents, carers, and/or disabled people are also disproportionately represented among this group. So are the young, with 27 per cent of people aged 18–34 behind on their bills compared to 4 per cent of people aged 55+ (2021: 17–19). These trends are sure to continue—and to continue being contested—as households in the UK and elsewhere face a 'cost of living crisis' fuelled by rising inflation and surging prices for fuel, energy, foodstuffs, and so on.

A similar story can be told about COVID-19 and indebtedness in many countries in the Global South. In India, the majority of the working population works in the informal economy, which is characterized by low earnings, precarious working conditions, and weak or non-existent social protections. There is also very little in the way of a social security net, which means that the population is highly dependent on day-to-day earnings for their ability to survive. One large-scale study showed that as the pandemic hit India and the government imposed lockdowns, two thirds of respondents lost employment, while those who continued to be employed saw drops in their earnings. Almost 80 per cent of households saw a reduction in food intake, more than 60 per cent did not have enough money to afford a week's worth of essentials, and a third took out loans to cover expenses during lockdown, mostly from moneylenders or their families or friends (Kesar et al. 2021). As occurred elsewhere, in India the COVID-19 crisis compounded already existing inequalities, with those racial, gender, caste, religious, and economic groups who were already the most disadvantaged facing the most deleterious consequences, and ending up in the most debt.

The COVID-19 pandemic struck at a moment where an unprecedented number of households in the Global South relied on microfinance to meet their everyday needs. The microfinance sector in Cambodia, for instance, is one of the fastest growing globally, growing from 300,000 borrowers in 2005 to an estimated 2.2 million in 2020 (Brickell et al. 2020: 2). Even before COVID-19, borrowers in Cambodia were experiencing problems with over-indebtedness, forcing families to reduce the amount of food they consume, take out new loans to service existing debts, migrate for work, or sell their land to repay loans, thereby reducing the possibility of using it to earn future income. As the pandemic unfolded, it impacted global supply chains, causing major economic downturns and extensive job losses. Cambodia relies heavily on the global garment industry as a source of employment, and the disruption to this industry caused mass unemployment, an increase in poverty, and an increase in borrowing that compounded the already high levels of private debt (2020: 2).

10.3.4 Debt and the self

Oftentimes, when major international organizations such as the IMF and state departments such as the US Treasury mention rising levels of household debt, they are ultimately concerned about what this means more broadly for 'the economy'. This is because high levels of debt may lead households to rein in everyday spending and/or lead to massive defaults, which then has knock-on effects throughout the financial system as it impacts asset-backed securities and related financial products. While this is important, GPE scholars attuned to in the everyday are equally interested in how financial relations shape the routines and practices of everyday life, including the work we do, the choices we make, the relationships we form, and even the way we understand ourselves.

For example, as many students will be acutely aware, having university-related debt may impact decisions such as what kind of job you look for,

where you live, whether or not you buy a car, and if/when you decide to get married and have children. Student debt is most pervasive in those countries that have high university fees that are expected to be paid for by individuals through savings and/or loans provided by public or private institutions that have to be repaid. This is less of a problem in places that offer publicly funded non-repayable grants, as occurs in some Scandinavian countries. Paying for university this way may lead you to *think* about your education differently, seeing it as something that you have purchased in the same way you purchase other goods or services in the market. It might lead you to think about your degree as a debt-financed investment or asset, something that will provide financial returns in the medium to long term.

Having student debt hanging over you may also foster a certain sense of burden, guilt, and/or shame. Maurizio Lazzarato (2011) writes about how the identities that people used to have as workers, consumers, producers, the unemployed, retirees, or welfare recipients are all being superseded by the persona of the 'debtor', which he sees as the neoliberal subject *par excellence*. He believes that the creditor-debtor relationship is the most important power relation in contemporary society, and that it produces a particular subjectivity: 'indebted man'. This has an important moral aspect to it, as people are conditioned to believe that debt is a moral failing, and they have a duty to honour their debts. This stands in tension with some of the arguments surveyed earlier that focus on the differences that exist between different types of debtors (see Section 10.3.2 above). Feminists have also challenged the idea that there is a singular universal debtor subject. Argentinian feminists Cavallero and Gago (2021: 4) write in their anti-debt manifesto that 'there is not a singular subjectivity of indebtedness that can be universalized nor a sole debtor-creditor relation that can be separated from concrete situations and especially from sexual, gender, racial, and locational difference'. This is because, as demonstrated in this section, debt does not lead to a flattening or a homogenization of those differences, but rather exploits them (Cavallero and Gago 2021: 4). This is not passively accepted, and people engage in everyday acts of resistance while mass campaigns advocate debt jubilees for individuals and poor countries alike.

10.4 Everyday money

In recent decades, the political economy of money has re-emerged as a topic of primary concern for scholars of GPE and related fields. It has long been established in GPE that 'monetary phenomena are always and everywhere political' (Kirshner 2003: 645). Traditionally, study of the GPE of money has focused on the policy choices of states, viewing choices made about how money is governed as inherently political decisions. Yet in the decades since the Global Financial Crisis of 2007–2008, the political economy of money has been recognized in increasingly broad terms. For instance, the rapid emergence and spread of new mobile payment technologies has changed how we think about how money is used by the huge proportion of the world's population who have access to internet-enabled mobile devices. This draws attention to the everyday politics of money, or how important choices about money are made at the level of the everyday.

In light of successive financial crises and waves of digital technological change, questions about how best to understand money, how it can be used, and who has power over its creation have become the subject of widespread public attention and scholarly debate. In turn, these drive new everyday political economy puzzles and analyses, such as questions of who benefits from new money forms, how emergent technologies alter the infrastructures that enable individuals and households to access and manage money, and the extent to which digital money can be used in new and innovative ways in everyday life.

This section departs from accounts of money typically found in GPE and economics textbooks that emphasize the functional aspects of money (that is, money as a medium of exchange, a unit of account, and a store of value). There is no reason to deny the partial usefulness of this depiction, but in order to engage the everyday political economy of money we need to interrogate the deeply political, social, and cultural dimensions of money that are often obscured in such accounts. The social and relational significance of money is lost if we do not go beyond a standard functional account of money (Zelizer 1997). Put another way, we need to better conceptualize money in a way that departs from the 'folk theory of money' (see Key Theory Box 10.4), influential as it is in public consciousness. As such this chapter draws attention to money primarily in terms of the *sites* and *practices* of money in everyday life.

The collapse of the Bretton Woods exchange rate system in the early 1970s is widely viewed as a pivotal moment in the history of international monetary politics (see Helleiner, Chapter 8). This was when many states moved away from the gold-dollar standard of the post-war era to an 'Information Standard', a floating exchange-rate system determined by market exchange of fiat currencies (James 1996). Yet, from the perspective of the everyday, we can also reflect on changes to how national currencies are thought about and used by individuals and households. In the rest of this section, we discuss three key trends: the rise of the 'cashless society', the emergence of 'FinTech' in retail money and banking, and cryptocurrencies.

10.4.1 The cashless society

A significant development in how currencies are used in everyday life is the remarkable rise of digital payments. The concept of the digital economy has been with us for some time, but the acceleration of the trend away from the use of hard cash (notes and coins) to cashless payments is no less than profound. We might think this is old news for a rich state with an 'advanced' or 'modern' economy. However, at a consumer level it is still a relatively recent phenomenon, with card payments in the UK for example only overtaking their cash purchase equivalents in 2017. Around the world, and especially in the Global South (see Case Study Box 10.5), the rise of cashless

KEY THEORY BOX 10.4 THE FOLK THEORY OF MONEY

There are three elements to the folk theory of money, which is a set of ideas and assumptions that permeate public consciousness about what money is, the role of a central bank, and how banks handle ordinary people's money (Braun 2016). The first 'myth' upheld by the folk theory is that all money is created equal. This is an intuitive thought given the way cash is routinely experienced. However, the quality of financial claims that circulate as money varies considerably depending on the issuer of those claims. In other words, the money system is not flat but hierarchical, and it is only because of the way the payments system works (in normal times) that money appears to be of equal quality. Put simply, the money that banks use to settle payments with each other is of a different and essentially sounder quality than the money people and businesses use to pay each other. Ordinary people do not have access to central bank money. When thinking of money as hierarchical, we might also consider how some national currencies (especially the US dollar) retain their acceptability as payment more easily than others in times of crisis, irrespective of the relative price of the currencies in question.

The second and related myth upheld by the folk theory is that banks act as intermediaries. This has been called the 'dogmatic notion of banking as a system of financial intermediation', that is, the idea that banks take in deposits from those with a surplus of money and lend part of these funds to people and businesses who need money (Sgambati 2016: 275). Together with the third myth of the folk theory—the idea that money is 'exogenous', that is, *only central banks* create money—this view offers an 'upside down' account of money and banking (Braun 2016: 1075). Put simply, when a bank makes a loan it expands its balance sheet (that is, it adds items to both the asset and the liability side) and in doing so it creates new money. The folk theory of money obscures this process, suggesting instead that the central bank directly controls the quantity of money in the system. In reality, central banks are compelled to provide the reserves banks require for the money they have already created through lending, and the limits to this lending are set not by the central bank, but by the demand for loans from people and businesses (Braun 2016: 1076). This has led many money activists to argue that credit money fuels debt growth, feeding into the dynamics outlined in Section 10.2.1.

Central banks, such as the Bank of England, have in recent years explicitly addressed the deficiencies of the folk theory of money, even going as far as to acknowledge that banks create money when they make a loan and that the central bank is not in control of the amount of money in circulation. Such unconventional disclosures are the result of rising public debate about the politics of money creation, including the consciousness-raising efforts of movements like Positive Money.[1] The folk theory of money may still dominate policy circles and prevalent understandings of money and banking, notably as taught in economics textbooks, but increased questioning of the folk theory is emblematic of the new everyday political economy of money in recent decades.

payments is radically altering the political economy of money at the level of the household and the everyday. For instance, demonetization in India is a significant episode for understanding the everyday politics of the move to a cashless society, showing how shifts in monetary form can have huge consequences for whole societies.

A decline in the use of cash has been identified by the Bank for International Settlements (BIS 2021) as a global phenomenon, especially since the onset of the COVID-19 pandemic. Both advanced industrialized countries and underdeveloped countries have witnessed sharp increases in cashless payments and a move away from cash transactions. In 2020, people in the former made almost twice as many cashless payments as people in the latter, but the decline in cash is observable in most countries (BIS 2021: 2). In Canada, for instance, the total volume of cash transactions decreased by 62 per cent between 2016 and 2021, while the total value of these transactions decreased by 44 per cent (Yun and Olorundaré 2022: 18). According to one report, '[t]he COVID-19 pandemic has ushered in the new digital payment norm. It includes the ongoing acceleration of digital and contactless payments usage and e-commerce purchases' (Yun and Olorundaré 2022: 4).

Digital payments infrastructures rely on people having a bank account, yet access is never equal. It is dependent on being able to document things like a recorded birthdate, identifiable parents, a state ID number, stable income, a fixed address, and so on. The World Bank estimates that there are approximately 2 billion adults who do not have a bank account and thus rely on cash. For advocates of digital money, especially payments firms, 'banking the unbanked' represents a business opportunity for expansion under the tropes of

[1] https://positivemoney.org/.

CASE STUDY BOX 10.5 DEMONETIZATION IN INDIA

In November 2016, the Indian government attempted to remove 86 per cent of banknotes from circulation. Overnight 500- and 1000-rupee banknotes were outlawed. The government's reasoning for this drastic action was wide-ranging but primarily centred on the aims of reducing the amount of counterfeit cash in circulation and cracking down on activities in the 'shadow economy'. Prime Minister Narendra Modi was also keen to stress the importance of promoting cashless payments as part of his vision of a 'Digital India'. The pursuit of a rapid demonetization policy meant the Indian state was further positioning itself as an active driver of the digital turn in financial inclusion.

The demonetization experiment was not smooth. Some estimates suggest that it cost India at least 1 per cent of its GDP and resulted in the loss of over 1.5 million jobs. The currency crunch induced by the policy lasted for several months and left tens of millions of people cashless or standing in line for hours each day in an attempt to deposit soon to be worthless banknotes. The human toll of the policy is not to be underestimated, causing around 150 million daily wage earners, agricultural labourers, and migrant and informal workers to lose their income for weeks in the initial aftermath. Women, the elderly, and disabled people were the worst hit by the shock, and it was directly linked to at least one hundred deaths. There can be few greater reminders that monetary policy has the potential to have a direct and even violent impact on everyday life. The fallout of the experiment was framed in terms of 'inconvenience' by backers of the Digital India concept, but many people resisted and protested demonetization as a violation of rights, particularly the poor and vulnerable populations most affected.

The case of demonetization in India also draws attention to longer-term changes in the everyday political economy of money (see Figure 10.3). Chief amongst these is the process of

Figure 10.3 Long queues of people form outside banks in Gurgaon, Delhi, waiting to exchange demonetized 500 and 1000 currency notes in exchange for new currency.

Source: Shutterstock.

'digital financialization', in which people are invited, or sometimes coerced, into new digital financial realms and subjectivities (Jain and Gabor 2020). The promotion of a cashless society by the Indian government serves to rapidly advance the digital payments sector and the number of people who use it. The key point about how such developments shift the everyday political economy of money is that the tech and FinTech firms in this sector do not generate revenue through the activity of facilitating payments so much as the business of collecting and monetizing mass customer data. Individuals and households have new forms of interaction with the worlds of retail money and finance when digital data about them becomes the stuff of monetization and marketization.

'modernization' and 'development' (see Section 10.2.2 above). For those more sceptical of the 'war on cash', the question of inclusion and the promise of digital money is more complex. For instance, the move to a cashless society might augment rather than reduce the digital divide witnessed in many countries along the lines of age, class, gender, race, and able-bodiedness. Those who cannot, or choose not to, live according to the 'normal' parameters of everyday digital financial citizenship will not necessarily be able to be full participants in the cashless society.

The replacement of cash by digital money is also an issue of freedom and democracy. Digital money transforms everyday payments into something that can be surveilled by state and market actors alike. Whereas hard cash is (for the most part) untraceable, digital money offers opportunities for increased state monitoring and control and for private firm revenue models built on data harvesting and analytics. Many commentators stress how a cashless society offers individuals opportunities and increased levels of financial inclusion, sometimes even access to formal finance (for example, consumer loans) based on using historic payments data to generate a credit score (see Section 10.2.2 above). On these grounds, 'money is data' in that it is reconfigured into a form of transactional data used for purposes other than payments (Westermeier 2020). Such dynamics lie at the heart of debates about the emergence of FinTech more broadly as a key site and set of practices in the everyday political economy of money.

10.4.2 **FinTech and money**

FinTech is a label typically applied to a set of digital financial technologies that have emerged in retail money and finance in recent decades. Advances in digital retail monetary and financial services have sparked debates about the nature of new forms of reintermediation through 'platforms' (Langley and Leyshon 2021). As a set of mass consumer products facilitated by digitally enabled infrastructures, the rise of FinTech has altered how many people engage with money in their daily lives. From buying groceries to paying a friend, from borrowing short-term credit to applying for a mortgage, from exchanging travel money to sending remittances around the world, there are numerous ways that FinTech has altered how people access and manage their money. The geographies of FinTech are unequal and variegated, and its spread and adoption around the world produces dramatic changes in the everyday political economy of money across the Global North and the Global South.

A key area of FinTech is mobile payments. These are typically viewed through the lens of their business case. From this perspective, providers—whether start-up firms, incumbent banks, or established technology brands—generate new retail money and banking products built on notions of digital disruption, increases in efficiency, and network effects. Consumers take advantage of these products such that access to services at low prices increases as compared to earlier forms of retail money and banking. By contrast, critics stress how mobile payments firms extract fees from their position of control over payments networks. While consumers may be attracted to the idea of escaping the vested interests of state-backed money, mobile payments firms do not so much challenge state money, and the banking system more generally, as they merely extract tolls from payments infrastructures (Dodd 2014: 370). Important contributions to GPE have also adopted a more nuanced view, resisting the instinct to understand mobile payments through the lens of a commodification of everyday experience. From this perspective, mobile payments are recognized as more diverse, at times even proliferative of

new market subjects able to reshape the consumption experience of using and managing money (Kremers and Brassett 2017).

GPE scholars have made sense of the broader rise of FinTech through an engagement with the theme of infrastructures (Bernards and Campbell-Verduyn 2019). In the area of money and payments, research on the impact of FinTech on remittance transfers is particularly illuminating. **Remittances** between individuals in the Global North and South, as well as domestic payments within underdeveloped countries, play a crucial role in many places, especially where people lack access to other types of formal credit and income. Here, FinTech is providing the 'often missing infrastructures of finance' and creating new opportunities and vulnerabilities for those who depend on remittances (Rodima-Taylor and Grimes 2019: 840). Other important work emphasizes how in a world dominated by modern credit money, cross-border transactions will always be dependent on state institutions to some extent, so no matter how far FinTech innovation progresses, the idea of a 'frictionless global infrastructure for payments' will remain a utopia (Brandl and Dieterich 2021). Future research in GPE is likely to continue to explore how FinTech serves to reshape the everyday political economy of money.

10.4.3 **Cryptocurrencies**

Blockchain-based cryptocurrencies have captured enormous public attention around the world since the publication of Satoshi Nakamoto's white paper outlining the blueprint for developing **blockchain** technology in the form of 'electronic cash' (Bitcoin) in 2008. In November 2021 the market capitalization of all cryptocurrencies briefly peaked at US$3 trillion—more than the GDP of 186 countries—before falling, though there is continuous price volatility compared to the US dollar. Enthusiasts claim there is revolutionary potential in cryptocurrencies to transform money and finance, since money built on a failsafe distributed ledger allows for 'decentralized' and 'stateless' economic interaction. Detractors point to the concentration of ownership of major coins, and the fact that the wild volatility in the price of cryptocurrencies such as Bitcoin makes it unsuitable for actual use as money. Put simply, the more a currency acts like a speculative asset the less it can be trusted as a store of value and a means of exchange. GPE scholars have taken a nuanced view, looking specifically for example at the underlying blockchain technologies behind crypto-currencies to better understand their implications for global governance (Campbell-Verduyn 2018b).

How might we understand the rise (and falls) of cryptocurrencies from an everyday perspective? One productive route is to consider the communities—made up of technological enthusiasts, professional investors, casual traders, monetary activists, ordinary people, and so on—who work to maintain and advance cryptocurrencies as a coherent site and set of practices of money (see Everyday GPE Box 10.6). Research in this area has identified a crucial paradox at the heart of cryptocurrencies like Bitcoin (Dodd 2018). On the one hand, Bitcoin depends on and fosters an ideology centred on the premise that money *does not* depend on social relations and trust. That is, Bitcoin is celebrated as a way of escaping the state and social institutions by offering a form of 'trust-free' money.

Yet, on the other hand, the communities that have grown up around Bitcoin are dependent on that *very same shared set of beliefs*. That is, the communities of Bitcoin, so central to its rise, are forged on an ideology built on the notion that cryptocurrencies can replace social relations. Put another way, 'Bitcoin will succeed as money to the extent that it fails as an ideology. The currency relies on that which the ideology under-pinning it seeks to deny, namely, the dependence of money upon social relations, and upon trust' (Dodd 2018: 37). An important implication of recognizing the social and everyday life of cryptocurrencies like Bitcoin is that the future of money is likely to be diverse, in the sense that actors other than the state and monetary policymakers are likely to contribute to increased levels of monetary pluralism.

That cryptocurrencies have emerged with such rapid speed and gained a place in global public

---

EVERYDAY GPE BOX 10.6 THE MASS ADOPTION OF 'CRYPTO'

In February 2022, the Super Bowl—the annual playoff champion game of the US National Football League (NFL)—was widely dubbed the 'Crypto Bowl' because the commercials shown to the approximately 100 million viewers were dominated by advertisements from the cryptocurrency industry. The Super Bowl is widely acknowledged as something of a barometer for American culture, constituting the single most important event for US advertisers in any given year. Almost half of the commercials were from cryptocurrency firms, which have also become more visible across the NFL in recent years by signing major stars and celebrities as brand ambassadors and paying teams to rename their stadiums. Cryptocurrencies had become mainstream.

Numerous celebrities and influencers have also endorsed cryptocurrency exchanges, which are essentially businesses that allow customers to trade cryptocurrencies with other digital assets, such as traditional state money. This brought even more mass exposure to 'crypto' in general and specific interest in a relatively small number of financial start-ups with speculative business models. NFL quarterback Tom Brady is one among many high-profile people who have had class action lawsuits filed against them for lending credibility to now collapsed cryptocurrency exchanges, such as FTX, which went bankrupt in November 2022.

The everyday politics of crypto are also highly gendered and racialized in places like the US. For instance, in 2021–2022 crypto trading and use was higher among US Black, Hispanic, and Asian adults (20 per cent) compared to white adults (13

per cent), while Black investors are more likely to own crypto than stocks or mutual funds (the opposite is the case for white investors). Black and Latino crypto enthusiasts have backed crypto on the grounds that it subverts the 'old money' system and has the potential to foster more equitable systems in economy and finance. American filmmaker and director Spike Lee, famous for making films that explore race relations, is one of many voices to describe crypto as 'positive' and 'inclusive' in contrast to exploitative old money. This messaging appeared in advertising for Coin Cloud, a firm that operates crypto ATMs and which filed for bankruptcy protection in February 2023.

Cryptocurrencies have made huge inroads into public consciousness, and mass adoption has taken place in many countries. Nigeria, for example, was home to more cryptocurrency trading in 2020 than almost anywhere else in the world (behind only the US and Russia in trading volumes). Multiple reasons explain the rise of non-state digital currencies in Nigeria, including the Central Bank of Nigeria's successive devaluations of the national currency (the naira) and restrictions on foreign exchange. In terms of mass awareness, cryptocurrency exchanges also witnessed a surge in interest during the End SARS mass protests in the country in October 2020, during which a government crackdown on organizers resulted in bank account freezes and people moving to use digital currencies instead. While many authorities around the world warn that cryptocurrencies are high-risk volatile 'investments' and in some jurisdictions even outlaw their use, people still engage with them for a multitude of reasons and with diverse goals in mind.

consciousness and popular culture—witness the mass adoption of 'crypto' and 'Crypto Bowl'—is perhaps unsurprising to GPE researchers who have long stressed the historical specificity of national currencies as the norm, and suggested that the diversification of monetary forms is to be expected over time (Seyfang 2000). Nonetheless, major cryptocurrencies like Bitcoin are still modelled on 'digital metallism'. That is, certain cryptocurrencies are designed *as if* they are like precious metals (typically gold), with a deflationary logic of finite supply and a libertarian claim to intrinsic or 'fundamental' value. In other words, digital metallism speaks to the idea that digital money can be conceptualized and used as if it conforms to the imagined supply and demand dynamics of a precious metal as a commodity, and as such speaks to a libertarian politics that seeks to enhance freedom from government and state control of social systems such as money. Looking to popular culture to unpack digital metallism and its associations with gold shows how everyday perceptions of how cryptocurrencies 'work' might serve to advance new forms of libertarianism. In this analysis, technical systems like blockchain become legitimized based on their supposed political neutrality and 'natural' foundations, and the gendered, racialized, and sexualized discursive practices that go into constructing the place of gold in many societies are potentially reproduced (Allon 2018: 226). As cryptocurrencies continue to gain a place within everyday perceptions of technological innovation and 'new' forms of money, they will still be part of longer-standing political debates about how to understand, organize, and resist money.

> decades. Mobile payments and remittances are two areas that have witnessed dramatic shifts at the everyday level.
>
> • Blockchain-based cryptocurrencies have garnered huge interest, despite the fact that for the most part they act as speculative assets as opposed to digital currency. Blockchain technologies are likely to continue to fuel debates about and engagement with non-state money.

10.5 Monetary governance in everyday life

GPE scholars have engaged in research on the governance of money for many decades. However, in recent years there has been a reinvigoration of study of central banks in particular, driven by greater recognition of their fundamental place in the world economy as major players who drive and condition change, especially since the financial crisis of 2007–2008 (Mehrling 2011). Research into central banking has produced important insights relevant for considering the contemporary everyday political economy of money, including how the actions of central banks serve to shape and make available certain sites and practices of money in everyday life (see Pauly, Chapter 9). By applying an everyday lens to monetary governance, this section aims to explore the intersections between monetary governance and the ways in which people engage with money at an everyday level. It does so by first exploring the everyday life of prices, followed by a consideration of the everyday political economy of money under conditions of 'unconventional' monetary policy since 2008.

10.5.1 The everyday life of prices

The value of the money in our digital wallet or the cash in our pocket matters a great deal. Yet money works best when its value (as in what it can buy) is not something that needs to be thought about, but can be taken for granted. It is during times when we are unsure about the value of money that a series of broader destabilizing decisions might be taken. We might refrain from a planned purchase, feel unable to meet a debt repayment, or try to demand more income from an employer. While this is an overly simplistic depiction of how money affects everyday decisions, in a broad sense we can see that money and monetary governance has something to do with trust

KEY POINTS

• Successive waves of financial crisis and digital technological change have in part driven changes in the everyday political economy of money. From an everyday perspective, money is more diverse and complex than is commonly recognized in the folk theory of money.

• The rapid shift away from cash to digital payments in many countries around the world alters how people use and understand money. A 'cashless society' produces new opportunities and vulnerabilities for people and households.

• FinTech innovation has increased the diversity of the power relations, sites, and practices of money in recent

and confidence. To function as money, something needs to inspire our trust as a store of value and our confidence in the idea that someone will accept it as payment, or as a means to settle a debt.

In recent decades, the pursuit of price stability has been one of the central pillars of economic policy around the world. An emphasis on **sound money**—money that neither depreciates nor appreciates (too rapidly)—has figured in the minds of monetary policymakers as fundamental to producing the stability required that in turn fosters trust and confidence in the money system. Yet maintaining trust and confidence in a social institution is no simple process. The orthodox approach to monetary policy has stressed the importance of a 'rules-based' agenda, one that communicates in an ostensibly apolitical manner the technical requirements of monetary policy in advance and then carefully and prudently uses monetary policy tools to govern through expectation management. Of course, such political 'neutrality' in the context of decision-making that carries huge societal consequences is highly questionable for many GPE scholars. To echo a theme mentioned in Section 10.4, 'inflation is always and everywhere a political phenomenon. All levels of inflation, high and low, are the outcome of political conflicts' (Kirshner 2001: 42).

Moreover, central bankers themselves are highly politicized actors, and gendered tropes associated with certain masculinities might even play a role in their capacity to perform the job of a central banker effectively. For instance, when Mark Carney was the governor of the Bank of England, political actors and the media often appealed to masculinized traits, such as his ability to act 'reasonably', to be ferocious when needed, and to 'steer the ship' of the sinking British economy, as reasons to support decisions taken by the Bank of England in the wake of economic turbulence post-2008. These tropes worked to depoliticize what many GPE scholars would understand to be political decisions about monetary policy, including regarding price stability (Key Concept Box 10.7), that have important redistributive dimensions (Clarke and Roberts 2016).

In governing expectations—those of ordinary people, households, firms, financial market actors, and so on—central banks should not be viewed as straightforwardly dictating to or manipulating passive bystanders at an everyday level. Indeed, GPE research has established that economic and political elites are constrained at least in part by everyday expectations about how the economy works (Seabrooke 2010). On the one hand, central banks have developed multiple means through which to govern expectations, including prioritizing simple rules and transparency, as well as engaging in novel communicative experiments (Holmes 2014). On the other hand, recent GPE research has drawn attention to the broader range of *practices* that are involved in contemporary monetary governance. This includes, for instance, the 'everyday practices through which workers, business owners and families respond to and act upon their faith (or lack of faith) in the current value of money', which may serve to either reinforce or undermine the prevailing monetary policy (Best 2019: 625). A key point stemming from this research is that we should not take the credibility of monetary governance as given or fixed and remember that it can be subjected to significant change, including change driven by the actions and expectations of everyday people.

Monetary governance can be challenged, resisted, and reinterpreted at the everyday level in multiple ways. As mentioned above, one of the drivers of mass interest in blockchain technologies, cryptocurrencies, and 'alternative finance' is distrust in national monies and a desire by ordinary people and monetary activists to seek out new money arrangements that challenge the financial status quo (Tooker and Clarke 2018). Since the financial crisis of 2007/8, this has occurred dramatically in rich states such as the US and the UK, but it is also a trend accelerating in poorer states where public distrust in state and financial institutions is often high, and digital technology firms promise people monetary stability and trust via technological solutionism.

Yet monetary governance is subject to everyday politics even where national fiat money remains the dominant currency in use. For instance, as consumers people challenge the success of interest rate hikes in combating inflation when their expectations about prices and wages do not conform to the intentions of monetary policymakers. As workers, people challenge monetary governance when they take collective industrial action to demand wage rises that keep pace with inflation. As mentioned above, high levels of inflation have been experienced in many countries around the world in recent years, leading some central bankers such as Andrew Bailey of the Bank of England to urge workers not to demand large pay rises (since in his view this could cause inflation to become further entrenched). In the UK, the central bank has

KEY CONCEPT BOX 10.7 PRICE STABILITY

Since the early 1980s, monetary policy has been defined primarily in terms of maintaining price stability. Central banks typically seek to achieve a specified annual rate of inflation. In other words, central banks use monetary policy (such as setting interest rates) to target a specific general rate of increase in a set of prices for goods and services over a given period. Inflation targeting is built on the ideas that maintaining price stability is key to supporting growth and broader stability in a capitalist world economy, and that central banks operate best under conditions of 'independence' from national governments (in theory, so that they are governed by appointed 'expert' technocrats rather than influenced by elected politicians, who may seek to manipulate monetary policy at certain times in order to gain electoral advantage). Rules-based monetary policy has come under significant strain during recent years of 'unconventional' policy (see Section 10.5.2), but it constitutes the orthodoxy against which other elements and changes to central bank activity are assessed.

In an absence of price stability, huge political and social effects are often felt. In particular, high food prices have long been thought to contribute to mass protest movements. The Arab Spring uprisings in the early 2010s had multiple complex social causes, but some commentators point to the idea that food price spikes cause the conditions under which riots and uprisings like these are more likely to emerge. The Food and Agricultural Organization of the UN produces a Food Price Index that measures monthly change in international prices for a basket of food commodities, which has been used to explore the relationship between rapidly rising food prices and political and social unrest.

The sharp move to inflation targeting by many central banks around the world in the 1990s and 2000s has also had varied and oftentimes destabilizing impacts on people and households at an everyday level. In Latin America, a number of countries found it difficult to establish the credibility of their monetary regimes, particularly as they came to be viewed by ordinary citizens as externally imposed conditions as set by the 'neoliberal' policy prescriptions of the IMF, which further contributed to broader financial instability. Moreover, radical inflation targeting in different parts of the world has been shown to contain significant gender biases, principally because low inflation targets may lead to unemployment in industries that employ disproportionate numbers of women (Braunstein and Heintz 2011), or because they serve to benefit creditors, who are more likely to be (well-off) men, at the cost of debtors (Young 2018). To be sure, sustained high levels of inflation cause harm to almost all members of society, and especially to those least able to bear the costs of rising prices for food and other necessary goods, so it is understandable that monetary policy targets price stability. At the same time, there are many other societal problems that cause harm—including unemployment, inequality, and climate change—which might also be relevant concerns for monetary policy, but the almost exclusive focus on price stability serves to prioritize it above all else, with huge political, social, and distributional consequences.

---

been subject to much criticism for such statements and from the popular press for monetary mismanagement, while the number of working days lost to strike action in 2022 was at its highest since the 1980s. Such episodes are important reminders of the political character of monetary governance, even in the face of formal central bank independence, which has been the norm in most countries since the 1990s.

10.5.2 **Living with 'unconventional' monetary policy**

Across a number of states in the Global North (in particular, the US, the UK, the euro area, and Japan), 'unconventional' monetary policy has become a lasting feature of monetary governance in recent decades. In response to the financial crisis of 2007–2008, and

continuing beyond the COVID-19 pandemic, central banks embarked on a series of novel measures that departed from previous norms. In short, these were the adoption of historically low interest rates, as well as asset purchases and targeted funding subsidies for banks that lend to businesses aimed at supporting the stability of the financial system and preserving the value of financial assets. More recently, and especially since the economic fallout from the pandemic, the IMF (2021) documents that more and more states in the Global South have pursued unconventional monetary policy as well, especially the adoption of asset purchase programmes.

A useful entry point into the everyday political economy of recent monetary policy is to contextualize the specific central bank actions within previous experiences of monetary policy change and

KEY CONCEPT BOX 10.8 THE ASSET ECONOMY

The 'asset economy' refers to a set of circumstances in which an economy comes to be defined by wage stagnation, on the one hand, and asset inflation (especially in property price inflation) on the other (Adkins, Cooper, and Konings 2020). The position of housing as a wealth-generating asset is emphasized in work that theorizes the asset economy because it plays such a pivotal role in configuring class position and life chances. There are links here to asset-based welfare (see Section 10.2.2).

The core tenets of monetary governance in recent decades, especially in rich countries but also witnessed in the actions of central banks in the Global South, serve to support asset price inflation as the primary means of securing financial stability and stimulating economic growth. The unconventional monetary policies of recent decades may even have become 'locked-in', since to roll back on them would undermine dominant debt-fuelled growth models. Under such conditions the everyday impact of the asset economy is likely to be experiences associated with greater inequality, since the wealth effect of asset ownership intensifies existing inequalities and produces new chasms between those able and unable to access housing and other assets.

experiment. For some scholars, the development of ostensibly extraordinary monetary policies is actually better conceptualized as a 'radical continuation' of previous state strategies for governing labour and ensuring debt discipline (Evemy, Yates, and Eggleston 2021: 833). On this view, with particular reference to Bank of England policies, 'unconventional' monetary policy should be understood as a key form of disciplining labour since it drives growth primarily through rising asset prices, such as in housing and supporting the asset economy more broadly, while at the same time still using inflation targeting as an incomes policy aimed at suppressing wage demands (see Key Concept Box 10.8). Linking back to Section 10.2.1, we can see how recent monetary policy fits with conditioning how people and households take on debt.

In many countries, over a decade of 'unconventional' monetary policy since 2008 continues to shape the everyday politics of monetary governance in significant ways. National economic growth driven by rising asset prices, especially in housing, and a dependence on household debt to sustain standards of living were further entrenched by central bank actions that attempted to secure confidence in financial markets. It is perhaps unsurprising that central banking appears to be 're-politicized' in some national contexts as ordinary people grapple with a continued dependence on debt, in part sustained by the post-2008 monetary settlement, which has now become even more difficult to navigate in the higher interest rate environment that has emerged in response to global inflationary pressures since 2021.

KEY POINTS

- The study of monetary governance is a crucial topic of concern for understanding the everyday political economy of money. Central bank policymaking in particular can be studied from an everyday perspective, given that the expectations and actions of everyday people and households are crucial determinants of the legitimacy and credibility of monetary governance.

- Price stability has been the primary goal of monetary policy in most states in recent years. This is understandable given the widespread harms caused by prolonged periods of inflation, yet at the same time the exclusive focus of monetary policy on price stability can serve to create other harms, inequalities, and vulnerabilities for everyday people and households.

- Since the Global Financial Crisis of 2007/8, both major world central banks and those in underdeveloped countries have experimented with 'unconventional' monetary policy. This has furthered inequalities based on asset ownership and increased the widespread dependence on debt in many countries.

10.6 Conclusion

'The everyday' can be used as a productive lens in GPE to explore finance. This chapter has mapped key issues and research that speak to the everyday political economy of debt and money in order to showcase the pay-off of using the everyday lens. Ordinary people and households are centred so as to better understand how the power relations, sites, and practices of everyday money and finance are constitutive of broader trends in the world economy. At the same time, the everyday lens can be used to draw attention to aspects of the political economy of money and finance that tend not to be privileged in standard GPE accounts. The major themes that have been used in this chapter are how and why households have come to rely on debt as part of everyday life, how this has unequal consequences, how the diverse uses of money are changing over time with variegated results, and how the governance of money often serves to reproduce an expansion of indebted life.

Future research in GPE and related fields is likely to continue to explore the everyday political economy of global finance in a multiplicity of ways. One direction for research that this chapter has attempted to reflect, but has only done so in part, is the important work done on documenting and understanding the everyday financial experiences of the vast majority of the world's population who live outside the Global North. After all, it is often in countries in the Global South where the rapid adoption of experimental financial technologies is having the most transformative impact, where new money forms shift and interact with the politics of fiat currencies that are less 'stable' than the major 'world currencies', and where lives and life chances are most subject to the disciplining and political negotiation of relations of debt. As this chapter has attempted to illustrate, relations of money and finance intersect with relations of class, race, gender, geography, and more, in complex and contested ways. Questions of who benefits, who loses, and what politics are reproduced or replaced are not straightforward to answer in attempts to study the everyday political economy of global finance. Still, however, the everyday of global finance demands a *global* political economy.

? 10.7 QUESTIONS

1. How do you understand the role of debt in contemporary society?

2. Can you think of any examples of how aspects of your everyday life have come to be financialized?

3. Who benefits and who loses when people come to rely on debt to meet more of life's necessities?

4. Why might the financial inclusion agenda be understood as a deeply political issue?

5. To what extent does a financial mode of thinking influence decisions in your everyday life?

6. When was the last time you made a payment in cash and what was it for?

7. How is FinTech shaping your involvement with the worlds of money, credit, and payment?

8. Do you see political potential in the rise of cryptocurrencies, or are they simply a speculative asset?

9. How do the views and actions of central banks shape everyday experiences?

10. To what extent does access to asset ownership affect everyday life chances?

≋ 10.8 FURTHER READING

Adkins, L., Cooper, M., and Konings, M. (2020), *The Asset Economy: Property Ownership and the New Logic of Inequality* (Cambridge: Polity). An important and timely mapping of how inequalities of asset ownership are driving social transformations in Anglo-capitalist societies.

Aitken, R. (2015), *Fringe Finance: Crossing and Contesting the Borders of Global Capital* (Abingdon, UK: Routledge). A powerful conceptualization and interrogation of the experiences of those populations who live on the 'fringes' of financial markets.

Cavallero, L., and V. Gago (2021), *A Feminist Reading of Debt* (trans. L. Mason-Deese) (London: Pluto Press). An anti-debt manifesto that renders visible the links between debt, gendered violence, and social reproduction, and shows how debt can be resisted in Latin America and beyond.

De Goede, M. (2005), *Virtue, Fortune, and Faith* (Minneapolis, MN: University of Minnesota Press). A cultural history of financial markets that questions assumptions about international finance's unchallenged position and exposes its ambiguous scientific authority.

Dodd, N. (2014), *The Social Life of Money* (Princeton, NJ: Princeton University Press). An essential and provocative social theory of money.

Elias, J., and Roberts, A. (eds.) (2018), *Feminist Global Political Economies of the Everyday* (London and New York: Routledge). An important and comprehensive volume showcasing the breadth and depth of feminist contributions to the study of everyday global political economy.

Langley, P. (2008), *The Everyday Life of Global Finance: Saving and Borrowing in Anglo-America* (Oxford: Oxford University Press). A pathbreaking exploration into the everyday political economy of global finance.

Martin, R. (2002), *Financialization of Daily Life* (Philadelphia, PA: Temple University Press). One of the earliest and most influential accounts of how cultural changes and policy priorities have led to the financialization of ever more aspects of daily life.

Montgomerie, J. (2019), *Should we Abolish Household Debts?* (Cambridge: Polity). An essential guide for understanding why we need to abolish household debt and how we can do it.

Soederberg, S. (2014a), *Debtfare States and the Poverty Industry: Money, Discipline and the Surplus Population* (London: Routledge). A considered theorization of money and debt that draws out the power relations at play in different aspects of the poverty industry in the US and Mexico.

CONTRIBUTOR NOTES

Chris Clarke is Reader in Political Economy at the University of Warwick. He has published on a range of topics associated with international political economy and finance. His first book is entitled *Ethics and Economic Governance: Using Adam Smith to Understand the Global Financial Crisis*, and he is currently writing a monograph on the political economy of FinTech.

Adrienne Roberts is Senior Lecturer in International Politics at the University of Manchester. She has published widely in the area of feminist international political economy, with a particular focus on the gendered relations of finance, debt, development, and trade. Her recent books include *Feminist Global Political Economies of the Everyday* (with Juanita Elias), *Handbook of the International Political Economy of Gender* (with Juanita Elias), and *Gendered States of Punishment and Welfare*.

PART IV
Resurgence of the State?

11

Ideologies of Globalism, Populism, and Economic Nationalism

Adam Harmes

Reader's guide

This chapter examines how political ideologies can help to explain the contemporary politics of globalization, anti-globalization, and global governance, including new forms of populism and economic nationalism. The first part of the chapter outlines the main ideologies of international relations and economic policy including liberal internationalism, progressivism, neoliberalism, populist conservatism, and, to a lesser extent, realism and neoconservatism. The second part of the chapter shows how these ideologies influenced the preferences of political actors and contributed to a globalization/anti-globalization sequence that has been strongly consistent across Anglo-American countries.

11.1 Introduction

The literature on global political economy (GPE) often identifies three broad eras in the modern history of the global economy. The first was the original period of free markets and economic globalization. It lasted from the early 1800s until the 1930s when the Great Depression led to the rise of government economic intervention and trade protectionism. The second era, which ran until the **stagflation** crisis of the 1970s, was characterized by more interventionist welfare states, greater restrictions on trade and capital flows, and an absence of economic globalization. In the third era, from the 1980s to the present, business interests and free market intellectuals mobilized against the welfare state through the promotion of more free market policies, including a return to free trade and economic globalization (for a discussion of these eras, see Helleiner, Chapter 8). This return to free markets, free trade, and globalization was highly contested among different political actors, and today, over a quarter of a century later, it remains contested. So much so that many wonder if we are on the cusp of another new era, one where the forces of populism, nationalism, and concerns over national security could lead to a resurgence of the state and a shift in the nature of economic globalization. To understand this political contestation and where it may lead, this chapter examines the ideologies, actors, and history that define the current debate.

11.2 Ideologies in the global political economy

Ideologies are competing sets of philosophical principles, often connected to underlying material interests, that can guide the policy preferences of different actors. For example, being a 'conservative' or 'progressive' means that you believe in a broad set of principles that will inform your views on different issues. Understanding ideologies is useful because—alongside other factors such as identity, institutional structures, public opinion, national interests, and other constraints—they can help to explain why different actors often support different policies. Traditionally, the GPE literature emphasized three main ideological approaches to economic policy: liberalism, nationalism, and

Marxism. Today, however, these terms can be more confusing than helpful. Liberalism can have multiple meanings (see Key Theory Box 11.1), nationalism can be associated with both free market and interventionist approaches, and Marxism is a term very few political actors in the Anglosphere actually use to describe their approach to economic policy. Beyond the Anglosphere, other ideologies and belief systems are often context dependent (see Key Theory Box 11.2).

11.2.1 Liberal internationalism

Liberal internationalism is a centre-left approach to foreign policy. It emphasizes democracy and human rights, international institutions and diplomacy, and using trade to promote interdependence and peace as well as prosperity. On economic policy, it supports a market economy and international trade, but also the use of government intervention to reduce inequality and deal with market failures such as recessions, financial crises, and environmental issues. This more interventionist approach to economic policy draws on Keynesian-welfare economics and is often referred to as 'embedded liberalism' in the GPE literature (see Watson, Chapter 2).

11.2.1.1 Early liberalism

The antecedents of liberal internationalism are usually traced back to the classical liberal thinkers of the eighteenth and nineteenth centuries. Economic liberals such as Adam Smith and David Ricardo made the case against **mercantilism** and **protectionism** and in favour of international trade on the grounds of economic efficiency and mutual gains. Other classical economic liberals, including John Stuart Mill and Richard Cobden, supported international trade and investment (**capital mobility**) for their ability to promote peace through economic interdependence and the transmission of democratic values. As Helleiner notes, 'economic liberals such as Mill and Cobden saw free trade primarily as a tool to strengthen a peaceful cosmopolitan world society. Free trade would foster peace, they argued, by creating ties of interdependence and spreading "civilization"' (2002: 313). Similarly, Immanuel Kant's 1795 essay *Perpetual Peace* highlighted the importance of domestic and international institutions. He argued that republican forms of government (essentially democracies) are less likely to fight each other and that an international federation

KEY THEORY BOX 11.1   VARIETIES OF LIBERALISM: ARE LIBERALS LEFT WING OR RIGHT WING?

In the academic literature, the term 'liberal' relates to the idea of 'liberalization' or 'to make free'. Liberalizing economic policy is about shifting to a more free market approach with less government intervention in the economy, including free trade, lower taxes, less redistribution through social programmes, and fewer regulations. This is why the early proponents of free market economics, such as Adam Smith and David Ricardo, are referred to as 'classical economic liberals' (for a discussion, see Watson, Chapter 2). It is also why the more contemporary intellectuals of free market economics, such as Friedrich Hayek and Milton Freidman, are referred to as 'neoliberals'. Other terms that are associated with the free market approach include libertarianism, laissez-faire economics, and supply-side economics. Today, the free market approach is generally advocated by more conservative right-of-centre political parties such as the Republicans in the US and the Conservatives in the UK and Canada. This is why the media will sometimes refer to the free market approach as 'fiscal conservatism'.

Liberalization can also apply to social policies such as abortion, LGBTQ rights, marijuana legalization, immigration, and others. When policies on these issues move in the direction of greater freedom, it is generally associated with the left side of the political spectrum where 'social liberals' have opposing views to 'social conservatives'. This is why in North America, where social policies and the so-called culture wars (see Everyday GPE

Box 11.5) have often been more polarized, the term 'liberal' is regularly used to refer to the left side of the spectrum, and not just on social issues. For example, you will frequently hear conservative politicians and media commentators in the US and Canada speak derisively about the 'liberal media' or 'tax-and-spend liberals'. In both cases, they are referring to left-of-centre media outlets and politicians, including those that advocate for more interventionist economic policies. These differences in terminology help to explain why Australia's Liberal Party is best viewed as a centre-right conservative party while Canada's Liberal Party is better described as centre-left.

Another occasion where liberalism is associated with the left side of the political spectrum is in the broader international relations (IR) literature. Here, **'liberal internationalism'** is viewed as the centre-left approach to foreign policy, with **'embedded liberalism'** being its economic component. Liberal internationalism emerged from the classical liberal focus on democracy and human rights, international institutions and diplomacy, and using trade to promote interdependence and peace as well as prosperity. Today, the liberal internationalist approach is associated with centre-left political parties such as the Democrats in the US, the Liberal Party in Canada, and the Labour Party in the UK. As a side note, the 'neoliberal institutionalism' described in many IR textbooks has nothing to do with the economic neoliberalism of Hayek and Friedman.

of free states would help to promote international cooperation and peace.

In these classical liberal ideas, we see the origins of key liberal internationalist principles such as international trade, economic interdependence, democracy promotion, and support for international cooperation through diplomacy and international institutions. As Held and McGrew note, 'liberal internationalists consider that political necessity requires, and will help bring about, a more cooperative world order. Three factors are central to this position: growing interdependence, democracy and global institutions' (2002: 101). These principles were then promoted in the early twentieth century by the so-called 'idealists'. Most prominent here was US President Woodrow Wilson and his 1918 'fourteen points' speech which outlined a set of peace proposals for the post-First World War era. This included the creation of a League of Nations as well as the promotion of free trade, international

law, sovereign equality, the right of self-determination for all states, anti-imperialism and an end to colonialism, and disarmament.

After the First World War, events such as the Great Depression, the failure of the League of Nations, and the onset of the Second World War all worked to further shape the development of liberal internationalism. On the economic side, the rise of Keynesian economics led to the more interventionist form of 'embedded liberalism'. This emerged in US President Roosevelt's Depression-era 'New Deal' social and regulatory programmes, the controls on the cross-border movement of capital contained in the 1944 Bretton Woods Agreement, and the rise of more interventionist welfare states after the Second World War. On the security side, the failure of the League of Nations and then the Second World War tempered the more idealistic aspects of Wilsonian liberalism. However, liberal support for a Kantian

KEY THEORY BOX 11.2 IDEOLOGIES BEYOND THE ANGLOSPHERE

Beyond the Anglosphere, other ideologies and belief systems can also be highly relevant to explaining and predicting the policy preferences of different actors and, through them, the specific policies implemented by governments. While a few examples are outlined here, the important point is that ideologies are numerous and context dependent. Therefore, it is necessary to examine which specific ideologies are relevant to the country and case being examined.

German ordoliberalism: In Germany, a prominent ideology is 'ordoliberalism'—a version of economic liberalism—which is also known as the 'Freiburg school' based on its founding at the University of Freiburg in the 1930s. Ordoliberalism believes that free market competition will produce socially beneficial outcomes, but only if the competition is truly free and fair. This is why ordoliberalism advocates for strong government regulation to ensure competition by preventing the emergence of monopolies and oligopolies. This differs from the neoliberal view, which believes that markets are more self-regulating and that government regulation, even to promote competition, will ultimately work to undermine economic freedom. As Cerny notes, 'Anglo-American neoliberals see the market as a "spontaneous order" with a minimal role for the state while Ordoliberals believe markets left to their own devices are prone to systemic anti-competitive cartellisation and rent-seeking by capitalists, labour unions and bureaucrats. Competition therefore must be promoted, enabled and enforced by a strong pro-competitive state' (2016: 78). At the same time, ordoliberalism also supports the notion of a 'social market economy', where social programmes focus on the creation of equal opportunity and social cohesion rather than redistribution.

China's leader-driven ideologies: In China, economic policy is based on the ideology of the Chinese Communist Party (CCP). However, this ideology has changed significantly across China's modern history and leaders. Most prominent was 'Mao Zedong Thought', or 'Maoism', which sought to apply Marxist-Leninism to an agricultural rather than industrial country. Mao Zedong was a founding member of the Chinese Communist Party, founded the People's Republic of China in 1949 after the civil war, and led China until 1976. Another major ideological milestone in China's history was the more pro-market ideology of 'Deng Xiaoping Theory', or 'Dengism'. Deng Xiaoping led China from 1978 to 1989 and was responsible for China's shift from communism to a socialist market economy. Today, the dominant ideology of the CCP has again shifted under the current leader Xi Jinping. The official ideology is now referred to as 'Xi Jinping Thought on Socialism with Chinese Characteristics for a New Era'. It argues for a 'great rejuvenation' to restore China's global prominence and it helps to explain the more assertive foreign policy pursued under Xi Jinping's leadership.

Islamic economics: In many Muslim countries, neoliberal economics can often compete with, or be modified by, a form of 'Islamic economics'. Different religious traditions have long helped to inform economic ideologies in the Anglo-American countries and around the world. In some Islamic countries, where church and state are not separated, the influence of religion, and thus Islamic economics, can be greater. Islamic economics is a more interventionist approach that seeks to adapt the moral principles outlined in the Quran to economic policy. An illustrative example would be the prohibition on Riba—the charging of interest on loans—and the role it has played in the rapid growth of Islamic banking.

---

federation of states re-emerged with the creation of the United Nations.

11.2.1.2 Contemporary liberal internationalism

Liberal internationalism evolved again with the end of the Cold War and the rise of the human development and human security agendas in the early 1990s. These concepts came to prominence, respectively, in the 1990 and 1994 Human Development Reports published by the United Nations Development Programme (UNDP). Both concepts sought to shift the focus of economics and security from an emphasis on national economies and state security to a more people-centred or human approach. Human development thus implied a focus on distribution as well as

growth. Similarly, human security meant a stronger concern with the 'root causes' of conflict and with security threats that had a more immediate impact on people as opposed to the sovereignty of states. It was this shifting focus from states to people that underpinned key liberal internationalist projects such as the ban on landmines, the Responsibility to Protect (R2P) doctrine, and the creation of the International Criminal Court (ICC).

Also important to liberal internationalism in the post-Cold War era has been the growing desire to manage the negative side-effects of free trade and globalization. This has led to an emerging 'global governance' agenda where international cooperation is viewed as the best way to manage global issues such as climate change, financial crises, and pandemics. On the negative side-effects of free trade, such as rising inequality within countries, liberal internationalists have generally preferred to work within the existing structure of free trade through national-level policies to attract jobs and investment. This includes a focus on human capital development through education and training programmes, the modernization of physical infrastructure, and a limited use of industrial policies where targeted tax breaks, subsidies, and other policies are used to attract business investment and jobs.

11.2.2 Progressivism

Progressivism is the left-wing and populist-leaning approach to economic and foreign policy. It emphasizes social justice, human rights, environmentalism, disarmament, and an opposition to neo-colonialism, imperialism, war, and militarism. On economic issues, it promotes a more interventionist approach that draws on Keynesian-welfare and socialist economics. Today, those advocating a progressive approach are found on the left side of the Democratic Party in the US, the Labour Parties in the UK and Australia, and the Liberal Party in Canada. They are also found among more specifically left-leaning parties, including the various Anglo-American green parties as well as the New Democratic Party in Canada.

In terms of IR and GPE, the progressive approach can be traced back to the early Marxists and socialists who focused on class conflict and who viewed imperialism, colonialism, and inter-imperialist wars as an outgrowth of capitalism's need for new markets and resources. In addition to Karl Marx, most prominent here is Vladimir Lenin's 1917 book *Imperialism: The Highest Stage of Capitalism*. After the Second World War, the progressive approach manifested itself in the new mass social movements of the 1960s and 1970s. These included the peace movement with its opposition to nuclear weapons and the Vietnam war, the environmental movement, the women's liberation movement, and the civil rights movement for racial equality.

In the Global South, forerunners of the progressive approach could be found in the various socialist-leaning national liberation, anti-colonial, and revolutionary movements that produced progressive icons such as Mahatma Gandhi in India, Nelson Mandela in South Africa, and Che Guevara in Latin America. In economics, many of these movements were informed by 'dependency theory' (see Bhagat, Chapter 14). In contrast to liberal 'modernization theory', dependency theory argued that the Global South did not benefit from its contact with the Global North because of 'declining terms of trade'. This was a situation where developing countries exported natural resources (that had less value added) and imported more expensive manufactured goods in a way that locked them into a structural form of under-development.

With the end of the Cold War and the onset of economic globalization, the progressive approach was most prominently represented in the so-called anti-globalization movement that opposed the return of free market economics and the signing of various free trade agreements. In 2001, the 9/11 terrorist attacks caused the focus of progressives to shift to the promotion of peace, civil liberties, anti-racism, and opposition to the US war in Iraq. Today, progressives have also come to support the emerging global governance agenda to deal with global issues and rising economic inequality. However, where liberal internationalists seek to work within the existing structure of free trade, progressives advocate for 'structural change'. A key example here is the notion of 'progressive' or 'inclusive trade', where minimum labour, environmental, and other standards are entrenched in trade agreements.

11.2.3 Neoliberalism

In the political economy literature, 'neoliberalism' refers to the more orthodox version of free market economics associated with economists Friedrich Hayek, Milton Freidman, and James Buchanan. It emphasizes individual freedom, small government, civil liberties, and restraint in foreign policy. Neoliberalism supports liberal social policies and is generally pro-choice on abortion, pro-LGBTQ rights, pro-immigration, and pro-drug legalization. It also supports restraint on matters of war and peace based on its concerns over the high taxes and curtailed civil liberties associated with a national security state. As Milton Friedman argued, 'war is a friend of the state' (cited in Preble 2016: 169). However, because neoliberalism places its greatest priority on economic policies—such as tax cuts, cuts to social programmes, deregulation, and free trade—its supporters are most often found within right-of-centre conservative parties. This is why, outside of academia, neoliberalism is usually referred to as 'libertarianism' or 'fiscal conservatism'. Economic neoliberalism is also quite distinct from the free market economics of classical economic liberals such as Adam Smith and David Ricardo. In fact, while many neoliberals trace their lineage to these classical thinkers, there are three key differences between the two approaches.

11.2.3.1 Differences between classical economic liberalism and neoliberalism

First, neoliberalism has a much more negative view of government intervention than classical economic liberalism. In particular, it views government as a self-interested and coercive 'leviathan' that seeks to maximize its own size rather than the public interest. Second, this negative view of government leads to a focus on economic freedom over efficiency and mutual gains, and individual choice over the regulation of market failures and morality. For example, in addition to viewing most wealth redistribution as a form of coercion, neoliberals oppose the correction of many market failures such as pollution and monopolies. On the one hand, they dispute the existence of many of the market failures identified by classical liberal and Keynesian-welfare economics. On the other hand, they doubt that government intervention can effectively correct market failures and, even if it could, they believe intervention should still be avoided in the interests of preserving individual freedom. Illustrating this difference with classical economic liberalism, free market economist Walter Block argued that 'Adam Smith should be seen as a moderate free enterpriser who appreciated markets but made many, many exceptions. He allowed government all over the place' (quoted in Heer 2001).

Third, neoliberalism also places a much greater emphasis on using constitutional and institutional mechanisms to 'lock-in' free market policies; a component of neoliberalism that Stephen Gill (1998) has described as the 'new constitutionalism'. In addition to Hayek, a key intellectual behind these lock-in mechanisms is economist James Buchanan, who founded the sub-field of economics known as 'constitutional economics'. The goal is to protect free market policies from politicians and the voting public by enshrining them in national constitutions and other forms of institutional design. Illustrating this view, neoliberal economist Barry Weingast notes that:

The fundamental political dilemma of an economic system is this: A government strong enough to protect property rights and enforce contracts is also strong enough to confiscate the wealth of its citizens. Thriving markets require not only the appropriate system of property rights and a law of contracts, but a secure political foundation that limits the ability of the state to confiscate wealth (1995: 1).

Source: Journal of Law, Economics, & Organization

Therefore, in the same way that constitutions protect the right to free speech, neoliberals want them to also protect property rights and economic freedoms by allowing laws that violate them to be overturned by the courts as 'unconstitutional'. This could include putting a balanced budget requirement or the phrase 'property rights' into the US Bill of Rights or the Canadian Charter of Rights and Freedoms. It could also include the use of **foreign investor protection agreements** (FIPAs) in international trade agreements, which allow corporations to sue governments if they feel their property rights have been violated. For neoliberals, free trade itself is also viewed as a form of institutional design that helps to lock-in free market policies. Specifically, free trade allows companies to move across borders in a way that creates 'policy competition' between countries (see Key Concept Box 11.3). This is a situation where countries have to compete for business investment and jobs by providing the free market policies that companies prefer.

11.2.4 **Populist conservatism**

By itself, the term 'populism' is not very useful. It generally refers to policies and political rhetoric that champion average citizens against the elites. However, which policies and which elites are emphasized can vary significantly depending on whether it is a left-wing or right-wing form of populism. Therefore, to understand populism as ideology, it is more useful to describe left-wing populism as 'progressivism' and right-wing populism as 'populist conservatism'. Since Brexit (the British exit from the European Union) and the election of Donald Trump in 2016, most references to the rise of populism are referring to populist conservatism.

Progressivism and populist conservatism do have some overlaps stemming from their populist roots. First, both believe that free trade agreements and economic globalization have hurt average people by shifting manufacturing jobs to developing countries and, in turn, by putting downward pressure on wages. Second, both also believe that military interventions

KEY CONCEPT BOX 11.3 POLICY COMPETITION

Policy competition is a dynamic that occurs when companies have the ability to move their factories and other investments across the borders of different political jurisdictions, as occurs under free trade. This then forces governments and unions in different territories to compete for jobs and investment by providing the types of free market policies that businesses prefer. When politicians and members of the business community argue that their country needs to be more 'competitive'—on taxes, regulations, intellectual property rights, etc.—this is a large part of what they are referring to. In the GPE literature, policy competition and its subvariants have also been described as 'tax competition', 'competitive deregulation', 'social dumping', the 'structural power of capital', and the '**race to the bottom**'. This last term definitely overstates the constraints imposed by policy competition, and there is an ongoing debate in the GPE literature over the extent to which it actually constrains progressive economic policies. What is interesting though is that both neoliberals and progressives have long believed that policy competition does impose these constraints.

Neoliberal support for policy competition: For example, the neoliberal approach to federalism—known as 'competitive federalism' or 'market-preserving federalism'—is explicitly based on the idea of creating policy competition between subnational governments within a country to lock-in free market policies (Harmes 2019). This approach to federalism has long been advocated by key neoliberal intellectuals including Friedrich Hayek, James Buchanan, and various free market think tanks such as the Cato Institute. As Hayek argued: 'Not only would the greater mobility between the states make it necessary to avoid

all sorts of taxation that would drive capital or labour elsewhere, but there would also be considerable difficulties with many kinds of indirect taxation [i.e. regulation]' (Hayek 1948: 270). The neoliberal Cato Institute think tank made a similar argument about economic globalization in a study titled 'International Tax Competition: A 21st-Century Restraint on Government'. As the authors argued, '[h]igh tax rates are more difficult to sustain in the new economic environment. That is particularly true for taxes on capital, which include taxes on business profits and taxes on individual receipts of dividends, interest, and capital gains . . . In our view, international tax competition may indeed hamper income redistribution, but that is a beneficial outcome because redistribution has progressed to a remarkably high degree in most industrial countries' (Edwards and De Rugy 2002: 3).

Progressive opposition to policy competition: In contrast, while progressives are normatively opposed to policy competition, they have long agreed that it imposes constraints. This is why Keynes sought to limit policy competition through the capital controls that were part of the post-Second World War Bretton Woods Agreement (Helleiner 1994). It is also why classical fiscal federalism theory sought to protect post-war welfare states through a form of cooperative federalism that deliberately aimed to limit policy competition. Since that time, at all levels, policy competition has been consistently supported by more conservative political parties, think tanks, and advocacy groups that are less in favour of redistributive policies, and consistently opposed by their more progressive counterparts (Harmes 2019).

---

in Iraq, Afghanistan, and elsewhere have hurt average families through the military lives lost and the sheer amount of money spent that they believe could have been better used at home. Third, based on these overlaps, progressive and populist conservative politicians can sometimes compete for some of the same voters. This mainly includes white working-class—often unionized—voters located in '**rust belt**' cities and suburbs who traditionally voted for progressives but have more recently migrated to populist conservatives. This is why the second choice of many Trump voters was progressive Bernie Sanders rather than establishment Republicans.

Populist conservativism, sometimes referred to as 'paleoconservatism' or 'conservative nationalism', has a long tradition in the Anglo-American countries. In addition to the swing voters mentioned above,

populist conservative voters are also strongly represented in small town and rural communities. They tend to be religious, socially conservative, nationalistic, anti-elitist, and isolationist. A more masculine and xenophobic culture also tends to inform their views (see GPE of the Everyday Box 11.5). A key subset of populist conservative voters, who are much more fundamentalist in their religious beliefs, are religious social conservatives. While they hold very similar policy preferences as other populist conservatives, they do differ on some issues and motivations.

The foreign policy of populist conservatism is **nationalism**, and this is based on both economic and cultural concerns. In the former case, populist conservatives, while sometimes pro-free market at the domestic level, tend to hold views that are opposed to free trade and immigration, both of which are viewed as hurting the economic interests of working families. This anti-trade, anti-immigration view came to national prominence in the US with Patrick Buchanan's 1992 run against George H. W. Bush for the Republican Party leadership nomination where he argued for a 'new nationalism' that would put 'America first'. Buchanan opposed the North American Free Trade Agreement (NAFTA) for its potential impact on American sovereignty, immigration, identity, and jobs.

11.2.5 Realism and neoconservatism

In terms of priorities, realism and neoconservatism tend to emphasize the 'high politics' of national security issues over the 'low politics' of the economy and environment. Despite this, they can both still exert an important influence over foreign economic policies.

11.2.5.1 Prescriptive realism as ideology

The prescriptive aspects of realism have been promoted by key standard bearers including Machiavelli, Friedrich List, E. H. Carr, Henry Kissinger, John Mearsheimer, Stephen Walt, and Barry Posen. As an ideology, realism most represents the foreign policy of moderate conservatism. As Rathbun observes, '[r]ealism has traditionally found a home on the right of the political spectrum among conservatives as part of their general skepticism about reform and change in both domestic and foreign affairs . . . Many prominent conservatives, such as George Will and William F. Buckley, have defined conservatism in terms identical to how Carr has defined realism, that of seeing the world as it is, not as it might or should be' (2008: 281). Thus, realism today advises states to accept the world as it is and to focus on promoting their national interests and security rather than values. On security matters, this implies strong defence spending for 'deterrence' combined with 'restraint' in the use of military force to avoid creating new enemies. Military action should be for the 'containment' of strategic rivals rather than regime change or democracy promotion. International organizations such as the UN are simply arenas of power politics, meaning that states should pick and choose their participation based solely on their national interests.

On economic matters, the GPE literature has traditionally linked realism with economic nationalism and protectionism. This traces back to Friedrich List's 1840 *The National System of Political Economy*, which argued that the goal of economic policy should be to support national power. However, as Helleiner has argued, what matters are the goals of promoting national unity, power, autonomy, and sovereignty and not the specific policies used to do so. In other words, foreign economic policies that are focused on the national interest 'can be associated with a wide range of policy projects, including the endorsement of liberal economic policies' (2002: 308). This is why realists often advise free trade for powerful states and protectionism and industrial policy for less powerful states. However, even when realists support free trade, they still believe that security should always trump trade. This means always producing strategic products (those needed in wars or pandemics) at home, not exporting military equipment and strategic technology to rival states, and not being economically dependent on potential rivals. It also means focusing more on relative gains than absolute gains in trade policy to avoid helping strategic competitors such as China to promote their relative economic development (see Scott, Chapter 12, for discussion).

11.2.5.2 Neoconservatism

As with realism, neoconservative foreign policy is also more focused on high politics. However, where realists emphasize national interests and restraint, neoconservatives are the foreign policy hawks who advocate for promoting Western values abroad through a muscular foreign policy. This contrast was evident in the post-9/11 years where neoconservatives in the George W. Bush administration supported the 2003 invasion of Iraq to promote regime change while most realists were opposed. Ideologically, neoconservatives are further to the right than realists in that they seek to promote moral clarity, civic virtue, and patriotism. On security issues, this means viewing the world in terms of good and evil, avoiding neutrality, and taking sides to support allies and confront enemies with military force.

On economic issues, neoconservatives overlap with, but are not the same as, neoliberals. They support the 'tough love' of free market policies to promote the virtues of employment and self-reliance. However, as outlined in Irving Kristol's *Two Cheers for Capitalism* (not three cheers), neoconservatives are also critical of the way that excessively free markets privilege individual self-interest over civic virtue, and decadence and hedonism over moral character. For neoconservatives, therefore, morality and security must always trump free markets and free trade. At the international level, this implies a more targeted approach to trade that supports democratic allies while avoiding trade with authoritarian regimes. On international organizations and global governance, neoconservatives view the UN as an unnecessary constraint on US power that only serves to dilute the 'moral clarity' of US foreign policy. Illustrating this view, US neoconservative John Bolton noted that '[f]or virtually every area of public policy there is a globalist proposal, consistent with the overall objective of reducing individual nation-state autonomy, particularly that of the United States' (Bolton 2000: 220).

KEY POINTS

- Ideologies are competing sets of philosophical principles that can guide the policy preferences of different actors.

- While ideologies can vary across countries, prominent ideologies in the Anglo-American countries include: liberal internationalism, progressivism, neoliberalism, populist conservatism, realism, and neoconservatism.

- Liberal internationalism and progressivism are centre-left and left approaches that support greater government intervention in the economy to reduce inequality and deal with market failures such as recessions, financial crises, and environmental issues.

- Neoliberalism and populist conservatism are centre-right and right approaches found within modern conservative parties. Where neoliberals support free markets and less government intervention, populist conservatives support economic nationalism and limits on immigration.

- Realism and neoconservatism are centre-right approaches that focus on national security rather than economic issues. While generally supportive of free markets and free trade, they believe that national security considerations should always guide foreign economic policy.

11.3 Neoliberal and liberal support for economic globalization

Ideologies can help to explain the contemporary politics of globalization, anti-globalization, and global governance, including new forms of populism and economic nationalism. This began with the return to free trade and capital mobility that started in the 1970s at the regional level and that was most strongly supported by neoliberal actors. This included free market

politicians, intellectuals, think tanks, and advocacy groups as well as large corporations, business lobby groups, and much of the business media. While partially about mutual gains and access to new markets, the effort to promote free trade was also strongly motivated by the desire to create policy competition between countries (see Key Concept Box 11.3). This was seen as a way to impose structural constraints on the welfare state and create pressures for the adoption of more free market policies within countries.

11.3.1 UK neoliberals and the Common Market

In the United Kingdom, the shift to free trade took the form of membership in the European Economic Community (EEC, or 'Common Market'). Here support for joining, and later staying in, the Common Market was strongest within the Conservative Party and the business community. These proponents of free market policies had initially viewed the EEC as a protectionist bloc that would undermine broader efforts for global free trade. Over time, however, many of them came to view the Common Market as a way to constrain the interventionist policies of a resurgent Labour Party. As one neoliberal think tank observed, 'Conservatives feared that the return to power of the Labour Party would push British society further to the left . . . They saw in the [EEC] a capitalist club . . . [and] a barrier to Socialism' (Holmes 1994).

Following Britain's entry in 1973, neoliberal support for the Common Market was further demonstrated in 1975 when the Labour government held a referendum—similar to the 'Brexit' referendum of 2016—on whether Britain should remain in the EEC. The Conservative Party, then under Margaret Thatcher, strongly supported the 'Yes' campaign to remain in the Common Market. Similarly, the business community, led by its national lobby group the Confederation of British Industry (CBI), participated on an unprecedented scale. It did so by providing financial support, advertising, and the mobilization of employees, customers, and suppliers in support of the campaign. A decade after the 'Yes' campaign won the referendum, neoliberal support for the Common Market continued with strong support for the proposed Single European Act (SEA). The SEA proposal, which aimed to expand the process of economic regionalization in Europe, had been led by the European Roundtable of Industrialists (ERT), Europe's premier business lobby group.

Figure 11.1 Margaret Thatcher and William Whitelaw during the Conservative Group for Europe press conference in 1975. Years later, Thatcher stated her opposition to a centralized Europe in her renowned Bruges speech, addressed in Section 11.7 in this chapter, with her famous statement 'We did not roll back the frontiers of the state of Britain, only to see them reimposed at a European level' (Thatcher 1988).

Source: Alamy.

11.3.2 **US and Canadian neoliberals and the push for free trade**

In North America, the push for regional free trade began in the early 1980s with the Canadian business community's lobbying of the Conservative government for a Canada–US Free Trade Agreement (CUFTA). Hinting at its constraining effects, Republican President Ronald Reagan described the CUFTA as an 'economic constitution for North America' (quoted in Cameron 1988: x). The US business community, particularly the American Coalition for Trade Expansion which grew out of the US Business Roundtable's committee on trade, also supported the agreement, which was signed in 1987. In Canada, the 1988 election became a referendum on free trade with the Conservative Party, free market think tanks, and the business community campaigning strongly in support. Most prominent in the latter case was the Canadian Alliance for Trade and Job Opportunities, a coalition of Canada's main business associations including the Business Council on National Issues, the Canadian Chamber of Commerce, the Canadian Exporters' Association, the Canadian Federation of Independent Businesses, and the Canadian Manufacturers' Association. According to one of the country's main national newspapers, these efforts represented

an 'unprecedented involvement by business in an election' (Van Alphen 1988).

With Canada–US free trade a reality, neoliberal politicians and the North American business community then worked to expand the deal to include Mexico under NAFTA, which came into effect in 1994. At the same time, a similar coalition was working to promote free trade at the more global level. This included strong lobbying by business groups in North America, Europe, and elsewhere to ratify the recently concluded Uruguay Round negotiations of the General Agreement on Tariffs and Trade (GATT). In the US, for example, business interests created the 'Alliance for GATT NOW' to lobby Congress and build public support for the deal through advertising, getting the endorsement of 450 leading economists, issuing press releases and op-eds, and the lobbying of journalists and newspaper editorial boards. In 1995, these efforts, and similar ones in other countries, led to the ratification of the deal and creation of the World Trade Organization (WTO) (on the history of international trade negotiations, see Trommer, Chapter 5).

Also important is that, by this point, support for free trade agreements had spread to the centrist factions within many left-of-centre political parties, including the US Democrats under Bill Clinton, the Liberal Party in Canada, and many within the UK Labour Party. Overall, the push for free trade was led by neoliberal actors and then supported by liberal internationalists. It was also supported, with some reservations related to China, by neoconservatives and realists who saw free trade as enhancing the economic power of the US and the West more generally. Together, these groups came to represent the 'pro' side in the debate over globalization.

KEY POINTS

- Neoliberals/libertarians supported free trade based on the way that policy competition would impose constraints on progressive economic policies. Liberal internationalists supported free trade based on the promise of market access and mutual gains as well as peace through interdependence and modernization.

- In the UK, the shift to free trade began with Britain's 1973 entry into the European Economic Community (EEC, or 'Common Market'), which was deepened in 1986 through the Single European Act (SEA). Support for the Common Market, including during a 1975 referendum, was strongest within the Conservative Party and the business community.

- In North America, the shift to free trade began with the 1989 Canada–US Free Trade Agreement (CUFTA), which was expanded to include Mexico in the 1994 North American Free Trade Agreement (NAFTA). Support for these agreements was strongest among right-of-centre political parties and the business community.

- At the global level, the shift to free trade is most symbolized by the conclusion of the Uruguay Round negotiations of the General Agreement on Tariffs and Trade (GATT) and the 1995 creation of the World Trade Organization (WTO). Centre-right parties and the business community were again the most prominent supporters.

11.4 Progressive and populist conservative anti-globalization

In contrast to neoliberals, liberal internationalists, and the business community, progressives and populist conservatives strongly opposed the new free trade deals. They both agreed that economic globalization would hurt the economic interests of blue-collar workers by creating an outflow of manufacturing jobs and downward pressure on wages. However, in contrast to progressives, populist conservatives were also very concerned about immigration for both economic and cultural reasons. Where free trade was seen as moving blue-collar jobs to low-wage developing countries, they viewed immigration as bringing in low-wage workers from developing countries to take jobs in Europe and North America. At the same time, they also viewed immigration as a threat to the white, Christian culture of many populist conservative voters.

11.4.1 Progressive and populist opposition to the Common Market

In the UK for example, since Britain first joined the Common Market in 1973 the Labour Party had been split over the issue, with centrists being in favour and progressives opposed. The latter's views reflected the concerns of the labour movement—and its national organization the Trades Union Congress (TUC)—about the constraining effects of policy competition. Highlighting this point, Silvia notes that the TUC

'officially opposed British membership in the European Community altogether, arguing that it restricted British economic autonomy to a degree that rendered impossible the implementation of the TUC's economic program. Informally referred to as "Keynesianism in one country", this program called for expansionary government spending and increased trade restrictions to restore full employment' (1991: 631).

The split in the Labour Party caused its leader Harold Wilson, who came to power in 1974, to promise to renegotiate the UK's relationship with the EEC and then put the results to a referendum. In many ways, this foreshadowed the emergence of a similar split in the Conservative Party and a similar promise by its leader, Prime Minister David Cameron, to hold the 2016 Brexit referendum. In the 1975 referendum, the division within the Labour Party was evident, with almost a third of the cabinet and many Labour Members of Parliament (MPs) campaigning for the 'No' side. Also campaigning on the 'No' side was the Trades Union Congress and a number of individual unions. For the TUC, the renegotiation did not address any of the fundamental issues they had with the Common Market. Illustrating this point, the TUC noted that:

The development of the Community since its inception has been largely directed to business rather than social goals, to the elimination of obstacles to free competition and harmonization of the commercial environment. The effect has been to increase the mobility of capital . . .enabling business to avoid more easily its obligations to employees, and undermining the countervailing influences which the trade union movement might be able to bring to bear . . . there is no denying that the operations of the Community in elevating freedom of competition as the ideal in the determination of economic and social objectives has made the task of the European trade union movement in securing equity more difficult (TUC 1975).

Source: TUC Trades Union Congress

Populist conservatives also strongly opposed Britain joining the European Economic Community. First, many populist conservative voters came from rural communities and were worried about how the EEC's Common Agricultural Policy would affect Britain's system of agricultural preferences with the Commonwealth. Second, concerns over immigration and national identity were also paramount. This view was represented most prominently by the anti-immigration Conservative Member of Parliament Enoch Powell. As

Gamble reports, in the choice between the nation and the market, 'Powell had no doubt about his choice. The nation came first. Its preservation was ultimately much more important to him than the particular economic and social arrangements that were instituted by government' (1990: 37). It was for this reason that Powell ultimately left the Conservative Party when he voted for Labour based on the promise to hold a referendum on the EEC. Powell then campaigned for withdrawal from the Common Market on the 'No' side during the 1975 referendum.

Five years after the 'No' campaign lost the referendum, progressive opposition to the Common Market continued. In 1980, with Margaret Thatcher and the Conservatives in power, progressives in the Labour Party gained influence with the election of the left-leaning Michael Foot as leader. From that point on, the official position of the Labour Party was to withdraw from the EEC if elected. Unsurprisingly, both the Labour Party and the labour movement were opposed to the 1983 proposal for a Single European Act. For them, it would only amplify the policy competition between countries and thus the constraints on interventionist economic policies. As Silvia reports: 'Many labour officials feared that [the SEA] would undermine the position of unions in Europe and could trigger an outbreak of competitive "social dumping" (a contest among Member States to gain an economic edge by offering businesses low wage costs, weak labour laws, and minimal government regulation) that would deteriorate into a relentless downward spiral in the level of wages, benefits, and workers' rights throughout Europe' (1991: 626).

11.4.2 Progressive and populist opposition to North American trade

In North America, similar concerns over policy competition caused progressives in the US and Canada to oppose both the CUFTA and NAFTA free trade agreements. In Canada, free trade proposals led to the creation of a key anti-CUFTA activist group, the Council of Canadians (COC). By 1987, the COC had created a broad anti-free trade coalition of trade unions, environmental groups, church groups, women's organizations, and Indigenous groups under the banner of the Pro-Canada Network (PCN). This network of progressive activists, along with the left-leaning Liberal and New Democratic parties, campaigned strongly against CUFTA in Canada's 1988 'free trade election'.

A short time later, the same coalition then campaigned against NAFTA alongside their US counterparts. Among progressives, NAFTA was even more concerning in terms of policy competition. Specifically, by expanding free trade to Mexico—a developing country with much lower wages, environmental regulations, and corporate taxes—the concern was that more and more companies would move south to take advantage of the lower costs. This, in turn, would put much greater pressure on workers and governments in Canada and the US to cut wages, regulations, and corporate taxes to compete for jobs and remain 'competitive'. Illustrating this view, an American Federation of Labor-Congress of Industrial Organizations (AFL-CIO) spokesperson told a US congressional hearing that 'A free trade agreement with Mexico, a country where wages and social protections are almost nonexistent when compared with our own, simply invites disaster for U.S. workers' (quoted in Mayer 1998: 45).

American populist conservatives shared this view and combined it with their ongoing concerns over immigration. Most prominent here was Patrick Buchanan's 1992 candidacy for the Republican Party nomination. Running against George H. W. Bush ('Bush senior'), Buchanan advocated for a 'new nationalism' that would put 'America first'. His approach was 'free markets at home protected by a high tariff wall' (1993: 25). Buchanan strongly opposed NAFTA and other trade negotiations based on their implications for US sovereignty, immigration, identity, and jobs. As he later remarked: 'Free trade is the serial killer of American manufacturing and the Trojan Horse of world government. It is the primrose path to the loss of economic independence and national sovereignty. Free trade is a bright shining lie' (2005: 171).

11.4.3 Progressive and populist opposition to GATT and the WTO

Throughout the 1990s, coalitions of anti-trade progressives became increasingly transnational as their focus shifted from regional trade agreements to the GATT negotiations and the creation of the World Trade Organization in 1995. By 1999, these efforts reached a tipping point with the so-called 'Battle of Seattle'. Over 50,000 protestors showed up in the west coast city to protest the WTO's most recent round of trade negotiations and express their concerns over the

negative impact of free trade and economic globalization. As Prakash observes: 'These groups believe
that because globalization favours mobile capital over
(relatively) non-mobile resources, it empowers few
but impoverishes many, both in developing and developed countries. They allege that capital mobility, both
portfolio and foreign direct investment, abet races-to-
the-bottom, forcing governments to lower labour and
environmental standards' (2002: 514). In this way, progressive concerns over policy competition were at the
heart of this emerging 'anti-globalization' movement.

By the end of the 1990s, these were the lines drawn
in the politics of economic globalization. Neoliberals
and liberal internationalists were on the 'pro' side of
the debate, while progressives and populist conservatives were on the 'anti-globalization' or 'economic
nationalist' side. As discussed in Scott, Chapter 12,
China joined the WTO in 2001, and over the fifteen
years that followed economic globalization became
more entrenched, and the effects of free trade began
to manifest themselves. As this occurred, it became
apparent that 'pro-' and 'anti-' globalization were not
very accurate terms. Rather than trade and globalization themselves, what neoliberal actors supported,
and progressives opposed, were the constraints
imposed by policy competition. This is why both
groups seemed to change their positions when the
debate over economic globalization came to include
the issue of social globalization.

KEY POINTS

- Progressive actors such as trade unions, environmental
  groups, and many left-of-centre political parties
  opposed the shift towards economic regionalization
  and globalization. Whether in the European Common
  Market, NAFTA, or more globally through the WTO, they
  worried that free trade would lead to a loss of well-paid
  manufacturing jobs. They also worried that, due to policy
  competition, free trade would put downward pressure on
  wages, environmental regulations, and the corporate taxes
  needed to fund social programmes.

- Populist conservatives also opposed free trade and
  economic globalization. In addition to the outflow of
  manufacturing jobs, they saw immigration as a tool to bring
  in low-wage workers from developing countries to take
  jobs in Europe and North America. Immigration was also
  seen as a threat to the white, Christian culture of many
  populist conservative voters.

11.5 The pros and cons of economic globalization

Economic globalization brought many benefits, but
also costs. In the Global South, lower wages, regulations, and corporate tax rates caused many companies
to relocate their factories to developing countries such
as China, India, Mexico, and others. This inflow of jobs,
in turn, pulled over a billion people out of poverty, led
to the emergence of a middle class in these states, and
helped to somewhat reduce the economic disparities
between the developed and developing worlds. At the
same time, developed countries were able to import
cheaper goods from around the globe, resulting in
lower prices and greater consumer choice. However,
for blue-collar workers in the developed world, the
job gains experienced by these countries often came at
their expense. Hundreds of thousands of well-paying,
unionized manufacturing jobs were lost as companies
shifted factories to the lower-cost developing world
(see Case Study Box 11.4). Moreover, in addition to the
jobs that left, the ability of companies to threaten to
relocate did create the policy competition that both
neoliberals and progressives had anticipated.

11.5.1 Policy competition and the 'retreat of the state' debate

In the GPE literature, there has long been a debate
over the so-called retreat of the state and the extent
to which globalization actually caused job losses and
forced countries to compete for investment with
lower wages, regulations, and corporate taxes. Much
of this debate got bogged down over broader questions about sovereignty, the future of the nation-state,
and whether the constraints imposed by policy competition would lead to a full-blown race to the bottom and/or a retrenchment of the welfare state. At
the same time, many of the empirical studies focused
on the somewhat separate issue of financial capital
mobility and on whether government spending had
declined or not. Less attention was paid to the impact
on union membership, wages, pension benefits, and
a shifting of the tax burden through declining corporate tax rates and rising consumption taxes. While this
extensive debate cannot be resolved here, a few points
can be made. Government spending has remained
resilient, welfare states have not retrenched, and different models of welfare states have not all converged

CASE STUDY BOX 11.4 MANUFACTURING IN ONTARIO, CANADA

In 2008, Conservative Prime Minister Stephen Harper held a media event at Electro-Motive Diesel (EMD), a locomotive manufacturing plant in London, Ontario, Canada. London is a small city two hours west of Toronto located in Canada's manufacturing heartland in the southwest of the province of Ontario. The Prime Minister's media event was held to showcase the government's new corporate tax cuts, which they said would help to attract business investment and jobs to Canada. In 2010, the Electro-Motive Diesel plant was purchased by Caterpillar Inc, a US manufacturer of construction, mining, and other heavy machinery. Around the same time, Caterpillar also purchased locomotive plants in Brazil, Mexico, and the US state of Indiana.

Towards the end of 2011, as EMD started negotiating a new contract with its unionized workers, Caterpillar demanded an unprecedented cut to the workers' pay and benefits. This included a roughly 50 per cent pay cut for over half the

workers, as well as the elimination of cost-of-living increases, retiree benefits, and the defined-benefit pension plan. The union refused and, on 31 December 2011, the company locked out the workers to put pressure on the union. After a month of picketing, protests, and the company refusing to alter its demands for pay and benefit cuts, Caterpillar announced it was closing the factory and moving the work to its other plants in Brazil, Mexico, and Indiana. This occurred at the same time Caterpillar was posting record profits. It also occurred only thirty-six hours after the Republican governor of Indiana signed new 'right-to-work' legislation designed to attract business investment by making it much harder for unions to organize. As one business columnist observed, the Caterpillar case 'tells the larger story of why middle-class incomes have flat-lined across North America over the past three decades' (Olive 2012).

on the lowest common denominator. This means that exaggerated claims about a race to the bottom or an end of the welfare state have simply not come to fruition.

At the same time, however, large numbers of developed country manufacturing jobs have moved offshore (see Case Study Box 11.4), union membership and corporate tax rates have declined, and economic inequality within countries has increased significantly. In terms of corporate taxes, for example, Clausing, Saez, and Zucman report that '[b]etween 1985 and 2019, the global average statutory corporate tax rate has fallen from 49 percent to 23 percent, largely due to the rise of international tax competition' (2021: 1). Illustrating a similar trend in US private sector union membership, a study by the progressive-leaning Economic Policy Institute found that membership fell from a peak of 35.7 per cent in 1953 down to only 6.2 per cent in 2019 (Mishel, Rhinehart, and Windham 2020: 9). Union membership has been more resilient in the public sector, although this is mainly because, unlike companies, governments cannot threaten to relocate. The decline of unions, in turn, contributed to the vast growth in the number of part-time, contract, and temporary jobs, as well as to the stagnating wages, reduced pension benefits, and rising inequality within countries that have come to characterize the current era of economic globalization.

Regardless of the debate in the academic literature, these trends would seem to be more than a coincidence. First, if policy competition does not impose constraints on interventionist policies, it raises the fairly significant puzzle of why so many neoliberal and progressive economists and practitioners—including Hayek, Keynes, Buchanan, Oates, and scores of think tanks, unions, and advocacy groups—have believed that it does for over two thirds of a century (see Key Concept Box 11.3). Second, these trends have become so apparent that even many neoliberal proponents of free trade have started to acknowledge its downsides, particularly for blue-collar workers. As one of many examples, Stephen Harper, the former Conservative Prime Minister of Canada and strong proponent of free trade, recently wrote that '[m]illions of workers in advanced countries have experienced wage stagnation, job losses or both. As one example, manufacturing employment has fallen by one-third in the U.S. since 1980'. Moreover, while recognizing there are various factors involved, he further noted that 'trade is also partly responsible for the loss of manufacturing jobs. It is silly to claim otherwise. Workers and communities can point to factories and jobs that still exist but are now located offshore' (Harper 2018: 43). Harper also acknowledged the clear connection between these trends and rising populism on both the progressive and conservative sides of the political spectrum.

11.6 From anti-globalization to progressive global governance

Based on their opposition to free trade agreements, progressives were often portrayed as being protectionist, economically nationalist, and anti-globalization. However, rather than being opposed to trade and globalization, most progressive actors were primarily opposed to policy competition and the constraints it would impose on interventionist economic policies. To prevent this, they initially advocated a type of economic nationalism to bring the economy back down to the level of national democratic control. But over time, as free trade became more entrenched, progressives shifted from economic nationalism to progressive global governance as their main strategy for limiting policy competition. In other words, rather than bringing the global or regional economy back down to the level of national democratic control by ending free trade, they would bring democratic control up to the level of the global or regional economy through the creation of minimum standards on taxes, labour, and the environment. This would offset policy competition by creating a 'floor' below which no state is allowed to go in trying to attract business investment and jobs.

11.6.1 **UK progressives shift from anti- to pro-Europe**

One of the first and most explicit examples of this shift happened when the TUC dropped its opposition to the European Common Market and its proposed extension through the Single European Act. It did so in response to a 1988 speech given by Jacques Delors, the president of the European Commission, to the TUC, three years after the SEA had first been proposed. Delors told them that '[i]t is impossible to build Europe only by deregulation . . . the social dimension is a vital element' (Delors 1988). In doing so, he proposed what would later become known as the European 'Social Charter', an agreement that would offset policy competition through the creation of minimum labour and social standards. For the Trades Union Congress, as well as progressive MPs in the Labour Party, the social charter proposal led to an immediate shift in their view on Europe. They came to accept that economic regionalization was going to occur with or without them and that their best strategy was to get on board and attempt to nudge it in a more progressive direction. As one study noted: 'The enthusiastic reception given to the Charter by trade unions suggests that it will assist them. It is noteworthy, in this connection, that the British Trades Union Congress (TUC) abruptly changed its anti-community stance in 1988 in response to the advantages it perceived as emanating from the establishment of a Community-wide plinth of social rights' (Addison and Siebert 1991: 618).

11.6.2 **North American progressives push for enforceable regional standards**

In North America, progressive groups attempted (unsuccessfully) to follow the European example by advocating for enforceable labour and environmental side agreements to the NAFTA. This became possible when President Bill Clinton, a Democrat, came to power in 1993. As Mayer reports, '[t]he prospect of side agreements raised hope among some U.S. labor and environmental activists that Clinton might push for new international standards in these areas, something of a "social charter" along the lines of standards established by the European Union' (1998: 168–169). As with the European Social Charter, progressive think tanks in the US and Canada explicitly wanted minimum standards to offset policy competition. For example, the US Economic Policy Institute argued that NAFTA should include a 'Social Charter which establishes the principle that trade should not be based on "social dumping", where poorer countries follow low-wage, low regulation strategies in order to increase exports' (Faux and Lee 1992). At the same time, many trade unions also supported side agreements and minimum standards to prevent any downward harmonization of labour and environmental protections due to policy competition.

11.6.3 The shift to progressive global governance

In the years that followed, the shift among progressives from economic nationalism to progressive global governance became more widespread. In 2003 for example, George Monbiot, a progressive activist and commentator with the UK's *Guardian* newspaper, wrote a prominent column titled 'I Was Wrong About Trade' (Monbiot 2003). The column argued that, instead of opposing economic globalization, progressives should work to promote a rules-based international economy. Similarly, a number of progressive scholars created detailed proposals for progressive forms of global governance through books such as *Taming Globalization, Civilizing Globalization, Global Covenant,* and *Making Globalization Work.* In 2002, several so-called anti-globalization activists created the International Forum on Globalization, which produced a report titled *A Better World Is Possible: Alternatives to Economic Globalization.* According to the *Financial Times* newspaper, the report 'set out an alternative agenda calling for new institutions of global governance under a reformed United Nations', and it provided 'a sense of what is becoming the unifying theme of an inchoate movement: the creation of democratic institutions of global governance' (Harding 2002).

Today, most progressive activists and politicians have abandoned economic nationalism and opposition to international trade. Instead, they promote progressive global governance through the creation of minimum standards to offset policy competition. As the British Trades Union Congress notes, 'we are calling for labour standards, in particular the [UN International Labour Organization's] core labour standards, to be included in all agreements . . . This position is supported by the entire international trade union movement including unions in both developed and developing countries' (TUC 2007). In Canada, this approach became prominent through Prime Minister Justin Trudeau's so-called inclusive approach to trade, which advocated for minimum standards related to labour and the environment, as well as gender and Indigenous rights. In the United States, the Biden administration led efforts to implement a

global minimum corporate tax, and a deal was signed by 176 countries in 2021. Overall, these examples demonstrate that progressives were more concerned with policy competition than with free trade and economic globalization themselves. Moreover, it is this concern that explains their shift from anti-globalization to pro-global governance. It also explains the opposite shift which occurred among neoliberals.

KEY POINTS

- As free trade became more entrenched, progressives shifted from economic nationalism to progressive global governance as their main strategy for limiting policy competition.

- Progressive global governance involves the creation of minimum standards on taxes, labour, and the environment that offset policy competition. They do so by creating a 'floor' below which no state is allowed to go in attracting business investment and jobs.

- Examples of progressive global governance include: the European Social Charter; the attempts to add enforceable labour and environmental side agreements to NAFTA and other trade agreements; international climate action deals; the Trudeau government's 'inclusive approach to trade'; and the Biden administration's global minimum corporate tax.

11.7 The new populism: Neoliberal and conservative nationalism

When progressive actors argued against free trade and economic globalization, neoliberals responded with an internationalist discourse that stressed mutual gains and market access while de-emphasizing their more controversial goal of policy competition. However, as progressives swung from anti-globalization to progressive global governance, neoliberals also switched their position on globalization to one that can be described as 'neoliberal nationalism' (Harmes 2012; 2019). Specifically, neoliberals began to use the language of nationalism and sovereignty to oppose progressive global governance because they knew it would offset policy competition. As they did so, their position began to somewhat overlap with the nationalist views of populist conservatives. In fact, neoliberal media outlets often used nationalism, xenophobia, and anti-immigration discourses to deflect blame for stagnating wages and rising inequality and to rally populist conservative voters against progressive global governance. It is this sequence of events that helps to explain the rise of populist conservatism that manifested itself in the UK's 2016 'Brexit' vote and the election of US President Donald Trump that same year. Importantly, the resurgence of both conservative and progressive forms of populism can be found around the world (see Case Study Box 11.6).

11.7.1 UK neoliberals shift from pro-Europe to Eurosceptic

In the UK, just as the European Social Charter caused the British Trades Union Congress and Labour Party to become pro-Europe, it also caused Prime Minister Margaret Thatcher and many British neoliberals to become very anti-Europe, or 'Eurosceptic'. Illustrating this point was Thatcher's famous 'Bruges speech'—given in Bruges, Belgium—where she outlined her opposition to the minimum social and labour standards contained in the Social Charter: 'We have not successfully rolled back the frontiers of the state in Britain', she argued, 'only to see them reimposed at the European level' (Thatcher 1988). For British neoliberals and much of the business community, the Bruges speech became a rallying cry against the European Union. It led to the creation of a new free market think tank—the Bruges Group—explicitly created 'to promote the idea of a less centralised European structure' (Bruges Group 2018).

The shift among neoliberals from pro-Europe to Eurosceptical also occurred among the free

---

EVERYDAY GPE BOX 11.5 RACE, GENDER, AND POPULISM: EVERYDAY IDEOLOGY AND THE US 'CULTURE WARS'

The increasing influence of both progressive and conservative forms of populism has contributed to a growing politicization of people's everyday lives and a growing polarization over issues related to race and gender. In people's daily activities, ideology has become more visible and visceral as more and more cultural issues—from immigration to bathrooms to school curriculums to police budgets to vaccinations—are viewed as existential battles between good and evil. Political parties on the left and right have often been unwilling to address the economic concerns of their voters for fear of alienating their respective business-oriented supporters. The result has been a greater relative priority given to identity politics as an alternative way to address the concerns of their parties' grassroots. Moreover, when combined with ideologically oriented media outlets, and social media echo chambers, these strategies have worked to amplify the more strident voices, and thus polarization, in the so-called culture wars.

On the right, President Trump's election demonstrated the growing influence of the populist conservative faction within the US Republican Party; an ideological faction that places much greater emphasis on cultural issues related to race and gender. Many populist conservative voters are white religious conservatives from small town and rural communities who view progressive social policies as a threat to their cultural and religious identity. On race-related issues, this can lead to strong opposition to immigration, multiculturalism, and diversity policies that they view as biased against them. On gender issues, the religiosity of these voters leads to a greater emphasis on opposing abortion, LGBTQ and trans rights, sex education, and what they see as an overreach on certain feminist issues. President Trump catered to these voters through a wide range of policies such as the so-called Muslim ban, restrictions on immigration, a promise to 'build the wall' on the US–Mexico border, and the appointment of strongly social conservative judges to the Supreme Court, a policy that resulted in the most significant change to abortion laws in modern US history. Along with conservative media outlets and other Republican politicians, President Trump has also amplified the concerns of these voters through a continuous framing of progressive policies on race and gender as a threat to their way of life. Attacks on 'wokeism', critical race theory, pronoun politics, and 'cancel culture' as well as social movements such as Black Lives Matter and #MeToo were all designed to mobilize populist conservative voters.

On the left, the growing influence of the progressive faction within the Democratic Party also contributed to a greater focus on issues of racial and gender equality and to the emergence of more strident positions on some of these issues. In part, this reflected the understandable impatience of many groups with the slow pace on some equality issues. It also reflected fears over the growing mobilization of populist conservatives and how this added greater urgency to their concerns. But as Democrats also gave greater priority to identity issues, their efforts contributed to a partisan action-reaction dynamic that amplified the culture wars and the politicization of everyday life. Therefore, while populist ideologies are essential to understanding the political economy of globalization and anti-globalization, they are also essential to understanding today's identity politics and the growing merger of ideology and identity (for a discussion on the intersections of identity and attitudes towards trade, see Guisinger, Chapter 6).

market-oriented media, with the Rupert Murdoch-owned outlets being the most prominent. As Daddow reports '[t]he medium might change from broadsheets to tabloids, but the Murdoch message has been the same: deregulated free markets are under threat from the existence of a powerful EU' (2012: 1230). In terms of the relationship between neoliberalism and populist conservatism, the Murdoch approach has been described as 'market populism' based on its use of populist discourse to promote free market policies. Highlighting this trend, Daddow notes that '[t]abloid coverage of European affairs took on a qualitatively different tone in Britain during the 1980s. It became more bombastic, injected a greater sense of urgency into the debates by presenting treaty reforms as existential threats to British sovereignty and identity' (2012: 1232). It was in this way that neoliberal opposition to the progressive aspects of the EU fanned the flames of populist conservative nationalism.

11.7.2 From neoliberal to populist conservative Euroscepticism

The rise of populist conservatism in Britain became most prominent with the emergence of the United Kingdom Independence Party (UKIP), whose entire purpose was to promote Britain's exit from the European Union. Tellingly, both its creator, historian Alan Sked, and its leader during the 2016 Brexit campaign, Nigel Farage, were former members of the neoliberal Bruges Group think tank. Significant for UKIP's growth was the 2008 'Great Recession' that began in the United States. By 2010, the recession led to a crisis of the euro, growing austerity measures, and ever larger bailouts of countries such as Greece by the EU. As the crisis and bailouts continued, the EU moved towards greater economic integration through various proposals for a fiscal union. In Britain, talk of a fiscal union further increased neoliberal and populist conservative opposition to the European Union. As one study by the UK House of Commons Library reported, '[t]he eurozone crisis and EU moves towards closer fiscal, as well as economic and political, union, have given rise to renewed questioning of the UK's relationship with the EU' (Miller 2012). This questioning manifested itself in the growing strength of UKIP as well as various motions, by Conservative backbench MPs, to hold a Brexit referendum.

11.7.3 Neoliberals, populist conservatives, and Brexit

In the run-up to the 2015 British election, many populist conservative voters had left the Conservative Party for UKIP and the Conservatives themselves became more divided. In response, Prime Minister David Cameron followed the same path as the Labour Prime Minister in 1974; he promised to hold a referendum on Europe if he won the election. The Conservatives did win re-election in 2015, and Cameron held the Brexit referendum in 2016. In many ways, the populism that had been amplified by neoliberal interests went farther than many of them had intended. The business community, for example, opposed the progressive aspects of the EU but did not want to leave the single market and, accordingly, they campaigned in favour of the 'Remain' side.

Neoliberal purists within the free market think tanks and advocacy groups, however, did support the 'Leave' campaign, along with UKIP, a large number of Conservative Party MPs, the tabloid press, and the populist former mayor of London (and later prime minister) Boris Johnson. To build public support for Brexit, the Leave campaign emphasized the populist rather than neoliberal arguments against the EU. This included taking a page from the UKIP playbook by focusing heavily on immigration issues to mobilize populist conservative voters; a strategy that was aided by the refugee crisis resulting from the Syrian civil war. Overall, Brexit originated in neoliberal opposition to the progressive governance of the EU and the use of nationalism and identity politics to mobilize populist conservative voters.

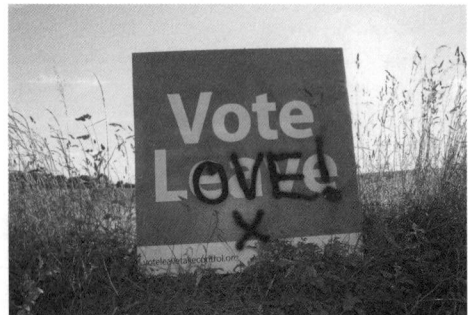

Figure 11.2 This sign shows the juxtaposition of both sides of public opinion in the Brexit 2016 referendum.

Source: Alamy.

11.7.4 **Neoliberal nationalism in the US**

In the United States, a similar combination of neo-liberal nationalism and populist conservatism ulti-mately contributed to the election of President Donald Trump in 2016. As in Europe, US neoliberals had grown increasingly concerned with the growing number of proposals related to progressive global governance, including international climate agree-ments, the Organization for Economic Cooperation and Development (OECD) Initiative on Harmful Tax Competition, and various regulations on business. Illustrating this view, Roger Bate of the prominent free market think tank the American Enterprise Insti-tute (AEI) argued:

. . . there has been a slow and now accelerating push for global governance, and away from the sovereignty of nation-states . . . The global governance institutions that pressure groups, bureaucrats and politicians promote include international treaties on numerous issues such as climate change, chemicals, and tobacco. There are also proposals pushed by powerful and respected international bodies for agreements on labour standards, environmental protection, and tax harmonization. These entail an entirely different form of globalization – one that is beginning to have a significant, and deleterious, effect (Bate 2004).

To discuss these concerns, the AEI held a key confer-ence in April of 2000 titled 'Trends in Global Gover-nance: Do They Threaten American Sovereignty?'.

As with progressives before them, US neoliberals were more focused on policy competition (and their desire to maintain it) than they were on protecting national sovereignty. Reflecting this view, they began to distinguish between good and bad forms of glo-balization and were selective in their concerns over sovereignty. For example, constraints on progressive governments due to free trade and policy competi-tion are viewed as acceptable, whereas attempts to offset these constraints through minimum standards are not. As the AEI's Jeremy Rabkin observes, 'the trading system is fundamentally compatible with tra-ditional notions of sovereignty' (1998: 86). However, climate treaties are, in contrast, 'by almost every cri-terion, a disturbing challenge to constitutional limi-tations on the treaty power' (1998: 80). Similarly, the AEI's Roger Bate further notes that 'It's tax harmo-nization that can lead to the greatest loss of national sovereignty' (Bate 2004).

11.7.5 **Neoliberals, populist conservatives, and the 'Tea Party'**

As in the UK, neoliberal actors and media outlets used market populism, nationalism, and identity politics to mobilize populist conservative voters against inter-ventionist policies, including those related to pro-gressive global governance. Significant here was the Rupert Murdoch-owned Fox News Channel, which framed issues such as immigration, environmental policy, and the 'culture wars' as threats to the liveli-hood and identity of populist conservative voters (see Everyday GPE Box 11.5). With the election of Presi-dent Obama, this growing fusion between neoliberals and populist conservatives led to the emergence of the 'Tea Party' protest movement and its growing influ-ence within the Republican Party. Significant funding for the Tea Party movement came from Americans for Prosperity, a prominent neoliberal advocacy group created and funded by the billionaire Koch brothers. In a similar fashion to neoliberals in the UK, the Tea Party movement used market populism to mobilize populist conservative voters. Also similar was that the populism fanned by neoliberal actors may have gone farther than they intended, with the neoliberal donors eventually being overtaken by the rise of populist conservatism and its manifestation in the election of President Donald Trump.

11.7.6 **Donald Trump and the rise of US populist conservatism**

The election of Donald Trump represented the ascendancy of populist conservatism in the United States. Trump's campaign revived Patrick Buchanan's 'America first' nationalism, with its strong concerns over immigration and trade and in which he continu-ously referred to NAFTA as 'a disaster'. His chief strat-egist, Steve Bannon, was the executive chair of the populist conservative news website Breitbart News. Bannon describes himself as an 'economic national-ist' who strongly opposes the 'globalist' agenda of free trade and pro-immigration policies because of their negative impact on the American working class and on US sovereignty and identity. As Bannon noted, '[t]he globalists gutted the American working class and created a middle class in Asia' (quoted in Wolff 2016). When President Trump took office, this economic nationalist position manifested itself in the US with-drawal from the Trans-Pacific Partnership (TPP) free

CASE STUDY BOX 11.6 POPULISM BEYOND THE ANGLOSPHERE

The resurgence of populism, in both its conservative and progressive forms, has not been limited to the Anglosphere countries. Prominent examples of right-wing populism include Jair Bolsanaro in Brazil, Viktor Orbán in Hungary, and Marine Le Pen in France. Prominent examples of left-wing populism include the Podemos party in Spain, Luiz Inácio Lula da Silva in Brazil, and the Syriza movement in Greece. Moreover, while these right and left forms of populism do share similarities with their Anglosphere counterparts, it is important to recognize that considerable differences exist between and among them. Therefore, as with ideologies in general, the causes and policy preferences of different populist movements must always be viewed as context dependent rather than universal.

In Latin America, populism has a long history and has often leaned towards the socialist left. This is why some have sought to contrast the 'inclusionary' left-wing populism of Latin America with the more 'exclusionary' right-wing form that became prominent in Europe after the 2008 Great Recession and the Syrian refugee crisis (Mudde and Kaltwasser 2013). However, this characterization does not really hold given that both right and left populisms are significant on both continents. Highlighting this in Latin America was the 2022 Brazilian election between the progressive Luiz Inácio Lula da Silva and the populist conservative Jair Bolsanaro.

Luiz Inácio Lula da Silva (often known as 'Lula') was a union leader and founder of the Workers' Party who first served as Brazil's president from 2003–2010. Like progressives more generally, he promoted left-of-centre economic policies including social programmes aimed at reducing poverty and increasing food security. He also sought to advance a more inclusive education system and reassert control over the country's regulatory agencies, which he claimed had become beholden to elite private interests. After a corruption conviction prevented him from continuing to run for office, da Silva returned to contest the 2022 election against right-wing incumbent Jair Bolsanaro. In doing so, he continued to advocate for a progressive agenda, including reversing previous cuts to public services and social programmes and asserting more control over oil resources as a way to lower energy prices, reduce inflation, and improve food security.

Lula's right-wing opponent, Jair Bolsanaro, had come to power in 2018 at a time when Brazil was plagued by economic crisis and the sitting president—Dilma Rousseff of the Workers' Party—had been impeached for corruption. Similar to populist conservatives elsewhere, Bolsanaro drew much of his support from evangelical Christians, who constituted about one third of Brazil's population, as well as many members and supporters of the military. His policies reflected a strongly populist

conservative agenda that was often compared to that of US President Donald Trump. On social issues, this included easing gun control restrictions, tough-on-crime justice policies, anti-abortion and LGBTQ+ rights, as well as freedom of religion and speech policies. On economic and foreign policy issues, Bolsanaro promoted privatization and social programme cuts, attacked international institutions, and offered strong support for Israel. Another similarity between Bolsanaro and Trump was that, when Bolsanaro lost the 2022 election, he made strong claims of election fraud and his supporters rioted in a manner similar to the 6 January storming of the US Congress by Trump supporters.

In Europe, the populism that emerged in the wake of the 2008 Great Recession and the 2015 Syrian refugee crisis also came in both conservative and progressive forms. In the former case, Hungary's Viktor Orbán became a prominent standard-bearer for the rise of populist conservatism in Europe. Orbán had been Prime Minister of Hungary from 1998–2002 and was later re-elected in 2010. Since that time, he has adopted many socially conservative policies, such as restricting LGBTQ+ rights, to promote his broader notion of 'Christian democracy'. He has also promoted nationalist and xenophobic policies to restrict immigration, increase the domestic birth-rate, and limit multiculturalism. Also in line with some tenets of populist conservatism has been Orbán's push towards authoritarianism and illiberal democracy. This included controversial and socially conservative changes to the Hungarian constitution, efforts to limit judicial independence, and greater constraints on the freedom of the press. Like Bolsanaro in Brazil, Orbán has been endorsed by prominent populist conservatives in the US, including Donald Trump, Trump-advisor Steve Bannon, and Fox News host Tucker Carlson.

On Europe's populist left, a similarly prominent example was Greece's Coalition of the Radical Left–Progressive Alliance party, more commonly known as Syriza. In the wake of the 2008 Great Recession and subsequent Greek debt crisis, Syriza was able to capitalize on growing popular opposition to the severe programme cuts and other austerity policies being implemented by the Greek government. For example, the party's popular support went from just under 5 per cent in 2009 to over 36 per cent when it won the 2015 election under its leader Alexis Tsipras. That year, as a key representative of Europe's growing anti-austerity populism, Tsipras was named one of *Time* magazine's 100 most influential people. Moreover, in addition to opposing austerity measures, Syriza used its four years in office to promote a broadly progressive agenda including secular and inclusive social policies, versions of progressive global governance, and strongly interventionist economic and environmental policies.

trade agreement, the 'trade war' with China, and in the renegotiation of NAFTA. It also manifested itself in Trump's various efforts to limit immigration, including his 'build the wall' proposal.

KEY POINTS

- As progressives swung from anti-globalization to progressive global governance, neoliberals also switched their position on globalization to one that can be described as 'neoliberal nationalism'.

- Neoliberal actors began to use the language of nationalism and sovereignty to rally populist conservative voters against progressive global governance because they knew it would offset policy competition.

- This sequence of events, combined with the Great Recession and growing concerns over immigration and identity, help to explain the UK's 'Brexit' vote and the election of US President Donald Trump in 2016.

- Rising inequality, the Great Recession, and concerns over immigration and identity also contributed to a surge of left and right populism beyond the Anglosphere countries.

11.8 Conclusion

This chapter examined how political ideologies can help to explain the contemporary politics of globalization, anti-globalization, and global governance, including new forms of populism and economic nationalism. It showed how the political competition between different ideological factions—including neoliberals, liberal internationalists, progressives, and populist conservatives—contributed to a globalization/anti-globalization sequence that has been strongly consistent across the Anglo-American countries.

This sequence started with support for economic globalization and regionalization among neoliberals and liberal internationalists and opposition among progressives and populist conservatives. Over time, as regional and global free trade and economic integration became more entrenched, a realignment occurred. Progressives shifted from anti-globalization to progressive global governance; a form of social globalization to offset the negative side-effects of economic globalization. While liberal internationalists also supported this agenda, neoliberals strongly opposed it, and they employed the language of populism to mobilize populist conservative voters against the 'globalist' agenda. As they did so, populist conservatives began to overtake the neoliberals, and this contributed to Brexit, the election of US President Donald Trump, and the rise of populism more broadly.

Between the economic nationalism of populist conservatives and the progressive global governance of progressives and liberal internationalists, there is clearly a strong challenge to the neoliberal form of globalization and the retreat of government economic intervention that came with it. At the same time, the national security concerns of realists and neoconservatives have been gaining in prominence. The rise and growing assertiveness of China, the COVID-19 pandemic, and the Russian invasion of Ukraine have all served to highlight some of the downsides of economic interdependence. What all of these trends imply is that any resurgence of the state in the years to come may be more about the return of government economic intervention—to manage rising inequality, global-level issues, and national security—than it is about the state as an institution. What they also imply is that an understanding of political ideologies, and the actors that promote them, will remain essential to explaining and predicting what the future may hold.

? 11.9 QUESTIONS

1. Which ideologies do different political parties in the Anglo-American countries represent?

2. What types of institutional, electoral, and other constraints do political parties face when trying to promote their ideological preferences?

3. What are the main differences between progressives, liberal internationalists, neoliberals, and populist conservatives on international trade?

4. What would neoconservatives and realists have done differently on trade and globalization? How could/should national security considerations influence foreign economic policy?

5. How do ideological differences and divisions play out in our everyday lives?

6. What is policy competition?

7. What is progressive global governance and how does it address the issue of policy competition?

8. What is neoliberal nationalism and how did it contribute to the rise of populist conservatism?

9. How has the growing influence of progressives and populist conservatives affected policies related to race and gender?

10. Is today's economic globalization reversible? What are the different scenarios that could cause a resurgence of the state?

11.10 FURTHER READING

Dueck, C. (2019), *Age of Iron: On Conservative Nationalism* (NYC: Oxford University Press). This book examines the long history and recent rise of populist (nationalist) conservatism in the US Republican party.

Freeden, M., Sargent, L. T., and Stears, M. (eds.) (2013), *The Oxford Handbook of Political Ideologies* (Oxford: Oxford University Press). This edited collection examines how ideologies have been studied and theorized in political science as well as a wide variety of contemporary political ideologies from across the spectrum and around the world.

Harmes A. (2019), *The Politics of Fiscal Federalism: Neoliberalism versus Social Democracy in Multilevel Governance* (Montreal: McGill-Queens University Press). This book provides a more detailed account of the themes covered in this chapter, including detailed cases on globalization/global governance, Brexit, North American regionalism, and the neoliberal and social democratic approaches to federalism and multilevel governance.

Held, D., and McGrew, A. (2007), *Globalization/Anti-Globalization* (Cambridge: Polity Press). This book examines the key debates over economic globalization and the ideologies and actors that participate in them.

Helleiner, E. (2023), *The Contested World Economy: The Deep and Global Roots of International Political Economy* (Cambridge: Cambridge University Press). This book examines the history and development of economic ideas and ideologies from around the world in a way that highlights the global diversity of economic thought.

Kaltwasser, C. R., Taggart, P. A., Espejo, P. O., and Ostiguy, P. (eds.) (2017), *The Oxford Handbook of Populism* (Oxford: Oxford University Press). This edited collection examines the nature, origins, and varieties of contemporary populism across different regions and policy issues.

Mansbach, R. W., and Ferguson, Y. H. (2021), *Populism and Globalization: The Return of Nationalism and the Global Liberal Order* (London: Palgrave Macmillan). This book examines the recent rise of conservative populism and its implications for globalization and the liberal world order.

Norris, P., and Inglehart, R. (2019), *Cultural backlash: Trump, Brexit, and Authoritarian Populism* (Cambridge: Cambridge University Press). This is one of the most cited books on the origins and varieties of contemporary populism across different countries.

Rupert, M. (2000), *Ideologies of Globalization: Contending Visions of a New World Order* (NYC: Psychology Press). This book examines the competition between left and right ideologies over the return to free trade and economic globalization in the 1980s and 1990s.

Stiglitz, J. E. (2017), *Globalization and its Discontents Revisited: Anti-globalization in the Era of Trump* (NYC: W. W. Norton & Company). This book is one of the most cited critiques of economic globalization by Nobel prize winning economist Joseph Stiglitz.

CONTRIBUTOR NOTE

Adam Harmes is an Associate Professor in the Department of Political Science at the University of Western Ontario. His most recent book is *The Politics of Fiscal Federalism: Neoliberalism vs Social Democracy in Multilevel Governance* (McGill-Queen's University Press, 2019).

12

China and the Global Political Economy

James Scott

Chapter contents

Reader's guide

The global political economy (GPE) is undergoing a moment of profound change and upheaval, precipitated by (among other things) the shifting of the centre of the global economy back towards Asia, where it had traditionally been until the shock of colonialism and European industrialization. Key states have greatly increased their influence over international affairs, particularly China as it has registered decades of sustained, rapid economic growth and come to dominate global manufacturing capacity. This chapter explores some of the challenges generated by China and the other so-called rising powers, including increased military and diplomatic confrontation, the erosion of core norms that underpin key institutions of economic governance such as the World Trade Organization (WTO), and the creation of new institutions that may undermine the existing framework of global economic governance. Such considerations enable us not only to reflect on the future of global political economy, but also question the basis of the existing set of approaches, norms, and institutions of global governance whom they were created to benefit and the extent of their claims to legitimacy.

12.1 Introduction

Perhaps no recent issue in global political economy (GPE) has generated so large a response, and one exhibiting as great a diversity of opinion, as that of the impact of the so-called **rising powers**. In 2001 the Goldman Sachs economist Jim O'Neill coined the acronym BRICs (with a small s) from Brazil, Russia, India, and China, setting out the potential they held for financial investors (O'Neill 2001), and subsequent years saw a deluge of research and comment on the impact that these countries were having on international affairs. O'Neill was one of the first to recognize the extent to which the centre of economic power was shifting away from the West, primarily eastward towards Asia.

In 2009 the states themselves set up the BRICS Forum, with a capital S from 2010 when South Africa was integrated into the group, which has given birth to a variety of economic and political institutions, including the BRICS Development Bank (subsequently renamed the New Development Bank) and the BRICS Credit Reserve Arrangement. The creation of these new institutions has sparked great debate about whether the existing global economic system centred on the United States (US) and the Bretton Woods Institutions (the World Bank and International Monetary Fund) is being directly challenged by the rising powers, or whether they will be complementary. That debate is mirrored in discussion of how the shift in economic muscle towards the BRICS has changed the political dynamics of the existing multilateral institutions, particularly the World Trade Organization (WTO), potentially rendering it all but defunct.

This chapter explores these debates, addressing the question of how the rising powers are impacting the GPE and the institutions that govern it. But it does so in a way that is mindful of the fact that these institutions are not neutral forums that are having their smooth operation disrupted by changing power dynamics. Rather, they are amalgams of ideas and power dynamics that have always worked to privilege some and marginalize others. The established Western powers are facing challenges to the ways in which their interests have been favoured. Throughout the chapter, the behaviour of the rising powers is juxtaposed with that of the established powers, as a means of exploring areas of continuity and difference. Through this we see the hypocrisy of some of the criticisms levelled at the likes of China.

Indeed, all too often, commentary on the rise of China, India, and Brazil has been shaped by preconceived ideas and prejudices, with China in particular presented as being a threat, working relentlessly to overthrow the Western order (Mawdsley 2008). As will be seen in more detail below, clear-headed analysis suggests that this characterization may at times be exaggerated. Nonetheless, China is also presenting significant challenges to the international system, particularly around the norms concerning the role of the state in the economy, the use of trade as a weapon of foreign policy, and fomenting regional security concerns.

The chapter unfolds as follows. Following this introduction, Section 12.2 examines the concept of 'rising powers' and whether the term continues to be (or indeed ever was) analytically meaningful. It also sets out why China warrants particular attention. Section 12.3 examines the global trade system and the ways in which Brazil, India, and China have affected the political dynamics of the WTO, focusing on the Doha Round negotiations. It then explores in more detail China's impact on the WTO, both within the Doha Round and beyond, and the contentious debates that have arisen thereon. Subsequently we turn away from the trade system to explore the new institutions of global governance that have been created by the BRICS, with a particular focus on the Asian Infrastructure and Investment Bank and China's associated Belt and Road Initiative. Again, the chapter examines the competing narratives that have arisen around this phenomenon and the need for great care in interpreting whether such actions are truly challenging to the existing world order. The penultimate section analyses the importance of getting those narratives right, and how the discourse surrounding China's rise can further inflame tensions. The final section concludes.

12.2 Problematizing the 'rising powers' concept

The whole notion of 'rising powers' has always been problematic from the moment it entered academic discourse, collapsing very disparate countries into a single category that arguably makes little analytical sense. Beginning with Jim O'Neill's early intervention, the rising power phenomenon came to be most closely associated with the BRICs (or BRICS, depending on whether South Africa was being included), but this was immediately subject to strong critique. Russia is not so much a rising power as an old power temporarily suppressed by the collapse of the Soviet Union, and is consequently analytically quite different to the others (Macfarlane 2006). In fact, a similar argument can be made for China, albeit on a longer timescale, which is recovering the pre-eminent economic position it held for many centuries until global order was disrupted by the industrial revolution and imperialism (Turner 2009). South Africa is economically incomparable to the likes of China and could perhaps be more usefully analysed within a grouping 'beyond the BRICs' (vom Hau, Scott, and Hulme 2012). In fact, as Figure 12.1 shows, economic weight within the BRICS is massively skewed towards China, which is the only country that has attained an economic status remotely similar to the Western powers. That said, as Figure 12.2 indicates, India is following in its wake, sustaining very high growth rates across the last ten years which, if maintained, will lead to it becoming another economic giant. Brazil and South Africa, by contrast, are achieving low rates of growth, or indeed negative growth in per capita income. Both are important regional actors but lack the economic weight to affect the global political economy deeply other than when acting in concert with the likes of China. For all of these reasons, it is of dubious analytical usefulness to lump these countries together as examples of a 'rising power' phenomenon.

Such considerations are compounded by the fact that more than twenty years have now passed since the BRICS term was first coined, and much has changed over that period. It makes little sense to see China in particular as 'rising' regardless of economic performance since it is now the second largest economy in the world and has surely in a sense 'risen'. Moreover, Russia's **neo-colonialist** invasion of Ukraine in 2022 demonstrates its willingness to profoundly shake the existing global order and operate against the most basic foundations of UN-based international law, including sovereign equality and the prohibition against the use of force (Snyder 2022). Other members of the BRICS, notably India and China, hold anti-colonialism as a core tenet of their national identities (albeit not so strongly as to outright condemn Russian actions in Ukraine) as a consequence of their histories with the British empire. Again, the diversity between the BRICS or 'rising powers' is such that using the term as a category of analysis is of dubious value. Its continued usage reflects as much as anything a hangover from the past, or the failure to identify a better term.

Figure 12.1 GDP, US$ billions, 2000 and 2021

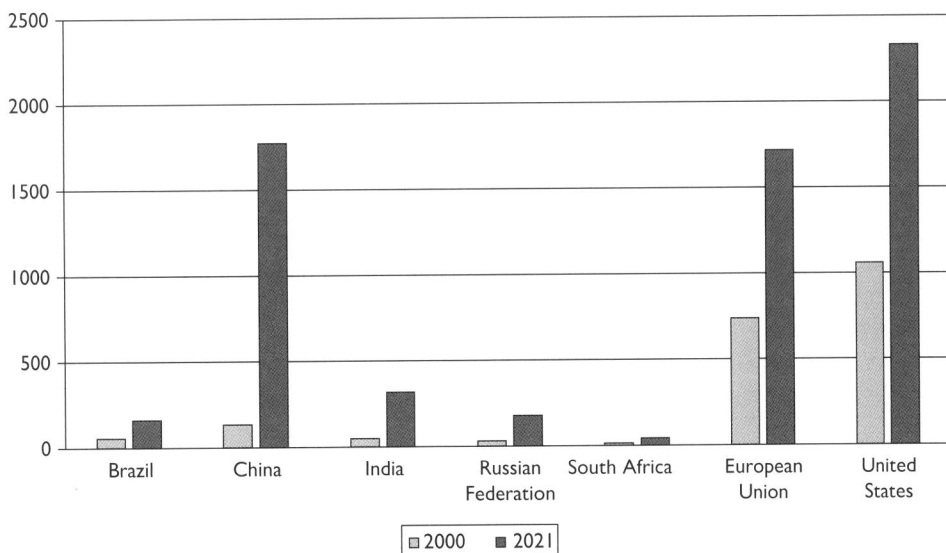

Source: World Bank data, available from https://data.worldbank.org/.

Figure 12.2 Growth rates in gross domestic product (GDP) and GDP per capita, 2012–2021 averages

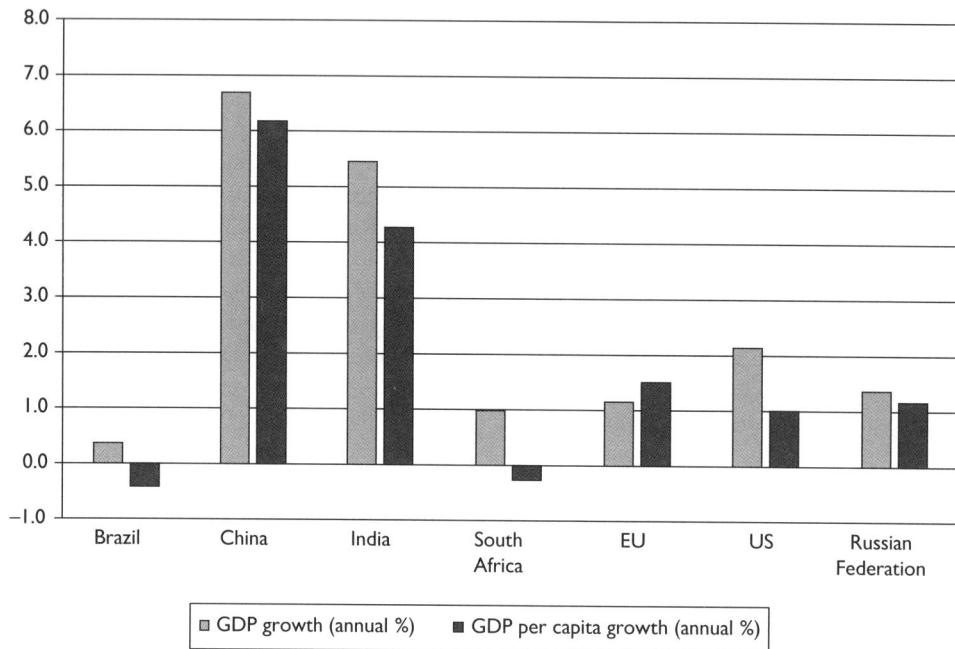

Source: World Bank data, available from https://data.worldbank.org/.

Given this diversity, the best approach is often to explore specific issue areas or specific countries. In that vein, this chapter focuses first on the multilateral trade system as a key area within global political economy that has been significantly impacted by the emergence of new powerful actors, focusing on China, India, and Brazil and the various ways in which they have sought to influence the direction of trade governance. The chapter then focuses on China and its creation of new institutions, as the country that has elicited the greatest academic attention. Nonetheless, the chapter does use the term 'rising powers' for ease of expression, but the caveats above should be borne in mind throughout.

KEY POINTS

- The concept of 'rising powers' is widely used but it is, and always has been, highly problematic.
- The BRICS set of countries is by far the most widely used group, though there is little that links them and it is analytically dubious.

- China stands out as having had the greatest impact on the global political economy, through its enormous size and sustained economic growth.
- Given the diversity, the best approach is often to look at specific issue areas and specific countries.

12.3 Rising powers in the multilateral trade system

Trade has been one of the areas of greatest tension brought about by the shift in economic weight towards the rising powers, particularly China. Here we will examine the WTO and its (ultimately failed) round of trade negotiations, the Doha Round, as a key site of tension, though space does not allow for a full examination of the institution (for which, see Trommer, Chapter 5). We see that Brazil, India, and China have had a significant impact on the WTO, though in different ways and to different degrees (see Hopewell 2016). In order to be able to apprehend that impact we must first outline the nature of the trade system as it was before the present-day rising powers emerged as key players.

The post-Second World War trade system was constructed around the General Agreement on Tariffs and Trade (GATT), which held eight rounds of trade negotiations between its inception in 1947 and its replacement by the WTO in 1995. These rounds followed a fairly consistent pattern, in which the most powerful, industrialized countries set the agenda, formed the nucleus of the negotiations, and largely dictated outcomes (Wilkinson 2014). Negotiations followed what has been called a concentric circle (Kwa 2003: 36) or pyramidal (Winham 1986: 174–175) approach. An inner core of the most powerful countries would come to a mutually acceptable agreement between themselves. That agreement would then be taken to a group of influential states and some concessions made to ensure their acquiescence. This process would continue through various groups of countries, with the concessions being made diminishing as the influence of those countries diminished. Where countries fitted into this structure would change depending on the issue being discussed, but the US and EEC/EU (from its creation in 1957) would always be in the innermost circle, often joined by Japan and Canada. These four formed the group known as the Quad and were the locus for much of the final, and most important, round of negotiations, the Uruguay Round (1986–1994). India and Brazil were tacitly afforded a position as leaders of the developing world and were included towards, but not in, the inner circle. The rest of the developing world was largely ignored.

This approach to negotiations unsurprisingly delivered highly unequal results, with the interests of the innermost, most powerful countries privileged over those of others. Each round was asymmetric in outcome, delivering greatest benefits to the industrialized countries and marginalizing the developing world, which grew increasingly disillusioned with the GATT (Wilkinson and Scott 2008). The Uruguay Round was particularly flawed. Despite being billed as a balance between the interests of the Global North and the Global South, it was tilted heavily towards the former. As Finger and Nogués (2002: 337, emphasis in original) argued, 'What the North *gave up* was, in real economics, of benefit to *the North* as well as to the South. This is the familiar GATT politics of using an international commitment to achieve useful but politically unpopular domestic reforms. What the South gave up was a benefit to the North but in many cases *a cost* to the

South. This is the politics of imperialism, of extracting from a less powerful party'.

12.3.1 The Doha Round

The Doha Round, officially known as the Doha Development Agenda, was the first round of negotiations launched by the WTO and was putatively aimed at redressing some of the inequalities of previous GATT agreements, particularly the Uruguay Round. However, once the talks were underway the US and EU defaulted to the traditional mode of negotiation, centred on finding a bilateral mutually agreeable framework agreement as per the concentric circle model explained above. This was particularly true in agriculture, which has always been the most intractable sector, facing the heftiest political obstacles to agreement. Many developing countries are highly competitive in agricultural goods, while most rich countries are not competitive and rely on a range of tariff protections and subsidies to ensure the viability of their domestic agricultural sectors. The US and EU tried to force through a deal that would have delivered minimal liberalization, repeating what they had managed to do in previous rounds (WTO 2003). Rather than bringing about the modification of agricultural protection, the deal being offered would have loosened existing rules on some subsidies employed by the US known as counter-cyclical payments and rowed back from the work programme agreed at Doha that mandated the phased elimination of export subsidies (see Denny and Osborn 2003).

India and Brazil played a central role in resisting the US–EU proposal, particularly at the WTO's Cancún Ministerial Conference of 2003, where they galvanized developing country resistance to the exclusion of their interests. This was done primarily through the creation of a new coalition of developing countries which came to be known as the Group of 20, or G20 (though sometimes referred to as the G20-Trade, or G20-T, to differentiate it from the unrelated Group of 20 Finance Ministers—on which see Helleiner, Chapter 8, and Pauly, Chapter 9), which was created specifically as a response to the US–EU text on agriculture. Developing countries have a long history of using coalitions in multilateral trade negotiations, but these have traditionally been highly fragile and ineffective (Narlikar 2003). The G20 broke that pattern, with Indian and Brazilian leadership managing to hold the coalition together in the face of concerted attempts to 'divide and rule' the group (Tussie and Narlikar 2003: 953). Moreover, the G20 was more proactive than previous coalitions, arriving in Cancún with a well-developed counter-proposal, primarily put together by Brazil, that sought to target US and EU subsidy regimes. The Ministerial became a battle between the developed countries and the developing countries, with the increased economic and political heft of Brazil and India helping them to stand firm and hold the coalition together. Unable to bridge that divide, the Cancún Ministerial ultimately collapsed.

This dramatically changed the WTO's political dynamic. As Hopewell (2016: 82) puts it: 'Under the leadership of Brazil and India, the emergence of the G20-T produced . . . a "tectonic shift" at the WTO. From that point onward, the US and EU realized it would be impossible to secure a Doha agreement without the assent of Brazil and India as representatives of the G20-T and the developing world more broadly'. After Cancún, the inner circle of negotiations was reformed into what became known as the New Quad, consisting of the US, EU, India, and Brazil, fundamentally transforming the politics of the WTO. A few years later, China was also integrated into this group.

Having a seat at the top-most negotiation table allowed Brazil, India, and China to counterbalance the tendencies of the US and EU to shape the Doha Round towards their own interests (Scott and Wilkinson 2011). It ensured that agriculture remained front and centre of the discussion and the extent of liberalization (or 'ambition' in WTO parlance) that would be expected in other sectors was benchmarked against the agricultural offers made by the US and EU. This was in direct challenge to the position taken by the US and EU, which were demanding quite the opposite. To understand this, we need to understand a little about how the WTO system works. The WTO does not set the tariffs of its member states. Rather, during WTO negotiations the members agree on bindings, or limits, for their tariffs and agricultural subsidies. They are free to choose to *apply* lower tariffs, or pay out lower subsidies, but they cannot exceed those bindings. The tariff and subsidy bindings (or bound rates as they are known) are lowered over successive rounds of negotiations, which has the effect of lowering the degree of latitude states face when setting their applied rates. This is the mechanism through which WTO members move progressively towards free trade. For a variety of reasons that do not concern us here, the

rich, industrialized countries typically have a large gap between their bound and applied rates of agricultural subsidies, while India and Brazil have a large gap between their bound and applied tariffs on industrial goods. China, incidentally, has almost no gap, as they had to agree to low tariff bindings when acceding to the WTO.

There were significant imbalances in what was on offer in the Doha Round. In agriculture, both the US and EU had offered only to reduce their bindings on agricultural subsidies to a little above their current applied level (that is, the total they were actually spending on subsidies each year), meaning that they would not have to reduce their actual subsidy programmes and could indeed expand them in certain areas. By contrast, they demanded that the likes of India and Brazil cut their bound tariffs on industrial goods sufficiently that the reductions would bite into applied rates, to ensure that real liberalization was achieved.

Such disparities between sectors and between the interests of the (often agricultural-based) developing world and the industrialized developed countries may seem hypocritical and perplexing, but this was the reality of each of the trade rounds undertaken within the GATT (Kim 2011; Wilkinson 2014). The negotiation process, based on competitive bargaining within the concentric circles process outlined above, all but ensured that the outcomes would favour the interests of the most powerful. The rapid economic growth seen in Brazil, India, and China and the consequent inclusion of them in the innermost negotiating circle has overturned that dynamic and ensured that the US and EU cannot dictate outcomes in the way they have (largely) previously been able to do.

Brazil, India, and China (the BICs) are not sufficiently powerful to force through their own package, but were able to block the unbalanced deal the US and EU had been pursuing. However, it is important to understand the nature of the challenge that the BICs presented to the WTO. Most notably, they did not directly challenge the neoliberal basis of the trade system. Rather, they sought to utilize that framework to their own ends, turning the tables, as it were, on the industrialized countries and exposing the hypocrisy of the US and EU preaching liberal trade to others while maintaining protectionism in agriculture and other non-competitive sectors such as textiles and clothing (Hopewell 2016). The BICs focused attention on that hypocrisy and used it to demand greater conformity with, not deviation from, the liberal rhetoric that the

US and EU espoused. This reflects the fact that the BICs had considerable interests in achieving further liberalization in certain sectors, since trade expansion has been a key factor driving their economic rise. Each had become a highly competitive exporter in a different area—Brazil in agricultural goods, India in services, and China in manufactures—and therefore had a strong interest in maintaining a fairly open trade system. That said, they also have defensive interests and have been forthright in defending these, leveraging the framing of the WTO talks as the 'Doha Development Agenda' (see Trommer, Chapter 5) to ensure that their interests, which they presented as being synonymous with the interests of the developing world as a whole (however problematic this claim may be), were at the forefront.

In this sense, the early concerns that the rising powers would have a revisionist or 'system challenging' agenda (see, for example, Johnston 2003) can be seen to be rather misplaced in the field of trade at least. The BICs have no interest in destroying the WTO or the trade system in general. Rather, they seek—as do *all* member states—wherever possible to shape the organization towards their interests while opposing moves to liberalize areas in which they are not competitive (Scott and Wilkinson 2013; Hopewell 2016).

However, despite the fact that the BICs were not seeking to radically change the fundamental tenets of the WTO, the altered political structures outlined above have had a profound impact on the organization and ultimately led it into a period of crisis. Neither side was willing to make the concessions needed to make progress in the talks, and in 2007 the Doha Round was declared by Director General Pascal Lamy to be at an impasse and was put on ice (see Blustein 2009).

12.3.2 **The aftermath and beyond**

In the 'blame game' that followed, the Western powers made it clear that they felt it was the lack of commitments by the rising powers that sealed the fate of the Doha Round. Susan Schwab, who had been US Trade Representative for much of the Doha Round negotiations, argued that the primary cause of the collapse was the 'failure to address the central question facing international economic governance today: What are the relative roles and responsibilities of advanced (or developed), emerging and developing countries?' (Schwab 2011: 105). The emerging powers, she argued, were 'hiding behind' the other developing countries by insisting that they were all one group and therefore the BICs should not be asked to take on greater commitments than the rest of the developing world (although **least developed countries** were not required to offer significant liberalization). This was untenable, Schwab argued, in the context of the rapid economic transformation and high degree of competitiveness the BICs had achieved. By contrast, Indian trade minister Kamal Nath argued that the collapse was the result of the US failing to make concessions, particularly in agriculture, claiming '[t]he US brought nothing to the table. They stuck to their old position' (BBC News 2006). Brazil likewise identified US intransigence as having prevented an agreement.

The point here is not to seek to determine the 'truth' between these positions or apportion blame between the actors. Rather, the point is to see the effect that the rising powers have had on WTO negotiations, and the way in which they changed the politics of the multilateral trade system. The state of affairs that characterized the GATT from the time of its creation in 1947 until the Uruguay Round (1986–1995), in which the major Western powers could use their economic and political weight to forge a deal that benefitted themselves more than others, notably the developing world, is over. The BICs have the capacity to prevent such an outcome. They, particularly China, are far too large not to include in the inner circle of the negotiations, and they are able to bolster their position further through positions as leaders of larger coalitions of developing countries. However, and to reiterate what was noted above, they have not used that position to seek to radically overturn the foundations of the WTO or to discard its liberal principles. Rather, they have redirected the focus of those principles away from the sectors that principally benefit the rich world towards areas in which the Western countries have been unwilling to liberalize, notably agriculture and the temporary migration of people in the service sector (Hopewell 2016). Partly as a consequence of this, the WTO has been unable to achieve a comprehensive trade agreement, and there is little prospect of one in the foreseeable future.

Much of the account in this section has concerned India and Brazil as they played important leadership roles in the Doha Round at a time when China was still new to the WTO, having joined only in 2001. The broader and continuing impact of China on the trade system deserves a closer examination on its own, to which the next section turns.

12.4 China in the WTO

China acceded to the WTO in 2001, after a long and at times acrimonious accession negotiation (for details, see Feng 2006). Under WTO rules, countries acceding must gain the approval of all existing members and must agree concessions to secure their support. China had to make extensive concessions, reflecting its size and growing competitiveness as an industrial powerhouse, committing to one of the most rapid processes of trade liberalization ever undertaken. Chinese tariffs were reduced to a lower level than comparable developing countries: it accepted tariff bindings on non-agricultural goods at an average of 9.1 per cent (from a pre-accession level of 42.9 per cent), while those on agricultural products were bound at an average of 15.7 per cent (from 54 per cent) (WTO 2005; also see WTO Tariff Profiles at www.wto.org). Key service sectors that had been closed to trade or investment, such as banking and insurance, were opened up. Indeed, in certain areas China had to take on obligations that went beyond those of the US and EU. For instance, China was required to eliminate all agricultural export subsidies, while the US and EU were required under the Uruguay Round Agreement on Agriculture only to limit their use below a certain threshold (Bergsten et al 2006: 36).

The established powers faced increasing trade competition from China, particularly in manufacturing, but were nonetheless keen to see it join the multilateral trade system. The expectation was that being brought into the multilateral trade system, built as it is on a foundational liberal-legal episteme (Hannah 2011), would force China to become a fully

market-based economy (Mavroidis and Sapir 2021). This would entail curtailing Beijing's interference in the 'free' operation of the market, notably the use of subsidies to chosen strategic industries and support for **state-owned enterprises**.

Despite the onerous nature of these concessions, China was willing to sign the agreement because it was using WTO accession as a means of locking in domestic reform. Put crudely for present purposes, two factions can be identified within China's domestic politics: one that favours greater movement towards market-based reform, and one composed of more conservative forces opposed to further global economic integration (Yong 2002). China's Premier at the time of accession, Zhu Rongji, was in the former group. He sought to use WTO accession as a means of locking in place pro-market reforms and bringing about further opening to the world economy. This is the frequently seen process of governments using international organizations as a means of overcoming domestic political resistance to the policies they want to enact. As Shaun Breslin has argued, WTO accession was intended as 'an external tool to *enforce* marketization and reform [at home], brought about by international globalizing elites wishing to lock China into multilateral trade norms and aiming to promote domestic political and economic change within China' (Breslin 2003: 214, emphasis in original). In addition, the political elite in Beijing were conscious of the perception around the world that China's rise constituted a threat to international peace and stability. Indeed, this view was so frequently expressed that it was given its own name, the China Threat Thesis—see Key Concepts Box 12.1—sparked particularly, though not exclusively, by influential thinkers drawing from various strands of realism—see Key Theory Box 12.2. They felt that active participation in global multilateral institutions would help dispel such fears and would fit closely with the official strategy of 'peaceful rise' (Li 2011: 338).

This conscious desire to blunt the China Threat Thesis was one reason for Beijing being relatively quiescent within the WTO following its accession. It was unwilling to show leadership and played a largely passive role in the Doha Round, initially even refusing to participate in the inner circle of the most powerful countries that characterizes the WTO's modus operandi. Where it felt its core interests were at stake China would be more assertive, but much of the time it simply supported any compromise that could be found between the more belligerent members,

KEY CONCEPT BOX 12.1 CHINA THREAT THESIS

The China Threat Thesis refers to the viewpoint that China's rise as a global power poses significant challenges and potential risks to the existing international order and the interests of other countries. It suggests that China's economic, military, and geopolitical ambitions may undermine the stability and security of the world.

This idea is perhaps most associated with realist thinkers, who have argued that conflict with China is all but inevitable as its influence increases (see Key Theory Box 12.2), but plenty of others concur, drawing from alternative perspectives (Friedberg 2005).

Proponents of the China Threat Thesis advocate for vigilance and assertiveness in countering what they perceive as China's challenges to the existing world order. They emphasize the need for countries to strengthen alliances, protect their economic interests, and promote democratic values and human rights as a means to manage and mitigate the potential risks associated with China's rise.

However, the China Threat Thesis is by no means universally accepted. Many emphasize the possibility of engaging and cooperating with China where possible and alleviating tensions through diplomatic channels where they arise. Furthermore, despite the recent attempts to partially decouple the US economy from that of China, particularly so as not to be overly reliant on China as a source of strategically important materials and goods, the two economies remain highly intertwined. Many European countries rely heavily on China for export growth, notably Germany, while millions of workers in China continue to be employed in manufacturing for export. Such interdependencies on both sides may help to avoid the catastrophe of a full-scale conflict.

KEY THEORY BOX 12.2 REALISM AND THE RISE OF CHINA

For some commentators, particularly those writing from some realist perspectives, conflict between rising powers and the established powers is all but inevitable. The logic of self-help and the competition between states for influence and regional or even global domination drive unavoidable tension between the interests of the presently dominant and those that seek to overturn existing power structures. A key thinker in this vein is John Mearsheimer (2005), who is among the most prominent offensive realist thinkers. Offensive realism forms a subcategory of thinkers who argue that the logic of anarchy demands that states must constantly strive for more power. The world is one of constant belligerence and conflict, driven by a dispassionate, rational calculation of how to achieve security. The 'Thucydides Trap' is endlessly appealed to within this tradition, referring to the rise of Athens, the alarm this set off in Sparta, and the emergence of the Peloponnesian Wars in response.

Realism is a highly varied tradition, however, loosely bound by some common themes and concepts but differing quite fundamentally on others. For example, defensive realists can be more sanguine about the likelihood of conflict. Defensive realism shares the common assumption that states must first and foremost secure themselves against external threats, but does not draw from this the conclusion that this demands ever increasing military build-up and an aggressively expressed, assertive foreign policy. They argue rather that once states have sufficient military power to protect themselves, there is no need to pursue more. Both China and the US have large stockpiles of nuclear weapons which would make any conflict between them suicidal. As such, realist assumptions and its focus on self-preservation—the central realist concern of the state—would caution China against any military action to secure dominance (Glaser 2011; Kirshner 2012).

Finally, classical realists (such as Hans Morgenthau and E. H. Carr) place less emphasis than either of the traditions explored above on structuralism: the idea that state behaviour is forever dictated by the structures of global politics. Instead, though concerned with the destabilizing effects of changes in the balance of power, they emphasize the role to be played by diplomacy and the incentive to avoid circumstances that lead to war. E. H. Carr, for instance, argued that the preservation of order and peace requires that 'sufficient concessions' are made by all parties, with 'the responsibility for seeing that these changes take place as far as possible in an orderly way [resting] as much on the defenders as on the challengers' (Carr 1939/1946: 91, 169, quoted in Kirshner 2012: 66).

Realism is just one lens to bring to understanding the impact of rising powers. The focus on it here is not meant to suggest that it deserves any particularly vaunted status, and the fact that realists can draw very different policy prescriptions concerning how to respond to changing power dynamics highlights the importance of looking beyond pure abstract reasoning and formulaic application of theories when seeking to respond to the issues explored in this chapter.

primarily the US and India. It was also in a process of learning how to operate within the WTO, building diplomatic knowledge and experience and slowly becoming more involved in core WTO activities, such as the dispute settlement system (DSM) (Scott and Wilkinson 2013).

This relative quietude has continued even as the US has pulled back from the WTO and from international leadership more generally, opening what might be seen as an opportunity for Beijing to step to the forefront of the organization and drive the agenda itself. China is, after all, now the largest single trading nation in the world. However, continued contestation between domestic interest groups noted above, a desire to maintain a dual identity as both a developing country and a technologically advanced, cutting-edge economy, and fluctuating focus on trade policy within the top echelons of the government (in what continues to be a very centralized political decision-making process) have made China reluctant to adopt the mantle of leadership within the WTO (Bishop and Xiaotong 2020). They have, it has been argued, followed the path of being 'neither the leading goat, nor the stumbling bloc' (China Ministry of Commerce 2006, quoted in Bishop and Xiaotong 2020: 760).

12.4.1 Integrating China's economic system into the WTO

That said, a more worrisome trend may also underlie Beijing's unwillingness to show leadership within the WTO, namely China's unwillingness to ensure that its economic system is consistent with the underlying tenets of the global trade system. Mavroidis and Sapir (2021), for instance, argue that China has failed to bring itself into full conformity with the *spirit* of WTO rules, despite formally being within the *letter* of the law. They focus on two key issues. First is the continued (and deepening) importance of state-owned enterprises (SOEs) to the Chinese economy. The unwritten ethos of the WTO assumes a broadly market-based economy, in which the bulk of economic activity is given over to the private sector, with the state's role restricted largely to the provision of infrastructure, regulation, and the rule of law in facilitating that activity. This is not explicitly written into WTO law. Rather, it reflects the Organization's foundational liberal–legal *episteme*, meaning the 'intersubjective, or taken-for-granted causal and evaluative assumptions about how the world works' that underpins all social endeavours

(Hannah 2011: 183–184). China's trading partners claim that SOEs receive substantial state support and are the means through which Beijing seeks to shape the economy and acquire competitiveness in strategic sectors. To take one example, in China's 2021 WTO Trade Policy Review, Japan raised its concern over 'the number of SOEs in industrial sectors, the significant roles they play in China's economy, and the public support they receive. Such a trend should be incompatible with China's goal of creating a market-oriented, law-based, and internationalized business environment' (WTO 2021: paragraph 4.130).

The second area of key concern raised by Mavroidis and Sapir is that of forced technology transfer, which relates to claims that the Chinese companies (both private and SOEs) impose deals on foreign businesses as a condition for accessing the Chinese market that require the handing over of technological know-how without the payment of royalties. This has, again, been a perennial complaint by China's critics, though it is denied by Beijing, which notes that its new 2020 Foreign Investment Law explicitly stipulates that technology transfer through administrative means is prohibited (WTO 2021: paragraph 2.25). How effective that law change has been is yet to be seen.

12.4.2 Emerging policy challenges

The two issues explored in the preceding section are somewhat unique to China (though other countries use SOEs, this is on a much more restricted basis), but elsewhere Beijing is following illiberal policies that mirror those practised by many Organization for Economic Cooperation and Development (OECD) countries but on a scale that is causing significant disruption to the global economy. Two such areas relate to the subsidization of agricultural and fisheries sectors (see Hopewell 2020). Agricultural subsidies have long been controversial, and contention over this topic could be said to have caused the failure of the Doha Round of WTO negotiations. At that time, this was largely a developed versus developing country battle (though it should be noted that any time such a characterization is employed on any WTO topic there is significant simplification taking place, though it nonetheless serves as a useful overview). Since the Doha Round's collapse in 2008, however, China's subsidy regimes have grown to the point where they are now the world's largest agricultural subsidizer in aggregate terms, transforming the politics of agricultural

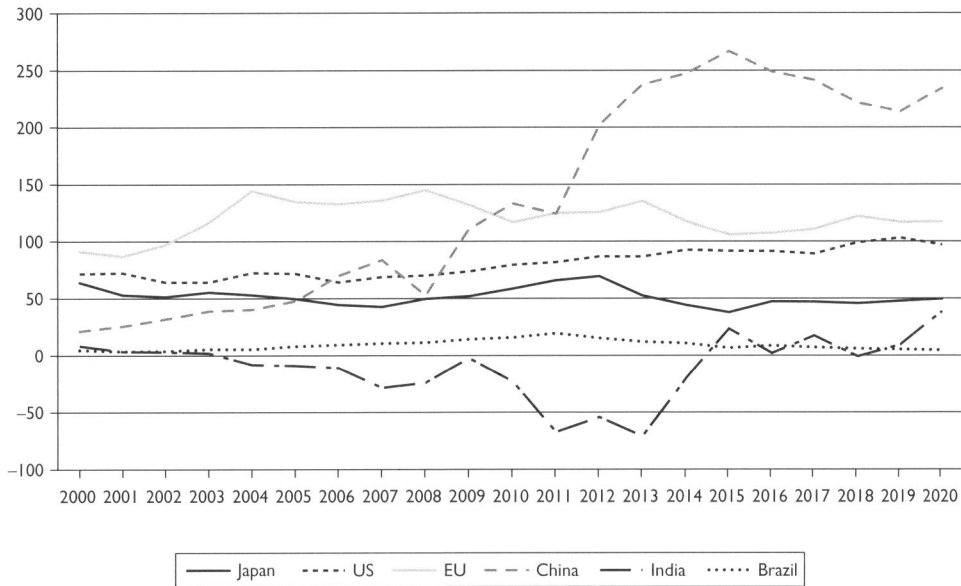

Figure 12.3 Total estimated agricultural support, millions euro

Source: OECD Data, www.oecd.org.

negotiations from the traditional Global North versus Global South orientation to one of China versus the United States (Hopewell 2019). Figure 12.3 illustrates the estimated total agricultural support paid to farmers for a selection of countries, showing the meteoric rise of China's subsidy programmes. It also shows that India and Brazil are relatively insignificant in this regard.

It is also worth noting that following the Uruguay Round Agreement on Agriculture, the US and EU have been shifting their policies away from the more distortionary forms of subsidy (those directly linked to either export or how much is produced, hence creating incentives to farmers to produce more and more), towards less distortionary forms (those that are 'delinked' from production, for example based on undertaking measures to protect wildlife). China's subsidy regime is concentrated in the more distortionary types of intervention—70 per cent of the total fell into this category in 2018–2020, compared to 33 per cent for the United States (OECD 2021). That said, China can point out that aggregate statistics may be misleading, since its population is so much larger than every other state (except India). Indeed, when the levels

of subsidies are measured as a percentage of farm receipts, China lies far below the levels seen in Japan and the EU (see Figure 12.4). This is because the large aggregate subsidies are being spread across many more farmers than seen in other countries.

Nonetheless, the sheer size of Beijing's subsidy programmes now makes China central to any future discussion of agricultural liberalization, transforming the politics of the situation. Any deal that does not include China and make significant cuts to its agricultural support would not deal with the problem of global market distortions in the sector. We return to this below.

The second issue is fisheries subsidies, which follow a similar pattern (Hopewell 2020). This has become an area of mounting international concern due to the effects of overcapacity in global fishing fleets and the associated problem of overfishing (see the Everyday GPE Box 12.3). Tackling fishery subsidies was included in the Sustainable Development Goals due to the importance of fish stocks to many communities around the world for livelihoods and nutrition, and the WTO was tasked with the creation of new global regulation to this end.

Figure 12.4 Producer support estimate, percentage of farm receipts

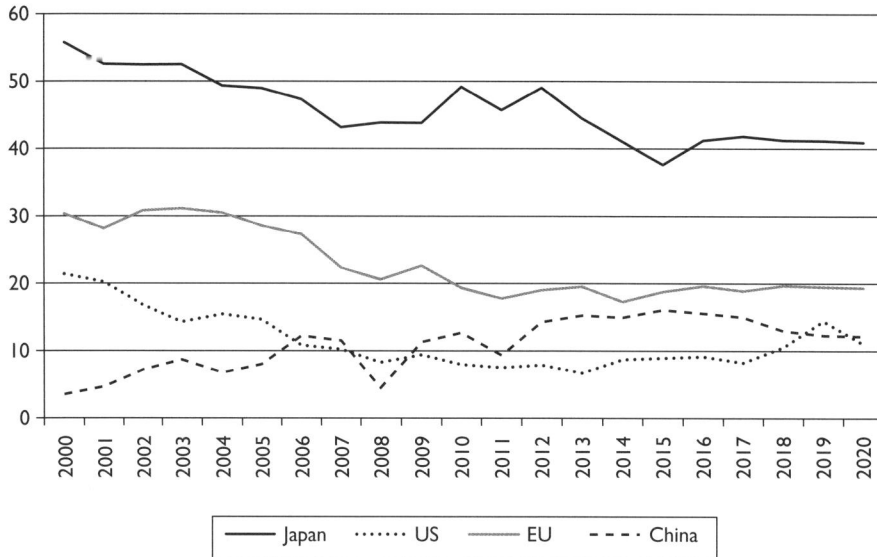

Source: OECD.

The lack of existing disciplines in WTO rules in this area has meant that it is relatively unrestricted, allowing China to build up huge support measures for its domestic fishing industry, with global consequences. They are far from alone, and as with agricultural subsidies Beijing is simply following in the footsteps of other wealthy countries. When the negotiations really got underway in the WTO in 2005, China had a significant fishing industry but paid no central government subsidies (Hopewell 2020: 95). Since then, however, Beijing has built a subsidy regime that accounts for 21 per cent of total global subsidies. The United States comes in second, but at less than half China's level. Furthermore, as Sumaila et al. (2019: 2) find in their comprehensive analysis, most 'subsidies provided by China . . . are classified as capacity-enhancing subsidies. In the case of the United States, beneficial subsidies dominate'. The Chinese fishing fleet catches around the same amount per year as the next seven countries combined, transforming a problem that was previously spread across the range of rich countries into one that is dominated by a single country.

That kind of dynamic would make the negotiation of disciplines difficult in any circumstances, because the effects of any agreement would inevitably fall on one country far more than others. This is exacerbated, however, by the fact that China identifies as a developing country within WTO negotiations and has demanded that it is able to make use of the full range of Special and Differential Treatment (SDT) provisions in any deal. SDT measures are included in all WTO agreements for the benefit of developing countries, as a means of lessening the commitments required of them and ensuring that they maintain a degree of policy space. China's stance on this has been argued to render the negotiations all but pointless (Hopewell 2022). Other users of fisheries subsidies, such as the US, Japan, EU, and South Korea, will never—and politically speaking could never—accept a deal that significantly cuts back their subsidy policies but leaves China's far greater subsidy programmes largely untouched because Beijing is able to make use of the flexibilities associated with SDT. A similar dynamic, though less extreme, is at play in the agriculture negotiations, in which granting SDT for China would make any deal politically unacceptable for the other parties involved.

For its part, China has no desire to engage in wholesale reform of its subsidy programmes in either area. Agricultural subsidies form a significant part of

EVERYDAY GPE BOX 12.3 FISHERIES, SUBSIDIES, AND FISH STOCKS

Since 1950, the amount of fish consumed per capita has doubled, while the global population has more than tripled (Our World in Data 2023). Numerous factors have contributed to this expansion. Humans have always lived close to fresh water sources, for obvious reasons, and partly as a consequence fish has formed a significant part of protein intake. Technological changes over the course of the nineteenth and twentieth centuries enabled larger fishing vessels which were able to go further out to sea for longer periods and ever more precise targeting of where fish can be found. Meanwhile, increased disposable income has enabled people to eat more of what they want rather than what they can afford, which has included the consumption of more fish.

Increased demand has been met through massive expansion in fish catches. Countries have sought to increase their capacity to capture more and more of the available fish stocks in what is a good example of the tragedy of the commons. Since nobody has ownership or control of fish stocks outside their exclusive economic zone (an area stretching to 200 miles from any state's coast which the 1982 UN Convention on the Law of the Sea designates as for their commercial use), and since fish stocks typically will migrate across large areas, each country has an incentive to catch as much as possible.

Governments have responded by increasing subsidies to their fishing sectors to ensure that they can compete and to enable them to capture more of this global market. Global fisheries subsidies are estimated to have reached US$35.4 billion in 2018,

of which US$22.2 billion were subsidies aimed at increasing the capacity of the fishing fleet (Sumaila et al. 2019). The impact of all this growth in fishing capacity has been that fish stocks are increasingly over-exploited—officially around a third of global fish stocks are over-exploited. Some are collapsing, or have collapsed. Southern bluefin tuna stocks have fallen by around 85 per cent since 1950 (Our World in Data 2023).

Compounding the problem is rampant illegal fishing, where fishing vessels enter areas that they are not allowed to fish in, or catch more than their allowed quota where stock management agreements are in place. Inevitably, the countries that have least capacity to protect their fishing waters and the interests of their fishing communities are poor countries. Somalia forms a telling example of the consequences. In the early 1980s Somali waters were still the preserve for their domestic, small-scale fishing fleet, but by the 2000s those fishers accounted for only around a quarter of the total catch, the rest being taken by foreign vessels, often illegally. The resulting collapse in the capacity of Somali fishers to make a living led them to turn their marine skills elsewhere, driving the sudden explosion in piracy off the Somali coast. With international ships being taken hostage, disrupting international commerce, an international effort was put in place to police the waters and the Somali government was pressured to arrest pirates. These efforts brought the problem of Somali piracy to an end, with attacks falling to close to zero by around 2013, but the problems caused by illegal fishing, depleted fish stocks, and the role these play in driving poverty and destroying livelihoods in Somalia remain.

attempts by Beijing to ensure that rural communities, where there is still widespread absolute poverty, are not left behind during the period of rapid economic growth. Fisheries subsidies perform several functions. One is to satisfy the rising demand for fish by a growing middle class, but there are also larger considerations at play. Beijing wants to build its deep-sea capacity not just to supply fish from further afield (since its coastal waters have seen fish stocks collapse due to overutilization), but also to support two other strategic purposes. First, China has, as Zhang Hongzhou (2015: 11) puts it, 'been deliberately encouraging its fishermen to undertake fishing activities in disputed waters in order to assert China's maritime claims in the South and East China Seas'. An illustration of this is the incident around the Whitsun Reef (see Case Study Box 12.4). Second, subsidies support the development of a strong domestic shipbuilding industry and pool of

skilled mariners, both of which facilitate the building of a strong navy.

12.4.3 Where does the threat to the WTO lie: China or the US?

Section 12.4.2 suggests a rather bleak assessment of China's impact on the WTO. Though initially China was quiescent in the organization, it has, critics suggest, emerged to become a formidable blocking force on achieving future agreements in core areas of WTO activity. It is widely argued that the WTO's negotiation function is in crisis (see, for example, Steger 2009; Wilkinson 2017). While some of the reasons for that predate the full emergence of China as a global economic superpower, as we have seen above China is increasingly identified as being a major reason for global trade negotiations to be stalled, due to their

CASE STUDY BOX 12.4 CONTESTATION IN THE SOUTH CHINA SEA

As China has become more economically and militarily powerful, it has sought to enable the projection of power in its immediate region. One element of this strategy has been to enforce claims on islands within the South China Sea to use as military bases, and to build new islands on shallow reefs. Such activities have been highly contentious among the other states in the region, since the islands and reefs in question have competing claims. The most keenly contended, perhaps, are the Spratly Islands, which are disputed by China, the Philippines, Vietnam, Malaysia, Taiwan, and Brunei among others, and lie among several important trade routes, fishing grounds, and potential oil and gas fields. China has unilaterally declared that it has sovereignty over all islands within what it calls the nine-dash line, demarcating almost all the waters of the South China Sea, arguing that it has exercised jurisdiction over the islands for centuries, as evidenced by historical documents and maps. This was, however, rejected in 2016 by the Permanent Court of Arbitration in the Hague. China rejected the ruling and declared that it would not recognize the Court's jurisdiction. In reality, sovereignty over the various islands is unclear and highly contested. For example, the second largest island, known as Pagasa, was snatched from Taiwan by the Philippines in 1971 when the Taiwanese troops stationed there left to seek shelter from an incoming typhoon (Wingfield-Hayes 2023).

China has sought to impose its control over islands and reefs regardless of legal rulings. In 2021 two Chinese fishing vessels 'swarmed' the Whitsun Reef in the Spratlies, currently formally controlled by the Philippines, in what has been interpreted as an attempt by Beijing to assert de facto control of the territory, changing the reality on the ground regardless of legal rulings

(Reed and Shepherd 2021). Elsewhere, in what is perhaps aptly known as Mischief Reef, China has been using the world's largest ocean-going dredgers to pump millions of tonnes of sand to raise the reef above sea level, creating new islands on which to build military bases, despite these falling well within the Philippines' internationally recognized 200-mile exclusive economic zone (Wingfield-Hayes 2023).

As China grows it is becoming more assertive. On one level this is to be expected. China is the world's largest goods exporter, so it has a core interest in ensuring that it can protect its shipping. The US has played a role since the end of the Second World War in keeping shipping lanes open for commerce, but as relations between the US and China become ever more tense it is unsurprising that Beijing is seeking ways to ensure that the US is not in a position to disrupt Chinese ships in the area should hostilities emerge.

It should also be noted that the US has itself made use of rather contestable claims to sovereignty over islands for similar purposes. One example is the Chagos Islands in the Indian Ocean. Originally considered to be part of Mauritian territory, when the UK granted Mauritius independence in 1968 it carved out the Chagos Islands as a separate British Indian Ocean Territory, which it then leased to the US for use as a military base. The population was forcibly removed and has been seeking restitution from the UK ever since (Evers and Kooy 2011). The displaced islanders have won multiple court cases brought by Mauritius against the UK, in the UN's International Tribunal for the Law of the Sea in 2021 and the International Court of Justice in 2019, but the UK has refused to hand over sovereignty (Harding 2021).

rampant use of subsidies to achieve strategic economic objectives and failure to transition towards being a full market economy.

However, as ever, caution is required when interpreting the current malaise in the WTO and when attributing responsibility for it to specific countries. Aside from the issue of fishery subsidies, China's role in the WTO is not as destructive as claimed by its critics. It is worth noting that China has faced many challenges in the WTO's Dispute Settlement Mechanism (DSM) but has always brought itself into compliance with any adverse ruling (Mavroidis and Sapir 2021). No disputant has been awarded the option of retaliation against China for non-compliance with panel rulings, suggesting a strong compliance record. It has been argued that this is not the full story, that Beijing avoids

implementing the full letter of adverse rulings, engaging instead in what has been termed 'paper compliance' without fundamentally reforming the aspects of its economic system that conflict with WTO rules (Webster 2014). But it is worth noting that other major economic powers, such as the US and EU, also do not always bring their laws into compliance with adverse DSM rulings. For example, the EU ignored the determination that its ban on hormone treated beef contravened WTO law, choosing to pay compensation to the US instead. Likewise, when US farm subsidies were challenged by Brazil, it similarly chose to pay compensation rather than comply with the ruling. It also refuses to amend its anti-dumping laws despite repeatedly losing disputes on the subject. In this sense, China is doing nothing fundamentally different to the other major powers (Scott and Wilkinson 2022). It broadly conforms with any rulings made against it but where those cases impinge on what it considers to be core areas of interest it finesses the subject. That is what all major powers do.

Furthermore, whatever the effect China is having on the negotiating function of the WTO, it is undeniable that a far greater immediate threat to the organization comes from the US, the chief architect of the system. In recent years, the US has deliberately brought about the collapse of the Appellate Body—the highest 'court' within the DSM, to which initial findings can be appealed—by vetoing the appointment of new members to the supposed seven-strong team of judges. This means that the dispute process has been effectively rendered non-functional, since any finding from the lower Panel stage can be appealed by the losing state to the Appellate Body, where it languishes without the chance of progress. It is worth noting that while the hostility of the Trump administration to the WTO is well catalogued, this sabotaging of the WTO's DSM started under the Obama administration and has continued through Trump's and into the Biden administration (see Kuijper 2017).

Similarly, while China may push against the boundaries of what is permissible within the WTO, it is again the US that has engaged in a trade war that threatens to undermine the whole basis of the multilateral trade system. The tariffs unilaterally implemented by Trump against China were clearly illegal within WTO law, and Biden has shown little inclination to reverse them. Though stopping short of pulling out of the organization, as Trump at times threatened, the US has nonetheless placed the WTO in a prolonged existential crisis. Whatever complaints may be raised against China's interpretation and implementation of WTO law, it cannot be said to have undermined the WTO system in anything like the manner of the US.

The US has justified these actions as necessitated by the failure of the WTO to deal with China's actions and perceived 'cheating'. As US Trade Representative in the Trump administration Robert Lighthizer put it, '[t]he sheer scale of [China's] co-ordinated efforts to develop their economy, to subsidize, to create national champions, to force technology transfer, and to distort markets in China and throughout the world is a threat to the world trading system that is unprecedented. The WTO and its predecessor, the [GATT], were not designed to successfully manage mercantilism on this scale' (quoted in Donnan 2017).

12.4.4 Problems of de-industrialization and appropriate policy responses

Whatever the merits of Lighthizer's argument, the strong actions against China have been popular domestically in the US, reflecting the perceived effect that imports from China have had on US jobs (see also Guisinger, Chapter 6). The latest research has given some vindication to the idea that some segments of the US have suffered due to the rise of China and its highly competitive manufacturing. One influential contribution has been made by Autor, Dorn, and Hanson (2013), who looked at the impact of increased trade between China and the US at the level of individual districts and found that those areas where Chinese trade had achieved greatest penetration of the market had also caused higher unemployment and reduced wages. While the rise of China might have been a benefit to the US overall, bringing with it new export opportunities and cheaper consumer goods, the costs were (as they tend to be with trade adjustments) localized in specific regions that were reliant on manufacturing-based employment. Further work found that such areas took at least a decade to adjust (Autor, Dorn, and Hanson 2016) (see Figure 12.5).

However, while the economic pain felt in those areas is very real, in the continuing to-and-fro of the debate it should be noted that care is needed when attributing blame to China. First, while the rise of China has unquestionably exacerbated the process of de-industrialization of areas of the established industrialized countries, even Autor, Dorn, and Hanson (2013) found that increased competition from China accounted for only around a quarter of the lost industrial jobs in the US. The primary cause is technological advancement driving productivity growth, allowing more to be manufactured by a smaller workforce. As Adam Posen, president of the Peterson Institute for International Economics, has argued:

After much debate, economists have agreed on an upper-bound estimate of the number of U.S. manufacturing jobs that were lost as a result of Chinese competition after 1999: two million, at most, out of a workforce of 150 million. In other words, from 2000 to 2015, the China shock was responsible for displacing roughly 130,000 workers a year. That amounts to a sliver of the average churn in the U.S. labor market, where about 60 million job separations typically take place each year (Posen 2021: 30).

Source: Foreign affairs.

Figure 12.5 Abandoned factory in Detroit, Michigan

Source: Shutterstock.

As Posen goes on to argue, governments have a range of policy tools available to them to help workers cope with economic dislocations, whether driven by globalization or other forces, but have not always been good at implementing them. The United States in particular does not do well in this regard. It spends only around a tenth as much as European countries on helping unemployed people find new jobs and offers little protection to workers in terms of unemployment benefits that would give them the time to find a new job (Posen 2021: 40). The stakes for individuals when facing losing their jobs are consequently much higher. Where there are generous unemployment payments and better retraining opportunities, the effects of lost jobs are not as acute and the political opposition to trade and globalization consequently less sharp (Katzenstein 2016). The US could offer this, but chooses not to. This is not China's fault.

12.4.5 Coercive diplomacy

While some of the blame for trade disruption directed towards China may be exaggerated, there are also examples of Beijing acting entirely outside of the basic norms of the international trade system, creating major new trade barriers targeted towards punishing those by which it feels aggrieved. One example occurred in 2020, when Australia incensed Beijing by calling for an investigation into the origins of the COVID-19 outbreak in Wuhan. China responded by closing its market overnight to Australian barley exports, which had been running at AU\$1 billion a year, subsequently extending the ban

to beef, wine, wheat, and a range of other agricultural commodities, alongside instructing Chinese importers to stop purchasing Australian coal and liquified natural gas (Wilson 2021). A similar experience was felt by Norway when the Nobel Committee awarded the 2010 Peace Prize to Liu Xiaobo, a Chinese human rights activist. China responded by immediately closing its market to many Norwegian exports. Such actions have been termed '**coercive diplomacy**', with Beijing using the immense size of its market and the reliance of many countries on Chinese exports to punish countries for (sometimes rather minor) actions that China dislikes (Hanson, Currey, and Beattie 2020).

To summarize overall, what should be clear from the discussion above is that great care is needed when interpreting the impact of the likes of India, Brazil, and China on the global trade system. It is certainly the case that the rise of large and economically powerful states has made the process of negotiating global trade deals harder, but it would be simplistic to attribute this to any intransigence on the part of those rising powers. Rather, it is a consequence of the unwillingness of the established economic powers, particularly the US, EU, and Japan, to live up to their rhetoric on free trade and open their own markets in areas in which they do not have a comparative advantage. China has faced particular criticism for its policies, particularly the role of the state in the economy. The argument made by the United States and others is that China's economic system, coupled with the WTO's inability to enforce required changes on Beijing, has resulted in trade tensions and China's reluctance to genuinely embrace liberalization, thereby hindering the possibility of new trade agreements.

While it is certainly true that China has implemented large-scale subsidy systems in key sectors, notably here agriculture and fisheries, it must be borne in mind that they are doing little different to other rich, industrialized states. In agriculture particularly, the problems created by China's subsidies are less to do with their generosity than with the fact that China is such a large country in terms of population. With fisheries, there are real global problems being created by China's building up of fishing capacity, which are contributing to overfishing around the world. But again, it should be noted that the Western powers cannot take a moral high ground here, having done plenty themselves in contribution to this problem. This reflects a more general conclusion: that whatever problems

China and the other rising powers may or may not be causing, they are doing little that is fundamentally different to the other major powers. The trade system is competitive, with economic and political power central to the process of bargaining over commercial agreements (Wilkinson 2014). The rising powers are doing little more than pushing for agreements in areas in which they have a competitive advantage, while resisting liberalization in sectors in which they do not. Nonetheless, Beijing has also implemented significant, unilateral trade restrictions when feeling aggrieved by the actions of trade partners.

KEY POINTS

- When China joined the WTO many hoped that it would shift its economy decisively towards being fully market based. This has not happened.

- Some argue that China's political economy model is incompatible with the fundamental principles of the WTO. Nonetheless, China largely complies with WTO rulings. The US has arguably done more to disrupt the global trade system in recent years.

- It is unquestionable that China's emergence as a major centre for global manufacturing has had some adverse impacts on certain groups within the West, but the extent of this is often exaggerated and is exacerbated by wider policy failures within those countries.

- Tensions have also been mounting in the South China Sea, where China is seeking to exert greater influence, and China has increasingly used its large market size to punish countries for actions that displease Beijing.

12.5 New BRICS institutions

The rising powers have not just been affecting the existing institutions of global governance, they have also set about creating new institutions with them at the centre (see Figure 12.6). As before, and as we will explore below, this has given rise to very different narratives and interpretations of why these institutions have been created, what their impact will be, and whether they pose a direct challenge to the existing international order. Here we explore some of the key new institutions, the Contingent Reserve Arrangement (CRA) and the New Development Bank (NDB), before focusing in greater detail on the Asian Infrastructure and Investment Bank (AIIB) and the role it plays in China's Belt and Road Initiative.

Figure 12.6 Fortaleza, Brazil. Chinese President Xi Jinping delivers a speech during the 6th BRICS summit in Fortaleza, Brazil, 15 July 2014.

Source: Alamy.

The CRA and the NDB (originally known as the BRICS Development Bank) were set up in 2014 at a meeting of the BRICS in Fortaleza, Brazil, and came into force a year later following ratification of the founding agreements. They were immediately widely interpreted as directly challenging the IMF and World Bank, respectively (for example, *The Economist* 2014; Reisen 2015).

The CRA mirrors the role of the IMF. It is designed to offer access to credit when one of the BRICS member states falls into liquidity problems and needs access to foreign reserves. It has US$100 billion of capital, with China putting in US$41 billion of that total, while Brazil, Russia, and India each contribute US$18 billion and South Africa the remaining US$5 billion. This distribution reflects the fact that within the BRICS China dominates economically (as seen above in Figure 12.1), even when it has little desire to dominate politically. Indeed, other members, notably India, are wary of giving China too great an influence (Chin 2014: 372). The idea behind the CRA is often interpreted as helping the BRICS avoid having to go to the IMF in times of economic crisis, thereby avoiding the harsh conditionality that comes with an IMF bailout—a concern that has been on the minds of all emerging countries since the IMF's mismanagement of the Asian financial crisis of 1997 (Stiglitz 2002).

The details, however, paint a more nuanced picture. Access to the initial 30 per cent of each country's allocated funds is largely automatic, but if a member wants to access more than that threshold it becomes conditional on them having an existing IMF agreement in place (*The Economist* 2014). As such, the extent to which the CRA can be said to challenge the IMF is rather moot, leading Barry Eichengreen, one of the foremost commentators on the global monetary system, to declare the CRA to be 'empty symbolism' with no future (Eichengreen 2014). As noted by Biziwick, Cattaneo, and Fryer (2015: 317), for critics on the left the CRA may even make things worse in the sense that it will tend 'to smooth rather than challenge the process of financial globalization', legitimizing the status quo by giving the appearance of challenging prevailing power structures without actually doing so.

The NDB, as noted above, was created at the same time as the CRA. Where the CRA may be seen as the BRICS counterpart to the IMF, the NDB is the counterpart to the World Bank, created to address the 'challenges of infrastructure development due to insufficient long-term financing and foreign direct investment' faced by developing countries (Republic of South Africa 2013, quoted in Chin 2014: 367). The declaration goes on to specify that the NDB will 'supplement the existing efforts of multilateral and regional financial institutions', in a clear attempt to frame the Bank as not being a direct challenge to the World Bank and associated regional development banks. As with all BRICS institutions, there was considerable political wrangling over the balance between the various members, particularly the extent of control China would have. The BRICS institutions have had to balance a strong desire to do things differently from, and have a more equitable structure than, the IMF and World Bank with the fact that China inevitably dominates economically. The ensuing tensions were largely overcome, however, and the NDB has departed from the established practice of all major institutions of global governance and instituted a principle of equality, with equal voting weights between members despite China having put in more capital, and a consensus decision-making system that ensures that Beijing cannot dominate (Luo and Yang 2021). Despite early analysis suggesting that the NDB could grow to provide roughly the same amount of lending per year as the World Bank (Reisen 2015), growth in membership has been slow, with only four new members as of 2022 (Bangladesh, Egypt, the United Arab Emirates, and Uruguay).

12.5.1 The Asian Infrastructure and Investment Bank

The AIIB, the third major new institution created by the rising powers in 2015, has grown at a far faster pace, beginning with fifty-seven signatories but increasing by 2022 to ninety-one full and fourteen prospective members (AIIB 2022). Notably, signatories to the AIIB include a range of Western countries, including the UK, Germany, and the Netherlands, which were among the founding members, while France joined in 2016 and Canada in 2018. This has happened despite perceived opposition from the US, and the inability of the US to prevent its close allies from joining the AIIB has been interpreted as signalling an important shift in where political power lies globally, with Washington no longer able to control the Western alliance. Former US Treasury Secretary Larry Summers, for instance, argued that 'the combination of China's effort to establish a major new institution and the failure of the US to persuade dozens of its traditional allies, starting with Britain, to stay out of it [could signal] the moment the United States lost its role as the underwriter of the global economic system' (Summers 2015), though it should be noted that there is debate over quite how strong US opposition to the project ever was (Freeman 2019).

The AIIB was created initially with a capital stock of US$100 billion, with China providing US$29.8bn of that. Unlike the NDB, voting rights are not equal. Rather, they are based on a formula that includes financial contribution, size of economy, an equal basic vote tally, and an additional 600 votes for each founding member (Chin 2016: 13). From this, China has a 30.34 per cent vote share and crucially a veto over major decisions, where a super majority of three quarters of votes is required. Beijing had signalled repeatedly that it would be willing to forgo veto power if either the US or Japan were to join as founding members, but neither took up the offer (Chin 2016: 13).

China has a special relationship with the AIIB outside of merely having a veto. The AIIB has been deeply intertwined with China's **Belt and Road Initiative** (BRI), Xi Jinping's flagship foreign economic policy (Callaghan and Hubbard 2016). The BRI is an ambitious project to expand infrastructure across the Asian region, including through networks of roads and railways, ports, power grids, pipelines, and more. Over US$1.4 trillion of investments have been committed so far, making the BRI over eleven times the size of the Marshall Plan in current dollars (Yang et al. 2018: 56). The overall purpose is to link China to the European market by road and sea, across sixty-five countries. It is 'essentially a new global architecture designed by

China to frame its new role as a leading world power' (Zhang, Alon, and Letterman 2018: 2).

Mirroring what we have seen before in this chapter, reaction to the creation of these new institutions spans the fullest possible breadth. On the one hand they are responding to a clear need for more infrastructure investment in Asia and across the developing world, with an estimated US$1 trillion a year shortfall in global infrastructure investment (Suchodolski and Demeulemeester 2018). As such, arguably there is no competition with existing multilateral investment banks. Furthermore, China's immense internal infrastructure investment over recent decades has meant that it has developed highly competitive skills in delivering such projects, but there are few opportunities left within China for putting them to use. The AIIB/BRI allows it to turn those skills to assisting the development of the wider region. This is a positive agenda that flows from China's phenomenal economic growth and will enable it to spread that prosperity to the region through improving trade and cooperation (Callaghan and Hubbard 2016; Chin 2016). Beijing realized that further regional economic integration relied less on the reduction of tariffs, which are already relatively low by historical standards, and more on the lack of appropriate infrastructure. All this may be in China's direct interests rather than being pure altruism, but that is to be expected. The Marshall Plan, for instance, was partly self-interest on the part of the US to provide Europe with sufficient US dollars to keep buying American goods (Gardner 1956).

12.5.2 **Debt trap diplomacy**

Critics, however, argue that the creation of these institutions is serving far more nefarious purposes. Some claim that China is engaging in 'debt-trap diplomacy' (see Bräutigam 2020). The idea is that China deliberately seeks to saddle developing countries with unsustainable debts to increase their dependence on Beijing, providing it with leverage or even allowing China to take over key infrastructure when debtor states default—see Key Concept Box 12.5. Chinese lending is made without the strict monitoring requirements and policy conditions demanded by the traditional multilateral lenders to try to ensure that the money lent is used appropriately and repayable (though the appropriateness of the World Bank and IMF conditionality is highly contested—see Bhagat, Chapter 14). This

may encourage countries to take on too much debt that cannot ultimately be repaid. Former US Secretary of State Rex Tillerson made this accusation when he characterized Chinese infrastructure lending as 'predatory economics' (Tillerson 2017).

12.5.3 **Failure to reform the IMF and World Bank**

One final element in the creation of the CRA, NDB, and AIIB that is worthy of note is the widely held view that a significant motivation behind their establishment lay in the failure to reform the voting structures of the World Bank and the IMF to give China (and other rising powers, but primarily China) a number of votes commensurate with its economic position. Tortuous negotiations between 2002 and 2010 resulted in minimal changes—an increase of 1.64 percentage points in voting share for China, 0.13 for India, and 0.17 for Brazil. Even after this, large disparities remain in the extent to which the size of each economy translates into voting rights. This can be seen by examining the ratio of voting share to GDP following the 2010 changes. That ratio is 0.71 for the US, 0.80 for Germany, 0.93 for Japan, but significantly lower at 0.43 for China, indicating that China was not given voting rights that reflected the size of its economy (Vestergaard and Wade 2015: 185). Even then, the US took five years to ratify the changes that had been agreed as the process got held up in Congress. The lesson for China was clear. They were not going to be given an equal seat at the table, so they set about creating alternative organizations.

KEY POINTS

- The BRICS, led by China, have created a number of new organizations that may be challenging the Bretton Woods Institutions.

- The AIIB is the most important of these and is closely bound up with China's Belt and Road Initiative.

- It has become commonplace to accuse China of debt trap diplomacy. However, such accusations are contestable and frequently do not stand up to scrutiny.

- Part of the reason for China wanting to create new institutions is that the Western powers have blocked reform of the World Bank and the IMF to give China greater influence, commensurate with its economic size.

KEY CONCEPT BOX 12.5 DEBT TRAP DIPLOMACY IN ACTION

The Hambantota port in Sri Lanka makes an interesting example, often held up as the example of Chinese debt diplomacy par excellence (for example, see Parker and Chefitz 2018) (see Figure 12.7). Built using a Chinese loan initially of only US$361 million in 2007, the port was a commercial failure from the start, necessitating a further loan of US$1.9 billion to upgrade the port and build a nearby airport (widely referred to as 'the world's emptiest'). This failed to turn around the viability of the port, and by 2017 the Sri Lankan government was mired in debt, with the Hambantota port a huge white elephant. Unable to maintain its debt repayments, Sri Lanka secured a further US$1.1 billion from China, giving Beijing in return a ninety-nine-year lease on the port—a debt for equity swap that provided China with a strategically important new naval hub in the region.

However, as ever, care is needed. Despite Western media and political commentators repeating this narrative widely, the details are contested (see, among others, Bräutigam 2020; Jones and Hameiri 2020). China did not push this project; it was driven by Sri Lanka itself, in particular the powerful Rajapaksa family following the election of Mahinda Rajapaksa, who was from Hambantota. The port was then opened too early, at a time chosen to celebrate the president's birthday but before it was ready to begin commercial operations. While Beijing had provided lending for the port, when Sri Lanka's financial problems came to a head in 2016 only around 10 per cent of its total debt was owed to China, with most owed to more traditional dollar-based international lenders. The injection of money by China through the debt for equity swap was to help repay this—it flowed into the Sri Lankan economy and then immediately out again to Western lenders—and was initiated by Colombo, not Beijing. Furthermore, raising money through selling off Sri Lankan infrastructure was being encouraged by the IMF and World Bank as a means of dealing with the impending debt crisis. Claims that Hambantota will further China's military reach are also questionable, not least because usage by military vessels was forbidden in the lease agreement. All in all, there was no overall Chinese grand strategy that locked Sri Lanka into debt in order to advance its geostrategic ambitions. The case was an example of 'messy real-world dynamics' rather than coherent strategy (Jones and Hameiri 2021).

Figure 12.7 Aerial view of Hambantota International Port premises in Hambantota District, Sri Lanka.

Source: Shutterstock.

12.6 Competing narratives

What we see across both the issue areas examined here—the WTO and the creation of new international institutions—is the prevalence of competing narratives that surround the rising powers, particularly China. All too often events are interpreted through a polarizing lens that distorts more than it illuminates. Actions by China are presented in a negative light, portraying Beijing as a nefarious actor that damages the international system, while Western states are seen positively, as supporters of the international system and its rules (Mawdsley 2008; Bräutigam 2020). Western lending to the Global South is seen as furthering development, while Chinese lending is 'debt trap diplomacy'. When China seeks to protect its core economic interests in the WTO it is seen as undermining the whole system, while continued protection of non-competitive sectors by Western states (particularly agriculture and textiles and clothing) is seldom seen in the same way.

This is not to say that there are no problems with what the rising powers have been doing with their new-found economic and political power. As noted above, the subsidy regimes that China is building in agriculture and fisheries are deeply problematic and have serious consequences for the environment and for the economic prospects of other developing countries. Even more concerning are Chinese actions in the South China Sea over the various contested islands and posturing towards Taiwan, which could spill over into outright war.

For some commentators, particularly those writing from a realist perspective, conflict between the rising powers and the established powers is all but inevitable, as set out in Key Theory Box 12.2. The logic of self-help and the tensions created by changing power dynamics see greatest threat of conflict, whether deliberate or inadvertent (Gilpin 1981).

However, others are more sanguine, and the problem outlined above of unjustifiably negative interpretations of the behaviour of the rising powers is pertinent here. Predictions of conflict can become a self-fulfilling prophecy, exacerbating tensions, precluding cooperation, and preventing the kinds of global governance reforms that would forestall discord. Treating China as inherently different, as trying to overthrow the liberal regime and engaging in various nefarious grand strategies, will push Beijing towards actions that conform with this view.

China's rise to being roughly on an economic par with the US was always going to radically alter global politics and with it the systems of governing that economy. Some areas of conflict were inevitable, particularly given that China's domestic political-economic system is very different to those of the dominant Western states, notably with regard to the strong role of the state in many areas of the economy. But these tensions have been exacerbated by the failure of the West to accommodate China's rise.

As noted at the start, crystal ball gazing is difficult and can be dangerous. The narratives constructed around the rising powers, particularly China, will contribute to structuring the future and determining the extent to which that rise fractures global politics and economics in problematic and potentially perilous ways. Perhaps China will be a threat to the rules-based system of economic governance, and there is plenty of evidence that can be marshalled in favour of this possibility. Perhaps it will not, and there is also plenty of evidence that can be marshalled in favour of this alternative possibility. Dealing with such complexity demands a keen focus on case studies and particular disputes, alongside an open-minded approach that recognizes that issues are seldom black and white.

KEY POINTS

- Great caution is required in passing judgement on the actions of China or the other rising powers.

- Too often, China's actions are interpreted in a highly negative way when similar actions by Western powers are not.

- Some key thinkers have presented the rise of China as inevitably leading to conflict. This is analytically questionable and unhelpful as it could become a self-fulfilling prophecy.

- The issues arising from the emergence of China and the other rising powers are seldom as black and white as often made out. Care and nuance are needed.

12.7 Conclusion

This chapter has looked at two key areas of GPE that have been affected by the rising powers, namely trade and the creation of new development institutions. Brazil and India have risen to be powerful voices in the WTO, changing the dynamics of the organization and ending the previous dominance of the established industrialized countries. Though they continue to be relatively small economically compared to the global behemoths of the US, EU, and China, India and Brazil have leveraged their positions as leaders of the developing world to increase their influence. Crucially, they have not used that position to undermine the core tenets of the trade system, not least because trade has been an essential factor driving their economic growth. Rather, they have turned the liberal framework of the WTO back against the EU and US, highlighting their hypocrisy in advocating liberalization while maintaining protection of key sectors, and refusing to agree to further expansion of the trade agenda until that duplicity is addressed.

China's role in the WTO has been highly contentious. Some have argued that Beijing's state-led development policies and refusal to move towards a wholly market-based economy have all but killed the WTO, rendering its negotiation function defunct and challenging its future viability. And it is certainly the case that some areas of negotiation within the WTO are becoming harder to tackle because China dominates the problem and has little incentive to reach an agreement. This is particularly the case with fisheries subsidies.

Yet as we have also seen, there is always another side to the story, and criticism of China is all too often simplistic and lacking balance. Arguably, all WTO members are doing exactly the same thing: broadly operating within WTO law, with derogations where this conflicts with deeply embedded domestic programmes, while advocating liberalization in sectors in which they are competitive and resisting liberalization in sectors in which they are not. The major powers, whether rising or established, all closely fit this mould.

We have also seen that the rising powers, again most of all China, have engaged in the creation of new institutions of global governance, which have been similarly contentious. Where some see them as directly challenging the existing Western-centred institutions of the IMF and World Bank, others emphasize the potential complementarity between the Bretton Woods Institutions and the NDB, AIIB, and CRA. Nobody at present can fully determine where the truth lies within this debate, though it is clear that some of the evidence being marshalled in support of the idea that China is engaging in 'debt-trap diplomacy' is rather questionable. Picking through these competing narratives requires detailed, careful, empirical work, undertaken in a manner that is mindful of the biases prevalent in debates surrounding challenges to the Western powers.

? 12.8 QUESTIONS

1. Does the term 'rising powers' continue to have meaning given the fact that China, for instance, is the second largest economy in the world and is surely already 'risen'?

2. Has it ever made analytical sense to lump these countries into a single group given their heterogeneity?

3. What are the different strategies to securing greater global influence that Brazil, India, and China have utilized?

4. To what extent were the rising powers responsible for the collapse of the WTO's Doha Development Agenda?

5. To what extent is the rise of China challenging the World Bank and IMF?

6. Is China presenting a normative challenge to global political economy? If so, what are the alternative norms that it is pushing?

7. Is conflict with China inevitable? What would mitigate the risk?

8. To what extent does China have to be accommodated in the current structures of global economic governance? What are the benefits of doing so? What are the drawbacks?

9. Has the US or China done most to undermine the WTO system in recent years?

≋ 12.9 FURTHER READING

Bishop, M. L., and Xiaotong, Z. (2020), 'Why is China a Reluctant Leader of the World Trade Organization?', *New Political Economy*, 25/5: 755–772. Examines why China has not adopted a level of leadership in the WTO commensurate with its status as the world's largest trading nation.

Bräutigam, D. (2020), 'A Critical Look at Chinese "Debt-Trap Diplomacy": The Rise of a Meme', *Area Development and Policy*, 5/1: 1–14. An informed and concise critical analysis of the claims about China pursuing 'debt-trap diplomacy'.

Chin, G. T., and Gallagher, K. P. (2019), 'Coordinated Credit Spaces: The Globalization of Chinese Development Finance', *Development and Change* 50/1: 245–274. Examines China's emergence as a provider of finance for other countries, including through the AIIB, and how this differs from Western-led financing.

Hopewell, K. (2016), *Breaking the WTO: How Emerging Powers Disrupted the Neoliberal Project* (Stanford: Stanford University Press). Hopewell provides an excellent analysis of the role of China, India, and Brazil in the WTO and how their emergence disrupted the status quo.

Hopewell, K. (2020), *Clash of Powers: US–China Rivalry in Global Trade Governance* (Cambridge, MA: Cambridge University Press). The difficult relationship between the US and China will shape the world trade system in the foreseeable future. This book sets out some of the tensions between the two and the challenges China presents to the normative basis of the current system.

Jones, L., and Zeng, J. (2019), 'Understanding China's "Belt and Road Initiative": Beyond "Grand Strategy" to a State Transformation Analysis', *Third World Quarterly* 40/8: 1415–1439. This, and other work by the same authors, offers an important corrective to the tendency to view China as a unified state in which policy is driven from the top down. They highlight the need to examine China's internal political dynamics to understand its foreign policy.

Lesage, D., and Van de Graaf, T. (eds.) (2015), *Rising Powers and Multilateral Institutions.* (Basingstoke: Palgrave). This edited book provides a set of chapters looking at how a range of global institutions are being affected by the rising powers.

Mearsheimer, J. J. (2005), 'China's Unpeaceful Rise', *Current History*, 105/690: 160–162. Though criticized from many directions, this short article has been highly influential in shaping thinking about the rise of China and the likelihood of conflict and remains worth reading.

Posen, A. S. (2021), 'The Price of Nostalgia: America's Self-Defeating Economic Retreat', *Foreign Affairs*, 100/3: 28–43. How the West reacts to the shift in economic and political weight towards Asia is crucial not just for shaping the domestic effects of that process, but also the international consequences. This article provides a readable and critical examination of that reaction within the US.

Scott, J., and Wilkinson, R. (2022), 'China and the WTO, Redux: Making Sense of Two Decades of Membership', *Journal of World Trade*, 56/1: 87–110. This article analyses China's impact on the WTO after twenty years of membership, and the extent to which criticisms of China's behaviour are warranted.

CONTRIBUTOR NOTE

James Scott is Reader in International Political Economy in the Department of Political Economy at King's College London. He works on global governance, with a primary focus on trade, and mainly with regard to the relationship between trade governance and development. James has published widely across the fields of trade, global governance, International Political Economy, and development. He coedited the books *Trade, Poverty, Development: Getting beyond the WTO's Doha Deadlock* (2013) and *Expert Knowledge in Global Trade* (2015).

PART V

Development and Inequality

13

The Political Economy of Global Inequality

Erin Lockwood

Chapter contents

Reader's guide

The global political economy is characterized by tremendous disparities in wealth and income both within and between countries. Patterns of inequality have their origins in both historical institutions, like colonial extraction, as well as contemporary institutions, like the liberal trading order and financial capitalism. Although typically measured in economic terms, the consequences of global inequality go well beyond wealth and income to affect political institutions, labour conditions, and migration pressures and restrictions. However, not everyone agrees that global inequality is inherently a bad thing: some approaches to global justice emphasize absolute measures of economic wellbeing, such as GDP growth or declines in the number of people living in poverty, over relative concepts like levels of inequality. Nonetheless, many scholars and practitioners would prefer to reduce the level of global inequality in practice, and this chapter concludes with an overview of some policies that have been proposed as partial solutions.

13.1 Introduction

When asking audiences to think about global inequality, economist Dani Rodrik (2019) sometimes asks people to engage in the following thought experiment: Assuming you only care about your own income, would you rather be a rich person in a poor country or a poor person in a rich country? Here, we understand 'rich person' as someone having an income in the top 5 per cent of their national income distribution, 'poor person' as someone having an income in the bottom 5 per cent of their national income distribution, 'rich country' as a country with a per capita income falling in the top 5 per cent of the global distribution, and 'poor country' as a country with a per capita income falling in the bottom 5 per cent of the global distribution. From the perspective of your expected income, there is a correct answer to this question: It is far better to be a poor person in a rich country than a rich person in a poor country. The representative (adjusted for purchasing power) annual income for a poor person in a rich country is about US$13,000, whereas the representative income for the latter is about $5,039. This disparity reflects the disproportionate impact that one's country of residence has on determining one's material wellbeing. Indeed, while everyone's annual income is determined by many factors (education, profession, race, gender, skill, etc.), economist Branko Milanovic (2015) estimates that, at the global level, somewhere around 70 per cent of the variation in individual income can be explained by just one piece of data: the country where you live. The observation that so much of one's material wellbeing is determined by a factor almost entirely outside of one's control has profound implications for both migration politics, as discussed in Section 13.3.3, and for how we think about the ethics of global inequality, as discussed in Section 13.4.

We can account for 90 per cent of variation in individual income in a given ventile of the global distribution by looking at just two factors: class (where a person falls in their national income distribution) and location (the country they live in) (Milanovic 2015). The proportion in which these two factors have affected the global distribution of income has shifted over time. Historically, prior to the first wave of economic globalization in the mid-nineteenth century, class was the dominant determinant of average incomes at the global level. With the advent of industrialization and the colonial domination of non-industrialized countries by industrialized

colonizers, income gaps between the former and the latter began to widen. For much of the twentieth century, national location came to have a much greater impact on one's income than class (Bourguignon and Morrisson 2002). Today, there is reason to think that that trend may be once more reversing, as rising inequality in rich countries has led to a resurgence of class-based inequality (Chancel and Piketty 2021). The global distribution of wealth is even more unequal than the global distribution of income: the poorest 50 per cent of the world owns only 2 per cent of the world's total wealth, and the top 10 per cent owns 76 per cent of all wealth (Chancel and Piketty 2021).

While some level of inequality in any society is likely inevitable, contemporary global economic inequality is, in no small part, the result of both historical and contemporary political decisions, institutionalized in international economic institutions, practices, and norms, about how income and wealth should be apportioned. Many of the other topics discussed in this textbook—colonial extraction, trade, finance, development—have profound implications for the global distribution of material resources. If the causes of global inequality are political, so too are its consequences, insofar as income and especially wealth are sources of power in national and international politics.

Why are the world's wealth and income so unequally distributed? What role do historical forces play in structuring today's distribution, and how much of an impact do contemporary economic institutions of trade, finance, and development have in this equation? Does inequality matter, politically and ethically? Is it really such a bad thing? If we decide it does matter, what tools and policies are available to reduce global economic inequality? This chapter will provide an overview of some of the answers scholars have given to these questions.

13.2 Measuring global inequality

Measuring global income inequality is important for several reasons: measuring inequality accurately is a prerequisite for making any statistical claims about the causes and consequences of changes in inequality over time; being able to track changes in inequality matters for envisioning and implementing effective redistributive policies; and knowing how unequal a society is may affect our ethical judgements about whether that society is structured justly or not. So, just how unequal is the global distribution of income? Answering that question is not straightforward, and different measurements tell us different stories about how inequality has changed over the past century and a half.

13.2.1 Relative and absolute measures of global inequality

Before we attempt to measure *global* inequality, it is helpful to know some basic concepts used in measuring inequality more generally. The first of these is the **Gini coefficient**, a statistical measure of the dispersion of incomes within a society (see Key Concept Box 13.1).

Frequently, when thinking about the global political economy of inequality, we want to be able to talk about changes in inequality over time. A second important concept in the context of measuring inequality is the difference between **relative inequality** and **absolute inequality**. To understand the difference, we can work through an example comparing the annual income of two imagined individuals in a developing country in 1986 versus 2016 (see Figure 13.3).

Suppose the representative daily income of a poor person in that county in 1986 was about US$0.10, and the representative daily income of a rich person in 1986 was about US$0.80. By 2016, suppose that the representative daily income of a poor person had increased to US$10, while the representative income of a rich person had increased to US$80. Would you say inequality had increased in that country over this period? Answering this question depends on whether you are thinking in relative or absolute terms. Relative inequality measures the ratio of two incomes (that is, how many times richer is A than B?). Absolute inequality measures the difference between two incomes (that is, how much more money does A make than B?). In relative terms, inequality has remained unchanged in our imaginary developing economy: each person's income has increased one hundredfold, and a rich person still makes roughly eight times what a poor person does. But in absolute terms, the gap has widened dramatically: from a difference of US$0.70 to a difference of US$70. People may disagree about whether relative or absolute inequality is a better way of accounting for this change, but generally speaking we tend to use relative measures (like the Gini coefficient) to account for

---

KEY CONCEPT BOX 13.1 THE GINI COEFFICIENT

The Gini coefficient is a single number that captures the level of inequality within a society, making it a useful way to compare levels of inequality across time and space. The Gini coefficient is calculated using the Lorenz curve, which depicts the percentage of income or wealth (on the y axis) held by a given percentile of the distribution of a population (on the x axis). The 45° line depicts a perfectly equal distribution of income, and as the Lorenz curve approaches 90°, the distribution of income becomes less and less equal (see Figure 13.1). The Gini coefficient is the area between the Lorenz curve and the 45° line of perfect equality as a percentage of the total area below the line of perfect inequality. The Gini coefficient ranges between 0 (in a perfectly equal distribution) and 1 (in a society where all the income is held by one person) (see Figure 13.2).

Most countries have a Gini coefficient somewhere between 0.2 and 0.7. For example, according to 2020 Organization for Economic Cooperation and Development (OECD) data, Norway, a state with strong redistributive policies, had a Gini coefficient of 0.263, whereas Mexico's Gini coefficient was 0.420. The United States has a Gini coefficient of 0.378. Outside of the OECD, some states have even higher Gini coefficients. The

World Bank estimates Brazil's Gini coefficient to be 0.489, and South Africa's is 0.63. The global Gini coefficient—an estimate of how unequal the distribution of incomes is at the global level—is even higher; Hellebrandt and Mauro (2015) estimate the global Gini coefficient for income to be 0.649, and the global distribution of wealth, rather than income, is even higher yet, estimated at 0.922 (Davies et al. 2017).

The Gini coefficient is not the only statistical measure of inequality within a population; other measures capture the ratio between the income of the top 20 per cent and bottom 20 per cent of the population or various other segments of the income distribution. Alternative measures of inequality can be useful in cases where we want to know more about *how* a population's inequality changed over time. For instance, one way that inequality can increase is if the rich get richer and the poor get poorer. But inequality can also increase if both the rich and the poor get richer, as long as the rich are getting richer faster than the poor are getting richer. The Gini coefficient cannot capture this kind of nuance. Nonetheless, the Gini coefficient (sometimes rendered as the Gini index) is widely used as a means of comparing levels of inequality between countries.

Figure 13.1 The Lorenz curve

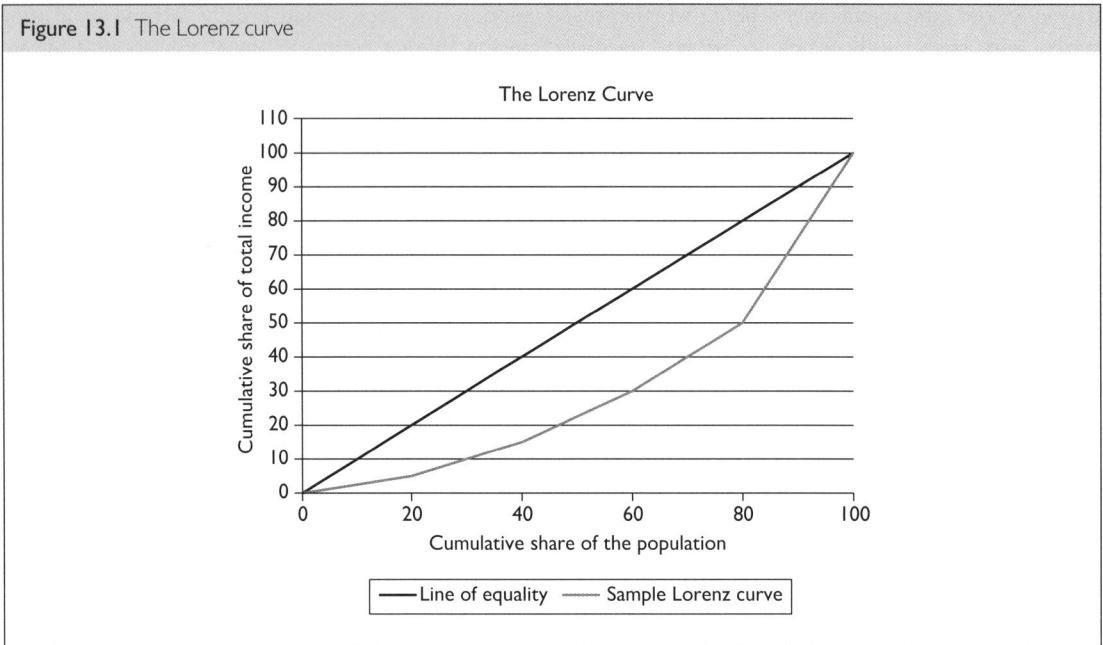

The Lorenz Curve

— Line of equality ⸺ Sample Lorenz curve

Figure 13.2 Calculating the Gini coefficient

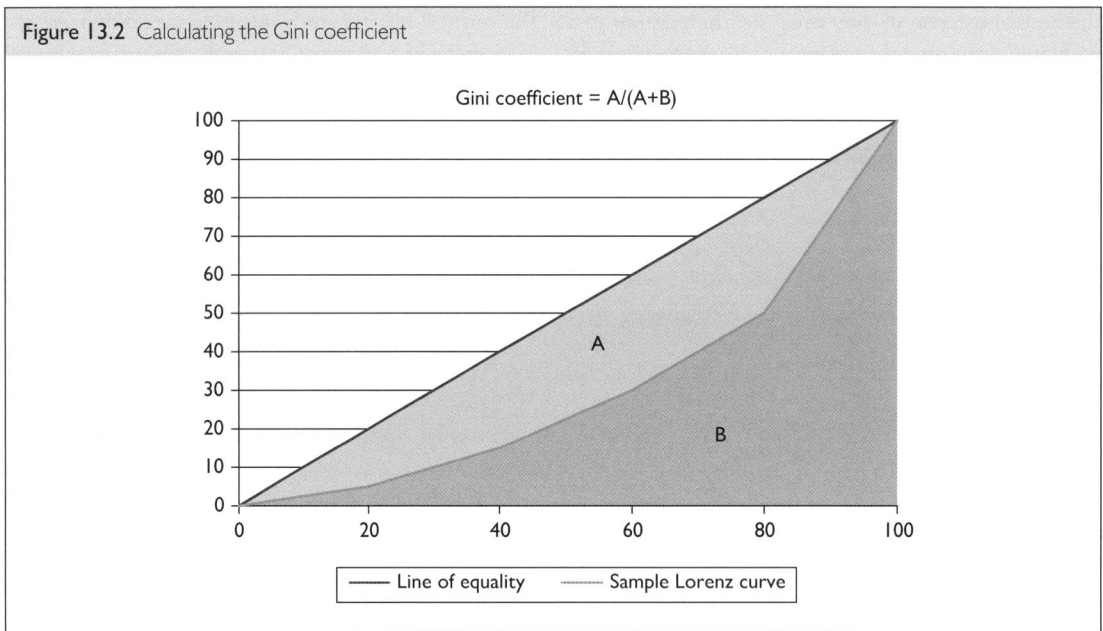

Gini coefficient = A/(A+B)

— Line of equality ⸺ Sample Lorenz curve

changes in inequality over time. All economic growth tends to increase absolute inequality, but the same is not true for relative inequality, and we often want to be able to distinguish between economic growth that exacerbates relative inequality versus economic growth that ameliorates relative inequality.

13.2.2 Three approaches to measuring global inequality

We want to be able to talk about *global* inequality—not just whether particular countries' income distributions are becoming more or less equal over time,

Figure 13.3 Absolute versus relative income inequality

Income growth in a representative developing country, 1986–2016

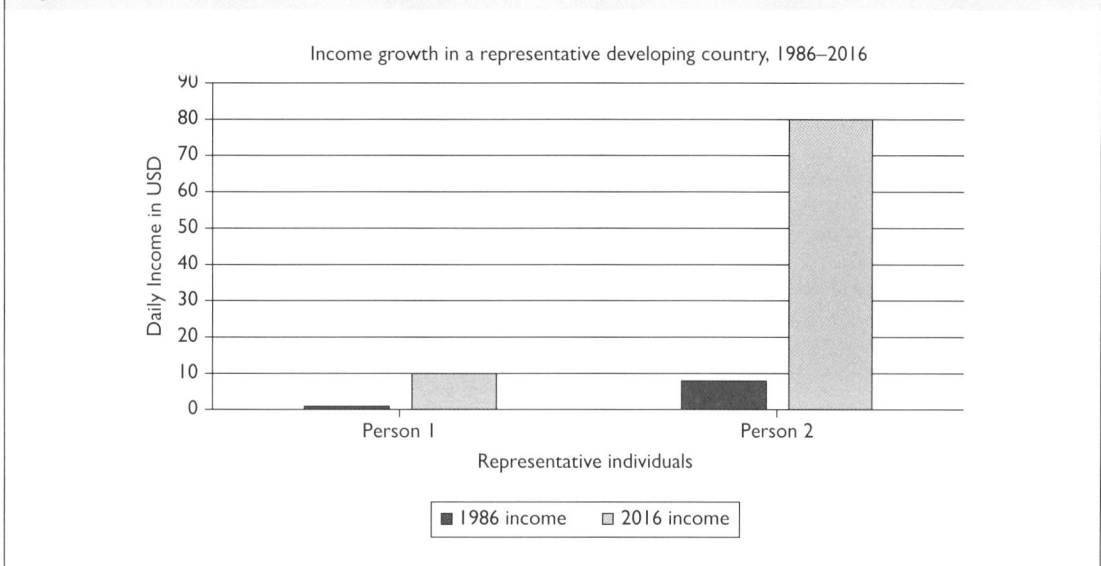

Representative individuals

■ 1986 income   □ 2016 income

but whether the world as a whole is. That is, we want a Gini coefficient for the whole world that we can track over time. But how should this global Gini be calculated? Economist Branko Milanovic (2005: 7–12) distinguishes among three approaches to calculating global inequality. The first of these uses the per capita gross domestic product (GDP) of each country in the world to calculate the global Gini coefficient; rather than each person in a country being one unit of observation as in a national Gini coefficient, this measurement treats each country's per capita GDP as a unit of observation. The problem with this approach is that countries have wildly different populations. Using this concept means that an increase in the average income in Iceland (population 372,520) would have the same impact on the global Gini as an increase in the average income in India (population 1.4 billion). To correct for this, a second approach weights each country's per capita GDP by population. The problem with this approach is that, as we know from our discussion of national Gini coefficients, countries have very different national income distributions. Per capita GDP only tells us about the average income—nothing about the distribution.

The third approach to calculating global inequality is intended to account for differences both among and within countries. Rather than treating each country as an observation, this approach imagines we could line up all 8.1 billion people on earth according to their

income and calculate the global Gini coefficient on this basis. This is a measure of *interpersonal* **global inequality**, rather than international (between-nation) inequality. The challenge with such an approach is that we do not have reliable data about every single individuals' income; there is no global household income survey. The best approximations are national income statistics, based on household surveys of representative samples of a given country's population. There are significant data limitations to calculating a true global interpersonal measure of inequality: states vary in their capacity to collect income data; sample sizes used in national income accounting vary widely; the survey data national estimates are based on are conducted at irregular and varying intervals; national statistics omit both the bottom of the distribution (for example, unhoused people) and the top of the distribution (the very rich generally underreport their true income). Moreover, correcting for differences in price levels among all the world's countries adds a further complication (see Key Concept Box 13.2) Nonetheless, economists Christopher Lakner and Branko Milanovic (2016) have used historical and contemporary household survey data, coupled with purchasing power parity exchange rates, to generate income distribution data for more than one hundred countries from the late 1980s until the present. While limited, these data nonetheless give us some idea of the depth and extent of global interpersonal inequality.

KEY CONCEPT BOX 13.2 PURCHASING POWER PARITY

One significant problem in aggregating national economic statistics, like household income, at the global level is that price levels vary significantly among countries. While we can use exchange rates to normalize household income statistics into a common currency (for example, convert CFA francs into US dollars), it is still the case that one US dollar will purchase very different baskets of goods in, for example, Sweden and Mali. To account for this, we need what are called purchasing power parity (PPP) exchange rates—that is, exchange rates that tell us how much of one currency you would need to purchase an equivalent basket of goods in another currency.

The PPP exchange rate between global currencies and the home currencies of low-income countries will often be quite different than the official exchange rate since price levels are generally lower in low-income countries. For example, the average official exchange rate between Indonesia and the US in 2021 was 14,308 rupiah to one US dollar. But the PPP exchange rate in 2021 was 4,758 rupiah to one US dollar. That means that while you would have needed 14,308 rupiah to purchase a US dollar, you would only have needed 4,758 rupiah in Indonesia to purchase the same amount of goods and services that one US dollar could buy in the United States.

KEY POINTS

- An important statistical measure of inequality is the Gini coefficient, which ranges from 0 (perfectly equal) to 1 (perfectly unequal).

- When thinking about how global inequality has changed over time, we can use either relative or absolute measures, but relative measures are more common.

- There are multiple ways to conceptualize and measure 'global inequality' because there is important variation both among individuals within a given country and among countries themselves.

- A measure of global interpersonal income inequality best accounts for inequality within and between countries, but there are limitations to calculating this measure.

13.3 History of global inequality

Now that we know something about how to measure global income inequality, we can turn to the questions of whether it has increased or decreased historically and what has caused these changes. Global income inequality today is very high; by some estimates, the global Gini coefficient is higher than any individual country's Gini coefficient (Hellebrandt and Mauro 2015: 13). But does this mean that inequality is at an all-time high? How have the major economic changes of the past two centuries affected global inequality? As you might guess from the preceding section's discussion of multiple measures of inequality, the answer in part depends on how you measure inequality. But recent efforts to amass high-quality income data going back to the mid-nineteenth century have

provided us with the ability to chart patterns in the history of global inequality (Chancel and Piketty 2021; Chancel et al. 2022). As Figure 13.4 depicts, global inequality as measured by the unweighted Gini coefficient increased throughout the nineteenth century, declined during the world wars and interwar years, and began to increase again from about 1960 onwards, peaking in 2000 and decreasing in the first decades of the twenty-first century. There is not one parsimonious explanation for this trajectory, but this section of the chapter will tell you some of what we know about the political economy behind this graph.

13.3.1 Colonial origins of inequality

No society has a perfectly equal distribution of resources, and the world as a whole is no exception. Nonetheless, we should understand global inequality not as an unfortunate inevitability, but rather as the result of identifiable political choices, practices, and norms. In particular, the divergence between rich and poor countries today can be traced back to colonial and imperial practices on which industrialization and the first wave of globalization were founded.

Central to the practice of European colonialism is what is known as the 'colonial contract' (Mills 1997: 25), a series of formal and informal institutions established by colonizing powers that legitimated European domination in the colonies. Rooted in white supremacy, the colonial contract included a set of economic practices between colonies and the metropole, inducing dependence of the colony on the metropole by limiting imports from and exports to third countries and preventing colonies from producing

Figure 13.4 Global income inequality: Gini index, 1820–2020

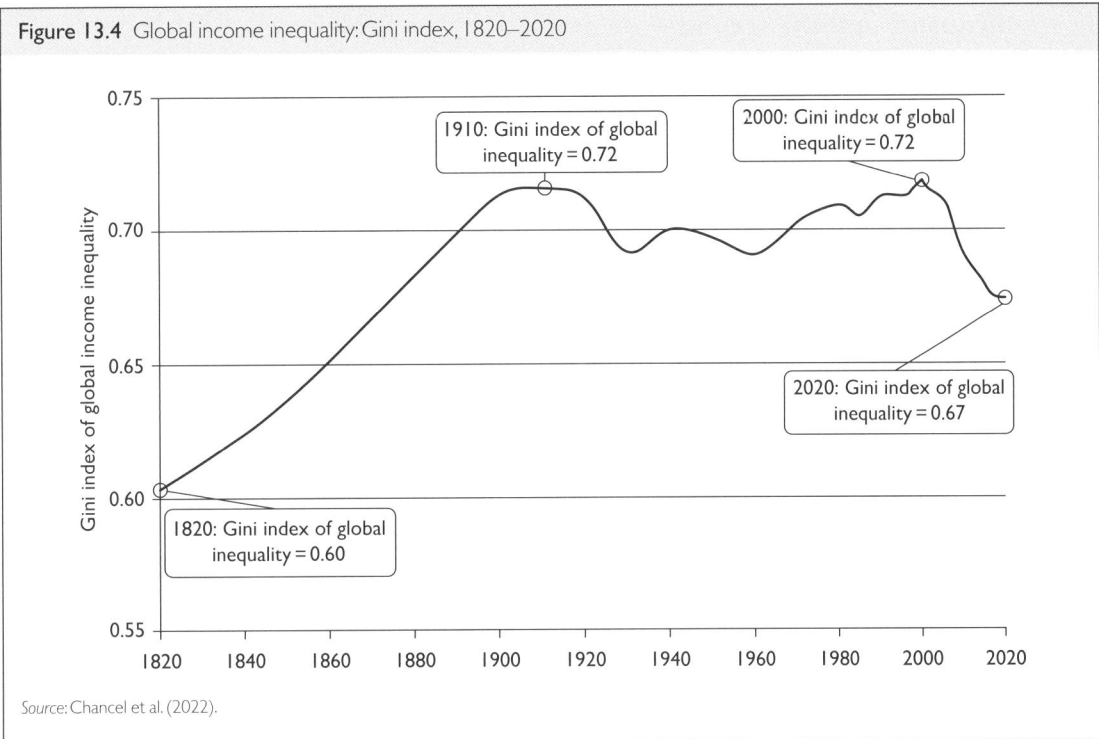

Source: Chancel et al. (2022).

manufactured goods that would compete with those produced in the metropole. As a result, as colonizing powers grew richer their colonies were prohibited from industrializing, dependent on low-value commodity exports, and stripped of their resources. Fuelled by these imperial dynamics, estimates of global inequality show a clear increase from 1820 to 1910 (Chancel and Piketty 2021).

The hierarchical domination of the colonial contract was heightened even further through the close imbrication of the Atlantic slave trade with European economic development. While economic historians debate about how to quantify the contribution of slavery to European economic development (Williams 1994; Eltis and Engerman 2000), the labour of enslaved people produced much of the raw material that fuelled American and European industrialization. For example, until 1861 almost all of the cotton used in industrial production was grown by enslaved workers in the American South (Beckert and Rockman 2016). Profits from slave labour were invested in banks, textile factories, and infrastructure (Berry 2017), and the risks of the slave trade and the commodification of human bodies were closely linked to the development of private credit, securitized assets, and the modern insurance industry (Baucom 2005), financial technologies that contributed to the economic development of countries participating in the slave trade, even as legacies of slavery and its aftermath have produced a massive and enduring racial wealth gap in the United States (Desmond 2019).

These practices of exploitation and domination cast long shadows. Acemoglu, Johnson, and Robinson (2001) have found that extractive colonial institutions, premised on the often violent expropriation of human and natural resources, persisted after decolonization. Elites who retained power after decolonization tended to benefit from these institutions, which both heighted inequality between elites and the masses within postcolonial states (within-country inequality) and were causally associated with lower per capita GDPs in comparison to post-colonial states where colonizers established (and post-colonial governments inherited) institutions more similar to those of the metropole. As discussed in Section 13.2.3, scholars disagree about how much latitude post-colonial states have to escape the detrimental legacies of colonialism, but there can be little doubt that this history is crucial context to understanding contemporary patterns of global inequality, both within and between states.

13.3.2 **Inequality and the second wave of globalization**

Most of what we know about how global income inequality has changed over time focuses on the second half of the twentieth century through the present, and especially on the period from roughly 1980 to the present. This period tracks major changes in economic globalization dating from the end of the Second World War: the advent of the liberal international economic order and international organizations like the International Monetary Fund (IMF), World Bank, and the General Agreement on Tariffs and Trade (GATT) / the World Trade Organization (WTO); the rise and fall of the Bretton Woods monetary order and proliferation of floating exchange rates; a dramatic increase in international capital mobility from the 1970s onwards; the globalization of production; the dominance and subsequent retrenchment of the Washington Consensus paradigm for international development (see Trommer, Chapter 5, Helleiner, Chapter 8, and Bhagat, Chapter 14). All of these changes, and more, have affected the global distribution of income both within and among states.

How has twentieth-century globalization affected the global income distribution? Measured in absolute terms, global inequality increased dramatically between 1975 and 2010 (Niño-Zarazúa et al. 2017). Measured in relative terms, the picture is more complicated.

Using the first approach to measuring global inequality, per capita GDP unweighted by population, global inequality as measured by the Gini coefficient increased markedly over the second half of the twentieth century before starting to fall around the year 2000. But the second approach, in which each country's GDP is weighted by its population, shows that global inequality has declined steadily over the second half of the twentieth century and more sharply after 1990. Why has global inequality increased according to the first measure and decreased according to the second? The answer lies in the rapid economic growth of China and India, two very populous countries whose high growth rates dominate the data when we use weighted Gini coefficients. In fact, almost all of the decrease in global inequality measured according to per capita GDPs can be accounted for by China's economic rise (Milanovic 2003). Recall that the measure of economic inequality that comes closest to capturing inequality both among and within countries is

to measure the global interpersonal Gini coefficient. When we take national income distributions into account, the picture becomes fuzzier. Even as the past four decades have been characterized by rapidly rising incomes in many countries (and especially in some of the most populous ones), leading to a decline in population-weighted between-country inequality, within-country inequality began to increase during this period for the first time since the late nineteenth and early twentieth centuries (Chancel and Piketty 2021). As a result, interpersonal income inequality as measured by a global Gini coefficient has remained relatively constant over this time. Figure 13.5 depicts the changes in inequality since 1950 according to each of these three approaches.

Going beyond the Gini coefficient helps us understand how the economic growth of the most recent wave of globalization has been distributed. Branko Milanovic's '**elephant curve**' (Figure 13.6)—so called because its shape resembles an elephant's head and trunk—is one way of visualizing this. This graph (a growth incidence curve) depicts the percentage gain in real household income for different parts of the global income distribution between 1988 and 2008. For example, we can see that real incomes for people in the 50th percentile of the global income distribution grew by about 80 per cent during this period. People in the 99th percentile also saw a large growth in their incomes. In contrast, growth was quite low—under 20 per cent and occasionally even negative—for people between the 75th and 95th percentiles. This graph shows us that the 'winners' from the past decades of globalization and attendant global growth have been people in the middle class of emerging economies (point A on Figure 13.6) and the very rich—the global top 1 per cent, which roughly corresponds to anyone making more than US$65,000 a year (point C on Figure 13.6). (You'll note that the global top 1 per cent includes many people in rich countries who would not be in the top 1 per cent of their national income distributions). In contrast, people in the bottom half of rich countries' income distributions (those in the 80th and 90th deciles globally) have seen very low rates of growth over the past decades.

Why does it matter whether global inequality has increased or decreased? As Martin Ravaillon (2018) explains, the conclusions we draw in answer to this question have important political consequences. If we determine, based on relative measures, that global inequality has fallen in the wake

Figure 13.5 Changes in global inequality, according to three measures

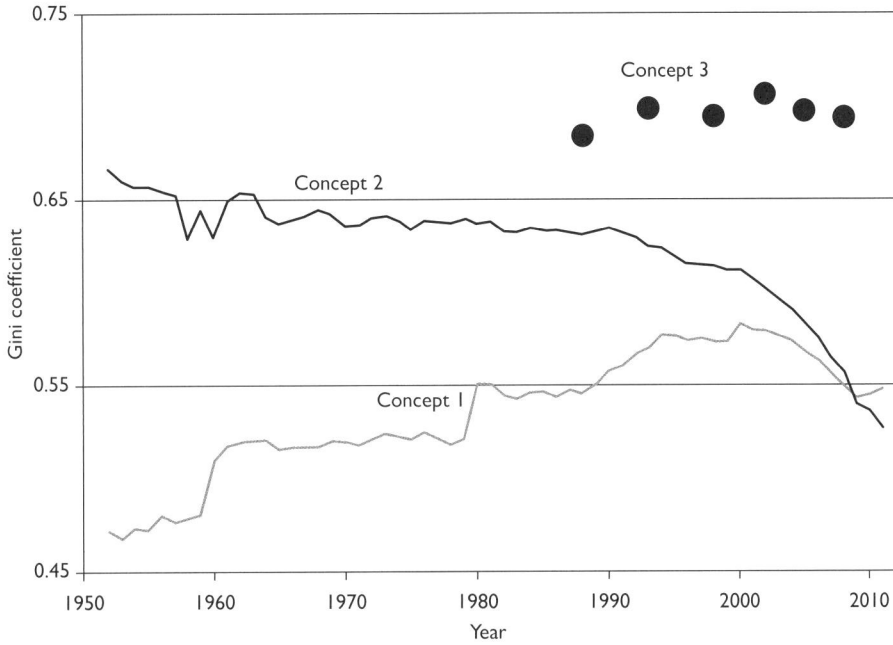

Source: Milanovic (2013).

Figure 13.6 Relative gain in real per capita income by global income level, 1988–2008

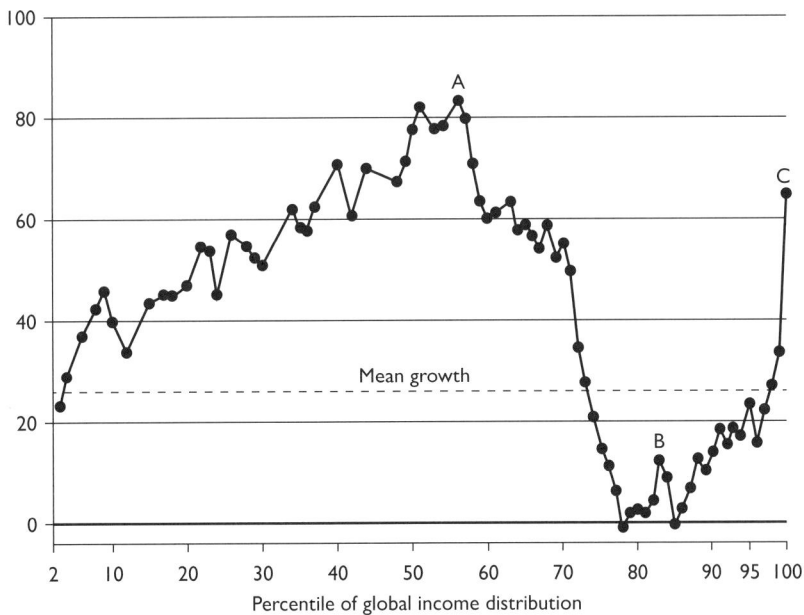

Source: Milanovic (2016).

of globalization and liberal economic policies, then there is little justification for pushing for greater regulation and redistribution to reduce global inequality. We might conclude that globalization has been a dramatic success in terms of both raising incomes and lowering inequality. But if we look at absolute measures—or want to look at the world beyond China's and India's very high growth rates—we might temper our judgement of globalization's gains. Looking at interpersonal measures of inequality reveals a more nuanced depiction of the winners and losers (in purely economic terms) from the past decades of globalization.

13.3.3 Explaining global inequality

Scholars of global political economy have sought to explain the uneven gains from globalization in various ways. In the 1950s and 1960s, American economists were optimistic about developing countries' growth prospects, assuming that as international markets liberalized and capital markets opened, capital would flow from rich countries, where returns were relatively low, to poor countries, where returns were higher. According to **modernization theory**, this influx of foreign capital and production technology would jump-start growth in poor countries, allowing them to follow the same path to prosperity that industrialized countries had followed in the nineteenth century. However, this has only been unevenly the case at best. Some poor countries have remained very poor while others have seen very high rates of economic growth.

What accounts for these uneven growth rates? Many explanations emphasize either structure (that is, states' location within hierarchical patterns of exchange) or agency (that is, the policy choices of leaders in terms of things like trade liberalization, capital market openness, and national fiscal and monetary policy). Explanations that emphasize structure are consistent with **world-systems theory,** with its emphasis on states' structural position within global systems of exchange and extraction (see Key Theory Box 13.3). These approaches to world politics fell out of favour in the Global North in the 1980s and 1990s as Asian economies grew very quickly, integrating into the global economy with a heavy dose of state intervention. For some observers, the export-led economic growth of previously very poor states—coupled with low long-run growth rates in states that adopted policies like import-substitution industrialization—undermined world-systems theory's central claim that developing states were trapped in structurally unequal relations.

In the wake of structuralist explanations for the persistent gaps between countries, explanations that instead emphasize the impact of policy choice on states' economic trajectories came to dominate scholarship on the topic of global inequality (see, for example, Krueger 1990). These explanations aligned with what have historically been the priorities of international economic institutions like the WTO,

---

KEY THEORY BOX 13.3 WORLD-SYSTEMS THEORY AND DEPENDENCY THEORY

World-systems theory is an approach to studying global political economy that takes the international division of labour among capital-rich and capital-poor countries and regions as foundational to understanding key outcomes in world politics. According to this theory, the global political economy is hierarchically structured, with the industrialized 'core' persistently benefitting at the expense of countries and regions in the periphery and semi-periphery whose economies are dominated by the production and extraction of raw materials. World-systems theory developed as a critique of modernization theory (see Bhagat, Chapter 14), which assumed that developing states would follow more or less the same path to industrialization that rich countries had. In contrast, world-systems theory built on dependency theory, which argued that developing countries cannot easily replicate rich countries' path towards industrialization because of the structure of global markets. Dependency theory was rooted in what is known as the Prebisch-Singer thesis, the idea that developing countries face declining terms of trade over time: the price of the primary goods and raw materials they export tends to remain constant or even decline as the price of manufactured goods imported from rich countries increases, entrenching developing countries in poverty and preventing them from 'catching up'. A core implication of both dependency theory and world-systems theory is that the structure of global capitalism produces a persistently unequal balance of economic power between rich and poor countries. For a discussion on the relevance of dependency theory to global political economy today, see Kvangraven (2020).

World Bank, and IMF. During the 1990s and early 2000s, these organizations embraced what is known as the **Washington Consensus**, variously encouraging and pressuring poor states into adopting liberal market policies (for example, trade liberalization, open capital markets, cuts to government spending and taxes) as a condition for receiving access to international markets, loans, and development finance. But as much as the growth of many Asian economies in the 1980s and 1990s challenged the core of dependency theory, the failure of the Washington Consensus to produce sustained growth in poor countries challenged the idea that liberalizing economic institutions was sufficient to close the gap between rich and poor countries.

We do not have one simple explanation for why some countries' economies have grown rapidly and others have not. We know that states' choice of economic institutions matter, but we also know that states are not completely free to choose their institutions and policies. Contemporary inequalities have their roots in colonial and post-colonial patterns of exploitation and coercion.

13.4 Consequences of global inequality

Thus far, we have mainly talked about global inequality in terms of economic measures: income, wealth, and growth rates. But global inequality has consequences that extend far beyond individual and national income. Because income and especially wealth are closely linked with political power, global inequality has profound implications for structures and relations of power at the global level. Economic inequality is deeply intertwined with inequalities of race, gender, and national origin, and global inequality has consequences across nearly all domains of international politics, from health to the environment to security. This section explores some of those consequences in the areas of politics and capital accumulation, labour governance, and migration.

13.4.1 **Wealth and political inequality**

Societies with highly unequal distributions of income and wealth tend to be accompanied by unequal political institutions as well. Sometimes the reasons for this are fairly straightforward: rent-seeking by governments concentrates resources in the hands of elites, and successfully running for elected office in competitive democracies requires varying (but often very high) levels of resources and elite connections. As a result, the people who would benefit the most from redistributive policies that would bring down inequality tend to be excluded from the very institutions that would authorize that redistribution (see Figures 13.7 and 13.8).

The work of Thomas Piketty (2017) helps us understand another mechanism through which wealth inequality tends to produce unequal political systems that in turn perpetuate economic inequality. Drawing on historical evidence from capital-rich countries, Piketty identifies what he terms a 'central contradiction' in capitalist economies: the average annual rate of return to capital investments consistently is greater than the rate of economic growth. Profits, dividends, interest, rents, and other forms of income from capital grow faster than income from labour, the form of income the vast majority of people rely on globally. Piketty (2017: 544–545) additionally finds that returns to capital are not evenly distributed: the more capital you

---

KEY POINTS

- Colonial practices of domination and expropriation drove global inequality sharply upwards during the nineteenth century. Legacies of those practices continue to shape the global distribution of wealth and income today.

- Twentieth-century globalization has had multiple effects on the global distribution of income. While gaps between rich and poor countries remain huge, the growth of populous countries like China and India has driven down inequality when we weigh observations by population.

- When we look at the global interpersonal distribution of income, we see that globalization has produced clear winners (the middle of the global income distribution, corresponding roughly to the middle-class in emerging economies; the global top 1 per cent) and losers (the top ventiles of the global distribution, corresponding roughly to the lower class in rich countries).

- Scholars have attempted to theorize the relationship between globalization and inequality in different ways, placing varying amounts of emphasis on the importance of global structures of economic hierarchy and the policy choices of leaders in poor countries in explaining the divergence between rich and poor countries.

Figure 13.7 Makoko, a fishing community in Lagos, grapples with severely neglected living conditions exacerbated by its location atop heavily contaminated water, standing in stark contrast to the neighbouring areas of Lagos and juxtaposed against the luxury housing development project Eko Atlantic, designed for the high-income population.

Source: Shutterstock.

Figure 13.8 Ikoyi, situated across the Lagos Lagoon on Lagos Island, stands as one of the most affluent and prosperous districts within Lagos.

Source: Shutterstock.

have, the higher your average returns, since wealthier people have a greater ability to take on risk and can afford more sophisticated investment and wealth management services. As a result, inequality is a structural feature of capitalist economies. Absent very strong redistributive policies, like taxes on capital gains, inheritance, and financial transactions, those who earn their living from capital investments will get richer much faster than those for whom wages are a primary source of income. Those who benefit from this system have little incentive to change it. This dynamic can help us understand, at least in part, why within-country inequality has been increasing since about 1980, when capital market openness took hold globally, bolstered by pressure from international lenders and developers to liberalize national economies (Chancel et al. 2022).

Piketty's research focuses on returns to capital and wealth accumulation within national economies, but we know that concentrations of wealth are very high at the global level as well—recall that the global Gini coefficient for wealth is even higher than the global Gini for income (Davies et al. 2017). As with income inequality, between-country inequality accounts for a significant portion (estimated at 79 per cent) of that variation. Much like highly unequal national economies often struggle to implement redistributive policies that would tamp down inequality due to the close relationship between political and economic inequality, the same is also true at the global level. The absence of effective global governance around tax sheltering and financial regulation means that the very high levels of returns to capital are seldom redistributed either nationally or globally, but instead remain highly concentrated (see Murphy 2001). This can happen through a couple of pathways.

Wealthy businesses and individuals in high-tax jurisdictions are frequently able to take profits to **'offshore' tax havens**—foreign jurisdictions with lax tax policies—to avoid paying taxes. This is often perfectly legal (though not always—we call that money laundering). Tax havens are often thought of as microstates like the Seychelles, British Virgin Islands, and Liechtenstein, but they are not always: Australia, Switzerland, and the Netherlands also function as tax havens in some contexts (Sharman 2017). Tax havens can shelter bank accounts, insulating capital from taxation in the capital holder's home country, but they can also shelter companies, frequently referred to as **shell companies**. These are companies that exist entirely or almost entirely on paper—they don't have a physical office or staff within the country where they are incorporated, and they are used to facilitate financial transactions, shield assets from national regulators, avoid taxes, and sometimes to launder money. Tax havens and shell companies hinder the ability of states in both rich and poor countries to redistribute the income and wealth of the richest individuals. Efforts to regulate these practices, even when implemented, can sometimes have unintended consequences.

While national anti-money laundering laws have proliferated in the past decades, J. C. Sharman (2011) finds that these policies have largely been ineffective at cracking down on untraceable shell companies.

Instead, they have worked to the advantage of large rich states whose lax tax policies go unchecked and to the detriment of poor small states who are frequently targets of these laws, further widening the gap between rich and poor countries and concentrating wealth in the hands of the very rich.

13.4.2 Inequality and global labour governance

Global inequality does not just benefit holders of capital; it also frequently harms the interests of workers. On the one hand, the second wave of globalization has led to a dramatic increase in income and fall in poverty. In 2015, World Bank President Jim Yong Kim announced that the proportion of the world's population living in poverty had fallen below 10 per cent, calling this 'the best news story in the world' (*The Economist* 2015). On the other hand, however, the international division of labour between capital-rich and capital-poor countries means that the kinds of jobs available to people in rich and poor countries are often very different and unequally compensated. For certain kinds of jobs—those deemed (often pejoratively) 'low skilled'—it is cheaper for multinational corporations (MNCs) headquartered in rich countries to outsource labour to countries where labour is relatively abundant and cheap. Many countries implement policies to attract lucrative manufacturing contracts by establishing **special economic zones**, which are often characterized by lax labour laws and enforcement, in addition to tax breaks and weak environmental protections. When poor countries compete for foreign capital on the basis of low labour costs, there is a **race to the bottom** in terms of labour standards. Mosley and Uno (2007) find that MNCs' investments do not always lead to this race to the bottom, but when MNCs prioritize economic efficiency over things like labour quality and minimizing worker turnover, labour standards degrade.

The consequences of this race to the bottom are profound. Weak labour protections mean that workers in low-wage sectors are not just poorly compensated for their work, but also vulnerable to both economic and physical harm, in the form of exploitation, wage theft, suppressed bargaining rights, and exposure to higher rates of industrial accidents and workplace fires (see Gore, Chapter 7). There are many examples of these harms in traditional labour-intensive sectors of the global economy. One example, garment manufacturing, is discussed in Everyday GPE Box 13.4. At the

EVERYDAY GPE BOX 13.4 THE COST OF CHEAP CLOTHES

We live in a world of fast fashion. Whether it is the demise of skinny jeans, the ever evolving sneaker economy, or the return to styles from the 1990s, trends can shift on a dime, and consumers expect to be able to purchase the latest fashions for cheap to keep up. Take a look at the label of the clothes you have on as you are reading this. Where were they made? If they come from a major brand, it is likely they were made in China, Bangladesh, Vietnam, or India, countries where labour is comparatively cheap and labour and environmental protections weak. Such countries have a comparative advantage in garment manufacturing and some, like Bangladesh, are highly dependent on it: 84 per cent of Bangladesh's export earnings in 2019–2020 came from garment exports (Swazan, Sharif, and Das 2022). This dependence comes at a high cost: even if they wanted to improve working conditions, such states can ill-afford to do so, lest the global brands which subcontract with their factories take their business elsewhere. The combination of competitive pressures to keep wages low and highly volatile demand from MNCs operating in the fast fashion sector mean that working conditions in the garment industry are extremely poor. The industry relies on 'just-in-time' production to create and meet demand for trendy products; firms keep very low inventories and expect clothing to be produced very quickly. As a result of this volatile demand for labour, workers are often confronted with periods of long and demanding work days, alternating with times of no work at all. Conditions are often especially perilous for female workers. Garment manufacturing is a female-dominated industry, and MNCs' recruitment and employment practices often exploit local gender inequalities to reinforce a gendered division of labour that relegates women to low-wage work (Elias 2004).

In addition to the low wages (the minimum wage in Bangladesh is 32 cents an hour), working conditions in garment factories are often hazardous. There is little incentive to maintain health and safety standards, and production often occurs in crowded rooms with too few exits, dangerous wiring, and crumbling architecture. Industrial 'accidents'—the foreseeable result of these conditions—are all too common. Between 2006 and 2012, more than 500 Bangladeshi garment workers died in factory fires. Then in November 2012, the Tazreen Fashions factory burned, killing at least 117 people and injuring 200 more. Just five months later, in 2013, an eight-story-high factory building in Dhaka's Rana Plaza collapsed, crushing workers within it, killing more than 1,133 people and injuring 2,500 in the deadliest garment industry accident in modern history.

The perils of cheap clothes are not limited to Bangladesh. The Chinese fast fashion company Shein takes many of these trends to an extreme. The company sells very cheap, mostly polyester clothes online, and uses a sophisticated internal software system that collects real-time data about sales and aggressively advertises popular items online, often via social media influencers on TikTok. The 6,000 Chinese factories Shein contracts with are expected to produce a massive amount of clothing very quickly in response to the company's identification of trends online—but at a high cost to workers and their safety. A 2022 investigation of Shein by Channel 4 found that workers in some of its suppliers' factories were working seventeen-hour days, receiving a base salary of only 4,000 yuan (about US$556) a month, and only receiving one day off a month. In response to this investigation and other reports, Shein admitted that some of its suppliers had violated labour laws and partnered with private auditing firms to monitor its supply chain. However, in his study of private compliance auditors, Richard Locke (2013) found that auditors have limited time and resources to conduct their assessments and tend to focus on highly visible safety issues to the exclusion of issues related to wages, harassment, collective bargaining rights, and contract violations. Moreover, because they are employed by MNCs, they have little incentive to report on labour rights violations.

Like factory audits, the ability of international private governance agreements to improve labour conditions is limited. In the aftermath of the Rana Plaza collapse, multinational apparel companies created both binding and non-binding agreements to better monitor labour conditions within their supply chains. The 2013 Accord on Fire and Building Safety in Bangladesh was a five-year legally binding agreement between brands and trade unions to improve safety in factories via inspections and enforcement. While over 200 brands signed on, most North American companies like Gap and Walmart did not (Ahlquist and Mosley 2021). The Center for Global Workers' Rights found that during the five years the original Accord was in place, safety violations in 1,600 factories were corrected, improving working conditions—at least in this respect—for 2.5 million workers. However, wages in Bangladesh remain very low, and labour organizing is highly suppressed. Although a transition accord was signed in 2018, it will eventually hand over inspections and enforcement to an arm of the Bangladeshi government, where many members of parliament are themselves factory owners, underscoring once more the misalignment of incentives and power in supply chain governance.

extreme, competitive pressure to keep production costs low and attract foreign investment can create incentives for countries to overlook or even promote forced labour (see Gore, Chapter 7). In the Ghanaian cocoa industry, for example, the dominant business model for cocoa production relies on forced labour, with women workers disproportionately vulnerable to this form of exploitation (for example, see LeBaron and Gore 2020).

CASE STUDY BOX 13.5 INEQUALITY AND THE CHATGPT SUPPLY CHAIN

When OpenAI's artificial intelligence app ChatGPT launched in late 2022, it promised to revolutionize how we seek information and produce written content. Despite some concerns about factual inaccuracies in its responses, ChatGPT generated a huge amount of media coverage and popular interest. By early 2023, OpenAI was valued at US$29 billion. But while ChatGPT is expected to help generate US$200 million in revenue in 2023 and US$1 billion by 2024 (Dastin, Hu, and Paresh 2022), these profits are premised, in part, on the poorly compensated labour of Kenyan workers hired to sift through large amounts of graphic, explicit, and offensive content in an effort to hone ChatGPT's marketability.

ChatGPT produces textual responses to users' prompts, which can take the form of queries for information, instructions to produce poems or stories, or other genres of writing. The app is based on a generative large language model which was trained on a massive dataset of text scraped from the Internet. Instead of reproducing that text verbatim in response to users' queries the way a traditional search engine would, ChatGPT generates novel responses based on a predictive model of what a likely sequence of words in response to that query would be. Because it has been trained on a dataset that contains no shortage of violent, offensive, sexually explicit, and racist content, early iterations of the app were prone to reproducing that content. In order to make the product marketable, OpenAI needed to develop a filter to prevent ChatGPT from generating offensive content. But manually eliminating offensive content from its training data set of billions of words would be impossible: there is simply no way for humans to read through all that text in a timely manner. The alternative was to develop an additional AI that would detect and discard offensive content. But to do that, the AI would need a training set of offensive content to learn from.

We are accustomed to thinking about supply chains for physical products (see, for example, Everyday GPE Box 13.4; Gore,

Chapter 7), but technological products have supply chains too. In the case of ChatGPT, developers needed to supply their AI with a dataset of offensive content. To do so, they subcontracted with Sama, a firm that employs workers, often for very low wages, in labour-abundant countries to label data for tech companies. According to an investigation by *TIME* magazine, workers in Kenya earning less than US$2 an hour combed through graphic content, including child sexual abuse, murder, suicide, torture, and incest in order to make ChatGPT a more marketable product for OpenAI (Perrigo 2023). According to *TIME*'s investigation, workers read and labelled around 200 passages of offensive text in a nine-hour shift, describing the work as mentally scarring and traumatic. Sama employees who worked to fulfil content moderation contracts with other tech companies such as Meta echo these descriptions of the work involved. Although Sama employees were offered counselling due to the traumatic nature of their work, workers found these services unhelpful and rare, trading off with pressures to be more productive. Sama eventually cancelled its work for OpenAI early, citing an OpenAI pilot project to collect and label images, some of which, like the textual passages Sama employees worked with, were extremely graphic and explicit in nature.

The consequences of Sama terminating its contract with OpenAI reveal the precarious position workers in poor countries are often placed in: although the workers involved no longer had to spend every day combing through disturbing content, they also lost the US$70/month bonus they had been receiving for working with explicit content, and some lost their jobs entirely. In a report on social media giants' outsourcing of content moderation to low-wage workers in poor countries, Paul Barrett (2020) argues that outsourcing this work via layers of subcontracting relationships marginalizes workers at the bottom of technology companies' supply chains and creates plausible deniability for companies' responsibility towards those workers (see also Roberts 2021) (for further discussion of the GPE of digital technology, including AI, see Girard, Chapter 17).

Nor is labour exploitation solely the domain of manufacturing and commodity supply chains: technological companies, too, rely on an unequal global division of labour (see Case Study Box 13.5).

The causes of labour exploitation in global supply chains are multiple, but broadly characterized by a misalignment of incentives and power. The actors with the greatest incentives to improve working conditions are the most disempowered, while those best in a position to improve labour standards have little incentive to do so. Workers in low-wage sectors in

poor countries are disempowered by both global and national forces: they frequently have few alternative employment opportunities and have highly constrained or no collective bargaining rights that might enable them to exert leverage over their employers. Some blame surely lies with their employers, but here too the hierarchical structure of global supply chains means that factory owners have few good options: improving working conditions would raise labour costs, driving contracts elsewhere. The same is true of governments in labour-abundant countries, given the race to the bottom logic discussed above. The actors with the greatest power to improve poor working conditions are MNCs themselves: they could choose to award contracts to jurisdictions and factories with better working conditions (even if these come at a higher cost), though they too are somewhat constrained by the consumer demand they helped to create. Acting individually, consumers have relatively little power to improve labour conditions, but collective action in the form of organized consumer pressures can, under some circumstances, be effective. At the global level, economic and political inequalities are closely intertwined in ways that systematically disadvantage labour, even as they continue to reward capital.

13.4.3 Income inequality and the unmet demand for immigration

If wages and working conditions are often so undesirable in capital-poor economies, why do workers not simply move to rich countries? Indeed, pressure to migrate—and the concomitant enforcement of policies to limit movement across national borders—is another important consequence of global inequality (see Figure 13.9).

There is a close relationship between global inequality and migration patterns and policies. Recall from the introduction to this chapter that nationality accounts for a significant amount of variation in global interpersonal inequality. While many things affect a given individual's income—gender, race, education, profession, ability—citizenship dominates these other variables at the global level. Where you live, in no small part, determines your economic fortunes. In economic terms, being born in a rich country is an unearned rent, a benefit citizens of rich countries enjoy that bears no relation to their labour or life choices. Political theorist Ayelet Shachar (2009) refers to this random distribution of life chances on the basis of citizenship as the '**birthright lottery**', arguing that citizenship should be thought of as a form of property inheritance—and as generating similar redistributive obligations.

Economists have attempted to estimate the size of this rent, or premium, for various pairs of countries. Milanovic (2015: 133), for example, estimates that, controlling for all other factors, being born in the US rather than the Democratic Republic of the Congo multiplies one's income ninety-three times. Michael Clemens, Claudio Montenegro, and Lant Pritchett (2008; 2019) estimate the cross-border wage differentials for 'observationally equivalent workers', finding, for example, that a Peruvian-born, Peruvian-educated, urban-dwelling 35-year-old man with nine years of schooling working in the US would make roughly 3.8 times as much as the same worker working

Figure 13.9 Mexico–US border fence separating the city of Tijuana (top left) and the Otay Mountain Wilderness reserve located in San Diego, California

Source: Alamy.

in Peru. Pritchett (2006) performs a similar analysis for forty-two pairs of countries, finding wage differentials as high as 15.45 for observationally equivalent workers in Yemen and the US, meaning that the same worker could increase their income fifteen times over simply by moving from Yemen to the United States. In historical terms, the wage gaps between immigrant-sending and immigrant-destination countries today are several times higher than they were in the late nineteenth and early twentieth centuries, when immigration rates were much higher (Pritchett 2006).

And yet, despite these dramatic wage differentials, cross-border migration today is rare: only about 3.6 per cent of the global population lives outside of the country where they were born (McAuliffe and Triandafyllidou 2021). Barriers to migration today are much higher than they were in previous eras of globalization. What percentage of people would move to countries with higher prevailing wages if they could? This is a very challenging question to answer, since our answers depend on comparing the world as it is today to a counterfactual world with open borders—a world that would likely differ from ours in many more respects than migration restrictions. Moreover, estimates must take into account not only the incentives to migrate in the form of wage gaps, but also the costs of moving internationally. Using European immigration data from the first wave of globalization in the late nineteenth century as a reference point suggests that labour mobility today is likely lower than it could be by a factor of between 2 and 5 due to host-country barriers to migration (Pritchett 2006: 69). Another approach to measuring the unmet demand for immigration based on cross-border wage differentials relies on survey data. In 2006, the World Bank conducted a survey of young people aged 15–24 in seven developing countries which included the question, 'If it were possible for you legally to move to another country to work, would you?' There was significant variation in response based on national origin and gender, but across nearly all demographics fewer than half of respondents said they would be unwilling to move, either permanently or temporarily (Blanchflower and Shadforth 2009).

While estimates vary according to methodology, global income inequality has produced a tremendous unmet demand for migration, even as barriers to migration perpetuate that inequality. The World Bank (2018) estimates that doubling the number of immigrants in high-income countries would result in an annual income gain of US$1.4 trillion—far more than we stand to gain from further reductions in barriers to the transnational flow of capital and goods. Indeed, reducing barriers to migration is likely the single most effective policy for reducing global income inequality. Migration increases migrant workers' own wages, but it also generates income for sending states via **remittances**, transfers of money by foreign workers to their home country. Remittances are an increasingly important transnational flow of capital, facilitated by international efforts to reduce the costs of sending money back to countries of origin and by online service providers. Remittances represent a significant source of income—up to 25–30 per cent of total GDP in some cases—for receiving countries, and have been found to do more to reduce poverty in developing countries than domestically generated income (Adams and Page 2005). But while reducing barriers to migration would likely substantially reduce global inequality, immigration is a deeply politically fraught topic, involving xenophobia, nationalism, and a mix of both legitimate and deeply misinformed economic concerns related to the impact of immigration on prevailing wages.

The unmet demand for immigration also gives immigrant-receiving states and employers a high degree of leverage over migrant workers, exposing migrant workers to exploitation and poor working conditions. For example, under the Gulf states' kafala system, employers must sponsor migrant workers' visas and in turn exert a high degree of control over migrant workers' entry and exit from the country, ability to find another job, housing, and banking. More generally, migrant workers frequently face limited rights to organize and unionize, and female workers in particular are vulnerable to trafficking and sexual exploitation.

KEY POINTS

- Economic inequality generates consequences with profound implications for every major area of international politics, because wealth and income are tightly intertwined with political power.

- The unequal distribution of wealth in particular skews political institutions at both the national and global level to prioritize the interests of the wealthy. In the absence of strong redistributive policy, the returns to capital grow faster than the returns to labour, and holders of capital have strong incentives to shield their wealth from taxation via the use of tax havens and shell corporations.

- Countries that are relatively labour-abundant and capital-poor face considerable pressure to keep wages low to attract foreign investment. Insofar as it is costly to enforce high labour standards, working conditions in such countries are frequently very poor.

- Layers of subcontracting relationships between MNCs in rich countries and vulnerable workers in poor countries make holding actors in global supply chains accountable for labour rights violations very challenging.

- Global inequality manifests in cross-border wage differentials which create a huge amount of pressure for people to move to a new country in search of a higher income, while barriers to the free movement of labour keep inequality high.

- The scarcity of opportunities to work abroad puts migrant workers in a vulnerable position, and their wages, ability to find a new job, and ability to leave the country may be curtailed by their employer.

13.5 Ethics of global inequality

Global inequality is real, it is very high, and it has profound consequences across a range of areas of global politics. But does this mean that global inequality itself is unethical or unjust? If we think inequality today is too high, what amount of inequality would be preferable? Is there some level of inequality that is normatively acceptable or even desirable? Would inequality still be bad if everyone had sufficient resources to live a healthy and productive life? The answers to these questions are not straightforward and depend on how we think of justice in the global political economy. But how we answer them matters a great deal for what, if anything, we choose to do to reduce global inequality. This section sketches out some arguments for and against the injustice of global economic inequality, before turning to the question of who is responsible for responding to global inequality.

13.5.1 Global inequality is unjust: Cosmopolitanism and distributive justice

Many people's initial reaction to hearing about high levels of global inequality is to think that this is a bad thing. But why might we think this? One possible argument is that global inequality is unjust because it

generates unjust consequences. As Section 13.3.3 discusses, global economic inequality has profound consequences for politics, labour, and migration. But how do we know if those consequences are unjust? After all, the same forces that have fuelled global inequality have also fuelled economic growth and a dramatic improvement in standards of living in some countries. One theory that offers an answer to that question is **cosmopolitanism**, a theory of justice that argues that we owe all fellow human beings an equal duty in virtue of our shared humanity, and that the demands of justice do not depend on race, gender, or nationality (see Key Theory Box 13.6). Cosmopolitan theorists, like Peter Singer, might argue that global inequality is unjust insofar as it causes suffering to many people—workers in poor countries, migrant workers, those suffering from the excesses of climate change fuelled by economic growth, etc. That global inequality has also generated benefits for those at the top of the wealth and income distributions would do little to offset cosmopolitan condemnations of global inequality, because according to this theory there is no justification for valuing the interests of the wealthy and powerful over the interests of the poor and vulnerable.

A second possible ethical argument against global inequality can be found in political philosopher John Rawls' (1971) theory of distributive justice. To figure out whether a given set of practices for distributing resources was just or not, Rawls used a thought experiment called the **original position**. The idea of the original position was that members of a political community should choose distributive principles from behind a veil of ignorance. Rawls asks us to imagine that we do not know what our class, status, gender, ethnicity, preferences, religion, or values will be at the point where we are born into a society. What principles for allocating resources would you choose from behind this veil? The answer, he argued, was to choose principles that would produce the highest payoff for the least advantaged person in society—you would want to choose a society where even if you were the worst off, you would still be comfortable. Under this framework, economic inequalities are only justified if they benefit the least well-off: those at the bottom of the income or wealth distribution must be better off in an unequal distribution than they would be in a more equal distribution.

How does global economic inequality measure up to this standard? If you did not know what country you would be born into, would you be comfortable

KEY THEORY BOX 13.6 COSMOPOLITANISM

Cosmopolitanism is an ethical approach that argues that the demands of justice derive from an equal duty which we owe to all fellow human beings. Central to cosmopolitanism is the idea of a universal community of world citizens. This universal community is an ideal to be worked towards rather than a description of empirical reality, with different theorists envisioning different pathways towards this ideal. When faced with ethical dilemmas, we sometimes confront a choice between what is best for us or those who are like us in some way and what is best for people far away, who we have never met and likely never will. Cosmopolitan theorists argue that for judgements to count as moral judgements, they must be universalizable, that is, they must apply to all people, without regard to those people's attributes or characteristics. Simply put, there is no moral difference between a Bangladeshi factory worker and a Canadian university student. Although partiality for 'our own'—whether that be our family, co-nationals, or people who share some demographic characteristics with us—may seem obvious or natural, cosmopolitan theorists would argue that this way of thinking is dangerous and unethical. Such partiality paves the way to racism, sexism, dehumanization, and, at the extreme, policies of ethnic violence and mass atrocities.

Cosmopolitan thinkers argue against the allocation of privilege and resources on the basis of nationality, contending that nobody chooses to be born into the political community that they are in and that others' needs are often more pressing than our fellow citizens'. Although other approaches to global justice prioritize the nation-state as the appropriate actor for enacting redistributive policies (see Section 13.4.2), cosmopolitanism regards the demands of justice as truly global. Cosmopolitan utilitarian philosopher Peter Singer (2004) writes, 'Whatever it is we value about political equality, including the opportunity to participate in decisions that affect us, globalization means that we should value equality between societies and at the global level, at least as much as we value political equality within one society'.

Cosmopolitanism has had real-world impacts. International institutions, like the International Criminal Court, envision individuals as having rights under international law that supersede the principle of state sovereignty. International relief efforts like the International Red Cross and Red Crescent are premised on the alleviation of human suffering without regard to nationality, and in fact derive their legitimacy from this cosmopolitan principle.

with the current distribution of resources globally? The answer is likely no. Recall that the largest predictor of income at the global level is nationality, something people have very little control over. From behind Rawls' veil of ignorance, we probably would not choose 'luck' or 'chance' as a rule for allocating income globally. Because the vast majority of global variation in income is attributable to luck—what Shachar (2009) terms 'the birth-right lottery'—current levels of global inequality are an unjust allocation of global resources.

We can also ask whether the least well-off in the global economy are better off than they would be in a more equal distribution of income and wealth at the global level. Here too, the answer is likely no. While it is certainly possible to argue that economic globalization has made both poor people and poor countries better off than they would be in a world of autarky, this argument is more difficult to sustain as it pertains to the specific—and very high—levels of inequality globalization has produced. We can quite easily imagine an even slightly more equal distribution of resources that would improve the lives of the most

vulnerable and exploited workers without fundamentally altering patterns of global growth.

13.5.2 Global inequality is not unjust

Rawlsian principles of distributive justice give us one possible argument against global inequality, but Rawls himself would go on to argue that these principles only hold within particular (liberal) societies, not globally. In his 1993 book *The Law of Peoples*, Rawls argued that imposing a veil of ignorance at the global level would be to assume that all societies share certain liberal principles—namely, that resources should not be allocated on the basis of gender, race, or other inherent characteristics. Because we cannot assume that non-liberal societies share these commitments, the principles of distributive justice do not apply globally.

Rawls did not argue that global inequality was not unjust, simply that his theory of justice could not be used to judge the global distribution of resources. Other thinkers, however, have made a stronger argument against the idea that global inequality is an injustice. Political philosopher Thomas Nagel (2005), for example, argues that nation-states are the only actors with the political legitimacy to enact redistributive justice, and that there is no comparable actor at the global level—no institution that can levy taxes and invest tax revenue in redistributive programmes that would lower global wealth and income inequality. Nagel argues that justice can only be accomplished if there is a government and some measure of equality among citizens because the demands of justice depend on collective action and ultimately on law backed with legitimate force. Because the international system is anarchical, inequality may be regarded as immoral or as a pressing humanitarian concern, but it cannot be considered a matter of justice. Does this mean global justice is impossible? In the absence of very strong supranational institutions, yes. Nagel does hold open the possibility that such institutions could be established, but he argues that the only way they would ever be established is if they reflected the interests of powerful states. Such institutions would therefore likely heighten inequality before they could be transformed into institutions capable of distributing global resources justly.

For Rawls and Nagel, the key question regarding global inequality and justice is the level at which the demands of distributive justice apply. For other thinkers, economic inequality itself is simply not a moral or ethical concern. Harry Frankfurt (2015), for instance, makes the case for what he calls the 'doctrine of sufficiency', which holds that what is morally important is that each person has enough that they are able to pursue the kind of life they want and that they are content without having any more money than they currently have. That some people might have more— even much more—money than others is not unjust or immoral, as long as everyone has at least enough. For Frankfurt, poverty and extreme deprivation are indeed unjust, but inequality is only immoral to the extent that it violates the doctrine of sufficiency. Does global inequality violate this doctrine? In its current form, the answer is almost certainly yes: many people at the bottom—and even in the middle—of the global income distribution do not have enough resources to live the kind of comfortable and flourishing lives that Frankfurt envisions. But that does not mean that global inequality is always inherently unjust.

Frankfurt could envision a just world in which everyone's basic needs and wants were met and some people were still much richer than others. Something akin to this logic animates policymakers, scholars, and public commentators who defend economic globalization on the basis of falling poverty rates and economic growth, regarding these developments as more morally consequential than the rising inequality that has accompanied them. For those, like Steven Pinker (2018: 97–120), who believe that increases in the average standard of living should dominate distributional concerns, global inequality is not an injustice, but simply a by-product of vast improvements in the human condition.

13.5.3 Who is responsible for responding to global inequality?

Not everyone will agree that global inequality is a moral or ethical problem. However, for those who do hold this position, a further question presents itself: Who is responsible for fixing it? As we know from the discussion of labour abuses in global supply chains (Section 13.2.2) and the ways that economic inequality reinforces unequal political institutions (Section 13.2.1), there is often a mismatch between actors who have the power to make the world more equal and those who have an incentive to do so. It is difficult to know who to blame for the harms of inequality in the complex network of workers, factory owners, local firms, MNCs, consumers, financial institutions, international institutions, and investors that make up the global economy.

Philosopher Iris Marion Young (2004) developed what is known as a **social connection model** for thinking about the allocation of responsibility within the unjust structures that perpetuate global inequality. Young argued that global inequality results from unjust structural processes, and that rather than trying to figure out which individual actors are to blame for things like labour rights violations in poor countries or the exploitation of migrant workers, we need to consider how actors are structurally connected to these unjust structures. For Young, the key question is not, for example, whether it is consumers' fault or multinational corporations' fault that garment manufacturing is fraught with labour abuses. Instead, the key question is who can and should contribute to fixing those injustices looking forwards. So, who should take up that responsibility? Young says that anyone who participates in and benefits from structural injustices has a responsibility to work with others to remedy those injustices. That responsibility is not evenly distributed; Young's social connection model argues that our level of responsibility varies based on how closely connected we are to an injustice, how much power we have to change the unjust structural process, and how much we benefit from injustices and inequalities.

Young's approach to thinking about responsibility for inequality differs from both cosmopolitanism and from Rawls' and Nagel's location of redistributive authority within the nation-state. While cosmopolitanism is premised on a flattening of ethical distinctions between individuals, Young makes the case that those who are more closely connected to an injustice have a greater responsibility to act. But unlike Rawls and Nagel, who assign primary responsibility for enacting justice to the nation-state, Young demands that all of us—consumers, workers, investors, states, bankers, and CEOs—examine our relationship to inequality and injustice and act collectively to ensure a more just world.

KEY POINTS

- Not everyone agrees that global inequality is a bad thing.

- Those who argue that global inequality is unjust often do so from the starting point of cosmopolitanism, which argues that our duties to other people do not depend on shared nationality or other characteristics, or from a Rawlsian conception of distributive justice, which argues that a just distribution of resources is one that ensures that even the least well-off person has enough.

- Those who argue that global inequality is not unjust may take the position that only nation-states are responsible for remedying injustice through redistribution. They may also take the position that inequality in and of itself is not a problem; it only becomes a moral concern when it leads to people not having enough resources to live the lives they would choose to lead.

- Scholars disagree on the question of who is responsible for the injustices that global inequality produces. Young's social connection model challenges us to think about how we are connected to the economic and political structures that generate inequality and injustice and to act collectively to repair those harms.

13.6 Conclusion: Responding to global inequality

Global economic inequality is not a topic that lends itself to easy answers. While we know that the world is tremendously unequal, going beyond this observation requires careful analysis. Measuring global inequality is fraught with methodological challenges and choices, making it difficult to definitively say whether global inequality has increased or decreased in pace with globalization. Global inequality has complex causes that involve a mix of both unequal structures, many of them with their origins in colonial domination, and more recent policy choices concerning trade, investment, and migration. Tracing the consequences of global inequality for wealth and political power, labour, and migration involves disentangling complex relationships between money and power at both the national and international level. And reasonable people may disagree about the conditions under which global inequality is a problem and about the appropriate level of inequality in the global economy. These are, at their heart, political questions: how we answer them involves choices about whose interests should be prioritized, whose voices amplified, and what kind of world we envision as desirable.

Any attempt to respond to global inequality is likely to be similarly complex and politically contentious. Mitigating inequality inevitably involves redistribution, and redistributive practices necessarily create winners and losers. (While it is true that, historically, significant decreases in inequality have been produced by war and catastrophe, neither of these is an appealing proposal for redressing inequality.) If we want to reduce global inequality, we face many difficult choices as to how to accomplish this. The policies that are most likely to be effective, like liberalizing migration, are also the most politically fraught. More incremental approaches, like increasing growth rates in poor countries, also entail redistribution insofar as they would likely involve a net transfer of capital from rich countries to poor countries. Moreover, higher growth rates in poor countries do not guarantee a more equitable national income distribution and may even increase within-country inequality. Taxes on capital and the repatriation of wealth are difficult to achieve in a world where capital-holders are disproportionately represented in national and international governance.

But while global inequality does not lend itself to easy answers, this chapter has attempted to show how the conceptual and theoretical tools of global political economy can help make sense of a complicated topic.

? 13.7 QUESTIONS

1. On what basis might someone argue that global inequality has been increasing over the past fifty years? Why might some disagree with this conclusion? Your answer should reference specific approaches to measuring global inequality.

2. How have colonial-era institutions shaped the global distribution of income today?

3. Scholars disagree about the role globalization and market liberalization have played in global income distribution. Why might someone argue that globalization has generally been a good thing for workers in developing economies? Why might someone disagree?

4. How does global inequality leave workers vulnerable to exploitation?

5. How do economic and political inequalities reinforce each other in international politics? Discuss with respect to the use of offshore tax havens and shell corporations.

6. How has global inequality increased pressure for migration? What are some consequences of the unmet demand for immigration and how do those in turn shape the global distribution of income?

7. Many people would argue that current levels of global inequality are too high. Is there some level of inequality that would be acceptable or is inequality always a problem?

8. Is global inequality likely to increase or decrease in the future? What practices, institutions, or trends are likely to affect the global income and wealth distribution going forwards?

≋ 13.8 FURTHER READING

Atkinson, A. (2015), *Inequality: What Can Be Done?* (Cambridge, MA: Harvard University Press.) This book, by British economist Anthony Atkinson, argues that wealth and income inequality are a pressing policy concern, rejecting the often-made claim that policy should focus exclusively on inequality of opportunity, not on inequality of outcome. Atkinson proposes a series of policies targeting technology, employment, social security, capital sharing, and taxation, aimed at reducing inequality in an era of globalization.

Boushey, H., Bradford, D. J., and Steinbaum, M. (eds.) (2017), *After Piketty: The Agenda for Economics and Inequality* (Cambridge, MA: Harvard University Press). This is a collection of essays responding to Thomas Piketty's *Capital in the Twenty-First Century*. The essays explore and critique Piketty's discussion (and sometimes exclusion) of power, slavery, and the nature of capital, the impact of technology, gender, and trends in the Global South, while examining the implications of Piketty's arguments for the social sciences beyond economics.

Elias, J. (2004), *Fashioning Inequality? The Multinational Company and Gendered Employment in a Globalizing World* (Farnham, UK: Ashgate Publishing). Juanita Elias' book is based on a case study of a British garment manufacturing MNC and examines how employment and recruitment practices exploit and reproduce local gendered and ethnic divisions within Malaysia, where the MNC has invested in manufacturing.

Held, D., and Kaya A. (eds.) (2007), *Global Inequality: Patterns and Explanations* (Cambridge: Polity). This book is a collection of chapters by economists and other social scientists examining global inequality in terms of its measurement, trends and patterns, implications for global governance, and policymaking.

Lockwood, E. (2021), 'The International Political Economy of Global Inequality', *Review of International Political Economy*, 28/2: 421–445. This article argues that the field of International Political Economy (IPE; referred to as GPE in this volume) should foreground global economic inequality due to the inescapably political nature of its causes and consequences. It outlines a research agenda for doing so, emphasizing the relevance of IPE's conceptual tools to many as-yet unanswered questions concerning the impact and development of global inequality in world politics.

Milanovic, B. (2016), *Global Inequality: A New Approach for the Age of Globalization* (Cambridge: Belknap Press). Milanovic's book relies on novel household income data sets to examine the forces that have impacted the global distribution of income over the past centuries. This book examines the relationship between patterns of within- and between-country inequality, introducing the elephant curve discussed in this chapter and considering potential policy responses to these trends.

Nagel, T. (2005), 'The Problem of Global Justice', *Philosophy and Public Affairs*, 33/2: 113–147. Nagel examines the relationship between justice and sovereignty to consider whether global justice is possible in the absence of world government, ultimately arguing (drawing on Hobbes and Rawls) that, while there is a humanitarian obligation to address global poverty and suffering, the demands of justice—insofar as they concern inequality as opposed to suffering—rely on the sovereign nation-state and therefore are only meaningful at the national, rather than global, level.

Parks, B. C., and Roberts, J. T. (2006), *A Climate of Injustice: Global Inequality, North-South Politics, and Climate Policy* (Cambridge, MA: MIT Press). This book tackles the question of who should take action to address climate change, focusing on the inequalities inherent in historical and contemporary emissions patterns between rich and poor countries, differential capacity to effectively mitigate the climate crisis, and the profound gulf between those who will suffer the most from the climate crisis and those with the resources to insulate themselves from its worst effects. They argue that an effective global climate agreement is impossible without addressing underlying economic inequalities between the Global North and South.

Piketty, T. (2014), *Capital in the Twenty-First Century* (trans. A. Goldman) (Cambridge: Belknap Press). Piketty develops an argument, grounded in detailed economic history, about how in the absence of robust redistributive policy capitalism will inevitably produce an ever widening gap between those whose income derives from capital and those whose income comes from labour. Piketty argues that the outcome of these dynamics is patrimonialism—a society dominated politically by the very wealthy, given the close relationship between wealth and political power.

Pritchett, L. (2006), *Let Their People Come: Breaking the Gridlock on International Labor Mobility* (Washington, D.C.: Center for Global Development). Pritchett's report for the Center for Global Development examines migration from the perspective of international development, focusing on the huge income differentials for workers in rich and poor countries and the resulting unmet demand for cross-border migration. Pritchett examines the tension between this pressure to migrate and the power of anti-immigration sentiment and policy in rich countries, ultimately arguing that the gains from greater labour mobility far outweigh the risks and developing a proposal for mutually beneficial bilateral migration agreements between rich and poor countries.

Shachar, A. (2009), *The Birthright Lottery: Citizenship and Global Inequality* (Cambridge, MA: Harvard University Press). This book compares birth-right citizenship in rich countries as a form of property inheritance—an unearned entitlement legally passed down to an arbitrarily privileged group of recipients. She argues that just as inherited property is rightly taxed and the gains redistributed, birth-right citizenship in wealthy countries generates similar redistributive obligations, and that states should expand their membership boundaries accordingly.

Sharman, J. C. (2006), *Havens in a Storm: The Struggle for Global Tax Regulation* (Ithaca, NY: Cornell University Press). This book focuses on the efforts of rich countries in the OECD to stem the offshore flow of capital to tax haven states—small countries with low taxes and favourable regulatory environments for capital. Sharman is interested in how very small states were able to stave off global regulatory efforts to crack down on tax havens by strategically deploying reputational discursive resources aimed at persuading an international audience that the OECD was acting hypocritically and in anti-competitive ways by targeting tax havens.

Singer, P. (2004), *One World: The Ethics of Globalization* (New Haven, CN: Yale University Press). This book focuses on ethical issues related to climate change, global trade, humanitarian intervention, and foreign aid, arguing that in each case a global ethic is more just and appropriate than the nationalist and state-centric lenses that tend to dominate foreign policymaking and international relations.

Young, I. M. (2004), 'Responsibility and Global Labor Justice', *The Journal of Political Philosophy*, 12/4: 365–388. In this article, Young develops a theory of political responsibility that is intended to respond to the complexities of inequalities of power and privilege within global injustices. She focuses on global apparel manufacturing supply chains to argue that, in contrast to a legalistic liability model of responsibility, everyone who has a connection to these supply chains has some responsibility to improve working conditions in the factories where clothes are produced, and that these responsibilities vary with people's power and privilege within these networks of connection.

CONTRIBUTOR NOTE

Erin Lockwood is an Assistant Professor in the Department of Political Science at the University of California, Irvine. Her research explores how private financial authority is exercised and the politicization of global inequality, including the intersection between both domains. Her work is published in the *Review of International Political Economy*, *New Political Economy*, and *Theory and Society*.

14

The Global Political Economy of Development

Ali Bhagat

Chapter contents

Reader's guide

Since the Second World War the planet has made some major advances in the betterment of human life at the cost of accelerated climatic change and through uneven means of development. We have witnessed a reduction in child mortality, a rise in literacy and education, and by some measures the fewest people live in extreme poverty than they ever have before, causing many economists and development practitioners to laud the success of modern capitalist development. Despite some of these accomplishments we continue to live in a world where inequality on the multiple axes of health, income, environment, gender, education, technology, finance, shelter, food, water, and various other issues concerning access persist. These problems concerning development have motivated various institutions like the United Nations, the International Monetary Fund and the World Bank, governments, non-governmental organizations, private sector actors, and everyday people to organize resources and deal with these problems with mixed and contested results. Indeed, little to no consensus exists on what global development is, who it is meant to be for, where and when it should take place, and, in fact, whether it should take place at all. Without a doubt, we live in an increasingly interconnected world where the relationship between globalization and development is fraught. This chapter interrogates some of these concerns and is centred around a key question: who benefits and why from globalized development? In exploring this question, the chapter is divided into three main sections. First, we look at various ideas and theories of development which include modernization theory, dependency, neoliberalism, and critical approaches to development. Second, we explore the history of globalization-led development since the Second World War to the present day. In the final section, we pay attention to two contemporary issues—the Great Recession and the Global Refugee Crisis—in order to understand the crisis-prone tendencies of globalization and its linkages to everyday practices in global political economy.[1]

14.1 Introduction

What is development? This is a central question that many instructors in development studies or global political economy (GPE) classes pose to their undergraduate students. The answer still has little to no consensus and often depends on the paradigm and worldview of the individual or organization that desires to address various development-related social and economic issues. Ideas like 'poverty alleviation' or 'solving world hunger' often spring to mind. Development is also a process that is encapsulated by conceptions of progress from a stage of poverty to an eventual age of global prosperity fuelled by economic growth. This leads us to the key question that drives this chapter: who benefits and why from globalized development?

In asking this question, we are implicitly also interrogating the various power relations that govern and manage development policies and practices today. These might take the form of rich and powerful states, global corporations, and international organizations (IOs). Development could also occur from the grass-roots through civil society organizations, local governments, and the actions of everyday people, at least since the 1980s. However, the dominant development agenda fits under an overarching policy platform of **neoliberalism** which can be defined by commitments to the reduction of government intervention, social welfare retrenchment—that is, a commitment to austerity in governance—economic growth, and trade and financial liberalization. Progress for the purposes of economic growth is the central idea that guides mainstream development policy.

In understanding development, and attempting to complicate its core notions of progress, I am reminded of the eminent philosopher V. Y. Mudimbe's writing on Africa's colonial library—an abstraction that refers to the wide array of artwork, texts, writing, and representations of (and on) Africa from many social science disciplines that have produced knowledge about the continent framing it as one of extreme difference, especially in relation to the so-called Euro-American West (see Key Concept Box 14.1).

While Mudimbe's colonial library centres knowledge in Africa, we can extend the concept of the colonial library to include many countries in the Global South that now seemingly require Western intervention. The way we write about and conceive of development is important to pay attention to. Many countries in the Global South have been forged through anti-colonial struggle but have since been incorporated into the global capitalist system. In turn, former Western colonial states have reframed their relationships with former colonies through trade and development assistance, leaving questions of neo-colonialism, asymmetric power relations, and the ongoing subservience of the so-called former colonies still in question (see Singh, Chapter 15, on North–South relations).

The world has taken some strides to reduce poverty and improve the lives of people in the Global North and Global South alike. A UN report (2015) suggests that the percentage of people living in extreme poverty fell from 47 to 14 between 1990 and 2015; primary school enrolment rate rose from 83 to 91 per cent between 2000 and 2015; and more women have gained parliamentary representation and joined the workforce than ever before. The same report also highlights various problems including climate change, gender inequality, widespread inequality between rich and poor households, and conflict (United Nations 2015). Moreover, even in states that are seeing economic growth, the benefits of globalization—defined by Giddens (2003)

---

[1] Many thanks are owed to Nicola Phillips for inspiring this chapter due to her work on the political economy of development in previous iterations of this textbook.

KEY CONCEPT BOX 14.1 THE COLONIAL LIBRARY

The colonial library is a paradox, a place of immensely violent knowledge production but also an ever present referent that continues to contextualize scholarship about Africa today. In relation to the production of knowledge about Africa, Mudimbe powerfully questions, 'Who is speaking about it? Who has the right and the credentials to produce it, describe it, comment upon it, or at least present opinions about it?' (Mudimbe 1988: 3). This concept is important as it contextualizes the ways that theories of development are produced and reproduced and how these powerful ideas shape development. Indeed, an imagined conception of Africa is often the fantasized site of development—a continent that is continually portrayed as homogenous, poor, and requiring urgent international attention whether it be due to conflict, hunger, or migration. The colonial library is not a real place, but it is a 'collection' of multiform representations about Africa that emerge from colonization and Western-produced knowledge. As political scientist Zubairu Wai reminds us, the colonial library not only justified the monstrosities of the Atlantic slave trade and various forms of

colonial violence, but it has also formed the basis of knowledge that even contemporary African scholars must continue to interrogate and, in some ways, reproduce (Wai 2015: 263). We have to be cautious about homogenizing stories of the developing world, colonies, and the post-colony as sites of abject poverty that require Western intervention. When thinking about various theories of development we must consider why they exist in the first place and whose interests they serve. Moreover, the colonial library urges us to think beyond neat boundaries that confine places and people to static positions in history. As queer theorist Keguro Macharia (2016: 188) writes, 'I am not really sure I have anything to say about area studies—about the maps of the world it created, about the maps of the world it still uses, about how it assembles knowledge, about the academy's complicity in it . . .'. The colonial library, the academy, and the multitude of actors that comprise the development industry rest on imaginations of interventions and their various strengths. As students of global political economy, we might meditate on what it means to engage in development at all.

---

as the intensification of worldwide social relations that link local happenings to global events—are felt unevenly and disadvantage the working and non-working poor. Indeed, there has been no silver bullet for the challenges posed by uneven economic growth and poverty, despite different approaches that have dominated development policy in the late twentieth and early twenty-first centuries. Collectively we can refer to these various approaches to development as global development agendas or 'the global development agenda', which is popularized by international institutions led by the United Nations (UN), International Monetary Fund (IMF), and the World Bank with increased participation from many global corporations. Missing in these economic growth and anti-poverty platforms are the linkages to colonial history and the ways that the development paradigm came to be in the first place.

Despite the language of global community and widespread international commitments to many causes of development, the global development agendas starting after the Second World War have yet to address the most glaring issues of material and social insecurity. Take for instance the fact that according to the United Nations High Commissioner for Refugees (UNHCR) more people are forcibly displaced than ever before, or, as the World Health Organization (WHO)

states, that between 2030 and 2050 250,000 people per year will die from malnutrition, malaria, diarrhoea, and heat stress. These ominous challenges ensure that urgent action is necessary for human life to sustain itself while also ensuring that the global development agenda dominated by international organizations, Western states, and global corporations is here to stay.

In order to target various issues of global poverty—a global condition where communities cannot access basic goods or services such as water, shelter, food, healthcare, sanitation, and education—the United Nations along with other organizations unveiled the Millennium Development Goals (MDGs), which were meant to hinge global development policies in eight key areas (including approximately eighteen targets or sub-goals): extreme poverty and hunger, universal primary education, gender equality, child mortality, maternal health, transmittable diseases like HIV/AIDS and malaria, environmental sustainability, and global partnerships for development. Despite some gains in gender equality, primary education, and reducing communicable diseases, the MDGs were not achieved and have since been replaced by the Sustainable Development Goals (SDGs), also known as the Global Goals Agenda 2030, where an expanded seventeen goals are meant to be achieved by the year 2030.

These goals parallel and expand upon the MDGs and also include efforts to eradicate poverty entirely, protect land and sea environments, create economic growth and full employment, and deepen partnerships with the private sector, among other areas targeting water, energy, climate change, and urbanization (UN 2022). Missing in these goals, however, is any attention to the ways that power operates in the global political economy. For instance, it is not inconceivable that goals of economic growth and infrastructure development might also result in negative impacts on the climate (see Ervine, Chapter 16, for discussion). The influence of corporations might overemphasize economic growth and reduce the capacity of states to provide welfare for their citizens. The global development agenda remains pro-growth and follows a neoliberal model of development leading us once again to our key question: who benefits and why from globalization-led development?

14.2 Theories of development

In the introduction of this chapter, you might have already gleaned that the UN and its related organizations define development and progress through the MDGs or SDGs. Similarly, the IMF states that 'development needs to be economically, socially, and environmentally sustainable. The IMF helps countries around the world achieve the SDGs by working with them to develop the foundation for strong, sustainable economic growth, job creation and poverty reduction . . . it helps create a stable economic and monetary ecosystem e.g., efficient tax structure, sustainable debt, reliable data, sound regulatory framework which enables transparency, stimulates private sector development and leads to greater and more equitable economic growth' (IMF 2022b). The IMF is of course a financial institution, and we can see from this definition that economic growth through fiscal responsibility is a core aim for the IMF in the developing world.

In contrast, the International Labour Organization (ILO)'s conception of development surrounds their 'Decent Work Agenda', which centres collective bargaining and labour relations where decent work 'sums up the aspirations of people in their working lives. It involves opportunities for work that is productive and delivers a fair income, security in the workplace and social protection for families, better prospects for personal development and social integration, freedom for

people to express their concerns, organize and participate in the decisions that affect their lives and equality of opportunity and treatment for all men and women' (ILO 2023). Both the IMF and the ILO are international organizations with very different mandates; however, what we are also seeing are two competing conceptions of what matters as development. The IMF focuses on economic growth and financial regulation, thereby favouring the private sector in facilitating fiscal responsibility and transparency. In contrast, the ILO is concerned with labour relations and therefore sees development as the material improvement in the lives of everyday working (and non-working) people.

The academic debate on development is similarly unsettled. As we saw above, the various organizations that comprise the global development agenda seem to diagnose the central issues of development differently. This is similar in scholarly conceptions of development too. For example, Nobel prize winning economist Amartya Sen argues that development should be defined as freedom—the removal of poverty, government oppression and other forms of social deprivation, intolerance, and repression (Sen 1991). In contrast, post-development scholars such as Arturo Escobar argue that strategies and discourses of development produce the exact opposite of their intentions, namely underdevelopment, poverty, exploitation, and oppression (Escobar 2011). While there might be some scholarly consensus that development might employ the aspects of a good society or what H. W. Arndt (1987) calls an 'everyman's utopia' [sic], there is little agreement about how this can be achieved.

The global development agenda is marked by two important ideas that guide domestic and international development policy. From the end of the Second World War until the early 1980s, the United States and other countries followed a Keynesian model of economics. To simplify, a hallmark of Keynesian economics is the role of the government, which should actively influence the economy. In recessions governments should spend money to stimulate demand. This model eventually became critiqued for stifling private sector growth, government over-expenditure, and the overreach of the state—particularly in the US. These critiques, along with the Vietnam War and an oil crisis that we will discuss in Section 14.2.3 of this chapter, give way to the neoliberal era, which hinged on economic growth through the liberalization of financial markets, export-oriented growth, and the dismantling of big government (see also Helleiner, Chapter 8, for discussion). These two big ideas are in the foreground where the development theories discussed in this section emerge.

This section will cover four important theoretical strands: modernization, structuralism and dependency, neoliberalism, and critical approaches to development which include race, gender, and post-development theories. Each of these groups of theories defines and diagnoses the problems associated with development differently. They are concerned either with solving development or critiquing the failures of major trends in development.

14.2.1 Modernization

The first mainstream theory of development we will look at is modernization. Modernization theory emerged in the post-Second World War era and in the context of the Cold War. The GPE was being reshaped due to the security interests of the Soviet Union and the United States. This meant that both blocs recognized the importance of the so-called Third World where the US, in particular, wanted to prevent the spread of communism. This meant recognizing countries of the world that at one point considered themselves part of a **Non-Aligned Movement**—a movement spearheaded by India and Yugoslavia at the United Nations on the principles of territorial integrity, non-aggression, non-interference in domestic politics, and a commitment to peace. Central to non-alignment was abstaining from violence and big military pacts; however, both major powers in the Cold War had much to gain in terms of their security interests by forging allies in the 'Third World'.

Modernization thus appears as a way for the US to frame development through a narrative of progress. The roots of this theory can be found in sociologist Max Weber's writings on *The Protestant Ethic and the Spirit of Capitalism* (1905). Weber (2005: 96) famously argues, 'in the last resort the factor which produced capitalism is the rational permanent enterprise, rational accounting, rational technology and rational law, but again not these alone. Necessary were the complementary factors, the rational spirit, the rationalization of the conduct of life in general and a rationalistic economic ethic'. The implications of this approach influenced other modernization theorists who sought to theorize why capitalism 'takes off' in some societies and not others, and thus these theories offer various solutions to the problems of 'underdevelopment'. The

theories are divided into cultural or political theories and more economistic conceptions of modernization.

One such economistic theorist of modernization is Walt Whitman Rostow (1960), who describes various stages of a linear mechanism of development in his famous book *The Stages of Economic Growth: A Non-Communist Manifesto*. In his public life, Rostow was a National Security Advisory to US President Lyndon B. Johnson. He had a hand in crafting US foreign policy in the 1960s and was an ardent supporter of the US going to war with Vietnam. It goes without saying that theories like modernization which appear banal and economistic in their texts have real-world implications for war, security, and power. Rostow's modernization theory is presented with cherry-picked historical examples and abstract empirical ideas—these wield power and shape the world, forming a colonial library of what development *should* look like by inventing the category of development in and of itself. In answering who benefits from globalized development, an analysis of Rostow's modernization theory presents a clear answer: US political, economic, and security interests (see Key Theory Box 14.2).

With regard to cultural-institutional approaches to modernization, Bert Hoselitz (1957) and others emphasized the institutional basis of liberal democracies that should form the bedrock of sound development policy and economic growth. For example, Hoselitz's article *Non-Economic Factors in Economic Development* attempts to explain why Western European countries 'take off'. Hoselitz's reasons include the presence of rule of law, the development of universal standards as opposed to tribal or caste-based judicial adjudication, and the ability for Western societies to be achievement-oriented as opposed to stalled in the struggles of kinship and religion. These cultural or institutional arguments return with the advent of neoliberal theory as we will see below; however, it is important to point out that the portrayal of developing countries in both variations of modernization theory is negative and backwards, where the problem of development can only be solved by a commitment to capitalist-oriented growth and Western institutions.

14.2.2 Structuralism and dependency

While modernization theories paint a rosy picture of all the countries marching towards some sort of advanced capitalist industrial future of mass consumption, critics of modernization starting as early

KEY THEORY BOX 14.2 MODERNIZATION THEORY

Modernization theory forms the meta-narrative of development as we know it today. Development is often twinned with progress, and modernization theorists view progress through capitalist development—this has not changed in our current-era development paradigm either. Rostow describes modernization as the ability for all countries to evolve through various hierarchical states of development so long as they are able to maintain certain cultural and political conditions. Indeed, Rostow provides a meta-theory of development where traditional societies—defined by Rostow as immersed in 'pre-Newtonian' science and technology—can transform themselves into societies of high mass consumption where real income rises and a large number of people are able to afford more than basic needs such as food, shelter, and clothing (1960: 4–10). This transition occurs in five stages of economic growth: (1) traditional societies that are influenced by markets or other external factors embody agrarian economies, limited technological development, and a static socio-economic structure; (2) the pre-conditions of take-off occur through the exploitation of land and extractive industry; (3) these societies then hit the take-off stage when they develop a manufacturing sector, and this requires the installation of infrastructure and a socio-political elite; (4) from take-off to the drive to maturity requires an investment in manufacturing that exceeds 10 per cent of national income and the social development of modern institutions; (5) with a wide industrial and commercial base societies can then transform themselves into high mass-consumption societies by finding their comparative advantage and engaging in global trade. The key implication of Rostow's theory is the equation of modernity with American or Western capitalism and the framing of developing countries as backwards and requiring capitalist intervention. Development is understood as linear and hinged to patterns of production and consumption.

as the 1940s emphasize that global structures of trade, finance, and production debilitate the aspirations of development in the Global South. The structuralist and dependency theorists who originated in Latin America were less concerned with the great power politics of the US and the USSR and were instead considering the material implications of industry, economic growth, and everyday life in states that were ignored by the West—Latin American countries were not prospering through the spread of capitalism. The rise of structuralism and dependency as critique emerged from an engagement with Marxist ideas of exploitation and, as such, critique of the capitalist mode of production that denigrated the Global South to a position of global precarity (see Key Theory Box 14.3). While structuralism and dependency have similar theoretical backgrounds, it is important to note that the former's key contribution to development was a nationalized policy directive known as **import substitution industrialization (ISI).** In contrast, dependency produced a more radical critique of development based on a **New International Economic Order** vis-à-vis a transition to socialism (see Singh, Chapter 15). These different policy prescriptions notwithstanding, the key argument of both structuralism and dependency approaches to development is that the global

capitalist system is designed to exploit developing countries of their natural resources for the purposes of profit maximization, keeping them in a permanent state of underdevelopment.

As discussed in Chapter 15, Raúl Prebisch is perhaps the most important thinker when it comes to structuralism, where he highlights that a reliance on raw material exports in former colonies leads to a widening gap between the Global North and Global South. With his contemporary Hans Singer, Prebisch argues that the price of primary commodities—raw materials—declines in comparison to manufactured goods; this is known as the Prebisch-Singer thesis (see also Lockwood, Chapter 13). This thesis implies that the trade system devalues the labour and exports of goods coming from developing countries who do not have manufacturing sectors. As such, the structuralists influenced policies that focused on homegrown manufacturing as opposed to an overreliance on imports. Ultimately, ISI policies failed for a multitude of reasons discussed in Section 14.3; however, these policies emerged in a moment of globalization where South–South interaction and an international discussion of socialism were being taken seriously, particularly by leaders like Jawaharlal Nehru of India, Dr Kwame Nkrumah of Ghana, and Gamal Abdel Nasser of Egypt, to name a few.

The work on structuralism was furthered by a key theorist of dependency—Andre Gunder Frank—who wrote extensively about the creation of underdevelopment by colonial and pillaging states. Frank famously stated, '[u]nderdevelopment is not due to the survival of archaic institutions and the existence of capital shortage in regions that have remained isolated from the stream of world history. On the contrary, underdevelopment was and still is generated by the very same historical process which also generated economic development: the development of capitalism itself' (Frank 1989: 6). Another influential thinker in the dependency tradition is Samir Amin, who highlights that underdeveloped countries can be characterized by the predominance of agriculture in their economies, a local elite which holds the interest of foreign capital, and low wages for the majority of people, and that these so-called satellite economies are incapable of achieving high development on their own accord. For Amin (1974), capitalism could only result in **uneven development**.

In sum, the economies and regions that had the closest ties to metropole states (through colonial connections and empire) were the most likely to be seen as underdeveloped today. Here, the language and material reality of development come into the fore view. Underdevelopment only exists as a category of development because richer and more powerful states have created this form of development through historical extraction. When one country is seen as underdeveloped, the global development agenda of economic growth through trade and raw material extraction can swoop in as a saving strategy. If a country is to modernize according to theorists like Rostow and Hoselitz, then they have to engage in uneven trade relationships with the metropole. Moreover, these countries are only discovered to be underdeveloped because they were formerly colonized and extraction had taken place at a wide scale, for example, the looting of gold and silver in Latin America by the Spanish and Portuguese. Hence, theories of modernization that treat all countries on an equal footing are devoid of an analysis of power and history by way of colonialism, slavery, and dependency.

While dependency, underdevelopment, and their Marxist critiques provide crucial insights in relation to how we should think about the global political economy, many of these ideas fell out of vogue by the 1980s. Namely, dependency is critiqued for being too structuralist and economically deterministic—it also misses social nuances and does not allow for much political agency amidst changing power dynamics in an international system.

Returning to our key question 'Who benefits and why?', it is perhaps worth thinking about power and class politics with particular attention to the relations between the Global North and South. The allure of socialism arrived at a moment where many countries in the world were decolonizing. The era of the Cold War was a material and ideological battle for hearts and minds between the US and the USSR. While these ideas around dependency were undoubtedly important in understanding the exploitative nature of capitalism on a world scale, one view of the failures of dependency theory and its resulting policies could be that dependency theorists underemphasized or were not able to foresee the power of global finance which came to dominate the global economy with the advent of neoliberal policies. Another potential critique of dependency could be that the allure of capitalist high-consumption society was powerful for both states and societies where manufacturing in the Global South could not keep pace with the domestic demand for exports. In addition, the sheer ideological and material power of the US cannot be discounted in delegitimizing dependency. By the 1980s—with what is called the Washington Consensus—powerful state actors, global financial and trade institutions, and even everyday people living in countries oriented to socialism were buying into a globalization-led future.

Despite these historical changes, we might still consider the ways that dependency theory provides us with some valuable insights to analyse our contemporary GPE. For example, we could understand uneven development through an analysis of global supply chains (which rely on cheap labour and raw commodity extraction) (LeBaron 2020a; Gore, Chapter 7), the concentration of financial power in the Global North (Pauly, Chapter 9), and the ongoing extraction of racialized labour from formerly colonized states. It is also equally important to consider that the advent of the neoliberal doctrine alters the power dynamics of the global economy by doing away with Keynesian models that were dominant since the Second World War. In this sense, dependency and structuralism have moved away from mainstream policy relevance towards providing an analytical tool kit for critical development scholars.

KEY THEORY BOX 14.3 DEPENDENCY AND UNDERDEVELOPMENT

Dependency theory is the antithesis to modernization. Taken together we can view two meta-narratives of developments. Modernization theorists see development as progress, and dependency theorists argue that development is extractive and creates underdevelopment in a global capitalist system. For instance, Frank describes a relationship between metropoles (core) and satellites (periphery) and the comprador bourgeoisie (semi-periphery in Wallerstein 1974). In his neo-Marxist view, various nations of the world are linked together due to the unfolding of global capitalism. Major Western nations like the United States or the United Kingdom are unequivocally metropoles that exploit resource-rich countries like Argentina and Brazil. Countries in the developing world supply raw materials to metropole economies which are in turn enriched by manufacturing processes that do not take place in the Global South. In Frank's view the majority of value in the global commodity chain is added outside the site of raw material extraction. This is possible because of an important class of indigenous elites in periphery nations which he calls the comprador bourgeoisie. These sub-level elites facilitate the extraction of raw materials in satellite states, all the while pocketing some profit for themselves. Dependency is later taken up by Immanuel Wallerstein in what he calls world-systems theory (see Lockwood, Chapter 13, Key Theory Box 13.3). Wallerstein updates dependency to highlight that workers all over the world—not just in the core but in the core and periphery alike—are exploited by the capitalist system for the purposes of surplus value extraction (profit). In this system, the labour of workers in the periphery is disproportionately transferred to the core.

14.2.3 Neoliberalism

As we will see through this chapter, the socio-economic upheaval and uncertainty that dominated the 1970s and early 1980s gave way to a new development agenda that broke with the Keynesian model of development that had guided policy and praxis for decades prior. Neoclassical economics provided a touchstone set of theories for thinking about development. Theorists of neoliberalism draw heavily on Adam Smith and David Ricardo to rationalize existing policing like free trade, market expansion, and the reduction of the welfare state (see Key Theory Box 14.4). Without a doubt, neoliberalism is the single most important set of theoretical principles that governs contemporary development policy today.

Neoliberalism comes to light in a particular context of a renewed Cold War in the 1980s and coincides with the rise of Ronald Reagan in the US and Margaret Thatcher in the United Kingdom. It is not shocking that Reagan's version of neoliberalism showed deep scepticism about the US welfare state and targeted particularly Black women as welfare queens who were draining the public system (Haney-Lopez 2014). In general, neoliberalism can be understood as a mode of regulation that centres austerity. Although neoliberalism is an incredibly slippery concept which is difficult to define, it is important to remember that its general predisposition to austerity economics is centred on courting the interests of the private sector. Cuts to social spending, public services, and infrastructure are meant to indicate a commitment to the reduction of government debt in favour of creating an environment that protects the corporate actors. Both Thatcher and Reagan found that government intervention created too much distortion and instead believed in entrepreneurial freedom, private property rights, free trade, and rule by free market. While the neoliberal state is often portrayed as a lean state with little government intervention, the police and military have always been funded exceptionally well. The neoliberal state is thus a very strong state when it comes to military intervention and the policing of crime, particularly of Indigenous, Black, Latinx, and other minority communities in the US and other so-called multicultural societies (Wacquant 2010). Similarly, Thatcher's idea that individuals are responsible for their own wellbeing created the explicit targeting of queer communities in the heyday of the HIV/AIDS crisis in Great Britain. It is thus not coincidental that the neoliberal era has given rise to such phenomena as the **prison industrial complex**, global border violence, intensified forced labour, lack of intervention for communicable diseases, and all forms of wealth inequality around the world today despite its various failures in terms of economic policy.

As Marxist economic geographer David Harvey writes, 'neoliberalism . . . is a theory of political economic practices that proposes that human well-being can best be advanced by liberating individual entrepreneurial freedoms and skills within an institutional framework characterized by strong private property

KEY THEORY BOX 14.4 INVISIBLE HAND AND COMPARATIVE ADVANTAGE

Two central ideas underpin today's neoliberal doctrine: the invisible hand that rests on Smith's work and **comparative advantage** which is based on the ideas of Ricardo. These two concepts provide the justification for neoliberal policies including structural adjustment programmes and market-oriented growth based on trade and financial liberalization. Briefly, Smith's concept of the invisible hand is part of a laissez-faire ('allow to do' in French) approach to government, that is to say, let the market find its own equilibrium without intervention. That said, as discussed by Watson in Chapter 2, Smith is often mischaracterized by neoliberals and might hang his head in shame with becoming a beacon of thinking for the political right (see also Harmes, Chapter 11, for discussion). For instance, Smith's metaphor of the invisible hand was in fact a warning against **merchant-dominant monopolies** that captured the state and its politicians. Equally, he saw politicians as corrupt and equally bad at allocating resources. As such, the invisible hand of the market appears as a way to allocate resources and create wealth for citizens outside of these forces of corruption—far removed from the neoliberal doctrine that champions the private sector. All this said, the way that neoliberal economists like Friedrich Hayek, Ludwig von Mises, and Milton Friedman have used Smith has given these concepts a decontextualized and secondary meaning that has been adapted to contemporary development dilemmas.

Ricardo's theorization of comparative advantage is another key concept that buttresses a global development agenda hinged on production and free trade. In brief, comparative advantage rests on the idea that states are better off when they produce goods at lower opportunity costs as compared to others. Even when a country has an absolute advantage at producing all other goods than another country, it still makes sense to trade based on what each country is comparatively better at producing. For example, Ricardo famously illustrated that England cheaply manufactured textiles while Portugal could easily produce wine. Even if England had an absolute advantage at producing both goods, as time went on both countries would realize that they could produce the cheaper item at home while trading for the more costly one. The implications of this theory for a contemporary global development agenda meant that homegrown industries that dominated the post-Second World War world could be replaced with more focused industries based on a country's comparative advantage. Poorer nations, particularly in Africa, could produce raw materials while richer nations could get these raw goods for a cheaper price while providing these poorer countries with much needed imports. The opening up of all markets to trade via the reduction of domestic inefficiencies in state welfare sutures the concepts of the invisible hand and comparative advantage together as a dominant development policy.

rights, free markets, and free trade. The role of the state is to create and preserve the institutional framework appropriate to such practices . . . It must . . . set up those military, defence, police, and legal structures and functions required to secure private property rights and guarantee, by force, if need be, the proper functioning of markets' (Harvey 2005: 64–76). Hardly weak and non-interventionist, the neoliberal states of the 1980s and 1990s functioned to punish the poor for the purposes of economic growth while filling the coffers of corporate elites.

In sum, neoliberal thinking has led to global development policies of market deregulation, **austerity** on multiple scales of development, privatization, and economic growth (above all) as the most important metric of development. The belief in **trickle-down economics** and a reduction of the state's welfare policies became known as the **Washington Consensus**. In the Global South, the 1980s brought an era of structural adjustment (see Key Concept Box 14.5) where countries were given loans accompanied by conditionalities to slash welfare and commit to neoliberal-led growth

models. World Bank President Lewis Preston used the phrase 'the bitter medicine of structural adjustment' to refer to the fact that structural adjustment was painful to enact for many countries as people would suffer job losses, vulnerability, and high costs of goods and services; however, this 'medicine' was worth swallowing for the prospects of long-term economic growth.

By the late 1990s and 2000s, even the seemingly unshakeable international financial institutions (IFIs)—the IMF and the World Bank—which were bastions of economic growth, started questioning the validity of the Washington Consensus and the effectiveness of SAPs. This was due to the fact that the Asian Tiger economies (South Korea, Taiwan, Singapore, Hong Kong) were experiencing high growth with state intervention, and countries in Africa and Latin America—forced to undergo structural adjustment—were still lagging behind. More recently, an IMF-backed report (2016) highlights, the opening up of the economy to foreign capital inflows has increased the risk of a financial crisis and worsened inequality. This is an important finding because it illustrates that

---

KEY CONCEPT BOX 14.5 STRUCTURAL ADJUSTMENT PROGRAMMES (SAPS)

The era of structural adjustment emerged in the 1980s, with the central purpose being to stabilize economies in the Global South. The IMF and World Bank provided loans and financial assistance to developing countries on the basis of conditionalities. These conditionalities committed developing countries to neoliberalizing their economies namely through enacting austerity measures like cuts in social spending. At the same time, states were meant to capitalize on their comparative advantage and open up their markets to free trade, putting neoliberal policies in sharp relief with **import-substitution industrialization (ISI)** policies of the past.

Through the bolstering of free market policies, the key legacy of structural adjustment programmes (SAPs) was placing lots of power in the hands of the private sector. Through the privatization of state-owned enterprises, reduction of taxes, and the removal of red tape for Global North corporations to enter new markets, the era of structural adjustment placed economic growth as the most important priority and indicator of development. This occurred at a cost to labour (and labour organization), as people all over the world were made more vulnerable through a downward pressure on wages and cuts to essential state services.

---

even the key actors that shaped the neoliberal world are starting to see some cracks in their vision of unfettered economic growth based on deregulation of trade and financial markets.

In questioning the Washington Consensus, the global development agenda moved away from 'fixing the economy' of developing nations vis-à-vis structural adjustment to emphasizing a good governance agenda where markets needed a solid bedrock of a transparent government focused on anti-corruption, democratic values, and a trustworthy public sector in order to create long-standing economic growth. Douglas North's (1991) conception of neo-institutionalism—getting the institutions right—provided new theoretical insights for the IFIs and other neoliberal states to intervene in the Global South. Put simply, developing states were considered too corrupt and could not possibly create the environment for economic growth to take place. Importantly, the meta-narrative of modernization never disappears. Belief in free markets, the flourishing of corporations, and austere economics still characterizes many of the policy recommendations by IFIs. Even if SAPs were failing, the key tenets of neoliberal-led development do not disappear. Although neoliberalism has been the mainstream of development policy, other theories of development continue to challenge this dominant approach.

14.2.4 **Racial capitalism, post-development, and gendered approaches**

The theories in this section are placed together because they are outside the mainstream of development approaches and challenge the bedrock of the development agenda. While there are many intellectual differences, debates, and contentions within these umbrella categories, there is also cross-pollination among them. Karl Marx, Antonio Gramsci, Maria Mies, Silvia Federici, Cedric Robinson, and Arturo Escobar are some of the thinkers associated with this subsection. While giving ample room to explore all these theories exceeds the boundaries of an introductory chapter on the global political economy of development, it is important to keep in mind the ways that these critical approaches challenge extant doctrines of development.

One impactful critique of development that has gained recent traction comes from Cedric Robinson's influential book *Black Marxism* (1983). Robinson famously contends that all capitalism is **racial capitalism** and suggests that capitalism's history involves the enslavement of Africans and the extraction of their resources, centring former colonies rather than Europe and the US as the reason that capitalism has flourished. Robinson represents a new wave of critical theory that is grounded in Marx's analysis of exploitation and capital accumulation but also pays attention to colonial linkages and social difference. Race takes centre stage in Robinson's analysis because the very foundation of capitalist development rests on sourcing low or unpaid labour in order to create a production-driven economy.

Scholars in this new wave of Marxian analysis critique theories of development in modernization, dependency, and neoliberal traditions together. For example, even the works of Wallerstein and Polanyi centre the West as the place where development takes off; however, less attention is paid to the colonial linkages that bring development and capitalism itself into existence. Gurminder Bhambra (2020) argues that, 'colonialism is constitutive to the emergence and development of capitalism . . . the purpose of this is to orient our conceptual understandings of capitalism away from the primary focus on the capital-labour relation to demonstrate how other forms of appropriation were not simply in existence (as is recognized), but how these other forms disrupt the teleology attributed to "labour" and thus the centrality of class to our analysis. This has a further consequence of providing a global account of the emergence and configuration of the world we share; moving beyond Eurocentred explanations that fail to acknowledge the significance of forms of colonial appropriation and displacement'. In this view, the global development agenda is, as it has always been, another iteration of colonial expansion. To be understood fully, scholars and practitioners must take seriously the combined violence of colonialism, race, and class together.

Another alternative to mainstream development sits in the critiques of post-development or post-colonial scholars who emphasize the ways that Western ways of thinking and writing about the non-West are better understood as part of a colonial ideology rather than an actual lived reality of people and places in the Global South. Mudimbe's work introduced at the beginning of this chapter on the colonial library is one illustration of this type of critique. Indeed, as Mudimbe reminds us, the colonial library in the African context provides an inescapable representation of Africa that guides our imaginary. In the context of global development, the colonial library includes not only countries in Africa, Latin America, and South and Central Asia, but also the representations and erasures of Indigenous groups in countries like the US, Canada, Australia, and New Zealand. Far from development happening 'over there', Mudimbe and other post-colonial scholars remind us that the images and representations of development say a lot (if not more) about the West too.

In a similar vein, Escobar argues that the knowledge produced about development represents a cultural tool of the West for the purposes of domination and hegemony. We could apply this to a theory like modernization. For example, the linear model of development as the sole way to think, know, and act out development based on capital accumulation and production shows us what values and tools the West sees as most useful. For Escobar, the West is creating a world in its own image, one that chooses profit and growth over human lives. These sorts of representations become hegemonic and are internalized by practitioners and policymakers from the Global South too. The fixation on neoliberal economics is another example of powerful ideas ascending to an unchallenged mainstream position. As Edward Said (1978) powerfully reminds us in *Orientalism*, the orient is created by the intersection of ideas, images, and representations of some imagined territory 'over there'. By rendering something 'oriental', the West creates a project of development. Through a post-development or post-colonial lens the entire project of development is brought into question, paving the way for non-structuralist, non-Western, and, thus, bottom-up solutions to the problems of development that are grounded in local communities.

Finally, we turn to some gendered critiques of development, and of capitalism more largely, that will draw our theoretical considerations to a close. Gendered approaches to development are not a monolith, and they cut across the various theoretical positions presented here. While women (and various gendered considerations) are mostly ignored by the grand narratives of development, the position of women is often used to blame or praise various countries as being too traditional or insufficiently advanced. The allure and metanarrative of modernization theory does not disappear when we consider gender.

Much of the critical work on gender and development falls in the Marxist-feminist or post-development camp of theory. Diane Elson (1995) argues that development practice is inseparable from male bias and, at best, simply adds women and stirs without considering the gendered experiences of women in the Global South. Moreover, Elson emphasizes that class and capitalism are central to understanding the predicament of women. In a similar vein, Silvia Federici (2004) makes a compelling argument in *Caliban and the Witch* that women's bodies were the first sites of primitive accumulation that gave rise to the labour force ready for capitalist exploitation. In colonizing the womb (and persecuting women who exercised their sexuality, freedom, and self-survival as witches), capitalists were able to discipline women's labour in the household without which capitalism could not function. In so doing, Federici twins feminist resistance with the resistance to capitalism itself. The household becomes a central site of oppression where women in the Global South must not only be responsible for formal work, but return home to take care of their children, male partners, and communities, a situation often named the double or triple burden (Mies 1986/2014; Elson 1995; see also Hannah and Hinton, Chapter 4). Maria Mies (1986/2014) suggests that through a process called 'housewifization', women's labour becomes increasingly devalued and is thus viewed as subsistence and therefore unproductive work. For Elson, Federici, and Mies, patriarchy and class are central to the way that capitalism functions.

These Marxist-feminist views are often critiqued for essentializing the category of gender. Post-colonial scholars such as Chandra Mohanty (2003) warn against Western feminism's ability to universalize the experiences of 'Third World' women. Both liberal and Marxist feminists tend to reduce women in the Global South to a single collective 'other' waiting for intervention and liberation. In homogenizing women as a category of analysis, Western feminists strip away the heterogeneity of place, culture, ethnicity, and sexuality, thereby minimizing the particular for the imagined universal. As Mohanty (1988: 74) writes, 'it is only by understanding the contradictions inherent in women's location within various structures that effective political action and challenges can be devised'. Beyond adding women and stirring, contemporary critical development scholarship is starting to consider gender and sexuality not as essentialized categories, but rather as features embedded under multiple layers of oppression and resistance (Bhagat 2018; Gore 2022). Gendered critiques emerge as another way to challenge the mainstream theories of development and emphasize the blind spots towards women and other sexual and gender minorities in development policy. Indeed, the theoretical vantage points introduced in this subsection point out the ways that race, gender, class, and colonialism are central to the critiques of development in contemporary capitalism.

While the theory section of this chapter is by no means an exhaustive account of the various intricacies in the ways that we think about development, it does provide an overview of the meta-narratives that guide development policy, as we will see in the next major section of this chapter. In general, there were three main theoretical categories covered here: liberalism/mainstream development theories that included modernization and neoliberalism; Marxist theories which included dependency, racial capitalism, and Marxist feminism; and post-colonial theories which continue to critique both liberal and Marxist views for their

contribution in the colonial library of the Global South. The answer to our key question—who benefits and why from globalization-led development?—depends on which theoretical viewpoint you arrive from. For instance, Marxist-feminists might argue that a male-dominated capitalist society is always in the driver's seat of every global development agenda. Meanwhile, modernization theorists might suggest that the pursuit of progress is in itself virtuous and that development can, and should, benefit all. In the end, the mainstream conceptions of development—modernization and neoliberalism—implement policies that are pro-globalization, and the various development dilemmas that arise from these policies are thus a result of globalization itself to some degree. In what follows we will look at how some of these big ideas have played out in the historical unfolding of development since the end of the Second World War.

KEY POINTS

- Modernization and dependency form two important meta-narratives of development. The former emphasizes progress, and the latter is more concerned with uneven capitalist development.

- Neoliberalism emerged as a challenge to Keynesian orthodoxy. It is based on welfare retrenchment and a commitment to export-oriented growth via trade and financial liberalization, deregulation, austerity, and privatization.

- Identity and its intersections with capitalism form the basis of alternative ideas of development. Critiques through theories of racial or colonial capitalism emphasize the ways that contemporary development is shaped by colonial histories. Gendered critiques in both Marxist and post-colonial thought highlight the importance of gender as a governing feature of development and the burden that **heteropatriarchy** places on the marginalized poor.

- Post-development scholarship challenges development as a concept through the various discourses that portray the Global South as perennially inferior and deserving of aid. In this view, development is portrayed as a project for capitalist interests amidst erasures of local organization, Indigenous sovereignty, and ongoing colonialism.

14.3 Globalization-led development

The previous section detailed various viewpoints of development and it is now important for us to see how some of these theoretical strands can be translated to development policy and its lived realities. We start after the Second World War because here we see the rise of global institutions and internationally driven development strategies take shape. The era of the Cold War also coincides with formal decolonization in parts of Africa and Asia. Undoubtedly, the end of the Second World War also revealed many advances in technology, spurring an era of accelerated globalization and wide-scale interconnectivity in terms of trade, finance, production, and communications technologies (see Girard, Chapter 17). We will study this era in three key historical periods: Keynesianism and import-substitution industrialization; the Washington Consensus; and the post-Washington Consensus era. Our key question, 'who benefits and why from globalization-led development?', still lingers here in the background as we should always remember to interrogate who has power and how it is wielded as it pertains to development. The story of globalization is also one of US-backed economic and cultural dominance, and while the policies and approaches to development are not the same through time, the locus of power remains in Western hands.

14.3.1 Keynesianism, decolonization, and import-substitution (mid-1940s to early 1980s)

The post-war development era is characterized by two major movements: formal decolonization in African and Asian states (Latin American decolonization occurred in the 1800s) and the formation of the Bretton Woods Institutions which include the IMF, the International Bank for Reconstruction and Development (IBRD), and a precursor to the World Trade Organization (WTO) called the General Agreement on Tariffs and Trade (GATT) (see Helleiner, Chapter 8 for a detailed discussion of Bretton Woods). The formation of these organizations coincides with a historical sea change where the explicit racism of the West's civilizing or plundering missions of colonization is transformed to a commitment to modernization and economic progress through which these former colonies could eventually become nations of mass consumption in the image of the US and Western Europe. It is important to remember that the liberal interventionist organizations that formed in the early 1940s were also acting to contain the spread of communism and the Soviet Union. Recall, Rostow's version of modernization is a rebuttal of Marx and

communism—without its own colonial empire the US started to fund decolonization and rebuilding projects around the world.

The structural context of an emerging liberal-capitalist world order does not delegitimize actual anti-colonial movements in countries like Algeria, India, Ghana (Gold Coast), and Indonesia, to name a few countries that officially overthrew their colonial oppressors. Indeed, the Non-Aligned Movement briefly discussed earlier came to fruition in this era because its founding members—Jawaharlal Nehru (India), Gamal Abdel Nasser (Egypt), Kwame Nkrumah (Ghana), H. Sukarno (Indonesia), and Josip Broz Tito (Yugoslavia)—were committed to being neither capitalist nor communist and wanted to forge new pathways for development (see Singh, Chapter 15) (see Figure 14.1).

This moment of decolonization involved a radical commitment by many states in the developing world to overthrow the West and resist neo-colonialism and interference. Fidel Castro's speech at the United Nations best sums up anti-colonial resistance, particularly against the US, and the language of dependency theory is very apparent in what follows: 'We are, and always shall be for everything that is just: against colonialism, exploitation, monopolies, militarism, the armaments race, and warmongering . . . The United States government cannot be on the side of the Algerian people; it cannot be on the side of the Algerian people because it is allied to metropolitan France . . . It cannot be on the side of the workers who are demanding better living conditions in all parts of the world, because it is allied to monopolies. It cannot be on the side of the colonies which want their freedom because it is allied to the colonizers' (Castro 1960).

Evidently, three competing models of development were being actively contested in the post-war era: the modernization (capitalist world order) of the US and Western Europe, the **socialist development approach**—based on central planning and state ownership of the means of production—of the Soviet Union, and a non-aligned movement of recently decolonized countries. At the same time, Keynesian ideas and the allure of US-backed development assistance were actively reshaping development. Keynesianism succeeded in creating a social contract between labour and capital by muting some of capitalism's most egregiously anti-labour tendencies. Keynesianism had implications for national economies and the new development infrastructure which John Maynard Keynes helped establish in the early 1940s.

Figure 14.1 Founder members of the Non-Aligned Movement

Source: Wilson Center

Domestically, the Keynesian era is associated with the welfare state where citizens are supported through government programmes. Internationally, trade and finance were governed through the IMF, IBRD, and the GATT so that capital did not obliterate the economies of the developing world. As Leys (1996: 6–7) argues, '[c]apital was not allowed to cross frontiers without government approval, which permitted governments to determine domestic interest rates, fix the exchange rate of the national currency, and tax and spend as they saw fit to secure national economic objectives'. In addition, the Bretton Woods Agreements of 1944 pegged the US dollar to the value of gold, and, in turn, all other currencies were pegged to the US dollar, preventing speculative currency devaluation. The IMF monitored exchange rates, and the IBRD was meant to manage funds for development assistance, particularly for those nations that faced devastation following the Second World War. The Keynesian international system was meant to create global stability while allowing developing nations to modernize and support their own economies. That said, the Bretton Woods Institutions initially formed to assist Western Europe and the US, and it was not until the 1960s that the IMF and World Bank turned their attention to the Global South. There were incredible power differences baked into the formation of these institutions—voting rights, language, and who received a seat at the negotiation table. To be sure, the Bretton Woods model was driven by, and favoured, the US, and developing countries had very little bargaining power (for an extensive discussion of Bretton Woods, see Helleiner, Chapter 8).

All this said, developing countries did challenge the mainstream development trajectories touted by modernization theorists in the US. For instance, you might recall our discussion of the Prebisch-Singer thesis in the preceding section where the thinkers argued that raw materials were volatile and lost their value in comparison to manufactured goods in the Global North. As such, it was important for developing countries to manage their own economies and produce homegrown, high-value goods. We can see the direct influence of structuralism and dependency in the real world through a set of policies called import-substitution industrialization. ISI policies existed to de-link developing countries from advanced economies by levying tariffs and quotas on non-domestic imports while subsidizing domestic industries. The underlying argument runs counter to Ricardian comparative advantage—dependency theorists were especially concerned with the fact that advanced economies were only able to get to their stage of development through some type of protectionism. The ISI model allowed developing countries to control **foreign direct investment** (**FDI**) and protect their economies from being flooded with imports. Although ISI was successful predominantly in Latin America, the rules of the international financial system never favoured this model of development.

In many ways, ISI and Keynesianism fell apart due to a series of circumstances that cast major doubt on the ways that development was taking place. These included the quadrupling of international oil prices due to an embargo by the Organization of Petroleum Exporting Countries (OPEC), the costly war on Vietnam that depleted US gold reserves, and, in turn, the end of the dollar-gold peg where the US dollar was de-linked from the fixed price of gold in 1971. The world was witnessing a structural change in the global economy from fixed to floating exchange rates. This is because there were many more US dollars floating around in the world than the US could back by gold—a central reason why President Richard Nixon ended the dollar-gold peg. The OPEC-driven oil crisis led to low economic growth and high inflation (**stagflation**) in the world economy, which the Keynesian model was unable to explain. Indeed, inflation and recession were considered mutually exclusive phenomena; however, when a commodity such as oil rises sharply, these two events occur at once. At the same time, the ISI model was failing not only due to the persistent presence of transnational corporations in Latin American countries, but also because of massive amounts of debt that developing countries accrued due to volatile commodity prices and borrowing for various infrastructure and development projects in the 1960s and 1970s. The presence of stagflation delegitimized Keynesian economics and paved the way for a new model of economic development known as neoliberalism.

Importantly, when we return to our question of 'who benefits', the US and Western Europe continue to guide the hand of development in their favour. The Global South remains indebted, unevenly developed, and a perennial arena for Western intervention. The established notions of economic growth, progress, and consumption rooted in modernization remain unchallenged with the advent of neoliberalism. In effect, any semblance of social protection is removed in favour of a market and export-oriented model of development.

14.3.2 **The Washington Consensus, structural adjustment, and the Asian Financial Crisis (1980s to late 1990s)**

The death knell of the ISI model of development was a major debt crisis in 1982 that started in Mexico and spread through Latin America, leading to the era of structural adjustment (see Key Concept Box 14.5). By the end of 1978, combined debt in Latin America amounted to US$159 billion, and this reached US$327 billion by 1981 (FDIC 1997). The 1982 debt crisis is a near-perfect illustration of the uneven power relations between the Global North (particularly the US) and the Global South. Latin American countries defaulted on their loans not because of poor fiscal management, but because the US, backed by the Chair of the Federal Reserve Paul Volcker, raised interest rates from 13.7 per cent in April of 1979 to nearly 20 per cent in 1981. When interest rates rise so sharply, the cost of borrowing money (holding US dollar debt in the case of Mexico for example) leads to an economic collapse. Mexico toppled first, followed by sixteen other Latin American countries and eleven other developing countries elsewhere in the world. The cumulative effect of the tumultuous 1970s was a new development agenda called the Washington Consensus.

The Washington Consensus (WC) broadly refers to free market reforms supported by the IFIs—the World Bank and the IMF—and the US Treasury. While the 1970s might have put US structural dominance in the international financial system in question, the 1980s, vis-à-vis the Washington Consensus, illustrates US hegemony in the global financial system. Neoliberalism eviscerates any semblance of the welfare state and aims to pull the state away from managing the economy. The WC is hinged to policy prescriptions such as fiscal discipline, reduction of spending in welfare areas like health, infrastructure, education, tax reform, trade, and financial liberalization, breaking down the barriers for FDI, privatization, and private property rights, and full-scale economic deregulation. Based on neo-classical economic theories like comparative advantage, developing countries could no longer protect and bolster their own industries and had to open up to free trade, making long-term growth and the development of their own industries highly challenging.

The WC is enforced by the IFIs through what is known as structural adjustment. In the aftermath of the 1982 debt crisis, Latin American and African countries in particular were highly indebted and needed loans to pay off their debts and spur economic growth. These loans were given out with strict conditionalities based on three core principles: deregulation, privatization, and liberalization of trade and financial markets. The World Bank and the IMF employed a 'one-size-fits-all' model to structural adjustment, taking an ahistorical and economically reductive model. By the mid- to late 1990s, the IFIs were attempting to figure out the successes and failures of conditional loans. In an important paper by David Dollar and Jakob Svensson (2000) evaluating many SAPs, we can see the ways that developing countries are blamed for improper implementation, corruption, and poor transparency. Importantly, the theoretical underpinnings of neoliberalism and the WC remain unchallenged—the theory is always right, but it is social reality that is blamed for poor implementation.

The WC started to unravel not only because of sluggish growth in Latin America and Africa, but also because of the stronger performance of the Asian Tiger economies that did not embrace WC policies on a full scale and instead opted for a more government-guided approach to development. That said, the Tigers had their own financial collapse in 1997, known as the East Asian Financial Crisis (see Pauly, Chapter 9). Two important aspects are worth keeping in mind when understanding the causes of the Asian Financial Crisis: financial liberalization—the removal of barriers for **foreign portfolio investments (FPIs)**—and the change from fixed to floating exchange rates. Financial liberalization benefitted both London and New York as leading financial hubs of the world, and the Tiger economies were opened up for highly liquid finance capital to pour into these economies. While this injection of finance could be used for all sorts of infrastructure projects and to grease the wheels of a growing economy, the lack of capital controls also allowed finance capital to flow in and out of a country unfettered.

In simple terms, when investors in Wall Street lost confidence in a currency like the Thai baht it created a domino effect where millions of dollars of FPI left the Thai and later other Tiger economies, known as the phenomenon of capital flight. This occurred because in the mid-1990s the US raised its interest rates to curtail inflation, causing a lot of **hot money** to flow into the US economy and disincentivizing the Southeast Asian economies as the best countries to invest in. Hot money mainly comes from financial actors attempting to capitalize on financial gains, and in the case of the US this caused an appreciation of the US dollar. The Tiger economies were pegged to the US dollar in order to encourage the flow of hot money into their own economies throughout the 1990s, which contributed to the Asian miracle in the first place. However, with the US dollar rising in the late 1990s, the currencies in the Tiger economies which were pegged to the US dollar rose too. When currencies appreciate the costs of imports rise—you can buy more things with a stronger dollar, for example—however, export-dependent economies like the Tiger economies are inevitably damaged because of their rising export costs making their goods less competitive in the global political economy. These factors spooked Wall Street and other investors, causing capital flight and the toppling of the economies of South Korea, Indonesia, and Thailand, but throughout other parts of South and East Asia as well vis-à-vis widespread currency depreciation.

The aftermath of this crisis involved a bailout from the IMF of around US$120 billion to South Korea, Indonesia, and Thailand, and the return of conditionalities based on the reduction of government spending, raising interest rates, and a new commitment to end crony capitalism and anti-corruption (Glassman and Carmody 2000). This paved the way for the post-Washington Consensus era, where the IFIs and other international organizations like the United Nations are focused on fixing governments in order to align with a neoliberal mindset of market-oriented governance.

14.3.3 Post-Washington Consensus, good governance, and corporate social responsibility (2000 to present?)

The Asian Financial Crisis and the various failures of structural adjustment called the WC into question. Some might argue that the post-2000s have led to an era called the post-Washington Consensus (PWC). Whether we should refer to this era as 'post' continues to be debated as many of the policies, tenets, and ideas behind the WC drive policy. Private interests, economic growth, and austerity in public expenditure continually play out, even in so-called advanced economies of the US, UK, and Canada. Nevertheless, left-leaning governments in Latin America, for instance, did challenge the WC, and current policies that target inequality, poverty, climate change, and social issues above economic growth are part of political platforms in many countries.

It is important not to discount the efforts of Indigenous, peasant, working-class, and landless workers all over the world who fought against austerity imposed by the IMF and World Bank for two decades. For instance, 50,000 people took to the streets of Seattle in the year 2000, where Waldon Bello, in his article *2000: The Year of Global Protests Against Globalization*, writes 'most of them [50,000 protestors and delegates from the global South] were united by one thing: their opposition to the expansion of a system that promoted corporate-led globalization at the expense of social goals like justice, community, national sovereignty, cultural diversity, and ecological sustainability' (2000: 1). It is important to flag the relevance of post-development scholars, as the early 2000s reflected many active contestations against the global development agenda imposed by the forces of globalization (IFIs, the US, and Western conceptions of development). As we see in Case Study Box 14.6, the development trajectory became more human-centric while continuing to persist with capitalist-oriented development. For example, the critiques of development launched by feminists could no longer be ignored.

The World Bank and the IMF also paid attention to this backlash led by social movements in developing countries, and these movements partly caused the IFIs to reframe their commitments to economic growth and austerity. This is evident in a now famous speech by James Wolfensohn, the ninth President of the World Bank. He says, ' . . . for development to be real and effective, we need local ownership and local participation. Gone are the days when development can be done behind closed doors in Washington or Western capitals or any capital for that matter'. This seems like a step in the right direction, bringing forth a multistakeholder approach to development which includes private sector actors, NGOs, IFIs and IOs, governments, and everyday citizens. However, the emphasis

---

CASE STUDY BOX 14.6 WOMEN IN DEVELOPMENT (WID), WOMEN AND DEVELOPMENT (WAD), GENDER AND DEVELOPMENT (GAD)

This case study illustrates the changing nature of women's role in development that parallels the various global development agendas we have looked at so far. The Women in Development model (WID) coincided with modernization theorists of the 1960s where women's inclusion in workplaces of the Global South was seen to be a potential avenue for economic growth and a cultural move away from traditionalism. In addition, the UN started to unveil women-centric development policies focused on family planning, reproduction, and industrial labour. However, the various problems of patriarchy like traditional gender roles, a lack of income, a lack of power in communities and households, and improper legislation emphasized that just adding women to job markets and focusing on family planning would not alleviate women's poverty. In effect, WID policies end up being non-confrontational, ahistorical, and blind to the class, gender, and cultural dimensions of everyday life.

Critiques of WID by Marxist and socialist feminists gave way to a new gendered perspective called Women and Development (WAD), which paralleled the critiques of dependency theory. Two variants of WAD emerged: 'dependency feminism', which emphasizes that the inequality between men and women is a result of global capitalist accumulation, and 'global patriarchy', which eschews class analysis for gendered and embodied violence. Indeed, the WAD approaches together emphasized that the sexual division of labour including both reproduction and low-wage work in the Global South was a result of heteropatriarchal capitalism—a system which reinforces gender and sexual inequality over liberation for the purposes of profit. While these critiques offered an important corrective to WID, they were subsumed in the Washington Consensus which focused on democracy, women's equality, and a human rights perspective devoid of a class analysis. Like dependency, the WAD approach is minimized by a switch to market-oriented governance.

With the advent of neoliberalism, a new gendered critique emerged from WAD called the Gender and Development (GAD) approach. Evidently, WID, WAD, and GAD have distinct theoretical lineages. WID is grounded in liberal feminism, WAD in Marxist and socialist approaches, and GAD in post-development theories. Central to the GAD approach is an understanding of feminism outside Western constructions and diktats. Mohanty's (1988) critique exemplifies the ways that women in the Global South could create their own alternatives to development, calling greater attention to the lived realities of class, race, gender, caste, ethnicity, sexuality, and other relations of power. The GAD approach is diametrically opposed to the economic inclusion of women in low-wage industries and instead points out the triple burden that women face. Not only are women responsible for working formal underpaid jobs, but they also disproportionately serve their communities and their households—the modernization of women's roles has in fact led to more work, further highlighting the failures of one-size-fits-all development (Momsen 2009).

of institutions and fixing governments that forms the backbone of the new development agenda is revealed through the following excerpt: 'We have learned that development is possible not inevitable. That growth is necessary but not sufficient to ensure poverty reduction. We have learned that we must take the social and structural hand in hand with the macroeconomic and the financial . . . leaders of developing and transition economies must reaffirm their commitments to carry out their promises for good governance, equality, and growth' (1999: 2–11).

The question of 'who benefits and why' is still pertinent. While the PWC might reflect on a softer, more participatory approach to neoliberalism, the changes seem to be more in appearance and discourse than deep challenges to the core principles of neoliberal governance. To quote my own introductory class in global political economy, the engine of the proverbial neoliberal car never changes, only the body receives an uplift and cosmetic upgrade.

In the so-called PWC, the IFIs have moved away from structural adjustment programmes and reframed economic growth reforms as Poverty Reduction Strategy Papers (PRSPs) based on macroeconomic, structural, and social policies under the umbrella of 'pro-poor growth' or 'participatory development'. The PWC era might seem like it is bringing the state back into development; however, the market-oriented nature of development focused on progress and economic growth has not disappeared. For deregulation, privatization, and liberalization to take place, the IFIs realize that they need governments, NGOs, private sector actors, and everyday citizens to cooperate. The central aim of the PWC is to create a viable landscape for business and economic growth to take place. The failures of Latin America and Africa had little to do with neoliberal models and everything to do with illegitimate and corrupt governments, at least according to the IFIs. The PWC thus sees an era of good governance. These good governance principles are based on the rule of law, transparency, accountability, and anti-corruption measures. Undoubtedly, states should aspire to follow these principles; however, the focus on corruption fails to account for the violence of neoliberal globalization.

Missing in the PRSPs is any indication that widescale economic crises such as the Asian Financial Crisis occurred because capital was allowed to flow in and out of countries unfettered. Similarly, the entire neoliberal experiment which abandoned the Keynesian social contract between labour and capital remains unquestioned. Instead, the IFIs lean into a softer development approach based on accountability and transparency that also extends to corporations. The Labour Party of Tony Blair, for example, championed a third way approach which remained steadfast in its commitments to market-oriented governance but also focused on social justice on the grounds of gender, race, sexuality, and other identities meant to unify progressives in the Global North. This type of third way politics makes its way into the global development agenda of the PWC too.

In 2005, the UN adopted the Global Compact government framework, which is a 'voluntary value system and principles-based approach to doing business'. Key principles include not committing human rights abuses, eliminating forced and child labour, emphasizing anti-corruption and transparency, and taking some form of environmental responsibility. These principles do not include specific details on fair wages, carbon emissions, or specific steps to fighting corruption beyond bribery and extortion. The most important aspect of the Global Compact is its voluntary nature. Corporations can choose to govern their businesses with some respect to these values and principles; however, these are not legally binding (Soederberg 2007).

Although the PWC is intended to be a softer and more participatory set of regulations that undoubtedly further neoliberal ideas of free market governance, the result is the reification of corporate power and more corporate influence in the Global South. Over 9,500 companies have signed on to the UN Global Compact; however, the voluntary nature of these programmes has implied highly uneven labour standards and even fewer improvements in the standards of living of the working poor. The PWC thus coincides with the rise of **corporate social responsibility (CSR)** strategies that align broadly with the SDGs introduced in the beginning of this chapter. Over the years, these have included Starbucks selling plastic Ethos Water bottles where a percentage of the sales goes to clean water access in developing countries, Ikea's commitment to sustainable materials and recycling, and Coca Cola spending 1 per cent of its annual operating income on various causes such as water access for refugees.

These campaigns seem benign at first glance; however, CSR can generate more profit for companies (Bhardwaj et al. 2018) without much commitment or impact to profit margins. As Soederberg (2007) eloquently sums up, ' . . . the Global Compact is in essence a neoliberal strategy that is highly exclusionary, corporate-led attempt to legitimate and thus reproduce the growing social power of TNCs across the world . . . ' (2007: 500). While CSR appears benevolent, it also masks the hidden violence of production in global supply chains and the ways in which the self-regulatory nature of CSR undercuts the ability of states in the Global South to regulate their own economies. As LeBaron (2020b) reminds us, 'study after study has found that tools like social auditing and ethical certification are profoundly flawed and ineffective when its comes to the worst forms of labour exploitation . . . Research reveals corporate fairytales for what they are: enthralling stories that are very unlikely to be true' (see also Gore, Chapter 7).

In many ways this section provides us with some key insights in order to answer our initial question of 'who benefits and why from globalization-led development?' Capitalist development since the end of the Second World War has favoured the interests of elites primarily in the US and other Global North countries while creating, at best, uneven growth in the Global South. We have observed three major trends marked by dramatic crises. The Keynesian era came to an end due in part to the oil crisis of the 1970s and created dramatic structural change in the world economy due to the abandonment of the gold standard and a move away from ISI. The hard neoliberalism of structural adjustment followed suit and, in this era, we saw a commitment to economic growth above all, with austerity as a key measure of development. This era too was punctuated by the 1982 debt crisis of Latin America and then later the Asian Financial Crisis. The third era, known as the PWC, represented a softer and more participatory approach to neoliberalism; however, the commitments to markets never disappear amidst governance strategies of accountability, transparency, and anti-corruption. In short, the engine of the car does not change, and power continues to rest in the hands of global elites and in the interests of the US and its allies. What we can learn from the history of development and how these various development strategies have unfolded so far is that capitalist development is crisis prone and structural one-size-fits-all models have led to ongoing periodic failures. In the last major section of this chapter, we will explore some contemporary socio-economic crises of development.

KEY POINTS

- Since the 1940s global development has been marked by transition and crises starting with Keynesian welfare states and import-substitution industrialization. Marked by oil and debt crises, the neoliberal era based on export-oriented growth replaced Keynesian ideas by the early 1980s. Structural adjustment and the rise of Asian Tigers challenged this neoliberal status quo of the Washington Consensus which—due to the Asian Financial Crisis of 1997—was replaced by the post-Washington Consensus.

- The US played a central role in driving many of the key changes that transitioned global development from one era to the next. This US and Western dominance has always been contested, as we see in the era of decolonization and the Non-Aligned Movement, as well as the push against austerity and globalization which eventually led to the breakdown of the Washington Consensus.

- The UN, the World Bank, and the IMF are also key institutions that have enacted policies like structural adjustment, loan conditionalities, and the buttressing of corporate social responsibility, starting in the 1980s. These organizations, too, reiterate the implicit dominance of former colonial states and attempt to shape the global political economy with growth-driven solutions based on market-oriented techniques of governance.

14.4 Crisis-prone globalization

In this final section we will explore some interrelated crises that blur the distinctions between the Global North and Global South. In many ways, these distinctions are part of a colonial library that justifies intervention in the developing world. Increasingly, however, the racialized and marginalized poor in the Global North are feeling the burdens of welfare retrenchment and uneven development. We will explore two contemporary moments in the global economy to tease out the ways that globalization is inherently crisis prone: financial inclusion, and the ongoing crisis of global displacement.

The PWC was punctuated by the Great Recession of 2008, which was a subprime lending-based housing crisis which started in the US. The causes and consequences of this crisis once again emphasized the structural power of the US. This had worldwide effects, potentially resulting in a staggering US$2 trillion loss of global economic growth. The Great Recession illustrates the ways that national, regional, and global levels of the political economy are intertwined. As mentioned in the introduction, globalization connects the everyday lives of people in distant countries to one another, and the crisis caused by subprime lending is one such example. In brief, the Great Recession was precipitated by mortgage lending to the poor at subprime rates. The prime rate is what commercial banks charge their more creditworthy customers, and lending at subprime means that the poor were able to enter into the housing market at very low interest rates—customers qualified for mortgages based on low monthly payments, where the majority of these clients opted for variable rate mortgages. The US Federal Reserve eventually pushed up interest rates, placing a downward pressure on housing demand and causing home prices to fall. The majority of the poor—who borrowed at subprime rates but held variable rate mortgages—now found the monthly costs unaffordable, and this resulted in foreclosures, evictions, and massive unemployment.

While largely concentrated in the Global North, the subprime mortgage crisis illustrates the perils of **financial inclusion** of the poor, which is at the heart of participatory development in the new global development agenda of the PWC. Importantly, while financial inclusion through access to credit might seem like a benevolent action by various creditors and the IFIs, the subprime crisis illustrates how lending to the poor lined the pockets of commercial banks and various investors. In the Global South, the PWC also represented the era of microfinance, hailed by the IFIs as a poverty reduction strategy where the poor are given small loans without the need of collateral. According to the UN, financial inclusion is a key aspect of achieving SDGs of economic growth and women's equality; however, even the IFIs have acknowledged that the benefits to the poor are uneven, as microfinance lenders find it difficult to target (and make a return on their investment) if they lend to the poorest of the poor (IMF 2020).

As Soederberg (2014a) argues, credit and debt are ubiquitous features of contemporary neoliberal development, with credit card debt, student loans, payday loans, and microcredit loans replacing state-led welfare as assistance to the poor. The Global South is characterized by many people who survive in the informal sector. With a lack of viable formal job opportunities, development policy has upheld the notion that entrepreneurialism (that is, starting a small business) is a viable solution to escape poverty. This dream of entrepreneurialism makes people reliant on small loans. In short, financial inclusion strategies through instruments of credit and debt attempt to solve extant crises of globalization, including insecure housing and work, as well as the lack of access to resources like education.

These vectors of development also appear as crucial aspects of refugee governance in an era of heightened global displacement (see Everyday GPE Box 14.7)

EVERYDAY GPE BOX 14.7 MOBILE MONEY AND DIGITAL INFRASTRUCTURES IN KENYA

We are all familiar with the use of credit cards to pay for everyday items, and some of us might even use Apple or Google Pay from our phones to make quick purchases. Credit cards are of course debt instruments where everyday people are charged high interest rates for their purchases, allowing credit card companies to have a steady revenue stream. The equivalent to credit cards for the poor in the Global South has been microloans, mostly for the purposes of entrepreneurialism but often used as a cash stream for poor people to use on food, education, shelter repair, and other survival costs, indebting some of the most precarious people on the planet. Refugees in Kenyan camps like Dadaab and Kakuma and in the major city of Nairobi until recently were reliant on international aid, part-time work, entrepreneurial survival, or piecemeal forms of assistance from NGOs. These forms of assistance for refugees are still dominant.

However, Mastercard and Western Union have recently seen refugees as a viable population for financial inclusion.

Kenya was a pioneering country for the innovation of mobile-based money transfers called M-Pesa. This is a ubiquitous banking and payment feature found all over the country through which people can pay for transactions and make deposits on their cellular devices. In a report titled 'Kakuma as a Marketplace' (2018), the International Finance Corporation characterizes refugees in the Kakuma camp as a potentially profitable and self-determined entrepreneurial population. In a bid for financial inclusion, refugees could be brought into banking relationships through mobile money networks, thereby formalizing their small-scale businesses and turning the camp into a viable marketplace. The act of using mobile money services might

EVERYDAY GPE BOX 14.7 MOBILE MONEY AND DIGITAL INFRASTRUCTURES IN KENYA (continued)

seem benign; however, corporations like Mastercard see these as revenue streams for transaction fees—the more people use this type of digital infrastructure, the more money a company like Mastercard can skim from each transaction. Indeed, both Mastercard and Western Union (2017) promote the Kakuma refugee camp as a place where the combined digital infrastructures of mobile money, digital vouchers, and card-based solutions could promote self-reliance for host communities.

For instance, the head of customer relations at Western Union claims that '[r]efugees across the world want to be empowered to break the chains of dependence and rebuild their lives in meaningful ways' (Bloomberg News 2017). What we are seeing is a neoliberalized form of refugee assistance based on credit

as opposed to welfare—a side effect of a reduction in global aid money to countries with long-term displacement crises like Kenya. Through our GPE analysis we can see how something as mundane as a payment method is actually wrapped into extant logics of neoliberal development where the poor are now a revenue stream (Soederberg 2014a; Bhagat and Roderick 2020), regardless of the fact that they have no basic citizenship rights in Kenya. Refugees are often portrayed as limbo groups relying on assistance; however, the big corporate actors understand that the displaced work and survive and need financial access of some sort to do so. Missing in these solutions are long-term and sustainable welfare policies—credit and debt are seen to step in as a form of assistance instead.

Figure 14.2 There are three Dadaab refugee camps: Dagahaley, Ifo, and Hagadera. The camps formed in the 1990s and have since developed commercial hubs connecting Kenya and Somalia by the north-west. By 2020, Dadaab registered 218,873 refugees and asylum seekers. In 2021 the Dadaab camp was set to be closed by June 2022, generating a crisis in resettling the population of those camps who in some cases were forced to return to Somalia. Dadaab camp Ifo II was reopened in January 2023, receiving between 400 to 500 people daily, most of them seeking asylum from Somalia.

Source: UNHCR Innovation Service

---

due to conflict, climate change, and economic impoverishment (Figure 14.2). Thus far we have looked at the systemic and dynamic ways that Western and elite influences have shaped globalization. However, since the 'Syrian refugee crisis' in 2015, the presence of refugees and other forcibly displaced people has reworked the imaginary of nationhood and development. In many ways, the Global South has become intertwined with the Global North, and, since 2015, we have also witnessed the rise of jingoistic and populist governments that have focused on the threats posed by racialized migrants.

Displacement has reached unprecedented levels, with 103 million forcibly displaced people worldwide by mid-2022 (UNHCR 2023). These numbers are matched with scores of people losing their lives crossing the Mediterranean Sea or facing long-term encampment in various countries like Greece, Kenya, Uganda, and Bangladesh. The notion of strong and secure borders as a development strategy emerged in the US with the Donald Trump Presidency, in the UK with the rise of Brexit and Boris Johnson as Prime Minister, as well as various countries in the EU which pivoted towards anti-migrant policies, spurring political campaigns where race and nation were (and are) central (for discussion see Harmes, Chapter 11).

Underpinning these racial sentiments are very material concerns surrounding labour, shelter, and political belonging. Decades of neoliberal restructuring has meant that homelessness and unemployment has impacted many. At the same time, the perceived influx of migrants has allowed the political right to centre nationhood and citizenship as primary concerns for those who truly belong in the West. Refugees and migrants are portrayed as outcasts who steal jobs, resources, and the Western way of life (see Guisinger, Chapter 6, and Harmes, Chapter 11, for discussion). Indeed, the crisis of refugees has much more to do with affordable housing and securing long-term and sustainable work than it does with the so-called existential and destabilizing threat of migrants.

The fact remains that welfare retrenchment has led to more draconian measures of governance where refugees have to prove that they are authentic and deserving of asylum. At the same time, while laws in the West as defined by the United Nations and the UNHCR seem progressive, the question of what happens to migrants when they arrive in major urban centres remains an open one.

Questions of global displacement point us to the ways that GPE is an embodied, everyday, and urban experience. While we have seen many crises unfold since the Second World War, the world has now entered an era of chronic global displacement that blurs the lines between the Global North and Global South. No longer is the South a development project. Instead, the very material dimensions of poverty, inequality, and resource access are in every major city across the planet. With the emerging threat of climate change, globalization has resoundingly failed to create common solutions which could mitigate the single largest threat to humanity. All this said,

alternatives to globalization-led development and neoliberalism in particular have been actively contested the world over. While this chapter cannot do these social movements justice, it is important to highlight that movements like Occupy Wall Street, Black Lives Matter, and recent climate justice movements have gained traction on a global stage. These movements challenge racism, gender hierarchies, class inequality, and the destruction of our planet; however, it is important to note that neoliberalism is able to subsume these projects and protests into marketable and profitable diversity- and inclusivity-based development agendas.

14.5 Conclusion

We shall conclude this chapter by returning to one of the key concepts mentioned in the introduction: the colonial library. In many ways, the knowledge produced about development and the Global South itself retells a structural story that centres the West as the producer of knowledge and the rest of the world as receiver of that knowledge. While I have made efforts here to point out the inherent power relations and introduce readers to some various theories that emerge from non-Western scholars, there is more work to be done in our thinking of the global political economy. Our central question has been who benefits and why from globalization-led development? The answer to this question remains ambiguous depending on the scale, location, and viewpoint of your argument. However, I have maintained that the unfolding of global development, even in its Keynesian iterations, has benefitted the US, other former colonial states, and global elites. We saw evidence of this argument time and time again, even in the most seemingly benign situations. For example, refugees in seemingly isolated and distant camps are not free from the financial penetration of companies like Mastercard and Western Union. We have also seen that many radical movements like decolonization, non-alignment, and anti-globalization protests have involved a milieu of actors who challenge global development and its colonial linkages. That said, even more participatory models of development still favour the meta-narratives of pro-growth and modernization, which continue to lurk in the background of policy prescriptions that have characterized neoliberal development since the 1980s.

Global development is a study of transitions and crises. In order to understand these tendencies of globalization-led development we explored four sets of theories under the umbrella terms of modernization, dependency, neoliberalism, and critical approaches. These approaches helped us contextualize big trends in development policy like Keynesianism and ISI, the Washington Consensus and its features of deregulation, liberalization, and privatization, and the post-Washington Consensus characterized by participatory development and corporate social responsibility. Each of these historical trends was marked by a type of economic and political crisis. Keynesian welfare states were seen as economically wasteful domestically amidst the OPEC-driven oil crisis and the reduction of US gold reserves which led to the Washington Consensus. The debt crisis of 1982 which started in Mexico solidified the age of structural adjustment, and fiscal austerity emerged as a key goal for developing states. In turn, the Washington Consensus fell apart—at least to some degree—due to the uneven economic growth in countries that had adopted structural adjustment policies. The Asian Tiger economies were using a much more state-guided strategy of growth and were outperforming expectations until these markets collapsed in 1997. There was relative international stability until 2008 when the subprime mortgage crisis took off. All these crises illustrate the perils of global interconnectivity, financial liberalization, and the reduction of state capacity in managing markets. The solutions, however, remain oriented to the private sector and call for greater transparency, accountability, and good governance; however, the role of globalization-led development remains unchecked.

At present we are sitting on the precipice of catastrophe, as several crises seem to be looming and operating in tandem. Since 2010 we have seen the Eurozone crisis, the so-called European refugee crisis, the COVID-19 pandemic, and an unavoidable climate crisis that is sure to upend life as we know it. Even through COVID-19 we have seen oil shocks, a reassertion of US–Russia conflict, a depression in wages, high inflation, and severe disruption in global supply chain production networks. This past decade has also illustrated the rise of the alt-right (or neo-fascist right) along with global movements like Black Lives Matter, where race and inequality are no longer exiled debates but are in fact central to the ways that people live their lives. Indeed, a new era of critical scholarship is shedding more light on the historical linkages of colonial capitalism, thereby emphasizing the ways in which old weapons of tyranny and oppression are masked by seemingly benign actors like foreign states and corporations who are yet still complicit in stealing land and resources from the Global South. New theoretical directions are pointing us to the embodied nature of race, class, and sexuality in GPE. Various contemporary crises are also illustrating the ever blurry lines between the Global North and Global South where the project of development has arrived at every major metropolitan city world over.

While there are undoubtedly new challenges in global development, the existential questions surrounding what development is and who it is for remain. Students and practitioners alike must think clearly and critically about how to approach these tensions surrounding race, class, various identities, and contemporary capitalism. Is development still for global elites, or is an egalitarian future possible despite imminent threats to global stability?

? 14.6 QUESTIONS

1. How does the colonial library shape our understanding of development?

2. How do you define development? Is it progress? If so, for whom?

3. What makes modernization theory a meta-narrative of global development?

4. What are the key differences between modernization and dependency theories?

5. What are the key differences between Marxist-feminist and post-colonial feminist theories?

6. How did neo-classical economics impact the Washington Consensus?

7. What were some similarities and differences between the Washington Consensus and the post-Washington Consensus?

8. What were the causes and consequences of the 1982 debt crisis and the 1997 Asian Financial Crisis?

9. In what ways can we use post-development theories to critique neoliberalism?

10. Who benefits and why from globalization-led development?

14.7 FURTHER READING

Bello, W. (2008), *Deglobalization: Ideas for a New World Economy* (London: Zed Books). This book covers the short history of key development institutions—the IMF, World Bank, WTO, and Group of Seven (G7)—and their various failures. Read this for an understanding of economic globalization and new ways to reform this system.

Bhagat, A. (2023), 'Queer Global Displacement: Social Reproduction, Refugee Survival, and Organised Abandonment in Nairobi, Cape Town, and Paris', *Antipode*, 21/1: 1–21. This article would be interesting to students who want a deeper understanding of global displacement in the context of political economy and sexuality. This article combines three cases linking Global North to Global South with a focus on the experiences of queer refugees who struggle to access housing, work, and nationhood. This type of analysis points to literature relevant to the political economy of development that links structural constraints like states and borders to the lived experiences of people.

Ferguson, J. (2015), *Give A Man A Fish: Reflections on the New Politics of Distribution* (Durham: Duke University Press). James Ferguson goes beyond liberal and Marxist theories of development to explore the rise of social welfare programmes in South Africa. The book is important reading as it interrogates whether neoliberalism has led to the death of social welfare and whether conditions of social equality could be resuscitated. It challenges the two major readings of neoliberalism provided in this chapter.

Fridell, G. (2007), *Fair Trade Coffee: The Prospects and Pitfalls of Market-driven Social Justice* (Toronto: University of Toronto Press). This book is essential for students interested in a grounded analysis of a commodity chain and its relations with neoliberal-led development. This book challenges positive readings of fair trade and interrogates its potential for social development. It examines whether fair trade initiatives are actually socially just or work to line the pockets of corporate elites.

LeBaron, G. (2020a), *Combatting Modern Slavery: Why Labour Governance is Failing and What We Can Do About It* (London: Polity). This book is essential reading for students who are interested in labour, modern slavery, and the political economy of global supply chains. Similar to themes in this chapter, the book challenges neoliberal conceptions of corporate power (and their failures) even when lots of money is spent on corporate-led anti-slavery campaigns.

Oswin, N. (2019), *Global City Futures: Desire and Development in Singapore* (Athens: University of Georgia Press). Students interested in the ways that sexuality and development are interconnected should read Natalie Oswin's book on Singapore, which challenges the city-state's position as a model of economic growth. Oswin's argument rests on the politics of intimacy and what they can tell us about development.

Peck, J., and Theodore, N. (2015), *Fast Policy: Experimental Statecraft at the Thresholds of Neoliberalism* (Minneapolis: University of Minnesota Press). This book explores globalization and the interconnections between Global North and Global South, spanning fieldwork on six continents. It focuses on the often neglected urban dimensions of two important policies: conditional cash transfers and participatory budgeting.

Soederberg, S. (2020), *Urban Displacements: Governing Surplus and Survival in Global Capitalism* (London: Routledge). This book provides a critical political economy analysis of low-income housing in three major European cities. It is important reading because it centres cities in global political economy and analyses housing as a key vector of social inequality. The book also highlights the importance of race, gender, and social reproduction as features of urban poverty.

Tawakkol, L. (2023), 'Capitalizing on Crises: The EBRD, Jordanian State and Joint Infrastructure Fixes', *Review of International Political Economy*: 1–23. This article furthers our understanding of financial institutions by examining the role of the European Bank for Reconstruction in the Middle East. It highlights the conditionalities, concerns, and major questions of EBRD involvement in Jordan amidst a so-called refugee crisis. In reading this piece, students might consider whether we have broken away from the Washington Consensus over the last three years or whether loan conditionalities and neoliberal reform, as policy tools, are here to stay.

Wacquant, L. (2009), *Punishing the Poor: The Neoliberal Government of Social Insecurity* (Durham, NC: Duke University Press). Students who are interested in the prison industrial complex and its linkages to neoliberalism will find this book essential reading. Wacquant coins the term prisonfare to refer to the system in which the US (in particular) penalizes poverty in the context of precarious employment and welfare retrenchment. It is essential reading for a deeper understanding of the neoliberal state.

CONTRIBUTOR NOTE

Ali Bhagat is an Assistant Professor of Racial Equity and Public Policy in the School of Public Policy at Simon Fraser University. His book, *Governing the Displaced: Race and Ambivalence in Global Capitalism*, is forthcoming with Cornell University Press (2024). He has published in journals relevant to international political economy, global development, and geography such as *Review of International Political Economy*, *New Political Economy*, and *Antipode*.

15

The Global Political Economy of North–South Relations: A View from the South

J. P. Singh

Chapter contents

Readers' guide

All global interactions are shaped through collective or 'cultural' understandings among groups of international actors such as nation-states, international organizations, or international thinkers about the terms of interaction. At the end of the Second World War, colonial countries overwhelmingly influenced the terms and meanings of North–South interactions. This chapter provides a history of these interactions with a focus on international organizations, mostly in the United Nations system, where these cultural understandings were institutionalized. North–South relations have now evolved to feature divisions among prosperous countries regarding the terms of engagement with the South and considerable variety in development—a departure from the 'industrialization and modernization' approaches that were dominant in the immediate post-colonial period. Cultural elites in the colonizing countries dominated the post-war understandings, while contemporary understandings can feature local actors and transnational solidarities. The chapter also details three current challenges for Global North–South relations including the future of multilateralism, emergent forms of global solidarity, and current development aspirations.

15.1 Introduction

During the colonial days, Britain would boast that the sun never set on its empire. The 'National Curriculum' in British high schools now hardly teaches the history or the problematic legacy of this empire that can be dated back to the establishment of the East India Company in 1600 (Goodfellow 2019). The legacy, nevertheless, continues at an everyday level in colonial-era British statues, linguistic expressions linked to colonialism, and in current forms of racism and xenophobia. Seen from the colonies, this history was not that of freedom and democracy—but illiberalism and violence. Nationalists in colonized countries in the 1930s and 1940s likened colonial occupation and history to that of the Nazis in Germany (Césaire 2001; Sanghera 2021; Elkins 2022). Winston Churchill was a reviled name in colonial India: just as allies pushed against the Nazis, the Bengal famine took place under his watch and neglect with an official death toll of 1.5 million people (Sen 1982). It is not easy to acknowledge past wrongs: Shashi Tharoor's recent book argued that India's gross domestic product (GDP) was nearly one quarter of the world's total when the Mughal Empire finally collapsed in the mid-nineteenth century, but was barely 3 per cent of the world's total when the British left India in the mid-twentieth century (Tharoor 2016). Colonial violence left many legacies. The controversies in the United States about not teaching critical race theory in its classrooms follow directly from the country's dark past and present history of racism and slavery. While estimates vary, the drastic depopulation of Indigenous populations in the Americas since 1492 is now generally confirmed through bioarcheology and anthropological genetics: 'The contours of Indigenous depopulation were shaped not only by disease but also by complex colonial factors including violence, forced labor, exorbitant taxation, malnutrition, and dislocation' (Liebmann 2021: 58).

The histories being taught in Anglo-American classrooms that ignore questions of colonialism and race find their counterpart in the understandings in international relations and in global political economy (GPE), which until quite recently were dominated with paradigms that arose from the Global North and reflected its preferred forms of storytelling or narration (see Hannah and Hinton, Chapter 4). The early history of international relations was obsessed with questions of race and the management of the colonies. At the beginning of the twentieth century, international relations meant international race relations (Vitalis 2015). The prominent journal *Foreign Affairs* had its origins as the *Journal of Race Development* between 1910–1919, though it did feature anti-racism contributors such as W. E. B. Du Bois (Henderson 2013). Post-war international relations may have ignored race because as colonies became independent they did not need to be managed, and because questions of domination and interdependence took on other guises, as this chapter explains later. In the global political economy of North–South relations, the liberal models predicated prosperity through the replication of the European industrial experience in the Global South with industrialization, modernization, and international trade (Rostow 1960). The radical and Marxian versions extended European models of unequal exchange and class relations to the Global South, or the 'periphery' (Brewer 1990). Both liberal and radical Global South scholars contributed to, and amended, the European narratives (Bhagwati 1958; Cardoso and Faletto 1979), but they also resurrected or reimagined historical and cultural understandings that challenged the world-views of 'Northern' scholars (Escobar 1995).

This chapter reframes the history of North–South relations with a view towards how post-colonial countries regarded North–South multilateral relations and international development, the latter generally relegated to the back end of most texts in global political economy. The current text is different in that it starts with a chapter on race, empire, and colonialism, and non-Western perspectives are central claims throughout the text. Nominally, the lopsidedness with which North–South relations are regarded is not hard to understand. High-income countries, often understood as the Global North, account for about 15 per cent of the world's population, but 63 per cent of world GDP.[1] To the rich belong the spoils.

The next section in this chapter provides a brief theoretical reprise of the global political economy of North–South relations as a lens for understanding cultural understandings from a theoretical perspective. The subsequent section roughly corresponds to the history of North–South relations in the post-Second World War era. For focus, North–South

---

[1] For current data, see World Bank (n.d.), 'Data', available at https://data.worldbank.org/.

relations are refracted through post-war international organizations in trade and development that have been central to the global political economy of these interactions. The first subsection revisits the convergences and divergences among Global North and South scholars, but with real history in mind. The subsection thereafter deals with the era of exclusion and marginalization lasting until the early 1960s when post-war international organizations both constituted and regulated the conduct of the Global South, but at the behest of the Global North. A second era documents the **advocacy** and **bloc diplomacy** that began with the creation of an international organization that represented the Global South's interests: the United Nations Conference on Trade and Development (UNCTAD), created in 1964 under the leadership of Argentinian economist Raúl Prebisch. A third era starting in the late 1980s documents inclusion and participation by the developing world in international organizations. The final section of this chapter addresses current issues and challenges in North–South relations and the strategies that the Global South adopts. The terms Global South and the developing world are used interchangeably in this chapter, but the former signifies more of an oppositional position to the former colonial powers and the prosperous countries of the industrialized world.

Cultural narratives are stories, and as such feature narrators and characters. Like in the novels from the nineteenth century, the story of the Global South in global political economy was initially told in third person from the perspective of an omniscient narrator or the cultural elite in the Global North. Anthropologist Arturo Escobar (1995: 130) calls these 'developmentalist regimes of representation' that not only represented reality, but constituted it. The everyday practice of North–South relations in the twenty-first century means that the story is difficult to narrate without some reflexivity to the context of a narrator (see Everyday GPE Box 15.1). Reflexivity here connotes being cognizant of both the historical context and the power of being the narrator. A provocative example in the new narration is Zambian-born Dambisa Moyo (2009), whose book *Dead Aid* questioned the motivations and mechanisms of foreign donors to highlight both the paternalism and ineffectiveness in foreign aid. **Paternalism** here refers to infantilizing the developing world and assuming for oneself the parental or care-taking role.

15.2 Global political economy theories and North–South relations

North–South relations are presented in this chapter as cultural narratives about people slowly gaining consciousness and agency to change their circumstances (see Hannah and Hinton, Chapter 4, for a broader framing on cultural political economy). The theory and method derive inspiration from disciplines such as anthropology, cultural studies, and sociology, but economics and global political economy are catching up (Shiller 2017; Singh 2017a). Cultural narratives are about collectively held meanings about identities and processes. Brazilian educator Paulo Freire (2018) noted that overcoming oppression means finding a cultural voice for the oppressors to name their world. In the North–South relations cultural narrative, the world was named for the people of the developing world. A process of consciousness awakening has meant not just that the formerly colonized people find a voice, but also that those who were colonizers gain a consciousness of their past (see Watson, Chapter 2, for racist ideas that existed historically in Great Britain). Recent international relations scholarship also now represents the world as narratives: 'Narratives are seen as being vital in the construction of a political actor's identity and their understanding in the world' (Miskimmon et al. 2017: 5).

In fashioning cultural narratives, theory from and about the Global South has converged around or readapted dominant perspectives in global political economy. It has also departed in its understandings, especially in the importance given to cultural narratives in what is now known as post-colonial studies. The convergences and divergences are now discussed separately below, but for the purposes of brevity, the liberal and radical versions are emphasized.

The history of North–South relations in the next subsection shows how Global South scholars both agreed with and departed from the dominant cultural narrative regarding exchange and industrialization. Early contributions from the Argentinian economist Raúl Prebisch (1950) or Indian-born economist Jagdish Bhagwati (1958) questioned whether the pursuit of comparative advantage through exports of primary commodities could result in economic growth. With high price elasticity of primary goods, meaning high production leads to lower prices, the developing world would be worse off through international trade. The situation was even worse because developed countries

EVERYDAY GPE BOX 15.1 'PRABHAT PHERI' OR MORNING ROUNDS

The anti-colonial movement to oust the British from South Asia resonated with people at an everyday level through the moral economy of rituals such as 'prabhat pheri', or morning rounds, which brought groups of a dozen or more people to roam the streets singing nationalist songs, or later hymns, as the British sought to ban nationalist songs. Mahatma Gandhi, the leader of the Indian nationalist movement, especially encouraged the practice in the 1930s as the opposition to British Raj grew stronger. The songs were often about solidarity, dignity, and 'swadeshi', or self-reliance—and everyone was encouraged to join regardless of social and economic inequality. For the parbhat pheri, people generally wore clothes made out of home-spun cotton or 'khadi' that the nationalist leaders had popularized, and they spoke eloquently against raw cotton exports from India to the textile mills of Britain. The songs, even when drawing upon religious content, were secular in the South Asian sense of speaking across communities. I grew up in post-colonial India when 'prabhat pheri' became a morning ritual to celebrate Gandhi's birthday on 2 October. We dressed in khadi and roamed the streets singing the nationalist songs. Gandhi's favourite was a song that features the following lines: 'You are variously called God or Allah; award wisdom to everyone, O God'. The songs provided dignity, solidarity, and suggested a self-sufficient way forwards. Post-colonial India followed an industrialization strategy based on self-sufficiency, and this was not just a reflection of European industrialization experience with a Keynesian twist, but also movements such as 'swadeshi' that had roots in Indian political thought (Vajpeyi 2012). Wearing cotton and singing songs of solidarity provided a unique voice to people who had been oppressed and divided for centuries through caste, religious domination, patriarchy, and foreign rule. In 2022, as India headed into the 75th anniversary of its independence, there were calls from opposition politicians to revive prabhat pheri. The context for revival includes the diminishing of Gandhian legacy with the rise of extremist Hindu movements in India (see Figure 15.1).

Nationalist songs providing dignity and solidarity are not unique to India. Freedom songs from apartheid South Africa are a

Figure 15.1 Mohandas Karamchand Gandhi (1869–1948)

Source: Alamy.

powerful example. At a more general level, ethno-musical traditions are increasingly examined for helping people find a cultural voice, not just through music but also the physical involvement of bodies, whether in a prabhat pheri in India or a tango in Argentina, although anthropologists also make us aware that all cultures or cultural voices represent their own power relations and exclusions (for further reading on India, see Subramanian 2020; for global contexts, see Radano and Olaniyan 2016).

discouraged indigenous industry in the developing world through higher tariffs on exports that added value to primary products (see Key Concept Box 15.4). Economist T. N. Srinivasan (2019) further warned in the 1960s that the preferential carve-outs for the developing world in the global trading system would marginalize the developing world and force it to receive 'crumbs from the rich man's table' (2019: 27).

Global South scholars in the liberal tradition now point out the problematic assumptions about race and gender in liberal theories of trade and development. For example, liberal models paid insufficient attention to how the poor and the marginalized (including gender) may participate in political economic activities (Banerjee and Duflo 2012). They also showed how carve-outs and marginalization from the trading system carry racist and paternalistic cultural assumptions (Singh 2017b). At a broader emancipatory level, Amartya Sen (2000) cites both Eastern and Western emancipatory traditions to show that development is about dignity and freedom and the capacity to change one's circumstances in life.

Working within the confines of radical and Marxian traditions, Global South scholars reimagined the way capitalism and class would function in North–South relations. Theories of imperialism had already accorded attention to the international division of labour. Economists such as Egyptian-French Samir Amin deepened it further to describe the basis of what would later become dependency and world systems theories that relegated peripheral economic and cultural positions to the Global South (Amin 1972; 1989). The strongest enunciation of dependency came from Brazilian academics Cardoso and Faletto (1979). Dependency theory conceived the unequal exchange further through core and peripheral regions of the global economy (see Bhagat, Chapter 14, for a full explanation). Interestingly, Henrique Cardoso, one of the main exponents of dependency theory, was elected President of Brazil 1995–2002. This is not an aberration: many of the post-colonial leaders such as Julius Nyerere of Tanzania, Kwame Nkrumah of Ghana, Leopold Senghor of Senegal, or Jawaharlal Nehru of India were educated in socialist traditions of the day. Their genius lay in adapting these radical narratives to local cultures. The 'everyday' life of radical thought in the Global South was not in academic trenches, but in the reality of its politics that adapted these Western traditions to local cultural dignities. Testaments include Leopold Senghor's pioneering writing on Negritude or Black consciousness and struggle in Africa, or Jawaharlal Nehru's autobiographical *Discovery of India*. Ideas of radical struggle, including race, would further find articulation through activist-intellectuals such as Argentina's Che Guevarra, Brazil's Paulo Freire, Afro-Caribbean's Frantz Fanon, and South Africa's John Steven Biko. Accounts in global political economy that neglect such 'praxis' need to re-examine their cultural assumptions that assign production of knowledge to elite academic presses and journals. Subaltern scholars such as Rana-jit Guha and Gayatri Spivak have also called attention to cultural ideologies that ignored the position of the post-colonial 'subject' or prevented them from articulating their experience (Guha et al. 1997; Spivak 2015).

Global political economy from the Global South is a counter cultural narrative to the theoretical imaginaries of the Global North. Edward Said's *Orientalism* is an exemplar, though not strictly confined to GPE alone (Said 1978). *Orientalism* showed how the dominant intellectual views about the East or the Orient in Western academic thought ran parallel to Occident's cultural assumptions about the colonized being an inferior set of people (see Figure 15.2). Academic thought further strengthened this 'othering'. The Western subject was constituted as rational and civilized, while the Eastern as 'irrational and depraved'. Scholars working within these traditions have underscored, among other things, the cultural marginalization of gender, race, class, caste, and sexuality in these narratives (for examples, see Ling 2002; Geeta and Nair 2003). As with praxis of theoretical traditions in the Global South, to understand the counter-cultural global political economy narrative the readers must study everyday cultural representations and practices. My own forays include gender and Islam (Singh 2016) and post-colonial literatures and cultural media (Singh 2014).

KEY POINTS

- Drawing inspiration from disciplines such as anthropology, cultural studies, sociology, economics, and global political economy, North–South relations can be understood as cultural narratives—collectively held meanings about identities and processes—which allow people to gain consciousness and agency to change their circumstances.

- Global South scholars have converged and departed from dominant perspectives in global political economy, particularly emphasizing cultural narratives in post-colonial studies and highlighting issues of race, gender, and marginalization.

- The history of North–South relations challenges the dominant cultural narrative on exchange and industrialization, questioning the pursuit of comparative advantage and exposing the marginalization of the developing world in the global trading system.

- Working within radical and Marxian traditions, Global South scholars reimagine capitalism, class, and the international division of labour in North–South relations, highlighting the theories of imperialism, dependency, and world systems, as well as the adaptation of radical narratives to local cultural contexts.

Figure 15.2 Western views on the so-called *Orient* highly impacted the arts in the nineteenth century, creating an image that still lasts in current portraits of the Middle East in movies and the collective imaginary. Famous paintings like this from Eugene Delacroix represented women as 'odalisques', noble-women, and slaves, portraying women from the eyes of Western travellers and romantics.

Source: Alamy.

15.3 A history of North–South cultural narratives

The cultural perspectives from the Global South can be understood through praxis, which is theory as practice, as seen through the history of North–South relations. This section distils the cultural praxis that created post-war multilateral institutions, which represented the pinnacle of North–South interactions. The negotiations in the 1940s leading up to the creation of the United Nations and its specialized and affiliated agencies are remarkable for their imagination in responding to the need for an international order that would avoid conflict and war. They are equally remarkable for having largely marginalized the developing world, which was then either colonized or emerging from this experience.

15.3.1 Exclusion and marginalization

Until recently, dominant GPE explanations or narratives, at least in North America, about the creation of the post-war international institutions such as the

United Nations tended to oscillate between the power of a few to create these institutions versus interdependence among international actors, chiefly states, that led to forms of institutionalized cooperation at the global level (Carr 1964; Keohane and Nye Jr 1977; see Key Theory Box 15.2). The Global South barely featured in these narratives, except as one affected by global conditions or interactions that were created elsewhere. Critical theory perspectives rooted in historical materialist and class conditions also did not assign any significant agency to the Global South (Singh 2023). A counter-narrative, with historical corrections, that has been around but has gained renewed currency recently revises the existing narratives in GPE to show how the marginalization of the developing world was intentional, and bordered on racism.

Rooted in forms of consciousness and agency in the Global South, the counter-narrative, which can be called post-colonial, cuts across various conceptualizations that already exist in GPE. For example, when post-colonial countries in the 1950s questioned the terms of trade explained below, their stance was compatible with liberal theories of trade. It would also be wrong to assume that the developing countries were unaware of what post-war institutions held for them. Here's a quote from Indian philosopher Sarvapelli Radhakrishnan, later India's President from 1962–1967, who spoke at the United Nations Educational, Scientific, and Cultural Organization (UNESCO)'s first General Assembly in 1946: 'We must give the disinherited people the breath of an everlasting spirit, the sense of a liberating faith, which is distinct from the intellectual narrowness and rigidity of revelatory creeds which would accept no standards as valid save the explicit prescription of canonical texts' (Radhakrishnan 1949). Mahatma Gandhi, when asked what he thought of Western civilization, had famously replied that it would be a good idea. Just as the elite in the Western world were aware of their habits of domination, the cultural elite from the developing world were equally aware of the terms of engagement to which they were being subjected, and held them to be unfair and unjust. Resurrecting these histories is important: when liberal policy perspectives assume that the developing world would benefit from (exclusionary) terms created in the North, or critical theory assumes that people in the developing world are unaware of the terms to which they are being subjected, both contain elements of paternalism, if not being outright patronizing in assuming that most oppressed people are unaware of their own subjugation.

The United Nations charter was signed in San Francisco on 26 June 1945, and fifty-one states met in January 1946 for the first meetings. Although a brainchild of President Franklin D. Roosevelt, the UN rested on earlier ambitions and initiatives. This included the League of Nations, which was created in 1920 and formally disbanded in 1946 when many of its agencies were absorbed into the UN system. The original signatories to the UN charter included several developing countries, but the negotiations were mostly among the allied nations. China, Russia, the United States, and the United Kingdom drew up the draft of the UN charter at a conference in Dumbarton Oaks, Washington, D.C., in August 1944. Innis Claude (1959) provides an account of the UN creation reflecting pragmatism at the UN about accommodating powerful states in the world, while advancing an idealism about the future of humanity. The interests of great powers were foremost represented through the Security Council and the veto given to its five permanent members. However, an expansive General Assembly granted each member-state a right to vote.

Lurking underneath the power and idealism of the UN creation may have been some sinister men and motives. The racism of 'internationalists' such as President Woodrow Wilson, the force behind the League of Nations, and President Franklin D. Roosevelt (FDR) continues to be unearthed. The Atlantic Charter in 1941 was an initiative between the US and the UK and spelled out the plans for the international order. The British architect was Winston Churchill, who certainly held the colonies in low esteem. On the US side, FDR's Secretary of State Cordell Hull thought that democracy and civilization belonged to the West, and hardly mentions the colonies in his expansive memoirs (Hull 1948). The creation of the UN also involved well-known racists such as Jan Smuts of South Africa. Historian Mark Mazower (2012) notes that the United Nations was conceived as a set of institutions to continue imperialism by other means: 'A democratic imperial order had been preserved, thanks to the formation of the UN, even as fascist militarism had been defeated. The world of civilizing inferior races, and keeping them in order, could continue' (2012: 21).

Despite its chequered history, the creation of the UN was a bold step—institutions, once created, can have a history and trajectory of their own, and the world now sees the UN as a pre-eminent global governance body, albeit not without its faults. Its charter starts with four aims: cessation of war, faith in human rights, respect for international law, and 'to promote social progress and better standards of life'. This last feature, conceived mostly as an addendum, about ending war through prosperity and with European post-war reconstruction in mind, uniquely brought economic and social matters to the forefront of global governance (Jolly et al. 2009; Hanhimäki 2015). The UN Economic and Social Council became the umbrella body of the agencies and programmes associated with these goals. In practice, most of the post-war economic and social development work was done through specialized UN agencies, and three economic bodies commonly known as the Bretton Woods Institutions.

The Bretton Woods Institutions, named after the negotiations starting in 1942 at this place in New Hampshire, were mostly a creation of the allied powers to govern international trade and monetary flows and to set up agencies for post-war economic reconstruction. The three 'sisters' that resulted from these negotiations were the International Monetary Fund, the International Bank for Reconstruction and Development (IBRD), and a trade organization that emerged in 1947 and became known as the General Agreement on Tariffs and Trade (GATT) (see Trommer, Chapter 5, and Helleiner, Chapter 8, for details on these institutions). Richard Gardner (1980) provides a colourful account of these negotiations where the US wanted to assert its pre-eminent power to shape the global order, while the UK was loathe to give up its (former) leadership role.

Harry Dexter White, chief economist at the Treasury, led the US team while the famous economist John Maynard Keynes led the UK side. The IBRD would be chiefly involved in the task of European reconstruction in the decade following its creation, while the IMF governed the rules for exchange rates, with a leading role for the dollar in a system that affixed the rate for one ounce of gold to the dollar (US$35 for an ounce of gold in 1958); all the other world currencies were tied to the dollar. Keynes had envisioned a world currency instead of the dollar, but the Americans prevailed in the negotiations. The voting in both the World Bank and the IMF is weighted in favour of members making the highest percentage of contributions. Therefore, the US and Western Europe (and soon Japan) controlled these agencies, and the US could exercise its influence from its nearly 25 per cent vote share to shape the institutions with its market-oriented interests and economists educated at US universities.

The history of the trading system is slightly more complicated, but chiefly obeyed the interests of the US and the UK (see Trommer, Chapter 5). The post-war trading organization was to be something more ambitious than GATT but, fearing rejection, President Truman did not submit the charter to US Congress. A set of generalized agreements on tariffs and trade became the *de facto* trade organization, with the first tariff-cutting negotiations held in Geneva in 1947. During the lead up to GATT, the developing countries had argued for **infant industry** protections to help grow their domestic manufacturing capabilities (see Key Concept Box 15.3). Most of their demands were

---

KEY CONCEPT BOX 15.3 INFANT INDUSTRY AND IMPORT-SUBSTITUTION INDUSTRIALIZATION (ISI)

These two concepts address industrialization strategies in the post-colonial world. Infant industry policies sought to both incentivize and protect emerging industries. Emergent industries could not compete with industrial products from the developed world; therefore tariff protection was deemed necessary to make them grow, and this was one of the major demands from the developing world at the GATT negotiations. **Import-substitution industrialization (ISI)**, as the name implies, emphasized domestic industry over imports, but often through manufacture of products that were domestically feasible and appropriate. For example, China prioritized bicycles over automobiles. In practice, both strategies were difficult and endowed post-colonial states and bureaucracies with enormous power, which was often misused and led to inefficient and even

corrupt practices. Brazil's devolution into the Branco regime's military dictatorship in 1964 was related to the failures of the government with its ISI strategy. In India, the ISI strategy came to be known as 'license-quota-permit Raj' that replaced the British empire, and its failures were masked with populist rhetoric from the government. On the positive side, ISI endowed many parts of the developing world with a manufacturing and infrastructural base that they had previously lacked. This included diversification into agro-industries, and manufacturing such as autos and textiles and garments. Although the so-called East Asian Miracle is understood through export-led growth, underlying this growth was ISI, which included textile and electronic manufacturing in South Korea, and intermediate goods in Taiwan.

overlooked, and the GATT included ambiguous and challenging language that made it difficult for developing countries to safeguard their manufacturing industries. Instead, the UK made tariff preferences for products from its colonies an overriding objective of the trade negotiations. In 1938, Britain's trade with its colonies was substantive; the export share was 49.9 per cent, and 40.4 per cent of total imports came from colonies (Feis 1945: 668). The US viewed the need for **imperial preferences** variously as a protectionist ploy and as continuation of empire, but eventually gave into the British and other similar demands from European colonial powers. In any case, the US was also not sympathetic to any position taken by representatives from the developing world.

It soon emerged that the trading system was highly biased against the developing world. Economists Raúl Prebisch and Hans Singer pointed out that by being relegated to producing primary commodities, the developing world was subjected to **high price elasticities**: the more they produced, the less they earned (Prebisch 1950; Singer 1950). Economist Jagdish Bhagwati (1958) noted the implication was 'immiserizing growth' that would not make the developing world better off. A powerful commission appointed at GATT, known as Committee III, issued a report that came to be known as the Haberler Report, after its chairperson Harvard economist Gottfried Haberler, which powerfully critiqued the global trading practices that were biased against the developing world (General Agreement on Tariffs and Trade 1958). The developing world also saw the writing on the wall for even imperial preferences: new leaders of post-colonial countries considered the Treaty of Rome in 1958 and the Common Agricultural Policy (CAP) of a budding European Economic Community (EEC) as measures that would discriminate against developing world's exports, especially in agriculture.

In the meantime, most of the developing world adopted the so-called **modernization approach** to development, which equated industrialization with economic growth and progress. The strategy was in part rooted in the Western industrial experience and in part blessed and promoted through UN agencies, though as we just read, these blessings lacked teeth: the GATT actively discriminated against the developing world's advocacy (and plans) for industrialization. The modernization approach was deeply flawed on other counts. At a governance level, it assumed that there were institutions such as a fully functioning state that could implement these strategies. At a conceptual level, it entrusted the task of development to technocrats educated and housed at agencies in the Global North who assumed that there were 'backward societies' that were 'underdeveloped' with tradition-bound populations who were waiting for the Global North's technocrats to transform their lives (Ferguson 1990; Escobar 1995). This reasoning was also part of the 'authoritarian high modernism' that vested great authorities in states to direct the human condition (Scott 1998).

The developing world's elite was neither docile nor stupid. It was aware of the inimical terms of trade and had actively supported an infant-industry strategy to provide teeth to a domestic growth agenda. The latter could be connected to modernization, but its roots were equally in their history and need for self-sufficiency. The developing world was also coming of age through the sheer act of decolonization, and new members were being added to the UN system. Both the US and the Soviet Union initially vetoed members that were seen as allied to the other side's interests. By 1955, only nine new members were added. But in 1955, sixteen new members joined, and the membership grew rapidly thereafter (it stood at 193 in 2022 and 117 in 1965, the latter figure more than double the number from the time of the UN's creation). That same year in 1955, twenty-nine newly independent countries met for the Asian-African Conference in Bandung, Indonesia, and declared an independent path forwards for themselves, through what became the **Non-Aligned Movement** (**NAM**), formally launched in 1961.[2]

> ### KEY POINTS
>
> - Post-war multilateral institutions chiefly reflected cultural understandings of the Global North.
> - The creation of the post-war international order resulted from negotiations among powerful allied states in the Second World War.

---

[2] In practice NAM was never truly non-aligned, with members that were sympathetic towards one great power or the other. However, the Bandung conference and NAM are important for the consciousness and articulation of the Global South's interests at a very early time.

- The Bretton Woods Institutions—the IMF, the World Bank and, later, the GATT—influenced trade and development agendas in developing countries.
- The terms of international trade were biased against the developing world, and developing countries' calls for infant-industry protections were ignored.
- The chief development approach was the modernization approach, which sought to replicate the Western industrialization experience in the developing world.

15.3.2 Advocacy and bloc diplomacy

The cultural understandings of the multilateral system began to be challenged in the 1950s through the collective or cultural advocacy from, or on behest of, the Global South. Designed in the 1940s, the multilateral system was biased against the Global South's economic and social interests, and came with an in-built historical paternalism from the Global North. Even studies such as the Haberler Report pointed out how the terms of trade were biased against the developing world. With the growing ranks of post-colonial countries, empowered now with technical studies, advocacy to reform the multilateral system grew in the 1960s and began to result in institutional changes that were a departure from extant practice.

Institutions represent collective aspirations and ideas. The big institutional changes from Global South advocacy were the creation of the United Nations Conference on Trade and Development (UNCTAD) in 1964 and the United Nations Development Program (UNDP) in 1965: over time, UNCTAD became associated with the developing world's trade interests, and UNDP offered a more expansive and inclusive definition of development than the modernization approach. The terms of trade debate, spearheaded by Raúl Prebisch, was fundamental to the creation of UNCTAD. A 1962 resolution in the UN General Assembly called for a conference on trade and development in 1963. Prebisch became the first Secretary-General of the organization from 1964–1969. His studies of terms of trade set off a wave of others, especially those dealing with tariff differentials, which pointed out how the terms of trade were further biased against the developing world (see Key Concept Box 15.4).

UNCTAD sought to create fairer terms of trade for the developing world, mostly through coalitional pressures and technical studies. UNCTAD support was fundamental to the creation in June 1964 of a developing world trade coalition known as the G-77, which continues to exist with 134 members in 2022. The G-77 offered solidarity to the developing world and practised bloc diplomacy, or the ability to present a singular position in negotiations to apply pressure (Narlikar 2003). UNCTAD's technical studies rooted in economic logic and data provided an evidence-based and ideas-led forum for the developing world's concerns. The International Trade Centre was created in 1968 as a joint organization of the GATT and UNCTAD to collect data and research trade issues. UNCTAD was not an alternative to the GATT, but a way to bring pressure on the GATT from the developing world. A pre-eminent trade economist wrote: 'Although it did not seem so at the time, developing countries actually used the UNCTAD threat with a great deal of caution and patience' (Hudec 2011: 40). For example, advocacy through UNCTAD led GATT

KEY CONCEPT BOX 15.4 TARIFF DIFFERENTIALS

Tariff differentials refer to the differences in tariffs between raw materials and goods with value added. Lower tariffs for raw materials and higher tariffs for value added to raw materials would constitute a tariff differential on a similar product line. Trade economists found in the 1960s that developing countries faced higher tariffs if they added value to their primary commodities in agriculture or extracted minerals. For example, one study showed that cocoa beans imported into the EEC faced a tariff of 9 per cent, which increased to 27 per cent if the beans were processed as powder (Curzon 1965: 229–230). Such tariff differentials kept the developing world poor and at the lower end of the production value chain for the product.

In the example just provided, cacao producers have an incentive to export beans rather than develop chocolate factories that could ostensibly compete with chocolate producers in Europe. The work on tariff differentials also built on findings in the Haberler Report (Balassa 1965; Grubel and Johnson 1967). The developing world was worse off than just tariff differentials: its comparative advantage in trade was in agricultural and textile products. These products faced not just tariff differentials, but also quantitative restrictions on exports from the developing world, starting with the Common Agricultural Policy (CAP) of the European Union in 1962 and the Multi-Fibre Arrangement from the GATT, following more than a decade of other restrictions, in 1974.

to adopt Articles XXXVI–XXXVIII as a 'Chapter on Trade and Development'.

In the late 1960s, developing countries' collective position shifted from seeking protections for its infant industries to advocating for preferential treatment for its products through limited access in developed country markets with minimal tariffs. Certainly UNCTAD and Raúl Prebisch supported such preferences. But the effects of preferences were hotly debated: minimal access was not free trade access, and in economic terms guarantees of such access would set up inefficiencies in production. The limited access offered to the developing world further weakened through a trade practice that emerged in the 1970s and came to be known as the Generalized System of Preferences (GSP), which provided for many contingencies and exceptions (Erb 1974; Dos Santos and Cunha 2005). GSP was voluntary. The enabling clause of 1979—formally the Decision on Differential and More Favorable Treatment Reciprocity and Fuller Participation of Developing Countries—negotiated at the close of GATT's Tokyo Trade Round (1974–1979), integrated GSP into the GATT trading system to enable market access for limited amounts of products on a non-reciprocal and non-discriminatory basis. Although GSP became central to North–South trade relations, its impact was minimal and, as mentioned, may have been economically harmful. One study calculated that GSP exports to developed countries were only 2 per cent

higher than what they would have been without these preferences. Further, the Global North had made sure that developing world export products such as agriculture and textiles were off the table at GATT negotiations. Limited access through the GSP created a side bargain rather than a trading bargain for increasing the amount of exports for which the Global South had some advantage in production (see Key Theory Box 15.5). Over time, the GSP was also used manipulatively by the 'donor' countries, such as the US, as a tool to coerce the developing world to endorse the Global North's foreign policy objectives in general.

Over time, a set of provisions emerged in the GATT that became known as 'Special and Differential Treatment' (SDT) for developing country products and trade policies. SDT included longer time periods for implementing trade provisions, reduced obligations for providing access to their markets, and incorporated GSP provisions. SDT has become controversial as China and India have sought to benefit from them as developing countries, but with large shares of global markets—14.7 per cent and 1.7 per cent respectively of total merchandise exports for China and India. In 2020, the Trump administration in the US revoked India's GSP provisions.

In the 1970s, a broader movement developed at the United Nations and called for an examination and transformation of North–South economic relations, in what came to be known as the calls for a

---

KEY THEORY BOX 15.5 PRINCIPAL SUPPLIER AND TRADE THEORY

New trade theory shows empirically that trade takes place because there are large firms with economies of scale that reflect an underlying comparative advantage in production of goods (Krugman 1987). In other words, trade bargains on tariffs are often struck among principal suppliers of commodities. The implication is that developing countries with small-scale producers cannot compete, and this reason is often cited in international trade for developing countries' small trade portfolios. However, many developing countries are large-scale agriculture producers, and were kept out of agricultural markets to protect agriculture in the Global North. In GATT, these bargains were often called 'Green Room' processes, named after the wallpaper in the GATT building in Geneva, where the US, the EU, and a few other principal suppliers such as Japan would meet to hammer out trade bargains that were then passed along to other countries. Great powers deliberately kept agriculture off the rounds of trade negotiations at the GATT. A similar case can be made for textiles, which since the

1960s had been governed through a 'Multi-Fibre Arrangement' that provided a limited amount of import access to developing country textiles. Principal supplier theory not only ignores power, but also economics: product specificity is important for trade, and in many specific products the developing world was the principal supplier. The developing world did not shape the trade agreements that governed the principal supply of minerals from Africa, or sugar and cotton from Brazil.

New-new trade theory demonstrates that the most innovative firms in an economy with a great degree of specialization participate in international trade (Bernard et al. 2007). The developing world's firms face two binds here: one, they are often stuck at the lower ends of a value chain where the high value-added part of the commodity chain is in the developed world; second, in order to be a principal supplier, countries must court (or even submit to) principal powers in global political economy.

New International Economic Order (NIEO). The movement received support from UNCTAD and was pushed forwards through the developing world coalition known as G 77. A special session of the United Nations was convened in 1974. NIEO sought both justice and self-reliance, and supported redistributive claims in the international economy. A cultural counterpart to NIEO was the call for a New World Communication and Information Order (NWICO), launched formally at the 1976 Colombo meeting of the Non-Aligned Movement, to redress how the developing world was represented in global media and information flows dominated by Global North agencies (Frau-Meigs and Nicey 2012). The MacBride Commission report *Many Voices, One World* in 1980 also pushed developing countries towards self-reliant communication infrastructures that included media, broadcasting, and telecommunications. Communication and cultural representation factors thus ran parallel to and informed the political economies of trade and development. Especially for development purposes, radio and broadcasting were often prioritized (Singh 1999).

Meanwhile, the overall development agenda continued to follow the modernization and ISI strategies described earlier. By the 1960s, the IBRD, or the World Bank, also moved from the 'R' of reconstruction in Europe to the 'D' of development in the Global South. In 1960, the World Bank created the International Development Association, which focused on providing concessional loans to the least developed countries. The World Bank staffers were mostly development economists and practitioners and reflected the dominance of the market-based perspectives, not least because of the influence of the United States that reserved the power to appoint the organization's president. In 1968, Robert McNamara, fresh off the conflict in Vietnam as Presidents Kennedy and Johnson's Secretary of Defense (1961–1968), was appointed World Bank president and served until 1981. However, he brought a socially liberal, expansive agenda, along with business management practices, to the World Bank. The Bank's lending increased from US$1 billion in 1961 to US$13 billion in 1981. His key agenda items were poverty eradication, best outlined in a speech he gave in Nairobi in 1973 where he emphasized ending absolute poverty, and focus on rural areas and small-shareholder agriculture (World Bank 1973). This was clearly a departure from industrialization thinking, but not without precedent. ISI strategies had begun

to backfire, and post-colonial states were beginning to discover that rural areas, where a majority of the developing world's population lived, could not be ignored. The 1964 military coup in Brazil, following social unrest, partly reflected the failure of industrialization in the country. In the late 1960s, the Indian government shifted to a pro-agriculture strategy. Prime Minister Indira Gandhi's 1971 election campaign slogan was 'garibi hatao', or eradicate poverty, perhaps an influence on McNamara's 1973 speech. Whatever the reasonableness or trickle-up of these strategies, remember that for a quarter of a century development and industrialization had been imagined in the minds of global technocrats far removed from the agricultural lands of the Global South.

Development also began to be imagined in a wholly different way through a new agency, the UNDP, created out of merging existing programmes like the UN Special Fund and the Expanded Program. The UNDP offered more of a human-centred perspective that slowly began to offer an alternative to the World Bank's approach embedded in economic growth. A chief architect of this approach was Pakistani economist and finance minister (1985–1988) Mahbub ul Haq, who during the 1970s had worked at the World Bank on its strategy for least developed countries. In 1990, the UNDP began to publish its annual flagship Human Development Report (HDR), which provided a different perspective from the World Bank's annual World Development Report (WDR). The WDR chiefly held national GDP and per capita income to be the main indicators of development. HDR took into account income growth but also included social entitlements such as education and life expectancy. The entitlements reflected Amartya Sen's capabilities perspective on development, as the freedoms or capabilities people have to better the circumstances of their life (Sen 2000). Martha Nussbaum's extension of this work into gender empowerment is noteworthy (Nussbaum 2000).

The narratives of trade and development, as seen above, ran parallel to each other. Both trade and development were imagined in international organizations with academics and practitioners educated in the Global North. Economists such as Prebsich, Sen, and ul Haq were also educated in elite schools in the Global North but, coming from the Global South, they provided perspectives that were not always rooted in the Western economic growth experience. They also understood the increasing advocacy from the post-colonial countries to change the way global North–South relations were imagined. Prebisch led the creation of the UNCTAD, and ul Haq changed the development approach through the UNDP. The stage was now set for the developing world to play more of an assertive role in global processes that affected them.

KEY POINTS

- Global South advocacy utilized bloc diplomacy and technocratic studies that resulted in new UN organizations and greater responsiveness to their concerns in existing ones, such as the poverty reduction agenda at the World Bank.

- Some of the measures and institutions created in the 1960s and 1970s that continue to exist include the G-77 bloc, Special and Differential Treatment (SDT), and UN organizations such as UNCTAD and UNDP.

- The Global South's advocacy was cultural—it sought to reimagine and represent its assigned position in the multilateral trade, finance, and development orders.

15.3.3 **Participation and inclusion**

Global South advocacy began to pay off in the 1980s, but with the past narrative of the Global North's domination being challenged, contested, and transfigured in market-based terms. A market-driven approach became dominant in both development and trade, with twists. In trade, developing countries pushed for more market access for their products, along with SDT, while in development the ISI strategy was replaced variously with market-based and export-led approaches. At the same time, local and national participation began to influence policies both in trade and development.

The **Washington Consensus**, as it came to be known in 1989 after economist John Williamson coined the term, brought together the World Bank, the International Monetary Fund, and the US Treasury Department into pushing for markets, deregulation, and liberalization. However, it is a narrative stretch to argue that this market-based **neoliberalism**, as it is sometimes almost pejoratively labelled, arose only from Washington. It reflected as much the grassroots consequences of the high-modernist ideology of ISI as it did the strategy rethink in Washington. Further, while the Washington Consensus was a departure from state-led initiatives, it also revealed continuities: like previous global efforts, it also reflected a top-down strategy being pushed through global agencies. The Washington Consensus set off a wave of privatizations and liberalization both in the developing world and also in the former Soviet bloc, as the latter disintegrated after the fall of the Berlin Wall in 1989.

Interestingly, in the 1990s a parallel approach developed at the World Bank and other UN agencies that sought to be more culturally sensitive and involve local people as stakeholders in decision-making (see Key Concept Box 15.6). There were several precedents to participatory approaches, one of the most important being the Latin American school of participatory action research (PAR), traced back to Brazilian educator Paulo Freire (2018) who sought to replace the top-down 'embankment' pedagogies of development with a more 'dialogic' problem-solving approach (Singh 2008a). By 1999, the World Bank and IMF had pioneered the use of Poverty Reduction Strategy Papers (PRSPs), as a precondition for debt relief.

KEY CONCEPT BOX 15.6 PARTICIPATION AND DELIBERATION IN DEVELOPMENT

The participatory turn in international development, starting in the 1990s, sought to be more inclusive of people affected by the development projects that would impact their daily lives. Simple forms of participation would entail 'stakeholder' consultations. Deliberation involves giving of public reasons, problem-solving, and arriving at solutions that were unavailable to participants prior to their communication interactions. The deliberation perspective is associated with German philosopher Habermas' notion of the 'public sphere', where 'communicative action' among participants in an inclusive fashion leads to problem-solving (Habermas 1979; Mackie 2006). Amartya Sen (2012) argues that deliberative contexts in the developing world do not resemble the formal deliberations that Habermas outlines; the basis of deliberation must be located in local cultural circumstances. Similarly, anthropologist Arjun Appadurai (2004) points to the 'capacity to aspire' through a combination of local/global imaginaries and solidarities. Theorists also point out the sheer implausibility of idealized deliberation where elite capture and power hierarchies are common' (Cooke and Kothari 2001).

PRSPs had to be prepared with broad participation from communities, stakeholders, and policymakers. However, such broad participation is difficult to implement, and ignores existing power relations (Cooke and Kothari 2001). A number of the World Bank's exercises in participation were purely performative without substance. The manual on participatory techniques assigns a huge role to experts to carry out participatory evaluations, while populations appear in various stakeholder roles (Rietbergen-McCracken and Narayan-Parker 1998). Since then, development thought has moved slowly towards outlining and trying to replicate more sophisticated forms of participation, such as the participatory budgeting exercises in Porto Allegre, Brazil (Baiocchi et al. 2013; Curato et al. 2017), or participation through party organizations in India (Auerbach 2019; Auerbach and Thachil 2023).

Another current approach to development being pushed through global development agencies also takes local culture seriously but employs scientific methodologies to test effects of interventions through techniques developed in medicine for randomized controlled trials (RCTs). The RCT technique, for which Banerjee and Duflo (2012) received the Nobel prize in economics, allows for isolation of local or culturally sensitive interventions whose effects are first studied through trials in which a set of people receive the treatment (the incentive) while the placebo (controlled) group does not. RCTs respond to the critique

that development interventions from the North were often poorly designed and did not consider local cultures and incentives. In practice, RCTs need resources and time, and are difficult to replicate across contexts.

An unlikely place to find organic participatory politics may be at the GATT and its successor organization in 1995, the World Trade Organization (WTO) (Singh 2015) (see Key Theory Box 15.7). Take the example of the multilateral trade negotiations from the GATT between 1986–1994 that came to be known as the Uruguay Round, thus named for the country where the round was launched in September 1986. While the Global South did not 'win' many concessions, the possible implications of the round's outcomes were deeply felt among societal actors globally. For example, the Uruguay Round delivered the Agreement on Agriculture (AoA); while limited in its benefits to the Global South, the AoA connected agricultural coalitions in GATT with farmers in their national constituencies. Competitive farmers in Argentina favoured an export-led strategy, which led to Argentina joining the liberal Cairns group at GATT. Other countries, such as the G77 group, favoured SDTs. However, both coalitions wanted market access in the Global North. The intellectual property provisions also led to participatory politics in the Global South. Indian farmers protested intellectual property provisions that would have patented, with minimal innovation, seeds that were already in the public domain. Thus, participatory

---

KEY THEORY BOX 15.7 THEORIES OF INTERNATIONAL NEGOTIATION

Theories of negotiation demonstrate that negotiation processes make a difference to expectations about international interactions. This is different from known GPE paradigms where negotiations and diplomacy are hardly ever assigned any major role: outcomes are explained through power structures (realism), or through convergence and socialization of actors' interests (liberalism and constructivism). In the realist version, preponderant powers can ignore demands from the Global South (Krasner 1985). In the liberal version, economic actors know their interests and preferred outcomes in advance and negotiations merely pave the way for a realization of those interests. Scholars working on North–South negotiations have shown how negotiations processes allow developing world agency for action that they otherwise would not have. The basic concept in negotiation theory is the Best Alternative to a Negotiated Agreement (BATNA) (Lax 1986). Even a small or a weak country with a better alternative than one they would

receive from a negotiated agreement need not acquiesce to a great power at a negotiation. Tiny Vanuatu walked out of accession talks for joining the WTO when they faced pressures from powers such as the US, EU, and Australia, which made them realize that they were better off without the WTO (Gay 2005). Bettering one's alternatives includes doing so through negotiation tactics such as coalition-building, trade-offs and linkages, agenda-setting, and technocratic strategies (Odell 2006; Singh 2008b). Of these, coalition-building is a major aspect of multilateral negotiations, and this chapter provides several examples such as those from G-77 and NIEO advocacy (also see Narlikar 2003). Technocratic strategies through the production of information and knowledge, such as those leading to the creation of the UNCTAD, are also detailed in this chapter. An example of agenda-setting would be the initiative taken by the developing world to recognize intangible cultural heritage (see Everyday GPE Box 15.8).

politics played a role in trade policies from farmers in Argentina to protest against emerging intellectual property provisions in India.

Throughout the Uruguay Round, a shift emerged in public health provisions, aiming to challenge the dominance of patents held predominantly by Global North countries. This shift was fuelled by strident advocacy and protests in the Global South. Notably, the now defunct Doha Round, which commenced in November 2001, was pivotal. It introduced a public health declaration that aimed to initiate negotiations concerning compulsory licensing. This mechanism was proposed to empower developing countries, allowing them to navigate around patents owned by Global North entities during critical public health crises. In practice such patents have not been granted due to opposition from pharmaceutical firms (Sell 2010). Most recently, during the COVID-19 pandemic, developing countries again advocated for compulsory licensing of the COVID-19 vaccines, but ran into stiff opposition from pharmaceutical companies such as Pfizer, and the German government has refused to go along with a relaxation of intellectual property provisions (for further discussion of the WTO, health, and COVID-19, see Trommer, Chapter 5).

Having presented a history of the cultural narratives of trade and development, Table 15.1 summarizes

Table 15.1 Development organizations and their narratives

	WTO	World Bank	UNDP	UNESCO
Main objectives	Trade liberalization	Development loans	Technical assistance	Culture of Peace
Main narrative	Trade causes growth	Institutions and markets cause growth	Human development	Cultural and human rights approaches
Theoretical exemplars	Neo-classical trade theory	Institutional political economy, randomization	Amartya Sen, Mehbub Ul Haque, Martha Nussbaum	UN Commission on Culture and Development, Thomas Pogge
Subsidiary narrative	Special and differential treatment, capacity-building	Community development, participatory development	Markets and technology, instruments of change	Think tank of the world
Practices	Negotiating and enforcing rules	Ideas bank, development project implementation	Ideas bank, development project implementation	Norm-making
Main practitioners	Economists, governments ministries	Economists, few social scientists, government ministries, NGOs	Economists, development scholars, UN bureaucrats, government officials, few NGOs	Intellectuals, UN bureaucrats, government agencies, few NGOs

---

EVERYDAY GPE BOX 15.8 INTANGIBLE CULTURAL HERITAGE

Did you know that Tango from Argentina, Batik from Indonesia (see Figure 15.3), Maqqam singing from Central Asia, or Congolese rumba that inform the lives of people living in these places are part of global cultural heritage? Formally, these practices comprise intangible cultural heritage (ICH) and are listed with the United Nations Educational, Scientific, and Cultural Organization. The 2003 UNESCO Convention on the Safeguarding of Intangible Cultural Heritage speaks to 'living' cultural heritage, as opposed to 'monumental' heritage that UNESCO has recognized with its World Heritage Program. The initiative for safeguarding ICH came from the developing world: in the 1970s from Latin American countries, and at the turn of the century from several African states who also received support from Japan and UNESCO Director-General

EVERYDAY GPE BOX 15.8 INTANGIBLE CULTURAL HERITAGE (continued)

Kōichirō Matsuura. ICH safeguards culturally inherited processes rather than the product itself, such as those that would continue to produce Tango in Argentina or Vedic chants in India. Importantly, to get inscribed on the UNESCO ICH list, the process starts with communities deciding what is of value to them, rather than international authorities such as the World Heritage Commission. ICH generated considerable enthusiasm, such as among anthropologists, for the recognition of everyday culture and the participatory processes involved in inscription. Critics note that ICH in practice relies heavily on national governments and UNESCO officials, and that even local cultural products can mask oppressive practices: for example, Vedic chants from Kerala were limited to male Brahmins; Argentinian Tango arose out of colonial conquest.

Figure 15.3 Indonesian batik is a hand-dyed technique for silk and cotton garments that surrounds the lives of Indonesians from their childhood, as they are carried in batik slings, to their last moments, as funerals and rites of death also employ batik. The designs are crafted with lines and dots of hot wax, soaking the cloth in one colour, removing the wax, and repeating to achieve different colours. There is a wide range of patterns inspired by Arabic, Chinese, and Japanese cultures. Their patterns and craftmanship express Indonesian identity, as their creativity, and spirituality.

Source: Shutterstock.

four of the international organizations discussed most in this chapter. There are many other international organizations that are relevant, of course. Therefore, the table is representative of the differences among narratives in international institutions. For example, the IMF and IBRD are often mentioned together as Bretton Woods Institutions (for further discussion, see Helleiner, Chapter 8). The differences described in the table are important from the perspective of developing countries and their interests in particular issues.

KEY POINTS

- The creation of post-war multilateral institutions, such as the United Nations, largely marginalized the developing world despite their imagination and response to the need for an international order that avoids conflict and war.

- The dominant explanation for the creation of these institutions focused on the power of a few and interdependence among states, largely ignoring the perspectives and agency of the Global South.

- The counter-narrative suggests that the marginalization of the developing world was intentional and bordered on racism, with historical corrections challenging existing narratives in international relations.
- The United Nations Charter was signed in 1945, primarily through negotiations among the allied nations, and aimed to promote peace, human rights, and social progress.
- The Bretton Woods Institutions, including the International Monetary Fund and the International Bank for Reconstruction and Development, were created by the allied powers to govern international trade and monetary flows, with voting power predominantly held by the United States and Western Europe.

15.4 Current challenges

At the turn of the century, the Global South was, to use Paulo Freire's terms, increasingly naming its world with a cultural voice. This Global South had come a long way since the 1940s when its docility and obedience was assumed among multilateral institutions and North–South interactions were top-down to shape the destiny of newly independent post-colonial states. While the Global South may have more agency and choice now, there are also old and new challenges that limit their aspirations. The multilateral system itself seems to be weakening, just as global solidarities are increasing. Old and new development aspirations now also arise out of varied interests and divisions among the Global South.

15.4.1 **Crisis of multilateralism**

The post-war multilateral system when created was deeply flawed but over time, through advocacy and continuing interactions, made way for inclusion and participation from the developing world. However, just when the multilateral system began to deliver a few positive results, it began to break down in the last two decades. In trade, the Doha Development Agenda, or the multilateral round of trade negotiations that started in November 2001, was called off by 2015. The United States blamed China and India for their intransigence on agricultural issues. By 2019, the Appellate Body of the World Trade Organization's vaunted Dispute Settlement Mechanism (DSM) came to a halt as the United States blocked the appointment of judges as their terms expired. By December 2019, the two judges left were below the quorum needed, and DSM became non-functional (see Trommer, Chapter 5, for details).

In development, UN-affiliated organizations have dealt with reduction or threat of reduction to budgets, especially through the Coronavirus pandemic, while rival organizations either supported from businesses or emerging powers have unhinged the former centres of power. These include new multilateral development banks such as the New Development Bank (NDB) and the India Brazil South Africa (IBSA) Fund (Roy 2022). There are also new sources of development finance that are corporate funded, such as the Gates Foundation, microfinance loans such as through the Grameen Foundation, and crowdsourcing platforms such as Kiva that now include socially responsive impact investments. The development landscape intersecting North–South interactions is much more variegated and diffused than it was in the 1950s.

The breakdown and transformation of the multilateral system also means the clash of two extant cultural narratives about multilateralism. In one narrative, the great powers mostly benefit from the multilateral system while supporting its institutions with resources. In this narrative, the Global South benefits from trade measures in the margins and is the net recipient of development ideas and efforts conceived in global organizations under *de facto* control of the Global North. If the balance begins to tip away from the benefactors, they pull out, as is the case at the WTO. Reforming and revisioning this version of the multilateral system might require compromise and restraint on the part of the Global South, including rolling back their expectations and benefits. In international negotiations on trade, the compromises from the developing world and its emerging powers are not forthcoming. Within this narrative, a more granular analysis could also permit reform and marginal change (Singh and Woolcock 2022). Major chunks of the multilateral system remain in place, and arguably there is no downward spiral: the total amount from the UN Scale of Assessments has risen from US$1.3 trillion in 2002 to US$3.2 trillion for 2022, and there's no marked decline either in the number of intergovernmental organizations that exist, hovering around 5,000 since the early 2000s (Union of International Associations 2021; UNGA 2022). This allows for some reform within the UN system.

The second cultural narrative is harder to assess. It includes multiple players including emergent great powers such as China, and a proliferation of new non-governmental multilateral organizations. Ostensibly, the developing world can fare better in a scenario when there are two multilateralisms to play off each other, but this could equally be two forms of manipulation instead of one. In Internet governance debates, the developing world has complained of US domination, but the alternative proposed with support from China, and empowering the International Telecommunication Union, would impose severe costs on global civil society. The question of the efficacy (and manipulation) through Chinese development aid is equally debatable.

15.4.2 Current forms of international solidarity

The crisis of multilateralism must also be understood in the context of global forms of solidarity that intersect the Global North and Global South. Unfortunately, though, these global forms of solidarity present a cultural battle between cosmopolitanism and parochialism (Kahler 2020). Parochial, populist, and protectionist parties have been on the rise in many countries in the Global North and Global South (see Harmes, Chapter 11). The reasons vary from economic to cultural: the economic explanation explains the shift among populations to the right after the loss of jobs from manufacturing competition, but this explanation only holds in the Western world (Broz et al. 2021). The cultural explanation prefaces racism, ethnocentrism, and the longing for authoritarian solutions for complex problems (Norris and Inglehart 2019). Populist 'strongman' leaders in the Global South have included Jair Bolsonaro in Brazil, Andrés Manuel López Obrador (AMLO) in Mexico, Narendra Modi in India, and Recep Tayyip Erdoğan in Turkey: all of them cracked down on progressive human rights policies, and unleashed violence on multiple minorities in their countries.

Populist authoritarianism, nevertheless, is coupled with increasing cosmopolitan and progressive politics through solidarities such as the global environmental movement, Black Lives Matter and #MeToo protests, support for Ukraine over Russian aggression in 2022 and, to some extent, positive attitudes towards refugees and immigrants in many societies.

The implications of global solidarities and parochialisms for global trade and development are mixed. New types of initiatives have brought together the Global North and Global South. Most importantly, the cultural imagination about the developing world that was limited to the elite in the Global North, mostly governments and technocrats, has now been widened to include civil society and market actors. The total value of the microfinance market was estimated to be US$156.7 billion in 2020 and is expected to grow to US$304.3 by 2026, though 42.5 per cent of the total in 2020 was in East Asia (Globe Newswire 2022). Nevertheless, contrast the microfinance total with US$169.2 billion in official development assistance from the Global North's prosperous countries, such as the Development Assistance Committee (DAC) (Organization for Economic Cooperation and Development 2021). Some of the microfinance and 'inclusive finance' efforts have involved large banks from the Global North such as Mastercard, which has a large presence in Sub-Saharan Africa. Even microfinance organizations such as KIVA and Grameen Foundation now feature funds and returns for socially responsive investments. Crowdsourcing, microfinance, and inclusive finance efforts have benefitted from artificial intelligence technologies that have informed FinTech.

In trade, the picture remains mixed (see Case Study Box 15.9). With new trade initiatives at a halt, world trade has grown but more slowly than before, and the Coronavirus pandemic since 2020 has brought up deglobalization concerns about the resilience of global value chains. International trade has grown from US$18.3 trillion in 2011 to US$22.3 trillion in 2021, but contrast the US$4 trillion increase in this decade with the US$12.1 trillion increase from 2001–2011 (WTO 2022f). Institutional forms that support global civil society have grown even as the growth of intergovernmental organizations has stalled. Figure 15.4 shows the growth of international NGOs, which in the twenty-first century only slowed down during the financial crisis in 2007–2008 and the Coronavirus pandemic in 2020.

15.4.3 Development aspirations

A grand narrative starting in 2000 has pushed a remarkable global agenda in development in a new direction. This agenda, created through the United Nations, outlined eight Millennium Development Goals (MDGs) for the world community from 2000–2015, and then seventeen Sustainable Development Goals (SDGs) for 2015–2030 (for full exposition, see

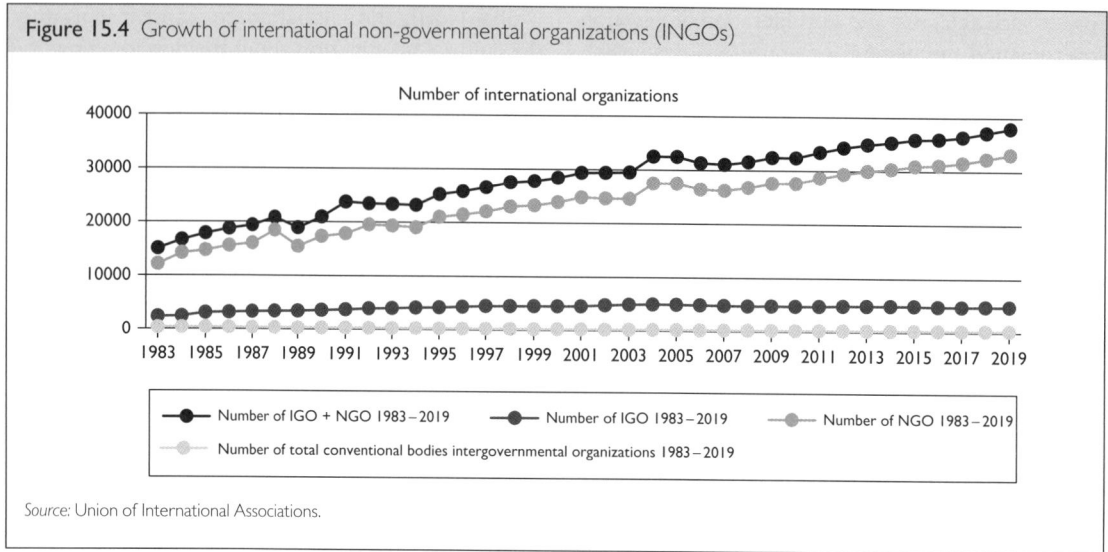

Figure 15.4 Growth of international non-governmental organizations (INGOs)

Number of international organizations

Legend:
- Number of IGO + NGO 1983–2019
- Number of IGO 1983–2019
- Number of NGO 1983–2019
- Number of total conventional bodies intergovernmental organizations 1983–2019

Source: Union of International Associations.

Bhagat, Chapter 14). The grandness of the ambition behind MDGs and SDGs can be discerned in several aspects: global benchmarking, involvement of private and public actors, increasing rates of participation from global civil society, and an agenda that cuts across the entire UN and its affiliated agencies. Hulme (2012) notes that the MDGs struck a balance between neoliberal and human development efforts. Fukuda-Parr and Hulme (2011: 27) note that the balances struck on formulating these goals 'were sensitive to the demands for political expediency: to come up with a list that would be accepted by nearly 200 governments'. For the MDGs the goals were: poverty reduction, universal education, gender equality, child health, maternal health, ending HIV / AIDS and other diseases, and global partnerships. The SDGs listed in Table 15.2 preserved the MDGs but added in goals related to equality, energy and climate action, innovation and industry, and the institutional framework within which the goals work (see Case Study Box 15.10 for a discussion of the importance of trade in services for development).

Underlying the formation of the MDGs and the SDGs was global summitry and norm entrepreneurship. Norms are global values that are shared and accepted among a variety of global actors. Finnemore and Sikkink (1998) note there are norm cycles spanning a value chain from their creation, diffusion to adoption. Norm champions or entrepreneurs are often needed to persuade global actors to adopt a norm. Fukuda-Parr and Hulme (2011) trace MDGs back to the 1990 World Summit for Children and the Copenhagen Declaration at the World Social Summit in 1995 for mobilizing a set of norm entrepreneurs who began to plan this global agenda. The issue of development was raised at the G8 Okinawa Summit in July 2000, and in September 2000 nearly 200 heads of state met at the UN for a Millennium Declaration that led to the MDGs. The Millennial Project was launched in 2002. The SDGs were launched in 2015 with greater input and participation from global development communities.

The MDGs and SDGs present a mixed story of resource mobilization and success stories. One of the goals behind the agenda-setting was to push the donor states to fulfil their self-declared obligation to donate 0.7 per cent of the gross national income towards official development assistance. In 2021 the DAC average was 0.33 per cent, and only five countries went over 0.7 per cent (Luxembourg, Norway, Sweden, Germany, and Denmark). Both the MDGs and SDGs have been far more successful in meeting their expectations in East Asia, partially in Latin America, and much less so in Sub-Saharan Africa. Table 15.2 summarizes the mixed results for SDGs (see also Bhagat, Chapter 14, for details on SDGs). However, the biggest success of the SDGs may be in the global mobilization and awareness that has gone into this effort.

Table 15.2 Sustainable Development Goals (SDGs)

SDGs	Notes
1. No Poverty	Between 1993 to 2017, global population increased from 5.3 billion to 7.5 billion, but absolute poverty decreased from 1.9 billion to 689 million.
2. Zero Hunger	Hunger on decline since 2010, climbed in 2019 with 690 million experiencing hunger. Numbers increased during the pandemic.
3. Good Health & Well-Being	COVID-19 exposed the vulnerabilities and disparities of heath-care systems worldwide. There are 0.3 physicians per 1,000 people in low-income countries, and 3 per 1,000 in high-income countries.
4. Quality Education	There was 90% primary age enrolment in low- and middle-income countries, but they rated low on learning.
5. Gender Equality	Women have gained the right to vote but gender inequalities continue on numerous indicators from labour force participation and wages to domestic violence.
6. Clean Water & Sanitation	71% of the households in 2017 had access to clean water, up from 61% in 2000.
7. Affordable & Clean Energy	In 2018, 789 million had no electricity, and 2.8 billion no access to cooking fuels or technologies.
8. Decent Work & Economic Growth	Agriculture generated 60% of the employment in low-income and 3% in high-income countries. The pandemic increased unemployment by hundreds of millions.
9. Industry, Innovation, & Infrastructure	Wide disparities in infrastructures. Sixty million lack access to an all-season road in Ethiopia and Nigeria. Less than 25% of the population had access to Internet in South Asia and Sub-Saharan Africa.
10. Reduced Inequalities	This goal aims to increase share of gross national product (GNP) for bottom 40% of population. Some countries do, others don't. In Brazil the bottom 40% receive 16% of the GNP.
11. Sustainable Cities & Communities	A third of the world's urban population lives in slums. India and China account for 75% of total decreases in life expectancy due to pollution.
12. Responsible Production and Consumption	Most food loss in developing countries occurs at production and distribution stages. In rich countries, it's at the consumption stage.
13. Climate Action	Between 2010–2019, floods affected 710 million people, and droughts affected 653 million.
14. Life Below Water	Fish provide food sustenance to 1 billion people, but over 35% of stock is over-fished.
15. Life on Land	Efforts to control land degradation and deforestation. Sixteen and a half million hectares were deforested between 2010–2015, especially in Brazil and Indonesia.
16. Peace, Justice, & Strong Institutions	A variety of indicators exhibit overall governance, but also issues such as transparency, budgets, and levels of violence.
17. Partnerships for the Goals	Includes foreign direct investment (FDI), official development assistance (ODA), and remittances. In many countries, remittances are greater than ODA.

CASE STUDY BOX 15.9 TRADE AND DEVELOPMENT THROUGH SERVICES

Agriculture and manufacturing sectors showcase prominently in describing the trade and development of North–South interactions in the twentieth century. In national income accounts, agriculture and industry are the primary and secondary accounts. The last thirty years have also featured a sector that was long cast as 'tertiary' but is now seen as increasingly important: namely, the 'services' sector that provides intangible products to the population. These include communications, education, finance, health, transportation, and tourism. Services also include the current emphasis on information technologies, communication, and artificial intelligence—collectively known as the fourth industrial revolution (see Girard, Chapter 17). The content of the SDGs reveals the importance of services. Interestingly, the UNDP's Human Development Index includes 'services' indicators such as education and health to measure the prosperity and capabilities of a country.

The importance of services for the developing world were part of a learning process at the Uruguay Round of trade talks (1986–1994). The United States and the European Community led the way for the General Agreement on Trade in Services that emerged from the Uruguay Round. In the US, a powerful services coalition of businesses such as airlines, banks, and telecommunications pushed for this agreement. The developing world was cast as striking a 'Faustian bargain' in opening up its services markets in exchange for concessions in agriculture and manufacturing (Ostry 2008). A closer look shows that the developing world began to wake up to its own potential services advantages at the Uruguay Round. The most notable example is India, which opposed the services agenda at the beginning of the Uruguay Round, but strongly supported it when it ended (Singh 2008b). India is now the seventh largest services exporter among the WTO members, and that includes its information technology and culture industry (film) exports. However, smaller cases are important. Costa Rica capitalized on its educated

workforce to attract major industries such as Intel. Both Costa Rica and Mauritius pioneered sustainable tourism strategies in the 1990s. Several Caribbean states have opened health facilities, not coincidentally close to the US border, to offer inexpensive healthcare as part of a growing trend to capitalize on 'health tourism'. It is hard to imagine innovations such as Kenya's mobile money platform M-Pesa without accompanying developments in mobile telephony and finance. Technically, when a country provides a service to a foreigner within its borders, it counts as an export. International students at any university are consuming an education export from the country where they study.

The World Trade Organization has pushed for the liberalization of services sectors, and can count it as one of its few success stories. Even as the Doha Round was failing, countries carried out 'autonomous liberalization' of their services sectors for reasons ranging from attracting foreign investments and collaboration to pushing their domestic providers (in health or education) towards reform. In 2013, WTO members signed a Trade in Services Agreement (TiSA).

Services liberalization and services-led development have also been critiqued. Many countries privatized and sold off their services providers to foreign investors without strictly calculating the returns or benefits to consumers (Raghavan 2002; Kelsey 2008). For example, Costa Rica was pressured to open its insurance market to US providers, even though traditionally in Costa Rica the insurance sector played a social role—providing health and education benefits to members—that went beyond its financial role. Arguably developing countries are ill-positioned to devote resources to services when most of their populations live in rural areas and are involved in agriculture. However, these debates have also helped to clarify the importance of services for development. After all, the fourth industrial revolution is of immense importance to agriculture, from the use of crop sensors to deal with weather and soil, to algorithms that can inform and coordinate global value chains in agricultural goods.

KEY POINTS

- The Global South has gained more agency and choice in shaping its own destiny, but it faces both old and new challenges that limit its aspirations.

- The multilateral system, including trade negotiations and development organizations, has been weakened in the last two decades, leading to a breakdown in international cooperation.

- Two cultural narratives about multilateralism exist: one that benefits the great powers and controls global

organizations, and another involving multiple players and new non-governmental multilateral organizations.

- The crisis of multilateralism is influenced by global forms of solidarity and parochialism, with the rise of populist and protectionist parties in both the Global North and Global South.

- The implications of global solidarities and parochialisms for global trade and development are mixed, with growth in initiatives involving civil society and market actors, but slower growth in international trade and concerns about global value chains' resilience.

15.5 Conclusion

This chapter presents Global North–South relations as cultural narratives with elements and ideas shared among groups of actors. Narratives feature actor agency: that of the Global South is important for this chapter. The story of North–South relations starts in a post-colonial era when the South is largely marginalized and easily acquiesced to the way trade and development are imagined through the force of global institutions.

Two thematic cautions are necessary. First, this chapter uses the terms Global South and Global North as cultural heuristics for the way poor or prosperous countries respectively imagined themselves in global political interactions. However, the Global South and Global North are not homogeneous entities: this chapter points to divisions among them but keeps the terms to also point out the starkly different historical origins of their poverty or prosperity. Second, while this chapter celebrates cultural voices and consciousness, it shares the anthropological caution that all cultures are inclusionary and exclusionary and carry power hierarchies. While the cultural perspective provided here is mostly celebratory of Global South efforts, it also points out places where it fails, such as in the rise of populist autocracies.

Agency in political action must feature both consciousness of one's condition and then political strategy. When seen from the Global South perspective, the consciousness of its condition is easily seen—from its early advocacy for infant-industry protections to the betrayals in international trade. In fact, the Global North appears delusional in this narrative, attributing virtue to itself even through heinous acts of colonialism and in designing post-war institutions that *de facto* excluded the developing world or perpetuated its historical economic conditions, such as production of primary products.

The developing world's advocacy for itself has, in hindsight, included an impressive array of diplomatic and negotiation tools: coalition-building, production of sophisticated technical knowledge and reports, and leadership for its cause through a host of intellectual and political leaders. Standard histories of North–South negotiations often miss the importance of this diplomatic history when assigning an inferior or subsidiary role to the Global South.

The bloc diplomacy from the Global South that provided a collective voice and gains through the UN and the GATT/WTO system is now diffused, but at a time when the developing world can not be cowered into the type of submission that was foisted upon it in the early history of North–South relations. Domination is not so easily undone. Just as the Global South has begun making gains, great powers such as the United States have begun to side step the multilateral order or bring to a halt the work of the World Trade Organization. When the strong cannot get what they want, they throw hissy-fits!

Despite the seeming unravelling of multilateral institutions, North–South interactions in international development now include multiple actors, initiatives, and imaginaries. This is a far cry from the cultural and technocratic elite in the Global North that created international development initiatives in the 1950s and 1960s. Development finance in the current era extends far beyond official development assistance to include a host of market, civil society, and government organizations.

The strongest agency that is likely to survive in the future is that of new global solidarities that cojoin the North and the South through common purposes and endeavours. The solidarity is fragile, though, and must confront the rise of autocratic populism. Nevertheless, such solidarity, to borrow words from Nobel laureate Rabindranath Tagore, may represent 'ever widening thought and action'.

? 15.6 QUESTIONS

1. In what ways was the Global South marginalized and excluded in global political economy in the post-war era?

2. What collective strategies did the Global South adopt to advocate for itself in international interactions?

3. How effective were the Global South's advocacy and diplomatic strategies?

4. Are Global North–South interests irreconcilable?

5. In what ways can the Global North and Global South work together in the future? Is it mutually beneficial for them to do so?

6. In what ways are international trade and development inextricably linked for the Global South?

7. Given the record of past global trade and development efforts, what kinds of strategies are practicable and desirable for the Global South in the future?

8. What mistakes, in your opinion, did the Global South make in its interactions with the Global North? How would you have corrected them?

9. Given the COVID-19 pandemic and focus on resilient global values chains, how can the developing world benefit in the future?

10. How can sustainable development goals be better refined and implemented?

11. Do services offer a viable strategy for trade and development? In what ways do they not?

15.7 FURTHER READING

Appadurai, A. (2004), 'The Capacity to Aspire', in M. W. Vijayendra Rao (ed.), *Culture and Public Action* (Stanford, CA: Stanford University Press): 59–84. This book argues for the importance of 'culture' for capacity building and poverty reduction. The author explains that culture is a dialogue between traditions and aspirations, and that policymakers can utilize this dialogue to promote a culture of aspiration and self-guided poverty reduction.

Escobar, A. (1995), *Encountering Development: The Making and Unmaking of the Third World* (Princeton, NJ: Princeton University Press). Through an illustrative case study, Auturo Escobar shows how the economization of development issues acts to continue the legacy of colonial control. Instead, Escobar argues that development should undergo a more pluriversal approach, integrating traditional knowledges and cultural experiences in the process.

Freire, P. (2018), *Pedagogy of the Oppressed*, 4th edn. (London: Bloomsbury Publishing). Through this book, Friere seeks to empower those in marginalized and oppressed groups to liberate themselves from their oppression, and provides tangible methods of doing so.

Hudec, R. E. (2011), 'Developing Countries in the GATT Legal System', *Trade Policy Research Centre* (Cambridge: Cambridge University Press). This book offers a clear insight into the interplay of 'developed' and 'underdeveloped' countries in the international trade regime. Robert E. Hudec's contribution to trade discourse is an important guide to how current and future trade policy must adapt to the needs of the developing world.

Krasner, S. D. (1985), *Structural Conflict: The Third World Against Global Liberalism* (Berkeley, CA: University of California Press). Through this critical account, Steven D. Krasner challenges the economistic interpretation of the seemingly anti-liberal view held by the South, instead arguing that North–South conflicts originate from structural asymmetries and power imbalances.

Said, E. (1978), *Orientalism* (New York: Vintage Books). Through this first-of-its-kind account of orientalism, or the scholarship of the Eastern world by Western scholars, Said shows how the paternalizing accounts of the East maintain the imperialistic status quo.

Sen, A. (2000), *Development as Freedom*, 1st edn. (New York: Anchor Books). The book offers accounts of modern economic poverty, social deprivation, and political tyranny or cultural authoritarianism in the Global South to describe the unfreedom of those who reside under these conditions. Sen argues that shifting the goal of development to be the promotion of freedom and social values will sustain these outcomes.

Singh, J. P., and Woolcock, M. (2022), 'The Future of Multilateralism and Global Development' a collection of essays published in the journal *Global Perspectives*. By summarizing key insights of a recent critical assessment of multilateralism, this book highlights specific ways for political, policy, and procedural challenges to be addressed through higher levels of inclusion for South-based multilateralism. The essays are open source and can be found here: https://online.ucpress.edu/gp/collection/8658/Future-of-Multilateralism-and-Global-Development.

Srinivasan, T. N. (2019), *Developing Countries and the Multilateral Trading System: From GATT to the Uruguay Round and the Future* (Boulder, CO: Westview Press). Focusing on the interactions between developed and developing countries, this book provides a historical account of the Uruguay Round and how North–South relations have affected matters relating to the global trading system since the GATT years.

Vitalis, R. (2015), *White World Order, Black Power Politics: The Birth of American International Relations* (Ithaca, NY: Cornell University Press). By focusing on the historic examples of race development and international relations (IR), the author shows how race has always been fundamental in the study of IR, and that the erasure of race relations in IR has invariably sustained the current White world order.

CONTRIBUTOR NOTE

J. P. Singh is Distinguished University Professor at George Mason University, USA, and Richard von Weizsäcker Fellow with the Robert Bosch Academy, Berlin. He works at the intersection of technology, culture, and political economy in global contexts, examining transformative impacts from the provision of telephone services in poor countries to the use of artificial intelligence in global value chains in cutting-edge industries. J. P. has consulted or advised international organizations such as the British Council, UNESCO, the World Bank, and the World Trade Organization, and has conducted field research in thirty-six countries.

PART VI

Contemporary Issues

16

The Political Economy of the Environment

Kate Ervine

Chapter contents

Reader's guide

The global community is confronted with an unprecedented array of overlapping environmental crises that threaten large segments of humanity and non-human species. The impacts remain highly uneven, with nations and communities least responsible for contemporary ecological problems already paying the highest cost. With widespread climate disruption projected to intensify in the coming years and decades, marked by deadly heat waves, wildfires, floods, droughts, crop losses, sea level rise, and the forced displacement of populations worldwide, the need for effective and democratic governance is critical. How governments and various actors respond, however, depends heavily on a range of factors, including prevailing relations of power connected to the global political economy of advanced capitalism. This chapter has been developed to provide the reader with an introduction to the dominant debates and points of disagreement that influence how environmental crises are explained, and what this implies for the types of responses that follow and their potential for effectiveness. Particular attention is paid to how uneven development in the global political economy since the colonial era has profoundly shaped issues of inequality and ecological decline, such that the two are deeply interconnected. This implies that effective and meaningful responses to planetary crises will also need to respond to the deep injustices and inequalities that mark the contemporary period.

16.1 Introduction

The study of global political economy (GPE) in many ways remains wedded to its traditional thematic areas of analysis: trade, production, finance, the role of the state, and globalization. While important work is being done to show how colonial legacies and unequal relations of power along classed, racialized, and gendered lines shape the global political economy, too often the environment is treated separately and distinctly in our analyses. In many cases this has resulted in a failure to see how the environment itself is part of, and central to, the functioning of the GPE, along with its impacts on people and the planet. The stunning growth of the global economy since the Industrial Revolution has depended heavily on extracting ever growing amounts of materials and resources from the natural world, with researchers estimating 2020 as the year in which materials and objects made by humans, at roughly 30 billion tonnes per year, weighed more than all living biomass on Earth (Elhacham et al. 2020). The sheer scale of extractive activities connected to a range of global economic sectors, including energy, industry, agriculture, fishing, mining, forestry, technology, transportation, and construction, has led to the rapid degradation of diverse ecosystems and ecological processes around the world. Those same activities annually produce stunning levels of waste that ends up in oceans and waterways, in the atmosphere and the air we breathe, and in the ecosystems and land we depend on for our survival as a species. As the depth and severity of overlapping environmental crises around the world intensify, many observers now refer to our current era as the Anthropocene, a new geological epoch displacing 11,700 years of the Holocene and suggesting that the impacts of human activity on the planet are so pervasive that there no longer exist any areas, anywhere, that are free from human influence.

While students and scholars interested in the political economy of the environment may appreciate how the concept of the Anthropocene draws our attention to the role of human activity in producing specific environmental crises and in disrupting broader and interrelated ecological systems and relationships, they may also note its shortcomings as an explanatory concept. By focusing heavily on an undifferentiated humanity and its assumed destructiveness, important questions that are central to the study of GPE are not asked. For example: What is the relationship between nature and capitalist relations of production and social reproduction, and how do these relationships lead to environmental degradation and crises? Who maintains control over these relationships and who decides? How do the power relations embedded in this system of production shape the governance of environmental problems and the types of actions taken or not? How do histories of colonialism and contemporary inequalities and oppressions shape the environmental impacts of and on individuals, communities, and nations?

As the global community enters an era of environmental extremes, marked by a rupture with the stable ecological conditions that allowed for human society to evolve on this planet, providing answers to these questions lies at the heart of GPE research. Doing so also prepares us to engage more fully with core debates on the future of economic growth, historical responsibility, the right to development, over-consumption, green transformations, and environmental justice. This chapter begins with an overview of contemporary environmental crises before moving on to consider competing explanations of the causes of environmental harm, along with the types of interventions that are proposed in response. This is followed by an analysis of how historical and contemporary injustices and inequalities shape the landscape of environmental harm and ecological breakdown, while considering what they imply for fair and equitable solutions to a range of ecological problems. Finally, a case study of climate governance draws many of the chapter's themes together.

16.2 Contemporary environmental crises

The deteriorating state of ecosystems and ecological processes across the globe has been well understood for many decades, supported by increasingly robust scientific research. It is only much more recently, however, that the environment has moved beyond its historical status for many as a niche issue. Driven especially by the severity, speed, cost, and visibility of climate-related disasters worldwide, governments, global institutions, and private companies have had to publicly engage the issue. Whether effective and genuine or not, this engagement has been driven further by popular awareness and citizen mobilization as the immediate costs and future threats of climate break-down intensify.

An abbreviated survey of global environmental problems paints a troubling picture. Climate change, or climate breakdown, results predominantly from the combustion of fossil fuels which release carbon dioxide (CO_2), a heat trapping gas, into the atmosphere when burned. Land use and land use change account for a much smaller share of atmospheric warming. As a result of these activities, it is estimated that at the time of writing the global temperature has warmed to approximately 1.2° Celsius above pre-industrial levels, leading worldwide to more frequent and severe climate disruptions (Newclimate Institute 2022). The global insurance industry estimated economic losses of US$329 billion in 2021 from extreme weather and climate-related events, only 38 per cent of which were insured. Of these insured losses, 71 per cent were located in the United States (Aon 2022: 4, 8). This figure likely underestimates the full monetary cost of these disasters given the absence of precise data from some parts of the world; however, it underscores the fact that the majority of individuals globally, including those who bear little to no responsibility for climate breakdown, have no recourse to financial compensation in the wake of climate disasters. This represents a major flashpoint between developing and developed countries in global climate negotiations, a point to which we will return later in this chapter.

The scientific consensus is that climate-related events and disasters, including flooding, tropical cyclones, wildfires, heatwaves, and severe storms, will continue to increase annually as the planet warms. The same is projected for slow-onset climate events, including droughts, sea level rise, biodiversity loss, ocean acidification, glacial melt, and desertification, with an estimated 3.3 to 3.6 billion people currently living in conditions that are 'highly vulnerable to climate change' (Pörtner et al. 2022: 35). Climate breakdown poses threats to human health; to livelihoods and social reproduction; to global food security; to the ability and opportunity to work; to human rights and equity; to physical infrastructure and the coordination of societal networks; to economic and political systems; and to national sovereignty, cultures, and identities. Already climate breakdown is forcibly displacing populations worldwide—in 2020 approximately 30.7 million people were internally displaced within their own countries, 98 per cent resulting from weather and climate hazards (IFRC 2021: 7). Projections for 2050

show that, in the absence of effective climate action, internal climate-induced displacement will increase to over 216 million (Cement et al. 2021: xv), with much higher numbers of climate refugees globally, a category for which no legal recognition exists.

Climate breakdown in turn intersects with a range of additional globally significant environmental crises. In 2011 researchers published findings showing that the world is now undergoing a sixth mass extinction event, defined as a situation in which extinction rates lead to more than 75 per cent of species disappearing over a geologically short timeframe (Barnosky et al. 2011: 52). The last mass extinction, which killed off the dinosaurs, took up to 2.5 million years and ended 65 million years ago. It was the result of cataclysmic global cooling after an asteroid struck the Yucatán Peninsula. The current mass extinction is distinct for a number of reasons. First, unlike all previous mass extinctions, the current one is being driven by human activities, including resource exploitation and extraction, habitat destruction and fragmentation, the introduction of non-native species, the direct killing of species, and climate change (Barnosky et al. 2011: 51). Second, the current mass extinction could be so severe that extinction rates comparable to those that occurred in all previous mass extinctions combined, and which spanned hundreds of thousands to millions of years, could be reached in as little as 300 years (Barnosky et al. 2011: 55). In addition to its intrinsic values, biodiversity is critical to the functioning of ecological systems globally, and thus to supporting human societies. From the health of soils, pollinators, agricultural systems, the global food supply, forests and their ability to sequester carbon, regulate the global climate, and provide energy, and ecosystems that purify water or mediate natural hazards, biodiversity is essential to supporting all life on Earth.

Beyond climate breakdown and biodiversity loss, it is estimated that air pollution worldwide reduces average global life expectancy by 2.2 years. This is much higher for some countries, particularly in South Asia, with India estimated at almost 5 years and Bangladesh at almost 7 years (Greenstone et al. 2022: 6–7). Microplastics are now pervasive in countless aspects of our existence, including in the air we breathe, the water we drink, and the food we eat, with our bodies and those of non-human species now prime sites for the accumulation of chemical-laden microplastics. Additionally, microplastics have been found in extremely remote environments, including the deep ocean, snow in the Antarctic, and the top of Mount Everest (Osborne 2022). Plastic waste is extensive in garbage patches in the oceans, with the highest concentrations of plastics per km² surpassing 1 million pieces (Egger et al. 2020: 1). Some researchers have suggested that given the ubiquity of plastics worldwide, their long-term persistence in the environment, and their planetary movement, the framework of a global plastic cycle, like those of carbon, nitrogen, and phosphorous, is needed to assist research and improve our understanding of the implications of so much plastic (Zhu 2021).

The environmental crises described thus far provide a snapshot of the mounting problems that threaten the planet's ecological integrity. From industrial and chemically intensive agriculture, overfishing, hazardous and toxic waste, habitat destruction, climate breakdown, and more, the planetary conditions necessary to support healthy human societies, let alone equitable and just human development, are being undermined. The impacts are also highly uneven (see Figure 16.1); extreme heat illustrates this point. Beginning in March 2022 in India and Pakistan, a severe heat wave lasting three months led to persistent temperatures averaging around 47°C, with the Pakistani city of Jacobobad, home to approximately 300,000 residents, recording temperatures of 51°C on more than one occasion (Ghazi 2022). Jacobobad is one of two cities worldwide that has experienced a wet-bulb temperature of 35°C, the point at which humidity and thus moisture in the air is too high for sweat to evaporate from the human body, necessary to cool it. This is considered the physiological 'upper limit for survivability' (Raymond et al. 2020: 1). Severe heat extremes are compounded by high concentrations of poverty and persistent power cuts and water shortages, leaving people, and especially the poor, with few to no options to cool themselves. Evidence from coastal and sub-tropical locations globally shows a doubling in the frequency of extreme and dangerous humid heat since 1979, much faster than predicted by climate models, and a phenomenon predicted to increase further over the coming decades (Raymond et al. 2020: 1). Deadly heat thus highlights the complex factors that mediate how different groups experience ecological crisis, thus helping to focus issues central to the study of political economy, including power, justice, and equity.

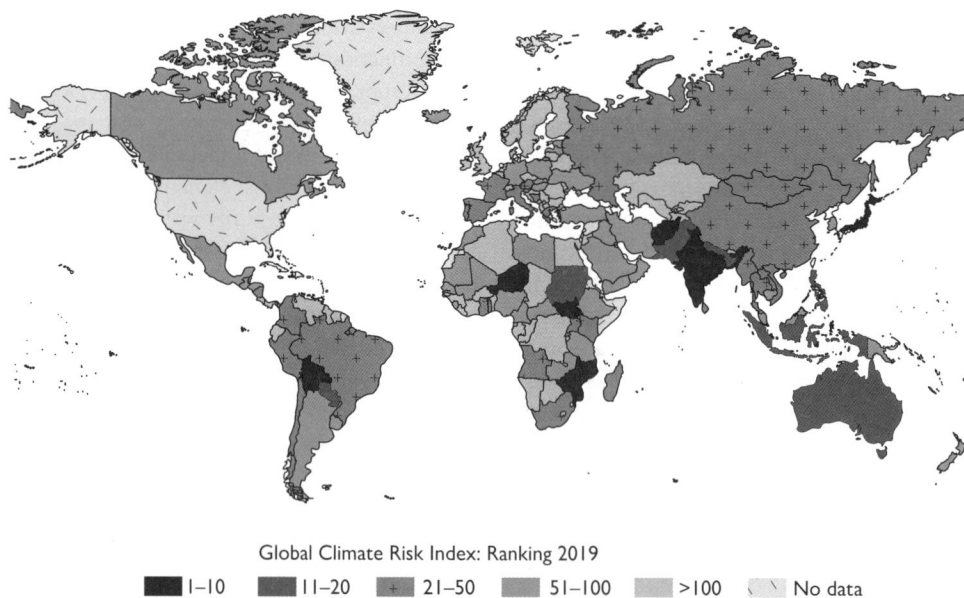

Figure 16.1 Human impacts (fatalities) and economic losses from climate-related events, 2019

Global Climate Risk Index: Ranking 2019

1–10   11–20   21–50   51–100   >100   No data

Highest impact: 1–10; lowest impact: >100 (Eckstein et al., 2021).

Source: https://www.germanwatch.org/de/19777.

Moreover, GPE research offers important tools to understand the ways in which contemporary environmental crises are themselves interconnected as manifestations of globalized relations of production and social reproduction, both of which are profoundly ecological in their implications and outcomes. It is to an explanation of these points, and to an examination of the roots of contemporary ecological crises, that we now turn.

KEY POINTS

- Climate breakdown, biodiversity loss, pollution, plastics waste, and more provide evidence of rapidly deteriorating ecological conditions globally.

- In the absence of effective action, environmental crises will continue to intensify.

- The impacts of environmental crises are experienced unevenly across the globe, with the poor and those least responsible disproportionately impacted.

16.3 Explanations of globalized environmental problems

To respond effectively to globalized environmental problems, one must first understand what causes them. Theory can help in this respect, but it is useful to recall Robert Cox's assertion that '[t]heory is always *for* someone and *for* some purpose' (1981: 128—emphasis in original). Cox was a scholar of International Relations who wanted to explain why scholars studying the very same problems could come to very different conclusions, from which very different prescriptions would follow. He argued that theory is never neutral but is shaped by history, dominant relations of power, and political economic structures. Cox labelled those theories that naturalize the existing world order of global capitalism, its power relations and its institutions, and that claim to be value-neutral and to offer objective truths, as 'problem-solving'. He explained that by naturalizing these things, problem-solving theories did not allow for the possibility that they might be implicated in producing the problems we are trying to explain. For Cox, this meant that problem-solving theories tend to support the status quo and those actors that have a vested interest in maintaining it (Cox 1981: 128–130). In contrast, he framed 'critical theory' as theory that denaturalizes the existing world order

and that highlights its historical specificity. By problematizing global capitalism, its political economic structures, its relations of power and institutions, and the dominant ideas that support it, Cox suggested that critical theory opens the door to examining how the current world order may produce and sustain particular problems. It also opens space for considering solutions that challenge this order and that, in doing so, carry with them emancipatory potential (Cox 1981: 130; see also Hannah and Hinton, Chapter 4). The distinction between problem-solving and critical theories provides a helpful framework to consider competing explanations of the causes of globalized environmental problems and the responses that flow from them.

16.3.1 Problem-solving perspectives and global environmental problems

In response to the question 'what causes global environmental problems?', problem-solving perspectives and theories offer a range of responses, a selection of which are reviewed here. For some, emphasis is placed on underdevelopment and poverty as major causes of environmental degradation. This perspective gained prominence with the publication in 1987 of *Our Common Future* by the World Commission on Environment and Development. Also known as the Brundtland Report, *Our Common Future* acknowledged significant global threats to the world's biosphere. On the one hand, it argued that poverty in the Global South, from a lack of development, leads the poor to 'destroy their immediate environment in order to survive'. It continued: 'they will cut down forests; their livestock will overgraze grasslands; they will overuse marginal lands; and in growing numbers they will crowd into congested cities' (World Commission on Environment and Development 1987: 28). Moreover, poor terms of trade and a dependence on the exportation of primary products whose prices are volatile on international markets and low relative to manufactured goods lead developing countries to overexploit their natural resources (World Commission on Environment and Development 1987: 36). While on the one hand the Report acknowledged that economic growth in industrialized countries had been resource-intensive and environmentally damaging, it noted that efficiency gains in energy and resource use per unit of output was mediating the impact, as would work to emit fewer pollutants. It cautioned, however, that this progress would be offset by increased per capita energy and materials use in developing countries, due to increases in population and per capita incomes (World Commission on Environment and Development 1987: 32).

Overall, *Our Common Future* called for 'a new era' of economic growth to eliminate poverty in the Global South, reducing its unsustainable burden on the global biosphere. Since economic growth had historically produced environmental harm, however, this new era was to be guided by the concept of sustainable development, defined as 'development that meets the needs of the present without compromising the ability of future generations to meet their own needs' (see Key Concept Box 16.1) (World Commission on Environment and Development 1987: 43). The Environmental Kuznets Curve (EKC) is often used to bolster calls for increased economic growth to address environmental harm. The original Kuznets Curve, developed by economist Simon Kuznets in the 1950s, posits an initial increase in inequality as economies develop, followed by a subsequent decline. Similarly, the inverted U-shape of the EKC suggests an initial increase in environmental harm with economic growth, followed by a drop as per capita incomes surpass a particular threshold and financial, institutional, and technological capacities increase (Grossman and Krueger 1991). Overall, if poverty and underdevelopment are identified as the problems, economic growth is offered as the solution. According to this perspective, however, it must be better than what preceded it, in line with the principles of sustainability.

Another problem-solving explanation of environmental harm identifies market failures related to **negative externalities** as the problem, drawing on neo-classical economics and public choice theory to support this perspective (Coase 1960). A negative externality is said to occur when the adverse impacts of productive activities are not factored into the price of production. Rather, the cost is externalized, leaving society to pay for the harm. A common example used to illustrate this is that of CO_2 emissions from industrial production, which then cause global warming. Economists argue that until the full cost of emitting CO_2 is internalized in the cost of production, producers will have no incentive to change their behaviours. To correct this so-called market failure, economists call for the pricing of carbon and other pollution, asserting that as it becomes more expensive, companies will look for greener and thus cheaper alternatives (Stavins 2017). The global growth of emissions trading schemes (ETS) that create a market for buying and selling the right to emit provides an example. Within a national jurisdiction, an ETS entails a government capping allowable emissions, creating allowances equivalent to the cap, and requiring emitters to surrender allowances equivalent to their emissions each year. ETSs are framed as the most cost-effective mechanisms to price carbon, since companies that can lower their emissions with greater ease can sell excess allowances to those that cannot, for example fossil fuel and energy-intensive companies. By allowing the latter to purchase emission reductions on the market in place of making more costly reductions at the source, proponents argue that ETSs reconcile economic growth with climate action. Overall, price signals, it is argued, will incentivize a generalized low- to zero-carbon transition, with prices themselves determined via supply and demand (Ervine 2018).

The same logic supports calls to create markets in environmental services which, instead of pricing negative externalities, seek to establish market values and thus prices for ecosystems and the services they provide. Attempts to estimate the value of global ecosystem services have arrived at figures well above global gross domestic product (GDP), with one prominent effort estimating US$125–$146 trillion per year in 2011 (Costanza et al. 2014). Using biodiversity as an example, proponents of this approach argue that even though biodiversity is essential to supporting human survival on this planet, there is little incentive to conserve it in the absence of a visible market value. Eco-tourism and the harvesting of non-timber forest products are examples of efforts to put a market value on intact biodiversity. The logic here suggests that as long as economic activities that produce environmental harms are valued more than conservation—activities like logging, mining, and clearcutting to make way for industrial monoculture plantations—biodiversity will not stand a chance. Creating markets in biodiversity, or for other ecosystem services, is said to level the playing field. By also emphasizing the possibility of biodiversity's sustainable economic use as a means of achieving alternative local livelihoods, such that the poor no longer need to overuse, overgraze, and cut the forest, efforts to create markets for ecosystem services find common ground with those that emphasize poverty and underdevelopment as key drivers of environmental degradation.

The well-known concept of the '**tragedy of the commons**', introduced by Garrett Hardin in an article of the same name in 1968, provides support to the approaches discussed in this section. In his article, Hardin asked the reader to imagine a common pasture free to be used by all. In this scenario, he argued, individual herdsmen (sic), as rational actors, were incentivized to maximize their individual gains by adding additional cattle to the pasture to graze, from which they could reap the economic rewards. Hardin suggested that in a world of finite resources and limits, rational self-interest and the freedom to pursue it 'brings ruin to all' (Hardin 1968). The metaphor of the tragedy of the commons is frequently referenced in approaches to environmental management that call for the expansion of private property rights. For them, once access and the right to use the land and its resources are restricted to the private property owner, the problem of collective overuse is eliminated. This allows for the internalization of the negative externalities that arise when no one is responsible for paying the cost of overuse. The application of this logic extends beyond visible examples of land and the resources upon it; in an ETS property rights are embedded in the carbon allowance that confers the right to emit, for example.

Overall, the problem-solving approaches reviewed here, and which are influential in contemporary global governance forums, share some basic premises. Most importantly, in response to environmental degradation all propose in one way or another an expansion and strengthening of capitalist markets and social relations. This aligns closely to the rise of neoliberalism since the 1980s, which has emphasized free markets, free trade, and deregulation, arguing that markets, when freed from government interventions that are said to distort them, are best positioned to produce the greatest good for the greatest number. Thus, if poverty and poor terms of trade are the problems, economic growth and the removal of protectionist barriers to trade are required; if market failures that produce negative externalities are the problem, more markets and better pricing are required; if overuse and overexploitation are the problem, private property and new markets are required.

While many of these responses are based on observable conditions, it is important to highlight what distinguishes them from critical theory such that they are grouped within the problem-solving category. For example, it is true that the poor may be forced to engage in environmentally damaging activities to survive. However, a problem-solving approach does not ask why individuals are poor in the first place,

or what circumstances led to their poverty; poverty is simply taken as a given. It is also true that many developing countries experience poor terms of trade and heavily exploit the natural resource base for export purposes. However, a problem-solving approach does not consider global power relations and histories of colonialism and imperialism to understand how underdevelopment was produced or the enduring legacies of these processes (Gunder Frank 1966; Bhagat, Chapter 14). Nor does it consider the role played by neoliberal structural adjustment policies in the 1980s which emphasized commodity-driven export-led development in developing countries, led to high levels of competition between these countries for global market space, and depressed commodity prices as a result; underdevelopment is simply taken as a given.

It is also true that in some instances environmental harm, for example air pollution, has declined with high incomes, consistent with the EKC. However, the empirical evidence suggests that these cases are very limited (Stern 2017). By generalizing the experience of one and applying it to the whole, known as a **fallacy of composition**, problem-solving approaches utilizing the EKC to call for increased economic growth do not probe the relationship between economic growth and environmental degradation in a broader and systematic fashion. This is despite sufficient evidence questioning the assumptions of the EKC and showing increased levels of environmental degradation with economic growth and rising incomes (Stern 2017).

It is also true that overfishing in the world's oceans and the steady increase in CO_2 emissions since the onset of the industrial era are leading to collapsing ecological systems, and thus provide examples that appear to confirm Hardin's tragedy of the commons. However, problem-solving approaches that utilize it do not probe the complexity of actually existing property regimes and resource management strategies around the world. What the tragedy of the commons actually described was an open-access context in which institutions and rules for using and managing resources are absent. There are very few real-world examples of this open-access context; common property regimes, on the other hand, entail complex sets of rules regarding who can use resources, when, and how, with access strictly managed (Ostrom 1990; Bryant and Bailey 1997: 161). Proposals to privatize common property ignore abundant evidence detailing the highly effective management of common property resources by local communities globally. Additionally, they ignore the negative environmental consequences of eliminating common property regimes, referred to as a '**tragedy of enclosure**' by some, when property rights shift to the state or private actors who exploit resources for large-scale commercial purposes. This undermines many of the institutional arrangements through which local actors sustainably manage common property resources, while also forcing them onto marginal lands once access to the lands and resources necessary to meet livelihood needs are lost (Bryant and Bailey 1997: 159–168). On this latter point, we can see how the failure to ask what makes individuals poor is a critical oversight of approaches that identify poverty as the cause of environmental degradation.

Two additional points are worth raising with respect to the tragedy of the commons. First, Hardin subscribed to a model of human behaviour that understands humans as self-interested utility maximizers whose decisions are based on cost-benefit analysis. This is '**homo economicus**', or economic man (sic). While examples of this type of behaviour, often framed as 'selfish', are amply available, critics note that those who subscribe to such a perspective ignore the ways in which humans are also cooperative, caring, community-focused, and selfless (Fineman and Dougherty 2005). By accepting Hardin's version of who humans are, whether explicitly or implicitly, problem-solving perspectives do not probe how social relations of production and power might influence behaviours, nor do they probe the historical specificities of homo economicus, an individual that encapsulates behaviours that are highly valued in a capitalist economic system. On the question of values more specifically, problem-solving perspectives that accept this view of human nature often fall into the trap of assuming that in the absence of a market price, nature and ecosystem services have no value, or that the values we do ascribe to them are insufficient to make them worth saving.

Finally, Hardin's work was deeply problematic on the relationship between population and environmental degradation. Hardin, an American who drew on neo-Malthusian ideas in much of his work, blamed the poor, immigrants, and non-Europeans for 'overbreeding' and thus threatening the planet's ecological integrity. His article on the tragedy of the commons included a section titled 'freedom to breed is intolerable', suggesting that the Universal Declaration of Human Rights, which enshrines the right of families to determine family size, should be rejected (Hardin 1968: 1246). Hardin was thus an ardent critic of the welfare state for supporting those

that would 'overbreed', arguing against immigration and aid to poor countries where birth rates outpaced those of wealthier nations and advocating for a **lifeboat ethics** that claims it is better to let some people die in a context of resource scarcity, in order to save the whole. This position was articulated in his 1974 article 'Lifeboat Ethics: The Case Against Helping the Poor'. Hardin's deeply problematic and racist views on the poor, immigrants, and minorities cannot be separated from his metaphor of the tragedy of the commons, since it was those same individuals that he associated most closely with 'overbreeding' globally. Furthermore, this position implies that women's bodies and the reproductive patterns of poor women, often Brown and Black, are dangerous, posing some of the greatest threats to the future of the planet. While asking questions about the Earth's carrying capacity relative to the human population is fair, if it is done without simultaneously probing and historicizing relations of power globally, or questioning the distribution of wealth and resource use patterns globally, or asking who produces and who consumes what, an emphasis on population frequently becomes a classed, gendered, and racialized instrument that blames the poor for global ecological collapse. When this happens, the results throughout history have often been deadly, marked by profound human rights abuses which are often channelled through multiple forms of oppression (Peluso and Watts 2001; Neumann 2004).

16.3.2 Critical perspectives on global environmental problems

If problem-solving approaches advance capitalism as a framework for action in response to global environmental problems, theories and approaches that can be classified as 'critical' start with a critique of capitalism and its historical evolution, arguing that its imperatives and the social relations of power specific to it are anti-ecological. The central claim of many critical perspectives is that a deep contradiction exists between the needs of a capitalist economic system and those of a nature capable of sustaining just and liveable futures for all (Harvey 1996; Castree and Braun 1998; O'Connor 1998). Critical approaches thus set to work to explain why this is the case and what it is about capitalism that stands it in opposition to nature. The most influential approaches in this vein include those within the traditions of Marxist- and Gramscian-inspired global political economy and political ecology (see Key Theory Box 16.2).

As a point of departure, critical perspectives often begin by considering *nature* in capitalism. From the clothes you wear, the food you eat, the electronics you own, to this book you are reading, none could exist without the resources and services we get from nature. Indeed, nature is essential to capitalism and its ability to produce the vast and growing range of goods and services we consume, even if we may not see the nature in them. As the late Marxist political economist Neil Smith wrote, 'the universal production of nature was written into the DNA of capitalist ambition' (Smith 2007: 22). When nature enters into capitalist circuits of production, it is not as resources critical to supporting the healthy functioning of ecosystems or the cultural vibrancy of communities, but as factors of production that impose costs on producers. For this to happen, nature is remade in the form of the commodity—something produced for sale in the market. Karl Polanyi's important insight that nature is a '**fictitious commodity**' (1957) helps us to think critically about the implications of transforming nature into commodities to be bought and sold in markets for profit. As he implied, nature, as trees, soils, seeds, animals, minerals, and more, exists within and as part of dynamic ecosystems, performing critical functions to sustain the ecological integrity of those systems. The process of remaking nature as commodity, however, entails carving up and breaking down living systems, what Raj Patel and Jason W. Moore describe as a 'web of life', so that nature can be put to the work of making money (Patel and Moore 2017). Yet treating living systems as commodities does not diminish the functions they must perform; it simply degrades and destroys them. In this context, asking who controls nature and for what purpose is central to critical perspectives on capitalism and nature. Moreover, by analysing the relationship between capitalism and nature, and its implications and consequences, critical global political economy approaches lay the groundwork for transcending siloed approaches to environmental problems, for example climate change *or* biodiversity loss, that prevent us from perceiving them as symptoms of a broader planetary ecological crisis connected to the global political economy (Katz-Rosene and Paterson 2018).

In turn, the profit motive, which drives capitalist classes to extract as much profit, or surplus value, as possible from the goods and services produced, is identified as a primary source of ecological harm under capitalism. As a system of production, capitalism needs nature, it needs lots of it, and it needs it as cheap as possible. If nature costs too much, for example the cotton to produce a shirt or the wood required to manufacture a table, profit margins shrink. Profit maximization thus entails widening to the greatest possible extent the distance between the cost of producing a good and the price for which it can be sold. Patel and Moore argue that this dynamic requires us to theorize 'cheapness' as an intentional strategy within capitalism, whereby nature is instrumentalized and valued only insofar as it supports profitability (Patel and Moore 2017). As we will discuss later, histories of colonial violence and extractivism are intimately connected to these processes, with capitalist classes harnessing their political-economic and material power to secure continued access to the nature and wealth of colonized peoples.

Also central to the critique of capitalism as anti-ecological is a focus on its growth imperative. The

KEY CONCEPT BOX 16.1 SUSTAINABILITY

The concept of sustainability is contested. The Brundtland Report's definition of sustainable development (see above) called for an economic growth-based model to meet the needs of the poor. The UN's Sustainable Development Goals of 2015 call for global economic growth of 3 per cent per year, and up to 7 per cent in the poorest countries, implying that without economic growth, basic needs cannot be met, nor environmental protection achieved (Hickel 2019). Critical observers contend that a growth-based model is one that instrumentalizes nature as an economic good, rooted in hierarchies of domination and extractivism which are then central to colonial, racial, and patriarchal violence (Banerjee 2003). This runs counter to Indigenous perspectives on sustainability, for example, that understand the natural world as a source of life, sustenance, and meaning; that advance models of reciprocity and responsibility between humans and non-human species; that foster an ethic of humility and generosity in being; and that call for the impacts of decisions to be evaluated seven generations into the future (Corntassel 2014: 69). The concept of 'Buen Vivir', or living well, has its roots in South American perspectives that combine Indigenous knowledge with political critiques of modernity and capitalism, emphasizing the health of the collective over the individual, and harmony between humans and nature (Chuji et al. 2019).

significance of growth is most visible when it is threat-ened, as is the case with the continued impacts of the COVID-19 pandemic and the global economic fallout from Russia's invasion of Ukraine. In the absence of growth, wages and incomes contract, jobs disappear, government budgets are slashed, inequality and suffer-ing increase, and profits dry up. The pursuit of growth is thus central to capitalist economies, with firm competi-tion for market shares, for new and growing consumer bases, for shareholder investment, and more, producing a system that operates as though ecological limits do not exist. Critical analyses often start with the Industrial Revolution and the inception of the age of economic growth to map out the deep interconnections between economic growth and environmental decline. It was during the Industrial Revolution that capitalist rela-tions of production took off, starting in Britain in the eighteenth century, with growth rates beginning their dramatic ascent into the nineteenth and twentieth cen-turies. While the availability of data in the 1800s was limited, estimates put total world GDP, a measure of all goods and services produced in a country or globally over a year, at just over $694 billion in 1820, measured in 1990 US dollars. By 1950 world GDP had increased to over $5.3 trillion measured in 1990 US dollars, while in 2021 it was estimated at $96.1 trillion in current US dollars (OECD 2006: 173; World Bank 2022a). Critical perspectives on the environment remind us that these stunning levels of economic growth have depended not only on cheap nature, but also on capital's ability to exploit and produce ever increasing quantities of nature—recall here the research estimating 2020 as the year in which materials and objects made by humans surpassed the weight of all living biomass on Earth (Elhacham et al. 2020).

This research also highlights the centrality of fos-sil energy to driving growth during the Industrial Revolution and into the present. Energy is central to capitalism—it produces electricity, powers machines, transports goods, and more. Fossil energy derived from coal, oil, and gas is deeply entrenched in modern soci-ety, fulfilling the requirements of capitalist accumula-tion 'almost perfectly', according to Altvater (2006: 41). There are a number of reasons for this. First, with industrialization, fossil energy's high energy return on energy input (EROEI), starting with coal, meant that smaller quantities of energy had to be invested to pro-duce greater quantities of usable energy to power fac-tories and machines. This is changing today with the growth of renewables that can efficiently convert solar

and wind energy to usable energy, for example, but fos-sil energy's entrenchment throughout the nineteenth and twentieth centuries, the power relations that it gave rise to, and the path dependencies it has created make it incredibly difficult to displace (Altvater 2006). Second, as industrialization proceeded, fossil energy freed produc-ers from rooted energy sources that tied production to particular places—for example, rivers from which water was drawn to power cotton mills. Rootedness limited accumulation and production: rivers could be far from cities and the flexibilities of cheap surplus labour popu-lations, while weather and seasonal variation meant that water as an energy source was unreliable (Malm 2016: 165–193). Overall, these strategic advantages have entrenched fossil energy as the preferred source of power to meet the twin objectives of growth and profitability. But it has come with immense ecological consequences.

While extracting and burning fossil fuels produces significant localized environmental harm, its combus-tion, as noted earlier, also releases CO_2, a heat-trapping gas that can remain in the atmosphere for hundreds to thousands of years. With the onset of industrial capi-talism in the mid-1700s, concentrations of atmospheric CO_2 began a dramatic ascent, rising from 278 parts per million (ppm) in 1750 to approximately 419 ppm at the time of writing, a level scientists say is its highest in 3.6 million years (Scripps Institution of Oceanog-raphy 2022; NOAA 2021). A review of historical data beginning in the 1700s reveals an almost perfect cor-relation between increasing economic growth, fossil fuel combustion, CO_2 emissions, and atmospheric concentrations of CO_2. Research thus reveals the dis-proportionate contribution of the fossil fuel industry to climate breakdown: between 1965–2017, twenty state- and investor-owned fossil fuel companies were responsible for 35 per cent of global CO_2 and methane emissions, the latter of which is also a heat-trapping gas (Heede 2019); and between 1988–2019, one hun-dred fossil fuel companies were responsible for 70 per cent of global greenhouse gas emissions (Griffin 2017).

In sum, critical perspectives on the environment start with capitalism, its growth imperative and that of profit maximization, and the role of cheap nature and fossil fuels in facilitating both, to understand the pro-liferation of contemporary interconnected ecological crises. A final consideration has to do with the tendency under capitalism to commodify existence. To under-stand what is meant by this, ask yourself what sustains human life. Obvious answers include food, water, shel-ter, and clothing. Now ask yourself how you are able to access these things. While your response may appear self-evident, and thus natural, critical perspectives point out that the issue of how humans access the necessities of life is in fact historically contingent and contextually specific. They would highlight the fact that within a capitalist system, access to many of the things required for human survival is mediated through market relations and contingent on one's ability to pay for them. This is because, under a capitalist system, many of the necessities of life become commodities—things produced for sale on the market. Degrees of **commodification** vary from country to country and within countries, but the general trend under global capitalism has been for the progressive expansion globally of the commodification of life's necessities. Land, food, housing, clothing—large segments of the human population across the world can only access these things if they have the money to pay for them, with money serving as the medium through which exchange takes place. Critical perspectives note that acquiring that money therefore requires humans to sell their labour, with humans thus treated like any other commodity that is bought and sold in a market. Moreover, capitalist classes, who Marx called the bourgeoisie, also have an incentive to keep labour costs low, like those of nature, in order to increase rates of profitability. This treatment has thus been foundational to many of the moral, ethical, and political economic critiques of the capitalist economic system (Polanyi, 1957; Marx 1976). In addition to arguing that land, and thus nature, is a fictitious commodity, Polanyi argued the same for labour given that humans

were never created for sale in markets. For Polanyi, treating humans as such, and normalizing the idea that survival is a market good, threatens the very fabric of society. At the same time, by structurally tying one's survival to an economic system whose imperatives have led to the dramatic overexploitation of the planet's ecological systems, capitalism requires labourers to 'collaborate in the destruction of nature' (Peet et al. 2011: 15). This constrains the space available to challenge the system since our own survival depends on its success, measured not by planetary and human wellbeing, but on rates of unsustainable growth and profitability.

Overall, by prioritizing the capitalist economic system as an analytical focal point, critically informed perspectives on the environment seek to understand how its core imperatives and social relations produce contemporary ecological crises; how these same imperatives create obstacles to meaningful action to address environmental harms; and how they then shape many of the dominant governance approaches in response to crises like climate breakdown and biodiversity loss such that they fail to challenge this system, the power relations it has created, and the vested interests that seek to maintain it (see Everyday GPE Box 16.3). Before looking more closely at the question of environmental governance, an examination of the relationship between global capitalism, colonialism, inequality, and ecological harm is provided to show how the analytical lens provided by critical analyses can be extended to better contextualize the overlapping issues that shape environmental harm and how the world responds to it.

KEY THEORY BOX 16.2 POLITICAL ECOLOGY

Political ecology represents a range of theoretical perspectives and approaches that seek to politicize the environment. What does this mean? Take the problem of biodiversity loss and the need for conservation. For some, biodiversity loss is a problem of too many people in biodiverse areas; nature must thus be protected from them. Ideas of nature here connect closely to ideas of the pristine, and wilderness, such that it is assumed humans do not belong in them. Scholars have shown, however, that our ideas about nature are in fact political, with policies intended to protect an imagined pristine nature from people often leading to the forced displacement of Indigenous populations, the poor, and those whose claims to nature conflict with more powerful actors (Peluso 1993; Cronon 1995). For others, when poor people are blamed for biodiversity loss, for example, when they cut trees to grow crops, frequently the

source of their poverty is not explored. In Chiapas, Mexico, for example, conservation policies to protect the Lacandon Jungle during the 1980s to the present have often focused on changing the behaviours of poor people without asking what made them poor and shaped how they interacted with the environment. This means that a highly unequal land tenure regime, begun during the colonial era and that concentrated the best lands and political and economic power with elites, was ignored. So too was the impact of neoliberal free trade agreements like the North American Free Trade Agreement (NAFTA) that flooded Mexico with cheap subsidized corn from the US, forcing small farmers to clear more land to compete (Ervine 2010; Gálvez 2018). These examples show us how the environment and ecological problems are profoundly political. Political ecology perspectives emerged first in the 1970s and sought

> **KEY THEORY BOX 16.2 POLITICAL ECOLOGY (continued)**
>
> to apply the tools of political economy to an understanding of environmental change and ecological problems specifically. Blaikie and Brookfield, whose early analysis of soil degradation in the developing world showed that farmers were forced to overwork their land due to capitalist market structures and power relations, defined political ecology as bringing together the 'concerns of ecology with a broadly defined political economy' (1987: 17). Early political ecologists thus shifted the focus from identifying population growth, poverty, or largely apolitical factors as the sources of ecological problems, to analysing how political and economic structures and classed power relations produced ecological harm. In this respect, they
>
> prioritized questions about control over and access to resources to uncover how these forces manifested into particular ecological problems (Blaikie and Brookfield 1987; Bryant and Bailey 1997). From its early roots, political ecology has evolved to incorporate a range of theoretical traditions, while also expanding to consider, among other things, how multiple structures of oppression along gendered, racialized, and classed lines, and with respect to knowledge/power regimes, intersect to influence who has access to and control over resources and how these relationships produce particular ecological problems, while simultaneously shaping the responses that follow (Mollett and Faria 2013; Gill 2021).

> **KEY POINTS**
>
> - Problem-solving approaches to explaining environmental harm take the existing world order as a given, seeking to ensure that it continues to operate smoothly in the face of ecological disruption. They are thus understood as supporting the status quo and the relations of power specific to it.
>
> - Critical approaches to explaining environmental harm emphasize the contingency of world orders and highlight the role of the capitalist economy and its social and power relations in producing ecological disruption.
>
> - To understand capitalism's anti-ecological tendencies, critical approaches examine the implications of nature's commodification, the capitalist imperatives of growth and profitability, the role of fossil fuels in powering the economic system, and the consequences of commodifying existence.

16.4 Inequality and injustice in global environmental problems

We live in a highly unequal world (see Lockwood, Chapter 13). Oxfam estimates that at the end of 2021, the world's ten richest men owned more than the bottom 3.1 billion people; that the share of wealth captured by the world's top 1 per cent since 1995 was twenty times greater than the bottom 50 per cent; and that the carbon emissions of the world's top twenty billionaires were, on average, 8,000 times greater than the world's poorest billion. Oxfam calls this 'economic violence', emerging from the structure of the global

economy and related policy and political decisions that favour the wealthy (Ahmed et al. 2022: 6,10,12). The final figure hints at the interrelationship between economic violence and ecological violence, with political economy perspectives on the environment noting that the global economy, inequality, and environmental harm are mutually and historically constituted. A review of some key figures helps to illustrate this point.

Ecological footprint accounting measures how much nature is required to produce all that humanity consumes, and to absorb its waste. The measure indicates that a deficit occurs when demands for nature and its services exceed its ability to regenerate sustainably. This measure is used to calculate the arrival of Earth Overshoot Day, the date on which Earth's biocapacity is insufficient to meet humanity's demands. When first calculated in 1971, Earth Overshoot Day fell on 25 December; in 2022 it fell on 28 July (Global Footprint Network 2022b). The Ecological Footprint Network estimates that 1.75 Earths would be needed to accommodate current demands placed upon nature. These demands are, however, highly uneven. Table 16.1 provides data for a selection of countries to illustrate this point.

On average wealthier countries and individuals consume far more of the world's nature and produce far more waste than lower-income countries and individuals. Some of the reasons for this are obvious—greater wealth permits greater consumption. However, critical perspectives on the environment suggest that to understand the disproportionate wealth of some nations and individuals, and thus their greater ecological burden, it

Table 16.1 Ecological footprints and global inequality

Country	How many Earths needed to accommodate demands (2022)[1]	Per capita ecological footprint—gha (2018)[2]	National Overshoot Day (2022)[3]	GDP per capita (2021—current US $s)[4]	Vulnerability to climate change—2020 ranking[5]
United States	5.1	8.1	13 March	$69,287.5	23
Canada	5.1	8.1	13 March	$52,051.4	8
Australia	4.5	7.1	23 March	$59,934.1	16
Germany	3.0	4.7	4 May	$50,801.1	4
China	2.4	3.8	1 June	$12,556.3	68
South Africa	2.4	3.8	1 June	$6,994.2	83
Fiji	1.7	2.7	5 August	$5,086.0	96
Brazil	1.6	2.6	12 August	$7,518.8	66
Mexico	1.5	2.4	31 August	$9,926.4	84
Guatemala	1.1	1.8	14 November	$5,025.6	105
Egypt	1.2	1.8	11 November	$3,876.4	100
Ecuador	1.1	1.7	6 December	$5,934.9	105
Indonesia	1.1	1.7	3 December	$4,291.8	107
Jamaica	1.0	2.8	20 December	$4,586.7	88
India	0.8	1.2	None	$2,277.4	132
Central African Republic	0.8	1.2	None	$511.5	175
Nigeria	0.7	1.1	None	$2,085.0	129
Bangladesh	0.6	0.9	None	$2,503.0	154
Afghanistan	0.4	0.7	None	$516.7 (2020)	168
World	1.75	2.8	28 July	$12,262.9	

[1] Number of Earths needed if all of humanity consumed at levels of country listed (Global Footprint Network 2022d);
[2] Measured in global hectares (gha) per person (Global Footprint Network 2022c);
[3] Measures when Earth Overshoot Day would occur if humanity's consumption levels matched those in country listed (Global Footprint Network 2022a);
[4] (World Bank 2022c);
[5] Vulnerability ranks countries on a scale of 1/182, on exposure, sensitivity, and ability to adapt to climate change's negative impacts (Nd-Gain 2022).

is necessary to consider how the imperatives of global capitalism also drove the history of colonial and imperial expansion and exploitation, thereby structuring the global political economy and its power relations to the advantage of the colonizers (see Case Study Box 16.4).

Scholars of **racial capitalism** and **environmental racism** highlight further that colonialism and the post-colonial condition are racial projects wherein racial identity legitimates whose lands, resources, and bodies are exploited disproportionately, and whose suffering is

EVERYDAY GPE BOX 16.3 MOBILITY

Global transportation, including for personal mobility, shipping, and aviation, accounts for 37 per cent of global CO_2 emissions from end-use sectors, relying more heavily on fossil fuels than any other sector worldwide. It is estimated that in 2022 there were over 1.4 billion personal automobiles worldwide, including cars, trucks, vans, and sport utility vehicles. Ownership is highly unequal, however. On the high end, vehicles per capita in the United States are 0.89 per person, 0.88 in New Zealand, and 0.79 in Canada. This can be contrasted with per capita rates in Nigeria of 0.05 per person, 0.023 in Vietnam, 0.02 in Pakistan, and 0.004 in the Democratic Republic of the Congo (Hedges and Company 2022). The correlation between wealth, environmental and climate impact, and automobility is well established, posing important questions about the future of personal transportation in a world of climate breakdown. From an economic standpoint, the automobile industry is significant. In 2021 its revenues were US$2.7 trillion, with an estimated 80 million motor vehicles manufactured, including 21.4 million in China, the world's largest producer, with Japan second at 6.62 million. Countries like Germany and the United States produce fewer vehicles, with 3.1 million and 1.56 million, respectively, in 2021; however, leading automakers globally are headquartered predominantly in the Global North (Statista 2022). Tackling transportation emissions is central to dealing with climate change, yet the wealth and power of the industry, the revenue provided to governments, the jobs provided to citizens, and the centrality of personal automobility to everyday life have made this difficult. On the latter point, personal automobility, despite its many problems, comes with notions of freedom, status, and progress. Many people love to drive and love what it symbolizes. Given this complexity, problem-solving solutions to dealing with transportation are common. In the European Union, its Renewable Energy Directive of 2009 created an artificial market for biofuels, allowing food-based fuels made from wheat and vegetable oils, for example, to be blended with gasoline to lower its carbon content. At the time of writing, the EU used for biofuels 10,000 tonnes of wheat per day, equivalent to 15 million loaves of bread, and burned over 17,000 tonnes of rapeseed and sunflower oil per day, equivalent to almost 19 million bottles of cooking oil. Palm and soy oils are significant as well, both linked to deforestation in Indonesia and South America. Biofuels are considered a false solution for many reasons, including the fact that they divert food crops to fuel, exacerbating global hunger and poverty. Russia's invasion of Ukraine has amplified this; Ukraine accounts for more than 40 per cent of global sunflower oil exports, with the war squeezing supply and leading to extreme inflation. Importing countries and poor populations are being hit the hardest (Transport and Environment 2022a; Transport and Environment 2022b). As governments around the world have enacted biofuels legislations, the current global food crisis and the role of biofuels in it provides an opportunity to imagine what accessible public transportation for all could look like, promising far greater reach and impact compared to the personal vehicle.

considered acceptable (Waldron 2018; Gill 2021; Bhagat, Chapter 14).

European colonial and imperial projects were heavily extractive and brutal. While nature in the Global South and settler colonies was exploited for the land, raw materials, and agricultural goods needed to develop the European powers, colonized societies and communities were devastated by war, disease, forced labour, and more, with an estimated 15 million Africans forced into the transatlantic slave trade during its existence. The magnitude of extraction, prefaced on racial and ecological violence, meant that European nations achieved their own wealth, power, and development by under-developing the colonized (Du Bois 1946; Fanon 1963; Rodney 1972; Galeano 1973). Not only did these patterns of global extraction and wealth accumulation help to lay the foundation for countries of the Global North to dominate the global political economy and institutions of global governance; they also established what Ulrich Brand and Markus Wissen have called an '**imperial mode of living**' (2021). Begun during the colonial era, the imperial mode of living today, they argue, maintains the prosperity of populations in the Global North by ensuring that nature and people in the Global South can be exploited as cheaply as possible. This is made possible through processes of unequal exchange that devalue resources and labour in the Global South, creating significant price differentials in international trade. Recent estimates suggest that between 1990–2015 unequal exchange between North and South represented a drain of US$242 trillion from Southern nations (Hickel et al. 2022). While steady access to cheap nature, cheap commodities, cheap labour, and

CASE STUDY BOX 16.4 MINING AND COLONIAL EXTRACTIVISM IN A GREEN TRANSITION

As the transition to zero-carbon energy sources accelerates globally, the demand for minerals deemed critical to advancing green energy technologies is growing dramatically. Cobalt, copper, graphite, lithium, and nickel are amongst some of the most important, with geopolitical tensions growing as nations, employing discourses of national security, vie for control of strategic reserves to support industrial development in solar, wind, electric vehicles, and battery storage systems. Problem-solving perspectives on energy and green transitions tend to narrow their analyses to questions of energy switching—from fossil fuels to renewables, and to those related to electrification in transportation systems—while leaving broader questions of consumption, equity, justice, and power unexamined. Revisiting the case of mobility, with a focus on *electromobility*, helps to illustrate these points. Around the world governments are implementing electric vehicle mandates; for example, the European Union, Canada, and the US states of California and New York have introduced rules requiring all passenger vehicles sold by 2035 to be electric, with the US government's 2022 Inflation Reduction Act investing heavily in the electrification of that country's transportation system (Riofrancos et al. 2023). Projections for the United States alone estimate that 50 per cent of car sales by 2030 will be electric, with demand projections through to 2050 pegging lithium requirements to meet market demand at triple the current quantity produced for the global market (Riofrancos et al. 2023). With China capturing roughly 60 per cent of the global electric vehicle market in 2022 (Mckerracher 2022), demand for lithium in that nation is projected to continue its rapid growth in the years and decades to come. Lithium is a light metal that is essential to the production of batteries. While it is fairly abundant globally, lithium's extraction from brines, or salt water, is the most profitable method given current

technological conditions (Hernandez and Newell 2022: 946), reminding us of Patel and Moore's discussion of cheap nature and the role of cheapness as a capitalist strategy for increasing profitability (Patel and Moore 2017). This has meant that South America's 'lithium triangle', containing significant salt flats and spanning rural territories in Argentina, Bolivia, and Chile, has become a site of intense geopolitical interest as nations and companies compete for control of the area's 'white gold'. As highlighted by Hernandez and Newell (2022: 951), however, global struggles for control over and access to lithium in these nations are reproducing familiar patterns of colonial exploitation and ecologically unequal exchange. Regarding the former, they detail how the narrative of the lithium triangle, bolstered by the 'drive to electromobility in the Global North', discursively and singularly constructs the region as a 'commodity supply zone' devoid of communities, cultures, and complex ecosystems. As a result, the rights of the region's Indigenous peoples to land, water, and alternative ways of living and being are sacrificed, so that the growth of electric vehicle (EV) markets and personal automobility, particularly in the Global North, can continue unabated (Hernandez and Newell 2022). This problem-solving approach that relies on individual automobility with a simple energy switch has been challenged by recent research, however. It has shown that by investing heavily in electrified public transportation to reduce car dependency, limiting the size of EV batteries, and aggressively recycling, lithium demand in 2050 in the US, based on high growth scenarios, could be reduced by as much as 92 per cent (Riofrancos et al. 2023). Indeed, while mining and extraction are inevitable activities in our globalized world, Hernandez and Newell remind us that it is possible to imagine a decolonized transition that challenges the current growth model, its relations of power, and the social and ecological harm that it continues to produce.

cheap goods facilitates destructive patterns of hyper-consumption concentrated in the Global North, Brand and Wissen argue that it also stabilizes social relations in the North by keeping the cost of living artificially low and externalizing a significant share of the ecological and social costs of this mode of living onto the world's poorest members.

The data provided in Table 16.2 illustrates the inequalities embedded in the imperial mode of living. Importantly, it reveals patterns of demand and

consumption in wealthy nations that, through historically rooted networks of global trade, production, and finance, depend on channelling an unequal share of the world's nature to those countries and their citizens—we would need 5.1 Earths if all of humanity were to replicate the demands placed on nature by the average Canadian or American. As a result, wealthy nations bear a much greater responsibility for ecological collapse and climate breakdown. For example, it is estimated that one country, the United

Table 16.2 Historical Responsibility for Carbon Emissions

	Share of global population	Cumulative CO$_2$ emissions— 1850–2021[1]
23 Rich countries	12%	50%
Remaining 150+ countries	88%	48%

Source: (Popovich and Plumer 2021).
[1] CO$_2$ emissions from fossil fuel burning and cement.

States, is responsible for almost 25 per cent of cumulative historical CO$_2$ emissions; that twenty-three rich countries with only 12 per cent of the global population are responsible for 50 per cent of cumulative historical CO$_2$ emissions; and that over 150 countries with 88 per cent of the global population are responsible for the rest, including China, which accounts for 13.9 per cent, and India, accounting for 3.2 per cent (see Table 16.2).

Concepts like **ecological debt** and **climate debt** have been developed to call attention to these historical inequalities, suggesting that the Global North owes a large debt to the Global South and the world's poor based on its disproportionate exploitation of the world's ecological resources, its equally disproportionate contribution to environmental harms, and the disproportionate burden that is carried by those least responsible for these problems (Martinez-Alier 2002). Applied to climate breakdown, for example, repayment would require the Global North to drastically lower its emissions so that the remaining carbon space within which CO$_2$ can be emitted while also limiting warming to 1.5°C above pre-industrial levels is reserved for those countries and peoples who have yet to use their fair share and whose right to development is threatened by climate disasters and persistent poverty. It would also require the Global North to provide meaningful finance and technology to the Global South to support low- to zero-carbon development, pay for adaptation to climate change, and pay for the loss and damage caused by slow onset climate change and climate disasters. As we will see, however, persistently high emission levels in the Global North and chronic and significant shortfalls in climate finance to the South, with the North's refusal until 2022 to even acknowledge the need for loss and damage financing under the Paris Agreement, show that the Global North has been unwilling to acknowledge its historical ecological and climate debt to the Global South (see Key Concept Box 16.5). The next section will review these points in more detail with a case study of global climate governance.

KEY CONCEPT BOX 16.5 COMMON BUT DIFFERENTIATED RESPONSIBILITIES AND RESPECTIVE CAPABILITIES

Article 3(1) of the UNFCCC states: 'The Parties should protect the climate system for the benefit of present and future generations of humankind, on the basis of equity and in accordance with their common but differentiated responsibilities and respective capabilities. Accordingly, the developed country Parties should take the lead in combatting climate change and the adverse effects thereof' (United Nations 1992). This principle of common but differentiated responsibilities and respective capabilities (CBDR-RC) has been central to the global climate governance regime since its inception. Notably, it meant that developing countries did not have legally binding emission reduction requirements under the Kyoto Protocol. Nevertheless, Northern nations have failed to take seriously their historical responsibility for climate breakdown with respect to emission reductions and climate finance. In 2009 rich countries committed to providing US$100 billion in climate finance per year by 2020 to developing countries, split equally between mitigation and adaptation. Observers note that the US$100 billion figure has no grounding in actual financial requirements, which are far higher. Data shows that by 2020 only US$83 billion had been provided; 70 per cent was in the form of loans; and only approximately 25 per cent went to adaptation (Oxfam 2021). Debt-based finance is considered particularly scandalous, running counter to the spirit of CBDR-RC and the concept of climate debt whereby Northern nations owe the South for their disproportionate contribution to global climate breakdown. Moreover, the US$100 billion figure was not intended to finance the losses and damages caused by climate disasters, despite the scale of their costs. Hurricane Maria, a category 5 storm, hit the Caribbean

KEY CONCEPT BOX 16.5 COMMON BUT DIFFERENTIATED RESPONSIBILITIES AND RESPECTIVE CAPABILITIES (continued)

island of Dominica in 2017. In a nation whose per capita CO_2 emissions were 1.9 tonnes per person in 2014, damages of US$1.37 billion represented 226 per cent of the nation's GDP, with 70 per cent of livelihoods destroyed (see Figure 16.2) (Richards and Schalatek 2017: 6). Oxfam notes that in 2000 approximately 36 per cent of humanitarian appeals to the UN were connected to extreme weather events; that figure had risen to 78 per cent by 2021 (see Figure 16.3). Following years of coordinated and tireless mobilization, Southern nations achieved a historic victory in November 2022 at the UN climate change meeting in Sharm El-Sheikh, Egypt, when they forced rich nations to agree to the creation of a Loss and Damage Fund to support vulnerable countries. Nevertheless, many anticipate that negotiations to operationalize the Fund, and to determine levels and sources of funding, will be framed by a deeply contentious politics as Northern nations seek to minimize their responsibility while simultaneously failing to strengthen their emission reduction commitments such that the need for loss and damage funding could be minimized into the future (Pflieger 2023).

Figure 16.2 In September 2017, Hurricane Maria devastated the island of Dominica in the Caribbean, destroying houses and interrupting essential services such as water and electricity.

Source: Shutterstock.

Figure 16.3 Proportion of UN humanitarian appeals involving extreme weather

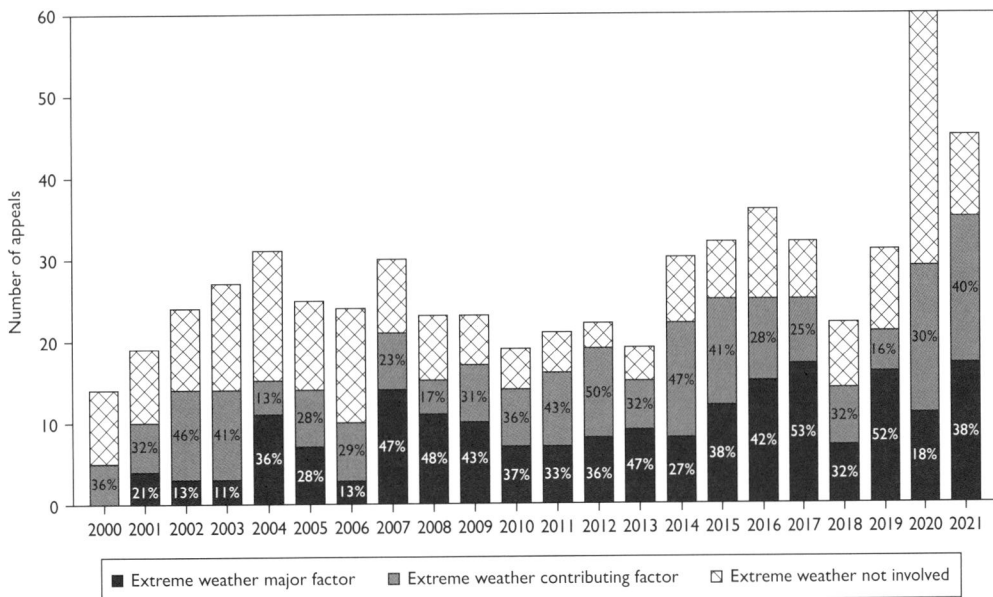

Source: Image reproduced from 'Footing the Bill: Fair Finance for Loss and Damage in an Era of Escalating Climate Impacts' (2022), with the permission of Oxfam, Oxfam House, John Smith Drive, Cowley, Oxford OX4 2JY, UK, www.oxfam.org.uk. Oxfam does not necessarily endorse any text or activities that accompany the materials.

16.5 Governing global climate breakdown

Climate breakdown represents a profoundly complex problem, making governance equally complex. The overlapping material imperatives of continued economic growth and profitability on a finite planet; the centrality of fossil fuels to supporting these imperatives; the Global North's historical and continued use of a disproportionate share of the world's remaining carbon space and the normalization of high-carbon lifestyles and consumption patterns amongst the world's wealthier classes; the Global South's right to development and the fulfilment of the livelihood needs of the world's poor; increasing disunity between the world's Least Developed Countries (LDCs) and Small Island Developing States (SIDS) versus so-called emerging economies like China, India, and Brazil whose emissions have grown significantly in recent decades; the growing complexity of global supply chains and trade networks and debates over production versus consumption-based emissions and who should take responsibility; the concentration of political economic power with actors whose vested interests support the status quo and the rise of global neoliberalism; each of these interact to simultaneously shape global climate action and limit its effectiveness. Table 16.3 shows that as efforts globally to govern climate change have intensified, emissions of CO_2 have steadily increased; by 2018

they were 60 per cent higher than in 1990 (Stoddard et al. 2021: 656).

With the establishment of the United Nations Framework Convention on Climate Change (UNFCCC) in 1992, global negotiations began amongst member parties, of which there are now 198, with the goal of 'preventing dangerous human interference with the climate system' (UNFCC 2022). The UNFCCC held its first annual meeting, known as the Conference of the Parties (COP), in 1995, with the Kyoto Protocol adopted in 1997. With 192 parties, Kyoto's first commitment period ran from 2008–2012 and included legally binding emission reduction targets of an average of 5.2 per cent below 1990 levels for industrialized nations. Notably, the United States, then the world's largest emitter, never ratified the Protocol, while Canada withdrew under the Conservative government of Stephen Harper in 2011, with both nations citing the lack of emission reduction targets for developing countries. However, this exemption was specific to Kyoto's first commitment period only, based on the principle of CBDR-RC (see Key Concept Box 16.5). While a second commitment period to run from 2013–2020 was approved with the Doha Amendment in 2012, it lacked the necessary instruments of approval until October 2020 and only entered into force with 147 parties in December 2020. At that point, the Paris Agreement of 2015 was set to take effect, with parties agreeing on its Rulebook for implementation in 2018 and required to submit updated voluntary climate plans for the post-2020 period, known as Nationally Determined Contributions (NDCs). Unlike the Kyoto Protocol, the Paris Agreement lacks legally binding emission reduction commitments, with a stated goal of limiting warming to 'well-below 2°C' above pre-industrial levels, and an aspirational target of 1.5°C. Critics suggest the Agreement represents 'dangerous incrementalism' that is not fit for purpose given the urgency of climate breakdown (Allan 2019). Analysis shows that at the time of writing current NDCs would lead to average warming of 2.0°C, that actual policies and action would result in average warming of 2.7°C (see Figure 16.4), and that governments globally have fossil fuel production plans in place for 2030 that are double the permissible levels needed for the 1.5°C limit (SEI et al. 2021: 4). A closer examination of climate change mitigation can help us to better understand persisting ineffectiveness in the global climate regime.

Table 16.3 Climate governance milestones and rising emissions

Climate governance milestone	Year	Global annual GDP growth (%)	Annual global CO_2 emissions (fossil fuels and industry)—billions of tonnes	Atmospheric concentrations of CO_2—parts per million (ppm)
Creation of Intergovernmental Panel on Climate Change (IPCC)	1988	4.6%	22.10	350.93
IPCC releases First Assessment Report on the science of climate change	1990	2.9%	22.75	353.72
United Nations Framework Convention on Climate Change (UNFCCC) established	1992	2.1%	22.57	355.9
First Conference of the Parties—UNFCCC; IPCC Second Assessment Report (SAR)	1995	3.1%	23.45	360.23
Kyoto Protocol—UNFCCC	1997	3.9%	24.30	363.17
IPCC Third Assessment Report (TAR)	2001	2%	25.45	370.38
IPCC Fourth Assessment Report (AR4)	2007	4.5%	31.49	382.89
Copenhagen Accord—UNFCCC	2009	−1.3%	31.61	386.42
IPCC Fifth Assessment Report (AR5)	2014	3.1%	35.53	397.45
Paris Agreement—UNFCCC	2015	3.1%	35.50	399.58
IPCC Special Report on 1.5°C of Warming	2018	3.3%	36.65	407.58
COP 26—UNFCCC, Glasgow	2021	5.8%	36.4	416.45
IPCC Sixth Assessment Report (AR6)	2021/2022	2022 forecast—3.6%	No data	418.30 (25 July 2022)

Sources: (European Environment Agency 2019; Ritchie and Roser 2022; Scripps Institution of Oceanography 2022; World Bank 2022b).

16.5.1 | **Climate change mitigation**

Climate change mitigation refers to actions taken to limit or reduce greenhouse gas emissions. The IPCC's 2018 Special Report on the impacts of 1.5°C of warming noted that limiting warming to that level requires 'rapid and far-reaching transitions in energy, land, urban and infrastructure (including transport and buildings), and industrial systems' that are 'unprecedented in scale' and 'imply deep emissions reductions in all sectors' (IPCC 2018). For a 50 per cent chance of limiting warming to 1.5°C, researchers note that no new fossil fuel production facilities can be built, calculating a remaining carbon budget from fossil fuels of 361 billion tonnes, which would be exhausted in 9.8 years at current emission rates (Calverley and

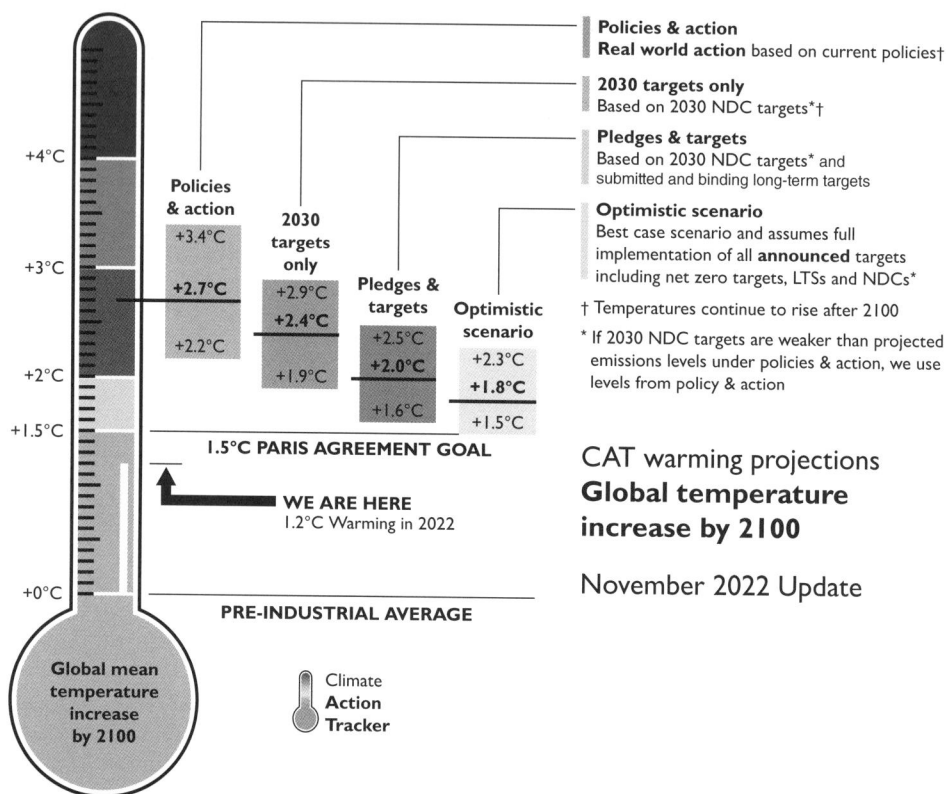

Figure 16.4 Climate Action Tracker thermometer

Source: Climate Analytics.

Anderson 2022: 19). When accounting for historical responsibility, equity, country dependence on fossil fuel production, and capacity to transition, they note coal production must be phased out by 2030 in developed countries, and by 2040 in developing countries. Oil and gas production must be phased out by 2034 in the wealthiest producing nations, by 2043 for middle-income countries, and by 2050 in the poorest countries (Calverley and Anderson 2022: 6). This roadmap for operationalizing CBDR-RC in a global fossil fuel phaseout allots a significant proportion of the world's remaining carbon space to poorer countries and peoples (see Case Study Box 16.6). Beyond historical responsibility, the capacity of rich countries to phase out production is significant given their wealth, high levels of development (what some would call over-development), and diversified economies. In contrast, close to 1 billion people, largely in the Global

South, lack access to electricity, while countries like Iraq, Congo, South Sudan, Brunei, and Gabon depend on oil and gas for over 50 per cent of national GDP (Calverley and Anderson 2022: 40).

In practice, Northern countries continue to operate in ways largely inconsistent with an equity-based carbon budget and a 1.5°C goal. In 2020, G20 countries provided direct subsidies of US$584 billion to fossil fuels, and between January 2020 and March 2021, COVID-19 recovery packages in G7 countries included US$189 billion for fossil fuels, with only 1 in every 10 dollars benefitting energy efficiency or renewable energy (Geddes et al. 2020; Dufour et al. 2021: iii). The potential for profiting from fossil fuels continues to drive investment as well: between 2015 and 2021, the world's sixty largest banks, many headquartered in the Global North, provided US$4.6 trillion in fossil fuel financing, while research shows global oil sector profits of US$52 trillion between 1970 and 2020, with

CASE STUDY BOX 16.6 JUSTICE IN RENEWABLE ENERGY

Transitioning from fossil to renewable energy sources is a core challenge in limiting warming to 1.5°C. Figure 16.5 shows the growth in renewables since 2012. By the end of 2020, however, modern renewables accounted for only 12.6 per cent of global total final energy consumption, with growth considered too low relative to fossil fuels. Critical perspectives note that questions of energy are about much more than the source, however (Newell 2021). In particular, access to energy is essential to human wellbeing, with the current capitalist model of energy provision commodifying and privatizing energy for profit. This means that even when it is available, far too many cannot afford it, especially poor, racialized, and Indigenous communities, while there is no accountability in decisions on its provisioning, impacts, and use. Social movements globally argue that the concept of '**energy democracy**' must be central to a renewables transition. At a minimum, energy democracy implies a shift to clean energy sources; energy's decommodification and universal access; the creation of fair and living wage jobs in the sector; and community ownership and democratic decision-making (Fairchild and Weinrub 2017). On this final point, observers argue that energy justice, entailing 'the equitable distribution of benefits and burdens', must guide policymaking (Baker 2020: 147). The expansion of wind power in the state of Oaxaca, Mexico, illustrates how renewable energy and climate policy can in fact reinforce and expand existing classed and racialized inequalities. Oaxaca's Isthmus of Tehuantepec has experienced rapid wind energy development since the 1990s, with the government, supported by the World Bank, citing the need for renewable energy to fight climate change. Working with private companies, including Walmart and Coca Cola, the government began a process of developing wind farms to attract private investment and to supply private companies with wind energy. By 2020 Oaxaca had over 130 wind turbines spanning 5,000 hectares, providing 62 per cent of Mexico's wind energy. With high levels of poverty in the state, and with Oaxaca's many Indigenous populations lacking access to electricity and basic services, renewable energy could have been part of a strategy to redress historical inequalities. However, Indigenous and local communities were not consulted, in breach of the United Nations Declaration on the Rights of Indigenous Peoples and

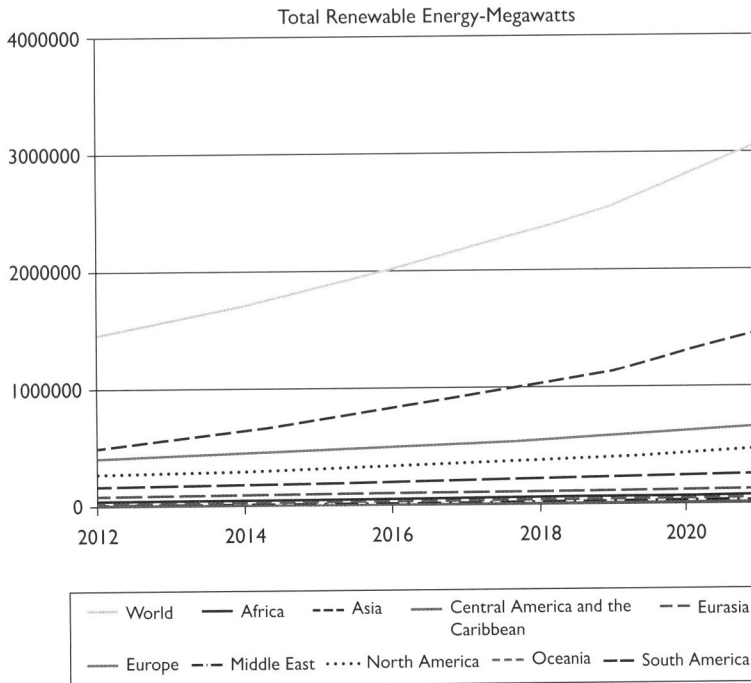

Figure 16.5 The growth in renewable energy capacity

Source: IRENA.

the principle of Free, Prior, and Informed Consent; their lands were appropriated; few to no local benefits were realized; and opposition has led to violence against community activists and even death. The case of Oaxaca is not unique and thus provides

a cautionary tale regarding the siting of infrastructure, human rights, justice, and power compelling us to ask: who and what is energy for, who decides, and who benefits? (Siamanta and Dunlap 2019; Baker 2020; Newell 2021)

the annual average of US\$1 trillion expected to double in 2022 as oil companies earn record profits amidst the cost of living crisis following Russia's invasion of Ukraine and COVID-19-related supply chain issues (Carrington 2022; Banking on Climate Chaos 2022). The power of the sector profoundly shapes climate politics, with the fossil fuel industry having the largest delegation at the UNFCCC's COP 26 in Glasgow in 2021.

The contours of the existing global political economy and its power relations have thus led to a preponderance globally of neoliberal problem-solving approaches to climate change mitigation. While climate science calls for unprecedented transformation and deep emission reductions, these approaches insulate the fossil-fuelled growth model with strategies and policies that shift responsibility in time and space. While positive actions progress worldwide, problem-solving approaches threaten to overwhelm their achievements by sustaining business as usual. Carbon markets, or emissions trading schemes, provide an example (see Key Concept Box 16.7). At the time of writing there were twenty-five ETSs worldwide covering 17 per cent of global greenhouse gas (GHG) emissions, with a further twenty-two under development (ICAP 2022). The largest by coverage is China's national ETS, followed by the European

Union's, with national (that is, UK, New Zealand, South Korea, Mexico, Kazakhstan, etc.), and sub-national (that is, California and the Regional Greenhouse Gas Initiative in the US; Quebec in Canada; Tokyo and Saitama in Japan, etc.) ETSs operating worldwide. As already noted, ETSs allows emitters to purchase emission reductions on the market in place of making more costly reductions at the source, generating significant criticism since emitters can delay deep cuts to emissions in the present required by a science-based carbon budget. Moreover, critical analyses have documented a number of general trends in ETS design that undermine effectiveness. First, caps are set too high, creating an oversupply of allowances and depressing prices. Second, provisions allow emitters to purchase carbon offsets to meet their requirements, adding additional supply and inflating the cap further. Third, allowances are distributed for free to heavy emitters, citing threats to competitiveness and carbon leakage concerns wherein production shifts to higher carbon jurisdictions lacking carbon prices, thereby shielding them from the carbon price and removing a large source of demand from the market (Ervine 2018). In the EU ETS, operating since 2005, industrial emitters continue to receive 94 per cent of allowances for free, preventing deep

KEY CONCEPT BOX 16.7 CARBON PRICING—EMISSIONS TRADING VERSUS TAXES

As governments around the world move to put a price on carbon, they typically choose between carbon taxes or emissions trading systems, or a mix of the two. As discussed in this chapter, emissions trading systems, also known as cap-and-trade, entail governments setting a cap on allowable emissions within a particular jurisdiction. It then creates allowances equivalent to the cap, measured in tonnes of CO_2 equivalent, which are then auctioned or given for free to emitters who must comply with the new cap by turning in allowances that are equivalent to their emissions for the period in question. Instead of a fixed price, the price is determined on the market, with polluters able to purchase, or trade, allowances in the market. Carbon taxes, in contrast, entail governments putting

a price on carbon emissions that must then be paid for each tonne of CO_2 emitted. Proponents of cap-and-trade schemes argue that they are preferable to taxes as the cap, in theory, will ensure the system's environmental integrity. Critics note that caps are frequently set too high, however, with low and highly volatile prices undermining effectiveness. This leads others to support taxation as an alternative given the fixed price and the stability that comes with it (Ervine 2018: 77–78). Still others argue that direct government regulation can be much more effective than carbon pricing, since pricing is intended to nudge behavioural changes, with the poor and lower-income individuals disproportionately burdened. Indeed, carbon pricing fits well within a problem-solving framework.

decarbonization, and heavy industries have earned over €50 billion in 'windfall profits' selling free allowances on the market and by passing their cost, which they did not pay, on to consumers (Amaral 2021; Jacques Delors Institute 2022). Research shows the limited impact of the EU ETS, achieving average annual emission reductions between 0 per cent to 1.5 per cent since 2005 (Green 2021). World Bank data shows that of sixty-eight carbon pricing instruments, including tax systems, operating globally, less than 4 per cent have prices consistent with a 1.5°C goal (World Bank 2022d: 9).

Critical analyses highlight that the limited impact in carbon pricing and carbon markets is by design. Many of the world's largest oil companies lobby aggressively for emissions trading while opposing climate action and regulations that would restrict fossil fuel production. Powerful business lobbies like the International Emissions Trading Association (IETA), representing some of the most polluting companies worldwide, advocate for carbon markets and against direct regulations, working closely with national governments, UN bodies including the UNFCCC, international financial institutions like the World Bank, and large environmental non-governmental organizations, helping to draft global rules for carbon trading, first for the Kyoto Protocol and now for the Paris Agreement (Ervine 2018). Article 6 of the Paris Agreement sets the parameters to facilitate carbon trading globally, building on Kyoto's 'flexible mechanisms' which included emissions trading between governments, and carbon offsetting, primarily through the Clean Development Mechanism (CDM). The CDM allowed countries in the Global South to undertake projects that, in theory, avoid future emissions. Examples include building renewable energy projects instead of fossil-energy projects; capturing methane from landfills; installing technology to capture GHGs from industrial processes; and planting trees that sequester carbon. In the case of a wind energy project to displace coal-fired electricity, for example, the offset project developer would estimate future emissions under a business-as-usual scenario that uses coal, followed by an estimate of future emissions with wind energy instead. The difference between the two, or the quantity of emissions to be avoided by developing the wind energy project, measured in tonnes of CO_2 equivalent (tCO_2e), could then be sold as carbon offsets, each worth one tCO_2e. However, to qualify to sell offsets, project developers would need to demonstrate that the project was not viable without offset money. The reward for offset purchasers in the Global North, in turn, was that they could then count these offsets as actual emission reductions under the Kyoto Protocol.

The critiques of carbon offsetting for mitigation are extensive. From the complexity of calculating potential avoided emissions to the tendency to over-inflate estimates to earn more offsets, evidence has shown that offsets often lack environmental integrity (Haya 2019; Badgley et al. 2021). For example, an EU-commissioned review of CDM projects found that an estimated 85 per cent of projects reviewed and 73 per cent of available offsets between 2013 and 2020 lacked environmental integrity according to the CDM's own standards (Cames et al. 2016). This suggested that as the largest purchaser of CDM offsets to meet its Kyoto targets, at 1.4 billion by 2017, the EU had helped to undermine the regime's effectiveness. Additionally, like ETSs, offsetting allows heavy emitters to purchase emission reductions on the market in place of making reductions at the source. Some observers highlight that the money paid for offsets under the CDM channelled large sums of climate finance to actors in the Global South for low-carbon projects; this is true. However, finance was contingent on purchasers in the Global North being able to count offsets towards their own emission reduction requirements. For many, this underscores the North's failure to honour the principle of CBDR-RC, with offsetting tying finance to the North getting something in return; shifting the responsibility to lower emissions onto actors and communities in the Global South; and delaying the real work of lowering emissions aggressively in the North. Described as **carbon colonialism** by some, critics contend that offsetting maintains a disproportionate share of the world's remaining carbon space for the Global North so that its lifestyles and emissions can continue.

Offsetting will continue under the Paris Agreement, while the global voluntary market in carbon offsetting, which allows polluters to voluntarily purchase offsets, has seen dramatic growth in recent years, with proponents projecting its value will reach over US$50 billion by 2030. In this, offsetting is set to play a major role in countries and companies meeting their 'net-zero' targets. Net-zero does not imply emissions of actual zero; rather, offsets or negative emissions technologies (NET) that remove CO_2 from the atmosphere are used to reduce remaining emissions to zero. Most NETs remain unproven at scale. By November 2021 over 140 countries had made net-zero pledges covering 90 per cent of global emissions, often targeting 2050.

An analysis of these commitments by Climate Action Tracker showed that targets covering a mere 6 per cent of global emissions were considered adequate, with no country having adequate short-term policies in place to meet their target. This led them to conclude a major 'credibility gap' existed, with net-zero paying 'lip service' to climate action (Climate Action Tracker 2021). Similar findings have been found for companies. The oil major Shell has a 2050 net-zero target; however, analysis shows that it plans to rely on offsets from tree planting, called a 'nature-based solution' (NBS), with its global scenario for limiting warming to 1.5°C implying land equivalent to the size of Brazil would be needed for tree planting (Gabbattis 2021). This raises important questions: whose lands will be used so that Shell and other major emitters can continue to produce oil and gas, and who decides? All of these strategies must be contextualized within the IPCC's warning in 2018 that deep emissions reductions and transformative climate action are required in the present in order to avoid catastrophic climate breakdown. As problem-solving approaches, emissions trading, carbon offsetting, and net zero commitments provide examples of strategies and frameworks that allow for a delay in climate action, often far into the future, and a shifting of responsibility onto others. While they are not the only strategies being employed by a range of actors globally, including national governments, networks of cities, institutions and organizations, and a range of movements, their influence, breadth, and reach, connected to dominant relations of power within the global political economy, threaten to overshadow what meaningful action is occurring. This is in part because CO_2 is a cumulative problem—once emitted, its impacts will be felt for generations. It is thus that critical attention must be paid to developing strategies and responses that offer effective near-term action and that uphold the principles of equity and responsibility in doing so.

KEY POINTS

- Alongside the growth in global efforts to govern climate breakdown since the 1990s, greenhouse gas emissions have continued to increase.

- Unlike the Kyoto Protocol which had a legally binding emissions reduction target for countries in the Global North, the Paris Agreement has voluntary commitments

from states, known as Nationally Determined Contributions.

- Emissions trading, carbon offsetting, and net-zero targets can be theorized as problem-solving approaches to addressing climate change that provide ways for emitters to avoid deep emissions reductions in the short term, in line with equity-based carbon budgets.

16.6 Conclusion

As ecological breakdown brings with it new crises and disasters on a weekly basis it seems, and as global governance efforts appear unable to adequately respond, actors and movements around the world are working towards meaningful change that can redefine humanity's relationship with the planet and each other. The principle of a '**just transition**' has gained traction in recent years, and while contestation exists over how it might be defined, its most progressive version entails a move away from today's extractive economy that reduces nature to commodities and exploits it for profit, with wealth and power accruing to a small minority committed to a colonial mindset and militarism to defend their interests, to a living and regenerative economy that invests in communities, promotes cooperation over commodification, and prioritizes the wellbeing of people and the planet (Mascarenhas-Swan 2017: 47). Ideas like degrowth are gaining traction, challenging an ideology of limitless economic growth that denies planetary boundaries, and advocating instead for rethinking our relationship with nature and each other so that we redefine notions of the good life and wellbeing. Youth the world over have organized to draw attention to the future that will be theirs; one that in the absence of meaningful action promises insecurity and devastation that will surely be experienced unevenly, those least responsible paying the heaviest cost. Activists organize for fossil fuel divestment, energy democracy, public and patient green finance, green jobs, and regenerative agriculture, using legal tools to sue companies and governments that fail to uphold their commitments to ensuring a liveable future for all or that breach public trust, while the movement for a global Fossil Fuel Non-Proliferation Treaty gains momentum, endorsed globally by twelve nation states (including Tuvalu and Vanuatu), over ninety cities and sub-national governments, 3,000 scientists and academics, over 552,000 individuals, and over 2,418 organizations.[1] Indeed, there is much that is happening throughout the world. Defining the pathway forwards will be caught in many ways between problem solving and critical approaches, with the risk of eco-apartheid, wherein the wealthy and powerful insulate themselves from ecological collapse and the social dislocation that this entails, all too real. As Russia's invasion of Ukraine has made tragically clear, our dependence on fossil energy threatens more than the health of the ecosystems that sustain human societies. Asking who owns the future, for what ends, and who benefits, are some of the most pressing questions now before us. Our ability to answer them and reflect on their implications will be important for choosing pathways forwards rooted in justice and equity.

[1] Fossil Fuel Non-Proliferation Treaty: https://fossilfueltreaty.org/home.

16.7 QUESTIONS

1. What are the main differences between problem-solving and critical approaches to explaining environmental problems?

2. Why do critical approaches to explaining environmental problems start with an analysis of capitalism and its imperatives?

3. What should be included in a definition of sustainability?

4. What do we learn from examining ecological footprints between nations and peoples?

5. To what extent has the concept of common but differentiated responsibilities and respective capabilities influenced global climate governance? Has it been effective?

6. Why is it important to examine the role of fossil fuels in contributing to climate breakdown and what role do they play in shaping climate governance?

7. How do the principles of energy democracy differ from dominant approaches to providing people with energy?

8. What is an imperial mode of living, and what are the implications for the politics of climate change action?

9. Do you think carbon offsetting is an appropriate way to counteract climate change? Why or why not?

10. How would you characterize the relationship between nature and capitalism?

16.8 FURTHER READING

Adow, M. (2021), *Mobilizing Resources Urgently for Climate Action: Overcoming Longstanding Challenges and Learning from Covid-19* (Brussels: Heinrich Boll Stiftung). Focuses on climate finance and pathways to ensuring adequate levels of finance to the Global South.

Ajl, M. (2022), *A People's Green New Deal* (London: Pluto Press). Develops a framework for a 'People's Green New Deal' rooted in degrowth, anti-imperialism, and agro-ecology.

Bryant, R. L., and Bailey, S. (1997), *Third World Political Ecology* (London and New York: Routledge). Provides an introduction to the field of political ecology, focusing on the Global South.

Ervine, K. (2018), *Carbon* (Basingstoke: Polity). Examines the political economy of climate breakdown and dominant responses to it, including carbon trading.

Fairchild, D., and Weinrub, A. (eds.) (2017), *Energy Democracy: Advancing Equity in Clean Energy Solutions* (Washington, D.C.: Island Press). An edited volume that examines the concept of energy democracy in theory and practice, focusing on case studies from the United States.

Kallis, G. (2018), *Degrowth* (Newcastle upon Tyne: Agenda Publishing). Provides an overview of the key ideas underpinning the theory and science of degrowth.

Katz-Rosene, R., and Paterson, M. 2018, *Thinking Ecologically about the Global Political Economy* (London: Routledge). Advances a framework for integrating ecological thinking into political economy scholarship and analyses.

Kothari, A., Salleh, A., Escobar, A., Demaria, F., and Acosta, A. (eds.) (2019), *Pluriverse: A Post-Development Dictionary* (New Delhi: Tulika Books). An edited volume providing short essays on transformative alternatives, rooted in just ecologies, to dominant development models.

Newell, P. (2021), *Power Shift: The Global Political Economy of Energy Transitions* (Cambridge: Cambridge University Press). Provides a detailed political economy account of the challenges of achieving a global energy transition to achieve a zero-carbon economy.

Nirmal, P., and Rocheleau, D. (2019), 'Decolonizing Degrowth in the Post-Development Convergence: Questions, Experiences, and Proposals from Two Indigenous Territories', *Environment and Planning E: Nature and Space*, 2: 465–492. Harnesses decolonial and feminist critiques to build a broader decolonial degrowth movement rooted in multiple diversities and ways of being.

Trebeck, K., and Williams, J. (2019), *The Economics of Arrival: Ideas for a Grown Up Economy* (Bristol: Policy Press). Challenges the dominant growth paradigm that shapes contemporary capitalism, offering a framework for an inclusive, just, and ecologically informed economy.

CONTRIBUTOR NOTE

Kate Ervine is an Associate Professor in the Department of Global Development Studies at Saint Mary's University and a Faculty Associate with SMU's School of the Environment. Her publications include *Carbon* (Polity Press), *Beyond Free Trade: Alternative Approaches to Trade, Politics and Power* (coedited with Gavin Fridell; Palgrave Macmillan), and the short documentary film *The Carbon Cage* (with Duy Linh Tu; Scientific American).

17

The Global Political Economy of Digital Technology

Tyler Girard

Chapter contents

Reader's guide

This chapter explores how the digital transformation of the global economy creates new forms of power, new political cleavages, and new coalitions. The first part of the chapter explains the technologies and firm dynamics at the centre of this transformation, as well as the new analytical tools and concepts being used to explain these changes. The chapter then explores the digital transformation across three interrelated areas. The fragmentation of national and global governance initiatives for artificial intelligence is contrasted with the emergence of the European Union (EU) as a global standard setter in data and privacy governance. The chapter then unpacks the disruption of labour markets and shifting political cleavages caused by the digitization of global trade, as well as the creation of new points of conflict in global trade governance. Finally, the chapter concludes with an assessment of the disruptive impact of technology firms and cryptocurrency on global finance.

17.1 Introduction

New digital technologies have fundamentally changed how we communicate and work, how businesses engage in international trade, and even how we think about the nature and role of finance. Rapid improvements in the storage and use of digital information have led to new business models and extraordinary forms of corporate power. Indeed, 'Big Technology' (Big Tech) firms located in the United States (such as Facebook, Amazon, Apple, and Google[1]) and China (such as Huawei, Alibaba, and Tencent) have become ubiquitous in the lives of people throughout the world. Moreover, these firms are increasingly scrutinized as part of political debates over human rights, economic inequality, and corporate power. The many changes associated with new digital technologies have prompted a shared sense among scholars that social, political, and economic relations are experiencing a fundamental shift, even if disciplines differ in their preferred language to analyse and communicate this shift. In the aftermath of the COVID-19 pandemic, the digital transformation of the global economy has further accelerated as people across the world increased their dependency on existing and new technologies (McNamara and Newman 2020). However, the field of global political economy has arguably overlooked many of these changes, leading to multiple calls for greater engagement by scholars of global politics (Atal 2021; Srivastava 2021).

This chapter examines the global political economy of digital technology and, in so doing, makes two fundamental claims. First, the disruptive effects of new digital technologies on political and economic relations cannot be fully understood in isolation, but instead requires a broad understanding of how these changes are interwoven across different domains in the global economy. Second, idealistic representations of these changes often obscure the exercise of power and the creation of new political cleavages and coalitions.

To provide a shared understanding of the key components of the digital transformation, the chapter begins by mapping the central new technologies in this process, as well as the conceptual tools that have been developed to provide analytical traction on these issues. The chapter then unpacks the politics of the digital disruption across three substantive areas. First, the regulation of artificial intelligence (AI) and of data and privacy are crucial sites of global conflict yet have followed very different regulatory trajectories so far. Second, the global exchange of digital data, the expansion of digital services trade, and the reconfiguration of labour relations have created important new political cleavages. Third, financial technology (FinTech) and Big Tech firms have challenged existing firms and regulatory frameworks in global finance, while cryptocurrencies have ascended from fringe finance to mainstream debates.

17.2 Power in the digital global economy

The transformation of the digital economy has not just introduced new everyday technologies and types of firms, but also demanded new analytical tools to help make sense of our experiences. Despite the attention within this chapter and in public debates on the most recent developments, it is important to recognize that this process has been unfolding over decades. Indeed, Zysman and Newman (2006) argued that evolving digital technologies in the 2000s were disrupting both national and global political orders. Nevertheless, the commodification of digital data and the development of cloud computing, artificial intelligence, and blockchain have led to changes in the global economy that are distinct from earlier periods. Moreover, changing economic and socio-political relations have led to important debates about the nature of capitalism in this era and governance through and by algorithms.

17.2.1 Mapping the digital transformation

Central to the digital revolution is how we think about, how we collect, and how we use massive amounts of digital *data*. Data can be understood as a representation of the world, which then provides the building blocks for the creation of information and knowledge. This can include things like numbers, text, images, and sounds, which are used to represent features of

---

[1] The corporate structures of Facebook and Google have changed in recent years, such that Facebook and Google were reorganized as part of corporations named Meta and Alphabet (respectively). For simplicity, this chapter uses the terms Facebook and Google and does not emphasize this change in structure.

the world and human behaviours. While the economic and political importance of data is not new, the creation and storage of digital 'big data' suggests we have entered a distinct 'data revolution' (Kitchin 2014). Everything we do with digital technology, from the way we move a cursor on a screen to how often we visit a webpage, can be recorded, shared, and analysed. The transformation of data into a capitalized property is a process variously conceptualized as **commodification** or as **assetization** (Beauvisage and Mellet 2020; Bilić et al. 2021; Birch et al. 2021) and serves to extract data from its original context in a manner that benefits particular groups: 'Commodifying data, detaching the data from the individuals or contexts that produced it, gives it an instrumental (often for-profit) characteristic, often placing it in a closed economic system and under the control of specific groups or individuals' (Haggart 2021: 21). This is a crucial point. To paraphrase Robert Cox: digital data is always for someone and for some purpose.

The economic value of digital data is often likened to commodities (for example, oil). However, Weymouth (2023) argues that data differs from oil and other commodities in several important ways. Individual data are not inherently valuable and typically only gain value when compiled with others' data and analysed collectively. To date, there is also a lack of property rights over individuals' data. Data are also not public goods. Data are non-rivalrous, insofar as the use and reproduction of data is nearly costless, but data remain excludable through user exclusions and restrictions. Data are often non-fungible, which is to say that different types of data are often not interchangeable (that is, data gathered in one setting may not be useful for analysis in a different setting). From a political perspective, the most important feature of data is its deeply *personal* nature: 'Data on individuals can be collected, transferred, and analyzed to reveal deeply personal attributes, behaviors, and preferences in ways that can make it an ideal input into businesses' digital marketing strategies' (Weymouth 2023: 10). These features of data have profound implications for designing regulations and for global regulatory cooperation.

In conjunction with the commodification of personal data is the advancement in new digital technologies, many (though not all) of which were developed to generate value from this data. While an exhaustive account is beyond the scope of this chapter, I focus on three especially prominent technologies: cloud computing, artificial intelligence, and blockchain.

The study of these technologies also sets the stage for identifying the power dynamics embedded within the digital transformation of the global economy.

First, the collection of massive amounts of digital data requires new systems to manage and analyse this data on a global scale. **Cloud computing** provides one solution to this challenge. While a single definition of cloud computing does not exist, Microsoft (a major provider of cloud computing services) offers an accessible definition (Microsoft 2022): '[C]loud computing is the delivery of computing services—including servers, storage, databases, networking, software, analytics, and intelligence—over the Internet ("the cloud") to offer faster innovation, flexible resources, and economies of scale'. As a type of infrastructure, cloud computing is integral to the pooling of data for subsequent analysis (including the use of artificial intelligence) and the cross-border flow of data. This also helps firms to reduce costs since they do not need to acquire and manage the physical, local computing infrastructure. While cloud computing can be entirely owned and operated by third-party service providers (for example, Microsoft providing cloud computing services to a firm, known as a 'public cloud'), these services can also be used exclusively by a single organization (known as a 'private cloud'). Of particular importance to the study of global political economy, cloud computing is central to the development of new global digital value chains (DVCs) (for a discussion of global value chains, see, Gore Chapter 7) and cross-border data flows (see Sections 17.3.2 and 17.4.2).

The second innovation is **artificial intelligence (AI)**. AI broadly refers to any technology designed to reproduce high-order levels of human intelligence (Mayo 2021). In other words, it goes beyond performing predetermined tasks (for example, a calculator performing arithmetic is not AI); instead, AI typically relies on algorithms to engage in some level of analysis or interpretation that begins to approximate human reasoning. As a subset of AI, 'machine learning' relies on algorithms to identify patterns and predict outcomes using vast amounts of data. A simple example of this is a spam trap used by any email provider: an algorithm predicts whether incoming messages are spam based on the language or image patterns identified in previous emails. While machine learning for the purposes of filtering spam emails is relatively benign, AI is used in increasingly sophisticated and varied contexts, from the automation of financial services (such as investment and lending decisions; see Section 17.5.1) to self-driving cars, language translation, and military weapons (Dafoe 2018; Gallego and Kurer 2022).

The third innovation is **blockchain**. Campbell-Verduyn (2018b: 1) describes blockchains as 'digital sequences of numbers coded into computer software that permit the secure exchange, recording, and broadcasting of transactions between individual users operating anywhere in the world with Internet access'. Blockchains combine digital encryption technologies with algorithms to enable permanent recordkeeping among a decentralized network of users. Central to the development and use of blockchain is the idea of *trust* (Casey and Vigna 2018). Traditional accounting systems are typically managed by a centralized institution that others trust to maintain an accurate record of account (for example, banks maintaining the record of transactions conducted through a savings account). Blockchains eliminate the need for trust in a centralized authority through their decentralized systems of account: each user in the network maintains identical copies of the ledger, which can only be (simultaneously) updated or changed following a set of rules (an algorithm called a 'consensus protocol'). While often associated with Bitcoin, a type of cryptocurrency that uses blockchain, blockchain and bitcoin are not synonymous (for more on Bitcoin and cryptocurrency, see Section 17.5.2). Instead, blockchain applications range from real estate and insurance to supply chain monitoring (see Section 17.4.1)—virtually any activity requiring secure recordkeeping. By disrupting the traditional structures of authority in the global economy, blockchains raise a host of pressing questions central to the study of global governance and global political economy (Campbell-Verduyn 2018a).

The massive increase and commodification of data, combined with a variety of technology advances, have led to the creation of new types of businesses and business models. In particular, much of the debate has focused on the rapid expansion and dominance of Big Tech firms. These multinational companies are overwhelmingly based in two countries: the United States (for example, Facebook, Amazon, Apple, Netflix, Google, and Microsoft) and China (for example, Huawei, Alibaba, and Tencent). As of April 2022, the market capitalization of Apple, Microsoft, Google, and Amazon each exceeded US$1 trillion, and the growth of these firms has only accelerated through the pandemic. While Big Tech firms vary with respect to the roles they serve in the contemporary global economy—from Amazon's control of distribution

networks for goods and services to Google's control of online information and advertising to Facebook's control of social networks and media—they each share an outsized role in the economy and our daily lives.

There are several important characteristics of these firms. At their core, many emerged as intermediary platforms that solve basic coordination problems in market exchanges (Langley and Leyshon 2017). That is to say, they help economic actors (buyers and sellers) find each other. In turn, these firms have occupied central roles as intermediaries in complex economic and social systems. This includes online marketplaces linking buyers and sellers of goods (for example, Amazon), services (for example, Uber, AirBnb), and labour (for example, Upwork, TaskRabbit, Fiverr), social media and the sharing of user-generated content (for example, YouTube, Facebook, Twitter), and even crowdfunding and **peer-to-peer (P2P) lending** (for example, Kickstarter, Lending Club). In doing so, technology firms generate enormous **network effects** (Key Concept Box 17.1), which then contribute to increasing **market concentration** (Key Concept Box 17.2). Beyond serving as intermediary platforms, we also need to recognize the relationship between revenue creation, data commodification, and new digital technologies. The 'deal' offered by many technology companies to consumers is free access to unparalleled digital products and services in exchange for users' data—their search history, their browsing history, a record of how they navigate websites and digital content, etc. Using this data, firms can build complex profiles of its users, provide targeted advertisements with unprecedented precision, and license the information to third parties (Weymouth 2023). This business model is associated with the often used saying: 'If you're not paying for it, you are the product'.

17.2.2 **New forms of capitalism, governance, and power**

How can we make sense of these changes? There are competing narratives and frameworks that are used to understand the digital transformation. On the one hand, 'conventional narratives' emphasize the inclusivity of platform firms (for example, enabling lower-cost entry for workers and firms), the high-quality products and services through which platform firms acquire massive market share, and the flexibility and independence afforded to users and workers who rely

KEY CONCEPT BOX 17.1 NETWORK EFFECTS

Network effects (or network externalities) occur when the value of a product or service increases as the number of people who also use that product or service increases. These effects are especially common in technology and communications sectors and can help firms that benefit from network effects become dominant (or even a monopoly). The operation of network effects becomes clear when we consider social media. If you and all your friends have social media accounts with different platforms, you are strongly limited in your ability to communicate with each other. As more and more of you create accounts with the same platform, it becomes easier to communicate with each other and the value of that platform increases. For more information, see Krugman and Wells (2018).

KEY CONCEPT BOX 17.2 MARKET STRUCTURE, COMPETITION, AND MONOPOLIES

Central to the study of markets is their structure, often understood as a spectrum between competitive markets (or a state of perfect competition) and monopolistic markets. In competitive markets, there are many buyers and sellers of a product or service, which prevents any individual actor from affecting the market price of the product or service. More formally, perfect competition requires both many producers (none of whom control a large share of the market) and consumers to treat the products and services of producers as equivalent. At the other extreme, monopolies occur when there is a single producer whose products and services have no close substitutes. Oligopolies fall in the middle, where there are a small number of firms that constitute the market.

Why does market structure matter? Properly functioning markets require competition. Governments use regulation and competition (or anti-trust) policy to combat the ability of oligopolistic firms to collude to set market prices or, alternatively, to prevent or break up monopolistic firms. Many of the central debates around Big Tech are animated by conflicting views of the type of market in which technology firms participate and whether technology firms operate as monopolies. For more information, see Krugman and Wells (2018).

on platform firms (Pasquale 2016). At the centre of this understanding is a constantly expanding market rationality, whereby new digital commodities and digital markets are created. Further, this narrative relies heavily on an 'idealist discourse' and 'techno-utopianism' whereby the language and values used to promote technological disruption often mimic the language and values found in community or grassroots movements (Liang et al. 2022). For example, the 'sharing economy' is used to describe economic activities involving peer-to-peer collaboration and consumption (for example, Uber for shared transportation, WeWork for shared office space, or Fiverr for labour freelancing).

On the other hand, a variety of critical frameworks and concepts challenge the idealism associated with conventional narratives. More specifically, they help us to identify how power is exercised and the ways in which the benefits and costs of the digital transformation are unequally distributed. The commodification of data and capacity of firms and governments to monitor individual behaviour with unprecedented precision is characterized by Zuboff (2019) as a new form of **surveillance capitalism**. Other scholars instead focus on the central role of platforms and platform business models within the digital economy, arguing that we are witnessing the development of the platform economy or **platform capitalism** (Srnicek 2017; Kenney and Zysman 2020; Langley and Leyshon 2021; 2017). From this perspective, the centrality of platforms as intermediaries in new types of socio-political relations leads to dramatic shifts in how we understand and create *value* and who benefits from or controls this value. As discussed in Section 17.2.1, data undergoes a process of commodification through which platform intermediaries create and extract value from digital information. As central intermediaries, these firms both disproportionately benefit from the data commodification process and, through economies of scale and market concentration, contribute to growing social and economic inequality.

Others have called attention to the specific role of **algorithmic governance** in the digital economy. The promise of algorithms as a tool of governance depends on a particular type of rationality, one that legitimates processes of data commodification and heralds improved decision-making (Aradau and Blanke 2022). Across a variety of domains, including economic activity, crime, border control, and humanitarianism, algorithms are used to reconfigure existing governance structures. In turn, they can exacerbate hierarchies and social divisions, reinforce existing inequalities, and disrupt traditional ideas of authority. Indeed, Srivastava (2021: 3) powerfully captures the dual nature inherent in this new form of governance: '[A]lgorithmic governance reflects both the use of algorithms *by* authorities and algorithms *as* authorities'. In turn, this has important consequences for issues that are central to the study of the global political economy, namely the exercise of authority by new private governors and the expansion of relations between states and firms (Srivastava 2021).

Finally, the unique attributes of Big Tech may generate distinct forms of corporate power. Across both liberal pluralist and Marxist scholarship, the exercise of power by firms has been variously conceptualized as *structural* power and *instrumental* power. That is to say, policymakers may anticipate and respond to the preferences of businesses due to the privileged position of firms in the structure of global capitalism. Alternatively, firms may secure favourable policy or regulatory arrangements through strategic and direct political engagement. However, Big Tech firms uniquely combine economic scale and direct relationships with millions (or even billions) of consumers. This results in what Culpepper and Thelen (2020) have conceptualized as **platform power**. Big Tech firms can mobilize public opinion in ways that create an advantage for them in regulatory conflicts. So long as citizens value the consumer benefits derived from the products and services offered by Big Tech more than they value other concerns (for example, privacy), such firms can overcome formidable opposition from incumbent firms, interest groups, and politicians.

KEY POINTS

- Cloud computing, artificial intelligence, blockchain, and data commodification have enabled new types of products, services, and business models.

- These changes have led to new types of economic relations and power that challenge traditional analytical tools and concepts.

- Platform firms are often able to combine these technologies, their massive scale, and their intimate relationships with consumers in a way that facilitates a unique type of political influence called 'platform power'.

17.3 Regulating digital disruptions

The global scale of the digital transformation transcends national boundaries. This new era of 'digital globalization'—the integration of national digital economies (Weymouth 2023)—stands to disrupt traditional power structures and regulatory models. While the following sections in this chapter unpack in greater detail the power politics of digital technology associated with global trade and finance, here I explore the key logics underpinning global cooperation, regulatory harmonization, and the creation of national regulatory regimes (for a more detailed overview of global cooperation and conflict, see Aggarwal and Dupont, Chapter 3). Regulating these firms is no easy feat since there are few straightforward answers to which sectors they operate in, their role in the market and global economy, and whether they are ultimately public or private actors (Atal 2021: 337). Yet, in this rapidly changing space, it is possible we are witnessing a shift towards greater state intervention in ways that will fundamentally challenge existing models and strategies of technology firms. Not only will states, international organizations, firms, and civil society organizations compete to establish dominant ideas and norms that will inform the design of regulation, but the implementation of these interventions will also have important distributional consequences for economic and political power. This section focuses on the new and fragmented approaches to governing AI and the emergence of the European Union (EU) as a global leader in data and privacy governance.

17.3.1 **Artificial intelligence**

Artificial intelligence (AI) enables the exercise of private authority and transforms state–firm relations in ways that necessitate a global response. As discussed in Section 17.2.2, private actors exercise considerable authority through opaque algorithms and AI, which allow technology firms to shape individual behaviour, automate governance decisions, and (in some cases) perpetuate different forms of discrimination and harm. The digital markets within which technology firms operate are truly global—millions (and even billions) of people around the world participate in the same social media platforms or use the same online search engines. As such, many of the risks associated with AI, including economic concentration and inequality, artificially curated information and media environments, and mass surveillance and repression, cannot be effectively addressed by a single country (Dafoe 2018, Schmitt 2022). To date, however, the global landscape of regulatory initiatives remains fragmented, with a wide variety of approaches being pursued at the international and national levels. This fragmentation has resulted in the creation of multiple and varied national arrangements, which encompass different institutional logics and public–private interactions (Radu 2021). One way in which this can be seen is through the Organization for Economic Cooperation and Development (OECD) AI Policy Observatory, which provides an interactive tool for exploring more than 700 AI policy initiatives across sixty countries (https://oecd.ai/en/dashboards). These policy instruments span national strategies, new regulations (and regulatory bodies), and industrial policies to provide funding, coordination, and logistical support.

Notwithstanding the failure (to date) to firmly establish an AI governance regime at the global level, there are a number of preliminary efforts to address this governance gap. To distinguish between different approaches, Schmitt (2022) offers a useful framework consisting of whether initiatives are state or non-state led and whether initiatives are contained within existing governance architectures or are instead implemented through new instruments. Bearing in mind that regulatory initiatives can have different aims (for example, targeting specific AI applications or promoting general principles for AI ethics), this framework offers a starting point for deciphering the global regulatory landscaping and the distribution of power among states, firms, and civil society organizations.

On the one hand, efforts to establish an AI regime within existing structures can be both state-led (for example, G20) and non-state led (for example, OECD). Following public commitments to 'ethical AI' by the G20 in 2019 and 2020, some have called for the primacy of the G20 in AI governance. Such arguments resemble similar claims of G20 primacy in global economic governance at its creation. As suggested by Pomares and Abdala (2020: 92): 'By engaging in this debate and leading the conversation, the G20 has the potential of becoming the spinal column of a new architecture for the 21st century and ensure a better future for all'. By comparison, the OECD AI Principles (adopted in May 2019) have gained greater

traction and aim to both shape national policymaking while also encouraging international cooperation (Ulnicane et al. 2022).

On the other hand, a variety of new governance initiatives have been introduced by both state and non-state actors. The Global Partnership for AI (GPAI) was proposed in 2017 and overcame opposition from the Trump administration (who feared it would primarily impede American firms) when the administration was convinced the GPAI would help limit China's influence in global AI governance (Schmitt 2022). As a standalone initiative with a permanent secretariat and relatively broad membership (twenty-five member states), the GPAI aims to promote the OECD AI Principles and facilitate international collaboration around AI development and ethical use. By comparison, the Partnership on AI (PAI), established in 2016, is an attempt at industry self-regulation by major American technology firms (for example, Apple, Google, Facebook, and Microsoft). It primarily operates as a platform for knowledge sharing and the identification of best practices.

In the absence of a clearly established global regime for AI governance, the proliferation of initiatives can mask the underlying power politics, result in the competing AI regimes, and create favourable conditions for technology firms to shape the rules that govern their activities. It might also enable authoritarian regimes to further use AI to expand and consolidate state power, namely as a tool of oppression to help maintain control over domestic populations (although such efforts are not infallible; see Harari 2018; and Zeng 2016). As explained in greater detail by Harmes in Chapter 11, neoliberal social forces typically support the state-constraining effects of policy competition, which in this case can result in unfavourable conditions, such as fewer limits on how firms design and use AI. By establishing new forms of industry self-regulation (such as the Partnership on AI), technology firms may also effectively prevent greater international cooperation and more direct and unfavourable state interventions. Indeed, the risks of private regulation are well established in many other areas of global political economy. Moreover, a reliance on principles or best practices rather than formal regulatory frameworks and accompanying enforcement mechanisms, regardless of the jurisdiction (national or global), may ultimately reinforce the power of technology firms.

17.3.2 **Data and privacy regulation**

In contrast to the dynamics around AI governance, the global politics around data and privacy governance are more strongly influenced by the EU and the cross-national privacy coalitions seeking to constrain technology firms (for details about the New Interdependence Approach that guides much of this research, see Key Theory Box 17.3). In particular, the EU has emerged as a key global regulator and standard setter through the 'Brussels effect'. As Bradford (2020: 25) argues, the combination of market size, regulatory capacity, and political choices has enabled the EU to externalize its standards across other jurisdictions. This is not to suggest that the EU is able to impose standards across the world in *all* areas related to digital technology; rather, as outlined below, the Brussels

effect is especially prominent in the areas of data and privacy governance.

A major step towards regulating data and privacy was the creation of the EU's General Data Protection Regulation (GDPR). When it entered into force in 2018, it replaced the existing Privacy Directive to provide a single, standardized privacy architecture. The GDPR contains many notable features that distinguish it from other attempts at data and privacy governance (Farrell and Newman 2019a; Bradford 2020). It limits the type and quantity of data that can be collected, requires all entities to ensure the security and integrity of data (a crucial point that animates digital trade politics; see Section 17.4.2), and enshrines new obligations like the 'right to be forgotten' (allowing data subjects to request the erasure of their data) and 'privacy by

---

KEY THEORY BOX 17.3 THE NEW INTERDEPENDENCE APPROACH

In the context of high levels of integration between national economies, how will global regulatory disputes be resolved and whose interests will be represented in the new rules? While traditional explanations in global political economy often point to the relative market power of competing states or veto points created by national institutions, these approaches suffer from several shortcomings. In particular, they often treat one 'level' (domestic or international) as fixed or study bargaining as if it occurs in set jurisdictions that are independent of each other (that is, 'methodological nationalism'). The New Interdependence Approach (NIA) is an emerging framework for exploring the relationships between interdependence, power, and cross-national coalitions (Farrell and Newman 2014; 2015; 2016; 2019a). More specifically, the NIA is used to examine how political processes produce the rules that govern global market actors and the institutional configurations at the domestic level.

The NIA rests on three pillars. First, *rule-overlap* is created when economic integration leads to incompatible sets of rules, which in turn make conflicting demands on market actors (especially multinational firms) and destabilize domestic coalitions and bargains. This dynamic is also associated with the extraterritorial effects of regulatory regimes, as the rules in one jurisdiction (often the US or EU due to their market size) can affect the development of rules in other jurisdictions around the world. Second, globalization creates *opportunity structures* for privileged actors to form cross-national coalitions and exert pressure through new venues (for example, new international organizations or regulatory networks). This can both strengthen or disrupt existing political cleavages and lead to new forms of

coalitional politics. Third, domestic and international institutions unevenly constrain or empower different actors. The resulting *asymmetric power* leads to different strategies for defending domestic institutional arrangements or instead seeking their reform.

Temporal sequencing is central to the specific mechanisms of institutional change within the NIA. More specifically, the timing of institutional change in one jurisdiction can change the bargaining strength and available political strategies in other jurisdictions. For instance, regulators who are the 'first-mover' in an issue area can develop greater expertise and authority, creating an advantage when engaging with their peers in other countries. Alternatively, the development of new rules in other jurisdictions can empower select actors to then seek institutional reforms at home.

Taken together, the NIA draws attention to the strategies of actors, particularly sub-state actors, in ongoing processes of political conflict and institutional change across multiple levels and jurisdictions. While not dismissing the nation-state entirely, the NIA draws attention to a broader set of actors, processes, and questions that are integral to contemporary global political economy. Moreover, the NIA helps reveal the critical role of regulatory capacity—that is, the ability of regulators (as sub-state actors) to create and enforce market rules. Notwithstanding important critiques of the limited applications of the NIA beyond the Global North (Farrell and Newman 2015) and the under-theorization of capitalism and the state within the NIA (Hameiri 2020), the NIA offers an important set of tools for interrogating institutional change within processes of digital globalization.

design' (requiring firms to proactively design products and services to meet GDPR obligations). Perhaps most importantly, the GDPR was also designed with enforcement concerns at the forefront: it requires the creation of national independent data protection authorities who, in collaboration with a European Data Protection Board, can sanction non-compliant firms with fines of up to 20 million euros or 4 per cent of the firm's global revenue from the previous financial year (whichever is higher). The transformative nature of the GDPR led to considerable lobbying and both private and public political conflict. More than 3,000 amendments were introduced during the legislative process. Foreign governments, firms, and business groups sought to weaken the GDPR by reducing the compliance costs and limiting its scope. By comparison, domestic and international civil society organizations sought to strengthen privacy protections and ensure adequate enforcement mechanisms.

Alongside the GDPR, European courts have further expanded the scope of citizens' privacy rights. In contrast to other jurisdictions, where data and privacy are firmly embedded within market discourses and mechanisms (for example, the United States), privacy is situated within Europe's human rights framework (beginning with the 1950 European Convention on Human Rights). Perhaps most famously, Max Schrems, an Austrian lawyer and privacy activist, has been at the centre of multiple judicial challenges to the business practices of technology firms. For example, Schrems successfully challenged both the US–EU Safe Harbour Agreement and its successor, the EU–US Privacy Shield, which were intended to govern transatlantic data transfers (Farrell and Newman 2019a; Bradford 2020). These court challenges have threatened the business models on which Big Tech often relies by contesting (among other things) whether customers' personal data could be used to target advertising. As described in Section 17.2.1, this would fundamentally undermine the ability of platform firms to commodify data and use different types of artificial intelligence to profit from that data.

Compounding the regulatory challenges to technology firms created by the GDPR and European courts, the EU has recently embarked on a wide-ranging overhaul of its regulatory framework. More specifically, the proposed Digital Markets Act (DMA) and Digital Services Act (DSA) will 'represent the furthest reaching expansion of platform regulation in OECD countries to date' (Cioffi et al. 2022: 9). Together, the

DMA and DSA will target platform firms that operate as 'gatekeepers' and specific types of platform behaviours. Although neither act has been finalized nor implemented, it is abundantly clear that technology firms view the DMA and DSA as a significant threat to the status quo. Corporate lobbying has increased dramatically since the initial announcement of the DMA and DSA, including both private advocacy and public campaigns (Lomas 2022). Importantly, this is not to suggest that lobbying by technology firms has been unified; rather, there remain competing interests even among technology firms, leading to diverging regulatory priorities and preferences between firms. Reflecting the dramatically changing landscape, there is even speculation—fuelled in part by company filings with the US Securities and Exchange Commission—that both Facebook and Instagram could exit the European market altogether due to increased compliance costs and data privacy regulations challenging their established business models (Hetzner and Kahn 2022).

Notwithstanding the fluidity of the situation, we are witnessing a rapid shift towards the global harmonization of data and privacy regulation due to the interventions of the EU. Illustrating this point, Bradford (2020: 140) notes how quickly this effect was observed among technology firms after the implementation of the GDPR: 'US Fortune 500 companies had spent approximately $7.8 billion on GDPR compliance by May 2018, averaging $16 million per company. Regardless of the costs involved, many US companies are adjusting their global business practices to reflect European norms, making data privacy one of the most powerful examples of the Brussels Effect'. We can also observe this dynamic through the creation of EU-style data protection standards across Africa, Asia, and Latin America—failure to do so would jeopardize the ability of firms to transfer data between the EU and those jurisdictions. These protections have not come without resistance from other countries; indeed, the US has characterized such protections as disguised protectionism, and there are broader conflicts over data sovereignty and data colonization (see Section 17.3.2). The move to regulate technology firms has also enabled new political strategies for civil society organizations and the creation of cross-national alliances. For example, Jang and Newman (2022) argue that the ability of NGOs to bring third-party complaints under the GDPR enables NGOs to mobilize public attention in new ways and pursue greater enforcement of the GDPR by directly pressuring regulators. The ability of the EU to not only transform the regulation of digital technology internally but also create new global standards is changing how firms operate and how power is distributed among states, firms, and civil society organizations.

KEY POINTS

- The governance of artificial intelligence is fragmented at global and national levels. Intergovernmental organizations, individual countries, firms, and civil society organizations are competing to establish new structures for regulating AI.

- The fragmentation in AI governance creates advantages for firms to seek out weaker regulatory environments or pursue forms of self-regulation.

- The governance of data and privacy is strongly influenced by the European Union. The market size and regulatory capacity of the EU creates pressure on firms and jurisdictions to abide by EU standards.

- To date, multinational technology firms and associated interest groups have been unable to stop the development of new and increasingly stringent technology regulations in the EU.

17.4 The digital transformation of global trade politics

Transformations associated with new digital technologies have profound implications for global labour markets and the structure of international trade. Digitalization and artificial intelligence change the way we work and the types of jobs that are created, resulting in new political cleavages, policy preferences, and political coalitions. Further, the commodification of data (see Section 17.2.1) and the creation of new business models also challenge the rules and institutions that constitute global trade governance. These shifts are intimately connected to the exercise of power in global trade politics and the uneven distribution of benefits and costs from the digital transformation.

17.4.1 Robots, automation, and the reorganization of labour

The increasing sophistication of digital technologies—particularly artificial intelligence and digital communication tools—have combined with the expansion of platform firms to produce fundamental shifts in the organization of labour. In some instances, this has accelerated a longer process of economic dislocation due to automation or introduced new forms of labour (and precarity) through 'gig' work and the 'sharing' economy. Moreover, new types of offshoring are expanding the scope of these processes to include workers and occupations that may have been considered 'safe' a few decades ago. For instance, Baldwin (2019) suggests that the combination of new telecommunications technologies and increasing access to digital infrastructures across the world will enable people to live in one country but work in the office of another—a form of labour called 'telemigration' (see Figure 17.1).

What are the political consequences of these labour market changes? Current research approaches this question in two ways (Gingrich and Kuo 2022). First, the loss of employment or the downgrading in the types of jobs that people hold can spur calls for redistributive policies or greater employment protections. For example, workers concerned with job risks related to digitization may prefer policies designed to slow down the pace of technological change rather than implement new forms of digital protectionism (Gallego et al. 2022). While such 'pocketbook' concerns may partially explain the policy preferences of those affected by automation and digitization, it may also be the case that the loss of relative 'status' among these workers drives support for nationalist appeals (Kurer 2020). Further, workers negatively affected by digital technologies and automation may lack a clear understanding of who (or what) is at fault. For instance, American workers who are at greater risk of job loss due to automation are more likely to oppose free trade and support immigration restrictions (Wu 2021; Guisinger, Chapter 6).

A second change is the political realignments associated with digital disruptions of labour markets. There is some evidence that the realignment can produce new cross-class coalitions. Focusing on those who hold 'routine' occupations—jobs that require well defined and repetitive tasks (for example, bookkeeping)—Thewissen and Rueda (2019: 194) identify 'the possibility of cross-class coalitions in support of a redistributive welfare state between low-wage individuals in nonroutine occupations and high-wage individuals holding routine occupations'. However, as summarized by Gallego and Kurer (2022: 2): 'The most consistent finding of the literature is that those who

Figure 17.1 'Telemigration' and international remote working have changed the way companies recruit employees, broadening the search thanks to the support of new technologies that allow real-time work from distant geographical areas.

Source: Shutterstock.

lose out to technological innovation turn against the political status quo in general and toward the populist radical right in particular'. Such parties have been well positioned in Europe to capitalize on the perceived economic vulnerability created by increasing automation and technological change (Im et al. 2019; Milner 2021). In some ways, this backlash resembles the dynamics associated with globalization and international trade more generally. The benefits of technological innovations are widely distributed in the form of new and/or cheaper products and services. The costs, however, tend to be more concentrated in certain industries and occupations. Importantly, this research suggests that the traditional tools of government for compensating or protecting labour—such as early retirement benefits, labour market regulations, and expanding public services—may have little effect on the growth in support for anti-establishment political parties and right-wing populism (Kurer 2020). In other words, the digital transformation of labour markets may lead to greater support for redistributive or compensatory government policies; nevertheless, enacting these policies will not necessarily prevent political realignments and the emergence of new political cleavages.

In addressing the question of 'who benefits?' in the reorganization of labour markets, it is crucial to also consider how these changes intersect with the gendered (as well as racialized and class-based) performance of labour. Consider, for example, how automation, digitalization, and **telemigration** may have differential effects for men and women in labour markets. On the one hand, women already experience many unique labour market risks, marginalization, and precarity, which may limit the effect of digital disruption on their policy preferences and voting behaviour (Gingrich and Kuo 2022). Yet, as illustrated in Figure 17.2, the gendered composition of labour is far from equal in occupations predicted to be at the greatest risk of offshoring in the near future. While roughly 87 per cent of bookkeeping, accounting, and auditing clerks employed in the United States in 2019 were female, this pattern was nearly reversed for computer support specialists (73 per cent of whom were male). This division extends more broadly to the feminization of digital labour markets associated with digital platforms and the 'gig economy'. As Gregg and Andrijasevic (2019: 3) note, 'Gig work is the flipside of the mythical white, male "brogrammer" or software developer enjoying the comforts and benefits of large multinational tech firms'. The celebration of worker 'flexibility' and the growing number of self-employed contractors (such as those working for ride-hailing apps, food delivery services, or freelance task or project services) often exacerbates the precarity of those employed in these roles and perpetuates the unpaid performance of social reproduction (see Hannah and Hinton, Chapter 4) (see Figure 17.2).

Figure 17.2 Service-Sector Occupations Most Vulnerable to Offshoring. Service-sector occupations predicted to be most vulnerable to offshoring identified by Baldwin and Dingel (2021). Percentages indicate gender composition within occupation. Occupation ordering determined by total employment. Data Source: Data USA (https://datausa.io/)

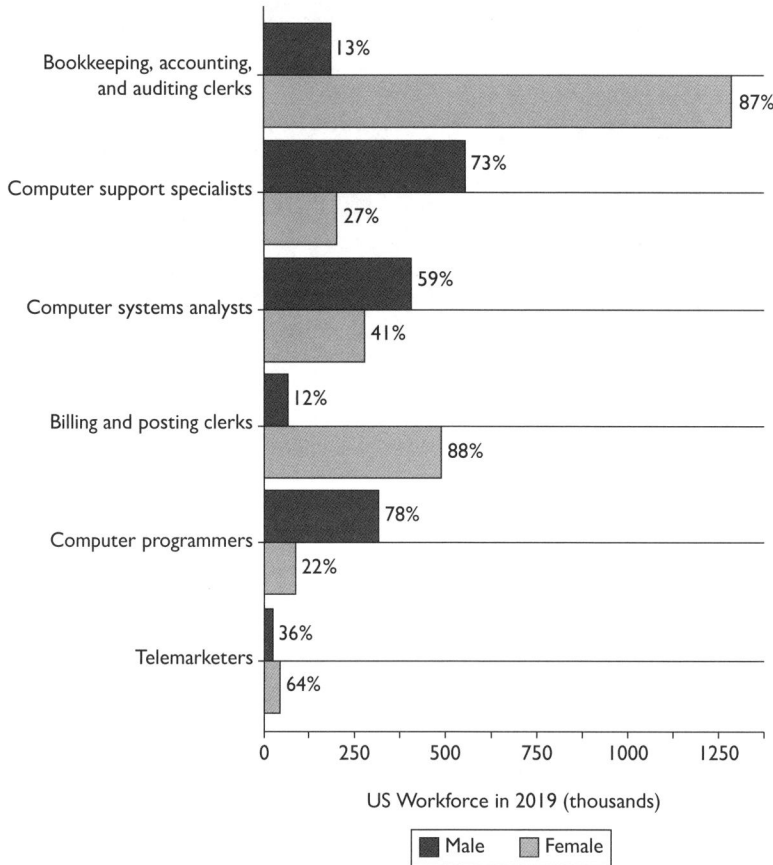

17.4.2 **Integrating digital trade in global trade governance**

In addition to the reorganization of labour, the digitization of trade has deep implications for the structure and politics of global trade governance. According to one estimate from the McKinsey Global institute, cross-border data flows contributed US$2.8 trillion to the global economy in 2014 and were forecast to reach US$11 trillion by 2025 (Meltzer 2019: S28). However, we have also witnessed a backlash to the development of digital trade. Restrictions of cross-border data flows— a new form of digital protectionism—have increased dramatically since 2010. According to one estimate, there are currently 133 restrictions in 104 countries (Weymouth 2023). The expansion of digital trade

has challenged the adequacy of current international arrangements to provide effective governance while also creating new points of conflict between Global North and South states.

A major source of tension is that the World Trade Organization (WTO; the main international institution for the governance of international trade; see Trommer, Chapter 5) does not currently possess the rules or norms for governing digital trade (Meltzer 2019; Weymouth 2023). For instance, the General Agreement on Trade in Services (GATS) was negotiated long before the emergence of modern digital technologies and technology firms. Not only is it often unclear whether digital trade falls under the umbrella of 'goods' or 'services', but it is also unclear if GATS even covers new digital technologies and services (for example, cloud computing). As summarized by Weymouth (2023: 53–54): 'The general consensus is that international rules for digital trade need to be established, and that the WTO is late to the game'.

Central to current debates about the cross-border flow of digital data is a tool known as **data localization**. Data localization requirements can take several forms, including 'measures that do not permit the transfer of data outside national borders; measures that allow cross-border transfers but require a copy to be maintained domestically; and requirements such as to obtain the prior consent of data providers before personal data can be transferred overseas' (Meltzer 2019: S35). These rules directly affect the ability of firms to use cloud computing technologies and services for the cross-border transfer and use of digital data. An example of this is the European GDPR (see Section 17.3.2), which prohibits firms (like Facebook or Google) from transferring the data of European citizens to other jurisdictions *unless* those jurisdictions have equivalent privacy protections. In the absence of an updated trade regime that addresses the specific challenges of digital technologies, efforts to limit data localization requirements have fallen to regional or bilateral agreements (for example, the United States–Mexico–Canada Agreement).

Data localization requirements can be driven by several factors that are not mutually exclusive. Opponents, including firms, free market or free trade interest groups, and negatively affected states, decry data localization as a form of digital protectionism. While data localization can be used to protect domestic firms or industries, it can also be used to secure privacy rights (as in the case of the GDPR) and combat cyber crime. Moreover, the question of 'who benefits from digital data?' has animated increasingly prominent debates over digital sovereignty and new forms of digital colonialism (see Key Theory Box 17.4). Rather than view Global South states as lacking agency in questions of data governance, there is growing evidence of data localization debates as intense sites of contestation and resistance. For instance, several developing countries refused to sign the 2019 G20 declaration on cross-border data flows, India has trumpeted its regulatory model as a template for other countries in the Global South, and some states (for example, Indonesia) have pursued data localization requirements amidst intense US diplomatic pressure and lobbying from Big Tech firms (Hicks 2019). In fact, this resistance to digital colonialism has motivated the development of new

digital ID capitalism models by countries across the Global South. In contrast to data commodification processes led by firms (especially Big Tech), digital ID capitalism refers to a state-driven model of digital data creation, management, and distribution (Hicks 2020).

The impact of technology on global trade governance can also be seen in the adoption of artificial intelligence and blockchain to aid supply chain monitoring. On the one hand, AI is being integrated across industries to improve the efficiency of global supply chains. It does so through more precise forecasting of such factors as consumer demands, equipment maintenance requirements, and traffic and shipping conditions. In addition to the economic payoff for firms, the use of AI in supply chains is also promoted as enhancing the environmental sustainability of global trade by, for example, reducing waste (for example, more efficient transportation routes) and preventing accidents (for example, spills due to equipment failure). Yet this may not only significantly oversell the extent to which AI contributes to sustainability goals, but also help firms resist more transformative measures to improve sustainability by reducing the costs associated with current business practices (Dauvergne 2020). On the other hand, blockchain has been increasingly promoted as a tool for improving supply chain monitoring and governance (see Everyday GPE Box 17.5). In particular, the features of blockchain appear ideally suited for the task: a decentralized, transparent accounting of each link in the supply chain. However, this too may oversell the transformative potential of blockchain for improving issues like sustainability and labour rights, since these tools ultimately reinforce existing forms of private and market-based governance (Bernards et al. 2020: 525): '[B]lockchain applications for supply chain governance leave market-based forms of governance rooted in "disclosure" and soft standards largely intact, both in terms of the actors involved and the standards being enforced'.

17.5 Technological disruption in global finance

Perhaps one of the most visible manifestations of the digital revolution is found in the changing nature of financial markets. This change is not simply the shift towards greater use of digital services by retail banks and remittance networks; rather, the emergence of financial technology (FinTech) and Big Tech firms

KEY THEORY BOX 17.4 DIGITAL COLONIALISM

To what extent can processes of data commodification and digital transformation be separated from historical and ongoing systems of colonial dominance? While critical theories of global political economy offer important insights into the extractive logics of capitalism and digital technologies, recent work aims to recentre analyses within the historical evolution of colonial economic systems. In so doing, a new framework of digital colonialism (Couldry and Mejias 2019; Kwet 2019; Couldry and Mejias 2021) helps to expand our understanding of the relationship between digital technology, colonialism, and capitalism.

The structure of the global digital economy is argued to reinforce the dominance of Western states and technology firms in three major ways (Pinto 2018). First, Western states and firms possess extensive control over physical digital resources (for example, hardware, servers, and data) and human capital (for example, experts in information technology, advanced research institutions). Second, the financial capital required to fund technological research and development is heavily concentrated among Western states and firms. Third, the international and domestic legal architecture strongly favours Western states and firms and inhibits the development of domestic industry in the Global South. This is accomplished through such tools as existing (for example, the WTO Agreement on Trade-Related Aspects of Intellectual Property Rights) and new (for the example, the Trans-Pacific Partnership) trade agreements.

These features of the global digital economy combine to reinforce the economic dominance of Big Tech and Western states. Indeed, Western technology firms may become the sole provider of digital infrastructure, products, and services in Global South states. In turn, this enables data commodification and the extraction of value from Global South populations en masse, as well as the accumulation of profits among a concentrated group of firms. This process of accumulation by dispossession is intimately connected to colonial systems of oppression.

Situating technology firms and Western states within the framework of digital colonialism also helps to reveal sites of resistance and contestation throughout the world. For instance, movements to promote the development and use of open-source software provide an important alternative

for digital technology users. Such movements seek to counter the network effects and the opportunities for data extraction on which the business models of Western technology firms depend. Resistance is also found in the development of state technology policies that deliberately seek to protect citizens' fundamental rights while fostering local research and development. Finally, activists, civil society organizations, and policymakers are contesting the ideologies that legitimate the extraction, surveillance, and exploitation that constitute contemporary digital colonialism to create a more just digital society.

The digital colonialism framework sheds new light on the asymmetric power relations and systems of exploitation that are deeply intertwined with digital globalization. There are important opportunities for further development of the digital colonialism framework, especially with respect to South–South imperialism (given the potential reach of Chinese Big Tech firms like Baidu, Alibaba, and Tencent; Kwet, 2019), the uneven development of data colonialism across the Global South, and advocacy for Indigenous data sovereignty within settler-colonial states (Walter et al. 2021) (see Figure 17.3).

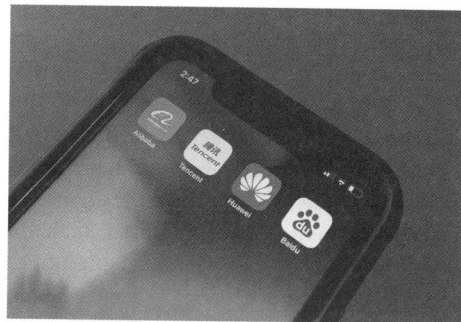

Figure 17.3 Baidu, Alibaba, and Tencent (also known as BAT) are three leading Chinese internet companies focused on e-commerce, search, and games and instant messaging, respectively.

Source: Shutterstock

as competitors to traditional financial service providers and the creation of (and growing interest in) cryptocurrencies have upset the status quo in global finance. This section builds on earlier chapters (Helleiner, Chapter 8; Clarke and Roberts, Chapter 10)

by unpacking the connections between the key components of the digital transformation—data commodification, cloud computing, artificial intelligence, and blockchain—and the changing political cleavages and regulatory conflicts in finance.

EVERYDAY GPE BOX 17.5 BLOCKCHAIN AND THE GLOBAL COFFEE TRADE

In 2018, Coda Coffee Co (Denver, US) unveiled what was marketed as the world's first blockchain-traced coffee (Comunicaffe 2018; Phillips 2018). In coordination with bext360, a Denver-based technology firm that provides digital technology solutions for monitoring global supply chains, Coda Coffee Co customers were able to scan a QR code on the coffee bags in Denver and instantly see a record of its journey from the original coffee beans in Uganda. This was made possible by the adaptation of blockchain technology. Blockchain is perhaps most famous for its use in cryptocurrency, but ultimately provides a digital and decentralized accounting system. In the context of global coffee supply chains, the use of blockchain provided a transparent record of the supply chain that produced the coffee on the shelves of Coda Coffee Co. In practical terms, this required Great Lakes Coffee (a coffee exporter in Uganda) to install a new machine provided by bext360 (called the 'bextmachine') at the washing stations on its farms. The machine evaluated the coffee cherries and produced a special blockchain token that was used to record the farmer's identity, the characteristics of the coffee cherries, and (ultimately) each step of the commodity through the supply chain.

This example provides a brief glimpse into the complex relationship between the consumption decisions of everyday individuals (in this case, their coffee purchases), private governance, global supply chains, and digital technology.

Advocates of the use of blockchain in global supply chains point to its potential to improve supply chain monitoring in a way that not only reduces firm costs, but also strengthens private fair trade certification regimes. While not a panacea, this use of blockchain might ultimately contribute to more equitable and sustainable coffee supply chains.

However, there are also ways in which this characterization of the impact of blockchain misses key power dynamics. In particular, the digital surveillance of global supply chains may also contribute to the undermining of labour standards in Global South countries and a misperception that the problems associated with the digital transformation are unique to the Global North. As Atal (2022) points out, the costs of using these new technologies are largely borne by suppliers in the Global South (who, in turn, cut the wages of labourers). This can exacerbate market concentration in global supply chains as only those firms that can afford to implement these technologies are able to participate in associated certification programs. Further, the adoption of such surveillance technologies within global supply chains has enabled workplace surveillance techniques that often pre-date similar systems in the 'gig economies' of the Global North. Taking these dynamics into account illuminates a far more complicated picture of the transformative potential of digital technologies that underpin the purchase of a cup of coffee.

KEY POINTS

- Digital disruptions to labour markets have resulted in new types of economic precarity, which often exacerbate existing racial and gendered inequalities, and new types of political cleavages and coalitions.

- The existing architecture of global trade governance may be poorly suited to overseeing the expansion of digital trade.

- Efforts to limit cross-border data flows through data localization policies have created new trade conflicts between the Global North and South.

- By extracting value (and profits) from data generated by people throughout the Global South, the practices of Big Tech firms are characterized by some as part of a new form of digital colonialism.

17.5.1 **FinTech and Big Tech**

Both FinTech and Big Tech firms are challenging existing business models and structures in global finance. FinTech is a catch-all term for technologies and technology firms that seek to disrupt traditional financial services. The range of activities encompassed by FinTech firms is extensive, including nearly everything from electronic payments to applications for credit to retail investing and cryptocurrency exchanges. Moreover, FinTech firms can be organized around a traditional business-to-customer model (for example, providing a digital bank account or payment service) or, alternatively, mirror the platform model seen in Big Tech (for example, peer-to-peer lending) (Langley and Leyshon 2021). Unlike smaller FinTech firms, Big Tech typically benefits from massive captive consumer bases, enormous cash reserves, and established expertise in digital innovation. In a speech delivered to a conference on regulating Big Tech, Agustín Carstens (General Manager, Bank for International Settlements) remarked that 'big techs were virtually non-existent in financial services only a decade ago', yet they control 94 per cent of mobile payments in China (Carstens 2021). By 2019, the combined global credit volume of FinTech and Big Tech was nearly US$800 billion, the majority of which was controlled by Big

Tech firms (Cornelli et al. 2021). Importantly, much of the 'credit boom' is found in areas outside of the Global North, particularly in Asia and Africa.

There are several factors that may give FinTech and Big Tech firms a competitive advantage over established financial institutions (Vives 2019). First, technology firms benefit from dramatically reduced personnel and infrastructure costs. Unlike traditional financial institutions, which are typically organized around extensive branch networks to reach customers, technology firms instead rely on mobile phones and other electronic devices to provide digital products and services. Moreover, these firms are better able to adapt to and adopt new technologies in the absence of legacy information and technology systems. Second, and relatedly, technology firms are often better equipped to reach individuals and businesses that have historically been excluded from retail services, which allows these firms to benefit from and contribute to the global financial inclusion agenda. Especially in contexts outside of the Global North, this has led to a rapid increase in financial inclusion. Third, technology firms can capture, manage, and use digital financial data at a massive scale. This is especially the case for Big Tech, who can combine customers' financial data with data collected from other services. Using cloud computing and artificial intelligence, technology firms can more precisely target their products and services to individual customers (for example, by tailoring the interest rates on credit products to the specific individual). In short, the network effects and market concentration that have been integral to the rise of digital technology firms in the global economy more generally provide similar advantages as these firms enter global finance.

Notwithstanding these advantages, the evidence for the realized disruption by FinTech and Big Tech firms is mixed. On the one hand, FinTech firms have experienced rapid growth and investment over the past decade, and regulators have facilitated the disruptive efforts of technology firms in several ways. According to some estimates, the total amount invested in Fin-Tech since 2015 is more than US$500 billion (Shrier and Pentland 2022: 7). Especially in the contexts of digital payments and digital lending, a variety of FinTech firms have experienced rapid growth. Stripe, an online payment processing FinTech, has a market valuation of nearly US$100 billion and processed more than US$640 billion in payments in 2021 alone (Wilhelm 2022). As highlighted at the beginning of this section, the growth of both FinTech and Big Tech firms in global finance has increasingly attracted the attention of national and global regulators.

Notwithstanding these disruptive achievements, there are two major reasons to contest the 'success story'. First, both FinTech and Big Tech firms are often integrated into—rather than displacing—or work with incumbent firms. For example, robo-advisors (digital platforms that use algorithms to replace human financial advisor services) were once viewed as a FinTech innovation that would revolutionize asset management and retail investment services. Indeed, a 2016 Deloitte report speculated that the assets under management (AUM) for robo-advisory services would surpass US$16 trillion by 2025—more than three times larger than the AUM for BlackRock, the largest asset manager in the world (Deloitte Consulting 2016). But instead of broadly displacing incumbent wealth management services, successful robo-advisors have often been purchased by incumbent firms and integrated within existing services (Rosenbaum 2022).

Focusing further on the effects of and governance by financial technologies, the second reason to question the 'success story' is how such digital technologies can reinforce existing structures of power and exploitation. The shift from traditional models of lending to either peer-to-peer platform models or models that rely on algorithms to make lending decisions has perpetuated many of the same types of credit discrimination that have long existed in global finance while also exacerbating over-indebtedness throughout the world (Clarke 2019). Indeed, a growing body of research provides clear evidence that these platforms perpetuate different forms of gender and racial discrimination in lending across a variety of contexts. In a process described by Friedline (2021) as 'digital redlining', the discriminatory and exclusionary effects of FinTech can mirror historical redlining practices (where Black and Brown consumers were deliberately excluded from the mortgage lending market). The consequence of digital redlining is to increase the costs of financial services for historically marginalized communities and reinforce racial and geographic segregation in digital markets.

From a regulatory perspective, there has often been broad support for the technological disruption of finance across jurisdictions. Firms, business associations, and think tanks regularly participate in benchmarking exercises to jointly produce global rankings of the most 'innovative' and 'supportive'

FinTech jurisdictions (for example, the Global Fintech Index produced by Findexable). One illustration of the extent to which governments are actively encouraging FinTech is the creation of regulatory 'sandboxes'. These regulatory tools allow qualifying firms to avoid particular regulations (for example, an otherwise necessary licence) in order to have greater freedom in the development and testing of new products and services. While countries like the United Kingdom and Singapore have been praised as 'pioneers' for their efforts (Brett 2017), this rosy depiction may obscure who exercises power in these arrangements and how risks are conceptualized and managed. Brown and Piroska (2021) highlight the many ways in which the input of financial experts is privileged over other societal groups and the manner in which 'sandboxes' serve as a form of 'riskwashing', thereby masking the extent of and control over financial risks. Despite concerns about market competition, data governance, and financial stability, national regulators and global standard setting bodies have also broadly embraced policy experimentation to manage the entrance of Big Tech into global finance rather than seeking to interrupt this process. For example, the extreme concentration of cloud computing services for financial institutions (four Big Tech firms provide almost two thirds of global cloud computing services) has sparked considerable debate about the adequacy of existing regulatory frameworks, but not more direct forms of state intervention.

The promotion of FinTech has also coincided with the development of the global financial inclusion agenda. Along with other new entrants to financial markets, such as telecommunications firms offering new types of mobile money, FinTech firms have contributed to the ambiguity of the global agenda while seeking to shape it in favourable ways (Girard 2021). Indeed, the promotion of FinTech (and financial inclusion more generally) often defies monolithic accounts, as broader societies can exercise considerable agency in the development and use of these digital technologies (Singh 2019). However, in many contexts, intense lobbying by incumbent firms and potential regulatory capture is viewed as a key barrier to the disruptive potential of FinTech firms (Shrier and Pentland 2022). These political conflicts between banks, technology firms, FinTech firms, telecommunications firms, and regulators mark a distinct shift in the regulatory politics of finance. Moreover, the data commodification and extraction associated with FinTech and the financial inclusion agenda has also raised concerns about

the extension of digital financialization and the coercive role of the state (Jain and Gabor 2020).

17.5.2 Cryptocurrency

After more than a decade of development and promotion as a type of fringe finance, cryptocurrencies arguably reached a tipping point by 2021–2022. Beginning in early 2021, the value of Bitcoin increased dramatically, reaching highs of nearly US$70,000 per Bitcoin. By November 2021, cryptocurrency markets hit an all-time high of US$2.9 trillion (Singh 2022). Cryptocurrency television advertisements frequently featured major celebrity endorsements, and high-profile social media influencers promoted a range of cryptocurrency investment opportunities. Even the world's biggest institutional investors (such as BlackRock) began pouring money into crypto markets (Wintermeyer 2021). These developments have required national regulators and global standard-setting bodies to reconsider the adequacy of regulatory frameworks and traditional understandings of finance.

Cryptocurrencies use blockchain (see Section 17.2.1) to produce a form of private money, creating a digital manifestation of libertarian ideas about currency that can be traced to Frederich Hayek (Campbell-Verduyn 2018a). The first cryptocurrency, called Bitcoin, was created by an anonymous individual (known as Satoshi Nakamoto) in 2008 amidst the global financial crisis. Bitcoin provided users with a decentralized, peer-to-peer system of record-keeping and transacting. According to proponents, this would dramatically reduce (or eliminate) the role of governments and central banks in financial markets. In short, Bitcoin (and cryptocurrencies more generally) operate as a type of digital currency without centralized political control. The initial popularity of Bitcoin spurred the creation of other types of cryptocurrencies, which are often referred to as **altcoins**. Cryptocurrencies can vary in terms of their particular features, such as the specific rules they use to construct the blockchain (for example, the 'consensus protocols') or the use of 'smart contracts' to automatically execute the terms of a contract using an algorithm. Further, some cryptocurrencies (known as **stablecoins**) are designed such that their value is fixed to a different asset (for example, the US dollar). For example, the commonly used Tether stablecoin can theoretically be exchanged for 1 US dollar at any time. Consequently, stablecoins bear many similarities to fixed exchange rate systems (see Helleiner, Chapter 8).

Perhaps *the* central challenge to regulating cryptocurrency markets is definitional: is cryptocurrency appropriately regulated as a *currency* or as an *asset*? This is not a trivial question. To properly function as a currency, Bitcoin (and other cryptocurrencies) must provide a medium of exchange, a store of value, and a unit of account (see Figure 17.4). In other words, currencies must facilitate transactions, hold their value over time, and provide a common valuation of exchanged goods or services. The combination of wild fluctuations in value and cumbersome and costly transaction platforms have thus far undermined the claims that cryptocurrency is the currency of the future. Of course, this has not hindered its rise in popularity, or even stopped politicians from experimenting with formally integrating cryptocurrencies into national economies (see Case Study Box 17.6).

Figure 17.4 Bitcoin, as the most established cryptocurrency, had a great impact on global finance and trade and the establishment of traditional currencies.

Source: Shutterstock.

CASE STUDY BOX 17.6 BITCOIN IN EL SALVADOR

On 7 September 2021, El Salvador became the first country in the world to make Bitcoin legal tender. This meant that Bitcoin had the same legal status as the US dollar (since the US dollar is used in lieu of a national currency in El Salvador) and that all payments—including those between customers and businesses or even tax payments to the government—could be conducted using Bitcoin. All it required was a smartphone and an internet connection.

The decision was not without controversy. For example, both the International Monetary Fund and the World Bank expressed scepticism and even rejected requests from El Salvador to assist with the implementation of the policy (BBC News 2021). Among Bitcoin supporters, making Bitcoin legal tender was a widely celebrated step towards greater legitimation of Bitcoin (and other cryptocurrencies) as *currencies*.

What factors drove this decision by the government? In short, the answer is remittances, financial inclusion, and the reliance on the US dollar (Arslanian et al. 2021). First, El Salvador relies heavily on international remittances (money sent home from family and friends living outside of the country); in fact, remittances constitute roughly 20 per cent of El Salvador's gross domestic product (GDP) (BBC News 2021). Bitcoin could potentially reduce many of the costs associated with remittances. Second, Bitcoin could improve financial inclusion in El Salvador. As many people in El Salvador do not have access to formal financial services, Bitcoin (and associated cryptocurrency wallets) may help

address this problem. Third, widespread adoption of Bitcoin would reduce the country's reliance on the US dollar as the only medium of exchange.

While the full effects of the decision remain to be seen, there are early indications that it has not only failed to incentivize wider adoption and use of Bitcoin within El Salvador, but it has also laid bare the key flaws of cryptocurrencies as *currencies*. Media coverage shared stories of everyday people possessing little understanding of cryptocurrency, struggling to use the Bitcoin wallet developed by the government (called 'Chivo'), and losing interest due to wild fluctuations in the price of Bitcoin (McDonald 2022). The limited adoption of Bitcoin as a currency has been corroborated by academic studies of the new policy. For example, Alvarez et al. (2022) conducted a nationally representative survey of individuals in El Salvador to assess Bitcoin's usage and effects in the broader population. Despite being heavily promoted by the government, including a significant financial incentive for adopting the Chivo wallet (US$30, equivalent to 0.7 per cent of annual income per capita), approximately 40 per cent of all Chivo wallet downloads occurred in September 2021 and virtually no downloads were recorded in the first two months of 2022. Further, there was little evidence of widespread use of Bitcoin for remittances or day-to-day transactions. While El Salvador and other national (and sub-national) governments continue to experiment with cryptocurrencies as currencies, the evidence thus far points to a far more limited role for cryptocurrency than that envisioned by its early promoters.

As a result, the governance of cryptocurrencies has often been situated within existing financial regulations—notwithstanding tremendous variation across countries (Hammond and Ehret 2022)—and remains a point of intense conflict between and among policymakers, interest groups, and investors.

The ambiguity and risk of cryptocurrency was further revealed as cryptocurrencies (and businesses involved in promoting or facilitating cryptocurrencies) experienced widespread devaluations in 2022 and 2023. Perhaps most famously, FTX (a cryptocurrency exchange worth US$40 billion) collapsed in November 2022, and a cofounder is awaiting trial for fraud (Lawson 2023). Indeed, the collapse of FTX was likened to a 'Lehman Brothers moment' for the cryptocurrency industry (see Pauly, Chapter 9). We can also see important elements of the fallout through celebrity endorsements of cryptocurrency (see Everyday GPE Box 10.6). In the aftermath of the devaluations, many of the same celebrities faced lawsuits for their role in promoting 'unregistered securities' (Redbord 2023).

While states may have been slow to respond to the development of cryptocurrency markets, that is not to suggest that states are unable to assert their authority in this domain. Consider, for example, the rise and fall of Facebook's stablecoin experiment called Diem (originally Libra). Launched in 2019 with initial support from a wide range of firms, including Visa, Mastercard, Lyft, and Spotify, Diem was envisioned as a US dollar-backed stablecoin that could be used to conduct payments globally (Gooding 2022). Yet, widely reported regulator hostility effectively ended the experiment before its official launch. The reasons behind this opposition were extensive, ranging from Facebook's repeated failures to adequately address user privacy concerns and misinformation, to fears that the size and reach of Facebook could enable Diem to challenge US-dollar primacy, to concerns over potential bank run risks if reserves were inadequate (BBC News 2022; Gooding 2022). Regardless of whether each individual concern was well grounded, the result was a reassertion of state power over cryptocurrency development and Big Tech's foray into global finance.

KEY POINTS

- FinTech and Big Tech firms are forcing incumbent financial institutions to adapt their products and services and policymakers to adapt their regulatory frameworks.

- Globally, FinTech, and Big Tech have drawn support from policymakers in part due to their ability to facilitate greater financial inclusion.

- Despite the growing popularity of cryptocurrencies in mainstream markets, there is limited evidence for their success as a currency.

- Especially in the aftermath of widespread cryptocurrency devaluations in 2022–2023, regulators are increasingly attuned to the risks posed by cryptocurrencies as financial assets.

17.6 Conclusion

This chapter examines the digital transformation of the global economy. Through the emergence of new technologies—cloud computing, artificial intelligence, and blockchain—and the commodification of data at massive scales, new business models and technology firms are disrupting traditional social, political, and economic relations. In turn, scholars have developed new analytical tools and concepts to explain the resulting shift in power and the creation of new political cleavages and coalitions. Given how new digital technologies and technology firms link together multiple domains in the global economy, this chapter demonstrates how a broad view is required to understand the interwoven points of political conflict.

To unpack the digital transformation, this chapter explores three distinct but related areas. First, the governance of artificial intelligence remains fragmented at the national and global levels, but the European Union has emerged as a global standard setter in data and privacy governance due to its regulatory capacity and political entrepreneurship. Second, the digital transformation has introduced new forms of labour relations and sources of conflict in global trade governance, which have often exacerbated the precarity of labour and geopolitical conflict between the Global North and Global South. Third, the entrance of FinTech and Big Tech firms into global finance, along with the mainstreaming of cryptocurrency, has created new types of financial risk and power relations among regulators, firms, and interest groups.

From the perspective of incumbent firms and regulators, these changes have often required extensive adaptation. Technology firms have been adept at navigating in 'grey spaces' of old regulatory frameworks and masking their market and political power under the guise of innovation, convenience, and solutionism.

Moreover, historically marginalized communities in both the Global North and Global South have often borne the costs of this disruption through more precarious forms of labour, greater surveillance, and different types of algorithmic discrimination. Far from a panacea, the digital transformation has instead amplified many political and economic inequalities and divisions. However, from the perspective of technology firms, there are early indicators of a shift towards re-embedding technology in society through the regulatory power of the state. For students of global political economy, the digital transformation is a defining feature of the contemporary global economy. Interrogating these changes will be vital to identifying the conditions for greater global cooperation and the creation of more equitable digital economies.

17.7 QUESTIONS

1. How do multinational technology firms benefit from network effects and why does this matter for the structure of markets?

2. Should we treat data like other types of commodities (for example, oil)?

3. What is cloud computing and why is it central to the politics of data localization?

4. What are the main differences between the global regulation of artificial intelligence and the global regulation of data and privacy?

5. How do digital technologies affect different types of workers? Why does this matter for understanding political responses?

6. What is digital offshoring and why might it affect men and women differently?

7. Are 'FinTech' and 'Big Tech' firms likely to replace banks?

8. Are cryptocurrencies assets or currencies? Why? Does the classification matter?

9. To what extent has the development of 'Big Tech' changed who has power in the global economy?

17.8 FURTHER READING

Atal, M. R. (2021), 'The Janus Faces of Silicon Valley', *Review of International Political Economy*, 28/2: 336–350. Provides an insightful overview of the many identities that large, multinational technology firms hold simultaneously and how this 'shape shifting' helps mitigate efforts to constrain their power.

Baldwin, R. (2019), *The Globotics Upheaval: Globalization, Robotics, and the Future of Work* (Oxford: Oxford University Press). A provocative account of how digital technologies are reshaping the global economy and the potential political consequences of these changes.

Campbell-Verduyn, M. (ed.) (2018a), *Bitcoin and Beyond: Cryptocurrencies, Blockchains, And Global Governance* (New York: Routledge). An edited volume that unpacks the many ways in which new digital technologies, especially cryptocurrencies and blockchain, intersect with global governance.

Cioffi, J. W., Kenney, M. F., and Zysman, J. (2022), 'Platform Power and Regulatory Politics: Polanyi for the Twenty-First Century', *New Political Economy*, 27/2: 1–17. An assessment of the rise of platform firms and the political response through the lens of a 'Polanyian' double-movement, with a particular emphasis on the regulatory reforms in the European Union.

Culpepper, P. D., and Thelen, K. (2020), 'Are We All Amazon Primed? Consumers and the Politics of Platform Power', *Comparative Political Studies*, 53/2: 288–318. Theorizes a new type of business power—platform power—that differs from structural or instrumental power and helps to explain the unique political influence of platform firms.

Friedline, T. (2021), *Banking on a Revolution: Why Financial Technology Won't Save a Broken System* (Oxford: Oxford University Press). A detailed account of the 'everyday' consequences of new financial technologies, including their limited capacity to disrupt financial systems and their role in ongoing processes of racialized exploitation.

Gallego, A., and Kurer, T. (2022), 'Automation, Digitalization, and Artificial Intelligence in the Workplace: Implications for Political Behavior', *Annual Review of Political Science*, 25: 463–484. A broad review of contemporary research on how changes in digital technology in the workplace affect various types of political behaviour.

Li, W. Y. (2023), 'Regulatory Capture's Third Face of Power', *Socio-Economic Review*, mwad002: 1–29. An empirically rich and theoretically nuanced examination of how technology industry lobbyists helped create the idea of 'digital trade' and reshaped trade policy in their interests.

Srivastava, S. (2023), 'Algorithmic Governance and the International Politics of Big Tech', *Perspectives on Politics*, 21/3: 989–1000. An incisive account of how the emergence of 'Big Tech' and algorithmic governance intersects with the study of authority and state-corporate relations.

Weymouth, S. (2023), *Digital Globalization* (Cambridge: Cambridge University Press). An agenda-setting and accessible overview of digital globalization, with an emphasis on cross-border data flows, digital trade, and policy responses.

CONTRIBUTOR NOTE

Tyler Girard is an Assistant Professor in the Department of Political Science at Purdue University. His work broadly explores the political economy of digital technologies and the promotion of global norms and agendas. His research is published in such journals as the *American Political Science Review* and the *Review of International Political Economy*, among others.

Glossary

Absolute advantage Where a country produces one or more goods or services at lower cost than other countries.

Absolute inequality A way of measuring changes in inequality that compares the difference in income, in dollar terms, between two segments of the distribution over time.

Adverse incorporation A concept used to analyse how processes of social and economic inclusion shape the experiences of marginalized groups. Rather than solely focusing on exclusion, it highlights the negative or 'adverse' impacts of people's incorporation into economic and social systems.

Algorithmic governance The use of algorithms—a set of computational instructions or procedures to perform a specific task—as a distinct tool in governance processes.

Altcoins Any type of cryptocurrency that is not Bitcoin.

American Civil War Fought between the Union armies of the North and the Confederate armies of the South, the latter representing the states that had seceded from the Union over the Federal Government's insistence that slavery would not be permitted in expanded territories to the West; it lasted for four years from 1861 to 1865.

Anti-Corn Law League Founded in 1836, but becoming a nationwide movement in 1838, it showcased the new phenomenon of middle-class political campaigning in early Victorian Britain; its activities were specifically against the Corn Laws, the system of price protection for agricultural produce that a parliament of landowners had instituted in its own interest.

Artificial intelligence Any technology designed to reproduce high-order levels of human intelligence.

Asset-based welfare This concept describes the ways in which certain countries, primarily the Anglo (or English-speaking) countries, but also some European and East Asian countries, have promoted the individual accumulation of assets (such as houses, stocks, bonds, financial securities, pension plans, and more) to sustain economic and social development, with supporters claiming this fosters personal responsibility and poverty reduction, while opponents contend it transfers responsibilities to citizens, reinforces inequalities, and contributes to excessive household debt.

Assetization At the most general level, 'assetization' refers to the process of turning 'things' (for example, knowledge, data, nature, etc.) into 'assets'—something that grants the owner some type of economic benefit thereafter.

Austerity In the context of neoliberal-led development, austerity refers to reductions in social welfare and government spending. It is a fundamental logic of neoliberal governance which characterizes contemporary global politics.

Balance of payments An account of a country's transactions with foreign countries and international institutions in a specific period. Transactions are divided into current account, which consists of the balance of trade in goods and services plus profits and interest on overseas assets less those paid to foreign owners of domestic assets, plus net transfers such as worker remittances, and the capital account, which consists of inflows and outflows of money for investment, and for grants and loans (and their repayment). The balance of payments is an accounting identity: the entries in the account should sum to zero with, for example, any imbalances on the current account being offset by net movements of capital.

Bank for International Settlements (BIS) Set up in 1930 and located in Basel, Switzerland, the BIS facilitates financial relations and policymaking among many of the world's central banks.

Beggar thy neighbour An economic policy that benefits one country at the expense of others, often through protectionist measures or currency devaluation.

Belt and Road Initiative (BRI) A large-scale infrastructure and development project led by China, aiming to enhance connectivity and economic cooperation between Asia, Europe, and Africa through the construction of networks of roads, railways, ports, and other infrastructure projects.

Birth-right lottery Political theorist Ayelet Shachar's term for the observation that life chances are distributed randomly on the basis of citizenship.

Bloc diplomacy The ability to build coalitions and to present a singular position in negotiations to apply pressure.

Blockchain Blockchain combines digital encryption technologies with algorithms to enable permanent record-keeping among a decentralized network of users.

Bound rates The WTO works by requiring member states to bind their tariffs and subsidies at specific levels. They are free to apply lower rates, but cannot exceed the bound rates. Over time, negotiations reduce the bound rates and thereby reduce trade barriers.

Bourgeois Related to the bourgeoisie, middle-class people who were spared the hardship of labouring during a time of largely subsistence wages, and were usually assumed to have materialistic values that were satisfied through the labour of others.

Bretton Woods The site of the 1944 United Nations Monetary and Financial Conference (the Mount Washington Hotel in the New Hampshire village of Bretton Woods). This conference marked the birth of the IMF and the World Bank. 'Bretton Woods' is often used as shorthand for post-war international financial regimes.

Capital accumulation In Marxist and critical political economy, capital accumulation refers to the ability of capitalists to profit through the exploitation of workers. Capitalists maximize their wealth by continually reinvesting their profits back into the means of production to increase output and productivity.

Capital controls Restrictions placed by governments on private actors moving funds into or out of the territories they control.

Capital mobility A situation that is the financial equivalent to free trade where an absence of capital controls allows financial investments (capital) to be mobile across different political jurisdictions.

Carbon colonialism The shifting of the responsibility to lower emissions onto actors and communities in the Global South; thereby allowing actors in the Global North to delay and avoid the aggressive emission reductions that historical responsibility requires.

Carrying trade Profit-making strategies focused on merchants transporting goods other people have made to where their customer base is located.

Central bank digital currencies A digital payment instrument denominated in the national unit of account, which is a direct liability of the central bank.

China shock The impact of rising Chinese exports on manufacturing employment in the United States and Europe after China's accession to the World Trade Organization in 2001 being concentrated in local labour markets.

Cloud computing The provision of computing infrastructures and resources (for example, data storage, analytics, etc.), through the Internet ('the cloud').

Cobdenite A political position involving passionate endorsement of free trade, named after the Anti-Corn Law League's founder, Richard Cobden.

Coercive diplomacy Involves leveraging economic measures, strategic pressure, or threats to influence the behaviour or policies of other states' markets without resorting to direct military action, aiming to achieve its geopolitical or economic objectives.

Colonial contract A series of formal and informal institutions established by colonizing powers that legitimated European dominance in the colonies, including economic practices intended to induce dependency of the colony on the metropole by restricting trade and manufacturing.

Colonial trade Refers to a system of trade established under colonial relationships between the imperial country and its dependent territories overseas. It typically entails the exchange of primary products obtained in the colonies and manufactured and industrial products obtained in the imperial country. As a central mechanism of the colonial economy, colonial trade encouraged the industrial development of the imperial countries. Following the decolonization movement, many former imperial countries maintained the colonial trade preference system on which colonial trade was, in part, based.

Commodification Highlights processes of enclosure and privatization within a capitalist society as a prerequisite for the buying and selling of commodities. Under capitalism, access to many of the things required for human survival is mediated through market relations and contingent on one's ability to pay for them.

Common pool of resources Goods that cannot be withheld from those that do not pay for them, and whose consumption comes at the expense of other potential consumers.

Comparative advantage Where a country is relatively more efficient at producing at least one product vis-à-vis others, even though it may lack absolute advantage in producing that good or service. Production according to comparative advantage enables specialization in relatively more efficient production, thereby increasing aggregate levels of economic welfare.

Comparative disadvantage The inability of a state to produce a good more efficiently than another state due to scarcity of resources or technological disadvantage.

Competitive advantages The competitive strength of an economy that derives from the capacity of its firms in various sectors. Whether government intervention can enhance an economy's competitive advantage remains a matter of considerable controversy.

Conditionality The stipulation by lenders of conditions that borrowers must meet if they are to continue to receive instalments of their loans.

Continuum of unfreedom A range from decent work to the most extreme forms of exploitation and abuse.

Coordination games A type of game that typically has multiple Nash Equilibria, some of which are more preferred by one or more players.

Corporate social responsibility (CSR) Typically defined as a business model whereby companies integrate social and environmental concerns into their business operations and interactions with stakeholders. This is contrasted with a business model that only prioritizes financial profit.

Cosmopolitanism A theory of justice that argues that we owe all fellow human beings an equal duty in virtue of our shared humanity and that the demands of justice do not depend on race, gender, nationality, or other shared characteristics.

Cryptocurrencies Cryptocurrencies use blockchain to produce a form of private money, which provides users with a decentralized, peer-to-peer system of record-keeping and transacting.

Currency pegs Refers to fixed exchange rate regimes in which a country's currency is tied or 'pegged' to another currency or a specific value, typically maintained through central bank interventions.

Current account payments *See* **balance of payments**.

Customs unions Agreements between two or more countries to trade freely between themselves, and to adopt a common tariff on imports from countries outside the customs union.

Data localization Data localization laws can take different forms, but often require companies to domestically store and process the digital data they collect from people. These laws restrict the cross-border transfer of data and can be viewed as a type of digital protectionism.

Debtfare states Debtfare is a social structure in which fundamental necessities like housing, education, and healthcare are increasingly commodified, necessitating indebtedness for access, rather than being universally provided as essential public goods.

Debt Trap Diplomacy A foreign policy strategy of making loans to developing countries with the intention of gaining strategic advantages or exerting influence over them when they cannot repay.

Decolonization An intellectual strategy with two dimensions: first, to demonstrate that Europe was not the source of all global knowledge; second, to demonstrate that the knowledge that was generated during the European Enlightenment was shot through with often unacknowledged assumptions about the 'normality' of empire.

Denomination rents Economic benefits or profits that arise from having control over the issuance or denomination of a particular currency.

Dialectical A method of reasoning or argumentation that involves examining and reconciling different and/or contradictory points of view.

Digital ID capitalism A specific model of data generation and commercial exploitation whereby state agencies create digital data through state services and work with businesses to commercialize the data.

Discourse A system of written and verbal communication that is embedded in and shaped by prevailing power structures. For Foucault it is a 'historically contingent social system that produces knowledge and meaning'.

Dollarization The adoption by foreign countries of the US dollar as their national currency.

East India Company In India more often known as the Company Bahadur, or the Honourable Company, it was chartered in 1600 under a royal seal of approval by Elizabeth I, and it traded cotton, silk, tea, sugar, salt, indigo dye, saltpetre, spices, and opium; it increasingly took on sovereign executive powers until being replaced by direct British rule in 1858.

Ecological debt and climate debt Suggests that the Global North owes a large debt to the Global South and the world's poor based on its disproportionate exploitation of the world's ecological resources since the colonial era and into the present, its equally disproportionate contribution to environmental harms, and the disproportionate burden that is carried by those least responsible for these problems.

Economic globalization The condition whereby more and more economic activity takes place across and beyond national borders, leaving the impression of increasingly interconnected global markets.

Economic union(s) A common market that has also adopted common monetary and fiscal policies.

Elephant curve A growth incidence curve that depicts the percentage gain in real household income for different parts of the global income distribution; so called because its shape resembles an elephant's head and trunk.

Embedded liberalism A concept put forwards by John Gerard Ruggie, following Karl Polanyi, to capture the compromise in the Bretton Woods economic regimes between liberalization and the pursuit of domestic social and political objectives.

Enabling Clause Formally, the 1979 Decision on Differential and More Favourable Treatment, Reciprocity and Fuller Participation of Developing Countries, it legitimizes Special and Differential Treatment in the trade regime for Least Developed Countries.

Energy democracy An energy democracy implies a shift to clean energy sources; energy's decommodification and universal access; the creation of fair and living wage jobs in the sector; and community ownership and democratic decision-making.

Entrepôt Usually a port city, but any place that develops economically as a centre for importing and exporting goods.

Environmental racism Developed by Dr Robert D. Bullard with respect to the US, the concept of environmental racism highlights how racialized communities are disproportionately harmed by environmental problems, including the siting of polluting industries. It highlights further that colonialism and the post-colonial condition are racial projects wherein racial identity legitimates whose lands, resources, and bodies are exploited disproportionately, and whose suffering is considered acceptable.

European Stability Mechanism (ESM) Established in 2012 by the European states using the euro as their currency, this intergovernmental organization is based in Luxembourg. Along with the European Central Bank, it provides last-resort lending to euro members unable to refinance their debts in capital markets at sustainable rates. On the basis of its own capital reserves and guarantees from its most creditworthy members, it sells bonds to international investors and passes the proceeds on to troubled members under conditions designed to restore their own creditworthiness. It succeeded the European Financial Stability Facility, which was set up on a temporary basis to help stabilize European markets during the crisis of 2010.

Factor endowments The amount of land, labour, and capital that a country possesses and can exploit for the domestic production of goods.

Factors of production Primary factors of production are traditionally defined as land (natural resources), labour (workers), and capital (money) necessary for the production of goods and services. More recently, some economists have extended the definition to include technology or entrepreneurship. Alternatively, some models distinguish between skilled labour and unskilled labour.

Fallacy of composition Generalizing the experience of one and applying it to the whole.

Feminism A political position which advocates for gender equality for all and which challenges and seeks to redress historical and systemic inequalities based on gender.

Fictitious commodity A concept developed by Karl Polanyi (1957) to highlight that nature and humans can never be real commodities which, by definition, are produced for sale on the market. He warned of the dangers of reducing living beings to the logic of the market.

Financial inclusion The access to and use of retail financial services, including bank accounts, payment services, credit, and insurance, by all individuals and businesses in society.

Financial intermediaries An institution that facilitates a financial transaction between two parties.

FinTech Short for financial technology, the term encompasses innovative digital solutions and technologies revolutionizing financial services, ranging from mobile payment platforms and online banking to cryptocurrency and investment apps.

Fiscal policy Government policies on taxation and expenditure.

Flight capital Also known as hot money, refers to large-scale and rapid movements of funds and assets from one country to another, often seeking to evade unfavourable economic, political, or regulatory conditions or instability.

Foreign direct investment (FDI) An investment made by a company or entity in one country that gives it a controlling interest in a company or entity based in another country.

Foreign investor protection agreement (FIPA) A type of international investment agreement that allows corporations to directly sue governments for policies which they believe hurts their profitability and violates trade and investment agreements.

Free trade areas Agreements between two or more countries to remove tariff and non-tariff barriers on trade between themselves.

Fundamental disequilibrium Refers to persistent and substantial imbalances in a country's economic fundamentals such as its balance of payments, exchange rates, or fiscal policies, which can lead to long-term economic instability.

Gender A set of socially constructed ideas and assumptions 'describing what men and women ought to be' as opposed to sex, which is biologically determined. Gender provides a signifying or governing code that tells people what it means to be a man or a woman in the world, and which behaviours are appropriate and inappropriate, even as these binaries are being challenged in new ways. These codes are shaped by culture and vary across time and space. Gender not only informs peoples' everyday practices, but also their political practices, including those who are engaged in governing the GPE.

General Agreement on Tariffs and Trade (GATT) A 1947 agreement that became the principal component of the international trade regime following the failure of the international community to establish the ITO. Its provisions were incorporated into the WTO when it was established in 1995.

Gini coefficient A statistical measure of the dispersion of incomes within a society, ranging from 0 (a perfectly equal distribution) to 1 (in a society where all income is held by a single person).

Global poverty A global condition where communities cannot access basic goods or services such as water, shelter, food, healthcare, sanitation, and education.

Gold standard A monetary system in which the money supply is linked directly to the country's holdings of gold; citizens are usually entitled to exchange banknotes for gold. An international gold standard is an international monetary system in which the value of all currencies is set in terms of a unit of gold, and settlement of trade imbalances occurs through the transfer of gold reserves.

Grand narratives The term grand narrative, coined by French philosopher Jean-François Lyotard, refers to a meta-narrative or a story that includes mini-stories. In the context of the United Nations development goals, for example, the grand narrative includes poverty, hunger, human rights, climate change, and political institutions. For Lyotard, modernity, with its ideological promises of emancipation and progress, was a grand narrative. Post-structuralist sociological and philosophical thought often warns against 'meta-narratives' that provide an overarching unity to disparate social and historical forces. Therefore, the term 'grand narrative' here connotes both the ambition and the possible folly of designing global development goals.

Gross domestic product (GDP) The total value of goods and services produced by an economy in a specific time period.

Hegemony Often in international relations treated as a synonym for dominance, whereby a dominant state, institution, or ideology is described as being hegemonic, but in its original form following Gramsci the condition of hegemony also requires the consent of the subordinate to be governed in that way.

Heteropatriarchy Refers to the intersecting oppressions of gender and sexuality where male-dominated power structures and heterosexual norms influence laws, culture, and the global political economy.

Homo economicus Latin for 'economic man', this is a term used in economic theories to describe humans as rational and self-interested beings capable of deciding the optimal strategy for pursuing their goals (usually assumed to be the accumulation of wealth).

Hot money Related to foreign portfolio investments (FPI) where short-term capital flows quickly move in and out of a country in the form of investments in financial assets like stocks, bonds, and currency trading.

Imperial federation The proposal to unite all of Britain's colonial territories within a single political structure, so that local decision-making would persist on strictly local issues but common concerns would be resolved centrally.

Imperialism A global economic system in which a small number of powerful countries forced their own interests on the management of less powerful countries' economies.

Imperial mode of living Patterns of global extraction, exploitation, and wealth accumulation, begun during the colonial era and persisting into the present, that have helped to lay the foundation for countries of the Global North to dominate the global political economy and institutions of global governance.

Imperial preference A system of asymmetric tariffs, whereby goods originating within the empire could be traded at a lower tariff than those originating outside the empire.

Import-substitution industrialization A strategy pursued by less developed economies to promote industrialization by domestic production of goods previously imported (usually undertaken behind high levels of tariff protection).

Inclusive club goods Goods that can be withheld from those who do not pay for them, and whose consumption does not reduce their availability to other potential consumers. Examples include cable television and access to copyrighted works.

Industrialization Usually treated as the period of economic time that followed the Industrial Revolution of the eighteenth and nineteenth centuries, the word also refers to the societal transformation to an economic order based on industrial production.

Infant industry promotion Based on the idea that recently established industries require protection until they are able to produce efficiently and withstand import competition from more advanced economies.

Informal economy All economic activities by workers and economic units that are—in law or in practice—not covered or insufficiently covered by formal arrangements.

Intellectual history An approach to the interpretation of historical ideas in which much of the focus is on understanding the context out of which those ideas arose.

Interdependence A network of relationships among actors that is costly for any of the actors to break.

Intermediation *See* **financial intermediaries**.

International Bank for Reconstruction and Development (IBRD) (World Bank) (known as the World Bank) The original component of the World Bank group, created at the Bretton Woods conference in 1944. Subsequently, two other institutions, the International Finance Corporation (1956) and the International Development Association (1960) were added to the group. Most writers today simply refer to the group of institutions as the 'World Bank'.

International financial institutions (IFIs) The World Bank and the IMF.

International gold standard *See* **gold standard**.

International Monetary Fund (IMF) An institution of 189 members as of early 2016, providing extensive technical assistance and short-term flows of stabilization finance to any of those members experiencing temporarily distressed finances.

International Trade Organization (ITO) Intended to be the third of the major post-war international economic institutions alongside the World Bank and the IMF, the ITO was stillborn when the US Congress failed to ratify the Havana Charter.

Interpersonal global inequality An approach to measuring global inequality that takes as the unit of observation the actual or estimated income of individuals rather than relying on per capita GDP; it takes into account both within-country and between-country inequality.

Intersectional/Intersectionality An intersectional approach considers differences and inequalities along multiple axes, including those of class, caste, race, ethnicity, nationality, citizenship status, sexuality, age, and more.

Intra-industry trade International trade in products from the same sector.

Invisible hand Arguably the most famous phrase in the whole history of economic thought, said to signify Adam Smith's commitment to the idea of self-regulating markets, but an interpretation for which there is scant textual evidence in *The Wealth of Nations*.

Involuntariness Refers to a worker's 'free and informed consent' to take a job and their freedom to exit it at any time.

Just transition principle A move away from today's extractive economy that reduces nature to commodities and exploits it for profit, with wealth and power accruing to a small minority committed to a colonial mindset and militarism to defend their interests, to a living and regenerative economy that invests in communities, promotes cooperation over commodification, and prioritizes the wellbeing of people and the planet.

Least developed countries A UN-designated group of fifty low-income countries, membership of which is defined by per capita GDP under US$750, weak human assets (a composite index of health, nutrition, and education indicators), and high economic vulnerability (a composite index based on instability of export earnings, dependence on a limited number of primary product exports, and overall size of the economy). The UN can 'graduate' countries from the category when they meet the thresholds of two of the three criteria (over US$900 per capita GDP) for two successive years.

Lender of last resort A financial institution, usually the central bank, that is charged with the responsibility of providing loans to other financial institutions when they need an injection of cash—and no other institution is willing to lend to them.

Liberal internationalism The centre-left approach to foreign policy and international relations that emphasizes democracy and human rights, international institutions and diplomacy, and using trade to promote interdependence and peace as well as prosperity.

Lifeboat ethics A concept that claims it is better to let some people die in a context of resource scarcity, in order to save the whole. Garrett Hardin used it to argue against support for the world's poor, who he blamed for environmental crises.

Liquidity International liquidity comprises the total gold and foreign exchange reserves and Special Drawing Rights (that is, all international reserves acceptable to other countries) held by all countries in the international financial system.

Longue durée An approach to history pioneered by the Annales School, in which the emphasis is placed explicitly on the long term.

Market concentration The degree to which a market is controlled by a small number of firms.

Menace Threat of penalty, which may take various forms, such as 'penal sanctions' and 'direct or indirect coercion, such as physical violence, psychological threats or the non-payment of a wage'.

Mercantilism An economic theory that measures the wealth of a nation in terms of profitable trade balances, encouraging an asymmetric approach to trade regulation that incentivizes exports but disincentivizes imports.

Merchant-dominated monopolies A phrase used by Adam Smith to refer to a small group of merchants or traders controlling a market. Smith was a critic of monopolies and believed in free and open markets as a moral position which could ensure that a few greedy people did not dominate the rest.

Metropole The imperial centre in the relationship between a colonizing country and those people it colonizes (e.g., Britain's self-image as the 'Mother Country' of the British Empire).

Mobility The ease with which factors of production can move from one sector to another.

Modernization theory An economic theory that held that inflows of foreign capital and production technology would jump-start growth in poor countries, allowing them to follow the same path to industrialization that rich countries followed in the nineteenth and early twentieth centuries.

Modern slavery An umbrella term used to encompass a range of exploitative practices and relations, including slavery, forced labour, and human trafficking. It became popular in development studies in the late 1990s and has since gained widespread traction.

Monetary policy Government policies on the money supply, the rate of interest, and the exchange rate.

Moral hazards The creation of a situation in which individuals or institutions are encouraged to act irresponsibly because of the guarantees (implicit or explicit) that others provide for them.

Most-favoured-nation (MFN) The principle of non-discrimination, enshrined in Article I of the GATT/WTO, that members must give all other members the most favourable trade treatment they offer to any member.

Multifibre agreement (MFA) A multilateral agreement (1974–1994), a form of OMA, limiting the exports of textiles and clothing by LDCs to industrialized countries. Industrialized countries agreed to phase out the MFA over a ten-year period, as part of the GATT Uruguay Round negotiations.

Multilateralism Policy coordination by three or more states on the basis of principles that specify appropriate conduct.

Multinational corporation (MNC) Companies that have a presence in more than one country and which use the different institutional structures in those countries to organize their activities—from basic decisions about production to how best to limit their tax payments—so as to make the highest possible level of profit (*see* also **transnational corporation**).

Multilateral enterprises *See* multinational corporation (MNC); transnational corporation.

Nash equilibrium In game theory, a situation where all participants are pursuing their best possible strategy, given the strategies that other players have chosen; in other words, no player can improve their situation by changing their own strategy.

Nationalism An ideology that advocates for whichever policies best promote the interests of a specific ethnic group (ethnic nationalism) or state (civic nationalism).

Navigation Acts Seventeenth- and eighteenth-century legal statutes through which Britain tried to transpose its naval dominance into commercial dominance, limiting the amount of tradeable cargo that non-British ships could bring through British waters while allowing British ships unrestricted access.

Negative externality Said to occur when the adverse impacts of productive activities are not factored into the price of production. Rather, the cost is externalized, leaving society to pay for the harm.

Negative news bias A theory that human cognition's negativity bias—the tendency of humans to react more strongly to negative than positive information—manifests in media's overrepresentation of negative news stories.

Neo-colonialism Defined broadly, neo-colonialism refers to powerful states imposing colonial-like economic exploitation or political control on the less powerful. The term was originally coined to characterize the continued domination of ex-colonies by the colonial Western powers even after independence.

Neoliberal capitalism A contemporary variant of capitalism that is underpinned by neoliberal ideas and policies.

Neoliberalism Defined by commitments to the reduction of government intervention, and social welfare retrenchment, that is, a commitment to austerity in governance, economic growth, and the reduction of trade and financial barriers. Progress for the purposes of economic growth is the central idea that guides mainstream development.

Network effects Any situation in which the value of the product or service increases as more people also use that product or service.

Network externalities A situation where the value or utility of a product or service increases as more people use it.

New constitutionalism A concept put forwards by Stephen Gill to describe neoliberal/libertarian efforts to lock in free market policies, regardless of the government in power, through the use of constitutional and institutional mechanisms.

New International Economic Order (NIEO) A list of demands by less developed economies in the 1970s that proposed a radical restructuring of international economic regimes.

Newly Industrializing Economies (NIEs) or Countries (NICs) Term originally applied to the 'Gang of Four' economies of East Asia (Hong Kong, Korea, Singapore, Taiwan) that experienced rapid economic growth from the late 1960s. Subsequently sometimes applied to selected rapidly growing Southeast Asian and Latin American economies.

Non-Aligned Movement In the context of the Cold War, the Non-Aligned Movement (NAM) refers to countries that were not aligned with either the US or the Soviet Union and included India, Egypt, Indonesia, Ghana, and Yugoslavia. These countries (and others) were called the 'Third World' as they were not part of the 'First' or 'Second World'—a term which is now derogatory.

Offshore tax havens Foreign jurisdictions with lax tax policies where wealthy businesses and individuals can shield their wealth from taxation in their home countries.

Orderly marketing arrangement (OMA) An agreement between an importing country and one or more exporting countries whereby the latter pledge to limit their exports of particular products. This was outlawed by the GATT Uruguay Round Agreements.

Original position Political philosopher John Rawls' idea that if members of a political community were to choose distributive principles from behind a veil of ignorance, that is, as if they did not know what their class, status, gender, ethnicity, preferences, religion, or values would be upon being born into a society, they would choose principles that produced the highest payoff for the least advantaged in society.

Outsourcing A business practice in which a company passes key tasks, operations, or elements of service provision over to a third party, often as a cost-cutting measure.

Pareto-optimal outcome Where no actor can be better off without making others worse off. In Pareto-suboptimal (instead of Pareto-deficient) situations, other outcomes could increase some actors' welfare without decreasing that of others.

Paternalism The practice of infantilizing the developing world and assuming for oneself the parental or care-taking role.

Peer-to-peer lending A form of lending in which borrowers access credit directly from individuals or investors, thereby eliminating banks as the intermediary.

Platform capitalism A distinct type of social, technical, and economic relations centred around digital platforms and platform firms. In particular, the study of platform capitalism focuses on the distinct, intermediary role of digital platforms in solving coordination problems among different types of actors (for example, consumers and producers) and the associated changes in how markets are structured and how power is distributed.

Platform power A form of business power, distinct from structural or instrumental power, that is exercised by platform firms who achieve both sufficient scale and intimate relations with consumers (users).

Pluralism An approach that acknowledges the value of multiple perspectives and approaches and advocates for tolerance, open dialogue, and exchange of viewpoints.

Portfolio investment The acquisition of interest-bearing foreign securities (either government bonds or company stocks and shares) that do not in themselves give the investor management control over the foreign concern.

Price elasticity The responsiveness of the quantity demanded or supplied of a good or service to changes in its price, indicating the sensitivity of consumers or producers to price fluctuations.

Prison industrial complex The interconnected networks of corporations, government, and other entities that profit from prison labour and incarceration, particularly in the context of the US.

Private goods Goods and services that can be withheld from those who do not pay for them, and that cannot be used by others without additional production taking place.

Privatized Keynesianism A concept used to denote a shift in how demand is stimulated in economies. Whereas Keynesian policies usually entail the government taking on additional debt that is spent to stimulate the economy in times of need, this newer model relies on households taking on debt to stimulate it.

Proletarian Related to the proletariat, working-class people who sought to provide for their families by selling their labour, but typically received nothing more than subsistence wages for it.

Property rights The legal right of owners of resources to be paid for their usage; for example, fees paid to patent or copyright owners.

Protectionism or Protectionist policies Policies that are designed to enhance the trading position of domestic producers by lowering the price of their goods vis-à-vis those of foreign competitors. Home-produced goods can be made more cheaply if the government is prepared to subsidize production, while overseas-produced goods will be more expensive for final consumers if the government forces their producers to pay an import fee called a tariff.

Public goods Goods that cannot be withheld from consumers who do not pay for them, and whose consumption does not reduce their availability to other consumers. Examples include national security and street lighting.

Race to the bottom The idea that, in a globalized economy, some governments will attempt to increase their attractiveness to investors by offering minimal requirements on, for example, environmental and labour standards and taxation.

Racial capitalism A term first used by Cedric Robinson in his influential book *Black Marxism* (1983). Robinson contends that capitalism is built on racial ordering, established first in Europe's internal relations before developing alongside capitalist expansion to empires and colonies, and driving economic growth in Western states. In this respect, all capitalism is racial capitalism.

Rational choice theory A theory of human behaviour that assumes that social activity reflects the behaviours of individuals who are acting rationally to pursue their interests.

Reciprocity The principle in international trade that countries benefitting from trade liberalization by others should offer equivalent (but not necessarily identical) concessions in return.

Regime A set of international governing arrangements (including rules, norms, and procedures) that are intended to regularize the behaviour of state and non-state actors, and control its effects.

Regulatory and tax arbitrage Business practices that take advantage of differences in regulations or taxation rules across diverse jurisdictions to avoid certain costs or lower overall expenses in order to bolster net earnings. Common tactics involve relocating certain operations, taking advantage of legal loopholes, or booking payments outside the country where actual goods and services are produced or delivered. The avoidance of higher costs in such ways is typically not illegal, as evasion would be. But it does often lead to accusations of unfairness. (*Also see* **Race to the bottom**.)

Relative inequality A way of measuring changes in inequality that compares the ratio of the incomes of two segments of the distribution across time.

Remittances The transfer of money by individuals or groups of people working in one country to people in their home country. These money transfers are often sent by migrants who have sought work in a foreign country and are sending money back to family in their home country.

Ricardian science In the early nineteenth century, English-speaking economic theorists coalesced around what they took to be David Ricardo's vision: an economy oriented towards free trade and based on the equitable distribution of rewards between landlords, bosses, and workers.

Rising powers Also often referred to as 'emerging powers', rising powers are states that are significantly increasing their influence in global or regional affairs, often through achieving sustained, high rates of economic growth. There is no agreed list of which countries fall into this category in the contemporary era, and there is debate about whether it is still appropriate to consider the likes of China 'rising' rather than having already risen.

Robinsonade Popular story of the nineteenth century based on plot of Daniel Defoe's *Robinson Crusoe*, where the victims of a shipwreck have to make their lives anew on an island setting.

Rust belt A term used to describe a series (or 'belt') of northeastern US states where the once-dominant manufacturing sector began to decline (or 'rust') from the late 1970s onwards.

Safeguards Provisions enabling countries with problems in specific sectors or their economy more generally to seek temporary exemptions from some of their obligations in the trade regime.

Shell companies Companies that exist entirely or almost entirely on paper which exist to facilitate financial transactions, shield assets from national regulators, avoid taxes, and sometimes launder money.

Single undertaking The principle within the GATT/WTO that members must accept all parts of an agreement rather than signing on selectively to individual components. The effect is that in WTO negotiations, 'Nothing is agreed until everything is agreed'.

Social connection model Political theorist Iris Marion Young's approach to thinking about the allocation of responsibility within unjust global structures; it holds that anyone who participates in and benefits from structural injustices has a responsibility to work with others to remedy those injustices and that our level of responsibility varies based on proximity, power, and privilege.

Socialist Development Approach A development strategy that emphasizes state intervention in the economy through policies like nationalization of industries, land reform, and public service provisions such as education, healthcare, housing.

Social reproduction Processes associated with the biological reproduction of the species, the reproduction of the labour force (including subsistence, education, and training), and the reproduction and provisioning of caring needs.

Social structure The dynamic interplay of material factors, institutions, and ideas that shape patterns of social and international relations, reflecting underlying power dynamics and historical contexts.

Sociotropic politics An assumption that an individual's decision-making extends past self-interests to incorporate group interests, generally defined by geography (for example local community or nation).

Sound money Money that neither depreciates nor appreciates (too rapidly).

Sovereign debt The total amount of money that a national government owes to external creditors or domestic lenders.

Sovereign wealth funds Pools of foreign currency reserves managed by governments for profit. According to the Sovereign Wealth Fund Institute, a private agency established to monitor SWFs, the total assets of SWFs in 2016 exceeded US$7.25 trillion. Their assets are more than double those of all hedge funds combined.

Special and differential treatment (SDT) Exemptions for LDCs from some of the obligations imposed on other members of the trade regime.

Special Drawing Rights An international reserve asset created by the IMF in 1969. Over 200 billion SDRs (equivalent to US$285 billion) have been created; these were distributed by the IMF to member countries in proportion to the size of their IMF quota. The SDR is based on a basket of five major currencies (the Chinese renminbi, the euro, the Japanese yen, and the US dollar).

Special economic zones Geographic areas within countries that are characterized by lax labour laws and enforcement, tax breaks, and weak environmental protections to attract foreign direct investment.

Stablecoins A type of cryptocurrency in which the value is fixed ('pegged') to the value of a different asset, often either a specific type of fiat money (for example, the US dollar) or a different cryptocurrency, to help maintain a stable price.

Stagflation A situation where economic stagnation (low growth) and high inflation emerge at the same time, as occurred most prominently in many developed countries in the 1970s.

State-owned enterprises Companies that are either wholly or partially owned by the government. They play a significant role in the economy of a number of countries, operating in various sectors and industries. The government's involvement can mean that such enterprises receive financial and other benefits that undercut normal market forces.

Sterilize Efforts by monetary authorities to counter the impact of international monetary flows on domestic economic activity by issuing/selling financial instruments to reduce or increase the domestic money supply.

Structural adjustment programmes (SAPs) These are often designed in association with the IFIs, and are pursued by countries experiencing debt problems. They usually include privatization of assets, reductions in government expenditure to reduce budgetary deficits, trade liberalization, encouragement of foreign investment, and currency devaluation.

Structural Inequalities Inequalities are structural when they are baked into the ideas and institutions that comprise a given world order (such as capitalism) and they are material when they produce different life chances for different categories of people.

Sunk costs Costs that are difficult for investors to recover; for example, investment in physical infrastructure, plant, and machinery.

Surveillance capitalism Refers to the commodification of personal data and the associated changes in digital infrastructures, market structures, and individual behaviours that enable firms to engage in mass (digital) surveillance.

Tariff Reform A protectionist British policy proposal of the early twentieth century, designed to discriminate against cheap imports, which were accused of overwhelming domestic markets to the detriment of local firms and local jobs.

Telemigration The practice of living in one country while working remotely in another.

Temptation to free ride A situation in which actors are tempted to contribute less than their appropriate share to the cost of the goods or services from which they benefit.

Terms of trade The price of a country's exports relative to the price of its imports.

The everyday The mundane practices and routines of everyday life including child and elderly care, cooking dinner, going to school, and buying clothes.

Third Great Debate The inter-paradigm debate in International Relations in the 1970s and 1980s, which pitted liberals against realists against radicals in the search for more rigorous theoretical foundations for the field.

Trade creation Where a preferential trade agreement leads to the replacement of domestic production by lower-cost imports from a party to the trade agreement.

Trade diversion Where a preferential trade agreement leads to the displacement of goods previously imported from a non-preferred trading partner by imports from a party to the preferred agreement (because the preferential imports now enter the local market at a reduced tariff).

Trade-Related Aspects of Intellectual Property Rights (TRIPs) A Uruguay Round WTO agreement that establishes minimum levels of protection that governments must give to the intellectual property of fellow WTO members.

Trade-Related Investment Measures (TRIMs) The title of a Uruguay Round WTO agreement that prohibits governments from applying measures that discriminate against foreign companies or foreign products; for example, requirements that foreign investors must source a certain value of their inputs locally ('local content' requirements) or export a certain value of their output ('trade balancing' requirements).

Tragedy of enclosure Challenging the idea of the 'tragedy of the commons', the idea of the tragedy of enclosure suggests that environmental destruction emerges when local actors lose access to collectively managed common property, with privatization facilitating large-scale commercial exploitation.

Tragedy of the commons Garrett Hardin, in a paper published in *Science* in 1968, first put forwards the idea that when individuals are freely able to access resources, they will necessarily overuse and overexploit them in the pursuit of self-interest.

Transaction costs The costs other than the nominal price that are involved in trading goods and services, for example costs of search and information, bargaining and decision-making, and policing and enforcement. High transaction costs are often viewed as a significant example of externalities.

Transatlantic slave trade The transatlantic slave trade was practised from approximately 1500 until the 1870s. At least 12–15 million people are estimated to have fallen victim to the transatlantic slave trade. It is also known as the 'Middle Passage' in the so-called triangular trade, whereby European merchants would ship slaves from Africa to the Americas, would return to Europe with primary products such as cotton, sugar, tobacco, and indigo dye produced in the Americas, often through the forced labour of the enslaved peoples, and would then ship European-made manufactured and industrial products into Africa.

Transnational corporations (TNCs) Companies that engage in FDI; that is, which own, control, and manage assets in more than one country (*see also* **MNCs**).

Trickle-down economics A de-bunked economic theory also known as 'supply-side economics' that argues that the economic benefits and wealth will 'trickle-down' to all other members of society. The theory suggests that tax cuts for the rich and corporate elite will eventually lead to economic prosperity for all.

Triffin dilemma Yale University economist Robert Triffin pointed out in a 1960 book that the Bretton Woods monetary system rested on the confidence of other countries in the gold exchange standard—that is, their belief that they could convert their dollar holdings into gold—yet, the capacity of the US to guarantee this conversion was being undermined by dollar outflows that were the principal source of new liquidity in the system. If outflows stopped, the system would have insufficient liquidity; if they continued, confidence in the system would be undermined.

Uneven development Refers to the uneven distribution of wealth and resources between countries, regions, and/or cities with special reference to

historical legacy, colonialism, social structures, and economic policies.

Voluntary export restraints An agreement between an exporting and an importing country under which the exporting country agrees to limit the total (value or volume of) exports of particular products. Outlawed by the GATT Uruguay Round Agreements.

Washington Consensus An approach to international development in the 1990s and early 2000s embraced by international economic organizations that pushed poor countries to adopt liberal market policies as a condition for receiving access to international markets, loans, and development finance.

White man's burden A phrase occasionally in use before Rudyard Kipling brought it to wider attention in an imperialist poem of 1899, it invoked the moral responsibility to bring civilization to currently uncivilized people, which in turn was often cited in the late nineteenth century as a justification for empire.

World-systems theory A social and economic theory that takes the international division of labour among capital-rich and capital-poor countries and regions as foundational to understanding key outcomes in world politics; it divides the world into an industrialized core which persistently benefits at the expense of countries and regions in the periphery and semi-periphery whose economies are dominated by the production and extraction of raw materials.

Writing back Taking the characters of a classic novel but subverting its original plot lines by allowing those who were previously silenced to talk about their experiences of the world.

References

Aalbers, M. (2008), 'The Financialization of Home and Mortgage Markets', *Competition and Change*, 12/2: 148–166.

Abbas, R. (2016), 'Internal Migration and Citizenship in India', *Journal of Ethnic and Migration Studies*, 42/1: 150–168.

Abbott, F. M. (2002), 'The Doha Declaration on the TRIPS Agreement and Public Health: Lighting a Dark Corner at the WTO', *Journal of International Economic Law*, 5/2: 469–505.

Abbott, K. W., and Snidal, D. (2000), 'Hard and Soft Law in International Governance', *International Organization*, 54/3: 421–456.

Abdelal, R. (2007), *Capital Rules: The Construction of Global Finance* (Cambridge, MA: Harvard University Press).

Abdelal, R. (2022), 'Of Learning and Forgetting: Centrism, Populism, and the Legitimacy Crisis of Globalization', in P. J. Katzenstein and J. Kirshner (eds.), *The Downfall of the American Order?* (Ithaca, NY: Cornell University Press), 105–123.

Abdelal, R., Blyth, M., and Parsons, C. (eds.) (2010), *Constructing the International Economy* (Cornell: Cornell University Press).

Abu-Lughod, L. (1990), 'The Romance of Resistance: Tracing Transformations of Power through Bedouin Women', *American Ethnologist*, 17/1: 41–55.

Acemoglu, D., Johnson, S., and Robinson, J. (2001), 'The Colonial Origins of Comparative Development: An Empirical Investigation', *American Economic Review*, 91/5: 1369–1401.

Acharya, A. (2014), 'Global International Relations (IR) and Regional Worlds: A New Agenda for International Studies', *International Studies Quarterly*, 58/4: 647–659.

Adams R., and Page, J. (2005), 'Do International Migration and Remittances Reduce Poverty in Developing Countries?', *World Development*, 33/10: 1645–1669.

Addison, J. T., and Siebert, W. S. (1991), 'The Social Charter of the European Community: Evolution and Controversies', *ILR Review*, 44/4: 597–625.

Adkins, L., Cooper, M., and Konings, M. (2020), *The Asset Economy: Property Ownership and the New Logic of Inequality* (Cambridge: Polity).

Adler, E., and Bernstein, S. (2005), 'Knowledge in Power: The Epistemic Construction of Global Governance', in M. Barnett and R. Duvall (eds.), *Power in Global Governance* (Cambridge: Cambridge University Press).

Agarwala, P. N. (1983), *The New International Economic Order: An Overview* (Oxford: Pergamon Press).

Aggarwal, V. K. (1985), *Liberal Protectionism: The International Politics of Organized Textile Trade* (Berkeley, CA: University of California Press).

Aggarwal, V. K. (1994), 'Comparing Regional Cooperation Efforts in Asia-Pacific and North America', in A. Mack and J. Ravenhill (eds.), *Pacific Cooperation: Building Economic and Security Regimes in the Asia-Pacific Region* (Sydney: Allen & Unwin).

Aggarwal, V. K. (ed.) (1998), *Institutional Designs for a Complex World: Bargaining, Linkages and Nesting* (Ithaca, NY: Cornell University Press).

Aggarwal, V. K., and Dupont, C. (1999), 'Goods, Games and Institutions', *International Political Science Review*, 20/4: 393–409.

Aggarwal, V. K., and Dupont, C. (2002), '"Goods, Games, and Institutions": A Reply', *International Political Science Review*, 23/4: 402–10.

Aggarwal, V. K., and Govella, K. (eds.) (2013), *Linking Trade and Security* (Berlin: Springer).

Aggarwal, V. K., Keohane, R. O., and Yoffie, D. B. (1987), 'The Dynamics of Negotiated Protectionism', *American Political Science Review*, 81/2: 345–366.

Aggarwal, V. K., and Marple, T. (2020), 'Digital Currency Wars? US–China Competition and Economic Statecraft', *Global Asia*, 15/4: 79–85.

Aggarwal, V. K., and Reddie, A.W. (2021), 'Economic Statecraft in the 21st Century: Implications for the Future of the Global Trade Regime', *World Trade Review*, 20/2: 137–151.

Ahlquist, J. S., and Mosley, L. (2021), 'Firm Participation in Voluntary Regulatory Initiatives: The Accord, Alliance, and US Garment Importers from Bangladesh', *Review of International Organization*, 16/2: 317–343.

Ahmed, N. et al. (2022), *Inequality Kills: The Unparalleled Action Needed to Combat Unprecedented Inequality in the Wake of COVID-19* (Oxford: Oxford University Press).

AIIB (Asian Infrastructure Investment Bank) (2022), 'Members and Prospective Members of the Bank', https://www.aiib.org/en/about-aiib/governance/members-of-bank/index.html.

Aitken, R. (2015), *Fringe Finance: Crossing and Contesting the Borders of Global Capital* (Abingdon: Routledge).

Aitken, R. (2022), 'Mediating and Mapping Climate Change Risk: Micro-Insurance and Earth Observation', *Journal of Cultural Economy*, 15/4: 468–487.

Aiyar, S. et al. (2023), *Geoeconomic Fragmentation and the Future of Multilateralism* (Washington, D.C.: International Monetary Fund), https://www.imf.org/-/media/Files/Publications/SDN/2023/English/SDNEA2023001.ashx.

Ajdacic, L., Heemskerk, E., and Garcia-Bernardo, J. (2021), 'The Wealth Defence Industry: A Large-Scale Study on Accountancy Firms as Profit Shifting Facilitators', *New Political Economy*, 26/4: 690–706.

Alami, I. et al. (2022), 'International Financial Subordination: A Critical Research Agenda', *Review of International Political Economy*, 30/4: 1360–1386.

Alatas, S. H. (1977), *The Myth of the Lazy Native* (London: Routledge).

Alcantara, C., and Dick, C. (2017), 'Decolonization in a Digital Age: Cryptocurrencies and Indigenous Self-Determination in Canada', *Canadian Journal of Law and Society*, 32/1: 19–35.

Alimahomed-Wilson, J., and Reese, E. (2021), 'Surveilling Amazon's Warehouse Workers: Racism, Retaliation, and Worker Resistance amid the Pandemic', *Work in the Global Economy*, 1/1–2: 55–73.

Allan, J. I. (2019), 'Dangerous Incrementalism of the Paris Agreement', *Global Environmental Politics*, 19: 4–11.

Allen, M. (2003), 'Some Lessons from the Argentine Crisis: A Fund Staff View', in J. J. Teunissen and A. Akkerman (eds.), *The Crisis That Was Not Prevented: Lessons for Argentina, the IMF, and Globalisation* (The Hague: FONDAD).

Allen, W., and Moessner, R. (2010), 'Central Bank Co-operation and International Liquidity in the Financial Crisis of 2008–9', BIS Working Papers, 310, Bank for International Settlements.

Allon, F. (2015), 'Everyday Leverage, or Leveraging the Everyday', *Cultural Studies*, 29/5–6: 687–706.

Allon, F. (2018), 'Money after Blockchain: Gold, Decentralised Politics and the New Libertarianism', *Australian Feminist Studies*, 33/96: 223–243.

Alt, J. E., and Gilligan, M. (1994), 'The Political Economy of Trading States: Factor Specificity, Collective Action Problems and Domestic Political Institutions', *Journal of Political Philosophy*, 2/2: 165–192.

Altan-Olcay, Ö. (2022), 'Feminist International Political Economy in Europe', in M. Stern and A. E. Towns (eds.), *Feminist IR in Europe. Trends in European IR Theory* (New York, NY: Palgrave Macmillan).

Altvater, E. (2006), 'The Social and Natural Environment of Fossil Capitalism', in L. Panitch and C. Leys (eds.), *Socialist Register 2007: Coming to Terms with Nature* (Monmouth: The Merlin Press).

Alvarez, F. E., Argente, D., and Van Patten, D. (2022), 'Are Cryptocurrencies Currencies? Bitcoin as Legal Tender in El Salvador', Working Paper 29968, National Bureau of Economic Research.

Amaral, K. (2021), *Europe's Industry Polluters make €50 in Carbon Market Windfall Profits* (Brussels: Carbon Market Watch).

American National Election Studies (1986–2012), 'Time Series Study Data Set', *Center for Political Studies* (Ann Arbor, MI: the University of Michigan), http://ww.electionstudies.org.

American National Election Studies (2010), 'Time Series Cumulative Data File Dataset', Stanford University and the University of Michigan, http://www.electionstudies.org.

Amin A. (2009), *The Social Economy: International Perspectives on Economic Solidarity* (London: Zed Books).

Amin, S. (1972), 'Underdevelopment and Dependence in Black Africa—Origins and Contemporary Forms', *The Journal of Modern African Studies*, 10/4: 503–524.

Amin, S. (1974), *Accumulation on a World Scale* (Sussex. Harvester Press).

Amin, S. (1989), *Eurocentrism* (New York, NY: Monthly Review Press).

Amsden, A. H. (1989), *Asia's Next Giant: How Korea Competes in the World Economy* (Oxford: Oxford University Press).

Andrees, B. (2014), 'Why Definitions Matter', *International Labour Organization*, 3 February, http://www.ilo.org/global/about-the-ilo/newsroom/news/WCMS_234854/lang--en/index.htm.

Andrews, D. (1994), 'Capital Mobility and State Autonomy', *International Studies Quarterly*, 38/2: 193–218.

Anner, M. (2017), 'Monitoring Workers' Rights: The Limits of Voluntary Social Compliance Initiatives in Labor Repressive Regimes', *Global Policy*, 8/3: 56–65.

Aon, P. (2022), *2021 Weather, Climate and Catastrophe Insight* (London: Aon, plc).

Apostolou, A., Al-Haschimi, A., and Ricci, M. (2022), 'Financial Risks in China's Corporate Sector: Real Estate and Beyond', ECB Economic Bulletin, Issue 2/2022, https://www.ecb.europa.eu/pub/economic-bulletin/articles/2022/html/ecb.ebart202202_01~48041a563f.en.html.

Appadurai, A. (2004), 'The Capacity to Aspire', in M. W. Vijayendra Rao (ed.), *Culture and Public Action* (Stanford, CA: Stanford University Press), 59–84.

Applebaum, A. (2021), *The Twilight of Democracy* (New York, NY: Knopf Doubleday).

Aradau, C., and Blanke, T. (2022), *Algorithmic Reason: The New Government of Self and Other* (Oxford: Oxford University Press).

Arndt, H. (1987), *Economic Development: The History of an Idea*, 1st edn. (Chicago, IL: University of Chicago Press).

Arnoldi, J. (2009), *Risk* (Cambridge: Polity).

Arslanian, H. et al. (2021), *El Salvador's Law: A Meaningful Test for Bitcoin* (Hong Kong: PricewaterhouseCoopers).

Arunachalam, R. (2011), *The Journey of Indian Micro-Finance* (Chennai: AAPTI Publications).

Arup, C. (2000), *The New World Trade Organization Agreements: Globalizing Law through Services and Intellectual Property* (Cambridge: Cambridge University Press).

Atal, M. R. (2021), 'The Janus Faces of Silicon Valley', *Review of International Political Economy*, 28/2: 336–350.

Atal, M. R. (2022), 'The Origins of Surveillance Capitalism: Monopoly Power, Labor Control and Digital Surveillance in Global Supply Chains', Working Paper.

Auerbach, A. M. (2019), *Demanding Development: The Politics of Public Goods Provision in India's Urban Slums* (Cambridge: Cambridge University Press).

Auerbach, A. M., and Thachil, T. (2023), *Migrants and Machine Politics: How India's Urban Poor Seek Representation and Responsiveness* (Princeton, NJ: Princeton University Press).

Austen-Smith, D., and Wallerstein, M. (2006), 'Redistribution and Affirmative Action', *Journal of Public Economics*, 90/10–11: 1789–1823.

Autor, D. H., Dorn, D., and Hanson, G. H. (2013), 'The China Syndrome: Local Labor Market Effects of Import Competition in the United States', *American Economic Review*, 103/6: 2121–2168.

Autor, D. H., Dorn, D., and Hanson, G. H. (2016), 'The China Shock: Learning from Labor-Market Adjustment to Large Changes in Trade', *Annual Review of Economics*, 8: 205–240.

Autor, D., Dorn, D., Hanson, G., and Majlesi, K. (2017), 'Importing Political Polarization? The Electoral Consequences of Rising Trade Exposure', *Economics Unpublished Paper*, (Cambridge, MA: MIT Press), http://www.ddorn.net/papers/ADHM-PoliticalPolarization.pdf.

Axelrod, R., and Keohane, R. O. (1986), 'Achieving Cooperation under Anarchy: Strategies and Institutions', *World Politics*, 38/1: 226–254.

Ba, H. (2021), 'Hegemonic Instability: Complex Interdependence and the Dynamics of Financial Crisis in the Contemporary International System', *European Journal of International Relations*, 27/2: 369–402.

Bachrach, P., and Baratz, M. S. (1970), *Power and Poverty: Theory and Practice* (Oxford: Oxford University Press).

Bacon, C. M. (ed.) (2008), *Confronting the Coffee Crisis: Fair Trade, Sustainable Livelihoods and Ecosystems in Mexico and Central America* (Cambridge, MA: MIT Press).

Badgley, G. et al. (2021), 'Systematic Over-Crediting in California's Forest Carbon Offsets Program', *Global Change Biology*, 28/4: 1433–1445.

Baiocchi, G., Graizbord, D., and Rodríguez-Muñiz, M. (2013), 'Actor-Network Theory and the Ethnographic Imagination: An Exercise in Translation', *Qualitative Sociology*, 36/4: 323–341.

Bair, J. (2010), 'On Difference and Capital: Gender and the Globalization of Production', *Signs*, 36/1: 203–226.

Baker, A. (2005), 'Who Wants to Globalize? Consumer Tastes and Labor Markets in a Theory of Trade Policy Beliefs', *American Journal of Political Science*, 494: 924–938.

Baker, A. (2018), 'Macroprudential Regimes and the Politics of Social Purpose', *Review of International Political Economy*, 25/3: 293–316.

Baker, S. H. (2020), 'Fighting for a Just Transition', *NACLA Report on the Americas,* 52: 144–151.

Bakker, I. (2003), 'Neoliberal Governance and the Reprivatization of Social Reproduction', in I. Bakker and S. Gill (eds.), *Power, Production, and Social Reproduction* (New York, NY: Palgrave Macmillan).

Bakker, I. (2007), 'Social Reproduction and the Constitution of a Gendered Political Economy', *New Political Economy*, 12/4: 541–556.

Bakker, I., and Gill, S. (eds.) (2003), *Power, Production, and Social Reproduction* (New York, NY: Palgrave Macmillan).

Balassa, B. (1965), 'Tariff Protection in Industrial Countries: An Evaluation', *Journal of Political Economy*, 73/6: 573–594.

Baldwin, R. (2012), 'Global Supply Chains: Why They Emerged, Why They Matter, and Where They are Going', in D. K. Elms and P. Low (eds.), *Global Value Chains in a Changing World* (Geneva: World Trade Organization, Fung Global Institute, and Temasek Foundation Centre for Trade and Negotiations).

Baldwin, R. (2019), *The Globotics Upheaval: Globalization, Robotics, and the Future of Work* (Oxford: Oxford University Press).

Baldwin, R., and Dingel, J. I. (2021), 'Telemigration and Development: On the Offshorability of Teleworkable Jobs', Working Paper No. w29387, National Bureau of Economic Research.

Baldwin, R. E. (2011), *21st Century Regionalism: Filling the Gap between 21st Century Trade and 20th Century Trade Rules*, Policy Insight No. 56 (London: Centre for Economic Policy Research), https://cepr.org/system/files/publication-files/103072-policy_insight_56_21st_century_regionalism_filling_the_gap_between_21st_century_trade_and_20th_century_trade_rules.pdf.

Baldwin, R. E. (2016), 'The World Trade Organization and the Future of Multilateralism', *Journal of Economic Perspectives*, 30/1: 95–116.

Bales, K. (2005), *Understanding Global Slavery: A Reader* (Oakland, CA: University of California Press).

Bales, K. (2012), *Disposable People: New Slavery in the Global Economy, Updated with a New Preface*, 3rd edn. (Oakland, CA: University of California Press).

Ball, T. (2010), 'Competing Theories of Character Formation: James vs John Stuart Mill', in G. Varouxakis and P. Kelly (eds.), *John Stuart Mill—Thought and Influence: The Saint of Rationalism* (London: Routledge).

Banerjee, A., and Duflo, E. (2012), *Poor Economics: A Radical Rethinking of the Way to Fight Global Poverty* (New York: Public Affairs).

Banerjee, S. B. (2003), 'Who Sustains Whose Development? Sustainable Development and the Reinvention of Nature', *Organization Studies*, 24: 143–180.

Banking on Climate Chaos (2022), *Banking on Climate Chaos: Fossil Fuel Finance Report 2022*, https://www.bankingonclimatechaos.org/#downloads-panel.

Bannerji, A., and Hussain, Z. (2018), 'India Tea Workers Live in "Appalling" Conditions on $2 a Day: Report', *Reuters*, 22 May, https://www.reuters.com/article/us-india-tea-workers-idUSKCN1IN29P.

Bano, M. and Sakurai, K. (eds.) (2015), *Shaping Global Islamic Discourses: The Role of Al-Azhar, Al-Medina, and Al-Mustafa* (Edinburgh: Edinburgh University Press).

Barajas, A. et al. (2020), 'Financial Inclusion: What have We Learned So Far? What Do We Have to Learn?', Working Paper 20/157, IMF, https://www.imf.org/en/Publications/WP/Issues/2020/08/07/Financial-Inclusion-What-Have-We-Learned-So-Far-What-Do-We-Have-to-Learn-49660.

Barber, W. (1975), *British Economic Thought and India, 1600–1858* (Oxford: Clarendon Press).

Barlow, P., van Schalkwyk, M. C., McKee, M., Labonté, R., and Stuckler, D. (2021), 'COVID-19 and the Collapse of Global Trade: Building an Effective Public Health Response', *The Lancet Planetary Health*, 5(2): 102–107.

Barnosky, A. D. et al. (2011), 'Has the Earth's Sixth Mass Extinction Already Arrived?', *Nature*, 471: 51–57.

Barrett, P. M. (2020), 'Who Moderates the Social Media Giants? A Call to End Outsourcing', *NYU Stern Center for Business and Human Rights*, June, https://static1.squarespace.com/static/5b6df958f8370af3217d4178/t/5ed9854bf618c710cb55be98/1591313740497/NYU+Content+Moderation+Report_June+8+2020.pdf.

Barrientos, S. (2013), '"Labour Chains": Analysing the Role of Labour Contractors in Global Production Networks', *Journal of Development Studies*, 49/8: 1058–1071.

Barrientos, S. (2014), 'Gendered Global Production Networks: Analysis of Cocoa–Chocolate Sourcing', *Regional Studies*, 48/5: 791–803.

Barrientos, S. (2022), 'Regional Value Chains in the Global South: Governance Implications for Producers and Workers?', *Cambridge Journal of Regions, Economy, and Society*, 15/2: 437–443.

Barrientos, S., Gereffi, G., and Rossi, A. (2011), 'Economic and Social Upgrading in Global Production Networks: A New Paradigm for a Changing World', *International Labour Review*, 150/3–4: 319–340.

Barrientos, S., Kothari, U., and Phillips, N. (2013), 'Dynamics of Unfree Labour in the Contemporary Global Economy', *Journal of Development Studies*, 49/8: 1037–1041.

Bastia, T., and McGrath, S. (2011), 'Temporality, Migration and Unfree Labour: Migrant Garment Workers', *Manchester Papers in Political Economy*, Working Paper No. 6, (Manchester: University of Manchester Press), https://www.escholar.manchester.ac.uk/uk-ac-man-scw:146037.

Bate, R. (2004), 'Taxing Times: The Fight for National Sovereignty in Europe', *National Review Online*, 6 May, on file with author.

Baucom, I. (2005), *Specters of the Atlantic: Capital, Slavery, and the Philosophy of History* (Durham, NC: Duke University Press).

Bazbauers, A., and Engel, S. (2021), *The Global Architecture of Multilateral Development Banks* (London: Routledge).

BBC News (2006), 'In Quotes: The Doha Deadlock', 26 July, *BBC News*, news.bbc.co.uk/2/hi/business/5216080.stm.

BBC News (2021), 'World Bank Rejects El Salvador Request for Bitcoin Help', *BBC News*, 17 June, https://www.bbc.com/news/business-57507386.

BBC News (2022), 'Facebook-Funded Cryptocurrency Diem Winds Down', *BBC News*, 1 February, https://www.bbc.com/news/technology-60156682.

Beaulieu, E., Yatawara, R. A., and Wang, W. G. (2005), 'Who Supports Free Trade in Latin America?', *World Economy*, 28/7: 941–957.

Beauvisage, T., and Mellet, K. (2020), 'Datassets: Assetizing and Marketizing Personal Data', in K. Birch and F. Muniesa (eds.), *Assetization: Turning Things into Assets in Technoscientific Capitalism* (Cambridge, MA: MIT Press), 75–95.

Beckert, S., and Rockman, S. (eds.) (2016), *Slavery's Capitalism: A New History of American Economic Development* (Philadelphia, PA: University of Pennsylvania Press).

Bedford, K., and Rai, S. (2010), 'Feminists Theorize International Political Economy', *Signs: Journal of Women in Culture and Society*, 36/1: 1–18.

Béland, D., and Cox, R. H. (2016), *Ideas and Politics in Social Science Research* (Oxford: Oxford University Press).

Bello, W. (2000), '2000: The Year of Global Protest', *Global Policy Forum*, https://archive.globalpolicy.org/ngos/advocacy/protest/2001/03092000.htm.

Bergsten, C. F. et al. (2006), *China: The Balance Sheet: What the World Needs to Know about the Emerging Superpower* (New York: Public Affairs).

Bernanke, B. (2015), *The Courage to Lead: A Memoir of a Crisis and its Aftermath* (New York, NY: Norton).

Bernard, A. B., Jensen, J. B., Redding, S. J., and Schott, P. K. (2007), 'Firms in International Trade', *Journal of Economic Perspectives* 21/3: 105–130.

Bernards, N., and Campbell-Verduyn, M. (2019), 'Understanding Technological Change in Global Finance through Infrastructures', *Review of International Political Economy*, 26/5: 773–789.

Bernards, N. et al. (2020), 'Interrogating Technology-led Experiments in Sustainability Governance', *Global Policy*, 11/4: 523–531.

Bernstein, E. (2007), 'The Sexual Politics of the "New Abolitionism"', *Differences*, 18/3: 128–151.

Berry, D. R. (2017), 'The Ubiquitous Nature of Slave Capital', in H. Boushey et al. (eds.), *After Piketty: The Agenda for Economics and Inequality* (Cambridge, MA: Harvard University Press).

Best, J. (2005), *The Limits of Transparency: Ambiguity and the History of International Governance* (Ithaca, NY: Cornell University Press).

Best, J. (2014), *Governing Failure: Provisional Expertise and the Transformation of Global Development Finance* (Cambridge: Cambridge University Press).

Best, J. (2019), 'The Inflation Game: Targets, Practices and the Social Production of Monetary Credibility', *New Political Economy*, 24/5: 623–640.

Best, J., Hay, C., LeBaron, G., and Mügge, D. (2021), 'Seeing and Not-Seeing Like a Political Economist: The Historicity of Contemporary Political Economy and its Blind Spots', *New Political Economy*, 26/2: 217–228.

Best, J., and Patterson, M. (2009), *Cultural Political Economy* (London: Routledge).

Betz, T., Fortunato, D., and O'Brien, D. (2021), 'Women's Descriptive Representation and Gendered Import Tax Discrimination', *American Political Science Review*, 115/1: 307–315.

Beviglia Zampetti, A., and Tran-Nguyen, A-N. (2004), *Trade and Gender: Opportunities and Challenges for Developing Countries* (Geneva: UNCTAD), https://policycommons.net/artifacts/77230/trade-and-gender/.

Bhagat, A. (2018), 'Forced (Queer) Migration and Everyday Violence: The Geographies of Life, Death, and Access in Cape Town', *Geoforum*, 89/Spring: 155–163.

Bhagat, A., and Roderick, L. (2020), 'Banking on Refugees: Racialized Expropriation in the FinTech Era', *Environment and Planning A: Economy and Space*, 52/8: 1498–1515.

Bhagwati, J. (1958), 'Immiserizing Growth: A Geometrical Note', *The Review of Economic Studies*, 25/3: 201–205.

Bhambra, G. K. (2020), 'Colonial Global Economy: Towards a Theoretical Reorientation of Political Economy', *Review of International Political Economy*, 28/2: 307–322.

Bhardwaj, P. et al. (2018), 'When and How is Corporate Social Responsibility Profitable?', *Journal of Business Research*, 84/1: 206–219.

Bhattacharya, T. (2017), 'Introduction: Mapping Social Reproduction Theory', in T. Bhattacharya (ed.), *Social Reproduction Theory: Remapping Class, Recentering Oppression* (London: Pluto Press).

Bhattacharyya, G. (2018), *Rethinking Racial Capitalism* (Landham, MD: Rowman & Littlefield).

Bigelow, G. (2003), *Fiction, Famine, and the Rise of Economics in Victorian Britain and Ireland* (Cambridge: Cambridge University Press).

Bilić, P., Prug, T., and Žitko, M. (2021), *The Political Economy of Digital Monopolies: Contradictions and Alternatives to Data Commodification* (Bristol: Bristol University Press).

Birch, K., Cochrane, D., and Ward, C. (2021), 'Data as Asset? The Measurement, Governance, and Valuation of Digital Personal Data by Big Tech', *Big Data & Society*, 8/1: 1–15.

BIS (Bank for International Settlements) (2021), 'Covid-19 Accelerated the Digitalisation of Payments', Red Book Statistics, https://www.bis.org/statistics/payment_stats/commentary2112.pdf.

BIS (Bank for International Settlements) (2022), *Annual Report* (Basle: Bank for International Settlements).

Bishop, M. L., and Xiaotong, Z. (2020), 'Why is China a Reluctant Leader of the World Trade Organization?', *New Political Economy*, 25/5: 755–772.

Biziwick, M., Cattaneo, N., and Fryer, D. (2015), 'The Rationale for and Potential Role of the BRICS Contingent Reserve Arrangement', *South African Journal of International Affairs*, 22/3: 307–324.

Blackhurst, R. (1998), 'The Capacity of the WTO to Fulfill its Mandate', in A. O. Krueger (ed.), *The WTO as an International Organization* (Chicago, IL: University of Chicago Press).

Blaikie, P., and Brookfield, H. (1987), *Land Degradation and Society* (London: Methuen).

Blanchflower, D. G., and Shadforth, G. (2009), 'Fear, Unemployment and Migration', *The Economic Journal*, 119/535: F136–F182.

Bloomberg News (2017), 'Mastercard and Western Union Explore Digital Model for Refugee Camps', *Bloomberg News*, 20 June 2017.

Blustein, P. (2005), *And the Money Kept Rolling In (and Out): Wall Street, the IMF, and the Bankrupting of Argentina* (New York: Public Affairs).

Blustein, P. (2009), *Misadventures of the Most Favored Nations: Clashing Egos, Inflated Ambitions, and the Great Shambles of the World Trade System* (New York: Public Affairs).

Blustein, P. (2016), *Off Balance: The Travails Institutions That Govern the Global Financial System* (Waterloo: CIGI).

Blyth, M. (1997), 'Any More Bright Ideas? The Ideational Turn of Comparative Political Economy', *Comparative Politics*, 29/1: 229–250.

Blyth, M. (2002), *Great Transformations: Economic Ideas and Institutional Change in the Twenty First Century* (Cambridge: Cambridge University Press).

Blyth, M. (ed.) (2009), *Routledge Handbook of International Political Economy (IPE): IPE as a Global Conversation* (London: Routledge).

Bolton, J. R. (2000), 'Should We Take Global Governance Seriously', *Chicago Journal of International Law*, 1: 205–221.

Boohoo Group PLC (2020), 'Annual Reports and Accounts 2020', https://www.boohooplc.com/sites/boohoo-corp/files/all-documents/result-centre/2020/boohoo-com-plc-annual-report-2020-hyperlink.pdf.

Bordo, M., and B. Eichengreen (2002), 'Crises Now and Then', Working Paper w8716, National Bureau of Economic Research.

Bordo, M., Eichengreen, B., and Irwin, D. A. (1999), 'Is Globalization Today Really Different than Globalization a Hundred Years Ago?', Working Paper 7195, National Bureau of Economic Research.

Borrows, J., and Schwartz, R. (eds.) (2020), *Indigenous Peoples and International Trade: Building Equitable and Inclusive International Trade and Investment Agreements* (Cambridge: Cambridge University Press).

Boughton, J. (2001), *Silent Revolution: The International Monetary Fund, 1979–1989* (Washington, D.C.: International Monetary Fund).

Boughton, J. (2012), *Tearing Down Walls: The International Monetary Fund, 1990–1999* (Washington, D.C.: International Monetary Fund).

Bourguignon, F., and Morrisson, C. (2002), 'Inequality Among World Citizens: 1820–1992', *American Economic Review*, 92/4: 727–744.

Brace, L., and O'Connell Davidson, J. (2018), 'Slavery and the Revival of Anti-Slavery Activism', in L. A. Brace and J. O'Connell-Davidson (eds.), *Revisiting Slavery and Antislavery: Towards a Critical Analysis* (London: Palgrave Macmillan), 3–4.

Bradford, A. (2020), *The Brussels Effect: How the European Union Rules the World* (Oxford: Oxford University Press).

Brand, U., and Wissen, M. (2021), *The Imperial Mode of Living: Everyday Life and the Ecological Crisis of Capitalism* (New York, NY: Verso).

Brandl, B., and Dieterich, L. (2021), 'The Exclusive Nature of Global Payments Infrastructures: The Significance of Major Banks and the Role of Tech-Driven Companies', *Review of International Political Economy*, 30/2: 535–557.

Brantlinger, P. (1996), *Fictions of State: Culture and Credit in Britain, 1694–1994* (Ithaca, NY: Cornell University Press).

Brassett, J., Elias, J., Rethel, L., and Richardson, B. (2023), *I-PEEL: The International Political Economy of Everyday Life* (Oxford: Oxford University Press).

Braun, B. (2016), 'Speaking to the People? Money, Trust, and Central Bank Legitimacy in the Age of Quantitative Easing', *Review of International Political Economy*, 23/6: 1064–1092.

Braunstein, E., and Heintz, J. (2011), 'Central Banks, Employment and Gender in Developing Countries', in B. Young, I. Bakker, and D. Elson (eds.), *Questioning Financial Governance from a Feminist Perspective* (London and New York: Routledge), 90–109.

Braunstein, J. (2019), *Capital Choices: Sectoral Politics and the Variation of Sovereign Wealth* (Ann Arbor, MI: University of Michigan Press).

Bräutigam, D. (2020), 'A Critical Look at Chinese "Debt-Trap Diplomacy": The Rise of a Meme', *Area Development and Policy*, 5/1: 1–14.

Breslin, S. (2003), 'Reforming China's Embedded Socialist Compromise: China and the WTO', *Global Change, Peace, and Security*, 15/3: 213–229.

Brett, L. (2017), 'What Makes a Successful FinTech Hub in the Global FinTech Race?', *Deloitte Inside Magazine*, 16: 11–17.

Brewer, A. (1990), *Marxist Theories of Imperialism: A Critical Survey* (London: Routledge).

Brickell, K., Picchioni, F., Natarajan, N., Guermond, V., Parsons, L., Zanello, G., and Bateman, M. (2020), 'Compounding Crises of Social Reproduction: Microfinance, Over-indebtedness and the COVID-19 Pandemic', *World Development*, 136: 105087.

Brooks, R., and Simon, R. (2007), 'Subprime Debacle Traps Even Very Credit-Worthy', *The Wall Street*

Journal, 3 December, https://www.wsj.com/articles/SB119662974358911035.

Brooks, S. (2019), 'The Politics of Regulatory Design in the Sovereign Debt Restructuring Regime', *Global Governance*, 25: 393–417.

Brown, A. G. (2003), *Reluctant Partners: A History of Multilateral Trade Cooperation, 1850–2000* (Ann Arbor, MI: University of Michigan Press).

Brown, E., and Piroska, D. (2021), 'Governing FinTech and FinTech as Governance: The Regulatory Sandbox, Riskwashing, and Disruptive Social Classification', *New Political Economy*, 27/1: 19–32.

Brown, M. (2010), *Civilizing the Economy: A New Economics of Provision* (Cambridge: Cambridge University Press).

Brown, V. (1994), *Adam Smith's Discourse: Canonicity, Commerce and Conscience* (London: Routledge).

Broz, J. L. (2015), 'The Politics of Rescuing the World's Financial System: The Federal Reserve as a Global Lender of Last Resort', *Korean Journal of International Studies*, 13/2: 323–351.

Broz, J. L., Frieden, J., and Weymouth, S. (2021), 'Populism in Place: The Economic Geography of the Globalization Backlash', *International Organization*, 75/2: 464–494.

Bruges Group (2018), 'The Bruges Group', http://www.brugesgroup.com/about/the-bruges-group.

Brummer, C. (2012), *Soft Law and the Global Financial System* (Cambridge: Cambridge University Press).

Brutger, R., and Guisinger, A. (2022), 'Labor Market Volatility, Gender, and Trade Preferences', *Journal of Experimental Political Science*, 9/2: 189–202.

Brutger, R., and Li, S. (2019), 'Institutional Design, Information Transmission, and Public Opinion: Making the Case for Trade', *Journal of Conflict Resolution*, 66/10: 1735–1930.

Brutger, R., and Rathbun, B. (2021), 'Fair Share? Equality and Equity in American Attitudes Toward Trade', *International Organization*, 75/3: 880–900.

Brutger, R., and Strezhnev, A. (2022), 'International Investment Disputes, Media Coverage, and Backlash Against International Law', *Journal of Conflict Resolution*, 66/6.

Bryan, D., Martin, R., and Rafferty, M. (2009), 'Financialization and Marx: Giving Labor and Capital a Financial Makeover', *Review of Radical Political Economics*, 41/4: 458–472.

Bryan. S. (2010), *The Gold Standard at the Turn of the Twentieth Century* (New York, NY: Columbia University Press).

Bryant, R. C. (2003), *Turbulent Waters: Cross-Border Finance and International Governance* (Washington, D.C.: Brookings Institution).

Bryant, R. L. and Bailey, S. (1997), *Third World Political Ecology* (London and New York: Routledge).

Buchanan, P. J. (1993), 'America First—NAFTA Never', *Washington Post National Weekly Edition*, 15–21 November.

Buchanan, P. J. (2005), *Where the Right Went Wrong: How Neoconservatives Subverted the Reagan Revolution and Hijacked the Bush Presidency* (New York, NY: St. Martin's Griffin).

Bunting, A., and Quirk, J. (2018), 'Contemporary Slavery as More Than Rhetorical Strategy? The Politics and Ideology of a New Political Cause', in A. Bunting and J. Quirk (eds.), *Contemporary Slavery: The Rhetoric of Global Human Rights Campaigns* (Ithaca, NY: Cornell University Press), 3–5.

Busch, M. L., and Reinhardt, E. (2000), 'Geography, International Trade, and Political Mobilization in U.S. Industries', *American Journal of Political Science* 44/4: 703–719.

Caceres, C. et al. (2017), 'Drivers of Capital Flows and the Role of the Investor Base in Latin America', in *Regional Economic Outlook: Western Hemisphere: Tale of Two Adjustments* (Washington, D.C.: IMF), 81–108.

Callaghan, M., and Hubbard, P. (2016), 'The Asian Infrastructure Investment Bank: Multilateralism on the Silk Road', *China Economic Journal*, 9/2: 116–139.

Calleo, D. (1987), *Beyond American Hegemony* (New York, NY: Basic Books).

Calverley, D., and Anderson, K. (2022), 'Phaseout Pathways for Fossil Fuel Production Within Paris-compliant Carbon Budgets', IISD Research Report, (Winnipeg, MB: IISD).

Calvo, G. A., and Talvi, E. (2005), 'Sudden Stop, Financial Factors and Economic Collapse in Latin America: Learning from Argentina and Chile', Working Paper 11153, National Bureau of Economic Research.

Cameron, D. (1988), *The Free Trade Deal* (Toronto, ON: James Lorimer & Company).

Cames, M. et al. (2016), 'How Additional is the Clean Development Mechanism? Analysis of the Application of Current Tools and Proposed Alternatives',

Paper Prepared for DG CLIMA (Berlin: Oeko Institute).

Cammack, P. (2021), 'Blind Spots in IPE. What's Worth Reading', https://whatsworthreading.weebly.com/blind-spots-in-ipe.html.

Campbell-Verduyn, M. (ed.) (2018a), *Bitcoin and Beyond: Cryptocurrencies, Blockchains, and Global Governance* (New York: Routledge).

Campbell-Verduyn, M. (2018b), 'Introduction: What are Blockchains and How are they Relevant to Governance in the Global Political Economy?', in M. Campbell-Verduyn (ed.), *Bitcoin and Beyond: Cryptocurrencies, Blockchains, and Global Governance* (New York: Routledge), 1–24.

Campbell-Verduyn, M., Rodima-Taylor, D., and Hütten, M. (2022), 'Technology, Small States and the Legitimacy of Digital Development', *Journal of International Relations and Development*, 24: 455–482.

Capling, A. (2001), *Australia and the Global Trade System: From Havana to Seattle* (Cambridge: Cambridge University Press).

Capling, A., and Low, P. (2010), 'The Domestic Politics of Trade Policy-making: State and Non-State Actor Interactions and Forum Choice', in A. Capling and P. Low (eds.), *Governments, Non-State Actors and Trade Policy-Making* (Cambridge: Cambridge University Press), 4–28.

Cardoso, F. H., and Faletto, E. (1979), *Dependency and Development in Latin America* (Berkeley, CA: University of California Press).

Carnegie, A., and Gaikwad, N. (2022), 'Public Opinion on Geopolitics and Trade: Theory and Evidence', *World Politics*, 74/2: 167–204.

Carr, E. H. (1939/1946), *The Twenty Years' Crisis, 1919–1939* (New York, NY: Harper Perennial).

Carré, E., and Le Maux, L. (2020), 'The Federal Reserve's Dollar Swap Lines and the European Central Bank during the Global Financial Crisis of 2007–09', *Cambridge Journal of Economics*, 44: 723–747.

Carrington, D. (2022), 'Revealed: Oil Sector's "Staggering" $3bn-a-day Profits for Last 50 Years', *The Guardian*, 21 July, https://www.theguardian.com/environment/2022/jul/21/revealed-oil-sectors-staggering-profits-last-50-years.

Carstens, A. (2021), 'Regulating Big Tech in the Public Interest', Speech at the BIS Research Conference, 6–7 October (Bern: Bank for International Settlements).

Casey, M. J., and Vigna, P. (2018), 'In Blockchain We Trust', 9 April 2018, *MIT Technology Review*, https://www.technologyreview.com/2018/04/09/3066/in-blockchain-we-trust/.

Castell Roldán, E. Z., and Alvarez Anaya, Y. A. (2022), 'Migration and Dependency: Mexican Countryside Proletarianization and the Seasonal Agricultural Worker Program', *Dialectical Anthropology*, 46/2: 163–182.

Castree, N., and Braun, B. (1998), 'The Construction of Nature and Nature of Construction: Analytical and Political Tools for Building Survivable Futures', in N. Castree and B. Braun (eds.), *Remaking Reality: Nature at the Millennium* (New York: Routledge).

Castro, F. (1960), 'Speech Delivered to the UN General Assembly' (New York, United Nations).

Castro, F. (1996), 'Cuba and the End of Apartheid', *Socialism and Democracy,* 10/1: 1–5.

Cavalcanti, T. V., Mohaddes, K., and Raissi, M. (2012), 'Commodity Price Volatility and the Sources of Growth', Working Paper 12, International Monetary Fund.

Cavallero, L., and V. Gago (2021), *A Feminist Reading of Debt*, trans. L. Mason-Deese (London: Pluto Press).

Çelikkol, A. (2011), *Romances of Free Trade: British Literature, Laissez-Faire, and the Global Nineteenth Century* (Oxford: Oxford University Press).

Cement, V. et al. (2021), *Groundswell Part 2: Acting on Internal Climate Migration* (Washington, DC: The World Bank).

Cerny, P. (1994), 'The Dynamics of Financial Globalization', *Policy Sciences* 27/4: 319–342.

Cerny, P. G. (2016), 'In the Shadow of Ordoliberalism: The Paradox of Neoliberalism in the 21st Century', *European Review of International Studies*, 3/1: 78–91.

Césaire, A. (2001), *Discourse on Colonialism* (New York, NY: NYU Press).

Chakravartty, P., and da Silva, D. F. (2012), 'Accumulation, Dispossession, and Debt: The Racial Logic of Global Capitalism—An Introduction', *American Quarterly*, 64/3: 361–385.

Chancel L., and Piketty, T. (2021), 'Global Inequality 1820–2020: The Persistence and Mutation of

Extreme Inequality', *Journal of the European Economic Association*, 19/6: 3025–3062.

Chancel, L., Piketty, T., Saez, E., and Zucman, G. (eds.) (2022), *World Inequality Report 2022*. Harvard University Press. https://wir2022.wid.world/www-site/uploads/2021/12/WorldInequalityReport2022_Full_Report.pdf.

Charnovitz, S. (2003), 'Trade and Climate: Potential Conflicts and Synergies', *Beyond Kyoto: Advancing the International Effort Against Climate Change*, 141: 143.

Chen, J-G. (2017), 'Yan Fu's *Wealth of Nations*: A Victorian Adam Smith in Late Qing China', *Adam Smith Review*, 9: 145–168.

Chey, H. K. (2012), 'Theories of International Currency and the Future of the World Monetary Order', *International Studies Review*, 14/1: 51–77.

Chiang, C., Kuo, J. M., Naoi, M., and Liu, J. (2020), 'What do Voters Learn from Foreign News? Emulation, Backlash, and Public Support for Trade Agreements', Working Paper 27497, National Bureau of Economic Research.

Chimni, B. S. (2006), 'The World Trade Organization, Democracy and Development: A View from the South', *Journal of World Trade*, 40/1: 5–36.

Chin, G. (2014), 'The BRICS-led Development Bank: Purpose and Politics beyond the G20', *Global Policy*, 5/3: 366–374.

Chin, G. (2016), 'Asian Infrastructure Investment Bank: Governance Innovation and Prospects', *Global Governance*, 22/1: 11–26.

China Ministry of Commerce (2006), 'Debriefing on the WTO Hong Kong Ministerial', 13 January, on file with author.

Christiensen, Z. (2021), 'Poverty Trends: Global, Regional and National', Development Initiatives Factsheet, https://devinit.org/documents/1100/Poverty_trends_-_global_regional_and_national_-_November_2021.pdf.

Chuang, J. (2014), 'Exploitation Creep and the Unmaking of Human Trafficking Law', *American Journal of International Law*, 108/4: 609.

Chuji, M., Rengifo, G., and Gudynas, E. (2019), 'Buen Vivir', in A. Kothari, et al. (eds.), *Pluriverse* (New Delhi: Tulika Books).

Chwieroth, J. M. (2010), *Capital Ideas: The IMF and the Rise of Financial Liberalization* (Princeton, NJ: Princeton University Press).

Cioffi, J. W., Kenney, M. F., and Zysman, J. (2022), 'Platform Power and Regulatory Politics: Polanyi for the Twenty-First Century', *New Political Economy*, 27/2: 1–17.

Ciofu, S. M., and Stefanuta, N. (2016), 'TTIP, the Bullied Kid of Twitter', *Georgetown Public Policy Review*, 14.

Claessens, S., and Kose, M. A. (2013), 'Financial Crises: Explanations, Types, and Implications', IMF Working Paper, International Monetary Fund, https://www.imf.org/external/pubs/ft/wp/2013/wp1328.pdf

Clapp, J. (2020), *Food*, 2nd edn. (Cambridge: Polity Press).

Clarke, C. (2019), 'Platform Lending and the Politics of Financial Infrastructures', *Review of International Political Economy*, 26/5: 863–885.

Clarke, C., and Roberts, A. (2016), 'Mark Carney and the Gendered Political Economy of British Central Banking', *The British Journal of Politics and International Relations*, 18/1: 49–71.

Claude, I. L. (1959), *Swords into Plowshares; The Problems and Progress of International Organization*, 2nd edn. (New York: Random House).

Clausing, K. A., Saez, E., and Zucman, G. (2021), 'Ending Corporate Tax Avoidance and Tax Competition: A Plan to Collect the Tax Deficit of Multinationals', *UCLA School of Law*, Law-Economics Research Paper, No. 20–12.

Clemens, M. A., Montenegro, C. E., and Pritchett, L. (2008), 'The Pace Premium: Wage Differences for Identical Workers across the US Border', World Bank Policy Research Paper No. 4671 (Washington, DC: World Bank).

Clemens, M. A., Montenegro, C. E., and Pritchett, L. (2019), 'The Place Premium: Bounding the Price Equivalent of Migration Barriers', *Review of Economics and Statistics*, 101/2: 201–213.

Climate Action Tracker (2021), 'Glasgow's 2030 Credibility Gap: Net Zero's Lip Service to Climate Action', *Climate Action Tracker Publication*, https://climateactiontracker.org/publications/glasgows-2030-credibility-gap-net-zeros-lip-service-to-climate-action/.

Cline, W. R. (ed.) (1983), *Trade Policy in the 1980s* (Washington, D.C.: Institute for International Economics).

Coase, R. H. (1960), 'The Problem of Social Cost', *Journal of Law and Economics*, 3: 1–44.

Coburn, E. (2019), 'Trickle-Down Gender at the International Monetary Fund: The Contradictions of "Femina Economica" in Global Capitalist Governance', *International Feminist Journal of Politics*, 21/5: 768–788.

Cohen, B. (2015), *Currency Power* (Princeton: Princeton University Press).

Cohen, B. (2017), 'The IPE of Money Revisited', *Review of International Political Economy*, 24/4: 657–680.

Cohen, B. (2018), *Currency Statecraft* (Chicago, IL: University of Chicago Press).

Cohen, B. J. (2008), *International Political Economy: An Intellectual History* (Princeton, NJ: Princeton University Press).

Cohen, D. A., and Babey, S. H. (2012), 'Contextual Influences on Eating Behaviors: Heuristic Processing and Dietary Choices', *Obesity Reviews: An Official Journal of the International Association for the Study of Obesity*, 13/9: 766–779.

Colantone, I., and Stanig, P. (2018a), 'The Trade Origins of Economic Nationalism: Import Competition and Voting Behavior in Western Europe', *American Journal of Political Science*, 62/4: 936–953.

Colantone, I., and Stanig, P. (2018b), 'Global Competition and Brexit', *American Political Science Review*, 112/2: 201–218.

Comunicaffe (2018), 'bext360 and Coda Coffee Release the World's First Blockchain-Traced Coffee', Comunicaffe, 23 April, https://www.comunicaffe.com/bext360-and-coda-coffee-release-the-worlds-first-blockchain-traced-coffee/.

Conway, E. (2014), *The Summit* (London: Pegasus Books).

Conybeare, J. A. C. (1980), 'International Organization and the Theory of Property Rights', *International Organization*, 34/3: 307–334.

Conybeare, J. A. C. (1984), 'Public Goods, Prisoners' Dilemmas and the International Political Economy', *International Studies Quarterly*, 28/1: 5–22.

Cooke, B., and Kothari, U. (eds.) (2001), *Participation: The New Tyranny?* (London: Zed Books).

Cooper, R. N. (1972), 'Economic Interdependence and Foreign Policy in the Seventies', *World Politics*, 24/2: 159–181.

Cooper, R. N. (1975), 'Prolegomena to the Choice of an International Monetary System', *International Organization*, 29/1: 63–97.

Copelovitch, M., and Singer, D. (2020), *Banks on the Brink: Global Capital, Securities Markets, and the Political Roots of Financial Crises* (Cambridge: Cambridge University Press).

Cornelli, G. et al. (2021), 'Fintech and Big Tech Credit: What Explains the Rise of Digital Lending?', *CESifo Forum*, 22/2: 30–34.

Cornes, R., and Sandler, T. (1996), *The Theory of Externalities, Public Goods, and Club Goods*, 2nd edn. (Cambridge: Cambridge University Press).

Corntassel, J. (2014), 'Our Ways Will Continue On: Indigenous Approaches to Sustainability', in T. Mitchell (ed.), *The Internationalization of Indigenous Rights: UNDRIP in the Canadian Context* (Waterloo: CIGI).

Costanza, R. et al. (2014), 'Changes in the Global Value of Ecosystem Services', *Global Environmental Change*, 26: 152–158.

Couldry, N., and Mejias, U. A. (2019), 'Data Colonialism: Rethinking Big Data's Relation to the Contemporary Subject', *Television & New Media*, 20/4: 336–349.

Couldry, N., and Mejias, U. A. (2021), 'The Decolonial turn in Data and Technology Research: What is at Stake and Where is it Heading?', *Information, Communication & Society*, 26/4: 786–802.

Cox, R. W. (1981), 'Social Forces, States and World Orders: Beyond International Relations Theory', *Millennium*, 10/2: 126–155.

Cox, R. W. (1987), *Production, Power, and World Order: Social Forces in the Making of History* (New York, NY: Columbia University Press).

Cox, R. W. (1996), *Approaches to World Order* (Cambridge: Cambridge University Press).

Cox, R. W. (1999), 'Civil Society at the Turn of the Millennium: Prospects for an Alternative World Order', *Review of International Studies*, 25/1: 3–28.

Craig, L., and Mullan, K. (2011), 'How Mothers and Fathers Share Childcare: A Cross-National Time-Use Comparison', *American Sociological Review*, 76: 834–861.

Crane, A., LeBaron, G., Allain, J., and Behbahani, L. (2019), 'Governance Gaps in Eradicating Forced Labor: From Global to Domestic Supply Chains', *Regulation & Governance*, 13/1: 86–106.

Cristea, M. (2022), 'Nestlé Announces Full-Year Results for 2021 and Reports an Organic Growth of 7.5%', *Business Review*, https://business-review.eu/lifestyle/food-and-drinks/nestle-announces-full-year-results-for-2021-and-reports-an-organic-growth-of-7-5-228135.

CRL (Centre for Responsible Lending) (2007), 'Subprime Lending: A Net Drain on Homeownership', 27 March, CRL Issue Paper No. 14 (Durham, NC: Center for Responsible Lending).

Cronon, W. (1995), 'The Trouble with Wilderness: Or, Getting Back to the Wrong Nature', in W. Cronon (ed.), *Uncommon Ground: Toward Reinventing Nature* (New York: W. W. Norton).

Croome, J. (1995), *Reshaping the World Trading System: A History of the Uruguay Round* (Geneva: World Trade Organization).

Crouch, C. (2009), 'Privatised Keynesianism: An Unacknowledged Policy Regime', *The British Journal of Politics and International Relations*, 11/3: 382–399.

Culpepper, P. D., and Thelen, K. (2020), 'Are We All Amazon Primed? Consumers and the Politics of Platform Power', *Comparative Political Studies*, 53/2: 288–318.

Curato, N., Dryzek, J. S., Ercan, S. A., Hendriks, C. M., and Niemeyer, S. (2017), 'Twelve key Findings in Deliberative Democracy Research', *Daedalus*, 146/3: 28–38.

Curthoys, A., and Mitchell, J. (2018), *Taking Liberty: Indigenous Rights and Settler Self-Government in Colonial Australia, 1830–1890* (Cambridge: Cambridge University Press).

Curzon, G. (1965), *Multilateral Commercial Diplomacy: The General Agreement on Tariffs and Trade and its Impact on National Commercial Policies and Techniques* (New York, NY: Praeger).

Czarnezki, J. J., Homant, A., and Jeans, M. (2014), 'Greenwashing and Self-Declared Seafood Ecolabels', *Tulane Environmental Law Journal*, 28/1: 37–52.

Daddow, O. (2012), 'The UK Media and "Europe": From Permissive Consensus to Destructive Dissent', *International Affairs*, 88/6: 1219–1236.

Dadush, U. (2022), 'The Future of Global Value Chains and the Role of the WTO', Working Paper No. ERSD-2022-11, World Trade Organization.

Dafermos, Y., Gabor, D., and Michell, J. (2021), 'The Wall Street Consensus in Pandemic Times: What Does It Mean for Climate-Aligned Development?', *Canadian Journal of Development Studies*, 42/1–2: 238–251.

Dafoe, A. (2018), *AI Governance: A Research Agenda* (Oxford: Centre for the Governance of AI, Future of Humanity Institute, and University of Oxford).

Dahl, R. A. (1963), Modern Political Analysis (Englewood Cliffs, NJ: Prentice-Hall).

Dannreuther, C. and Kessler, O. (2017), 'Racialized Future: On Risk, Race and Finance', *Millennium: Journal of International Studies*, 45/3: 356–379.

Dastin, J., Hu, K., and Paresh, D. (2022), 'Exclusive: ChatGPT Owner OpenAI Projects $1 Billion in Revenue by 2024', *Reuters*, December, https://www.reuters.com/business/chatgpt-owner-openai-projects-1-billion-revenue-by-2024-sources-2022-12-15/.

Datta, M. N. and Bales, K. (2013), 'Slavery in Europe: Part 1, Estimating the Dark Figure', *Human Rights Quarterly*, 354: 817–829.

Dauvergne, P. (2020), 'Is Artificial Intelligence Greening Global Supply Chains? Exposing the Political Economy of Environmental Costs', *Review of International Political Economy*, 29/3: 1–23.

Davidson, C., Matusz, S., and Nelson, D. (2006), 'Fairness and the Political Economy of Trade', *World Economy*, 29/8: 989–1004.

Davies, J. B., Lluberas, R., and Shorrocks, A. F. (2017), 'Estimating the Level and Distribution of Global Wealth, 2000–2014', *Review of Income and Wealth*, 63/4: 731–759.

Davies, T. (ed.) (2019), *Routledge Handbook of NGOs and International Relations* (Abingdon: Routledge).

Dawson, M. (2004), *The Consumer Trap: Big Business Marketing in American Life* (Champaign, IL: University of Illinois Press).

De Cecco, M. (1974), *Money and Empire* (Oxford: Blackwell).

De Goede, M. (2000), 'Mastering Lady Credit: Discourses of Financial Crisis in Historical Perspective', *International Feminist Journal of Politics*, 2/1: 58–81.

De Goede, M. (2005), *Virtue, Fortune, and Faith* (Minneapolis, MN: University of Minnesota Press).

de Oliveira, F. A., and Kvangraven, I. H. (2023), 'Back to Dakar: Decolonizing International Political

Economy through Dependency Theory', *Review of International Political Economy*, 30/5.

Dean, A. (2015), 'The Gilded Wage: Profit-Sharing Institutions and the Political Economy of Trade', *International Studies Quarterly*, 59/2: 316–329.

Dedeoglu S. (2010), 'Visible Hands—Invisible Women: Garment Production in Turkey', *Feminist Economics*, 16/4: 1–32.

Dedrick, J., Kraemer, K. L., and Linden, G. (2011), 'The Distribution of Value in the Mobile Phone Supply Chain', *Telecommunications Policy*, 35/6: 505–521.

Del Felice, C. (2014), 'Power in Discursive Practices: The Case of the STOP EPAs Campaign', *European Journal of International Relations*, 20/1: 145–167.

Delautre, G. (2017), 'The Distribution of Value Added among Firms and Countries: The Case of the ICT Manufacturing Sector', *Working Paper* 16 (Geneva: ILO), http://www.ilo.org/global/research/publications/working-papers/WCMS_544190/lang--en/index.htm.

Delmas, M. A., and Burbano, V. C. (2011), 'The Drivers of Greenwashing', *California Management Review*, 54/1: 64–87.

Deloitte Consulting (2016), *The Expansion of Robo-Advisory in Wealth Management* (Berlin: Deloitte).

DeLong, J. B. (2022), *Slouching Towards Utopia: An Economic History of the Twentieth Century* (New York, NY: Basic Books).

Delors, J. (1988), '1992: The Social Dimension', Address by Jacques Delors, President of the Commission of the European Communities to the Trades Union Congress at Bournemouth, UK, 8 September, http://europa.eu/rapid/press-release_SPEECH-88-66_en.htm.

Denny, C., and Osborn, A. (2003), 'Farm Deal puts WTO Talks at Risk: Washington-Brussels Pact Angers Developing World by Backtracking on Subsidies', *The Guardian*, 14 August.

DeRock, D. (2021), 'Hidden in Plain Sight: Unpaid Household Services and the Politics of GDP Measurement', *New Political Economy*, 26/1: 20–35.

Deshingkar, P., Abrar, C. R., Sultana, M. T., Haque, K. N. H., and Md Reza, S. (2019), 'Producing Ideal Bangladeshi Migrants for Precarious Construction Work in Qatar', *Journal of Ethnic and Migration Studies*, 45/14: 2723–2738.

Desmond, M. (2019), 'In Order to Understand the Brutality of American Capitalism, You Have to Start at the Plantation', *New York Times Magazine*, August, https://www.nytimes.com/interactive/2019/08/14/magazine/slavery-capitalism.html.

Development Initiatives (2023), 'Economic Poverty Trends: Global, Regional and National Factsheet', *devinit.org*, https://devinit.org/documents/1285/Economic_poverty_factsheet_February_2023_JRJ2Y4f.pdf.

Deville J. (2015), *Lived Economies of Default: Consumer Credit, Debt Collection, and the Capture of Affect* (Abingdon: Routledge).

DG Trade (2015), 'Client and Supplier Countries of the EU28 in Merchandise Trade', on file with author.

DiCaprio, A., and Trommer, S. (2010), 'Bilateral Graduation: The Impact of EPAs on LDC Trade Space', *Journal of Development Studies*, 46/9: 1607–1627.

Dicken, P. (2015), *Global Shift: Mapping the Changing Contours of the World Economy*, 7th edn. (Thousand Oaks, CA: Sage).

Dilley, A. R. (2008), 'The Economics of Empire', in S. E. Stockwell (ed.), *The British Empire: Themes and Perspectives* (Oxford: Blackwell): 101–130.

Dirlik, A. (2002), 'Rethinking Colonialism: Globalization, Postcolonialism, and The Nation', *Interventions*, 4/3: 428–448.

Dodd, N. (2014), *The Social Life of Money* (Princeton, NJ: Princeton University Press).

Dodd, N. (2018), 'The Social Life of Bitcoin', *Theory, Culture, and Society*, 35/3: 35–56.

Dollar, D., and Svensson, J. (2000), 'What Explains the Success or Failure of Structural Adjustment Programmes?', *The Economic Journal*, 110: 894–917.

Domínguez-Villalobos, L., and Brown-Grossman, F. (2010), 'Trade Liberalization and Gender Wage Inequality in Mexico', *Feminist Economics*, 16/4: 53–79.

Doner, R. F., Noble, G. W., and Ravenhill, J. (2021), *The Political Economy of Automotive Industrialization in East Asia* (Oxford: Oxford University Press).

Donnan, S. (2017), 'Fears for Global Trade as Trump Fires First Shots to Kneecap WTO', *Financial Times*, 10 November, https://www.ft.com/content/5afbd914-a2b2-11e7-8d56-98a09be71849.

Dorn, F., Fuest, C., and Potrafke, N. (2022), 'Trade Openness and Income Inequality: New Empirical Evidence', *Economic Inquiry*, 60/1: 202–223.

Dos Santos, N. B., and Cunha, R. (2005), 'Generalized System of Preferences in General Agreement on Tariffs and Trade/World Trade Organization: History and Current Issues', *Journal of World Trade*, 39/4.

Dow, S. (2019), '"Such Brutality": Tricked into Slavery in the Thai Fishing Industry', *The Guardian*, 21 September, https://www.theguardian.com/world/2019/sep/21/such-brutality-tricked-into-slavery-in-the-thai-fishing-industry.

Doyal, L. (1995), *What Makes Women Sick? Gender and the Political Economy of Health* (Palgrave Macmillan).

Drache, D., and Froese, M. D. (2022), *Has Populism Won? The War on Liberal Democracy*, (Toronto, ON: ECW Press).

Drescher, S. (2002), *The Mighty Experiment: Free Labor versus Slavery in British Emancipation* (Oxford: Oxford University Press).

Drezner, D. (2001), 'Globalization and Policy Convergence', *International Studies Review*, 3/1: 53–78.

Drezner, D. W. (2007), *All Politics is Global: Explaining International Regulatory Regimes* (Princeton, NJ: Princeton University Press).

Drezner, D. W. (2014), *The System Worked: How the World Stopped Another Great Depression* (Oxford: Oxford University Press).

Du Bois, W. E. B. (1946), *The World and Africa: An Inquiry into the Part Which Africa has Played in World History* (New York, NY: International Publishers).

Du Bois, W. E. B. (2003/2007), *The Souls of Black Folk* (Oxford: Oxford University Press).

Dufour, L. et al. (2021), *Cleaning up their Act? G7 Fossil Fuel Investments in a Time of Green Recovery* (Teddington, UK: Tearfund).

Duina, F. (2007), 'The Social Construction of Free Trade', *The Social Construction of Free Trade* (Princeton, NJ: Princeton University Press).

Dupont, C. (1998), 'European Integration and APEC: The Search for Institutional Blueprints', in V. K. Aggarwal and C. Morrison (eds.), *Asia-Pacific Crossroads: Regime Creation and the Future of APEC* (New York, NY: St Martin's Press).

Dupont, C., and Hefeker, C. (2001), 'Integration Linkages: Between Trade-Offs and Spillovers', Paper Presented at the 4th Pan-European IR Conference, Canterbury, 8–10 September.

Düppe, T. (2011), *The Making of the Economy: A Phenomenology of Economic Thought* (New York, NY: Lexington).

Dutta, M. (2021), 'Becoming "Active Labour Protestors": Women Workers Organizing in India's Garment Export Factories', *Globalizations*, 18/8: 1420–1435.

Dymski G. (2009), 'Racial Exclusion and the Political Economy of the Subprime Crisis', *Historical Materialism*, 17/2: 149–179.

Eagleton-Pearce, M. (2016), *Neoliberalism: The Key Concepts* (Abingdon: Routledge).

Eckel, C. C., and Grossman, P. J. (2008), 'Men, Women and Risk Aversion: Experimental Evidence', *Handbook of Experimental Economics Results*, 1: 1061–1073.

Eckstein, D., Künzel, V., and Schäfer, L. (2021), 'Global Climate Risk Index 2021', Briefing Paper, Germanwatch.

Edge, R. M., and J. N. Liang (2019), 'New Financial Stability Governance Structures and Central Banks', Hutchins Centre Working Paper No. 50 (Washington, DC: Brookings Institution).

Edmond, R. (1997), *Representing the South Pacific: Colonial Discourse from Cook to Gaugin* (Cambridge: Cambridge University Press).

Edwards, C., and De Rugy, V. (2002), 'International Tax Competition: A 21st-Century Restraint on Government', Policy Analysis No. 431 (Washington, DC: Cato Institute), https://object.cato.org/pubs/pas/pa431.pdf.

Edwards, S. (2005), 'Capital Controls, Sudden Stops and Current Account Reversals', Working Paper 11170, National Bureau of Economic Research.

Egger, M., Sulu-Gambari, F., and Lebreton, L. (2020), 'First Evidence of Plastic Fallout from the North Pacific Garbage Patch', *Scientific Reports*, 10.

Ehrlich, S., and Maestas, C. (2010), 'Risk Orientation, Risk Exposure, and Policy Opinions: The Case of Free Trade', *Political Psychology*, 31/5: 657–684.

Eichengreen, B. (ed.) (1985), *The Gold Standard in Theory and History* (New York, NY: Methuen).

Eichengreen, B. (ed.) (1992), *Golden Fetters: The Gold Standard and the Great Depression: 1919–1939* (Oxford: Oxford University Press).

Eichengreen, B. (2011), *Exorbitant Privilege* (Oxford: Oxford University Press).

Eichengreen, B. (2014), 'Do the BRICs Need Their Own Development Bank?', *The Guardian*, 14 August.

Eichengreen, B. J., and Bordo, M. D. (2002), 'Crises Now and Then: What Lessons from the Last Era of Financial Globalization?', Working Paper 8716, National Bureau of Economic Research.

Elhacham, E. et al. (2020), 'Global Human-Made Mass Exceeds all Living Biomass', *Nature*, 588: 442–444.

Elias, J. (2004), *Fashioning Inequality? The Multinational Company and Gendered Employment in a Globalizing World* (Farnham, UK: Ashgate Publishing).

Elias, J. (2010), 'Locating the Everyday in International Political Economy: That Roar Which Lies on the Other Side of Silence', *International Studies Review*, 12/4: 603–609.

Elias, J. (2011), 'Critical Feminist Scholarship and IPE', in S. Shields, et al. (eds.), *Critical International Political Economy: Dialogue, Debate and Dissensus* (London: Palgrave Macmillan), 99–113.

Elias, J., and Roberts, A. (2016), 'Feminist Global Political Economies of the Everyday: From Bananas to Bingo', *Globalizations*, 13/6: 787–800.

Elias, J., and Roberts, A. (eds.) (2018), *Feminist Global Political Economies of the Everyday* (London and New York: Routledge).

Elkins, C. (2022), *Legacy of Violence: A History of the British Empire* (Toronto, ON: Knopf).

Elsig, M., and Dupont, C. (2012), 'Persistent Deadlocks in Multilateral Trade Negotiations: The Case of Doha', in A. Narlikar, M. Daunton, and R. M. Stern (eds.), *The Oxford Handbook on the World Trade Organization* (Oxford: Oxford University Press).

Elson, D. (1995), *Male Bias in the Development Process*, 1st edn. (Manchester: Manchester University Press).

Elson, D. (2012), 'Social Reproduction in the Global Crisis: Rapid Recovery or Long-lasting Depletion?', in P. Utting, S. Razavi, and R. V. Buchholz (eds.), *The Global Crisis and Transformative Social Change* (London: Palgrave Macmillan), 63–80.

Elson, D. (2013), 'Economic Crises from the 1980s to the 2010s', in S. M. Rai and G. Wayeln (eds.), *New Frontiers in Feminist Political Economy* (London: Routledge), 189–212.

Elson, D., and Çağatay, N. (2000), 'The Social Content of Macroeconomic Policies', *World Development*, 28/7: 1347–1364.

Eltis, D., and Engerman, S. (2000), 'The Importance of Slavery and the Slave Trade to Industrializing Britain', *The Journal of Economic History*, 60/1: 123–144.

Eni, R., Phillips-Beck, W., Achan, G. K., Lavoie, J. G., Kinew, K. A., and Katz, A. (2021), 'Decolonizing Health in Canada: A Manitoba First Nation Perspective', *International Journal for Equity in Health*, 20/1: 206.

Enloe, C. (2013), *Seriously! Investigating Crashes and Crises as if Women Mattered* (Berkeley, CA: University of California Press).

Epstein, G. (2005), 'Introduction: Financialization and the World Economy', in G. Epstein (ed.), *Financialization and the World Economy* (North Hampton, NH: Edward Elgar Publishing Limited).

Erb, G. (1974), 'The Developing Countries in the Tokyo Round', in J. W. Howe (ed.), *The US and the Developing World: Agenda for Action 1974* (New York, NY: Praeger).

Ervine, K. (2010), 'Participation Denied: The Global Environment Facility, its Universal Blueprint, and the Mexico-Mesoamerican Biological Corridor in Chiapas', *Third World Quarterly*, 31: 773–790.

Ervine, K. (2018), *Carbon* (Basingstoke: Polity).

Escobar, A. (1995), *Encountering Development: The Making and Unmaking of the Third World* (Princeton, NJ: Princeton University Press).

Escobar, A. (2011), *Encountering Development: The Making and Unmaking of the Third World*, 3rd edn. (Princeton, NJ: Princeton University Press).

Espey, J., Harper, C., and Jones, N. (2010), 'Crisis, Care and Childhood: The Impact of Economic Crisis on Care Work in Poor Households in the Developing World', *Gender & Development*, 18/2: 291–307.

Espinoza, J., and Fleming, S. (2023), 'EU Opens Subsidy Race with US to Fight Exodus of Green Projects', *Financial Times*, 9 March 2023.

Etherington, N. (1984), *Theories of Imperialism: War, Conquest and Capital* (London: Croom Helm).

European Commission (2019), *EU-China: A Strategic Outlook* (Brussels: High Representative of the Union for Foreign Affairs and Security Policy), https://eur-lex.europa.eu/legal-content/EN/TXT/PDF/?uri=CELEX:52019JC0005.

European Commission (2021), *Joint EU–US Statement on a Global Arrangement on Sustainable Steel and Aluminium* (Brussels: European Union), https://ec.europa.eu/commission/presscorner/detail/en/ip_21_5724.

European Commission (2023), *China: EU Trade Relations with China* (Brussels: European Commission),https://policy.trade.ec.europa.eu/eu-trade-relationships-country-and-region/countries-and-regions/china_en.

European Environment Agency (2019), *Trends in Atmospheric Concentrations of CO2 (ppm) between 1800–2017* (Copenhagen: EEA), https://www.eea.europa.eu/data-and-maps/daviz/atmospheric-concentration-of-carbon-dioxide-5#tab-chart_5_filters=%7B%22rowFilters%22%3A%7B%7D%3B%22columnFilters%22%3A%7B%22pre_config_polutant%22%3A%5B%22CO2%20(ppm)%22%5D%7D%7D.

European Stability Mechanism (ESM) (2019), *Safeguarding the Euro in Times of Crisis* (Luxembourg: Publications Office of the European Union).

Eurostat (2023), 'China-EU—International Trade in Goods Statistics', February 2023, https://ec.europa.eu/eurostat/statistics-explained/index.php/China-EU_-_international_trade_in_goods_statistics.

Evans, A. (2017), 'Patriarchal Unions = Weaker Unions? Industrial Relations in the Asian Garment Industry', *Third World Quarterly*, 38/7: 1619–1638.

Evemy, J., Yates, E., and Eggleston, A. (2021), 'Monetary Policy as Usual? The Bank of England's Extraordinary Monetary Policies and the Disciplining of Labour', *New Political Economy*, 26/5: 832–850.

Evers, S. J. T. M., and Kooy, M. (2011), *Eviction from the Chagos Islands: Displacement and Struggle for Identity Against Two World Powers* (Leiden and Boston: Brill).

Fairchild, D., and Weinrub, A. (2017), 'Introduction', in A. D. Fairchild and A. Weinrub (eds.), *Energy Democracy: Advancing Equity in Clean Energy Solutions* (Washington, D.C.: Island Press).

Fairtrade (2023), 'Home', Fairtrade Canada, https://fairtrade.ca/.

Fanon, F. (1963), *The Wretched of the Earth* (New York, NY: Grove Press).

FAO (Food and Agriculture Organization) (2003), *Trade Reforms and Food Security: Conceptualising the Linkages* (Rome: FAO).

FAO (Food and Agriculture Organization) (2022), *Food Outlook—Biannual Report on Global Food Markets* (Rome: FAO).

Farrell, H., and Newman, A. L. (2014), 'Domestic Institutions Beyond the Nation-State: Charting the New Interdependence Approach', *World Politics*, 66/2: 331–363.

Farrell, H., and Newman, A. L. (2015), 'The New Politics of Interdependence', *Comparative Political Studies*, 48/4: 497–526.

Farrell, H., and Newman, A. L. (2016), 'The New Interdependence Approach: Theoretical Development and Empirical Demonstration', *Review of International Political Economy*, 23/5: 713–736.

Farrell, H., and Newman, A. L. (2019a), *Of Privacy and Power: The Transatlantic Struggle Over Freedom and Security* (Princeton, NJ: Princeton University Press).

Farrell, H., and Newman, A. L. (2019b), 'Weaponized Interdependence: How Global Economic Networks Shape State Coercion', *International Security* 44/1: 42–79.

Faux, J., and Lee, T. (1992), 'The Effect of George Bush's NAFTA on American Workers: Ladder Up or Ladder Down?' (Washington, D.C.: Economic Policy Institute), https://www.epi.org/publication/epi_virlib_briefingpapers_1992_effecto/.

(FCIC) Financial Crisis Inquiry Commission (2011), 'The Financial Crisis Inquiry Report: Final Report on the Causes of the Financial and Economic Crisis in the United States', FCIC https://www.govinfo.gov/content/pkg/GPO-FCIC/pdf/GPO-FCIC.pdf.

FDIC (Federal Deposit Insurance Corporation) (1997), 'Chapter 5: The LDC Debt Crisis', in *History of the 80s*, https://www.fdic.gov/bank/historical/history/vol1.html.

Federici, S. (2004), *Caliban and the Witch* (Brooklyn, NY: Autonomedia).

Feenstra, R. C., and Hanson, G. H. (1996), 'Globalization, Outsourcing, and Wage Inequality', *American Economic Review*, 86/2: 240–245.

Feis, H. (1945), 'The Future of British Imperial Preferences', *Foreign Affairs*, 24/4: 661–674.

Feng, H. (2006), *The Politics of China's Accession to the World Trade Organization: The Dragon Goes Global* (London and New York: Routledge).

Ferguson, J. (1990), *The Anti-Politics Machine: 'Development', Depoliticization, and Bureaucratic Power in Lesotho* (Cambridge: Cambridge University Press).

Ferguson, L. (2015), 'This Is Our Gender Person. The Messing Business of Working as a Gender Expert in International Development', *International Feminist Journal of Politics*, 17/3: 380–397.

Ferrín, M., Fraile, M., and García-Albacete, G. M. (2019), 'Adult Roles and the Gender Gap in Political Knowledge: A Comparative Study', *West European Politics*, 42/7: 1368–1389.

Fineman, M., and Dougherty, T. (eds.) (2005), *Feminism Confronts Homo Economicus: Gender, Law, and Society* (Ithaca, NY: Cornell University Press).

Finger, J. M., and Nogués, J. J. (2002), 'The Unbalanced Uruguay Round Outcome: The New Areas in Future WTO Negotiations', *World Economy*, 25/3: 321–340.

Finlayson, J. A., and Zacher, M. (1981), 'The GATT and the Regulation of Trade Barriers: Regime Dynamics and Functions', *International Organization*, 35/4: 561–602.

Finnemore, M., and Sikkink, K. (1998), 'International Norm Dynamics and Political Change', *International Organization*, 52/4: 887–917.

Fioretos, O. (2016), 'Retrofitting Financial Globalization', in T. Rixen, L. Viola, and M. Zürn (eds.), *Explaining Institutional Development in World Politics* (Oxford: Oxford University Press).

Fischer, S. (2000), *On the Need for an International Lender of Last Resort* (Princeton, NJ: International Economics Section, Department of Economics, Princeton University).

Fischer, J. (2016), *Islam, Standards, and Technoscience: In Global Halal Zones* (Abingdon: Routledge).

Flandreau, M., and Zumer, F. (2004), *The Making of Global Finance, 1880–1913* (Paris: OECD Development Centre).

Fordham, B. O., and Kleinberg, K. B. (2012), 'How can Economic Interests Influence Support for Free Trade?', *International Organization*, 66/2: 311–328.

Foucault, M. (1970), *The Archeology of Knowledge* (New York, NY: Harper Collins).

France24 (2022), 'Google Parent Alphabet Nearly Doubles Annual Profit', *France 24*, 2 February, https://www.france24.com/en/business/20220202-google-parent-alphabet-nearly-doubles-annual-profit.

Francis-Devine, B., (2021), 'Coronavirus: Impact on Household Debt and Savings, House of Commons Library', 6 July, https://researchbriefings.files.parliament.uk/documents/CBP-9060/CBP-9060.pdf.

Frank, A. G. (1969), *Capitalism and Underdevelopment in Latin America: Historical Studies of Chile and Brazil* (New York: Monthly Review Press).

Frank, A. G. (1989), 'The Development of Underdevelopment', *Monthly Review*, 41/2: 1–36.

Frankel, J. A. (1997), *Regional Trading Blocs in the World Economic System* (Washington, D.C.: Institute for International Economics).

Frankel, J. A. (2005), 'Contractionary Currency Crashes in the Developing Countries', Working Paper 117, Center for International Development at Harvard University.

Frankfurt, H. (2015), *On Inequality* (Princeton, NJ: Princeton University Press).

Franklin, J. et al. (2021), 'Household Debt and Covid', 25 June, Bank of England Quarterly Bulletin 2021 Q2, https://www.bankofengland.co.uk/quarterly-bulletin/2021/2021-q2/household-debt-and-covid.

Fraser, N. (2009), 'Feminism, Capitalism and the Cunning of History', *New Left Review*, 56: 97–117.

Frau-Meigs, D., and Nicey, J. (2012), *From NWICO to WSIS: 30 Years of Communication Geopolitics-Actors and Flows, Structures and Divides* (Bristol: Intellect Books).

Freedgood, E. (1999), 'Banishing Panic: Harriet Martineau and the Popularization of Political Economy', in M. Woodmansee and M. Osteen (eds.) *The New Economic Criticism: Studies at the Intersection of Literature and Economics* (London: Routledge).

Freeman, C. (2019), 'Constructive Engagement? The US and the AIIB', *Global Policy*, 10/4: 667–676.

Freire, P. (2018), *Pedagogy of the Oppressed* (London: Bloomsbury Publishing).

Fridell, G. (2014), 'Fair Trade Slippages and Vietnam Gaps: The Ideological Fantasies of Fair Trade Coffee', *Third World Quarterly*, 35/7: 1179–1194.

Fridell, G., Gross, Z., and McHugh, S. (eds.) (2021), *The Fair Trade Handbook: Building a Better World, Together* (Winnipeg, MB: Fernwood Publishing).

Fridell, M., Hudson, I., and Husdon, M. (2021), 'Uneven Outcomes: The Tensions, Contradictions, and Challenges in the Search for Fair Trade', in G. Fridell, Z. Gross, and S. McHugh (eds.), *The Fair Trade Handbook: Building a Better World, Together* (Winnipeg, MB: Fernwood Publishing).

Friedberg, A. L. (2005), 'The Future of US-China Relations: Is Conflict Inevitable?', *International Security*, 30/2: 7–45.

Frieden, J. (2006), *Global Capitalism: Its Fall and Rise in the Twentieth Century* (New York, NY: W. W. Norton).

Frieden, J. A. (1991), 'Invested Interests: The Politics of National Economic Policies in a World of Global Finance', *International Organization*, 45/4: 425–451.

Friedline, T. (2021), *Banking on a Revolution: Why Financial Technology Won't Save a Broken System* (Oxford: Oxford University Press).

Friedman, M. (1957), *A Theory of the Consumption Function* (Princeton, NJ: Princeton University Press).

Friedmann, H., and McMichael, P. (1989), 'Agriculture and the State System: The Rise and Decline of National Agricultures, 1870 to the Present', *Sociologia Ruralis*, 29/2: 94–117.

Friman, R., and Andreas, P. (eds.) (1999), *The Illicit Global Economy and State Power* (Lanham, MD: Rowman & Littlefield).

Fröbel, F., Heinrichs, J., and Kreye, O. (1978), 'The New International Division of Labour', *Social Science Information*, 17/1: 123–142.

Froud, J. et al. (2000), 'Shareholder Value and Financialization: Consultancy Promises, Management Moves', *Economy and Society*, 29/1: 80–110.

Frundt, H. J. (2009), *Fair Bananas! Farmers, Workers, and Consumers Strive to Change an Industry* (Tuscon, AZ: University of Arizona Press).

Fudge, J. (2018), 'Modern Slavery, Unfree Labour and the Labour Market: The Social Dynamics of Legal Characterization', *Social & Legal Studies*, 27/4: 414–434.

Fudge, J. (2019), '(Re)Conceptualising Unfree Labour: Local Labour Control Regimes and Constraints on Workers' Freedoms', *Global Labour Journal*, 10/2.

Fukuda-Parr, S., and Hulme, D. (2011), 'International Norm Dynamics and the End of Poverty: Understanding the Millennium Development Goals', *Global Governance* 17/1: 17–36.

Funabashi, Y. (1988), *Managing the Dollar: From the Plaza to the Louvre* (Washington, D.C.: Institute for International Economics).

Furlong, A., Aarup, S. A., and Horti, S. (2022), 'Who Killed the COVID Vaccine Waiver?', *Politico*, https://www.politico.eu/article/covid-vaccine-poor-countries-waiver-killed/.

G20 (Group of 20) (2022), 'G20 Bali Leaders' Declaration: The Bali Summit', 16 November 2022.

Gabbattis, J. (2021), 'Shell Says New "Brazil-sized" Forest Would Be Needed to Meet 1.5C Climate Goal', *Carbon Brief*, https://www.carbonbrief.org/analysis-shell-says-new-brazil-sized-forest-would-be-needed-to-meet-1-5c-climate-goal/.

Gabor, D., and Brooks, S. (2017), 'The Digital Revolution in Financial Inclusion: International Development in the FinTech Era', *New Political Economy*, 22/4: 423–436.

Gaikwad, N., and Suryanarayan, P. (2019), 'Attitudes Toward Globalization in Ranked Ethnic Societies', *SSRN*, 3 June 2019, http://dx.doi.org/10.2139/ssrn.3398262.

Galeano, E. (1973), *Open Veins of Latin America: Five Centuries of the Pillage of a Continent* (New York, NY: Monthly Review Press).

Gallagher, A. T. (2017), 'What's Wrong with the Global Slavery Index?', *Anti-Trafficking Review*, 8: 90–112.

Gallagher, K. (2015), *Ruling Capital: Emerging Markets and the Reregulation of Cross-Border Finance* (Ithaca, NY: Cornell University Press).

Gallagher, K., and R. Kozul-Wright (2022), *The Case for a New Bretton Woods* (Cambridge: Polity Press).

Gallego, A., Kuo, A., Manzano, D., and Fernández-Albertos, J. (2022), 'Technological Risk and Policy Preferences', *Comparative Political Studies*, 55/1: 60–92.

Gallego, A., and Kurer, T. (2022), 'Automation, Digitalization, and Artificial Intelligence in the Workplace: Implications for Political Behavior', *Annual Review of Political Science*, 25: 1–22.

Gálvez, A. (2018), *Eating NAFTA: Trade, Food Policies, and the Destruction of Mexico* (Oakland, CA: University of California Press).

Gamble, A. (1990), 'The Great Divide', *Marxism Today*, 31/3: 34–37.

Gamble, A., and Payne, A. (eds.) (1996), *Regionalism and World Order* (New York, NY: St Martin's Press).

Gamble A., and Prabhakar, R. (2005), 'Assets and Poverty', *Theoria: A Journal of Social and Political Theory*, 107: 1–18.

Gardner, R. N. (1956), *Sterling Dollar Diplomacy: Anglo-American Collaboration in the Reconstruction of Multilateral Trade* (Oxford: Oxford University Press).

Gardner, R. N. (1969), *Sterling–Dollar Diplomacy: The Origins and the Prospects of our International Economic Order*, 2nd edn. (New York, NY: McGraw-Hill).

Gardner, R. N. (1980), 'Sterling-Dollar Diplomacy in Current Perspective', in *Sterling-Dollar Diplomacy in Current Perspective*, 3rd edn. (Columbia: Columbia University Press).

Garrett, G., and Lange, P. (1996), 'Internationalization, Institutions, and Political Change', *International Organization*, 49/4: 627–655.

GATT (General Agreement on Tariffs and Trade) (1958), 'Trends in International Trade', *Report by a Panel of Experts* (Geneva: GATT).

Gay, D. (2005), 'Vanuatu's Suspended Accession Bid: Second Thoughts', in P. Gallagher, P. Low, and A. L. Stoler (eds.), *Managing the Challenges of WTO Participation: 45 Case Studies* (Cambridge: Cambridge University Press), 590–606.

Geddes, A., et al. (2020), *Doubling Back and Doubling Down: G20 Scorecard on Fossil Fuel Funding* (Winnipeg, MB: International Institute for Sustainable Development).

Geeta, C., and Nair, S. (2003), *Power, Postcolonialism and International Relations* (London: Routledge).

Geithner, T. (2014), *Stress Test: Reflections on Financial Crises* (New York, NY: Crown).

Gender and Trade Coalition (n.d.), 'Unity Statement', https://sites.google.com/regionsrefocus.org/gtc/unity-statement.

Gereffi, G., and Fernandez-Stark, K. (2016), *Global Value Chain Analysis: A Primer*, 2nd edn. (Durham, NC: Duke University Center on Globalization, Governance and Competitiveness), https://dukespace.lib.duke.edu/server/api/core/bitstreams/fd7a47de-df3b-4a75-9749-e5113e28def3/content.

Germain, R. (1997), *The International Organization of Credit* (Cambridge: Cambridge University Press).

Gandhi, G. (2019), *The Oxford India Gandhi: Essential Writings* (Oxford: Oxford University Press).

Ghazi, S. H. (2022), 'Here's What It's Like Living in One of the World's Hottest Cities', *Vice*, 14 June, https://www.vice.com/en/article/88q4pg/jacobabad-climate-change-heat-wave-extreme-weather.

Ghosh, A., Ostry, J., and Qureshi, M. (2018), *Taming the Tide of Capital Flows* (Cambridge, MA: The MIT Press).

Giddens, A. (2003), *Runaway World: How Globalization is Reshaping our Lives*, 1st edn. (London: Routledge).

Gilens, M. (1999), *Why Americans Hate Welfare: Race, Media, and the Politics of Antipoverty Policy* (Chicago, IL: University of Chicago Press).

Gill, B. S. (2021), 'A World in Reverse: The Political Ecology of Racial Capitalism', *Politics*, 43/2.

Gill, S. (1990), *American Hegemony and the Trilateral Commission* (Cambridge: Cambridge University Press).

Gill, S. (1998), 'New Constitutionalism, Democratisation and Global Political Economy', *Pacifica Review: Peace, Security & Global Change*, 10/1: 23–38.

Gill, S. (2000), 'Toward a Postmodern Prince? The Battle in Seattle as a Moment in the New Politics of Globalisation', *Millennium Journal of International Studies*, 29/1: 131–141.

Gill, S. (2002), 'Constitutionalizing Inequality and the Clash of Globalizations', *International Studies Review*, 4/2: 47–65.

Gill, S., and Cutler, C. (eds.) (2014), *New Constitutionalism and World Order* (Cambridge: Cambridge University Press).

Gill, S., and Law, D. (1989), 'Global Hegemony and the Structural Power of Capital', *International Studies Quarterly*, 33/4: 475–499.

Gilmore, R. W. (2007), Golden Gulag: Prisons, Surplus, Crisis, and Opposition in Globalizing California (Berkeley: University of California Press).

Gilpin, R. (1975), *U.S. Power and the Multinational Corporation* (London: Macmillan).

Gilpin, R. (1981), *War and Change in World Politics* (Cambridge: Cambridge University Press).

Gilpin, R. (1987), *The Political Economy of International Relations* (Princeton, NJ: Princeton University Press).

Gingrich, J., and Kuo, A. (2022), 'Gender, Technological Risk, and Political Preferences', in M. R. Busemeyer, A. Kemmerling, P. Marx, and K. Van Kersbergen (eds.), *Digitalization and the Welfare State* (Oxford: Oxford University Press).

Girard, T. (2021), 'Participatory Ambiguity and the Emergence of the Global Financial Inclusion Agenda', *Review of International Political Economy,* 29/5: 1690–1722.

Gjesvik, L. (2022), 'Private Infrastructure in Weaponized Interdependence', *Review of International Political Economy*, 30/2: 1–25.

Glaser, C. (2011), 'Will China's Rise Lead to War? Why Realism Does Not Mean Pessimism', *Foreign Affairs*, 90/2: 80–91.

Glassman, J., and Carmody, P. (2000), 'Structural Adjustment in East and Southeast Asia: Lessons from Latin America', *Geoforum*, 32/1: 77–90.

Global Footprint Network (2022a), *Country Overshoot Days* (Geneva: Global Footprint Network), https://www.overshootday.org/newsroom/country-overshoot-days/.

Global Footprint Network (2022b), *Earth Overshoot Day* (Geneva: Global Footprint Network), https://www.overshootday.org/.

Global Footprint Network (2022c), *Global Footprint Data* (Geneva: Global Footprint Network), https://data.footprintnetwork.org/#/.

Global Footprint Network (2022d), *How Many Earths? How Many Countries?* (Geneva: Global Footprint Network), https://www.overshootday.org/how-many-earths-or-countries-do-we-need/.

Global Trade Alert (2021), 'Global Dynamics', https://www.globaltradealert.org/global_dynamics/area_all/year-to_2021.

Globe Newswire (2022), 'Global Microfinance Market Report 2022: Market to Surpass 300 Billion by 2026', *Research and Markets*, 25 March, https://www.globenewswire.com/news-release/2022/03/25/2410223/28124/en/Global-Microfinance-Market-Report-2022-Market-to-Surpass-300-Billion-by-2026-Focus-on-Providing-Access-to-the-Unbanked-and-Alleviate-Property-Propels-Growth.html.

Godwin, C. (2021), 'US Lawmakers Introduce Bills Targeting Big Tech', *BBC News*, https://www.bbc.com/news/technology-57450345.

Goidel, K., Procopio, S., Terrell, D., and Wu, D. H. (2010), 'Sources of Economic News and Economic Expectations', *American Politics Research*, 38/4: 759–777.

Goldstein, J. and Keohane, R. O. (eds.) (1993) *Ideas and Foreign Policy: Beliefs, Institutions, and Political Change* (Ithaca, NY: Cornell University Press).

Gomez, G. (2015), *Argentina's Parallel Currency* (London: Routledge).

Goodfellow, M. (2019), 'Put our Colonial History on the Curriculum—Then We'll Understand Who We Really Are', *The Guardian*, https://www.theguardian.com/commentisfree/2019/dec/05/britain-colonial-history-curriculum-racism-migration.

Goodhart, C. (2011), *The Basel Committee on Banking Supervision* (Cambridge: Cambridge University Press).

Goodhart, C., and Illing, G. (eds.) (2002), *Financial Crises, Contagion, and the Lender of Last Resort* (Oxford: Oxford University Press).

Gooding, M. (2022), 'Diem is Dead. What next for Stablecoins?', *Tech Monitor*, 28 January, https://techmonitor.ai/technology/emerging-technology/facebook-diem-stablecoin-cryptocurrency.

Goodman, J., and Pauly, L. (1993), 'The Obsolescence of Capital Controls? Economic Management in an Age of Global Markets', *World Politics*, 46/1: 50–82.

Gore, E. (2022), 'Understanding Queer Oppression and Resistance in the Global Economy: Towards a Theoretical Framework for Political Economy', *New Political Economy*, 27/2: 296–311.

Gould, H. (2016), 'Vulnerable and Exploited: 7 Things We Learned about Migrant Labour in Palm Oil', *The Guardian*, 10 June, https://www.theguardian.com/sustainable-business/2016/jun/10/vulnerable-exploited-7-things-we-learned-about-migrant-labour-in-palm-oil.

Gowa, J. (1983), *Closing the Gold Window* (Ithaca, NY: Cornell University Press).

Grabel, I. (2015), 'The Rebranding of Capital Controls in an Era of Productive Incoherence', *Review of International Political Economy*, 22/1: 7–43.

Grabel, I. (2017), *When Things Don't Fall Apart: Global Financial Governance and Developmental Finance in An Age of Productive Incoherence* (Cambridge, MA: MIT Press).

Graeber, D. (2011), *Debt: The First 5,000 Years* (New York, NY: Melville House).

Grande, E., and Pauly, L. (eds.) (2005), *Complex Sovereignty: Reconstituting Political Authority in the Twenty-first Century* (Toronto, ON: University of Toronto Press).

Green, J. F. (2021), 'Does Carbon Pricing Reduce Emissions? A Review of Ex-Post Analyses', *Environmental Research Letters*, 16/4.

Green, M. (2019), 'China's Debt Diplomacy: How Belt and Road Threatens Countries' Ability to Achieve Self-Reliance', *Foreign Policy*, 25 April, https://foreignpolicy.com/2019/04/25/chinas-debt-diplomacy/.

Greenstone, M., Hasenkopf, C., and Lee, K. (2022), 'Air Quality Life Index', AQLI Annual Report, June 2022 (Chicago, IL: Air Quality Life Index).

Gregg, M., and Andrijasevic, R. (2019), 'Virtually Absent: The Gendered Histories and Economies of Digital Labour', *Feminist Review*, 123/1: 1–7.

Grey, S., and Patel, R. (2015), 'Food Sovereignty as Decolonization: Some Contributions from Indigenous Movements to Food System and Development Politics', *Agriculture and Human Values*, 32/3: 431–444.

Griffin, P. (2009), *Gendering the World Bank: Neoliberalism and the Gendered Foundations of Global Governance* (London: Palgrave Macmillan).

Griffin, P. (2017), *CDP Carbon Majors Report 2017* (London: CDP).

Griffin, P. (2019), 'The Everyday Practices of Global Finance: Gender and Regulatory Politics of "Diversity"', *International Affairs* 95/6: 1215–1233.

Grossman, G. M., and Helpman, E. (1995), 'The Politics of Free-Trade Agreements', *American Economic Review*, 85: 667–690.

Grossman, G. M., and Krueger, A. B. (1991), 'Environmental Impacts of a North American Free Trade Agreement', *NBER Working Paper*, 3914.

Grubel, H. G., and Johnson, H. G. (1967), 'Nominal Tariffs, Indirect Taxes and Effective Rates of Protection: The Common Market Countries 1959', *The Economic Journal*, 77/308: 761–776.

Guha, R. et al. (1997), *Dominance without Hegemony: History and Power in Colonial India* (Cambridge, MA: Harvard University Press).

Guisinger, A. (2009), 'Determining Trade Policy: Do Voters Hold Politicians Accountable?', *International Organization*, 63/3: 533–557.

Guisinger, A. (2017), *American Opinion on Trade: Preferences without Politics* (Oxford: Oxford University Press).

Guisinger, A., and Kleinberg, K. B. (2023), 'The Unlevel Playing Field: Gender, Discrimination, and Global Attitudes toward Trade', *Foreign Policy Analysis* 19/4.

Gunawardana, S. J. (2018), 'Industrialization, Feminization and Mobilities', in J. Elias and A. Roberts (eds.), *Handbook on the International Political Economy of Gender* (Cheltenham: Edward Elgar Publishing), 440–455.

Gunder Frank, A. (1966), 'The Development of Underdevelopment', *Monthly Review*, 18: 17–31.

Guthman, J. (2019), *Wilted: Pathogens, Chemicals, and the Fragile Future of the Strawberry Industry* (Oakland, CA: University of California Press).

Haagh, L. (2019), *The Case for Universal Basic Income* (Cambridge: Polity).

Haas, E. B. (1980), 'Why Collaborate? Issue-Linkage and International Regimes', *World Politics*, 32/3: 357–405.

Haas, P. M. (1992), 'Introduction: Epistemic Communities and International Policy Coordination', *International Organization*, 46/1: 1–35.

Habermas, J. (1979), *Communication and the Evolution of Society* (Boston, MA: Beacon Press).

Hacker, J. S. (2004), 'Privatizing Risk without Privatizing the Welfare State: The Hidden Politics of Social Policy Retrenchment in the United States', *American Political Science Review,* 98/2: 243–260.

Hagan, S. (2016), 'Expanding the IMF's Regulatory Authority—Incrementally', *Journal of International Economic Law*, 19: 375–377.

Hagan, S. (2020), 'Sovereign Debt Restructuring: The Centrality of the IMF's Role', Working Paper 20–13, Peterson Institute for International Economics.

Haggart, B. (2021), 'The Government's Role in Constructing the Data-driven Economy', in *Data Governance in the Digital Age: Special Report* (Waterloo: Centre for International Governance Innovation).

Hakelberg, L. (2020), *The Hypocritical Hegemon* (Ithaca, NY: Cornell University Press).

Hakelberg, L., and Rixen, T. (2021), 'Is Neoliberalism Still Spreading? The Impact of International Cooperation on Capital Taxation', *Review of International Political Economy*, 28/5: 1142–1168.

Hall, D. (2023), 'On "Blind Spots" in (International) Political Economy', *Review of International Political Economy*, 30/1: 384–399.

Hall, H. K., Kao, C., and Nelson, D. (1998), 'Women and Tariffs: Testing the Gender Gap Hypothesis in a Downs-Mayer Political-Economy Model', *Economic Inquiry* 36/2: 320–332.

Hall, S. (1979), 'The Great Moving Right Show', *Marxism Today*, January: 14–20.

Hall, S. (1989), 'Cultural Identity and Cinematic Representation', *Framework: The Journal of Cinema and Media*, 36: 68–81.

Hall, S. (1996), 'Race, Articulation, and Societies Structured in Dominance', in H. A. Baker, Jr., M. Diawara and R. Lindborg, (eds.), *Black British Cultural Studies Reader* (Chicago, IL: University of Chicago Press), 16–61.

Hall, S., du Gay, P., and Hall, S. (eds.) (2011), 'Introduction: Who Needs Identity?', in *Questions of Cultural Identity* (London: Sage).

Hally, S. M. (2016), 'Everyday Family Experiences of the Financial Crisis', *Journal of Economic Geography*, 16: 305–330.

Hameiri, S. (2020), 'Institutionalism Beyond Methodological Nationalism? The New Interdependence Approach and the Limits of Historical Institutionalism', *Review of International Political Economy*, 27/3: 637–657.

Hammond, S., and Ehret, T. (2022), *Cryptocurrency Regulations by Country* (London: Thomson Reuters).

Haney-Lopez, I. (2014), *Dog Whistle Politics: How Coded Racial Appeals have Reinvented Racism and Wrecked the Middle Class* (Oxford: Oxford University Press).

Hanhimäki, J. M. (2015), *The United Nations: A Very Short Introduction* (Oxford: Oxford University Press).

Hannah, E. (2016), *NGOs and Global Trade: Non-State Voices in EU Trade Policymaking* (Abingdon and New York: Routledge).

Hannah, E., Roberts, A., and Trommer, S. (2018), 'Can Gender Quality Give the WTO Renewed Purpose?', Opencanada.org, https://www.open canada.org/features/can-gender-equality-give-wto-renewed-purpose/.

Hannah, E., Roberts, A., and Trommer, S., (2021), 'Towards a Feminist Global Trade Politics', *Globalizations, Special Issue*, 18/1: 70–85.

Hannah, E., Roberts, A., and Trommer, S. (2022), 'Gender in Global Trade: Transforming or Reproducing Trade Orthodoxy?', *Review of International Political Economy*, 29/4: 1368–1393.

Hannah, E., Roberts, A., and Trommer, S. (2023), 'Feminist Interventions in Trade Governance', in M. Sawer, L. A. Banaszak, J. True, and J. Kantola (eds.), *Handbook of Feminist Governance* (Northampton, MA: Edward Elgar Publishing).

Hannah, E., Ryan, H., and Scott, J. (2017), 'Power, Knowledge and Resistance: The Revolutionary Potential of IGOs in Global Trade Governance?', *Review of International Political Economy*, 24/5: 741–775.

Hannah, E., Scott, J., and Trommer, S., (2015), *Expert Knowledge in Global Trade* (Abingdon: Routledge, Global Institutions Series).

Hannah, E. N. (2011), 'NGOs and the European Union: Examining the Power of Epistemes in the EC's TRIPS and Access to Medicines Negotiations', *Journal of Civil Society*, 7/2: 179–206.

Hannah, E. N. (2014), 'The Quest for Accountable Governance: Embedded NGOs and Demand Driven Advocacy in the International Trade Regime', *Journal of World Trade*, 48/3: 457–479.

Hansard (1805), *Debate in the House of Commons on the Second Reading of the Bill for the Abolition of the Slave Trade* (London: HMSO).

Hanson, F., Currey, E., and Beattie, T. (2020), 'The Chinese Communist Party's Coercive Diplomacy', *Analysis and Policy Observatory Policy Report*, https://apo.org.au/node/307991.

Harari, Y. N. (2018), 'Why Technology Favors Tyranny', *The Atlantic*, October 2018, https://www.theatlantic.com/magazine/archive/2018/10/yuval-noah-harari-technology-tyranny/568330/.

Hardin, G. (1968), 'The Tragedy of the Commons', *Science,* 162: 1243–1248.

Harding, A. (2021), 'UN Court Rules UK has no Sovereignty over Chagos Islands', 28 January, www.bbc.co.uk/news/world-africa-55848126.

Harding, J. (2002), 'Capitalism's Critics Urge New Global Institutions', *Financial Times*, 2 February, https://www.businesshumanrights.org/en/capitalisms-critics-urge-new-global-institutions.

Harker, C., and Martin, L. L. (2012), 'Familial Relations: Spaces, Subject, and Politics', *Environment and Planning A*, 44: 768–775.

Harmes, A. (2011), 'The Limits of Carbon Disclosure: Theorizing the Business Case for Investor Environmentalism', *Global Environmental Politics*, 11/2: 98–119.

Harmes, A. (2012), 'The Rise of Neoliberal Nationalism', *Review of International Political Economy*, 19/1: 59–86.

Harmes A. (2019), *The Politics of Fiscal Federalism: Neoliberalism versus Social Democracy in Multilevel*

Governance (Montreal, QC: McGill-Queens University Press).

Harper, S. J. (2018), *Right Here Right Now: Politics and Leadership in the Age of Disruption* (Toronto, ON: Signal, McClelland & Stewart).

Harvey, D. (1996), *Justice, Nature, and the Geography of Difference* (Oxford: Blackwell Publishing).

Harvey, D. (2005), *A Brief History of Neoliberalism,* 1st edn. (Oxford: Oxford University Press).

Harvey, D. I., Kellard, N. M., Madsen, J. B., and Wohar, M. E. (2010), 'The Prebisch-Singer Hypothesis: Four Centuries of Evidence', *The Review of Economics and Statistics*, 92/2: 367–377.

Haufler, V. (1997), *Dangerous Commerce* (Ithaca, NY: Cornell University Press).

Hawkins, D. G., Lake, D. A., Nielson, D. L., and Tierney, M. J. (eds.) (2006), *Delegation and Agency in International Organizations* (Cambridge: Cambridge University Press).

Hay, C. (2019), 'Brexistential Angst and the Paradoxes of Populism: On the Contingency, Predictability and Intelligibility of Seismic Shifts', *Political Studies*, 68/1: 187–206.

Haya, B. (2019), *The California Air Resources Board's U.S. Forest Offset Protocol Underestimates Leakage* (Berkeley, CA: University of California).

Hayek, F. V. (1948), 'The Economic Conditions of Interstate Federalism', reprinted in F. V. Hayek (ed.) (1980), *Individualism and the Economic Order* (Chicago: Chicago University Press), 255–272.

Heckscher, E. (1949), 'The Effect of Foreign Trade on the Distribution of Income', in S. Howard Ellis and L. A. Metzler (eds.), *Readings in the Theory of International Trade*, Volume 4 (Philadelphia, PA: Blakiston Company).

Hedges and Company (2022), 'How Many Cars Are There in the World in 2022', https://hedgescompany.com/blog/2021/06/how-many-cars-are-there-in-the-world.

Heede, R. (2019), *Carbon Majors: Update of Top Twenty Companies 1965–2017* (Snowmass, CO: Climate Accountability Institute).

Heer, J. (2001), 'Adam Smith and the Left', *National Post*, 3 December.

Hefner, R. W. (2006), 'Islamic Economics and Global Capitalism', *Society*, 44/16: 16–22.

Held, D., and McGrew, A. (2002), *Globalization/Anti-Globalization* (Cambridge: Polity Press).

Heldring, L., and Robinson, J. A. (2018), 'Colonialism and Development in Africa', in C. Lancaster and N. van de Walle (eds.), *The Oxford Handbook of the Politics of Development* (Oxford: Oxford University Press).

Hellebrandt, T., and Mauro, P. (2015), 'The Future of the Worldwide Income Distribution', Peterson Institute for International Economics Working Paper, 15/7.

Helleiner, E. (1994), *States and the Reemergence of Global Finance: From Bretton Woods to the 1990s* (Ithaca, NY: Cornell University Press).

Helleiner, E. (2000), 'Think Globally, Transact Locally: Green Political Economy and the Local Currency Movement', *Global Society*, 14/1: 35–52.

Helleiner, E. (2002), 'Economic Nationalism as a Challenge to Economic Liberalism?: Lessons from the 19th Century', *International Studies Quarterly*, 46: 307–329.

Helleiner, E. (2003), *The Making of National Money* (Ithaca, NY: Cornell University Press).

Helleiner, E. (2006), *Towards North American Monetary Union?* (Montreal, QC: McGill, Queen's University Press).

Helleiner, E. (2014a), *Forgotten Foundations of Bretton Woods: International Development and the Making of the Postwar Order* (Ithaca, NY: Cornell University Press).

Helleiner, E. (2014b), *The Status Quo Crisis: Global Financial Governance after the 2008 Crisis* (Oxford: Oxford University Press).

Helleiner, E. (2019), 'The Life and Times of Embedded Liberalism', *Review of International Political Economy*, 26/6: 1112–1135.

Helleiner, E. (2022), 'Silences of Bretton Woods', mimeo.

Helleiner, E. (2023), *The Contested World Economy: The Deep and Global Roots of International Political Economy* (Cambridge: University of Cambridge Press).

Helleiner, E., and Wang, H. (2018), 'Limits to the BRICS' Challenge: Credit Rating Reform and Institutional Innovation in Global Finance', *Review of International Political Economy*, 25/5: 573–595.

Henderson, E. A. (2013), 'Hidden in Plain Sight: Racism in International Relations Theory', *Cambridge Review of International Affairs*, 26/1: 71–92.

Henning, C. R. (2017), *Tangled Governance: International Regime Complexity, the Troika, and the Euro Crisis* (Oxford: Oxford University Press).

Henning, C. R. (2020), *Regional Financial Arrangements and the International Monetary Fund* (Waterloo: Centre for International Governance Innovation).

Herbst, J. I. (2014), *States and Power in Africa: Comparative Lessons in Authority and Control* (Princeton, NJ: Princeton University Press).

Hernandez, D. S. and Newell, P. (2022), 'Oro Blanco: Assembling Extractivism in the Lithium Triangle', *Journal of Peasant Studies*, 49: 945–968.

Herrmann, R. K., Tetlock, P. E., and Diascro, M. N. (2001), 'How Americans Think About Trade: Reconciling Conflicts Among Money, Power, and Principles', *International Studies Quarterly*, 45/2: 191–218.

Hetzner, C., and Kahn, J. (2022), 'Meta Threatens to Pull the Plug on Facebook and Instagram in Europe over Data Privacy Dispute', *Fortune*, 9 February, https://fortune.com/2022/02/09/meta-european-withdrawal-warning-gdpr-us-surveillance-ceo-daily/.

Hickel, J. (2019), 'The Contradiction of the Sustainable Development Goals: Growth versus Ecology on a Finite Planet', *Sustainable Development*, 27: 873–884.

Hickel, J., Dorninger, C., Wieland, H., and Suwandi, I. (2022), 'Imperialist Appropriation in the World Economy: Drain from the Global South through Unequal Exchange, 1990–2015', *Global Environmental Change*, 73/102467.

Hicks, J. (2019), '"Digital Colonialism": Why Some Countries Want to Take Control of Their People's Data from Big Tech', *The Conversation*, 26 December, https://theconversation.com/digital-colonialism-why-some-countries-want-to-take-control-of-their-peoples-data-from-big-tech-123048.

Hicks, J. (2020), 'Digital ID Capitalism: How Emerging Economies are Re-inventing Digital Capitalism', *Contemporary Politics*, 26/3: 330–350.

Hill Collins, P. and S. Bilge (2016), *Intersectionality* (Malden: Polity Press).

Hinton, L. (2022), 'Discursive Power: Trade Over Health in CARICOM Food Labelling Policy', *Frontiers in Communication*, 6/796425.

Hirschman, A. O. (1945), *National Power and the Structure of Foreign Trade* (Berkeley, CA: University of California Press).

Hirschman, A. (1978), *The Passions and the Interests: Political Arguments for Capitalism before Its Triumph* (Princeton, NJ: Princeton University Press).

Hiscox, M. J. (1999), 'The Magic Bullet? The RTAA, Institutional Reform, and Trade Liberalization', *International Organization*, 53/4: 669–698.

Hiscox, M. J. (2001), 'Class versus Industry Cleavages: Inter-Industry Factor Mobility and the Politics of Trade', *International Organization*, 55/1: 1–46.

Hiscox, M. J. (2002), *International Trade and Political Conflict: Commerce, Coalitions, and Mobility* (Princeton, NJ: Princeton University Press).

Hiscox, M. J., and Burgoon, B. A. (2004), 'The Mysterious Case of Female Protectionism: Gender Bias in Attitudes toward International Trade', *Weatherhead Center for International Affairs* (Boston, MA: Harvard University), http://www.tinyurl.com/meb2eqm.

Hiss, S. (2013), 'The Politics of the Financialization of Sustainability', *Competition and Change* 17/3: 234–247.

Hobson, J. M., and Seabrooke, L. (2007), *Everyday Politics of the World Economy* (Cambridge: Cambridge University Press).

Hoekman, B. (2011), 'Proposals for WTO Reform: A Synthesis and Assessment', *Minnesota Journal of International Law*, 20: 324.

Hoekman, B., and Kostecki, M. (2009), *The Political Economy of the World Trading System: The WTO and Beyond*, 3rd edn. (Oxford: Oxford University Press).

Hoekman, B., and Kostecki, M. (1995), *The Political Economy of the World Trading System* (Oxford: Oxford University Press).

Hoekman, B., and Mavroidis, P. C. (2021), 'WTO Reform: Back to the Past to Build for the Future', *Global Policy*, 12: 5–12.

Hoffmann, S. (1995), 'The Politics and Ethics of Military Intervention', *Survival*, 37/4: 29–51.

Hofmann C., Osnago, A., and Ruta, M. (2017), 'Horizontal Depth: A New Database on the Content of Preferential Trade Agreements', Policy Research Working Paper 7981, World Bank.

Hollis, H. (2002), 'The Rhetoric of Jane Marcet's Popularizing Political Economy', *Nineteenth-Century Contexts*, 24/4: 379–396.

Holmes, D. R. (2014), *Economy of Words: Communicative Imperatives in Central Banks* (Chicago, IL: Chicago University Press).

Holmes, M. (1994), 'The Conservative Party and Europe', *Bruges Group Paper No. 17*, on file with author.

Hongzhou, Z. (2015), 'China's Fishing Industry: Current Status, Government Policies, and Future Prospects', *China as a Maritime Power Conference* (Arlington, TX), https://www.cna.org/archive/CNA_Files/pdf/china-fishing-industry.pdf.

Hopewell, K. (2016), *Breaking the WTO: How Emerging Powers Disrupted the Neoliberal Project* (Stanford, CA: Stanford University Press).

Hopewell, K. (2019), 'US-China Conflict in Global Trade Governance: the new Politics of Agricultural Subsidies at the WTO', *Review of International Political Economy*, 26/2: 207–231.

Hopewell, K. (2020), *Clash of Powers: US–China Rivalry in Global Trade Governance* (Cambridge: Cambridge University Press).

Hopewell, K. (2022), 'Emerging Powers, Leadership, and South–South Solidarity: The Battle Over Special and Differential Treatment at the WTO', *Global Policy*, 13/4: 469–482.

Horowitz, D. L. (2000), *Ethnic Groups in Conflict, Updated Edition with a New Preface* (California: University of California Press).

Hoselitz, B. (1957), 'Noneconomic Factors in Economic Development', *The American Economic Review*, 47/2: 28–41.

Hossein, C. S. (2019), 'A Black Epistemology for the Social and Solidarity Economy: The Black Social Economy', *Review of Black Political Economy*, 46/3: 209–229.

Hossein, C. S., Austin, S. D., and Edmonds, K. (eds.) (2023), *Beyond Racial Capitalism: Cooperatives in the Global South* (Oxford: Oxford University Press).

Hossein, C. S., and Christabell, P. J. (eds.). (2022), *Community Economies in The Global South: Case Studies About Rotating Savings and Credit Associations and Economic Cooperatives* (Oxford: Oxford University Press).

Hossein, C. S., and Pearson, M. (2023), 'Black Feminists in the Third Sector: Here Is Why We Choose to Use the Term Solidarity Economy', *Review of Black Political Economy*, 50/2: 1–27.

Huang, Y., and Meyer, M. (2022), 'Digital Currencies, Monetary Sovereignty, and US–China Power Competition', *Policy and Internet*, 14: 324–347.

Hudec, R. E. (1975), *The GATT Legal System and World Trade Diplomacy* (New York, NY: Praeger).

Hudec, R. E. (2011), *Developing Countries in the GATT Legal System* (Cambridge: Trade Policy Research Centre & Cambridge University Press).

Hudec, R. E., Kennedy, D., and Sgarbossa, M. (1993), 'A Statistical Profile of GATT Dispute Settlement Cases: 1948–1989', *Minnesota Journal of Global Trade*, 2/1: 1–25.

Hull, C. (1948), *The Memoirs of Cordell Hull*, vols. 1–2 (New York, NY: Macmillan).

Hulme, D. (2012), *Global Poverty: How Global Governance is Failing the Poor* (New York, NY: Routledge).

Hume, D. (1748), 'Of National Characters', in D. Hume, *Essays: Moral, Political and Literary*, (reprint, 2007; New York, NY: Cosimo).

Husain, Z., Mukherjee, D., and Dutta, M. (2012), 'Self-Help Groups and Empowerment of Women: Self-Selection or Actual Benefits?', *Journal of International Development*, 26/4: 422–437.

ICAP (International Carbon Action Partnership) (2022), *Emissions Trading Worldwide: Status Report 2022* (Berlin: ICAP).

IFRC (International Federation of Red Cross and Red Crescent Societies) (2021), *Displacement in a Changing Climate: Localized Humanitarian Action at the Forefront of the Climate Crisis* (Geneva: International Federation of Red Cross and Red Crescent Societies).

IISD (International Institute for Sustainable Development) (2020), WTO Members Highlight Benefits and Drawbacks of E-Commerce Moratorium, https://sdg.iisd.org/news/wto-members-highlight-benefits-and-drawbacks-of-e-commerce-moratorium/#:~:text='%20The%20members%20state%20that%2C%20according,the%20extension%20of%20the%20moratorium.

Ikenberry, G. J. (2018), 'The End of Liberal International Order?', *International Affairs*, 94/1: 7–23.

Ikenberry, G. J. (2001), *After Victory* (Princeton, NJ: Princeton University Press).

Ikenberry, G. J. (2011), 'The Future of the Liberal World Order: Internationalism After America', *Foreign Affairs*, 90/3: 56–68.

Ikenberry, G. J. (2020), *A World Safe for Democracy: Liberal Internationalism and the Crises of Global Order* (New Haven, CT: Yale University Press).

ILO (International Labour Organization) (2009), *Gender Equality at the Heart of Decent Work* (Geneva: International Labour Organization).

ILO (International Labour Organization) (2012) *ILO Indicators of Forced Labour* (Geneva: ILO), https://www.ilo.org/global/topics/forced-labour/publications/WCMS_203832/lang--en/index.htm.

ILO (International Labour Organization) (2013), *Caught at Sea—Forced Labour and Trafficking in Fisheries* (Geneva: ILO), http://www.ilo.org/global/topics/forced-labour/publications/WCMS_214472/lang--en/index.htm.

ILO (International Labour Organization) (2014), *Wages and Working Hours in the Textiles, Clothing, Leather and Footwear Industries* (Geneva: ILO), http://www.ilo.org/sector/Resources/publications/WCMS_300463/lang--en/index.htm.

ILO (International Labour Organization) (2015), *World Employment and Social Outlook 2015: The Changing Nature of Jobs* (Geneva: ILO), https://www.ilo.org/wcmsp5/groups/public/---dgreports/---dcomm/---publ/documents/publication/wcms_368626.pdf.

ILO (International Labour Organization) (2017), *Global Estimates of Modern Slavery: Forced Labour and Forced Marriage* (Geneva: ILO and Walk Free), http://www.ilo.org/global/publications/books/WCMS_575479/lang--en/index.htm.

ILO (International Labour Organization) (2018), *Women and Men in the Informal Economy: A Statistical Picture*, 3rd edn. (Geneva: ILO), http://www.ilo.org/global/publications/books/WCMS_626831/lang--en/index.htm.

ILO (International Labour Organization) (2019a), *Business and Forced Labour* (Geneva: ILO), https://www.ilo.org/empent/areas/business-helpdesk/WCMS_DOC_ENT_HLP_FL_EN/lang--en/index.htm.

ILO (International Labour Organization) (2019b), 'Decent Work in Global Supply Chains: An Internal Research Review', *Working Paper* 49 (Geneva: ILO). http://www.ilo.org/global/research/publications/working-papers/WCMS_723274/lang--en/index.htm.

ILO (International Labour Organization) (2019c), *The Working Poor—or How a Job Is No Guarantee of Decent Living Conditions* (Geneva: ILO).

ILO (International Labour Organization) (2021), *Building Forward Fairer: Women's Rights to Work and Work at the Core of the COVID-19 Recovery* (Geneva: ILO).

ILO (International Labour Organization) (2022a), *Resolution Concerning Decent Work and the Social and Solidarity Economy* (Geneva: ILO), https://www.ilo.org/wcmsp5/groups/public/---ed_norm/---relconf/documents/meetingdocument/wcms_848633.pdf.

ILO (International Labour Organization) (2022b), *Global Estimates of Modern Slavery: Forced Labour and Forced Marriage* (Geneva: ILO, Walk Free, and IOM), https://www.ilo.org/wcmsp5/groups/public/---ed_norm/---ipec/documents/publication/wcms_854733.pdf.

ILO (International Labour Organization) (2022c), *What Is Forced Labour, Modern Slavery and Human Trafficking?* (Geneva: ILO), https://www.ilo.org/global/topics/forced-labour/definition/lang--en/index.htm.

ILO (International Labour Organization) (2023), 'Decent Work', *2030 Agenda for Sustainable Development*, https://www.ilo.org/global/topics/decent-work/lang--en/index.htm.

Im, Z. J., Mayer, N., Palier, B., and Rovny, J. (2019), 'The "Losers of Automation": A Reservoir of Votes for the Radical Right?', *Research & Politics,* 6/1: 1–7.

IMF (International Monetary Fund) (2009), *World Economic Outlook* (Washington, DC: International Monetary Fund, October).

IMF (International Monetary Fund) (2012a), *World Economic Outlook*, Special Feature: Commodity Market Review (Washington, D.C.: International Monetary Fund).

IMF (International Monetary Fund) (2012b), *The Liberalization and Management of Capital Flows: An Institutional View* (Washington, D.C.: International Monetary Fund).

IMF (International Monetary Fund) (2016), 'Neoliberalism: Oversold?', *Finance & Development,* 53/2: 38–41.

IMF (International Monetary Fund) (2017), *World Economic Outlook April 2017* (Washington, D.C.: International Monetary Fund), https://www.imf.org/en/Publications/WEO/Issues/2017/04/04/world-economic-outlook-april-2017.

IMF (International Monetary Fund) (2020), 'Financial Inclusion: What Have We Learned So Far? What Do We Have to Learn?', WP/20/157, August, https://www.imf.org/-/media/Files/Publications/WP/2020/English/wpiea2020157-print-pdf.ashx.

IMF (International Monetary Fund) (2021) 'Unconventional Monetary Policies in Emerging Markets and Frontier Countries', Working Paper No. 2021/014, https://www.imf.org/en/Publications/WP/Issues/2021/01/22/Unconventional-Monetary-Policies-in-Emerging-Markets-and-Frontier-Countries-50013.

IMF (International Monetary Fund) (2022a), *Regional Economic Outlook: Asia and the Pacific* (Washington, D.C.: International Monetary Fund), https://www.imf.org/-/media/Files/Publications/REO/APD/2022/October/English/text.ashx.

IMF (International Monetary Fund) (2022b). 'Capacity Development', https://www.imf.org/external/np/ins/english/capacity_about.htm#:~:text=Development%20needs%20to%20be%20economically,job%20creation%20and%20poverty%20reduction.

IMF (International Monetary Fund) (2023), *World Economic Outlook Update January 2023* (Washington, D.C.: International Monetary Fund), https://www.imf.org/-/media/Files/Publications/WEO/2023/Update/January/English/text.ashx.

Inikori, J. E. (1981), 'Under-Population in Nineteenth Century West Africa: The Role of the Export Slave Trade', *African Historical Demography II*, 30/3: 283–313.

IPCC (International Panel on Climate Change) (2018), *Headline Statements—IPCC SR1.5*, https://www.ipcc.ch/sr15/resources/headline-statements/ (Geneva: IPCC).

IRENA (International Renewable Energy Agency) (2022), *Renewable Energy Statistics 2022* (Abu Dhabi: IRENA), https://www.irena.org/publications/2022/Jul/Renewable-Energy-Statistics-2022.

Irwin, D. (2003), 'Explaining America's Surge in Manufacturing Exports, 1880–1913', *Review of Economics and Statistics*, 85/2: 364–376.

Irwin, D. (2011), *Peddling Protectionism: Smoot-Hawley and the Great Depression* (Princeton, NJ: Princeton University Press).

Irwin, D., and Kroszner, R. S. (1997), 'Interests, Institutions and Ideology in the Republican Conversion to Trade Liberalization, 1934–45', Working Paper 6112, National Bureau of Economic Research.

ISSP Research Group (2015), International Social Survey Programme: National Identity III—ISSP 2013 Data Set, *GESIS Data Archive* (Cologne: ISSP).

Jackson, R. H. (1993), 'The Weight of Ideas in Decolonization: Normative Change in International Relations', in J. Goldstein and R. O. Keohane (eds.), *Ideas and Foreign Policy: Beliefs, Institutions and Political Change* (Ithaca, NY: Cornell University Press).

Jacques Delors Institute (2022), *No More Free Lunch: Ending Free Allowances in the EU ETS to Benefit Innovation* (Paris: Jacques Delors Institute).

Jaffee, D. (2014), Brewing Justice: Fair Trade Coffee, Sustainability, and Survival, Updated *Edition with a New Preface and Final Chapter* (Oakland, CA: University of California Press).

Jaffee, D., Kloppenburg, J. R., and Monroy, M. B. (2004), 'Bringing the "Moral Charge" Home: Fair Trade within the North and within the South', *Rural Sociology*, 69/2: 169–196.

Jain, S., and Gabor, D. (2020), 'The Rise of Digital Financialisation: The Case of India', *New Political Economy*, 25/5: 813–828.

James, H. (1996), *International Monetary Cooperation Since Bretton Woods* (Washington, DC: IMF and Oxford: Oxford University Press).

Jang, W., and Newman, A. L. (2022), 'Enforcing European Privacy Regulations from Below: Transnational Fire Alarms and the General Data Protection Regulation', *Journal of Common Market Studies*, 60/2: 283–300.

Janow, M. E. and Mavroidis, P. C. (2019), 'Digital Trade, E-Commerce, the WTO and Regional Frameworks', *World Trade Review* 18/1: S1–S7.

Jentleson, B. (2022), *Sanctions: What Everyone Needs to Know* (Oxford: Oxford University Press).

Johnson, A. (2016), *From Convergence to Crisis: Labor Markets and the Instability of the Euro* (Ithaca, NY: Cornell University Press).

Johnson, J., and Barnes, A. (2015), 'Financial Nationalism and Its International Enablers: The Hungarian Experience', *Review of International Political Economy*, 22/3: 535–569.

Johnston, A. I. (2003), 'Is China a Status Quo Power?', *International Security* 27/4: 5–56.

Jolly, R., Emmerij, L., and Weiss, T. G. (2009), *UN Ideas that Changed the World* (Bloomingtom, IN: Indiana University Press).

Jones, C. (2010), 'Materializing Piety: Gendered Anxieties about Faithful Consumption in Contemporary

Urban Indonesia', *American Ethnologist*, 37/4: 617–637.

Jones, E., and Kira, B. (2020), 'It's Time to Talk Digital Trade', *UK Trade Policy Observatory Blog*, https://blogs.sussex.ac.uk/uktpo/2020/11/13/its-time-to-talk-digital-trade/.

Jones, L., and Hameiri, S. (2020), *Debunking the Myth of 'Debt-trap Diplomacy': How Recipient Countries Shape China's Belt and Road Initiative* (London: Chatham House).

Jones, L., and Hameiri, S. (2021), *Fractured China* (Cambridge: Cambridge University Press).

Justman, S. (1991), *The Hidden Text of Mill's Liberty* (London: Rowman and Littlefield).

Kahler, M. (2020), 'Cosmopolitans and Parochials: Economy, Culture, and Political Conflict', in J. P. Singh (ed.) *Cultural Values in Political Economy* (Stanford, CA: Stanford University Press).

Kahler, M. et al. (2018), *Global Governance to Combat Illicit Financial Flows: Measurement, Evaluation, Innovation* (New York: Council on Foreign Relations).

Kalaitzake, M. (2017), 'Death by a Thousand Cuts: Financial Political Power and the Case of the European Financial Transaction Tax', *New Political Economy*, 22/6: 709–726.

Kamugisha, A. (2019), *Beyond Coloniality: Citizenship and Freedom in the Caribbean Intellectual Tradition* (Bloomington, IN: Indiana University Press).

Kapstein, E. B. (1994), *Governing the Global Economy: International Finance and the State* (Cambridge, MA: Harvard University Press).

Kapur, D., and McHale, J. (2003), 'Migration's New Payoff', *Foreign Policy*, 139: 49–57.

Katzenstein, P. J. (2016), *Small States in World Markets*, (Ithaca, NY: Cornell University Press).

Katzenstein, P. J. (2022), *Uncertainty and Its Discontents* (Cambridge: Cambridge University Press).

Katz-Rosene, R., and Paterson, M. (2018), *Thinking Ecologically about the Global Political Economy* (London: Routledge).

Kay, J., and M. King (2020), *Radical Uncertainty* (New York, NY: W. W. Norton).

Keck, M. E., and Sikkink, K. (1998), *Activists Beyond Borders* (Ithaca, NY: Cornell University Press).

Kellstedt, P. M. (2000), 'Media Framing and the Dynamics of Racial Policy Preferences', *American Journal of Political Science*, 44/2: 245–260.

Kellstedt, P. M. (2003), *The Mass Media and the Dynamics of American Racial Attitudes*. (Cambridge: Cambridge University Press).

Kelsey, J. (2008), *Serving Whose Interests?: The Political Economy of Trade in Services Agreements* (New York, NY: Routledge-Cavendish).

Kempadoo, K. (2005), 'From Moral Panic to Global Justice: Changing Perspectives on Trafficking', in K. Kempadoo, J. Sanghera, and B. Pattanaik (eds.), *Trafficking and Prostitution Reconsidered: New Perspectives on Migration, Sex Work, and Human Rights* (Boulder, CO: Paradigm).

Kempadoo, K. (2015), 'The Modern-Day White (Wo) Man's Burden: Trends in Anti-Trafficking and Anti-Slavery Campaigns', *Journal of Human Trafficking*, 1/1: 8–20.

Kempadoo, K. (2017), '"Bound Coolies" and Other Indentured Workers in the Caribbean: Implications for Debates about Human Trafficking and Modern Slavery', *Anti-Trafficking Review*, 9: 48–63.

Kenney, M., and Zysman, J. (2020), 'The Platform Economy: Restructuring the Space of Capitalist Accumulation', *Cambridge Journal of Regions, Economy, and Society*, 13/1: 55–76.

Keohane, R. O. (1984), *After Hegemony: Cooperation and Discord in the World Political Economy* (Princeton, NJ: Princeton University Press).

Keohane, R. O. (1997), 'Problematic Lucidity: Stephen Krasner's "State Power and the Structure of International Trade"', *World Politics*, 50/1: 150–170.

Keohane, R. O., and Nye Jr, J. S. (eds.) (1972), *Transnational Relations and World Politics* (Cambridge, MA: Harvard University Press).

Keohane, R. O., and Nye Jr, J. S. (1977), *Power and Interdependence: World Politics in Transition* (Boston, MA: Little Brown and Company).

Kesar, S. et al. (2021), 'Pandemic, Informality, and Vulnerability: Impact of Covid-19 on Livelihoods in India', *Canadian Journal of Development Studies/Revue Canadienne d'études du Développement*, 42/1–2: 145–164.

Keucheyan, R. (2018), 'Insuring Climate Change: New Risks and the Financialization of Nature', *Development and Change*, 49/2: 484–501.

Keynes, J. M. (1925), *The Economic Consequences of Mr. Churchill* (London: L. and V. Woolf).

Kim, S. Y. (2011), *Power and Governance of Global Trade: From the GATT to the WTO* (Ithaca, NY: Cornell University Press).

Kinder, D. R., and Roderick Kiewiet, D. (1981), 'Sociotropic Politics: The American Case', *British Journal of Political Science*, 11/2: 129–161.

Kindleberger, C. P. (1951), 'Group Behavior and International Trade', *Journal of Political Economy*, 59/1: 30–46.

Kindleberger, C. P. (1973), *The World in Depression, 1929–39* (Berkeley, CA: University of California Press).

Kindleberger, C. P. (1978), *Manias, Panics, and Crashes: A History of Financial Crises* (New York, NY: Basic Books).

Kirshner, J. (1995), *Currency and Coercion* (Princeton, NJ: Princeton University Press).

Kirshner, J. (2001), 'The Political Economy of Low Inflation', *Journal of Economic Surveys*, 15/1: 41–70.

Kirshner, J. (ed.) (2003), *Monetary Orders* (Ithaca, NY: Cornell University Press).

Kirshner, J. (2003), 'Money is Politics', *Review of International Political Economy*, 10/4: 645–660.

Kirshner, J. (2012), 'The Tragedy of Offensive Realism: Classical Realism and the Rise of China', *European Journal of International Relations*, 18/1: 53–75.

Kirshner, J. (2014), *American Financial Power after the Financial Crisis* (Ithaca, NY: Cornell University Press).

Kitchin, R. (2014), *The Data Revolution: Big Data, Open Data, Data Infrastructures and Their Consequences* (London: SAGE Publications).

Klaver, C. (2003), *A/moral Economics: Classical Political Economy and Cultural Authority in Nineteenth-Century England* (Columbus, OH: Ohio State University Press).

Klein, N. (2015), *This Changes Everything: Capitalism vs. the Climate* (New York, NY: Simon and Schuster).

Kleinberg, K. B., and Fordham, B. O. (2018), 'Don't Know Much about Foreign Policy: Assessing the Impact of "Don't Know" and "No Opinion" Responses on Inferences about Foreign Policy Attitudes', *Foreign Policy Analysis*, 14/3: 429–448.

Knaack, P. and Katada, S. (2013), 'Fault Lines and Issue Linkages at the G20', *Global Policy*, 4/3: 236–246.

Knight, F. (1921), *Risk, Uncertainty and Profit* (Chicago, IL: University of Chicago Press).

Knight, J. (1992), *Institutions and Social Conflict* (Cambridge: Cambridge University Press).

Koopman, R., Powers, W., Wang, Z., and Wei, S.-J. (2010), 'Give Credit Where Credit Is Due: Tracing Value Added in Global Production Chains', Working Paper 16426, National Bureau of Economic Research, http://www.nber.org/papers/w16426.pdf.

Koremenos, B., Lipson, C., and Snidal, D. (2001), 'The Rational Design of International Institutions', *International Organization*, 55/4: 761–799.

Kranke, M., and Yarrow, D. (2018), 'The Global Governance of Systemic Risk: How Measurement Practices Tame Macroprudential Politics', *New Political Economy*, 24/6: 816–832.

Krasner, S. D. (1976), 'State Power and the Structure of International Trade', *World Politics*, 28/3: 317–347.

Krasner, S. D. (ed.) (1983), *International Regimes* (Ithaca, NY: Cornell University Press).

Krasner, S. D. (1985), *Structural Conflict: The Third World Against Global Liberalism* (Berkley, CA: University of California Press).

Krasner, S. D. (1991), 'Global Communications and National Power: Life on the Pareto Frontier', *World Politics*, 43/3: 336–366.

Kremers, R., and Brassett, J. (2017), 'Mobile Payments, Social Money: Everyday Politics of the Consumer Subject', *New Political Economy*, 22/6: 645–660.

Krippner, G. (2005), 'The Financialization of the American Economy', *Socio-Economic Review*, 3/2: 173–208.

Kristiansen, K., Lindkvist, T., and Myrdal, J. (eds.) (2018), *Trade and Civilisation: Economic Networks and Cultural Ties, from Prehistory to the Early Modern Era* (Cambridge: Cambridge University Press).

Krueger, A. O. (1990), 'Government Failures in Development', *Journal of Economic Perspectives*, 4/3: 9–23.

Krueger, A. O. (2002), *A New Approach to Sovereign Debt Restructuring*, Pamphlet Series (Washington, DC: International Monetary Fund).

Krugman, P., and Helpman, E. (1985), *Market Structure and Foreign Trade* (Brighton: Wheatsheaf Press).

Krugman, P., and Wells, R. (2018), *Microeconomics* (New York, NY: Worth Publishers).

Krugman, P. R. (1987), 'Is Free Trade Passé?', *Journal of Economic Perspectives*, 1/2: 131–144.

Kuijper, P. J. (2017), 'The US Attack on the WTO Appellate Body', *Legal Issues of Economic Integration*, 45/1: 1–12.

Kurer, T. (2020), 'The Declining Middle: Occupational Change, Social Status, and the Populist Right', *Comparative Political Studies*, 53/10–11: 1798–1835.

Kurzer, P. (1993), *Business and Banking* (Ithaca, NY: Cornell University Press).

Kushi, S., and McManus, I. P. (2018), 'Gendered Costs of Austerity: The Effects of Welfare Regime and Government Policies on Employment across the OECD, 2000–2013', *International Labour Review* 157/4: 557–587.

Kvangraven, I. H. (2020), 'Beyond the Stereotype: Restating the Relevance of the Dependency Theory Research Programme', *Development and Change*, 52/1: 76–112.

Kwa, A. (2003), *Power Politics in the WTO*, 2nd edn. (Thailand: Focus on the Global South).

Kwan, C. H. (2020), 'The China–US Trade War: Deep-Rooted Causes, Shifting Focus and Uncertain Prospects', *Asian Economic Policy Review*, 15: 55–72.

Kwet, M. (2019), 'Digital Colonialism: US Empire and the New Imperialism in the Global South', *Race & Class*, 60/4: 3–26.

Lafferty, G. (2000), 'The Dynamics of Change: Class, Politics and Civil Society—from Marx to Post-Marxism', *Democracy & Nature*, 6/1: 19–26.

Lake, D. A. (2009), *Hierarchy in International Relations* (Ithaca, NY: Cornell University Press).

Lake, D. A. (2009), 'Open Economy Politics: A Critical Review', *Review of International Organizations*, 4/3: 219–244.

Lakner, C., and Milanovic, B. (2016), 'Global Income Distribution: From the Fall of the Berlin Wall to the Great Recession', *The World Bank Economic Review*, 30/2: 203–232.

Langley, P. (2008), *The Everyday Life of Global Finance: Saving and Borrowing in Anglo-America* (Oxford: Oxford University Press).

Langley, P., and Leyshon, A. (2017), 'Platform Capitalism: The Intermediation and Capitalization of Digital Economic Circulation', *Finance and Society*, 3/1: 11–31.

Langley, P., and Leyshon, A. (2021), 'The Platform Political Economy of FinTech: Reintermediation,

Consolidation and Capitalisation', *New Political Economy*, 26/3: 376–388.

Langley, P., and Morris, J. (2020), 'Central Banks: Climate Governors of Last Resort?', *Environment and Planning A*, 52/8: 1471–1479.

Larue, L. (2022), 'The Case Against Alternative Currencies', *Politics, Philosophy and Economics*, 21/1: 75–93.

Lawrence, R. Z. (1996), *Regionalism, Multilateralism, and Deeper Integration* (Washington, D.C.: Brookings Institution).

Lawson, A. (2023), 'Sam Bankman-Fried Received $2.2bn from FTX-linked Entities, Say Court Filings', *The Guardian*, 16 March, https://www.theguardian.com/business/2023/mar/16/sam-bankman-fried-received-22bn-from-ftx-linked-entities-say-court-filings.

Lax, D. A. (1986), *The Manager as Negotiator: Bargaining for Cooperation and Competitive Gain* (London: Collier Macmillan).

Lazzarato, M. (2011), *The Making of the Indebted Man: An Essay on the Neoliberal Condition*, trans. Joshua David Gordon (Semiotext; reprint edition).

Leamer, E. (1984), *Sources of International Comparative Advantage* (Cambridge, MA: MIT Press).

LeBaron, G. (2015), 'Unfree Labour Beyond Binaries', *International Feminist Journal of Politics*, 17/1: 1–19.

LeBaron, G. (2020a), *Combatting Modern Slavery: Why Labour Governance is Failing and What We Can Do About It*, 1st edn. (London: Polity).

LeBaron, G. (2020b), 'Opinion: It's Time to Stop Believing Corporate Fairy Tales about Modern Slavery', *Thomson Reuters Foundation News*, 30 July, https://news.trust.org/item/20200730072924-uxgwe/.

LeBaron, G., Edwards, R., Hunt, T., Sempéré, C., and Kyritsis, P. (2022), 'The Ineffectiveness of CSR: Understanding Garment Company Commitments to Living Wages in Global Supply Chains', *New Political Economy*, 27/1: 99–115.

LeBaron, G., and Gore, E. (2020), 'Gender and Forced Labour: Understanding the Links in Global Cocoa Supply Chains', *Journal of Development Studies*, 56/6: 1095–1117.

LeBaron, G., Howard, N., Thibos, C., and Kyritsis, P. (2018), 'Confronting Root Causes: Forced Labour in Global Supply Chains', *openDemocracy*,

Sheffield Political Economy Research Institute (SPERI), https://www.opendemocracy.net/en/beyond-trafficking-and-slavery/confronting-root-causes/.

LeBaron, G., and Lister, J. (2022), 'The Hidden Costs of Global Supply Chain Solutions', *Review of International Political Economy*, 29: 669–695.

LeBaron, G., Lister, J., and Dauvergne, P. (2017), 'Governing Global Supply Chain Sustainability through the Ethical Audit Regime', *Globalizations*, 14/6: 958–975.

LeBaron, G., Mügge, D., Best, J., and Hay, C. (2021), 'Blind Spots in IPE: Marginalized Perspectives and Neglected Trends in Contemporary Capitalism', *Review of International Political Economy*, 28/2: 283–294.

LeBaron, G., and Phillips, N. (2019), 'States and the Political Economy of Unfree Labour', *New Political Economy*, 24/1: 1–21.

Lee, A. (1764), 'An Essay in Vindication of the Continental Colonies of America', from a Censure of Mr Adam Smith, in *The Theory of Moral Sentiments*, with Some Reflections on Slavery in General by an American (London: Becket and De Hondt).

Lerche, J. (2011), 'The Unfree Labour Category and Unfree Labour Estimates: A Continuum within Low-End Labour Relations', *Manchester Papers in Political Economy* No. 10 (Manchester: University of Manchester), 1–45.

Lewis, C. (2020), 'Boohoo & COVID-19: The People behind the Profit', *Labour Behind the Label*, https://labourbehindthelabel.org/report-boohoo-covid-19-the-people-behind-the-profit/.

Leys, C. (1996), *The Rise and Fall of Development Theory*, 4th edn. (Bloomington and Indianapolis, IN: Indiana University Press).

Li, M. (2011), 'Rising from Within: China's Search for a Multilateral World and its Implications for Sino-US Relations', *Global Governance*, 17/3: 331–351.

Li, W. Y. (2023), 'Regulatory Capture's Third Face of Power', *Socio-Economic Review*, 1–29.

Li, Y. W. V. (2018), *China's Financial Opening* (London: Routledge).

Liang, Y., Aroles, J., and Brandl, B. (2022), 'Charting Platform Capitalism: Definitions, Concepts and Ideologies', *New Technology, Work and Employment*, 37/1: 1–20.

Liebmann, M. (2021), 'Colonialism and Indigenous Population Decline in the Americas', in L. M. Panich and S. L. Gonzalez (eds.), *The Routledge Handbook of the Archaeology of Indigenous-Colonial Interaction in the Americas* (London: Routledge).

Lindert, P. H., and Williamson, J. (2001), 'Globalization and Inequality: A Long History', World Bank Annual Conference on Development Economics, Europe, 25–27 June.

Ling, L. (2002), *Postcolonial International Relations: Conquest and Desire between Asia and the West* (London: Palrave Macmillan).

Lipscy, P., and Lee, H. (2019), 'The IMF As a Biased Global Insurance Mechanism', *International Organization*, 73: 35–64.

Liu, Y., Garrido, J., and Delong, C., (2020), 'Private Debt Resolution Measures in the Wake of the Pandemic', *IMF Special Series on COVID-19* (Washington, DC: International Monetary Fund).

Locke, R. (2013), *The Promise and Limits of Private Power: Promoting Labor Standards in a Global Economy* (Cambridge: Cambridge University Press).

Lockwood, E. (2015), 'Predicting the Unpredictable: Value-at-risk, Performativity, and the Politics of Financial Uncertainty', *Review of International Political Economy*, 22/4: 719–756.

Logan, D. (2007), 'The Redemption of a Heretic: Harriet Martineau and Anglo-American Abolitionism', in K. K. Sklar and J. B. Stewart (ed.) *Women's Rights and Transatlantic Antislavery in the Era of Emancipation* (New Haven, CT: Yale University Press).

Logan, D. (2016), *Harriet Martineau, Victorian Liberalism, and the Civilizing Mission* (London: Routledge).

Lohmann, S. (1997), 'Linkage Politics', *Journal of Conflict Resolution*, 41/1: 38–67.

Lomas, N. (2022), 'Report Reveals Big Tech's Last Minute Lobbying to Weaken EU Rules', 22 April, *TechCrunch*, https://techcrunch.com/2022/04/22/google-facebook-apple-eu-lobbying-report/.

Lopez-Acevado and Robinson (2016), Stitches to Riches?: Apparel Employment, Trade, and Economic Development in South Asia'. Directions in Development: Poverty, World Bank Group, https://openknowledge.worldbank.org/entities/publication/05ab7228-e4fc-587a-86de-28f0aea12545

Low, P., Marceau, G., and Reinaud, J. (2012), 'Interface between the Trade and Climate Change Regimes: Scoping the Issues', *Journal of World Trade*, 46: 485.

Lowenstein, R. (2001), *When Genius Failed: The Rise and Fall of Long-Term Capital Management* (London: Fourth Estate).

Lü, X., Scheve, K., and Slaughter, M. J. (2012), 'Inequity Aversion and the International Distribution of Trade Protection', *American Journal of Political Science* 56/3: 638–654.

Lukes, S. (1974), *Power: A Radical View* (London: Macmillan).

Luo, H., and Yang, L. (2021), 'Equality and Equity in Emerging Multilateral Financial Institutions: The Case of the BRICS Institutions', *Global Policy*, 12/4: 482–508.

Luo, Y. (2022), 'Illusions of Techno-Nationalism', *Journal of International Business Studies*, 53: 550–567.

Luxton, M. (2018), 'The Production of Life Itself: Gender, Social Reproduction and IPE', in J. Elias and A. Roberts (eds.), *Handbook on the International Political Economy of Gender* (Cheltenham: Edward Elgar), 37–49.

MacFarlane, S. N. (2006), 'The "R" in BRICs: Is Russia an Emerging Power?', *International Affairs*, 82/2: 41–57.

Macharia, K. (2016), 'On Being Area-Studied: A Litany of Complaint', *GLQ: A Journal of Lesbian and Gay Studies*, 22/2: 183–190.

MacKenzie, J. (1984), *Propaganda and Empire: The Manipulation of British Public Opinion, 1880–1960* (Manchester: Manchester University Press).

Mackie, G. (2006), 'Does Democratic Deliberation Change Minds?', *Politics, Philosophy & Economics*, 5/3: 279–303.

Maddison, A. (1989), *The World Economy in the 20th Century* (Paris: Development Centre of the Organisation for Economic Co-operation and Development).

Maddison, A. (2001), *The World Economy: A Millennial Perspective* (Paris: Development Centre of the Organisation for Economic Co-operation and Development).

Mader, P., Mertens, D., and van der Zwan, N. (eds.) (2020), *The Routledge International Handbook of Financialization* (London: Routledge).

Magee, S. P., Brock, W. A., and Young, L. (eds.) (1989), *Black Hole Tariffs and Endogenous Policy Theory: Political Economy in General Equilibrium* (Cambridge: Cambridge University Press).

Maggi, G. (1999), 'The Role of Multilateral Institutions in International Trade Cooperation', *American Economic Review*, 89/1: 190–214.

Majeed, J. (1992), *James Mill's* The History of British India *and Orientalism* (Oxford: Clarendon).

Malm, A. (2016), *Fossil Capital: The Rise of Steam Power and the Roots of Global Warming* (London: Verso).

Maniates, M. (2002), 'Individualization: Plant a Tree, Buy a Bike, Save the World?', in T. Princen, M. Maniates, and K. Conca (eds.), *Confronting Consumption* (Boston, MA: MIT Press), 43–66.

Maniates, M. (2014), 'Sustainable Consumption—Three Paradoxes', *GAIA—Ecological Perspectives for Science and Society*, 23/3: 201–208.

Manjapra, K. (2018), 'Plantation Dispossessions: The Global Travel of Agricultural Racial Capitalism', in S. Beckert, and C. Desan (eds.), *American Capitalism: New Histories* (New York, NY: Columbia University Press), 361–387.

Mansfield, E. D., and Mutz, D. C. (2009), 'Support for Free Trade: Self-Interest, Sociotropic Politics, and Out-Group Anxiety', *International Organization*, 63: 425–457.

Mantena, K. (2010), *Alibis of Empire: Henry Maine and the Ends of Liberal Imperialism* (Princeton, NJ: Princeton University Press).

Manuel, A., and Derrickson, G. C. R. M. (2021), *Unsettling Canada: A National Wake-up Call*, 2nd edn. (Toronto, ON: Between the Lines).

Marcet, J. (1816), *Conversations on Political Economy* (London: Longman).

Marcet, J. (1819), *Conversations on Natural Philosophy* (Boston: Lincoln & Edmands).

Marcet, J. (1833), *John Hopkins's Notions on Political Economy* (London: Longman).

Marcet, J. (1858), *Mrs. Marcet's Story-Book. Being a Selection from the Stories Contained in her Books for Little Children* (London: Longman).

Marcus, N. (2018), *Austrian Reconstruction and the Collapse of Global Finance, 1921–1931* (Cambridge, MA: Harvard University Press).

Margulis, M. E. (2017), 'The Forgotten History of Food Security in Multilateral Trade Negotiations', *World Trade Review,* 16/1: 25–57.

Martill, B. (2017), 'International Ideologies: Paradigms of Ideological Analysis and World Politics', *Journal of Political Ideologies*, 22/3: 236–255.

Martin, L. L. (1992), 'Interests, Power, and Multilateralism', *International Organization*, 46/4: 765–792.

Martin, R. (2002), *Financialization of Daily Life* (Philadelphia, PA. Temple University Press).

Martineau, H. (1832/1834), *Illustrations of Political Economy* (London: Leonard C. Bowles).

Martineau, H. (1838/2020), *How to Observe: Morals and Manners* (Frankfurt: Outlook Verlag).

Martineau, H. (1845), *Dawn Island. A Tale* (Manchester: Gadsby).

Martinez-Alier, J. (2002), *The Environmentalism of the Poor: A Study of Ecological Conflicts and Valuation* (Northampton: MA, Edward Elgar).

Martinez-Diaz, L. (2009), *Globalizing in Hard Times: The Politics of Banking-Sector Opening in the Emerging World* (Ithaca, NY: Cornell University Press).

Marx, K. (1976), *Capital, Volume 1: A Critique of Political Economy* (London: Penguin).

Mascarenhas-Swan, M. (2017), 'The Case for a Just Transition', in *Energy Democracy: Advancing Equity in Clean Energy Solutions* (Washington, D.C.: Island Press).

Maskus, K. E. (2000), *Intellectual Property Rights in the Global Economy* (Washington, DC: Institute for International Economics).

Matthijs, M., and McNamara, K. (2015), 'The Euro Crisis' Theory Effect', *Journal of European Integration*, 37/2: 229–245.

Maurer, S. (2012), *The Dispossessed State: Narratives of Ownership in Nineteenth-Century Britain and Ireland* (Baltimore, MR: Johns Hopkins University Press).

Mavroidis, P. C., and Sapir, A. (2021), *China and the WTO: Why Multilateralism Still Matters* (Princeton, NJ: Princeton University Press).

Mawdsley, E. (2008), 'Fu Manchu versus Dr Livingstone in the Dark Continent? Representing China, Africa and the West in British Broadsheet Newspapers', *Political Geography*, 27/5: 509–529.

Mayda, A. M., and Rodrik, D. (2005), 'Why Are Some People (And Countries) More Protectionist Than Others?', *European Economic Review*, 49: 1393–1430.

Mayer, F. W. (1998), *Interpreting NAFTA: The Science and Art of Political Analysis* (New York: Columbia University Press).

Mayo, W. (2021), 'What Is Artificial Intelligence?', *Forbes*, 7 October, https://www.forbes.com/sites/ forbestechcouncil/2021/10/07/what-is-artificial-intelligence/?sh=4982c18b1890.

Mayoux, L. (2000), 'Micro-Finance and the Empowerment of Women: A Review of the Key Issues', Social Finance Working Paper No. 23 (Geneva: ILO).

Mazower, M. (2012), *Governing the World: The History of an Idea, 1815 to the Present* (New York, NY: Penguin Books).

McArthur, C., and S. Edelman (2017), 'The Housing Crisis of 2008', *CAP Report*, 13 April (Washington, D.C.: Center for American Progress).

McAuliffe, M., and Triandafyllidou A. (eds.) (2021), *World Migration Report 2022* (Geneva: International Organization for Migration).

McCall Smith, J. (2000), 'The Politics of Dispute Settlement Design: Explaining Legalism in Regional Trade Pacts', *International Organization*, 54/1: 137–180.

Mcdonald, M. (2022), 'The Infuriating Reality of Traveling with Bitcoin in the World's Crypto Capital', *Bloomberg*, https://www.bloomberg.com/features/2022-bitcoin-travel-problems/.

McDowell, D. (2019), 'The (Ineffective) Financial Statecraft of China's Bilateral Swap Agreements', *Development and Change*, 50/1: 122–143.

McDowell, D. (2023), *Bucking the Buck: US Financial Sanctions and the International Backlash Against the Dollar* (Oxford: Oxford University Press).

McDowell, L. (1997), *Capital Culture* (Oxford: Basil Blackwell).

McGinnis, M. D. (1986), 'Issue Linkage and the Evolution of International Cooperation', *Journal of Conflict Resolution*, 30/1: 141–170.

McGrath, S. (2013), 'Fuelling Global Production Networks with Slave Labour?: Migrant Sugar Cane Workers in the Brazilian Ethanol GPN', *Geoforum*, 44: 32–43.

McGrath, S. (2017), 'Unfree Labor', in *International Encyclopedia of Geography* (London: Wiley).

McGrath, S., and Strauss, K. (2015), '"Unfreedom and Workers" Power: Ever-Present Possibilities', in K. van der Pijl (ed.), *Handbook of the International Political Economy of Production* (Cheltenham: Edward Elgar Publishing), 299–317.

McKeen-Edwards, H., and Porter, T. (2013), *Transnational Financial Associations and the Governance of Global Finance: Assembling Power and Wealth* (Abingdon: Routledge).

McKerracher, C. (2022), 'China Has Shot at Seizing 60% Share of Global EV Sales This Year', *Bloomberg,* https://www.bloomberg.com/news/articles/2022-11-15/china-has-shot-at-seizing-60-share of global ev sales this year.

McMichael, P. (2013), *Food Regimes and Agrarian Questions* (Halifax, NS: Fernwood Publishing).

McNamara, K. (1998), *The Currency of Ideas* (Ithaca, NY: Cornell University Press).

McNamara, K. R., and Newman, A. L. (2020), 'The Big Reveal: COVID-19 and Globalization's Great Transformations', *International Organization,* 74/S1: E59–E77.

Mearsheimer, J. J. (1990), 'Back to the Future: Instability in Europe after the Cold War', *International Security,* 15/1: 5–56.

Mearsheimer, J. J. (2005), 'China's Unpeaceful Rise', *Current History,* 105/690: 160–162.

Mehrling, P. (2011), *The New Lombard Street: How the Fed Became the Dealer of Last Resort* (Princeton, NJ: Princeton University Press).

Mehta, U. S. (1990), 'Liberal Strategies of Exclusion', *Politics and Society,* 18/4: 427–454.

Melitz, M. J., and Redding, S. J. (2015), 'New Trade Models, New Welfare Implications', *American Economic Review,* 105/3: 1105–1146.

Melossi, E. (2021), '"Ghetto Tomatoes" and "Taxi Drivers": The Exploitation and Control of Sub-Saharan African Migrant Tomato Pickers in Puglia, Southern Italy', *Journal of Rural Studies,* 88: 491–499.

Meltzer, J. P. (2019), 'Governing Digital Trade', *World Trade Review,* 18/S1: S23–S48.

Mende, J. (2019), 'The Concept of Modern Slavery: Definition, Critique, and the Human Rights Frame', *Human Rights Review,* 20/2: 229–248.

Mennillo, G. (2022), *Credit Rating Agencies* (Newcastle: Agenda).

Merling, L., and Ramos, L. (2022), 'In Turbulent Times the IMF Can Safeguard Financial Stability by Fully Embracing Capital Controls', *Initiative for Policy Dialogue,* 14 June, https://policydialogue.org/opinions/capital-flows_merling-ramos/.

METI (Ministry of Economy, Trade and Industry, Japan) (2000), 'The Economic Foundations of Japanese Trade Policy: Promoting a Multi-layered Trade Policy', Ministry of Economy, Trade and Industry, Tokyo, www.meti.go.jp/english/report/data/g00Wconte.pdf.

Mezzadri, A. (2016), 'Class, Gender and the Sweatshop: On the Nexus between Labour Commodification and Exploitation', *Third World Quarterly,* 37/10: 1877–1900.

Microsoft (2022), 'What is Cloud Computing?', https://azure.microsoft.com/en-us/overview/what-is-cloud-computing/#benefits.

Mies, M. (2014), *Patriarchy and Accumulation on a World Scale: Women in the International Division of Labour,* 3rd edn. (London: Bloomsbury).

Milanovic, B. (2003), 'The Two Faces of Globalization: Against Globalization As We Know It', *World Development,* 31/4: 667–683.

Milanovic, B. (2005), *Worlds Apart: Measuring International and Global Inequality* (Princeton, NJ: Princeton University Press).

Milanovic, B. (2012), 'Global Income Inequality by the Numbers: in History and Now: An Overview', Policy Research Working Paper Series 6259, World Bank, https://openknowledge.worldbank.org/server/api/core/bitstreams/10deadc9-f4b4-5c9b-b241-7c173f01d67c/content.

Milanovic, B. (2015), 'Global Inequality of Opportunity: How Much of Income is Determined by Where We Live', *Review of Economics and Statistics,* 97/2: 452–460.

Mill, J. (1809), 'Review of de Guignes', *Edinburgh Review,* 14/28, 407–429.

Mill, J. (1817), *History of British India: Volume 1* (London: Baldwin, Cradock, and Joy).

Mill, J. (1820), 'Government', in J. Mill (1992) *Political Writings,* edited by T. Ball (Cambridge: Cambridge University Press).

Mill, J. (1823), 'Colony', in Encyclopaedia Britannica (1823), *Supplement to the Encyclopaedia Britannica* (London: Innes).

Mill, J. S. (1843), 'Of Ethology, or the Science of the Formation of Character', in John Stuart Mill (1843/2002), *A System of Logic, Ratiocinative and Inductive* (Honolulu: University Press of the Pacific).

Mill, J. S. (1850), 'The Negro Question', *Fraser's Magazine,* 41/360: 25–31.

Mill, J. S. (1859), 'A Few Words on Non-Intervention', *Fraser's Magazine,* 60/360: 766–776.

Mill, J. S. (1862), *The Contest in America* (Boston, MA: Little, Brown, and Company).

Mill, J. S. (1868), *England and Ireland* (London: Longman).

Mill, J. S. (1963a), *Collected Works of John Stuart Mill: The Later Letters, 1849–1873* (Toronto, ON: University of Toronto Press).

Mill, J. S. (1963b), *Collected Works of John Stuart Mill: Newspaper Writings* (Toronto: University of Toronto Press).

Mill, J. S. (1970), *Principles of Political Economy, with Some of their Applications to Social Philosophy* (Harmondsworth: Penguin).

Miller, V. (2012), 'The UK and Europe: Time for a New Relationship?', House of Commons Library Standard Note SN/IA/6393, 24 July, http://researchbriefings.parliament.uk/ResearchBriefing/Summary/SN06393.

Mills, C. W. (1997), *The Racial Contract* (Ithaca, NY: Cornell University Press).

Milner, H. V. (2021), 'Voting for Populism in Europe: Globalization, Technological Change, and the Extreme Right', *Comparative Political Studies,* 54/13: 2286–2320.

Minsky, H. (1986), *Stabilizing an Unstable Economy* (New Haven, CN: Yale University Press).

Mishel, L., Rhinehart, L., and Windham, L. (2020), 'Explaining the Erosion of Private-Sector Unions' (Washington, D.C.: Economic Policy Institute, epi.org/215908), 1–65.

Miskimmon, A., O'loughlin, B., and Roselle, L. (2017), *Forging the World: Strategic Narratives and International Relations* (Ann Arbor, MI: University of Michigan Press).

Mitchell, B. R. (1992), *International Historical Statistics: Europe 1750–1988*, 3rd edn. (London: Macmillan).

Mitchell, B. R. (1993), *International Historical Statistics: The Americas 1750–1988*, 2nd edn. (London: Macmillan).

Mody, A. (2018), *Euro Tragedy* (Oxford: Oxford University Press).

Mohanty, C. (1988), 'Under Western Eyes: Feminist Scholarship and Cultural Discourses', *Feminist Review*, 30: 61–88.

Mohanty, C. (2003), '"Under Western Eyes" Revisited: Feminist Solidarity through Anticapitalist Struggles', *Signs: Journal of Women in Culture and Society*, 28/2: 499–535.

Mollett, S., and Faria, C. (2013), 'Messing with Gender in Feminist Political Ecology', *Geoforum,* 45: 116–125.

Momsen, J. (2009), *Gender and Development*, 3rd edn. (London: Routledge).

Monbiot, G. (2003), 'I Was Wrong About Trade', *The Guardian*, 24 June, https://www.theguardian.com/world/2003/jun/24/globalisation.politics.

Montgomerie, J. (2009), 'The Pursuit of (Past) Happiness? Middle-class Indebtedness and American Financialisation', *New Political Economy*, 14/1: 1–24.

Montgomerie, J. (2013), 'America's Debt Safety-net', *Public Administration*, 91/4: 871–888.

Montgomerie, J. (2019), *Should We Abolish Household Debts?* (Cambridge: Polity).

Montgomerie J., and Büdenbender, M. (2015), 'Round the Houses: Homeownership and Failures of Asset-Based Welfare in the United Kingdom', *New Political Economy*, 20/3: 386–405.

Montgomerie, J., and Tepe-Belfrage, D. (2016), 'Caring for Debts: How the Household Economy Exposes the Limits of Financialisation', *Critical Sociology,* 43/4–5: 653–668.

Montgomerie, J., and Young, B. (2011), 'Home is Where the Hardship is: Gender and Wealth (Dis) Accumulation in the Subprime Boom', CRESC Working Paper Series, Working Paper No. 79.

Morrison, O. (2021), 'Europe-Wide Eco-Label Scheme Set for Launch in 2022 as Industry Joins Forces to Launch Pilot', Foodnavigator-Usa.Com, 28 June, https://www.foodnavigator-usa.com/Article/2021/06/28/Europe-wide-eco-label-scheme-set-for-launch-in-2022-as-industry-joins-forces-to-launch-pilot.

Morse, E. L. (1976), *Modernization and the Transformation of International Relations* (New York: Free Press).

Morse, J. (2021), *The Bankers' Blacklist* (Ithaca, NY: Cornell University Press).

Mörth, U. (2014), 'Organizational Legitimation in the Age of Governing by Numbers: The Case of Regulatory Partnerships on ESG issues and Financial Decisions', *Globalizations*, 11/3: 369–384.

Moschella, M. (2017), 'International Finance', in J. K. Cogan et al. (eds.), *The Oxford Handbook of International Organizations* (Oxford: Oxford University Press), Ch. 17.

Moschella, M. (2024), *Unexpected Revolutionaries: How Central Banks Made and Unmade Economic Orthodoxy* (Ithaca, NY: Cornell University Press).

Mosley, L. (2003), *Global Capital and National Governments* (Cambridge: Cambridge University Press).

Mosley, L., and Uno, S. (2007), 'Racing to the Bottom or Climbing to the Top? Economic Globalization and Collective Labor Rights', *Comparative Political Studies*, 40/8: 923–948.

Mott, H., Stephenson, M., and De Henau, J. (2018), 'Exploring the Economic Impact of Brexit on Women', *UK Women's Budget Group*, https://wbg.org.uk/wp-content/uploads/2018/03/Economic-Impact-of-Brexit-on-women-briefing-FINAL-for-print.pdf.

Moyo, D. (2009), *Dead Aid: Why Aid is Not Working and How There is a Better Way for Africa* (New York, NY: Farrar, Straus, and Giroux).

Mudde, C., and Rovira Kaltwasser, C. (2013), 'Exclusionary vs. Inclusionary Populism: Comparing Contemporary Europe and Latin America', *Government and Opposition*, 48/2: 147–174.

Mudde, C., and Rovira Kaltwasser, C. (2013), 'Studying Populism in Comparative Perspective: Reflections on the Contemporary and Future Research Agenda', *Comparative Political Studies*, 51/13: 1667–1693.

Mudimbe, V. Y. (1988), *The Invention of Africa: Gnosis, Philosophy, and the Order of Knowledge*, 1st edn. (Bloomington, IN: Indiana University Press).

Mügge, D. (2016), 'Studying Macroeconomic Indicators as Powerful Ideas', *Journal of European Public Policy*, 23/3: 410–427.

Mügge, D. (2017), '40.3 Million Slaves? Four Reasons to Question the New Global Estimates of Modern Slavery', Beyond Trafficking and Slavery Policy Brief No. 1, *openDemocracy*, https://cdn2.opendemocracy.net/media/documents/Mugge_4_reasons_to_question_GEMS.pdf

Mundell, R. (1961), 'A Theory of Optimum Currency Areas', *American Economic Review* 51/3: 657–665.

Murau, S., Pape, F., and Pforr, T. (2022), 'International Monetary Hierarchy through Emergency US-dollar Liquidity', *Competition & Change*, 1–21.

Murphy, C., and Rojas de Ferro, C. (1995), 'Introduction', *Review of International Political Economy*, Special Issue: The Power of Representation in International Political Economy, 2/1: 63–69.

Murphy, C. N. (2001), 'Political Consequences of the New Inequality', *International Studies Quarterly*, 45/3: 347–356.

Murphy, C. N., and Tooze, R. (eds.) (1991), *The New International Political Economy* (Boulder, CO: Lynne Rienner Publishers).

Musthaq, F. (2021), 'Dependency in a Financialized Global Economy', *Review of African Political Economy*, 48/167: 15–31.

Muthu, S. (2008), 'Adam Smith's Critique of International Trading Companies: Theorizing "Globalization" in the Age of Enlightenment', *Political Theory*, 36/2: 185–212.

Mutz, D. C., and Kim, E. (2017), 'How Ingroup Favoritism Affects Trade Preferences', *International Organization*, 71/4: 827–850.

Mutz, D., Mansfield, E. D., and Kim, E. (2021), 'The Racialization of International Trade', *Political Psychology*, 42/4: 555–573.

Nagel, T. (2005), 'The Problem of Global Justice', *Philosophy and Public Affairs*, 33/2: 113–147.

Naoi, M., and Kume, I. (2011), 'Explaining Mass Support for Agricultural Protectionism: Evidence from a Survey Experiment During the Global Recession', *International Organization*, 65/4: 771–795.

Naqvi, N. (2021), 'Renationalizing Finance for Development: Policy Space and Public Economic Control in Bolivia', *Review of International Political Economy*, 28/3: 447–478.

Narlikar, A. (2003), *International Trade and Developing Countries: Bargaining Coalitions in the GATT and WTO* (London: Routledge).

Narlikar, A. (2022), 'How Not to Negotiate: The Case of Trade Multilateralism', *International Affairs*, 98/5: 1553–1573.

ND-GAIN (Notre Dame Global Adaptation Initiative) (2022), *Vulnerability Index* (Notre Dame: Notre Dame Global Adaptation Initiative), https://gain-new.crc.nd.edu/ranking/vulnerability.

Nelson, S., and Katzenstein, P. (2014), 'Uncertainty, Risk, and the Financial Crisis of 2008', *International Organization*, 68/2: 361–392.

Nembhard G. J. (2014), 'Community-Based Asset Building and Community Wealth', *The Review of Black Political Economy*, 41/2: 101–117.

Neumann, R. P. (2004), 'Moral and Discursive Geographies in the War for Biodiversity in Africa', *Political Geography*, 23: 813–837.

Newclimate Institute (2022), 'The CAT Thermometer', https://climateactiontracker.org/global/cat-thermometer/.

Newell, P. (2021), *Power Shift: The Global Political Economy of Energy Transitions* (Cambridge: Cambridge University Press).

NGFS (Network for Greening the Financial System) (2019), *A Call for Action: Climate Change as a Source of Financial Risk* (Paris: NGFS Secretariat).

Niemi, R. G., Bremer, J., and Heel, M. (1999), 'Determinants of State Economic Perceptions', *Political Behavior*, 21/2: 175–193.

Niño-Zarazúa, M., Roope, L., and Tarp, F. (2017), 'Global Inequality: Relatively Lower, Absolutely Higher', *Review of Income and Wealth*, 63/4: 661–684.

Nkrumah, K. (1966), *Neo-Colonialism: The Last Stage of Imperialism* (New York: International Publishers).

NOAA (National Oceanic and Atmospheric Administration) (2021), 'Despite Pandemic Shutdowns, Carbon Dioxide and Methane Surged in 2020', *NOAA Research News,* https://research.noaa.gov/article/ArtMID/587/ArticleID/2742/Despite-pandemic-shutdowns-carbon-dioxide-and-methane-surged-in-2020.

Nordhaus, W. (2015), 'Climate Clubs: Overcoming Free-Riding in International Climate Policy', *American Economic Review*, 105: 1339–1370.

NordiCity (2022), 'The Missing Pillar: Culture's Contribution to the UN Sustainable Development Goals', *The British Council*, https://www.british-council.org/arts/culture-development/our-stories/common-sense-community.

Norloff, C. et al. (2020), 'Global Monetary Order and the Liberal Order Debate', *International Studies Perspectives*, 21: 109–153.

Norris, P., and Inglehart, R. (2019), *Cultural Backlash: Trump, Brexit, and Authoritarian Populism* (Cambridge: Cambridge University Press).

North, D. (1991), 'Institutions', *Journal of Economic Perspectives*, 5/1: 97–112.

Nunn, N. (2008), 'The Long-Term Effects of Africa's Slave Trades', *Quarterly Journal of Economics*, 123: 139–176.

Nussbaum, M. (2000), 'Women's Capabilities and Social Justice', *Journal of Human Development*, 1/2: 219–247.

NYCCLC (New York City Central Labor Council) (2021), 'Bezos Faces Backlash for Comments on Amazon Workers', *New York City Central Labor Council, 23 July,* https://www.nycclc.org/news/2021-07/bezos-faces-backlash-comments-amazon-workers.

O'Connell, W. D., and Elliott, C. (2023), 'States and New Markets: The Novelty Problem in the IPE of Finance', *Review of International Political Economy*, 30/2: 403–420.

O'Connell Davidson, J. (2013), 'Troubling Freedom: Migration, Debt, and Modern Slavery', *Migration Studies*, 1/2: 176–195.

O'Connor, J. (1998), *Natural Causes: Essays in Ecological Marxism* (New York: Guilford Press).

O'Neill, J. (2001), 'Building Better Global Economic BRICs', Global Investment Research, Goldman Sachs, www.goldmansachs.com/intelligence/archive/building-better.html.

O'Rourke, K., and Sinnott, R. (2001), 'The Determinants of Individual Trade Policy Preferences: International Survey Evidence', *Brookings Trade Forum*: 157–206.

Oatley, T. (2017), 'Open Economy Politics and Trade Policy', *Review of International Political Economy*, 24/4: 699–717.

Odell, J. (1982), *US International Monetary Policy* (Princeton, NJ: Princeton University Press).

Odell, J. S. (2006), *Negotiating Trade: Developing Countries in the WTO and NAFTA* (Cambridge: Cambridge University Press).

OECD (Organization for Economic Co-Operation and Development) (2006), *The World Economy: A Millennial Perspective* (Paris: OECD Development Centre).

OECD (Organization for Economic Co-Operation and Development) (2020), 'Statistical Insights: How did the First Wave of the COVID-19 Pandemic affect the Household Sector and Public Finances?', statistical-insights-how-did-the-first-wave-of-the-covid-19-pandemic-affect-the-household-sector-and-public-finances.htm.

OECD (Organization for Economic Co-Operation and Development) (2021), *Agricultural Policy Monitoring and Evaluation 2021: Addressing the Challenges Facing Food Systems* (Paris: OECD).

OECD (Organization for Economic Co-Operation and Development) (2021), Official Development

Assistance (ODA), https://www.oecd.org/dac/financing-sustainable-development/development-finance-standards/official-development-assistance.htm.

OECD (Organization for Economic Co-Operation and Development) (2023), *Digital Trade*, https://www.oecd.org/trade/topics/digital-trade/.

Offer, A. (1989), *The First World War: An Agrarian Interpretation* (Oxford: Clarendon Press).

Officer, L. H. (2001), 'Gold Standard', *EH.Net Encyclopedia*, 1 October, http://eh.net/encyclopedia/gold-standard/.

Ogle, V. (2017), 'Archipelago Capitalism: Tax Havens, Offshore Money and the State, 1950s-1970s', *American Historical Review*, 122/5: 1431–1458.

Okou, C., Spray, J. D., and Unsal, F. (2022), 'Africa Food Prices are Soaring Amid High Import Reliance', Blog Post, International Monetary Fund, 27 September 2022, https://www.imf.org/en/Blogs/Articles/2022/09/26/africa-food-prices-are-soaring-amid-high-import-reliance.

Olive, D. (2012), 'Why Caterpillar has the Upper Hand in London Plant Lockout', *Toronto Star*, 3 January.

Osborne, M. (2022), 'In a First, Microplastics Are Found in Fresh Antarctic Snow', *Smithsonian Magazine*, https://www.smithsonianmag.com/smart-news/in-a-first-microplastics-are-found-in-fresh-antarctic-snow-180980264/.

Ostrom, E. (1990), *Governing the Commons: The Evolution of Institutions for Collective Action* (Cambridge: Cambridge University Press).

Ostrom, E. (2000), 'Reformulating the Commons', *Swiss Political Science Review*, 6/1: 29–52.

Ostrom, E. (2003), 'How Types of Goods and Property Rights Jointly Affect Collective Action', *Journal of Theoretical Politics*, 15/3: 239–270.

Ostry, S. (1997), *The Post-Cold War Trading System: Who's on First* (Chicago, IL: University of Chicago Press).

Ostry, S. (2008), 'The Uruguay Round North-South Grand Bargain: Implications for Future Negotiations', in D. L. Kennedy and J. D. Soutwick (eds.), *The Political Economy of International Trade Law: Essays in Honor of Robert E Hudec* (Cambridge: Cambridge University Press), 285–300.

Our World in Data (2023), 'Fish and Seafood Consumption per Capita, 2020', ourworldindata.org/grapher/fish-and-seafood-consumption-per-capita.

Oxfam (2020), 'Time to Care? Unpaid and Underpaid Care Work and the Global Equality Crisis', Oxfam Briefing Paper January 2020, *Oxfam International*, https://oxfamilibrary.openrepository.com/bitstream/handle/10546/620928/bp-time-to-care-inequality-200120-en.pdf.

Oxfam (2021), *Poorer Nations Expected to Face up to $75 billion Six-Year Shortfall in Climate Finance* (Oxford: Oxfam International).

Oye, K. A. (1992), *Economic Discrimination and Political Exchange: World Political Economy in the 1930s and 1980s* (Princeton, NJ: Princeton University Press).

Paarlberg, R. L. (1997), 'Agricultural Policy Reform and the Uruguay Round: Synergistic Linkage in a Two-Level Game', *International Organization*, 51/3: 413–444.

Pagliari, M. S., and Hannan, S. (2017), 'The Volatility of Capital Flows in Emerging Markets: Measures and Determinants', IMF Working Paper 17/41, IMF.

Pahre, R. (1999), *Leading Questions: How Hegemony Affects the International Political Economy* (Ann Arbor, MI: University of Michigan Press).

Palan, R. (2006), *The Offshore World: Sovereign Markets, Virtual Places and Nomad Millionaires*, 2nd edn. (Ithaca, NY: Cornell University Press).

Palan, R., Murphy, R., and Chavagneux, C. (2009), *Tax Havens* (Ithaca, NY: Cornell University Press).

Palen, M-W. (2014), 'Adam Smith as Advocate of Empire, c.1870–1932', *Historical Journal*, 57/1: 179–198.

Palmeter, D. N., and Mavroidis, P. C. (1999), Dispute Settlement in the World Trade Organization: Practice and Procedure (The Hague: Kluwer).

Pape, F. (2022), 'Governing Global Liquidity: Federal Reserve Swap Lines and the International Dimension of US Monetary Policy', *New Political Economy*, 27/3: 455–472.

Parker, S., and Chefitz, G. (2018), *Debtbook Diplomacy: China's Strategic Leveraging of its Newfound Economic Influence and the Consequences for US Foreign Policy*, (Cambridge, MA: Belfer Centre for Science and International Affairs).

Pasquale, F. (2016), 'Two Narratives of Platform Capitalism', *Yale Law & Policy Review*, 35/1: 309–319.

Patalano, R. (2019), 'Surplus Country Adjustment: Revising the Post-World War II Scarce Currency

Clause', *Cambridge Journal of Economics*, 43/5: 1149–1182.

Patel, R. (2009), 'Food Sovereignty', *Journal of Peasant Studies*, 36/3: 663–706.

Patel, R., and Moore, J. W. (2017), *A History of the World in Seven Cheap Things* (Oakland, CA: University of California Press).

Paterson, B. (2009), 'Transformismo at the WTO', in M. McNally and J. Schwarzmatel (eds.), *Gramsci and Global Politics: Hegemony and Resistance* (Abingdon and New York: Routledge).

Paterson, M. (2001), 'Risky Business: Insurance Companies in Global Warming Politics', *Global Environmental Politics*, 1/4: 18–42.

Pattberg, P. (2017), 'The Emergence of Carbon Disclosure: Exploring the Role of Governance Entrepreneurs', *Environment and Planning C*, 35/8: 1437–1455.

Pauly, L. (1988), *Opening Financial Markets* (Ithaca, NY: Cornell University Press).

Pauly, L. W. (1997), *Who Elected the Bankers? Surveillance and Control in the World Economy* (Ithaca, NY: Cornell University Press).

Pauly, L. W. (2009), 'The Old and the New Politics of International Financial Stability', *Journal of Common Market Studies*, 47/5: 955–975.

Pauly, L. W., and Jentleson, B. (eds.) (2014), *Power in a Complex Global System* (Abingdon: Routledge).

Peet, R., Robbins, P., and Watts, M. (2011), 'Global Nature', in R. Peet, P. Robbins, and M. Watts (eds.), *Global Political Ecology* (London: Routledge).

Peluso, N. (1993), 'Coercing Conservation? The Politics of State Resource Control', *Global Environmental Change*, 199–217.

Peluso, N. L., and Watts, M. (eds.) (2001), *Violent Environments* (Ithaca, NY: Cornell University Press).

Perelman, M. (2000), *The Invention of Capitalism: Classical Political Economy and the Secret History of Primitive Accumulation* (Durham, NC: Duke University Press).

Perrigo, B. (2023) 'Exclusive: OpenAI used Kenyan Workers on less than $2 per hour to make ChatGPT less toxic', *TIME,* January, https://time.com/6247678/openai-chatgpt-kenya-workers/.

Perroni, C., and Whalley, J. (1994), 'The New Regionalism: Trade Liberalization or Insurance?', Working Paper 4626, National Bureau of Economic Research.

Peterson, S. (2006), 'How (the meaning of) Gender Matters in Political Economy', *New Political Economy*, 10/4: 499–521.

Petrou, K. (2021), *Engine of Inequality: The Fed and the Future of Wealth in America* (Hoboken, NJ: Wiley).

Petry, J., Fichtner, J., and Heemskerk, E. (2021), 'Steering Capital: The Growing Private Authority of Index Providers in the Age of Passive Asset Management', *Review of International Political Economy*, 28/1: 152–176.

Pew Research Center for the People and the Press. Pew Research Center (Spring 2017), Global Attitudes Survey, 2017 [Dataset]. Roper #31116604, Version 2. D3 Systems/Kantar Public UK/ORB International/Princeton Survey Research Associates International/Voices! Research & Consultancy [producer]. Cornell University, Ithaca, NY: Roper Center for Public Opinion Research [distributor]. doi:10.25940/ROPER-31116604.

Pflieger, G. (2023), 'COP27: One Step on Loss and Damage for the Most Vulnerable Countries, No Step for the Fight Against Climate Change', *PLOS Climate,* 2: 1–3.

Phillips, E. E. (2018), 'Bringing Blockchain to the Coffee Cup', *The Wall Street Journal*, 15 April, https://www.wsj.com/articles/bringing-blockchain-to-the-coffee-cup-1523797205.

Phillips, N. (2011), 'Unfree Labour and Adverse Incorporation in Global Production Networks', Working Paper 176, Chronic Poverty Research Centre.

Phillips, N. (2013), 'Unfree Labour and Adverse Incorporation in the Global Economy: Comparative Perspectives on Brazil and India', *Economy and Society*, 2/2: 171–196.

Phillips, N. (2017), 'Power and Inequality in the Global Political Economy', *International Affairs*, 93/2: 429–444.

Piketty T. (2014), *Capital in the Twenty-First Century* (Cambridge, MA: Harvard University Press).

Piketty, T. (2017). *Capital in the Twenty-first Century*, trans. A. Goldhammer (Cambridge, MA: Belknap Press).

Pinker, S. (2018), *Enlightenment Now: The Case for Science, Reason, Humanism, and Progress* (New York, NY: Viking).

Pinto, R. Á. (2018), 'Digital Sovereignty or Digital Colonialism', *SUR-International Journal on Human Rights*, 15/27: 15–27.

Piper, N., Rosewarne, S., and Withers, M. (2017), 'Migrant Precarity in Asia: "Networks of Labour Activism" for a Rights-Based Governance of Migration', *Development and Change*, 48/5: 1089–1110.

Pipkin, S., and Fuentes, A. (2017), 'Spurred to Upgrade: A Review of Triggers and Consequences of Industrial Upgrading in the Global Value Chain Literature', *World Development*, 98: 536–554.

Pitts, J. (2005), *A Turn to Empire: The Rise of Imperial Liberalism in Britain and France*, (Princeton, NJ: Princeton University Press).

Polanyi, K. (1944), *The Great Transformation: The Political and Economic Origins of our Time* (New York, NY: Farrar & Reinhart).

Polanyi, K. (1957), *The Great Transformation: The Political and Economic Origins of our Time*, 2nd edn. (Boston, MA: Beacon).

Pomares, J., and Abdala, M. B. (2020), 'The Future of AI Governance: The G20's Role and the Challenge of Moving Beyond Principles', *Global Solutions Journal*, 5: 84–93.

Popovich, N., and Plumer, B. (2021), 'Who Has the Most Historical Responsibility for Climate Change?', *New York Times*, 12 November, https://www.nytimes.com/interactive/2021/11/12/climate/cop26-emissions-compensation.html.

Porter, C., Méheut, C., Gebrekidan, S., and Apuzzo, M. (2022), 'The Ransom: A Look Under the Hood', *New York Times*, 20 May, https://www.nytimes.com/2022/05/20/world/americas/haiti-bibliography.html.

Pörtner, H. et al. (eds.) (2022), *Climate Change 2022: Impacts, Adaptation, and Vulnerability. Contribution of Working Group II to the Sixth Assessment Report of the Intergovernmental Panel on Climate Change* (Cambridge: Cambridge University Press).

Posen, A. S. (2021), 'The Price of Nostalgia: America's Self-Defeating Economic Retreat', *Foreign Affairs*, 100/3: 28–43.

Power, A. (2018), 'Regional Politics of an Urban Age: Can Europe's Former Industrial Cities Create a New Industrial Economy to Combat Climate Change and Social Unraveling?', *Palgrave Commun*, 4/97: 1–15.

Prakash, A. (2002), 'Beyond Seattle: Globalization, the Nonmarket Environment and Corporate Strategy', *Review of International Political Economy*, 9/3: 513–537.

Prebisch, R. (1950), 'Crecimiento, Desequilibrio y Disparidades: Interpretación del Proceso de Desarrollo Económico', *Estudio Económico de América Latina*, Naciones Unidas Comisión Económica para América Latina y el Caribe (CEPAL), Working Paper 1110, July.

Prebisch, R. (1963), *Towards a Dynamic Development Policy for Latin America* (New York: United Nations).

Prebisch, R. (1970), *Change and Development: Latin America's Great Task* (Washington, D.C.: Inter-American Development Bank).

Preble, C. A. (2016), 'Libertarians and Foreign Policy: The Individual, the State, and War', *The Independent Review*, 21/2: 167–179.

Preeg, E. H. (1970), *Traders and Diplomats: An Analysis of the Kennedy Round under the General Agreement on Tariffs and Trade* (Washington, D.C.: Brookings Institution).

Pritchett, L. (2006), *Let Their People Come: Breaking the Gridlock on International Labor Mobility* (Washington, D.C.: Center for Global Development).

Prügl, E. (2012), '"If Lehman Brothers had been Lehman Sisters . . .": Gender and Myth in the Aftermath of the Financial Crisis', *International Political Sociology*, 6/1: 21–35.

Prügl, E. (2017), 'Neoliberalism with a Feminist Face: Crafting a New Hegemony at the World Bank', *Feminist Economics*, 23/1: 30–53.

Prügl, E. (2020), 'Feminist Methodology between Theory and Praxis', *Review of International Studies*, 46/3: 304–314.

Prügl, E. (2021), 'Untenable Dichotomies: De-Gendering Political Economy', *Review of International Political Economy*, 28/2: 295–306.

Prügl, E., and True, J. (2014), 'Equality means Business? Governing Gender through Transnational Public-Private Partnerships', *Review of International Political Economy*, 21/6: 1137–1169.

Public Citizen (2012), 'Obama, Romney and Congressional Candidates Nationwide Used Trade-Themed Ads to Appeal to U.S. Majority Opposing Trade Status Quo, Reinforcing Public Anger and Building Expectations for Reform',

7 November, https://www.citizen.org/news/obama-romney-and-congressional-candidates-nationwide-used-trade-themed-ads-to-appeal-to-u-s-majority-opposing-trade-status-quo-reinforcing-public-anger-and-building-expectations-for-reform/.

Pun, N. et al. (2016), 'Apple, Foxconn, and Chinese Workers' Struggles from a Global Labor Perspective', *Inter-Asia Cultural Studies*, 17/2: 166–185.

Putnam, R. D., and Bayne, N. (1987), *Hanging Together: Cooperation and Conflict in the Seven-Power Summits* (Cambridge, MA: Harvard University Press).

Pytkowska, J. (2020), *Microfinance in Europe: Survey Report 2020 Edition* (Brussels: European Microfinance Network and Microfinance Centre).

Quaglia, L. (2022), 'Financial Systems', in J. Pevehouse and L. Seabrooke (eds.), *The Oxford Handbook of International Political Economy* (Oxford: Oxford University Press).

Quarter, J., Mook, L., and Armstrong, A. (2017), *Understanding the Social Economy: A Canadian Perspective*, 2nd edn. (Toronto, ON: University of Toronto Press).

Rabkin, J. (1998), *Why Sovereignty Matters* (Washington, D.C.: AEI Press).

Radano, R., and Olaniyan, T. (2016), *Audible Empire: Music, Global Politics, Critique* (Durham, NC: Duke University Press).

Radhakrishnan, S. S. (1949), 'Reflections on Our Age', *Lectures Delivered at the Opening Session of UNESCO at the Sorbonne University, Paris* (New York, NY: Colombia University Press).

Radu, R. (2021), 'Steering the Governance of Artificial Intelligence: National Strategies in Perspective', *Policy and Society*, 40/2: 178–193.

Raghavan, C. (2002), *Developing Countries and Services Trade: Chasing a Black Cat in a Dark Room, Blindfolded* (Penang: Third World Network).

Rajaram, P. K. (2018), 'Refugees as Surplus Population: Race, Migration and Capitalist Value Regimes', *New Political Economy*, 23/5: 627–639.

Ramchandani, A. (2018), 'Forced Labor Is the Backbone of the World's Electronics Industry', *The Atlantic*, 28 June, https://www.theatlantic.com/business/archive/2018/06/malaysia-forced-labor-electronics/563873/#.

Ramos, L., Gallagher, K., Stephenson, C., and Monasterolo, I. (2022), 'Climate Risk and IMF Surveillance Policy: A Baseline Analysis', *Climate Policy*, 22/3: 371–388.

Rankin, K. (2001), 'Governing Development: Neoliberalism, Microcredit, and Rational Economic Woman', *Economy and Society*, 30/1: 18–37.

Rasillo, X. B. (2021), 'Alternative Economies, Digital Innovation and Commoning in Grassroots Organisations: Analysing Degrowth Currencies in the Spanish region of Catalonia', *Environmental Policy and Governance*, 31/3: 175–185.

Rathbun, B. C. (2008), 'Does One Right Make a Realist? Conservatism, Neoconservatism, and Isolationism in the Foreign Policy Ideology of American Elites', *Political Science Quarterly*, 123/2: 271–299.

Rathgeber, E. (1990), 'WID, WAD, GAD: Trends in Research and Practice', *Journal of Developing Areas*, 24/4: 489–502.

Rauchway, E. (2015), *The Money Makers* (New York, NY: Basic Books).

Ravenhill, J. (1995), 'Competing Logics of Regionalism in the Asia-Pacific', *Journal of European Integration*, 18/2–3: 179–199.

Ravenhill, J. (2001), *APEC and the Construction of Asia-Pacific Regionalism* (Cambridge: Cambridge University Press).

Ravenhill, J. (2004), 'Back to the Nest? Europe's Relations with the African, Caribbean and Pacific Group of Countries', in V. K. Aggarwal and E. A. Fogarty (eds.), *EU Trade Statistics: Between Regionalism and Globalization* (Basingstoke: Palgrave Macmillan).

Ravenhill, J. (2014), 'Global Value Chains and Development', *Review of International Political Economy*, 21: 264–274.

Rawls, J. (1971), *A Theory of Justice* (Cambridge, MA: Belknap Press).

Ray, S. (2000), *En-Gendering India: Woman and Nation in Colonial and Postcolonial Narratives* (Durham, NC: Duke University Press).

Raymond, C., Matthews, T., and Horton, R. M. (2020), 'The Emergence of Heat and Humidity too Severe for Human Tolerance', *Science Advances*, 6.

Redbord, A. (2023), 'Tom Brady and Other A-Listers Sued For Fumbling FTX Endorsements', *Forbes*, 1 February 2023, https://www.forbes.com/sites/ariredbord/2023/02/01/tom-brady-and-other-a-listers-fumble-ftx-endorsements-but-will-they-be-held-liable/?sh=4cab9f197d8c.

Reed, J., and Shepherd, C. (2021), 'Manila Confronts Beijing's "Utter Disregard" for Law in South China Sea', *Financial Times*, 9 April, https://www.ft.com/content/1ec532e8-2ed0-44ea-82ce-942b74b9b8d3.

Reich, R. (1987), 'The Rise of Techno-Nationalism', *The Atlantic Monthly*: 62–69.

Reinhart, C., and Rogoff, K. (2009), *This Time is Different: Eight Centuries of Financial Folly* (Princeton, NJ: Princeton University Press).

Reinhart, C., and Trebesch, C. (2016), 'The International Monetary Fund: 70 Years of Reinvention', *Journal of Economic Perspectives*, 30/1: 3–28.

Reisen, H. (2015), 'Will the AIIB and the NDB help Reform Multilateral Development Banking?', *Global Policy*, 6/3: 297–304.

Republic of South Africa (2013), 'Fifth BRICS Summit Declaration and Action Plan', *Fifth BRICS Summit* (Durban, South Africa) https://www.mea.gov.in/bilateral-documents.htm?dtl/21482.

Rethel, L. (2019), 'Corporate Islam, Global Capitalism, and the Performance of Economic Moralities', *New Political Economy*, 24/3: 350–364.

Rho, S., and Tomz, M. (2017), 'Why Don't Trade Preferences Reflect Economic Self-Interest?', *International Organization*, 71/S1: S85–S108.

Ricardo, D. (1817), *On the Principles of Political Economy, and Taxation* (Cambridge: Cambridge University Press).

Richards, J. A., and Schalatek, L. (2017), *Not a Silver Bullet: Why the Focus on Insurance to Address Loss and Damage Is a Distraction from Real Solutions* (Washington, D.C.: Heinrich Boll).

Rietbergen-McCracken, J., and Narayan-Parker, D. (1998), *Participation and Social Assessment: Tools and Techniques*, Vol. 1 (Washington, DC: World Bank Publications).

Riley, J. (1998), 'Mill's Political Economy: Ricardian Science and Liberal Utilitarian Art', in J. Skorupski (ed.), *The Cambridge Companion to Mill* (Cambridge: Cambridge University Press).

Riofrancos, T. et al. (2023), 'Achieving Zero Emissions with More Mobility and Less Mining', *Climate and Community Project*, https://www.climateandcommunity.org/more-mobility-less-mining.

Ritchie, H., and Roser, M. (2022), 'CO2 Emissions', *Our World in Data Global Change Data Lab*, https://ourworldindata.org/co2-emissions.

Robbins, L. (1984), *An Essay on the Nature and Significance of Economic Science*, 3rd edn. (London: Macmillan).

Roberts, A. (2013), 'Financing Social Reproduction: The Gendered Relations of Debt and Mortgage Finance in 21st Century America', *New Political Economy*, 18/1: 21–42.

Roberts, A. (2015), 'The Political Economy of Transnational Business Feminism: Problematizing the Corporate-Led Gender Equality Agenda', *Review of International Political Economy*, 17/2: 209–231.

Roberts, A., and Soederberg, S. (2012), 'Gender Equality as Smart Economics? A Critique of the 2012 World Development Report', *Third World Quarterly*, 33/5: 949–968.

Roberts, A., Trommer, S., and Hannah, E., (2019), 'Gender Impacts of Trade and Investment Agreements', Policy Briefing prepared for the UK Women's Budget Group, https://wbg.org.uk/wp-content/uploads/2019/09/FINAL-.pdf.

Roberts, C., Armijo, L., and Katada, S. (2018), *The BRICS and Collective Financial Statecraft* (Oxford: Oxford University Press).

Roberts, N. (2015), *Freedom as Marronage* (Chicago, IL: University of Chicago Press).

Roberts, S. T. (2021), *Behind the Screen: Content Moderation in the Shadows of Social Media* (New Haven, CN: Yale University Press).

Robin, T. (2019), 'Our Hands at Work: Indigenous Food Sovereignty in Western Canada', *Journal of Agriculture, Food Systems, and Community Development*, 9/b: 85–99.

Robin (Martens), T., Dennis, M. K., and Hart, M. A. (2020), 'Feeding Indigenous People in Canada', *International Social Work*, 65/4.

Robinson, C. (1983), *Black Marxism: The Making of the Black Radical Tradition* (Chapel Hill, NC: University of North Carolina Press).

Robinson, C. J. (2000), *Black Marxism: The Making of the Black Radical Tradition*, 2nd edn. (Chapel Hill, NC: University of North Carolina Press).

Robinson, J., and Heldring, L. (2013), 'Colonialism and Development in Africa', *Centre for Economic*

Policy Research, https://cepr.org/voxeu/columns/colonialism-and-development-africa.

Rodima-Taylor, D., and Grimes, W W (2019), 'International Remittance Rails as Infrastructures: Embeddedness, Innovation and Financial Access in Developing Economies', *Review of International Political Economy*, 26/5: 839–862.

Rodney, W. (1972), *How Europe Underdeveloped Africa* (London: Bogle-L'Ouverture Publications).

Rodrik, D. (2006), 'The Social Cost of Foreign Exchange Reserves', Working Paper 11952, National Bureau of Economic Research.

Rodrik, D. (2011), *The Globalization Paradox* (Oxford: Oxford University Press).

Rodrik, D. (2017), 'Economics of the Populist Backlash', *Centre for Economic Policy Research*, https://voxeu.org/article/economics-populist-backlash.

Rodrik, D. (2019), 'Is it Better to be Poor in a Rich Country or Rich in a Poor Country?', *Project Syndicate*, September, https://www.weforum.org/agenda/2019/09/truth-income-gaps-in-between-countries/.

Rogaly, B. (2021), 'Commentary: Agricultural Racial Capitalism and Rural Migrant Workers', *Journal of Rural Studies*, 88: 527–531.

Rogers, C., and Clarke, C. (2016), 'Mainstreaming Social Finance: The Regulation of the Peer-to-Peer Lending Marketplace in the United Kingdom', *British Journal of Politics and International Relations*, 18/4: 930–945.

Rogowski, R. (1987), 'Political Cleavages and Changing Exposure to Trade', *American Political Science Review*, 81/4: 1121–1137.

Rommerskirchen, C. (2019), *EU Fiscal Policy Coordination in Hard Times: Free Riders on the Storm* (Oxford: Oxford University Press).

Rommerskirchen, C., and Snaith, H. (2017), 'Bringing Balance to the Force? A Comparative Analysis of Institutionalisation Processes in the G20's Mutual Assessment Process and the EU's Macroeconomic Imbalances Procedure', *New Political Economy*, 23/4: 391–406.

Rosecrance, R. (1986), *The Rise of the Trading State: Commerce and Conquest in the Modern World* (New York, NY: Basic Books).

Rosenbaum, E. (2022), 'Robo-Advisor Dream of Disrupting Wall Street Wealth is not Working out Exactly as Planned', *CNBC*, 27 January, https://www.cnbc.com/2022/01/27/roboadvisor-disruption-of-wall-street-wealth-is-not-working-out.html.

Rossi, A. (2013), 'Does Economic Upgrading Lead to Social Upgrading in Global Production Networks? Evidence from Morocco', *World Development*, 46: 223–233.

Rostow, W. W. (1960), *The Stages of Growth: A Non-Communist Manifesto*, 1st edn. (Cambridge: Cambridge University Press).

Rothschild, E. (2010), 'The Theory of Moral Sentiments and the Inner Life', *Adam Smith Review*, 5: 25–36.

Rothschild, E. (2011), *The Inner Life of Empires: An Eighteenth-Century History* (Princeton, NJ: Princeton University Press).

Roy, A. (2014), *The NGO-ization of Resistance*, https://towardfreedom.org/story/archives/globalism/arundhati-roy-the-ngo-ization-of-resistance/.

Roy, I. (2022), *Southern Multilateralism: Comparing the Influence of the New Development Bank and the IBSA Fund on the Liberal International Order* (Berkley, CA: Global Perspectives at the University of California Press).

Ruggie, J. G. (1982), 'International Regimes, Transactions, and Change: Embedded Liberalism in the Postwar Economic Order', *International Organization*, 36/2: 379–415.

Ruggie, J. G. (1992), 'Multilateralism: The Anatomy of an Institution', *International Organization*, 46/3: 561–598.

Sabet, S. (2013), 'What's in a Name? Isolating the Effect of Prejudice on Individual Trade Preferences', American Political Science Association 2013 Annual Meeting, 29 August, Chicago, IL (New York, NY: Social Science Research Network), 1–35.

Said, E. (1978), *Orientalism: Western Concepts of the Orient* (New York, NY: Pantheon).

Sakamoto, T. (2017), 'Adam Smith's Dialogue with Rousseau and Hume: Yoshihiko Uchida and the Birth of *The Wealth of Nations*', *Adam Smith Review*, 9: 127–144.

Samman A., and Sgambati, S. (2022), 'Financial Eschatology and the Libidinal Economy of Leverage', *Theory, Culture & Society*, 40/3: 103–121.

Samuels, R. J. (1993), *'Rich Nation, Strong Army': National Security and the Technological Transformation of Japan* (Ithaca, NY: Cornell University Press).

Samuelson, P. A. (1949), 'International Factor-Price Equalization Once Again', *Economic Journal*, 59/234: 181–197.

Sandler, T. (1992), *Collective Action: Theory and Applications* (Ann Arbor, MI: University of Michigan Press).

Sanghera, S. (2021), *Empireland: How Imperialism has Shaped Modern Britain* (London: Penguin).

Sau, A. (2021), 'On Cultural Political Economy: A Defence and Constructive Critique', *New Political Economy*, 26/6: 1015–1029.

Scheve, K., and Slaughter, M. (2001), 'What Determines Individual Trade Policy Preferences?' *Journal of International Economics*, 54: 267–292.

Schmidheiny, S., and Zorraquin, F. (1996), *Financing Change* (Cambridge, MA: MIT Press).

Schmitt, L. (2022), 'Mapping Global AI Governance: A Nascent Regime in a Fragmented Landscape', *AI and Ethics*, 2/2: 303–314.

Schubert, A. (1992), *The Credit-Anstalt Crisis of 1931* (Cambridge: Cambridge University Press).

Schwab, S. C. (2011), 'After Doha: Why the Negotiations are Doomed and What we Should do About It', *Foreign Affairs*, 90/3: 104–117.

Schwartz, H. (2009), *Subprime Nation* (Ithaca, NY: Cornell University Press).

Schwecke, S. (2022), *Debt, Trust, and Reputation: Extra-Legal Finance in Northern India* (Cambridge: Cambridge University Press).

Schweinberger, T. (2022), 'How Promise Breaking in Trade Rhetoric Shapes Attitudes Toward Bilateral US-China Trade Cooperation', *Business and Politics*, 1/28.

Scott, J. (1998), *Seeing Like a State: How Certain Schemes to Improve the Human Condition Have Failed* (New Haven, CT: Yale University Press).

Scott, J., and Wilkinson, R. (2011), 'The Poverty of the Doha Round and the Least Developed Countries', *Third World Quarterly*, 32/4: 611–627.

Scott, J., and Wilkinson, R. (2013), 'China Threat? Evidence from the WTO', *Journal of World Trade*, 47/4: 761–782.

Scott, J., and Wilkinson, R. (2022), 'China and the WTO, Redux: Making Sense of Two Decades of Membership', *Journal of World Trade*, 56/1: 87–110.

Scripps Institution of Oceanography (2022), *Keeling Curve* (San Diego, CA: Scripps Institution of Oceanography and UC San Diego), s://keeling-curve.ucsd.edu/.

Seabrooke, L. (2010), 'What Do I Get? The Everyday Politics of Expectations and the Subprime Crisis', *New Political Economy*, 15/1: 51–70.

SEI, IISD, ODI, E3G, and UNEP (2021), 'The Production Gap Report 2021', http://www.productiongap.org/2021report.

Sell, S., and A. Prakash (2004), 'Using Ideas Strategically: The Contest between Business and NGO Networks in Intellectual Property Rights', *International Studies Quarterly*, 48/1: 143–175.

Sell, S. K. (2010), 'TRIPS was Never Enough: Vertical Forum Shifting, FTAs, ACTA, and TPP', *Journal of Intellectual Property Law*, 18/447: 447–478.

Selwyn, B. (2019), 'Poverty Chains and Global Capitalism', *Competition & Change*, 23/1: 71–97.

Sen, A. (1982), *Poverty and Famines: An Essay on Entitlement and Deprivation* (Oxford: Oxford University Press).

Sen, A. (1991), 'Welfare, Preference, and Freedom', *Journal of Econometrics*, 50/1–2: 15–29.

Sen, A. (2000), *Development as Freedom*, 1st edn. (New York, NY: Anchor Books).

Sen, A. (2009), *The Idea of Justice* (Cambridge, MA: Belknap Press).

Sen, A. (2012), *The Argumentative Indian: Writings on Indian history, Culture and Identity* (New Delhi: Penguin Books India).

Sen, S. (2004), 'Liberal Empire and Illiberal Trade: The Political Economy of "Responsible Government" in Early British India', in K. Wilson (ed.), *A New Imperial History: Culture, Identity and Modernity in Britain and the Empire, 1660–1840* (Cambridge: Cambridge University Press).

Seyfang, G. (2000), 'The Euro, the Pound and the Shell in our Pockets: Rationales for Complementary Currencies in a Global Economy', *New Political Economy*, 5/2: 227–246.

Sgambati, S. (2016), 'Rethinking Banking. Debt Discounting and the Making of Modern Money as Liquidity', *New Political Economy*, 21/3: 274–290.

Sgambati S. (2022), 'Who Owes? Class Struggle, Inequality and the Political Economy of Leverage in the 21st Century', *Finance and Society*, 8/1: 1–21.

Shachar, A. (2009), *The Birthright Lottery: Citizenship and Global Inequality* (Cambridge, MA: Harvard University Press).

Shadlen, K. (2005), 'Exchanging Development for Market Access? Deep Integration and Industrial Policy under Multilateral and Regional-Bilateral Trade Agreements', *Review of International Political Economy*, 12/5: 750–775.

Shapiro, J. S. (2021), 'The Environmental Bias of Trade Policy', *Quarterly Journal of Economics*, 136/2: 831–886.

Sharman, J. C. (2011), *The Money Laundry: Regulating Criminal Finance in the Global Economy* (Ithaca, NY: Cornell University Press).

Sharman, J. C. (2017), 'Illicit Global Wealth Chains after the Financial Crisis: Micro-states and an Unusual Suspect', *Review of International Political Economy*, 24/1: 30–55.

Shemirani, M. (2016), *Sovereign Wealth Funds and International Political Economy* (London: Routledge).

Shen, J. (2020), 'Internal Migration in China', in M. Bell, A. Bernard, E. Charles-Edwards, and Y. Zhu (eds.), *Internal Migration in the Countries of Asia* (Cham, SW: Springer), 51–75.

Shepherd, L. (2022), '(Why) Gender Matters in Global Politics', in L. Shepherd and C. Hamilton (eds.), *Gender Matters in Global Politics: A Feminist Introduction to International Relations* (Abingdon: Routledge).

Shields, S. et al. (2011), *Critical International Political Economy: Dialogue, Debate and Dissensus* (London: Palgrave Macmillan).

Shih, V. (2017), 'Financial Instability in China: Possible Pathways and their Likelihood', *Mercator Institute for China Studies Paper*, 20 October.

Shiller, R. J. (2017), 'Narrative Economics', *American Economic Review*, 107/4: 967–1004.

Shilliam, R. (2021), *Decolonizing Politics: An Introduction* (Cambridge: Polity Press).

Shrier, D. L., and Pentland, A. (2022), 'Fintech Foundations: Convergence, Blockchain, Big Data, and AI', in D. L. Shrier and A. Pentland (eds.), *Global Fintech: Financial Innovation in the Connected World* (Cambridge, MA: MIT Press).

Siamanta, Z. C., and Dunlap, A. (2019), 'Wind Energy Development as a Capitalist Trojan Horse in Crete, Greece and Oaxaca, Mexico', *ACME*, 18: 925–955.

Siddiqi, M. N. (2006), 'Shariah, Economics and the Progress of Islamic Finance: The Role of Shariah Experts', paper presented to Pre-Forum Workshop, Seventh Harvard Forum on Islamic Finance, ://www.siddiqi.%20com/mns/Role_of_Shariah_Experts.htm.

Sien, I. A. R. (2007), 'Beefing up the Hormones Dispute: Problems in Compliance and Viable Compromise Alternatives', *Georgetown Law Journal*, 95: 565–590.

Siles-Brügge, G. (2013), 'The Power of Economic Ideas: A Constructivist Political Economy of EU Trade Policy', *Journal of Contemporary European Research*, 9/4.

Siles-Brügge, G. (2014), 'Explaining the Resilience of Free Trade: The Smoot-Hawley Myth and the Crisis', *Review of International Political Economy*, 21/3: 535–574.

Silvia, S. J. (1991), 'The Social Charter of the European Community: A Defeat for European Labour', *ILR Review*, 44/4: 626–643.

Sinclair, T. (1994), 'Between State and Market', *Policy Sciences*, 27/4: 447–466.

Sinclair, T. (2021), *To the Brink of Destruction: America's Rating Agencies and Financial Crisis* (Ithaca, NY: Cornell University Press).

Singer, D. (2007), *Regulating Capital: Setting Standards for the International Financial System* (Ithaca, NY: Cornell University Press).

Singer, H. W. (1950), 'The Distribution of Trade Between Investigating and Borrowing Countries', *American Economic Review*, 40: 531–548.

Singer, P. (2004), *One World: The Ethics of Globalization* (New Haven, CN: Yale University Press).

Singh, A., and Zammit, A. (2000), 'International Capital Flows: Identifying the Gender Dimension', *World Development*, 28/7: 1249–1268.

Singh, J. P. (1999), *Leapfrogging Development?: The Political Economy of Telecommunications Restructuring* (Albany, NY: State University of New York Press).

Singh, J. P. (2008a), 'Paulo Freire: Possibilities for Dialogic Communication in a Market-driven Information Age', *Information, Communication & Society*, 11/5: 699–726.

Singh, J. P. (2008b), *Negotiation and the Global Information Economy* (Cambridge: Cambridge University Press).

Singh, J. P. (2014), 'Development Remix: Representing Poverty, Culture, and Agency in the Developing World', *International Studies Perspectives*, 15/3: 243–256.

Singh, J. P. (2015), 'Global Institutions and Deliberations: Is the World Trade Organization More Participatory than UNESCO?', in P. Heller and V. Rao (eds.), *Deliberation and Development: Rethinking the Role of Voice and Collective Action in Unequal Societies* (World Bank Publications), 192–222.

Singh, J. P. (2016), 'A Subaltern Performance: Circulations of Gender, Islam, and Nation in India's Song of Defiance', *Arts and International Affairs*, 1.

Singh, J. P. (2017a), 'Beyond Neoliberalism: Contested Narratives of International Development', in B. O. Alistair Miskimmon and L. Roselle (eds.), *Forging the World: Strategic Narratives and International Relations* (Ann Arbor, MI: The University of Michigan Press), 134–163.

Singh, J. P. (2017b), *Sweet Talk: Paternalism and Collective Action in North–South Trade Relations* (Stanford, CA: Stanford University Press).

Singh, J. P. (2019), 'Development Finance 2.0: Do Participation and Information Technologies Matter?', *Review of International Political Economy*, 26/5: 886–910.

Singh, J. P. (ed.) (2020), *Cultural Values in Political Economy* (Stanford, CA: Stanford University Press).

Singh, J. P. (2021), 'Race, Culture, and Economics: An Example from North–South Trade Relations', *Review of International Political Economy*, 28/2: 323–335.

Singh, J. P. (2023), 'Critical Theory and its Critique of Liberalism', in C. Thies (ed.), *Handbook of International Relations* (Cheltenham: Edward Elgar Publishing).

Singh, J. P., and Woolcock, M. (2022), *The Future of Multilateralism and Global Development* (Berkeley, CA: Global Perspectives at the University of California Press).

Singh, M. (2022), 'Crypto Assets Shed $800 billion in Market Value in a Month', *Reuters*, 10 May, https://www.reuters.com/business/finance/crypto-assets-shed-800-bln-market-value-month-2022-05-10/.

Singh, N. P. (2022), 'Black Marxism and the Antinomies of Racial Capitalism', in C. Nealon, and C. Lye (eds.), *After Marx: Literature, Theory, and Value in the Twenty-First Century* (Cambridge: Cambridge University Press), 33–39.

Skidelsky, R. (2009), *Keynes: The Return of the Master* (New York: Public Affairs).

Skorupski, J. (2021), *Being and Freedom: On Late Modern Ethics in Europe* (Oxford: Oxford University Press).

Smith, A. (1759/1982), *The Theory of Moral Sentiments*, Glasgow Edition of the Works and Correspondence of Adam Smith, D. D. Raphael, and A. L. Macfie (eds.) (Indianapolis, IN: Liberty Fund).

Smith, A. (1776/1981), *An Inquiry into the Nature and Causes of the Wealth of Nations*, Glasgow Edition of the Works and Correspondence of Adam Smith, R. H. Campbell and A. Skinner (eds.) (Indianapolis, IN: Liberty Fund).

Smith, A. (1982), *Lectures on Jurisprudence*, Glasgow Edition of the Works and Correspondence of Adam Smith, R. L. Meek, D. D. Raphael, and P. G. Stein (eds.) (Indianapolis, IN: Liberty Fund).

Smith, N. (2007), 'Nature as Accumulation Strategy', in L. Panitch and C. Leys (eds.), *Socialist Register 2007: Coming to Terms with Nature* (London: The Merlin Press Ltd).

Snidal, D. (1985a), 'The Limits of Hegemonic Stability Theory', *International Organization*, 39/4: 579–614.

Snidal, D. (1985b), 'Coordination versus Prisoners' Dilemma: Implications for International Cooperation and Regimes', *American Political Science Review*, 79/4: 923–942.

Snyder, T. (2022), 'Ukraine Holds the Future: The War Between Democracy and Nihilism', *Foreign Affairs*, 101/5: 124–141.

Soederberg, S. (2007), 'Taming Corporations or Buttressing Market-Led Development? A Critical Assessment of the Global Compact', *Globalizations*, 4/4: 500–513.

Soederberg, S. (2014a), *Debtfare States and the Poverty Industry: Money, Discipline and the Surplus Population*, 1st edn. (London: Routledge).

Soederberg, S. (2014b), 'Student Loans, Debtfare and the Commodification of Debt: The Politics of Securitization and the Displacement of Risk', *Critical Sociology*, 40/5: 689–709.

Spatafora, N., and Tytell, I. (2009), 'Commodity Terms of Trade: The History of Booms and Busts', Working Paper 205, International Monetary Fund.

Spero, J. (1980), *The Failure of the Franklin National Bank* (New York, NY: Columbia University Press).

Spilker, G., Bernauer, T., and Umaña, V. (2016), 'Selecting Partner Countries for Preferential Trade Agreements: Experimental Evidence from Costa Rica, Nicaragua, and Vietnam', *International Studies Quarterly*, 60/4: 706–718.

Spivak, G. C. (2015), 'Can the Subaltern Speak?', in *Colonial Discourse and Post-colonial Theory* (London: Routledge), 66–111.

Srinivasan, T. N. (2019), *Developing Countries and the Multilateral Trading System: From GATT to the Uruguay Round and the Future* (Boulder, CO: Westview Press).

Srivastava, S. (2021), 'Algorithmic Governance and the International Politics of Big Tech', *Perspectives on Politics*, 1–12.

Srnicek, N. (2017), *Platform Capitalism* (Malden, MA: Polity Press).

Stasavage, D. (2003), *The Politics of a Common Currency* (Aldershot: Ashgate).

Statista (2022), *Automotive Industy Worldwide* (New York: Statista), https://www.statista.com/topics/1487/automotive-industry/#editorialPicks.

Stavins, R. (2017), *An Economic View of the Environment*, http://www.robertstavinsblog.org.

Steger, D. P. (ed.) (2009), *Redesigning the World Trade Organization for the Twenty-First Century* (Waterloo, ON: Wilfrid Laurier University Press).

Steil, B. (2018), *The Marshall Plan* (New York: Simon and Schuster).

Stein, A. A. (1982), 'Coordination and Collaboration: Regimes in an Anarchic World', *International Organization*, 36/2: 294–324.

Steinberg, D. (2015), *Demanding Devaluation* (Ithaca, NY: Cornell University Press).

Steiner, N. D. (2018), 'Attitudes Towards the Transatlantic Trade and Investment Partnership in the European Union: The Treaty Partner Heuristic and Issue Attention', *European Union Politics*, 19/2: 255–277.

StepChange (2020), 'Coronavirus and Personal Debt: A Financial Recovery Strategy for Households',

StepChange Debt Charity, June 2020, https://www.stepchange.org/Portals/0/assets/pdf/coronavirus-policy-briefing-stepchange.pdf.

Stern, D. I. (2017), 'The Environmental Kuznets Curve after 25 Years', *Journal of Bioeconomics*, 19: 7–28.

Stiglitz, J. E. (2002), *Globalization and its Discontents* (Toronto, ON: Penguin Publishing).

Stockhammer, E. (2004), 'Financialisation and the Slowdown of Accumulation', *Cambridge Journal of Economics*, 28/5: 719–741.

Stoddard, I. et al. (2021), 'Three Decades of Climate Mitigation: Why Haven't We Bent the Global Emissions Curve?', *Annual Review of Environment and Resources*, 46: 653–689.

Stokes, B. (2018), 'Americans, Like Many in Other Advanced Economies, Not Convinced of Trade's Benefits', Pew Research Center Report, s://www.pewresearch.org/global/2018/09/26/americans-like-many-in-other-advanced-economies-not-convinced-of-trades-benefits/.

Stolper, W. F., and Samuelson. P. A. (1941), 'Protection and Real Wages', *Review of Economic Studies*, 9/1: 58–73.

Strange, M. (2013), *Writing Global Trade Governance: Discourse and the WTO* (London: Routledge).

Strange, S. (1970), 'International Economics and International Relations: A Case of Mutual Neglect', *International Affairs*, 46/2: 304–315.

Strange, S. (ed.) (1984), *Paths to International Political Economy* (Routledge Revivals).

Strange, S. (1986), *Casino Capitalism* (Oxford: Basil Blackwell).

Strange, S. (1988), *States and Markets* (London: Pinter).

Strange, S. (1996), *The Retreat of the State: The Diffusion of Power in the World Economy* (Cambridge: Cambridge University Press).

Strange, S. (1998), *Mad Money* (Ann Arbor: University of Michigan Press).

Strange, S. (1998), 'Protectionism and World Politics', *International Organization*, 39/2: 233–259.

Strauss, K., and Fudge, J. (2014), 'Temporary Work, Agencies, and Unfree Labor: Insecurity in the New World of Work', in J. Fudge and K. Strauss (eds.), *Temporary Work, Agencies, and Unfree Labor: Insecurity in the New World of Work* (New York, NY: Routledge).

Strauss, K., and McGrath, S. (2017), 'Temporary Migration, Precarious Employment and Unfree Labour Relations: Exploring the "Continuum of Exploitation" in Canada's Temporary Foreign Worker Program', *Geoforum*, 78: 199–208.

Subacchi, P. (2017), *The People's Money* (New York, NY: Columbia University Press).

Subacchi, P. (2020), *The Cost of Free Money* (New Haven, CT: Yale University Press).

Subramanian, L. (2020), *Singing Gandhi's India-Music and Sonic Nationalism* (New Delhi: Roli Books Private Limited).

Suchodolski, S. G., and Demeulemeester, J. M. (2018), 'The BRICS Coming of Age and the New Development Bank', *Global Policy*, 9/4: 578–586.

Sumaila, U. R., Ebrahim, N., Schuhbauer, A., Skerritt, D., Li, Y., Kim, H. S., Mallory, T. G., Lam, V. W. L., and Pauly, D. (2019), 'Updated Estimates and Analysis of Global Fisheries Subsidies', *Marine Policy*, 109/103695.

Summers, L. H. (2015), 'Time US Leadership Woke up to New Economic Era', http://larrysummers.com/2015/04/05/time-us-leadership-woke-up-to-new-economic-era/.

Svartzman, R., and Althouse, J. (2020), 'Greening the International Monetary System? Not Without Addressing the Political Ecology of Global Imbalances', *Review of International Political Economy*, 29/3: 844–869.

Swazan, I., Sharif, I., and Das, D. (2022), 'Bangladesh's Emergency as a Ready-Made Garment Export Leader: An Examination of the Competitive Advantages of the Garment Industry', *International Journal of Global Business and Competitiveness*, 17: 62–174.

Swider, S. (2015), 'Building China: Precarious Employment Among Migrant Construction Workers', *Work, Employment and Society*, 29/1: 41–59.

Tarrow, S. (2005), 'The Dualities of Transnational Contention: "Two Activist Solitudes" or a New World Altogether?', *Mobilization: An International Quarterly*, 10/1: 53–72.

Taylor, M. (1987), *The Possibility of Cooperation* (Cambridge: Cambridge University Press).

Taylor, M. (2012), 'The Antinomies of "Financial Inclusion": Debt, Distress and the Workings of Indian Microfinance', *Journal of Agrarian Change*, 12/4: 601–610.

Temin, D. M. (2022), 'Development in Decolonization: Walter Rodney, Third World Developmentalism, and "Decolonizing Political Theory"', *American Political Science Review*, 1–14.

Tharoor, S. (2016), *An Era of Darkness: The British Empire in India* (New Delhi: Aleph Book Company).

Thatcher, M. (1988), 'Speech to the College of Europe ("The Bruges Speech")', Belfry, Bruges, 20 September, http://www.margaretthatcher.org/document/107332.

The Economist (2014), 'An Acronym with Capital: Setting up Rivals to the IMF and World Bank is Easier than Running them', *The Economist*, 9 July, http://www.economist.com/news/finance-and-economics/21607851-setting-up-rivals-imf-and-world-bank-easier-running-them-acronym.

Thewissen, S., and Rueda, D. (2019), 'Automation and the Welfare State: Technological Change as a Determinant of Redistribution Preferences', *Comparative Political Studies,* 52/2: 171–208.

Thiong'o, N. W. (1986), *Decolonising the Mind: The Politics of Language in African Literature* (Rochester, NY: Boydell & Brewer Inc).

Thistlethwaite, J., and Paterson, M. (2016), 'Private Governance and Accounting for Sustainability Networks', *Environment and Planning C*, 34/7: 1197–1221.

Thomson Reuters (2015), *State of the Global Islamic Economy Report 2015–16* (Dubai: Dubai the Capital of Islamic Economy).

Thurbon, E. (2016), *The Developmental Mindset* (Ithaca, NY: Cornell University Press).

Tickner, J. A., and Sjøberg, L., (eds.) (2011), *Feminism and International Relations: Conversations about the Past, Present, and Future* (London: Routledge).

Tillerson, R. (2017), 'Defining Our Relationship with India for the Next Century: An Address by U.S. Secretary of State Rex Tillerson', https://www.csis.org/analysis/defining-our-relationship-india-next-century-address-us-secretary-state-rex-tillerson.

Tilley, L., and Shilliam, R. (2018), 'Raced Markets: An Introduction', *New Political Economy*, 23/5: 534–543.

Tobin, S. (2016), *Everyday Piety. Islam and Economy in Jordan* (Ithaca, NY: Cornell University Press).

Tooker, L., and Clarke, C. (2018), 'Experiments in Relational Finance: Harnessing the Social in

Everyday Debt and Credit', *Theory, Culture & Society*, 35/3: 57–76.

Tooze, A. (2019), *Crashed: How a Decade of Financial Crisis Changed the World* (London: Penguin).

Tooze, R. and Murphy, C. (1996), 'The Epistemology of Poverty and the Poverty of Epistemology in IPE: Mystery, Blindness and Invisibility', *Millennium: Journal of International Studies*, 25/3: 681–707.

Transport and Environment (2022a), *Food not Fuel: Part One* (Brussels: Transport and Environment).

Transport and Environment (2022b), *Food Not Fuel: Part Two* (Brussels: Transport and Environment).

Trautmann, T. (1997), *Aryans and British India* (Los Angeles, CA: University of California Press).

Trentmann, F. (2008), *Free Trade Nation: Commerce, Consumption, and Civil Society in Modern Britain* (Oxford: Oxford University Press).

Triffin, R. (1960), *Gold and the Dollar Crisis* (New Haven, CN: Yale University Press).

Trommer, S. (2014), *Transformations in Trade Politics: Participatory Trade Politics in West Africa* (Abingdon: Routledge).

Trommer, S. (2015), 'Trade Policy Communities, Expert Language and the Dehumanization of World Trade', in E. Hannah, J. Scott, and S. Trommer (eds.), *Expert Knowledge in Global Trade* (London: Routledge), 63–82.

Trommer, S. (2017), 'The WTO in an Era of Preferential Trade Agreements: Thick and Thin Institutions in Global Trade Governance', *World Trade Review* 16/3: 501–526.

Trommer, S. (2022), 'Trade, Health and Social Reproduction in a COVID World', *Globalizations*, 19/3: 397–407.

TUC (Trades Union Congress) (1975), 'European Community: Renegotiation and the Referendum: The TUC View', April (London: Trades Union Congress) http://www.cvce.eu/content/publication/2002/2/25/57a89ee3-d3ab-4089-a443-3fc179a2fc3c/publishable_en.pdf, 1–9.

TUC (Trades Union Congress) (2007), 'Put Labour Standards and Development at the Heart of EU Trade Agreements' (London: Trades Union Congress), https://www.tuc.org.uk/research-analysis/reports/put-labour-standards-and-development-heart-eu-trade-agreements/.

Tuck, E., and Yang, K. W. (2012), 'Decolonization is Not a Metaphor', *Decolonization: Indigenity, Education & Safety* 1/1: 1–40.

Tucker, K. (2014), 'Participation and Subjectification in Global Governance: NGOs, Acceptable Subjectivities and the WTO', *Millennium: Journal of International Studies*, 42/2: 376–396.

Turner, O. (2009), 'China's Recovery: Why the Writing was Always on the Wall', *Political Quarterly*, 80/1: 111–118.

Tussie, D., and Narlikar, A. (2003), 'The G20 at the Cancún Ministerial: Developing Countries and their Evolving Coalitions in the WTO', *World Economy*, 27/7: 947–1148.

UIA (Union of International Associations) (2021), 'Yearbook of International Organizations', *UIA*, https://uia.org/yearbook.

Ulnicane, I., et al. (2022), 'Governance of Artificial Intelligence: Emerging International Trends and Policy Frames', in M. Tinnirello (ed.), *The Global Politics of Artificial Intelligence* (New York: CRC Press), 29–56.

UN (United Nations) (1974), World Food Conference. Note by the Secretary-General. Document E/5587.

UN (United Nations) (1978), *Transnational Corporations in World Development: A Re-examination* (New York: United Nations Commission on Transnational Corporations).

UN (United Nations) (1992), *United Nations Framework Convention on Climate Change* (New York: United Nations General Assembly).

UN (United Nations) (2006), *Building Inclusive Financial Sectors for Development* (New York: UN Press).

UN (United Nations) (2015), 'The Millennium Development Goals', https://www.un.org/millenniumgoals/2015_MDG_Report/pdf/MDG%202015%20rev%20(July%201).pdf (Geneva: United Nations).

UN (United Nations) (2017a), 'Cooperatives in Social Development', Report of the Secretary General, 22 July, https://acrobat.adobe.com/id/urn:aaid:sc:VA6C2:4dafb012-d120-42ce-8ccc-dac737ac4daf.

UN (United Nations) (2017b), *World Economic and Social Survey 2017: Reflecting on Seventy Years of Development Policy Analysis* (New York: United Nations) https://www.un.org/development/desa/dpad/wp-content/uploads/sites/45/publication/WESS_2017-FullReport.pdf.

UN (United Nations) (2022), 'The 17 Goals', *Department of Economic and Sustainable Development*, https://sdgs.un.org/goals.

UNCTAD (United Nations Conference on Trade and Development) (1982), *Assessment of the Results of the Multilateral Trade Negotiations* (Geneva: UNCTAD).

UNCTAD (United Nations Conference on Trade and Development) (2001), *World Investment Report: Promoting Linkages* (Geneva: UNCTAD).

UNCTAD (United Nations Conference on Trade and Development) (2009), *World Investment Report 2009: Transnational Corporations, Agricultural Production and Development* (Geneva: UNCTAD).

UNCTAD (United Nations Conference on Trade and Development) (2012), *Excessive Commodity Price Volatility: Macroeconomic Effects on Growth and Policy Options* (Geneva: UNCTAD).

UNCTAD (United Nations Conference on Trade and Development) (2017), *Beyond Austerity: Towards a Global New Deal*, Trade and Development Report 2017, https://unctad.org/system/files/official-document/tdr2017_en.pdf (Geneva: United Nations).

UNCTAD (United Nations Conference on Trade and Development) (2019), *Commodity Dependence: A Twenty-Year Perspective* (Geneva: UNCTAD).

UNCTAD (United Nations Conference on Trade and Development) (2021), 'Escaping from the Commodity Dependence Trap through Technology and Innovation', *Commodities and Development Report* (Geneva: UNCTAD).

UNCTAD (United Nations Conference on Trade and Development) (2022a), *Impact of the Covid-19 Pandemic on Trade and Development: Lessons Learned*, https://unctad.org/system/files/official-document/osg2022d1_en.pdf (Geneva: United Nations).

UNCTAD (United Nations Conference on Trade and Development) (2022b), *World Investment Report 2022: International Tax Reforms and Sustainable Development* (New York and Geneva: United Nations).

UNDP (United Nations Development Programme) (2011), *Towards Human Resilience: Sustaining MDG Progress in an Age of Economic Uncertainty* (New York: UNDP).

UNFCC (2022), *What is the United Nations Framework Convention on Climate Change?* (Bonn: UNFCCC).

UNGA (United Nations General Assembly) (2013), 'World Commodity Trends and Prospects', *Report of the Secretary General*, A/68/204 (New York: United Nations).

UNGA (United Nations General Assembly) (2022), 'Regular Budget and Working Capital Fund', https://www.un.org/en/ga/contributions/budget.shtml (Geneva: UN General Assembly).

(UNHCR) United Nations High Commissioner for Refugees (2023), 'Refugee Data Finder', https://www.unhcr.org/refugee-statistics/#:~:text=Forcibly%20displaced%20people%20worldwide,103%20million%20at%20mid%2D2022 (Geneva: United Nations).

United States Trade Representative (2020), *Report on the Appellate Body of the World Trade Organization*, https://ustr.gov/sites/default/files/Report_on_the_Appellate_Body_of_the_World_Trade_Organization.pdf (Washington, DC: Office of the United States Trade Representative).

United States Trade Representative (2021), 'United States—Certain Measures on Steel and Aluminum Products (DS548)', *Integrated Executive Summary of the United States of America*, https://ustr.gov/sites/default/files/enforcement/DS/DS548/US.Integrated.Exec.Summary.fin.(DS548).pdf (Washington, D.C.: Office of the United States Trade Representative).

UNODC (United Nations Office on Drugs and Crime) (2000), *Protocol to Prevent, Suppress and Punish Trafficking in Persons, Especially Women and Children*, https://www.ohchr.org/sites/default/files/ProtocolonTrafficking.pdf (Geneva: United Nations).

US Census Bureau (2023), 'Trade in Goods with China', https://www.census.gov/foreign-trade/balance/c5700.html.

Vajpeyi, A. (2012), *Righteous Republic: The Political Foundations of Modern India* (Cambridge, MA: Harvard University Press).

Van Alphen, T. (1988), 'Backers Plan Final Ad Blitz for Free Trade', *Toronto Star*, 17 November.

van Dormael, A. (1978), *Bretton Woods: The Birth of a Monetary System* (London: Macmillan).

van Staveren, I. (2002), 'Global Finance and Gender', in J. A. Scholte (ed.), *Civil Society and Global Finance* (London: Routledge).

van Staveren, I., Elson, D., Grown, C., and Çagatay, N. (2007), *The Feminist Economics of Trade* (Routledge).

Vasudevan, R. (2020), 'Libra and Facebook's Money Illusion', *Challenge*, 63/1: 21–39.

Vestergaard, J., and Wade, R. (2012), 'The Governance Response to the Great Recession: The "Success" of the G20', *Journal of Economic Issues*, 46: 481–489.

Vestergaard, J. and Wade, R. (2015), 'Protecting Power: How Western States Retain Their Dominant Voice in the World Bank's Governance', in D. Lesage and T. Van de Graaf (eds.), *Rising Powers and Multilateral Institutions* (Basingstoke: Palgrave MacMillan).

Vía Campesina (2007), *Declaration of Nyéléni*, Selingue, Mali: Forum for Food Sovereignty, 27 February, https://nyeleni.org/en/declaration-of-nyeleni/.

Viner, J. (1948), 'Power Versus Plenty', *World Politics*, 1/1: 1–29.

Viner, J. (1950), *The Customs Union Issue* (New York, NY: Carnegie Endowment for International Peace).

Vitalis, R. (2015), *White World Order, Black Power Politics: The Birth of American International Relations* (Ithaca, NY: Cornell University Press).

Vives, X. (2019), 'Digital Disruption in Banking', *Annual Review of Financial Economics*, 11: 243–272.

Vom Hau, M., Scott, J., and Hulme, D. (2012), 'Beyond the BRICs: Alternative Strategies of Influence in the Global Politics of Development', *European Journal of Development Research*, 24/2: 187–204.

Wacquant, L. (2010), 'Crafting the Neoliberal State: Workfare, Prisonfare, and Social Insecurity', *Sociological Forum*, 25/2: 197–220.

Wade, R. (1990), *Governing the Market: Economic Theory and the Role of Government in East Asian Industrialization* (Princeton, NY: Princeton University Press).

Wade, R. H. (2016), 'Industrial Policy in Response to the Middle-income Trap and the Third Wave of the Digital Revolution', *Global Policy*, 7: 469–480.

Wade, R. H. (2018), 'The Developmental State: Dead or Alive?', *Development and Change*, 49: 518–546.

Wai, Z. (2015), 'On the Predicament of Africanist Knowledge: Mudimbe, Gnosis and the Challenge of the Colonial Library', *International Journal of Francophone Studies*, 18/2–3: 263–290.

Waldron, I. (2018), *There's Something in the Water: Environmental Racism in Indigenous and Black Communities* (Black Point, MB: Fernwood Publishing).

Wallerstein, I. (1974), 'Dependence in an Interdependent World: The Limited Possibilities of Transformation within the Capitalist World Economy', *African Studies Review*, 17/1: 1–26.

Wallerstein, I. (1974), *The Modern World System* (New York, NY: Academic Press).

Walter, M., Kukutai, T., Carroll, S. R., and Rodriguez-Lonebear, D. (eds.) (2021), *Indigenous Data Sovereignty and Policy* (New York, NY: Routledge).

Waltz, K. N. (1979), *Theory of International Politics* (Reading, MA: Addison Wesley).

Watson, M. (2014), 'The Historical Roots of Theoretical Traditions in Global Political Economy', in J. Ravenhill (ed.), *Global Political Economy*, 4th edn. (Oxford: Oxford University Press), 25–49.

Watson, M. (2018), 'Crusoe, Friday and the Raced Market Frame of Orthodox Economics Textbooks', *New Political Economy*, 23/5: 544–559.

Watson, M. (2020), 'The Historical Roots of Theoretical Traditions in Global Political Economy', in J. Ravenhill (ed.), *Global Political Economy*, 6th edn. (Oxford: Oxford University Press).

Watson, M. (2022), 'The Place of Glasgow in *The Wealth of Nations*: Caught between Biography and Text, Philosophical and Commercial History', *History of Political Economy*, 54/5: 975–990.

Waylen, G. (2006), 'You Still Don't Understand: Why Troubled Engagements Continue between Feminists and (Critical) IPE', *Review of International Studies*, 32/1: 145–164.

Webb, D. (2022), *Progress on UK Free Trade Agreement Negotiations*, https://researchbriefings.files.parliament.uk/documents/CBP-9314/CBP-9314.pdf (London: House of Commons Library).

Weber, H. (2004), 'The "New Economy" and Social Risk: Banking on the Poor?', *Review of International Political Economy*, 11/2: 356–386.

Weber, M. (2005), *Protestant Ethic and the Spirit of Capitalism,* 1st edn. (London: Routledge).

Webster, T. (2014), 'Paper Compliance: How China Implements WTO Decisions', *Michigan Journal of International Law*, 35/3: 525–578.

WEF (World Economic Forum) (2020) *Global Gender Gap Index* (Geneva: World Economic Forum).

WEF (World Economic Forum) (2022), 'Unlocking the Social Economy: Towards an Inclusive and Resilient Society', Insight Report, May, https://www3.weforum.org/docs/WEF_Unlocking_the_Social_Economy_2022.pdf.

Weingast, B. (1995), 'The Economic Role of Political Institutions: Market-Preserving Federalism and Economic Development', *Journal of Law, Economics, & Organization*, 11/1: 1–31.

Weiss, T. G., Carayannis, T., and Jolly, R. (2009), 'The "Third" United Nations', *Global Governance*, 15/1: 123–142.

Wendt, A. (1995), 'Constructing International Politics', *International Security*, 20/1: 71–81.

Wendt, A. (1999), *Social Theory of International Politics* (Cambridge: Cambridge University Press).

Westermeier, C. (2020), 'Money is Data—the Platformization of Financial Transactions', *Information, Communication & Society*, 23/14: 2047–2063.

Weymouth, S. (2023), *Digital Globalization* (Cambridge: Cambridge University Press).

Wigglesworth, R., and Agnew, H. (2022), 'BlackRock Passes $10tn Milestone', *Financial Times*, 15 January.

Wigglesworth, R., Ivanova, P., and Smith, C. (2022), 'Will There Be a Backlash Against the Dollar?' *Financial Times*, 8 April.

Wilhelm, A. (2022), 'Is Stripe Cheap at $95 Billion?', 12 April, *TechCrunch*, https://techcrunch.com/2022/04/12/is-stripe-cheap-at-95-billion/.

Wilkinson, R. (2009), 'Language, Power and Multilateral Trade Negotiations', *Review of International Political Economy*, 16/4: 597–619.

Wilkinson, R. (2014), *What's Wrong with the WTO and How to Fix It* (Hoboken, NK: Wiley & Sons).

Wilkinson, R. (2017), 'Back to the Future: "Retro" Trade Governance and the Future of the Multilateral Order', *International Affairs*, 93/5: 1131–1147.

Wilkinson, R., and Scott, J. (2008), 'Developing Country Participation in the GATT: A Reassessment', *World Trade Review*, 7/3: 473–510.

Williams, E. (1994), *Capitalism and Slavery* (North Carolina: University of North Carolina Press).

Williams, J. (2021), 'Fair Trade, Firsthand: Connecting Northern Consumers with Southern Producers', in G. Fridell, Z. Gross, and S. McHugh (eds.), *The Fair Trade Handbook: Building a Better World, Together* (Black Point, NS: Fernwood Publishing), 137–147.

Williamson, O. E. (1975), *Markets and Hierarchies, Analysis and Anti-Trust Implications: A Study in the Economics of Internal Organization* (New York, NY: Free Press).

Wilson, J. (2021), 'Australia Shows the World What Decoupling from China Looks Like', *Foreign Policy*.

Wingfield-Hayes, R. (2023), 'Holding Out Against China in a Row over Reefs', *BBC News*, 16 February, https://www.bbc.co.uk/news/world-asia-64634814.amp.

Winham, G. (1986), *International Trade and the Tokyo Round Negotiation* (Princeton, NJ: Princeton University Press).

Winham, G. R. (1998), 'Explanations of Developing Country Behaviour in the GATT Uruguay Round Negotiation', *World Competition*, 21/3: 109–134.

Wintermeyer, L. (2021), 'Institutional Money Is Pouring Into The Crypto Market And Its Only Going To Grow', *Forbes*, 12 August, https://www.forbes.com/sites/lawrencewintermeyer/2021/08/12/institutional-money-is-pouring-into-the-crypto-market-and-its-only-going-to-grow/?sh=4deb36f01459.

Wolff, M. (2016), 'Ringside with Steve Bannon at Trump Tower as the President-Elect's Strategist Plots "An Entirely New Political Movement"', *Hollywood Reporter*, 18 November, http://www.hollywoodreporter.com/news/steve-bannon-trump-tower-interview-trumps-strategist-plots-new-political-movement-948747.

Wood, A. (2018), 'The 1990s Trade and Wages Debate in Retrospect', *The World Economy*, 41: 975–999.

Woodward, D., Drager, N., Beaglehole, R., and Lipson, D. (2002), 'Globalization, Global Public Goods and Health', in J. A. Casa et al. (eds.), *Trade in Health Services: Global, Regional, and Country Perspectives* (Pan American Health Organization).

Worker Rights Consortium (2013), 'Global Wage Trends for Apparel Workers, 2001–2011', (New York: Workers Rights Consortium), https://www.workersrights.org/research-report/global-wage-trends-for-apparel-workers-2001-2011/.

World Bank (1973), 'President McNamara Nairobi Speech 1973', https://www.worldbank.org/en/archive/history/past-presidents/robert-strange-mcnamara.

World Bank (2008), *Finance for All? Policies and Pitfalls in Expanding Access* (Washington, DC: IBRD).

World Bank (2011), *Global Economic Prospects* (Washington, D.C.: World Bank).

World Bank (2018), 'Moving for Prosperity: Global Migration and Labor Markets', Policy Research Report (Washington D.C.: World Bank), https://openknowledge.worldbank.org/server/api/core/bitstreams/4ab45187-53ee-550c-8638-4fef04d30599/content.

World Bank (2020), *Women, Business and the Law 2020* (Washington, D.C.: IBRD).

World Bank (2022a), *GDP (Current US$)* (Washington, D.C.: World Bank), https://data.worldbank.org/indicator/NY.GDP.MKTP.CD.

World Bank (2022b), *GDP Growth (annual %)* (Washington, D.C.: World Bank), https://data.worldbank.org/indicator/NY.GDP.MKTP.KD.ZG.

World Bank (2022c), *GDP Per Capita* (Washington, D.C.: World Bank), https://data.worldbank.org/indicator/NY.GDP.PCAP.CD.

World Bank (2022d), *State and Trends of Carbon Pricing 2022* (Washington, D.C.: World Bank).

World Bank (2023), 'Gross Savings (% of GDP)', https://data.worldbank.org/indicator/NY.GNS.ICTR.ZS?order=wbapi_data_value_2011%20wbapi_data_value%20wbapi_data_value-first&sort=desc.

World Commission on Environment and Development (1987) *Our Common Future* (Oxford: Oxford University Press).

World Food Programme (2023), *A Global Food Crisis* (Rome: WFP), https://www.wfp.org/global-hunger-crisis.

WTO (World Trade Organization) (2001), *World Trade Report* (Geneva: WTO).

WTO (World Trade Organization) (2003), 'Agriculture Framework Agreement—Proposal by the EU and US', JOB/3/157.

WTO (World Trade Organization) (2005), 'Statement by HE Mr Bo Xilai, Minister of Commerce: Hong Kong Ministerial Conference', 14 December, WT/MIN/05/ST/59.

WTO (World Trade Organization) (2019), 'Participation in Regional Trade Agreements', https://www.wto.org/english/tratop_e/region_e/rta_participation_map_e.htm.

WTO (World Trade Organization) (2020a), 'Trade Falls Steeply in First Half of 2020', Press Release 858 (Geveva: WTO), https://www.wto.org/english/news_e/pres20_e/pr858_e.htm.

WTO (World Trade Organization) (2020b), 'Waiver from Certain Provisions of the TRIPS Agreement for the Prevention, Containment and Treatment of COVID-19', Communication from India and South Africa. IP/C/W/669.

WTO (World Trade Organization) (2020c), 'Work Programme on Electronic Commerce, The E-Commerce Moratorium: Scope and Impact', Communication from India and South Africa, WT/GC/W/798.

WTO (World Trade Organization) (2021), 'Trade Policy Review: China, Minutes of the Meeting', 20 and 22 October, WT/TPR/M/415.

WTO (World Trade Organization) (2022a), 'WTO Data', https://data.wto.org/en.

WTO (World Trade Organization) (2022b), *World Trade Report: Climate Change and International Trade* (Geneva: WTO).

WTO (World Trade Organization) (2022c), 'Trade and Climate Change', Information Brief 1 (Geneva: WTO).

WTO (World Trade Organization) (2022d), 'Trade and Climate Change', Information Brief 2 (Geneva: WTO).

WTO (World Trade Organization) (2022e), Ministerial Decision on the TRIPS Agreement, adopted by the General Council on 17 June, WTO/MIN/22/30.

WTO (World Trade Organization) (2022f), 'Evolution of Trade under the WTO: Handy Statistics', https://www.wto.org/english/res_e/statis_e/trade_evolution_e/evolution_trade_wto_e.htm#:~:text=As%20of%202022%2C%20world%20trade,at%20an%20average%20of%209%25.

WTO (World Trade Organization) (2023), 'Overview of the WTO Secretariat', https://www.wto.org/english/thewto_e/secre_e/intro_e.htm.

Wu, N. (2021), 'Misattributed Blame? Attitudes Toward Globalization in the Age of Automation', *Political Science Research and Methods*, 10/3: 470–487.

Wynter, S. (2003), 'Unsettling the Coloniality of Being/Power/Truth/Freedom: Towards the Human, After Man, Its Overrepresentation—An Argument', *CR: The New Centennial Review*, 3/3: 257–337.

Yang, X., Lewis, D. J., Roddy, S., and Moise, D. (2018), 'One Belt, One Road, One World: Where is US Business Connectivity?', in W. Zhang, I. Alon, and C. Lattemann (eds.), *China's Belt and Road Initiative: Changing the Rules of Globalization* (Cham: Palgrave Macmillan).

Yong, W. (2002), 'China's Stakes in WTO Accession: The Internal Decision-making Process', in H. Holbig and R. Ash (eds.), *China's Accession to the World Trade Organization: National and International Perspectives* (New York, NY: Routledge-Curzon).

Young B. (2018), 'Financialization, Unconventional Monetary Policy and Gender Inequality', in Elias J. and Roberts, A. (eds.), *Handbook on the International Political Economy of Gender* (Cheltenham: Edward Elgar), 241–251.

Young, I. M. (2004), 'Responsibility and Global Labor Justice', *The Journal of Political Philosophy*, 12/4: 365–388.

Yun, S. and Olorundaré, A. (2022), 'Rebound and Grow: Canadian Payment Methods and Trends Report 2022', Payments Canada, https://payments.ca/sites/default/files/PaymentsCanada_Canadian_Payment_Methods_and_Trends_Report_2022_En_0.pdf.

Zeleza, P. T. (1997), *A Modern Economic History of Africa: The Nineteenth Century, Volume 1* (Nairobi: East African Publishers).

Zelizer, V. A. (1997), *The Social Meaning of Money: Pin Money, Paychecks, Poor Relief, and Other Currencies* (Princeton, NJ: Princeton University Press).

Zeng, J. (2016), 'China's Date with Big Data: Will it Strengthen or Threaten Authoritarian Rule?', *International Affairs*, 92/6: 1443–1462.

Zhang, W., Alon, I., and Lattemann, C., (eds.) (2018), *China's Belt and Road Initiative: Changing the Rules of Globalization* (Cham: Palgrave Macmillan).

Zhu, X. (2021), 'The Plastic Cycle—An Unknown Branch of the Carbon Cycle', *Frontiers in Marine Science*, 7.

Zimmermann, H. (2002), *Money and Security* (Cambridge: Cambridge University Press).

Zuboff, S. (2019), *The Age of Surveillance Capitalism: The Fight for a Human Future at the New Frontier of Power* (New York, NY: Hachette Book Group).

Zürn, M. (2018), *A Theory of Global Governance: Authority, Legitimacy, and Contestation* (Oxford: Oxford University Press).

Zysman, J., and Newman, A. L. (eds.) (2006), *How Revolutionary was the Digital Revolution?: National Responses, Market Transitions, and Global Technology* (Stanford, CA: Stanford University Press).

Index

Tables, figures, and boxes are indicated by an italic *t, f,* and *b* following the page number.